OPERATIONS MANAGEMENT

OPERATIONS MANAGEMENT

Eighth edition

Nigel Slack
Alistair Brandon-Jones
Robert Johnston

Harlow, England • London • New York • Boston • San Francisco • Toronto • Sydney • Auckland • Singapore • Hong Kong
Tokyo • Seoul • Taipei • New Delhi • Cape Town • São Paulo • Mexico City • Madrid • Amsterdam • Munich • Paris • Milan

Pearson Education Limited
Edinburgh Gate
Harlow CM20 2JE
United Kingdom
Tel: +44 (0)1279 623623
Web: www.pearson.com/uk

First published under the Pitman Publishing imprint 1995 (print)
Second edition (Pitman Publishing) 1998 (print)
Third edition 2001 (print)
Fourth edition 2004 (print)
Fifth edition 2007 (print)
Sixth edition 2010 (print)
Seventh edition 2013 (print and electronic)
Eighth edition published 2016 (print and electronic)

ISBN: 978 1 292 09867 8 (print)
      978 1 292 09871 5 (PDF)
      978 1 292 17190 6 (ePub)

British Library Cataloguing-in-Publication Data
A catalogue record for the print edition is available from the British Library

Library of Congress Cataloging-in-Publication Data
A catalog record for the print edition is available from the Library of Congress

10 9 8 7 6 5 4 3 2 1
20 19 18 17 16

Cover image © Karin Hildebrand Lau / Alamy Stock Photo

Print edition typeset in 9.25/12 Charter ITC Std by 76
Printed in Slovakia by Neografia

NOTE THAT ANY PAGE CROSS REFERENCES REFER TO THE PRINT EDITION

Brief contents

Contents

Part One

DIRECTING THE OPERATION 3

Part Three

DELIVER

Chapter 10:
Planning and control

Chapter 11:
Capacity management

Supplement to Chapter 11:
Analytical queuing models

Chapter 12:
Supply chain management

Chapter 13:
Inventory management

Chapter 14:
Planning and control systems

Guide to 'operations in practice', examples, short cases and case studies

Chapter	Location	Company/example	Region	Sector/activity	Company size
1 Operations management		Lego	Europe	Manufacturing	Large
		Torchbox	UK	Web design	Small
		MSF	Global	Charity	Large
		Pret a Manger	Global	Hospitality	Medium
		Formule 1	Europe	Hospitality	Large
		Ski Verbier Exclusive	Europe	Hospitality	Small
		Hewlet Packard		Manufacturing	Large
		To be a great operations manager...	Global	N/A	N/A
		Concept design services	General	Design/manufacturing/distribution	Medium
2 Operations performance		Novozymes	Europe	Pharmaceutical	Large
		Patagonia	Global	Garments	Large
		Holcim	Global	Cement/aggregates	Large
		Quality Street	Global	Confectionary	Large
		The Golden Hour	General	Healthcare	N/A
		UPS	Global	Distribution	Large
		Mymusli	German	Web retail	Small
		Aldi	Europe	Retail	Large
		Foxconn	Taiwan	Manufacturing	Large
		The Penang Mutiara	Malaysia	Hospitality	Medium
3 Operations strategy		SSTL	UK/ Space	Aerospace	Medium
		Apple retail	Global	Retail	Large
		Amazon	Global	Web retail	Large
		Apple supply operations	Global	Manufacturing	Large
		Nokia	Global	Telecomm	Large
		Sometimes any plan is better than no plan	Europe	Military	Large
		McDonalds	Global	Hospitality	Large
4 Product and service innovation		Apple iPhone	Global	Design	Large
		Kodak	Global	Manufacturing	Smaller
		Square watermelons	Global	Agriculture	Various
		IKEA	Global	Design/ Retail	Large
		Dyson	Global	Manufacturing	Large
		The circular economy	Global	Sustainability	Various
		Dreddo Dan's	Global	Snack food	Large

Chapter	Location	Company/example	Region	Sector/activity	Company size
5 The structure and scope of operations		ARM and Intel	Global	Design and Design/ manufacturing	Large
		Hollywood studios	USA	Creative	Large
		Surgery and shipping	India/Global	Healthcare/transportation	Large
		Counting clusters	Various	Various	Various
		HTC	Taiwan	Design/manufacturing	Large
		Samsun	Korea	Manufacturing	Large
		Aarens Electronic	Netherlands	Manufacturing	Medium
6 Process design		Changi airport	Singapore	Air travel	Large
		Fast food	Global	Hospitality	Large
		Ecover	Europe	Manufacturing	Large
		Sands Film Studio	UK	Creative	Small
		Space4 housing	UK	Construction	Medium
		Sainsbury's	UK	Retail	Large
		Shouldice hospital	Canada	Healthcare	Small
		Action response	UK	Charity	Small
7 Layout and flow		Volkswagen	Germany	Manufacturing	Large
		Google	USA	Technology	Large
		Factory flow helps surgery	UK	Healthcare	Medium
		Apple's shop	UK	Retail	Large
		Cadbury's	UK	Manufacturing/ entertainment	Large
		Nestlé	Global	Manufacturing	Large
		Office cubicles	Various	Design	Various
		Zodiac	France / Global	Manufacturing	Medium
		The Event Hub	UK	Policing	Medium
8 Process technology		I Robot	Global	Various	Various
		Technology or people?	Various	Various	Various
		QB house	Asia	Hairdressing	Medium
		Marmite	UK	Food	Large
		Technology failures	UK	Technology	Large
		Who's in the cockpit?	Global	Various Airlines	Various
		Rochem	UK	Food processing	Medium
9 People in operations		W L Gore	Global	Manufacturing	Large
		High customer contact jobs	USA	Air travel	Large
		McDonald's	Global	Hospitality	Large
		Yahoo	USA	Technology	Large
		Music while you work	Global	Various	Various
		Grace faces (three) problems	UK	Legal	Medium
10 Planning and control		Joanne manages the schedule	UK	Retail	Medium
		Operations control at Air France	Global	Airline	Large
		Uber	Global	Technology platform	Large
		Can airline passengers be sequenced?	General	Airports	Various
		The hospital triage system	Global	Healthcare	Various
		The life and times of a chicken sandwich (part 1)	UK	Food processing	Medium

Chapter	Location	Company/example	Region	Sector/activity	Company size
11 Capacity management		Heathrow	UK	Airports	Large
		Panettone	Italy	Food processing	Large
		Amazon	Global	Retail	Large
		Lowaters	UK	Horticulture	Medium
		Demand management	USA	Public	Large
		Baseball games	USA	Leisure	Medium
		Blackberry hill farm	UK	Leisure	Small
12 Supply chain management		Ocado	UK	Retail	Large
		The North Face	Global	Garment manufacture	Large
		Apple	Global	Technology	Large
		The tsunami effect	Asia	Various	Various
		Levi Strauss	Global	Garment manufacture	Large
		Seven-Eleven Japan	Japan	Retail	Large
		Supplying fast fashion	Global	Garment design/ manufacture/ retail	Large
13 Inventory management		National Health Service Blood and Transplant service	UK	Public sector	Large
		Energy inventory	Global	Power generation	Large
		Treasury wines	Australia	Wine production	Large
		Gritting roads	Europe	Public sector	Large
		Flame electrical	South Africa	Wholesale	Small
		Amazon	Global	Retail	Large
		Supplies4medics	Europe	Retail	Medium
14 Planning and control systems		Butchers pet care	UK	(Dog) food production	Medium
		SAP and its partners	Global	Systems developers	
		The life and times of a chicken salad sandwich (part 2)	UK	Food production	Medium
		What a waste	USA	Recycling	Large
		Psycho sports	N/A	Manufacturing	Small
15 Lean operations		Jamie's lean meals	UK	Domestic food preparation	N/A
		Pixar adopts lean	USA	Creative	Large
		Toyota	Global	Auto production	Large
		Waste reduction in airline maintenance	N/A	Air transport	N/A
		Andon's in Amazon	Global	Retail	Large
		Torchbox	UK	Web design	Small
		St Bridget's Hospital	Sweden	Healthcare	Medium
16 Improvement		Sonae Corporation	Portugal	Retail	Large
		The checklist manifesto	N/A	Healthcare	Various
		6Wonderkinder	Germany	App developer	Small
		Improvement at Heineken	Netherlands	Brewer	Large
		6Sigma at Wipro	India	Outsourcers	Large
		Learning from Formula 1	UK	Transport	Various
		Reinventing Singapore's libraries	Singapore	Public sector	Medium

Chapter	Location	Company/example	Region	Sector/activity	Company size
17 Quality management		TNT Express	Global	Transport	Large
		Victorinox	Switzerland	Manufacturing	Large
		Four Seasons	Global	Hospitality	Large
		Magic moments	UK	Photography	Small
		Ryanair's	Europe	Airline	Large
		Millbrook Proving Ground	UK	Auto testing	Medium
		Quick Food Products	UK	Food production	Small
		Fat finger syndrome	Global	Finance	Various
		Deliberate defectives	Canada	Manufacturing	Large
		Preston plant	Canada	Manufacturing	Medium
18 Managing risk and recovery		Tesco	UK	Retail	Large
		Findus	Europe	Food production	Large
		G4S	UK	Outsourcer	Large
		The rise of the micromort	N/A	Various	Various
		Is failure designed-in to airline operations?	Netherlands	Airline	Large
		General motors	USA	Auto manufacture	Large
		Slagelse Industrial Services	Denmark	Manufacturing	Medium
19 Project management		Disney	Global	Leisure	Large
		Vasa's first voyage	Sweden	Military	N/A
		Halting the growth of malaria	Global	Healthcare	Large
		The Scottish Parliament Building	UK	Construction	Large
		United Photonics	Malaysia	Development	Large

Preface

Introduction - Operations may not run the World, but it makes the World run

Operations management is *important*. It is concerned with creating the services and products upon which we all depend. And all organizations produce some mixture of services and products, whether that organization is large or small, manufacturing or service, for profit or not for profit, public or private. Thankfully, most companies have now come to understand the importance of operations. This is because they have realized that effective operations management gives the potential to improve both efficiency and customer service simultaneously. But more than this, operations management is *everywhere*, it is not confined to the operations function. All managers, whether they are called Operations or Marketing or Human Resources or Finance, or whatever, manage processes and serve customers (internal or external). This makes, at least part of their activities 'operations'.

Operations management is also *exciting*. It is at the centre of so many of the changes affecting the business world – changes in customer preference, changes in supply networks brought about by internet-based technologies, changes in what we want to do at work, how we want to work, where we want to work, and so on. There has rarely been a time when operations management was more topical or more at the heart of business and cultural shifts.

Operations management is also *challenging*. Promoting the creativity that will allow organizations to respond to so many changes is becoming the prime task of operations managers. It is they who must find the solutions to technological and environmental challenges, the pressures to be socially responsible, the increasing globalization of markets and the difficult- to-define areas of knowledge management.

The aim of this book

This book provides a clear, authoritative, well-structured and interesting treatment of operations management as it applies to a variety of businesses and organizations. The text provides both a logical path through the activities of operations management and an understanding of their strategic context.

More specifically, this text is:

- *Strategic* in its perspective. It is unambiguous in treating the operations function as being central to competitiveness.
- *Conceptual* in the way it explains the reasons why operations managers need to take decisions.
- *Comprehensive* in its coverage of the significant ideas and issues which are relevant to most types of operation.
- *Practical* in that the issues and challenges of making operations management decisions *in practice* are discussed. The 'Operations in practice' feature, which starts every chapter, the short cases that appear through the chapters, and the case studies at the end of each chapter, all explore the approaches taken by operations managers in practice.
- *International* in the examples that are used. There are over 110 descriptions of operations practice from all over the world.
- *Balanced* in its treatment. This means we reflect the balance of economic activity between service and manufacturing operations. Around seventy-five per cent of examples are from organizations that deal primarily in services and twenty-five per cent from those that are primarily manufacturing.

Who should use this book?

This book is for anyone who is interested in how services and products are created.

- *Undergraduates* on business studies, technical or joint degrees should find it sufficiently structured to provide an understandable route through the subject (no prior knowledge of the area is assumed).
- *MBA students* should find that its practical discussions of operations management activities enhance their own experience.
- *Postgraduate students* on other specialist Master's degrees should find that it provides them with a well-grounded and, at times, critical approach to the subject.

Distinctive features

Clear structure

The structure of the book uses the '4Ds' model of operations management that distinguishes between the strategic decisions that govern the *direction* of the operation, the *design* of the processes and operations that create products and services, planning and control of the *delivery* of products and services, and the *development*, or improvement of operations.

Illustrations-based

Operations management is a practical subject and cannot be taught satisfactorily in a purely theoretical manner. Because of this we have used examples and short 'operations in practice' cases that explain some of the issues faced by real operations.

Worked examples

Operations management is a subject that blends qualitative and quantitative perspectives; 'worked examples' are used to demonstrate how both types of technique can be used.

Critical commentaries

Not everyone agrees about what is the best approach to the various topics and issues with operations management. This is why we have included 'critical commentaries' that pose alternative views to the one being expressed in the main flow of the text.

Summary answers to key questions

Each chapter is summarized in the form of a list of bullet points. These extract the essential points that answer the key questions posed at the beginning of each chapter.

Case studies

Every chapter includes a case study suitable for class discussion. The cases are usually short enough to serve as illustrations, but have sufficient content also to serve as the basis of case sessions.

Problems and applications

Every chapter includes a set of problem-type exercises. These can be used to check out your understanding of the concepts illustrated in the worked examples. There are also activities that support the learning objectives of the chapter that can be done individually or in groups.

Selected further reading

Every chapter ends with a short list of further reading that takes the topics covered in the chapter further, or treats some important related issues. The nature of each further reading is also explained.

To the Instructor . . .

Teaching and learning resources for the 8th edition

New for the eighth edition

This 8th Edition is different. In fact, it's the biggest set of changes that we have made between editions. We have been consulting widely with our users, who have very kindly contributed to advising us on how we should further improve both the structure and content of the book. First the structure – we have retained the '4Ds' structure (direct, design, delivery and development) that has proved to be exceptionally popular, but we have shifted two chapters that were in the 'design' section into the 'direct' section. Our users, quite rightly, pointed out that 'design innovation' and 'the structure and scope of operations' (what was called 'Supply network design' in previous editions) were both fundamental and strategic, and so therefore should be included in the first part of the book. We have done this and made both chapters more strategic. We have also moved two chapters (Quality management and Project management) into the 'Development' section on the grounds that they are both increasingly seen as part of operations improvement. In terms of the content, we have included various aspects of sustainability and Corporate Social Responsibility in each chapter rather than separating the issue out at the end of the book. The issues covered are just too important to be segregated in that way. Needless to say, as usual, we have tried to keep up to date with the (increasingly) rapid changes taking place in the (wonderful) world of operations.

Specifically, the 8th edition includes the following key changes:

- There are now more than 110 of the popular 'Operations in Practice' examples throughout the book, over 40 per cent of which are new.

- The importance of sustainability and Corporate Social Responsibility (CSR) has been emphasised further, and included throughout the book.
- We have even further strengthened the emphasis on the idea that 'operations management' is relevant to every type of business and all functional areas of the organization.
- Many new ideas in operations management have been incorporated, including the 'three level' approach to performance, the relationship between innovation, creativity and design, crowdsourcing, ideas management, business ecosystems, triadic relationships, office layout, telecommuting and organisational 'ambidexterity'. However, we have retained the emphasis on the foundations of the subject.
- Six of the 19 cases at the end of the chapter are new (but the old ones are still available on the website), and provide an up-to-date selection of operations issues.
- The book has been visually redesigned to aid learning. Instructor's resources A completely new instructor's manual is available to lecturers adopting this textbook, together with PowerPoint presentations for each chapter and a Testbank of assessment questions. Visit www.pearsoned.co.uk/slack to access these. Most importantly, a new set of online resources to enable students to check their understanding, practise key techniques and improve their problem-solving skills now accompanies the book.

To the Student . . .

Making the most of this book

All academic textbooks in business management are, to some extent, simplifications of the messy reality that is actual organizational life. Any book has to separate topics, in order to study them, which in reality are closely related. For example, technology choice impacts on job design that in turn impacts on quality management; yet, for simplicity, we are obliged to treat these topics individually. The first hint therefore in using this book effectively is to look out for all the links between the individual topics. Similarly with the sequence of topics: although the chapters follow a logical structure, they need not be studied in this order. Every chapter is, more or less, self-contained. Therefore study the chapters in whatever sequence is appropriate to your course or your individual interests. But because each part has an introductory chapter, those students who wish to start with a brief 'overview' of the subject may wish first to study Chapters 1, 6, 10 and 16 and the chapter summaries of selected chapters. The same applies to revision – study the introductory chapters and summary answers to key questions.

The book makes full use of the many practical examples and illustrations that can be found in all operations. Many of these were provided by our contacts in companies, but many also come from journals, magazines and newspapers. So if you want to understand the importance of operations management in every-day business life look for examples and illustrations of operations management decisions and activities in newspapers and magazines. There are also examples which you can observe every day. Whenever you use a shop, eat a meal in a restaurant, borrow a book from the library or ride on public transport, consider the operations management issues of all the operations for which you are a customer.

The case exercises and study activities are there to provide an opportunity for you to think further about the ideas discussed in the chapters. Study activities can be used to test out your understanding of the specific points and issues discussed in the chapter and discuss them as a group, if you choose. If you cannot answer these you should revisit the relevant parts of the chapter. The case exercises at the end of each chapter will require some more thought. Use the questions at the end of each case exercise to guide you through the logic of analysing the issue treated in the case. When you have done this individually try to discuss your analysis with other course members. Most important of all, every time you analyse one of the case exercises (or any other case or example in operations management) start off your analysis with the two fundamental questions:

- How is this organization trying to compete (or satisfy its strategic objectives if a not-for-profit organization)?
- What can the operation do to help the organization compete more effectively?

Ten steps to getting a better grade in operations management

I could say that the best rule for getting a better grade is to be good. I mean really, really good! But, there are plenty of us who, while fairly good, don't get as good a grade as we really deserve. So, if you are studying operations management, and you want a really good grade, try following these simple steps:

Step 1 Practise, practise, practise. Use the Key questions and the Problems and applications to check your understanding.

Step 2 Remember a few **key models**, and apply them wherever you can. Use the diagrams and models to describe some of the examples that are contained within the chapter.

Step 3 Remember to use both **quantitative and qualitative analysis.** You'll get more credit for appropriately mixing your methods: use a quantitative model to answer a quantitative question and vice versa, but qualify this with a few well-chosen sentences.

Step 4 There's always a *strategic* **objective** behind any operational issue. Ask yourself, 'Would a similar operation with a different strategy do things differently?' Look at the 'Operations in practice' pieces in the book.

Step 5 Research widely around the topic. Use websites that you trust – we've listed some good websites at the end of the book. You'll get more credit for using references that come from genuine academic sources.

Step 6 Use **your own experience.** Every day, you're experiencing an opportunity to apply the principles of operations management. Why is the queue at the airport check-in desk so long? What goes on behind the 'hole in the wall' of your bank's ATM machines?

Step 7 Always answer the question. Think 'what is really being asked here? What topic or topics does this question cover?' Find the relevant chapter or chapters, and search the Key questions at the beginning of each chapter and the Summary at the end of each chapter to get you started.

Step 8 Take account of the three tiers of accumulating marks for your answers.

(a) First, demonstrate your knowledge and understanding. Make full use of the text to find out where you need to improve.
(b) Second, show that you know how to illustrate and apply the topic. The Case studies and 'Operations in practice' sections give you hundreds of different examples.
(c) Third, show that you can discuss and analyse the issues critically. Use the Critical commentaries within the text to understand some of the alternative viewpoints.

Generally, if you can do (a) you will pass; if you can do (a) and (b) you will pass well, and if you can do all three, you will pass with flying colours!

Step 9 Remember **what** the issue is about, but also **understand why!** Read the text until you really understand why the concepts and techniques of operations management are important, and what they contribute to an organization's success. Your new-found knowledge will stick in your memory, allow you to develop ideas, and enable you to get better grades.

Step 10 Start now! Don't wait until two weeks before an assignment is due. GOOD LUCK!

Nigel Slack

About the authors

Nigel Slack is an Emeritus Professor of Operations Management and Strategy at Warwick University, an Honorary Professor at Bath University and an Associate Fellow of Said Business School, Oxford University. Previously he has been Professor of Service Engineering at Cambridge University, Professor of Manufacturing Strategy at Brunel University, a University Lecturer in Management Studies at Oxford University and Fellow in Operations Management at Templeton College, Oxford. He worked initially as an industrial apprentice in the hand-tool industry and then as a production engineer and production manager in light engineering. He holds a Bachelor's degree in Engineering and Master's and Doctor's degrees in Management, and is a Chartered Engineer. He is the author of many books and papers in the operations management area, including *The Manufacturing Advantage*, published by Mercury Business Books, 1991, and *Making Management Decisions* (with Steve Cooke), 1991, published by Prentice Hall, *Service Superiority* (with Robert Johnston), published in 1993 by EUROMA, *The Blackwell Encyclopedic Dictionary of Operations Management* (with Michael Lewis) published by Blackwell, *Operations Strategy* together with Michael Lewis, the fourth edition published by Pearson in 2014 and *Perspectives in Operations Management (Volumes I to IV)* also with Michael Lewis, published by Routledge in 2003, *Operations and Process Management*, with Alistair Brandon-Jones, Robert Johnston and Alan Betts, now in its 4th Edition 2015. He has authored numerous academic papers and chapters in books. He also acts as a consultant to many international companies around the world in many sectors, especially financial services, transport, leisure and manufacturing. His research is in the operations and manufacturing flexibility and operations strategy areas.

Alistair Brandon-Jones is a Professor in Operations and Supply Management and Associate Dean for Post-Experience Education at the University of Bath School of Management, He was formerly a Reader at Manchester Business School, an Assistant and Associate Professor at Bath School of Management and a Teaching Fellow Warwick Business School, where he also completed his PhD. His other books include *Operations and Process Management*, *Essentials of Operations Management*, and *Quantitative Analysis in Operations Management*. Alistair is an active empirical researcher focusing on e-enabled operations and supply management, healthcare operations, and professional services. This work, supported by a range of grants, has been published in many leading management journals. Alistair has consulting and executive development experience with organizations around the world, in various sectors including petrochemicals, health, financial services, manufacturing, defence, and government. In addition, he has won several university, national, and international awards for teaching excellence.

Acknowledgements

During the preparation of the eighth edition of this book (and previous editions) we have received an immense amount of help from friends and colleagues in the Operations Management community. In particular everybody who has attended one of the regular 'faculty work-shops' deserves thanks for the many useful comments. The generous sharing of ideas from these sessions has influenced this and all the other OM books that we prepare. Our thanks go to everyone who attended these sessions and other colleagues. It is, to some extent, invidious to single out individuals – but we are going to. We thank Pär Åhlström of Stockholm School of Economics, James Aitken of University Of Surrey, Yongmei Bentley of the University Of Bedfordshire, Helen Benton of Anglia Ruskin University, Ran Bhamra, Loughborough University, Tony Birch of Birmingham City University, Abhijeet Ghadge of Heriot Watt University, Professor Sven Åke Hörte of Lulea University of Technology, Eamonn Ambrose of University College, Andrea Benn of University of Brighton, Dublin, Mattia Bianchi of the Stockholm School of Economics John K Christiansen of Copenhagen Business School, Philippa Collins of Heriot-Watt University, Henrique Correa of Rollins College, Florida, Paul Coughlan of Trinity College Dublin, Simon Croom of the University of San Diego, Stephen Disney of Cardiff University, Doug Davies of University of Technology, Sydney, Tony Dromgoole of the Irish Management Institute, J.A.C. de Haan of Tilburg University, Carsten Dittrich of the University of Southern Denmark, David Evans of Middlesex University, Ian Evans of Sunderland University, Paul Forrester of Keele University, Ian Graham of Edinburgh University, Ian Fouweather of Bradford University, Alan Harle of Sunderland University, Norma Harrison of Macquarie University, Catherine Hart of Loughborough Business School, Steve Hickman of University Of Exeter, Chris Hillam of Sunderland University, Ian Holden of Bristol Business School, Matthias Holweg, Oxford University, Mickey Howard of Exeter University, Kim Hua Tan of the University Of Nottingham, Stavros Karamperidis of Heriot Watt University, Tom Kegan of Bell College of Technology, Hamilton, Denis Kehoe of Liverpool University, Mike Lewis of Bath University, Xiaohong Li of Sheffield Hallam University, John Maguire of the University of Sunderland, Charles Marais of the University of Pretoria, Peter McCullen of University Of Brighton, Roger Maull, Exeter University, Bart McCarthy, Nottingham University, Harvey Maylor of Cranfield University, John Meredith Smith of EAP, Oxford, Michael Milgate of Macquarie University, Keith Moreton of Staffordshire University, Chris Morgan of Cranfield University, Adrian Morris of Sunderland University, Andy Neely of Cambridge University, Steve New of Oxford University, John Pal of Manchester Business School, Antony Potter of Manchester Business School, Gary Priddis of University of Brighton, Sofia Salgado Pinto of the Católica Porto Business School, Peter Race of Henley College, Reading University, Gary Ramsden of University Of Lincoln, Steve Robinson of Southampton Solent University, James Rowell of University Of Buckingham, Frank Rowbotham of University Of Birmingham, Ian Sadler of Victoria University, Hamid Salimian of University of Brighton, Sarah Schiffling of University of Lincoln, Andi Smart, Exeter University, Amrik Sohal of Monash University, Nigel Spinks of the University Of Reading, Rui Soucasaux Sousa of the Católica Porto Business School, Alex Skedd of Northumbria Business School, Martin Spring of Lancaster University, Dr Ebrahim Soltani of the University of Kent, R. Stratton of Nottingham Trent University, James Stone, Aston University, Dr. Nelson Tang of the University of Leicester, David Twigg of Sussex University, Helen Valentine of the University of the West of England, Professor Roland van Dierdonck of the University of Ghent, Dirk Pieter van Donk of the University of Groningen, Arvind Upadhyay of University of Brighton, Vessela Warren of University Of Worcester, Bill Wright of Bpp Professional, Ying Xie of Anglia Ruskin University, Maggie Zeng of Gloucestershire University and Li Zhou of University Of Greenwich University.

Our academic colleagues at both Warwick Business School, Bath School of Management have also helped, both by contributing ideas and by creating a lively and stimulating work environment. At Warwick, thanks go to, Nicola Burgess, Mehmet Chakkol, Max Finne, Emily Jamieson, Mark Johnson, Pietro Micheli, Rhian Silvestro, and Chris Voss. At Bath, thanks go to Brian Squire, Chris Archer-Brown, Maria Battarra, Emma Brandon-Jones, Günes Erdogan, Marco Formentini, Emmanuel Fragniere, Andrew Graves, Jooyoung Jeon, Richard Kamm, Mike Lewis, Sheik Meeran, Dimitris

Paraskevopoulos, Tony Roath, Jens Roehrich, Christos Vasilakis, and Baris Yalabik.

Our late friend and colleague, Bob Johnston contributed both expertise and wisdom to earlier editions of this book. We still miss his intelligence, insight and support.

We were lucky to receive continuing professional and friendly assistance from a great publishing team. Especial thanks to Kate Brewin, Caitlin Lisle, Tim Parker, Kelly Miller, Kay Holman, Neville Hankins, Lucy Chantler, Isobel McLean, Frances Topp and Sasmita Sinha.

Finally, to our families, who both supported and tolerated our nerdish obsession, thanks are inadequate, but thanks anyway to Angela and Kathy, and Emma and Noah.

Nigel Slack
Alistair Brandon-Jones

Publisher's acknowledgements

We are grateful to the following for permission to reproduce copyright material:

Figures

Figure 2.11b from Spidergram to check on police forces, *The Times*, 10/07/2002 (Miles, A. and Bladwin, T.) reproduced with permission; Figure 3.15 adapted from *Operations Strategy*, 4 ed., Pearson Education (Slack N. and Lewis M.A. 2015) reproduced with permission; Figure 5.6 from *Operations and Process Management: Principles and Practice for Strategic Impact*, Pearson Education (Slack, Nigel, Brandon-Jones, A., Johnston, R. and Betts, A. 2012) reproduced with permission; Figure 7.6 from For Toyota, patriotism and profits may not mix, *Wall Street Journal*, 29/11/2011 (Dawson, C.) reprinted with permission of Wall Street Journal, Copyright © 2011 Dow Jones & Company, Inc. All Rights Reserved Worldwide. License numbers 3841860034292 and 3841860323322; Figure 8.4 from Unilever UK, Reproduced with kind permission of Unilever PLC and group companies; Figure 9.7 adapted from A new strategy for job enrichment, *California Management Review*, Vol. 17 (3) (Hackman, J.R., Oldham, G., Janson, R. and Purdy, K. 1975) republished with permission of University of California Press, permission conveyed through Copyright Clearance Center, Inc.; Figure 12.6 adapted from What is the right supply chain for your product?, *Harvard Business Review*, March-April, pp. 105–116 (Fisher, M.C. 1997), reprinted by permission of Harvard Business Review. Copyright ©1997 by Harvard Business Publishing; all rights reserved; Figure 12.10 adapted from Purchasing must become supply management, *Harvard Business Review*, September (Kraljic, Peter 1983), reprinted by permission of Harvard Business Review. Copyright ©1983 by Harvard Business Publishing; all rights reserved; Figure 15.7 from *Applying Lean in Offices, Hospitals, Planes and Trains*, Presentation at The Lean Services Summit, Amsterdam, June 24 (2004) p. 30, McKinsey & Company, www.mckinsey.com. Copyright © 2004 McKinsey & Company. All rights reserved. Reprinted by permission; Figure 15.12 adapted from C.A. Voss and A. Harrison, Strategies for implementing JIT, in, *Just-in-Time Manufacture,* IFS/Springer-Verlag (Voss, C.A. (ed.) 1987) Copyright © 1987 Springer; Figure 17.4 adapted from A conceptual model of service quality and implications for future research, *Journal of Marketing*, Vol. 49, Fall, pp. 41-50 (Parasuraman, A., Zeithaml, V.A. and Berry, L.B. 1985), American Marketing Association; Figure 19.4 from *Reinventing Project Management: The Diamond Approach to Successful Growth and Innovation*, Harvard Business School Press (Shenhar, A.J. and Dvir, D. 2007) reprinted by permission of Harvard Business Review Press. Copyright © 2007 by the Harvard Business Publishing Corporation; all rights reserved.; Figure 19.6 adapted from *Managing Sensitive Projects: A Lateral Approach,* English version by Cutrin, T. and Etcheber, P. Routledge, NY (D'Herbemont, O. and César B 1998) republished with permission of Routledge Publishing Inc. Permission conveyed through Copyright Clearance Center, Inc.; Figure 19.19 adapted from *Collaboration, Integrated Information, and the Project Life Cycle in Building Design and Construction and Operation*, Construction Users Roundtables (CURT).

Tables

Table S9.2 adapted from *Principles of Motion Economy: Revisited, Reviewed and Restored*, Proceedings of the Southern Management Association Annual Meeting (Atlanta, GA 1983) (Barnes, F.C. 1983) p. 298; Tables 9.3 and 9.4 from J.L. Kobrick and B.J. Fine, Climate and human performance, in, *The Physical Environment and Work* John Wiley (Oborne, D.J. and Gruneberg, M.M. (eds.) 1983) reproduced with permission of Wiley in the format Book via Copyright Clearance Center; Table 15.1 adapted from *What is the Theory of Constraints, and How Does it Compare to Lean Thinking?* The Lean Enterprise Institute (Rattner, S. 2009) Copyright © 1999 Sergio Rattner. All rights reserved.

Text

Case Study on pages 346–49 adapted from *Operations and Process Management*, 3rd ed., Pearson Education (Slack, N., Brandon-Jones, A., Johnston, R. and Betts, A. 2012) © Pearson Education Limited 2006, 2009, 2012; Box on page 470 adapted from My way - IT at Butcher's Pet Care, *Engineering and Technology Magazine*, Vol. 4 (13) (Allan K.); Box on pages 499–500 written and supplied by Janina Aarts and Mattia Bianchi, Department of Management and Organization, Stockholm School of

Economics, reproduced with permission; Box on page 534 adapted from Case study by Professors Rui Sousa and Sofia Salgado Pinto, Católica Porto Business School, Portugal; Case Study on pages 568-69 from Professors Robert Johnson, Warwick Business School, Chai Kah Hin and Jochen Wirtz, National University of Singapore, and Christopher Lovelock, Yale University.

Photos

The publisher would like to thank the following for their kind permission to reproduce their photographs:

(Key: b-bottom; c-centre; l-left; r-right; t-top)

123RF.com: Andrew Mayovskyy 628br, Igor Zakharevich 634; **Alamy Images:** 360b 539cr, AF Archive 501tr, Agencja Fotograficzna Caro 218tr, Arcaid Images 663tr, Asif's Photography 218br, Roger Bamber 352tr, David Burton 584br, Chih-Chung Johnny Chang 132tr, Clivestock 188cr, Cultura Creative 60br, David J. Green 457br, Karin Hildebrand Lau 180c, 314c, Matthew Horwood 89b, Bstar Images 25tr, Justin Kase 401tr, Lucia Lanpur 258cr, Mediablitzimages 136tr, Trevor Mogg 83b, Numb 479cr, Helen Sessions 419tr, Adrian Sherratt 9bl, Tetra Images 29b, Mikhail Tolstoy 33t, Peter Treanor 582tr, Urbanmyth 184tr, Mark Waugh 586tr, Julie Woodhouse 51tr, Andrew Woodley 71tr, Zoonar GmbH 512; **Alistair Brandon-Jones:** 370tr, 470tr; **Andy Maluche/Photographers Direct:** 252tr; **Bridgeman Art Library Ltd:** Look and Learn 648br; **Corbis:** Nur Photo / Zakir Hossain Chowdury 405, Monty Rakusen 510br, Michael Spooneybarger 639tr; **Courtesy of Cadbury plc:** 227; **Digital Vision:** 443tr; **Fotolia.com:** Maridav 159br, Tan Kian Khoon 100cr; **Getty Images:** AFP / Lee Celano 12c, AFP / Roberto Schmidt 54br, AFP / Romeo Gacad 9bc, Bloomberg / Chris Ratcliffe 18c, Bloomberg / Jason Alden 59tr, Bloomberg / Junko Kimura-Matsumoto 326tr, Bloomberg / Philipp Schmidli 45br, Caiaimage / Robert Daly 525tr, Look / Hendrik Holler 371tr, Ian McNichol 621, Tetra Images 180b, 314b, 530c, 530b, Ron Vesely 372cr, Paul Zimmerman 499br; **Imagemore**

Co., Ltd: 465tr; **Reproduced with the kind permission of Société des Produits Nestlé S.A.:** 229tr; **Newlife Paints Ltd:** 129tr; **PhotoDisc:** 433tr, 484br; **Press Association Images:** AP / Eckehard Schulz 272tr; **Rex Shutterstock:** Amer Ghazzal 53tr; **Sands Films Studio:** 193cr; **Shutterstock.com:** Haider Y. Abdulla 346tr, Alphaspirit 287, 514br, Aaron Amat 676tc, Andresr 575br, Anyunov 644tl, ArchMan 196br, Anna Baburkina 617tr, Blend Images 232br, Anna Bogush 441tr, Buruhthan 50br, 51br, 54cr, 56cr, 58br, Vladimir Caplinskij 166tr, Roberto Caucino 43br, Chen WS 487tr, Ant Clausen 190tl, Creations 505tr, Digital Storm 250tr, T P Feller 5r, Iakov Filimonov 234tr, Gabriel12 186br, Karel Gallas 384tr, Angelo Giampiccolo 322tr, Arina P Habich 436tr, Hadrian 50tl, 51cl, 54tl, 56tl, 58cl, Indianstockimages 9c, Stuart Jenner 9cl, 551br, Jezper 357tr, JHDT Productions 296tr, Jimmi 248tr, Justasc 416tr, Matej Kastelic 97c, Robert Kneschke 590cr, Ktsdesign 115c, Blaz Kure 50tr, 51cr, 54tr, 56tr, 58cr, Lamarinx 190bl, Lightspring 150, Liunian 191bl, Dmitry Lobanov 56, Luchunyu 192bl, Ludinko 451br, SV Luma 333tr, Robyn Mackenzie 537tr, Marques 278, Michaeljung 192c, Stuart Monk 224br, Monkey Business Images 163tr, 478tr, Natursports 564br, 650tr, Sergey Nivens 40tr, Nucleartist 156tr, Ollyy 201tr, 298tr, Pathdoc 267br, Sean Pavone 425tr, Phovoir 212tr, Potstock 192cl, Raimundas 142tr, Rido 111tr, Michael Rolands 50bl, 51bl, 54cl, 56cl, 58bc, Shadow216 647, StockLite 146cr, Stockphoto mania 151tr, Stokkete 534tr, Supergenijalac 9tl, 191cl, Jordan Tan 318br, Graham Taylor 241tr, Cappi Thompson 403br, Anatoly Tiplyashin 104br, Toria 11tr, TravnikovStudio 330br, VectorLifestylepic 568tr, Vipubadee 578tr, Valentyn Volkov 122tr, 543, Tatyana Vyc 191tl, Ingrid W 221tr, Wavebreakmedia 302cr, www.BillionPhotos.com 575tr, Yeko Photo Studio 337cr, Zurijeta 293br; **Ski Verbier Exclusive Ltd:** 25br; **The Kobal Collection:** Paramount Pictures 269cr

Cover images: *Front:* **Alamy Images:** Karin Hildebrand Lau c; **Getty Images:** Tetra Images

All other images © Pearson Education

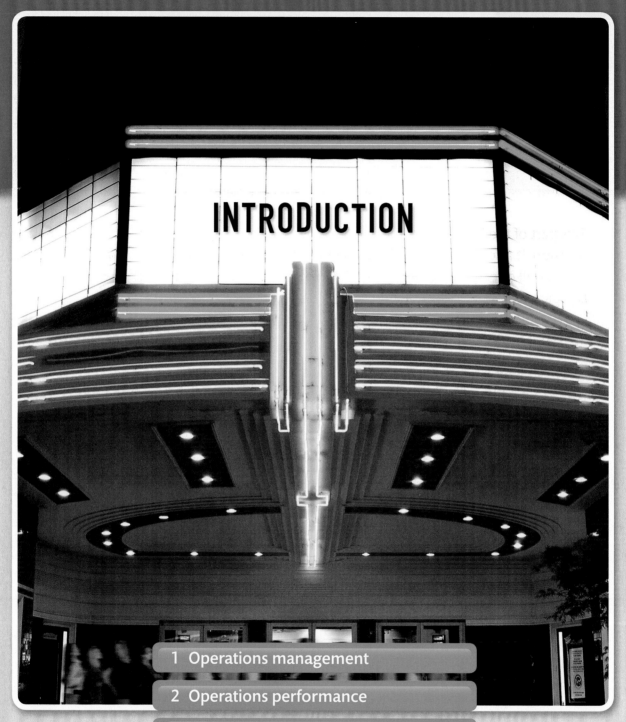

INTRODUCTION

Part One
DIRECTING THE OPERATION

This part of the book introduces the idea of 'operations' and the operations function. It also examines the fundamental activities and decisions that shape the overall direction and strategy of the operations function. The chapters in this part are:

- Chapter 1 Operations management – This introduces the common ideas that describe the nature and role of operations and processes in all types of organization.
- Chapter 2 Operations performance – This identifies how the performance of the operations function can be judged.
- Chapter 3 Operations strategy – This examines how the activities of the operations function can have an important strategic impact.
- Chapter 4 Product and service innovation – This looks at how innovation can be built into the product and service design process.
- Chapter 5 The structure and scope of operations – This describes the major decisions that determine how and the extent to which an operation adds value through its own activities.

1

Operations management

Key questions

> What is operations management?

> Why is operations management important in *all* types of organization?

> What is the input–transformation–output process?

> What is the process hierarchy?

> How do operations and processes differ?

> What do operations managers do?

INTRODUCTION

Operations management is about how organizations create and deliver services and products. Everything you wear, eat, sit on, use, read or knock about on the sports field comes to you courtesy of the operations managers who organized its creation and delivery. Every book you borrow from the library, every treatment you receive at the hospital, every service you expect in the shops and every lecture you attend at university – all have been created by operations. While the people who supervised their creation and delivery may not always be called operations managers, that is what they really are. And that is what this book is concerned with – the tasks, issues and decisions of those operations managers who have made the services and products on which we all depend. This is an introductory chapter, so we will examine what we mean by 'operations management', how operations processes can be found everywhere, how they are all similar yet different, and what it is that operations managers do (see Fig. 1.1).

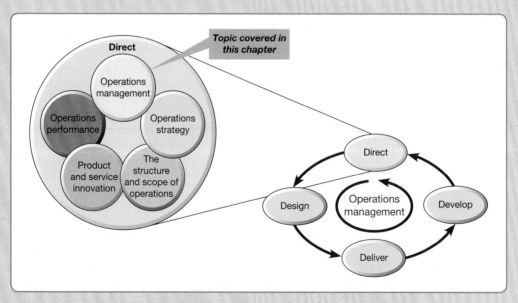

Figure 1.1 This chapter examines operations management

WHAT IS OPERATIONS MANAGEMENT?

Operations management is the activity of managing the resources that create and deliver services and products. The operations function is the part of the organization that is responsible for this activity. Every organization has an operations function because every organization creates some types of services and/or products. However, not all types of organization will necessarily call the operations function by this name. (Note in addition that we also use the shorter terms 'the operation' or 'operations' interchangeably with the 'operations function'.) Operations managers are the people who have particular responsibility for managing some, or all, of the resources that make up the operations function. Again in some organizations, the operations manager could be called by some other name. For example, he or she might be called the 'fleet manager' in a distribution company, the 'administrative manager' in a hospital, or the 'store manager' in a supermarket.

necessarily

> ✳ **Operations principle**
>
> All organizations have 'operations' that produce some mix of services and products.

OPERATIONS IN PRACTICE	Lego: building a creative experience[1]

'We want any child playing with LEGO® bricks to have a high quality play experience, and in addition we also want to make a positive impact through the way we operate – from our focus on business ethics to reducing our impact on the environment,' says Jørgen Vig Knudstorp, CEO of the LEGO Group.

Of all businesses, the toy business is one of the world's trickiest. Difficult to forecast, unfailingly subject to fickle kids' latest fads and subject to constant technological innovation. Yet The LEGO Group, a privately held, family-owned company with headquarters in Billund, Denmark, has, in recent years, thrived in the business, becoming one of the most reputable companies in the world, according to the Reputation Institute, and one of the leading manufacturers of play materials. It is a success founded on a deceptively simple idea. One LEGO brick is unremarkable, but put one or two together and possibilities start to emerge. With another few bricks the number of things you can create rises exponentially. For example, there are more than 915 million possible ways of arranging six standard four-by-two bricks, and with the approximately 4,200 different elements in the LEGO range and 58 different colours together with various decorations, the total number of active combinations is many more. And, however many bricks you assemble, irrespective of what colour or set they are from, your pieces will always fit together perfectly. All of the basic LEGO elements use the same method to stick together. They have studs on top that are slightly bigger than and tubes on the inside. Pressing the bricks together produces an 'interference fit' that provides a temporary joint without the use of an additional fastener. But this

Source: Shutterstock.com: T P Feller

principle does depend on the elements being made to very high levels of precision and quality, which explains the company's motto, 'Only the best is good enough'.

Ole Kirk Kristiansen, a Danish carpenter, who started selling wooden toys as a way of earning extra money, founded the company in 1932. These included wooden toy bricks, the forerunners of the plastic bricks, which are now so successful that it is estimated that there are now 86 bits of LEGO for every person on the planet. Bricks, and other LEGO 'elements', are manufactured at the group's factories in Denmark, Hungary, The Czech Republic and Mexico, locations that have been chosen to be near their key markets in Europe and the USA. These sites have been expanded to cope with increased demand, together with new factories built in Nyiregyhaza in Hungary and Jiaxing in China. Products made in these factories serve a global market. The aim, according to Bali Padda, Executive Vice President and

Chief Operations Officer of the LEGO Group, is to *'build a stable manufacturing base around the world, ultimately making sure that LEGO products are available to children and their parents when and where they want them'.* And it is the company's operations processes that are central to maintaining its reputation for quality, and its ability to produce millions of elements profitably and sustainably.

The process starts at the main warehouse that contains the silos holding raw plastic granulates. At the Billund operation, 60 tonnes of plastic is processed every 24 hours. The silos are linked to the moulding machines by a complex arrangement of tubes. The moulding stage is particularly important, because every LEGO piece must be made to a demanding level of precision, with tolerances as small as 10 micrometres. At each machine, the plastic is heated and pumped into the mould through a main channel, which divides into a number of narrower channels, each corresponding to a single brick. Water is used to cool the moulds, which can produce up to 32 bricks, and, when the plastic has solidified (only a couple of seconds), they release the bricks into containers. These moulds are expensive, and each element requires its own mould. The average cost of a mould is around €80,000 with some costing more than €360,000. A sensor detects when a container is full and a robot trolley is automatically sent. The robots travel between the machines, picking up boxes and leaving empty ones so production can be continued. The automation means that few people are required for the process. The robots transport the boxes to conveyors, which move them into the storage area where robotic cranes stack them until they are needed. From there some pieces go to the 'decoration' stage where they are individually painted. Decoration is the most expensive part of the LEGO process. Other pieces go straight to packing, where the LEGO sets take their final form. In the packaging process the pieces go into a machine that separates them individually, counts them using optical sensors, and places them in their box. The automatic movement system knows exactly how much a box should weigh at any stage and as the packing process continues, high-precision scales monitor the weight of the box. Any deviation, even of a few micrograms, sets off an alarm. At the end of the process the boxes are sealed shut, automatically weighed to ensure there are no missing components, checked by a worker trained to look for things like plastic bags sticking out of the box, packed by a robot six to a case, and finally sent off for distribution.

Quality assurance staff perform frequent inspections and tests on the various LEGO elements, such as drop, torque, tension, compression, bite and impact tests to make sure the toys are robust and safe. Only about 18 of every million LEGO elements produced, (that is 0.00002 per cent) fail to pass the tests. In addition, throughout the process, the company tries to achieve high levels of environmental sustainability. Plastic is extensively recycled in the factory. All scrap, for example the plastic that fills the channels that take the hot plastic into moulds, or faulty pieces that escape from automated handling, are ground up and used back into the production process. Similarly, the transparent plastic that is used to clean the channels when the production colour is changed in a moulding machine are also ground up and sold to other companies that produce other plastic products.

The LEGO example illustrates how important the operations function is for any company whose reputation depends on producing safe, high-quality, sustainable and profitable products or services. Its operations, like its market, are globally located, it is meticulous about ensuring that its processes operate to precise quality standards, and it has invested heavily in process technology that reduces the environmental impact of its operations and the cost of its products. Of course, exactly what is involved in producing products and services will depend to some extent on the type of organization of which the operations function is a part. Table 1.1 shows some of the activities of the operations function for various types of organization.

Operations in the organization

The operations function is central to the organization because it creates and delivers services and products, which is its reason for existing. The operations function is one of the three core functions of any organization. These are:

Table 1.1 Some activities of the operations function in various organizations

Internet service provider	Fast food chain	International aid charity	Furniture manufacturer
Maintain and update hardware	Locate potential sites for restaurants	Provide aid and development projects for recipients	Procure appropriate raw materials and components
Update software and content	Provide processes and equipment to produce burgers etc.	Provide fast emergency response when needed	Make sub-assemblies
Respond to customer queries	Maintain service quality	Procure and store emergency supplies	Assemble finished products
Implement new services	Develop, install and maintain equipment	Be sensitive to local cultural norms	Deliver products to customers
Ensure security of customer data	Reduce impact on local area, and packaging waste		Reduce environmental impact of products and processes

- the marketing (including sales) function – which is responsible for communicating the organization's services and products to its markets in order to generate customer requests;
- the product/service development function – which is responsible for coming up with new and modified services and products in order to generate future customer requests;
- the operations function – which is responsible for the creation and delivery of services and products based on customer requests.

In addition, there are the support functions which enable the core functions to operate effectively. These include, for example, the accounting and finance function, the technical function, the human resources function and the information systems function. Remember that different organizations will call their various functions by different names and will have a different set of support functions. Almost all organizations, however, will have the three core functions, because all organizations have a fundamental need to sell their products and services, meet customer requests for services and products, and come up with new services and products to satisfy customers in the future.

> **✳ Operations principle**
> Operations managers need to co-operate with other functions to ensure effective organizational performance.

In practice, there is not always a clear division between the three core functions or between core and support functions. This leads to some confusion over where the boundaries of the operations function should be drawn. In this book we use a relatively broad definition of operations. We treat much of the product/service development, technical and information systems activities and some of the human resources, marketing, and accounting and finance activities as coming within the sphere of operations management. We view the operations function as comprising all the activities necessary for the day-to-day fulfilment of customer requests within the constraints of environmental and social sustainability. This includes sourcing services and products from suppliers and delivering services and products to customers.

It is fundamental to modern management that functional boundaries should not hinder efficient internal processes. Figure 1.2 illustrates some of the relationships between operations and other functions in terms of the flow of information between them. Although it is not comprehensive, it gives an idea of the nature of each relationship. However, note that the support functions have a different relationship with operations than the other core functions. Operations management's responsibility to support functions is primarily to make sure that they understand operations' needs and help them to satisfy these needs. The relationship with the other two core functions is more equal – less of '*this is what we want*' and more '*this is what we can do currently – how do we reconcile this with broader business needs?*'

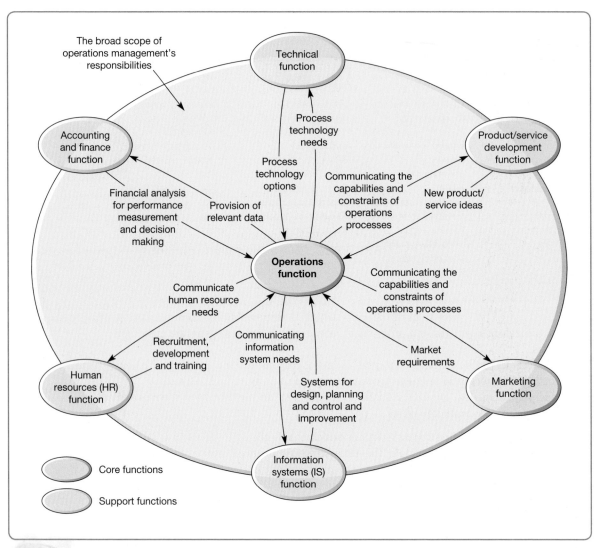

Figure 1.2 The relationship between the operations function and other core and support functions of the organization

WHY IS OPERATIONS MANAGEMENT IMPORTANT IN *ALL* TYPES OF ORGANIZATION?

In some types of organization it is relatively easy to visualize the operations function and what it does, even if we have never seen it. For example, most people have seen images of an automobile assembly. But what about an advertising agency? We know vaguely what these agencies do – they create the advertisements that we see in magazines and on television – but what is their operations function? The clue lies in the word 'create'. Any business that creates something must use resources to do so, and so must have an operations activity. Also the automobile plant and the advertising agency do have one important element in common: both have a higher objective – to make a profit from creating and delivering their products or services.

Yet not-for-profit organizations also use their resources to create and deliver services, not to make a profit, but to serve society in some way. Look at the following examples of what operations management does in five very different organizations and some common themes emerge.

Source: Shutterstock.com: Supergenijalac

Automobile assembly factory – *Operations management uses machines to efficiently assemble products that satisfy current customer demands*

Source: Shutterstock.com: Stuart Jenner

Physician (general practitioner) – *Operations management uses knowledge to effectively diagnose conditions in order to treat real and perceived patient concerns*

Source: Shutterstock.com: Indianstockimages

Management consultant – *Operations management uses people to effectively create the services that will address current and potential client needs*

Source: Getty Images: AFP / Romeo Gacad

Disaster relief charity – *Operations management uses ours and our partners' resources to speedily provide the supplies and services that relieve community suffering*

Source: Alamy Images: Adrian Sherratt

Advertising agency – *Operations management uses our staff's knowledge and experience to creatively present ideas that delight clients and address their real needs*

Start with the statement from the 'easy to visualize' automobile plant. Its summary of what operations management does is: '*Operations management uses machines to efficiently assemble products that satisfy current customer demands.*' The statements from the other organizations were similar, but used slightly different language. Operations management used not just machines but also *'knowledge, people, our and our partners' resources',* and *'our staffs' experience and knowledge',* to *'efficiently* (or *effectively,* or *creatively) assemble* (or *produce, change, sell, move, cure, shape, etc.) products* (or *services* or *ideas) that satisfy* (or *match* or *exceed* or *delight) customer* (or *client* or *citizens'* or *society) demands* (or *needs* or *concerns* or *even dreams).'*

So whatever terminology is used there is a common theme and a common purpose to how we can visualize the operations activity in any type of organization – small or large, service or manufacturing, public or private, profit or not-for-profit. Operations management uses *'resources* to *appropriately create outputs* that *fulfil defined market requirements'* (*see* Fig. 1.3). However, although the essential nature and purpose of operations management is the same in any type of organization, there are some special issues to consider, particularly in smaller organizations and those whose purpose is to maximize something other than profit.

Operations management in the smaller organization

Operations management is just as important in small organizations as it is in large ones. Irrespective of their size, all companies need to create and deliver their service and products efficiently and effectively. However, in practice, managing operations in a small or medium-size organization has its own set of problems. Large companies may have the resources to dedicate individuals to specialized tasks but smaller companies often cannot, so people may have to do different jobs as the need arises. Such an informal structure can allow the company to respond quickly as opportunities or problems present themselves. But decision making can also become confused as individuals' roles overlap. Small companies may have exactly the same operations management issues as large ones but they can be more difficult to separate from the mass of other issues in the organization. However, small operations can also have significant advantages; the short case on Torchbox illustrates this.

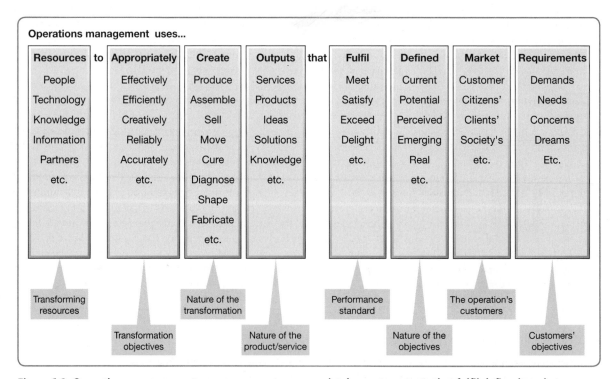

Figure 1.3 Operations management uses resources to appropriately create outputs that fulfil defined market requirements.

We may take it for granted, yet browsing websites, as part of your studies, your job, or your leisure, is an activity that we all do – probably every day, probably many times each day. So it is important. All organizations need to have a web presence if they want to sell products and services, interact with their customers, or promote their cause. And, not surprisingly, there is a whole industry devoted to designing websites so that they have the right type of impact. In fact, taken over the years, web development has been one of the fastest growing industries in the world. But it is also a tough industry. Not every web design company thrives, or even survives beyond a couple of years. To succeed, web designers need technology skills, design capabilities, business awareness and operational professionalism. One that has succeeded is Torchbox, an independently owned web design and development company based in Oxfordshire. Founded back in 2000, it now employs 30 people, providing 'high-quality, cost-effective, and ethical solutions for clients who come primarily, but not exclusively, from the charity, non-governmental organisations and public sectors'.

Co-founder and Technical Director Tom Dyson has been responsible for the technical direction of all major developments. 'There are a number of advantages about being a relatively small operation', he says. 'We can be hugely flexible and agile, in what is still a dynamic market. But at the same time we have the resources and skills to provide a creative and professional service. Any senior manager in a firm of our size cannot afford to be too specialised. All of us here have their own specific responsibilities; however, every one of us shares the overall responsibility for the firm's general development. We can also be clear and focused on what type of work we want to do. Our ethos is important to us. We set out to work with clients who share our commitment to environmental sustainability and responsible, ethical business practice; we take our work, and that of our clients, seriously. If you're an

Source: Shutterstock.com: Toria

arms dealer, you can safely assume that we're not going to be interested.'

Nevertheless, straightforward operational effectiveness is also essential to Torchbox's business. 'We know how to make sure that our projects run not only on time and to budget', says Olly Willans, also a co-founder and the firm's Creative Director, 'but we also like to think that we provide an enjoyable and stimulating experience – both for our customers' development teams and for our staff too. High standards of product and service are important to us: our clients want accessibility, usability, performance and security embedded in their web designs, and of course, they want things delivered on-time and on-budget. We are in a creative industry that depends on fast-moving technologies, but that doesn't mean that we can't also be efficient. We back everything we do with a robust feature-driven development process using a kanban project management methodology which helps us manage our obligations to our clients.'

The 'kanban' approach used by the Torchbox web development teams originated from car manufacturers like Toyota (it is fully explained in Chapter 15). 'Using sound operations management techniques helps us constantly to deliver value to our clients', says Tom Dyson. 'We like to think that our measured and controlled approach to handling and controlling work helps ensure that every hour we work produces an hour's worth of value for our clients and for us.'

Operations management in not-for-profit organizations

Terms such as 'competitive advantage', 'markets' and 'business', which are used in this book, are usually associated with companies in the for-profit sector. Yet operations management is also relevant to organizations whose purpose is not primarily to earn profits. Managing the operations in an animal welfare charity, hospital, research organization or government department is essentially the same as in commercial organizations. Operations have to take the same decisions – how to create and deliver service and products, invest in technology, contract out some of their activities, devise performance measures, improve their operations performance, and so on. However, the strategic objectives of not-for-profit organizations may be more complex and involve a mixture of political, economic, social or environmental objectives. Because of this there may be a greater chance of operations decisions being made under conditions of conflicting objectives. So, for example, it is the operations staff in a children's welfare department who have to face the conflict between the cost of providing extra social workers and the risk of a child not receiving adequate protection. Nevertheless the vast majority of the topics covered in this book have relevance to all types of organization, including non-profit ones, even if the context is different and some terms may have to be adapted.

MSF operations provide medical aid to people in danger[3]

Médecins Sans Frontières (MSF; also called Doctors Without Borders) is an independent humanitarian organization providing medical aid where it is most needed, regardless of race, religion, politics or gender, and raising awareness of the plight of the people it helps in countries around the world. Its core work takes place in crisis situations – armed conflicts, epidemics, famines and natural disasters such as floods and earthquakes. The teams deliver both medical aid (including consultations with a doctor, hospital care, nutritional care, vaccinations, surgery, obstetrics and psychological care) and material aid (including food, shelter, blankets, etc.). Each year, MSF sends around 3,000 doctors, nurses, logisticians, water and sanitation experts, administrators and other professionals to work alongside around 25,000 locally hired staff. It is one of the most admired and effective relief organizations in the world. But no amount of fine intentions can translate into effective action without superior operations management. As MSF says, it must be able to react to any crisis with 'fast response, efficient logistics systems, and efficient project management'.

Source: Getty Images; AFP / Lee Celano

MSF makes every effort to respond quickly and efficiently to crises around the world. Its response procedures are continuously being developed to ensure that it reaches those most in need as quickly as possible. The process has five phases: proposal, assessment, initiation, running the project, and closing. The information that prompts a possible mission can come from governments, the international community, humanitarian organizations such as the United Nations, financial bodies such as the Humanitarian Aid Department of the European Commission (ECHO), or MSF teams already present in the region. Once the information has been checked and validated, MSF sends a team of medical and logistics experts to the crisis area to carry out a quick evaluation. The team assesses the situation, the number of people affected, and the current and future needs, and sends a proposal back to the MSF office. When the proposal is approved, MSF staff start the process of selecting personnel, organizing materials and resources, and securing project funds. Initiating a project involves sending technical equipment and resources to the area. In large crises, aircraft fly in all the necessary materials so that the work can begin immediately. Thanks to its pre-planned processes, specialized kits and the emergency stores, MSF can distribute material and equipment within 48 hours, ready for the response teams to start work as soon as they arrive. Most MSF projects generally run for somewhere between 18 months and three and a half years. Whether an emergency response or a long-term healthcare project, the closing process is roughly similar. Once the critical medical needs have been met (which could be after weeks, months or years depending on the situation), MSF begins to close the project with a gradual withdrawal of staff and equipment. At this stage, the project closes or is passed on to an appropriate organization. MSF will also close a project if risks in the area become too great to ensure staff safety.

Whether it is dealing with urgent emergencies, when material might need to be on an aircraft within 24 hours, or a long-running programme where a steady supply of equipment and drugs is vital, everything MSF does on the ground depends on an efficient logistics system. It is based on the principle that MSF staff should always have exactly the right materials for the job at hand. So MSF has developed and produced pre-packaged disaster kits

ready for transport within hours, including a complete surgical theatre the size of a small conference table and an obstetrics kit the size of a two-drawer file. There is an ongoing process of revising the kits every time a new drug or medical tool becomes available.

To make sure it is reacting as quickly as possible, MSF has four logistical centres based in Europe and East Africa plus stores of emergency materials in Central America and East Asia. These purchase, test and store equipment so that aircraft can be loaded and flown into crisis areas within 24 hours. The pre-packaged disaster kits are custom-cleared within the logistics centres, ready for flight. But not all supplies are needed quickly. If it is not a dire emergency, MSF reduces its costs by shipping the majority of material and drugs by sea. Because of this, it is vital to monitor stock levels and anticipate future needs so that orders can be placed up to three months in advance of expected requirements.

The new operations agenda

Over the last few years, changes in the business environment have had a significant impact on the challenges faced by operations managers. Some of them are in response to changes in the nature of the demand side. Many (although not all) industries have experienced increasing cost-based competition while simultaneously their customers' expectations of quality and variety have increased. Markets have become more global, sometimes meaning a demand for a higher variety, or even totally customized products and services. Rapidly developing (often digital) technologies are leading to more frequent, new product/service introductions. Customers have increased ethical and environmental sensitivity. Also, the impact of new process technologies, in both manufacturing and service, is having a dramatic effect, radically altering the operating practices of almost every industry. This leads to operations having to change the way they create their products and services, serve their customers, relate to stakeholders and involve their workforce. Just as importantly, globalized supply markets are opening new options in how operations source input goods and services. Very few businesses have not at least considered purchasing from outside their own geographic area. But while bringing opportunities for cost savings, a bigger supply market also brings new problems of long supply chains, supply vulnerability and reputational risk. All this has led to new pressures for which the operations function has needed to develop responses. Figure 1.4 identifies just some of the operations responses to these business pressures. (If you do not recognize some of the terms in Figure 1.4, do not worry – we will explain them throughout the book.) These responses form a major part of a *new agenda* for operations. Parts of this agenda are trends which have always existed but have accelerated, such as globalization and increased cost pressures. Part of the agenda involves seeking way to exploit new technologies, most notably the Internet. Of course, the items in Figure 1.4 are not comprehensive, nor are they universal. But very few operations functions will be unaffected by at least some of these issues.

> **✳ Operations principle**
>
> Operations management is at the forefront of coping with, and exploiting, developments in business and technology.

WHAT IS THE INPUT–TRANSFORMATION–OUTPUT PROCESS?

All operations create and deliver service and products by changing *inputs* into *outputs* using an 'input–transformation–output' process. Figure 1.5 shows this general transformation process model that is the basis of all operations. Put simply, operations are processes that take

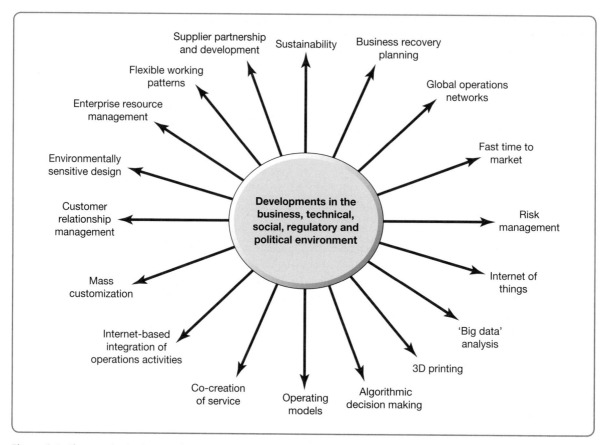

Figure 1.4 Changes in the business environment are shaping a new operations agenda

in a set of input resources which are used to transform something, or are transformed themselves, into outputs of services and products. And although all operations conform to this general input–transformation–output model, they differ in the nature of their specific inputs and outputs. For example, if you stand far enough away from a hospital or a car plant, they might look very similar, but move closer and clear differences do start to emerge. One is a service

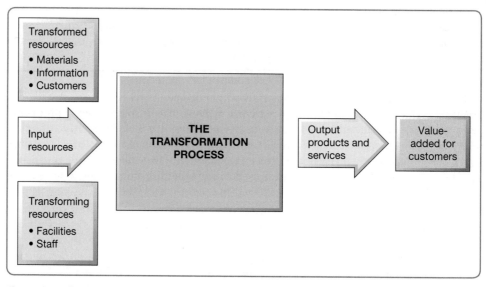

Figure 1.5 All operations are input-transformation-output processes

operation delivering 'services' that change the physiological or psychological condition of patients, the other is a manufacturing operation creating and delivering 'products'. What is inside each operation will also be different. The hospital contains diagnostic, care and therapeutic processes whereas the motor vehicle plant contains metal forming machinery and assembly processes. Perhaps the most important difference between the two operations, however, is the nature of their inputs. The hospital transforms the customers themselves. The patients form part of the input to, and the output from, the operation. The vehicle plant transforms steel, plastic, cloth, tyres and other materials into vehicles.

> **❋ Operations principle**
>
> All processes have inputs of transforming and transformed resources that they use to create products and services.

Inputs to the process

One set of inputs to any operation's processes is transformed resources. These are the resources that are treated, transformed or converted in the process. They are usually a mixture of the following:

- **Materials** – operations which process materials could do so to transform their *physical properties* (shape or composition, for example). Most manufacturing operations are like this. Other operations process materials to change their *location* (parcel delivery companies, for example). Some, like retail operations, do so to change the *possession* of the materials. Finally, some operations *store* materials, such as warehouses.
- **Information** – operations which process information could do so to transform their *informational properties* (that is, the purpose or form of the information); accountants do this. Some change the *possession* of the information, for example market research companies sell information. Some *store* the information, for example archives and libraries. Finally, some operations, such as telecommunication companies, change the *location* of the information.
- **Customers** – operations which process customers might change their *physical properties* in a similar way to materials processors: for example, hairdressers or cosmetic surgeons. Some *store* (or more politely *accommodate*) customers: hotels, for example. Airlines, mass rapid transport systems and bus companies transform the *location* of their customers, while hospitals transform their *physiological state*. Some are concerned with transforming their *psychological state*, for example most entertainment services such as music, theatre, television, radio and theme parks. But customers are not always simple 'passive' items to be processed. They can also play a more active part in many operations and processes. For example, they create the atmosphere in a restaurant; they provide the stimulating environment in learning groups in education; they provide information at check-in desks; and so on. When customers play this role it is usually referred to as 'co-production' because the customer plays a vital part in the provision of the product/service offering.

> **❋ Operations principle**
>
> Transformed resource inputs to a process are materials, information or customers.

Some operations have inputs of materials *and* information *and* customers, but usually one of these is dominant. For example, a bank devotes part of its energies to producing printed statements by processing inputs of material, but no one would claim that a bank is a printer. The bank also is concerned with processing inputs of customers at its branches and contact centres. However, most of the bank's activities are concerned with processing inputs of information about its customers' financial affairs. As customers, we may be unhappy with badly printed statements and we may be unhappy if we are not treated appropriately in the bank. But if the bank makes errors in our financial transactions, we suffer in a far more fundamental way. Table 1.2 gives examples of operations with their dominant transformed resources.

The other set of inputs to any operations process is transforming resources. These are the resources which act upon the transformed resources. There are two types which form the 'building blocks' of all operations:

Table 1.2 Dominant transformed resource inputs of various operations

Predominantly processing inputs of materials	Predominantly processing inputs of information	Predominantly processing inputs of customer
All manufacturing operations	Accountants	Hairdressers
Mining companies	Bank headquarters	Hotels
Retail operations	Market research company	Hospitals
Warehouses	Financial analysts	Mass rapid transports
Postal services	News service	Theatres
Container shipping line	University research unit	Theme parks
Trucking companies	Telecoms company	Dentists

- facilities – the buildings, equipment, plant and process technology of the operation;
- staff – the people who operate, maintain, plan and manage the operation. (Note that we use the term 'staff' to describe all the people in the operation, at any level.)

The exact nature of both facilities and staff will differ between operations. To a five-star hotel, its facilities consist mainly of 'low-tech' buildings, furniture and fittings. To a nuclear-powered aircraft carrier, its facilities are 'high-tech' nuclear generators and sophisticated electronic equipment. Staff will also differ between operations. Most staff employed in a factory assembling domestic refrigerators may not need a very high level of technical skill. In contrast, most staff employed by an accounting company are, hopefully, highly skilled in their own particular 'technical' skill (accounting). Yet although skills vary, all staff can make a contribution. An assembly worker who consistently misassembles refrigerators will dissatisfy customers and increase costs just as surely as an accountant who cannot add up. The balance between facilities and staff also varies. A computer chip manufacturing company, such as Intel, will have significant investment in physical facilities. A single chip fabrication plant can cost in excess of \$5 billion, so operations managers will spend a lot of their time managing their facilities. Conversely, a management consultancy firm depends largely on the quality of its staff. Here operations management is largely concerned with the development and deployment of consultant skills and knowledge.

> **✳ Operations principle**
>
> All processes have transforming resources of facilities (equipment, technology, etc.) and people.

Outputs from the process

Products and services are different. Products are usually tangible things whereas services are activities or processes. A car or a newspaper or a restaurant meal is a product, whereas a service is the activity of the customer using or consuming that product. Some services do not involve products. Consultancy advice or a haircut is a processes (though some products may be supplied in support of the service, such as a report or a hair gel). Also, while most products can be stored, at least for a short time, service only happens when it is consumed or used. So accommodation in an hotel room for example will perish if it is not sold that night, a restaurant table will remain empty unless someone uses it that evening.

Most operations produce both products and services

Some operations create and deliver just services and others just products, but most operations combine both elements. Figure 1.6 shows a number of operations (including some described as examples in this chapter) positioned in a spectrum from 'pure' products to 'pure' service. Crude oil producers are concerned almost exclusively with the product which comes from their oil wells. So are aluminium smelters, but they might also deliver some services such as technical

Figure 1.6 The output from most operations is a mixture of products and services. Some general examples are shown here together with some of the operations featured as 'operations in practice' examples in this chapter

advice. Services in these circumstances are called facilitating services. To an even greater extent, machine tool manufacturers deliver facilitating services such as technical advice and applications engineering. The services delivered by a restaurant are an essential part of what the customer is paying for. It is both a manufacturing operation which creates and delivers meals and a provider of service in the advice, ambience and service of the food. An information systems provider may create software 'products', but primarily it is providing a service to its customers, with facilitating products. Certainly, a management consultancy, although it produces reports and documents, would see itself primarily as a service provider. Finally, pure services solely create and deliver services, a psychotherapy clinic, for example. Of the 'Operations in practice' examples in this chapter, LEGO (or at least the part of the LEGO Group we described in this chapter) produces tangible products, and Pret A Manger both creates and 'serves' its products. It therefore has substantial service content. Médecins Sans Frontières supplies physical aid in emergencies, but also intangible advice and medical help.

> ✳ **Operations principle**
> Most operations produce a mixture of tangible products and intangible services.

Torchbox's customers receive no physical product but are paying for the design and functionality of the website designs. Likewise, hotels such as Formule 1 are close to being pure services, although they both have some tangible elements such as food.

Increasingly the distinction between services and products is difficult to define and not particularly useful. Software has moved from being primarily a product (sold on a disk) to an intangible download when sold over the Internet to an even less tangible rental or subscription service based 'in the cloud'. A restaurant meal is both a product and also a service as it is delivered and consumed. Indeed we would argue that *all* operations are service providers which may create and deliver products as part of the offering to their customers. This is why

> ✳ **Operations principle**
> Whether an operation produces tangible products or intangible services is becoming increasingly irrelevant. In a sense all operations produce service for their customers.

operations management is important to all organizations. Whether they see themselves as manufacturers or service providers is very much a secondary issue.

Customers

Customers may be an input to many operations (see earlier) but they are also the reason for their existence. If there are no customers (whether business customers, users or consumers), there will be no operation. So it is critical that operations managers are aware of customers' needs, both current and potential. This information will determine what the operation has to do and how it has to do it (the operation's strategic performance objectives) which in turn defines the service/product offering to be designed, created and delivered.

OPERATIONS IN PRACTICE

Customer service at Pret A Manger[4]

Pret A Manger is proud of its customer service. *'We'd like to think we react to our customers' feelings (the good, the bad, the ugly) with haste and absolute sincerity'*, it says. *'Pret customers have the right to be heard. Do call or email. Our UK Managing Director is available if you would like to discuss Pret with him. Alternatively, our CEO hasn't got much to do; hassle him!'*

It is a bold approach to customer service, but Pret has always been innovative. Described by the press as having 'revolutionized the concept of sandwich making and eating', Pret A Manger opened its first shop in London and now has over 260 shops in the UK, New York, Hong Kong and Tokyo. It says that its secret is to focus continually on the quality of its food and of its service. Pret avoids the chemicals and preservatives common in most 'fast' food. *'Many food retailers focus on extending the shelf life of their food, but that's of no interest to us. We sell food that can't be beaten for freshness. At the end of the day, we give whatever we haven't sold to charity to help feed those who would otherwise go hungry.'* Pret A Manger shops have their own kitchen where fresh ingredients are delivered every morning, with food prepared throughout the day. The team members serving on the tills at lunchtime will have been making sandwiches in the kitchen that morning. *'We are determined never to forget that our hardworking people make all the difference. They are our heart and soul. When they care, our business is sound. If they cease to care, our business goes down the drain. In a retail sector where high staff turnover is normal, we're pleased to say our people are much more likely to stay around! We work hard at building great teams. We take our reward schemes and career opportunities very seriously. We don't work nights (generally), we wear jeans, we party!'*

Customer feedback is regarded as being particularly important at Pret. Examining customers' comments for improvement ideas is a key part of weekly management meetings, and of the daily team briefs in each shop.

Source: Getty Images: Bloomberg / Chris Ratcliffe

Moreover, staff at Pret are rewarded in cash for being nice to customers. They collect bonuses for delivering outstanding customer service. Every week, each Pret outlet is visited by a secret shopper who scores the shop on such performance measures as speed of service, product availability and cleanliness. In addition the mystery shopper rates the 'engagement level' of the staff; questions include, 'Did servers connect with eye contact, a smile and some polite remarks?' Assessors score out of 50. If the store gets 43 points or more every team member receives an extra payment for every hour worked; and if an individual is mentioned by the mystery shopper for providing outstanding service, he or she gets an extra payment. *'The emphasis on jollity and friendliness has been a winner'*, said James Murphy of the Future Foundation, a management consultant. *'In the highly competitive sandwich market, that's been a big contributor to their success.'* But not everyone agrees with using mystery shoppers. *'It is the equivalent of asking one customer in a shop what they thought at that exact moment, and then planning an entire store-improvement strategy around the one piece of feedback'*, says Jeremy Michael of the Service Management Group, another consultancy.

WHAT IS THE PROCESS HIERARCHY?

So far we have discussed operations management, and the input–transformation–output model, at the level of 'the operation'. For example, we have described 'the web designer', 'the bank', 'the sandwich shop', 'the disaster relief operation', and so on. But look inside any of these operations. One will see that all operations consist of a collection of processes (though these processes may be called 'units' or 'departments') interconnecting with each other to form a network. Each process acts as a smaller version of the whole operation of which they form a part, and transformed resources flow in between them. In fact, within any operation the mechanisms that actually transform inputs into outputs are these processes. A 'process' is an arrangement of resources and activities that transform inputs into outputs that satisfy (internal or external) customer needs. They are the 'building blocks' of all operations, and they form an 'internal network' within an operation. Each process is, at the same time, an internal supplier and an internal customer for other processes. This 'internal customer' concept provides a model to analyse the internal activities of an operation. It is also a useful reminder that, by treating internal customers with the same degree of care as external customers, the effectiveness of the whole operation can be improved. Table 1.3 illustrates how a wide range of operations can be described in this way.

Within each of these processes is another network of individual units of resource such as individual people and individual items of process technology (machines, computers, storage facilities, etc.). Again transformed resources flow between each unit of transforming resource. So any business, or operation, is made up of a network of processes and any process is made up of a network of resources. But also any business or operation can itself be viewed as part of a greater network of businesses or operations. It will have operations that supply it with the services and products it needs and unless it deals directly with the end consumer, it will supply customers who themselves may go on to supply their own customers. Moreover, any operation could have several suppliers, several customers and may be in competition with

> ✳ **Operations principle**
>
> A process perspective can be used at three levels: the level of the operation itself, the level of the supply network and the level of individual processes.

Table 1.3 **Some operations described in terms of their processes**

Operation	Some of the operation's processes
Airline	Passenger check-in assistance, baggage drop, security/seat check, board passengers, fly passengers and freight around the world, flight scheduling, in-flight passenger care, transfer assistance, baggage reclaim, etc.
Department store	Source merchandise, manage inventory, display products, give sales advice, sales, aftercare, complaint handling, delivery service, etc.
Police service	Crime prevention, crime detection, information gathering/collating, victim support, formally charging/detaining suspects, managing custody suites, liaising with court/justice system, etc.
Ice cream manufacturer	Source raw materials, input quality checks, prepare ingredients, assemble products, pack products, fast-freeze products, quality checks, finished goods inventory, etc.

other operations creating similar services or products to itself. This network of operations is called the supply network. In this way the input–transformation–output model can be used at a number of different 'levels of analysis'. Here we have used the idea to analyse businesses at three levels: the process, the operation and the supply network. But one could define many different 'levels of analysis', moving upwards from small to larger processes, right up to the huge supply network that describes a whole industry.

This idea is called the hierarchy of operations and is illustrated for a business that makes television programmes and videos in Figure 1.7. It will have inputs of production, technical and administrative staff, cameras, lighting, sound and recording equipment, and so on. It transforms these into finished programmes, music videos, etc. At a more macro level, the business itself is part of a whole supply network, acquiring services from creative agencies, casting agencies and studios, liaising with promotion agencies, and serving its broadcasting company customers. At a more micro level within this overall operation there are many

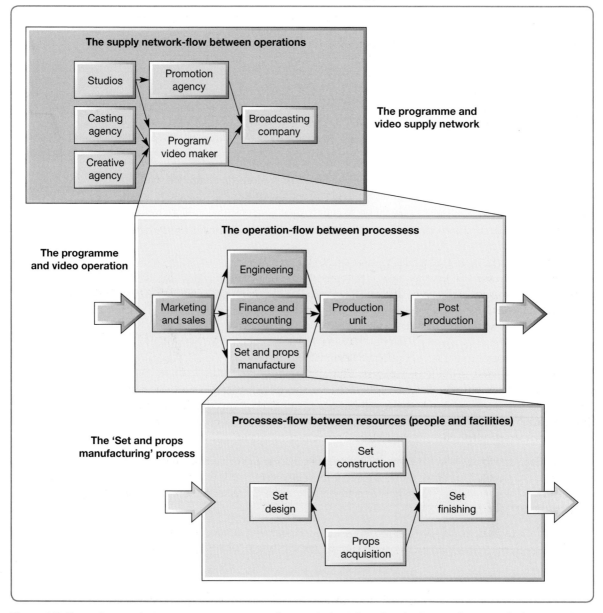

Figure 1.7 Operations and process management requires analysis at three levels: the supply network, the operation and the process

individual processes: workshops manufacturing the sets; marketing processes that liaise with potential customers; maintenance and repair processes that care for, modify and design technical equipment; production units that shoot the programmes and videos; and so on. Each of these individual processes can be represented as a network of yet smaller processes, or even individual units of resource. So, for example, the set manufacturing process could comprise four smaller processes: one that designs the sets, one that constructs them, one that acquires the props, and one that finishes (paints) the set.

Operations management is relevant to all parts of the business

The example in Figure 1.7 demonstrates that it is not just the operations function that manages processes; all functions manage processes. For example, the marketing function will have processes that create demand forecasts, processes that create advertising campaigns and processes that create marketing plans. These processes in the other functions also need managing using similar principles to those within the operations function. Each function will have its 'technical' knowledge. In marketing, this is the expertise in designing and shaping marketing plans; in finance, it is the technical knowledge of financial reporting. Yet each will also have a 'process management' role of producing plans, policies, reports and services. The implications of this are very important. Because all managers have some responsibility for managing processes, they are, to some extent, operations managers. They all should want to give good service to their (often internal) customers, and they all will want to do this efficiently. So, operations management is relevant for all functions, and all managers should have something to learn from the principles, concepts, approaches and techniques of operations management. It also means that we must distinguish between two meanings of 'operations':

> **✳ Operations principle**
>
> All parts of the business manage processes so all parts of the business have an operations role and need to understand operations management principles.

- 'Operations' as a function, meaning the part of the organization which creates and delivers services and products for the organization's external customers.
- 'Operations' as an activity, meaning the management of the processes within any of the organization's functions.

Table 1.4 illustrates just some of the processes that are contained within some of the more common non-operations functions, the outputs from these processes and their 'customers'.

Business processes

Whenever a business attempts to satisfy its customers' needs it will use many processes, both in its operations and in its other functions. Each of these processes will contribute some part to fulfilling customer needs. For example, the television programme and video

Table 1.4 **Some examples of processes in non-operations functions**

Organizational function	Some of its processes	Outputs from its processes	Customer(s) for its outputs
Marketing and sales	Planning process Forecasting process Order taking process	Marketing plans Sales forecasts Confirmed orders	Senior management Sales staff, planners, operations Operations, finance
Finance and accounting	Budgeting process Capital approval processes Invoicing processes	Budgets Capital request evaluations Invoices	Everyone Senior management, requesters External customers
Human resources management	Payroll processes Recruitment processes Training processes	Salary statements New hires Trained employees	Employees All other processes All other processes
Information technology	Systems review process Help desk process System implementation project processes	System evaluation Systems advice Implemented working systems and aftercare	All other processes in the business

> ✳ **Operations principle**
>
> Processes are defined by how the organization chooses to draw process boundaries.

production company, described previously, creates and delivers two types of 'product'. Both of these involve a slightly different mix of processes within the company. The company decides to reorganize its operations so that each product is created from start to finish by a dedicated process that contains all the elements necessary for its production, as in Figure 1.8. So customer needs for each product are entirely fulfilled from within what is called an 'end-to-end' business process. These often cut across conventional organizational boundaries. Reorganizing (or 're-engineering') process boundaries and organizational responsibilities around these business processes is the philosophy behind business process re-engineering (BPR) which is discussed further in Chapter 16.

HOW DO OPERATIONS AND PROCESSES DIFFER?

Although all operations processes are similar in that they all transform inputs, they do differ in a number of ways, four of which, known as the four Vs, are particularly important:

- The volume of their output.
- The variety of their output.
- The variation in the demand for their output.
- The degree of visibility which customers have of the creation of their output.

The volume dimension

Let us take a familiar example. The epitome of high-volume hamburger production is McDonald's, which serves millions of burgers around the world every day. Volume has important implications for the way McDonald's operations are organized. The first thing you notice is the repeatability of the tasks people are doing and the systemization of the work where

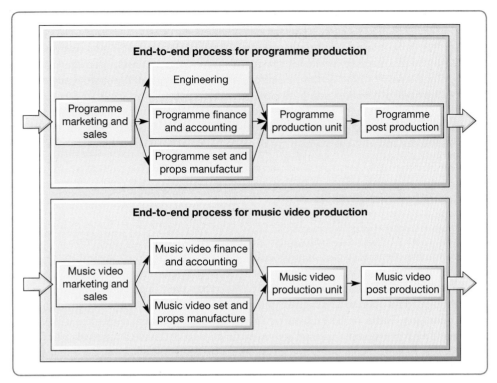

Figure 1.8 The television and video company divided into two 'end-to-end' business processes, one dedicated to creating programmes and the other dedicated to creating music videos

standard procedures are set down specifying how each part of the job should be carried out. Also, because tasks are systematized and repeated, it is worthwhile developing specialized fryers and ovens. All this gives *low unit costs*. Now consider a small local cafeteria serving a few 'short-order' dishes. The range of items on the menu may be similar to the larger operation, but the volume will be far lower, so the repetition will also be far lower and the number of staff will be lower (possibly only one person) and therefore individual staff are likely to perform a wider range of tasks. This may be more rewarding for the staff, but less open to systemization. Also, it is less feasible to invest in specialized equipment. So the cost per burger served is likely to be higher (even if the price is comparable).

The variety dimension

A taxi company offers a relatively high-variety service. It is prepared to pick you up from almost anywhere and drop you off almost anywhere. To offer this variety it must be relatively *flexible*. Drivers must have a good knowledge of the area, and communication between the base and the taxis must be effective. However, the cost per kilometre travelled will be higher for a taxi than for a less customized form of transport such as a bus service. Although both provide the same basic service (transportation), the taxi service has a higher variety of routes and times to offer its customers, while the bus service has a few well-defined routes, with a set schedule. If all goes to schedule, little, if any, flexibility is required from the bus operation. All is standardized and regular, which results in relatively low costs compared with using a taxi for the same journey.

The variation dimension

Consider the demand pattern for a successful summer holiday resort hotel. Not surprisingly, more customers want to stay in summer vacation times than in the middle of winter. At the height of 'the season' the hotel could be full to its capacity. Off-season demand, however, could be a small fraction of its capacity. Such a marked variation in demand means that the operation must change its capacity in some way, for example by hiring extra staff for the summer. The hotel must try to predict the likely level of demand. If it gets this wrong, it could result in too much or too little capacity. Also, recruitment costs, overtime costs and under-utilization of its rooms all have the effect of increasing the hotel's costs operation compared with a hotel of a similar standard with level demand. A hotel which has relatively level demand can plan its activities well in advance. Staff can be scheduled, food can be bought and rooms can be cleaned in a *routine* and *predictable* manner. This results in a high utilization of resources and unit costs which are likely to be lower than those hotels with a highly variable demand pattern.

The visibility dimension

Visibility is a slightly more difficult dimension of operations to envisage. It means how much of the operation's activities its customers experience, or how much the operation is exposed to its customers. Generally, customer-processing operations are more exposed to their customers than material- or information-processing operations. But even customer-processing operations have some choice as to how visible they wish their operations to be. For example, a retailer could operate as a high-visibility 'bricks and mortar', or a lower visibility web-based, operation. In the 'bricks and mortar', high-visibility operation, customers will directly experience most of its 'value-adding' activities. Customers will have a relatively *short waiting tolerance*, and may walk out if not served in a reasonable time. Customers' perceptions, rather than objective criteria, will also be important. If they perceive that a member of the operation's staff is discourteous to them, they are likely to be dissatisfied (even if the staff member meant no discourtesy), so high-visibility operations require staff with good customer contact skills. Customers could also request services or products which clearly would not be sold in such a shop, but because the customers are actually in the operation they can ask what they like! This is called high received variety. This makes it difficult for high-visibility operations to achieve high productivity of resources, so they tend to be relatively high-cost operations. Conversely, a web-based retailer, while not a pure low-contact operation, has far lower visibility. Behind its website, it can be more 'factory-like'. The *time lag* between the order being placed and the items ordered by the customer being retrieved and dispatched does not have to be minutes, as in the shop, but can be hours or even days. This allows the tasks of finding the items, packing and dispatching them to be *standardized* by staff who need few customer contact skills. Also, there can be relatively *high staff utilization*. The web-based organization can also centralize its operation on one (physical) site, whereas the 'bricks and mortar' operation needs many shops close to centres of demand. Therefore, the low-visibility web-based operation will have lower costs than the shop.

> ✳ **Operations principle**
>
> The way in which processes need to be managed is influenced by volume, variety, variation and visibility.

Mixed high- and low-visibility processes

Some operations have both high- and low-visibility processes within the same operation. In an airport, for example, some activities are totally 'visible' to its customers such as information desks answering people's queries. These staff operate in what is termed a front-office environment. Other parts of the airport have little, if any, customer 'visibility', such as the baggage handlers. These rarely seen staff perform the vital but low-contact tasks, in the back-office part of the operation.

The implications of the four Vs of operations processes

All four dimensions have implications for the cost of creating and delivering services and products. Put simply, high volume, low variety, low variation and low customer contact all help to keep processing costs down. Conversely, low volume, high variety, high variation and high customer contact generally carry some kind of cost penalty for the operation. This is why

Two very different hospitality operations

Ski Verbier Exclusive

It is the name of the company that gives it away: Ski Verbier Exclusive Ltd is a provider of 'upmarket' ski holidays in the Swiss winter sports resort of Verbier. With 23 years' experience of organizing holidays, Ski Verbier Exclusive looks after luxury properties in the resort that are rented from their owners for letting to Ski Verbier Exclusive's clients. The properties vary in size and the configuration of their rooms, but the flexibility to reconfigure the rooms to cater for the varying requirements of client groups is important. 'We are very careful to cultivate as good a relationship with the owners, as we are with our clients that use our holiday service', says Tom Avery, Joint founder and Director of the company. 'We have built the business on developing these personal relationships, which is why our clients come back to us year after year (40% to 50% of clients are returners). We pride ourselves on the personal service that we give to every one of our clients; from the moment they begin planning their ski holiday, to the journey home. What counts is experience, expertise, obsessive eye for detail and the understated luxury of our chalets combined with our ability to customise client experience.' And client requests can be anything from organizing a special mountain picnic complete with igloos, to providing an ice sculpture of Kermit the Frog for a kids' party. The personal concierge service begins from the moment the client books. The company's specialist staff have all lived and worked in Verbier and take care of all details of the trip well in advance, from organizing airport transfers to booking a private ski instructor, from arranging private jet or helicopter flights to Verbier's local airport, to making lunch reservations in the best mountain restaurants. 'We cater for a small, but discerning market', says Tom. 'Other companies may be bigger, but with us it's our personal service that clients remember.' However, snow does not last all the year round. The company's busiest period is mid-December to mid-April. That is when all the properties that the company manages are full. The rest of the year is not so busy,

Source: Alamy Images: Bstar Images

but the company does offer bespoke summer vacations in some of its properties. These can be either self-catering, or with the full concierge service that clients get in the ski season. 'We adapt to clients' requirements', says Tom. 'That is why the quality of our staff is so important. They have to be good at working with clients, be able to judge the type of relationship that is appropriate, and be committed to providing what makes a great holiday. That's why we put so much effort into recruiting, training and retaining our staff.'

Formule 1

Hotels are high-contact operations – they are staff-intensive and have to cope with a range of customers, each with a variety of needs and expectations. So, how

Source: Alamy Images: Ski Verbier Exclusive Ltd

can a highly successful chain of affordable hotels avoid the crippling costs of high customer contact? Formule 1, a subsidiary of the French Accor group, manages to offer outstanding value by adopting two principles not always associated with hotel operations – standardization and an innovative use of technology. Formule 1 hotels are usually located close to the roads, junctions and cities that make them visible and accessible to prospective customers. The hotels themselves are made from state-of-the-art volumetric prefabrications. The prefabricated units are arranged in various configurations to suit the characteristics of each individual site. All rooms are 9 square metres in area, and are designed to be attractive, functional, comfortable and soundproof. Most important, they are designed to be easy to clean and maintain. All have the same fittings, including a double bed, an additional bunk-type bed, a wash basin, a storage area, a working table with seat, a wardrobe and a television set. The reception of a Formule 1 hotel is staffed only from 6.30 am to 10.00 am and from 5.00 pm to 10.00 pm. Outside these times an automatic machine sells rooms to credit card users, provides access to the hotel, dispenses a security code for the room and even prints a receipt. Technology is also evident in the washrooms. Showers and toilets are automatically cleaned after each use by using nozzles and heating elements to spray the room with a disinfectant solution and dry it before it is used again. To keep things even simpler, Formule 1 hotels do not include a restaurant, as they are usually located near existing ones. However, a continental breakfast is available, usually between 6.30 am and 10.00 am, and of course on a 'self-service' basis!

the volume dimension is drawn with its 'low' end at the left, unlike the other dimensions, to keep all the 'low-cost' implications on the right. To some extent the position of an operation in the four dimensions is determined by the demand of the market it is serving. However, most operations have some discretion in moving themselves on the dimensions. Figure 1.9 summarizes the implications of such positioning.

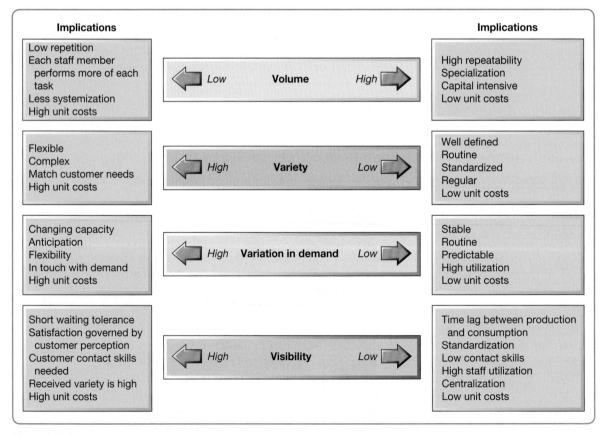

Implications		Implications
Low repetition Each staff member performs more of each task Less systemization High unit costs	**Low Volume High**	High repeatability Specialization Capital intensive Low unit costs
Flexible Complex Match customer needs High unit costs	**High Variety Low**	Well defined Routine Standardized Regular Low unit costs
Changing capacity Anticipation Flexibility In touch with demand High unit costs	**High Variation in demand Low**	Stable Routine Predictable High utilization Low unit costs
Short waiting tolerance Satisfaction governed by customer perception Customer contact skills needed Received variety is high High unit costs	**High Visibility Low**	Time lag between production and consumption Standardization Low contact skills High staff utilization Centralization Low unit costs

Figure 1.9 A typology of operations

Figure 1.10 illustrates the different positions on the dimensions of the Ski Verbier Exclusive operation and the Formule 1 hotel chain (*see* the 'Operations in practice' example above). At the most basic level, both provide the same basic service. They accommodate people. Yet they are very different: Ski Verbier Exclusive provides luxurious and bespoke vacations for a relatively small segment of the ski holiday market. Its variety of services is almost infinite in the sense that customers can make individual requests in terms of food and entertainment. Variation is high with four months of 100 per cent occupancy, followed by a far quieter period. Customer contact, and therefore visibility, are also very high (in order to ascertain customers' requirements and provide for them). All of this is very different from the Formule 1 branded hotels, whose customers usually stay one night, where the variety of services is strictly limited, and business and holiday customers use the hotel at different times, which limits variation. Most notably, though, customer contact is kept to a minimum. Ski Verbier Exclusive has very high levels of service, which means it has relatively high costs. Its prices therefore are not cheap – certainly not as cheap as Formule 1, which has arranged its operation in such a way as to provide a highly standardized service at minimal cost.

Figure 1.10 The four Vs profiles of two very different hospitality operations

WHAT DO OPERATIONS MANAGERS DO?

The exact details of what operations managers do will, to some extent, depend on the way an organization defines the boundaries of the function. Yet there are some general classes of activities that apply to all types of operation irrespective of whether they are service, manufacturing, private or public sector, and no matter how the operations function is defined. We classify operations management activities under the four headings: direct, design, deliver and develop.

- **Directing** the overall strategy of the operation. A general understanding of operations and processes and their strategic purpose and performance, together with an appreciation of how strategic purpose is translated into reality, are prerequisites to the detailed design of operations and process. This is treated in Chapters 1 to 5.
- **Designing** the operation's resources and processes. Design is the activity of determining the physical form, shape and composition of operations and processes in line with the services and products that they create. This is treated in Chapters 6 to 9.

- Planning and control process *delivery*. After being designed, the delivery of services and products from suppliers and through the total operation to customers must be planned and controlled. This is treated in Chapters 10 to 15.
- *Developing* process performance. Increasingly it is recognized that operations managers, or any process managers, cannot simply routinely deliver services and products in the same way that they always have done. They have a responsibility to develop the capabilities of their processes to improve process performance. This is treated in Chapters 16 to 19.

Operations management impacts environmental sustainability

It is worth noting at this point that many of the activities of operations managers have a huge impact on their organization's environmental sustainability. Environmental sustainability means (according to the Brundtland Report from the United Nations) *'meeting the needs of the present without compromising the ability of future generations to meet their own needs'*. Put more directly, it means the extent to which business activity negatively impacts the natural environment. It is clearly an important issue, not only because of the obvious impact on the immediate environment of hazardous waste, air, and even noise, pollution, but also because of the less obvious, but potentially far more damaging, issues around global warming.

It is important to operations managers because the pollution-causing disasters which make the headlines seem to be the result of a whole variety of causes – oil tankers run aground, nuclear waste is misclassified, chemicals leak into a river, or gas clouds drift over industrial towns. But in fact they all have something in common. They were all the result of an operations-based failure. Somehow operations procedures were inadequate. Less dramatic in the short term, but perhaps more important in the long term, is the environmental impact of products which cannot by recycled and processes which consume large amounts of energy. In fact many of operations management's environmental issues are concerned with waste. Operations management decisions in product and service design significantly affect the utilization of materials both in the short term and in long-term recyclability. Process design influences the proportion of energy and labour that is wasted as well as materials wastage. Planning and control may affect materials wastage (packaging being wasted by mistakes in purchasing, for example), but also affects energy and labour wastage. Improvement, of course, is dedicated largely to reducing wastage. Here environmental responsibility and the conventional concerns of operations management coincide. Reducing waste, in all its forms, may be environmentally sound but it also saves cost for the organization.

> ✳ **Operations principle**
>
> Operations management activities will have a significant effect on the sustainability performance of any type of enterprise

The model of operations management

We can now combine two ideas to develop the model of operations and process management that will be used throughout this book. The first is the idea that *operations* and the *processes* that make up both the operations and other business functions are transformation systems that take in inputs and use process resources to transform them into outputs. The second idea is that the resources both in an organization's operations as a whole and in its individual processes need to be managed in terms of how they are *directed*, how they are *designed*, how *delivery* is planned and controlled, and how they are *developed* and improved. Figure 1.11 shows how these two ideas go together. This book will use this model to examine the more important decisions that should be of interest to all managers of operations and processes.

> ✳ **Operations principle**
>
> Operations management activities can be grouped into four broad categories: directing the overall strategy of the operation, designing the operation's products, services and processes, planning and controlling delivery, and developing performance.

36 → 60

HP's recycling activities[5]

HP began recycling hardware as far back as 1987, when it was the only major computer manufacturer to operate its own recycling facility. Since then HP has recovered over 227 billion pounds (1.27 billion kilograms) of products for reuse or recycling. Its recycling programme seeks to reduce the environmental impact of its products, minimizing waste going to landfills by helping customers discard products conveniently in an environmentally sound manner. Recovered materials, after recycling, have been used to make various products, including auto body parts, clothes hangers, plastic toys, fence posts, and roof tiles.

HP has developed a standard for management of hardware at the end of its useful life to ensure the hardware is responsibly recycled or recovered. It also helps other electronics recyclers to work effectively with its products by providing disassembly instructions to them.

More than 75 per cent of its ink cartridges and 24 per cent of LaserJet toner cartridges are manufactured with what is known as 'closed loop' recycled plastic. This indicates that ink cartridges that include recycled plastic will contain 50–70 per cent recycled plastic and LaserJet toner cartridges that include recycled plastic will contain 10–20 per cent recycled plastic. HP sees its recycling service as providing an easy way to recycle. Its specially developed state-of-the-art processes are designed to make sure that computer hardware, empty HP printing supplies and other items are recycled responsibly. The HP recycling programme includes such customer-friendly features as recycling HP inkjet and LaserJet cartridges for free, recycling *any* brand of computer hardware, being able to use its online ordering tool to request recycling services, and recycling HP Large Format and Banner Media for free.

To be a great operations manager you need to...[6]

So, you are considering a career in operations management, and you want to know, 'is it for you?' What skills and personal qualities will you need to make a success of the job as well as enjoying yourself as you progress in the profession? Well, the first thing to recognize is that there are many different roles encompassed within the general category of 'operations management'. Someone who makes a great risk control system designer in an investment bank may not thrive as a site manager in a copper mine. A video game project manager has a different set of day-to-day tasks when compared with a purchasing manager for a hospital. So the first skill you need is to understand the range of operations-related responsibilities that exist in various industries; and there is no better way to do this than by reading this book! However, there are also some generic skills that an effective operations manager must possess. Here are some of them. How many of them do you share?

- *Enjoys getting things done* – Operations management is about doing things. It takes energy and/or commitment to finishing tasks. It means hitting deadlines and not letting down customers, whether they are internal or external.

- *Understands customer needs* – Operations management is about adding value for customers. This means fully understanding what 'value' means for customers. It means 'putting yourself in the customer's place': knowing what it is like to be the customer, and knowing how to ensure that your services or products make the customer's life better

Source: Alamy Images: Tetra Images

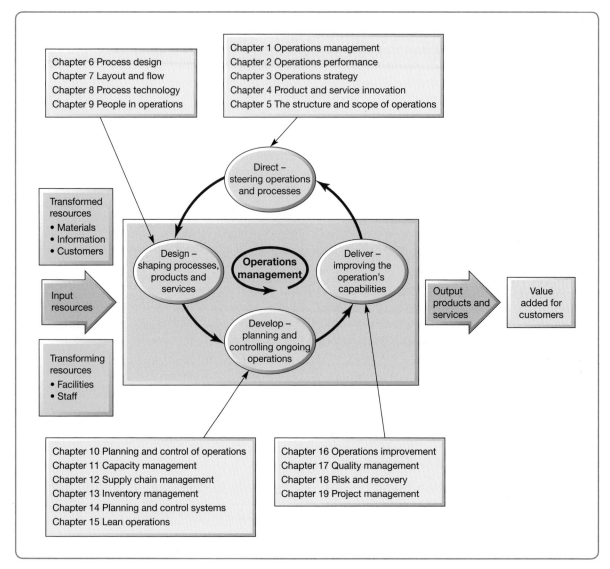

Figure 1.11 **A general model of operations management**

- *Communicates and motivates* – Operations management is about directing resources to produce services or products in an efficient and effective manner. This means articulating what is required and persuading people to do it. Interpersonal skills are vital. Operations managers must be 'people people'.

- *Learns all the time* – Every time an operations manager initiates an action (of any kind) there is an opportunity to learn from the result. Operations management is about learning, because without learning there can be no improvement, and improvement is an imperative for all operations.

- *Committed to innovation* – Operations management is always seeking to do things better. This means creating new ways of doing things, being creative, imaginative, and (sometimes) unconventional.

- *Knows his or her contribution* – Operations management may be the central function in any organization, but it is not the only one. It is important that operations managers know how they can contribute to the effective working of other functions.

- *Capable of analysis* – Operations management is about making decisions. Each decision needs to be evaluated (sometimes with very little time). This involves looking at both the quantitative and the qualitative aspects of the decision. Operations managers do not necessarily have to be mathematical geniuses, but they should not be afraid of numbers!
- *Keeps cool under pressure* – Operations managers often work in pressured situations. They need to be able to remain calm no matter what problems occur.

Critical commentary

The central idea in this introductory chapter is that all organizations have operations processes which create and deliver services and products and all these processes are essentially similar. However, some believe that by even trying to characterize processes in this way (perhaps even by calling them 'processes') one loses or distorts their nature, depersonalizes or takes the 'humanity' out of the way in which we think of the organization. This point is often raised in not-for-profit organizations, especially by 'professional' staff. For example, the head of one European 'Medical Association' (a doctors' trade union) criticized hospital authorities for expecting a *sausage factory service based on productivity targets*. No matter how similar they appear on paper, it is argued, a hospital can never be viewed in the same way as a factory. Even in commercial businesses, professionals, such as creative staff, often express discomfort at their expertise being described as a 'process'.

SUMMARY ANSWERS TO KEY QUESTIONS

❭ What is operations management?

- Operations management is the activity of managing the resources which are devoted to the creation and delivery of service and products. It is one of the core functions of any business, although it may not be called operations management in some industries.
- Operations management is concerned with managing processes. And all processes have internal customers and suppliers. But all management functions also have processes. Therefore, operations management has relevance for all managers.

❭ Why is operations management important in *all* types of organization?

- Operations management uses the organization's resources to create outputs that fulfil defined market requirements. This is *the* fundamental activity of any type of enterprise.
- Operations management is increasingly important because today's business environment requires new thinking from operations managers.

❭ What is the input–transformation–output process?

- All operations can be modelled as input–transformation–output processes. They all have inputs of transforming resources, which are usually divided into 'facilities' and 'staff', and transformed resources, which are some mixture of materials, information and customers.
- Most operations create and deliver a combination of services and products, rather than being a 'pure' service or 'product' product operation.

❭ What is the process hierarchy?

- All operations are part of a larger supply network which, through the individual contributions of each operation, satisfies end customer requirements.
- All operations are made up of processes that form a network of internal customer–supplier relationships within the operation.
- End-to-end business processes that satisfy customer needs often cut across functionally based processes.

❭ How do operations and processes differ?

- Operations and processes differ in terms of the volume of their outputs, the variety of outputs, the variation in demand for their outputs, and the degree of 'visibility' they have.
- High volume, low variety, low variation and low customer 'visibility' are usually associated with low cost.

❭ What do operations managers do?

- Responsibilities can be classed in four categories – direct, design, deliver and develop:
  - Direct includes understanding relevant performance objectives, setting an operations strategy, managing innovation and the scope of the operation.
  - Design includes the design of the operation and its processes and its resources.
  - Delivery includes the planning and controlling of the activities of the operation.
  - Develop includes the improvement of the operation over time.
- Increasingly operations managers have a responsibility for an operations environmental performance.

Design house partnerships at Concept Design Services

'I can't believe how much we have changed in a relatively short time. From being an inward looking manufacturer, we became a customer focused "design and make" operation. Now we are an integrated service provider. Most of our new business comes from the partnerships we have formed with design houses. In effect, we design products jointly with specialist design houses that have a well-known brand, and offer them a complete service of manufacturing and distribution. In many ways we are now a "business-to-business" company rather than a "business-to-consumer" company.' (Jim Thompson, CEO, Concept Design Services (CDS))

CDS had become one of Europe's most profitable homeware businesses. Originally founded in the 1960s, the company had moved from making industrial mouldings, mainly in the aerospace sector, and some cheap 'homeware' items such as buckets and dustpans, sold under the 'Focus' brand name, to making very high-quality (expensive) stylish homewares with a high 'design value'.

The move into 'Concept' products

The move into higher margin homeware had been masterminded by Linda Fleet, CDS's Marketing Director, who had previously worked for a large retail chain of paint and wallpaper retailers.

'Experience in the decorative products industry had taught me the importance of fashion and product development, even in mundane products such as paint. Premium-priced colours and new textures would become popular for one or two years, supported by appropriate promotion and features in lifestyle magazines. The manufacturers and retailers who created and supported these products were dramatically more profitable than those who simply provided standard ranges. Instinctively, I felt that this must also apply to homeware. We decided to develop a whole co-ordinated range of such items, and to open up a new distribution network for them to serve up-market stores, kitchen equipment and specialty retailers. Within a year of launching our first new range of kitchen homeware under the "Concept" brand name, we had over 3000 retail outlets signed up, provided with point-of-sale display facilities. Press coverage generated an enormous interest which was reinforced by the product placement on several TV cookery and "lifestyle" programmes. We soon developed an entirely new market and within two years Concept products were providing over 75 per cent of our revenue and 90 per cent of our profits. The price realization of Concept products is many times higher than for the "Focus" range. To keep ahead we launched new ranges at regular intervals.'

The move to the design house partnerships

'Over the last four years, we have been designing, manufacturing and distributing products for some of the more prestigious design houses. This sort of business is likely to grow, especially in Europe where the design houses appreciate our ability to offer a full service. We can design products in conjunction with their own design staff and offer them a level of manufacturing expertise they can't get elsewhere. More significantly, we can offer a distribution service which is tailored to their needs. From the customer's point of view the distribution arrangements appear to belong to the design house itself. In fact they are based exclusively on our own call centre, warehouse and distribution resources.'

The most successful collaboration was with Villessi, the Italian designers. Generally it was CDS's design expertise which was attractive to 'design house' partners. Not only did CDS employ professionally respected designers, but also it had acquired a reputation for being able to translate difficult technical designs into manufacturable and saleable products. Design house partnerships usually involved relatively long lead times but produced unique products with very high margins, nearly always carrying the design house's brand.

'This type of relationship plays to our strengths. Our design expertise gains us entry to the partnership but we are soon valued equally for our marketing, distribution and manufacturing competence.' (Linda Fleet, Marketing Director)

Manufacturing operations

All manufacturing was carried out in a facility located 20 km from Head Office. Its moulding area housed large injection-moulding machines, most with robotic materials handling capabilities. Products and components passed to the packing hall, where they were assembled and inspected. The newer, more complex products often had to move from moulding to assembly and then back again for further moulding. All products followed the same broad process route but with more products needing several progressive moulding and assembly stages, there was an increase in 'process flow recycling' which was adding complexity. One idea was to devote a separate cell to the newer and more complex products until they had 'bedded in'. This cell could also be used for testing new moulds. However, it would need investment in extra capacity that would not always be fully utilized. After manufacture, products were packed and stored in the adjacent distribution centre.

'When we moved into making the higher margin Concept products, we disposed of most of our older, small injection-moulding machines. Having all larger machines allowed us to use large multi-cavity moulds. This increased productivity by allowing us to produce several products, or components, each machine cycle. It also allowed us to use high quality and complex moulds which, although cumbersome and more difficult to change over, gave a very high quality product. For example, with the same labour we could make three items per minute on the old machines, and 18 items per minute on the modern ones using multi moulds. That's a 600 per cent increase in productivity. We also achieved high dimensional accuracy, excellent surface finish, and extreme consistency of colour. We could do this because of our expertise derived from years making aerospace products. Also, by standardising on single large machines, any mould could fit any machine. This was an ideal situation from a planning perspective, as we were often asked to make small runs of Concept products at short notice.' (Grant Williams, CDS Operations Manager)

Increasing volume and a desire to reduce cost had resulted in CDS subcontracting much of its Focus products to other (usually smaller) moulding companies.

'We would never do it with any complex or Design House partner products, but it should allow us to reduce the cost of making basic products while releasing capacity for higher margin ones. However there have been quite a few "teething problems". Coordinating the production schedules is currently a problem, as is agreeing quality standards. To some extent it's our own fault. We didn't realise that subcontracting was a skill in its own right. And although we have got over some of the problems, we still do not have a satisfactory relationship with all of our subcontractors.' (Grant Williams, CDS Operations Manager)

Planning and distribution services

The distribution services department of the company was regarded as being at the heart of the company's customer service drive. Its purpose was to integrate the efforts of design, manufacturing and sales by planning the flow of products from production, through the distribution centre, to the customer. Sandra White, the Planning Manager, reported to Linda Fleet and was responsible for the scheduling of all manufacturing and distribution, and for maintaining inventory levels for all the warehoused items

'We try to stick to a preferred production sequence for each machine and mould so as to minimise set-up times by starting on a light colour, and progressing through a sequence to the darkest. We can change colours in 15 minutes, but because our moulds are large and technically complex, mould changes can take up to three hours. Good scheduling is important to maintain high plant utilisation. With a higher variety of complex products, batch sizes have reduced and it has brought down average utilisation. Often we can't stick to schedules. Short-term changes are inevitable in a fashion market. Certainly better forecasts would help...but even our own promotions are sometimes organised at such short notice that we often get caught with stockouts. New products in particular are difficult to forecast, especially when they are "fashion" items and/or seasonal. Also, I have to schedule production time for new product mould trials; we normally allow 24 hours for the testing of each new mould received, and this has to be done on production machines. Even if we have urgent orders, the needs of the designers always have priority.' (Sandra White)

Customer orders for Concept and design house partnership products were taken by the company's sales call centre located next to the warehouse. The individual orders would then be dispatched using the company's own fleet of medium and small distribution vehicles for UK orders, but using carriers for the Continental European market. A standard delivery timetable was used and an 'express delivery' service was offered for those customers prepared to pay a small delivery premium. However, a recent study had shown that almost 40 per cent of express deliveries were initiated by the company rather than customers. Typically this would be to fulfil deliveries of orders containing products out of stock at the time of ordering. The express delivery service was not required for Focus products because almost all deliveries were to five large customers. The size of each order was usually very large, with deliveries to customers' own distribution depots. However, although the organization of Focus delivery was relatively straightforward, the consequences of failure were large. Missing a delivery meant upsetting a large customer.

Challenges for CDS

Although the company was financially successful and very well regarded in the homeware industry, there were a number of issues and challenges that it knew it would have to address. The first was the role of the design department and its influence over new product development.

New product development had become particularly important to CDS, especially since it had formed alliances with design houses. This had led to substantial growth in both the size and the influence of the design department, which reported to Linda Fleet.

'Building up and retaining design expertise will be the key to our future. Most of our growth is going to come from the business which will be bought in through the creativity and flair of our designers. Those who can combine creativity with an understanding of our partners' business and design needs can now bring in substantial contracts. The existing business is important of course, but growth will come directly from these people's capabilities.' (Linda Fleet)

But not everyone was so sanguine about the rise of the design department.

'It is undeniable that relationships between the designers and other parts of the company have been under strain recently. I suppose it is, to some extent, inevitable. After all, they really do need the freedom to design as they wish. I can understand it when they get frustrated at some of the constraints which we have to work under in the manufacturing or distribution parts of the business. They also should be able to expect a professional level of service from us. Yet the truth is that they make most of the problems themselves. They sometimes don't seem to understand the consequences or implications of their design decisions or the promises they make to the design houses. More seriously they don't really understand that we could actually help them do their job better if the cooperated a bit more. In fact, I now see some of our design house partners' designers more than I do our own designers. The Villessi designers are always in my factory and we have developed some really good relationships.' (Grant Williams)

The second major issue concerned sales forecasting, and again there were two different views. Grant Williams was convinced that forecasts should be improved.

'Every Friday morning we devise a schedule of production and distribution for the following week. Yet, usually before Tuesday morning, it has had to be significantly changed because of unexpected orders coming in from our customers' weekend sales. This causes tremendous disruption to both manufacturing and distribution operations. If sales could be forecast more accurately we would achieve far high utilization, better customer service, and, I believe, significant cost savings.'

However, Linda Fleet saw things differently.

'Look, I do understand Grant's frustration, but after all, this is a fashion business. By definition it is impossible to forecast accurately. In terms of month-by-month sales volumes we are in fact pretty accurate, but trying to make a forecast for every week end every product is almost impossible to do accurately. Sorry, that's just the nature of the business we're in. In fact, although Grant complains about our lack of forecast accuracy, he always does a great job in responding to unexpected customer demand.'

Jim Thompson, the Managing Director, summed up his view of the current situation.

'Particularly significant has been our alliances with the Italian and German design houses. In effect we are positioning ourselves as a complete service partner to the designers. We have a world-class design capability together with manufacturing, order processing, order-taking and distribution services. These abilities allow us to develop genuinely equal partnerships which integrate us into the whole industry's activities.'

Linda Fleet also saw an increasing role for collaborative arrangements.

'It may be that we are seeing a fundamental change in how we do business within our industry. We have always seen ourselves as primarily a company that satisfies consumer desires through the medium of providing good service to retailers. The new partnership arrangements put us more into the "business to business" sector. I don't have any problem with this in principle, but I'm a little anxious as to how much it gets us into areas of business beyond our core expertise.'

The final issue which was being debated within the company was longer term, and particularly important.

'The two big changes we have made in this company have both happened because we exploited a strength we already had within the company. Moving into Concept products was only possible because we brought our high-tech precision expertise that we had developed in the aerospace sector into the homeware sector where none of our new competitors could match our manufacturing excellence. Then, when we moved into design house partnerships we did so because we had a set of designers who could command respect from the world class design houses with whom we formed partnerships. So what is the next move for us? Do we expand globally? We are strong in Europe but nowhere else in the world. Do we extend our design scope into other markets, such as furniture? If so, that would take us into areas where we have no manufacturing expertise. We are great at plastic injection moulding, but if we tried any other manufacturing processes, we would be no better than, and probably worse than, other firms with more experience. So what's the future for us?' (Jim Thompson, CEO CDS)

QUESTIONS

1 Why is operations management important in CDS?

2 Draw a four Vs profile for the company's products/ services.

3 What would you recommend to the company if it asked you to advise it in improving its operations?

1   Read the 'Operations in practice' case on Pret A Manger. (a) Identify the processes in a typical Pret A Manger shop together with their inputs and outputs. (b) Pret A Manger also supplies business lunches (of sandwiches and other take-away food). What are the implications for how it manages its processes within the shop? (c) What would be the advantages and disadvantages if Pret A Manger introduced 'central kitchens' that made the sandwiches for a number of shops in an area?

2   Compare and contrast Torchbox and Pret A Manger in terms of the way that they need to manage their operations.

3   Visit a hotel (other than Formule 1) and a sandwich or snack shop (other than Pret a Manger). Observe how each operation appears to work: for example, where customers go, how staff interact with them, how big it is, how the operation has chosen to use its space, what variety of products/services it offers, and so on. Think about how these shops are similar to Formule 1 and Pret a Manger, and how they differ.

4   Reread the 'Operations in practice' case on LEGO. LEGO also lends its name to a chain of LEGO-themed amusement parks aimed at younger children and families. Although the LEGO Group has a share in the parks, they are largely owned and operated by a theme park company – Merlin Entertainments. Visit the website for one of these theme parks (or visit an actual site if you want a day out) and compare the LEGO manufacturing operation with the theme park operations using the four Vs.

5   Visit and observe three restaurants. Compare them in terms of the four Vs. Think about the impact of volume, variety, variation and visibility on the day-to-day management of each of the operations and consider how each operation attempts to cope with its volume, variety, variation and visibility.

6   **(Advanced)** Find a copy of a financial newspaper (*Financial Times*, *Wall Street Journal*, *The Economist*, etc.) and identify one company which is described in the paper that day. Using the list of issues identified in Figure 1.4, what do you think would be the *new operations agenda* for this company?

SELECTED FURTHER READING

Anupindi, R. and Chopra, S. (2013) *Managing Business Process Flows*, 3rd edn, Pearson, Harlow.

Takes a 'process' view of operations; it is mathematical but rewarding.

Barnes, D. (2007) *Operations Management: An international perspective*, Cengage Learning, Boston, MA.

A text that is similar in outlook to this one, but with more of a (useful) international perspective.

Brandon-Jones, A. and Slack, N. (2008) *Quantitative Analysis in Operations Management*, Financial Times Prentice Hall, Harlow.

A useful short book covering some of the more advanced quantitative aspects of operations management.

Hall, J.M. and Johnson, M.E. (2009) When should a process be art, not science?, *Harvard Business Review*, March.

One of the few articles that looks at the boundaries of conventional process theory.

Hammer, M. and Stanton, S. (1999) How process enterprises really work, *Harvard Business Review*, **November–December.**

Hammer is one of the gurus of process design. This paper is typical of his approach.

Jacobs, F.R. and Chase, R.B. (2012) *Operations and Supply Chain Management*, **3rd edn, McGraw-Hill/Irwin, New York.**

There are many good general textbooks on operations management. This takes a supply chain perspective, though written very much for an American audience.

Johnston, R., Clark, E. and Shulver M. (2012) *Service Operations Management*, **4th edn, Pearson, Harlow.**

What can we say! A great treatment of service operations from the same stable as this textbook.

Slack, N. and Lewis, M.A. (eds) (2005) *The Blackwell Encyclopedic Dictionary of Operations Management*, **2nd ed, Blackwell Business, Oxford.**

For those who like technical descriptions and definitions.

Operations performance

Key questions

❯ Why is operations performance vital in any organization?

❯ How is operations performance judged at a societal level?

❯ How is operations performance judged at a strategic level?

❯ How is operations performance judged at an operational level?

❯ How can operations performance be measured?

❯ How do operations performance objectives trade off against each other?

INTRODUCTION

Operations are judged by the way they perform. However, there are many ways of judging performance and there are many different individuals and groups doing the judging. Also, performance can be assessed at different levels. So in this chapter we start by describing a very broad approach to assessing operations performance at a societal level that uses the 'triple bottom line' to judge an operation's social, environmental and economic impact. We then look at how operations performance can be judged in terms of how it affects an organization's ability to achieve its overall strategy. The chapter then looks at the more directly operational-level aspects of performance – quality, speed, dependability, flexibility and cost. Finally we examine how performance objectives trade off against each other. On our general model of operations management the topics covered in this chapter are represented by the area marked on Figure 2.1.

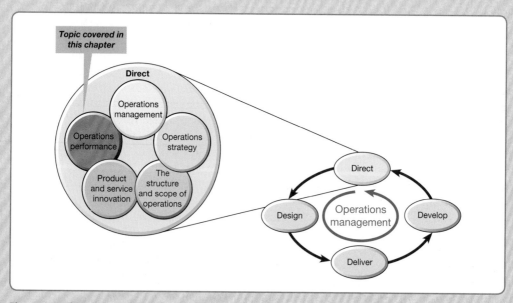

Figure 2.1 This chapter examines operations performance

WHY IS OPERATIONS PERFORMANCE VITAL IN ANY ORGANIZATION?

It is no exaggeration to view operations management as being able either to 'make or break' any business – not just because the operations function is large and, in most businesses, represents the bulk of its assets and the majority of its people, but because the operations function gives the power to compete by providing the ability to respond to customers and by developing the capabilities that will keep it ahead of its competitors in the future. But when things go wrong in operations, the reputational damage can last for years. For example, air travel depends on the smooth and efficient operation of airport terminals, so when Terminal 5 at London's Heathrow Airport first opened and there was chaos on its opening days, it was seen by many as one of the most public failures of basic operations management in the modern history of aviation. The problems included a lack of adequate training in new systems, confusing signage, slow baggage handling and a failure to understand how the terminal's individual processes needed to be integrated. It needed an extra 400 volunteer staff and courier companies to wade through the backlog of late baggage, and 200 flights in and out of the terminal were cancelled in its first three days. Now, the terminal works well and is popular with passengers, but it has taken time to shake off the poor reputation it gained in those first chaotic days.

So, to understand the importance of operations management, one must first understand why things can go wrong in operations and their impact. We will deal with the nature of operations failures in Chapter 18, but the first point to make is that when operations do go wrong it can be very obvious. Look at the various high-profile problems and disasters reported in the news. Very many of them are the direct result of poor operations management. From bank ATM failures that inconvenience an operation's customers, to air crashes that kill them, operations failures are both obvious and serious. Not that all operations failures have to be dramatic. One could argue that simply doing what has always been done is a failure to exploit opportunities to do things better. In this view, what is sometimes known as 'keeping the show on the road' rather than exploring chances for improvement is also a failure. However, do not think that operations management is just about avoiding failure; its contribution to an organization's overall success if far greater than that. Operations management can 'make' the organization in several ways. First, operations management is concerned with doing things better – better quality, better service, better responsiveness, better reliability, better flexibility, better cost, and better use of capital invested in facilities. And it is this focus on 'better', on improvement, that can potentially make operations the driver of improvement for the whole organization. Second, through the continual learning that can come from its improvement activities, operations management can build the 'difficult to imitate' capabilities that can have a significant strategic impact. (We will deal further with this issue in the next chapter on operations strategy.) Third, operations management is very much concerned with 'process', with how things are done. And there is a relationship between process and outcome. Good operations management is the best way to produce good products and services.

Of course, operations managers will always face new challenges, not only when they have major new projects to manage like Terminal 5, but also more generally as their economic, social, political and technological environment changes. Many of these decisions and challenges seem largely economic in nature. What will be the impact on our costs of adding a new product or service feature? Can we generate an acceptable return if we invest in new technology? Other decisions have more of a 'social' aspect. How do we make sure that all our suppliers treat their staff fairly? Yet others have an environmental impact. Are we doing enough to reduce our carbon footprint? What is more, the 'economic' decisions also have an environmental aspect to them. Will a new product feature make end-of-life recycling more difficult? Will the new technology increase pollution? Similarly the 'social' decisions must be made in the context of their economic consequences. Sure, we want suppliers to treat staff well, but we also need to

> ✳ **Operations principle**
>
> Operations management is fundamental to the sustainable success of any organization.

make a profit. And this is the great dilemma. How do operations managers try to be, simultaneously, economically viable while being socially and environmentally responsible? This is why we start our treatment of operations performance at the 'societal' level, looking at the 'triple bottom line'.

OPERATIONS IN PRACTICE   Novozymes[1]

It is not surprising perhaps that a company whose products help other firms to operate more sustainably should itself be keen to stress its own environmental and social performance. This certainly is true for Novozymes, the Denmark-based company, whose worldwide production of enzymes, micro-organisms, and biopharmaceutical ingredients help its customers in the household care, food and beverage, bioenergy, agriculture and pharmaceutical industries to *make more from less, while saving energy and generating less waste*. Novozymes is the world leader in what it terms 'bioinnovation', particularly in the field of enzyme production and application. Enzymes are proteins that, in nature, initiate biochemical reactions in all living organisms. It is enzymes that convert the food in our stomachs to energy and turn the falling leaves in the forest to compost. Novozymes' operations find enzymes in nature and optimize them so that they can replace harsh chemicals, accelerate its customers' production processes and minimize the use of scarce resources. These enzymes are widely used in many industries, including, for example, laundry and dishwashing detergents (where they remove stains and enable low-temperature washing), while other enzymes improve the quality of bread, beer and wine, or increase the nutritional value of animal feed. They are also used in the production of biofuels where they turn starch or cellulose from biomass into sugars that can be fermented to ethanol.

How does Novozymes judge its own performance? It is a commercial company with investors who expect a return on their investment, but the company also strives to balance good business for its customers and its shareholders with the impact it has on environmental and social change. In terms of the conventional financial performance of its operations, the company tracks revenues from its various markets as well as its raw materials costs, productivity improvements, investment in research and development, sales and administrative costs, as well as the effects of such operational factors as the product mix at its processing operations. Of course, Novozymes also monitors how good its operations are at interacting with customers and suppliers.

In terms of its environmental performance, Novozymes has two aspects to monitor. The first is its products and services' impact on its customers' performance. The company conducts peer-reviewed life cycle assessment (LCA)

Source: Shutterstock.com: Sergey Nivens

studies to document the environmental impact of its biosolutions for its customers and advise them on ways to reduce their CO_2 emissions. As regards its own operations, Novozymes attempts to reduce the consumption of natural resources (including water usage) every year and mitigate the negative environmental impact of its production processes. Likewise, the improvement in energy efficiency is driven by continuous process optimizations and the implementation of energy-saving projects at their global production sites. But all production processes produce waste and by-products, so Novozymes seeks continual improvement in the amount of waste and by-products that are sent for landfill or incineration. This has the double effect of reducing the cost of waste treatment as well as minimizing the company's environmental footprint. As a result of these efforts, the Dow Jones Sustainability Index, a global sustainability benchmark, has ranked Novozymes among the top 3 per cent of companies in the chemical industry sector.

The company also track several aspects of its social performance. These include: employee satisfaction and development, diversity and equal opportunities, occupational health and safety, compliance with human rights and labour standards, corporate citizenship efforts and business integrity. Perhaps most impressively, Novozymes sets long-term performance targets in key aspects of its performance that are integrated into incentive schemes throughout the organization. Long-term financial performance is measured conventionally through the rate of sales growth, profitability and the return on invested capital. However, in addition,

Novozymes also has a number of 'impact targets'. Within five years the company says that its aim is to:

- reach 6 billion people, especially in emerging markets, with its products that enhance sustainability;
- educate by providing knowledge of the potential of biology to 1 million people by training in factories, local-community outreach and involvement with universities and business schools;
- catalyse five global partnerships for change through high-impact partnerships with public and private organizations to create answers for a sustainable world;
- deliver 10 transformative innovations that change the lives of many people and fulfil sustainability goals.;
- save the world 100 million tons of CO_2 a year through customers applying its products;
- enable its employees to develop their skills.

Performance at three levels

Looking at the example of how Novozymes monitors and reports its performance demonstrates the point that 'performance' is not a straightforward or simple concept. First, it is multi-faceted in the sense that a single measure can never fully communicate the success, or otherwise, of something as complex as an operation. Several measures will always be needed to convey a realistic overview of the various aspects of performance. Second, performance can be assessed at different levels, from the broad, long-term, societal level of Novozymes' environmental monitoring, for example, to its more operational-level concerns over how it improves day-to-day efficiency, or how it serves its individual customers. In the rest of this chapter we will look at how operations can judge its performance at three levels:

- The broad, societal level, using the idea of the 'triple bottom line'.
- The strategic level of how an operation can contribute to the organization's overall strategy.
- The operational level, using the five operations 'performance objectives'.

These three levels of operations performance are illustrated in Figure 2.2.

HOW IS OPERATIONS PERFORMANCE JUDGED AT A SOCIETAL LEVEL?

No operation exists, or performs, in isolation. The decisions that are made within any operation and the way it goes about its day-to-day activities will affect a whole variety of 'stakeholders'. Stakeholders are the people and groups who have a legitimate interest in the operation's activities. Some stakeholders are internal, for example the operation's employees; others are external, for example customers, society or community groups and a company's shareholders. Some external stakeholders have a direct commercial relationship with the organization, for example suppliers and customers; others do not, for example industry regulators. In not-for-profit operations, these stakeholder groups can overlap. So, voluntary workers in a charity may be employees, shareholders and customers all at once. However, in any kind of organization, it is a responsibility of the operations function to understand the (sometimes conflicting) objectives of its stakeholders and set its objectives accordingly. Figure 2.3 illustrates just some of the stakeholder groups who would have an interest in how an organization's operations function performs. But although each of these groups, to different extents, will be interested in operations performance, they are likely to have very different views of which aspect of performance is important. Nevertheless, if one is to judge operations at a broad societal level, one must judge the impact it has on its stakeholders.

> ✳ **Operations principle**
>
> All operations decisions should reflect the interests of stakeholder groups.

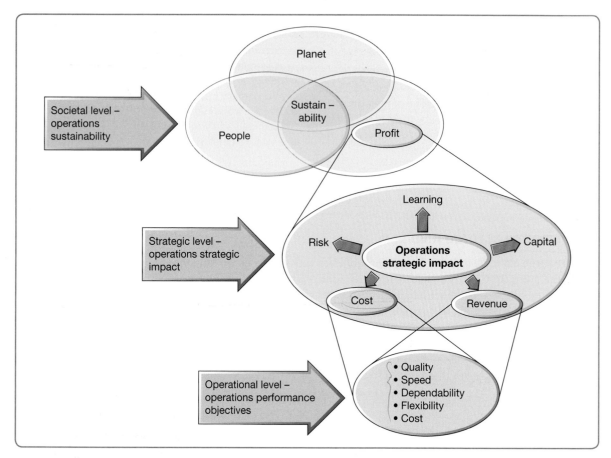

Figure 2.2 Three levels of operations performance

Corporate social responsibility (CSR)

This idea that operations should take into account their impact on a broad mix of stakeholders is often termed 'corporate social responsibility' (generally known as CSR). According to the UK government's definition: '*CSR is essentially about how business takes account of its economic, social and environmental impacts in the way it operates – maximizing the benefits and minimizing the downsides…Specifically, we see CSR as the voluntary actions that business can take, over and above compliance with minimum legal requirements, to address both its own competitive interests and the interests of wider society.*' A more direct link with the stakeholder concept is to be found in the definition used by Marks and Spencer, the UK-based retailer: '*Corporate Social Responsibility…is listening and responding to the needs of a company's stakeholders. This includes the requirements of sustainable development. We believe that building good relationships with employees, suppliers and wider society is the best guarantee of long-term success. This is the backbone of our approach to CSR.*'

The issue of how CSR objectives can be included in operations management's activities is of increasing importance, from both an ethical and a commercial point of view. It is treated several times at various points throughout this book.

The triple bottom line

One common term that tries to capture the idea of a broader approach to assessing an organization's performance is the 'triple bottom line'[2] (TBL, or 3BL), also known as 'people, plant and profit'. Essentially, it is a straightforward idea: simply that organizations should measure

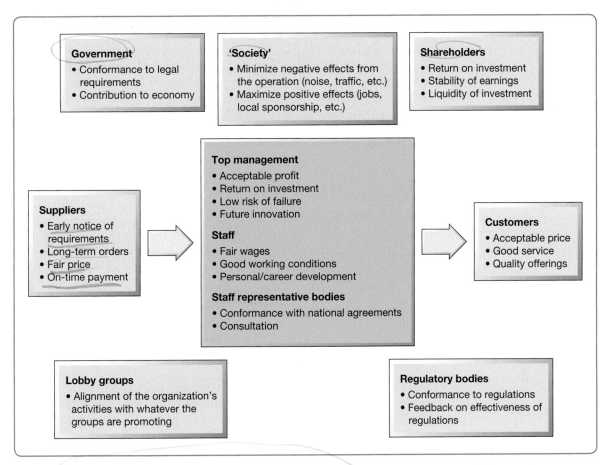

Figure 2.3 Stakeholder groups with typical operations objectives

Patagonia, a B Corp[3]

In most counties it is a principle that is enshrined in law: companies must look after the interests of their owners; in other words, their shareholders. But that is beginning to change. Since 2005 the UK, for example, has allowed people to form 'community interest companies' that have a broader set of objectives. Some argue that conventional 'for-profit firms' come under pressure to discard social goals in favour of increasing profits. Charities and 'non-profit firms' are constrained in their ability to raise capital when they need to grow. Similarly, in 2012 Yvon Chouinard, founder and owner of Patagonia Inc., the outdoor-clothing firm that designs, develops and markets clothing and gear for a wide range of outdoor sports, became the first business person to take advantage of a new law in California that gave businesses greater freedom to follow strategies which they believe benefit society as a whole rather than simply concentrating on maximizing profits. According to Mr Chouinard,

Source: Shutterstock.com: Roberto Caucino

Patagonia is one of the new 'benefit corporations' (usually called 'B Corps'). To meet the criteria as a B Corp, a firm should have a clear and unequivocal social and/or environmental mission, and a legal responsibility to respect the interests of workers, the community and the environment as well as its shareholders. It must also issue independently verified information on its social and environmental impact in addition to its financial results.

Patagonia's Mission Statement goes like this: 'Build the best product, cause no unnecessary harm, and use business to inspire and implement solutions to the environmental crisis.' The company uses environmentally sensitive materials (organic cotton, recycled and recyclable polyester, and hemp among them) and both sponsor and participate in a host of environmental initiatives that range from promoting wildlife corridors to combating genetic engineering. Its employees enjoy good benefits, including generous healthcare, subsidized day care, flexible work schedules and paid time off for environmental internships. Many employees share the company's values, care about quality and are active in environmental and community causes. But, like most clothing companies, Patagonia outsources its production. So how does it ensure that the company's values are also upheld in its supply chain? It is important, it says, to work with suppliers *'that share our values of integrity and environmentalism. In the past, we found we didn't have to make a lot of extra effort to achieve this. Our demand for high quality and our close relationships with the small number of factories we did business with pretty much assured it. It really is true that you can't make good products in a bad factory, and we did business with some of the world's best. They were, for the most part, efficient and well run. The people who worked in them tended to have a lot of experience. Despite high employee turnover elsewhere in the garment industry, these factories were able to retain employees because they paid them fairly and treated them humanely.'* Transparency is also important. In an effort to understand the social and environmental impacts of its supply chain, Patagonia launched its *Footprint Chronicles*, in which it traces the environmental and social impact of products from design through fibre creation to construction to shipment to its warehouse.

themselves not just on the traditional economic profit that they generate for their owners, but also on the impact their operations have on society (broadly, in the sense of communities, and individually, for example in terms of their employees) and the ecological impact on the environment. The influential initiative that has come out of this triple bottom line approach is that of 'sustainability'. A sustainable business is one that creates an acceptable profit for its owners, but minimizes the damage to the environment and enhances the existence of the people with whom it has contact. In other words, it balances economic, environmental and societal interests. This gives the organization its 'licence to operate' in society. The assumption underlying the triple bottom line (which is not universally accepted) is that a sustainable business is more likely to remain successful in the long term than one which focuses on economic goals alone. Only a company that produces a balanced TBL is really accounting for the total cost of running its operations.

> ✳ **Operations principle**
>
> Operations should judge themselves on the triple bottom line principle of people.

The social bottom line (People) – the social account, measured by the impact of the operation on the quality of people's lives

The idea behind the social bottom line performance is not just that there is a connection between businesses and the society in which they operate – that is self-evident. Rather it is that businesses should accept that they bear some responsibility for the impact they have on society and balance the external 'societal' consequences of their actions with the more direct internal consequences, such as profit. At the level of the individual, social bottom line performance means devising jobs and work patterns which allow individuals to contribute their talents without undue stress. At a group level, it means recognizing and dealing honestly with employee representatives. In addition, businesses are also a part of the larger community and, it is argued, should be recognizing their responsibility to local communities by helping to promote their economic and social well-being.

Some ways that operations can impact the social bottom line performance include the following:

- Customer safety from products and services
- Employment impact of an operation's location

- Employment implications of outsourcing
- Repetitive or alienating work
- Staff safety and workplace stress
- Non-exploitation of developing country suppliers.

The environmental bottom line (Planet) – the environmental account, measured by environmental impact of the operation

Environmental sustainability (according to the World Bank) means '*ensuring that the overall productivity of accumulated human and physical capital resulting from development actions more than compensates for the direct or indirect loss or degradation of the environment*'. Put more directly, it is generally taken to mean the extent to which business activity negatively impacts the natural environment. It is clearly an important issue, not only because of the obvious impact on the immediate environment of hazardous waste, air and even noise pollution, but also because of the less obvious, but potentially far more damaging, issues around global warming. Operations managers cannot avoid responsibility for environmental performance. It is often operational failures which are at the root of pollution disasters and operations decisions (such as product design) which impact on longer term environmental issues.

Some ways that operations can impact the environmental bottom line performance include the following:

- Recyclability of materials, energy consumption, waste material generation
- Reducing transport-related energy
- Noise pollution, fume and emission pollution
- Obsolescence and wastage
- Environmental impact of process failures
- Recovery to minimize impact of failures.

OPERATIONS IN PRACTICE

Holcim works with the 'triple bottom line'[4]

Holcim is a global company, based in Switzerland, and employs around 80,000 people, with production sites in around 70 countries. It is one of the world's leading manufacturers and distributors of cement and aggregates (for example, crushed stone, gravel and sand). It also supplies ready-mix concrete and asphalt as well as offering consulting, research, trading, engineering and other services. But, along with other companies in this sector, Holcim faces some considerable challenges in pursuing its sustainability objectives. After all, cement manufacture is an activity that has a significant impact on almost every aspect of sustainability and social responsibility. Concrete is the second most used resource in the world after water. As the chief ingredient in concrete, cement is therefore a key requirement of modern society, but its manufacture is a resource- and energy-intensive process. This possibly explains why Holcim put so much effort into its sustainable development strategies. It aspires, it says, '*to be the world's most respected and attractive company in our industry, creating value for all our stakeholders, by placing sustainable development at the core of our business strategy aims to enhance this value, safeguards our reputation*

Source: Getty Images: Bloomberg / Philipp Schmidli

and contributes to continued success'. Holcim's strategy and its approach to value creation attempts to integrate economic, environmental and social impacts using the 'triple bottom line' approach.

To achieve its triple bottom line business goals, Holcim has established a set of group-wide performance targets. But, before targets are met, the company aims to understand its current performance. Holcim does this by establishing consistent measurement and reporting techniques, as well as implementing management systems to monitor progress toward its goals. Yet CSR-related performance measurement systems should not, says Holcim, be separate from the more conventional business systems. To work effectively, CSR performance systems are integrated into overall business processes and supported by appropriate training.

The economic bottom line (Profit) – the economic account, measured by profitability, return on assets, etc., of the operation

The organization's top management represent the interests of the owners (or trustees, or electorate, etc.) and therefore are the direct custodians of the organization's economic performance. Broadly this means that operations managers must use the operation's resources effectively, and there are many ways of measuring this 'economic bottom line'. Finance specialists have devised various measures (such as return on assets etc.), that are beyond the scope of this book, to do this.

Some ways that operations can impact the financial bottom line performance include the following:

● Cost of producing products and services
● Revenue from the effects of quality, speed, dependability and flexibility
● Effectiveness of investment in operations resources
● Risk and resilience of supply
● Building capabilities for the future.

We will build on these 'economic bottom line' issues in the next section on judging operations performance at a strategic level.

HOW IS OPERATIONS PERFORMANCE JUDGED AT A STRATEGIC LEVEL?

Many (although not all) of the activities of operations managers are operational in nature. That is, they deal with relatively immediate, detailed and local issues. However, it is a central idea in operations management that the type of decisions and activities that operations

Critical commentary

The dilemma with using this wide range of triple bottom line, stakeholders or CSR to judge operations performance is that organizations, particularly commercial companies, have to cope with the conflicting pressures of maximizing profitability on the one hand, with the expectation that they will manage in the interests of (all or part of) society in general with accountability and transparency, on the other. Even if a business wanted to reflect aspects of performance beyond its own immediate interests, how is it to do it? According to Michael Jensen of Harvard Business School, 'At the economy-wide or social level, the issue is this: If we could dictate the criterion or objective function to be maximized by firms (and thus the performance criterion by which corporate executives choose among alternative policy options), what would it be? Or, to put the issue even more simply: How do we want the firms in our economy to measure their own performance? How do we want them to determine what is better versus worse?'[5] He also holds that using stakeholder perspectives gives undue weight to narrow special interests who want to use the organization's resources for their own ends. The stakeholder perspective gives them a spurious legitimacy which 'undermines the foundations of value-seeking behaviour'.

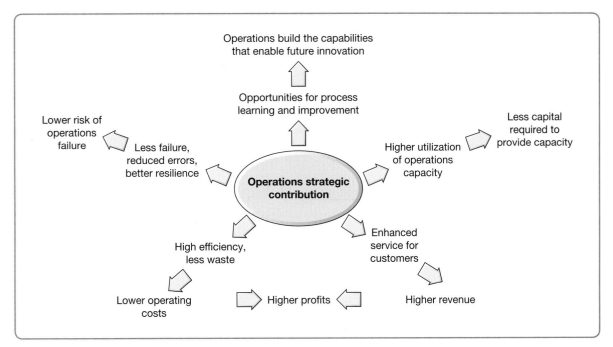

Figure 2.4 **Operations can contribute to financial success through low costs, increasing revenue, lowering risk, making efficient use of capital, and building the capabilities for future innovation**

managers carry out can also have a significant strategic impact. Therefore, if one is assessing the performance of the operations function, it makes sense to ask how it impacts the organization's strategic 'economic' position. We will examine that in more detail the way that operations management can think about the strategic role. But, at a strategic level, there are five aspects of operations performance that we identified as contributing to the 'economic' aspect of the triple bottom line that can have a significant impact, *see* Figure 2.4.

Let us start by looking at how operations affect profit. At a simple (and simplistic) level, profit is the difference between the costs of producing products and services and the revenue the organization secures from its customers in exchange. (In public sector operations an equivalent, although difficult to measure, performance metric could be 'welfare per unit of expenditure'.)

Operations management affects costs

It seems almost too obvious to state, but almost all the activities that operations managers regularly perform (and all the topics that are described in this book) will have an affect on the cost of producing products and services. Clearly the efficiency with which an operation purchases its transformed and transforming resources, and the efficiency with which it converts its transformed resources, will determine the cost of its products and services. And for many operations managers it is *the* most important aspect of how they judge their performance. Indeed, there cannot be many, if any, organizations that are indifferent to their costs.

Operations management affects revenue

Yet cost is not necessarily always the most important strategic objective for operations managers. Their activities also can have a huge effect on revenue. High-quality, error-free products and services, delivered fast and on time, where the operation has the flexibility to adapt to customers' needs, are likely to command a higher price and sell more than those with lower levels of quality, delivery and flexibility. And operations managers are directly responsible for issues such as quality, speed of delivery, dependability and flexibility, as we will discuss later in the chapter.

The main point here is that operations activities can have a significant effect on, and therefore should be judged on, the organization's profitability. Moreover, even relatively small improvements on cost and revenue can have a proportionally even greater effect on profitability. For example, suppose a business has an annual revenue of €1,000,000 and annual costs of €900,000, and therefore a 'profit' of €100,000. Now suppose that, because of the excellence of its operations managers in enhancing quality and delivery, revenue increases by 5 per cent and costs reduce by 5 per cent. Revenue now is €1,050,000 and costs €855,000. So profit is now €195,000. In other words, a 5 per cent change in cost and revenue has improved profitability by 95 per cent. But profit is not the only aspect of strategic performance that is affected by operations activities.

Operations management affects the required level of investment

How an operation manages the transforming resources that are necessary to produce the required type and quantity of its products and services will also have a strategic affect. If, for example, an operation increases its efficiency so that it can produce (say) 10 per cent more output, then it will not need to spend investment (sometimes called capital employed) to produce 10 per cent more output. Producing more output with the same resources (or sometimes producing the same output with fewer resources) affects the required level of investment.

Operations management affects the risk of operational failure

Well-designed and run operations should be less likely to fail. That is, they are more likely to operate at a predictable and acceptable rate without either letting customers down or incurring excess costs. And if they ever do suffer failures, well-run operations should be able to recover faster and with less disruption (this is called resilience).

> **✳ Operations principle**
>
> All operations should be expected to contribute to their business at a strategic level by controlling costs, increasing revenue, making investment more effective, reducing risks, and growing long-term capabilities.

Operations management affects the ability to build the capabilities on which future innovation is based

Operations managers have a unique opportunity to learn from their experience of operating their processes in order to understand more about those processes. This accumulation of process knowledge can build into the skills, knowledge and experience that allow the business to improve over time. But more than that, it can build into what are known as the 'capabilities' that allow the business to innovate in the future. We will examine this idea of operations capabilities in more detail in the next chapter.

HOW IS OPERATIONS PERFORMANCE JUDGED AT AN OPERATIONAL LEVEL?

Assessing performance at a societal level through the idea of the triple bottom line, and judging how well an operation is contributing to its general strategic objectives, are clearly important, particularly in the longer term. Both these levels form the backdrop to all operations decision making. But running operations at an operational day-to-day level requires a more tightly defined set of objectives. These are called operations 'performance objectives'. There are five of them and they apply to all types of operation. Imagine that you are an operations manager in any kind of business – a hospital administrator, for example, or a production manager in an automobile plant. What kinds of things are you likely to want to do in order to satisfy customers and contribute to competitiveness?

- You would want to do things right; that is, you would not want to make mistakes, and would want to satisfy your customers by providing error-free goods and services which are 'fit for their purpose'. This is giving a quality advantage.

- You would want to do things fast, minimizing the time between a customer asking for goods or services and the customer receiving them in full, thus increasing the availability of your goods and services and giving a **speed** advantage.
- You would want to do things on time, so as to keep the delivery promises you have made. If the operation can do this, it is giving a **dependability** advantage.
- You would want to be able to change what you do; that is, being able to vary or adapt the operation's activities to cope with unexpected circumstances or to give customers individual treatment. Being able to change far enough and fast enough to meet customer requirements gives a **flexibility** advantage.
- You would want to do things cheaply; that is, produce goods and services at a cost which enables them to be priced appropriately for the market while still allowing for a return to the organization; or, in a not-for-profit organization, give good value to the taxpayers or whoever is funding the operation. When the organization is managing to do this, it is giving a **cost** advantage.

> **✳ Operations principle**
> Operations performance objectives can be grouped together as quality, speed, dependability, flexibility and cost.

The next part of this chapter examines these five performance objectives in more detail by looking at what they mean for four different operations: a general hospital, an automobile factory, a city bus company and a supermarket chain.

Why is quality important?

Quality is consistent conformance to customers' expectations, in other words 'doing things right', but the things which the operation needs to do right will vary according to the kind of operation. All operations regard quality as a particularly important objective. In some ways quality is the most visible part of what an operation does. Furthermore, it is something that a customer finds relatively easy to judge about the operation. Is the product or service as it is supposed to be? Is it right or is it wrong? There is something fundamental about quality. Because of this, it is clearly a major influence on customer satisfaction or dissatisfaction. A customer perception of high-quality products and services means customer satisfaction and therefore the likelihood that the customer will return. Figure 2.5 illustrates how quality could be judged in four operations.

Quality inside the operation

When quality means consistently producing services and products to specification it not only leads to external customer satisfaction, but makes life easier inside the operation as well.

Quality reduces costs The fewer mistakes made by each process in the operation, the less time will be needed to correct the mistakes and the less confusion and irritation will be spread. For example, if a supermarket's regional warehouse sends the wrong goods to the supermarket, it will mean staff time, and therefore cost, being used to sort out the problem.

Quality increases dependability Increased costs are not the only consequence of poor quality. At the supermarket it could also mean that goods run out on the supermarket shelves with a resulting loss of revenue to the operation and irritation to the external customers. Sorting the problem out could also distract the supermarket management from giving attention to the other parts of the supermarket operation. This in turn could result in further mistakes being made.

> **✳ Operations principle**
> Quality can give the potential for better services and products, and save costs.

So, quality (like the other performance objectives, as we will see) has both an external impact, which influences customer satisfaction, and an internal impact, which leads to stable and efficient processes.

Quality could mean . . .

Hospital

- Patients receive the most appropriate treatment
- Treatment is carried out in the correct manner
- Patients are consulted and kept informed
- Staff are courteous, friendly and helpful

Source: Shutterstock.com: Hadrian

Automobile plant

- All parts are made to specification
- All assembly is to specification
- The product is reliable
- The product is attractive and blemish-free

Source: Shutterstock.com: Blaz Kure

Bus company

- The buses are clean and tidy
- The buses are quiet and fume-free
- The timetable is accurate and user-friendly
- Staff are courteous, friendly and helpful

Source: Shutterstock.com: Michael Rolands

Supermarket

- Goods are in good condition
- The store is clean and tidy
- Décor is appropriate and attractive
- Staff are courteous, friendly and helpful

Source: Shutterstock.com: Buruhthan

Figure 2.5 Quality means different things in different operations

---

Quality at Quality Street[6]

It has been a point of some debate for generations of children (and some adults): *'what is your favourite amongst the Quality Street assortment of chocolates?'* The world-famous brand of assorted chocolates is made in the same area of the UK where John Mackintosh first made this new type of sweet by mixing hard and soft caramel in 1890. But it was John Mackintosh's son who conceived and developed Quality Street in 1936. His idea (novel at the time) was to wrap each individual sweet separately and package them in a tin to preserve their quality. And Nestlé, which has owned the brand since 1988, has maintained this emphasis on quality. In fact, like all Nestlé products, Quality Street is made under the strict quality standards enshrined in the company's quality policy that outlines its commitment to *'build trust by offering products and services that match consumer expectation and preference'*. In other words, Nestlé understands that quality has a profound effect on how its products are viewed by consumers. As a food company (the largest in the world), it is also aware of its responsibility to comply with all food safety and regulatory requirements. *'I don't think most people are aware*

of the amount of work that goes into ensuring that the food they eat is safe', says John O'Brien, Head of the Food Safety and Integrity Research Programme at the Nestlé Research Center in Lausanne, Switzerland. *'It's only when something goes wrong that they sit up and take notice... Consumers rightly expect that the product they buy is safe to eat and contains what it says on the label'*, he said. *'But they also expect fewer preservatives on that label.'* At Quality Street the sweets are free from artificial colours, flavourings and preservatives, and since 2009, the packaging has been completely recyclable. The coloured wrappers are biodegradable and can be composted with garden waste, while the foil wrappers and the tin container can be recycled in the same way as cans. Yet, while consumer perception and particularly safety is of paramount concern at Quality Street, high-quality operations also have an impact on costs. One of Nestlé's quality policy is to *'gain a zero-defect, no-waste attitude by everyone in our company'*. Their 'Quality Management System' is used globally to guarantee compliance with quality standards and to create value for consumers. It is audited and verified by independent certification bodies to prove conformity to internal standards, laws and regulatory requirements. And quality is a priority throughout the whole supply chain. 'Quality by design' is built in during product development and the company's 'Supplier Code' sets minimum standards that it asks its suppliers, employees, agents and subcontractors to respect and to adhere to at all times. In the factory it applies internationally recognized good manufacturing practices (GMP) that cover all aspects of manufacturing, including standard operating procedures, people management and training, equipment maintenance, and handling of materials. Even when the chocolates get to the consumers, the company's worldwide consumer services organization allows them to respond immediately to any consumer enquiry, question or concern.

And the favourite Quality Street? Well several variants have been and gone, including Malt Toffee, Fruits of the Forest Cream, Almond Octagon and Gooseberry Cream. But of the 12 Quality Streets you will find in each tin today, one (admittedly unscientific) study claimed it was the Strawberry Cream.

Why is speed important?

Speed means the elapsed time between customers requesting products or services and their receiving them. Figure 2.6 illustrates what speed means for the four operations. The main benefit to the operation's (external) customers of speedy delivery of goods and services is that the faster they can have the product or service, the more likely they are to buy it, or the more

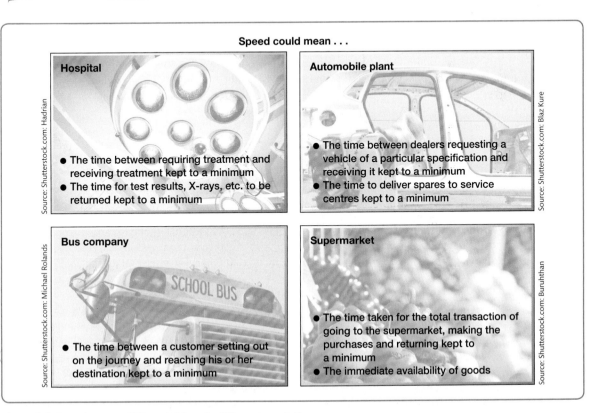

Figure 2.6 **Speed means different things in different operations**

they will pay for it, or the greater the benefit they receive (*see* the 'Operations in practice' case 'In "The Golden Hour" even two minutes counts').

Speed inside the operation

Inside the operation, speed is also important. Fast response to external customers is greatly helped by speedy decision making and speedy movement of materials and information inside the operation. And there are other benefits.

Speed reduces inventories Take, for example, the automobile plant. Steel for the vehicle's door panels is delivered to the press shop, pressed into shape, transported to the painting area, coated for colour and protection, and moved to the assembly line where it is fitted to the automobile. This is a simple three-stage process, but in practice material does not flow smoothly from one stage to the next. First, the steel is delivered as part of a far larger batch containing enough steel to make possibly several hundred products. Eventually it is taken to the press area, pressed into shape, and again waits to be transported to the paint area. It then waits to be painted, only to wait once more until it is transported to the assembly line. Yet again it waits by the trackside until it is eventually fitted to the automobile. The material's journey time is far longer than the time needed to make and fit the product. It actually spends most of its time waiting as stocks (inventories) of parts and products. The longer items take to move through a process, the more time they will be waiting and the higher inventory will be. This is an important idea which will be explored in Chapter 15 on lean operations.

Speed reduces risks Forecasting tomorrow's events is far less of a risk than forecasting next year's. The further ahead companies forecast, the more likely they are to get it wrong. The faster the throughput time of a process, the later forecasting can be left. Consider the automobile plant again. If the total throughput time for the door panel is six weeks, door panels are being processed through their first operation six weeks before they reach their final destination. The quantity of door panels being processed will be determined by the forecasts for demand six weeks ahead. If instead of six weeks, they take only one week to move through the plant, the door panels being processed through their first stage are intended to meet demand only one week ahead. Under these circumstances it is far more likely that the number and type of door panels being processed are the number and type that eventually will be needed.

> ✳ **Operations principle**
>
> Speed can give the potential for faster delivery of services and products, and save costs.

In 'The Golden Hour' even two minutes counts[7]

It is often called 'The Golden Hour'. It is the hour immediately following traumatic injury in which medical treatment to prevent irreversible internal damage and optimize the chance of survival is most effective. 'The Golden Hour' was first described by Dr R. Adams Cowley, at the University of Maryland Medical Center in Baltimore, from his personal experiences in Europe following the Second World War, and then in Baltimore in the 1960s, Dr Cowley recognized that the sooner trauma patients reached definitive care – particularly if they arrived within 60 minutes of being injured – the better their chance of survival. So of all the services that have to respond quickly to demand, few have more need of speed than the emergency services. In responding to road accidents especially, every second is critical. Major trauma is the leading cause of death in those under 45 years of age and is also a major cause of debilitating long-term injuries. Making full use of 'The Golden Hour' means speeding up three elements of the total time to treatment: the time it takes for the emergency services to find out the details of the accident, the time it takes them to travel to the scene of the accident, and the time it takes to get the casualty to appropriate treatment. That is why the London Air Ambulance service was delighted when a new tablet app saved their emergency team two minutes in responding to emergencies. Rather than having to take all the details of an emergency before they rushed to their helicopter, the app together with enhanced mobile communication allows them to set off immediately and receive the details on their tablet when they are in the air. But is getting airborne two minutes sooner really significant? It is, when one considers that, if starved of oxygen, a million brain cells can die every minute. It allows the service's advanced trauma doctors and paramedics to perform procedures to relieve pain, straighten broken limbs, even perform open-chest surgery to restart the heart, often within minutes of injury. Including trauma medics in the team, in effect, brings the hospital to the patient, wherever that may be. When most rescues are only a couple of minutes' flying time back to the hospital, speed can really saves lives. However, it is not always possible to land a helicopter safely at night (because of possible overhead wires and other hazards) so conventional ambulances will always be needed, both to get paramedics quickly to accident victims and to speed them to hospital. The London Air Ambulance service team works alongside the conventional Ambulance Service to provide rapid, effective treatment as soon as

Source: Rex Shutterstock: Amer Ghazzal

possible after injury. One increasingly common method of ensuring that ambulances arrive quickly at the accident site is to position them, not at hospitals, but close to where accidents are likely to occur. Computer analysis of previous accident data helps to select the ambulance's waiting position, and global positioning systems help controllers to mobilize the nearest unit.

Why is dependability important?

Dependability means doing things in time for customers to receive products or services exactly when they are needed, or at least when they were promised. Figure 2.7 illustrates what dependability means in the four operations. Customers might only judge the dependability of an operation after the product or service has been delivered. Initially this may not affect the likelihood that customers will select the service – they have already 'consumed' it. Over time, however, dependability can override all other criteria. No matter how cheap or fast a bus service is, if the service is always late (or unpredictably early) or the buses are always full, then potential passengers will be better off calling a taxi.

Dependability inside the operation

Inside the operation internal customers will judge each other's performance partly by how reliable the other processes are in delivering material or information on time. Operations where internal dependability is high are more effective than those which are not, for a number of reasons.

Dependability saves time Take, for example, the maintenance and repair centre for the city bus company. If the centre runs out of some crucial spare parts, the manager of the centre will need to spend time trying to arrange a special delivery of the required parts, and the resources allocated to service the buses will not be used as productively as they would have been without this disruption. More seriously, the fleet will be short of buses until they can be repaired and the fleet operations manager will have to spend time rescheduling services. So, entirely due to the one failure of dependability of supply, a significant part of the operation's time has been wasted coping with the disruption.

Dependability saves money Ineffective use of time will translate into extra cost. The spare parts might cost more to be delivered at short notice and maintenance staff will expect to be paid even when there is no bus to work on. Nor will the fixed costs of the operation, such as heating and rent, be reduced because the buses are not being serviced. The rescheduling of buses will probably mean that some routes have inappropriately sized buses and some

Dependability could mean . . .

Hospital
- Proportion of appointments which are cancelled kept to a minimum
- Keeping to appointment times
- Test results, X-rays, etc. returned as promised

Source: Shutterstock.com: Hadrian

Automobile plant
- On-time delivery of vehicles to dealers
- On-time delivery of spares to service centres

Source: Shutterstock.com: Blaz Kure

Bus company
- Keeping to the published timetable at all points on the route
- Constant availability of seats for passengers

Source: Shutterstock.com: Michael Rolands

Supermarket
- Predictability of opening hours
- Proportion of goods out of stock kept to a minimum
- Keeping to reasonable queuing times
- Constant availability of parking

Source: Shutterstock.com: Buruhthan

Figure 2.7 Dependability means different things in different operations

OPERATIONS IN PRACTICE   How UPS maintains its dependability[8]

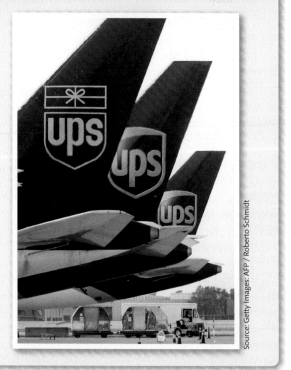

Source: Getty Images: AFP / Roberto Schmidt

What do you do when it is coming up to the biggest gift-giving time of the year, you are responsible for delivery and your aircraft that are vital for dependable delivery are grounded by a freak snowstorm a continent away, or mechanical problems, or an air traffic controllers dispute in France, or whatever? That is the problem facing all global parcel delivery companies; and it is made worse when customers blame you for any non-delivery. Generally freight operators have to absorb the cost when a delivery does not arrive on time, so weather, and other disruptions, directly affect their customer service, reputation and, ultimately, profitability. UPS, the largest express carrier and package delivery company in the world, reckons that each late shipment will cost it between $5 and $30 in revenue. And with almost 16 million packages and documents delivered worldwide every day it only takes a fraction of a percentage point to be late for the total cost of any lack of dependability to be huge.

So what does UPS do to minimize disruption to its delivery network when it is coming up to a peak demand time like Christmas and there is a possibility of bad weather? The obvious thing is to keep a constant watch very carefully on the weather forecast, and indeed UPS does have meteorologists and other staff who do this. But it also builds in a buffer of extra operational capacity. At UPS headquarters a 'hot status board' on the wall identifies cities and regions where the company has spare pilots and aircraft whose task is to 'rescue volume': that is, the spare resources are used to come to the aid of packages stuck somewhere. UPS says that this 'hot spares program' rescues more than 1 million packages annually and saves the company more than $20 million in revenue.

services could have to be cancelled. This will result in empty bus seats (if too large a bus has to be used) or a loss of revenue (if potential passengers are not transported).

Dependability gives stability The disruption caused to operations by a lack of dependability goes beyond time and cost. It affects the 'quality' of the operation's time. If everything in an operation is always perfectly dependable, a level of trust will have built up between the different parts of the operation. There will be no 'surprises' and everything will be predictable. Under such circumstances, each part of the operation can concentrate on improving its own area of responsibility without having its attention continually diverted by a lack of dependable service from the other parts.

> **✳ Operations principle**
>
> Dependability can give the potential for more reliable delivery of services and products, and save costs.

Why is flexibility important?

Flexibility means being able to change the operation in some way. This may mean changing what the operation does, how it is doing it, or when it is doing it. Specifically, customers will need the operation to change so that it can provide four types of requirement:

- product/service flexibility – the operation's ability to introduce new or modified products and services;
- mix flexibility – the operation's ability to produce a wide range or mix of products and services;
- volume flexibility – the operation's ability to change its level of output or activity to produce different quantities or volumes of products and services over time;
- delivery flexibility – the operation's ability to change the timing of the delivery of its services or products.

Figure 2.8 gives examples of what these different types of flexibility mean to the four different operations.

Mass customization

One of the beneficial external effects of flexibility is the increased ability of operations to do different things for different customers. So, high flexibility gives the ability to produce a high variety of products or services. Normally high variety means high cost (see Chapter 1). Furthermore, high-variety operations do not usually produce in high volume. Some companies have developed their flexibility in such a way that products and services are customized for each individual customer. Yet they manage to produce them in a high volume, mass production manner which keeps costs down. This approach is called mass customization. Sometimes this is achieved through flexibility in design. For example, Dell is one of the largest volume producers of personal computers in the world, yet allows each customer to 'design' (albeit in a limited sense) their own configuration. Sometimes flexible technology is used to achieve the same effect. Another example is Paris Miki, an upmarket eyewear retailer which has the largest number of eyewear stores in the world, which uses its own 'Mikissimes Design System' to capture a digital image of the customer and analyse facial characteristics. Together with a list of customers' personal preferences, the system then recommends a particular design and displays it on the image of the customer's face. In consultation with the optician the customer can adjust shapes and sizes until the final design is

Flexibility could mean . . .

Hospital
- Product/service flexibility – the introduction of new types of treatment
- Mix flexibility – a wide range of available treatments
- Volume flexibility – the ability to adjust the number of patients treated
- Delivery flexibility – the ability to reschedule appointments

Source: Shutterstock.com: Hadrian

Automobile plant
- Product/service flexibility – the introduction of new models
- Mix flexibility – a wide range of options available
- Volume flexibility – the ability to adjust the number of vehicles manufactured
- Delivery flexibility – the ability to reschedule manufacturing priorities

Source: Shutterstock.com: Blaz Kure

Bus company
- Product/service flexibility – the introduction of new routes or excursions
- Mix flexibility – a large number of locations served
- Volume flexibility – the ability to adjust the frequency of services
- Delivery flexibility – the ability to reschedule trips

Source: Shutterstock.com: Michael Rolands

Supermarket
- Product/service flexibility – the introduction of new goods or promotions
- Mix flexibility – a wide range of goods stocked
- Volume flexibility – the ability to adjust the number of customers served
- Delivery flexibility – the ability to obtain out-of-stock items (very occasionally)

Source: Shutterstock.com: Buruhthan

Figure 2.8 Flexibility means different things in different operations

566 quadrillion individual muesli mixes –now that's flexible[9]

The idea might sound somewhat unusual, but it has proved a great success. Three university students, Hubertus Bessau, Philipp Kraiss and Max Wittrock, in the small city of Passau, Germany, came up with the concept of mymuesli – the first web-based platform where you can mix your own organic muesli online, with a choice of 75 different ingredients. This makes it possible to create 566 quadrillion individual muesli mixes – and you can even name your own muesli. So, irrespective of whether you are a chocolate addict, a raisin hater or an athlete, this incredible variety will make it easy, says mymusli, for anyone to invent their all-time favourite muesli. 'We wanted to provide customers with nothing else but the perfect muesli', they say. 'Of course the idea of custom-mixing muesli online might sound wacky...but think about it – it's the breakfast you were always looking for.' All muesli is mixed in the Passau production site according to strict quality standards and hygiene law requirements. Ingredients are strictly organic, without additional sugar, additives,

Source: Shutterstock.com: Dmitry Lobanov

preservatives or artificial colours. On visiting the website customers first have to pick a muesli base (full nutritional information is provided). After this customers can add other basics and ingredients such as fruit, nuts and seeds and extras. And the company will deliver it direct by courier to your door! The name for the muesli (chosen by the customer) is printed on the can to make it even more personal. Names chosen by customers for their individual muesli mixes include 'reindeer food', 'donkey's breakfast', 'sweet dream', 'paradise meal' and, rather charmingly, 'darling's breakfast'. The company purchases its ingredients from selected suppliers and dealers throughout the world. One of mymuesli's great assets is the multitude of eccentric and exotic ingredients (from over 20 countries) included in the product range, like carrots, Tibetan goji-berries, cedar nuts or jelly babies. Philipp Kraiss, one of the company founders, is constantly on the lookout for 'new, crazy and tasty' muesli ingredients. During its first year mymuesli was awarded several business prizes (one of which was awarded by the *Financial Times* Germany), and has now grown to have annual sales worth over €1 million, with over 40 people working for the company. It has now expanded its operations to the UK. '*We seriously hope that mymuesli will find just as many friends here in the UK as in Germany and Austria*', says Max Wittrock, another of the three founding members. '*And we are looking forward to a great deal of feedback, so we can continue to improve our products. Last year thousands of e-mails and user replies in Germany really have helped us immensely with the project. Because after all*', Wittrock says, '*it is supposed to be a user-generated breakfast.*'

chosen. Within the store the frames are assembled from a range of pre-manufactured components and the lenses ground and fitted to the frames. The whole process takes around an hour. Another example is the mymuesli case.

Agility

Judging operations in terms of their agility has become popular. Agility is really a combination of all the five performance objectives but particularly flexibility and speed. In addition, agility implies that an operation and the supply chain of which it is a part (supply chains are described in Chapters 5 and 12) can respond to the uncertainty in the market. Agility means responding to market requirements by producing new and existing products and services fast and flexibly.

Flexibility inside the operation

Developing a flexible operation can also have advantages to the internal customers within the operation.

Flexibility speeds up response Fast service often depends on the operation being flexible. For example, if the hospital has to cope with a sudden influx of patients from a road accident, it clearly needs to deal with injuries quickly. Under such circumstances a flexible hospital which can speedily transfer extra skilled staff and equipment to the accident and emergency department will provide the fast service which the patients need.

Flexibility saves time In many parts of the hospital, staff have to treat a wide variety of complaints. Fractures, cuts or drug overdoses do not come in batches. Each patient is an individual with individual needs. The hospital staff cannot take time to 'get into the routine' of treating a particular complaint; they must have the flexibility to adapt quickly. They must also have sufficiently flexible facilities and equipment so that time is not wasted waiting for equipment to be brought to the patient. The time of the hospital's resources is being saved because they are flexible in 'changing over' from one task to the next.

Flexibility maintains dependability Internal flexibility can also help to keep the operation on schedule when unexpected events disrupt the operation's plans. For example, if the sudden influx of patients to the hospital requires emergency surgical procedures, routine operations will be disrupted. This is likely to cause distress and considerable inconvenience. A flexible hospital might be able to minimize the disruption by possibly having reserved operating theatres for such an emergency, and being able to bring in medical staff quickly who are 'on call'.

> ✳ **Operations principle**
> Flexibility can give the potential to create new, wider variety, differing volumes and differing delivery dates of services and products, and save costs.

Why is cost important?

To the companies that compete directly on price, cost will clearly be their major operations objective. The lower the cost of producing their goods and services, the lower can be the price to their customers. Even those companies which do not compete on price will be interested in keeping costs low. Every euro or dollar removed from an operation's cost base is a further euro or dollar added to its profits. Not surprisingly, low cost is a universally attractive objective. The case on everyday low prices at Aldi describes how one retailer keeps its costs down.

> **✳ Operations principle**
>
> Cost is always an important objective for operations management, even if the organization does not compete directly on price.

The ways in which operations management can influence cost will depend largely on where the operation's costs are incurred. The operation will spend its money on staff (the money spent on employing people), facilities, technology and equipment (the money spent on buying, caring for, operating and replacing the operation's 'hardware') and materials (the money spent on the 'bought-in' materials consumed or transformed in the operation). Figure 2.9 shows typical cost breakdowns for the hospital, car plant, supermarket and bus company.

Keeping operations costs down

All operations have an interest in keeping their costs as low as is compatible with the levels of quality, speed, dependability and flexibility that their customers require. The measure that this is most frequently used to indicate is productivity. Productivity is the ratio of what is produced by an operation (its output) to what is required to produce it (its input):

$$\text{Productivity} = \frac{\text{Output from the operation}}{\text{Input to the operation}}$$

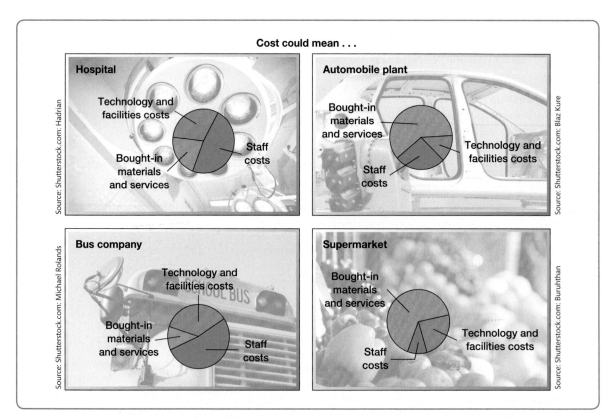

Figure 2.9 Cost means different things in different operations

Everyday low prices at Aldi[10]

Aldi is an international 'limited assortment' supermarket specializing in 'private label', mainly food products. It has carefully focused its service concept and delivery system to attract customers in a highly competitive market. The company believes that its unique approach to operations management makes it *'virtually impossible for competitors to match our combination of price and quality'*. And it has proved especially successful in meeting the increasingly price-conscious behaviour of customers. How has it done this? By challenging the norms of retail operations. They are deliberately simple, using basic facilities to keep down overheads. Most stores stock only a limited range of goods (typically around 700 compared with 25,000 to 30,000 stocked by conventional supermarket chains). The private label approach means that the products have been produced according to Aldi quality specifications and are only sold in Aldi stores. Without the high costs of brand marketing and advertising, and with Aldi's formidable purchasing power, prices can be 30 per cent below their branded equivalents. Other cost saving practices

Source: Getty Images: Bloomberg / Jason Alden

include open-carton displays which eliminate the need for special shelving, no grocery bags to encourage recycling as well as saving costs, multiple bar codes on packages (to speed up scanning) and using a 'cart rental' system which requires customers to return the cart to the store to get their coin deposit back.

Often partial measures of input or output are used so that comparisons can be made. So, for example, in the automobile industry productivity is sometimes measured in terms of the number of cars produced per year per employee. This is called a single-factor measure of productivity:

$$\text{Single-factor productivity} = \frac{\text{Output from the operation}}{\text{One input to the operation}}$$

This allows different operations to be compared excluding the effects of input costs. One operation may have high total costs per car but high productivity in terms of number of cars per employee per year. The difference between the two measures is explained in terms of the distinction between the cost of the inputs to the operation and the way the operation is managed to convert inputs into outputs. Input costs may be high, but the operation itself is good at converting them to goods and services. Single-factor productivity can include the effects of input costs if the single input factor is expressed in cost terms, such as 'labour costs'. Total factor productivity is the measure that includes all input factors.

$$\text{Multi-factor productivity} = \frac{\text{Output from the operation}}{\text{All inputs to the operation}}$$

Improving productivity One obvious way of improving an operation's productivity is to reduce the cost of its inputs while maintaining the level of its outputs. This means reducing the costs of some or all of its transformed and transforming resource inputs. For example, a bank may choose to locate its call centres to a place where its facility-related costs (for

Worked example

A health-check clinic has five employees and 'processes' 200 patients per week. Each employee works 35 hours per week. The clinic's total wage bill is £3,900 and its total overhead expenses are £2,000 per week. What is the clinic's single-factor labour productivity and its multi-factor productivity?

$$\text{Labour productivity} = \frac{200}{5} = 40 \text{ patients/employees/week}$$

$$\text{Labour productivity} = \frac{200}{5 \times 35} = 1.143 \text{ patients/labour hour}$$

$$\text{Multi-factor productivity} = \frac{200}{(3,900 + 2,000)} = 0.0339 \text{ patients/£}$$

example, rent) are cheaper. A software developer may relocate its entire operation to India or China where skilled labour is available at rates significantly less than in European countries. A computer manufacturer may change the design of its products to allow the use of cheaper materials. Productivity can also be improved by making better use of the inputs to the operation. For example, garment manufacturers attempt to cut out the various pieces of material that make up the garment by positioning each part on the strip of cloth so that material wastage is minimized. All operations are increasingly concerned with cutting out waste, whether it is waste of materials, waste of staff time, or waste through the under-utilization of facilities.

OPERATIONS IN PRACTICE

Can cost cutting go too far?[11]

There is a good reason why most electronic components are made in China. It is cheap. Companies such as Taiwan's Foxconn, which produces many of the world's computer, consumer electronics and communications products for customers such as Apple, Dell, Nokia and Sony, have perfected the art and science of squeezing cost out of their operations processes. But, can cost cutting conflict with respect for people (in a triple bottom line sense, see earlier). Although Foxconn is known for having an obsession with cutting its costs and has moved much of its manufacturing into China and other low-cost areas with plants in South-East Asia, Eastern Europe and Latin America, it has been criticized for pushing its workers too far. In the past there have been a cluster of suicides at its factories, with 18 workers throwing themselves from the tops of the company's buildings (14 people died) and violence between employees. The firm operates a huge industrial park, which it calls Foxconn City in Shenzhen, just across the border from Hong Kong, with 15 multi-storey manufacturing buildings, each devoted to one customer. This

is where the suicides took place. It prompted Foxconn to install safety nets in some of its factories and hire counsellors to help its workers.

However, Boy Lüthje of the Institute of Social Research in Frankfurt says that conditions at the firm are actually not that bad when compared with many competias

others. Food and lodging are free, as are extensive recreational facilities. But workers routinely put in overtime in excess of the 36 hours a month permitted under Chinese law and plenty of people seek jobs with the company. Moreover, the suicide rate at the company is lower than that among the general population in China. Yet the deaths raised questions about working conditions in electronics manufacturing in general and in particular at Foxconn. Nor was this the last time concern was raised over working conditions. In 2012 around 150 workers at Wuhan threatened to commit suicide by leaping from

their factory roof in protest at their working conditions. They were eventually coaxed down after two days on top of the three-floor plant by managers. '*We were put to work without any training, and paid piecemeal*', said one of the protesting workers. '*The assembly line ran very fast and after just one morning we all had blisters and the skin on our hand was black. The factory was also really choked with dust and no one could bear it.*' Some reports indicate that Foxconn is more advanced in designing its processes than many of its competitors, but it is run in a regimented fashion that it not always popular with workers.

Cost reduction through internal effectiveness Our previous discussion distinguished between the benefits of each performance objective externally and internally. Each of the various performance objectives has several internal effects, but *all of them* affect cost, so one important way to improve cost performance is to improve the performance of the other operations objectives (*see* Fig. 2.10):

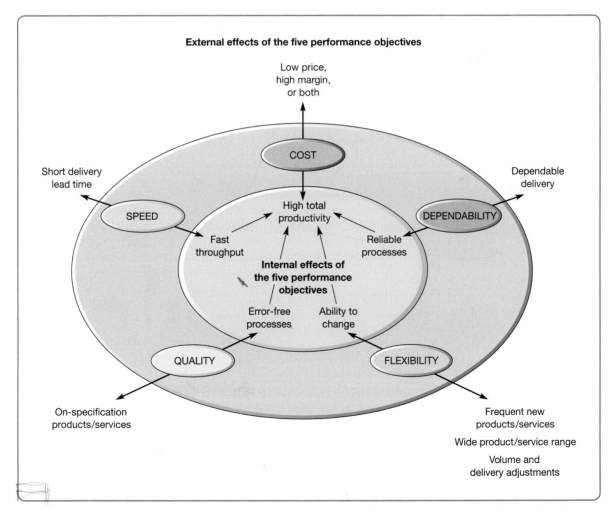

Figure 2.10 Performance objectives have both external and internal effects. Internally, cost is influenced by the other performance objectives

- High-quality operations do not waste time or effort having to redo things, nor are their internal customers inconvenienced by flawed service.
- Fast operations reduce the level of in-process inventory between micro operations, as well as reducing administrative overheads.
- Dependable operations do not spring any unwelcome surprises on their internal customers. They can be relied on to deliver exactly as planned. This eliminates wasteful disruption and allows the other micro operations to operate efficiently.
- Flexible operations adapt to changing circumstances quickly and without disrupting the rest of the operation. Flexible micro operations can also change over between tasks quickly and without wasting time and capacity.

Worked example

Slap.com is an Internet retailer of speciality cosmetics. It orders products from a number of suppliers, stores them, packs them to customers' orders, and then dispatches them using a distribution company. Although broadly successful, the business is very keen to reduce its operating costs. A number of suggestions have been made to do this. These are as follows:

- Make each packer responsible for his or her own quality. This could potentially reduce the percentage of mis-packed items from 0.25 per cent to near zero. Repacking an item that has been mis-packed costs €2 per item.
- Negotiate with suppliers to ensure that they respond to delivery requests faster. It is estimated that this would cut the value of inventories held by **slap.com** by €1,000,000.
- Institute a simple control system that would give early warning if the total number of orders that should be dispatched by the end of the day actually is dispatched in time. Currently 1 per cent of orders is not packed by the end of the day and therefore has to be sent by express courier the following day. This costs an extra €2 per item.

Because demand varies through the year, sometimes staff have to work overtime. Currently the overtime wage bill for the year is €150,000. The company's employees have indicated that they would be willing to adopt a flexible working scheme where extra hours could be worked when necessary in exchange for having the hours off at a less busy time and receiving some kind of extra payment. This extra payment is likely to total €50,000 per year.

If the company dispatch 5 million items every year and if the cost of holding inventory is 10 per cent of its value, how much cost will each of these suggestions save the company?

Analysis

Eliminating mis-packing would result in an improvement in quality. Currently 0.25 per cent of 5 million items are mis-packed. This amounts to 12,500 items per year. At €2 repacking charge per item, this is a cost of €25,000 that would be saved.

Getting faster delivery from suppliers helps reduce the amount of inventory in stock by €1,000,000. If the company is paying 10 per cent of the value of stock for keeping it in storage the saving will be €1,000,000 × 0.1 = €100,000.

Ensuring that all orders are dispatched by the end of the day increases the dependability of the company's operations. Currently, 1 per cent are late; in other words, 50,000 items per year. This is costing €2 × 50,000 = €100,000 per year which would be saved by increasing dependability.

Changing to a flexible working hours system increases the flexibility of the operation and would cost €50,000 per year, but it saves €150,000 per year. Therefore, increasing flexibility could save €100,000 per year.

So, in total, by improving the operation's quality, speed, dependability and flexibility, a total of €325,000 can be saved.

The polar representation of performance objectives

A useful way of representing the relative importance of performance objectives for a product or service is shown in Figure 2.11(a). This is called the polar representation because the scales which represent the importance of each performance objective have the same origin. A line describes the relative importance of each performance objective. The closer the line is to the common origin, the less important is the performance objective to the operation. Two services are shown, a taxi and a bus service. Each essentially provides the same basic service, but with different objectives. The differences between the two services are clearly shown by the diagram. Of course, the polar diagram can be adapted to accommodate any number of different performance objectives. For example, Figure 2.11(b) shows a proposal for using a polar diagram to assess the relative performance of different police forces in the UK.[12]

HOW CAN OPERATIONS PERFORMANCE BE MEASURED?

Having defined the three levels of operations performance, any business will need to measure how well, or badly, it is doing. This is performance measurement. It is the process of *quantifying action*, where measurement means the process of quantification and the performance of the operation is assumed to derive from actions taken by its management. Some kind of *performance measurement* is a prerequisite for judging whether an operation is good, bad or indifferent. Without performance measurement, it is impossible to exert any control over an operation on an ongoing basis, or to judge whether any improvement is being made.

Performance measurement, as we are treating it here, concerns three generic issues:

● What factors to include as performance measures?
● Which are the most important performance measures?
● What detailed measures to use?

What factors to include as performance measures?

Earlier in this chapter we explained how operations performance could be described at three levels: the societal level that included consideration of social and environmental factors as well as economic ones, the strategic level that included consideration of risk, capital and

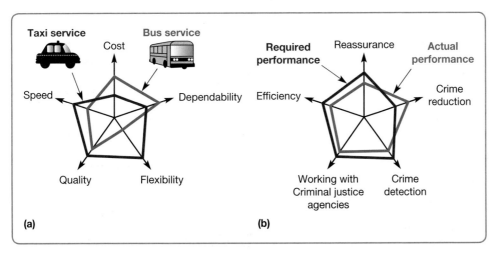

Figure 2.11 Polar representations of (a) the relative importance of performance objectives for a taxi service and a bus service, and (b) a police force's targets and performance

innovation capability issues as well as profitability, and the operational level that included the more directly operations-related factors of quality, speed, dependability, flexibility and cost. There are two important points to make here. First, sometimes these measures are aggregated into 'composite' measures that combine several measures, such as 'customer satisfaction', 'overall service level' or 'operations agility'. These more aggregated 'composite' performance measures help to present a picture of the overall performance of a business, although they may include some influences outside those that operations performance improvement would normally address (customer satisfaction may partly be a function of how a service is advertised, for example). Second, all of the factors at each level can be broken down into more detailed measures. Figure 2.12 gives examples of this. These more detailed performance measures are usually monitored more closely and more often, and although, by themselves, they provide a limited view of an operation's performance, taken together they do provide a more descriptive and complete picture of what should be and what is happening within the operation. In practice, most organizations will choose to use performance measures from all three levels.

Which are the most important performance measures?

One of the problems of devising a useful performance measurement system is trying to achieve some balance between having a few key measures on the one hand (straightforward and simple, but may not reflect the full range of organizational objectives), or, on the other hand, having many detailed measures (complex and difficult to manage, but capable of conveying many nuances of performance). Broadly, a compromise is often reached by making sure that there is a clear link between the operation's overall strategy, the most important (or 'key') performance indicators (often called KPIs) that reflect strategic objectives, and the bundle of detailed measures that are used to 'flesh out' each key performance indicator. Obviously, unless strategy is well defined then it is difficult to 'target' a narrow range of key performance indicators.

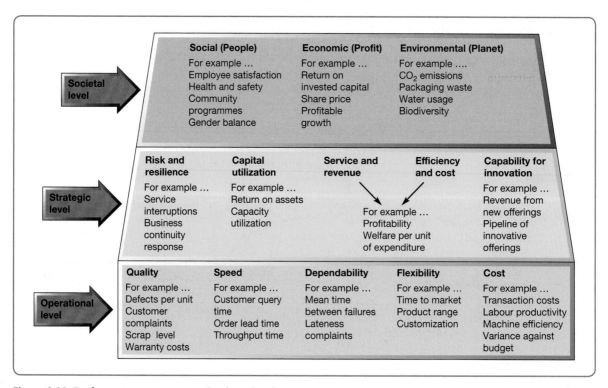

Figure 2.12 Performance measures at the three levels

What detailed measures to use?

The five performance objectives – quality, speed, dependability, flexibility and cost – are really composites of many smaller measures. For example, an operation's cost is derived from many factors which could include the purchasing efficiency of the operation, the efficiency with which it converts materials, the productivity of its staff, the ratio of direct to indirect staff, and so on. All of these measures individually give a partial view of the operation's cost performance, and many of them overlap in terms of the information they include. However, each of them does give a perspective on the cost performance of an operation that could be useful either to identify areas for improvement or to monitor the extent of improvement. If an organization regards its 'cost' performance as unsatisfactory, disaggregating it into 'purchasing efficiency', 'operations efficiency', 'staff productivity', etc., might explain the root cause of the poor performance. The 'operational' level in Figure 2.12 shows some of the partial measures which can be used to judge an operation's performance.

The balanced scorecard approach

Arguably, the best-known performance measurement approach, and one used by many organizations, is the 'balanced scorecard' devised by Kaplan and Norton: *'The balanced scorecard retains traditional financial measures. But financial measures tell the story of past events, an adequate story for industrial age companies for which investments in long-term capabilities and customer relationships were not critical for success. These financial measures are inadequate, however, for guiding and evaluating the journey that information age companies must make to create future value through investment in customers, suppliers, employees, processes, technology, and innovation.'*[13]

In the three-level framework used here, it lies across the strategic and operational levels. As well as including financial measures of performance, in the same way as traditional performance measurement systems, the balanced scorecard approach also attempts to provide the important information that is required to allow the overall strategy of an organization to be reflected adequately in specific performance measures. In addition to financial measures of performance, it also includes more operational measures of customer satisfaction, internal processes, innovation and other improvement activities. In doing so it measures the factors behind financial performance which are seen as the key drivers of future financial success. In particular, it is argued that a balanced range of measures enables managers to address the following questions (*see* Fig. 2.13):

- How do we look to our shareholders (financial perspective)?
- What must we excel at (internal process perspective)?
- How do our customers see us (the customer perspective)?
- How can we continue to improve and build capabilities (the learning and growth perspective)?

The balanced scorecard attempts to bring together the elements that reflect a business's strategic position, including product or service quality measures, product and service development times, customer complaints, labour productivity, and so on. At the same time it attempts to avoid performance reporting becoming unwieldy by restricting the number of measures and focusing especially on those seen to be essential. The advantages of the approach are that it presents an overall picture of the organization's performance in a single report, and, by being comprehensive in the measures of performance it uses, encourages companies to take decisions in the interests of the whole organization rather than sub-optimizing around narrow measures.

> *** Operations principle**
> Multi-dimensioned performance measurement approaches, such as the balanced scorecard, give a broader indication of overall performance.

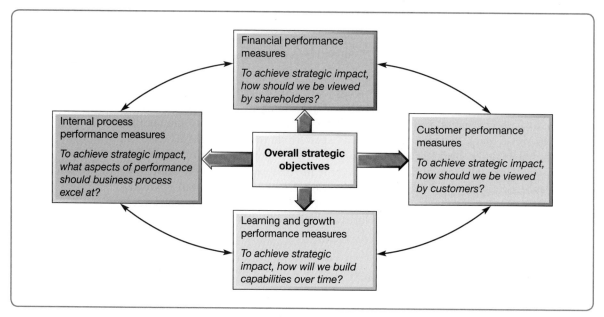

Figure 2.13 The measures used in the balanced scorecard

HOW DO PERFORMANCE OBJECTIVES TRADE OFF AGAINST EACH OTHER?

Earlier we examined how improving the performance of one objective inside the operation could also improve other performance objectives. Most notably better quality, speed, dependability and flexibility can improve cost performance. But externally this is not always the case. In fact there may be a 'trade-off' between performance objectives. In other words, improving the performance of one performance objective might only be achieved by sacrificing performance in another. So, for example, an operation might wish to improve its cost efficiencies by reducing the variety of products or services that it offers to its customers. 'There is no such thing as a free lunch' could be taken as a summary of this approach. Probably the best-known summary of the trade-off idea comes from Professor Wickham Skinner, who said: '*most managers will readily admit that there are compromises or trade-offs to be made in designing an airplane or truck. In the case of an airplane, trade-offs would involve matters such as cruising speed, take-off and landing distances, initial cost, maintenance, fuel consumption, passenger comfort and cargo or passenger capacity. For instance, no one today can design a 500-passenger plane that can land on an aircraft carrier and also break the sound barrier. Much the same thing is true in [operations].*'[14]

> **✳ Operations principle**
>
> In the short term, operations cannot achieve outstanding performance in all their operations objectives.

But there are two views of trade-offs. The first emphasizes 'repositioning' performance objectives by trading off improvements in some objectives for a reduction in performance in others. The other emphasizes increasing the 'effectiveness' of the operation by overcoming trade-offs so that improvements in one or more aspects of performance can be achieved without any reduction in the performance of others. Most businesses at some time or other will adopt both approaches. This is best illustrated through the concept of the 'efficient frontier' of operations performance.

Trade-offs and the efficient frontier

Figure 2.14(a) shows the relative performance of several companies in the same industry in terms of their cost efficiency and the variety of products or services that they offer to their customers. Presumably all the operations would ideally like to be able to offer very high

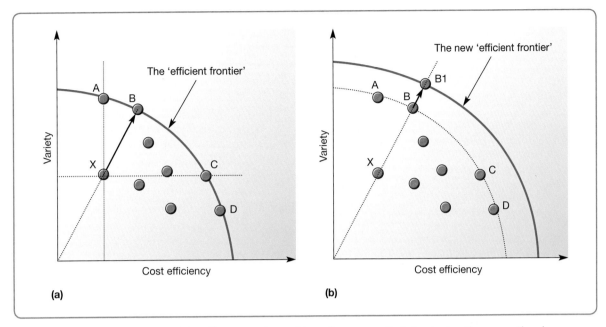

Figure 2.14 The efficient frontier identifies operations with performances that dominate other operations' performance

variety while still having very high levels of cost efficiency. However, the increased complexity that a high variety of product or service offerings brings will generally reduce the operation's ability to operate efficiently. Conversely, one way of improving cost efficiency is to limit severely the variety on offer to customers. The spread of results in Figure 2.14(a) is typical of an exercise such as this. Operations A, B, C, D all have chosen a different balance between variety and cost efficiency. But none is dominated by any other operation in the sense that another operation necessarily has 'superior' performance. Operation X, however, has an inferior performance because operation A is able to offer higher variety at the same level of cost efficiency and operation C offers the same variety but with better cost efficiency. The convex line on which operations A, B, C and D lie is known as the 'efficient frontier'. They may choose to position themselves differently (presumably because of different market strategies) but they cannot be criticized for being ineffective. Of course any of these operations that lie on the efficient frontier may come to believe that the balance they have chosen between variety and cost efficiency is inappropriate. In these circumstances they may choose to reposition themselves at some other point along the efficient frontier. By contrast, operation X has also chosen to balance variety and cost efficiency in a particular way but is not doing so effectively. Operation B has the same ratio between the two performance objectives but is achieving them more effectively.

> ✳ Operations principle
> Operations that lie on the 'efficient frontier' have performance levels that dominate those which do not.

However, a strategy that emphasizes increasing effectiveness is not confined to those operations that are dominated, such as operation X. Those with a position on the efficient frontier will generally also want to improve their operations effectiveness by overcoming the trade-off that is implicit in the efficient frontier curve. For example, suppose operation B in Figure 2.14(b) wants to improve both its variety and its cost efficiency simultaneously and move to position B1. It may be able to do this, but only if it adopts operations improvements that extend the efficient frontier. For example, one of the decisions that any supermarket manager has to make is how many checkout positions to open at any time. If too many checkouts are opened then there will be times when the checkout staff do not have any customers to serve and will be idle. The customers, however, will have excellent service in terms of little or no waiting time. Conversely, if too few checkouts are opened, the staff will be working all the time but customers will have to wait in long queues. There seems to be a direct trade-off between staff utilization (and therefore cost) and customer waiting time (speed of service). Yet even the supermarket manager might, for example, allocate a number of 'core' staff to operate the checkouts but also arrange for those other staff who are performing other jobs in the supermarket to be trained and 'on call' should demand suddenly increase. If the manager on duty sees a build-up of customers at the checkouts, these other staff could quickly be used to staff checkouts. By devising a flexible system of staff allocation, the manager can both improve customer service and keep staff utilization high.

> **❋ Operations principle**
>
> An operation's strategy improvement path can be described in terms of repositioning and/or overcoming its performance trade-offs.

This distinction between positioning on the efficient frontier and increasing operations effectiveness by extending the frontier is an important one. Any business must make clear the extent to which it is expecting the operation to reposition itself in terms of its performance objectives and the extent to which it is expecting the operation to improve its effectiveness in several ways simultaneously.

SUMMARY ANSWERS TO KEY QUESTIONS

〉 Why is operations performance vital in any organization?

- Operations management can either 'make or break' any business. In most businesses it represents the bulk of its assets.
- The positive effects of a well-run operation include a focus on improvement, the building of 'difficult to imitate' capabilities, and an understanding of the processes that are the building blocks of all operations.
- The negative effects of a poorly run operation include failures that are obvious to customers (and expensive for the organization), a complacency that leads to the failure to exploit opportunities for improvement.

〉 How is operations performance judged at a societal level?

- Operations decisions affect a variety of 'stakeholders'. Stakeholders are the people and groups who have a legitimate interest in the operation's activities.
- This idea that operations should take into account the impact on a broad mix of stakeholders is termed 'corporate social responsibility' (CSR).
- Performance at the societal level often uses the idea of the triple bottom line (TBL, or 3BL, also known as 'People, Planet and Profit'). It includes the social bottom line, the environmental bottom line and the economic bottom line.
- The social bottom line incorporates the idea that businesses should accept that they bear some responsibility for the impact they have on society and balance the external 'societal' consequences of their actions with the more direct internal consequences, such as profit.
- The environmental bottom line incorporates the idea that operations should accept that they bear some responsibility for the impact they have on the natural environment.
- The economic bottom line incorporates the conventional financial measures of performance derived from using the operation's resources effectively.

〉 How is operations performance judged at a strategic level?

- The type of decisions and activities that operations managers carry out can have a significant strategic impact.
- In particular, operations can affect economic performance in five ways:
  - It can reduce the costs.
  - It can achieve customer satisfaction through service.
  - It can reduce the risk of operational failure.
  - It can reduce the amount of investment that is necessary.
  - It can provide the basis for *future* innovation.

〉 How is operations performance judged at an operational level?

- The five 'performance objectives' that are used to assess the performance of operations at an operational level are quality, speed, dependability, flexibility and cost.
- Quality is important because:
  - By 'doing things right', operations seek to influence the quality of the company's goods and services.
  - Externally, quality is an important aspect of customer satisfaction or dissatisfaction.
  - Internally, quality operations both reduce costs and increase dependability.
- Speed is important because:
  - By 'doing things fast', operations seek to influence the speed with which goods and services are delivered.
  - Externally, speed is an important aspect of customer service.
  - Internally, speed both reduces inventories by decreasing internal throughput time and reduces risks by delaying the commitment of resources.
- Dependability is important because:
  - By 'doing things on time', operations seek to influence the dependability of the delivery of goods and services.
  - Externally, dependability is an important aspect of customer service.
  - Internally, dependability within operations increases operational reliability, thus saving the time and money that would otherwise be taken up in solving reliability problems and also giving stability to the operation.
- Flexibility is important because:
  - By 'changing what they do', operations seek to influence the flexibility with which the company produces goods and services.
  - Externally, flexibility can produce new products and services (product/service flexibility).
  - Externally, flexibility can produce a wide range or mix of products and services (mix flexibility).
  - Externally, flexibility can produce different quantities or volumes of products and services (volume flexibility).
  - Externally, flexibility can produce products and services at different times (delivery flexibility).
  - Internally, flexibility can help speed up response times, save time wasted in changeovers, and maintain dependability.

- Cost is important because:
  - By 'doing things cheaply', operations seek to influence the cost of the company's goods and services.
  - Externally, low costs allow organizations to reduce their price in order to gain higher volumes or, alternatively, increase their profitability on existing volume levels.
  - Internally, cost performance is helped by good performance in the other performance objectives.

❯ How can operations performance be measured?

- It is unlikely that for any operation a single measure of performance will adequately reflect the whole of a performance objective. Usually operations have to collect a whole bundle of partial measures of performance.
- The balanced scorecard (BSC) is a commonly used approach to performance measurement and incorporates measures related to:
  - How do we look to our shareholders (financial perspective)?
  - What must we excel at (internal process perspective)?
  - How do our customers see us (the customer perspective)?
  - How can we continue to improve and build capabilities (the learning and growth perspective)?

❯ How do operations performance objectives trade off against each other?

- Trade-offs are the extent to which improvements in one performance objective can be achieved by sacrificing performance in others. The 'efficient frontier' concept is a useful approach to articulating trade-offs and distinguishes between repositioning performance on the efficient frontier and improving performance by overcoming trade-offs.

CASE STUDY Operations objectives at the Penang Mutiara[15]

There are many luxurious hotels in the South-East Asia region but few can compare with the Penang Mutiara, a 440-room, top-of-the-market hotel which nestles in the lush greenery of Malaysia's Indian Ocean coast. Owned by Pernas–OUE of Malaysia and managed by Singapore Mandarin International Hotels, the hotel's general manager is under no illusions about the importance of running an effective operation. 'Managing a hotel of this size is an immensely complicated task', he says. 'Our customers have every right to be demanding. They expect first-class service and that's what we have to give them. If we have any problems with managing this operation, the customer sees them immediately and that's the biggest incentive for us to take operations performance seriously. Our quality of service just has to be impeccable. This means dealing with the basics. For example, our staff must be courteous at all times and yet also friendly towards our guests. And of course they must have the knowledge to be able to answer guests' questions. The building and equipment – in fact all the hardware of the operation – must support the luxury atmosphere which we have created in the hotel. Stylish design and top-class materials not only create the right impression but, if we choose them carefully, are also durable so the hotel still looks good over the years. Most of all, though, quality is about anticipating our guests' needs, thinking ahead so you can identify what will delight or irritate a guest.'

The hotel tries to anticipate guests' needs in a number of ways. For example, if guests have been to the hotel before, staff avoid their having to repeat the information they gave on the previous visit. Reception staff simply check to see if guests have stayed before, retrieve the information and take them straight to their room without irritating delays. Quality of service also means helping guests sort out their own problems. If the airline loses a guest's luggage en route to the hotel, for example, he or she will arrive at the hotel understandably irritated. *'The fact that it is not us who have irritated them is not really the issue. It is our job to make them feel better.'*

Speed, in terms of fast response to customers' requests is something else that is important. *'A guest just should not be kept waiting. If a guest has a request, he or she has that request now so it needs to be sorted out now. This is not always easy but we do our best. For example, if every guest in the hotel tonight decided to call room service and request a meal instead of going to the restaurants, our room service department would obviously be grossly overloaded and customers would have to wait an unacceptably long time before the meals were brought up to their rooms. We cope with this by keeping a close watch on how demand for room service is building up. If we think it's going to get above the level where response time to customers would become unacceptably long, we will call in staff from other restaurants in the hotel. Of course, to do this we have to make sure that our staff are multi-skilled. In fact we have a policy of making sure that restaurant staff can always do more than one job. It's this kind of flexibility which allows us to maintain fast response to the customer.'*

Dependability is also a fundamental principle of a well-managed hotel. *'We must always keep our promises. For example, rooms must be ready on time and accounts must be ready for presentation when a guest departs; the guests expect a dependable service and anything less than full dependability is a legitimate cause for dissatisfaction.'* It is on the grand occasions, however, when dependability is particularly important in the hotel. When staging a banquet, for example, everything has to be on time. Drinks, food, entertainment have to be available exactly as planned. Any deviation from the plan will very soon be noticed by customers. *'It is largely a matter of planning the details and anticipating what could go wrong. Once we've done the planning we can anticipate possible problems and plan how to cope with them, or better still, prevent them from occurring in the first place.'*

Flexibility means a number of things to the hotel. First of all it means that it should be able to meet a guest's requests. *'We never like to say NO! For example, if a guest asks for some Camembert cheese and we don't have it in stock, we will make sure that someone goes to the supermarket and tries to get it. If, in spite of our best efforts, we can't get any we will negotiate an alternative solution with the guest. This has an important side-effect – it greatly helps us to maintain the motivation of our staff. We are constantly being asked to do the seemingly impossible – yet we do it, and our staff think it's great. We all like to be part of an organization which is capable of achieving the very difficult, if not the impossible.'* Flexibility in the hotel also means the ability to cope with the seasonal fluctuations in demand. The hotel achieves this partly by using temporary part-time staff. In the back-office parts of the hotel this

is not a major problem. In the laundry, for example, it is relatively easy to put on an extra shift in busy periods by increasing staffing levels. However, this is more of a problem in the parts of the hotel that have direct contact with the customer. *'New temporary staff can't be expected to have the same customer contact skills as our more regular staff. Our solution to this is to keep the temporary staff as far in the background as we possibly can and make sure that our skilled, well-trained staff are the ones who usually interact with the customer. So, for example, a waiter who would normally take orders, service the food, and take away the dirty plates would in peak times restrict his or her activities to taking orders and serving the food. The less skilled part of the job, taking away the plates, could be left to temporary staff.'*

As far as cost is concerned, around 60 per cent of the hotel's total operating expenses go on food and beverages, so one obvious way of keeping costs down is by making sure that food is not wasted. Energy costs, at 6 per cent of total operating costs, are also a potential source of saving. However, although cost savings are welcome, the hotel is very careful never to compromise the quality of its service in order to cut costs. *'It is impeccable customer service which gives us our competitive advantage, not price. Good service means that our guests return again and again. At times, around half our guests are people who have been before. The more guests we have, the higher is our utilization of rooms and restaurants, and this is what really keeps cost per guest down and profitability reasonable. So in the end we've come full circle: it's the quality of our service which keeps our volumes high and our costs low.'*

QUESTIONS

1 Describe how you think the hotel's manager will:
   (a) make sure that the way he manages the hotel is appropriate to the way it competes for business;
   (b) implement any change in strategy;
   (c) develop his operation so that it drives the long-term strategy of the hotel.

2 The case describes how quality, speed, dependability, flexibility and cost impact the hotel's external customers. Explain how each of these performance objectives might have internal benefits.

1. The 'forensic science' service of a European country has traditionally been organized to provide separate forensic science laboratories for each police force around the country. In order to save costs, the government has decided to centralize this service in one large central facility close to the country's capital. What do you think are the external advantages and disadvantages of this to the stakeholders of the operation? What do you think are the internal implications to the new centralized operation that will provide this service?

2. The health clinic described in the worked example earlier in the chapter has expanded by hiring one extra employee and now has six employees. It has also leased some new health monitoring equipment which allows patients to be processed faster. This means that its total output is now 280 patients per week. Its wage costs have increased to £4,680 per week and its overhead costs to £3,000 per week. What are its single-factor labour productivity and its multi-factor productivity now?

3. A publishing company plans to replace its four proofreaders who look for errors in manuscripts with a new scanning machine and one proofreader in case the machine breaks down. Currently the proofreaders check 15 manuscripts every week between them. Each is paid €80,000 per year. Hiring the new scanning machine will cost €5,000 each calendar month. How will this new system affect the proofreading department's productivity?

4. Bongo's Pizzas have a service guarantee that promises you will not pay for your pizza if it is delivered more than 30 minutes from the order being placed. An investigation shows that 10 per cent of all pizzas are delivered between 15 and 20 minutes from order, 40 per cent between 20 and 25 minutes from order, 40 per cent between 25 and 30 minutes from order, 5 per cent between 30 and 35 minutes from order, 3 per cent between 35 and 40 minutes from order, and 2 per cent over 40 minutes from order. If the average profit on each pizza delivered on time is €1 and the average cost of each pizza delivered is €5, is the fact that Bongo's does not charge for 10 per cent of its pizzas a significant problem for the business? How much extra profit per pizza would be made if 5 minutes was cut from all deliveries?

5. *Step 1* – Look again at the figures in the chapter which illustrate the meaning of each performance objective for the four operations. Consider the bus company and the supermarket, and in particular consider their external customers.
   Step 2 – Draw the relative required performance for both operations on a polar diagram.
   Step 3 – Consider the internal effects of each performance objective. For both operations, identify how quality, speed, dependability and flexibility can help to reduce the cost of producing their services.

6. Visit the websites of two or three large oil companies such as Exxon, BP, Shell, Total, etc. Examine how they describe their policies towards their customers, suppliers, shareholders, employees and society at large. Identify areas of the company's operations where there may be conflicts between the needs of these different stakeholder groups. Discuss or reflect on how (if at all) such companies try and reconcile these conflicts.

7. Devise a performance measurement scheme for the performance of the course you are following.

SELECTED FURTHER READING

Bourne, M., Kennerley, M. and Franco, M. (2005) Managing through measures: a study of the impact on performance, *Journal of Manufacturing Technology Management*, vol. 16, issue 4, 373–395.

What it says on the tin.

Kaplan, R.S. and Norton, D.P. (2005) The balanced scorecard: measures that drive performance, *Harvard Business Review*, July–August.

The latest pronouncements on the balanced scorecard approach.

Neely, A. (2012) *Business Performance Measurement: Unifying Theory and Integrating Practice*, Cambridge University Press, Cambridge.

A collection of papers on the details of measuring performance objectives.

Pine, B.J. (1993) *Mass Customization*, Harvard Business School Press, Boston, MA.

The first substantial work on the idea of mass customization. Still a classic.

Savitz, A.W. and Weber, K. (2006) *The Triple Bottom Line: How Today's Best-Run Companies Are Achieving Economic, Social and Environmental Success – and How You Can Too*, Jossey-Bass, San Francisco.

Good on the triple bottom line.

Waddock, S. (2003) Stakeholder performance implications of corporate responsibility, *International Journal of Business Performance Management*, vol. 5, nos 2–3, 114–124.

An introduction to stakeholder analysis.

3

Operations strategy

Key questions

> What is strategy and what is operations strategy?

> What is the difference between a 'top-down' and a 'bottom-up' view of operations strategy?

> What is the difference between a 'market requirements' and 'operations resources' view of operations strategy?

> How can operations strategy form the basis for operations improvement?

> How can an operations strategy be formulated? The process of operations strategy

INTRODUCTION

No organization can plan in detail every aspect of its future actions; there is always some degree of uncertainty about what conditions will exist in the future. There will always have to be some adjustment to plans to accommodate circumstances. But simply always reacting to current, possibly short-term, issues can lead to constant changes in direction and the operation becoming volatile and unstable. That is why all organizations need the 'backdrop' of a well-understood strategic direction, so they know (at least, roughly) where they are heading and how they could get there. Once the operations function has understood its role in the business and after it has articulated its performance objectives, it needs to formulate a set of general principles which will guide its decision making. This is the operations strategy of the company. Yet the concept of 'strategy' itself is not straightforward; neither is operations strategy. This chapter considers four perspectives, each of which goes partway to illustrating the forces that shape operations strategy. Figure 3.1 shows the position of the ideas described in this chapter in the general model of operations management.

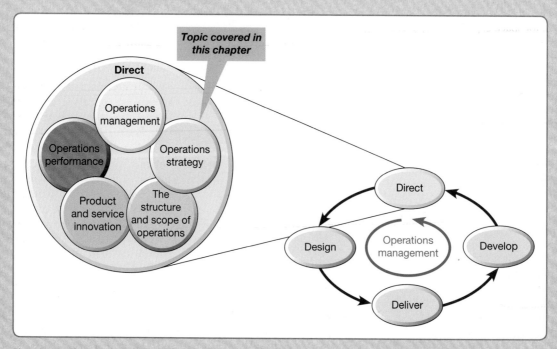

Figure 3.1 This chapter examines operations strategy

Changing the economics of space exploration[1]

You do not think of space satellites as cheap items, and of course they are not. They can be expensive – very expensive. And in the early days of space missions, this meant that only superpowers could afford to develop and launch them. The conventional wisdom was that space was such a hostile environment that satellites would have to be constructed using only specially developed components that could endure the severe conditions encountered in space. Satellites therefore would always be expensive items. Yet in the late 1970s this assumption was challenged by Sir Martin Sweeting, who then was studying for his PhD at the University of Surrey in the UK. The aerospace research team in the Electrical Engineering Department at the University of Surrey had built its first satellite (called UoSAT-1) using commercial off-the-shelf components. It was about as big as two microwave ovens, weighing in at 72 kg. By contrast, some of the huge satellites being launched by government space agencies were as large as a London double-decker bus. UoSAT-1 was launched in 1981 with the help of NASA, who had been persuaded to provide a free launch, piggybacking on the back of a mission to put a large scientific satellite into orbit. The team followed this up with a second satellite (UoSAT-2) built in just six months and launched in 1984. A year later Surrey Satellite Technology Limited (SSTL) was formed as a spinout company from the University of Surrey to transfer the results of its research into a commercial enterprise. The firm's vision was to open up the market for space exploration by pioneering the use of small and relatively cheap, but reliable, satellites built from readily available off-the-shelf components – then a revolutionary idea. Now SSTL is the world's leading small-satellite company and has delivered space missions for a whole range of applications including Earth observation, science, communications and in-orbit technology demonstration. The company is at the forefront of space innovation, exploiting advances in technologies and challenging conventions to bring affordable space exploration to international customers. The company, which has launched over 40 satellites, is based across four sites in South-East England, and employs more than 500 staff. Since 2014 SSTL has been an independent company within the Airbus defence and space group.

As the market for satellites developed, scientific and technological innovations have led to what has been called a 'democratisation' of space, with SSTL maintaining what it says is a 40 per cent share of the global export market for small affordable satellites. How has it achieved this success from such small beginnings? Well,

partly because it was an early player in the market having the vision to see that there would be a market for small satellites that could serve the ambitions of smaller countries, companies, research groups and even schools. As the company says, the small-satellite revolution started with SSTL. But in addition, it has always been innovative in finding ways of keeping the cost of building the satellites down to a minimum. SSTL pioneered the low-cost, low-risk approach to delivering operational satellite missions within short development timescales and with the capability that potential customers wanted. In the early 1980s, as the first microcomputers became commercially available, Sir Martin Sweeting speculated that it may be possible to use programmable technology to build small satellites that were 'intelligent' when compared with conventional large and expensive hard-wired satellites. It also would allow the satellite to be reprogrammed from the ground. Particularly important was the company's use of commercial off-the-shelf technology. Combined with a determination to learn something from each new project, a pragmatic approach to manufacture and low-cost operations, it enabled SSTL to keep costs as low as realistically possible. In effect, using industry-standard parts meant exploiting the (often enormous) investments by consumer electronics companies, auto part manufacturers and others who had developed complex components for their products. Even if this sometimes limited what a satellite could do, it provided the scale economies that would be impossible if SSTL were designing and making customized components from scratch. 'We were being parasitic, if you like', admits Sir Martin.

However, not all commercially available components made for terrestrial use are up to coping with conditions in space, which is a hugely important issue. Reliability is essential in a satellite. (It is difficult to repair them once in space.) And even though off-the-shelf components and systems have become increasing reliable, they must be rigorously tested to make sure that they are up to the severe conditions found in space. One of the key problems is how components react to the high levels of radiation in space. For example, different smartphone constituents (a regular source of components) react in different ways to radiation. Knowing which bits can be used and which cannot is an important piece of knowledge. Yet, although individual components and systems are often bought off the shelf, the company does most of its operations activities itself. This allows SSTL to provide a complete in-house design, manufacture, launch and operation service as well as a range of advice, analysis and consultancy services. *'What distinguishes us is our vertically integrated capability, from design and research to manufacturing and operations'*, says Sir Martin. *'We don't have to rely on suppliers, although of course we buy in components when that is advantageous.'* And innovation? It is still as important as it was at the company's start. Surrey University has retained a 1 per cent stake in the company because *'we wanted to cement the very close relationship between company and university'*, says Sir Martin. *'We work together on a number of research projects and staff flow back and forth between us.'*

WHAT IS STRATEGY AND WHAT IS OPERATIONS STRATEGY?

Surprisingly, 'strategy' is not particularly easy to define. Linguistically the word derives from the Greek word *strategos*, meaning 'leading an army'. And although there is no direct historical link between Greek military practice and modern ideas of strategy, the military metaphor is powerful. Both military and business strategy can be described in similar ways, and include some of the following:

- Setting broad objectives that direct an enterprise towards its overall goal.
- Planning the path (in general rather than specific terms) that will achieve these goals.
- Stressing long-term rather than short-term objectives.
- Dealing with the total picture rather than stressing individual activities.
- Being detached from, and above, the confusion and distractions of day-to-day activities.

Here, by strategic decisions, we mean those decisions which: are widespread in their effect on the organization to which the strategy refers; define the position of the organization relative to its environment; and move the organization closer to its long-term goals. But 'strategy' is more than a single decision; it is the *total pattern of the decisions* and actions that influence the long-term direction of the business. Thinking about strategy in this way helps us to discuss an organization's strategy even when it has not been explicitly stated. Observing the total pattern of decisions gives an indication of the *actual* strategic behaviour.

Operations strategy

Operations strategy concerns the pattern of strategic decisions and actions that set the role, objectives and activities of the operation. The term 'operations strategy' sounds at first like a contradiction. How can 'operations', a subject that is generally concerned with the day-to-day creation and delivery of goods and services, be strategic? 'Strategy' is usually regarded as the opposite of those day-to-day routine activities. But *'operations'* is not the same as *'operational'*. 'Operations' are the resources that create products and services. 'Operational' is the opposite of strategic, meaning day-to-day and detailed. So, one can examine both the operational *and* the strategic aspects of operations. It is also conventional to distinguish between the 'content' and the 'process' of operations strategy. The *content* of operations strategy is the specific decisions and actions that set the operations role, objectives and activities. The *process* of operations strategy is the method that is used to make the specific 'content' decisions.

> **❋ Operations principle**
>
> 'Operations' is not the same as 'operational'; it does have a strategic role.

From implementing to supporting to driving strategy

Most businesses expect their operations strategy to improve operations performance over time. In doing this they should be progressing from a state contributing very little to the competitive success of the business through to the point where they are directly responsible for its competitive success. This means that they should be able to, in turn, master the skills first to 'implement', then 'support' and then 'drive' operations strategy.

Implementing business strategy

The most basic role of operations is to implement strategy. You cannot, after all, touch a strategy; you cannot even see it; all you can see is how the operation behaves in practice. For example, if an insurance company has a strategy of moving to an entirely online service, its operations function will have to supervise the design of all the processes which allow customers to access online information, issue quotations, request further information, check credit details, send out documentation, and so on. Without effective implementation even the most original and brilliant strategy will be rendered totally ineffective.

Supporting business strategy

Support strategy goes beyond simply implementing strategy. It means developing the capabilities which allow the organization to improve and refine its strategic goals. For example, a mobile phone manufacturer wants to be the first in the market with new product innovations, so its operations need to be capable of coping with constant innovation. It must develop processes flexible enough to make novel components, organize its staff to understand the new technologies, develop relationships with its suppliers which help them to respond quickly when supplying new parts, and so on.

Driving business strategy

The third, and most difficult, role of operations is to drive strategy by giving it a unique and long-term advantage. For example, a specialist food-service company supplies restaurants with frozen fish and fish products. Over the years it has built up close relationships with its customers (chefs) as well as with its suppliers around the world (fishing companies and fish farms). In addition it has its own small factory which develops and produces a continual stream of exciting new products. In fact the whole company's success is based largely on these unique operations capabilities. The operation drives the company's strategy.

> **❋ Operations principle**
> Operations should try, progressively, to implement, support and drive strategy.

Hayes and Wheelwright's four stages of operations contribution

The ability of any operation to play these roles within the organization can be judged by considering the organizational aims or aspirations of the operations function. Professors Hayes and Wheelwright of Harvard University[2] developed a four-stage model which can be used to evaluate the role and contribution of the operations function. The model traces the progression of the operations function from what is the largely negative role of stage 1 operations to its becoming the central element of competitive strategy in excellent stage 4 operations. Figure 3.2 illustrates the four stages.

Stage 1: Internal neutrality

This is the very poorest level of contribution by the operations function. It is holding the company back from competing effectively. It is inward looking and, at best, reactive with very little positive to contribute towards competitive success. Paradoxically, its goal is 'to be ignored' (or, 'internally neutral'). At least then it is not holding the company back in any way. It attempts to improve by 'avoiding making mistakes'.

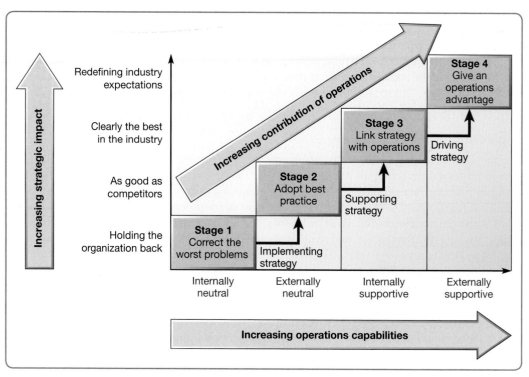

Figure 3.2 The four-stage model of operations contribution

Stage 2: External neutrality

The first step of breaking out of stage 1 is for the operations function to begin comparing itself with similar companies or organizations in the outside market (being 'externally neutral'). This may not immediately take it to the 'first division' of companies in the market, but at least it is measuring itself against its competitors' performance and trying to implement 'best practice'.

Stage 3: Internally supportive

Stage 3 operations are among the best in their market. Yet, stage 3 operations still aspire to be clearly and unambiguously the very best in the market. They achieve this by gaining a clear view of the company's competitive or strategic goals and supporting it by developing appropriate operations resources. The operation is trying to be 'internally supportive' by providing a credible operations strategy.

Stage 4: Externally supportive

Yet Hayes and Wheelwright suggest a further stage – stage 4 – where the company views the operations function as providing the foundation for its competitive success. Operations look to the long term. It forecasts likely changes in markets and supply, and it develops the operations-based capabilities which will be required to compete in future market conditions. Stage 4 operations are innovative, creative and proactive and are driving the company's strategy by being 'one step ahead' of competitors – what Hayes and Wheelwright call being 'externally supportive'.

Critical commentary

The idea that operations can have a leading role in determining a company's strategic direction is not universally supported. Both Hayes and Wheelwright's stage 4 of their four-stage model and the concept of operations 'driving' strategy not only imply that it is possible for operations to take such a leading role, but are also explicit in seeing it as a 'good thing'. A more traditional stance taken by some authorities is that the needs of the market will always be pre-eminent in shaping a company's strategy. Therefore, operations should devote all their time to understanding the requirements of the market (as defined by the marketing function within the organization) and devote themselves to their main job of ensuring that operations processes can actually deliver what the market requires. Companies can only be successful, they argue, by positioning themselves in the market (through a combination of price, promotion, product design and managing how products and services are delivered to customers) with operations very much in a 'supporting' role. In effect, they say, Hayes and Wheelwright's four-stage model should stop at stage 3. The issue of an 'operations resource' perspective on operations strategy is discussed later in the chapter.

Perspectives on operations strategy

Different authors have slightly different views and definitions of operations strategy. Between them, four 'perspectives' emerge:[3]

- Operations strategy is a top-down reflection of what the whole group or business wants to do.
- Operations strategy is a bottom-up activity where operations improvements cumulatively build strategy.
- Operations strategy involves translating market requirements into operations decisions (sometimes called the 'outside-in' perspective).
- Operations strategy involves exploiting the capabilities of operations resources in chosen markets (sometimes called the 'inside-out' perspective).

None of these four perspectives alone gives the full picture of what operations strategy is. But together they provide some idea of the pressures that go to form the content of operations strategy. First we will treat the top-down and bottom-up perspectives together, then the market requirements and operations resource perspectives together (*see* Fig. 3.3).

Figure 3.3 The four perspectives on operations strategy

WHAT IS THE DIFFERENCE BETWEEN A 'TOP-DOWN' AND 'BOTTOM-UP' VIEW OF OPERATIONS STRATEGY?

Top-down strategies

A large corporation will need a strategy to position itself in its global, economic, political and social environment. This will consist of decisions about what types of business the group wants to be in, what parts of the world it wants to operate in, how to allocate its cash between its various businesses, and so on. Decisions such as these form the corporate strategy of the corporation. Each business unit within the corporate group will also need to put together its own business strategy which sets out its individual mission and objectives. This business strategy guides the business in relation to its customers, markets and competitors, and also the strategy of the corporate group of which it is a part. Similarly, within the business, functional strategies need to consider what part each function should play in contributing to the strategic objectives of the business.

So, one perspective on operations strategy is that it should take its place in this hierarchy of strategies. Its main influence, therefore, will be whatever the business sees as its strategic direction. For example, a printing services group has a company that prints packaging for consumer products. The group's management figure that, in the long-term, only companies with significant market share will achieve substantial profitability. Its corporate objectives therefore stress market dominance. The consumer packaging company decides to achieve volume growth, even above short-term profitability or return on investment. The implication for operations strategy is that it needs to expand rapidly, investing in extra capacity (factories, equipment and labour) even if it means some excess capacity in some areas. It also needs to establish new factories in all parts of its market to offer relatively fast delivery. The important point here is that different business objectives would probably result in a very different operations strategy. The role of operations is therefore largely one of implementing or 'operationalizing' business strategy. Figure 3.4 illustrates this strategic hierarchy, with some of the decisions at each level and the main influences on the strategic decisions.

> **✳ Operations principle**
> Operations strategies should reflect top-down corporate and/or business objectives.

'Bottom-up' strategies

The 'top-down' perspective provides an orthodox view of how functional strategies *should* be put together. But in fact the relationship between the levels in the strategy hierarchy is more complex than this. When any group is reviewing its corporate strategy, it will also take into account the circumstances, experiences and capabilities of the various businesses that form the group. Similarly, businesses, when reviewing their strategies, will consult the individual functions within the business about their constraints and capabilities. They may also incorporate the ideas which come from each function's day-to-day experience. Therefore an alternative view to the top-down perspective is that many strategic ideas emerge over time from operational experience. Sometimes companies move in a particular strategic direction because the ongoing experience of providing products and services to customers at an operational level convinces them that it is the right thing to do. There may be no high-level decisions examining alternative strategic options and choosing the one which provides the best way forward. Instead, a general consensus emerges from the operational level of the organization.

> **✳ Operations principle**
> Operations strategy should reflect bottom-up experience of operational reality.

Suppose the printing services company described previously succeeds in its expansion plans. However, in doing so it finds that having surplus capacity and a distributed network of factories allows it to offer an exceptionally fast service to customers. It also finds that some customers are willing to pay considerably higher prices for such a responsive service. Its experiences lead the company to set up

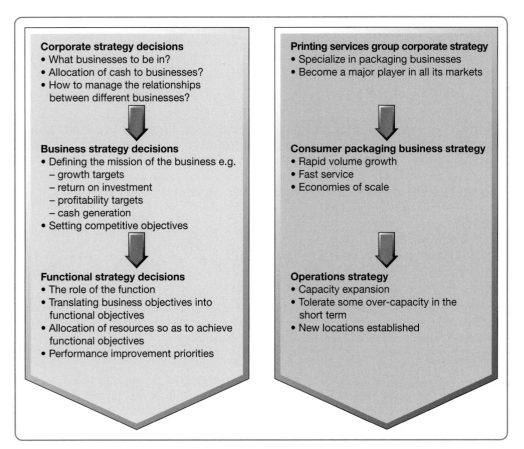

Corporate strategy decisions
• What businesses to be in?
• Allocation of cash to businesses?
• How to manage the relationships between different businesses?

Business strategy decisions
• Defining the mission of the business e.g.
  – growth targets
  – return on investment
  – profitability targets
  – cash generation
• Setting competitive objectives

Functional strategy decisions
• The role of the function
• Translating business objectives into functional objectives
• Allocation of resources so as to achieve functional objectives
• Performance improvement priorities

Printing services group corporate strategy
• Specialize in packaging businesses
• Become a major player in all its markets

Consumer packaging business strategy
• Rapid volume growth
• Fast service
• Economies of scale

Operations strategy
• Capacity expansion
• Tolerate some over-capacity in the short term
• New locations established

Figure 3.4 The top-down perspective of operations strategy and its application to the printing services group

a separate division dedicated to providing fast, high-margin printing services to those customers willing to pay. The strategic objectives of this new division are not concerned with high-volume growth but high profitability.

This idea of strategy being shaped by operational-level experience over time is sometimes called the concept of emergent strategies[4] (*see* Fig. 3.5). This view of operations strategy is perhaps more descriptive of how things really happen, but at first glance it seems less useful in providing a guide for specific decision making. Yet while emergent strategies are less easy to categorize, the principle governing a bottom-up perspective is clear: shape the operation's objectives and action, at least partly, by the knowledge it gains from its day-to-day activities. The key virtues required for shaping strategy from the bottom up are an ability to learn from experience and a philosophy of continual and incremental improvement.

Top-down and bottom-up perspectives on operations strategy can reinforce each other

The top-down and bottom-up perspectives are often seen as being diametrically opposite ways of looking at operations strategy, but they are not. In fact the two perspectives can be mutually reinforcing. This is how it can work. The top-down perspective sets the overall direction and objectives for operations decisions and activities. In fact, in order to implement top-down strategy, the day-to-day activities of the operation must be aligned with the strategy. So a way of judging operational day-to-day activities of an operation is to

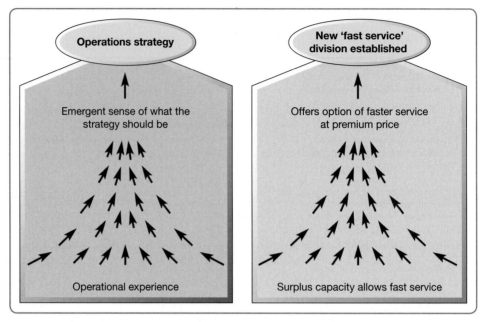

Figure 3.5 The 'bottom-up' perspective of operations strategy

check that they fully reflect the overall top-down strategy of the organization. But as we indicated in the last paragraph, the experience gained from day-to-day activities can be accumulated and built into capabilities that an organization could possibly exploit strategically. (We will expand this idea of 'capabilities' in the next section.) This idea of how top-down and bottom-up perspectives on operations strategy can reinforce each other is shown in Figure 3.6.

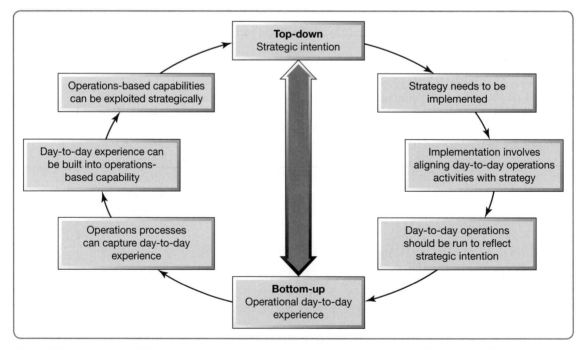

Figure 3.6 Top-down and bottom-up perspectives on operations strategy can reinforce each other

Apple's retail operations strategy[5]

One of the principles of operations strategy is that what operations do 'on the ground' should be aligned with what a business is trying to achieve in its market. The way Apple designs and runs its retail operations is a good example of this. (Later in this chapter we will look at Apple's supply strategy.) However, Apple has not always had a retail operations strategy, because Apple has not always sold its products through its own shops. It was back in 1990 when the late Steve Jobs, then Apple's boss, decided to build Apple Stores because conventional computer retailers were reluctant to stock his Mac computers. They said that the Apple brand was too weak (which, at the time, it was). The original Apple Stores were heavily influenced by Gap (the clothing retailer) and so many Gap employees moved to work for Apple that they joked about working for 'Gapple'. Yet, even with the experienced Gap retailers, Apple wanted to develop its own ideas. Consequently it built a 'prototype store' near its Californian headquarters and tested its retail concepts for a year before opening the first Apple Stores. This early learning period was important. It allowed Apple to come to the conclusion that the two key issues for its retail operations strategy were store location and the experience that customers would have within the stores.

First, store location: Apple has stores in some of the highest profile locations on Earth. This is expensive, but the large number of customers it attracts together with the Apple range of products allow the company to produce very high sales. In fact its sales productivity (sales per square metre) is above many luxury goods retailers such as Tiffany. Second, the customer experience: according to Ron Johnson, who built up Apple's shop network: 'People come to the Apple Store for the experience, and they're willing to pay a premium for that. There are lots of components to that experience, but maybe the most important is that the staff isn't focused on selling stuff, it's focused on building relationships and trying to make people's lives better. The staff is exceptionally well trained, and they're not on commission, so it makes no difference to them if they sell you an expensive new computer or help you make your old one run better so you're happy with it. Their job is to figure out what you need and help you get it, even if it's a product Apple doesn't carry. Compare that with other retailers where the emphasis is on encouraging customers to buy more, even if they don't want or need it. That doesn't enrich their lives, and it doesn't deepen the retailer's relationship with them. It just makes their wallets lighter.' Yet creating the customer experience is not a matter of chance – it is carefully designed into Apple's strategy. Employees are helped to cultivate their air of cool confidence through extensive training, and it is easier to be approachable and calm when there is little pressure to push sales. Training emphasizes the importance of problem solving rather than selling and treating customers with courtesy. For example, staff have been told never to correct a customer's mispronunciation of a product in case it is seen as patronizing. Of course, Apple's products are attractive and Apple customers are famously passionate about the brand, but if Apple products were the only reason for the stores' success, it is difficult to explain why customers flock to the stores to buy Apple products at full price when discount retailers sell them cheaper.

Source: Alamy Images: Trevor Mogg

WHAT IS THE DIFFERENCE BETWEEN A 'MARKET REQUIREMENTS' AND AN 'OPERATIONS RESOURCES' VIEW OF OPERATIONS STRATEGY?

Market-requirements-based strategies

No operation that continually fails to serve its markets adequately is likely to survive in the long term. Without an understanding of what markets require, it is impossible to ensure that the operation is achieving the right priority between its performance objectives (quality, speed, dependability, flexibility and cost).

The market influence on performance objectives

Operations seek to satisfy customers through developing their five performance objectives. For example, if customers particularly value low-priced products or services, the operation will place emphasis on its cost performance. Alternatively, a customer emphasis on fast delivery will make speed important to the operation. When it is important that products or services are delivered exactly when they are promised, the performance objective of dependability will be essential for the operation. When customers value products or services that have been adapted or designed specifically for them, flexibility will be vital, and so on. This list is not exhaustive; the key point is that whatever competitive factors are important to customers should influence the priority of each performance objective.

> ✳ **Operations principle**
>
> Operations strategy should reflect the requirements of the business's markets.

Order-winning and qualifying objectives

A particularly useful way of determining the relative importance of competitive factors is to distinguish between 'order-winning' and 'qualifying' factors.[6] Order-winning factors are those things which directly and significantly contribute to winning business. They are regarded by customers as key reasons for purchasing the product or service. Raising performance in an order-winning factor will either result in more business or improve the chances of gaining more business. Qualifying factors may not be the major competitive determinants of success, but are important in another way. They are those aspects of competitiveness where the operation's performance has to be above a particular level just to be considered by the customer. Performance below this 'qualifying' level of performance will possibly disqualify the company from being considered by many customers. But any further improvement above the qualifying level is unlikely to gain the company much competitive benefit. To order-winning and qualifying factors can be added less important factors which are neither order winning nor qualifying. They do not influence customers in any significant way. They are worth mentioning here only because they may be of importance in other parts of the operation's activities.

Figure 3.7 shows the difference between order-winning, qualifying and less important factors in terms of their utility or worth to the competitiveness of the organization. The curves illustrate the relative amount of competitiveness (or attractiveness to customers) as the operation's performance at the factor varies. Order-winning factors show a steady and significant increase in their contribution to competitiveness as the operation gets better at providing them. Qualifying factors are 'givens'; they are expected by customers and can severely disadvantage the competitive position of the operation if it cannot raise its performance above the qualifying level. Less important objectives have little impact on customers no matter how well the operation performs in them.

> ✳ **Operations principle**
>
> Competitive factors can be classified as order winners or qualifiers.

If, as is likely, an operation produces goods or services for more than one customer group, it will need to determine the order-winning, qualifying and less important competitive factors for each group. For example, Table 3.1 shows two 'product' groups in the banking industry. Here the distinction is drawn between the customers who are looking for banking services for their private and domestic needs (current accounts, overdraft facilities, savings accounts,

Figure 3.7 Order-winning, qualifying and less important competitive factors. Different customer needs imply different objectives

Table 3.1 Different banking services require different performance objectives

	Retail banking	Corporate banking
Products	Personal financial services such as loans and credit cards	Special services for corporate customers
Customers	Individuals	Businesses
Range of services offered	Medium but standardized, little need for special terms	Very wide range, many need to be customized
Changes to service design	Occasional	Continual
Delivery	Fast decisions	Dependable service
Quality	Means error-free transactions	Means close relationships
Volume per service type	Most services are high volume	Most services are low volume
Profit margins	Most are low to medium, some high	Medium to high
Competitive factors		
Order winners	Price	Customization
	Accessibility	Quality of service
	Ease of transaction	Reliability/trust
Qualifiers	Quality	Ease of transaction
	Range	Price
Less important		Accessibility
Internal performance	Cost	Flexibility
objectives	Speed	Quality
	Quality	Dependability

mortgage loans, etc.) and those corporate customers who need banking services for their (often large) organizations. These latter services would include such things as letters of credit, cash transfer services and commercial loans.

Worked example

'It is about four years now since we specialized in the small to medium firms' market. Before that we also used to provide legal services for anyone who walked in the door. So now we have built up our legal skills in many areas of corporate and business law. However, within the firm, I think we could focus our activities even more. There seem to be two types of assignment that we are given. About forty per cent of our work is relatively routine. Typically these assignments are to do with things like property purchase and debt collection. Both these activities involve a relatively standard set of steps which can be automated or carried out by staff without full legal qualifications. Of course, a fully qualified lawyer is needed to make some decisions, however most work is fairly routine. Customers expect us to be relatively inexpensive and fast in delivering the service. Nor do they expect us to make simple errors in our documentation, in fact if we did this too often we would lose business. Fortunately our customers know that they are buying a standard service and don't expect it to be customized in any way. The problem here is that specialist agencies have been emerging over the last few years and they are starting to undercut us on price. Yet I still feel that we can operate profitably in this market and anyway, we still need these capabilities to serve our other clients. The other sixty per cent of our work is for clients who require far more specialist services, such as assignments involving company merger deals or major company restructuring. These assignments are complex, large, take longer, and require significant legal skill and judgement. It is vital that clients respect and trust the advice we give them across a wide range of legal specialisms. Of course they assume that we will not be slow or unreliable in preparing advice, but mainly it's trust in our legal judgement which is important to the client. This is popular work with our lawyers. It is both interesting and very profitable. But should I create two separate parts to our business: one to deal with routine services and the other to deal with specialist services? And, what aspects of operations performance should each part be aiming to excel at?' (Managing Partner, Branton Legal Services)

Analysis

Table 3.2 has used the information supplied above to identify the order winners, qualifiers and less important competitive factors for the two categories of service. As the Managing Partner suspects, the two types of service are very different. Routine services must be relatively inexpensive and fast, whereas the clients for specialist services must trust the quality of advice and range of legal skills available in the firm. The customers for routine services do not expect errors and those for specialist services assume a basic level of dependability and speed. These are the qualifiers for the two categories of service. Note that qualifiers are not 'unimportant'. On the contrary, failure to be 'up to standard' at them can lose the firm business. However, it is the order winner which attracts new business. Most significantly, the performance objectives which each operations partner should stress are very different. Therefore there does seem to be a case for separating the sets of resources (for example, lawyers and other staff) and processes (information systems and procedures) that produce each type of service.

Table 3.2 **Competitive factors and performance objectives for the legal firm**

Service category	Routine services	Specialist services
Examples	Property purchase	Company merger deals
	Debt collection	Company restructuring
Order winner	Price	Quality of service
	Speed	Range of skills

Service category	Routine services	Specialist services
Qualifiers	Quality (conformance)	Dependability
	Speed	
Less important	Customization	Price
Operations partners	Cost	Quality of relationship
should stress	Speed	Legal skills
	Quality	Flexibility

The product/service life cycle influence on performance objectives

One way of generalizing the behaviour of both customers and competitors is to link it to the life cycle of the products or services that the operation is producing. The exact form of product/service life cycles will vary, but generally they are shown as the sales volume passing through four stages: introduction, growth, maturity and decline. The implication of this for operations management is that products and services will require different operations strategies in each stage of their life cycle (*see* Fig. 3.8).

Introduction stage

When a product or service is first introduced, it is likely to be offering something new in terms of its design or performance, with few competitors offering the same product or service. The needs of customers are unlikely to be well understood, so operations management needs to develop the flexibility to cope with any changes and be able to give the quality to maintain product/service performance.

	Introduction into market	Growth in market acceptance	Maturity of market, sales level off	Decline as market becomes saturated
Customers	Innovators	Early adopters	Bulk of market	Laggards
Competitors	Few/none	Increasing numbers	Stable numbers	Declining number
Likely order winners	Product/service specification	Availability	Low price Dependable supply	Low price
Likely qualifiers	Quality Range	Price Range	Range Quality	Dependable supply
Dominant operations performance objectives	Flexibility Quality	Speed Dependability Quality	Cost Dependability	Cost

Figure 3.8 The effects of the product/service life cycle on operations performance objectives

Growth stage

As volume grows, competitors may enter the growing market. Keeping up with demand could prove to be the main operations preoccupation. Rapid and dependable response to demand will help to keep demand buoyant, while quality levels must ensure that the company keeps its share of the market as competition starts to increase.

Maturity stage

Demand starts to level off. Some early competitors may have left the market and the industry will probably be dominated by a few larger companies. So operations will be expected to get the costs down in order to maintain profits or to allow price cutting, or both. Because of this, cost and productivity issues, together with dependable supply, are likely to be the operation's main concerns.

> **✳ Operations principle**
>
> Operations strategy objectives will change depending on the stage of the business's services and products.

Decline stage

After time, sales will decline with more competitors dropping out of the market. There might be a residual market, but unless a shortage of capacity develops, the market will continue to be dominated by price competition. Operations objectives continue to be dominated by cost.

The operations resources perspective

The fourth and final perspective we will take on operations strategy is based on a particularly influential theory of business strategy – the resource-based view (RBV) of the firm.[7] Put simply, the RBV holds that firms with an 'above-average' strategic performance are likely to have gained their sustainable competitive advantage because of the core competences (or capabilities) of their resources. This means that the way an organization inherits, or acquires, or develops its operations resources will, over the long term, have a significant impact on its strategic success. Furthermore, the impact of its 'operations resource' capabilities will be at least as great, if not greater, than that which it gets from its market position. So understanding and developing the capabilities of operations resources, although often neglected, is a particularly important perspective on operations strategy.

Resource constraints and capabilities

No organization can merely choose which part of the market it wants to be in without considering its ability to produce services and products in a way that will satisfy that market. In other words, the constraints imposed by its operations must be taken into account. For example, a small translation company offers general translation services to a wide range of customers who wish documents such as sales brochures to be translated into another language. A small company, it operates an informal network of part-time translators who enable the company to offer translation into or from most of the major languages in the world. Some of the company's largest customers want to purchase their sales brochures on a 'one-stop shop' basis and have asked the translation company whether it is willing to offer a full service, organizing the design and production, as well as the translation, of export brochures. This is a very profitable market opportunity, but the company does not have the resources, financial or physical, to take it up. From a market perspective, it is good business; from an operations resource perspective, it is not feasible.

However, the operations resource perspective is not always so negative. This perspective may identify *constraints* to satisfying some markets but it can also identify *capabilities* which can be exploited in other markets. For example, the same translation company has recently employed two new translators who have translation software skills, so now the company can offer a new 'fast-response' service which has been designed specifically to exploit the capabilities within the operations resources. Here the company has chosen to be driven by its resource capabilities rather than the obvious market opportunities.

As a publicly stated ambitious target it takes some beating: 'Amazon.com *strives to be*', it says, '*Earth's most customer-centric company.*' Founded by Jeff Bezos in 1995, the Amazon.com website started as a place to buy books, giving its customers what at the time was a unique customer experience. Bezos believed that only the Internet could offer customers the convenience of browsing a selection of millions of book titles in a single sitting. During its first 30 days of business, Amazon.com fulfilled orders for customers in 45 countries – all shipped from Bezos's Seattle-area garage. And that initial success has been followed by continued growth that is based on a clear strategy of technological innovation. Among its many technological innovations for customers, Amazon.com offers a personalized shopping experience for each customer, book discovery through 'Search Inside The Book', convenient checkout using '1-Click® Shopping', and community features like Listmania and Wish Lists that help customers discover new products and make informed buying decisions. In addition Amazon operates retail websites and offers programs that enable other retailers and individual sellers to sell products on their websites. It may not be glamorous, but Amazon has focused on what have been called 'the dull-but-difficult tasks' such as tracking products, managing suppliers, storing inventory and delivering boxes. Fulfilment By Amazon allows other companies to use Amazon's logistics capability including the handling of returned items, and access to Amazon's 'back-end' technology.

Amazon Web Services, its cloud computing business, provides the computing power for small and larger high-profile customers such as Spotify's digital music service, and Netflix's video streaming service. But, why should any business want to allow Amazon to have such control over its activities? Mainly because it allows entrepreneurs to create start-ups and established companies to expand their activities without the huge investment they would need to build appropriate infrastructure themselves. Amazon's large and efficient operations are also better value that smaller companies could achieve. Now, many prominent retailers work with Amazon Services to power their e-commerce offerings from end to end, including technology services, merchandizing, customer service, and order fulfilment. Offering business-to-business services is also good for Amazon. The problem with online retailing, said Bezos, is its seasonality. At peak times, such as Christmas, Amazon has far more computing capacity than it needs for the rest of the year. At low points it may be using as little as 10 per cent of its total capacity. Hiring out that spare capacity is an obvious way to bring in extra revenue. Its EC2 (Elastic Compute Cloud) service provides resizable computing capacity 'in the cloud'. It is designed, says Amazon, to make web-scale computing easier for developers: '*Amazon EC2's simple web service interface allows you to obtain and configure capacity with minimal friction. It provides you with complete control of your computing resources and lets you run on Amazon's*

Source: Alamy Images: Matthew Horwood

proven computing environment. Amazon EC2 reduces the time required to obtain and boot new server instances to minutes, allowing you to quickly scale capacity, both up and down, as your computing requirements change. Amazon EC2 changes the economics of computing by allowing you to pay only for capacity that you actually use. Amazon EC2 provides developers the tools to build failure resilient applications and isolate themselves from common failure scenarios.' Do not worry if you cannot follow the technicalities of Amazon's statement, it is aimed at IT professionals. The important point is that it is a business-to-business service based on the company's core competence of leveraging its processes and technology that can make retail operations ultra-efficient. However, some observers immediately criticized Amazon's apparent redefinition of its strategy. 'Why not', they said, 'stick to what you know, focus on your core competence of internet retailing?' Bezos's response was clear: 'We are sticking to our core competence. The only thing that's changed is that we are exposing it for (the benefit of) others.' At least for Jeff Bezos, Amazon is not so much an Internet retailer as a provider of Internet-based technology and logistics services.

Intangible resources

An operations resource perspective must start with an understanding of the resource capabilities and constraints within the operation. It must answer the simple questions: what do we have, and what can we do? An obvious starting point here is to examine the transforming and transformed resource inputs to the operation. These, after all, are the 'building blocks' of the operation. However, merely listing the type of *resources* an operation has does not give a complete picture of what it can do. Trying to understand an operation by listing its resources alone is like trying to understand an automobile by listing its component parts. To describe it more fully, we need to describe how the component parts form the internal mechanisms of the motor car. Within the operation, the equivalent of these mechanisms is its *processes*. Yet, even for an automobile, a technical explanation of its mechanisms still does not convey everything about its style or 'personality'. Something more is needed to describe these. In the same way, an operation is not just the sum of its processes. In addition, the operation has some intangible resources. An operation's intangible resources include such things as its relationship with suppliers, the reputation it has with its customers, its knowledge of its process technologies and the way its staff can work together in new product and service development. These intangible resources may not always be obvious within the operation, but they are important and have real value. It is these intangible resources, as well as its tangible resources, that an operation needs to deploy in order to satisfy its markets. The central issue for operations management, therefore, is to ensure that its pattern of strategic decisions really does develop appropriate capabilities within its resources and processes.

Strategic resources and sustainable competitive advantage

The 'resource-based' explanation of why some companies manage to gain sustainable competitive advantage is that they have accumulated better or more appropriate resources. Put simply, 'above-average' competitive performance is more likely to be the result of the core capabilities (or competences) inherent in a firm's resources than its competitive positioning in its industry. And resources can have a particularly influential impact on strategic success if they exhibit some or all of the following properties:[8]

- **They are scarce** – Unequal access to resources so that not all competing firms have scarce resources such as an ideal location, experienced engineers, proprietary software, etc., can strengthen competitive advantage. So, for example, if a firm did not have the good foresight (or luck) to acquire a strategic resource (such as a supply contract with a specialist supplier) when it was inexpensive, it will have to try and acquire it after it has become expensive (because other firms are also now wanting it).
- **They are not very mobile** – Some resources are difficult to move out of a firm. For example, if a new process is developed in a company's Stockholm site and is based on the knowledge and experience of the Stockholm staff, the process will be difficult (although not totally impossible) to sell to another company based elsewhere in Europe (or even Sweden

if the staff do not want to move). As a result, the advantages that derive from the processes resources are more likely to be retained over time.

- **They are difficult to imitate or substitute for** – These two factors help define how easily a resource-based advantage can be sustained over time. It is not enough only to have resources which are unique and immobile. If a competitor can copy these resources or, less predictably, replace them with alternative resources, then their value will quickly deteriorate. However, the less tangible are the resources and the more connected with the tacit knowledge embedded within the organization, the more difficult they are for competitors to understand and to copy.

Structural and infrastructural decisions

A distinction is often drawn between the strategic decisions which determine an operation's structure and those which determine its infrastructure. An operation's structural decisions are those which we have classed as primarily influencing design activities, while infrastructural decisions are those which influence the workforce organization and the planning and control, and improvement activities. This distinction in operations strategy has been compared with that between 'hardware' and 'software' in computer systems. The hardware of a computer sets limits to what it can do. In a similar way, investing in advanced technology and building more or better facilities can raise the potential of any type of operation. Within the limits which are imposed by the hardware of a computer, the software governs how effective the computer actually is in practice. The most powerful computer can only work to its full potential if its software is capable of exploiting its potential. The same principle applies with operations. The best and most costly facilities and technology will only be effective if the operation also has an appropriate infrastructure which governs the way it will work on a day-to-day basis. Figure 3.9 illustrates some typical structural and infrastructural decisions.

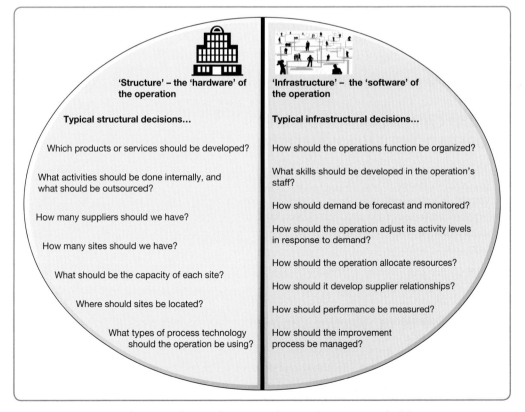

Figure 3.9 Some typical structural and infrastructural operations strategy decisions

Apple's supply operations strategy[9]

Earlier in this chapter we looked at Apple's retail operations strategy. Here we move on to how Apple supplies those, and other, retail outlets.

Behind the impressive corporate facade of Apple's Silicon Valley headquarters there are no factories churning out the millions of products that Apple sells every year. Apple, like most of its competitors, outsources its production to supplier operations around the world, mainly in the manufacturing powerhouses of South-East Asia. So does this mean that Apple's operations strategy is also outsourced along with its manufacturing? Not at all. What it does mean is that operations strategy for Apple is concerned with 'supply'. In other words, making sure that current products are always supplied fast enough to meet demand and new products always meet their launch dates. Over the years Apple has put together a remarkable supply network that is recognized as one of the most efficient in the world and, what is more important, gives them significant competitive advantage. The company's (outsourced) manufacturing, purchasing and supply logistics give it the ability to accomplish substantial new product launches without having to build up huge and expensive pre-launch stocks. In the words of Tim Cook, who developed Apple's operations strategy, 'nobody wants to buy sour milk.'

The way that Apple beats its competitors is to use its cash to secure exclusive deals on new component technologies (touchscreens, chips, LED displays, etc.). When a new component first comes out, it is usually very expensive to produce, and constructing a factory that can produce it in high volume is even more expensive. Combine this with the relatively small profit margin of many components and it becomes difficult for suppliers to make enough profit to guarantee that they can make an acceptable return on their investment. But, thanks to its successful stream of products, Apple can afford to pay for some or all of a supplier's construction cost of the new factory. In exchange the supplier gives exclusive rights to Apple for the new component over an agreed period. This has two advantages for Apple. First, it gives Apple access to new component technology months (or even years) before its rivals, allowing it to launch radical new products that are literally impossible for competitors to duplicate. Second, even when the exclusive agreement expires, Apple will often have negotiated a discounted price. So it can source the component at a lower cost from the supplier that is now the most experienced and skilled provider of those parts.

In summary, according to Marty Lariviere of Stanford University, '[Apple's operations strategy is to] *bet big on technology that lets them have distinctive products. With their limited product line and high volume, they can make commitments that other tech firms may shy away from. It also means that (if they are right) other firms are going to be hard pressed to catch up if Apple has locked up a large amount of supplier capacity.*'

HOW CAN OPERATIONS STRATEGY FORM THE BASIS FOR OPERATIONS IMPROVEMENT?

An operations strategy is not just about checking that a business's resources and processes are consistent with its overall strategy. As our earlier discussion of operations capabilities implied, it also can provide the foundation for improvement. And the objective of improvement is obvious – it tries to make things better! But how much better does better mean? And does this mean better in every way or better in some specific manner? This is why, in this section, we look at two models that use the market requirements and operations capabilities perspectives that we discussed earlier, to help answer these questions. First we examine the concept of the 'line of fit', then the 'importance–performance matrix'.

The 'line of fit' between market requirements and operations capabilities

At a strategic level, the whole purpose of operations improvement is to make operations performance better at serving its markets. In other words, there should be a fit between what an operation is trying to achieve in its markets (market requirements) and what it is good at doing (operations capabilities). Figure 3.10(a) illustrates this idea by showing diagrammatically

Figure 3.10 An operations improvement should achieve 'fit' between market requirements and operations performance, but deviation from the line of 'fit' between market requirements and operations performance can expose the operation to risk

the approximate alignment or 'fit' between an operation's performance and the requirements of its markets. The vertical dimension represents the level of market requirements that reflect the intrinsic needs of customers or their expectations. Moving along this dimension indicates a broadly enhanced level of market performance. The horizontal scale represents the level of the organization's operations capabilities. This includes such things as its ability to achieve its competitive objectives and the effectiveness with which it uses its resources. Moving along the dimension indicates a broadly enhanced level of operations capabilities and therefore operations performance. Be careful, however, in using this diagrammatic representation. It is a conceptual model rather than a practical tool. It is intended merely to illustrate some ideas around the concept of strategic improvement. In terms of the framework illustrated in Figure 3.10(a), improvement means three things:

> **✳ Operations principle**
>
> Operations strategy should aim for alignment or 'fit' between an operation's performance and the requirements of its markets.

1 **Achieving 'alignment'** – This means achieving an approximate balance between 'required market performance' and 'actual operations performance'. The diagonal line in Figure 3.10(a) therefore represents a line of fit with market requirements and operations capabilities in balance.

2 **Achieving 'sustainable' alignment** – It is not enough to achieve some degree of alignment to a single point in time. Equally important is whether operations processes could adapt to the new market conditions.

3 **Improving overall performance** – If the requirements placed on the organization by its markets are relatively undemanding, then the corresponding level of operations capabilities will not need to be particularly high. The more demanding the level of market requirements, the greater will have to be the level of operations capabilities. But most firms would see their overall strategic objectives as achieving alignment at a level that implies some degree of long-term competitive success. In Figure 3.10(a) point A represents alignment at a low level, while point B represents alignment at a higher level. The assumption in most firms' operations strategies is that point B is a more desirable position than point A because it is more likely to represent a financially successful position. High levels of market performance, achieved as a result of high levels of operations performance, being generally more difficult for competitors to match.

Deviating from the line of fit

During the improvement path (red dashed arrow) from A to B in Figure 3.10(a) it may not be possible to maintain the balance between market requirements and operations performance. Sometimes the market may expect something that the operation cannot (temporarily) deliver. Sometimes operations may have capabilities that cannot be exploited in the market. At a strategic level, there are risks deriving from any deviation from the 'line of fit'. For example, delays in the improvement to a new website could mean that customers do not receive the level of service they were promised. This is shown as position X in Figure 3.10(b). Under these circumstances, the risk to the organization is that its reputation (or brand) will suffer because market expectations exceed the operation's capability to perform at the appropriate level. At other times, the operation may make improvements before they can be fully exploited in the market. For example, the same online retailer may have improved its website so that it can offer extra services, such as the ability to customize products, before those products have been stocked in its distribution centre. This means that, although an improvement to its ordering processes has been made, problems elsewhere in the company prevent the improvement from giving value to the company. This is represented by point Y in Figure 3.10(b). In both instances, improvement activity needs to move the operation back to the line of fit.

A strategic view of operations improvement priorities

The idea of the line of fit is conceptually useful, but, as we mentioned earlier, not a practical tool. Yet one can use the idea of comparing market and operations perspectives to provide more direct guidance to operations managers. To do this we need to think about both market requirements and operations capabilities at a more focused and disaggregated level. So, rather than ask generally, 'what are the market requirements for our products and/or services?' one asks, 'how important are the competitive factors that characterise a product or service?' The intention is to gain an understanding of the relative importance to customers of the various competitive factors. For example, do customers for a particular product or service prefer low prices to a wide range? The needs and preferences of customers shape the *importance* of operations objectives within the operation. Similarly, rather than ask generally, 'what are our operations capabilities?' one asks, 'how good is our operation at providing the required level of performance in each of the competitive objectives?' But how good is our performance against what criteria? Strategically the most revealing point of comparison is with competitors. Competitors are the points of comparison against which the operation can judge its performance. From a competitive viewpoint, as operations improve their performance, the improvement which matters most is that which takes the operation past the performance levels achieved by its competitors. The role of competitors then is in determining achieved *performance*. (In a not-for-profit context, 'other similar operations' can be substituted for 'competitors'.)

Both importance and performance have to be brought together before any judgement can be made as to the relative priorities for improvement. Just because something is particularly important to its customers does not mean that an operation should necessarily give it immediate priority for improvement. It may be that the operation is already considerably better than its competitors at serving customers in this respect. Similarly, just because an operation is not very good at something when compared with its competitors' performance, it does not necessarily mean that it should be immediately improved. Customers may not particularly value this aspect of performance. Both importance and performance need to be viewed together to judge the prioritization of objectives:

> **✳ Operations principle**
>
> Improvement priorities are determined by importance for customers and performance against competitors or similar operations.

- **Judging importance to customers** – Earlier we introduced the idea of order-winning, qualifying and less important competitive factors, and one could take these three categories as an indication of the relative importance of each performance factor. But usually one needs to use a slightly more discriminating scale. One way to do this is to take our three broad categories of competitive factors – order winning, qualifying and less important – and divide each category into three further points representing strong, medium and weak positions. Figure 3.11(a) illustrates such a scale.

- **Judging performance against competitors** – At its simplest, a competitive performance standard would consist merely of judging whether the achieved performance of an operation is better than, the same or worse than that of its competitors. However, in much the same way as the nine-point importance scale was derived, we can derive a more discriminating nine-point performance scale, as shown in Figure 3.11(b).

The priority for improvement that each competitive factor should be given can be assessed from a comparison of their importance and performance. This can be shown on an importance–performance matrix that, as its name implies, positions each competitive factor according to its scores or ratings on these criteria. Figure 3.12 shows an importance–performance matrix divided into zones of improvement priority. The first zone boundary is the 'lower bound of acceptability' shown as line AB in the figure. This is the boundary between acceptable and unacceptable performance. When a competitive factor is rated as relatively unimportant (8 or 9 on the importance scale), this boundary will in practice be low. Most operations are prepared to tolerate performance levels which are 'in the same ball-park' as their competitors (even at the bottom end of the rating) for unimportant competitive factors. They only become concerned when performance levels are clearly below those of their competitors. Conversely, when judging competitive factors that are rated highly (1 or 2 on the importance scale) they will be markedly less sanguine at poor or mediocre levels of performance. Minimum levels of acceptability for these competitive factors will usually be at the lower end of the 'better than competitors' class. Below this minimum bound of acceptability (AB) there is clearly a need for improvement; above this line there is no immediate urgency for any improvement. However, not all competitive factors falling below the minimum line will be seen as having

Figure 3.11 Nine-point scales for judging importance and performance; the importance–performance matrix

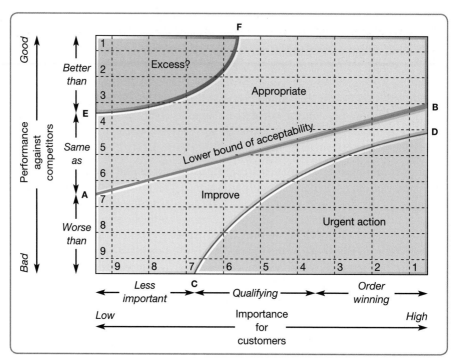

Figure 3.12 Priority zones in the importance–performance matrix

the same degree of improvement priority. A boundary approximately represented by line CD represents a distinction between an urgent priority zone and a less urgent improvement zone. Similarly, above the line AB, not all competitive factors are regarded as having the same priority. The line EF can be seen as the approximate boundary between performance levels which are regarded as 'good' or 'appropriate' on the one hand and those regarded as 'too good' or 'excess' on the other. Segregating the matrix in this way results in four zones which imply very different priorities:

- **The 'appropriate' zone** – Competitive factors in this area lie above the lower bound of acceptability and so should be considered satisfactory.
- **The 'improve' zone** – Lying below the lower bound of acceptability, any factors in this zone must be candidates for improvement.
- **The 'urgent-action' zone** – These factors are important to customers but performance is below that of competitors. The factors must be considered as candidates for immediate improvement.
- **The 'excess?' zone** – Factors in this area are 'high performing', but not important to customers. The question must be asked, therefore, whether the resources devoted to achieving such a performance could be used better elsewhere.

Worked example

EXL Laboratories is a subsidiary of an electronics company. It carries out research and development as well as technical problem-solving work for a wide range of companies, including companies in its own group. It is particularly keen to improve the level of service which it gives to its customers. However, it needs to decide which aspect of its performance to improve first. It has devised a list of the most important aspects of its service:

- **The quality of its technical solutions** – the perceived appropriateness by customers.
- **The quality of its communications with customers** – the frequency and usefulness of information.

- **The quality of post-project documentation** – the usefulness of the documentation which goes with the final report.
- **Delivery speed** – the time between customer request and the delivery of the final report.
- **Delivery dependability** – the ability to deliver on the promised date.
- **Delivery flexibility** – the ability to deliver the report on a revised date.
- **Specification flexibility** – the ability to change the nature of the investigation.
- **Price** – the total charge to the customer.

EXL assigns a score to each of these factors using the 1–9 scale described in Figure 3.12. After which EXL turned its attention to judging the laboratory's performance against competitor organizations. Although EXL has benchmarked information for some aspects of performance, it has to make estimates for the others. Both these scores are shown in Figure 3.13.

EXL Laboratories plotted the importance and performance ratings it had given to each of its competitive factors on an importance–performance matrix. This is shown in Figure 3.14. It shows that the most important aspect of competitiveness – the ability to deliver sound technical solutions to its customers – falls comfortably within the appropriate zone. Specification flexibility and delivery flexibility are also in the appropriate zone, although only just. Both delivery speed and delivery dependability seem to be in need of improvement as each is below the minimum level of acceptability for their respective importance positions. However, two competitive factors, communications and cost/price, are clearly in need of immediate improvement. These two factors should therefore be assigned the most urgent priority for

Figure 3.13 Rating 'importance to customers' and 'performance against competitors' on the nine-point scales for EXL Laboratories

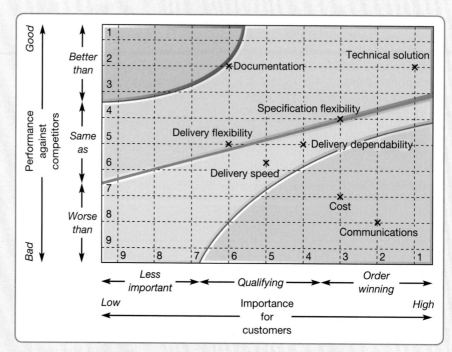

Figure 3.14 The importance–performance matrix for EXL Laboratories

improvement. The matrix also indicates that the company's documentation could almost be regarded as 'too good'.

The matrix may not reveal any total surprises. The competitive factors in the 'urgent-action' zone may be known to be in need of improvement already. However, the exercise is useful for two reasons:

- It helps to discriminate between many factors which may be in need of improvement.
- It gives purpose and structure to the debate on improvement priorities.

HOW CAN AN OPERATIONS STRATEGY BE PUT TOGETHER? THE PROCESS OF OPERATIONS STRATEGY

What is called the 'process' of strategy is concerned with 'how' strategies are put together. So the 'process of operations strategy' means the method that is used to determine what an operations strategy should be. It is not a simple task. Putting an operations strategy together and making it happen in practice is a complex and difficult thing to achieve. Even the most sophisticated organizations would probably admit that they do not always get it right. And although any simple step-by-step model of how to 'do' operations strategy will inevitably be a simplification of a messy reality, we will use a four-stage model to illustrate some of the elements of 'process'. This stage model is shown in Figure 3.15. It divides the process of operations strategy into formulation, implementation, monitoring and control.[10] These four stages are shown in Figure 3.15 as a cycle. This is because, in practice, strategies may be revisited depending on the experience gained from trying to make them happen.

> **✳ Operations principle**
>
> The process of operations strategy involves formulation, implementation, monitoring and control.

Figure 3.15 The stages of the process of operations strategy

Operations strategy formulation

The formulation of operations strategy is the process of clarifying the various objectives and decisions that make up the strategy, and the links between them. Unlike day-to-day operations management, formulating an operations strategy is likely to be only an occasional activity. Some firms will have a regular (for example, annual) planning cycle and operations strategy consideration may form part of this, but the extent of any changes made in each annual cycle is likely to be limited. In other words, the 'complete' process of formulating an entirely new operations strategy will be a relatively infrequent event. There are many 'formulation processes' which are, or can be, used to formulate operations strategies. Most consultancy companies have developed their own frameworks, as have several academics.

What should the formulation process be trying to achieve?

Before putting an operations strategy together, it is necessary to ask the question 'what should it be trying to achieve?' Clearly, it should provide a set of actions that, with hindsight, have provided the 'best' outcome for the organization. But that really does not help us. What do we mean by 'the best', and what good is a judgement that can only be applied in hindsight? Yet, even if we cannot assess the 'goodness' of a strategy for certain in advance, we can check it out for some attributes that could stop it being a success, as follows:

- **Is operations strategy comprehensive?** In other words, does it include all important issues? Business history is littered with companies that simply failed to notice the potential impact of, for instance, new process technology, or emerging changes in their supply network.
- **Is operations strategy coherent?** As a strategy evolves over time, tensions can emerge that threaten to pull the overall strategy in different directions. This can result in a loss of coherence. Coherence is when the choices made in each decision area all direct the operation in the same strategic direction, with all strategic decisions complementing and reinforcing each other in the promotion of performance objectives. For example, if new Internet-based remote diagnostic technology for heating systems is introduced which allows service engineers to customize their service advice to individual clients' needs, it would be 'incoherent' not to devise a new operating process which did not enable service staff to exploit the technology's potential, for example by emailing customers with service options before the service engineer visits.
- **Does operations strategy have correspondence?** The decisions pursued in each part of the strategy should correspond to the true priority of each performance objective. So, for example, if cost reduction is the main objective for an operation then its process technology investment decisions might err towards the purchase of 'off-the-shelf' (as opposed

to customized) equipment which would reduce the capital cost of the technology and may also imply lower maintenance and running costs. However, it is unlikely to be as flexible. Implicitly the strategy is accepting that cost is more important than flexibility. So, we would expect all other decisions to correspond with the same prioritization of objectives, for example: capacity strategies that exploit natural economies of scale; supply network strategies that reduce purchasing costs; performance measurement systems that stress efficiency and productivity; continuous improvement strategies that emphasize continual cost reduction; and so on.

- **Does operations strategy identify critical issues?** The more critical the decision, the more attention it deserves. Although no strategic decision is unimportant, in practical terms some decisions are more critical than others. The judgement over exactly what decisions are particularly critical is very much a pragmatic one which must be based on the particular circumstances of an individual firm's operations strategy. But they must be identified.

OPERATIONS IN PRACTICE | **Nokia, a failure to change**[11]

Only a few years ago Nokia was the king of the mobile phone business – and it was a good business to be in, with double-digit growth year on year. Nokia was omnipresent and all-powerful, a pioneer that had supplied the first mass wave of the expanding mobile phone industry. Nokia dominated the market in many parts of the world and the easily recognizable Nokia ring-tone echoed everywhere from boardrooms to shopping malls. So why did this, once-dominant, company eventually sink to the point where it was forced to sell its mobile communications business to Microsoft in 2013? The former Nokia CEO, Jormal Ollila, admitted that Nokia made several mistakes, but the exact nature of those mistakes is a point of debate among business commentators. Julian Birkinshaw, a professor at London Business School, dismisses some of the most commonly cited reasons. Did Nokia lose touch with its customers? Well, yes, but by definition that must hold for any company whose sales drop so drastically in the face of thriving competitors. Did it fail to develop the necessary technologies? No. Nokia had a prototype touchscreen before the iPhone was launched, and its smartphones were technologically superior to anything Apple, Samsung or Google had to offer for many years. Did it not recognize that the basis of competition was shifting from the hardware to the ecosystem? (A technology ecosystem in this case is a term used to describe the complex system of interdependent components that work together to enable mobile technology to operate successfully.) Not really. The 'ecosystem' battle began in the early 2000s, with Nokia joining forces with Ericsson, Motorola and Psion to create Symbian as a platform technology that would keep Microsoft at bay.

Source: Fotolia.com: Tan Kian Khoon

Where Nokia struggled was in relying on an operations strategy that failed to allocate resources appropriately and could not implement the changes that were necessary. As far as resource allocation was concerned, Nokia saw itself primarily as a hardware company rather than a software company. Its engineers were great at designing and producing hardware, but not the programs that drive the devices. They underestimated the importance of software (including, crucially, the apps that run on smartphones). Largely it was hardware rather than software experts who controlled its development process. By contrast, Apple had always emphasized that hardware and software were equally important. Yet while it was losing its dominance, Nokia was well aware of most of the changes occurring in the mobile communications market and the technology developments being actively pursued by competitors. Arguably, Nokia was not short of awareness, but it did lack the capacity to convert awareness into action. 'The failure of big companies to adapt to changing circumstances is one of the fundamental puzzles in the world of business', says Professor Birkinshaw. Occasionally, a genuinely 'disruptive' technology can wipe out an entire industry. But usually the sources of failure are less dramatic. Often it is a failure to implement strategies or technologies that have already been developed, an arrogant disregard for changing customer demands, or a complacent attitude towards new competitors.

Operations strategy implementation

Operations strategy implementation is the way that strategies are operationalized or executed. It means attempting to make sure that intended strategies are actually achieved. It is important because no matter how sophisticated the intellectual and analytical underpinnings of a strategy, it remains only a document until it has been implemented. But the way one implements any strategy will very much depend on the specific nature of the changes implied by that strategy and the organizational and environmental conditions that apply during its implementation. However, three issues are often mentioned by strategy practitioners as being important in achieving successful implementation:

- **Clarity of strategic decisions** – There is a strong relationship between the formulation stage and the implementation stage of operations strategy. The crucial attribute of the formulation stage is clarity. If a strategy is ambiguous it is difficult to translate strategic intent into specific actions. With clarity, however, it should be easier to define the intent behind the strategy, the few important issues that need to be developed to deliver the intent, the way that projects be led and resourced, who will be responsible for each task, and so on.
- **Motivational leadership** – Leadership that motivates, encourages and provides support is a huge advantage in dealing with the complexity of implementation. Leadership is needed to bring sense and meaning to strategic aspirations, maintain a sense of purpose over the implementation period, and, when necessary, modify the implementation plan in the light of experience.
- **Project management** – Implementation means breaking up a complex plan into a set of relatively distinct activities. Fortunately there is a well-understood collection of ideas of how to do this. It is called 'project management' and a whole chapter is devoted to this subject (Chapter 19).

Operations strategy monitoring

Especially in times when things are changing rapidly, as during strategic change, organizations often want to track ongoing performance to make sure that the changes are proceeding as planned. Monitoring should be capable of providing early indications (or a 'warning bell' as some call it) by diagnosing data and triggering appropriate changes in how the operations strategy is being implemented. Having created a plan for the implementation, each part of it has to be monitored to ensure that planned activities are indeed happening. Any deviation from what should be happening (that is, its planned activities) can then be rectified through some kind of intervention in the operation.

Operations strategy control

Strategic control involves the evaluation of the results from monitoring the implementation. Activities, plans and performance are assessed with the intention of correcting future action if that is required. In some ways this strategic view of control is similar to how it works operationally (which is discussed in Chapter 10), but there are differences. At a strategic level, control can be difficult because strategic objectives are not always clear and unambiguous. Ask any experienced managers; they will acknowledge that it is not always possible to articulate every aspect of a strategic decision in detail. Many strategies are just too complex for that. So, rather than adhering dogmatically to a predetermined plan, it may be better to adapt as circumstances change. And the more uncertain the environment, the more an operation needs to emphasize this form of strategic flexibility and develop its ability to learn from events.

OPERATIONS IN PRACTICE

Sometimes any plan is better than no plan[12]

There is a famous story that illustrates the importance of having some kind of plan, even if hindsight proves it to be the wrong plan. During manoeuvres in the Alps, a detachment of Hungarian soldiers got lost. The weather was severe and the snow was deep. In these freezing conditions, after two days of wandering, the soldiers gave up hope and became reconciled to a frozen death on the mountains. Then, to their delight, one of the soldiers discovered a map in his pocket. Much cheered by this discovery, the soldiers were able to escape from the mountains. When they were safe back at their headquarters, they discovered that the map was not of the Alps at all, but of the Pyrenees. What is the moral of the story? It is that a plan (or a map) may not be perfect but it gives a sense of purpose and a sense of direction. If the soldiers had waited for the right map they would have frozen to death. Yet their renewed confidence motivated them to get up and create opportunities.

Critical commentary

The argument has been put forward that strategy does not lend itself to a simple 'stage model' analysis that guides managers in a step-by-step manner through to the eventual 'answer' that is a final strategy. Therefore, the models put forward by consultants and academics are of very limited value. In reality, strategies (even those that are made deliberately, as opposed to those that simply 'emerge') are the result of very complex organizational forces. Even descriptive models such as the four-stage model described above in Figure 3.9 can do little more than sensitize managers to some of the key issues that they should be taking into account when devising strategies. In fact, they argue, it is the articulation of the 'content' of operation strategy that is more useful than adhering to some over-simplistic description of a strategy process.

SUMMARY ANSWERS TO KEY QUESTIONS

❯ What is strategy and what is operations strategy?

- Strategy is the total pattern of decisions and actions that position the organization in its environment and that are intended to achieve its long-term goals.
- Operations strategy concerns the pattern of strategic decisions and actions which set the role, objectives and activities of the operation.
- Operations strategy has content and process. The content concerns the specific decisions which are taken to achieve specific objectives. The process is the procedure which is used within a business to formulate its strategy.

〉 What is the difference between a 'top-down' and a 'bottom-up' view of operations strategy?

- The 'top-down' perspective views strategic decisions at a number of levels. Corporate strategy sets the objectives for the different businesses which make up a group of businesses. Business strategy sets the objectives for each individual business and how it positions itself in its marketplace. Functional strategies set the objectives for each function's contribution to its business strategy.
- The 'bottom-up' view of operations strategy sees overall strategy as emerging from day-to-day operational experience.

〉 What is the difference between a 'market requirements' and an 'operations resources' view of operations strategy?

- A 'market requirements' perspective of operations strategy sees the main role of operations as satisfying markets. Operations performance objectives and operations decisions should be primarily influenced by a combination of customers' needs and competitors' actions. Both of these may be summarized in terms of the product/service life cycle.
- The 'operations resources' perspective of operations strategy is based on the resource-based view (RBV) of the firm and sees the operation's core competences (or capabilities) as being the main influence on operations strategy. Operations capabilities are developed partly through the strategic decisions taken by the operation. Strategic decision areas in operations are usually divided into structural and infrastructural decisions. Structural decisions are those which define an operation's shape and form. Infrastructural decisions are those which influence the systems and procedures that determine how the operation will work in practice.

〉 How can operations strategy form the basis for operations improvement?

- An operations strategy can provide the foundation for improvement by achieving a fit between an operation's market requirements and its operations capabilities.
- A 'line of fit' diagram can illustrate this. It is a conceptual model intended to illustrate some ideas around the concept of strategic improvement.
- During improvement it may not be possible to maintain a balance between market requirements and operations performance. When markets expect something that the operation cannot deliver, or when operations have capabilities that cannot be exploited in the market, there are strategic risks deriving from the deviation from the 'line of fit'.
- The importance–performance matrix positions competitive factors according to their importance and the operation's success at achieving them to determine relative improvement priorities.

〉 How can an operations strategy be formulated? The process of operations strategy

- Putting an operations strategy together is called 'the process' of operations strategy.
- There are four stages in the process of operations strategy, which can be viewed as a cycle:
  - Formulation – which is the process of clarifying the various objectives and decisions that make up the strategy, and the links between them. This should produce strategies that are comprehensive, coherent, provide correspondence and prioritize the most critical activities or decisions.

- Implementation – the way that strategy is operationalized or executed. Three issues are often mentioned by strategy practitioners as being important in achieving successful implementation: the clarity of the strategy, the nature of the leadership provided by top management, and effective project management.

- Monitoring – involves tracking ongoing performance and diagnosing data to make sure that the changes are proceeding as planned and providing early indications of any deviation from the plan.

- Control – involves the evaluation of the results from monitoring the implementation so that activities, plans and performance can be assessed with the intention of correcting future action if that is required.

CASE STUDY

McDonald's: half a century of growth[13]

It is loved and it is hated. It is a shining example of how good-value food can be brought to a mass market. It is a symbol of everything that is wrong with 'industrialized', capitalist, bland, high-calorie and environmentally unfriendly commercialism. It is the best-known and most loved fast food brand in the world with more than 36,000 restaurants in 117 countries, providing jobs for 1.7 million staff and feeding 69 million customers per day (yes, per day!). It is part of the homogenization of individual national cultures, filling the world with bland, identical, 'cookie cutter', Americanized and soulless operations that dehumanize its staff by forcing them to follow ridged and over-defined procedures. But whether you see it as friend, foe, or a bit of both, McDonald's has revolutionized the food industry, affecting the lives of both the people who produce food and the people who eat it. It has also had its ups (mainly) and downs (occasionally) as markets, customers and economic circumstances change. Yet, even in the toughest times it has always displayed remarkable resilience. What follows is a brief (for such a large corporation) summary of its history.

Starting small

Central to the development of McDonald's is Ray Kroc, who by 1954 and at the age of 52 had been variously a piano player, a paper cup salesman and a multi-mixer salesman. He was surprised by a big order for eight multi-mixers from a restaurant in San Bernardino, California. When he visited the customer he found a small but successful restaurant run by two brothers Dick and Mac McDonald. They had opened their 'Bar-B-Que' restaurant 14 years earlier, and by the time Ray Kroc visited the brothers' operation it had a self-service drive-in format with a limited

menu of nine items. He was amazed by the effectiveness of their operation. Focusing on a limited menu including burgers, fries and beverages had allowed them to analyse every step of the process of producing and serving their food. Ray Kroc was so impressed that he persuaded the brothers to adopt his vision of creating McDonald's restaurants all over the USA, the first of which opened in Des Plaines, Illinois, in June 1955. However, later, Kroc and the McDonald brothers quarrelled, and Kroc bought them out. Now with exclusive rights to the McDonald's name, the restaurants spread, and in five years there were 200 restaurants through the USA. Yet through this, and later, expansions, Ray Kroc insisted on maintaining the same principles that he had seen in the original operation: *'If I had a brick for every time I've repeated the phrase Quality, Service, Cleanliness and Value, I think I'd probably be able to bridge the Atlantic Ocean with them.'*

Source: Shutterstock.com: Anatoly Tiplyashin

Priority to the process

Ray Kroc had been attracted by the cleanliness, simplicity, efficiency and profitability of the McDonald brothers' operation. They had stripped fast food delivery down to its essence and eliminated needless effort to make a swift assembly line for a meal at reasonable prices. Kroc wanted to build a process that would become famous for food of consistently high quality using uniform methods of preparation. His burgers, buns, fries and beverages should taste just the same in Alaska as they did in Alabama. The answer was the 'Speedee Service System', a standardised process that prescribed exact preparation methods, specially designed equipment and strict product specifications. The emphasis on process standardization meant that customers could be assured of identical levels of food and service quality every time they visited any store, anywhere. Operating procedures were specified in minute detail. The first operations manual prescribed rigorous cooking instructions such as temperatures, cooking times and portions. Similarly, operating procedures were defined to ensure the required customer experience, for example no food items were to be held more than 10 minutes in the transfer bin between being cooked and being served. Technology was also automated. Specially designed equipment helped to guarantee consistency using 'fool-proof' devices. For example, the ketchup was dispensed through a metered pump. Specially designed 'clam shell' grills cooked both sides of each meat patty simultaneously for a pre-set time. And when it became clear that the metal tongs used by staff to fill French-fry containers were awkward to use efficiently, McDonald's engineers devised a simple aluminium scoop that made the job faster and easier.

For Kroc, the operating process was both his passion and the company's central philosophy. It was also the foundation of learning and improvement. The company's almost compulsive focus on process detail was not an end in itself. Rather it was to learn what contributed to consistent high-quality service in practice and what did not. McDonald's always saw learning as important. It founded 'Hamburger University', initially in the basement of a restaurant in Elk Grove Village, Illinois. It had a research and development laboratory to develop new cooking, freezing, storing and serving methods. Also franchisees and operators were trained in the analytical techniques necessary to run a successful McDonald's. It awarded degrees in 'Hamburgerology'. But learning was not just for headquarters. The company also formed a 'field service' unit to appraise and help its restaurants by sending field service consultants to review their performance on a number of 'dimensions' including cleanliness, queuing, food quality and customer service. As Ray Kroc said, 'We take the hamburger business more seriously than anyone else. What sets McDonald's apart is the passion that we and our suppliers share around producing and delivering the highest-quality beef patties. Rigorous food safety and quality standards and practices are in place and executed at the highest levels every day.'

No story illustrates the company's philosophy of learning and improvement better than its adoption of frozen fries. French-fried potatoes had always been important for McDonald's. Initially, the company tried observing the temperature levels and cooking methods that produced the best fries. The problem was that the temperature during the cooking process was very much influenced by the temperature of the potatoes when they were placed in the cooking vat. So, unless the temperature of the potatoes before they were cooked was also controlled (not very practical) it was difficult to specify the exact time and temperature that would produce perfect fries. But McDonald's researchers discovered that, irrespective of the temperature of the raw potatoes, fries were always at their best when the oil temperature in the cooking vat increased by 3 degrees above the low-temperature point after they were put in the vat. So by monitoring the temperature of the vat, perfect fries could be produced every time. But that was not the end of the story. The ideal potato for fries was the Idaho Russet, which was seasonal and not available in the summer months. At other times an alternative (inferior) potato was used. One grower, who, at the time, supplied a fifth of McDonald's potatoes, suggested that he could put Idaho Russets into cold storage for supplying during the summer period. Unfortunately, all the stored potatoes rotted. Not to be beaten, he offered another suggestion. Why doesn't McDonald's consider switching to frozen potatoes? But the company was initially cautious about meddling with such an important menu item. However, there were other advantages in using frozen potatoes. Supplying fresh potatoes in perfect condition to McDonald's rapidly expanding chain was increasingly difficult. Frozen potatoes could actually increase the quality of the company's fries if a method of satisfactorily cooking them could be found. Once again McDonald's developers came to the rescue. They developed a method of air-drying the raw fries, quick frying, and then freezing them. The supplier, who was a relatively small and local supplier when he first suggested storing Idaho Russets, grew his business to supply around half of McDonald's US business.

Throughout its rapid expansion McDonald's focused on four areas: improving the product; establishing strong supplier relationships; creating (largely customized) equipment; and developing franchise holders. But also it was its strict control of the menu that provided a platform of stability. Although its competitors offered a relatively wide variety of menu items, McDonald's limited its to 10 items. As one of McDonald's senior managers at the time stressed, 'It wasn't because we were smarter. The fact that we were selling just ten items [and] had a facility that was small, and used a limited number of suppliers created an ideal environment.' Capacity growth (through additional stores) was also managed carefully. Well-utilized stores were important to franchise holders, so franchise opportunities were located only where they would not seriously undercut existing stores.

Securing supply

McDonald's says that it has been the strength of the alignment between the company, its franchisees and its suppliers (collectively referred to as the System) that has been the explanation for its success. But during the company's early years suppliers proved problematic. McDonald's approached the major food suppliers, such as Kraft and Heinz, but without much success. Large and established suppliers were reluctant to conform to McDonald's requirements, preferring to focus on retail sales. It was the relatively small companies who were willing to risk supplying what seemed then to be a risky venture. And as McDonald's grew, so did its suppliers, who also valued the company's less adversarial relationship. One supplier is quoted as saying, *'Other chains would walk away from you for half a cent. McDonald's was more concerned with getting quality. McDonald's always treated me with respect even when they became much bigger and didn't have to.'* Furthermore, suppliers were always seen as a source if innovation. For example, one of McDonald's meat suppliers, Keystone Foods, developed a novel quick-freezing process that captured the fresh taste and texture of beef patties. This meant that every patty could retain its consistent quality until it hit the grill. Keystone shared its technology with other McDonald's meat suppliers for McDonald's, and today the process is an industry standard. Yet, supplier relationships were also rigorously controlled. McDonald's routinely analysed its suppliers' products.

Fostering franchisees

McDonald's revenues consisted of sales by company-operated restaurants and fees from restaurants operated by franchisees. McDonald's views itself primarily as a franchisor and believe franchising is *'important to delivering great, locally-relevant customer experiences and driving profitability'.* However, it also believes that directly operating restaurants is essential to providing the company with real operations experience. Of the 36,000 restaurants in 117 countries, approximately 80 per cent were operated by franchisees. But where some restaurant chains concentrated on recruiting franchisees that were then left to themselves, McDonald's expected its franchisees to contribute their experiences for the benefit of all. Ray Kroc's original concept was that franchisees would make money before the company did, so he made sure that the revenues that went to McDonald's came from the success of the restaurants themselves rather from initial franchise fees.

Initiating innovation

Ideas for new menu items have often come from franchisees. For example, Lou Groen, a Cincinnati franchise holder, had noticed that in Lent (a 40-day period when some Christians give up eating red meat on Fridays and instead eat only fish or no meat at all) some customers avoided the traditional hamburger. He went to Ray Kroc with his idea for a 'Filet-o-Fish', a steamed bun with a shot of tartar sauce, a fish fillet, and cheese on the bottom bun. But Kroc wanted to push his own meatless sandwich, called the hula burge – a cold bun with a piece of pineapple and cheese. Groen and Kroc competed on a Lenten Friday to see whose sandwich would sell more. Kroc's hula burger failed, selling only six sandwiches all day while Groen sold 350 Filet-o-Fish. Similarly, the Egg McMuffin was introduced by franchisee Herb Peterson, who wanted to attract customers into his McDonald's stores all through the day, not just at lunch and dinner. He came up with the idea for the signature McDonald's breakfast item because he was reputedly *'very partial to eggs Benedict and wanted to create something similar'.*

Other innovations came from the company itself. When poultry became popular, Fred Turner, then the Chairman of McDonald's, had an idea for a new meal: a chicken finger-food without bones, about the size of a thumb. After six months of research, the food technicians and scientists managed to reconstitute shreds of white chicken meat into small portions that could be breaded, fried, frozen and then reheated. Test marketing of the new product was positive, and in 1983 they were launched under the name of Chicken McNuggets. These were so successful that within a month McDonald's became the second largest purchaser of chicken in the USA. Some innovations came as a reaction to market conditions. Criticized by nutritionists who worried about calorie-rich burgers and shareholders who were alarmed by flattening sales, McDonald's launched its biggest menu revolution in 30 years in 2003 when it entered the prepared salad market. McDonald's offered a choice of dressings for its grilled chicken salad with Caesar dressing (and croutons) or the lighter option of a drizzle of balsamic dressing. Likewise, moves towards coffee sales were prompted by the ever-growing trend set by big coffee shops like Starbucks.

Problematic periods

Food, like almost everything else, is subject to swings in fashion. Its is not surprising then that there have been periods when McDonald's has had to adapt. The period from the early 1990s to the mid-2000s was difficult for parts of the McDonald's Empire. Growth in some parts of the world stalled. Partly this was due to changes in food fashion, nutritional concerns and demographic changes. Partly it was because competitors were learning either to emulate McDonald's operating system, or to focus on one aspect of the traditional 'quick service' offering, such as speed of service, range of menu items, (perceived) quality of food, or price. Burger King promoted itself on its 'flame-grilled' quality. Wendy's offered a fuller service level. Taco Bell undercut McDonald's prices with its 'value-pricing' promotions. Drive-through specialists speeded up service times. Also, 'fast food' was developing a poor reputation in some quarters, and as its iconic brand, McDonald's was taking much of the heat. Similarly the company became a lightning rod for other questionable aspects of modern life that it was held to promote, from cultural imperialism, low-skilled jobs (called 'McJobs' by some critics), abuse of animals and the use of hormone-enhanced beef, to an attack on traditional (French) values (in France). A French farmer called Jose Bové (who was briefly imprisoned) got other farmers to drive their tractors through, and wreck, a half-built McDonald's.

Similarly, in 2015 McDonald's closed more stores in its US home market than it opened – for the first time in its 60-year history. Partly this was a result of the increase in so-called 'fast casual' dining, a trend that combined the convenience of traditional McDonald's-style service with food that was seen as more healthy, even if it was more expensive. Smaller rivals, such as Chipotle and Shake Shack, had started to take domestic market share.

Surviving strategies

Over recent years the company's strategy has been to become 'better, not just bigger', focusing on 'restaurant execution', with the goal of 'improving the overall experience for our customers'. In particular it has, according to some analysts, 'gone back to basics', a strategy used by McDonald's Chief Executive Officer, Steve Easterbrook, when he was head of the company's UK operation, where he redesigned the outlets to make them more modern, introduced coffee and cappuccinos, worked with farmers to raise standards and increased transparency about its supply chain. At the same time he participated fully and forcefully with the company's critics in the debate over fast food health concerns. But some analysts believe that the 'burger and fries' market is in terminal decline, and the McDonalds's brand is so closely associated with that market that further growth will be difficult.

QUESTIONS

1 How has competition to McDonald's changed over its existence?

2 What are the main operations performance objectives for McDonald's?

3 What are the most important structural and infrastructural decisions in McDonald's operations strategy, and how do they influence its main performance objectives?

PROBLEMS AND APPLICATIONS

1. Explain how the four perspectives of operations strategy would apply to SSTL (see the 'Operations in action' case at the start of this chapter).

2. Compare the operations strategies of a low-cost airline, such as Ryanair, and a full-service airline such as British Airways or KLM.

3. What do you think are the qualifying and order-winning factors for (a) a top of the range Ferrari, and (b) a Renault Clio?

4. What do you think are the qualifying or order-winning factors for Pret A Manger described in Chapter 1?

5. Search the Internet site of Intel, the best-known microchip manufacturer, and identify what appear to be its main structural and infrastructural decisions in its operations strategy.

6. **(Advanced)** A gliding club has a current membership of over 100 pilots, many of whom have their own gliders. In addition the club has a fleet of six gliders available to its members. The club also offers trial flights to members of the public – 'casual flyers' who can book flights in advance or just turn up and fly on a first-come, first-served basis. The club sells trial flight gift vouchers that are popular as birthday and Christmas presents. If the conditions are right the customer may get a longer flight, although at busy times the instructors feel under pressure to return to the ground to give another lesson. If the weather is poor the instructors still do their best to get people airborne, but they are restricted to a short two-minute flight. Club members are expected to stay all day to help each other and any casual flyers get airborne

while they wait their turn to fly. Casual flyers might have to stand and wait for some time until a club member has time to find out what they want. Even when a flight has been pre-booked casual flyers may then be kept waiting, on the exposed and often windy airfield, for up to two hours before their flight, depending on how many club members are present. Income from the casual flyers is small compared with membership income, but the club views casual flying as a 'loss leader' to generate club memberships. There is also some pressure from members to end trial flights because they reduce the number of flights members can have in a day. Some members have complained that they sometimes spend most of their day working to get casual flyers into the air and miss out on flying themselves.

(a) Evaluate the service to club members and casual flyers by completing a table similar to Table 3.1.

(b) Chart the five performance objectives to show the differing expectations of club members and casual flyers and compare these with the actual service delivered.

(c) What advice would you give to the club?

SELECTED FURTHER READING

Boyer, K.K., Swink, M. and Rosenzweig, E.D. (2006) Operations strategy research in the POMS journal, *Production and Operations Management*, vol. 14, issue 4, 442–449.

A survey of recent research in the area.

Braithwaite, A. and Christopher, M. (2015) *Business Operations Models: Becoming a Disruptive Competitor*, Kogan Page, London.

Aimed at practitioners, but authoritative and interesting.

Hayes, R.H., Pisano, G.P., Upton, D.M. and Wheelwright, S.C. (2005) *Pursuing the Competitive Edge*, Wiley, Hoboken, NJ.

The gospel according to the Harvard school of operations strategy. Articulate, interesting and informative.

Hill, A. and Hill, T. (2009) *Manufacturing Operations Strategy: Texts and Cases*, Palgrave Macmillan, Basingstoke.

Biased towards manufacturing, but well structured and readable.

Slack, N. and Lewis, M. (2015) *Operations Strategy*, 4th edn, Pearson, Harlow.

What can we say – just brilliant, it will change your life!

4 Product and service innovation

Key questions

❯ What is product and service innovation?

❯ What is the strategic role of product and service innovation?

❯ What are the stages of product and service innovation?

❯ What are the benefits of interactive product and service innovation?

INTRODUCTION

New product and service innovation is concerned with putting new ideas into practice by embedding them in services and products. Innovation is the act of introducing new ideas, design is about making those ideas practical. This is why the activity of product and service innovation and the activity of design are so closely linked. Both are important because products and services are often the first thing that customers see of a company. So they should have an impact. And although operations managers may not always have full responsibility for service and product innovation, they always have some kind of responsibility, if only to provide the information and advice upon which successful product or service development depends. But increasingly operations mangers *are* expected to take a greater and more active part in product and service innovation. Unless a service, however well conceived, can be implemented, and unless a product, however well designed, can be produced to a high standard, they can never bring their full benefits. Figure 4.1 shows where this chapter fits into the overall operations model.

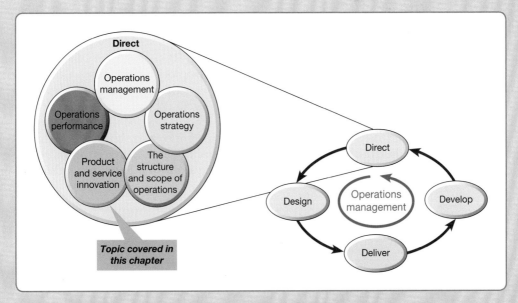

Figure 4.1 This chapter examines product and service innovation

WHAT IS PRODUCT AND SERVICE INNOVATION?

There are a number of terms that we will use in this chapter that have similar meanings, and are defined by different authorities in different ways, or overlap to some extent, and yet are related to each other. For example, what is 'innovation'? Is it the same as 'creativity'? How does 'design' relate to both terms? So a sensible first step might be to establish how we will be using these terms.

Innovation, design and creativity

Given that this chapter is about product and service innovation, we will start with what exactly *we* mean by 'innovation'. In fact there are many definitions. The term is notoriously ambiguous and lacks either a single definition or measure. It is *'a new method, idea, product, etc.'* (Oxford English Dictionary), *'change that creates a new dimension of performance'* (Peter Drucker, a well-known management writer), *'the act of introducing something new'* (American Heritage Dictionary), *'a new idea, method or device'* (Webster Online Dictionary), *'new knowledge incorporated in products, processes and services'*.[1] What runs through all these definitions is the idea of novelty and change. Innovation is simply about doing something new. But it is worth noting that the idea of innovation is both broader and more complete than that of 'invention'. An 'invention' is also something that is novel or unique (usually applied to a device or method), but it does not necessarily imply that the novel device or method has the potential to be practical, economic or capable of being developed commercially. Innovation goes further than 'invention'. It implies not just the novel idea, but also the process of transforming the idea into something that provides a return for an organization's customers, owners, or both. The study of innovation, what influences it, and how to manage it, is a huge subject and beyond the scope of this book. However, there is one particular attribute that is central to innovation – creativity. 'Creativity' is the ability to move beyond conventional ideas, rules or assumptions, in order to generate significant new ideas. It is a vital ingredient in innovation. It is seen as essential not just in product and service innovation, but also in the design and management of operations processes more generally.

> ✳ **Operations principle**
>
> The innovation activity is an important part of product and service design.

Partly because of the fast-changing nature of many industries, a lack of creativity (and consequently of innovation) is seen as a major risk.

So, if creativity is an essential ingredient of innovation, and innovation implies making novel ideas into practical, commercial form, what is the process that transforms innovative ideas into something more concrete? It is 'design'. Innovation creates the novel idea; design makes it work in practice. Design is to *'conceive the looks, arrangement, and workings of something. A design must deliver a solution that will work in practice.'* Design is also an activity that can be approached at different levels of detail. One may envisage the general shape and intention of something before getting down to defining its details (we will observe this later in this chapter when we examine the process of product and service design, and when we look at process design in Chapter 6). Figure 4.2 illustrates the relationship between creativity, innovation and design as we use the terms here. These concepts are intimately related, which is why we treat them in the same chapter. First we will look at some of the basic ideas that help to understand innovation.

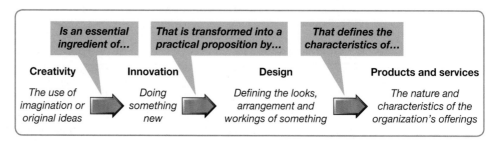

Figure 4.2 The relationship between creativity, innovation, and design

When Apple introduced the original iPhone, the world of smartphones was changed for ever. It was arguably one of the most influential products ever to be launched in the consumer technology market and set the benchmark for the (many) smartphones that came after it. It sold millions worldwide and helped to make Apple into the world's most valuable company. Yet how Apple and its visionary then leader, Steve Jobs, managed the innovation process remained something of a secret for years after the product's launch. Originally visualized as a tablet computer, work on the iPhone was initiated partly because of the success of the firm's earlier product, the iPod music player. It was the profound effect that the iPod had on the music industry that encouraged Apple to consider what other markets it could challenge. Yet, it was a technological breakthrough, the multi-touch display, which allowed the company to change course. As Steve Jobs said later, '*I had this idea about having a glass display, a multi-touch display you could type on. I asked our people about it. And six months later they came back with this amazing display. [When] we got inertial scrolling working and some other things, I thought, "my God, we can build a phone with this" and we put the tablet aside, and we went to work on the phone.*' But making the multi-touch display a working proposition was challenging for Apple's engineering team. The team had to create an entirely new way in which users could interact with their phones. There were many novel unsolved problems to overcome. Every single part of the design had to be rethought to adapt to touch. For example, engineers had to make scrolling work on the iPhone not only when a user's finger moved up and down, but also when a user's thumb moved in an arc across the screen. And there were many other obstacles to overcome, some which seemed almost insurmountable. Sir Jonathan Ive, Senior Vice-President of Design at Apple, has admitted that issues with the touchscreen were so difficult that it brought the project to the brink of being aborted. '*There were multiple times when we nearly shelved it because there were fundamental problems that we couldn't solve*', said Sir Jonathan. '*I would put the phone to my ear and my ear dialled a number. The challenge is that you have to then detect all sorts of ear shapes, chin shapes, skin colour and hairdos. We had to develop technology, basically a number of sensors, to inform the phone that "this is now going up to an ear, please deactivate the touchscreen".*'

Security during development was obsessively tight. For example, the senior Apple executive in charge of developing what would later become known as the iOS operating system was told that he could choose anyone

Source: Shutterstock.com: Rido

he wanted from within Apple to join the embryonic iPhone team, but he was not allowed to hire anybody from outside the company. He could not even convey to potential team members exactly what they would be working on, just that it was a new and exciting project and that they would have to '*work hard, give up nights, and work weekends for years*'. When the development team formed, it was located on a separate and secured floor on Apple's campus. The development area was 'locked down' with extensive use of badge readers and cameras. Team members might have to show their badges five or six times to gain access. Within Apple, the code name for the iPhone project was 'Project Purple' with the development area itself called the 'purple dorm' because the team worked continuously and so closely together that it felt 'like a college dorm'. It smelled like pizza.

The aesthetics of the iPhone were treated as being just as important as the iPhone technology. This was the responsibility of Apple's secretive industrial design group. Apple designer Christopher Stringer said that their objective was to create a '*new, original, and beautiful object* [that was] *so wonderful that you couldn't imagine how you'd follow it*'. The design group, Stringer explained, was composed of 16 'maniacal' individuals who shared one singular purpose – to '*imagine products that don't exist and guide them to life*'. Team members worked closely together, often gathering around a 'kitchen table' where they exchanged ideas, often in a 'brutally honest' way. To the designers, even the tiniest of details were important. They often would create up to 50 designs of a single component before moving on to computer-aided design modelling and the creation of physical mock-ups.

The fact that the Apple designers overcame several technology and production bugs during its development is partly a testament to the design team's belief, both in their technological skills and in their understanding of what people will buy. Yet Apple avoids conducting market research when designing its products, a policy introduced by Steve Jobs, its late chief executive. *'We absolutely don't do focus groups'*, said Ive. *'That's designers and leaders abdicating responsibility. That's them looking for an insurance policy, so if something goes wrong, they can say, well this focus group says that only 30 per cent of people are offended by this and, look, 40 per cent think it's OK. What a focus group does is that it will guarantee mediocrity.'*

The innovation S-curve

When new ideas are introduced in services, products or processes, they rarely have an impact that increases uniformly over time. Usually performance follows an S-shaped progression. So, in the early stages of the introduction of new ideas, although (often large) amounts of resources, time and effort are needed to introduce the idea, relatively small performance improvements are experienced. However, with time, as experience and knowledge about the new idea grow, performance increases. But as the idea becomes established, extending its performance further becomes increasingly difficult, *see* Figure 4.3(a). But when one idea reaches its mature, 'levelling-off' period, it is vulnerable to a further new idea being introduced which, in turn, moves through its own S-shaped progression. This is how innovation works, the limits of one idea being reached which prompts a newer, better idea, with each new S-curve requiring some degree of redesign, *see* Figure 4.3(b).

Incremental or radical innovation

An obvious difference between how the pattern of new ideas emerges in different operations or industries is the rate and scale of innovation. Some industries, such as telecommunications, enjoy frequent and often significant innovations. Others, such as house building, do have innovations, but they are usually less dramatic. So some innovation is radical, resulting in discontinuous, 'breakthrough' change, while other innovations are more incremental leading to smaller, continuous changes. Radical innovation often includes large technological advancements which may require completely new knowledge and/or resources making existing services and products obsolete and therefore non-competitive. Incremental innovation, by contrast, is more likely to involve relatively modest technological changes, built upon existing knowledge and/or resources so existing products and services are not fundamentally

(a) The basic S-shaped improvement in performance   **(b)** Innovation following multiple S-shaped curves

Figure 4.3 The S-shaped curve of innovation

changed. This is why established companies may favour incremental innovation because they have the experience of building up a significant pool of knowledge (on which incremental innovation is based). In addition, established companies are more likely to have a mindset that emphasizes continuity, perhaps not even recognizing potential innovative opportunities (see the 'Operations in practice' case on Kodak). New entrants to markets, however, have no established position to lose, nor do they have a vast pool of experience. They may be more likely to try for more radical innovation.

The Henderson–Clark model

Although distinguishing between incremental and radical innovation is useful, it does not fully make clear why some companies succeed or fail at innovation. Two researchers, Henderson and Clark,[3] looked at the question of why some established companies sometimes fail to exploit seemingly obvious incremental innovations. They answered this question by dividing the technological knowledge required to develop new products and services into 'knowledge of the components of knowledge' and 'knowledge of how the components of knowledge link together'. They called this latter knowledge 'architectural knowledge'. Figure 4.4 shows what has become known as the Henderson–Clark model. It refines the simpler idea of the split between incremental and radical innovation. In this model incremental innovation is built upon existing component and architectural knowledge, whereas radical innovation changes both component and architectural knowledge. Modular innovation is built on existing architectural knowledge, but requires new knowledge for one or more components. By contrast, architectural innovation will have a great impact upon the linkage of components (or the architecture), but the knowledge of single components is unchanged.

So, for example, in healthcare services, simple (but useful and possibly novel at the time) innovations in a primary-care (general practitioner) doctors' clinic, such as online appointment websites, would be classed as incremental innovation because neither any elements nor the relationship between them are changed. If the practice invests in a new diagnostic heart scanner, that element of their diagnosis task has been changed and will probably need new knowledge, but the overall architecture of the service has not been changed. This innovation

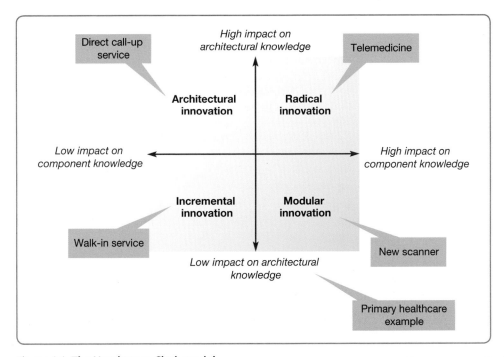

Figure 4.4 The Henderson–Clark model

would be classed as 'modular'. An example of architectural innovation would be the practice providing 'walk-in' facilities in the local city centre. It would provide more or less the same service as the regular surgery (no new components), but the relationship between the service and patients has changed. Finally, if the practice adopted some of the 'telemedicine' technology that monitors patient signs and can react to significant changes in patient condition, then this would be radical innovation. The components are novel (monitors) as is the overall architecture of the service (distance diagnosis).

WHAT IS THE STRATEGIC ROLE OF PRODUCT AND SERVICE INNOVATION?

Innovation is a risky business. Not every idea is transformed, or is capable of being incorporated into the design of a successful product or service. Sometimes this is because an innovative idea is just too challenging, at least with realistically available technology, or under prevailing market conditions. Sometimes the development cost is out of the reach of the business that had the original idea. Ideas may be abundant, but resources are limited. Yet despite the obstacles to successful innovation, almost all firms strive to be innovative. The reason is that there is overwhelming evidence that innovation can generate significant payback for the organizations that manage the incorporation of innovative ideas in the design of their products and services. What matters is the ability to identify the innovations and manage their transformation into effective designs so that they can sustain competitive advantage and/or generate social payback.

Design makes innovative ideas useful

It is worth repeating why design is so important. Good design takes innovative ideas and makes them practical. Good design also communicates the purpose of the product or service to its market, and brings financial rewards to the business. Product and service design, therefore, can be seen as starting and ending with the customer. So the design activity has one overriding objective: to provide products, services and processes which will satisfy the operation's customers. *Product* designers try to achieve aesthetically pleasing designs which meet or exceed customers' expectations. They also try to design a product which performs well and is reliable during its lifetime. Further, they should design the product so that it can be manufactured easily and quickly. Similarly, *service* designers try to put together a service which meets, or even exceeds, customer expectations. Yet at the same time the service must be within the capabilities of the operation and be delivered at reasonable cost.

Critical commentary

Remember that not all new services and products are created in response to a clear and articulated customer need. While this is usually the case, especially for products and services that are similar to (but presumably better than) their predecessors, more radical innovations are often brought about by the innovation itself creating demand. Customers do not usually know that they need something radical. For example, in the late 1970s people were not asking for microprocessors – they did not even know what they were. They were improvised by an engineer in the USA for a Japanese customer who made calculators. Only later did they become the enabling technology for the PC and after that the innumerable devices that now dominate our lives.

Design pays for itself[4]

There is an increasingly common acceptance that design can add very significant value to all types of organization. A growing number of books, articles, reports and blogs have looked at companies and the benefits that they have gained by taking the design process seriously. This interest in design is partly because of the success of companies like Apple (see the 'Operations in practice' case earlier in this chapter), which are regarded as excellent at design. Numerous authors have confirmed the impact of design on performance. One report from the Design Council in the UK has shown that, on average, for every £1 businesses invest in design, they gain over £4 net operating profit, over £20 net turnover and over £5 net exports.[5]

Design can add value to any organization. In particular, good design practice can:

- drive and operationalize innovation, increasing market share and opening up new markets;
- differentiate products and services, making them more attractive to customers, while increasing consistency in the company's range, and helping to ensure successful product launches;
- strengthen branding, so that products and services embody a company's values;
- reduce the overall costs associated with innovation, through more efficient use of resources, reduced project failure rate and faster time to market.

All of these benefits are strategic in that they very significantly affect the future of a business. As one company boss said, '*design is everything, because without it we have no business… There is intense competition, and anybody can design a decent product. They can't all design outstanding products. So, design is the differentiator.*'

OPERATIONS IN PRACTICE — The sad tale of Kodak and its digital camera[6]

Source: Shutterstock.com: Ktsdesign

The once mighty Eastman Kodak Company dominated the photographic and film markets for decades. But no longer: 30 years ago it employed over 140,000 people and made substantial profits; by 2010 it had shrunk to around 19,000, with regular quarterly losses. This dramatic fall from grace is usually put down to the company's failure to see the approach of digital photography or fully appreciate how it would totally undermine Kodak's traditional products. Yet, ironically, Kodak was more than ahead of its competitors than most people outside the company realized. It actually invented the digital camera. Sadly, though, it lacked the foresight to make the most of it. For years the company had, as one insider put it, '*too much technology in its labs rather than in the market*'.

It was back in 1975 when a newly hired scientist at Kodak, Steve Sasson, was given the task of researching how to build a camera using a comparatively new type of electronic sensor – the charged-coupled device (CCD). He found little previous research so he used the lens from a Kodak motion-picture camera, an ana- logue-to-digital converter, some CCD chips and some digital circuitry that he made himself. By December 1975 he had an operational prototype. Yet the advance was largely, although not completely, ignored inside the company. '*Some people talked about reasons it would never happen, while others looked at it and realized it was important*', he says. He also decided not to use the word 'digital' to describe his trial product. '*I proposed it as filmless photography, an electronic stills camera. Calling it "digital" would not have been an advantage. Back then "digital" was not a good term. It meant new, esoteric technology.*' Some resistance came from genuine, if mistaken, technical reservations. But others feared the magnitude of the changes that digital photography could bring. Objections '*were coming from the gut: a realization that* [digital] *would change everything – and threaten the company's entire film-based business model*'. Some see Kodak's reluctance to abandon its traditional product range as understandable. It was making vast profits and as late as 1999 it was making over $3 billion from film sales. Todd Gustavson, Curator of Technology at the George Eastman House Museum, says that '*Kodak was almost recession-proof until the rise of digital. A film-coating machine was like a device that printed money.*' So Kodak's first digital camera, the Quicktake, was licensed to and sold by Apple in 1994. In 2012 Kodak filed for bankruptcy protection.

The design activity is itself a process

Producing design innovations for products and services is itself a process that conforms to the input–transformation–output model described in Chapter 1. Although organizations will have their own particular ways of managing innovation and design, the design *process* itself is essentially very similar across a whole range of industries. It therefore has to be designed and managed like any other process. Broadly, the better the design process is managed, the better the products and service offering. Figure 4.5 illustrates the design activity as an input–transformation–output diagram. The transformed resource inputs will consist mainly of information in the form of market forecasts, market preferences, technical data, potential design ideas, and so on. It is these ideas and information that will be transformed in the design process into the final design. Transforming resource inputs includes the operations and design managers who manage the process, together with specialist technical staff with the specific knowledge necessary to solve design problems. They also may include suppliers, other collaborators, and even especially interested customer groups (sometimes called 'lead users') who are brought in to provide their expertise. Transforming resources may also include computer-aided design (CAD) equipment and software.

> ✻ **Operations principle**
>
> The design activity is a process that can be managed using the same principles as other processes.

Design process objectives

> ✻ **Operations principle**
>
> Innovation processes can be judged in terms of their levels of quality, speed, dependability, flexibility, cost and sustainability.

The performance of the design process can be assessed in much the same way as we would consider the products and services that result from it, namely in terms of quality, speed, dependability, flexibility and cost. Here we also include 'sustainability' as a design objective. It is, of course, included as part of the 'triple bottom line' objectives, as explained in Chapter 2, but because product and service design has such an influence on sustainability, we include it alongside our normal operational-level objectives. These performance objectives have just as much relevance for innovation as they do for the ongoing delivery of offerings once they are introduced to the market.

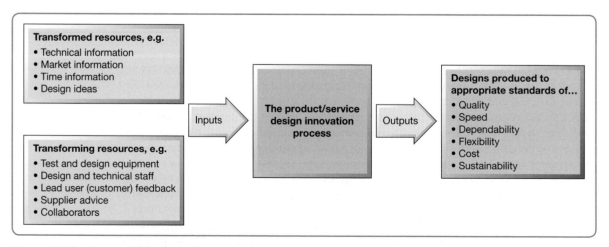

Figure 4.5 The design activity is itself a process

What does quality mean for the design process?

Design quality is not always easy to define precisely, especially if customers are relatively satisfied with existing product and service offerings. Many software companies talk about the 'I don't know what I want, but I'll know when I see it' syndrome, meaning that only when customers use the software are they in a position to articulate what they do or do not require. Nevertheless, it is possible to distinguish high- and low-quality designs (although this is easier to do in hindsight) by judging them in terms of their ability to meet market requirements. In doing this, the distinction between the specification quality and the conformance quality of designs is important. No business would want a design process that was indifferent to 'errors' in its designs, yet some are more tolerant than others. For example, in pharmaceutical development the potential for harm is particularly high because drugs directly affect our health. This is why the authorities insist on such a prolonged and thorough 'design' process (more usually called 'development' in that industry). Although withdrawing a drug from the market is unusual, it does occasionally occur. Far more frequent are the 'product recalls' that are relatively common in, for example, the automotive industry. Many of these are design related and the result of 'conformance' failures in the design process. The 'specification' quality of design is different. It means the degree of functionality, or experience, or aesthetics, or whatever the product or service is primarily competing on. Some businesses require product or service designs that are relatively basic (although free from errors), while others require designs that are clearly special in terms of the customer response they hope to elicit.

What does speed mean for the design process?

The speed of design matters more to some industries than others. For example, design innovation in construction and aerospace happens at a much slower pace than in clothing or microelectronics. However, rapid design innovation or 'time-based competition' has become the norm for an increasing number of industries. Sometimes this is the result of fast-changing consumer fashion. Sometimes a rapidly changing technology base forces it. Telecoms, for example, are updated frequently because their underlying technology is constantly improving. Yet, no matter what the motivation, fast design brings a number of advantages:

- Early market launch – an ability to innovate speedily is that product and service offerings can be introduced to the market earlier and thus earn revenue for longer, and may command price premiums.
- Starting design late – alternatively, starting the design process later may have advantages, especially where either the nature of customer demand or the availability of technology is uncertain and dynamic, so fast design allows design decisions to be made closer to the time when product and service offerings are introduced to the market.
- Frequent market stimulation – rapid innovations allow frequent new or updated offerings to be introduced into the market.

What does dependability mean for the design process?

Rapid design processes that cannot be relied on to deliver dependably are, in reality, not fast at all. Design schedule slippage can extend design times, but, worse, a lack of dependability adds to the uncertainty surrounding the innovation process. Conversely, processes that are dependable minimize design uncertainty. Unexpected technical difficulties, such as suppliers who themselves do not deliver solutions on time, customers or markets that change during the innovation process itself, and so on, all contribute to an uncertain and ambiguous design environment. Professional project management (see Chapter 19) of the innovation process can help to reduce uncertainty and prevent (or give early warning of) missed deadlines, process bottlenecks and resource shortages. However, external disturbances to the innovation process will remain. These may be minimized through close liaison with suppliers as well as market or environmental monitoring. Nevertheless, unexpected disruptions will always occur and the more innovative the design, the more likely they are to occur. This is why flexibility within the innovation process is one of the most important ways in which dependable delivery of new product and service offerings can be ensured.

What does flexibility mean for the design process?

Flexibility in the innovation process is the ability to cope with external or internal change. The most common reason for external change is because markets, or specific customers, change their requirements. Although flexibility may not be needed in relatively predictable markets, it is clearly valuable in more fast-moving and volatile markets, where one's own customers and markets change, or where the designs of competitors' offerings dictate a matching or leapfrogging move. Internal changes include the emergence of superior technical solutions. In addition, the increasing complexity and interconnectedness of product and service components in an offering may require flexibility. A bank, for example, may bundle together a number of separate services for one particular segment of its market. Privileged account holders may obtain special deposit rates, premium credit cards, insurance offers, travel facilities, and so on, together in the same package. Changing one aspect of this package may require changes to be made in other elements. So extending the credit card benefits to include extra travel insurance may also mean the redesign of the separate insurance element of the package. One way of measuring innovation flexibility is to compare the cost of modifying a design in response to such changes against the consequences to profitability if no changes are made. The lower the cost of modifying an offering in response to a given change, the higher is the level of flexibility.

What does cost mean for the design process?

The cost of innovation is usually analysed in a similar way to the ongoing cost of delivering offerings to customers. These cost factors are split up into three categories: the cost of buying the inputs to the process, the cost of providing the labour in the process, and the other general overhead costs of running the process. In most in-house innovation processes the latter two costs outweigh the former.

One way of thinking about the effect of the other innovation performance objectives on cost is shown in Figure 4.6. Whether caused by quality errors, an intrinsically slow innovation process, a lack of project dependability, or delays caused through inflexibility, the end result is that the design is late. Delayed completion of the design results in both more expenditure on the design and delayed (and probably reduced) revenue. The combination of these effects usually means that the financial break-even point for a new offering is delayed far more than the original delay in its launch.

What does sustainability mean for the design process?

The sustainability of a design innovation is the extent to which it benefits the 'triple bottom line' – people, planet and profit. When organizations carry out their design innovation activities, they should consider their objectives in relation to this triple bottom line. The design innovation process is particularly important in ultimately impacting the ethical, environmental and economic well-being of stakeholders. And incorporating sustainability criteria in the design process is increasingly common. Sometimes this is because of external pressures, such as new legislation, sometimes because of changing customer attitudes. For example, some innovation activity is particularly focused on the ethical dimension of sustainability. Banks have moved to offer customers ethical investments that seek to maximize social benefit as well as financial returns. Such investments tend to avoid businesses involved in weaponry, gambling, alcohol and tobacco, for example, and favour those promoting worker education, environmental stewardship and consumer protection. Other examples of ethically focused innovations include the development of 'fair-trade' products. Similarly, garment manufacturers may establish ethical trading initiatives with suppliers; supermarkets may ensure animal welfare for meat and dairy products; online companies may institute customer complaint charters.

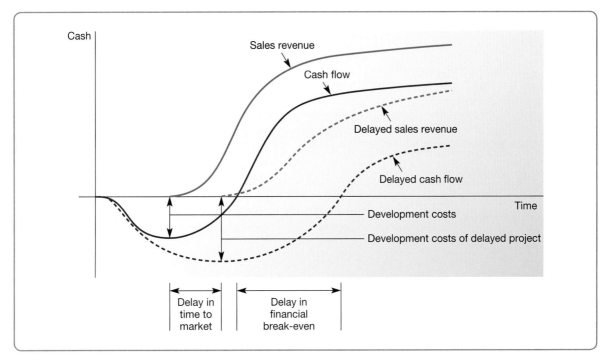

Figure 4.6 Delay in time to market of new innovations not only reduces and delays revenues, but also increases the costs of development. The combination of both of these effects usually delays the financial break-even point far more than the delay in the launch

Design innovation may also focus on the environmental dimension of sustainability. Critically examining the components of products towards a change of materials in the design could significantly reduce the environmental burden. Examples include the use of organic cotton or bamboo in clothing; wood or paper from managed forests used in garden furniture, stationery and flooring; recycled materials for carrier bags; and natural dyes in clothing, curtains and upholstery. Other innovations may be more focused on the use stage of an offering. The MacBook Air, for example, introduced an advanced power management system that reduced its power requirements. In the detergent industry, Unilever and Proctor & Gamble have developed products that allow clothes to be washed at much lower temperatures. Architecture firms are increasingly designing houses that can operate with minimal energy or use sustainable sources of energy such as solar panels. Some innovations focus on making product components within an offering easier to recycle or remanufacture once they have reached the end of their life. For example, some food packaging has been designed to break down easily when disposed of, allowing its conversion into high-quality compost. Mobile phones are often designed to be taken apart at the end of their life, so valuable raw materials can be reused. In the automotive industry, over 75 per cent of materials are recycled.

WHAT ARE THE STAGES OF PRODUCT AND SERVICE INNOVATION?

Fully specified designs rarely spring, fully formed, from a designer's imagination. The design activity will generally pass through several key stages. These form the sequence shown in Figure 4.7, although in practice designers will often recycle or backtrack through the stages. Nor is this sequence of stages descriptive of the stages used by all

> **✽ Operations principle**
> Design processes involve a number of stages that move an innovation from a concept to a fully specified state.

Figure 4.7 The stages of product/service design innovation

companies, yet most will use some stage model similar to this one. It moves from the concept generation stage to a screening stage, a preliminary design stage that produces a design to be evaluated and prototyped before reaching the final design.

Concept generation

This is where innovative ideas become the inspiration for new service or product concepts. And innovation can come from many different sources:

- **Ideas from customers** – Marketing, the function generally responsible for identifying new service or product opportunities, may use market research tools for gathering data from customers in a structured way to test out ideas or check services or products against predetermined criteria.
- **Listening to customers** – Ideas may come from customers on a day-to-day basis; from complaints, or from everyday transactions. Although some organizations may not see gathering this information as important (and may not even have mechanisms in place to facilitate it), it is an important potential source of ideas.
- **Ideas from competitor activity** – Most organizations follow the activities of their competitors. A new idea from a competitor may be worth imitating or, better still, improved upon. Taking apart a competitor's product or service to explore potential new ideas is called 'reverse engineering'. Some aspects of services may be difficult to reverse-engineer (especially 'back-office' services) as they are less transparent to competitors.
- **Ideas from staff** – The contact staff in a service organization or the salesperson in a product-oriented organization could meet customers every day. These staff may have good ideas about what customers like and do not like. They may have gathered suggestions from customers or have ideas of their own. One well-known example – which may be urban myth – is that an employee at Swan Vestas, the matchmaker, suggested having one instead of two sandpaper strips on the matchbox. It saved a fortune!
- **Ideas from research and development** – Many organizations have a formal research and development (R&D) function. As its name implies, its role is twofold. Research develops new knowledge and ideas in order to solve a particular problem or to grasp an opportunity. Development utilizes and operationalizes the ideas that come from research. And although 'development' may not sound as exciting as 'research', it often requires as much creativity and even more persistence. One product has commemorated the persistence of its development engineers in its company name. Back in 1953 the Rocket Chemical Company set out to create a rust-prevention solvent and degreaser to be used in the aerospace industry. It took them 40 attempts to get the water-displacing formula worked out. So that is what they called the product. WD-40 literally stands for Water Displacement, 40th attempt.

Open sourcing – using a 'development community'[7]

Not all 'products' or services are created by professional, employed designers for commercial purposes. Many of the software applications that we all use, for example, are developed by an open community, including the people who use the products. If you use Google, the Internet search facility, or use Wikipedia, the online encyclopaedia, or shop at

Amazon, you are using open-source software. The basic concept of open-source software is extremely simple. Large communities of people around the world, who have the ability to write software code, come together and produce a software product. The finished product is not only available to be used by anyone or any organization for free, but also regularly updated to ensure it keeps pace with the necessary improvements. The production of open-source software is very well organized and, like its commercial equivalent, is continuously supported and maintained. However, unlike its commercial equivalent, it is absolutely free to use. Over the last few years the growth of open source has been phenomenal, with many organizations transitioning over to using this stable, robust and secure software. With the maturity that open-source software now has to offer, organizations have seen the true benefits of using free software to drive down costs and to establish themselves on a secure and stable platform. Open source has been the biggest change in software development for decades and is setting new open standards in the way software is used. The open nature of this type of development also encourages compatibility between products. BMW, for example, was reported to be developing an open-source platform for vehicle electronics. Using an open-source approach, rather than using proprietary software, BMW can allow providers of 'infotainment' services to develop compatible, plug-and-play applications.

Crowdsourcing[8]

Closely related to the open sourcing idea is that of 'crowdsourcing'. Crowdsourcing is the process of getting work or funding, or ideas (usually online), from a crowd of people. Although in essence it is not a totally new idea, it has become a valuable source of ideas largely through the use of the Internet and social networking. For example, Procter & Gamble, the consumer products company, asked amateur scientists to explore ideas for a detergent dye whose colour changes when enough has been added to dishwater. Other uses of the idea involve government agencies asking citizens to prioritize spending (or cutting spending) projects.

Parallel-path approach

Because the likelihood of successful innovation coming from a single source of ideas is highly uncertain, it has been argued that firms could improve the odds of innovation success by using what is sometimes termed a 'parallel-path strategy'. This simply means utilizing a variety of different sources and approaches to generating ideas.

Traditionally, it was assumed that there was a trade-off between the depth and breadth of the usefulness of the ideas that can come from various sources. One could pursue a few sources of ideas in depth or a wide range of sources in a relatively shallow manner. In addition, the marginal cost of exploring a new source may increase as the number of sources examined increases. So, the breadth of knowledge sources also may be subject to diminishing marginal returns. However, more recent research[9] suggests that firms also may improve their odds of successful innovation by accessing a large number of knowledge sources.

Ideas management

Obtaining new product or service ideas (or indeed any innovative ideas) from employees was traditionally done through the use of paper-based 'suggestion schemes' where employees placed their ideas in a 'suggestion box'. Such schemes were often only partly effective, yielding few, low-quality ideas. Unless the running of the scheme was well resourced it could be difficult to guarantee that all ideas were evaluated consistently and quickly. Also, the scheme could lose credibility unless employees could track their ideas to confirm that they 'didn't just disappear'. However, the advent of 'idea management' software tools has overcome some of these difficulties. Ideas management systems are a type of enterprise software (often web-based) that can help operations to collect ideas from

It sounds like a joke, but it is a genuine product innovation motivated by a market need. It is green, square and comes originally from Japan. It is a square watermelon! Why square? Because Japanese grocery stores are not large and space cannot be wasted. Similarly a round watermelon does not fit into a refrigerator very conveniently. There is also the problem of trying to cut the fruit when it keeps rolling around. So an innovative farmer from Japan's south-western island of Shikoku solved the problem with the idea of making a cube-shaped watermelon which could easily be packed and stored. But there is no genetic modification or clever science involved in growing watermelons. It simply involves placing the young fruit into wooden boxes with clear sides. During its growth, the fruit naturally swells to fill the surrounding shape. Now the idea has spread from Japan. *'Melons are among the most delicious and refreshing fruit around but some people find them a problem to store in their fridge or to cut because they roll around'*, said Damien Sutherland, the exotic fruit buyer from Tesco, the UK supermarket. *'We've seen samples of these watermelons and they literally stop you in their tracks because they are so eye-catching. These square melons will make it easier than ever to eat because they can be served in long strips rather than in the crescent shape.'* But

Source: Shutterstock.com: Valentyn Volkov

not everyone liked the idea. Comments on news websites included: *'where will engineering every day things for our own unreasonable convenience stop? I prefer melons to be the shape of melons!'*; *'they are probably working on straight bananas next!'*; and *'I would like to buy square sausages then they would be easier to turn over in the frying pan. Round sausages are hard to keep cooked all over.'*

employees, assess them and, if appropriate, implement them quickly and efficiently. Such systems can track ideas all the way though from inception to implementation, making it much easier to understand important performance measures such as where ideas are being generated, how many ideas submitted are actually implemented, the estimated cost savings from submitted ideas and any new revenues generated by implemented ideas. Often ideas management systems are used to focus ideas on specific organizational targets and objectives, which it is claimed improved both the quality and quantity of ideas, when compared with 'open' suggestion schemes.

Concept screening

Not all concepts which are generated will necessarily be capable of further development into products and services. Designers need to be selective as to which concepts they progress to the next design stage. The purpose of the concept-screening stage is to evaluate concepts by assessing the worth or value of design options. This involves assessing each concept or option against a number of design criteria. While the criteria used in any particular design exercise will depend on the nature and circumstances of the exercise, it is useful to think in terms of three broad categories of design criteria:

- The feasibility of the design option – can we do it?
  - Do we have the skills (quality of resources)?
  - Do we have the organizational capacity (quantity of resources)?
  - Do we have the financial resources to cope with this option?

- The acceptability of the design option – do we want to do it?
  - Does the option satisfy the performance criteria which the design is trying to achieve? (These will differ for different designs.)
  - Will our customers want it?
  - Does the option give a satisfactory financial return?
- The vulnerability of each design option – do we want to take the risk? That is:
  - Do we understand the full consequences of adopting the option?
  - Being pessimistic, what could go wrong if we adopt the option? What would be the consequences of everything going wrong? (This is called the 'downside risk' of an option.)

The design 'funnel'

Applying these evaluation criteria progressively reduces the number of options which will be available further along in the design activity. For example, deciding to make the outside casing of a camera case from aluminium rather than plastic limits later decisions, such as the overall size and shape of the case. This means that the uncertainty surrounding the design reduces as the number of alternative designs being considered decreases. Figure 4.8 shows what is sometimes called 'the design funnel', depicting the progressive reduction of design options from many to one. But reducing design uncertainty also impacts the cost of changing one's mind on some detail of the design. In most stages of design the cost of changing a decision is bound to incur some sort of rethinking and recalculation of costs. Early on in the design activity, before too many fundamental decisions have been made, the costs of change are relatively low. However, as the design progresses the interrelated and cumulative decisions already made become increasingly expensive to change.

Preliminary design

Having generated an acceptable, feasible and viable product or service concept the next stage is to create a preliminary design. The objective of this stage is to have a first attempt at specifying the individual components or elements of the products and services, and the relationship between them, which will constitute the final offering.

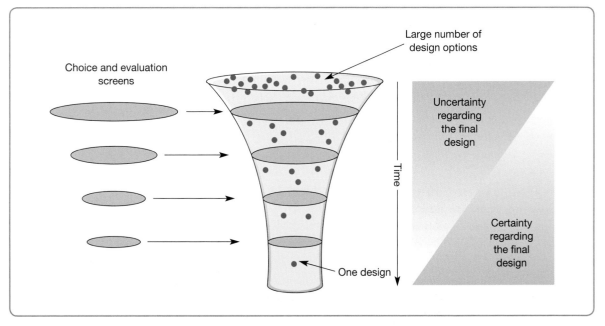

Figure 4.8 The design funnel – progressively reducing the number of possibilities until the final design is reached

Specifying the components of the design

The first task in this stage of design is to define exactly what will go into the product or service. This will require the collection of information about such things as the *constituent component parts* which make up the product or service package and the component (or product) structure, the order in which the component parts of the package have to be put together. For example, the components for a remote 'presentation' mouse may include the presentation mouse itself, a receiver unit and packaging. All these three items are made up of components, which are, in turn, made up of other components, and so on. A 'component structure' is the diagram that shows how these components all fit together to make the final product (*see* Fig. 4.9).

Reducing design complexity

Simplicity is usually seen as a virtue among designers of products and services. The most elegant design solutions are often the simplest. However, when an operation produces a variety of products or services (as most do) the range of products and services considered as a whole can become complex, which, in turn, increases costs. Designers adopt a number of approaches to reducing the inherent complexity in the design of their products or service range. Here we describe three common approaches to complexity reduction: standardization, commonality and modularization.

> ✳ **Operations principle**
>
> A key design objective should be the simplification of the design through standardization, commonality, modularization, and mass customization.

Standardization

Operations sometimes attempt to overcome the cost penalties of high variety by standardizing their products, services or processes. This allows them to restrict variety to that which has real value for the end customer. Often it is the operation's outputs which are standardized. Examples of this are fast food restaurants, discount supermarkets or telephone-based insurance companies. Perhaps the most common example of standardization is the clothes which most us of buy. Although everybody's body shape is different, garment manufacturers produce clothes in only a limited number of sizes. The range of sizes is chosen to give a reasonable fit for most body shapes. To suit all their potential customers and/or to ensure a perfect fit, garment manufacturers would have to provide an unfeasibly large range of sizes. Alternatively, they would need to provide a customized service. Both solutions

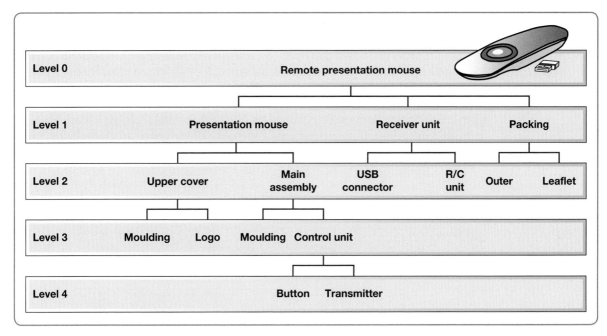

Figure 4.9 The component structure of a remote mouse

would have a significant impact on cost. This control of variety is an important issue with most companies. A danger facing established operations is that they allow variety to grow excessively. They are then faced with the task of *variety reduction*, often by assessing the real profit or contribution of each service or product. Many organizations have significantly improved their profitability by careful variety reduction. In order to overcome loss of business, customers may be offered alternative products or services which provide similar value.

Commonality

Using common elements within a product or service product can also simplify design complexity. Using the same components across a range of automobiles is a common practice. Likewise, standardizing the format of information inputs to a process can be achieved by using appropriately designed forms or screen formats. The more different product and services can be based on common components, the less complex it is to produce them. For example, the European aircraft maker, Airbus, has designed its aircraft with a high degree of commonality. This meant that 10 aircraft models ranging from the 100-seat A318 through to the world's largest aircraft, the A380 with over 500 seats, feature virtually identical flight decks, common systems and similar handling characteristics. In some cases, such as the entire A320 family, the aircraft even share the same 'pilot-type rating', which enables pilots with a single licence to fly any of them. The advantages of commonality for the airline operators include a much shorter training time for pilots and engineers when they move from one aircraft to another. This offers pilots the possibility of flying a wide range of routes from short haul to ultra-long haul and leads to greater efficiencies because common maintenance procedures can be designed with maintenance teams capable of servicing any aircraft in the same family. Also, when up to 90 per cent of all parts are common within a range of aircraft, there is a reduced need to carry a wide range of spare parts.

Modularization

The use of modular design principles involves designing standardized 'sub-components' of a product or service which can be put together in different ways. It is possible to create wide choice through the fully interchangeable assembly of various combinations of a smaller number of standard sub-assemblies; computers are designed in this way, for example. These standardized modules, or sub-assemblies, can be produced in higher volume, thereby reducing their cost. Similarly, the package holiday industry can assemble holidays to meet a specific customer requirement, from pre-designed and purchased air travel, accommodation, insurance, and so on. In education also there is an increasing use of modular courses which allow 'customers' choice but permit each module to have economical volumes of students.

OPERATIONS IN PRACTICE   **Innovative design from Dyson**[11]

In 1907 a janitor called Murray Spangler put together a pillowcase, a fan, an old biscuit tin, and a broom handle. It was a great innovation – the world's first vacuum cleaner – but not one that he ever capitalized on. One year later he had sold his patented idea to William Hoover whose company went on to dominate the vacuum cleaner market for decades, especially in its US homeland. Yet when Hoover's market share dropped significantly, it was because a futuristic looking and comparatively expensive rival product, the Dyson vacuum cleaner, had jumped from nothing to a position where it dominated the market. The product may have been new, but the company was not. The Dyson product dates back to 1978 when James (now Sir James) Dyson noticed how the air filter in the spray-finishing room of a company where he had been working was constantly clogging with power particles (just like a vacuum cleaner bag clogs with dust). So he designed and built an industrial cyclone tower, which removed the powder particles by exerting centrifugal forces. The question intriguing him was: '*Could the same principle work in a domestic vacuum cleaner?*' Five years and five *thousand* prototypes later he had a working design, since praised for its 'uniqueness and functionality'. However, existing vacuum cleaner manufacturers were not as impressed – two rejected the design outright. So Dyson started making his new design himself. Within a few years Dyson cleaners were, in the UK, outselling the rivals who had once rejected them. The aesthetics and functionality of the design help to keep sales growing in spite of a higher retail price. To Dyson, good '*is about looking at everyday things with new eyes and working out how they can be made better. It's about challenging existing technology.*' Then the Dyson engineers took the technology one stage further and developed core separator technology to capture even more microscopic dirt. Dirt now goes through three stages of separation. First, dirt is drawn into a powerful outer cyclone. Centrifugal forces fling larger debris

Source: Dyson

such as pet hair and dust particles into the clear bin at 500g (the maximum g-force the human body can take is 8g). Second, a further cyclonic stage, the core separator, removes dust particles as small as 0.5 microns from the airflow – particles so small you could fit 200 of them on this full stop. Finally, a cluster of smaller, even faster cyclones generates centrifugal forces of up to 150,000g, extracting particles as small as mould and bacteria.

Other innovations followed. The Dyson Airblade is an electric hand dryer that dries hands quicker (around 10 seconds) and uses less electricity than conventional hand dryers. Then came the Dyson Air Multiplier™: fans and fan heaters that work very differently to conventional fans and electric heaters. They do not have fast-spinning blades that chop the air and cause uncomfortable buffeting. Instead, they use Air Multiplier™ technology to draw in air and amplify it up to 18 times, producing an uninterrupted stream of smooth air. Sir James, who remains chief engineer and sole shareholder in Dyson, said the heater was part of the company's effort to turn itself into a *'broad-line technology company'* rather than being seen as only an appliance maker. *'I would not limit the company to particular areas of technology or markets. We are developing a range of technologies to improve both industrial and consumer products so that the people using them get a better experience than with the comparable items that currently exist.'*

Design evaluation and improvement

The purpose of this stage in the design innovation activity is to take the preliminary design and subject it to a series of evaluations to see if it can be improved before the service or product is tested in the market. There are a number of techniques that can be employed at this stage to evaluate and improve the preliminary design. Perhaps the best known is quality function deployment (QFD).

Quality function deployment

The key purpose of QFD is to try to ensure that the eventual innovation actually meets the needs of its customers. It is a technique that was developed in Japan at Mitsubishi's Kobe shipyard and used extensively by Toyota, the motor vehicle manufacturer, and its suppliers. It is also known as the 'house of quality' (because of its shape) and the 'voice of the customer' (because of its purpose). The technique tries to capture what the customer needs and how it might be achieved. Figure 4.10 shows a simple QFD matrix used in the design of a promotional USB data storage pen. The QFD matrix is a formal articulation of how the company sees the relationship between the requirements of the customer (the *whats*) and the design characteristics of the new product (the *hows*):

- The *whats*, or 'customer requirements', are the list of competitive factors which customers find significant. Their relative importance is scored, in this case on a 10-point scale, with *price* scoring the highest.
- The competitive scores indicate the relative performance of the product, in this case on a 1 to 5 scale. Also indicated are the performances of two competitor products.
- The *hows*, or 'design characteristics' of the product, are the various 'dimensions' of the design, which will operationalize customer requirements within the product or service.
- The central matrix (sometimes called the relationship matrix) represents a view of the interrelationship between the *whats* and the *hows*. This is often based on value judgements made by the design team. The symbols indicate the strength of the relationship. All the relationships are studied, but in many cases, where the cell of the matrix is blank, there is none.
- The bottom box of the matrix is a technical assessment of the product. This contains the absolute importance of each design characteristic.
- The triangular 'roof' of the 'house' captures any information the team has about the correlations (positive or negative) between the various design characteristics

Prototyping and final design

At around this stage in the design activity it is necessary to turn the improved design into a prototype so that it can be tested. It may be too risky to launch a product or service before testing it out, so it is usually more appropriate to create a 'prototype' (in the case of a product) or 'trial' (in the case of a service). Product prototypes include everything from clay models to computer simulations. Service trials may also include computer simulations but also the actual implementation of the service on a pilot basis. Many retailing organizations pilot new products and services in a small number of stores in order to test customers' reaction to them.

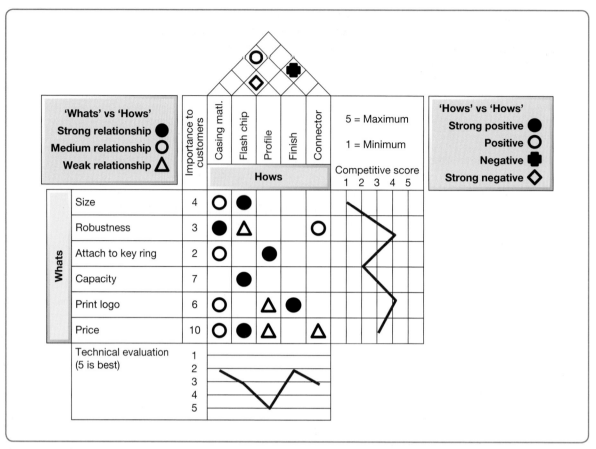

Figure 4.10 QFD matrix for a promotional USB data storage stick

Virtual reality-based simulations allow businesses to test new products and services as well as visualize and plan the processes that will produce them. Individual component parts can be positioned together virtually and tested for fit or interference. Even virtual workers can be introduced into the prototyping system to check for ease of assembly or operation.

Computer-aided design (CAD)

CAD systems provide the computer-aided ability to create and modify product drawings. These systems allow conventionally used shapes such as points, lines, arcs, circles and text to be added to a computer-based representation of the product. Once incorporated into the design, these entities can be copied, moved about, rotated through angles, magnified or deleted. The designs thus created can be saved in the memory of the system and retrieved for later use. This enables a library of standardized drawings of parts and components to be built up. The most obvious advantage of CAD systems is that their ability to store and retrieve design data quickly, as well as their ability to manipulate design details, can considerably increase the productivity of the design activity. In addition to this, however, because changes can be made rapidly to designs, CAD systems can considerably enhance the flexibility of the design activity, enabling modifications to be made much more rapidly. Further, the use of standardized libraries of shapes and entities can reduce the possibility of errors in the design.

Alpha and beta testing

A distinction that originated in the software development industry, but has spread into other areas, is that between the alpha and beta testing of a product or service. Most software products include both alpha *and* beta test phases, both of which are intended to uncover 'bugs' (errors) in the product. Not surprisingly alpha testing comes before beta testing. Alpha testing is essentially an *internal* process where the developers or manufacturers (or sometimes an outside agency that they have commissioned) examine the product for errors. Generally, it is also a private process, not open to the market or potential customers. Although it is intended to look for errors that otherwise would emerge when the product is in use, it is in effect performed in a virtual or simulated environment, rather than in 'the real world'. After alpha testing, the product is released for beta testing. Beta testing is when the product is released for testing by selected customers. It is an *external* 'pilot test' that takes place in the 'real world' (or near real world, because it is still a relatively small, and short, sample) before commercial production. By the time a product gets to the beta stage most of the worst defects should have been removed, but the product may still have some minor problems that may only become evident with user participation. This is why beta testing is almost always performed at the user's premises without any of the development team present. Beta testing is also sometimes called 'field testing', pre-release testing, customer validation, customer acceptance testing, or user acceptance testing.

OPERATIONS IN PRACTICE **Product innovation for the circular economy[12]**

Design innovation is not just confined to the initial conception of a product; it also applies to the end of its life. This idea is often called 'designing for the circular economy'. The 'circular economy' is proposed as an alternative to the traditional linear economy (or make–use–dispose as it is termed). The idea is to keep products in use for as long as possible, extract the maximum value from them while in use, and then recover and regenerate products and materials at the end of their service life. But the circular economy is much more than a concern for recycling as opposed to disposal. The circular economy examines what can be done right along the supply and use chain so that as few resources as possible are used, then (and this is the important bit) recover and regenerate products at the end of their conventional life. This means designing products for longevity, reparability, ease of dismantling and recycling.

Typical of the companies that have either adopted this idea, or been set up specially to promote it, is Newlife Paints, based on the south coast of England. It 'remanufactures' waste water-based paint back into a premium-grade emulsion. All products in the company's paint range guarantee a minimum 50 per cent recycled content, made up from waste paint diverted from landfill or incineration. The idea for the company began to take root in the mind of an industrial chemist, Keith Harrison. His garage was becoming a little unruly, after many years of do-it-yourself projects. Encouraged by his wife to clear out the mess, he realized that the stacked-up tins of paint represented a shocking waste. It was then that his search began for a sensible and environmentally responsible solution to waste paint. '*I kept

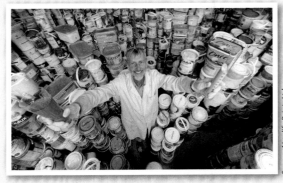

Source: Newlife Paints Ltd

thinking I could do something with it, the paint had an intrinsic value. It would have been a huge waste just to throw it away', said the former industrial chemist. Keith thought somebody must be recycling it, but no one was, and he set about finding a way to reprocess waste paint back to a superior-grade emulsion. After two years of research, he successfully developed his technology, which involves removing leftover paint from tins that have been diverted from landfill, and blending and filtering them to produce colour-matched new paints. The company has also launched a premium brand, aimed at affluent customers with a green conscience, called Reborn Paints, the development of which was partly funded by Akzo Nobel, maker of Dulux Paints. Although Keith started small (in his garage) he now licenses his technology to companies such as the giant waste company Veolia. '*By licensing we can have more impact and spread internationally'*, he says. He also points out that manufacturers could plan more imaginatively for the afterlife of their products. For example, simply adding more symbols to packs to assist sorting waste paints into types would help. 'At the moment we're fighting fires, *because the paints we pull out of the waste stream today were manufactured five or so years ago, when the circular economy was barely on the horizon'*, he says.

WHAT ARE THE BENEFITS OF INTERACTIVE PRODUCT AND SERVICE INNOVATION?

Treating each stage of design innovation as totally separate and sequential activities (as we have just done) is a little misleading. As we said earlier, it is common for companies to cycle back through stages, sometimes several times. Also it is increasingly common to break down the once ridged boundaries between each stage in the design innovation process. This applies especially to the boundary between the design of the product or service and the design of the process that will produce it.

It is generally considered a mistake to separate product and service design from process design. Operations managers should have some involvement from the initial evaluation of the concept right through to the production of the product or service and its introduction to the market. Merging the stages of the design innovation process is sometimes called 'interactive design'. The main benefit of merging stages is seen to be a reduction in the elapsed time for the whole design innovation activity, from concept through to market introduction. This is often called the time to market (TTM). The argument in favour of reducing time to market is that doing so gives increased competitive advantage. For example, if it takes a company five years to develop a product from concept to market, with a given set of resources, it can introduce a new product only once every five years. If its rival can develop products in three years, it can introduce its new product, together with its (presumably) improved performance, once every three years. This means that the rival company does not have to make such radical improvements in performance each time it introduces a new product, because it is introducing its new products more frequently. In other words, shorter TTM means that companies get more opportunities to improve the performance of their services or products.

Three factors in particular have been suggested which can significantly reduce time to market for a service or product:

- Simultaneous development of the various stages in the overall process.
- An early resolution of design conflict and uncertainty.
- An organizational structure which reflects the development project.

Simultaneous development

We described the design innovation process as essentially a set of individual, predetermined stages, each with a clear starting and an ending point. The implicit assumption is that one stage is completed before the next one commences. Indeed, this step-by-step, or sequential, approach has traditionally been the typical form of product/service development. It has some advantages. The process is easy to manage and control because each stage is clearly defined. In addition, each stage is completed before the next stage is begun, so each stage can focus its skills and expertise on a limited set of tasks. However, the main problem of the sequential approach is that it is both time consuming and costly. When each stage is separate, with a clearly defined set of tasks, any difficulties encountered during the design at one stage might necessitate the design being halted while responsibility moves back to the previous stage. This sequential approach is shown in Figure 4.11(a).

Yet often there is really little need to wait until the absolute finalization of one stage before starting the next. For example, perhaps while generating the concept, the evaluation activity

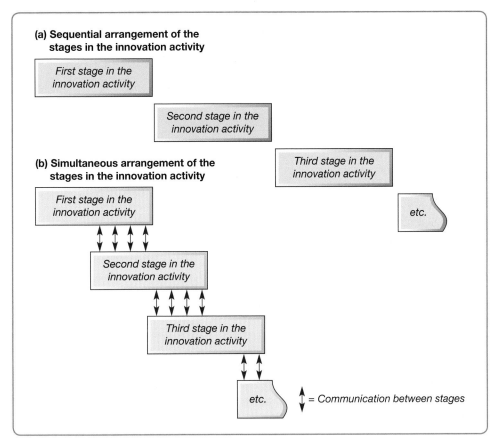

(a) Sequential arrangement of the stages in the innovation activity

First stage in the innovation activity

Second stage in the innovation activity

(b) Simultaneous arrangement of the stages in the innovation activity

Third stage in the innovation activity

First stage in the innovation activity

etc.

Second stage in the innovation activity

Third stage in the innovation activity

etc. ↕ = Communication between stages

Figure 4.11 (a) Sequential arrangement of the stages in the design activity; (b) simultaneous arrangement of the stages in the design activity

of screening and selection could be started. It is likely that some concepts could be judged as 'non-starters' relatively early on in the process of idea generation. Similarly, during the screening stage, it is likely that some aspects of the design will become obvious before the phase is finally complete. Therefore, the preliminary work on these parts of the design could be commenced at that point. This principle can be taken right through all the stages, one stage commencing before the previous one has finished, so there is simultaneous or concurrent work on the stages (*see* Fig. 4.11(b)). (Note that simultaneous development is often called simultaneous (or concurrent) engineering in manufacturing operations.)

> **✻ Operations principle**
> Effective simultaneous development reduces time to market.

OPERATIONS IN PRACTICE   **IKEA's slow development process[13]**

Most companies are obsessed with reducing the time to market (TTM) of their design process. Short TTM means lower development costs and more opportunities to hit the market with new designs. Some automobile companies have reduced the design time for their products to less than three years, while a new smartphone (a far more dynamic market) can be developed in as little as six months. So why does IKEA, the most successful homeware retailer ever, take five years to design its kitchens? Because, with the huge volumes that IKEA sells, development costs are small compared with the savings that can result from product designs that bring down the final price in its stores.

'It's five years of work into finding ways to engineer cost out of the system, to improve the functionality', IKEA's new Chief Executive, Peter Agnefjäll, said of the company's 'Metod' kitchen (which means 'Method' in English). Metod is a complex product. It has over a thousand different components. The kitchen is a product of IKEA's 'democratic design' process that ensures designs that will work in homes anywhere in the world – an important consideration when you sell about 1 million kitchens a year. Also, unlike some big-ticket purchases, consumer taste in home furnishing does not shift rapidly. 'We still hang paintings above the sofa and tend to have a TV in the corner', says IKEA Creative Director Mia Lundström. But even if trends do not materialize overnight, it is still important to spot emerging consumer preferences. A research team visits thousands of homes annually and compiles reports that look as far as a decade into the future. So without the imperative to change the product designs too

Source: Alamy Images: Chih-Chung Johnny Chang

frequently, product cost becomes a key driver. Rather than buy prefabricated components from outside sources, IKEA will develop its own if it keep costs down. For example, IKEA's designers created its own LED lighting system to light one of the kitchen drawers.

Early conflict resolution

Characterizing the design innovation activity as a whole series of decisions is a useful way of thinking about design. However, a decision, once made, need not totally and utterly commit the organization. For example, if a design team is designing a new vacuum cleaner, the decision to adopt a particular style and type of electric motor might have seemed sensible at the time the decision was made but might have to be changed later, in the light of new information. It could be that a new electric motor becomes available which is clearly superior to the one initially selected. Under those circumstances the designers might very well want to change their decision.

There are other, more avoidable, reasons for designers changing their minds during the design activity, however. Perhaps one of the initial design decisions was made without sufficient discussion among those in the organization who have a valid contribution to make. It may even be that when the decision was made there was insufficient agreement to formalize it, and the design team decided to carry on without formally making the decision. Yet subsequent decisions might be made as though the decision had been formalized. For

> *** Operations principle**
> The design process requires strategic attention early, when there is most potential to affect design decisions.

example, suppose the company could not agree on the correct size of electric motor to put into its vacuum cleaner. It might well carry on with the rest of the design work while further discussions and investigations take place on what kind of electric motor to incorporate in the design. Yet much of the rest of the product's design is likely to depend on the choice of the electric motor. The plastic housings, the bearings, the sizes of various apertures, and so on, could all be affected by this decision. Failure to resolve these conflicts and/or decisions early on in the process can prolong the degree of uncertainty in the total design activity. In addition, if a decision is made (even implicitly) and then changed later on in the process, the costs of that change can be very large. However, if the design team manages to resolve conflict early in the design activity, this will reduce the degree of uncertainty within the project and reduce the extra cost and, most significantly, time associated with either managing this uncertainty or changing decisions already made. Figure 4.12 illustrates two patterns of design changes through the life of the total design, which imply different time-to-market performances.

Figure 4.12 Sorting out problems early saves greater disruption later in the design activity

Project-based organizational structures

The total process of developing concepts through to market will almost certainly involve personnel from several different areas of the organization. To continue the vacuum cleaner example, it is likely that the vacuum cleaner company would involve staff from its research and development department, engineering, production management, marketing and finance. All these different functions will have some part to play in making the decisions which will shape the final design. Yet any design project will also have an existence of its own. It will have a project name, an individual manager or group of staff who are championing the project, a budget and, hopefully, a clear strategic purpose in the organization. The organizational question is which of these two ideas – the various organizational functions which contribute to the design or the design project itself – should dominate the way in which the design activity is managed?

Before answering this, it is useful to look at the range of organizational structures which are available – from pure functional to pure project forms. In a pure functional organization, all staff associated with the design project are based unambiguously in their functional groups. There is no project-based group at all. They may be working full-time on the project but all communications and liaisons are carried out through their functional manager. The project exists because of agreement between these functional managers. At the other extreme, all the individual members of staff from each function who are involved in the project could be moved out of their functions and perhaps even physically relocated to a task force dedicated solely to the project. The task force could be led by a project manager who might hold the entire budget allocated to the design project. Not all members of the task force necessarily have to stay in the team throughout the development period, but a substantial core might see the project through from start to finish. Some members of a design team may even be from other companies. In between these two extremes there are various types of matrix organization with varying emphasis on these two aspects of the organization (*see* Fig. 4.13). Although the 'task force' type of organization, especially for small projects, can sometimes be a little cumbersome, it seems to be generally agreed that, for substantial projects at least, it is more effective at reducing overall time to market.

Skunkworks[14] Encouraging creativity in design, while at the same time recognizing the constraints of everyday business life, has always been one of the great challenges of industrial design. One well-known organizational structure that is claimed to release the design and development creativity of a group has been called 'a Skunkworks'. It is usually taken to mean a small team who are taken out of their normal work environment and granted freedom

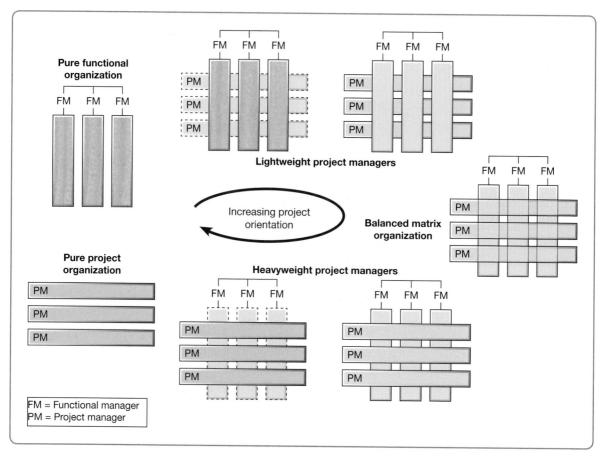

Figure 4.13 Organizational structures for the design innovation process

from their normal management activities and constraints – what we have called here a pure 'project-based' structure. It was an idea that originated in the Lockheed Aircraft Company in the 1940s, where designers were set up outside the normal organizational structure and given the task of designing a high-speed fighter. The experiment was so successful that the company continued with it to develop other innovative products. Since that time many other companies have used a similar approach, although 'Skunk Works' is a registered trademark of Lockheed Martin Corporation.

SUMMARY ANSWERS TO KEY QUESTIONS

〉 What is product and service innovation?

- Innovation is the act of introducing something new. Design is to 'conceive the looks, arrangement, and workings of something'. Creativity is the ability to move beyond conventional ideas, rules or assumptions, in order to generate significant new ideas. These three concepts are intimately related.

- The innovation S-curve describes the impact of an innovation over time, slow at first, increasing in impact, then slowing down before levelling off.

- Incremental and radical innovations differ in how they use knowledge. Radical innovation often requires completely new knowledge and/or resources making existing products and services obsolete. Incremental innovation builds upon existing knowledge and/or resources.
- The Henderson–Clark model goes further by distinguishing between 'knowledge of the components of innovation' and 'knowledge of how the components of innovation link together' (called architectural knowledge).

> ## What is the strategic role of product and service innovation?

- Good design takes innovative ideas and makes them practical.
- There is an increasingly common acceptance that design can add very significant value to all types of organization.
- Producing design innovations for products and services is itself a process that conforms to the input–transformation–output model described in Chapter 1.
- The performance of the design process can be assessed in the same way as any process, namely in terms of quality, speed, dependability, flexibility, cost and 'sustainability'.

> ## What are the stages of product and service innovation?

- *Concept generation* transforms an idea for a product or service into a concept which captures the nature of the product or service and provides an overall specification for its design.
- *Screening* the concept involves examining its feasibility, acceptability and vulnerability in broad terms to ensure that it is a sensible addition to the company's service or product portfolio.
- *Preliminary design* involves the identification of all the component parts of the product or service and the way they fit together. Typical tools used during this phase include component structures and flow charts.
- *Design evaluation and improvement* involve re-examining the design to see if it can be done in a better way, more cheaply or more easily. A typical technique used here is quality function deployment.
- *Prototyping and final design* involve providing the final details which allow the product or service to be produced. The outcome of this stage is a fully developed specification for the package of products and services, as well as a specification for the processes that will make and deliver them to customers.

> ## What are the benefits of interactive product and service innovation?

- Looking at the stages of design together can improve the quality of both product and service design and process design. It helps a design 'break even' on its investment earlier than would otherwise have been the case. It is particularly effective if managers:
  - Employ *simultaneous development* where design decisions are taken as early as they can be, without necessarily waiting for a whole design phase to be completed.
  - Ensure early *conflict resolution* which allows contentious decisions to be resolved early in the design process, thereby not allowing them to cause far more delay and confusion if they emerge later in the process.
  - Use a *project-based organizational structure* which can ensure that a focused and coherent team of designers is dedicated to a single design or group of design projects.

Developing 'Savory Rosti-crisps' at Dreddo Dan's

'Most people see the snack market as dynamic and innovative, but actually it is surprisingly conservative. Most of what passes for innovation is in fact tinkering with our marketing approach, things like special offers, promotion tie-ins and so on. We occasionally put new packs round our existing products and even more occasionally we introduce new flavors in existing ranges. Rarely though does anyone in this industry introduce something radically different. That is why "Project Orlando" is both exciting and scary.'

Monica Allen, the Technical Vice-President of PJT's Snack Division, was commenting on a new product to be marketed under PJT's best-known brand 'Dreddo Dan's Surfer Snacks'. The Dreddo Dan's brand made use of surfing and outdoor 'action-oriented youth' imagery, but in fact was aimed at a slightly older generation who, although aspiring to such a lifestyle, had more discretionary spend for the premium snacks in which the brand specialized. Current products marketed under the brand included both fried and baked snacks in a range of exotic flavours. The project, internally known as Project Orlando, was a baked product that had been 'in development' for almost three years but had hitherto been seen very much as a long-term development, with no guarantee of it ever making it through to market launch. PJT had several of these long-term projects running at any time. They were allocated a development budget, but usually no dedicated resources were associated with the project. Less than half of these long-term projects ever even reached the stage of being test marketed. Around 20 per cent never got past the concept stage, and less than 20 per cent ever went into production. However, the company viewed the development effort put into these 'failed' products as being worthwhile because it often led to 'spin-off' developments and ideas that could be used elsewhere. Up to this point 'Orlando' had been seen as unlikely ever to reach the test marketing stage, but that had now changed dramatically.

'Orlando' was a concept for a range of snack foods, described within the company as 'savory potato cookies'. Essentially they were 1½ inch discs of crisp, fried potato with a soft dairy-cheese-like filling. The idea of incorporating dairy fillings in snacks had been discussed within the industry for some time, but the problems of manufacturing such a product were formidable. Keeping the product crisp on the outside yet soft in the middle, while at the same time ensuring microbiological safety, would not be easy. Moreover, such a product would have to be capable of being stored at ambient temperatures, maintain its physical robustness and have a shelf life of at least three months.

Bringing Orlando products to market involved overcoming three types of technical problem. First, the formulation and ingredient mix for the product had to maintain the required texture yet be capable of being baked on the company's existing baking lines. The risk of developing an entirely new production technology for the offering was considered too great. Second, extruding the mixture into baking moulds while maintaining microbiological integrity (dairy products are difficult to handle) would require new extrusion technology. Third, the product would need to be packaged in a material that both reflected its brand image and kept the product fresh through its shelf life. Existing packaging materials were unlikely to provide sufficient shelf life. The first of these problems had, more or less, been solved in PJT's development laboratories. The second two problems now seemed less formidable because of a number of recent technological breakthroughs made by equipment suppliers and packaging manufacturers. This had convinced the company that Orlando was worth significant investment and it had been given priority development status by the company's board. Even so, it was not expected to come to the market for another two years and was seen by some as potentially the most important new product development in the company's history.

Source: Alamy Images: Mediablitzimages

The project team

Immediately after the board's decision, Monica had accepted responsibility to move the development forward. She decided to put together a dedicated project team to oversee the development. *'It is important to have representatives from all relevant parts of the company. Although the team will carry out much of the work themselves, they will still need the cooperation and the resources of their own departments. So, as well as being part of the team, they are also gateways to expertise around the company.'* The team consisted of representatives from marketing, the development kitchens (laboratories), PGT's technology centre (a development facility that served the whole group, not just the snack division), packaging engineers, and representative from the division's two manufacturing plants. All but the manufacturing representatives were allocated to the project team on a full-time basis. Unfortunately, manufacturing had no one who had sufficient process knowledge and who could be spared from their day-to-day activities.

Development objectives

Monica had tried to set the objectives for the project in her opening remarks to the project team members when they had first come together. 'We have a real chance here to develop an offering that not only will have major market impact, but will also give us a sustainable competitive advantage. We need to make this project work in such a way that competitors will find it difficult to copy what we do. The formulation is a real success for our development people, and as long as we figure out how to use the new extrusion method and packaging material, we should be difficult to beat. The success of Orlando in the marketplace will depend on our ability to operationalize and integrate the various technical solutions that we now have access to. The main problem with this type of offering is that it will be expensive to develop and yet, once our competitors realize what we are doing, they will come in fast to try and out-innovate us. Whatever else we do we must ensure that there is sufficient flexibility in the project to allow us to respond quickly when competitors follow us into the market with their own 'me-too' products. We are not racing against the clock to get this to market, but once we do make a decision to launch we will have to move fast and hit the launch date reliably. Perhaps most important, we must ensure that the crisps are 200 per cent safe. We have no experience in dealing with the microbiological testing which dairy-based food manufacture requires. Other divisions of PJT do have this experience and I guess we will be relying heavily on them.'

Monica, who had been tasked with managing the (now much expanded) development process, had already drawn up a list of key decisions she would have to take:

- **How to resource the innovation project** – The division had a small development staff, some of whom had been working on Project Orlando, but a project of this size would require extra staff amounting to about twice the current number of people dedicated to the innovation process.
- **Whether to invest in a pilot plant** – The process technology required for the new project would be unlike any of the division's current technology. Similar technology was used by some companies in the frozen food industry and one option would be to carry out trials at these (non-competitor) companies' sites. Alternatively, the Orlando team could build its own pilot plant which would enable it to experiment in-house. As well as the significant expense involve,

this would raise the problem of whether any process innovations would work when scaled up to full size. However, it would be far more convenient for the project team and allow its members to 'make their mistakes' in private.

- **How much development to outsource** – Because of the size of the project, Monica had considered outsourcing some of the innovation activities. Other divisions within the company might be able to undertake some of the development work and there were also specialist consultancies that operated in the food processing industries. The division had never used any of these consultancies before but other divisions had occasionally done so.
- **How to organize the innovation activities** – Currently the small development function had been organized around loose functional specialisms. Monica wondered whether this project warranted the creation of a separate department independent of the current structure. This might signal the importance of this innovation project to the whole division.

Fixing the budget

The budget to develop Project Orlando through to launch had been set at $30 million. This made provision to increase the size of the existing innovation team by 70 per cent over a 20-month period (for launch two years later). It also included enough funding to build a pilot plant which would allow the team the flexibility to develop responses to potential competitor reaction after the launch. So, of the $30m, around $18m was for extra staff and contracted-out innovation work, $7.5m for the pilot plant and $4.5m for one-off costs (such as the purchase of test equipment etc.). Monica was unsure whether the budget would be big enough. 'I know everyone in my position wants more money, but it is important not to under fund a project like this. Increasing our development staff by 70% is not really enough. In my opinion we need an increase of at least 90% to make sure that we can launch when we want. This would need another $5m, spread over the next 20 months. We could get this by not building the pilot plant I suppose, but I am reluctant to give that up. It would mean begging for test capacity on other companies' plants, which is never satisfactory from a knowledge-building viewpoint. Also it would compromise security. Knowledge of what we were doing could easily leak to competitors. Alternatively we could subcontract more of the research which may be less expensive, especially in the long run, but I doubt if it would save the full $5m we need. More important, I am not sure that we should subcontract anything which would compromise safety, and increasing the amount of work we send out may do that. No, it's got to be the extra cash or the project could overrun. The profit projections for the Orlando products look great [see Table 4.1], but delay or our inability to respond to competitor pressures would depress those figures significantly. Our competitors could get into the market only a little after us. Word has is that Marketing's

Table 4.1 Preliminary 'profit stream' projections for the Project Orlando offering, assuming launch in 24 months' time

Time period*	1	2	3	4	5	6	7
Profit flow ($m)	10	20	50	90	120	130	135

*Six-month periods.

calculations indicate a delay of only six months could not only delay the profit stream by the six months but also cut it by up to 30%.'

Monica was keen to explain two issues to the management committee when it met to consider her request for extra funding. First, that there was a coherent and well-thought-out strategy for the innovation project over the next two years. Second, that saving $5m on Project Orlando's budget would be a false economy.

QUESTIONS

1 How would you rank the innovation objectives for the project?

2 What are the key issues in resourcing this innovation process?

3 What are the main factors influencing the resourcing decisions?

4 What advice would you give Monica?

PROBLEMS AND APPLICATIONS

1 How would you go about evaluating the design of this book?

2 A company is developing a new app that will allow customers to track the progress of their orders. The website developers charge €10,000 for every development week and it is estimated that the design will take 10 weeks from the start of the design project to the launch of the website. Once launched, it is estimated that the new site will attract extra business that will generate profits of €5,000 per week. However, if the website is delayed by more than five weeks, the extra profit generated would reduce to €2,000 per week. How will a delay of five weeks affect the time when the design will break even in terms of cash flow?

3 How can the concept of modularization be applied to package holidays sold through an online travel agent?

4 One product where a very wide range of product types is valued by customers is that of domestic paint. Most people like to express their creativity in the choice of paints and other home decorating products that they use in their homes. Clearly, offering a wide range of paint must have serious cost implications for the companies which manufacture, distribute and sell the product. Visit a store which sells paint and get an idea of the range of products available on the market. How do you think paint manufacturers and retailers manage to design their services and products so as to maintain high variety but keep costs under control?

5 Some firms specialize in helping clients to innovate and design their products and services. One of the best known of these is IDEO (ideo.com). Look at the website and:
    (a) Identify the stages of design innovation that the firm goes through with its clients.
    (b) Assess its approach to design innovation. What does the firm believe are the most important aspects of successful new product and service development?
    (c) Why do you think IDEO is so willing to tell everyone how to go about the design innovation process? Isn't that giving away the firm's expertise for free?

SELECTED FURTHER READING

Bangle, C. (2001) The ultimate creativity machine: how BMW turns art into profit, *Harvard Business Review*, January, 47–55.

A good description of how good aesthetic design translates into business success.

Bruce, M. and Bessant, J. (2002) *Design In Business: Strategic innovation through design*, Financial Times Prentice Hall and The Design Council, Harlow.

Probably one of the best overviews of design in a business context available today.

Christensen, C. (1997) *The Innovator's Dilemma*, Harvard Business School Press, Boston, MA, 1997; Harper Business, New York, 2000.

A major influence on innovation theory.

Dyson, J. (1997) *Against the Odds: An autobiography*, Orion Business Books, London.

One of Europe's most famous designers gives his philosophy.

Kelly, T. (2002) *The Art Of Innovation: Success Through Innovation the IDEO Way*, Profile Books, London.

Ideas from IDEO, the best-known design and innovation consultancy.

Nambison, S. and Sawhney, M. (2007) A buyer's guide to the innovation bazaar, *Harvard Business Review*, June.

Provocative innovation ideas.

Rose, D. (2015) *Enchanted Objects: Innovation, Design, and the Future of Technology*, Scribner, New York.

An interesting look at how technology is (and will) impact on design.

Tidd, J. and Bessant, J. (2013) *Managing Innovation: Integrating Technological, Market and Organizational Change*, 5th edn, Wiley, Chichester.

The definitive textbook in the area.

5

The structure and scope of operations

Key questions

❯ What do we mean by the 'structure' and 'scope' of operations' supply networks?

❯ What configuration should a supply network have?

❯ How much capacity should operations plan to have?

❯ Where should operations be located?

❯ How vertically integrated should an operation's network be?

❯ How do operations decide what to do in-house and what to outsource?

INTRODUCTION

Both the structure and the scope of an operation's supply network are decisions that shape how the operation interacts with other operations, with its markets, with its suppliers – in fact with the world in general. After all, no operation exists in isolation. All operations are part of a larger and interconnected network of other operations. This is called the operation's *supply network*. It will include the operation's suppliers and customers. It will also include suppliers' suppliers and customers' customers, and so on. At a strategic level, operations managers are involved in deciding the shape and form of their network. This is called the *structure* of the network. It involves deciding the overall shape of the network, the location of each operation, and how big the parts of the network that the operation owns should be. And that is the next issue faced by all operations. Exactly how much of the network should the operation own? This is called the *scope* of the operation. Put another way, the scope of the operation defines what it is going to do itself and what it will buy in from suppliers. This chapter treats the issues related to both the structure and scope decisions (*see* Fig. 5.1).

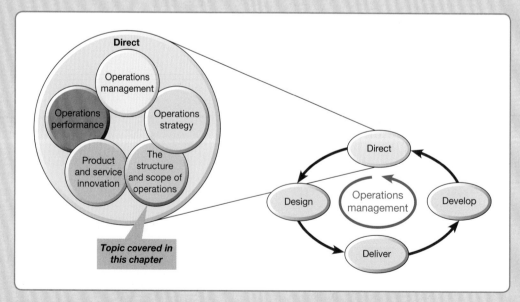

Figure 5.1 This chapter covers the topic of the structure and scope of operations

WHAT DO WE MEAN BY THE 'STRUCTURE' AND 'SCOPE' OF OPERATIONS' SUPPLY NETWORKS?

The 'structure' of an operation's supply network relates to the shape and form of the network. The scope of an operation's supply network relates to the extent that an operation decides to do the activities performed by the network itself, as opposed to requesting a supplier to do them. But before we examine these issues, we need to establish what we mean by 'a supply network': '*A supply network is an interconnection of organizations that relate to each other through upstream and downstream linkages between the different processes and activities that produce value in the form of products and services to the ultimate consumer.*'[1] In other words, a supply network is the means setting an operation in the context of all the other operations with which it interacts, some of which are its suppliers and its customers. Materials, parts, other information, ideas and sometimes people all flow through the network of customer–supplier relationships formed by all these operations. On its supply side an operation has its suppliers of parts, or information, or services. These suppliers themselves have their own suppliers which in turn could also have suppliers, and so on. On the demand side the operation has customers. These customers might not be the final consumers of the operation's products or services; they might have their own set of customers. On the supply side is a group of operations that directly supply the operation; these are often called first-tier suppliers. They are supplied by second-tier suppliers. However, some second-tier suppliers may also supply an operation directly, thus missing out a link in the network. Similarly, on the demand side of the network, 'first-tier' customers are the main customer group for the operation. These in turn supply 'second-tier' customers, although again the operation may at times supply second-tier customers directly. The suppliers and customers who have direct contact with an operation are called its immediate supply network, whereas all the operations that form the network of suppliers' suppliers and customers' customers, etc., are called the total supply network.

Figure 5.2 illustrates the total supply network for two operations. The first is a plastic homeware (kitchen bowls etc.) manufacturer. On the demand side it supplies products to wholesalers who supply retail outlets. However, it also supplies some retailers directly, bypassing a stage in the network – not an uncommon situation. As products flow from suppliers to customers, orders and information flow the other way from customers to suppliers. It is a two-way process with goods flowing one way and information flowing the other. But do not think that only manufacturers can be part of supply networks. The second illustration in Figure 5.2 shows a supply network centred on a shopping mall. It also has suppliers and customers who themselves have their own suppliers and customers.

OPERATIONS IN PRACTICE	Contrasting strategies on structure and scope: ARM versus Intel[2]

Nothing better illustrates the idea that there is more than one approach to competing in the same market than the contrasting business models of ARM and Intel in the microchip business. At one point in 2015, ARM's chip designs were to be found in almost 99 per cent of mobile devices in the world, while Intel dominates the PC and server markets. Yet ARM and Intel are very different companies, with different approaches to the structure and scope of their operations and, some claim, very different prospects for their future. They are certainly of a different size. In revenue terms Intel was around 50 times bigger than ARM. More interestingly, Intel is vertically integrated, both designing and manufacturing its own chips, while ARM is essentially a chip designer, developing intellectual property. It then licenses its processor designs to manufacturers such as Samsung, who in turn rely on subcontracting 'chip foundry' companies to do the actual manufacturing (ironically, including for Intel).

Intel's integrated supply network monitors and controls all stages of production, from the original design concept right through to manufacturing. Keeping on top of fast-changing (and hugely expensive – it can cost around $5 billion to build a new chip-making plant) operations requires very large investments. It is Intel's near

▶

monopoly (therefore high volume) of the server and PC markets that helps it to keep its unit prices high, which in turn gives it the ability to finance the construction of the latest semiconductor manufacturing equipment before its competitors. And having the latest manufacturing technology is important; it can mean faster, smaller and cheaper chips with lower power consumption. As one industry source put it, '*Intel is one of the few companies left with the financial resources to invest in state-of-the-art manufacturing research and development. Everyone else – including all the ARM licensees – have to make do with shared manufacturing, mainstream technology, and less-aggressive physics.*' By contrast, ARM's supply network strategy was a direct result of their early lack of cash. It did not have the money to invest in its own manufacturing facilities (or to take the risk of subcontracting manufacturing), so it focused on licensing its 'reference designs'. Reference designs provide the 'technical blueprint' of a microprocessor that third parties can enhance or modify as required. This means that partners can take ARM reference designs and integrate them in flexibly

Source: Shutterstock.com: Raimundas

to produce different final designs. And over the years a whole 'ecosystem' of tools has emerged to help developers build applications around the ARM design architecture. The importance of ARM's supply 'ecosystem' should not be underestimated. It is an approach that allows ARM's partners to be part of ARM's success rather than cutting them out of the revenue opportunities.

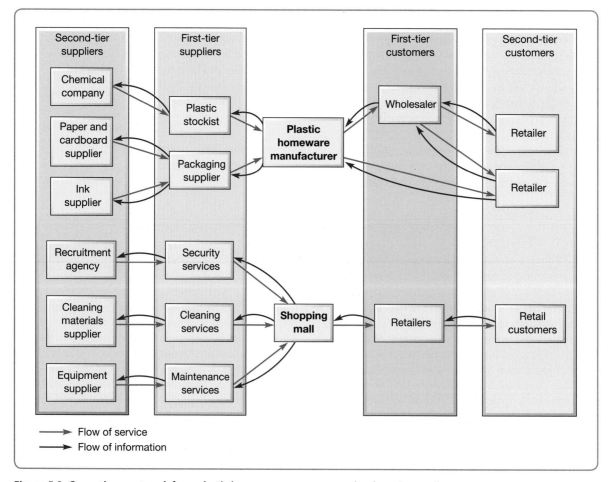

Figure 5.2 Operations network for a plastic homeware company and a shopping mall

Why is the structure and scope of an operation's supply network important?

So why is it important to stand back and look at the whole (or a large part) of a supply network rather than an individual operation? Here are three reasons:

- **It helps an understanding of competitiveness** – Immediate customers and immediate suppliers, quite understandably, are the main concern for companies. Yet sometimes they need to look beyond these immediate contacts to understand *why* customers and suppliers act as they do. Any operation has only two options if it wants to understand its ultimate customers' needs at the end of the network. It can rely on all the intermediate customers and customers' customers, etc., who form the links in the network between the company and its end customers. Alternatively, it can look beyond its immediate customers and suppliers. Relying on one's immediate network is seen as putting too much faith in someone else's judgement of things which are central to an organization's own competitive health.
- **It helps identify significant links in the network** – Not everyone in a supply network has the same degree of influence over the performance of the network as a whole. Some operations contribute more to the performance objectives that are valued by end customers. So an analysis of networks needs to understand the downstream and the upstream operations which contribute most to end customers' service. For example, the important end customers for domestic plumbing parts and appliances are the installers and service companies which deal directly with consumers. They are supplied by 'stock holders' who must have all parts in stock and deliver them fast. Suppliers of parts to the stock holders can best contribute to their end customers' competitiveness partly by offering a short delivery lead time but mainly through dependable delivery. The key players in this example are the stock holders. The best way of winning end customer business in this case is to give the stock holder prompt delivery, which helps keep costs down while providing high availability of parts.

> **✳ Operations principle**
> A supply network perspective helps to make sense of competitive, relationship and longer term operations issues.

- **It helps focus on long-term issues** – There are times when circumstances render parts of a supply network weaker than its adjacent links. High street music stores, for example, have been largely displaced by music streaming and downloading services. A long-term supply network view would involve constantly examining technology and market changes to see how each operation in the supply networks might be affected.

Structure and scope

So what do we mean by the structure and scope of an operation's supply network? The first point to make is that structure and scope are strongly related (which is why we treat them together). For example, look again at the supply network for the shopping mall in Figure 5.2. Suppose that the company that runs the mall is dissatisfied with the service that it is receiving from the firm that supplies security services. Also suppose that it is considering three alternatives. Option 1 is to switch suppliers and award the security contract to a competitor to the current security services supplier. Option 2 is to accept an offer from the company that supplies cleaning services to supply both security and cleaning services. Option 3 is to take over responsibility for security itself, hiring its own security staff who would be put on the mall's payroll. These options are illustrated in Figure 5.3. The first of these options changes neither the structure nor the scope of this part of the supply network. The shopping mall still has three suppliers and is doing exactly what it did before. All that has changed is that the mall's security services are being provided by another (hopefully better) supplier. However, option 1 changes the structure of the supply network (the mall now has only two suppliers, the combined cleaning and security supplier, and the maintenance supplier), but not the scope of what the mall does (it does exactly what it did before). Option 3 changes both the structure of the network (again, the mall has only two suppliers, cleaning and maintenance services) and the scope of what the mall does (it now also takes on responsibility for security itself).

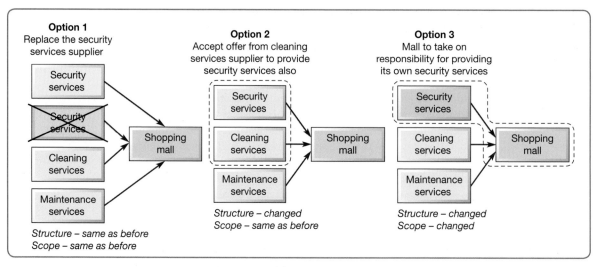

Figure 5.3 Three options for the shopping mall's supply network

So, decisions relating to structure and scope are often interrelated. But for simplicity we will treat them separately in this chapter.

The second point to make is that both structure and scope decisions are actually composed of a number of other 'constituent' decisions. These are shown in Figure 5.4. The structure of an operation's supply network is determined by three sets of decisions:

1 How should the network be configured?
2 What physical capacity should each part of the network have (the long-term capacity decision)?
3 Where should each part of the network be located (the location decision)?

The scope of an operation's activities within the network is determined by two decisions:

1 The extent and nature of the operation's vertical integration.
2 The nature and degree of outsourcing it engages in.

Note, however, that all of these decisions rely on forecasts of future demand that the supplement to this chapter explores in more detail.

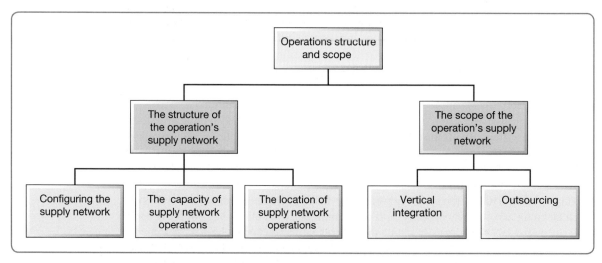

Figure 5.4 What determines an operation's structure and scope?

The final point to make here is that structure and scope decisions are undeniably strategic. Go back to the 'operations in practice' example on the contrasting strategies of ARM and Intel earlier in the chapter. Their (very different) approaches to the structure and scope of their operations have totally defined how each company does business in essentially similar markets. There are few decisions that are more strategic than which other businesses you are going to trade with (structure) and how much of the total activities in the supply network you are going to take responsibility for (scope). However, both structure and scope also have a more operational aspect. As we illustrated in Figure 5.3, an operation such as the shopping mall can change its supply arrangements in a relatively short-term manner, for example by simply changing its suppliers. We will treat the more operational day-to-day aspects of structure and scope in Chapter 12 on supply chain management.

WHAT CONFIGURATION SHOULD A SUPPLY NETWORK HAVE?

'Configuring' a supply network means determining its overall pattern. In other words, what should be the pattern, shape or arrangement of the various operations that make up the supply network? Even when an operation does not directly own, or even control, other operations in its network, it may still wish to change the shape of the network. This involves attempting to manage network behaviour by reconfiguring the network so as to change the nature of the relationships between them. Reconfiguring a supply network sometimes involves parts of the operation being merged – not necessarily in the sense of a change of ownership of any parts of an operation, but rather in the way responsibility is allocated for carrying out activities. The most common example of network reconfiguration has come through the many companies that have recently reduced the number of their direct suppliers. The complexity of dealing with many hundreds of suppliers may both be expensive for an operation and (sometimes more important) prevent the operation from developing a close relationship with a supplier. It is not easy to be close to hundreds of different suppliers.

Disintermediation

Another trend in some supply networks is that of companies within a network bypassing customers or suppliers to make contact directly with customers' customers or suppliers' suppliers. 'Cutting out the intermediaries' in this way is called disintermediation. An obvious example of this is the way the Internet has allowed some suppliers to 'disintermediate' traditional retailers in supplying goods and services to consumers. So, for example, many services in the travel industry that used to be sold through retail outlets (travel agents) are now also available direct from the suppliers. The option of purchasing the individual components of a vacation through the websites of the airline, hotel, car-hire operation, etc., is now easier for consumers. Of course, they may still wish to purchase an 'assembled' product from retail travel agents, which can have the advantage of convenience. Nevertheless the process of disintermediation has developed new linkages in the supply network.

Co-opetition

One approach to thinking about supply networks sees any business as being surrounded by four types of players: suppliers, customers, competitors and complementors. Complementors enable one's products or services to be valued more by customers because they also can have the complementor's products or services, as opposed to when they have yours alone. Competitors are the opposite; they make customers value your product or service less when they can have their product or service, rather than yours alone. Competitors can also be complementors and vice versa. For example, adjacent restaurants may see themselves as competitors for customers' business. A customer standing outside and wanting a meal will choose between the two of them. Yet in another way they are complementors.

Would that customer have come to this part of town unless there was more than one restaurant to choose from? Restaurants, theatres, art galleries, and tourist attractions generally, all cluster together in a form of co-operation to increase the total size of their joint market. It is important to distinguish between the way companies co-operate in increasing the total size of a market and the way in which they then compete for a share of that market. Customers and suppliers, it is argued, should have 'symmetric' roles. Harnessing the value of suppliers is just as important as listening to the needs of customers. Destroying value in a supplier in order to create it in a customer does not increase the value of the network as a whole. So, pressurizing suppliers will not necessarily add value. In the long term it creates value for the total network to find ways of increasing value for suppliers as well as customers. All the players in the network, whether they are customers, suppliers, competitors or complementors, can be both friends and enemies at different times. The term used to capture this idea is 'co-opetition'.

OPERATIONS IN PRACTICE   Virtually like Hollywood

As far as the scope and structure of supply networks are concerned, could that most ephemeral of all industries, Hollywood's film making business, hold messages for even the most sober of operations? It is an industry whose complexity most of us do not fully appreciate. The American writer Scott Fitzgerald said, *'You can take Hollywood for granted like I did, or you can dismiss it with the contempt we reserve for what we don't understand...not half a dozen men have ever been able to keep the whole equation of* [making] *pictures in their heads.'* The 'equation' involves balancing the artistic creativity and fashion awareness, necessary to cre-

Source: Shutterstock.com: StockLite

ate a market for its products, with the efficiency and tight operations practices which get films made and distributed on time. But although the form of the equation remains the same, the way its elements relate to each other has changed profoundly. The typical Hollywood studio once did everything itself. It employed everyone from the carpenters who made the stage through to the film stars. The film star Cary Grant (one of the biggest in his day) was as much of an employee as the chauffeur who drove him to the studio, though his contract was probably more restrictive. The finished products were rolls of film that had to be mass produced and physically distributed to the cinemas of the world. No longer. Studios now deal almost exclusively in ideas. They buy and sell concepts, they arrange finance, they cut marketing deals and, above all, they manage the virtual network of creative and not-so-creative talent that goes into a film's production. A key skill is the ability to put together teams of self-employed film stars and the small, technical specialist operations that provide technical support. It is a world that is less easy for the studios to control. The players in this virtual network, from film stars to electricians, have taken the opportunity to raise their fees to the point where, in spite of an increase in cinema attendance, returns are lower than at many times in the past. This opens up opportunities for the smaller, independent studios. One way to keep costs low is by using inexpensive, new talent. Technology could also help this process. Digital processes allow easier customization of the 'product' and also mean that movies can be streamed direct to cinemas and direct to individual consumers' homes.

The idea of the 'business ecosystem'[3]

An idea that is closely related to that of co-opetition in supply networks is that of the 'business ecosystem'. It can be defined as: *'An economic community supported by a foundation of interacting organizations and individuals – the organisms of the business world. The economic community produces goods and services of value to customers, who are themselves members of the ecosystem. The member organisms also include suppliers, lead producers, competitors, and other stakeholders. Over time, they coevolve their capabilities and roles, and tend to align themselves with the directions set by one or more central companies.'*[4]

One of the main differences between this idea and that of the supply network generally is the inclusion in the idea of the ecosystem of businesses that may have no or little direct relationship with the main supply network, yet exist only because of that network. They interact with each other, predominantly complementing or contributing significant components of the value proposition for customers. Many examples come from the technology industries. The innovative products and services that are developed in the technology sectors cannot evolve in a vacuum. They need to attract a whole range of resources, drawing in expertise, capital, suppliers and customers to create co-operative networks. For example, the app developers that develop applications for particular operating system platforms may not be 'suppliers' as such, but the relationship between them and the supply network that supplies the mobile device is mutually beneficial. Building an ecosystem of developers around a core product can increase its value to the end customer and by doing so complements the usage of the core product. Such an ecosystem of complementary products and services can also create significant barriers to entry for new competitors. Any possible competitors would not only have to compete with the core product, but also have to compete against the entire ecosystem of complementary products and services.

The terminology and metaphors used to describe business ecosystems are obviously based on that used to describe 'natural' biological systems, where elements in the 'ecosystem' affect and are affected by the others. This creates a constantly evolving set of relationships where, if they are to survive, businesses must be flexible, adaptable and preferably innovative. For an ecosystem to thrive, the relationships between elements (businesses in this case) must communicate, establish trust, share information, collaborate, experiment, and develop in a mutually supportive symbiotic manner. The comparison with the natural biological ecosystem is also important because it emphasizes that the relationships between things matter and that, to some extent, everything in a supply network touches everything else.

Describing supply networks – dyads and triads

The supply networks that were illustrated in Figure 5.2 are, of course, simplifications. Any realistic supply network diagram will be much more complex. There are many operations, all interacting in different ways, to produce end products and services. Because of this, and to understand them better, supply network academics and professionals often choose to focus on the individual interaction between two specific operations in the network. This is called a 'dyadic' (simply meaning 'two') interaction, or dyadic relationship, and the two operations are referred to as a 'dyad'. So if one wanted to examine the interactions that a focal operation had with one of its suppliers and one of its customers, one would examine the two dyads of 'supplier–focal operation' and 'focal operation–customer', *see* Figure 5.5(a). For many years most discussion (and research) on supply networks was based on dyadic relationships. This is not surprising as all relationships in a network are based on the simple dyad. However, more recently, and certainly when examining service supply networks, many authorities make the point that dyads do not reflect the real essence of a supply network. Rather, they say, it is triads, not dyads, that are the basic elements of a supply network, *see* Figure 5.5(b). No matter how complex a network, it can be broken down into a collection of triadic interactions. The idea of triads is especially relevant in service supply networks. Operations are increasingly outsourcing the delivery of some aspects of their service to specialist providers, who deal directly with customers on behalf of the focal operation (more usually called the 'buying operation', or just 'buyer' in this context). For example, Figure 5.5(b) illustrates the common example of an airline contracting a specialist baggage handling company to provide services to its customers on its behalf. Similarly, internal services are increasingly outsourced to form internal triadic relationships. For example, if a company outsources its IT operations, it is forming a triad between whoever is purchasing the service on behalf of the company, the IT service provider and the employees who use the IT services.

Thinking about supply networks as a collection of triads rather than dyads is strategically important. First, it emphasizes the dependence that organizations are placing on their suppliers' performance when they outsource service delivery. A supplier's service performance makes up an important part of how the buyer's performance is viewed. Second, the control that the buyer of the service has over service delivery to its customer is diminished in a triadic relationship. In a conventional supply chain, with a series of dyadic relationships, there is the opportunity to intervene before the customer receives the product or service. However, products or services in triadic relationships bypass the buying organization and go directly from provider to customer. Third, and partially as a consequence of the previous point, in triadic relationships the direct link between service provider and customer can result in power gradually transferring over time from the buying organization to the supplier that provides the service. Fourth, it becomes increasingly difficult for the buying organization to understand what is happening between the supplier and customer at a day-to-day level. It may not even be in the supplier's interests to be totally honest in giving performance feedback to the buyer. Finally, this closeness between supplier and customer, if it excludes the buyer, could prevent the buyer from building important knowledge. For example, suppose a specialist equipment manufacturer has outsourced the maintenance of its equipment to a specialist provider of maintenance services. The ability of the equipment manufacturer to understand how its customers are using the equipment, how the equipment is performing under various conditions, and how customers would like to see the equipment improved, is lost. The equipment manufacturer may have

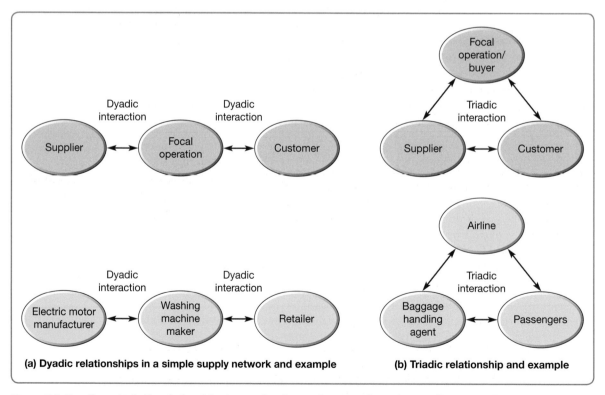

(a) Dyadic relationships in a simple supply network and example

(b) Triadic relationship and example

Figure 5.5 Dyadic and triadic relationships in two simple supply networks and examples outsourced the cost and trouble of providing maintenance services, but it has also outsourced the benefits and learning that come from direct interaction with customers.

HOW MUCH CAPACITY SHOULD OPERATIONS PLAN TO HAVE?

The next set of 'structure' decisions concerns the size or capacity of each part of the supply network. Here we will treat capacity in a general long-term sense. The specific issues involved in measuring and adjusting capacity in the medium and short terms are examined in Chapter 11.

The optimum capacity level

Most organizations need to decide on the size (in terms of capacity) of each of their facilities. A chain of truck service centres, for example, might operate centres that have various capacities. The effective cost of running each centre will depend on the average service bay occupancy. Low occupancy because of few customers will result in a high cost per customer served because the fixed costs of the operation are being shared between few customers. As demand, and therefore service bay occupancy, increase, the cost per customer will reduce. However, operating at very high levels of capacity utilization (occupancy levels close to capacity) can mean longer customer waiting times and reduced customer service. There may also be less obvious cost penalties of operating centres at levels close to nominal capacity. For example, long periods of overtime may reduce productivity levels as well as costing more in extra payments to staff; utilizing bays at very high utilization reduces maintenance and cleaning time that may increase breakdowns, reduce effective life, and so on. This usually means that average costs start to increase after a point which will often be lower than the theoretical capacity of the operation.

> ✽ **Operations principle**
> ALL types of operation exhibit economy of scale effects where operating costs reduce as the scale of capacity increases.

The blue curves in Figure 5.6 show this effect for the service centres of 5-, 10- and 15-bay capacity. As the nominal capacity of the centres increases, the lowest cost point at first reduces. This is because the fixed costs of any operation do not increase proportionately as its capacity increases. A 10-bay centre has less than twice the fixed costs of a 5-bay centre. Also the capital costs of constructing the operations do not increase proportionately to their capacity. A 10-bay centre costs less to build than twice the cost of a 5-bay centre. These two factors, taken together, are often referred to as economies of scale – a universal concept that applies (up to a point) to all types of operation. However, economies of scale do not go on for ever. Above a certain size, the lowest cost point on curves such as that shown in Figure 5.6 may increase. This occurs because of what are called diseconomies of scale, two of which are particularly important. First, complexity costs increase as size increases. The communications and co-ordination effort necessary to manage an operation tends to increase faster than capacity. Although not seen as a direct cost, this can nevertheless be very significant. Second, a larger centre is more likely to be partially underutilized because demand within a fixed location will be limited. The equivalent in operations that process physical items is transportation costs. For example, if a manufacturer supplies the whole of its European market from one major plant in Denmark, all supplies may have to be brought in from several countries to the single plant and all products shipped from there throughout Europe.

> ✽ **Operations principle**
> Diseconomies of scale increase operating costs above a certain level of capacity resulting in a minimum cost level of capacity.

Being small may have advantages

Although large-scale capacity operations will usually have a cost advantage over smaller units, there are also potentially significant advantages that can be exploited by small-scale operations. One significant research study showed that small-scale operations can provide significant advantages in the following four areas:

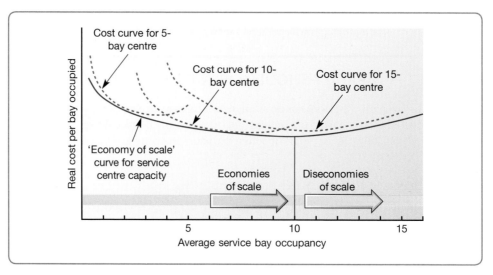

Figure 5.6 Unit cost curves for individual truck service centres of varying capacities

- They allow businesses to locate near to 'hot spots' that can tap into local knowledge networks. Often larger companies centralize their research and development efforts, losing touch with where innovative ideas area generated.
- They can respond rapidly to regional customer needs and trends by basing more and smaller units of capacity close to local markets.
- They can take advantage of the potential for human resource development by allowing staff a greater degree of local autonomy. Larger scale operations often have longer career paths with fewer opportunities for 'taking charge'.
- They can explore radically new technologies by acting in the same way as a smaller, more entrepreneurial rival. Larger, more centralized development activities are often more bureaucratic than smaller scale agile centres of development.

OPERATIONS IN PRACTICE	Economies of scale in heart surgery and shipping[5]

Do not think that the idea of economies of scale applies only to manufacturing operations. It is a universal concept. Here are just two examples.

In the 1,000-bed Narayana Hrudayalaya Hospital, in Bangalore, India, Dr Devi Shetty (who has been called the 'Henry Ford' of heart surgery) has created what, according to *Forbes* magazine, is the world's largest heart factory. It is a radical new approach, he says, and proves that economies of scale can transform the cost of cardiology. Dr Shetty calls his approach the 'Wal-Martisation' of surgery – referring to the high-volume approach of the world's largest supermarket chain, Wal-Mart. The hospital has 42 surgeons who perform 6,000 heart operations each year, including 3,000 on children. This makes the hospital the busiest facility of its type in the world. And it is needed; it is estimated that India

Source: Shutterstock.com: Lightspring

requires 2.5 million heart operations every year yet only 90,000 are performed. '*It's a numbers game,*' said Dr Shetty, who has performed 15,000 heart operations. '*Surgeons are technicians. The more practice they get, the more specialised they become and the better the results.*' The result is that costs are slashed and the hospital can be profitable even though many patients are poor. The hospital's charges for open-heart surgery are, on average, a tenth of the cost of the cheapest procedures in the USA. But even then, treatment is too expensive for many, so wealthier patients are charged more to subsidise the poorest.

The *Eleonora Maersk* is one of seven ships in her class that are owned my Maersk Lines, the world's biggest container-shipping company. They are among the biggest ships ever built, almost 400 metres long (the length of four football pitches). The *Eleonora Maersk* is also powerful; it has the largest internal combustion engine ever built, as powerful as 1,000 family cars, which enables it to move all its cargo from China to Europe in just over three weeks. Yet the ship is so automated that it requires only 13 people to crew it. On board, the ship can carry 15,000

Source: Shutterstock.com: Stockphoto mania

20-foot containers, each of which can hold 70,000 T-shirts. It is these economies of scale that allow a T-shirt made in China to be sent to the Netherlands for just 2.5 cents. And the economies of scale involved in building and running these ships mean that things will get bigger still. Hoping to drive costs down further, the ship's owners have ordered 20 even larger ships with a capacity of 18,000 20-foot containers, costing $200m each.

The timing of capacity change

Changing the capacity of any operation in a supply network is not just a matter of deciding on its optimum capacity. The operation also needs to decide when to bring new capacity 'on-stream'. For example, Figure 5.7 shows the forecast demand for a manufacturer's new product. In deciding *when* new capacity is to be introduced the company can mix the three strategies (also illustrated in Fig. 5.7):

> ※ **Operations principle**
>
> Capacity-leading strategies increase opportunities to meet demand. Capacity-lagging strategies increase capacity utilization.

- Capacity is introduced generally to lead demand – timing the introduction of capacity in such a way that there is always sufficient capacity to meet forecast demand.

Figure 5.7 (a) Capacity-leading and capacity-lagging strategies. (b) Smoothing with inventories means using the excess capacity in one period to produce inventory that supplies the under-capacity period

- Capacity is introduced generally to lag demand – timing the introduction of capacity so that demand is always equal to or greater than capacity.
- Capacity is introduced to sometimes lead and sometimes lag demand, but inventory built up during the 'lead' times is used to help meet demand during the 'lag' times. This is called 'smoothing with inventory'.

Each strategy has its own advantages and disadvantages. These are shown in Table 5.1. The actual approach taken by any company will depend on how it views these advantages and disadvantages. For example, if the company's access to funds for capital expenditure is limited, it is likely to find the delayed capital expenditure requirement of the capacity-lagging strategy relatively attractive. Of course, the third strategy, smoothing with inventory, is only appropriate for operations that produce products that can be stored. Customer-processing operations such as hotels cannot satisfy demand in one year by using rooms that were vacant the previous year.

Break-even analysis of capacity expansion

An alternative view of capacity expansion can be gained by examining the cost implications of adding increments of capacity on a break-even basis. Figure 5.8 shows how increasing capacity can move an operation from profitability to loss. Each additional unit of capacity results in a *fixed-cost break* that is a further lump of expenditure which will have to be incurred before any further activity can be undertaken in the operation. The operation is unlikely to be profitable at very low levels of output. Eventually, assuming that prices are greater than marginal costs, revenue will exceed total costs. However, the level of profitability at the point where the output level is equal to the capacity of the operation may not be sufficient to absorb all the extra fixed costs of a further increment in capacity. This could make the operation unprofitable in some stages of its expansion.

Table 5.1 The arguments for and against pure leading, pure lagging, and smoothing with inventory strategies of capacity timing

Advantages	Disadvantages
Capacity-leading strategies	
• Always sufficient capacity to meet demand, therefore revenue is maximized and customers satisfied • Most of the time there is a 'capacity cushion' that can absorb extra demand if forecasts are pessimistic • Any critical start-up problems with new operations are less likely to affect supply	• Utilization of the plants is always relatively low, therefore costs will be high • Risks of even greater (or even permanent) over-capacity if demand does not reach forecast levels • Capital spending on capacity will be early
Capacity-lagging strategies	
• Always sufficient demand to keep the operation working at full capacity, therefore unit costs are minimized • Over-capacity problems are minimized if forecasts prove optimistic • Capital spending on the operation is delayed	• Insufficient capacity to meet demand fully, therefore reduced revenue and dissatisfied customers • No ability to exploit short-term increases in demand • Under-supply position even worse if there are start-up problems with the new operations
Smoothing with inventory strategies	
• All demand is satisfied, therefore customers are satisfied and revenue is maximized • Utilization of capacity is high and therefore costs are low • Very short-term surges in demand can be met from inventories	• The cost of inventories in terms of working capital requirements can be high. This is especially serious at a time when the company requires funds for its capital expansion • Risks of product deterioration and obsolescence

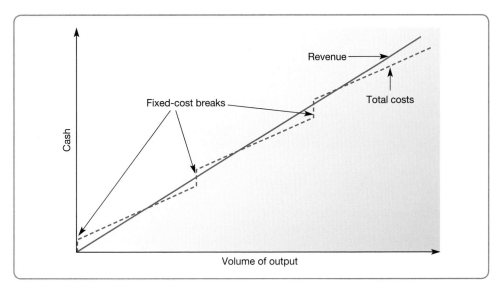

Figure 5.8 Repeated incurring of fixed costs can raise total costs above revenue

A specialist graphics company is investing in a new machine which enables it to make high-quality prints for its clients. Demand for these prints is forecast to be around 100,000 units in year 1 and 220,000 units in year 2. The maximum capacity of each machine the company will buy to process these prints is 100,000 units per year. They have a fixed cost of €200,000 per year and a variable cost of processing of €1 per unit. The company believes it will be able to charge €4 per unit for producing the prints.

Question
What profit is it likely to make in the first and second years?

$$\text{Year 1 demand} = 100{,}000 \text{ units; therefore company will need one machine}$$
$$\text{Cost of manufacturing} = \text{Fixed cost for one machine} + \text{Variable cost} \times 100{,}000$$
$$= €200{,}000 + (€1 \times 100{,}000)$$
$$= €300{,}000$$
$$\text{Revenue} = \text{Demand} \times \text{Price}$$
$$= 100{,}000 \times €4$$
$$= €400{,}000$$
$$\text{Therefore profit} = €400{,}000 - €300{,}000$$
$$= €100{,}000$$

$$\text{Year 2 demand} = 220{,}000; \text{ therefore company will need three machines}$$
$$\text{Cost of manufacturing} = \text{Fixed cost for three machines} + \text{Variable cost} \times 220{,}000$$
$$= (3 \times €200{,}000) + (€1 \times 220{,}000)$$
$$= €820{,}000$$
$$\text{Revenue} = \text{Demand} \times \text{Price}$$
$$= 220{,}000 \times €4$$
$$= €880{,}000$$
$$\text{Therefore profit} = €880{,}000 - €820{,}000$$
$$= €60{,}000$$

Note that the profit in the second year will be lower because of the extra fixed costs associated with the investment in the two extra machines.

WHERE SHOULD OPERATIONS BE LOCATED?

The location of each operation in a supply network is a key element in defining its structure and also will have an impact on how the network operates in practice. If any operation in a supply network gets the location wrong it can have a significant impact, not just on profits, but also on those of others in the network. For example, siting a data centre where potential staff with appropriate skills will not live will affect both its performance and the service it gives its customers. Location decisions will usually have an effect on an operation's costs as well as its ability to serve its customers (and therefore its revenues). Also, location decisions, once taken, are difficult to undo. The costs of moving an operation can be hugely expensive and the risks of inconveniencing customers very high. No operation wants to move very often.

Reasons for location decisions

Not all operations can logically justify their location. Some are where they are for historical reasons. Yet even the operations that are 'there because they're there' are implicitly making a decision not to move. Presumably their assumption is that the cost and disruption involved in changing location would outweigh any potential benefits of a new location. When operations do move, it is usually for one or both of two reasons – changes in demand or changes in supply:

- **Changes in demand** – A change in location may be prompted by customer demand shifting. For example, as garment manufacture moved to Asia, suppliers of zips, threads, etc., started to follow them. Changes in the volume of demand can also prompt relocation. To meet higher demand, an operation could expand its existing site, or choose a larger site in another location, or keep its existing location and find a second location for an additional operation; the last two options will involve a location decision. High-visibility operations may not have the choice of expanding on the same site to meet rising demand. A dry cleaning service may attract only marginally more business by expanding an existing site because it offers a local, and therefore convenient, service. Finding a new location for an additional operation is probably its only option for expansion.
- **Changes in supply** – The other stimulus for relocation is changes in the cost, or availability, of the supply of inputs to the operation. For example, a mining or oil company will need to relocate as the minerals it is extracting become depleted. The reason why so many software companies located in India was the availability of talented, well-educated, but relatively cheap staff.

The objectives of the location decision

The aim of the location decision is to achieve an appropriate balance between three related objectives:

- The spatially variable costs of the operation (spatially variable means that something changes with geographical location).
- The service the operation is able to provide to its customers.
- The revenue potential of the operation.

> **✳ Operations principle**
>
> An operation should only change its location if the benefits of moving outweigh the costs of operating in the new location plus the cost of the move itself.

In for-profit organizations the last two objectives are related. The assumption is that the better the service the operation can provide to its customers, the better will be its potential to attract custom and therefore generate revenue. In not-for-profit organizations, revenue potential might not be a relevant objective and so cost and customer service are often taken as the twin objectives of location. In making decisions about where to locate an operation, operations managers are concerned with minimizing spatially variable costs and maximizing revenue/customer service. Location affects both of these but not always equally. For example, customers may not care very much where some products are made, so location is unlikely to affect revenues significantly. However, the costs could be very greatly affected by location. Services, on the other hand, often have both costs and revenues affected by location. The location decision for any operation is determined by the relative strength of a number of factors, as follows:

- **Labour costs** – The costs of employing people with particular skills can vary between different regions and countries. Labour costs can be expressed in two ways. However, simple wage costs can be misleading when comparing locations in different countries. Labour costs must then also take into account the effects both of productivity differences and of differing currency exchange rates. Exchange rate variation can cause unit costs to change dramatically over time. Yet labour costs exert a major influence on the location decision, especially in industries (such as clothing) where labour costs, as a proportion of total costs, are relatively high.
- **Labour skills availability** – The skills abilities of a local population are clearly important. For example, 'science parks' are usually located close to universities because they hope to attract companies who are interested in using the skills available at the university.
- **Land costs** – The cost of acquiring or leasing the site itself can be relevant in location choice. Land and rental costs vary between countries, cities and districts. A retail operation, when choosing 'high street' sites, will pay a particular level of rent only if it believes it can generate a certain level of revenue from the site.
- **Energy costs** – Operations that use large amounts of energy, such as aluminium smelters, can be influenced in their location decisions by the availability of relatively inexpensive energy.
- **Transportation costs** – Transportation costs include both the cost of transporting inputs from their source to the operation and the cost of transporting outputs to customers. Almost all operations are concerned with the former, but not all operations transport goods to customers; rather, customers come to them (for example, hotels). Proximity to sources of *supply* dominates the location decision where the cost of transporting input materials is high or difficult. Food processing and other agricultural-based activities, for example, are often carried out close to growing areas. Conversely, transportation to *customers* dominates location decisions where this is expensive or difficult. Civil engineering projects, for example, are constructed mainly where they will be needed.
- **Community factors** – Community factors are those influences on an operation's costs that derive from the social, political and economic environment of its site: for example, tax rates, government financial assistance, political stability and corruption, language, local amenities, labour relations, environmental regulations and waste disposal, planning procedures, etc.
- **The suitability of the site itself** – Different sites may have different intrinsic characteristics that can affect an operation's ability to serve customers and generate revenue. For example, locate a luxury resort hotel next to a beach and it attracts custom. Move it a few kilometres away into the centre of an industrial estate and it rapidly loses its attraction.
- **Image of the location** – Some locations are firmly associated in customers' minds with a particular image: for example, advanced technology in Silicon Valley, fashion design houses in Milan and financial services in the City of London.
- **Convenience for customers** – This is often the most important factor when service is important to customers. Locating a general hospital, for instance, in the middle of the countryside may have many advantages for its staff, and even perhaps for its costs, but clearly would be very inconvenient to its customers (patients). So, hospitals are usually located close to centres of demand.

Counting clusters[6]

Similar companies with similar needs often cluster together in the same geographical area. Why? For a number of reasons. Michael Porter of Harvard Business School, the famous strategy professor and an authority on industrial clusters, says that firms' geographical proximity helps to promote economies of scale, learning and productivity, as well as boosting innovation and encouraging the growth of new supplier firms. This is a winning combination, according to Professor Porter, and accounts for the existence of such clusters around the world. Here are just a few examples.

Source: Shutterstock.com: Nucleartist

Financial services

These are clustered in relatively few centres globally, even after the turbulence in financial services. London, New York, Hong Kong, Singapore, Tokyo, Chicago and Zurich dominate the industry. According to Deutsche Bank, '*Big is beautiful – and will remain so.*' It is far easier to build on existing market strength than start afresh. Banks have to trade with each other and even in an increasingly globalized world being close helps. Combine this with good regulation and free markets and it becomes a significant competitive advantage.

High tech

These industries provide one of the most famous location clusters in the area south of San Francisco known as Silicon Valley, probably the most important intellectual and commercial hub of technological innovation. Yet other locations are developing. For example, Bangalore in India is fast becoming a cluster for the computer industry because of the ready availability of well-educated, low-cost English-speaking software technicians; it has now attracted more, and more sophisticated, business. Something similar is happening in Shanghai in China. '*Over the next ten years, China will become a ferociously formidable competitor for companies that run the entire length of the technology food chain*', says Michael J. Moritz, a Californian venture-capital firm. Even in

higher cost countries, new clusters are growing. One is around 'silicon roundabout', in East London, where old Victorian warehouses are home to a growing number of Web and technology start-ups, working on everything from online game design to streaming music services and general web services (Google has offices there). There was a history of start-ups in the area stretching back a couple of decades because of relatively low office rents, a creative atmosphere generated by an influx of artists and designers, London's world-class universities, art galleries and the kinds of cafés, bars, shops and clubs that help attract creative staff. So, again, the cluster developed for clear reasons and then grew because size and focus attract other companies.

Racing cars

These are mostly made in the UK, in particular in the areas of Oxfordshire or Northamptonshire. Most Formula One teams are based in the UK, as are many Indy Car teams. Even those who are not are likely to use British services. Motorsport is a flourishing cluster with around 4,500 firms working on building, maintaining, modifying and restoring cars, making engines and components, and providing technical and management services. Almost everything a racing team needs can be found without leaving the area.

HOW VERTICALLY INTEGRATED SHOULD AN OPERATION'S NETWORK BE?

The scope to which an operation controls its supply network is an issue that will shape the fundamental nature of any business. It determines the extent that an operation does things itself and the extent that it will rely on other operations to do things for it. This is often referred to as 'vertical integration', when it is the ownership of whole operations that is being decided, or 'outsourcing' when individual activities are being considered. We will look at the 'outsourcing' decision in the next section. Vertical integration is the extent to which an organization owns the network of which it is a part. It usually involves an organization assessing the wisdom of acquiring suppliers or customers. And different companies, even in the same industry, can make very different decisions over how much and where in the network they want to be. Figure 5.9 illustrates the (simplified) supply network for the wind turbine power generation industry. Original equipment manufacturers (OEMs) assemble the wind turbine nacelle (the nacelle houses the generator and gearbox). Towers and blades are often built to the OEM's specifications, either in-house or by outside suppliers. Installing wind turbines involves assembling the nacelle, tower and blades on site, erecting the tower and connecting to the electricity network. The extent of vertical integration varies by company and component. The three companies illustrated in Figure 5.9 have all chosen different vertical integration strategies. Company A is primarily a nacelle designer and manufacturer that also makes the parts. Company B is primarily an installer that also makes the tower and blades (but buys in the nacelle itself). Company C is primarily an operator that generates electricity and also designs and assembles the nacelles as well as installing the whole tower (but it outsources the manufacture of the nacelle parts, tower and blades).

An organization's vertical integration strategy can be defined in the following terms:

- **The direction of integration** – If a company decides that it should control more of its network, should it expand by buying one of its suppliers or should it expand by buying one of its customers? The strategy of expanding on the supply side of the network is sometimes called backward or 'upstream' vertical integration, and expanding on the demand side is sometimes called forward or 'downstream' vertical integration. Backward vertical integration, by allowing an organization to take control of its suppliers, is often used either to gain cost advantages or to prevent competitors gaining control of important suppliers. Forward vertical integration, on the other hand, takes an organization closer to its markets and allows more freedom for an organization to make contact directly with its customers, and possibly sell complementary products and services.

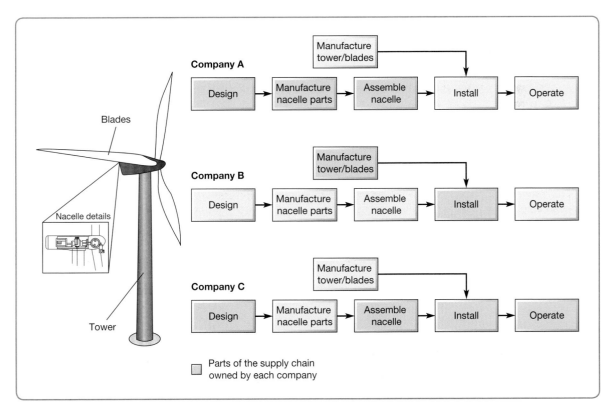

Figure 5.9 **Three companies operating in the wind power generation industry with different vertical integration positions**

- **The extent of the process span of integration** – Some organizations deliberately choose not to integrate far, if at all, from their original part of the network. Alternatively some organizations choose to become very vertically integrated. Take many large international oil companies, such as Exxon, for example. Exxon is involved with exploration and extraction as well as the refining of crude oil into a consumable product – gasoline. It also has operations that distribute and retail the gasoline (and many other products) to the final customer. This path (one of several for its different products) has moved the material through the total network of processes, all of which are owned (wholly or partly) by the one company.
- **The balance among the vertically integrated stages** – This is not strictly about the ownership of the network; it concerns the capacity and, to some extent, the operating behaviour of each stage in the network which is owned by the organization. It refers to the amount of the capacity at each stage in the network that is devoted to supplying the next stage. So a totally balanced network relationship is one where one stage produces only for the next stage in the network and totally satisfies its requirements. Less than full balance in the stages allows each stage to sell its output to other companies or buy in some of its supplies from other companies.

Figure 5.10 illustrates these three aspects of vertical integration.

The decision as to whether to vertically integrate in a particular set of circumstances is largely a matter of a business balancing the following advantages and disadvantages as they apply to it.

The perceived advantages of vertical integration

Although extensive vertical integration is no longer as popular as it once was, there are still companies who find it advantageous to own several sequential stages of their supply network. Indeed very few companies are anywhere close to 'virtual', with no vertical integration of stages whatsoever. What then are the reasons why companies still choose to vertically integrate? Most justifications for vertical integration fall into four categories:

- **It secures dependable access to supply or markets** – The most fundamental reasons for engaging in some vertical integration is that it can give more secure supply or bring a business closer to its customers. One reason why the oil companies which sell gasoline are also engaged in extracting it is to ensure long-term supply. In some cases there may not

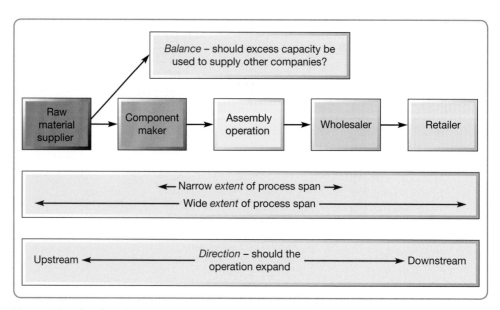

Figure 5.10 The direction, extent and balance of an operation's vertical integration

even be sufficient capacity in the supply market to satisfy the company. It therefore has little alternative but to supply itself. Downstream vertical integration can give a firm greater control over its market positioning. For example, Apple has always adopted a supply network model that integrates hardware and software with both its hardware and software designed by Apple.

- **It may reduce costs** – The most common argument here is that '*We can do it cheaper than our supplier's price*.' Such statements are often made by comparing the marginal direct cost incurred by a company in doing something itself against the price it is paying to buy the product or service from a supplier. But costs saving should also take into account start-up and learning costs. A more straightforward case can be made when there are technical advantages of integration. For example, producing aluminium kitchen foil involves rolling it to the required thickness and then 'slitting' it into the finished widths. Performing both activities in-house saves the loading and unloading activity and the transportation to another operation. Vertical integration also reduces the 'transaction costs' of dealing with suppliers and customers. Transaction costs are expenses, other than price, which are incurred in the process of buying and selling, such as searching for and selecting suppliers, setting up monitoring arrangements, negotiating contracts, and so on. If transaction costs can be lowered to the point where the purchase price plus transaction costs are less than the internal cost, there is little justification for the vertical integration of the activity.

- **It may help to improve product or service quality** – Sometimes vertical integration can be used to secure specialist or technological advantage by preventing product and service knowledge getting into the hands of competitors. The exact specialist advantage may be anything from the 'secret ingredient' in fizzy drinks through to a complex technological process. In either case the argument is the same: '*This process gives us the key identifying factor for our products and services. Vertical integration therefore is necessary to the survival of product or service uniqueness*.'

- **It helps in understanding other activities in the supply network** – Some companies, even those that are famous for their rejection of traditional vertical integration, do choose to own some parts of the supply network other than what they regard as core. So for example, McDonald's, the restaurant chain, although largely franchising its retail operations, does own some retail outlets. How else, it argues, could it understand its retail operations so well?

OPERATIONS IN PRACTICE

HTC moves downstream (and into problems)[7]

Moving to a different part of a supply network can be risky. Look at Taiwan's HTC. For years the firm had been one of the most important suppliers to better known brands. HTC was an 'original design manufacturer', or ODM, developing and building high-end 'smartphones' for better known Western mobile operators, including Verizon and Orange. It was a good business. HTC had built an enviable reputation as an innovative and reliable supplier of sophisticated hand-held computers and mobile phones. However, Peter Chou, the Chief Executive Officer of HTC, believed that the industry was changing. Chou could see the market becoming more difficult. Although still a profitable business, the margins from supplying other brands were shrinking. Chinese suppliers, with their lower labour costs, were providing stiff competition and customers had started to look

Source: Fotolia.com: Maridav

for rival suppliers. '*We needed to establish a new competency before we got into trouble*', explained Mr Chou. The way ahead, the company decided, was to move forward in the supply network and start developing its own brand. This new supply network strategy meant HTC had to develop new capabilities. More talent was recruited to strengthen its in-house design and software skills so that HTC products would have a unique look and feel. The company knew that the strategy was not without its risks. It meant investing in the marketing and sales operations that had, up till then, been the province of its customers. HTC also lost of much of its existing business, because some customers were reluctant to do business with a budding rival. Just as significant, the culture and objectives of the company had to move from *'efficiently implementing what had been decided by one's customers'* to one of *'constantly developing radical and innovative new ideas'*. And, indeed, it did prove difficult for the company. After a reasonable start in what was becoming an extremely competitive market, HTC sales of its own branded smartphones began to slump, as did its profits and share price. Some commentators said that the company had underestimated the operations and marketing skills that would be needed to succeed in its new business.

The perceived disadvantages of vertical integration

The arguments against vertical integration tend to cluster around a number of observed disadvantages of those companies that have practised vertical integration extensively. These are as follows:

- **It creates an internal monopoly** – Operations, it is argued, will only change when they see a pressing need to do so. Internal supply is less subject to the normal competitive forces that keep operations motivated to improve. If an external supplier serves its customers well, it will make higher profits; if not, it will suffer. Such incentives and sanctions do not apply to the same extent if the supplying operation is part of the same company.

- **You cannot exploit economies of scale** – Any activity that is vertically integrated within an organization is probably also carried out elsewhere in the industry. But the effort it puts into the process will be a relatively small part of the sum total of that activity within the industry. Specialist suppliers who can serve more than one customer are likely to have volumes larger than any of their customers could achieve doing things for themselves. This allows specialist suppliers to reap some of the cost benefits of economies of scale, which can be passed on in terms of lower prices to their customers.

- **It results in loss of flexibility** – Heavily vertically integrated companies by definition do most things themselves. This means that a high proportion of their costs will be fixed costs. They have, after all, invested heavily in the capacity that allows them to do most things in-house. A high level of fixed costs relative to variable costs means that any reduction in the total volume of activity can easily move the economics of the operation close to, or below, its break-even point.

- **It cuts you off from innovation** – Vertical integration means investing in the processes and technologies necessary to produce products and services in-house. But as soon as that investment is made the company has an inherent interest in maintaining it. Abandoning such investments can be both economically and emotionally difficult. The temptation is always to wait until any new technology is clearly established before admitting that one's own is obsolete. This may lead to a tendency to lag in the adoption of new technologies and ideas.

- **It distracts you from core activities (loss of focus)** – The final, and arguably most powerful, case against vertical integration concerns any organization's ability to be technically competent at a very wide range of activities. All companies have things that they need to be good at. And it is far easier to be exceptionally good at something if the company focuses exclusively on it rather than being distracted by many other things. Vertical integration, by definition, means doing more things, which can distract from the (few) particularly important things.

HOW DO OPERATIONS DECIDE WHAT TO DO IN-HOUSE AND WHAT TO OUTSOURCE?

Theoretically 'vertical integration' and 'outsourcing' are the same thing. Vertical integration is '*the extent to which an organization owns the network of which it is a part*'. Outsourcing is '*an arrangement in which one company provides services for another company that could also be, or usually have been, provided in-house*'.[8] It is based on the idea that no single business does everything that is required to produce its products and services. Bakers do not grow wheat or even mill it into flour. Banks do not usually do their own credit checking, but retain the services of specialist credit checking agencies that have the information systems and expertise to do it better. Outsourcing is also known as the 'do-or-buy' decision. It has become an important issue for most businesses. This is because, although most companies have always outsourced some of their activities, a larger proportion of direct activities is now being bought from suppliers. Also, many indirect and administrative processes are now being outsourced. This is often referred to as business process outsourcing (BPO). Financial service companies in particular are outsourcing some of their more routine back-office processes. In a similar way many processes within the HR function, from simply payroll services through to more complex training and development processes, are being outsourced to specialist companies. The processes may still be physically located where they were before, but the outsourcing service provider manages the staff and technology. The reason for doing this is often primarily to reduce cost. However, there can sometimes also be significant gains in the quality and flexibility of service offered.

What is the difference between vertical integration and outsourcing?

Very little really; it is largely a matter of scale and direction. Vertical integration is a term that is usually (but not always) applied to whole operations. So, buying a supplier because you want to deny its products to a competitor, or selling the part of your business that services your products to a specialist servicing company that can do the job better, is a vertical integration decision. Outsourcing usually applies to smaller sets of activities that have previously been performed in-house. Deciding to ask a specialist laboratory to perform some quality tests that your own quality control department used to do, or having your call (contact) centre taken over and run by a larger call centre company, are both outsourcing decisions.

Making the outsourcing decision

Outsourcing is rarely a simple decision. Operations in different circumstances with different objectives are likely to take different decisions. Yet the question itself is relatively simple, even if the decision itself is not: 'Does in-house or outsourced supply in a particular set of circumstances give the appropriate performance objectives that it requires to compete more effectively in its markets?' For example, if the main performance objectives for an operation are dependable delivery and meeting short-term changes in customers' delivery requirements, the key question should be: 'How does in-house or outsourcing give better dependability and delivery flexibility performance?' This means judging two sets of opposing factors – those which give the potential to improve performance, and those which work against this potential being realized. Table 5.2 summarizes some arguments for in-house supply and outsourcing in terms of each performance objective.

> ✳ **Operations principle**
> Assessing the advisability of outsourcing should include how it impacts relevant performance objectives.

Incorporating strategic factors into the outsourcing decision

Although the effect of outsourcing on the operation's performance objective is important, there are other factors that companies take into account when deciding if outsourcing an activity is a sensible option. For example, if an activity has long-term strategic importance

Table 5.2 How in-house and outsourced supply may affect an operation's performance objectives

Performance objective	'Do-it-yourself' in-house supply	'Buy-it-in' outsourced supply
Quality	The origins of any quality problems are usually easier to trace in-house and improvement can be more immediate but can be some risk of complacency	Supplier may have specialized knowledge and more experience, and may be motivated through market pressures, but communication more difficult
Speed	Can mean synchronized schedules which speeds throughput of materials and information, but if the operation has external customers, internal customers may be low priority	Speed of response can be built into the supply contract where commercial pressures will encourage good performance, but there may be significant transport/delivery delays
Dependability	Easier communications can help dependability, but if the operation also has external customers, internal customers may receive low priority	Late delivery penalties in the supply contract can encourage good delivery performance, but organizational barriers may inhibit in communication
Flexibility	Closeness to the real needs of a business can alert the in-house operation to required changes, but the ability to respond may be limited by the scale and scope of internal operations	Outsource suppliers may be larger with wider capabilities than in-house suppliers and more ability to respond to changes, but may have to balance conflicting needs of different customers
Cost	In-house operations do not have to make the margin required by outside suppliers so the business can capture the profits which would otherwise be given to the supplier, but relatively low volumes may mean that it is difficult to gain economies of scale or the benefits of process innovation	Probably the main reason why outsourcing is so popular. Outsourced companies can achieve economies of scale and they are motivated to reduce their own costs because it directly impacts their profits, but costs of communication and co-ordination with supplier need to be taken into account

to a company, it is unlikely to outsource it. For instance, a retailer might choose to keep the design and development of its website in-house even though specialists could perform the activity at less cost because it plans to move into web-based retailing at some point in the future. Nor would a company usually outsource an activity where it had specialized skills or knowledge. For example, a company making laser printers may have built up specialized knowledge in the production of sophisticated laser drives. This capability may allow it to introduce product or process innovations in the future. It would be foolish to 'give away' such capability. After these two more strategic factors have been considered, the company's operations performance can be taken into account. Obviously if its operations performance is already superior to any potential supplier, it would be unlikely to outsource the activity. But also, even if its performance was currently below that of potential suppliers, it might not outsource the activity if it feels that it could significantly improve its performance. Figure 5.11 illustrates this decision logic.

> ✳ **Operations principle**
>
> Assessing the advisability of outsourcing should include consideration of the strategic importance of the activity and the operation's relative performance.

Outsourcing and offshoring

Two supply network strategies that are often confused are those of outsourcing and offshoring. Outsourcing means deciding to buy in products or services rather than perform the activities in-house. Offshoring means obtaining products and services from

One of the best-known cautionary tales that illustrates the inherent dangers involved in subcontracting is that of how General Electric lost its microwave oven business. Although Japanese domestic appliance manufacturers, such as Matsushita and Sanyo, dominated the global microwave industry at the beginning of the 1980s, General Electric (GE) was enjoying reasonable success in the US market with its purpose-designed microwave oven plant in Maryland. However, GE soon came under price pressures from Japanese competitors. What seemed an obvious solution was to subcontract the production of some of its more basic models, where margins were relatively small. GE explored the idea of subcontracting these models to one of its main rivals, Matsushita, even though giving one of its main competitors such an advantage was considered risky. GE also found a small, but go-getting, Korean company which was already selling very simple (and very cheap) models in the USA. GE decided to continue making top-of-the-range models itself, subcontract its cheaper models to Matsushita, but also place a small order of 15,000 units of its cheaper models with the Korean company, partly to see whether it could cope with the order. Of course it also made sense for GE to send its own engineers to help the Korean company and ensure that quality standards would be maintained. The GE engineers found that, although the Korean company had little knowledge, it was very willing to learn. Eventually the Korean production line started producing reasonable-quality products, still at very low prices. Over

Source: Shutterstock.com: Monkey Business Images

time, the Korean company was given more and more orders by GE, who found that it was making more profit from the Korea-sourced products than those coming out of its Maryland plant. This became particularly important as the market continued to mature and costs came under increased pressure. The Maryland plant attempted to cut its own costs but this proved especially difficult with so much of its volume now subcontracted to the Korean company. In the end the Maryland plant was closed and GE withdrew entirely from the microwave oven (indeed the whole domestic appliance) market. And the Korean company? It was called Samsung, and within 10 years of starting to make them it became the world's largest manufacturer of microwave ovens.

operations that are based outside one's own country. Of course, one may both outsource and offshore as illustrated in Figure 5.12. Offshoring is very closely related to outsourcing and the motives for each may be similar. Offshoring to a lower cost region of the world is usually done to reduce an operation's overall costs as is outsourcing to a supplier which has greater expertise or scale, or both.

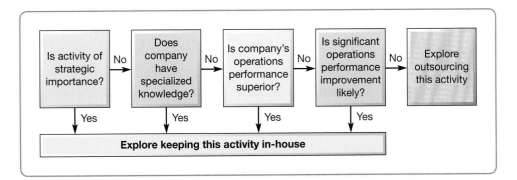

Figure 5.11 The decision logic of outsourcing

Figure 5.12 Offshoring and outsourcing are related but different

SUMMARY ANSWERS TO KEY QUESTIONS

❯ What do we mean by the 'structure' and 'scope' of operations' supply networks?

- The 'structure' of an operation's supply network relates to the shape and form of the network.

- The scope of an operation's supply network relates to the extent that an operation decides to do the activities performed by the network itself, as opposed to requesting a supplier to do them.

- The structure and scope of an operation's supply network is important because it helps an understanding of competitiveness, it helps identify significant links in the network, and it helps focus on long-term issues.

❭ What configuration should a supply network have?

- Even when an operation does not directly own other operations in its network, it may still wish to change the shape of the network by reconfiguring it so as to change the nature of the relationships.
- Changing the shape of the supply network may involve reducing the number of suppliers to the operation so as to develop closer relationships, and bypassing or disintermediating operations in the network.
- One may also use the idea of complementors that enable one's products or services to be valued more by customers because they also can have the complementor's products or services.
- An idea that is closely related to that of co-opetition in supply networks is that of the 'business ecosystem', defined as: 'An economic community supported by a foundation of interacting organizations and individuals.'

❭ How much capacity should operations plan to have?

- The amount of capacity an organization will have depends on its view of current and future demand. It is when its view of future demand is different from current demand that this issue becomes important.
- When an organization has to cope with changing demand, a number of capacity decisions need to be taken. These include choosing the optimum capacity for each site, balancing the various capacity levels of the operation in the network, and timing the changes in the capacity of each part of the network.
- Important influences on these decisions include the concepts of economy and diseconomy of scale.

❭ Where should operations be located?

- When operations change their location, their assumption is that the potential benefits of a new location will outweigh any cost and disruption involved in changing location. When operations do move, it is usually because of changes in demand and/or changes in supply.
- The factors that determine a location are such things as labour, land and utility costs, the image of the location, its convenience for customers and the suitability of the site itself.

❭ How vertically integrated should an operation's network be?

- The scope to which an operation controls its supply network is the extent that it does things itself as opposed to relying on other operations to do things for it. This is often referred to as 'vertical integration'.
- An organization's vertical integration strategy can be defined in terms of the direction of integration, the extent of integration, and the balance among the vertically integrated stages.
- The decision as to whether to vertically integrate is largely a matter of a business balancing the advantages and disadvantages as they apply to it.

- Outsourcing is 'an arrangement in which one company provides services for another company that could also be, or usually have been, provided in-house'.
- The difference between vertical integration and outsourcing is largely a matter of scale and direction.
- Like the vertical integration decision, it is often a matter of balancing advantages against disadvantages under particular circumstances.
- Assessing the advisability of outsourcing should also include consideration of the strategic importance of the activity and the operation's relative performance.

CASE STUDY   Aarens Electronic

Just outside Rotterdam in the Netherlands, Frank Jansen, the Chief Operating Officer of Aarens Electronic (AE), was justifiably proud of what he described as 'the most advanced machine of its type in the world, which will enable us to achieve new standards of excellence for our products requiring absolute cleanliness and precision'...and...'a quantum leap in harnessing economies of scale and new technology to provide the most advanced operation for years to come'. The Rotterdam Operation was joining AE's two existing operations in the Netherlands. They offered precision custom coating and laminating services to a wide range of customers, among the most important being Phanchem, to whom it supplied dry photoresist imaging films, a critical step in the manufacturing of microchips. Phanchem then processed the film further and sold it direct to microchip manufacturers

Source: Shutterstock.com: Vladimir Caplinskij

The Rotterdam Operation

The decision to build the Rotterdam Operation had been taken because the company believed that a new low-cost operation using 'ultra-clean' controlled environment technology could secure a very large part of Phanchem's future business – perhaps even an exclusive agreement to supply 100 per cent of its needs. When planning the new operation three options were presented to AE's Executive Committee:

(a) Expand an existing site by building a new machine within existing site boundaries. This would provide around 12 to 13 million square metres (MSM) per year of additional capacity and require around €19 million in capital expenditure.

(b) Build a new facility alongside the existing plant. This new facility could accommodate additional capacity of

around 15 MSM per year but, unlike option A, would also allow for future expansion. Initially this would require around €22 million of capital.

(c) Set up a totally new site with a much larger increment of capacity (probably around 25 MSM per year). This option would be more expensive, at least €30 million.

Frank Jansen and his team initially favoured option B but in discussion with the AE Executive Committee, opinion shifted towards the more radical option C. 'It may have been the highest risk option but it held considerable potential and it fitted with the AE Group philosophy of getting into high-tech specialised areas of business. So we went for it.' (Frank Jansen) The option of a very large, ultra-clean, state-of-the-art facility also had a further advantage – it could change the economics of the photoresist imaging industry. In fact, global demand and capacity did not immediately justify investing in such a large an increase in capacity. There was probably some over-capacity in the industry. But a large-capacity, ultra-clean-type operation could provide a level of quality at such low costs that, if there were over-capacity in the industry, it would not be AE's capacity that would by lying idle.

Designing the new operation

During discussions on the design of the new operation, it became clear that there was one issue that was underlying all the team's discussions – how flexible should the process be? Should the team assume that it was designing an operation that would be dedicated exclusively to the manufacture of photoresist imaging film, and ruthlessly cut out any technological options that would enable it to manufacture other products, or should the team design a more general-purpose operation that was suitable for photoresist imaging film, but could be also make other products? It proved a difficult decision. The advantages of the more flexible option were obvious. *'At least it would mean that there was no chance of me being stuck with an operation and no market for it to serve in a couple of year's time.'* (Frank Jansen) But the advantages of a totally dedicated operation were less obvious, although there was a general agreement that both costs and quality could be superior in an operation dedicated to one product.

Eventually the team decided to concentrate on a relatively non-flexible, focused and dedicated large machine. *'You can't imagine the agonies we went through when we decided not to make this a flexible machine. Many of us were not comfortable with saying, "This is going to be a photoresist machine exclusively, and if the market goes away we're in real trouble." We had a lot of debate about that. Eventually we more or less reached a consensus for focus but it was certainly one of the toughest decisions we ever made.'* (Frank Jansen) The capital cost savings of a focused facility and operating costs savings of up to 25 per cent were powerful arguments, as was the philosophy of total process dedication. *'The key word for us was focus. We wanted to be quite clear about what was needed to satisfy our customer in making this single type of product. As well as providing significant cost savings to us it made it a lot easier to identify the root causes of any problems because we would not have to worry about how it might affect other products. It's all very clear. When the line was down we would not be generating revenue! It would also force us to understand our own performance. At our other operations, if a line goes down, the people can be shifted to other responsibilities. We don't have other responsibilities here – we're either making it or we're not.'* (Frank Jansen)

When the Rotterdam Operation started producing, the team had tweaked the design to bring the capacity at start-up to 32 MSM per year. And notwithstanding some initial teething troubles it was, from the start, a technical and commercial success. Within six months a contract was signed with Phanchem to supply 100 per cent of Phanchem's needs for the next 10 years. Phanchem's decision was based on the combination of manufacturing and business focus that the Rotterdam team has achieved, a point stressed by Frank Jansen: *'Co-locating all necessary departments on the Rotterdam site was seen as particularly important. All the technical functions and the marketing and business functions are now on site.'*

Developing the supply relationship

At the time of the start-up, product produced in Rotterdam was shipped to Phanchem's facility near Frankfurt, Germany, almost 500 km away. This distance caused a number of problems including some damage in transit and delays in delivery. However, the relationship between AE and Phanchem remained sound, helped by the two companies' co-operation during the Rotterdam start-up. *'We had worked closely with them during the design and construction of the new Rotterdam facility. More to the point, they saw that they would certainly achieve cost savings from the plant, with the promise of more savings to come as the plant moved down the learning curve.'* (Frank Jansen) The closeness of the relationship between the two companies was a result of their staff working together. AE engineers were impressed by their customer's willingness to help out while they worked on overcoming the start-up problems. Similarly AE had helped Phanchem when it needed extra supplies at short notice. As Frank Jansen said, *'partly because we worked together on various problems the relationship has grown stronger and stronger.'*

In particular the idea of a physically closer relationship between AE and Phanchem was explored. *'During the negotiations with Phanchem for our 100 per cent contract there had been some talk about co-location but I don't think anyone took it particularly seriously. Nevertheless there was general agreement that it would be a good thing to do. After all, our success as Phanchem's sole supplier of coated photoresist was tied in to their success as a player in the global market: what was good for Phanchem was good for AE.'* (Frank Jansen) Several options were discussed within and between the two companies. Phanchem had, in effect, to choose between four options:

- Stay where it was, near Frankfurt.
- Relocate to the Netherlands (which would give easier access to port facilities) but not too close to AE (an appropriate site was available 30 km from Rotterdam).
- Locate to a currently vacant adjacent site across the road from AE's Rotterdam plant.
- Co-locate within an extension that could be specially built onto the AE plant at Rotterdam.

Evaluating the co-location options

Relatively early in the discussions between the two companies, the option of 'doing nothing' by staying in Frankfurt was discounted. Phanchem wanted to sell its valuable site near Frankfurt. The advantages of some kind of move were significant. The option of Phanchem moving to a site 30 km from Rotterdam was considered but rejected because it had no advantages over locating even closer to the Rotterdam plant. Phanchem also strongly considered building and operating a facility across the road from the Rotterdam plant. But eventually the option of locating in a building attached to AE's Rotterdam Operation became the preferred option. Co-location would have a significant impact on Phanchem's competitiveness by reducing its operating costs, enabling it to gain market share by offering quality film at attractive prices, thus increasing volume for AE. The managers at the Rotterdam plant also looked forward to an even closer operational relationship with the customer. 'Initially, there was some resistance in the team to having a customer on the same site as ourselves. No one in AE had ever done it before. The step from imagining our customer across the road to imagining them on the same site took some thinking about. It was a matter of getting used to the idea, taking one step at a time.' (Frank Jansen)

The customer becomes a paying guest

However, when Frank and the Rotterdam managers presented their proposal for extending the plant to the AE board the proposal was not well received. 'Leasing factory space to our customer seemed a long way from our core business. As one Executive Committee member said, we are manufacturers; we aren't in the real estate business. But we felt that it would be beneficial for both companies.' (Frank Jansen) And even when the proposal was eventually accepted, there was still concern over sharing a facility. In fact the Executive Committee insisted that the door between the two companies' areas should be capable of being locked from both sides. Yet the construction and commissioning of the new facility for Phanchem was also a model of co-operation. Now, all visitors to the plant are shown the door that had to be 'capable of being locked from both sides' and asked how many times they think it has been locked. The answer, of course, is 'never'.

QUESTIONS

1 What were the key structure and scope decisions taken by Aarens Electronic?

2 What were the risks involved in adopting a process design that was 'totally dedicated' to the one customer's needs?

3 What were the advantages and disadvantages of each location option open to Phanchem, and why do you think it eventually chose to co-locate with AE?

PROBLEMS AND APPLICATIONS

1 Visit the websites of companies that are in the paper manufacturing/pulp production/packaging industries. Assess the extent to which the companies you have investigated are vertically integrated in the paper supply chain that stretches from foresting through to the production of packaging materials

2 A private healthcare clinic has been offered a leasing deal where it could lease a CAT scanner at a fixed charge of €2,000 per month and a charge per patient of €6 per patient scanned. The clinic currently charges €10 per patient for taking a scan. (a) At what level of demand (in number of patients per week) will the clinic break even on the cost of leasing the CAT scan? (b) Would a revised lease that stipulated a fixed cost of €3,000 per week and a variable cost of €0.20 per patient be a better deal?

3 Revisit the 'operations in practice' example of the Hollywood movie business. Draw diagrams of the supply network for the industry (a) back in the days of studio power, and (b) the way the industry operates now.

4 Do the same thing for the music business, from the days when record labels controlled the business to the availability of streaming services.

5 How could universities adopt the practice of outsourcing more?

SELECTED FURTHER READING

Carmel, E. and Tjia, P. (2005) *Offshoring Information Technology: Sourcing and Outsourcing to a Global Workforce,* Cambridge University Press, Cambridge.

An academic book on outsourcing.

Corbett, M.F. (2010) *The Outsourcing Revolution: Why it Makes Sense and How to Do it Right,* Kaplan, Wokingham.

Not an academic book on outsourcing.

Cullen, S.K., Lacity, M. and Willcocks, L.P. (2014) *Outsourcing – All You Need To Know,* White Plume Publishing, Boston, MA.

Practical, interesting and intelligent.

Dell, M. (with Catherine Fredman) (1999) *Direct from Dell: Strategies that revolutionized an industry,* Harper Business, New York.

Michael Dell explains how his supply network strategy (and other decisions) had such an impact on the industry. Interesting and readable, but not a critical analysis!

Schniederjans, M.J. (1998) *International Facility Location and Acquisition Analysis,* Quorum Books, New York.

Very much one for the technically minded.

Vashistha, A. and Vashistha, A. (2006) *The Offshore Nation: Strategies for Success in Global Outsourcing and Offshoring,* McGraw Hill Higher Education, New York.

Another topical book on outsourcing.

Supplement to Chapter 5
Forecasting

INTRODUCTION

Some forecasts are accurate. We know exactly what time the Sun will rise at any given place on Earth tomorrow or one day next month or even next year. Forecasting in a business context, however, is much more difficult and therefore prone to error. We do not know precisely how many orders we will receive or how many customers will walk through the door tomorrow, next month, or next year. Such forecasts, however, are necessary to help managers make decisions about resourcing the organization for the future.

FORECASTING – KNOWING THE OPTIONS

Simply knowing that demand for your goods or services is rising or falling is not enough in itself. Knowing the rate of change is likely to be vital to business planning. A firm of lawyers may have to decide the point at which, in their growing business, they will have to take on another partner. Hiring a new partner could take months so they need to be able to forecast when they expect to reach that point and then when they need to start their recruitment drive. The same applies to a plant manager who will need to purchase new plant to deal with rising demand. The manager may not want to commit to buying an expensive piece of machinery until absolutely necessary but in enough time to order the machine and have it built, delivered, installed and tested. The same is so for governments, whether planning new airports or runway capacity or deciding where and how many primary schools to build.

The first question is to know how far you need to look ahead and this will depend on the options and decisions available to you. Take the example of a local government where the number of primary-age children (5–11 year olds) is increasing in some areas and declining in other areas within its boundaries. It is legally obliged to provide school places for all such children. Government officials will have a number of options open to them and they may each have different lead times associated with them. One key step in forecasting is to know the possible options and the lead times required to bring them about (*see* Table S5.1):

Table S5.1 **Options available and lead time required for dealing with changes in numbers of school children**

Options available	Lead time required
Hire short-term teachers	Hours
Hire staff	
Build temporary classrooms	
Amend school catchment areas	
Build new classrooms	
Build new schools	Years

1 Individual schools can hire (or lay off) short-term (supply) teachers from a pool not only to cover for absent teachers, but also to provide short-term capacity while teachers are hired to deal with increases in demand. Acquiring (or dismissing) such temporary cover may only require a few hours' notice. (This is often referred to as short-term capacity management.)

2 Hiring new (or laying off existing) staff is another option but both of these may take months to complete. (Medium-term capacity management.)

3 A shortage of accommodation may be fixed in the short to medium term by hiring or buying temporary classrooms. It may only take a couple of weeks to hire such a building and equip it ready for use.

4 It may be possible to amend catchment areas between schools to try to balance an increasing population in one area against a declining population in another. Such changes may require lengthy consultation processes.

5 In the longer term new classrooms or even new schools may have to be built. The planning, consultation, approval, commissioning, tendering, building and equipping process may take one to five years depending on the scale of the new build.

Knowing the range of options, managers can then decide the timescale for their forecasts; indeed several forecasts might be needed for the short term, medium term and long term.

IN ESSENCE FORECASTING IS SIMPLE

In essence forecasting is easy. To know how many children may turn up in a local school tomorrow you can use the number that turned up today. In the long term, in order to forecast how many primary-aged children will turn up at a school in five years' time one need simply look at the birth statistics for the current year for the school's catchment area, *see* Fig. S5.1.

However, such simple extrapolation techniques are prone to error and indeed such approaches have resulted in some local governments committing themselves to building schools which, five or six years later, when complete, had few children and other schools bursting at the seams with temporary classrooms and temporary teachers, often resulting in falling morale and declining educational standards. The reason why such simple approaches are prone to problems is that there are many contextual variables (*see* Fig. S5.2) which will have a potentially significant impact on, for example, the school population five years hence. For example:

1 One minor factor in developed countries, though a major factor in developing countries, might be the death rate in children between birth and 5 years of age. This may be dependent upon location with a slightly higher mortality rate in the poorer areas compared with the more affluent areas.

2 Another more significant factor is immigration and emigration as people move into or out of the local area. This will be affected by housing stock and housing developments, the ebb and flow of jobs in the area and the changing economic prosperity of the area.

3 One key factor which has an impact on the birth rate in an area is the amount and type of the housing stock. City centre tenement buildings tend to have a higher proportion of children per dwelling, for example, than suburban semi-detached houses. So not only will existing housing stock have an impact on the child population, but also will the type of housing developments under construction, planned and proposed.

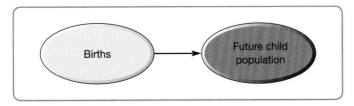

Figure S5.1 Simple prediction of future child population

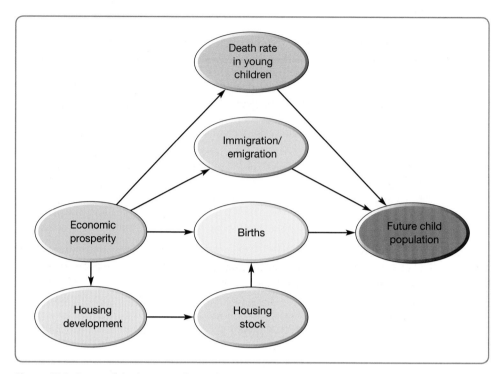

Figure S5.2 Some of the key causal variables in predicting child populations

APPROACHES TO FORECASTING

There are two main approaches to forecasting. Managers sometimes use qualitative methods based on opinions, past experience and even best guesses. There is also a range of qualitative forecasting techniques available to help managers evaluate trends, causal relationships and make predictions about the future. Also, quantitative forecasting techniques can be used to model data. Although no approach or technique will result in an accurate forecast, a combination of qualitative and quantitative approaches can be used to great effect by bringing together expert judgements and predictive models.

Qualitative methods

Imagine you were asked to forecast the outcome of a forthcoming football match. Simply looking at the teams' performance over the last few weeks and extrapolating it is unlikely to yield the right result. Like many business decisions, the outcome will depend on many other factors. In this case the strength of the opposition, their recent form, injuries to players on both sides, the match location and even the weather will have an influence on the outcome. A qualitative approach involves collecting and appraising judgements, options, even best guesses as well as past performance from 'experts' to make a prediction. There are several ways this can be done: a panel approach, the Delphi method and scenario planning.

Panel approach

Just as panels of football pundits gather to speculate about likely outcomes, so too do politicians, business leaders, stock market analysts, banks and airlines. The panel acts like a focus group allowing everyone to talk openly and freely. Although there is the great advantage of several brains being better than one, it can be difficult to reach a consensus, or sometimes the views of the loudest or highest status may emerge (the bandwagon effect). Although more reliable than one person's views, the panel approach still has the weakness that everybody, even the experts, can get it wrong.

Delphi method[1]

Perhaps the best-known approach to generating forecasts using experts is the Delphi method. This is a more formal method which attempts to reduce the influences from procedures of face-to-face meetings. It employs a questionnaire, emailed or posted to the experts. The replies are analysed, summarized and returned, anonymously, to all the experts. The experts are then asked to reconsider their original response in the light of the replies and arguments put forward by the other experts. This process is repeated several more times to conclude either with a consensus or at least a narrower range of decisions. One refinement of this approach is to allocate weights to the individuals and their suggestions based on, for example, their experience, their past success in forecasting, other people's views of their abilities. The obvious problems associated with this method include constructing an appropriate questionnaire, selecting an appropriate panel of experts and trying to deal with their inherent biases.

Scenario planning

One method for dealing with situations of even greater uncertainty is scenario planning. This is usually applied to long-range forecasting, again using a panel. The panel members are usually asked to devise a range of future scenarios. Each scenario can then be discussed and the inherent risks considered. Unlike the Delphi method, scenario planning is not necessarily concerned with arriving at a consensus but looking at the possible range of options and putting plans in place to try to avoid the ones that are least desired and taking action to follow the most desired.

Quantitative methods

There are two main approaches to qualitative forecasting, Time series analysis and causal modelling techniques.

Time series examine the pattern of past behaviour of a single phenomenon over time, taking into account reasons for variation in the trend in order to use the analysis to forecast the phenomenon's future behaviour.

Causal modelling is an approach which describes and evaluates the complex cause–effect relationships between the key variables (such as in Fig. S5.2).

Time series analysis

Simple time series plot a variable over time and then, by removing underlying variations with assignable causes, use extrapolation techniques to predict future behaviour. The key weakness with this approach is that it simply looks at past behaviour to predict the future, ignoring causal variables which are taken into account in other methods such as causal modelling or qualitative techniques. For example, suppose a company is attempting to predict the future sales of a product. The past three years' sales, quarter by quarter, are shown in Fig. S5.3(a). This series of past sales may be analysed to indicate future sales. For instance, underlying the series might be a linear upward trend in sales. If this is taken out of the data, as in Fig. S5.3(b), we are left with a cyclical seasonal variation. The mean deviation of each quarter from the trend line can now be taken out, to give the average seasonality deviation. What remains is the random variation about the trends and seasonality lines, Fig. S5.3(c). Future sales may now be predicted as lying within a band about a projection of the trend, plus the seasonality. The width of the band will be a function of the degree of random variation.

Forecasting unassignable variations The random variations which remain after taking out trend and seasonal effects are without any known or assignable cause. This does not mean that they do not have a cause, however, just that we do not know what it is. Nevertheless, some attempt can be made to forecast it, if only on the basis that future events will, in some way, be based on past events. We will examine two of the more common approaches to forecasting which are based on projecting forward from past behaviour. These are:

- moving-average forecasting;
- exponentially smoothed forecasting.

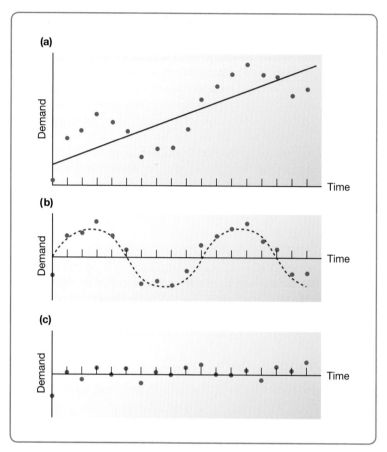

Figure S5.3 Time series analysis with (a) trend, (b) seasonality and (c) random variation

Moving-average forecasting The moving-average approach to forecasting takes the previous n periods' actual demand figures, calculates the average demand over the n periods, and uses this average as a forecast for the next period's demand. Any data older than the n periods plays no part in the next period's forecast. The value of n can be set at any level, but is usually in the range 4 to 7.

Example – Eurospeed parcels
Table S5.2 shows the weekly demand for Eurospeed, a European-wide parcel delivery company. It measures demand, on a weekly basis, in terms of the number of parcels which it is given to deliver (irrespective of the size of each parcel). Each week, the next week's demand is forecast by taking the moving average of the previous four weeks' actual demand. Thus if the forecast demand for week t is F_t and the actual demand for week t is A_t, then:

$$F_t = \frac{A_{t-1} + A_{t-2} + A_{t-3} + A_{t-4}}{4}$$

For example, the forecast for week 35 is:

$$F_{35} = (72.5 + 66.7 + 68.3 + 67.0)/4$$
$$= 68.8$$

Table S6.2 **Moving-average forecast calculated over a four-week period**

Week	Actual demand (thousands)	Forecast
20	63.3	
21	62.5	
22	67.8	
23	66.0	
24	67.2	64.9
25	69.9	65.9
26	65.6	67.7
27	71.1	66.3
28	68.8	67.3
29	68.4	68.9
30	70.3	68.5
31	72.5	69.7
32	66.7	70.0
33	68.3	69.5
34	67.0	69.5
35		68.6

Exponential smoothing There are two significant drawbacks to the moving-average approach to forecasting. First, in its basic form, it gives equal weight to all the previous n periods which are used in the calculations (although this can be overcome by assigning different weights to each of the n periods). Second, and more important, it does not use data from beyond the n periods over which the moving average is calculated. Both these problems are overcome by *exponential smoothing*, which is also somewhat easier to calculate. The exponential-smoothing approach forecasts demand in the next period by taking into account the actual demand in the current period and the forecast which was previously made for the current period. It does so according to the formula:

$$F_t = \alpha A_{t-1} + (1 - x)F_{t-1}$$

where α is the smoothing constant.

The smoothing constant α is, in effect, the weight which is given to the last (and therefore assumed to be most important) piece of information available to the forecaster. However, the other expression in the formula includes the forecast for the current period which included the previous period's actual demand, and so on. In this way all previous data has a (diminishing) effect on the next forecast.

Table S5.3 shows the data for Eurospeed's parcels forecasts using this exponential-smoothing method, where $\alpha = 0.2$. For example, the forecast for week 35 is:

$$F_{35} = 0.2 \times 67.0 + 0.8 \times 68.3 = 68.04$$

The value of α governs the balance between the *responsiveness* of the forecasts to changes in demand and the *stability* of the forecasts. The closer α is to zero, the more forecasts

Table S5.3 **Exponentially smoothed forecast calculated with smoothing constant $\alpha = 0.2$**

Week (t)	Actual demand (thousands) (A)	Forecast ($F_t = \alpha A_{t-1} + (1 - \alpha)F_{t-1}$) ($\alpha = 0.2$)
20	63.3	60.00
21	62.5	60.66
22	67.8	60.03
23	66.0	61.58
24	67.2	62.83
25	69.9	63.70
26	65.6	64.94
27	71.1	65.07
28	68.8	66.28
29	68.4	66.78
30	70.3	67.12
31	72.5	67.75
32	66.7	68.70
33	68.3	68.30
34	67.0	68.30
35		68.04

will be dampened by previous forecasts (not very sensitive but stable). Fig. S5.4 shows the Eurospeed volume data plotted for a four-week moving average, exponential smoothing with $\alpha = 0.2$ and exponential smoothing with $\alpha = 0.3$.

Causal models

Causal models often employ complex techniques to understand the strength of relationships between the network of variables and the impact they have on each other. Simple regression models try to determine the 'best-fit' expression between two variables. For example, suppose an ice cream company is trying to forecast its future sales. After examining previous demand, it figures that the main influence on demand at the factory is the average temperature of the previous week. To understand this relationship, the company plots demand against the previous week's temperatures. This is shown in Fig. S5.5. Using this graph, the company can make a reasonable prediction of demand, once the average temperature is known, provided that the other conditions prevailing in the market are reasonably stable. If they are not, then these other factors which have an influence on demand will need to be included in the regression model, which becomes increasingly complex.

These more complex networks comprise many variables and relationships each with their own set of assumptions and limitations. While developing such models and assessing the importance of each of the factors and understanding the network of interrelationships are beyond the scope of this text, many techniques are available to help managers undertake this more complex modelling and also feed back data into the model to further refine and develop it, in particular structural equation modelling.

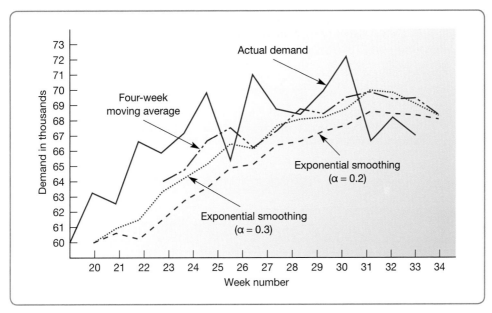

Figure S5.4 A comparison of a moving-average forecast and exponential smoothing with the smoothing constant $\alpha = 0.2$ and 0.3

The performance of forecasting models

Forecasting models are widely used in management decision making, and indeed most decisions require a forecast of some kind, yet the performance of this type of model is far from impressive. Hogarth and Makridakis,[2] in a comprehensive review of the applied management and finance literature, show that the record of forecasters using both judgement and sophisticated mathematical methods is not good. What they do suggest, however, is that certain

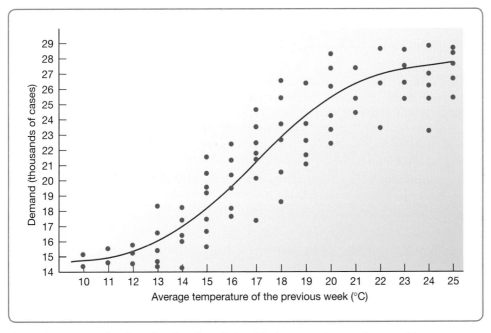

Figure S5.5 Regression line showing the relationship between the previous week's average temperature and demand

forecasting techniques perform better under certain circumstances. In short-term forecasting there is 'considerable inertia in most economic and natural phenomena. *Thus the present states of any variables are predictive of the short-term future (i.e. three months or less). Rather simple mechanistic methods, such as those used in time series forecasts, can often make accurate short-term forecasts and even out-perform more theoretically elegant and elaborate approaches used in econometric forecasting.*'[3]

Long-term forecasting methods, although difficult to judge because of the time lapse between the forecast and the event, do seem to be more amenable to an objective causal approach. In a comparative study of long-term market forecasting methods, Armstrong and Grohman[4] conclude that econometric methods offer more accurate long-range forecasts than do expert opinion or time series analysis, and that the superiority of objective causal methods improves as the time horizon increases.

SELECTED FURTHER READING

Hoyle, R.H. (ed.) (1995) *Structural Equation Modeling*, Sage, Thousand Oaks, CA.

For the specialist.

Hyndman, R.J. and Athanasopoulos, G. (2013) Forecasting: principles and practice, OTexts, https://www.otexts.org

A very good introduction, although technical at times.

Makridakis, S.G. (1998) *Forecasting*, 3rd edn, Wiley, New York.

A classic.

Maruyama, G.M. (1997) *Basics of Structural Equation Modeling*, Sage, Thousand Oaks, CA.

For the specialist.

Silver, N. (2013) *The Signal and the Noise: The Art and Science of Prediction*, Penguin, Harmondsworth.

A readable book on the meaning of forecasting and statistics. A miracle!

DESIGN

Part Two
DESIGNING THE OPERATION

This part of the book looks at how the resources and processes of operations are designed. By 'design' we mean how the overall shape and arrangement of transforming resources impact the flow of transformed resources as they move through the operation, and the nature of those transforming resources. And that is the order in which we treat the four key issues that concern the design of operations. The chapters in this part are:

- Chapter 6 Process design – This examines various types of process, and how these 'building blocks' of operations are designed.
- Chapter 7 Layout and flow – This looks at how different ways of arranging physical facilities affect the nature of flow through the operation.
- Chapter 8 Process technology – This describes how the effectiveness of operations is influenced by the fast-moving developments in process technology.
- Chapter 9 People in operations – This looks at the elements of human resource management that are traditionally seen as being directly within the sphere of operations management.

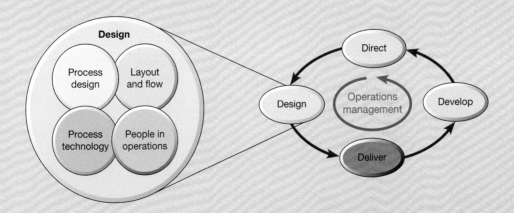

6

Process design

Key questions

❯ What is process design?

❯ What should be the objectives of process design?

❯ How do volume and variety affect process design?

❯ How are processes designed in detail?

INTRODUCTION

In Chapter 1 we described how all operations consist of a collection of processes (though these processes may be called 'units' or 'departments') that interconnect with each other to form an internal network. Each process acts as a smaller version of the whole operation of which they form a part, and transformed resources flow between them. We also defined a process as 'an arrangement of resources and activities that transform inputs into outputs that satisfy (internal or external) customer needs'. They are the 'building blocks' of all operations, and as such they play a vital role in how well operations operate. This is why process design is so important. Unless its individual processes are well designed, an operation as a whole will not perform as well as it could. And operations managers are at the forefront of how processes are designed. In fact all operations managers are designers. When they purchase or rearrange the position of a piece of equipment, or when they change the way of working within a process, it is a design decision because it affects the physical shape and nature of their processes, as well as its performance. This chapter examines the design of processes. Figure 6.1 shows where this topic fits within the overall model of operations management.

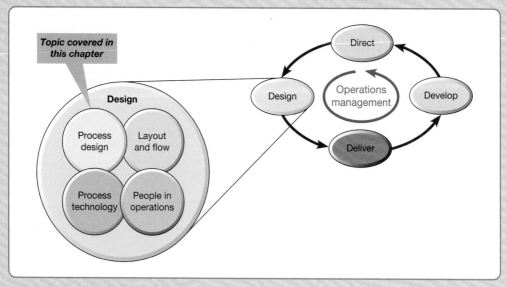

Figure 6.1 This chapter examines process design

WHAT IS PROCESS DESIGN?

To 'design' (as we explained in Chapter 4) is to conceive the looks, arrangement and workings of something *before it is created*. In that sense it is a conceptual exercise. Yet it is one that must deliver a solution that will work in practice. Design is also an activity that can be approached at different levels of detail. One may envisage the general shape and intention of something before getting down to defining its details. This is certainly true for process design. At the start of the process design activity it is important to understand the design objectives, especially at first, when the overall shape and nature of the process are being decided. The most common way of doing this is by positioning it according to its volume and variety characteristics. Eventually the details of the process must be analysed to ensure that it fulfils its objectives effectively. Yet, it is often only through getting to grips with the detail of a design that the feasibility of its overall shape can be assessed. But do not think of this as a simple sequential process. There may be aspects concerned with the objectives, or the broad positioning, of the process that will need to be modified following its more detailed analysis.

Process design and product/service design are interrelated

Often we will treat the design of products and services, on the one hand, and the design of the processes that make them, on the other, as though they were separate activities. Yet they are clearly interrelated. It would be foolish to commit to the detailed design of any product or service without some consideration of how it is to be produced. Small changes in the design of products and services can have profound implications for the way the operation eventually has to produce them. Similarly, the design of a process can constrain the freedom of product and service designers to operate as they would wish (*see* Fig. 6.2). This holds good whether the operation is producing products or services. However, the overlap between the two design activities is generally greater in operations that produce services. Because many services involve the customer in being part of the transformation process, the service, as far as the customer sees it,

> **✱ Operations principle**
> The design of processes cannot be done independently of the products and/or services that they are creating.

cannot be separated from the process to which the customer is subjected. Overlapping product and process design has implications for the organization of the design activity, as we discussed in Chapter 4. Certainly, when product designers also have to make or use the things

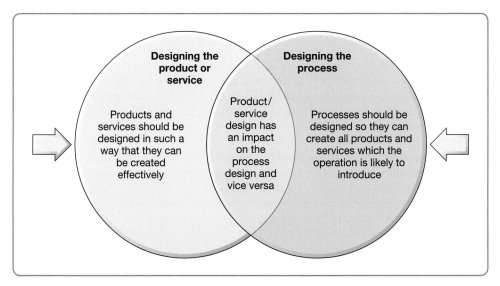

Figure 6.2 The design of products/services and processes are interrelated and should be treated together

that they design, it can concentrate their minds on what is important. For example, in the early days of flight, the engineers who designed the aircraft were also the test pilots who took them out on their first flight. For this reason, if no other, safety was a significant objective in the design activity.

Changi Airport[1]

Airports are complex operations – really complex. Their processes handle passengers, aircraft, crew, baggage, commercial cargo, food, security, restaurants and numerous customer services that all interact. The operations managers, who oversee the daily operations of an airport, must cope with Civil Aviation Administration rules and regulations, a huge number of airport service contracts, usually thousands of staff with a wide variety of specialisms, airlines with sometimes competing claims to service priority, customers who fly every week and others who have a family of seven with two baby strollers and fly once a decade. Also their processes are vulnerable to disruptions from late arrivals, aircraft malfunction, weather, the industrial action of workers two continents away, conflicts, terrorism and erupting volcanoes. Designing the processes that can operate under these conditions must be one of the most challenging operations tasks. So to win prizes for 'Best Airport' customer service and operating efficiency year after year have to be something of an achievement. Which is what the sixth busiest international airport, Changi Airport in Singapore, has done. As a major air hub in Asia, Changi serves more than 100 international airlines flying to some 300 cities in about 70 countries and territories worldwide. It handles almost 60 million passengers (that is roughly 10 times the size of Singapore's population). A flight takes off or lands at Changi roughly once every 90 seconds.

In 2017 Changi plans to open its new Terminal 4, which was started in 2013. The new US$1.03 billion T4 is expected to handle about 16 million passengers per year and will increase the airport's annual passenger handling capacity to 82 million. Every stage of the customers' journey through the terminal has been designed to be as smooth as possible. The aim of all the processes that make up the terminal is to provide fast, smooth and seamless flow for passengers. Each stage in the customer journey must have enough capacity to cope with anticipated demand. A new overhead bridge will be built across the airport boulevard connecting T4 with Singapore's highway system and enable the movement of cars, buses and airside vehicles. Two new car parks will accommodate up to 1,500 vehicles. The terminal will be internally connected to the new car parks via sheltered

Source: Alamy Images: Urbanmyth

links. Once passengers arrive at the two-storey terminal building they will pass through kiosks and automated options for self check-in, self bag tagging and self bag-drops. Their bags will then be transported to the aircraft via an advanced and automated baggage handling system. Similarly, automated options, including face recognition technology, will be used at immigration counters and departure-gate boarding. Biometric technology and fast and seamless travel (FAST) services are being implemented at the terminal to speed passenger throughput, reduce staffing and increase efficiency. After security checks, passengers find themselves in 15,000 m² of shopping, dining, liquor, tobacco, perfumery, cosmetics and other retail spaces. This space will implement a new walk-through retail concept. It will feature local, cultural and heritage-themed restaurants, as well as retail stores. The space also features a Central Galleria 300 m long, which will be a glazed open space that visually connects the departure, check-in, arrival and transit areas across the terminal. The emphasis on the aesthetic appeal of the terminal is something that Changi has long considered important. It already boasts a butterfly garden, orchid and sunflower gardens, as well as a koi pond.

The feelings of passengers using the terminal are an important part of its design. Mr Yam Kum Weng, Executive Vice-President of CAG, one of the companies helping to develop the design for the new terminal, said, *'T4 breaks new ground in passenger experience for travellers, while ensuring smooth and efficient operations for airlines and airport agencies. Architecturally, the design of T4 will be functional, and yet have its own distinct character compared to the other three terminals at Changi Airport. Our focus for the development of T4 will be on its interior and ensuring that the design and layout continues to be passenger-centric and user-friendly. It will offer what passengers want – a good range of leisure amenities, convenient facilities and attractive commercial offerings.'* And with so many different companies involved in the day-to-day operation of the airport it was vital to include as many stakeholders as possible during the design. Workshops were conducted with various stakeholders, including airlines, ground handlers, immigration and security agencies, retail and food and beverage operators, as well as other users to ensure that the T4 design met the needs of each party. The objective was to ensure that T4, when operational, could deliver a seamless and refreshing experience for travellers, and also be a place where staff will feel proud and motivated to work.

WHAT SHOULD BE THE OBJECTIVES OF PROCESS DESIGN?

The whole point of process design is to make sure that the performance of the process is appropriate for whatever it is trying to achieve. For example, if an operation competed primarily on its ability to respond quickly to customer requests, its processes would need to be designed to give fast throughput times. This would minimize the time between customers requesting a product or service and their receiving it. Similarly, if an operation competed on low price, cost-related objectives are likely to dominate its process design. Some kind of logic should link what the operation as a whole is attempting to achieve and the performance objectives of its individual processes. As when we examined product and service design innovation (see Chapter 4), we will include 'sustainability' as an operational objective of process design, even though it is really a far broader societal issue that is part of the organization's 'triple bottom line' (see Chapter 2). This is illustrated in Table 6.1.

> **✳ Operations principle**
>
> The design of any process should be judged on its quality, speed, dependability, flexibility, cost and sustainability performance.

Table 6.1 **The impact of strategic performance objectives on process design objectives and performance**

Operations performance objective	Typical process design objectives	Some benefits of good process design
Quality	Provide appropriate resources, capable of achieving the specification of product of services Error-free processing	Products and services produced to specification Less recycling and wasted effort within the process
Speed	Minimum throughput time Output rate appropriate for demand	Short customer waiting time Low in-process inventory
Dependability	Provide dependable process resources Reliable process output timing and volume	On-time deliveries of products and services Less disruption, confusion and rescheduling within the process
Flexibility	Provide resources with an appropriate range of capabilities Change easily between processing states (what, how, or how much is being processed?)	Ability to process a wide range of products and services Low cost/fast product and service change Low cost/fast volume and timing changes Ability to cope with unexpected events (e.g. supply or a processing failure)
Cost	Appropriate capacity to meet demand Eliminate process waste in terms of excess capacity, excess process capability, in-process delays, in-process errors, inappropriate process inputs	Low processing costs Low resource costs (capital costs) Low delay/inventory costs (working capital costs)
Sustainability	Minimize energy usage Reduce local impact on community Produce for easy disassembly	Lower negative environmental and societal impact

Operations performance objectives translate directly to process design objectives as shown in Table 6.1. But, because processes are managed at a very operational level, process design also needs to consider a more 'micro' and detailed set of objectives. These are largely concerned with flow through the process. When whatever is being 'processed' enters a process it will progress through a series of activities where its is 'transformed' in some way. Between these activities it may dwell for some time in inventories, waiting to be transformed by the next activity. This means that the time that a unit spends in the process (its throughput time) will be longer than the sum of all the transforming activities that it passes through. Also, the resources that perform the processes activities may not be used all the time because not all items will necessarily require the same activities and the capacity of each resource may not match the demand placed upon it. So neither the items moving through the process nor the resources performing the activities may be fully utilized. Because of this the way that items leave the process is unlikely to be exactly the same as the way they arrive at the process. It is common for more 'micro' performance flow objectives to be used that describe process flow performance. For example:

- Throughput rate (or flow rate) is the rate at which items emerge from the process, that is the number of items passing through the process per unit of time.
- Cycle time, or takt time, is the reciprocal of throughput rate; it is the time between items emerging from the process. The term 'takt' time is the same, but is normally applied to 'paced' processes like moving-belt assembly lines. It is the 'beat' or tempo of working required to meet demand.[2]
- Throughput time is the average elapsed time taken for inputs to move through the process and become outputs.
- The number of items in the process (also called the 'work-in-progress', or in-process inventory) as an average over a period of time.
- The utilization of process resources is the proportion of available time that the resources within the process are performing useful work.

OPERATIONS IN PRACTICE   Fast (but not too fast) food drive-throughs[3]

One of the most studied types of process is the 'fast food drive-through'. The quick service restaurant (QSR) industry reckons that the very first drive-through dates back to 1928 when Royce Hailey first promoted the drive-through service at his Pig Stand restaurant in Los Angeles. Customers would simply drive by the back door of the restaurant where the chef would come out and deliver the restaurant's famous 'Barbequed Pig' sandwiches. Today, drive-through processes are slicker, and far, far, faster. In fact there is intense competition to design the fastest and most reliable drive-through process. Starbuck's drive-throughs have strategically placed cameras at the order boards so that servers can recognize regular customers and start making their order even before it's placed. Burger King has experimented with sophisticated sound systems, simpler menu boards and see-through food bags to ensure greater accuracy

Source: Shutterstock.com: Gabriel12

(no point in being fast if you do not deliver what the customer ordered). These details matter. McDonald's reckons that its sales increase by 1 per cent for every six seconds saved at a drive-through. Perhaps the most remarkable experiment in making drive-through process times slicker is being carried out by McDonald's in the USA. On California's central coast 150 miles (240 km) from Los Angeles, a call centre takes orders remotely from 40 McDonald's outlets around the country. The orders are then sent back to the restaurants through the Internet and the food is assembled only a few metres from where the order was placed. It may only save a few seconds on each order, but that can add up to extra sales at busy times of the day.

Menu items must be easy to read and understand. Designing 'combo meals' (burger, fries and a cola), for example, saves time at the ordering stage. However, complex individual items that require customization meals can slow down the process, which is becoming an issue for operators as fashions move towards customized salads and sandwiches. Yet there are signs that, above a certain speed of service, other aspects of process performance become more important. As the chief operations manager at Taco Bell says, *'you can get really fast but ruin the overall experience, because now you're not friendly and now you're not taking the time to guarantee accuracy or make sure the products have been built the way you want them to be built. So there's a careful balance in there that we have to continually look at through our testing process, to make sure that the packaging we're providing, the product builds, the tools we give, the training we give, is such that it will support our current speed targets but allow us to continue to improve on our experience, on our accuracy, on our friendliness.'*

Standardization of processes

One of the most important process design objectives, especially in large organizations, concerns the extent to which process designs should be standardized. By standardization in this context we mean 'doing things in the same way' or, more formally, 'adopting a common sequence of activities, methods and use of equipment'. It is a significant issue in large organizations because, very often, different ways of carrying out similar or identical tasks emerge over time in the various parts of the organization. But why not allow many different ways of doing the same thing? That would give a degree of autonomy and freedom to individuals and teams to exercise their discretion. The problem is that allowing numerous ways of doing things causes confusion, misunderstandings and, eventually, inefficiency. In healthcare processes, it can even cause preventable deaths. For example, the Royal College of Physicians in the UK revealed that there were more than 100 types of charts that were used for monitoring patients' vital signs in use in UK hospitals.[4] This leads to confusion, it said. Potentially, thousands

> **❋ Operations principle**
>
> Standardizing processes can give some significant advantages, but not every process can be standardized.

of hospital deaths could be prevented if doctors and nurses used a standardized bed chart. Because hospitals can use different charts, doctors and nurses have to learn how to read new ones when they move. The Royal College recommended that there should be just one chart and one process for all staff that check on patients' conditions. Professor Derek Bell said, *'Developing and adopting a standardised early warning system will be one of the most significant developments in healthcare in the next decade.'*

Standardization is also an important objective in the design of some products and services, for similar reasons (see Chapter 4). The practical dilemma for most organizations is how to draw the line between processes that are required to be standardized and those that are allowed to be different.

Environmentally sensitive process design

With the issues of environmental protection becoming more important, process designers have to take account of 'green' (sustainability) issues. In many developed countries, legislation has already provided some basic standards. Interest has focused on some fundamental issues:

- *The sources of inputs* to a product or service. (Will they damage rainforests? Will they use up scarce minerals? Will they exploit the poor or use child labour?)

- *Quantities and sources of energy* consumed in the process. (Do plastic beverage bottles use more energy than glass ones? Should waste heat be recovered and used in fish farming?)
- *The amounts and type of waste material* that are created in the manufacturing processes. (Can this waste be recycled efficiently, or must it be burnt or buried in landfill sites?)
- *The life of the product itself.* If a product has a long useful life will it consume fewer resources than a short-life product?
- *The end of life of the product.* (Will the redundant product be difficult to dispose of in an environmentally friendly way?)

> ✳ **Operations principle**
>
> The design of any process should include consideration of ethical and environmental issues.

Designers are faced with complex trade-offs between these factors, although it is not always easy to obtain all the information that is needed to make the 'best' choices. To help make more rational decisions in the design activity, some industries are experimenting with *life cycle analysis*. This technique analyses all the production inputs, the life cycle use of the product and its final disposal, in terms of total energy used and all emitted wastes. The inputs and wastes are evaluated at *every* stage of a product or service's creation, beginning with the extraction or farming of the basic raw materials. The case 'Ecover's ethical operations design' demonstrates that it is possible to include ecological considerations in all aspects of product and process design.

OPERATIONS IN PRACTICE   **Ecover's ethical operations design[5]**

Source: Alamy Images: Clivestock

Ecover cleaning products, such as washing liquid, are famously ecological. In fact it is the company's whole rationale. *'We clean with care'*, says Ecover, *'whether you're washing your sheets, your floors, your hands or your dishes, our products don't contain those man-made chemicals that can irritate your skin.'* But it is not just its products that are based on an ecologically sustainable foundation. Ecover's ecological factories in France and Belgium also embody the company's commitment to sustainability. Whether it is the company's factory roof, its use of energy or the way it treats the water used in the production processes, Ecover points out that it does its best to limit environmental impact. For example, the Ecover factory operates entirely on green electricity – the type produced by wind generators, tidal generators and other natural sources. What is more, Ecover makes the most of the energy it does use by choosing energy-efficient lighting, and then only using it when needed. And, although the machinery used in the factories is standard for the industry, Ecover keeps its energy and water consumption down by choosing low-speed appliances that can multi-task and do not require water to clean them. For example,

the motors on the mixing machines can mix 25 tonnes of Ecover liquid while *'consuming no more electricity than a few flat irons'.* And Ecover has a *'squeezy gadget that's so efficient at getting every last drop of product out of the pipes, they don't need to be rinsed through'.* Ecover says that *'we hate waste, so we're big on recycling. We keep the amount of packaging used in our products to a minimum, and make sure whatever cardboard or plastic we do use can be recycled, re-used or re-filled. It's an ongoing process of improvement; in fact, we've recently developed a new kind of green plastic we like to call "Plant-astic" that's 100% renewable, reusable and recyclable - and made from sugarcane.'*

Even the building is ecological. It is cleverly designed to follow the movement of the Sun from east to west, so that production takes place with the maximum amount of natural daylight (good for saving power and good for working conditions). The factory's frame is built from pine rather than more precious timbers and the walls are constructed using bricks that are made from clay, wood pulp and mineral waste. They require less energy to bake, yet they are light, porous and insulate well. The factories' roofs are covered in thick, spongy Sedum (a flowering plant, often used for natural roofing) that gives insulation all year round. In fact it is so effective that they do not need heating or air-conditioning – the temperature never drops below 4°C and never rises above 26°C.

HOW DO VOLUME AND VARIETY AFFECT PROCESS DESIGN?

In Chapter 1 we saw how processes range from those producing at high volume (for example, credit card transaction processing) to a low volume (for example, funding a large complex takeover deal). Also processes can range from producing a very low variety of products or services (for example, in an electricity utility) to a very high variety (for example, in an architects' practice). Usually the two dimensions of volume and variety go together – but in a reversed way. So low-volume processes often produce a high variety of products and services, and high-volume operations processes often produce a narrow variety of products and services. Thus there is a continuum from low volume–high variety through to high volume–low variety, on which we can position processes. And within a single operation there could be processes with very different positions on this volume–variety spectrum. So, for example, compare the approach taken in a medical service during mass medical treatments, such as large-scale immunization programmes, with that taken in transplant surgery where the treatment is designed specifically to meet the needs of one person. In other words, no one type of process design is best for all types of requirement in all circumstances – different products or services with different volume–variety positions require different processes.

> * **Operations principle**
>
> The design of any process should be governed by the volume and variety it is required to produce.

Process types

The position of a process on the volume–variety continuum shapes its overall design and the general approach to managing its activities. These 'general approaches' to designing and managing processes are called process types. Different terms are used to identify process types depending on whether they are predominantly manufacturing or service processes, and there is some variation in the terms used. For example, it is not uncommon to find the 'manufacturing' terms used in service industries. Figure 6.3 illustrates how these 'process types' are used to describe different positions on the volume–variety spectrum.

Project processes

Project processes deal with discrete, usually highly customized products, often with a relatively long timescale between the completion of each item, where each job has a well-defined start and finish. Project processes have low volume and high variety. Activities involved in the process can be ill-defined and uncertain. Transforming resources may have to be organized especially for each item (because each item is different). The process may be complex, partly because the activities in such processes often involve significant discretion to act according to professional judgement. Examples of project processes include software design, movie production, most construction companies, and large fabrication operations such as those manufacturing turbogenerators.

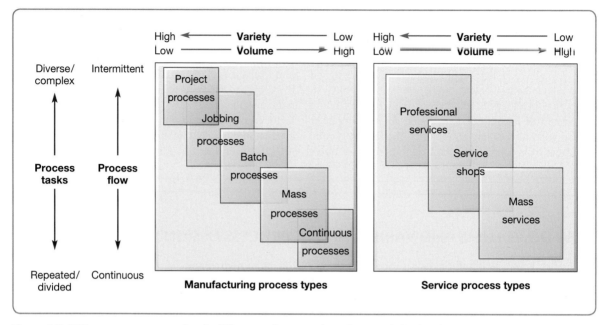

Figure 6.3 Different process types imply different volume–variety characteristics for the process

The major construction site shown in the picture is a project process. Each 'item' (building) is different and poses different challenges to those running the process (civil engineers)

Jobbing processes

Jobbing processes also deal with high variety and low volumes. However, while in project processes each item has resources devoted more or less exclusively to it, in jobbing processes each product has to share the operation's resources with many others. Resources will process a series of items but, although each one will require similar attention, they may differ in their exact needs. Many jobs will probably be 'one-offs' that are never repeated. Again, jobbing processes could be relatively complex; however, they usually produce physically smaller products and, although sometimes involving considerable skill, such processes often involve fewer unpredictable circumstances. Examples of jobbing processes include made-to-measure tailors, many precision engineers such as specialist toolmakers, furniture restorers, and the printer who produces tickets for the local social event.

This craftsman is using general-purpose wood-cutting technology to make a product for an individual customer. The next product made will be different (although maybe similar) for a different customer

Batch processes

Batch processes may look like jobbing processes, but do not have the same degree of variety. As the name implies, each time batch processes produce more than one item at a time. So each part of the process has periods when it is repeating itself, at least while the 'batch' is being processed. If the size of the batch is just two or three items, it is little different to jobbing. Conversely, if the batches are large, and especially if the products are familiar to the operation, batch processes can be fairly repetitive. Because of this, the batch type of process can be found over a wide range of volume and variety levels. Examples of batch processes include machine tool manufacturing, the production of some special gourmet frozen foods, and the manufacture of most of the component parts which go into mass-produced assemblies such as automobiles.

In this kitchen, food is being prepared in batches. All batches go through the same sequence (preparation, cooking and storage) but each batch is of a different dish

Mass processes

Mass processes are those which produce items in high volume and relatively narrow variety (narrow in terms of its fundamentals – an automobile assembly process might produce thousands of variants, yet essentially the variants do not affect the basic process of production). The activities of mass processes are usually repetitive and largely predictable. Examples of mass processes include frozen food production, automatic packing lines, automobile plants, television factories and DVD production.

The automobile plant is everyone's idea of a mass process. Each product is almost (but not quite) the same, and made in large quantities

Continuous processes

Continuous processes have even higher volume and usually lower variety than mass processes. They also usually operate for longer periods of time. Sometimes they are literally continuous in that their products are inseparable, being produced in an endless flow. They often have relatively inflexible, capital-intensive technologies with highly predictable flow and although products may be stored during the process, their predominant characteristic is of smooth flow from one part of the process to another. Examples of continuous processes include water processing, petrochemical refineries, electricity utilities, steel making and some paper making.

This continuous water treatment plant almost never stops (it only stops for maintenance) and performs only one task (filtering impurities). Often we only notice the process if it goes wrong

Professional services

Professional services are high-contact processes where customers spend a considerable time in the service process. These services can provide high levels of customization (the process being highly adaptable in order to meet individual customer needs). Professional services tend to be people based rather than equipment based, and usually staff are given considerable discretion in servicing customers. Professional services include management consultants, lawyers' practices, architects, doctors' surgeries, auditors, health and safety inspectors, and some computer field service operations.

Here consultants are preparing to start a consultancy assignment. They are discussing how they might approach the various stages of the assignment, from understanding the real nature of the problem through to the implementation of their recommended solutions. This is a process map, although a very high-level one. It guides the nature and sequence of the consultants' activities

Service shops

Service shops have levels of volume and variety (and customer contact, customization and staff discretion) between the extremes of professional and mass services (see next paragraph). Service is provided via mixes of front- and back-office activities. Service shops include banks, high street shops, holiday tour operators, car rental companies, schools, most restaurants, hotels and travel agents.

The health club shown in the picture has front-office staff who can give advice on exercise programmes and other treatments. To maintain a dependable service the staff need to follow defined processes every day

Mass services

Mass services have many customer transactions, involving limited contact time and little customization. Staff are likely to have a relatively defined division of labour and have to follow set procedures. Mass services include supermarkets, a national rail network, an airport, telecommunications service, library, television station, the police service and the enquiry desk at a utility. For example, one of the most common types of mass service is the call centre used by almost all companies that deal directly with consumers. Coping with a very high volume of enquiries requires some kind of structuring of the process of communicating with customers. This is often achieved by using a carefully designed enquiry process (sometimes known as a script).

> ✳ **Operations principle**
>
> Process types indicate the position of processes on the volume–variety spectrum.

This is an account management centre at a retail bank. It deals with thousands of customer requests every day. Although each customer request is different, they are all of the same type – involving customer accounts

Although the idea of process types can be useful, it is in many ways simplistic. In reality there is no clear boundary between process types. For example, many processed foods are manufactured using mass production processes but in batches. So, a 'batch' of one type of cake (say) can be followed by a 'batch' of a marginally different cake (perhaps with different packaging), followed by yet another, etc. Essentially this is still a mass process, but not quite as pure a version of mass processing as a manufacturing process that only made one type of cake. Similarly, the categories of service processes are likewise blurred. For example, a specialist camera retailer would normally be categorized as a service shop, yet it also will give sometimes very specialized, technical advice to customers. It is not a professional service like a consultancy of course, but it does have elements of a professional service process within its design. This is why the volume and variety characteristics of a process are sometimes seen as being a more realistic way of describing processes. The product–process matrix described next adopts this approach.

OPERATIONS IN PRACTICE

Sands Films Studio, jobbing costume makers[6]

Every film or television programme that is set in any period, other than the present day, needs costumes for its actors. And most films have a lot of characters, so that means a lot of costumes. Look at Sands Films Studio in London and you will see a well-established and permanent costume-making workshop. You will also see a typical 'jobbing' process. Sands Films provides a wide range of wardrobe and costume services. Its customers are the film, stage and TV production companies each of which has different requirements and time constraints. And because each project is different and has different requirements, the workshop's jobs go from making a single simple outfit to providing a wide variety of specially designed costumes and facilities over an extended production period. The facilities include most normal tailoring processes such as cutting, dyeing and printing, to varied specialist services such as corset and crinoline making as well as millinery (hats). During the design and making process actors often visit the workshop, which has been called an 'Aladdin's cave' of theatrical costumes. 'This is really where the actors come face to face with their character for the first time, and it's a fascinating process to watch,; Olivier Stockman, the company's Managing

Source: Sands Films Studio

Director, says. Making a costume can only start once a project has been approved and a costume designer appointed, although discussions with the workshop may have started prior to that. When the budget and the timing have been agreed, the designer can start to present ideas and finished design to the workshop. And although the processes in the workshop are well established, each costume requires different skills and so have different routes through the stages.

The product–process matrix

The most common method of illustrating the relationship between a process's volume–variety position and its design characteristics is shown in Figure 6.4. Often called the 'product–process' matrix,[7] it can in fact be used for any type of process whether producing products or services. The underlying idea of the product–process matrix is that many of the more important elements of process design are strongly related to the volume–variety position of the process. So, for any process, the tasks that it undertakes, the flow of items through the process, the layout of its resources, the technology it uses, and the design of jobs are all strongly influenced by its volume–variety position. This means that most processes should lie close to the diagonal of the matrix that represents the 'fit' between the process and its volume–variety position. This is called the 'natural' diagonal, or the 'line of fit'.

Moving off the natural diagonal

A process lying on the natural diagonal of the matrix shown in Figure 6.4 will normally have lower operating costs than one with the same volume–variety position that lies off the diagonal. This is because the diagonal represents the most appropriate process design for any volume–variety position. Processes that are on the right of the 'natural' diagonal would normally be associated with lower volumes and higher variety. This means that they are likely to be more flexible than seems to be warranted by their actual volume–variety position. That is, they are not taking advantage of their ability to standardize their activities. Because of this, their costs are likely to be higher than they would be with a

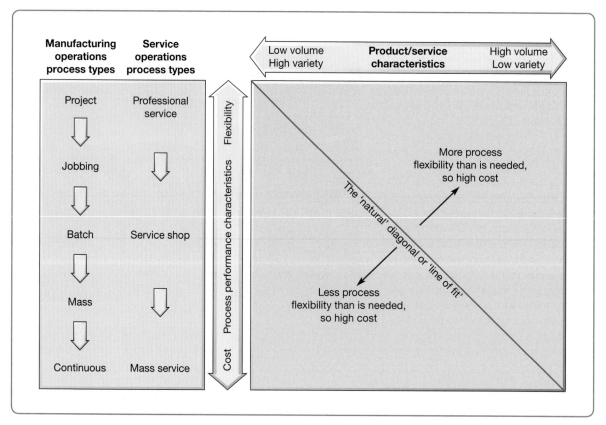

Figure 6.4 Deviating from the 'natural' diagonal on the product-process matrix has consequences for cost and flexibility

Source: Based on Hayes And Wheelwright[7]

process that was closer to the diagonal. Conversely, processes that are on the left of the diagonal have adopted a position that would normally be used for higher volume and lower variety processes. Processes will therefore be 'over-standardized' and probably too inflexible for their volume–variety position. This lack of flexibility can also lead to high costs because the process will not be able to change from one activity to another as readily as a more flexible process.[8] So a first step in examining the design of an existing process is to check if it is on the natural diagonal of the product–process matrix. The volume–variety position of the process may have changed without any corresponding change in its design. Alternatively, design changes may have been introduced without considering their suitability for the processes volume–variety position.

> ✱ **Operations principle**
> Moving off the 'natural diagonal' of the product–process matrix will incur excess cost.

Example

The 'meter installation' unit of a water utility company installed and repaired water meters. Each installation job could vary significantly because the requirements of each customer varied and because meters had to be fitted into different water pipe systems. When a customer requested an installation a supervisor would survey the customer's water system and inform the installation team. An appointment would then be made for an installer to visit the customer's location and install the meter. Then the company decided to install a new 'standard' remote-reading meter to replace the wide range of existing meters. This new meter was designed to make installation easier by including universal quick-fit joints that reduced pipe cutting and jointing during installation. As a pilot, it was also decided to prioritize those customers with the oldest meters and conduct trials of how the new meter worked in practice. All other aspects of the installation process were left as they were. However, after the new meters were introduced the costs of installation were far higher than forecast and the installers were frustrated at the waste of their time and the now relatively standardized installation job. So the company decided to change its process. It cut out the survey stage of the process because, using the new meter, 98 per cent of installations could be fitted in one visit, minimizing disruption to the customer. Just as significantly, fully qualified installers were often not needed, so installation could be performed by less expensive labour.

This example is illustrated in Figure 6.5. The initial position of the installation process is at point A. The installation unit was required to install a wide variety of meters into a very wide variety of water systems. This needed a survey stage to assess the nature of the job and the use of skilled labour to cope with the complex tasks. The installation of the new type of meter changed the volume–variety position for the process by reducing the variety of the jobs tackled by the process and increasing the volume it had to cope with. However, the process was not changed, so the design of the process was appropriate for its old volume–variety position, but not the new one. In effect it had moved to point B in Figure 6.5. It was off the diagonal, with unnecessary flexibility and high operating costs. Redesigning the process to take advantage of the reduced variety and complexity of the job (position C in Fig. 6.5) allowed installation to be performed far more efficiently.

HOW ARE PROCESSES DESIGNED IN DETAIL?

After the overall design of a process has been determined, its individual activities must be configured. At its simplest, this detailed design of a process involves identifying all the individual activities that are needed to meet the objectives of the process, and deciding on the sequence in which these activities are to be performed and who is going to do them.

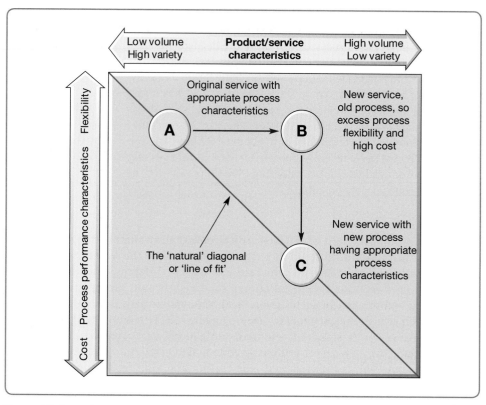

Figure 6.5 A product–process matrix with process positions from the water meter example

Space4 housing processes[9]

Productivity in house building is a problem. While most industries have made sometimes spectacular productivity gains, house building has actually been getting less productive. To add to the problem, a combination of population growth and rapid urbanization means that, in many countries, demand for housing is rising rapidly. But some companies are trying to remedy this by adopting new production methods. Space4 is one of these. It is a division of Persimmon, who are the UK's largest house builder. Its huge building in Birmingham (UK) contains what some believe could be the future of house building. It is more like the way you would expect an automobile to be made. It has a production line whose 90 operators, many of whom have automobile assembly experience, are capable of producing the timber-framed panels that form the shell of the new homes at a rate of a house every hour. The automated, state-of-the-art electronic systems within the production process control all

Source: Shutterstock.com: ArchMan

facets of the operation, ensuring that scheduling and operations are timely and accurate. There is a direct link between the CAD systems that design the houses and the manufacturing processes that make them, reducing the time between design and manufacture. The machinery itself incorporates automatic predictive and preventative maintenance routines that minimize the chances of unexpected breakdowns.

But not everything about the process relies on automation. Because of their previous automobile assembly experience, staff are used to the just-in-time, high-efficiency culture of modern mass production. After production, the completed panels are stacked in piles 3 metres high piles and are then fork-lifted into trucks prior to dispatch to building sites across the UK. Once the panels arrive at the building site, the construction workforce can assemble the exterior of a 1,200 sq. ft (112 m², average size) new home in a single day. Because the external structure of a house can be built in a few hours, and enclosed in a weatherproof covering, staff working on the internal fittings of the house, such as plumbers and electricians, can have a secure and dry environment in which to work, irrespective of external conditions. Furthermore, the automated production process uses a type of high-precision technology, which means there are fewer mistakes in the construction process on site. This means that the approval process from the local regulatory authority takes less time. This process, says Space4, speeds up the total building time from 12–14 weeks to 8–10 weeks.

There will, of course, be some constraints to this. Some activities must be carried out before others, and certain people or equipment can only do some activities. Nevertheless, for a process of any reasonable size, the number of alternative process designs is usually large. Because of this, process design is often done using some simple visual approach such as process mapping.

Process mapping

Process mapping simply involves describing processes in terms of how the activities within the process relate to each other. There are many techniques which can be used for *process mapping* (or process blueprinting, or process analysis, as it is sometimes called). However, all the techniques identify the different *types of* activity that take place during the process and show the flow of materials or people or information through the process.

Process mapping symbols

Process mapping symbols are used to classify different types of activity. And although there is no universal set of symbols, used all over the world for any type of process, there are some that are commonly used. Most of these derive either from the early days of 'scientific' management around a century ago (see Chapter 9) or, more recently, from information system flow charting. Figure 6.6 shows the symbols we will use here.

These symbols can be arranged in order, and in series or in parallel, to describe any process. For example, Figure 6.7 shows one of the processes used in a theatre lighting operation. The company hires out lighting and stage effects equipment to theatrical companies and event organizers. Customers' calls are routed to the store technician. After discussing their requirements, the technician checks the equipment availability file to see if the equipment can be supplied from the company's own stock on the required dates. If the equipment cannot be supplied in-house, customers may be asked whether they want the company to try to obtain it from other possible suppliers. This offer depends on how busy and how helpful individual technicians are. Sometimes customers decline the offer and a 'Guide to Customers' leaflet is sent to the customer. If the customer does want a search, the technician will call potential suppliers in an attempt to find available equipment. If this is not successful the customer is informed, but if suitable equipment is located it is reserved for delivery to the company's site. If equipment can be supplied from the company's own stores, it is reserved on the equipment availability file and the day before it is required a 'kit wagon'

> ✳ Operations principle
> Process mapping is needed to expose the reality of process behaviour.

Figure 6.6 Some common process mapping symbols

is taken to the store where all the required equipment is assembled, taken back to the workshop, checked, and if any equipment is faulty it is repaired at this point. After that it is packed in special cases and delivered to the customer.

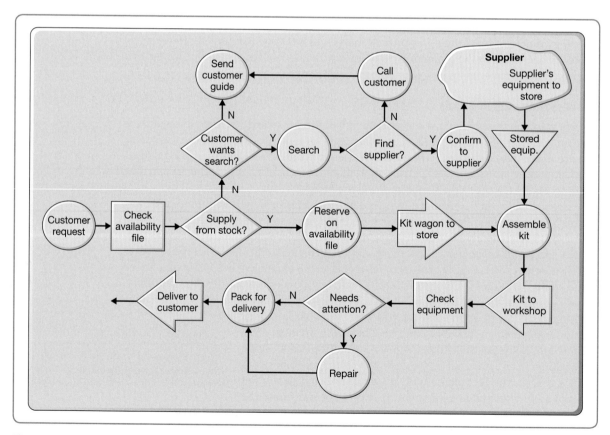

Figure 6.7 Process map for 'enquire to delivery' process at stage lighting operation

Different levels of process mapping

For a large process, drawing process maps at this level of detail can be complex. This is why processes are often mapped at a more aggregated level, called high-level process mapping, before more detailed maps are drawn. Figure 6.8 illustrates this for the total 'supply and install lighting' process in the stage lighting operation. At the highest level the process can be drawn simply as an input–transformation–output process with materials and customers as its input resources and lighting services as outputs. No details of how inputs are transformed into outputs are included. At a slightly lower or more detailed level, what is sometimes called an outline process map (or chart) identifies the sequence of activities but only in a general way. So the process of 'enquire to delivery' that is shown in detail in Figure 6.7 is here reduced to a single activity. At the more detailed level, all the activities are shown in a 'detailed process map' (the activities within the process 'install and test' are shown).

Although not shown in Figure 6.8, an even more 'micro' set of process activities could be mapped within each of the detailed process activities. Such a 'micro' detailed process map could specify every single motion involved in each activity. Some quick-service restaurants, for example, do exactly that. In the lighting hire company example most activities would not be mapped in any more detail than that shown in Figure 6.8. Some activities, such as 'return to base', are probably too straightforward to be worth mapping any further. Other activities, such as 'rectify faulty equipment', may rely on the technician's skills and discretion to the extent that the activity has too much variation and is too complex to

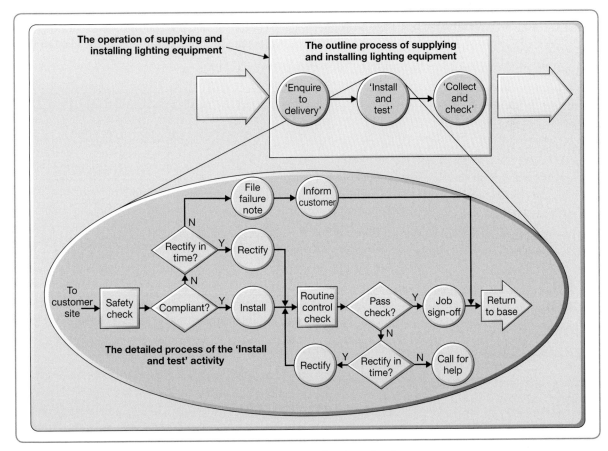

Figure 6.8 The 'supply and install' operations process mapped at three levels

map in detail. Some activities, however, may need mapping in more detail to ensure quality or to protect the company's interests. For example, the activity of safety checking the customer's site to ensure that it is compliant with safety regulations will need specifying in some detail to ensure that the company can prove it exercised its legal responsibilities.

Process visibility

It is sometimes useful to map such processes in a way that makes the degree of visibility of each part of the process obvious. This allows those parts of the process with high visibility to be designed so that they enhance the customer's perception of the process. Figure 6.9 shows yet another part of the lighting equipment company's operation: 'the collect and check' process. The process is mapped to show the visibility of each activity to the customer. Here four levels of visibility are used. There is no hard and fast rule about this; many processes simply distinguish between those activities that the customer *could* see and those that the customer could not. The boundary between these two categories is often called the 'line of visibility'. In Figure 6.9 three categories of visibility are shown. At the very highest level of visibility, above the 'line of interaction', are those activities that involve direct interaction between the lighting company's staff and the customer. Other activities take place at the customer's site or in the presence of the customer but involve less or no direct interaction. Yet further activities (the two transport activities in this case) have some degree of visibility because they take place away from the company's base and are visible to potential customers, but are not visible to the immediate customer.

Throughput time, cycle time and work-in-progress

So far we have looked at the more conceptual (process types) and descriptive (process mapping) aspects of process design. We now move on to the equally important analytical perspective. And the first stage is to understand the nature of, and relationship between, throughput time, cycle time and work-in-progress. As a reminder; throughput time is the elapsed time

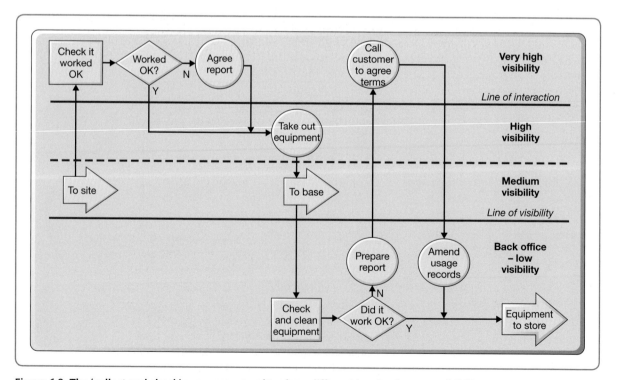

Figure 6.9 The 'collect and check' process mapped to show different levels of process visibility

Sometimes it gets embarrassing when customers see through the line of visibility. This happened when staff at Sainsbury's, a UK supermarket, mistakenly put up in its window a poster encouraging its workers to get customers to spend more. The poster, urging staff to get people to spend an extra 50p, appeared in a store in East London. It read: *'Fifty pence challenge – Let's encourage every customer to spend an additional 50p during each shopping trip between now and the year-end.'* Unfortunately, before the mistake was noticed, a customer took a picture and posted it on Twitter saying: *'.@sainsburys not sure this is supposed to be in your window'.* Quickly Sainsbury's tweeted back saying it should have remained behind closed doors and was meant for staff only. A spokesperson for Sainsbury's said: *'We often use posters to make store targets fun* *and achievable for our colleagues. They are intended for colleague areas in the store, but this one was mistakenly put on public display.'*

Source: Shutterstock.com: Ollyy

between an item entering the process and leaving it; cycle time is the average time between items being processed; and work-in-progress is the number of items within the process at any point in time. In addition the work content for each item will also be important for some analyses. It is the total amount of work required to produce a unit of output. For example, suppose that in an assemble-to-order sandwich shop, the time to assemble and sell a sandwich (the work content) is two minutes and that two people are staffing the process. Each member of staff will serve a customer every two minutes; therefore, every two minutes, two customers were being served and so on average a customer is emerging from the process every minute (the cycle time of the process). When customers join the queue in the process they become work-in-progress (sometimes written as WIP). If the queue is 10 people long (including that customer) when the customer joins it, he or she will have to wait 10 minutes to emerge from the process. Or put more succinctly:

> ✳ **Operations principle**
>
> Process analysis derives from an understanding of the required process cycle time.

$$\text{Throughput time} = \text{Work-in-progress} \times \text{Cycle time}$$

In this case: 10-minute wait = 10 people in the system × 1 minute per person

Little's law

This mathematical relationship (throughput time = work-in-progress × cycle time) is called Little's law. It is simple but very useful, and it works for any stable process. Little's law states that the average number of things in the system is the product of the average rate at which things leave the system and average time each one spends in the system. Or, put another way, the average number of objects in a queue is the product of the entry rate and the average holding time. For example, suppose it is decided that in a new sandwich assembly and sales process, the average number of customers in the process should be limited to around 10 and the maximum time a customer is in the process should be on average four minutes. If the time to assemble and sell a sandwich (from customer request to the customer leaving the process) in the new process has been reduced to 1.2 minutes, how many staff should be serving?

Putting this into Little's law:

$$\text{Throughput time} = 4 \text{ minutes}$$

And:

$$\text{Work-in-progress, WIP} = 10$$

So, since:

$$\text{Throughput time} = \text{WIP} \times \text{cycle time}$$

$$\text{Cycle time} = \frac{\text{Throughput time}}{\text{WIP}}$$

$$\text{Cycle time for the process} = \frac{4}{10} = 0.4 \text{ minutes}$$

That is, a customer should emerge from the process every 0.4 minutes, on average. Given that an individual can be served in 1.2 minutes:

$$\text{The number of servers required} = \frac{1.2}{0.4} = 3$$

> **✳ Operations principle**
>
> Little's law states that throughput time = work-in-progress × cycle time.

In other words, three servers would serve three customers in 1.2 minutes, that is one customer in 0.4 minutes.

Worked example

Mike was totally confident in his judgement: *'You'll never get them back in time'*, he said. *'They aren't just wasting time, the process won't allow them to all have their coffee and get back for 11 o'clock.'* Looking outside the lecture theatre, Mike and his colleague Dick were watching the 20 business people who were attending the seminar queuing to be served coffee and biscuits. The time was 10.45 am and Dick knew that unless they were all back in the lecture theatre at 11 o'clock there would be no hope of finishing his presentation before lunch. *'I'm not sure why you're so pessimistic'*, said Dick. *'They seem to be interested in what I have to say and I think they will want to get back to hear how operations management will change their lives.'* Mike shook his head: *'I'm not questioning their motivation'*, he said. *'I'm questioning the ability of the process out there to get through them all in time. I have been timing how long it takes to serve the coffee and biscuits. Each coffee is being made fresh and the time between the server asking each customer what they want and them walking away with their coffee and biscuits is taking 48 seconds. Remember that, according to Little's law, throughput equals work in process multiplied by cycle time. If the work in process is the 20 managers in the queue and cycle time is 48 seconds, the total throughput time is going to 20 multiplied by 0.8 minutes which equals 16 minutes. Add to that sufficient time for the last person to drink their coffee and you must expect a total throughput time of a bit over 20 minutes. You just haven't allowed long enough for the process.'* Dick was impressed: *'Er... what did you say that law was called again?'* *'Little's law'*, said Mike.

Worked example

Every year it was the same. All the workstations in the building had to be renovated (tested, new software installed, etc.) and there was only one week in which to do it. The one week fell in the middle of the August vacation period when the renovation process would cause minimum disruption to normal working. Last year the company's 500 workstations had all been renovated within one working week (40 hours). Each renovation last year took on average 2 hours and 25 technicians had completed the process within the week. This year there would be 530 workstations to renovate but the company's IT support unit had devised a faster testing and renovation routine that would take on average only 1½ hours instead of 2 hours. How many technicians will be needed this year to complete the renovation processes within the week?

Last year:

$$\text{Work-in-progress (WIP)} = 500 \text{ workstations}$$

$$\text{Time available } (T_t) = 40 \text{ hours}$$

$$\text{Average time to renovate} = 2 \text{ hours}$$

$$\text{Therefore throughput rate } (T_r) = 1/2 \text{ hour per technician}$$

$$= 0.5N$$

where N = Number of technicians

From Little's law:

$$\text{WIP} = T_t \times T_r$$

$$500 = 40 \times 0.5N$$

$$N = \frac{500}{40 \times 0.5}$$

$$= 25 \text{ technicians}$$

This year:

$$\text{Work in progress (WIP)} = 530 \text{ workstations}$$

$$\text{Time available} = 40 \text{ hours}$$

$$\text{Average time to renovate} = 1.5 \text{ hours}$$

$$\text{Throughput rate } (T_r) = 1/1.5 \text{ per technician}$$

$$= 0.67N$$

where N = Number of technicians

From Little's law:

$$\text{WIP} = T_t \times T_r$$

$$530 = 40 \times 0.67N$$

$$N = \frac{530}{40 \times 0.67}$$

$$= 19.88 \text{ (say 20) technicians}$$

Throughput efficiency

This idea that the throughput time of a process is different from the work content of whatever it is processing has important implications. What it means is that for significant amounts of time no useful work is being done to the materials, information or customers that are progressing through the process. In the case of the simple example of the sandwich process described earlier, customer throughput time is restricted to 4 minutes, but the work content of the task (serving the customer) is only 1.2 minutes. So, the item being processed (the customer) is only being 'worked on' for $1.2/4 = 30$ per cent of its time. This is called the throughput efficiency of the process.

In this case the throughput efficiency is very high, relative to most processes, perhaps because the 'items' being processed are customers who react badly to waiting. In most material and information transforming processes, throughput efficiency is far lower, usually in single percentage figures.

A vehicle licensing centre receives application documents, keys in details, checks the information provided on the application, classifies the application according to the type of licence required, confirms payment and then issues and mails the licence. It is currently processing an average of 5,000 licences for eight hours every day. A recent spot check found 15,000 applications that were 'in progress' or waiting to be processed. The sum of all activities that are required to process an application is 25 minutes. What is the throughput efficiency of the process?

$$\text{Work in progress} = 15000 \text{ applications}$$

$$\text{Cycle time} = \text{Time producing}$$

$$\frac{\text{Time producing}}{\text{Number produced}} = \frac{8 \text{ hours}}{5{,}000} = \frac{480 \text{ minutes}}{5{,}000} = 0.96 \text{ minutes}$$

From Little's law:

$$\text{Throughput time} = \text{WIP} \times \text{Cycle time}$$

$$= 15{,}000 \times 0.096$$

$$= 1{,}440 \text{ minutes} = 24 \text{ hours} = 3 \text{ days of working}$$

Although the process is achieving a throughput time of 3 days (which seems reasonable for this kind of process) the applications are only being worked on for 1.7 per cent of the time they are in the process.

Value-added throughput efficiency

The approach to calculating throughput efficiency that is described above assumes that all the 'work content' is actually needed. Therefore, work content is actually dependent upon the methods and technology used to perform the task. It may be also that individual elements of a task may not be considered 'value-added'. So, value-added throughput efficiency restricts the concept of work content to only those tasks that are literally adding value to whatever is being processed. This often eliminates activities such as movement, delays and some inspections.

For example, if, in the licensing worked example, of the 25 minutes of work content only 20 minutes was actually adding value, then:

$$\text{Value added throughput efficiency} = \frac{20}{1{,}440} = 1.39\%$$

Workflow[11]

When the transformed resource in a process is information (or documents containing information), and when information technology is used to move, store and manage the information, process design is sometimes called 'workflow' or 'workflow management'. It is defined as 'the automation of procedures where documents, information or tasks are passed between participants according to a defined set of rules to achieve, or contribute to, an overall business goal'. Although workflow may be managed manually, it is almost always managed using an IT system. The term is also often associated with business process re-engineering (see Chapters 1 and 16). More specifically, workflow is concerned with the following:

- Analysis, modelling, definition and subsequent operational implementation of business processes.
- The technology that supports the processes.
- The procedural (decision) rules that move information/documents through processes.
- Defining the process in terms of the sequence of work activities, the human skills needed to perform each activity and the appropriate IT resources.

Process bottlenecks

A bottleneck in a process is the activity or stage where congestion occurs because the work-load placed is greater than the capacity to cope with it. In other words, it is the most over-loaded part of a process. And as such it will dictate the rate at which the whole process can operate. For example, look at the simple process illustrated in Figure 6.10. It has four stages and the total amount of work to complete the work required for each item passing through the process is 10 minutes. In this simple case each of the four stages has the same capacity. In the first case (a) the 10 minutes of work is equally allocated between the four stages, each having 2.5 minutes of work. This means that items will progress smoothly through the process without any stage holding up the flow, and the cycle time of the process is 2.5 minutes. In the second case (b) the work has not been allocated evenly. In fact this is usually the case because it is difficult (in fact close to impossible) to allocate work absolutely equally. In this case stage 4 of the process has the greatest load (3 minutes). It is the bottleneck, and will constrain the cycle time of the process to 3 minutes.

Bottlenecks reduce the efficiency of a process because, although the bottleneck stage will be fully occupied, the other stages will be under-loaded. In fact the total amount of time invested in processing each item is four times the cycle time because, for every unit produced, all four stages have invested an amount of time equal to the cycle time. When the work is equally allocated between the stages, the total time invested in each product or service produced is $4 \times 2.5 = 10$ minutes. However, when work is unequally allocated, as illustrated, the time invested is $3.0 \times 4 = 12$ minutes. So, in total 2.0 minutes of time, 16.67 per cent of the total, is wasted. The activity of trying to allocate work equally between stages is called 'balancing', and the wasted time, expressed as a percentage, is called 'balancing loss'.

Balancing work time allocation

Allocating work to process stages must respect the 'precedence' of the individual tasks that make up the total work content of the job that the process is performing. The most common way of showing task precedence is by using a 'precedence diagram'. This is a representation of

Figure 6.10 The bottleneck is that part of the process that is the most overloaded relative to its capacity

the ordering of the elements, where individual tasks are represented by circles connected by arrows, which signify the ordering of the tasks. Figure 6.11 in the following worked example illustrates how precedence diagrams can be used.

Worked example

Karlstad Kakes (KK) is a manufacturer of speciality cakes, which has recently obtained a contract to supply a major supermarket chain with a speciality cake in the shape of a space rocket. It has been decided that the volumes required by the supermarket warrant a special production process to perform the finishing, decorating and packing of the cake. This line would have to carry out the elements shown in Table 6.2.

Table 6.2 The individual tasks that make up the total job of the finishing, decorating and packing of the cake

Task a: De-tin and trim	Task d: Clad in top fondant	Task g: Apply blue icing
Task b: Reshape	Task e: Apply red icing	Task h: Fix transfers
Task c: Apply base fondant	Task f: Apply green icing	Task i: To base and pack

Figure 6.11 shows the precedence diagram for the total job. The initial order from the supermarket is for 5,000 cakes a week and the number of hours worked by the factory is 40 per week. From this:

$$\text{The required cycle time} = \frac{40 \text{ hours} \times 60 \text{ minutes}}{4,000}$$

$$= 0.48 \text{ minutes}$$

$$\text{The required number of stages} = \frac{1.68 \text{ minutes (the total work content)}}{0.48 \text{ minutes (the required cycle time)}}$$

$$= 3.5 \text{ stages}$$

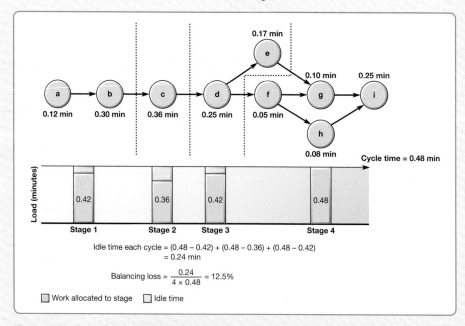

Figure 6.11 Precedence diagram for Karlstad Kakes with allocation of tasks to each stage

This means four stages.

Working from the left on the precedence diagram, tasks a and b can be allocated to stage 1. Allocating task c to stage 1 would exceed the cycle time. In fact, only task c can be allocated to stage 2 because including task d would again exceed the cycle time. Task d can be allocated to stage 3. Either task e or f can also be allocated to stage 3, but not both or the cycle time would be exceeded. In this case task e is chosen. The remaining tasks then are allocated to stage 4. The dashed lines in Figure 6.11 show the final allocation of tasks to each of the four stages.

Arranging the stages

All the stages necessary to fulfil the requirements of the process may not be arranged in a sequential 'single line'. For example, suppose a mortgage application process requires four stages working on the task to maintain a cycle time of one application processed every 15 minutes. One possible arrangement of the four stages would be to arrange them sequentially, each stage having 15 minutes' worth of work. However, (theoretically) the same output rate could also be achieved by arranging the four stages as two shorter lines, each of two stages with 30 minutes' worth of work each. Alternatively, following this logic to its ultimate conclusion, the stages could be arranged as four parallel stages, each responsible for the whole work content. Figure 6.12 shows these options.

This is a simplified example, but it represents a genuine issue. Should the process be organized as a single 'long thin' arrangement, or as several 'short fat' parallel arrangements, or somewhere in between? (Note that 'long' means the number of stages and 'fat' means the amount of work allocated to each stage.) In any particular situation there are usually technical constraints which limit either how 'long and thin' or how 'short and fat' the process can be, but there is usually a range of possible options within which a choice needs to be made. The advantages of each extreme of the 'long thin' to 'short fat' spectrum are very different and help to explain why different arrangements are adopted.

The advantages of the long thin arrangement include:

- *Controlled flow of items.* This is easy to manage.
- *Simple handling.* This is especially so if the items being processed are heavy, large or difficult to move.
- *Lower capital requirements.* If a specialist piece of equipment is needed for one task in the job, only one piece of equipment would need to be purchased; on short fat arrangements every stage would need one.
- *More efficient operation.* If each stage is performing only a small part of the total job, the person at the stage will have a higher proportion of direct productive work as opposed to the non-productive parts of the job, such as picking up tools and materials.

(This latter point is particularly important and is fully explained in Chapter 9 when we discuss job design.)

The advantages of the short fat arrangement include:

- *Higher mix flexibility.* If the process needs to work on several types of item, each stage or whole process could specialize in different types.
- *Higher volume flexibility.* As volume varies, stages can simply be closed down or started up as required; long thin arrangements would need rebalancing each time the cycle time changed.
- *Higher robustness.* If one stage breaks down or ceases operation in some way, the other parallel stages are unaffected; a long thin arrangement would cease operating completely.
- *Less monotonous work.* In the mortgage example, the staff in the short fat arrangement are repeating their tasks only every hour; in the long thin arrangement it is every 15 minutes.

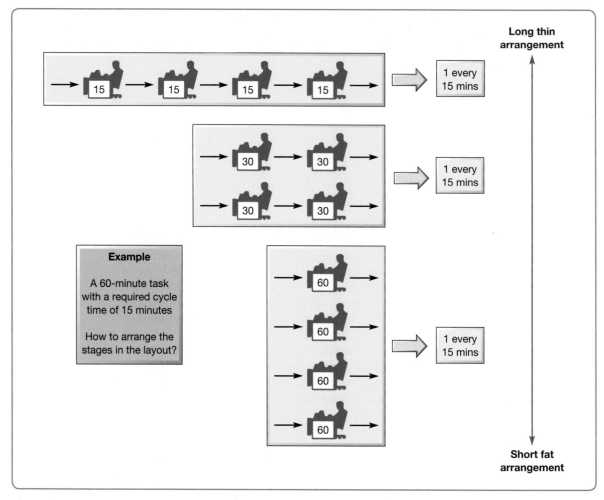

Figure 6.12 The arrangement of stages in a process can be described on a spectrum from 'long thin' to 'short fat'

The effects of process variability

So far in our treatment of process design we have assumed that there is no significant variability either in the demand to which the process is expected to respond, or in the time taken for the process to perform its various activities. Clearly, this is not the case in reality. So, it is important to look at the variability that can affect processes and take account of it.

There are many reasons why variability occurs in processes. These can include: the late (or early) arrival of material, information or customers; a temporary malfunction or breakdown of process technology within a stage of the process; the recycling of 'mis-processed' materials, information or customers to an earlier stage in the process; variation in the requirements of items being processed; etc. All these sources of variation interact with each other, but result in two fundamental types of variability:

● Variability in the demand for processing at an individual stage within the process, usually expressed in terms of variation in the inter-arrival times of items to be processed.
● Variation in the time taken to perform the activities (that is, process a unit) at each stage.

To understand the effect of arrival variability on process performance it is first useful to examine what happens to process performance in a very simple process as arrival time changes under conditions of no variability. For example, the simple process shown in Figure 6.13 is composed of one stage that performs exactly 10 minutes of work. Items arrive at the process at a constant and predictable rate. If the arrival rate is one unit every 30 minutes, then the process will be utilized for only 33.33 per cent of the time, and the items will never have to wait to be processed. This is shown as point A in Figure 6.13. If the arrival rate increases to one arrival every 20 minutes, the utilization increases to 50 per cent, and again the items will not have to wait to be processed. This is point B in Figure 6.13. If the arrival rate increases to one arrival every 10 minutes, the process is now fully utilized, but, because a unit arrives just as the previous one has finished being processed, no unit has to wait. This is point C in Figure 6.13. However, if the arrival rate ever exceeded one unit every 10 minutes, the waiting line in front of the process activity would build up indefinitely, as is shown as point D in Figure 6.13. So, in a perfectly constant and predictable world, the relationship between process waiting time and utilization is a rectangular function as shown by the red line in Figure 6.13.

However, when arrival and process times are variable, then sometimes the process will have items waiting to be processed, while at other times the process will be idle, waiting for items to arrive. Therefore the process will have a 'non-zero' average queue and also be under-utilized in the same period. So, a more realistic point is that shown as point X in Figure 6.13. If the average arrival time were to be changed with the same variability, the blue line in Figure 6.13 would show the relationship between average waiting time and process utilization. As the process moves closer to 100 per cent utilization, the higher the average waiting time will become. Or, to put it another way, the only way to guarantee very low waiting times for the items is to suffer low process utilization.

The greater the variability in the process, the more the waiting time utilization deviates from the simple rectangular function of the 'no variability' conditions that was shown in Figure 6.13. A set of curves for a typical process is shown in Figure 6.14(a). This phenomenon has important implications for the design of processes. In effect it presents three options to

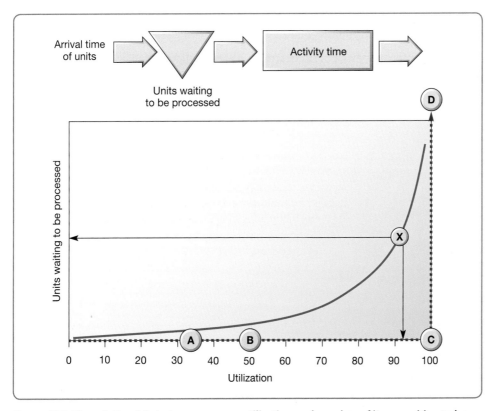

Figure 6.13 **The relationship between process utilization and number of items waiting to be processed for constant, and variable, arrival and process times**

Figure 6.14 The relationship between process utilization and number of items waiting to be processed for variable arrival and activity times

process designers wishing to improve the waiting time or utilization performance of their processes, as shown in Figure 6.14(b). Either:

- accept long average waiting times and achieve high utilization (point X);
- accept low utilization and achieve short average waiting times (point Y).

Or:

- reduce the variability in arrival times, activity times, or both, and achieve higher utilization and short waiting times (point Z).

To analyse processes with both inter-arrival and activity time variability, queuing or 'waiting line' analysis can be used. This is treated in the Supplement to Chapter 11. But do not dismiss the relationship shown in Figures 6.13 and 6.14 as some minor technical phenomenon. It is far more than this. It identifies an important choice in process design that could have strategic implications. Which is more important to a business: fast throughput time or high utilization of its resources? The only way to have both of these simultaneously is to reduce variability in its processes, which may itself require strategic decisions such as limiting the degree of customization of products or services, or imposing stricter limits on how products or services can be delivered to customers, and so on. It also demonstrates an important point concerned with the day-to-day management of process – the only way to guarantee absolutely 100 per cent utilization of resources is to accept an infinite amount of work-in-progress and/or waiting time.

> ✱ Operations principle
>
> Process variability results in simultaneous waiting and resource under-utilization.

OPERATIONS IN PRACTICE **Shouldice Hospital cuts variability[12]**

Shouldice Hospital is a Canadian hernia treatment hospital. Its approach to hernia treatment started when Dr Earle Shouldice, the founder, removed the appendix from a 7-year-old girl who refused to stay quietly in bed. In spite of her activity, no harm was done. In fact he found that encouraging post-operative activity could make recovery times shorter and more predictable. The hospital has a very standardized surgical procedure, called the 'Shouldice method', that all its surgeons follow strictly. Pre-surgery, Shouldice sends surveys to its patients asking for information that helps ensure that the patients are good candidates for the treatment Shouldice offers (this further helps reduce variability in process time). Shouldice requires patients to be at an acceptable weight appropriate to their height. Prospective patients who are overweight must lose weight. Patients enter the hospital the day before surgery and are given a briefing about the procedures to be followed the next day. The night before the operation is also intended as an opportunity for patients to come to know each other – Shouldice encourages patients to work together to promote recovery. The hospital schedules the surgeries in such a way that variability in the arrivals of customers is virtually non-existent. This means that Shouldice can operate in a routine and regular manner. This means that it can keep nearly all its beds full without creating customer waits. The procedure most commonly used at Shouldice involves sewing muscle layers together in an overlapping manner, a technique that is said to be particularly reliable. After discharge, Shouldice sends out an email newsletter to all of its patients that includes a questionnaire for Shouldice's post-operative follow-up programme, which shows that fewer than 1 per cent of patients have a recurrence after hernia repair. The questionnaire also helps the hospital to refine the knowledge that keeps its procedures reliable. So, by reducing the variability in its operations ('operations' in both senses of the word) the hospital has designed a set of processes that can both be highly utilized and reduce customer waiting time.

SUMMARY ANSWERS TO KEY QUESTIONS

❯ What is process design?

- Design is the activity which shapes the physical form and purpose of both products and services and the processes that produce them.
- The design activity is more likely to be successful if the complementary activities of product or service design and process design are coordinated.

❯ What should be the objectives of process design?

- The overall purpose of process design is to meet the needs of customers through achieving appropriate levels of quality, speed, dependability, flexibility and cost.
- The design activity must also take account of environmental issues. These include examination of the source and suitability of materials, the sources and quantities of energy consumed, the amount and type of waste material, the life of the product itself, and the end-of-life state of the product.

❯ How do volume and variety affect process design?

- The overall nature of any process is strongly influenced by the volume and variety of what it has to process.
- The concept of process types summarizes how volume and variety affect overall process design.
- In manufacturing, these process types are (in order of increasing volume and decreasing variety) project, jobbing, batch, mass and continuous processes. In service operations, although there is less consensus on the terminology, the terms often used (again in order of increasing volume and decreasing variety) are professional services, service shops and mass services.

- Processes are designed initially by breaking them down into their individual activities. Often common symbols are used to represent types of activity. The sequence of activities in a process is then indicated by the sequence of symbols representing activities. This is called 'process mapping'. Alternative process designs can be compared using process maps and improved processes considered in terms of their operations performance objectives.

- Process performance in terms of throughput time, work-in-progress and cycle time is related by a formula known as Little's law: throughput time equals work-in-progress multiplied by cycle time.

- Variability has a significant effect on the performance of processes, particularly the relationship between waiting time and utilization.

CASE STUDY

The Action Response Applications Processing Unit (ARAPU)

Introduction

Action Response is a London-based charity dedicated to providing fast responses to critical situations throughout the world. It was founded by Susan N'tini, its Chief Executive, to provide relatively short-term aid for small projects until it could obtain funding from larger donors. The charity receives requests for cash aid usually from an intermediary charity and looks to process the request quickly, providing funds where and when they are needed. 'Give a man a fish and you feed him today, teach him to fish and you feed him for life; it's an old saying and it makes sense but, and this is where Action Response comes in, he might starve while he's training to catch fish.' (Susan N'tini)

Nevertheless, Susan does have some worries. She faces two issues in particular. First, she is receiving complaints that funds are not getting through quickly enough. Second, the costs of running the operation are starting to spiral. She explains: 'We are becoming a victim of our own success. We have striven to provide greater accessibility to our funds; people can access application forms via the internet, by post and by phone. But we are in danger of losing what we stand for. It is taking longer to get the money to where it is needed and our costs are going up. We are in danger of failing on one of our key objectives: to minimize the proportion of our turnover that is spent on administration. At the same time we always need to be aware of the risk of bad publicity through making the wrong decisions. If we don't check applications thoroughly, funds may go to the "wrong" place and if the newspapers gets hold of the story we would run a real risk of losing the goodwill, and therefore the funds, from our many supporters.'

Susan held regular meetings with key stakeholders. One charity that handled a large number of applications for people in Nigeria told her of frequent complaints about

Source: Shutterstock.com: Phovoir

the delays over the processing of the applications. A second charity representative complained that when he telephoned to find out the status of an application, the ARAPU staff did not seem to know where it was or how long it might be before it was complete. Furthermore he felt that this lack of information was eroding his relationship with his own clients, some of whom were losing faith in him as a result: 'trust is so important in the relationship', he explained.

Some of Susan's colleagues, while broadly agreeing with her anxieties over the organization's responsiveness and efficiency, took a slightly different perspective. 'One of the really good things about Action Response is that we are more flexible than most charities. If there is a need and if they need support until one of the larger charities can step in, then we will always consider a request for aid. I would not like to see any move towards high process efficiency harming our ability to be open-minded and consider requests that might seem a little unusual at first.' (Jacqueline Horton, Applications Assessor)

Others saw the charity as performing an important counselling role. *'Remember that we have gained a lot of experience in this kind of short-term aid. We are often the first people that are in a position to advise on how to apply for larger and longer term funding. If we developed this aspect of our work we would again be fulfilling a need that is not adequately supplied at the moment.'* (Stephen Nyquist, Applications Assessor)

The Action Response Applications Processing Unit (ARAPU)

Potential aid recipients, or the intermediary charities representing them, apply for funds using a standard form. These forms can be downloaded from the Internet or requested via a special help line. Sometimes the application will come directly from an individual community leader but more usually it will come via an intermediary charity that can help the applicant to complete the form. The application is sent to ARAPU, usually by fax or post (some were submitted online, but few communities have this facility).

ARAPU employs seven applications assessors with support staff who are responsible for data entry, coding, filing and 'completing' (staff who prepare payment, or explain why no aid can be given). In addition, a board of non-paid trustees meets every Thursday, to approve the assessors' decisions. The unit's IT system maintained records of all transactions, providing an update on the number of applications received, approved, declined, and payments allocated. These reports identified that the unit received about 300 new applications per week and responded to about the same number (the unit operates a 35-hour week). But while the unit's financial targets were being met, the trend indicated that cost per application was increasing. The target for the turnaround of an application, from receipt of application to response, was 20 days, and although this was not measured formally, it was generally assumed that turnaround time was longer than this. Accuracy had never been an issue as all files were thoroughly assessed to ensure that all the relevant data was collected before the applications were processed. Productivity seemed high and there was always plenty of work waiting for processing at each section, with the exception that the 'completers' were sometimes waiting for work to come from the committee on a Thursday. Susan had conducted an inspection of all sections' in-trays that had revealed a rather shocking total of about 2,000 files waiting within the process, not counting those waiting for further information.

Processing applications

The processing of applications is a lengthy procedure requiring careful examination by applications assessors trained to make well-founded assessments in line with the charity's guidelines and values. Incoming applications are opened by one of the four 'receipt' clerks who check that all the necessary forms have been included in the application; the receipt clerks take about 10 minutes per application. These are then sent to the coding staff, in batches, twice a day. The five coding clerks allocate a unique identifier to each application and

key the information on the application into the system. The coding stage takes about 20 minutes for each application. Files are then sent to the senior applications assessor's secretary's desk. As assessors become available, the secretary provides the next job in the line to the assessor.

About 100 of the cases seen by the assessors each week are put aside after only 10 minutes of 'scanning' because the information is ambiguous, so further information is needed. The assessor returns these files to the secretaries, who write to the applicant (usually via the intermediate charity) requesting additional information, and return the file to the 'receipt' clerks who 'store' the file until the further information eventually arrives (usually between one and eight weeks). When it does arrive, the file enters the process and progresses through the same stages again. Of the applications that require no further information, around half (150) are accepted and half (150) declined. On average, those applications that were not 'recycled' took around 60 minutes to assess.

All the applications, whether approved or declined, are stored prior to ratification. Every Thursday the Committee of Trustees meets formally to approve the applications assessors' decisions. The committee's role is to sample the decisions to ensure that the guidelines of the charity are upheld. In addition the committee will review any particularly unusual cases highlighted by the applications assessors. Once approved by the committee, the files are then taken to the completion officers. There are three 'decline' officers whose main responsibility is to compile a suitable response to the applicant, pointing out why the application failed and offering, if possible, to provide helpful advice. An experienced declines officer takes about 30 minutes to finalize the file and write a suitable letter. Successful files are passed to the four 'payment' officers where again the file is completed, letters (mainly standard letters) are created and payment instructions are given to the bank. This usually takes around 50 minutes, including dealing with any queries from the bank about payment details. Finally the paperwork itself is sent, with the rest of the file, to two 'dispatch' clerks who complete the documents and mail them to the applicant. The dispatch activity takes, on average, 10 minutes for each application.

The feeling among the staff was generally good. When Susan consulted the team members, they said their work was clear and routine, but their life was made difficult by charities that rang in expecting them to be able to tell them the status of an application they had submitted. It could take staff hours, sometimes days, to find any individual file. Indeed two of the 'receipt' clerks now were working almost full-time on this activity. They also said that charities frequently complained that decision making seemed slow.

QUESTIONS

1 What objectives should the ARAPU process be trying to achieve?

2 What is the main problem with the current ARAPU processes?

3 How could the ARAPU process be improved?

PROBLEMS AND APPLICATIONS

1 Read again the description of fast food drive-through processes in the chapter. (a) Draw a process map that reflects the types of process described. (b) What advantage do you think is given to McDonald's through its decision to establish a call centre for remote order taking for some of its outlets?

2 A laboratory process receives medical samples from hospitals in its area and then subjects them to a number of tests that take place in different parts of the laboratory. The average response time for the laboratory to complete all its tests and mail the results back to the hospital (measured from the time that the sample for analysis arrives) is three days. A recent process map has shown that, of the 60 minutes that is needed to complete all the tests, the tests themselves took 30 minutes, moving the samples between each test area took 10 minutes, and double checking the results took a further 20 minutes. What is the throughput efficiency of this process? What is the value-added throughput efficiency of the process? (State any assumptions that you are making.) If the process is rearranged so that all the tests are performed in the same area, thus eliminating the time to move between test areas, and the tests themselves are improved to half the amount of time needed for double checking, what effect would this have on the value-added throughput efficiency?

3 The regional government office that deals with passport applications is designing a process that will check applications and issue the documents. The number of applications to be processed is 1,600 per week and the time available to process the applications is 40 hours per week.
   (a) What is the required cycle time for the process?
   (b) If the total work content of all the activities that make up the total task of checking, processing and issuing a passport is, on average, 30 minutes, how many people will be needed to meet demand?
   (c) The passport office has a 'clear desk' policy that means that all desks must be clear of work by the end of the day. How many applications should be loaded onto the process in the morning in order to ensure that every one is completed and desks are clear by the end of the day? (Assume a working day of 7.5 hours (450 minutes).)

4 Visit a drive-through, quick-service restaurant and observe the operation for half an hour. You will probably need a stopwatch to collect the relevant timing information. Consider the following questions:
   (a) Where are the bottlenecks in the service (in other words, what seems to take the longest time)?
   (b) How would you measure the efficiency of the process?
   (c) What appear to be the key design principles that govern the effectiveness of this process?
   (d) Using Little's law, how long would the queue have to be before you think it would be not worth joining the queue?

5 Reread the Shouldice Hospital example. How different would the operations issues be at an accident and emergency department?

SELECTED FURTHER READING

Chopra, S., Anupindi, R.,Deshmukh, S.D., Van Mieghem, J.A. and Zemel, E. (2012) *Managing Business Process Flows*, 3rd edn, Pearson, Englewood Cliffs, NJ.

An excellent, although mathematical, approach to process design in general.

Hammer, M. (1990) Reengineering work: don't automate, obliterate, *Harvard Business Review*, July–August.

This is the paper that launched the whole idea of business processes and process management in general to a wider managerial audience. Slightly dated but worth reading.

Hopp, W.J. and Spearman, M.L. (2001) *Factory Physics*, 2nd edn, McGraw-Hill, New York.

Very technical so do not bother with it if you are not prepared to get into the maths. However, some fascinating analysis, especially concerning Little's law.

Mahal, A. (2010) *How Work Gets Done: Business Process Management, Basics and Beyond*, Technics Publications, London.

Certainly not a critical look at process management, but an easily digestible coverage of 'how to do it'.

Smith, H. and Fingar, P. (2003) *Business Process Management: The Third Wave*, Meghan-Kiffer Press, Tampa, FL.

A popular book on process management from a BPR perspective.

7

Layout and flow

Key questions

❯ What is layout and how can it influence performance?

❯ What are the basic layout types used in operations?

❯ How does the appearance of an operation affect its performance?

❯ How should each basic layout type be designed in detail?

INTRODUCTION

The layout of an operation is concerned with the physical positioning of its people and facilities. It is often the first thing most of us would notice when we enter an operation because it determines what it looks like. Layout means deciding where to put all the facilities, desks, machines, equipment and people in the operation. It is also concerned with the physical appearance of an operation in a broader sense. It governs how safe, how attractive, how flexible and how efficient an operation is. It also determines how transformed resources – the materials, information and customers – flow through an operation. Relatively small changes in layout – moving displays in a supermarket, or the changing rooms in a sports centre, or the position of a machine in a factory - can affect the flow through the operation which, in turn, affects the costs and general effectiveness of the operation. Figure 7.1 shows the layout activity in the overall model of design in operations.

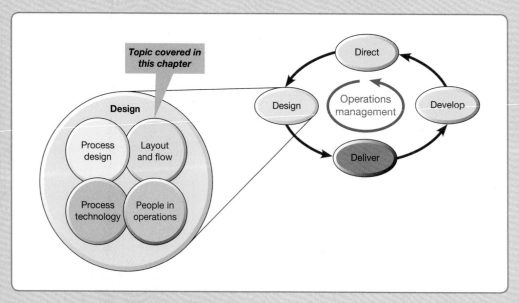

Figure 7.1 This chapter examines layout and flow

In this chapter we are going to do four things. First, we will look briefly at what operations managers are trying to achieve when they lay out (or usually re-lay out) their transforming resources. Second, we describe a number of recognized 'layout types'. These are derived largely from manufacturing, but we will use non-manufacturing examples to demonstrate how they can also be used for a whole range of operations. Third, we look at how the physical appearance of operations influences their effectiveness both for their customers and for the staff working in them. Finally, we look at just some of the (many) detailed techniques that help operations managers to design better layouts.

WHAT IS LAYOUT AND HOW CAN IT INFLUENCE PERFORMANCE?

The 'layout' of an operation or process means how its transforming resources are positioned relative to each other, how its various tasks are allocated to these transforming resources and the general appearance of the transforming resources. Together these three decisions will dictate the pattern and nature of how transformed resources progress through the operation or process (*see* Fig. 7.2). It is an important decision because, if the layout proves wrong, it can lead to over-long or confused flow patterns, customer queues, long process times, inflexible operations, unpredictable flow, high costs and a poor response for whoever is within the operation, whether they are customers or staff. In addition, a radical re-layout can cause disruption to ongoing operations, leading to possible customer dissatisfaction and/or lost operating time. So, because the layout decision can be difficult and expensive, operations managers are reluctant to do it too often. Therefore layout must start with a full appreciation of the objectives that the layout should be trying to achieve.

What makes a good layout?

To a large extent the objectives of any layout will depend on the strategic objectives of the operation, but there are some general objectives that are relevant to all operations. And before considering the various types of layout, it is useful to consider the objectives of the layout activity:

- **Inherent safety** – This is the prerequisite for any layout in any type of operation. All processes that might constitute any physical or other danger to either staff or customers should not be accessible to the unauthorized. Fire exits should be clearly marked with uninhibited access. Pathways should be clearly defined and not cluttered. All signage should be clear and unambiguous.

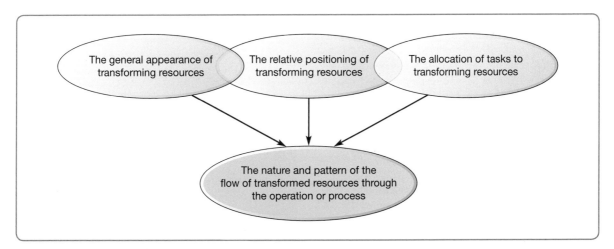

Figure 7.2 Layout involves the relative positioning of transforming resources within operations and processes, the allocation of tasks to the resources and their general appearance, which together dictate the nature and pattern of the flow of transformed resources through the operation or process

Volkswagen and Google pioneer new types of layouts[1]

The arrangement and physical appearance of operations in many industries are changing as the nature of competition changes and the needs of the people who work in them change. Here are two examples.

Source: Agencja Fotograficzna Caro

Volkswagen's transparent factory

Do not assume that the idea of the appearance of an operation applies only to high-contact service operations. VW's 'transparent factory' in the heart of Dresden in Germany certainly is visually impressive and does not look like a traditional automobile assembly plant. Inside the factory, which makes the very upmarket Phaeton sedan, the floors are expensive Canadian maple, the factory walls are made of clear glass (a loudspeaker outside imitates territorial bird sounds to keep birds from flying into the glass), and the workers all wear white coats and gloves; in fact the operation has the atmosphere of a research lab rather than a factory. Partly this is because the dirtier, noisier processes such as pressing, welding and the painting of steel bodies take place in another facility. Partly, though, it is because the facility is as much a customer relations and marketing device as it is a production plant. Thousands of visitors tour the plant each year. Its layout is visitor friendly and is designed to receive 250 tourists per day by advance reservation who are charged €5 each. Customers or prospective customers are not charged. The ground floor houses a restaurant, and on the lower level there is a simulator that allows visitors a virtual test drive of the Phaeton. Yet the transparent factory is also a serious manufacturing operation, producing an average of 44 Phaetons a day, most of which are destined for China, Germany and South Korea.

Google's revolutionary offices

Operations, and therefore operations layouts, are not confined to factories, warehouses, shops and other such workspaces. Many of us who work in operations actually work in offices. In financial services, government, call centres and the creative industries, all work for the most part sitting at their desks. (One estimate is that over 70 per cent of the UK's GDP is generated by people working in offices, though it is admittedly difficult to check.) So the layout of offices can affect operations performance for these industries just as much as layout can in a factory. And of all companies whose staff work in offices, Google, like many high-tech companies, is paying much more attention to its employees' work environment, the better to promote creativity and productivity. In fact, Google is famous for its innovative use

of its workspaces. This is because Google thrives on creativity and it believes that the designs of its offices will provide every employee with a space that will encourage creativity. Google put a lot of time and money into designing what it believes is the perfect work environment – one that can mix business with pleasure in the sense that the staff can relax and unwind during their breaks. The layouts of Google's offices are designed to promote creativity and collaboration. How people move about the space and who they meet and talk to are vital pieces of information that should contribute to any design. The information needs of the processes underlying activities are clearly an important driver of where the various departments of an organization are located. However, people sometimes are not fully aware of how they are interacting with one another, or with the space where they work. So, in addition to examining the formal needs of people's jobs, it is valuable to examine employee behaviour. For example, where do people actually spend the majority of their time? Where and when do the most productive meetings happen? Where and when do people make phone calls? When is the office at its emptiest? When is it most full (and noisy)?

Elliot Felix led the team that wrote Google's global design guidelines for its offices. '*Google was doubling in*

Source: Alamy Images: Asif's Photography

size every year and building new locations everywhere', he says. 'There was so much concern about what the ingredients of the offices should be and how they would all fit together cohesively for a consistent employee experience. We're never just talking about space. We're talking about culture, etiquette, and rituals. What a lot of people forget is that we imbue space with our values.' There's a rule at Google that nobody should be located more than 100 metres away from food. There are eco-friendly kitchens complete with healthy food sited at strategic locations around the buildings (that is, in addition to the cafeteria). There are quiet places, such as libraries and sometimes aquariums, if staff want somewhere quiet to relax or think through a problem. Some parts of the office look like an apartment, which appeals to those employees who like the idea of 'working from home' at the office. Designing these features in office buildings is partly a consequence of the long hours worked by many people in the high-tech industries. Offices must be equipped with areas for working and areas for relaxing (even if that means playing football, an approach championed by Google).

- **Security** – Similar to safety in some ways, facilities and layouts should ensure that anyone with malicious intent cannot gain access to staff, customers or property.
- **Length of flow** – The flow of materials, information or customers should be channelled by the layout so as to be appropriate for the objectives of the operation. In many operations this means minimizing the distance travelled by transformed resources. However, this is not always the case. In supermarkets, for example, layout objectives can include encouraging customers to 'flow' in particular ways that maximize sales.
- **Minimize delays** – Delays can, of course, be caused by over-long routes through the layout, as described above, but inconvenient placing of facilities, or insufficient capacity allocated to parts of the layout (that is, a bottleneck, *see* previous chapter), may also cause them.
- **Reduce work-in-progress** – Excessive work-in-progress can be caused by bottlenecks, but the layout of a process may be used deliberately to limit the ability of items to accumulate. This involves using what are called 'kanban squares' and are explained in Chapter 15.
- **Clarity of flow** – All flow of materials and customers should be well signposted, clear and evident to staff and customers alike. For example, hospital processes often rely on signposted routes with different coloured lines painted on the floor to indicate the routes to various departments.
- **Staff conditions** – Layouts should be arranged so that staff are located away from noisy or unpleasant parts of the operation. The layout should provide for a well-ventilated, well-lit and, where possible, pleasant working environment.
- **Communication** – Communication between staff can be particularly important for some types of operation, such as those in creative industries. The layouts of some operations are deliberately designed to promote the kind of chance meetings between staff that can lead to the formulation of creative ideas.
- **Management co-ordination** – Supervision and communication should be assisted by the relative location of staff, the use of communication devices and information points.
- **Accessibility** – All machines, plant or equipment should be accessible to a degree that is sufficient for proper inspection, cleaning and maintenance.
- **Use of space** – All layouts should achieve an appropriate use of the total space available in the operation (including height as well as floor space). This usually means minimizing the space used for a particular purpose, but sometimes can mean achieving an impression of spacious luxury, as in the entrance lobby of a high-class hotel.
- **Use of capital** – Capital investment should be minimized (consistent with other objectives) when finalizing layout.
- **Long-term flexibility** – Layouts need to be changed periodically as the needs of the operation change. A good layout will have been devised with the possible future needs of the operation in mind. For example, if demand is likely to increase for a product or service, has the layout been designed to accommodate any future expansion?

- **Image** – The layout of an operation can help to shape the image of an organization, both in its customer markets and in the labour market from which it recruits. The appearance of a layout can be used as a deliberate attempt to establish a company's brand.

As you see, there are many and various objectives to attempt to achieve during the layout activity. Some, such as safety, security and staff welfare, are absolutely required. Others may have to be compromised, or traded off with other objectives. For example, two processes may have need of the same piece of equipment and could quite feasibly share it. This would mean good use of the capital used to acquire that equipment. But both processes using it could mean longer and/or more confused process routes. Buying two pieces of equipment would under-utilize them, but give shorter distance travelled.

WHAT ARE THE BASIC LAYOUT TYPES USED IN OPERATIONS?

Most practical layouts are derived from only four basic layout types. These are:

- Fixed-position layout
- Functional layout
- Cell layout
- Line (sometimes called 'product') layout.

These layout types are loosely related to the process types described in Chapter 6. As Table 7.1 indicates, a process type does not necessarily imply only one particular basic layout.

Fixed-position layout

Fixed-position layout is in some ways a contradiction in terms, since the transformed resources do not move between the transforming resources. Instead of materials, information or customers flowing through an operation, the recipient of the processing is stationary and the equipment, machinery, plant and people who do the processing move as necessary. This could be because the product or the recipient of the service is too large to be moved conveniently, or it might be too delicate to move, or perhaps it could object to being moved. For example:

- *Motorway construction* – the product is too large to move.
- *Open-heart surgery* – patients are too delicate to move.
- *High-class service restaurant* – customers would object to being moved to where food is prepared.
- *Shipbuilding* – the product is too large to move.
- *Mainframe computer maintenance* – the product is too big and probably also too delicate to move, and the customer might object to bringing it in for repair.

Table 7.1 **Alternative layout types for each process type**

Manufacturing Process Type	Potential Layout Types		Service Process Type
Project	Fixed-position layout Functional layout	Fixed-position layout Functional layout Cell layout	Professional Service
Jobbing	Functional layout Cell layout		
Batch	Functional layout Cell layout	Functional layout Cell layout	Service Shop
Mass	Cell layout Product layout		
Continuous	Product layout	Cell layout Product layout	Mass Service

'Factory flow' helps surgery productivity[2]

Even surgery can be seen as a process, and, like any process, it can be improved. Normally patients remain stationary, with surgeons and other theatre staff performing their tasks around the patient. But this idea has been challenged by John Petri, a French consultant orthopaedic surgeon at a hospital in Norfolk in the UK. Frustrated by spending time drinking tea while patients were prepared for surgery, he redesigned the process so that now he moves continually between two theatres. While he is operating on a patient in one theatre, his anaesthetist colleagues are preparing a patient for surgery in another theatre. After finishing with the first patient, the surgeon 'scrubs up', moves to the second operating theatre and begins the surgery on the second patient. While he is doing this the first patient is moved out of the first operating theatre and the third patient is prepared (Fig. 7.3). This method of overlapping operations in different theatres allows him to work for five hours at a time rather than the previous standard session of three and a half hours. 'If you were running a factory', says the surgeon, 'you wouldn't allow your most important and most expensive machine to stand idle. The same is true in a hospital.' Currently used for hip and knee replacements, this layout would not be suitable for all surgical procedures. But since its introduction the surgeon's waiting list has fallen to zero and his productivity has doubled. 'For a small increase in running costs we are able to treat many more patients', said a spokesperson for the hospital management. 'What is important is that clinicians...produce innovative ideas and we demonstrate that they are effective.'

Source: Shutterstock.com: Ingrid W

① 7.20am Anaesthetist prepares patient for surgery in theatre one

Anaesthetist

② 8.00am Surgeon begins first hip operation in theatre one

③ 8.20am Halfway through first operation another anaesthetist prepares second patient in theatre two

④ 9.00am Surgeon finishes first operation, scrubs up and starts operating in theatre two

⑤ 9.20am Halfway through second operation third patient prepared in theatre one

Surgeon

THEATRE ONE

THEATRE TWO

Figure 7.3 'Assembly line' surgery

Functional layout

In functional layout, similar resources or processes are located together. This may be because it is convenient to group them together, or that the utilization of transforming resources is improved. It means that when products, information or customers flow through the operation, they will take a route from activity to activity according to their needs. Different products or customers will have different needs and therefore take different routes. Usually this makes the flow pattern in the operation very complex. Examples of functional layouts include:

- *Hospital* – some processes (for example, X-ray machines and laboratories) are required by several types of patient; some processes (for example, general wards) can achieve high staff and bed utilization.
- *Machining the parts which go into aircraft engines* – some processes (for example, heat treatment) need specialist support (heat and fume extraction); some processes (for example, machining centres) require the same technical support from specialist setter–operators; some processes (for example, grinding machines) get high machine utilization as all parts which need grinding pass through a single grinding section.
- *Supermarket* – some products, such as tinned goods, are convenient to restock if grouped together. Some areas, such as those holding frozen vegetables, need the common technology of freezer cabinets. Others, such as the areas holding fresh vegetables, might be together because, that way, they can be made to look attractive to customers (*see* the opening 'Operations in practice' case).

Like most functional layouts, a library has different types of user with different traffic patterns. The College library in Figure 7.4 has put its users into three categories, as follows (in fact very similar categories are used by retail customers):[3]

- **Browsers** – who seek interesting or useful materials by surfing the Internet, browsing shelves and examining items, and moving around slowly while assessing the value of items.
- **Destination traffic** – who have a specific purpose or errand and are not deterred from it by surroundings or other library materials.
- **Beeline traffic** – who concentrate on goals unconnected with personal use of the library, for example messengers, delivery staff or maintenance workers.

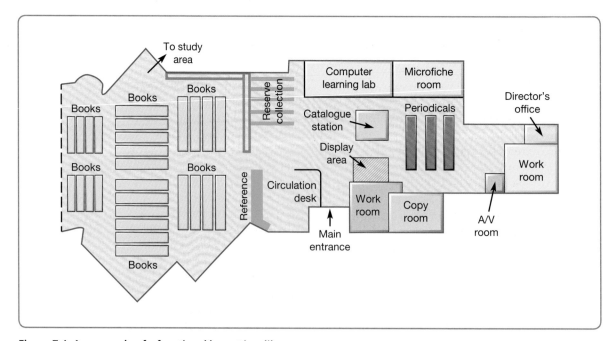

Figure 7.4 **An example of a functional layout in a library**

Based on studies tracking these different types of customer, the library derived the following guidelines for the layout of its library:

- Position displays and services that need to be brought to users' attention at the front of the facility.
- To the right of the entrance should be new acquisitions; items that might be selected on impulse and have no satisfactory substitutes; and items that require repeated exposure before users select them.
- On the left at the front should be items that probably will not be used unless there is maximum convenience for the user, such as the dictionary and the atlas and encyclopaedias.
- The circulation desk should be on the left of the entrance, the last thing the user passes before leaving.
- The rear of the library should house items for which user motivation is strong, such as classroom-assigned materials and meeting rooms, or for which the user is willing to spend time and effort obtaining, such as microfiche printouts.

Cell layout

A cell layout is one where the transformed resources entering the operation are pre-selected (or pre-select themselves) to move to one part of the operation (or cell) in which all the transforming resources, to meet their immediate processing needs, are located. The cell itself may be arranged in either a functional or line (*see* next section) layout. After being processed in the cell, the transformed resources may go on to another cell. In effect, cell layout is an attempt to bring some order to the complexity of flow that characterizes functional layout. Examples of cell layouts include:

- *Some computer component manufacture*– the processing and assembly of some types of computer parts may need a special area dedicated to the manufacturing of parts for one particular customer who has special requirements, such as particularly high-quality levels.
- *'Lunch' products area in a supermarket* – some customers use the supermarket just to purchase sandwiches, savoury snacks, cool drinks, yoghurt, etc., for their lunch. These products are often located close together so that customers who are just buying lunch do not have to search around the store.
- *Maternity unit in a hospital* – customers needing maternity attention are a well-defined group who can be treated together and who are unlikely to need the other facilities of the hospital at the same time that they need the maternity unit.

Although the idea of cell layout is often associated with manufacturing, the same principle can be, and is, used in services. In Figure 7.5 the ground floor of a department store is shown, comprising displays of various types of goods in different parts of the store. In this sense the predominant layout of the store is a functional layout. Each display area can be considered a separate process devoted to selling a particular class of goods – shoes, clothes, books, and so on. The exception is the sports shop. This area is a shop-within-a-shop area that is devoted to many goods that have a common sporting theme. For example, it will stock sports clothes, sports shoes, sports bags, sports magazines, sports books, sports equipment and gifts, and sports energy drinks. Within the 'cell' there are all the products that are also located elsewhere in the store. They have been located in the 'cell' not because they are similar goods (shoes, books and drinks would not usually be located together) but because they are needed to satisfy the needs of a particular type of customer. The store management calculate that enough customers come to the store to buy 'sports goods' in particular (rather than shoes, clothes, books, etc.) to devote an area specifically for them. The store is also aware that someone coming to the store with the intention of purchasing some sports shoes might also be persuaded to buy other sports goods if they are placed in the same area.

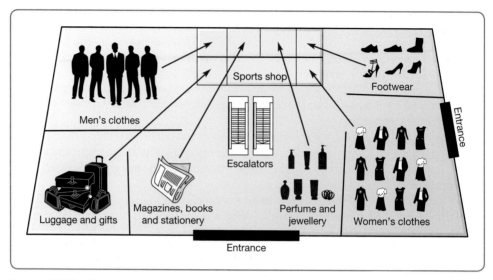

Figure 7.5 The floor plan of a department store showing the sports goods 'shop-within-a-shop cell' within the functional layout of the rest of the store

Line (product) layout

Line layout involves locating the transforming resources entirely for the convenience of the transformed resources. Each product, piece of information or customer follows a prearranged route in which the sequence of activities that are required matches the sequence in which

OPERATIONS IN PRACTICE

Apple's shop-within-a-shop in Harrods[4]

Apple has opened a string of over 300 Apple Stores all over the world in leading locations like London's Regent Street and Covent Garden, Grand Central Station and Fifth Avenue in New York, the Louvre in Paris, and the spectacular Beijing store with its 40-ft (12 m) curved glass exterior. These stores are large, beautifully architected, and in keeping with Apple's brand, the company. Then it was reported that Apple would be opening a store-within-a-store in one of the world's most famous department stores. Harrods is a huge 'upmarket' department store in the heart of London. It covers over five acres (20,000 m²) of land and the store itself features over 1 million square feet (93,000 m²) of selling space. Across this area are over 330 departments that cover clothing, technology accessories, and food. Commentators declared that the Apple brand would fit in well within the Harrods' surroundings, and the Harrods Apple Store, itself, would blend in nicely with the store's noted architecture. The Apple Store will feature most of what makes an Apple Store an Apple Store, like wooden tables and signage. Like most retail 'cells', all the products sold in the Apple Store in Harrods could be sold in other departments. But

Source: Shutterstock.com: Stuart Monk

they are collected together for another purpose. In this case the internal Apple Store supports the Apple brand yet does not inconvenience customers. In fact, for Apple fans, it is more convenient.

the processes have been located. The transformed resources 'flow' along a 'line' of processes according to their 'product' needs. This is why this type of layout is sometimes called flow or product layout. Flow is clear, predictable and therefore relatively easy to control. Usually, it is the standardized requirements of the product or service that lead to operations choosing line layouts. Examples of line layout include:

- *Automobile assembly* – almost all variants of the same model require the same sequence of processes.
- *Mass-immunization programme* – all customers require the same sequence of clerical, medical and counselling activities.
- *Self-service cafeteria* – generally the sequence of customer requirements (starter, main course, dessert and drink) is common to all customers, but layout also helps control customer flow.

But do not think that line layouts are not changing. Even Toyota, the best known of all automobile companies that routinely use this type of layout, is rethinking the assembly line. The appreciation of the Japanese yen has made it difficult for vehicles made in Japan to compete, and while Toyota, like other Japanese firms, has built factories in other parts of the world, if it still wants to manufacture in Japan, cost savings had to be made. Figure 7.6 shows just two of the ideas that Toyota is employing at its Miyagi factory in Japan to make assembly lines even more efficient.[5] The upper illustration shows how Toyota has positioned vehicles sideways rather than the conventional lengthways. A simple idea, but it has the advantage of shortening the line by 35 per cent (which saves on the cost of constructing the line and requires fewer steps by workers) and shortening the distance that workers have to walk between cars (which increases productivity). The lower illustration shows how, instead of the vehicle chassis hanging from overhead conveyor belts, they are positioned on raised platforms. This costs only half as much to construct and allows ceiling heights to be lowered, which is more space efficient and reduces heating and cooling costs by 40 per cent.

Figure 7.6 Contrasting arrangements in product (line) layout for automobile assembly plants

Source: From For Toyota, patriotism and profits may not mix, *Wall Street Journal*, 29/11/2011 (Dawson, C.), Reprinted with permission of Wall Street Journal, Copyright © 2011 Dow Jones & Company, Inc. All Rights Reserved Worldwide. License numbers 3841860034292 and 3841860323322.

Mixed layouts

Many operations either design themselves hybrid layouts which combine elements of some or all of the basic layout types, or use the 'pure' basic layout types in different parts of the operation. For example, a hospital would normally be arranged on functional layout principles – each department representing a particular type of function (the X-ray department, the surgical theatres, the blood-processing laboratory, and so on). Yet within each department, quite different layouts are used. The X-ray department is probably arranged in a functional layout, the surgical theatres in a fixed-position layout, and the blood-processing laboratory in a line layout.

Another example is shown in Figure 7.7. Here a restaurant complex is shown with three different types of restaurant and the kitchen which serves them all. The kitchen is arranged in a functional layout, with the various processes (food storage, food preparation, cooking processes, etc.) grouped together. The traditional service restaurant is arranged in a fixed-position layout. The customers stay at their tables while the food is brought to (and sometimes cooked at) the tables. The buffet restaurant is arranged in a cell-type layout with each buffet area having all the processes (dishes) necessary to serve customers with their starter, main course or dessert. Finally, in the cafeteria restaurant, all customers take the same route when being served with their meal. They may not take the opportunity to be served with every dish but they move through the same sequence of processes.

Cadbury's (see the 'Operations in practice' item) has chosen to use the line layout design for both the production of chocolates and the processing of its visitors. In both cases, volumes are large and the variety offered is limited. Sufficient demand exists for each standard 'product', and the operations objective is to achieve consistent high quality at low cost. Both operations have little volume flexibility, and both would be expensive to change.

What type of layout should an operation choose?

The importance of flow to an operation will depend on its volume and variety characteristics. When volume is very low and variety is relatively high, 'flow' is not a major issue. For example, in telecommunications satellite manufacture, a fixed-position layout is likely to be appropriate because each product is different and because products 'flow' through the operation very infrequently, so it is just not worth arranging facilities to minimize the flow of parts through the operation. With higher volume and lower variety, flow becomes an issue. If the variety is still high, however, an entirely flow-dominated arrangement is difficult because

Figure 7.7 A restaurant complex with all four basic layout types

Chocolate and customers both have a 'line' layout at Cadbury's[6]

Flow of chocolate in the factory

In the famous Cadbury's chocolate factory at Bournville, on the outskirts of Birmingham, UK, production processes are based on a *line layout*. This has allowed Cadbury's engineers to develop the technology to meet the technical and capacity requirements of each stage of the process. Consider, for example, the production of Cadbury's Dairy Milk bars. First, the standard liquid chocolate is prepared from cocoa beans, fresh milk and sugar using specialized equipment, connected together with pipes and conveyors. These processes operate continuously, day and night, to ensure consistency of both the chocolate itself and the rate of output. Next, the liquid is pumped through to the moulding department, where it is dispensed into a moving line of plastic moulds which form the chocolate bars and vibrate them to remove any trapped air bubbles. The moulds then move through a large refrigerator so the chocolate can harden. The moulded bars then pass directly to automated wrapping and packing machines, from where they go to the warehouse.

Flow of customers in the visitor attraction

Cadbury's also has a large visitor centre called 'Cadbury World' alongside the factory. It is a permanent exhibition devoted entirely to chocolate and the part Cadbury's has played in its fascinating history. The design is also based on a 'line' layout with a single route for all customers that promotes a smooth flow of customers, where possible avoiding bottlenecks and delays. Entry to the Exhibition Area is by timed ticket, to ensure a constant flow of input customers, who are free to walk around at their preferred speed, but are constrained to keep to the single track through the sequence of displays. On leaving this section, they are directed upstairs to the Chocolate Packaging Plant, where a guide escorts standard-sized batches of customers to the appropriate positions where they can see the packing processes and a video presentation. The groups are then led down to and around the Demonstration Area, where skilled employees demonstrate small-scale production of hand-made chocolates. Finally, visitors are free to roam unaccompanied through a long, winding path of the remaining exhibits.

Source: Courtesy of Cadbury plc

there will be different flow patterns. For example, the library in Figure 7.4 will arrange its different categories of books and its other services partly to minimize the average distance its customers have to 'flow' through the operation. But, because its customers' needs vary, it will arrange its layout to satisfy the majority of its customers (but perhaps inconvenience a minority). When the variety of products or services reduces to the point where a distinct 'category' with similar requirements becomes evident but variety is still not small, cell layout could become appropriate, as in the sports goods cell in Figure 7.5. When variety is relatively small and volume

> ❋ **Operations principle**
>
> Resources in low-volume–high-variety processes should be arranged to cope with irregular flow.

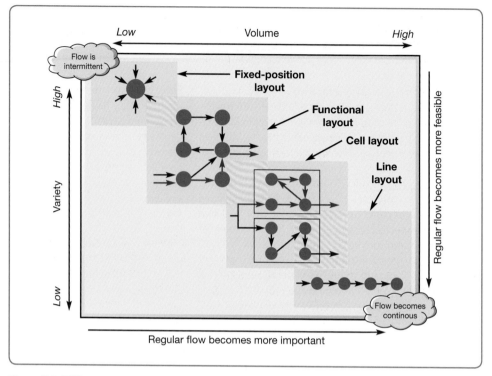

Figure 7.8 Different process layouts are appropriate for different volume–variety combinations

⁂ **Operations principle**

Resources in high-volume–low-variety processes should be arranged to cope with smooth, regular flow.

is high, flow can become regularized and a line layout is likely to be appropriate, as in an assembly plant. (*See* Fig. 7.8.)

Although the volume–variety characteristics of the operation will narrow the choice down to one or two layout options, there are other associated advantages and disadvantages, some of which are shown in Figure 7.9. However, the type of operation will also influence the relative importance of these advantages and disadvantages. For example, a high-volume television manufacturer may find the low-cost characteristics of a product layout attractive, but an amusement theme park may adopt the same layout type primarily because of the way it 'controls' customer flow.

OPERATIONS IN PRACTICE

Nestlé's flexible factories[7]

Nestlé is the largest food company in the world and has operations in almost 200 countries. It also has over 400 factories around the world, many of them in developing countries. Nestlé opened its first factory in Africa (a condensed milk production plant) in 1927. But factories are expensive to build, especially where infrastructure can be problematic and future demand uncertain. This is why Nestlé has created a blueprint for a new type of factory that can be built in half the time of a more traditional one for about 50–60 per cent of the cost.

The modular factory will be made of multiple, easy-to-assemble component sections designed to offer a highly flexible, simple and cost-effective solution for creating production sites in the developing world. Often, investing in these countries can be high risk, as they can lack infrastructure, reliable energy sources and building expertise, but the modular factory concept will enable Nestlé to establish a footprint rapidly, creating local jobs and being closer to its customers and its raw materials. *'The model is a real evolution from the traditional bricks and mortar factories of the past'*, Alfredo Fenollosa, Nestlé Technical Head for Asia, Oceania and Africa, said. *'Big companies traditionally build solid stuff but the lighter structure of this modular factory concept represents a real mindset change for Nestlé. We hope to be able to apply it soon in countries in Africa, and in some parts of Asia'*, he added.

The average Nestlé factory takes between 18 and 24 months and costs between SFr30m and 50m to build. The new modular factory could be complete, and up and running, in less than 12 months, at a cost of between SFr15m and 25m. The modular factory uses a series of purpose-built factory sections which can be brought, ready to use, directly to the site and connected to each other according to requirements. These could include, for example, a ready-to-use generator and boiler, a staff

canteen and changing rooms for factory employees. The factory can then be expanded, moved or its function transformed without having to start from scratch. The modular factory concept is designed to industrialize simple processes like repacking and mixing dry goods such as Maggi bouillon cubes, rather than creating more complex products.

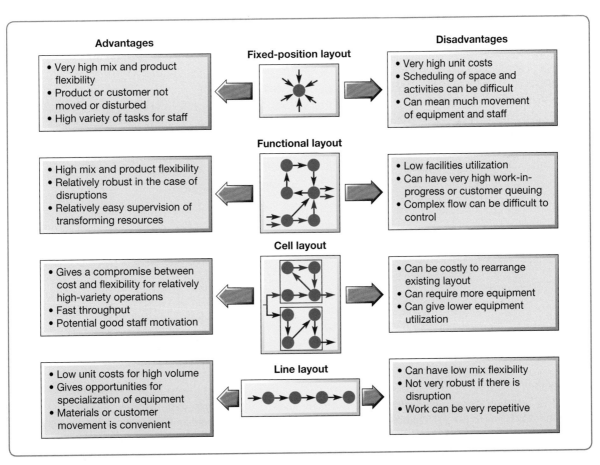

Figure 7.9 **Some advantages and disadvantages of layout types**

Cost analysis

Of all the characteristics of the various layout types, perhaps the most generally significant ones are the unit cost implications of layout choice. This is best understood by distinguishing between the fixed- and variable-cost elements of adopting each layout type.
For any particular product or service, the fixed costs of physically constructing a fixed-
position layout are relatively small compared with any other way of producing the same
product or service. However, the variable costs of producing each individual product or
service are relatively high compared with the alternative layout types. Fixed costs then
tend to increase as one moves from fixed-position, through process
and cell, to line layout. Variable costs per product or service tend to
decrease, however. The total costs for each layout type will depend
on the volume of products or services produced and are shown in
Figure 7.10(a). This seems to show that for any volume there is a
lowest cost basic layout. However, in practice, the cost analysis of
layout selection is rarely as clear as this. The exact cost of operating the layout is difficult to forecast and will probably depend on
many, often difficult to predict, factors. Rather than use thin lines to represent the cost
of layout as volume increases, broad bands, within which the real cost is likely to lie, are
probably more appropriate (*see* Fig. 7.10(b)). The discrimination between the different
layout types is now far less clear. There are ranges of volume for which any of two or three
layout types might provide the lowest operating cost. The less certainty there is over the
costs, the broader the cost 'bands' will be, and the less clear the choice will be. The prob-
able costs of adopting a particular layout need to be set in the broader context of advantages and disadvantages shown in Figure 7.9.

> ✳ **Operations principle**
>
> Different layout types have different
> fixed and variable costs which determine
> the appropriateness of layout for varying
> volume–variety characteristics.

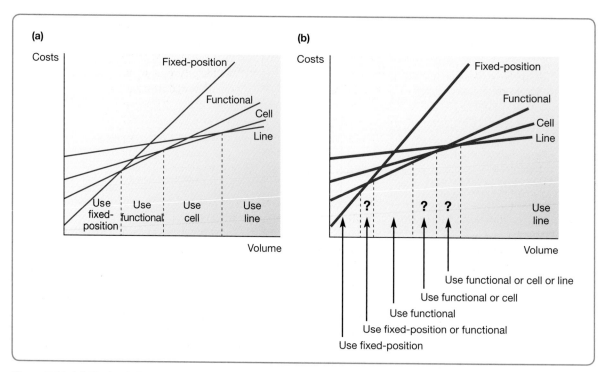

Figure 7.10 (a) The basic layout types have different fixed- and variable-cost characteristics which seem to
determine which one to use. (b) In practice the uncertainty about the exact fixed and variable costs of each layout
means the decision can rarely be made on cost alone

HOW DOES THE APPEARANCE OF AN OPERATION AFFECT ITS PERFORMANCE?

So far we have focused on the more evident 'pattern of flow' issues associated with layout. Yet the aesthetics of a layout (in other words, what it looks and feels like) is also important, particularly when customers experience the inside of an operation, as in high-visibility operations (see Chapter 1). In such operations the general look and feel of the operation will be as important, if not more important, than cost and distance criteria. Of course, the appearance of an operation must include how its facilities are arranged, but also increasingly it is recognized that the 'look and feel' of an operation can also have a significant effect on the staff of an operation, and therefore on its effectiveness and performance generally.

The effect of workplace design on staff

There are some obvious and basic aspects of workplace design that will affect anyone working there. These are such things as: Is it warm enough? Too warm? Sufficiently well lit to see adequately? Not too noisy? These are all the factors that deal with the physiological aspects of working – how we fit in with our physical working environment. Clearly, people who are cold, or irritated by their noisy environment, or straining to see what they are doing, will probably not be feeling, or working, particularly well. We look at these issues in Chapter 9 when we look at 'ergonomics'. But there are other factors associated with the design of a workplace that could affect staff attitudes, motivation and behaviour. This is why in recent years many companies have devoted resources to what goes into their workplaces and what they look like. Increasingly, special meeting zones, cappuccino bars, fish tanks, relaxing bean bags, games consoles, hammocks, ping-pong tables and other such features have been integrated into workspaces. Why is this?

The core of the argument for using these design features is that a workplace is more than simply the arrangement of facilities and the pattern of flow that it creates. It is also the furniture, the way space is used and even the colour of the paint on the walls. Some workplace designers would go further. The aesthetics of the workplace also reflects the culture of the organization. (There is no single authoritative definition of organizational culture, but generally it is taken to mean what it feels like to be part of an organization, 'the organization's climate'.)[8] Therefore, they argue, the appearance of a workplace should reflect the organization's culture. The key questions are: 'what does that workplace say about our culture?' and 'how can we create an environment that further promotes our culture?' What works for one company may be counter-cultural at another.[9] The Google headquarters in California (known as the Googleplex) is often cited as a good example of a workplace that reflects the company's culture.

Nevertheless, the question is how much difference do the aesthetics and components of the working environment make? In fact, according to Thomas Davenport, an expert in 'knowledge working', there is little evidence that anyone worked more productively because of these features. *'There's no clear relationship between knowledge worker performance and various appealing features of the work environment, though they may help slightly with recruiting and morale.'*[10] Rather, the proponents of improving the appearance of working environment say that the effect is subtler. It can encourage desired behaviours, in particular when the workplace reflects the activities and needs of the people working there. So, for example, flexible modular systems of furniture made up of a number of components can be changed to meet different needs as they arise. Screens can enclose a workstation if more privacy is needed, tables can be moved around for meetings, and so on. A study by Herman Miller[11] (an office furniture manufacturer) identified seven workspace attributes

> **✻ Operations principle**
>
> Layout should take into consideration the aesthetic appearance of the workplace and types of facilities available to staff.

that people value and which contribute to their satisfaction and (presumably) output. These were, in order of priority, a comfortable office, sufficient amount of work surface area, the flexibility to put their computer in the most suitable place, the capability to keep work within arm's reach, to contain sounds within the office, to keep out distracting noises from outside the office and to have 'visual privacy'.

The Allen curve

Arranging the facilities in any workplace will directly influence how physically close individuals are to each other. And this, in turn, influences the likelihood of communication between individuals. So, what effect does placing individuals close together or far apart have on how they interact? The work of Thomas J. Allen at the Massachusetts Institute of Technology first established how communication dropped off with distance. In 1984 his book, *Managing the Flow of Technology*, presented what has become known as the 'Allen curve'. It showed a powerful negative correlation between the physical distance between colleagues and their frequency of communication. The Allen curve estimated that we are four times as likely to communicate regularly with a colleague sitting 2 metres away from us as with someone 20 metres away, and 50 metres (for example, separate floors) marks a cut-off point for the regular exchange of certain types of technical information. But, as some experts have pointed out, the office is no longer just a physical place; email, remote conferencing and collaboration tools mean that colleagues can communicate without ever seeing each other. However, this appears not to be the case. One study[12] shows that so-called distance-shrinking technology actually makes close proximity more important, with both face-to-face and digital communications following the Allen curve. The study showed that engineers who shared a physical office were 20 per cent more likely to stay in touch digitally than those who worked elsewhere. Also, when they needed to collaborate closely, closely located colleagues emailed each other four times as frequently as colleagues in different locations.

OPERATIONS IN PRACTICE — Where did the office cubicle come from?[13]

Some people love them, many people loathe them; the office cubicle is rarely viewed as a neutral arrangement. But originally the man who invented the concept, Robert Propst, a designer working for the office-furniture firm Herman Miller, hoped it would bring flexibility and independence to the office environment. What he was reacting against was the then common arrangement of row after row of desks (a bit like a university examination room), where office workers toiled from 9 to 5, usually with a passageway of private, closed-off offices reserved for managers. In 1968 Propst proposed what was the first modular office system, called the 'Action Office 2'. Using his system, space could be divided up by wall-like vertical panels that could be slotted together in various ways. His original idea was that each employee could have a clamshell arrangement that gave him or her both privacy and a view. This would be furnished with desks of different heights (to prevent back strain). In addition, areas for informal meetings and coffee could be created.

Source: Shutterstock.com: Blend Images

Propst believed that the best way to arrange the 'walls' would be to join the panels at 120° angles. However, to his disappointment, office designers realized that they could squash more people into the available space if they arranged the 'walls' at 90° to form the classic cubicle. Propst also believed that people needed to stand as often as they sat (he was ahead of his time). So he created storage spaces located away from the cubicles to encourage workers to move about and encourage 'meaningful traffic'.

But cubicles were not universally popular. The unadorned open-plan arrangements were demotivating, but cubicles did not solve all their problems. Open-plan offices were noisy and distracting, but cubicles could be just as bad. Cubicles failed to block unwanted noise, and at the same time could block natural light. Cubicles could even make people behave badly according to researchers at Cornell University who found that employees in cubicles were more likely than those in open-plan offices to have loud (and long) conversations on the phone with visiting colleagues. This, they say, is possibly because cubicles 'mask the social cues such as facial expressions and body language that influence social interactions'. It makes it easier to consume an antisocially smelly lunch or have loud conversations on the phone, oblivious to their colleagues' reactions. But cubicles are still being used in offices around the world. One explanation for this is that privacy is so valued that office planners try to create the illusion of it. This seems to be borne out by the way people personalize their cubicles with, among other things, pictures, flowers and rugs, even, in some cases, curtains at the entrance, wallpaper, fairy lights and chandeliers.

The effect of workplace design on customers – servicescapes

If the appearance of an operation affects how its staff feel about working there, it certainly will also affect customers if they enter the workplace, as they do in 'high-visibility' operations. The term that is often used to describe the look and feel of the environment within an operation from a customer's perspective is its 'servicescape' (although it is sometimes also applied to how staff view their environment). There are many academic studies that have shown that the servicescape of an operation plays an important role, both positive and negative, in shaping customers' views.[14] The general idea is that ambient conditions, space factors, and signs and symbols in a service operation will create an 'environmental experience' for both employees and customers, and this environmental experience should support the service concept. The individual factors that influence this experience will then lead to certain responses (again, in both employees and customers). These responses can be put into three main categories:

> ✳ **Operations principle**
> Layout should include consideration of the look and feel of the operation to customers and/or staff.

- cognitive (what people think);
- emotional (what they feel); and
- physiological (what their body experiences).

However, remember that a servicescape will contain not only objective, measureable and controllable stimuli, but also subjective, immeasurable and often uncontrollable stimuli, which will influence customer behaviour. The obvious example is other customers frequenting an operation. As well as controllable stimuli such as the colour, lighting, design, space and music, the number, demographics and appearance of one's fellow customers will also shape the impression of the operation.

> **OPERATIONS IN PRACTICE** | **Facing the wrong way?[15]**

Some years ago, it was reported that a low-cost airline was to introduce standing-only sections on flights. Predictably there were some very vocal objections. The idea, however, turned out to be a joke. Yet it highlighted a serious issue: how can airlines reduce their costs (and therefore their fares) by packing more passengers onto the aircraft? Airbus has patented a design that uses fold-up seats resembling lines of bar stools or tractor-driver seats. Some industry commentators have suggested that airlines should consider shrinking the size of toilets and galleys. All are ideas to accommodate more passengers on board. One idea that has been suggested by Zodiac, a French supplier of airliner fittings, is to have passengers face each other on alternate seats that are hexagon shaped (*see* Fig. 7.11). This means that passengers will not have to compete for the armrest, but they will have to look at each other. Zodiac says it is trying to promote its thin, lightweight seating arrangement, not just to increase passenger density, but also to increase shoulder and leg room. Says Pierre-Antony Vastra, Vice-President of Zodiac, '*It's a different way of travelling, with people facing each other. We can have nice conversations.*' However, what has been called 'in-your-face' seating has met with significant opposition. *Wired Magazine* said, '*If you're around the sort of people one usually sits next to on airplanes, it would be horrible. At least if you're all facing the same direction, you can pretend they don't exist.*' Others called it '*the most atrocious idea for airplane seating design you've ever seen...like a sick joke*', while others doubted that the configuration would be safe because of the difficulty of evacuating alternating seats in an emergency.

Source: Shutterstock.com: Iakov Filimonov

Figure 7.11 Using 'hexagon' seats and requiring some passengers to face backwards could increase seating density, but would you be prepared to?

HOW SHOULD EACH BASIC LAYOUT TYPE BE DESIGNED IN DETAIL?

Once the basic layout type has been decided, the next step is to decide the detailed design of the layout. Detailed design is the act of operationalizing the broad principles that were implicit in the choice of the basic layout type.

Detailed design in fixed-position layout

In fixed-position arrangements the location of resources will be determined, not on the basis of the flow of transformed resources, but on the convenience of transforming resources themselves. The objective of the detailed design of fixed-position layouts is to achieve a layout for the operation which allows all the transforming resources to maximize their contribution to the transformation process by allowing them to provide an effective 'service' to the transformed resources. The detailed layout of some fixed-position layouts, such as building sites, can become very complicated, especially if the planned schedule of activities is changed frequently. Imagine the chaos on a construction site if heavy trucks continually (and noisily) drove past the site office, delivery trucks for one contractor had to cross other contractors' areas to get to where they were storing their own materials, and the staff who spent most time at the building itself were located furthest away from it. Although there are techniques that help to locate resources on fixed-position layouts, they are not widely used

Detailed design in functional layout

The detailed design of functional layouts is complex, as is flow in this type of layout. Chief among the factors which lead to this complexity is the very large number of different options. For example, in the very simplest case of just two work centres, there are only two ways of arranging these *relative to each other*. But there are 6 ways of arranging three centres and 120 ways of arranging five centres. This relationship is a factorial one. For N centres there are factorial N ($N!$) different ways of arranging the centres, where:

$$N! = N \times (N-1) \times (N-2) \times \ldots \times (1)$$

So for a relatively simple functional layout with, say, 20 work centres, there are $20! = 2.433 \times 10^{18}$ ways of arranging the operation. This combinatorial complexity of functional layouts makes optimal solutions difficult to achieve in practice. Most functional layouts are designed by a combination of intuition, common sense, and systematic trial and error.

> ✳ **Operations principle**
>
> Functional layouts are combinatorially complex; there are many alternative layouts.

The information for functional layouts

Before starting the process of detailed design in functional layouts there are some essential pieces of information which the designer needs:

- The area required by each work centre.
- The constraints on the shape of the area allocated to each work centre.
- The degree and direction of flow between each work centre (for example, number of journeys, number of loads or cost of flow per distance travelled).
- The desirability of work centres being close together or close to some fixed point in the layout.

The degree and direction of flow are usually shown on a flow record chart like that shown in Figure 7.12 in the worked example. This information could be gathered from routing information, or where flow is more random; as in a library for example, the information could be collected by observing the routes taken by customers over a typical period of time.

Minimizing distance travelled

In most examples of functional layout, the prime objective is to minimize the costs to the operation which are associated with flow through the operation. This usually means minimizing the total distance travelled in the operation, for example as in Figure 7.13 in the worked example. The effectiveness of the layout, at this simple level, can be calculated from:

$$\text{Effectiveness of layout} = \Sigma F_{ij} D_{ij} \quad \text{for all } i \neq j$$

where F_{ij} = the flow in loads or journeys per period of time from work centre i to work centre j

D_{ij} = the distance between work centre i and work centre j

The lower the effectiveness score, the better the layout.

The steps in determining the location of work centres in a functional layout is illustrated in the worked example on the Rotterdam Educational Group.

Rotterdam Educational Group (REG) is a company which commissions, designs and manufactures education packs for distance-learning courses and training. It has leased a new building with an area of 1,800 square metres, into which it needs to fit 11 'departments'. Prior to moving into the new building it conducted an exercise to find the average number of trips taken by its staff between the 11 departments. Although some trips are a little more significant than others (because of the loads carried by staff) it has been decided that all trips will be treated as being of equal value.

Step 1 – Collect information

The areas required by each department together with the average daily number of trips between departments are shown in the flow chart in Figure 7.12. In this example the direction of flow is not relevant and very low flow rates (less than five trips per day) have not been included.

Dimensions of the building = 30 metres × 60 metres

Figure 7.12 Flow information for Rotterdam Educational Group

Step 2 – Draw schematic layout

Figure 7.13 shows the first schematic arrangement of departments. The thickest lines represent high flow rates between 70 and 120 trips per day; the medium lines are used for flow rates between 20 and 69 trips per day; and the thinnest lines for flow rates between 5 and 19 trips per day. The objective here is to arrange the work centres so that those with the thick lines are closest together. The higher the flow rate, the shorter the line should be.

Step 3 – Adjust the schematic layout

If departments were arranged exactly as shown in Figure 7.13(a) the building which housed them would be of an irregular, and therefore high-cost, shape. The layout needs adjusting to take into account the shape of the building. Figure 7.13(b) shows the departments arranged in a more ordered fashion which corresponds to the dimensions of the building.

Step 4 – Draw the layout

Figure 7.14 shows the departments arranged with the actual dimensions of the building and occupying areas which approximate to their required areas. Although the distances between

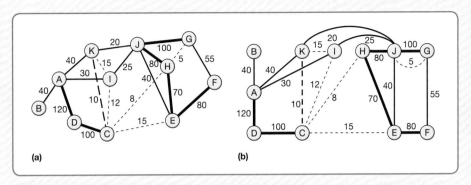

(a)   **(b)**

Figure 7.13 (a) Schematic layout placing centres with high traffic levels close to each other. (b) Schematic layout adjusted to fit building geometry

the centroids of departments have changed from Figure 7.14 to accommodate their physical shape, their relative positions are the same. It is at this stage that a quantitative expression of the cost of movement associated with this relative layout can be calculated.

Step 5 – Check by exchanging

The layout in Figure 7.14 seems to be reasonably effective but it is usually worthwhile to check for improvement by exchanging pairs of departments to see if any reduction in total flow can be obtained. For example, departments H and J might be exchanged, and the total distance travelled calculated again to see if any reduction has been achieved.

Figure 7.14 Final layout of building

Computer-aided functional layout design

The combinatorial complexity of functional layout has led to the development of several heuristic procedures to aid the design process. Heuristic procedures use what have been described as 'shortcuts in the reasoning process' and 'rules of thumb' in the search for a reasonable solution. They do not search for an optimal solution (though they might find one by chance) but rather attempt to derive a good sub-optimal solution. One such computer-based heuristic procedure is called CRAFT (Computerized Relative Allocation of Facilities Technique). The reasoning behind this procedure is that, whereas it is infeasible to evaluate factorial N ($N!$) different layouts when N is large, it is feasible to start with an initial layout and then evaluate all the different ways of exchanging two work centres.

There are:

$$\frac{N!}{2!(N-2)!}$$

possible ways of exchanging two out of N work centres. So for a 20 work-centre layout, there are 190 ways of exchanging two work centres.

Three inputs are required for the CRAFT heuristic: a matrix of the flow between departments; a matrix of the cost associated with transportation between each of the departments; and a spatial array showing an initial layout. From these:

- the location of the centroids of each department is calculated;
- the flow matrix is weighted by the cost matrix, and this weighted flow matrix is multiplied by the distances between departments to obtain the total transportation costs of the initial layout;
- the model then calculates the cost consequence of exchanging every possible pair of departments.

The exchange giving the most improvement is then fixed, and the whole cycle is repeated with the updated cost flow matrix until no further improvement is made by exchanging two departments.

Detailed design in cell layout

Figure 7.15 shows how a functional layout has been divided into four cells, each of which has the resources to process a 'family' of parts. In doing this the operations management has implicitly taken two interrelated decisions regarding:

- the extent and nature of the cells it has chosen to adopt;
- which resources to allocate to which cells.

Production flow analysis

The detailed design of cellular layouts is difficult, partly because the idea of a cell is itself a compromise between process and product layout. To simplify the task, it is useful to concentrate on either the process or product aspects of cell layout. If cell designers choose to

Figure 7.15 Cell layout groups the processes together which are necessary for a family of products/services

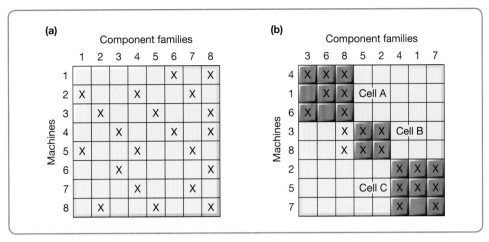

Figure 7.16 (a) and (b) Using production flow analysis to allocate machines to cells

concentrate on processes, they could use cluster analysis to find which processes group naturally together. This involves examining each type of process and asking which other types of processes a product or part using that process is also likely to need. One approach to allocating tasks and machines to cells is production flow analysis (PFA), which examines both product requirements and process grouping simultaneously. In Figure 7.16(a) a manufacturing operation has grouped the components it makes into eight families – for example, the components in family 1 require machines 2 and 5. In this state the matrix does not seem to exhibit any natural groupings. If the order of the rows and columns is changed, however, to move the crosses as close as possible to the diagonal of the matrix which goes from top left to bottom right, then a clearer pattern emerges. This is illustrated in Figure 7.16(b) and shows that the machines could conveniently be grouped together in three cells, indicated on the diagram as cells A, B and C. Although this procedure is a particularly useful way to allocate machines to cells, the analysis is rarely totally clean. This is the case here where component family 8 needs processing by machines 3 and 8 which have been allocated to cell B. There are some partial solutions for this. More machines could be purchased and put into cell A. This would clearly solve the problem but requires investing capital in a new machine that might be under-utilized. Or, components in family 8 could be sent to cell B after they have been processed in cell A (or even in the middle of their processing route if necessary). This solution avoids the need to purchase another machine but it conflicts partly with the basic idea of cell layout – to achieve a simplification of a previously complex flow. Or, if there are several components like this, it might be necessary to devise a special cell for them (usually called a remainder cell) that will almost be like a mini-functional layout. This remainder cell does remove the 'inconvenient' components from the rest of the operation, however, leaving it with a more ordered and predictable flow.

Detailed design in line layout

The nature of the line layout design decision is a little different to the other layout types. Rather than 'where to place what', product layout is concerned more with 'what to place where'. Locations are frequently decided upon and then work tasks are allocated to each location. So the 'layout' activity is very similar to aspects of process design, which we discussed in Chapter 6. The main product layout decisions are as follows:

- What cycle time is needed?
- How many stages are needed?
- How should the task-time variation be dealt with?
- How should the layout be balanced (bottlenecks reduced)?
- How should the stages be arranged ('long thin' layout to 'short fat layout')?

SUMMARY ANSWERS TO KEY QUESTIONS

❯ What is layout and how can it influence performance?

- The 'layout' of an operation or process is how its transforming resources are positioned relative to each other, how its various tasks are allocated to these transforming resources, and the general appearance of the transforming resources.

- These decisions will dictate the pattern and nature of the flow for transformed resources as they progress through the operation or process.

- The objectives of layout include: inherent safety, security, length of flow, minimizing delays, reducing work-in-progress, the clarity of flow, staff conditions, communication, management coordination, accessibility, the use of space, the use of capital, and long-term flexibility.

❯ What are the basic layout types used in operations?

- There are four basic layout types. They are fixed-position layout, functional layout, cell layout and line layout.

- Partly the type of layout an operation chooses is influenced by the nature of the process type, which in turn depends on the volume–variety characteristics of the operation. Partly also the decision will depend on the objectives of the operation. Cost and flexibility are particularly affected by the layout decision.

- The fixed and variable costs implied by each layout differ such that, in theory, one particular layout will have the minimum costs for a particular volume level. However, in practice, uncertainty over the real costs involved in layout make it difficult to be precise on which is the minimum cost layout.

❯ How does the appearance of an operation affect its performance?

- The general appearance and aesthetics of a layout affect how staff view the operation on which they work, and how customers behave.

- The communication between people reduces with the distance between them. This is called the 'Allen curve'.

- In addition to the conventional operations objectives that will be influenced by the feel and general impression of the layout design, this is often called the 'servicescape' of the operation.

❯ How should each basic layout type be designed in detail?

- In fixed-position layout the materials or people being transformed do not move but the transforming resources move around them. Techniques are rarely used in this type of layout, but some, such as resource location analysis, bring a systematic approach to minimizing the costs and inconvenience of flow at a fixed-position location.

- In functional layout all similar transforming resources are grouped together in the operation. The detailed design task is usually (although not always) to minimize the distance travelled by the transformed resources through the operation. Either manual or computer-based methods can be used to devise the detailed design.

- In cell layout the resources needed for a particular class of product are grouped together in some way. The detailed design task is to group the products or customer types such that convenient cells can be designed around their needs. Techniques such as production flow analysis can be used to allocate products to cells.

- In line (sometimes called 'product') layout, the transforming resources are located in sequence specifically for the convenience of products or product types. The detailed design of product layouts includes a number of decisions, such as the cycle time to which the design must conform, the number of stages in the operation, the way tasks are allocated to the stages in the line, and the arrangement of the stages in the line.

CASE STUDY   The event hub

Ross Richie, Loughborough University

The 'event hub' was new, shiny and fitted with the latest equipment. Chief Superintendent Janice Walker was looking forward to using it as the 'Silver Commander' of the Joint Service Command (JSC) at the forthcoming 'event'. An 'event' is a term that is used to describe a wide range of public occasions, ranging from the management of a football match, a public protest, a royal wedding through to a critical incident such as a terrorist attack. The management of an event is a highly structured and well-practised activity, bringing together many different bodies that have an interest in it. These could include, for example, the ambulance service, the police, transport authorities, security services and local authorities, among others.

Although event command structures (who reports to whom) were clearly defined, the design of each event was unique. The operationalized command structure needed to be sufficiently flexible to cater for all the different bodies that are represented 'on the ground' (OTG). These are the ambulances you may see outside a football ground or the lines of police officers escorting a demonstration. These OTG services have localized commanders, who have delegated tactical responsibility and are called the 'Bronze Commanders' regardless of whether they belong to the ambulance, police or fire services, or any other body. Bronze Commanders all report to the Silver Commander.

The command hub

All of the OTG services and commanders report back to a centralized intelligence and decision-making command hub. It is often located away from the event, co-ordinated through a vast array of visual and audio communication networks. Within the hub there are representatives from each of the Bronze command units providing direct communication and command links to each of the OTG resources. Also in the hub, there is the single strategic commander – called the 'Silver Commander'. In larger events,

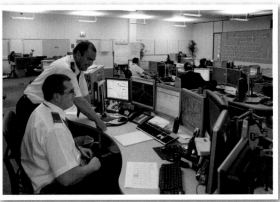

Source: Shutterstock.com: Graham Taylor

there may be as many as 80 different personnel in the command hub, co-ordinating between the Silver Commander and 15–20 OTG Bronze Commanders who, between them, manage more than 400 individual resources and assets.

The Silver Commander

Janice has acted as a Silver Commander before and knew that it was a highly pressured role, even though this time she would have a tactical advisor, a recorder (recording all decisions and actions), a communications officer and a runner in her support team. *'At some difficult phases of an Event, you may be making several critical decisions every minute. Silver Commanders have to assimilate a wide range of intelligence from many sources, match this with your resources and their locations, communicate your decisions to the OTG Bronze Commanders, and do all this within strict policy and legislative constraints.'*

In the upcoming event (a large protest march) Janice would have operational information inputs from:

- The Bronze command representatives.
- Their communications officer (who summarizes radio communications).

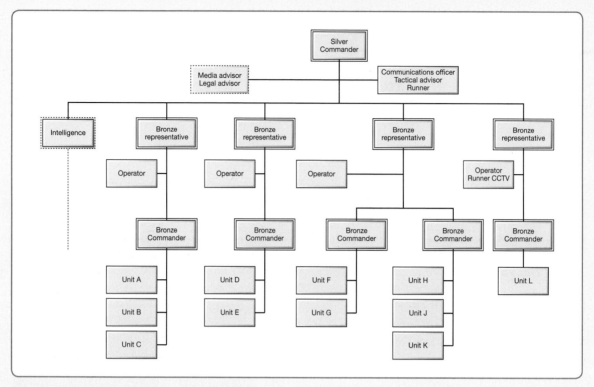

Figure 7.17 The chain of command for the event

- Intelligence feeds (from a specialist intelligence function).
- Any visual feeds, for example CCTV, policy logs, news and social media.

She would also have advisory inputs from tactical, media and legal advisors. These advisory inputs were usually more discursive than the information coming from the OTG operational units. In the hub, the Bronze representatives would have support teams of their own. In this event, for example, the local authority planned to have five CCTV operators to support their function, whereas the ambulance service representation was only a single officer. Figure 7.17 shows the organizational 'chain of command' for the event.

Hub layout

The bodies and services represented in the hub had varying requirements. For example, some of the intelligence functions needed to be sure that their computer screens would not be overlooked by other functions that were not security cleared to an appropriate level because of the sensitivity and secrecy of their information (such as the local authority representatives). This meant that they had been located in the far corner of the hub. Yet the intelligence functions would also need to get operational updates from the ambulance service and local authority to direct their intelligence gathering efforts. Janice was worried that, because of this, there would be a high degree of travelling between different functions in the room.

The layout of the hub is shown in Figure 7.18. One of the greatest points of interest in the room was the mapping screen, where a screen placed on the wall had special geographic information updated from all the OTG units. Both Bronze and Silver Commanders would probably need to view the real-time updates shown on this screen.

Janice, as Silver Commander, was allocated the only office in the hub. This was conventional practice because the Silver Commander needed a quiet place to go and consider his or her decisions and take confidential guidance from advisors.

Prior to the event, Janice had planned for 'update meetings' in the meeting room with 12 of her key personnel every two or three hours during the march. The meeting room was located 30 metres away from the hub, though in the same building. Also in the same building a secure area was provided for the wider intelligence functions. This was 10 metres away from the hub through two sets of locked doors. This provided a confidential area for the intelligence functions to operate without risk of information leakage.

Janice knew that events could be hectic, so in order to manage the busy room, and control the noise levels of the room, she had appointed a room manager who would sit in the centre of the room. The job of this officer would be to control movement within the room and intervene if noise levels became excessive.

What happened?

Janice was proved correct about its being hectic during the march. The first two hours of the protest went

Figure 7.18 The layout of the command hub

according to plan with good co-ordination within her team and between her team and the protest organizers. However, as the march progressed three things happened more or less concurrently. First, a splinter group from the march took a separate, non-agreed, route that required extra resources to police. Second, one of the people marching suffered a heart attack and needed emergency treatment and transport to the nearest hospital (difficult in the crowds). Third, an unexpected (and unauthorized), but small, counter-demonstration took place as the march passed a football stadium. And although the two sets of demonstrators were kept apart, there was raised tension and a need for extra monitoring of the situation. All of this resulted in an intense period of decision making and information gathering. Janice found herself continually moving between her office, the command teams and the screens, never spending more than a couple of minutes in one place. She was often followed by her tactical advisor, recorder and communications officer who had to run between her and their workstations, because their computers and radios were fixed to the desk.

To try and reduce the travel of her staff, finally Janice abandoned her office and moved her chair over to her 'Silver Commander's team' area, close to the information screen. However, the general noise levels in the room were interrupting discussions, and Janice's update meetings were also disturbing others in the room.

The move had a positive effect of unifying Janice and her team. However, now there was now a constant flow of Bronze representatives and media advisors to and from the area where Janice was sitting. Yet this was preferable to the earlier disruption caused by her moving around the room. She also made a further decision, which was not to consult the CCTV footage or the information screen, and moved her desk away from the screen area. 'It was information overload', said Janice. 'Using these boards, I don't need to micro-manage the resources, this is what my extended chain of command is in place to do.'

After several hectic hours, the event concluded successfully, with no injuries or serious incident, and with the operation being regarded as very successful. However, Janice had firm views on the new hub layout: 'The layout of the room hindered decision-making. The transfer of information on this kind of time critical operation is vital. There must be a better way of setting out the hub. It would not require much capital to re-design the area to reflect what we do. It could be more like a production process that takes into account the common transfer processes between each function.'

QUESTIONS

1 **What should an ideal design of an event centre be able to do?**

2 **Sketch out a layout for an event centre that would work better than the existing one.**

PROBLEMS AND APPLICATIONS

1. Reread the 'Operations in practice' case at the start of the chapter that describes the Volkswagen and Google operations. What do you think the main objectives of each layout were?

2. Visit and observe the flow of people in your library. Talk with the librarian (if you can) and make a list of the most important criteria that could be used if the library were to be redesigned.

3. The flow of materials through eight departments is shown in Table 7.2.
Assuming that the direction of the flow of materials is not important, construct a relationship chart, a schematic layout and a suggested layout, given that each department is the same size and the eight departments should be arranged four along each side of a corridor.

Table 7.2 **Flow of materials**

	D1	D2	D3	D4	D5	D6	D7	D8
D1	\	30						
D2	10	\	15	20				
D3		5	\	12	2		15	
D4		6		\	10	20		
D5				8	\	8	10	12
D6	3				2	\	30	
D7	3					13	\	2
D8				10	6		15	\

4. Sketch the layout of your local shop, coffee bar or sports hall reception area. Observe the area and draw on your sketch the movements of people through the area over a sufficient period of time to get over 20 observations. Assess the flow in terms of volume, variety and type of layout.

5. Visit a supermarket and observe people's behaviour. You may wish to try and observe which areas they move slowly past and which areas they seem to move past without paying attention to the products. (You may have to exercise some discretion when doing this; people generally do not like to be stalked round the supermarket too obviously.) If you were to redesign the supermarket what would you recommend?

SELECTED FURTHER READING

This is a relatively technical chapter and, as you would expect, most books on the subject are technical. Here are a few of the more accessible.

Karlsson, C. (1996) Radically new production systems, *International Journal of Operations and Production Management*, vol. 16, no. 11, 8–19.

An interesting paper because it traces the development of Volvo's factory layouts over the years.

Meyers, F.E. (2000) *Manufacturing Facilities Design and Material Handling*, Prentice Hall, Upper Saddle River, NJ.

Exactly what it says, thorough.

Rosenbaum, M.S. and Massiah, C. (2011) An expanded servicescape perspective, *Journal of Service Management*, vol. 22, issue 4, 471–490.

Academic but a good review of the research literature.

Van Meel, J., Martens, Y. and van Ree, H.J. (2010) *Planning Office Spaces: A Practical Guide for Managers and Designers*, Laurence King, London.

Exactly what the title says. A practical guide that includes both the 'flow' and the aesthetic aspects of office design.

White, J.A., White, J.A. Jr and McGinnis, L.F. (1998) *Facility Layout and Location: An Analytical Approach*, Prentice Hall Professional, Upper Saddle River, NJ.

One for the practitioners but including many quantitative techniques.

Wu, B. (1994) *Handbook of Manufacturing and Supply Systems Design*, Taylor & Francis, London.

A general treatment that includes layout and related subjects.

8

Process technology

Key questions

> What is process technology?

> What do operations managers need to know about process technology?

> How are process technologies evaluated?

> How are process technologies implemented?

INTRODUCTION

There is a lot of new process technology around. There can be few, if any, operations that have not been affected by the advances in process technology. And all indications are that the pace of technological development is not slowing down. This has important implications for operations managers because all operations use some kind of process technology, whether it is a simple Internet link or the most complex and sophisticated of automated factories. But whatever the technology, all operations managers need to understand what emerging technologies can do, in broad terms how they do it, what advantages the technology can give and what constraints it might impose on the operation. Figure 8.1 shows where the issues covered in this chapter relate to the overall model of operations management activities.

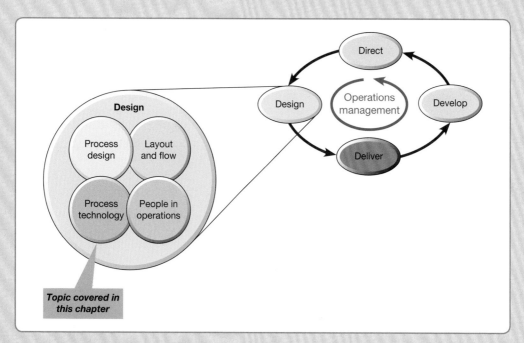

Figure 8.1 This chapter examines process technology

WHAT IS PROCESS TECHNOLOGY?

How operations managers deal with process technology is now one of the most important decisions that shape the capabilities of operations. This was not always the case, at least not for all operations. There used to be a simple division between those operations that used a lot of process technology, usually manufacturing operations, and those that used little or no process technology, usually service operations. But this is no longer true, and arguably has not been true for decades. High-volume services have for years understood the value of process technology. Online transactions for retail and other services are vital for their success. Yet even professional services such as legal and medical services can benefit from new and value-adding technologies (see the section on telemedicine later in this chapter).

So what do operations managers need to know about process technology? It must be important to them because they are continually involved in the choice, installation and management of process technology. But operations managers are not (or need not be) technologists as such. They do not need to be experts in engineering, computing, biology, electronics or whatever constitutes the core science of the technology. Yet they should be able to do three things. First, they need to understand the technology to the extent that they are able to articulate what it should be able to do. Second, they should be able to evaluate alternative technologies and share in the decisions of which technology to choose. Third, they must implement the technology so that it can reach its full potential in contributing to the performance of the operation as a whole. These are the three issues which this chapter deals with. This is illustrated in Figure 8.2 and forms the structure of the chapter.

Process technology defined

First, let us define what is meant by process technology. It is 'the machines, equipment, and devices that *create* and/or *deliver* products and services'. Process technologies range from milking machines to marking software, from body scanners to bread ovens, from mobile phones to milling machines. Disney World uses flight simulation technologies to create the thrill of space travel on its rides – just one in a long history of Disney Corporation and its 'imagineers' using technology to engineer the experience for their customers. In fact process technology is pervasive in all types of operations. Without it many of the products and services we all purchase would be less reliable, take longer to arrive and arrive unexpectedly, only be available in a limited variety, and be more expensive. Process technology has a very significant effect on quality, speed, dependability, flexibility and cost. That is why it is so important to operations managers, and that is why we devote a whole chapter to it. Even when technology seems peripheral to the actual creation of goods and services, it can play a key role in *facilitating* the

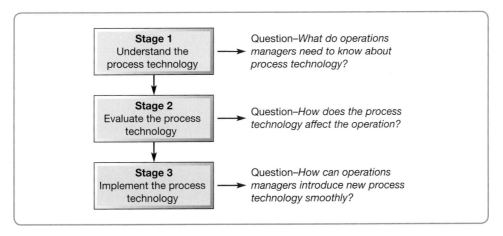

Figure 8.2 The three stages of process technology management

Back in 1920, a Czech playwright, Karel Capek, first coined the name 'robot' (it comes from the Slavonic word for 'work'). Since then, robots have moved from the stuff of science fiction to become a common, if not ubiquitous, element of mass production operations. There are more than a million industrial robots doing routine jobs on production lines. Robots do not take meal breaks, fall ill, complain or leave for better pay. They perform repetitive tasks cheaper than humans, give greater accuracy and repeatability, and can also be used where conditions are hazardous or uncomfortable for humans. Anyone who has seen the way that robots weld together automobile bodies, assemble complex products, or load and unload work pieces onto a machine cannot fail to recognize the impact that robotics has had on manufacturing operations since robots were first introduced in the 1960s.

Source: Shutterstock.com: Jimmi

But like most new process technologies, the effect of robotics on operations management practice can be both positive and negative, depending on one's perspective. (Film critics, who voted on Hollywood's 50 greatest good guys and 50 greatest baddies, included a robot – the Terminator – on both lists.) Certainly they can save humans from exposure to danger. Robots were used during the clear-up operation among the rubble of the Twin Towers in New York. 'Enough people have died here,' said a spokesperson for the emergency services. 'We don't want to risk any one.' Bomb disposal squads use specialized robots which can take at least some of the risk from what remains a hazardous job. Nuclear power stations are decommissioned using robots to move, dismantle and manipulate hazardous radioactive material. They are also becoming both cheaper and more versatile in their production role. For example, Canon has announced its plans to move towards fully automating its digital camera production. Decades ago, Canon, like other manufacturers, began using cell production with teams or a single worker assembling a major part of the product, rather than repeating a simple task (see Chapter 6). And over the years robots have been routinely used as part of production cells. Canon calls it a 'man–machine cell', and says that 'human involvement will be phased out in making some products'.

Only by substituting robots for people will production be kept in Japan, according to Canon, reversing the trend of Japanese manufacturers moving production to China, India and the rest of Asia, where labour costs are cheaper. 'When machines become more sophisticated, human beings can be transferred to do new kinds of work', Jun Misumi, a Canon spokesperson, said. But it is the nature of the interface between people and robots that is concerning some experts. Akihito Sano, a professor at Nagoya Institute of Technology, has stressed the need for some way in which workers can communicate effectively so that robotic technology can be fine-tuned to become more practical. He also says, reassuringly, that there will always be room for human intelligence and skill. 'Human beings are needed to come up with innovations on how to use robots. Going [totally] to a no-man operation at that level is still the world of science fiction.' Yet people have always been nervous that new process technologies will take away their jobs. (Capek's original play that gave robots their name described how, at first, they brought many benefits but eventually led to mass unemployment and unhappiness.) But there are some examples of a smooth introduction of robotics. Audi is said to have been successful in introducing industrial robots, partly because it asked its workers to suggest potential applications of robotics where they could both improve performance and then gave the same workers jobs supervising, maintaining and programming the robots. It may even be that robots can help defend manufacturing jobs in the rich world. For example, it has been pointed out that one reason why Germany has lost fewer such jobs than the UK is that it has five times as many robots for every 10,000 workers.

direct transformation of inputs to an operation. For example, the computer systems which run planning and control activities, accounting systems and stock control systems can be used to help managers and operators control and improve the processes. This type of technology is called indirect process technology. It is becoming increasingly important. Many businesses spend more on the computer systems which control their processes than they do on the direct process technology which acts on its material, information or customers.

Process technology and transformed resources

One common method of distinguishing between different types of process technology is by what the technology actually processes – materials, information or customers. We used this distinction in Chapter 1 when we discussed inputs to operations and processes.

Material-processing technologies

These include any technology that shapes, transports, stores, or in any way changes physical objects. It obviously includes the machines and equipment found in manufacturing operations (such as the robots described in the 'Operations in practice' case at the start of this chapter), but also includes trucks, conveyors, packing machines, warehousing systems and even retail display units. In manufacturing operations, technological advances have meant that the ways in which metals, plastics, fabric and other materials are processed have improved over time. Generally it is the initial forming and shaping of materials at the start, and the handling and movement through the supply network, that have been most affected by technology advances. Assembling parts to make products, although far more automated than it was once, presents more challenges.

Information-processing technology

Information-processing technology, or just information technology (IT), is the most common single type of technology within operations, and includes any device which collects, manipulates, stores or distributes information. Arguably, it is the use of Internet-based technology (generally known as e-business) that has had the most obvious impact on operations – especially those that are concerned with buying and selling activity (e-commerce). Its advantage was that it increased both reach (the number of customers who could be reached and the number of items they could be presented with) and richness (the amount of detail which could be provided concerning both the items on sale and customers' behaviour in buying them). Traditionally, selling involved a trade-off between reach and richness. The widespread adoption of Internet-based technologies effectively overcame this trade-off. Also, the Internet had equally powerful implications on many other operations management tasks.

Customer-processing technology

Although customer-processing operations were once seen as 'low technology', now process technology is very much in evidence in many services. In any airline flight, for example e-ticket reservation technology, check-in technology, the aircraft and its in-flight entertainment, all play vital parts in service delivery. Increasingly the human element of service is being reduced, with customer-processing technology used to give an acceptable level of service while significantly reducing costs. There are three types of customer-processing technologies. The first category includes active interaction technology such as automobiles, telephones, Internet bookings and purchases, fitness equipment and cash machines (ATMs). In all of these, customers themselves are using the technology to create the service. By contrast, aircraft, mass transport systems, moving walkways and lifts, cinemas and theme parks are passive interactive technology; they 'processes' and control customers by constraining their actions in some way. Some technology is 'aware' of customers but not the other way round: for example, security monitoring technologies in shopping malls or at national frontier customs areas. The objective of these 'hidden technologies' is to track customers' movements or transactions in an unobtrusive way.

Integrating technologies

Of course, some technologies process more than one type of resource. Many newer technologies process combinations of materials, people and customers. These technologies are called integrating technologies. Electronic point-of-sale (EPOS) technology, for example, processes shoppers, products and information.

OPERATIONS IN PRACTICE

Technology or people? The future of jobs[2]

Source: Shutterstock.com: Digital Storm

In his book, *The Power of Habit*, Charles Duhigg relates a story to demonstrate that human beings are more predictable than we sometimes like to think. A man walked into a supermarket to complain to the manager. The supermarket had been sending direct mail to the man's daughter containing discount vouchers for baby clothes and equipment. '*She is only in high school*', the father protested. The manager apologised profusely. It was the fault of a new program that predicted pregnancy based on the buying behaviour of their customers, he said. It was obviously a mistake and he was very sorry. A few days later, the man again visited the supermarket and said that it was his turn to apologise. His daughter was indeed pregnant and due to give birth due in a few months' time. The point of the story is that technology is increasing in sophistication to the extent that it is now capable of performing tasks that previously required skilled people making judgements based on insight and experience. Moreover, technology can often do those tasks better. A piece of software has replaced the marketing team trying to guess who to sell baby clothes to. So technology is not only replacing people, but also 'climbing the skills ladder all the time'.

Of course, technological advances have always had an impact on the type of jobs that are in demand by businesses, and, by extension, the type of jobs that are eliminated. So, much of the highly routine work of some mass manufacturing, or the type of standardized accounting processes that pay invoices, have been overtaken by the 'the robot and the spreadsheet'. Yet the type of work that is more difficult to break down into a set of standardized elements is less prone to being displaced by technology. The obvious examples of work that is difficult to automate are the types of management tasks that involve decision making based on judgement and insight, teaching small children, diagnosing complex medical conditions, and so on. However, the future may hold a less certain future for such jobs. As the convenience of data collection and analysis becomes more sophisticated, and process knowledge increases, it becomes easier to break more types of work down into routine constituents, which allows them to be automated. Carl Benedikt Frey and Michael Osborne, of the University of Oxford, maintain that the range of jobs that are likely to be automated is far higher than many assume, especially traditionally white-collar jobs such as accountancy, legal work, technical writing and (even) teaching. It is not simply that technology is getting cleverer; in addition it can exploit the capability to access far more data. Medical samples can be analysed cheaper and faster by image-processing software than by laboratory technicians, case precedents can be sourced by 'text-mining' programs more extensively than by para-legals, computers can even turn out news stories based on sports results or financial data. Frey and Osborne go so far as to estimate the probability that technology will mean job losses for certain jobs in the next two decades (bravely, because such forecasting is notoriously difficult). Among jobs most at risk are telemarketers (0.99, where 1.0 = certainty), accountants and auditors (0.94), retail salespersons (0.92), technical writers (0.89) and retail estate agents (0.86). Those jobs least likely to be replaced include actors (0.37), firefighters (0.17), editors (0.06), chemical engineers (0.02), athletic trainers (0.007) and dentists (0.004).

WHAT DO OPERATIONS MANAGERS NEED TO KNOW ABOUT PROCESS TECHNOLOGY?

Understanding process technology does not (necessarily) mean knowing the details of the science and engineering embedded in the technology. But it does mean knowing enough about the principles behind the technology to be comfortable in evaluating some technical information, capable of dealing with experts in the technology, and confident enough to ask relevant questions.

The four key questions

In particular the following four key questions can help operations managers to grasp the essentials of the technology:

> ✱ **Operations principle**
>
> Operations managers should understand enough about process technology to evaluate alternatives.

- What does the technology do which is different from other similar technologies?
- How does it do it? That is, what particular characteristics of the technology are used to perform its function?
- What benefits does using the technology give to the operation?
- What constraints or risks does using the technology place on the operation?

For example, return to the 'Operations in practice' case that discussed some developments in robotics. Now think through the four key questions.

- **What does the technology do?** Primarily used for handling materials, for example loading and unloading work pieces onto a machine, for processing where a tool is gripped by the robot, and for assembly where the robot places parts together. Some robots have some limited sensory feedback through vision control and touch control.
- **How does it do it?** Through a programmable and computer-controlled (sometimes multi-jointed) arm with an effector end piece which will depend on the task being performed.
- **What benefits does it give?** Can be used where conditions are hazardous or uncomfortable for humans, or where tasks are highly repetitive. Performs repetitive tasks at lower cost than using humans and gives greater accuracy and repeatability. Some robots are starting to mimic human abilities.
- **What constraints or risks does it impose?** Although the sophistication of robotic movement is increasing, robots' abilities are still more limited than popular images of robot-driven factories suggest. Not always good at performing tasks which require delicate sensory feedback or sophisticated judgement. The human–robot interface needs managing carefully, especially where robotics could replace human jobs.

Worked example

QB House speeds up the cut[3]

It was back in 1996 when Kuniyoshi Konishi became so frustrated by having to wait to get his hair cut, and then pay over 3,000 yen for the privilege, that he decided there must be a better way to offer this kind of service. 'Why not', he said, 'create a no-frills barbers shop where the customer could get a haircut in ten minutes at a cost of 1,000 yen [€7]?' He realized that a combination of technology and process design could eliminate all non-essential elements from the basic task of cutting hair. How is this done? Well, first, QB House's barbers never handle cash. Each shop has a ticket vending machine that accepts 1,000 yen bills (and gives no change!) and issues a ticket that the customer gives the barber in exchange for the haircut. Second, QB House does not take reservations. The shops do not even have telephones. Therefore, no

▶

receptionist is needed, or anyone to schedule appointments. Third, QB House developed a lighting system to indicate how long customers will have to wait. Electronic sensors under each seat in the waiting area and in each barber's chair track how many customers are waiting in the shop and different coloured lights are displayed outside the shop. Green lights indicate that there is no waiting, yellow lights indicate a wait of about 5 minutes, and red lights indicate that the wait may be around 15 minutes. This system can also keep track of how long it takes for each customer to be served. Fourth, QB has done away with the traditional Japanese practice of shampooing customers' hair after the haircut to remove any loose hairs. Instead, the barbers use QB House's own 'air wash' system where a vacuum cleaner hose is pulled down from the ceiling and used to vacuum the customer's hair clean. The QB House system has proved so popular that its shops (now over 200) can be found not only in Japan,

Source: Photographers Direct/Andy Maluche

but also in many other South-East Asian countries such as Singapore, Malaysia and Thailand. Each year almost 4,000,000 customers experience QB House's 10-minute haircuts.

Analysis

- **What does the technology do?** Signals availability of servers, so managing customers' expectations. It avoids hairdressers having to handle cash. Speeds service by substituting 'air wash' for traditional shampoo.
- **How does it do it?** Uses simple sensors in seats, ticket dispenser and air wash blowers.
- **What benefits does it give?** Faster service with predictable wait time (dependable service) and lower costs, therefore less expensive prices.
- **What constraints or risks does it impose?** Risks of customer perception of quality of service. It is not an 'indulgent' service. It is a basic, but value, service that customers need to know what to expect and how to use.

Emerging technologies – assessing their implications

The four questions are universal, in the sense that they can help to understand the implications for operations management of any new or emerging technology. By 'implications', we mean the natural consequence for the operation of adopting the technology. In other words, what would (or could) be the effects on the operation if the technology were included in the operation's transforming resources.

In the rest of this section we look at three technologies that, at the time of writing, were new(ish). One processes materials (3D printing), one processes information (the Internet of Things) and one processes customers (telemedicine). The intention is not to provide a comprehensive survey of technologies – that could be expanded into a whole book – nor is it to delve into technical details. Rather it is to demonstrate how operations managers have to look beyond the technology in order to start to understand their implications.

> ✳ **Operations principle**
>
> Emerging technologies can have a potentially significant impact on how operations are managed.

3D printing (additive manufacturing)

For decades and, in some industries, for centuries, producing physical products has been dominated by the principles of mass production. Standardized designs, repetitive processes and rigid, but productive process technology help to produce most of the items we use every day at (relatively) low cost. The downside of mass production was that variety and customization are difficult to achieve at the same time as economies of scale. However, a process technology called 3D printing (also known as 'additive manufacturing') could have the potential to change fundamentally the economics of manufacturing, and in doing so challenge the dominance of mass production. But 3D printing is not a new technology as such. Since the 1990s designers have been using the technology to make prototype products or parts quickly and cheaply prior to committing to the expense of equipping a factory to produce the real thing. Yet the technology has advanced to the point where it is used, not just to make prototypes, but to produce finished products for real customers.

A 3D printer produces a 3D object by laying down layer upon layer of material until the final form is obtained. This is why it is also known as 'additive manufacturing', because, starting from nothing, successive layers are built up. This contrasts with 'subtractive manufacturing' that starts with more material than an item requires and reduces it through cutting, drilling, squeezing and otherwise removing material until the finished form is reached. The process starts with a computer-based design which is 'digitally deconstructed' by software that takes a series of virtual digital slices through the design, details of which are sent to the 3D printer. Different materials can be used to build up the object from plastic to metals (and even food) and in various sizes limited only by the capacity of the printer.

Implications

The obvious implication of 3D printing is the effect it has on the economics of production, especially the economics of making small quantities of novel and/or complicated items economically. The technology's more enthusiastic proponents claim that, at last, the trade-off between speed and efficiency on the one hand, and flexibility and variety on the other, has been overcome. Most conventional process technology is at its most efficient when standardized products are made in large batches. But with 3D printing the cost of changing from one product to another is effectively zero. Also, because the technology is 'additive' it reduces waste significantly. Sometimes as much as 90 per cent of material is wasted in machining some aerospace parts, for example. It also enables a single 'experimental' item to be made quickly and cheaply, followed by another one after the design has been refined, as Ian Harris, from the Additive Manufacturing Consortium says: *'It adds up to a new industry which reduces immensely the gap between design and production. Manufacturers will be able to say to their customers, "Tell us what you want" and then they will be able to make specific products for them.'* Some commentators even believe that 3D printing will challenge the advantage of low-cost, low-wage countries. As labour costs become less important, it is argued, manufacturers will return to make items close to their market.

The Internet of Things[4]

Back in 1973 the Universal Product Code or bar code was developed to enable a part or product type to be identified when read by a bar-code scanner. Now bar codes are used to speed up checkout operations in most large supermarkets. However, they also have a role to play in many of the stages in the supply chain that delivers products to retail outlets. During manufacture and in warehouses bar codes are used to keep track of products passing through processes. But bar codes do have disadvantages. It is sometimes difficult to align the item so that the bar code can be read conveniently, items can only be scanned one by one and, most significantly, the bar code only identifies the *type* of item not a specific item itself. That is, the code identifies that an item is, say, a can of one type of drink rather than one specific can. Yet these drawbacks can be overcome through the use of automatic identification technologies such as radio frequency identification (RFID). Here an electronic product code (ePC) that is a unique number 96 bits long is embedded in a memory chip or smart tag. These tags are put on individual items so that each item has its own unique identifying code. At various points during its manufacture, distribution, storage and sale each smart tag can be scanned by a wireless radio frequency 'reader'. This can transmit the item's embedded identify code to a network such as the Internet. *See* Figure 8.3.

Over the last several years the full potential of RFID technology has risen to a more revolutionary level, and one which has some important implications for operations management. Embedding physical objects with sensors and actuators (from vehicles to pharmaceuticals), and connecting them using wireless networks and the protocol that connects the Internet, allows information networks and physical networks to merge to form what has become known as 'the Internet of Things' (IoT). SAP, the developer of enterprise resource systems, describes the Internet of Things as follows: '*A world where physical objects are seamlessly integrated into the information network, and where the physical objects can become active participants in business processes. Services are available to interact with these "smart objects" over the Internet, query and change their state and any information associated with them, taking into account security and privacy issues.*'[5]

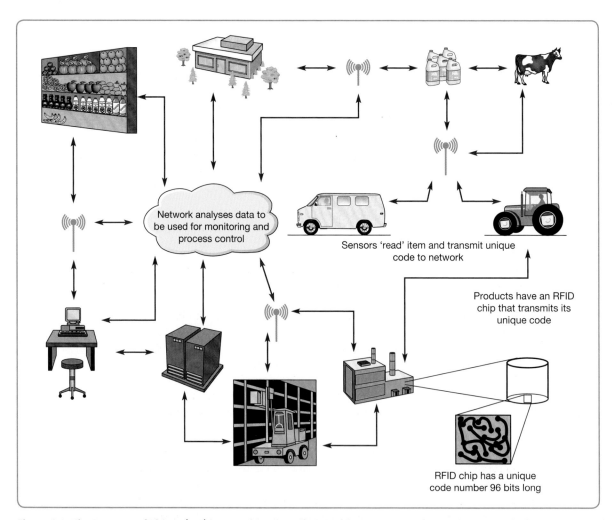

Figure 8.3 The Internet of Things (IoT) is a combination of RFID chips, sensors and Internet protocols that allows information on the location and state of physical objects to be networked

Implications

According to some authorities the IoT promises to create new ways of doing business, the potential to improve processes, and more possibilities to reduce costs and risks. Putting sensors on 'things' gives information networks the ability to generate huge volumes of current data that can both sense the environment and communicate between the 'things'. Operations managers can track and analyse the data to understand what is happening, even in complex systems, and respond quickly if necessary. This helps operations save significant amounts of money in lost, stolen or wasted products by helping manufacturers, distribution companies and retailers to pinpoint exactly the position and state of every item in the supply chain. So, for example, if a product had to be recalled because of a health-risk scare, the exact location of every potentially dangerous product could be immediately identified. Shoppers could easily scan a product to learn more about its characteristics and features while they are in the store, waiting at check-out counters could be eliminated because items will be scanned automatically by readers, the bill could even be automatically debited from your personal account as you leave the store. There are also potential benefits in tracking products after they leave the store. Data on how customers use products can be collected automatically and accurate recycling of waste materials could be made considerably easier. McKinsey, the consultants, see six distinct types of emerging applications with implications for operations managers. These implications fall into two broad categories: first, information and analysis and, second, automation and control.

Information and analysis Because IoT networks link data from products, equipment, processes and the operating environment, they will produce enhanced information and more sophisticated analysis, which can augment operations management decisions. In particular three aspects of information and analysis could be affected:

- *Knowing where things are* – tracking will be easier because the movements of products and their interactions with processes will be monitored in real time. For example, some insurance companies will install location sensors in customers' cars, allowing the insurer to base its fees on how a car is driven as well as where it travels.
- *Knowing what is happening* – the data from a large numbers of sensors, located in such infrastructural resources as roads and buildings, can report on conditions so that managers have an instantaneous awareness of events. For example, security systems can use sensor information from a combination of video, audio and vibration sensors to detect unauthorized entry to restricted areas.
- *Knowing what to do* – the IoT's storage and computing power, when combined with advanced decision support systems, could significantly enhance decision making. For example, in retailing, shoppers can be monitored as they move through stores. Sensors record how long customers loiter at individual displays and record what they ultimately buy. The resulting data can help to optimize retail layouts.

Automation and control Controlling any operation or process involves monitoring what is actually happening within the operation or process, comparing what is *actually* happening with what *should* be happening, then making any necessary interventions to correct any deviations from what should be happening. So monitoring and data collection are at the heart of the control activity, and monitoring and data are what the IoT is particularly good at. When information is fed back through a network to some kind of automation that can intervene and modify process behaviour, control can be exercised (theoretically at least) without human intervention. Again, three aspects could be affected:

- *Process optimization* – processes that can be controlled can be more easily optimized. For example, in some semi-continuous processes in pulp and paper manufacturing, the requirement for the temperature of lime kilns to be continually adjusted limits their productivity. Yet by embedding temperature sensors in the process the kiln's flame can be automatically adjusted to reduce temperature variance (and therefore increase quality) to near zero without frequent operator intervention.

- *Optimized resource usage* – knowing exactly how much resource is being used can help in reducing costs. For example, some energy companies are providing customers with 'smart' meters that give visual displays showing energy usage and the real-time costs of providing it. This allows domestic commercial customers to do things such as moving the use of energy-intensive processes away from peak energy demand periods to off-peak periods.
- *Fast reactions* – the most demanding use of the IoT involves rapid, real-time sensing of unpredictable circumstances and immediate responses governed by automated systems. The idea is for the IoT to imitate human decision makers' reactions, but at a faster and more accurate level. For example, it could be possible for a group of robots to clean up toxic waste spills when detected.

However, the IoT does pose problems. There are technical challenges in integrating RFID chips into physical objects in such a way that makes sure that information is accurately transmitted. And although, as volume has increased, the cost of such chips and sensors has fallen, cost is still a factor in adopting the technology. But perhaps the most contested issues are those relating to customer privacy in extending data capture from products beyond the checkout. It is this issue that particularly scares some civil liberties activists. Keeping track of items within a supply chain is a relatively uncontentious issue. Keeping track of items when those items are identified with particular individuals going about their everyday lives is far more problematic. So, beyond the checkout, for every arguably beneficial application there is also potential for misuse. For example, smart tags could drastically reduce theft because items could automatically report when they are stolen, their tags serving as a homing device to pinpoint their exact location. But similar technology could be used to trace any citizen, honest or not.

Telemedicine[6]

The technological breakthroughs in medical care reported in the press often focus on those dramatic 'miracle cures' which have undoubtedly improved the quality of medical care. Yet a whole collection of changes in medical process technology has also had a huge impact on the way healthcare operations manage themselves. In particular, telemedicine has challenged one of the most fundamental assumptions of medical treatment – that medical staff need to be physically present to examine and diagnose a patient. No longer; web-connected devices are now able to monitor an individual's health-related data and communicate the information to healthcare professionals located anywhere in the world. Doing this allows medical staff to be alerted to changing conditions as they occur, providing a status report of a person's health so that the appropriate care can be administered. Telemedicine generally refers to the use of information and communications technologies for the delivery of clinical care. Formally, telemedicine is the ability to provide interactive healthcare utilizing modern technology and telecommunications. It allows patients to virtually 'visit' physicians – sometimes live, maybe using video links; sometimes automatically in the case of an emergency; sometimes where patient data is stored and sent to physicians for diagnosis and follow-up treatment at a later time. Telemedicine may be as simple as two health professionals discussing a case over the telephone, or as complex as using diagnostic algorithms and video-conferencing equipment to conduct a real-time consultation between medical specialists in different countries. The first interactive telemedicine system was developed and marketed in the USA by MedPhone Corporation in 1989. It operated over standard telephone landlines and was used for remotely diagnosing and treating patients requiring cardiac resuscitation. A year later the company introduced a mobile cellular version.

Broadly, there are three types of telemedicine: store-and-forward, remote monitoring and interactive services.

- *Store-and-forward telemedicine* – involves acquiring medical data such as medical images, blood test results, dermatological data, biosigns, etc., and then transmitting this data to a (remote) medical specialist at a convenient time for assessment offline. Because this does not require the presence of both parties at the same time, there is no actual physical examination and sometimes no opportunity to collect a medical history. The store-and-forward process requires the clinician to rely on a medical record report and maybe audio/video information as a substitute for a physical examination.

- *Remote monitoring* – allows medical professionals to monitor a patient remotely using various technological devices. This method is primarily used for managing chronic (long-lasting) diseases or specific conditions, such as heart disease. Because monitoring can be almost continuous, remote monitoring services can provide better, or at least comparable, health outcomes to traditional physician–patient interactions. In addition, they could be more convenient for both patient and doctor.

- *Interactive telemedicine* – involves real-time interactions between patient and provider. These could include online communication, telephone conversations and facilitated home visits by a non-specialist. This type of telemedicine is similar to traditional face-to-face visits by a physician, and normal activities such as history review, physical examination, psychiatric evaluations, etc., can be performed, at least partially.

Implications

For communities in remote or isolated areas telemedicine can be particularly beneficial. Where previously no, or only a partial (or delayed), service was possible, it allows medical services to be delivered. This is particularly important in developing countries. Known as 'Primary Remote Diagnostic Visits', a doctor uses devices to remotely examine and treat a patient. Telemedicine can also be useful in facilitating communication between a general practitioner and a specialist. All doctors need to seek advice. The easier, faster and cheaper it is to get this advice, the more likely they are to do it. The approach can also make use of decision support diagnostic systems, which give accurate and consistent diagnoses. The quality of medical care in terms of accuracy of diagnosis and appropriateness of treatment is therefore enhanced by 'virtually' bringing specialist expertise to patients. New knowledge, improved medical practice, novel pharmaceuticals, the latest guidelines, and so on, can all be communicated more effectively. Monitoring patients at home using standard equipment like blood pressure monitors and transmitting the information to a carer provides the basis for a faster emergency service. This is certainly true for situations where a physician is needed but no physician is present, such as on a passenger aircraft. For example, telemedicine kits are regularly used by pilots, cabin crew and other attending staff – non-medical experts who may have to deal with possible medical emergencies. They can use the kits to collect and transmit the data that would normally be collected in a hospital emergency room. This enables doctors, at a remote advice service, to help manage the medical emergency, make sure the right decisions are made and determine what treatment can be carried out and whether a diversion or medical evacuation is necessary.

Just as important in a world where some healthcare costs are likely to increase substantially, telemedicine has the potential to bring substantial cost savings. Requiring patients to visit physicians at their surgeries or hospitals is costly for the patient. Requiring doctors to visit patients at home can be even more expensive. Connecting through telemedicine reduces these costs dramatically. Patients having convenient access to medical advice may make fewer visits to the hospital. It is also family centred in the sense that the patient's family life and work are less disrupted. More significantly, nurses can see up to 15 patients in four hours, whereas, visiting them in their home, they can see only 5 or 6 patients a day. Even when the costs of the technology are taken into account, telemedicine can represent a significant cost saving. Similarly, telemedicine can make the outsourcing of medical services easier. Primary-care physicians routinely outsource some services. For example, they take blood samples but send them to a specialist laboratory for analysis. With the more extensive use of telemedicine the data required for diagnostic decisions (for example, X-ray images) can be processed by a large-scale (therefore less expensive) specialist facility, possibly in a less expensive part of the world.

But there are issues with the adoption of telemedicine technology. One study[7] found that there were three major barriers to the adoption of telemedicine in emergency and critical-care units. The first of these is the regulatory environment in some regions. Medicine must be (of course) a regulated activity, but the difficulty and cost of obtaining permission and/or licences, especially when multiple states and multiple facilities are involved, can be prohibitive. Second, there can be a lack of acceptance by whoever pays for medical care, whether this is government or commercial insurance companies. This creates a major financial barrier because it puts the payment responsibility upon the hospital or healthcare system. Third, there may be cultural barriers, with some physicians unable or unwilling to adapt clinical procedures for telemedicine applications.

HOW ARE PROCESS TECHNOLOGIES EVALUATED?

> **✳ Operations principle**
>
> Process technologies can be evaluated in terms of their fit with process tasks, their effect on performance and their financial impact.

The most common technology-related decision in which operations managers will be involved is the choice between alternative technologies. It is an important decision because process technology can have a significant effect on the operation's long-term strategic capability; no one wants to change expensive technologies too frequently. This means that the characteristics of alternative technologies need to be evaluated so that they can be compared. Here we use three sets of criteria for evaluation:

- Does the technology fit the processing task for which it is intended?
- How does the technology improve the operation's performance?
- Does the technology give an acceptable financial return?

OPERATIONS IN PRACTICE

Love it or hate it, Marmite's energy recycling technology[8]

For those readers who live in regions of the world where Marmite is not a big seller, Marmite is 'a nutritious savoury spread that contains B vitamins, enjoyable in a sandwich, on toast, bread or even as a cooking ingredient'. It is not to everyone's taste, which is why it is advertised with the line 'you'll either love it or hate it'. But behind the clever advertising, Marmite, which is part of Unilever, the large food company, is a pioneer in recycling the leftovers from its production process to energy at the factory where it is made. The factory is in Burton upon Trent in the UK and every year around 18,000 tonnes of solidified Marmite deposit is left adhering to the surfaces of the machines and handling equipment that are used to produce the product. For years this residue was cleaned off and then either flushed into the sewerage system or sent to landfill sites. Then Unilever installed an anaerobic digester. This is a composter that uses the waste by-product where it is digested by microbes that feed on the waste. As they do, they release methane which is burned in a boiler connected to a generator

Source: Alamy Images: Lucia Lanpur

that produces power. The system also captures the waste heat that comes through the exhaust and helps heat the factory's water system. *See* Figure 8.4. But the Marmite example is just one part of Unilever's 'Sustainable Living Plan', first published in 2010. Since then it has published an update every year on the progress it is making globally and nationally towards meeting its Sustainable Living Plan targets.

Figure 8.4 Waste product recycling at Marmite

The major material used in the process is waste material produced during the manufacture of Marmite paste. A large proportion of this waste is substances 'driven off' during the evaporation stage.

This waste is a mixture of materials generated during the manufacture of Marmite paste.

The methane in 'bio-gas' is supplied to the site boiler house where it is burnt to produce steam

Steam, produced by burning bio-gas, provides power for the factory. It heats the product stream and lowers evaporator pressure.

Unilever publishes its performance against its Sustainable Living Plan targets as falling into three categories. The first is *'areas where we are making genuinely good progress'*. These included sustainable sourcing, nutrition and eco-efficiency (including the Marmite project). The second category is *'areas where we have had to consider carefully how to reach our targets but are now ready to scale up'*. For instance, a programme to increase the recycling rates of aerosols, encouraging more local councils to collect aerosols kerbside. *'However'*, the report admitted, *'we have more to do, working in partnership with industry, Government and NGOs to help to increase recycling and recovery rates.'* The third category is *'areas where we are finding it difficult to make progress and will need to work with others to find solutions'*. This included targets that require a change in consumer behaviour, such as encouraging people to eat foods with lower salt levels or reducing the use of heated water in showering and washing clothes.

Amanda Sourry, Unilever UK and Ireland Chairman, said: *'The old view of growth at any cost is unacceptable; today the only responsible way to do business is through sustainable growth. It's for this reason that the Unilever Sustainable Living Plan is not just a bolt-on strategy, it's our blue-print for the future. Today's progress update shows that we've made some fantastic steps forward, particularly in the areas of sustainable sourcing, health and nutrition and reducing greenhouse gases. Just one year into the decade-long plan, we are proud of our achievements so far but there's still much more to do.'*

Does the process technology fit the processing task?

Different process technologies will be appropriate for different types of operations, not just because they process different transformed resources, but also because they do so at different levels of volume and variety. High-variety–low-volume processes generally require process technology that is *general purpose*, because it can perform the wide range of processing activities that high variety demands. High-volume–low-variety processes can use technology that is more *dedicated* to its narrower range of processing requirements. Within

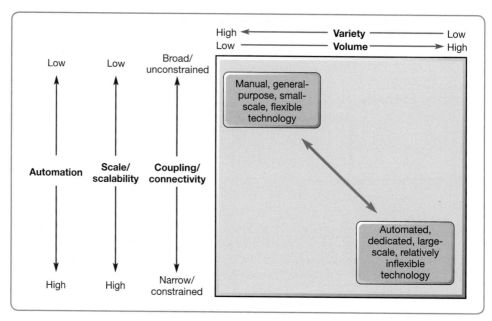

Figure 8.5 Different process technologies are important for different volume–variety combinations

the spectrum from general-purpose to dedicated process technologies three dimensions in particular tend to vary with volume and variety. Figure 8.5 illustrates these three dimensions of process technology:

- Its degree of 'automation'.
- The capacity of the technology to process work, that is its 'scale' or 'scalability'.
- The extent to which it is integrated with other technologies; that is, its degree of 'coupling' or 'connectivity'.

The degree of automation of the technology

To some extent, all technology needs human intervention. It may be minimal, for example the periodic maintenance interventions in a petrochemical refinery. Conversely, the person who operates the technology may be the entire 'brains' of the process, for example the surgeon using keyhole surgery techniques. The ratio of technological to human effort it employs is sometimes called the capital intensity of the process technology. Generally processes that have high variety and low volume will employ process technology with lower degrees of automation than those with higher volume and lower variety. For example, investment banks trade in highly complex and sophisticated financial 'derivatives', often customized to the needs of individual clients, and each may be worth millions of dollars. The back office of the bank has to process these deals to make sure that payments are made on time, documents are exchanged, and so on. Much of this processing will be done using relatively general-purpose technology such as spreadsheets. Skilled back-office staff are making the decisions rather than the technology. Contrast this with higher volume, lower variety products, such as straightforward equity (stock) trades. Most of these products are simple and straightforward and are processed in very high volume of several thousand per day by 'automated' technology.

The scale/scalability of the technology

There is usually some discretion as to the scale of individual units of technology. For example, the duplicating department of a large office complex may decide to invest in a single, very large, fast copier, or alternatively in several smaller, slower copiers distributed around the operation's various processes. An airline may purchase one or two wide-bodied aircraft or a larger number of smaller aircraft. The advantage of large-scale technologies is that they can usually process items cheaper than small-scale technologies, but usually need high volume and can cope only with low variety. By contrast, the virtues of smaller scale technology are often the nimbleness and flexibility that are suited to high-variety, lower volume processing. For example, four small machines can between them produce four different products simultaneously (albeit slowly), whereas a single large machine with four times the output can produce only one product at a time (albeit faster). Small-scale technologies are also more robust. Suppose the choice is between three small machines and one larger one. In the first case, if one machine breaks down, a third of the capacity is lost, but in the second, capacity is reduced to zero. The advantages of large-scale technologies are similar to those of large-capacity increments discussed in Chapter 4.

The equivalent to scale for some types of information-processing technology is *scalability*. By scalability we mean the ability to shift to a different level of useful capacity quickly, and cost-effectively. Scalability is similar to absolute scale in as much as it is influenced by the same volume–variety characteristics. IT scalability relies on consistent IT platform architecture and the high process standardization that is usually associated with high-volume and low-variety operations.

The coupling/connectivity of the technology

Coupling means the linking together of separate activities within a single piece of process technology to form an interconnected processing system. Tight coupling usually gives fast process throughput. For example, in an automated manufacturing system products flow quickly without delays between stages, and inventory will be lower – it cannot accumulate when there are no 'gaps' between activities. Tight coupling also means that flow is simple and predictable, making it easier to keep track of parts when they pass through fewer stages, or information when it is automatically distributed to all parts of an information network. However, closely coupled technology can be both expensive (each connection may require capital costs) and vulnerable (a failure in one part of an interconnected system can affect the whole system). The fully integrated manufacturing system constrains parts to flow in a predetermined manner, making it difficult to accommodate products with very different processing requirements. So, coupling is generally more suited to relatively low variety and high volume. Higher variety processing generally requires a more open and unconstrained level of coupling because different products and services will require a wider range of processing activities.

> **✳ Operations principle**
>
> Process technology in high-volume and low-variety processes is relatively automated, large scale and closely coupled when compared with that in low-volume and high-variety processes.

How does the technology improve the operation's performance?

In Chapters 2 and 3, we identified the five operations *performance objectives*. So a sensible approach to evaluating the impact of any process technology on an operation is to assess how it affects the quality, speed, dependability, flexibility and cost performance of the operation. For example, consider a warehouse that stores spare parts which it packs and distributes to its customers. It is considering investing in a new 'retrieval and packing' system which converts sales orders into 'retrieval lists' and uses materials-handling equipment automatically to pick up the goods from its shelves and bring them to the packing area. The market requirements evaluation for this warehouse might be as follows:

- **Quality** – The impact on quality could be the fact that the computerized system is not prone to human error, which may previously have resulted in the wrong part being picked off the shelves.
- **Speed** – The new system may be able to retrieve items from the shelves faster than human operators can do safely.

- **Dependability** – This will depend on how reliable the new system is. If it is less likely to break down than the operators in the old system were likely to be absent (through illness etc.), then the new system may improve dependability of service.
- **Flexibility** – New service flexibility is not likely to be as good as the previous manual system. For example, there will be a physical limit to the size of products able to be retrieved by the automatic system, whereas people are capable of adapting to doing new things in new ways. Mix flexibility will also be poorer than was previously the case, for the same reason. Volume (and perhaps delivery) flexibility, however, could be better. The new system can work for longer hours when demand is higher than expected or deadlines are changed.
- **Cost** – The new system is certain to require fewer direct operatives to staff the warehouse, but will need extra engineering and maintenance support. Overall, however, lower labour costs are likely.

Does the technology give an acceptable financial return?

Assessing the financial value of investing in process technology is in itself a specialized subject. And while it is not the purpose of this book to delve into the details of financial analysis, it is important to highlight one important issue that is central to financial evaluation: while the benefits of investing in new technology can be spread over many years into the future, the costs associated with investing in the technology usually occur up front. So we have to consider the time value of money. Simply, this means that receiving €1,000 now is better than receiving €1,000 in a year's time. Receiving €1,000 now enables us to invest the money so that it will be worth more than the €1,000 we receive in a year's time. Alternatively, reversing the logic, we can ask ourselves how much would have to be invested now to receive €1,000 in one year's time? This amount (lower than €1,000) is called the net present value of receiving €1,000 in one year's time.

For example, suppose current interest rates are 10 per cent per annum; then the amount we would have to invest to receive €1,000 in one year's time is:

$$€1,000 \times \frac{1}{(1.10)} = €909.10$$

So the present value of €1,000 in one year's time, *discounted for the fact that we do not have it immediately*, is €909.10. In two years' time, the amount we would have to invest to receive €1,000 is:

$$€1,000 \times \frac{1}{(1.10)} \times \frac{1}{(1.10)} = €1,000 \times \frac{1}{(1.10)^2} = €826.50$$

The rate of interest assumed (10 per cent in our case) is known as the discount rate. More generally, the present value of €x in n years' time, at a discount rate of r per cent, is:

$$€\frac{x}{(1+r/100)^n}$$

Worked example

The warehouse which we have been using as an example has been subjected to a costing and cost savings exercise. The capital cost of purchasing and installing the new technology can be spread over three years, and from the first year of its effective operation, overall operations cost savings will be made. Combining the cash that the company will have to spend and the savings that it will make, the cash flow year by year is shown in Table 8.1.

Table 8.1 Cash flows for the warehouse process technology

Year	0	1	2	3	4	5	6	7
Cash flow (€000s)	−300	30	50	400	400	400	400	0
Present value (discounted at 10%)	−300	27.27	41.3	300.53	273.21	248.37	225.79	0

However, these cash flows have to be discounted in order to assess their 'present value'. Here the company is using a discount rate of 10 per cent. This is also shown in Table 8.1 The effective life of this technology is assumed to be six years:

Total cash flow (sum of all the cash flows) = €1.38 million

However:

Net present value (NPV) = €816,500

This is considered to be acceptable by the company.

Calculating discount rates, although perfectly possible, can be cumbersome. As an alternative, tables are usually used such as the one in Table 8.2.

So now the net present value is:

$$P = DF \times FV$$

where:

DF = the discount factor from Table 8.2

FV = future value

To use the table, find the vertical column and locate the appropriate discount rate (as a percentage). Then find the horizontal row corresponding to the number of years it will take to receive the payment. Where the column and the row intersect is the present value of €1. You can multiply this value by the expected future value, in order to find its present value.

Table 8.2 Present value of €1 to be paid in future

Years	3.0%	4.0%	5.0%	6.0%	7.0%	8.0%	9.0%	10.0%
1	€0.970	€0.962	€0.952	€0.943	€0.935	€0.926	€0.918	€0.909
2	€0.942	€0.925	€0.907	€0.890	€0.873	€0.857	€0.842	€0.827
3	€0.915	€0.889	€0.864	€0.840	€0.816	€0.794	€0.772	€0.751
4	€0.888	€0.855	€0.823	€0.792	€0.763	€0.735	€0.708	€0.683
5	€0.862	€0.822	€0.784	€0.747	€0.713	€0.681	€0.650	€0.621
6	€0.837	€0.790	€0.746	€0.705	€0.666	€0.630	€0.596	€0.565
7	€0.813	€0.760	€0.711	€0.665	€0.623	€0.584	€0.547	€0.513
8	€0.789	€0.731	€0.677	€0.627	€0.582	€0.540	€0.502	€0.467
9	€0.766	€0.703	€0.645	€0.592	€0.544	€0.500	€0.460	€0.424
10	€0.744	€0.676	€0.614	€0.558	€0.508	€0.463	€0.422	€0.386
11	€0.722	€0.650	€0.585	€0.527	€0.475	€0.429	€0.388	€0.351
12	€0.701	€0.626	€0.557	€0.497	€0.444	€0.397	€0.356	€0.319
13	€0.681	€0.601	€0.530	€0.469	€0.415	€0.368	€0.326	€0.290
14	€0.661	€0.578	€0.505	€0.442	€0.388	€0.341	€0.299	€0.263

Years	3.0%	4.0%	5.0%	6.0%	7.0%	8.0%	9.0%	10.0%
15	€0.642	€0.555	€0.481	€0.417	€0.362	€0.315	€0.275	€0.239
16	€0.623	€0.534	€0.458	€0.394	€0.339	€0.292	€0.252	€0.218
17	€0.605	€0.513	€0.436	€0.371	€0.317	€0.270	€0.231	€0.198
18	€0.587	€0.494	€0.416	€0.350	€0.296	€0.250	€0.212	€0.180
19	€0.570	€0.475	€0.396	€0.331	€0.277	€0.232	€0.195	€0.164
20	€0.554	€0.456	€0.377	€0.312	€0.258	€0.215	€0.179	€0.149

Worked example

A healthcare clinic is considering purchasing a new analysis system. The net cash flows from the new analysis system are as follows:

Year 1: –€10,000 (outflow of cash)
Year 2: €3,000
Year 3: €3,500
Year 4: €3,500
Year 5: €3,000

Assuming that the real discount rate for the clinic is 9 per cent, using the net present value table (Table 8.2), demonstrate whether the new system would at least cover its costs. Table 8.3 shows the calculations. It shows that, because the net present value of the cash flow is positive, purchasing the new system would cover its costs, and will be (just) profitable for the clinic.

Table 8.3 **Present value calculations for the clinic.**

Year	Cash flow		Table factor		Present value
1	(€10,000)	×	1.000	=	(€10,000.00)
2	€3,000	×	0.917	=	€2,752.29
3	€3,500	×	0.842	=	€2,945.88
4	€3,500	×	0.772	=	€2,702.64
5	€3,000	×	0.708	=	€2,125.28
			Net present value	=	€526.09

HOW ARE PROCESS TECHNOLOGIES IMPLEMENTED?

Implementing process technology means organizing all the activities involved in making the technology work as intended. No matter how potentially beneficial and sophisticated the technology, it remains only a prospective benefit until it has been implemented successfully. So implementation is an important part of process technology management. Yet it is not always straightforward to make general points about the implementation process because it is very context dependent. That is, the way one implements any technology will very much depend on its specific nature, the changes implied by the technology and the organizational conditions that apply during its implementation. In the remainder of this chapter we look at four particularly important issues that affect technology implementation: the way technology is planned over the long term, the idea of resource and process 'distance', the need to consider customer acceptability, and the idea that if anything can go wrong, it will.

Technology planning in the long-term – technology roadmapping

However operations managers are involved with the development of process technologies, it is likely to be in consultation and collaboration with other parts of the firm. It is also likely to be in the context of some kind of formal planning process such as technology roadmapping. A technology roadmap (TRM) is an approach that provides a structure that attempts to assure the alignment of developments (and investments) in technology, possible future market needs, and the new development of associated operations capabilities. Motorola originally developed the approach in the 1970s so that it could support the development of its products and its supporting technologies. Bob Galvin, then Motorola's CEO, defined a TRM as: '*an extended look at the future of a chosen field of inquiry composed from the collective knowledge and imagination of the brightest drivers of change in that field*'. A TRM is essentially a process that supports technology development by facilitating collaboration between the various activities that contribute to technology strategy. It allows technology managers to define their firm's technological evolution in advance by planning the timing and relationships between the various elements that are involved in technology planning. For example, these 'elements' could include the business goals of the company, market developments or specific events, the component products and services that constitute related offerings, product/service and process technologies, the underlying capabilities that these technologies represent, and so on. Figure 8.6 shows the generic form of technology roadmaps, while Figure 8.7 shows an example of a TRM for the development of products/services, technologies and processes for a facilities management service.

The benefits of TRMs are mainly associated with the way they bring together the significant stakeholders involved in technology strategy and various (and often differing) perspectives

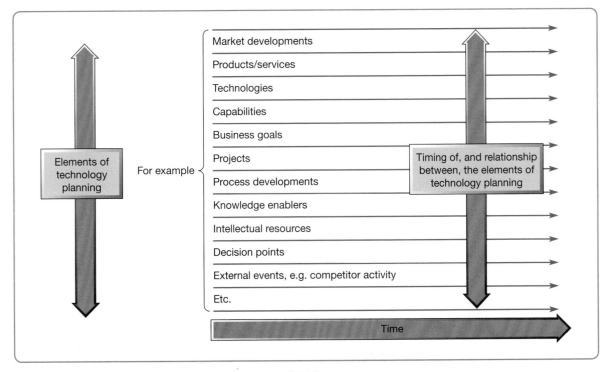

Figure 8.6 The generic form of a technology roadmap (TRM)

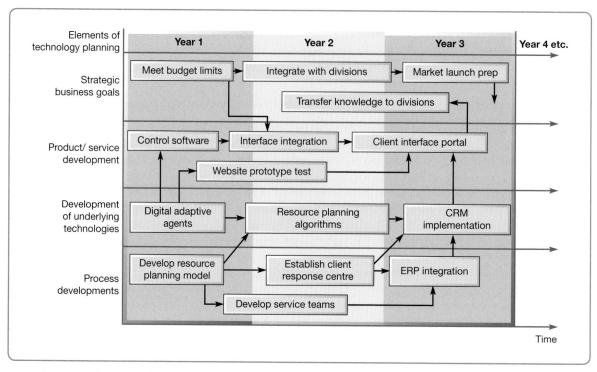

Figure 8.7 Simplified example of a TRM for the development of products/services, technologies, and processes for a facilities management service

they have. The approach forms a basis for communication, and possibly consensus. After all, it does tackle some fundamental questions that concern any technology strategy. Why do we need to develop our technology? Where do we want to go with our technological capabilities? How far away are we from that objective? How can we get to where we want to be? In what order should we do things? By when should development goals be reached? Yet TRMs do not offer any solutions to any firm's technological strategic options; in fact they need not offer options or alternative technology trajectories. They are essentially a narrative description of how a set of interrelated developments should (rather than will) progress. Because of this they have been criticized as encouraging over-optimistic projections of the future. Nevertheless, they do provide, at the very least, a plan against which technology strategy can be assessed.

Resource and process 'distance'

The degree of difficulty in the implementation of process technology will depend on the degree of novelty of the new technology resources and the changes required in the operation's processes. The less that the new technology resources are understood (influenced perhaps by the degree of innovation), the greater their 'distance' from the current technology resource base of the operation. Similarly, the extent to which an implementation requires an operation to modify its existing processes, the greater the 'process distance'. The greater the resource and process distance, the more difficult any implementation is likely to be. This is because such distance makes it difficult to adopt a systematic approach to analysing change and learning from mistakes. Those implementations which involve relatively little process or resource 'distance' provide an ideal opportunity for organizational learning. As in any classic scientific experiment, the more variables that are held constant, the more confidence you have in determining cause and effect. Conversely, in an implementation where the resource and process 'distance' mean

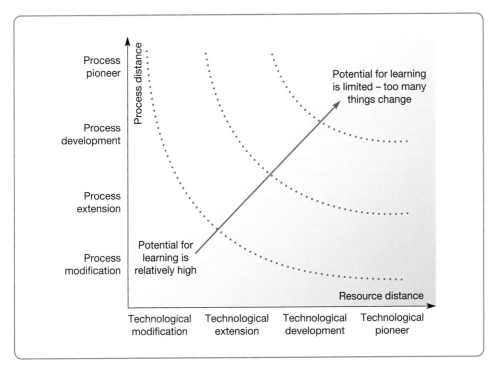

Figure 8.8 Learning potential depends on both technological resource and process 'distance'

that nearly everything is 'up for grabs', it becomes difficult to know what has worked and what has not. More importantly, it becomes difficult to know why something has or has not worked.[9] This idea is illustrated in Figure 8.8.

Not enough people choose 'Choose and Book'

It was a technology project that was 10 years in the making. The 'Choose and Book' system should have transformed the way in which patients and their 'General Practitioner' (GP) physicians could select an outpatient hospital appointment at a convenient date and time in the UK's National Health Service (NHS). The aim was to speed up the process and cut out the need for costly paperwork. Yet in 2014 it was quietly dropped despite costing £356m during the 10 years that it had been struggling to establish itself. It was taken as another example of the difficulties of introducing new technology systems into such a huge and complex organization. An investigation by the UK's House of Commons' Public Accounts Committee was told by NHS staff that, although some GPs liked the 'Choose and Book' system, many did not. Moreover, not all outpatient appointment slots were available on the system, which limited its usefulness. Many patients and doctors found 'Choose and

Book' complicated and time consuming. One GP, Sarah Wollaston, said, '*the system suits patients who were good with technology but not those who were less so. Doctors often did not have time to log on to it during appointments with their patients.*' A Member of Parliament

said: 'It's another NHS cock up. A system designed for use by GPs but only used by half of them...has been quietly dropped, so quietly that even most of the NHS seems unaware. In the middle of all of this are patients. Choose and Book was supposed to speed things up but the evidence we heard in committee showed this was not so in most cases.' Despite the failure of 'Choose and Book' (or only partial success) the government department that oversees the NHS decided to replace it with a potentially even more expensive e-referral scheme, saying that the new e-referral system would use different technology and have additional features as well as being available on mobile apps. A spokesperson said, 'we are aiming to have 100% electronic referrals within the next five years – sooner than that if we can make it. That will cut out a lot of these errors.' It was also reported that the idea of making it compulsory for GPs to use the replacement system when it comes on-stream, with an inbuilt incentive and penalty scheme for doctors and hospitals, was being considered.

The BBC's Digital Media Initiative

The BBC is one of the best-known broadcasters in the world, with an unrivalled reputation for the quality of some of its programmes. Sadly, its reputation for introducing new technology is less exemplary. Among its more spectacular failures was its Digital Media Initiative (DMI). The DMI was an endeavour by the BBC to dispense with videotapes and create a kind of 'internal YouTube' of archive content that staff could access, upload, edit and then air from their computers. When the project was originally envisaged, creating a single TV programme could involve 70 individual video-handling processes. DMI was meant to halve that. The project cost almost £100 million and lasted five years before it was scrapped. The flaws in the technology were exposed during the BBC's coverage of the state funeral of Margaret Thatcher, a well-known ex-Prime Minister. The DMI was supposed to create a production system linked to the BBC's huge broadcasting archive, but instead of streamlining access to old video footage, video editors were unable to access archive footage to use in news reports from their computers in Central London. Instead they had to transport videotapes there using taxis and the underground network from the archive storage facility in north-west London. Admitting that to continue with the project would be 'throwing good money after bad', the BBC suspended its chief technology officer. One BBC manager called the DMI project 'the axis of awful', while another said, 'The scale of the project was just too big, and it got out of hand.' Anthony Fry, a member of the BBC's governing body, said that the project had 'generated little or no assets for the corporation. This is because much of the software and hardware which has been developed could only be used by the BBC if the project were completed, which, due to technological difficulties and changes to business needs ...[was not possible]. Tony Hall, the BBC's Director General, said that off-the-shelf tools 'that simply didn't exist five years ago' had now become available and they could do the same job as some elements of the DMI. Professors Elizabeth Daniel of the Open University Business School and John Ward of Cranfield School of Management, commenting on the BBC DMI case, said, 'it is not the biggest or the worst IT project failure in the public or private sectors and, without organizations' implementing measures to guard against them, it will almost certainly not be the last'. While at first glance, they say, it seems the BBC's Digital Media Initiative project suffered from the challenges encountered in many other large IT projects, there are some aspects of the BBC operation and culture that may have exacerbated them. The organization appears to have reacted slowly to concerns raised at senior level, there was an inability to identify that things were going wrong and then to act impartially. The failure of the DMI was regarded as an IT failure, not of the BBC, and, most worrying, there was a culture which apparently did not allow staff involved to be given a voice, so, unable to feed their concerns about projects into review processes, they were instead reduced to privately voicing them.

Customer acceptability

When an operation's customers interact with its process technology it is essential to consider the customer interaction when evaluating it. If customers are to have direct contact with technology, they must have some idea of how to operate it. Where customers have an active interaction with technology, the limitations of their understanding of the technology can be the main constraint on its use. For example, even some domestic technology such as smart TVs cannot be used to their full potential by most owners. Other customer-driven technologies can face the same problem, with the important addition that if customers cannot use technologies such as Internet banking, there are serious commercial consequences for a bank's customer service. Staff in manufacturing operations may require several years of training before they are given control of the technology they operate. Service operations may not have the same opportunity for customer training. Walley and Amin[11] suggest that the ability of the operation to train its customers in the use of its technology depends on three factors: complexity, repetition, and the variety of tasks performed by the customer. If services are complex, higher levels of 'training' may be needed; for example, the technologies in theme parks and fast food outlets rely on customers copying the behaviour of others. Frequency of use is important because the payback for the 'investment' in training will be greater if the customer uses the technology frequently. Also, customers may, over time, forget how to use the technology, but regular repetition will reinforce the training. Finally, training will be easier if the customer is presented with a low variety of tasks. For example, vending machines tend to concentrate on one category of product, so that the sequence of tasks required to operate the technology remains consistent.

In other cases the technology may not be trusted by customers because it is technology and not a person. Sometimes we prefer to put ourselves in the care of a person, even if their performance is inferior to a technology. For example, the use of robot technologies in surgery has distinct advantages over conventional surgery, but in spite of the fact that the surgeon is in control, it is viewed with suspicion by some patients and physicians. When robot surgeons operate without any direct human control, rather than simply mirroring the movement of human surgeons, resistance is likely to be even greater. Similarly the idea of pilotless aircraft is difficult to 'sell' to customers; see the 'Who's in the cockpit?' case.

OPERATIONS IN PRACTICE

Who's in the cockpit?[12]

Modern aircraft fly on automatic pilot for most of their time, certainly more than most passengers realize. 'Most people are blissfully unaware that when an aircraft lands in mist or fog, it is a computer that is landing it', says Paul Jackson of *Jane's All The World's Aircraft*. 'It is the only sensible thing to do', agrees Ken Higgins of Boeing. 'When auto pilots can do something better than a human pilot, we obviously use auto pilots.' Generally this means using auto pilots to do two jobs. First, they can take control of the aircraft during the long and (for the pilot) monotonous part of the flight between take-off and landing. Automatic pilots are not prone to the tedium or weariness which can affect humans and which can cause pilot error. The second job is to make landings, especially when visibility is poor because of fog or light conditions. The auto pilot communicates with automatic equipment on the ground which allows the aircraft to be landed, if necessary, under conditions of zero visibility. In fact, automatic landings when visibility is poor are safer than when the pilot is in control. Even in the unlikely event of one of the aircraft's two engines failing, an auto pilot can land it safely. This means that, on some flights, the auto pilot is switched on within seconds of the aircraft wheels leaving the ground and then remains in charge throughout the flight and the landing. One of the few reasons not to use the auto pilot is if the pilot is training or needs to log up the required number of landings to keep licensed.

Source: The Kobal Collection: Paramount Pictures

As yet, commercial flights do not take off automatically, mainly because it would require airports and airlines to invest in extra guidance equipment which would be expensive to develop and install. Also take-off is technically more complex than landing. More things could go wrong and some situations (for example, an engine failure during take-off) require split-second decision making from the pilot. Industry analysts agree that it would be technically feasible to develop automatic take-off technology that met required safety standards, but it could be prohibitively expensive.

Yet some in the airline industry believe that technology could be developed to the point where commercial flights can do without a pilot on the aircraft entirely. This is not as far-fetched as it seems. In April 2001 the Northrop Grumman Global Hawk, an 'unmanned aerial vehicle' (UAV), completed the first entirely unmanned flight of the Pacific when it took off from California and landed nearly 24 hours later in South Australia. The Global Hawk made the journey without any human intervention whatsoever. 'We made a historic flight with two clicks of the mouse', said Bob Mitchell of Northrop Grumman. The first mouse click told the aircraft to take off; the second, made after landing, told it to switch of its engine. UAVs are used for military reconnaissance purposes but enthusiasts point out that most aircraft breakthroughs, such as the jet engine and radar, were developed for military use before they found civilian applications. However, even the enthusiasts admit that there are some significant problems to overcome before pilotless aircraft could become commonplace. The entire commercial flight infrastructure from air traffic control through to airport control would need to be restructured, a wholly automatic pilotless aircraft would have to be shown to be safe, and, perhaps most important, passengers would have to be persuaded to fly in them. If all these objections could be overcome, the rewards are substantial. Airlines' largest single cost is the wages of its staff (far more than fuel costs or maintenance costs etc.) and, of all staff, pilots are by far the most costly. Automated flights would cut costs significantly, but no one is taking bets on its happening soon!

Anticipating implementation problems

The implementation of any process technology will need to account for the 'adjustment' issues that almost always occur when making any organizational change. By adjustment issues we mean the losses that could be incurred before the improvement is functioning as intended. But estimating the nature and extent of any implementation issues is notoriously difficult. This is particularly true because, more often than not, Murphy's law seems to prevail. This law is usually stated as: 'if anything can go wrong, it will'. This effect has been identified empirically in a range of operations, especially when new types of process technology are involved. Specifically discussing technology-related change (although the ideas apply to almost any implementation), Bruce Chew of the Massachusetts Institute of Technology[13] argues that adjustment 'costs' stem from unforeseen mismatches between the new technology's capabilities and needs and the existing operation. New technology rarely behaves as planned, and as changes are made their impact ripples throughout the organization. Figure 8.9 is an example of what Chew calls a Murphy curve. It shows a typical pattern of performance reduction (in this case, quality) as a new process technology

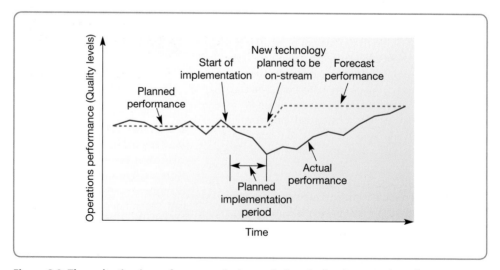

Figure 8.9 The reduction in performance during and after the implementation of a new process reflects 'adjustments costs'

is introduced. It is recognized that implementation may take some time; therefore allowances are made for the length and cost of a 'ramp-up' period. However, as the operation prepares for the implementation, the distraction causes performance actually to deteriorate. Even after the start of the implementation this downward trend continues and it is only weeks, indeed maybe months, later that the old performance level is reached. The area of the dip indicates the magnitude of the adjustment costs, and therefore the level of vulnerability faced by the operation.

SUMMARY ANSWERS TO KEY QUESTIONS

❭ What is process technology?

- Process technologies are the machines, equipment or devices that help operations to create or deliver products and services. Indirect process technology helps to facilitate the direct creation of products and services.

❭ What do operations managers need to know about process technology?

- Operations managers do not need to know the technical details of all technologies, but they do need to know the answers to four key questions: What does it do? How does it do it? What advantages does it give? What constraints does it impose?
- Process technologies can also be classified according to the transformed resources that they process, namely material-processing technologies, information-processing technologies and customer-processing technologies. In addition some technologies process more than one type of resource; they are called integrating technologies.
- An important element in understanding process technologies is to understand the implications they hold for the operations where they will be used.

❭ How are process technologies evaluated?

- All technologies should be appropriate for the activities that they have to undertake. In practice this means making sure that the degree of automation of the technology, the scale or scalability of the technology, and the degree of coupling or connectivity of the technology fit the volume and variety characteristics of the operation.
- All technologies should be evaluated by assessing the impact that the process technology will have on the operation's performance objectives (quality, speed, dependability, flexibility and cost).
- All technologies should be evaluated financially. This usually involves the use of some of the more common evaluation approaches, such as net present value (NPV).

❭ How are process technologies implemented?

- Implementing process technology means organizing all the activities involved in making the technology work as intended.
- A technology roadmap (TRM) is an approach that provides a structure that attempts to assure the alignment of developments (and investments) in technology, possible future market needs, and the new development of associated operations capabilities.

- The resource and process 'distance' implied by the technology implementation will indicate the degree of difficulty.
- Customer acceptability may be a barrier to implementation in customer-processing technologies.
- It is necessary to allow for the adjustment costs of implementation.

CASE STUDY

Rochem Ltd

Dr Rhodes was losing his temper. *'It should be a simple enough decision. There are only two alternatives. You are only being asked to choose a machine!'*

The Management Committee looked abashed. Rochem Ltd was one of the largest independent companies supplying the food-processing industry. Its initial success had come with a food preservative used mainly for meat-based products and marketed under the name of 'Lerentyl'. Other products were subsequently developed in the food colouring and food container coating fields, so that now Lerentyl accounted for only 25 per cent of total company sales, which were now slightly over £10 million.

Source: Press Association Images: AP / Eckehard Schulz

The decision

The problem over which there was such controversy related to the replacement of one of the process units used to manufacture Lerentyl. Only two such units were used; both were 'Chemling' machines. It was the older of the two Chemling units which was giving trouble. High breakdown figures, with erratic quality levels, meant that output-level requirements were only just being reached. The problem was: should the company replace the ageing Chemling with a new Chemling, or should it buy the only other plant on the market capable of the required process, the 'AFU' unit? The Chief Chemist's staff had drawn up a comparison of the two units, shown in Table 8.4.

The body considering the problem was the newly formed Management Committee. The committee consisted of the

Table 8.4 **A comparison of the two alternative machines**

	Chemling	AFU
Capital cost	£590,000	£880,000
Processing costs	Fixed: £15,000/month	Fixed: £40,000/month
	Variable: £750/kg	Variable: £600/kg
Design capacity	105 kg/month	140 kg/month
	98 ± 0.7% purity	99.5 ± 0.2% purity
Quality	Manual testing	Automatic testing
Maintenance	Adequate but needs servicing	Not known – probably good
After-sales services	Very good	Not known – unlikely to be good
Delivery	Three months	Immediate

four senior managers in the firm: the Chief Chemist and the Marketing Manager, who had been with the firm since its beginning, together with the Production Manager and the Accountant, both of whom had joined the company only six months earlier.

What follows is a condensed version of the information presented by each manager to the committee, together with their attitudes to the decision.

The Marketing Manager

The current market for this type of preservative had reached a size of some £5 million, of which Rochem Ltd supplied approximately 48 per cent. There had, of late, been significant changes in the market – in particular, many of the users of preservatives were now able to buy products similar to Lerentyl. The result had been the evolution of a much more price-sensitive market than had previously been the case. Further market projections were somewhat uncertain. It was clear that the total market would not shrink (in volume terms) and best estimates suggested a market of perhaps £6 million within the next three or four years (at current prices). However, there were some people in the industry who believed that the present market only represented the tip of the iceberg.

Although the food preservative market had advanced by a series of technical innovations, 'real' changes in the basic product were now few and far between. Lerentyl was sold in either solid powder or liquid form, depending on the particular needs of the customer. Prices tended to be related to the weight of chemical used, however. Thus, for example, the current average market price was approximately £1,050 per kg. There were, of course, wide variations depending on order size etc.

'At the moment I am mainly interested in getting the right quantity and quality of Lerentyl each month and although Production has never let me down yet, I'm worried that unless we get a reliable new unit quickly, it soon will. The AFU machine could be on line in a few weeks, giving better quality too. Furthermore, if demand does increase (but I'm not saying it will), the AFU will give us the extra capacity. I will admit that we are not trying to increase our share of the preservative market as yet. We see our priority as establishing our other products first. When that's achieved, we will go back to concentrating on the preservative side of things.'

The Chief Chemist

The Chief Chemist was an old friend of Dr Rhodes and together they had been largely responsible for every product innovation. At the moment, the major part of his budget was devoted to modifying basic Lerentyl so that it could be used for more acidic food products such as fruit. This was not proving easy and as yet nothing had come of the research, although the Chief Chemist remained optimistic.

'If we succeed in modifying Lerentyl the market opportunities will be doubled overnight and we will need the extra capacity. I know we would be taking a risk by going for the AFU machine, but our company has grown by gambling on our research findings, and we must continue to show faith. Also the AFU technology is the way all similar technologies will be in the future. We have to start learning how to exploit it sooner or later.'

The Production Manager

The Lerentyl Department was virtually self-contained as a production unit. In fact, it was physically separate, located in a building a few yards detached from the rest of the plant. Production requirements for Lerentyl were currently at a steady rate of 190 kg per month. The six technicians who staffed the machines were the only technicians in Rochem who did all their own minor repairs and full quality control. The reason for this was largely historical since, when the firm started, the product was experimental and qualified technicians were needed to operate the plant. Four of the six had been with the firm almost from its beginning.

'It's all right for Dave and Eric [Marketing Manager and Chief Chemist] to talk about a big expansion of Lerentyl sales; they don't have to cope with all the problems if it doesn't happen. The fixed costs of the AFU unit are nearly three times those of the Chemling. Just think what that will do to my budget at low volumes of output. As I understand it, there is absolutely no evidence to show a large upswing in Lerentyl. No, the whole idea [of the AFU plant] is just too risky. Not only is there the risk. I don't think it is generally understood what the consequences of the AFU would mean. We would need twice the variety of spares for a start. But what really worries me is the staff's reaction. As fully qualified technicians they regard themselves as the elite of the firm; so they should, they are paid practically the same as I am! If we get the AFU plant, all their most interesting work, like the testing and the maintenance, will disappear or be greatly reduced. They will finish up as highly paid process workers.'

The Accountant

The company had financed nearly all its recent capital investment from its own retained profits, but would be taking out short-term loans the following year for the first time for several years.

'At the moment, I don't think it wise to invest extra capital we can't afford in an attempt to give us extra capacity we don't need. This year will be an expensive one for the company. We are already committed to considerably increased expenditure on promotion of our other products and capital investment in other parts of the firm, and Dr Rhodes is not in favour of excessive funding from outside the firm. I accept that there might eventually be an upsurge in Lerentyl demand but, if it does come, it probably won't be this year and it will be far bigger than the AFU can cope with anyway, so we might as well have three Chemling plants at that time.'

1 How do the two alternative process technologies (Chemling and AFU) differ in terms of their scale and automation? What are the implications of this for Rochem?

2 Remind yourself of the distinction between feasibility, acceptability and vulnerability discussed in Chapter 4. Evaluate both technologies using these criteria.

3 What would you recommend the company should do?

PROBLEMS AND APPLICATIONS

1 In the early part of this chapter, three technologies are described: 3D printing, the Internet of Things, and Telemedicine. Try to describe the technologies by answering the 'four key questions' that are also described.

2 A new machine requires an investment of €500,000 and will generate profits of €100,000 for 10 years. Will the investment have a positive net present value assuming that a realistic interest is 6 per cent?

3 A local government housing office is considering investing in a new computer system for managing the maintenance of its properties. The system is forecast to generate savings of around £100,000 per year and will cost £400,000. It is expected to have a life of seven years. The local authority expects its departments to use a discount rate of 0.3 to calculate the financial return on its investments. Is this investment financially worthwhile?

4 In the problem above, the local government's finance officers have realized that their discount rate has been historically too low. They now believe that the discount rate should be doubled. Is the investment in the new computer system still worthwhile?

5 A new optical reader for scanning documents is being considered by a retail bank. The new system has a fixed cost of €30,000 per year and a variable cost of €2.5 per batch. The cost of the new scanner is €100,000. The bank charges €10 per batch for scanning documents and it believes that the demand for its scanning services will be 2,000 batches in year 1, 5,000 batches in year 2, 10,000 batches in year 3, and then 12,000 batches per year from year 4 onwards. If the realistic discount rate for the bank is 6 per cent, calculate the net present value of the investment over a five-year period.

SELECTED FURTHER READING

Arthur, W.B. (2010) *The Nature of Technology: What It Is and How It Evolves*, Penguin, Harmondsworth.

Popular science in a way, but very interesting on how technologies evolve.

Brain, M. (2001) *How Stuff Works*, Wiley, New York.

Exactly what it says. A lot of the 'stuff' is product technology, but the book also explains many process technologies in a clear and concise manner without sacrificing relevant detail.

Brynjolfsson, E. and McAfee, A. (2014) *The Second Machine Age: Work, Progress, and Prosperity in a Time of Brilliant Technologies*, W. W. Norton, New York.

This is one of the most influential recent books on how technology will change our lives.

Carr, N.G. (2000) Hypermediation: 'Commerce and Clickstream', *Harvard Business Review*, January–February.

Written at the height of the Internet boom, it gives a flavour of how Internet technologies were seen.

Chew, W.B., Leonard-Barton, D. and Bohn, R.E. (1991) Beating Murphy's Law, *Sloan Management Review*, vol. 5, Spring.

One of the few articles that treats the issue of why everything seems to go wrong when any new technology is introduced. Insightful.

Cobham, D. and Curtis, G. (2004) *Business Information Systems: Analysis, Design and Practice*, Financial Times Prentice Hall, Harlow.

A good solid text on the subject.

Evans, P. and Wurster, T. (1999) *Blown to Bits: How the new economics of information transforms strategy*, Harvard Business School Press, Boston, MA.

Interesting exposition of how Internet-based technologies can change the rules of the game in business.

9

People in operations

Key questions

❯ Why are people so important in operations management?

❯ How do operations managers contribute to human resource strategy?

❯ How can the operations function be organized?

❯ How do we go about designing jobs?

❯ How are work times allocated?

INTRODUCTION

Operations management is often presented as a subject the main focus of which is on technology, systems, procedures and facilities – in other words, the non-human parts of the organization. This is not true of course. On the contrary, the manner in which an organization's human resources are managed has a profound impact on the effectiveness of its operations function. In this chapter we look especially at the elements of human resource management which are traditionally seen as being directly within the sphere of operations management. These are how operations managers contribute to human resource strategy, organization design, job design, and the allocation of 'work times' to operations activities. The more detailed (and traditional) aspects of these last two elements are discussed further in the supplement on work study at the end of this chapter. Figure 9.1 shows how this chapter fits into the overall model of operations activities.

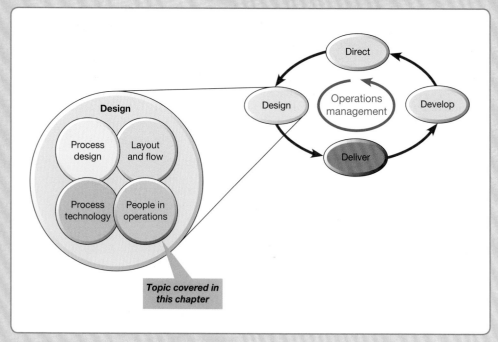

Figure 9.1 This chapter examines people in operations

WHY ARE PEOPLE SO IMPORTANT IN OPERATIONS MANAGEMENT?

To say that an organization's human resources are its greatest asset is something of a cliché. Yet it is worth reminding ourselves of the importance of the abilities, attitudes and culture of the people who make up the operations function. It is, after all, where most 'human resources' are to be found. It follows that it is operations managers who are most involved in the leadership, development and organization of human resources. In this chapter we examine some of the issues that most directly affect, or are affected by, operations management; these are illustrated in Figure 9.2. But the influence of operations management on the organization's staff is not limited to the topics covered in this chapter. Almost everything discussed in this book has a 'people' dimension. Yet, in some chapters, the human perspective is particularly important. In addition to this chapter, Chapters 16 and 17, for example, are concerned largely with how the contribution of the operation's staff can be harnessed. In essence the issues covered in this chapter define how people go about their working lives. It positions their expectations of what is required of them, and it influences their perceptions of how they contribute to the organization. It defines their activities in relation to their work colleagues and it channels the flows of communication between different parts of the operation. But, of most importance, it helps to develop the culture of the organization – its shared values, beliefs and assumptions.

> ✳ **Operations principle**
>
> Human resources aspects are especially important in the operations function, where most 'human resources' are to be found.

Operations culture

What do we mean by culture in the context of the operations function? There is a wealth of academic or popular literature that treats the concept of organizational culture, but no single authoritative definition has emerged. Nevertheless most of us know roughly what is meant by 'culture' in an organization. It is what it feels like to be part of it – what is assumed about how things get done rather than is necessarily formally articulated. It is, in the words of one well-known writer on the subject, *'the way we do things around here'* or *'the organisation's climate'*.[1] But the idea of 'organizational' culture can also apply to a single function like the operations function. In fact there is considerable interest among researchers and practitioners in overcoming the cultural differences between different functions that can sometimes lead to what has been called 'cultural fragmentation'. Even though there may be elements of an organization's culture that are shared across all parts of the enterprise, different functions are very likely to have their own subcultures.

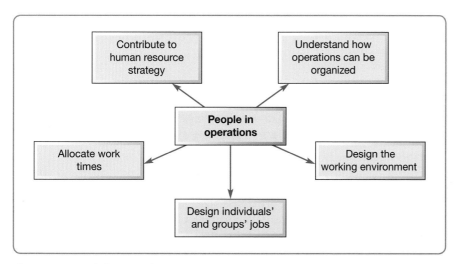

Figure 9.2 People in operations

Most famous for its high-performance fabrics such as Gore-Tex, W.L. Gore also has an enviable reputation as being one of the best companies to work for wherever it operates. In a recent 'Best Companies to work for' list its associates (the company does not use the term 'employees') gave it the very top marks for 'feeling you can make a difference'. More than half of its staff have been with the firm for at least a decade, a consequence of its philosophy ('to make money and have fun') and its unique organizational culture and job design practices. Few in the company have any formal job titles, or job descriptions. There are no managers, only leaders and associates, people are paid 'according to their contribution' and staff help to determine each other's pay – ideas which seem revolutionary yet are based on the company's founding principles from over 50 years ago. Started by Bill and Vieve Gore in the basement of their home in Delaware, it has now become a global business with facilities in more than 45 locations around the world. Its skilled staff develop, manufacture and sell a range of innovative products, virtually all of which are based on just one material (expanded polytetrafluoroethylene) which was discovered by Bob Gore (the founders' son) in 1969. It now has approximately 8,000 associates in its four main divisions (textiles, electronic, medical and industrial products) and annual revenues of over \$2 billion.

Gore's approach to how it works with its staff is at the heart of the company's success. On almost every level Gore is different to other global companies. Associates are hired for general work areas rather than specific jobs, and with the guidance of their 'sponsors' (not bosses), and as they develop experience, they commit to projects that match their skills. Teams organize around opportunities as they arise, with associates committing to the projects that they have chosen to work on, rather than having tasks delegated to them. Project teams are small, focused, multi-disciplined, and foster strong relationships between team members. Personal initiative is encouraged, as is 'hands-on' innovation, which involves those closest to a project in its decision making. There are, says Gore, no traditional organizational charts, no chains of command, no predetermined channels of communication. Instead, team members communicate directly with each other and are accountable to the other members of their team. Groups are led by whoever is the most appropriate person at each stage of a project. Leaders are not appointed by senior management; they 'emerge' naturally by demonstrating special knowledge, skill or experience that advances

Source: Shutterstock.com: Marques

a business objective. Everyone's performance is assessed using a peer-level rating system. Even the group's CEO (one of the few people with a title), Terri Kelly, 'emerged' in this way. When the previous CEO retired, no shortlist of preferred candidates was interviewed; instead, along with board discussions, a wide range of associates were invited to nominate people they would be willing to follow. 'We weren't given a list of names – we were free to choose anyone in the company', she says. 'To my surprise, it was me.'

The explicit aim of the company's culture is to 'combine freedom with co-operation and autonomy with synergy'. Everyone can earn the credibility to define and drive projects. Sponsors help associates chart a course in the organization that will offer personal fulfilment while maximizing their contribution to the enterprise. Associates adhere to four basic guiding principles, originally expressed by Bill Gore:

● Fairness to each other and everyone with whom we come in contact.
● Freedom to encourage, help, and allow other associates to grow in knowledge, skill, and scope of responsibility.
● The ability to make one's own commitments and keep them.
● Consultation with other associates before undertaking actions that could impact the reputation of the company.

This degree of personal commitment and control by associates would not sit happily with a large 'corporate'-style organization. It is no surprise, then, that Gore has unusual notions of economies of scale. Bill Gore believed in the need 'to divide so that you can multiply'. So when units grow to around 200 people, they are usually split up, with these small facilities organized in clusters or campuses. Ideally a dozen or so sites are close enough to permit good communication and knowledge exchange, but can still be intimate yet separate enough to promote a feeling of ownership. Bill Gore also believed that people come to work to be innovative and had a desire to invent great products. This, he said, 'would be the glue holding the company together', rather than the official procedures other companies rely on. And at Gore's Livingstone plant in Scotland the story of 'the breathable bagpipes' is used to illustrate this type of creative innovation generated from the company's culture of trust that allows people to follow their passion. The story goes that an associate who worked in Gore's filter bags department at Livingstone was also a keen exponent of his national instrument – the bagpipes. By day he would be working on filter systems, in the evening he would play his bagpipes. It occurred to him that the physical properties of the product he was putting together during the day could make a synthetic bag for the pipes he played in the evening. Traditionally, bagpipes have a bag made from sheepskin or cow leather which fills up with moisture and becomes a smelly health hazard. He recognized that if you added Gore-Tex, it would be breathable and it would be dry. He put a prototype together, tried it, and it worked. So he decided to spend time developing it, created a team to develop it further, and now almost all Scottish bagpipes have a Gore-Tex bag in them.

Believe, know and behave

Culture is difficult to explain. As was said of one organization with a particularly strong culture (a university as it happens), *'From the outside looking in, you can't understand it. From the inside looking out, you can't explain it.'*[3] As far as the operations function is concerned, it is best summed up by what the operations team *believes*, what it *knows* and how it *behaves*. It is these three elements of operations culture – belief, knowledge and behaviour – which provide the foundations for how it contributes to the business and how capable it is to improve over time:

- **What operations believe** – By 'operations belief', we mean what the people within the operations function accept as self-evident. For example, do operations believe that they have a responsibility to understand fully all other functions' strategies and their implications for operations; do they develop capabilities within their operations resources and processes that offer a unique and long-lasting strategic advantage?
- **What operations should know** – What should the operations team know? Obviously it should understand the underlying principles that govern how operations and processes work. Only with a thorough understanding of the objectives, concepts, tools and techniques of operations management will the operations function ever contribute fully to the success of any business.
- **How operations should behave** – The way operations managers should behave is not fundamentally different from any effective manager. The popular and academic literature have for decades been full of 'key behaviours' for effective leadership, and they do not seem to have changed much for years: 'Don't micromanage your team, empower them while still being available for advice.' 'Be a coach to your team.' 'Be clear and results-oriented, but help the team to see how they can achieve them.' 'Have a clear vision and strategy.' 'Always communicate; both ways – and listen to your team.' 'Support open discussion and listen to the team's concerns.' All of which are may be obvious, but make good managerial sense.

HOW DO OPERATIONS MANAGERS CONTRIBUTE TO HUMAN RESOURCE STRATEGY?

Human resource strategy is the overall long-term approach to ensuring that an organization's human resources provide a strategic advantage. It involves two interrelated activities. First, identifying the number and type of people that are needed to manage, run and develop the organization so that it meets its strategic business objectives. Second, putting in place the programmes and initiatives that attract, develop and retain appropriate staff. It is an essential activity. Here is what Accenture, one of the top consultancies in the world, has to say about it[4]: *'Attention to people is more critical than ever…a company's workforce has become increasingly important to business success – so much so that most senior executives now view people and workforce issues as a critical competitive differentiator and one of their top agenda items…A superior workforce – supported by highly effective, flexible and business-oriented HR and learning organizations – will be essential to achieving these objectives and taking greater strides toward high performance.'*

Developing the specific details of an HR strategy is outside the scope of this book. Yet one set of issues is directly relevant: that is, how can operations managers make sure that they are well served by, and contribute to, the strategy?

An influential contribution to the strategic role of HR comes from Dave Ulrich,[5] at the University of Michigan. His assumption is that traditional HR departments are often inadequate at fulfilling a meaningful strategic role. He proposes four elements to the HR activity: being a 'strategic partner' to the business, administering HR procedures and processes, being an 'employee champion', and being a 'change agent'. Table 9.1 explains each role and suggests how operations managers can be associated with each role.

It is important to recognize the interdependence of all the activities in Table 9.1. Managers may focus only on whatever of these activities currently demands attention. But, just as in the operations function generally, people issues are inter-reliant. There is little point in attempting, for example, to develop a more egalitarian team-based structure and then fail to change the organization's training or reward procedures. This is why a strategic perspective aimed at identifying the relationship between all four roles is necessary, and why the first step in developing an HR strategy is to understand the organization's overall strategy. In particular, key questions are: What are the implications of the strategy for HR? And how can the people in the organization contribute to successfully achieving the strategy?

Work-related stress

The idea that there is a link between HR strategy and the incidence of stress at work is not new. Even some of the early 'scientific management' pioneers accepted that working arrangements should not result in conditions that promoted stress. Now it is generally accepted that stress

Table 9.1 Ulrich's HR roles and their relevance to operations managers

HR role	What it involves	Relevance to operations management (OM)
Strategic partner	Aligning HR and business strategy: 'organizational diagnosis', staff planning, environmental monitoring, etc.	OM integrates operations strategy with HR strategy. OM both specifies its long-term skills requirements and relies on HR to supply/develop them informed by labour market forecasts, succession planning, etc.
Administrative expert	Running the organization's HR processes and 'shared services': payroll, appraisal, selection and recruitment, communication, etc.	OM is largely an 'internal customer' for HR's processes. OM must be clear in its requirements with agreed service levels mutually negotiated. Note that OM should also be able to advise HR on how to design and manage its processes efficiently and effectively
Employee champion	Listening and responding to employees: 'providing resources to employees', conciliation, career advice, grievance procedures, etc.	OM and HR must develop a good working relationship and clear procedures to deal with any 'emergency' issues that arise. Also OM must be sensitive to feedback from HR on how it manages day-to-day operations
Change agent	Managing transformation and change: 'ensuring capacity for change', management development, performance appraisal, organization development, etc.	OM and HR are jointly responsible for operations improvement activities. HR has a vital role in all the cultural, developmental and evaluation activities associated with improvement

can seriously undermine the quality of people's working lives and, in turn, their effectiveness in the workplace. Here stress is defined as 'the adverse reaction people have to excessive pressures or other types of demand placed on them'.[6] In addition to the obvious ethical reasons for avoiding work-related stress, there are also business-related benefits, such as the following:

- Staff feel happier at work, their quality of working life is improved and they perform better.
- Introducing improvements is easier when 'stress' is managed effectively.
- Employment relations: problems can be resolved more easily.
- Attendance levels increase and sickness absence reduces.

Table 9.2 illustrates some of the causes of stress at work and what operations managers can do about it.

HOW CAN THE OPERATIONS FUNCTION BE ORGANIZED?

There are two issues here. The first is 'how should the total set of processes and resources that produce products and services be organized?' The second is 'how should operations managers, who make the decisions about operations, position themselves relative to the rest of the operations function'? We will look at the first issue by examining some common forms of organizational structures, and the second by examining the role of operations 'decision making'. First, though, it is worth looking at how 'organizations' can be described.

Perspectives on organizations[7]

How we illustrate organizations says much about our underlying assumptions of what an 'organization' is and how it is supposed to work. For example, the illustration of an organization as a conventional 'organogram' implies that organizations are neat and controllable with unambiguous lines of accountability. But this is rarely the case. In fact taking such a

Table 9.2 **Causes of stress at work and what could be done about it**

Causes of stress	What can be done about it
Staff can become overloaded if they cannot cope with the amount of work or type of work they are asked to do	Change the way the job is designed, training needs and whether it is possible for employees to work more flexible hours
Staff can feel disaffected and perform poorly if they have no control or say over how and when they do their work	Actively involve staff in decision making, the contribution made by teams, and how reviewing performance can help identify strengths and weaknesses
Staff feel unsupported: levels of sick absence often rise if employees feel they cannot talk to managers about issues that are troubling them	Give staff the opportunity to talk about the issues causing stress, be sympathetic and keep them informed
A failure to build relationships based on good behaviour and trust can lead to problems related to discipline, grievances and bullying	Check the organization's policies for handling grievances, unsatisfactory performance, poor attendance and misconduct, and for tackling bullying and harassment
Staff will feel anxious about their work and the organization if they do not know their role and what is expected of them	Review the induction process, work out an accurate job description and maintain a close link between individual targets and organizational goals
Change can lead to huge uncertainty and insecurity	Plan ahead so change is not unexpected. Consult with employees so they have a real input, and work together to solve problems

mechanistic view may be neither appropriate, nor desirable. Seeing an organization as though it was unambiguously machine-like is just one of several metaphors commonly used to understand organizations. One well-known analysis by Gareth Morgan proposes a number of 'images' or 'metaphors' which can be used to understand organizations, as follows:

- **Organizations are machines** – The resources within organizations can be seen as 'components' in a mechanism whose purpose is clearly understood. Relations within the organization are clearly defined and orderly, processes and procedures that should occur usually do occur, and the flow of information through the organization is predictable. Such mechanical metaphors appear to impose clarity on what is actually messy organizational behaviour. But, where it is important to impose clarity (as in much operations analysis) such a metaphor can be useful, and is the basis of the 'process approach' used in this and similar books.
- **Organizations are organisms** – Organizations are living entities. Their behaviour is dictated by the behaviour of the individual humans within them. Individuals, and their organizations, adapt to circumstances just as different species adapt to the environment. This is a particularly useful way of looking at organizations if parts of the environment (such as the needs of the market) change radically. The survival of the organization depends on its ability to exhibit enough flexibility to respond to its environment.
- **Organizations are brains** – Like brains, organizations process information and make decisions. They balance conflicting criteria, weigh up risks and decide when an outcome is acceptable. They are also capable of learning, changing their model of the world in the light of experience. This emphasis on decision making, accumulating experience and learning from that experience is important in understanding organizations. They consist of conflicting groups where power and control are key issues.
- **Organizations are cultures** – An organization's culture is usually taken to mean its shared values, ideology, pattern of thinking and day-to-day ritual. Different organizations will have different cultures stemming from their circumstances and their history. A major strength of seeing organizations as cultures is that it draws attention to their shared 'enactment of reality'. Looking for the symbols and shared realities within an organization allows us to see beyond what the organization says about itself.
- **Organizations are political systems** – Organizations, like communities, are governed. The system of government is rarely democratic, but nor is it usually a dictatorship. Within the mechanisms of government in an organization are usually ways of understanding alternative philosophies, ways of seeking consensus (or at least reconciliation) and sometimes ways of legitimizing opposition. Individuals and groups seek to pursue their aims through the detailed politics of the organization. They form alliances, accommodate power relationships and manage conflict. Such a view is useful in helping organizations to legitimize politics as an inevitable aspect of organizational life.

Forms of organizational structure

There are many different ways of defining 'organizational structure'; here it is seen as the way in which tasks and responsibilities are divided into distinct groupings, and how the responsibility and co-ordination relationships between the groupings are defined. Most organizational designs attempt to divide an organization into discrete parts that are given some degree of authority to make decisions within their part of the organization. All but the very smallest of organizations needs to delegate decision making in this way; it allows specialization so decisions can be taken by the most appropriate people. The main issue is what dimension of specialization should be used when grouping parts of the organization together. There are three basic approaches to this:

- Group resources together according to their *functional purpose* – so, for example, sales, marketing, operations, research and development, finance, etc.

- Group resources together by the *characteristics of the resources themselves* – this may be done, for example, by clustering similar technologies together (extrusion technology, rolling, casting, etc.). Alternatively, it may be done by clustering similar skills together (audit, mergers and acquisitions, tax, etc.). It may also be done according to the resources required for particular products or services (chilled food, frozen food, canned food, etc.).
- Group resources together by the *markets* which the resources are intended to serve – again this may be done in various ways. Markets may be defined by location, with distinct geographical boundaries (North America, South America, Europe and the Middle East, South-East Asia, etc.). Alternatively, markets may be defined by the type of customer (small firms, large national firms, large multinational firms, etc.).

There are an almost infinite number of possible organizational structures. However, some pure types of organization have emerged that are useful in illustrating different approaches to organizational design, even if, in their pure form, they are rarely found:

- **The U-form organization** – The unitary form, or U-form, organization clusters its resources primarily by their functional purpose. Figure 9.3(a) shows a typical U-form organization with a pyramid management structure, each level reporting to the managerial level above. Such structures can emphasize process efficiency above customer service and the ability to adapt to changing markets. But the U-form keeps together expertise and can promote the creation and sharing of technical knowledge. The problem then with the U-form organization is not so much the development of capabilities, but the flexibility of their deployment.
- **The M-form organization** – This form of organizational structure emerged because the functionally based structure of the U-form was cumbersome when companies became

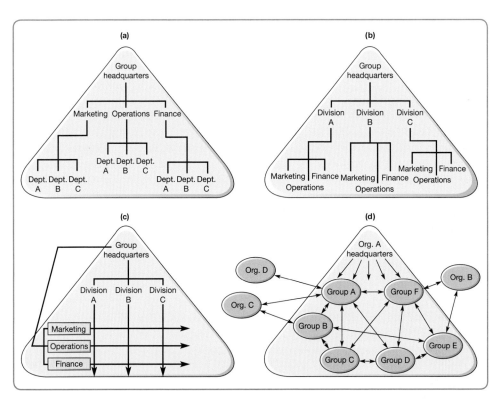

Figure 9.3 (a) U-form organizations give prominence to functional groupings of resources. (b) The M-form separates the organization's resources into separate divisions. (c) Matrix form structures the organization's resources so that they have two (or more) levels of responsibility. (d) N-form organizations form loose networks internally between groups of resources and externally with other organizations

large, often with complex, markets. It groups together either the resources needed for each product or service group, or, alternatively, those needed to serve a particular geographical market, in separate divisions. The separate functions may be distributed throughout the different divisions (*see* Fig. 9.3(b)), which can reduce economies of scale and operating efficiency. But it does allow each individual division to focus on the specific needs of their markets.

- **Matrix forms** – Matrix structures are a hybrid, usually combining the M-form with the U-form. In effect, the organization has simultaneously two different structures (*see* Fig. 9.3(c)). In a matrix structure each resource cluster has at least two lines of authority, for example both to the division and to the functional groups. While a matrix organization ensures the representation of all interests within the company, it can be complex and sometimes confusing.
- **The N-form organization** – The 'N' in N-form stand for 'network'. In N-form organizations, resources are clustered into groups as in other organizational forms, but with more delegation of responsibility for the strategic management of those resources. N-forms have relatively little hierarchical reporting and control. Each cluster of resources is linked to the others to form a network, with the relative strength of the relationships between clusters changing over time, depending on circumstances (*see* Fig. 9.3(d)). Senior management set broad goals and attempt to develop a unifying culture but do not 'command and control' to the same extent as in other organizational forms.

Operations 'developers' – 'staff' and 'line' roles

Traditionally, it was common to distinguish between two types of roles in organizations. People occupying classic 'staff' positions had a monitoring, planning, shaping and 'developing' role. They are the ones who are charged with building up the company's operations strategic capability. It is a task that needs some organizational 'space' to be performed effectively. It is certainly not a task that co-exists easily with the hectic and immediate concerns of running an operation on a day-to-day basis. These people constitute what could be termed the 'operations developers' or 'central operations'. They perform what are called (slightly confusingly) 'staff' roles. By contrast, people occupying 'line' roles are those who run the day-to-day operations. Theirs is partly a reactive role, one that involves finding ways round unexpected problems: reallocating resources, adjusting processes, solving quality problems, and so on. They need to look ahead only enough to make sure that resources are available to meet targets. Theirs is the necessary routine. Knowing where the operation is heading, keeping it on budget and pulling it back on course when the unexpected occurs – no less valuable a task than the developer's but very different.

While these descriptions are clearly stereotypes, they do represent two types of operations task. The issue, for organizational design, is whether it is wise to separate them organizationally. It may cause more problems than it solves. Although it allows each to concentrate on their different jobs, it also can keep apart the two sets of people who have most to gain by working together. Here is the paradox: the development role does need freedom from the immediate pressures of day-to-day management but it is crucial that it understands the exact nature of these pressures. What makes the operation distinctive? Where do the problems occur? What improvements would make most difference to the performance of the operation? These are questions answered only by living with the operation, not cloistered away from it. Similarly, the day-to-day operations manager has to interpret the workings of the operation, collect data, explain constraints and educate developers. Without the trust and co-operation of each, neither set of managers can be effective.

Four types of operations developer role

We can use the dimensions which define the perspectives on operations strategy described in Chapter 3 to examine the role that operations developers play within the operations function:

- **Top down or bottom up?** If operations developers have a predominantly top-down view of the world, they are likely to take a programmatic approach to activities, emphasizing the implementation of overall company strategy. Conversely, if they take a bottom-up view, they are more likely to favour a more emergent model of operations development where individual business operations together contribute to the overall building of operations expertise.

- **Market requirements or operations resource focus?** If operations developers take a market requirements view of operations development, they are likely to focus on the explicit performance achieved by each part of the operations function and how far that performance serves to satisfy the operation's customers. An operations resource focus, on the other hand, emphasizes the way in which each part of the operation function develops its competences and successfully deploys them in its marketplaces.

We can use these two dimensions to define a typology of how the operations developer role could work, as shown in Figure 9.4. It classifies operations developers into four pure types called governors, curators, trainers and facilitators – a typology. Although, in practice, the central operations function of most businesses is a combination of these pure types, usually one type predominates.

- **Operations developers as governors** – The term 'governor' is used to describe an agent of a central authority, interpreting operations strategy and arbitrating over any disputes. The term is also used to denote the mechanism that sets clear goals for each part of the operation, judges their performance and, if performance is not to target, wants to know the reason why.
- **Operations developers as curators** – Operations developers can be concerned primarily with performance against market requirements without being top down. They may take a more emergent view by acting as the repository of performance data and ideas regarding operations practice for the company as a whole. The term 'curator' is used to capture this idea. Operations developers therefore will be concerned with collecting performance information, examples of best practice, and so on. They will also be concerned with disseminating this information so that operations managers in different parts of the business can benchmark themselves against their colleagues and, where appropriate, adopt best practice from elsewhere.
- **Operations developers as trainers** – Moving from the market requirements to the operations resources emphasis shifts the focus more to the development of internal capabilities. If the mindset of operations developers is top down their role becomes 'trainers', who

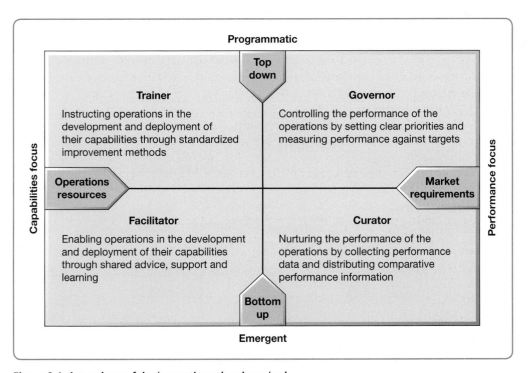

Figure 9.4 A typology of the 'operations developer' role

develop clear objectives, usually derived from overall company strategy, and devise effective methods of developing the various parts of the overall operation. And because the needs of individual parts of the operation may differ, 'trainer' operations developers may devise improvement methodologies that can, to some extent, be customized.

- **Operations developers as facilitators** – In some ways this final type of operations developer role is the most difficult to operate effectively. They are again concerned with the development of operations capabilities but do so by acting as facilitators of change rather than instructors. Their role is to advise, support and generally aid the development and deployment of capabilities through a process of mentoring the various parts of the operation. They share responsibility with day-to-day operations managers in forming a community of operations practice. Implicit in this type of operations developer role is the acceptance of a relatively long-term approach to operations development.

HOW DO WE GO ABOUT DESIGNING JOBS?

Job design is concerned with how we structure each individual's job, the team to which they belong (if any), their workplace and their interface with the technology they use. In this section we deal with what is usually considered to be the central people-related responsibility of operations managers – job design. It is a huge topic and we can only deal with some of the influences on, and approaches to, it.

The influences on job design that we deal with here are illustrated in Figure 9.5.

The decisions of job design

Job design involves a number of separate yet related elements:

- **What tasks are to be allocated to each person in the operation?** Producing goods and services involves a whole range of different tasks which need to be divided between the people who staff the operation. Different approaches to the division of labour will lead to different task allocations.
- **What is the best method of performing each job?** Every job should have an approved (or best) method of completion. And although there are different ideas of what is 'best', it is generally the most efficient method that fits the task, and does not unduly interfere with other tasks.

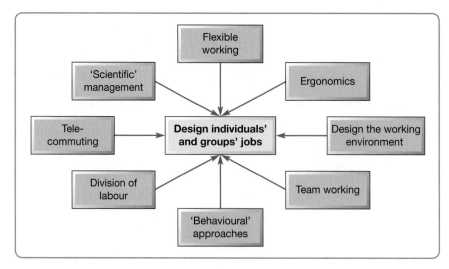

Figure 9.5 The main influences on job design, work time allocation and the design of the working environment

- **How long will it take and how many people will be needed?** Work measurement helps us calculate the time required to do a job, and therefore how many people will be needed.
- **How do we maintain commitment?** Understanding how we can encourage people and maintain job commitment is, arguably, the most important of the issues in job design. This is why behavioural approaches, including empowerment, team work and flexible working are at the core of job design.
- **What technology is available and how will it be used?** Many operational tasks require the use of technology. Not only does the technology need to be appropriately designed, but also so does the interface between the people and the hardware.
- **What are the environmental conditions of the workplace?** The conditions under which jobs are performed will have a significant impact on people's effectiveness, Although often considered a part of job design, we treat it separately in this chapter.

OPERATIONS IN PRACTICE

The stress of high customer contact jobs[8]

Those jobs that are on the front line of dealing directly with customers (particularly a lot of customers, all the time, of all different types) can be particularly stressful. Not all customers will be reasonable, patient, courteous or even sane. The people who have these high customer contact roles need support, training and perhaps a special aptitude. And there is plenty of advice for staff that have to deal with customers who are angry because they feel that the level of service they have received is inadequate. Such advice usually includes such things as: acknowledge the (perceived) problem, try to put yourself in the position of the complainer, get the all facts straight, and try to rectify the problem. Not easy, but if complaints can be resolved to the satisfaction of the customer, there can be significant benefits. Some surveys indicate that 90 per cent of customers whose complaints are resolved are happy to use the service again, and may even go on to become advocates for the service. Nevertheless, maintaining tolerance and politeness in the face of some particularly difficult customers can be more than even experienced staff can bear. That certainly was the case with Steven Slater, formerly an air steward on the US airline JetBlue. He was working on a flight to New York and had to arbitrate when a female passenger began arguing with a male passenger about space in the overhead luggage compartment during boarding. The female passenger swore at Mr Slater and pulled down the compartment door on his head. Later, when the aircraft landed, she seemingly refused to follow his request to remain in her seat and got up to take her bag from the overhead locker while the aircraft was still taxiing. Again, the woman allegedly swore at Mr Slater. It was then that his patience ran out in a

Source: Shutterstock.com: Alphaspirit

particularly dramatic fashion. He went to the intercom and broadcast to everybody on board: *'To the passenger who just called me a motherf*****: F*** you. I've been in this business for 28 years and I've had it.'* He then collected his hand-luggage (and two beers from the trolley) opened the cabin door, activated the inflatable chute, announced *'to those of you who have shown dignity and respect for 20 years, have a great ride'* and slid out of the (fortunately stationary) aircraft onto the runway. As a way to give up your job, it is not recommended. He was later arrested and charged with criminal mischief and reckless endangerment.

Task allocation – the division of labour

Any operation must decide on the balance between using specialists or generalists. This idea is related to the division of labour – dividing up the total task into smaller parts, each of which is accomplished by a single person or team. It was first formalized as a concept by the economist Adam Smith in his *Wealth of Nations* in 1746. Perhaps the epitome of the division of labour is the assembly line, where products move along a single path and are built up by operators continually repeating a single task. This is the predominant model of job design in most mass-produced products and in some mass-produced services (fast food, for example). There are some *real advantages* in division-of-labour principles:

- *It promotes faster learning*. It is obviously easier to learn how to do a relatively short and simple task than a long and complex one. This means that new members of staff can be quickly trained and assigned to their tasks when they are short and simple.
- *Automation becomes easier*. Dividing a total task into small parts raises the possibility of automating some of those small tasks. Substituting technology for labour is considerably easier for short and simple tasks than for long and complex ones.
- *Reduced non-productive work*. This is probably the most important benefit of division of labour. In large, complex tasks the proportion of time spent picking up tools and materials, putting them down again and generally finding, positioning and searching can be very high indeed. For example, one person assembling a whole motor car engine would take two or three hours and involve much searching for parts, positioning, and so on. Around half of the person's time would be spent on these reaching, positioning, finding tasks (called non-productive elements of work). Now consider how a motor car engine is actually made in practice. The total job is probably divided into 20 or 30 separate stages, each staffed by a person who carries out only a proportion of the total. Specialist equipment and materials handling devices can be devised to help them carry out their job more efficiently. Furthermore, there is relatively little finding, positioning and reaching involved in this simplified task. Non-productive work can be considerably reduced, perhaps to under 10 per cent, which would be very significant to the costs of the operation.

However, there are also serious drawbacks to highly divided jobs:

- *Monotony*. The shorter the task, the more often operators will need to repeat it. Repeating the same task, for example every 30 seconds, eight hours a day and five days a week, can hardly be called a fulfilling job. As well as any ethical objections, there are other, more obviously practical objections to jobs which induce such boredom. These include the increased likelihood of absenteeism and staff turnover, the increased likelihood of error and even deliberate sabotage of the job.
- *Physical injury*. The continued repetition of a very narrow range of movements can, in extreme cases, lead to physical injury. The overuse of some parts of the body (especially the arms, hands and wrists) can result in pain and a reduction in physical capability. This is sometimes called repetitive strain injury (RSI).
- *Low flexibility*. Dividing up a task into many small parts often gives the job design a rigidity which is difficult to change under changing circumstances. For example, if an assembly line has been designed to make one particular product but then has to change to manufacture a quite different product, the whole line will need redesigning. This will probably involve changing every operator's set of tasks, which can be a long and difficult procedure.
- *Poor robustness*. Highly divided jobs imply materials (or information) passing between several stages. If one of these stages is not working correctly, for example because some equipment is faulty, the whole operation is affected. On the other hand, if each person is performing the whole of the job, any problems will only affect that one person's output.

> **✽ Operations principle**
>
> There are both positive and negative effects of the division of labour, but it is still a significant factor in job design.

Designing job methods – scientific management

The term 'scientific management' became established in 1911 with the publication of the book of the same name by Fredrick Taylor (this whole approach to job design is sometimes referred to, pejoratively, as Taylorism). In this work he identified what he saw as the basic tenets of scientific management:[9]

- All aspects of work should be investigated on a scientific basis to establish the laws, rules and formulae governing the best methods of working.
- Such an investigative approach to the study of work is necessary to establish what constitutes a 'fair day's work'.
- Workers should be selected, trained and developed methodically to perform their tasks.
- Managers should act as the planners of the work (analysing jobs and standardizing the best method of doing the job) while workers should be responsible for carrying out the jobs to the standards laid down.
- Co-operation should be achieved between management and workers based on the 'maximum prosperity' of both.

The important thing to remember about scientific management is that it is not particularly 'scientific' as such, although it certainly does take an 'investigative' approach to improving operations. Perhaps a better term for it would be 'systematic management'. It gave birth to two separate, but related, fields of study: method study, which determines the methods and activities to be included in jobs; and work measurement, which is concerned with measuring the time that should be taken for performing jobs. Together, these two fields are often referred to as work study and are explained in detail in the supplement to this chapter.

Critical commentary

Even in 1915, criticisms of the scientific management approach were being voiced. In a submission to the United States Commission on Industrial Relations, scientific management is described as:

- being in 'spirit and essence a cunningly devised speeding up and sweating system';
- intensifying the 'modern tendency towards specialization of the work and the task';
- condemning 'the worker to a monotonous routine';
- putting 'into the hands of employers an immense mass of information and methods that may be used unscrupulously to the detriment of workers';
- tending to 'transfer to the management all the traditional knowledge, the judgement and skills of workers';
- greatly intensifying 'unnecessary managerial dictation and discipline';
- tending to 'emphasize quantity of product at the expense of quality'.

Two themes evident in this early criticism do warrant closer attention. The first is that scientific management inevitably results in standardization of highly divided jobs and thus reinforces the negative effects of excessive division of labour previously mentioned. Second, scientific management formalizes the separation of the judgemental, planning and skilled tasks, which are done by 'management', from the routine, standardized and low-skill tasks, which are left for 'operators'. Such a separation, at the very least, deprives the majority of staff of an opportunity to contribute in a meaningful way to their jobs (and, incidentally, deprives the organization of their contribution). Both of these themes in the criticisms of scientific management lead to the same point: that the jobs designed under strict scientific management principles lead to low motivation among staff, frustration at the lack of control over their work, and alienation from the job.

Designing the human interface - ergonomic workplace design

Ergonomics is concerned primarily with the physiological aspects of job design. Physiology is about the way the body functions. It involves two aspects: first, how a person interfaces with their immediate working area; second, how people react to environmental conditions. We will examine the second aspect of ergonomics later in this chapter. Ergonomics is sometimes referred to as human factors engineering or just 'human factors'. Both aspects are linked by two common ideas:

- There must be a fit between people and the jobs they do. To achieve this fit there are only two alternatives. Either the job can be made to fit the people who are doing it, or, alternatively, the people can be made (or perhaps less radically, recruited) to fit the job. Ergonomics addresses the former alternative.
- It is important to take a 'scientific' approach to job design, for example collecting data to indicate how people react under different job design conditions and trying to find the best set of conditions for comfort and performance.

Anthropometric aspects

Many ergonomic improvements are primarily concerned with what are called the anthropometric aspects of jobs – that is, the aspects related to people's size, shape and other physical abilities. The design of an assembly task, for example, should be governed partly by the size and strength of the operators who do the job. The data which ergonomists use when doing this is called anthropometric data. Because we all vary in our size and capabilities, ergonomists are particularly interested in our range of capabilities, which is why anthropometric data is usually expressed in percentile terms. Figure 9.6 illustrates the idea. This shows the idea of size (in this case height) variation. Only 5 per cent of the population are smaller than the person on the extreme left (5th percentile), whereas 95 per cent of the population are smaller than the

> **✳ Operations principle**
>
> Ergonomic considerations in job design can prevent excessive physical strain and increase efficiency.

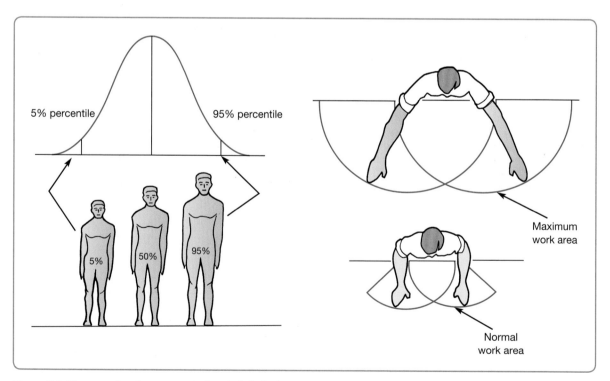

Figure 9.6 The use of anthropometric data in job design

person on the extreme right (95th percentile). When this principle is applied to other dimensions of the body, for example arm length, it can be used to design work areas. Figure 9.6 also shows the normal and maximum work areas derived from anthropometric data. It would be inadvisable, for example, to place frequently used components or tools outside the maximum work area derived from the 5th percentile dimensions of human reach.

Designing for job commitment – behavioural approaches to job design

Jobs that are designed purely on division of labour, scientific management or even purely ergonomic principles can alienate the people performing them. Job design should also take into account the desire of individuals to fulfil their needs for self-esteem and personal development. This is where motivation theory and its contribution to the behavioural approach to job design is important. This achieves two important objectives of job design. First, it provides jobs which have an intrinsically higher quality of working life – an ethically desirable end in itself. Second, because of the higher levels of motivation it engenders, it is instrumental in achieving better performance for the operation, in terms of both the quality and the quantity of output. This approach to job design involves two conceptual steps: first, exploring how the various characteristics of the job affect people's motivation; second, exploring how individuals' motivation towards the job affects their performance at that job.

Typical of the models which underlie this approach to job design is that by Hackman and Oldham shown in Figure 9.7.[10] Here a number of 'techniques' of job design are recommended in order to affect particular core 'characteristics' of the job. These core characteristics are held to influence various positive 'mental states' towards the job. In turn, these are assumed to give certain performance outcomes. In Figure 9.7 some of the 'techniques' (which Hackman and Oldham originally called 'implementing concepts') need a little further explanation:

- Combining tasks means increasing the number of activities allocated to individuals.
- Forming natural work units means putting together activities which make a coherent whole.
- Establishing client relationships means that staff make contact with their internal customers directly.
- Vertical loading means including 'indirect' activities (such as maintenance).
- Opening feedback channels means that internal customers feed back perceptions directly.

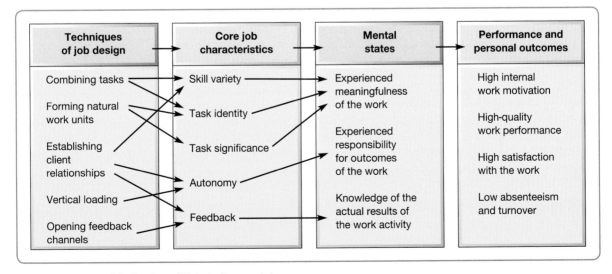

Figure 9.7 A typical 'behavioural' job design model

Hackman and Oldham also indicate how these techniques of job design shape the core characteristics of the resulting job and, further, how the core characteristics influence people's 'mental states'. Mental states are the attitudes of individuals towards their jobs – specifically, how meaningful they find the job, how much responsibility and control they feel they have over the way the job is done, and how much they understand about the results of their efforts. All of these mental states influence people's performance at their job in terms of their motivation, quality of work, satisfaction with their work, turnover and absenteeism.

Job rotation

If increasing the number of related tasks in the job is constrained in some way, for example by the technology of the process, one approach may be to encourage job rotation. This means moving individuals periodically between different sets of tasks to provide some variety in their activities. When successful, job rotation can increase skill flexibility and make a small contribution to reducing monotony. However, it is not viewed as universally beneficial either by management (because it can disrupt the smooth flow of work) or by the people performing the jobs (because it can interfere with their rhythm of work).

Job enlargement

The most obvious method of achieving at least some of the objectives of behavioural job design is by allocating a larger number of tasks to individuals. If these extra tasks are broadly of the same type as those in the original job, the change is called job enlargement. This may not involve more demanding or fulfilling tasks, but it may provide a more complete and therefore slightly more meaningful job. If nothing else, people performing an enlarged job will not repeat themselves as often, which could make the job marginally less monotonous. So, for example, suppose that the manufacture of a product has traditionally been split up on an assembly line basis into 10 equal and sequential jobs. If that job is then redesigned so as to form two parallel assembly lines of five people, the output from the system as a whole would be maintained but each operator would have twice the number of tasks to perform. This is job enlargement. Operators repeat themselves less frequently and presumably the variety of tasks is greater, although no further responsibility or autonomy is necessarily given to each operator.

Job enrichment

Job enrichment means not only increasing the number of tasks, but also allocating extra tasks which involve more decision making, greater autonomy and greater control over the job. For example, the extra tasks could include maintenance, planning and control, or monitoring quality levels. The effect is both to reduce repetition in the job and to increase autonomy and personal development. So, in the assembly line example, each operator, as well as being allocated a job which is twice as long as that previously performed, could also be allocated responsibility for carrying out routine maintenance and such tasks as record keeping and managing the supply of materials. Figure 9.8 illustrates the difference between what are called horizontal and vertical changes. Broadly, horizontal changes are those which extend the variety of *similar* tasks assigned to a particular job. Vertical job changes are those which add responsibilities, decision making or autonomy to the job. Job enlargement implies movement only on the horizontal scale, whereas job enrichment certainly implies movement on the vertical scale and perhaps on both scales.

Empowerment

Empowerment is an extension of the *autonomy* job characteristic prominent in the behavioural approach to job design. However, it is usually taken to mean more than autonomy. Whereas autonomy means giving staff the *ability* to change how they do their jobs, empowerment means giving staff the *authority* to make changes to the job itself, as well as how

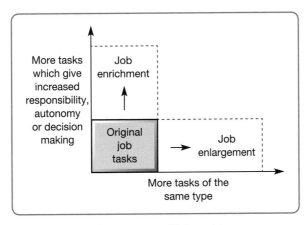

Figure 9.8 Job enlargement and job enrichment

it is performed. This can be designed into jobs to different degrees.[11] At a minimum, staff could be asked to contribute their suggestions for how the operation might be improved. Going further, staff could be empowered to redesign their jobs. Further still, staff could be included in the strategic direction and performance of the whole organization. The *benefits* of empowerment are generally seen as providing fast responses to customer needs (including dissatisfied customers), employees who feel better about their jobs and who will interact with customers with more enthusiasm, promoting 'word-of-mouth' advertising and customer retention. However, there are *costs* associated with empowerment, including higher selection and training costs, perceived inequity of service and the possibility of poor decisions being made by employees.

Team working

A development in job design which is closely linked to the empowerment concept is that of team-based work organization (sometimes called self-managed work teams). This is where staff, often with overlapping skills, collectively perform a defined task and have a high degree

---

McDonald's lets families share job

In what was thought to be the first contract of its type in the UK, McDonald's, the quick-service restaurant chain, announced that it was to allow family members to cover each other's jobs. Under the deal members of the same family working in the same outlet would be able to work each other's shifts without giving any prior notice or getting a manager's permission. The company said that it hoped the contracts would *'encourage people to become fully trained and fully rotatable'*. But that the main aim was to *'cut absenteeism and improve staff retention'*. *'It's great'*, said one McDonald's employee. *'Depending on how we feel in a morning, we decide which one of us wants to go in and work.'* Although the scheme is currently limited to family members only, McDonald's said that it might consider extending it to cover friends who work at the same restaurant.

Source: Shutterstock.com: Zurijeta

of discretion over how they actually perform the task. The team would typically control such things as task allocation between members, scheduling work, quality measurement and improvement, and sometimes the hiring of staff. To some extent most work has always been a group-based activity. The concept of team work, however, is more prescriptive and assumes a shared set of objectives and responsibilities. Groups are described as teams when the virtues of working together are being emphasized, such as the ability to make use of the various skills within the team. Teams may also be used to compensate for other organizational changes such as the move towards flatter organizational structures. When organizations have fewer managerial levels, each manager will have a wider span of activities to control. Teams which are capable of autonomous decision making have a clear advantage in these circumstances. The benefits of team work can be summarized as:

- improving productivity through enhanced motivation and flexibility;
- improving quality and encouraging innovation;
- increasing satisfaction by allowing individuals to contribute more effectively;
- making it easier to implement technological changes in the workplace because teams are willing to share the challenges this brings.

Critical commentary

Team work not only is difficult to implement successfully, but also can place undue stress on the individuals who form the teams. Some teams are formed because more radical solutions, such as total reorganization, are being avoided. Teams cannot compensate for badly designed organizational processes, nor can they substitute for management's responsibility to define how decisions should be made. Often teams are asked to make decisions but are given insufficient responsibility to carry them out. In other cases, teams may provide results but at a price. The Swedish car maker Volvo introduced self-governing teams in the 1970s and 1980s which improved motivation and morale but eventually proved prohibitively expensive. Perhaps most seriously, team work is criticized for substituting one sort of pressure for another. Although teams may be autonomous, this does not mean they are stress-free. Top-down managerial control is often replaced by excessive peer pressure, which is in some ways more insidious.

Flexible working

The nature of most jobs has changed significantly over the last 25 years. New technologies, more dynamic marketplaces, more demanding customers and a changed understanding of how individuals can contribute to competitive success have all had their impact. Also changing is our understanding of how home life, work and social life need to be balanced. Alternative forms of organization and alternative attitudes to work are being sought which allow, and encourage, a degree of flexibility in working practice which matches the need for flexibility in the marketplace. From an operations management perspective, three aspects of flexible working are significant: skills flexibility, time flexibility and location flexibility.

- **Skills flexibility** – A flexible workforce that can move across several different jobs could be deployed (or deploy themselves) in whatever activity is in demand at the time. In the short term, staff at a supermarket may be moved from warehouse activities to shelf replenishment in the store or to the checkout, depending on what is needed at the time. In the longer term sense, multi-skilling means being able to migrate individuals from one skill set to another as longer term demand trends become obvious. So, for example, an engineer who at one time maintained complex equipment by visiting the sites where such equipment was installed may now perform most of his or her activities by using remote computer diagnostics and 'help line' assistance. The implication of job flexibility is that a greater emphasis must be placed on training, learning and knowledge management. Defining what knowledge and experience are required to perform particular tasks and translating these into training activities are clearly prerequisites for effective multi-skilling.

- **Time flexibility** – Not every individual wants to work full-time. Many people, often because of family responsibilities, only want to work for part of their time, sometimes only during specific parts of the day or week (because of childcare responsibilities etc.). Likewise, employers may not require the same number of staff at all times. They may, for example, need extra staff only at periods of heavy demand. Bringing both the supply of staff and the demand for their work together is the objective of 'flexible time' or flexi-time working systems. These may define a *core* working time for each individual member of staff and allow other times to be accumulated flexibly. Other schemes include annual hours schemes, one solution to the capacity management issue described in Chapter 11.

- **Location flexibility** – The sectoral balance of employment has changed. The service sector in most developed economies now accounts for between 70 and 80 per cent of all employment. Even within the manufacturing sector, the proportion of people with indirect jobs (those not directly engaged in making products) has also increased significantly. One result of all this is that the number of jobs which are not 'location-specific' has increased. Location-specific means that a job must take place in one fixed location. So a shop worker must work in a shop and an assembly line worker must work on the assembly line. But many jobs could be performed at any location where there are communication links to the rest of the organization. The realization of this has given rise to what is known as telecommuting, teleworking, 'flexible working', 'home working', mobile working, and creating the 'virtual office'. See the 'Operations in practice' case of telecommuting (or not) at Yahoo.

Critical commentary

There is always a big difference between what is technically possible and what is organizationally feasible. Telecommuting does have its problems. In particular, those types that deny individuals the chance to meet with colleagues often face difficulties. Problems can include the following:

- *Lack of socialization* – offices are social places where people can adopt the culture of an organization as well as learn from each other. It is naive to think that all knowledge can be codified and learnt formally at a distance.

- *Effectiveness of communication* – a large part of the essential communication we have with our colleagues is unplanned and face to face. It happens on 'chance meet' occasions, yet it is important in spreading contextual information as well as establishing specific pieces of information necessary to the job.

- *Problem solving* – it is still often more efficient and effective informally to ask a colleague for help in resolving problems than formally to frame a request using communications technology.

- *It is lonely* – isolation among mobile or home workers is a real problem. For many of us, the workplace provides the main focus for social interaction. A computer screen is no substitute.

Yahoo clamps down on telecommuting[12]

When Marissa Mayer, the new boss of Yahoo, ruled that employees of the company could no longer work from home, but must come into the office to work, it was met with horror throughout Silicon Valley, and beyond. The news also prompted a debate about how much freedom employees should be given to decide how, when and where they should do their jobs. Perhaps most surprising was that Ms Mayer's decision seemed to go against the trend, especially in hi-tech companies, to allow and even encourage a degree of what had become known as 'telecommuting' (defined as 'the practice of working from home for a business and communicating through the use of a personal computer and communication systems'). Surveys had recently shown that home-based working in some industries, especially information systems, engineering and science, was rising particularly quickly. Also, given that many of these technology firms produced the hardware and software that make working from home possible, it seemed only sensible to let their employees use them. As one headline read, 'The "9 to 5" mentality is dead'. And it is not surprising that telecommuting is popular; it has a number of advantages for firms. First, it is popular with (most) staff, so it helps retain (and gain access to a larger pool of) talent. It also is said to improve productivity by avoiding the sometimes distracting work environment. And, of course, because staff spend less time in the office, there can be substantial overhead savings.

Source: Shutterstock.com; JHDT Productions

Which is possibly why Yahoo's decision was greeted with such criticism ('An epic fail', 'Hypocrite', 'Idiotic' were just some of the reactions). But it was not a fear that her employees were sitting around in their pyjamas all day that had prompted her decision to send the memo to Yahoo employees banning telecommuting. The leaked memo said that 'the habit has slowed the firm down and *made it harder to have serendipitous meetings that can give birth to new ideas*' and it was the innovation that came from these meetings that the firm required. '*We can all feel the energy and buzz in our offices*', the memo explained. Yahoo's defenders say that their staff are highly skilled people, such as designers and programmers, who needed more face time with colleagues. Quite simply, for Yahoo, the costs of telecommuting were greater than its benefits. And there are some widely accepted disadvantages of telecommuting. Working from home can be isolating, for staff and for managers who will need to put effort into keeping in touch. In fact, telecommuting can be difficult when employees require constant supervision. There is also the question of accountability. It is difficult to judge whether staff really are working rather than watching daytime TV. Nevertheless a blanket ban on working from home is still unusual in hi-tech industries. And within a year of Yahoo's original decision, there were some indications that, under certain circumstances, telecommuting was once more being permitted.

How should the working environment be designed?

The aspect of ergonomics that we examined earlier was concerned with how a person interfaces with the physical aspects of their immediate working area, such as its dimensions. But the subject also examines how people interface with their working environment. By this we mean the temperature, lighting, noise environment, and so on. It will obviously influence the way they are performed. Working conditions which are too hot or too cold, insufficiently illuminated or glaringly bright, excessively noisy or irritatingly silent, will all influence the way jobs are carried out. Many of these issues are often covered by occupational health and safety legislation which controls environmental conditions in workplaces throughout the world. A thorough understanding of this aspect of ergonomics is necessary to work within the guidelines of such legislation.

> ✳ **Operations principle**
>
> Designing working environments is an important part of job design.

Working temperature

Predicting the reactions of individuals to working temperature is not straightforward. Individuals vary in the way their performance and comfort vary with temperature. Furthermore, most of us judging 'temperature' will also be influenced by other factors such as humidity and air movement. Nevertheless, some general points regarding working temperatures provide guidance to job designers:

- Comfortable temperature range will depend on the type of work being carried out, lighter work requiring higher temperatures than heavier work.
- The effectiveness of people at performing vigilance tasks reduces at temperatures above about 29°C; the equivalent temperature for people performing light manual tasks is a little lower.
- The chances of accidents occurring increase at temperatures which are above or below the comfortable range for the work involved.

Illumination levels

The intensity of lighting required to perform any job satisfactorily will depend on the nature of the job. Some jobs which involve extremely delicate and precise movement, surgery for example, require very high levels of illumination. Other, less delicate jobs do not require such high levels. Table 9.3 shows the recommended illumination levels (measured in lux) for a range of activities.

Noise levels

The damaging effects of excessive noise levels are perhaps easier to understand than some other environmental factors. Noise-induced hearing loss is a well-documented consequence of working environments where noise is not kept below safe limits. The noise levels of various activities are shown in Table 9.4. When reading this list, bear in mind that the recommended (and often legal) maximum noise level to which people can be subjected over the working day is 90 decibels (dB) in the UK (although in some parts of the world the legal level is lower than this). Also bear in mind that the decibel unit of noise is based on a logarithmic scale, which means that noise intensity doubles about every 3 dB. In addition to the damaging effects of high levels of noise, intermittent and high-frequency noise can also affect work performance at far lower levels, especially on tasks requiring attention and judgement.[13]

Table 9.3 **Examples of recommended lighting levels for various activities**[14]

Activity	illuminance (lx)
Normal activities in the home, general lighting	50
Furnace rooms in glass factory	150
General office work	500
Motor vehicle assembly	500
Proofreading	750
Colour matching in paint factory	1,000
Electronic assembly	1,000
Close inspection of knitwear	1,500
Engineering testing inspection using small instruments	3,000
Watchmaking and fine jewellery manufacture	3,000
Surgery, local lighting	10,000–50,000

Table 9.4 **Noise levels for various activities**

Noise	Decibels (dB)
Quiet speech	40
Light traffic at 25 metres	50
Large busy office	60
Busy street, heavy traffic	70
Pneumatic drill at 20 metres	80
Textile factory	90
Circular saw – close work	100
Riveting machine – close work	110
Jet aircraft taking off at 100 metres	120

Music while you work?[15]

Background music at work is not new. It has been used in the workplace for centuries. As far back as the Industrial Revolution orchestras and singers would be hired occasionally to perform for workers in the quieter factories. Later, in the 1940s, the BBC launched a radio programme called *Music While You Work*. Broadcasting twice a day, it was made especially for factory workers. Artists who were booked for the show were told to '*play material with an upbeat rhythm that would keep the workers' attention*', in the belief that it would improve productivity. But playing music at work is not always free. In the UK, for example, the law requires businesses that play any recorded music in public to get licences from the Performing Right Society (PRS), which collects fees and pays royalties to composers and their publishers. Listening to a device through headphones, however, is free. But does music help or hinder?

Some bodies definitely think that it helps. Musicworks (which is an organization supported by the PRS, so it is not exactly independent) cites studies that show that music in the workplace promotes positive mood, can build team spirit, improves alertness and can reduce the number of workplace accidents. It can also, they say, cut the number of sick days and increase workplace productivity. One study by Teresa Lesiuk at the University of Miami found that IT specialists who listened to music completed tasks more quickly and came up with better ideas than those who did not. But not everyone is convinced. '*If people need a high level of concentration, it could be a distraction*', says Dr Carolyn Axtell, at the Institute of Work Psychology. '*When people choose to listen there can be positive effects – it can be relaxing and help manage other distractions such*

Source: Shutterstock.com: Ollyy

as noise. But when it's imposed, they can find it annoying and stressful.' However, individuals can differ in their reaction to music and problems occur when colleagues clash. '*You can look away if you don't want to see something, but you can't close your ears*', she says.

In another study researchers at London University studied the apparently common practice of surgeons playing music in the operating theatre (playlists ranged from gentle classical music, through heavy metal, to electronic dance music). Patients did not complain, being anaesthetized, but other members of the surgical team were not always happy. Music could damage communication in a surgical team, preventing team members from hearing instructions. Even worse, when sound levels are uneven and a new track blasts out unexpectedly, or when a surgeon turns up the volume when his or her favourite song comes on, other team members can be disturbed. But notwithstanding the sometimes conflicting findings from researchers, some themes do emerge:

- How 'immersive' a task is makes a difference when evaluating music's effectiveness in increasing productive output. 'Immersive' refers to the variability and creative demand of the task. Creating an entirely original piece of work from scratch that demands a lot of creativity is 'immersive'. Performing more routine tasks such as answering emails is not. When the task is routine, clearly defined and repetitive, music is probably useful for most people.
- Music affects your mood. Apparently, it is not the background noise of the music itself, but rather the improved mood that your favourite music creates that is the reason for the increase in productivity. In one study, IT specialists who listened to music completed their tasks more quickly and came up with better ideas than those who did not, because the music improved their mood.
- In open-plan offices where background chatter can be too much for some people to handle, headphones can help some people.
- Music does not help learning. It has a negative effect on absorbing and retaining new information, because it demands too much of your attention.
- Listening to music with lyrics, especially interesting and/or new lyrics, detracts from performing immersive tasks. Listening to lyrics activates the language centre of your brain, so trying to perform other language-related tasks is particularly difficult.

(Full disclosure: most of this book was written while listening to music.)

Ergonomics in the office

As the number of people working in offices (or office-like workplaces) has increased, ergonomic principles have been applied increasingly to this type of work. At the same time, legislation has been moving to cover office technology such as computer screens and keyboards. For example, European Union directives on working with display screen equipment require organizations to assess all workstations to reduce the risks inherent in their use, plan work times for breaks and changes in activity, and provide information and training for users. Figure 9.9 illustrates some of the ergonomic factors which should be taken into account when designing office jobs.

Figure 9.9 Ergonomics in the office environment

HOW ARE WORK TIMES ALLOCATED?

Without some estimate of how long it takes to complete an activity, it will not be possible to know how much work to allocate to teams or individuals, to know when a task will be completed, to know how much it costs, to know if work is progressing according to schedule, and many other vital pieces of information that are needed to manage any operation. Without some estimate of work times, operations managers are 'flying blind'. At the same time it does not need much thought before it becomes clear that measuring work times must be difficult to do with any degree of accuracy, or confidence. The time you take to do any task will depend on how skilled you are at the task, how much experience you have, how energetic or motivated you are, whether you have the appropriate tools, what the environmental conditions are, how tired you are, and so on. So, at best, any 'measurement' of how long a task will, or should, take will be an estimate. It will be our 'best guess' of how much time to allow for the task. That is why we call this process of estimating work times 'work time allocation'. We are allocating a time for completing a task because we need to do so for many important operations management decisions. For example, work times are needed for:

- planning how much work a process can perform (its capacity);
- deciding how many staff are needed to complete tasks;
- scheduling individual tasks to specific people;
- balancing work allocation in processes (see Chapter 7);
- costing the labour content of a product or service;
- estimating the efficiency or productivity of staff and/or processes; and
- calculating bonus payments (less important than it was at one time).

Notwithstanding the weak theoretical basis of work measurement, understanding the relationship between work and time is clearly an important part of job design. The advantage of structured and systematic work measurement is that it gives a common currency for the evaluation and comparison of all types of work. So, if work time allocation is important, how should it be done? In fact, there is a long-standing body of knowledge and experience in this area. This is generally referred to as 'work measurement', although, as we have said, 'measurement' could be regarded as indicating a somewhat spurious degree of accuracy. Formally, work measurement is defined as 'the process of establishing the time for a qualified worker, at a defined level of performance, to carry out a specified job'. Although not a precise definition, generally it is agreed that a *specified job* is one for which specifications have been established to define most aspects of the job. A *qualified worker* is 'one who is accepted as having the necessary physical attributes, intelligence, skill, education and knowledge to perform the task to satisfactory standards of safety, quality and quantity'. Standard performance is 'The rate of output which qualified workers will achieve without over-exertion as an average over the working day provided they are motivated to apply themselves to their work.'

The techniques of work measurement

At one time, work measurement was firmly associated with an image of the 'efficiency expert', 'time and motion' man, or 'rate fixer', who wandered around factories with a stopwatch, looking to save a few cents or pennies. And although that idea of work measurement has (almost) died out, the use of a stopwatch to establish a basic time for a job is still relevant, and used in a technique called 'time study'. Time study and the general topic of work measurement are treated in the supplement to this chapter.

As well as time study, there are other work measurement techniques in use. They include the following:

- *Synthesis from elemental data* – is a work measurement technique for building up the time for a job at a defined level of performance by totalling element times obtained previously from the studies in other jobs containing the elements concerned or from synthetic data.

- *Predetermined motion–time systems (PMTS)* – is a work measurement technique whereby times established for basic human motions (classified according to the nature of the motion and the conditions under which it is made) are used to build up the time for a job at a defined level of performance.
- *Analytical estimating* – is a work measurement technique which is a development of estimating whereby the time required to carry out the elements of a job at a defined level of performance is estimated from knowledge and experience of the elements concerned.
- *Activity sampling* – is a technique in which a large number of instantaneous observations are made over a period of time of a group of machines, processes or workers. Each observation records what is happening at that instant and the percentage of observations recorded for a particular activity or delay is a measure of the percentage of time during which that activity or delay occurs.

Critical commentary

The criticisms aimed at work measurement are many and various. Among the most common are the following:

- All the ideas on which the concept of a standard time is based are impossible to define precisely. How can one possibly give clarity to the definition of qualified workers, or specified jobs, or especially a defined level of performance?

- Even if one attempts to follow these definitions, all that results is an excessively rigid job definition. Most modern jobs require some element of flexibility, which is difficult to achieve alongside rigidly defined jobs.

- Using stopwatches to time human beings is both degrading and usually counter-productive. At best it is intrusive, at worst it makes people 'objects for study'.

- The rating procedure implicit in time study is subjective and usually arbitrary. It has no basis other than the opinion of the person carrying out the study.

- Time study, especially, is very easy to manipulate. It is possible for employers to 'work back' from a time which is 'required' to achieve a particular cost. Also, experienced staff can 'put on an act' to fool the person recording the times.

SUMMARY ANSWERS TO KEY QUESTIONS

❭ Why are people so important in operations management?

- Human resources are any organization's, and therefore any operation's, greatest asset. Often, most 'human resources' are to be found in the operations function.

❭ How do operations managers contribute to human resource strategy?

- Human resource strategy is the overall long-term approach to ensuring that an organization's human resources provide a strategic advantage. It involves identifying the number and type of people that are needed to manage, run and develop the organization so that it meets its strategic business objectives, and putting in place the programmes and initiatives that attract, develop and retain appropriate staff.

- One can take various perspectives on organizations. How we illustrate organizations says much about our underlying assumptions of what an 'organization' is. For example, organizations can be described as machines, organisms, brains, cultures or political systems.
- The relationship between the 'staff' and 'line' roles in operation can be modelled using the four perspective on operations strategy that were discussed in Chapter 3.
- There are an almost infinite number of possible organizational structures. Most are blends of two or more 'pure types', such as the U-form, the M-form, matrix forms, the N-form.

〉 **How do we go about designing jobs?**

- There are many influences on how jobs are designed. These include the division of labour, scientific management, method study, work measurement, ergonomics, behavioural approaches, including job rotation, job enlargement and job enrichment, empowerment, team working, and flexible working (including 'telecommuting').

〉 **How are work times allocated?**

- The best known method is time study, but there are other work measurement techniques including synthesis from elemental data, predetermined motion-time systems (PMTS), analytical estimating and activity sampling.

CASE STUDY | **Grace faces (three) problems**

Grace Whelan, Managing Partner of McPherson Charles, was puzzled. Three of her most successful teams seemed to be facing similar problems with their staff, even though each team had very different tasks, processes and types of staff. Every year the firm surveyed its entire staff in order to gauge their views, levels of satisfaction with their jobs and development needs. It was the results from the latest survey that surprised Grace. *'The results of the survey are really unanticipated. Only last year everything seemed fine. Now staff morale has evidently slumped in all three teams. Yet the partners who lead all of these teams are first class. Outstanding lawyers and good leaders.'*

McPherson Charles, based in Bristol in the West of England, had grown rapidly to be one of the biggest law firms in the region, with 21 partners and around 400 staff. Three years previously the firm had reorganized into 15 teams each headed by a 'lead partner' and specializing in practising one type of law. It had proved to be a good organizational structure, which encouraged teams to organize themselves appropriately for the type of clients that they dealt with. In particular three teams had flourished under

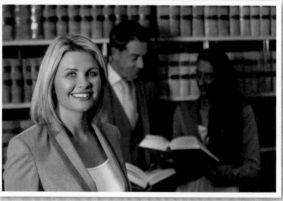
Source: Shutterstock.com: Wavebreakmedia

this structure: 'family law', 'property' and 'litigation'. Now it was these very teams whose staff were showing signs of dissatisfaction.

Before the results of the survey were published to all staff, Grace knew that she would need to have worked out some kind of response to the issues raised. She decided to go and see each of the lead partners in the three teams. The first person she decided to talk to was Simon Reece, who led the family law team. Before doing so she explained what his team did.

Family law

'They are called the "family law" team but basically what they do is to help people through the trauma of divorce, separation and break up. Their biggest "high value" clients come to them because of word of mouth recommendation. Last year they had almost a hundred of these "high value" clients and they all valued the personal touch that they were able to give them, getting to know them well and spending time with them to understand the, often "hidden" aspects of their case. Of course, not all their clients are the super-rich. About a third of the annual family law income comes from about 750 relatively routine divorce and counseling cases.'

Simon was blunt about the declining levels of staff satisfaction in his team. 'The problem is that working with the "high value" clients is just more fun and more rewarding than the routine "bread and butter" work. So my people who do that kind of work, usually the more experienced ones, don't want to take on the routine stuff. With "high value" cases you have to be able to untangle the personal issues from the business ones. Interviewing these clients cannot be rushed. They tend to be wealthy people with complex assets. We will often have to drop everything and go off half way round the world to meet and discuss their situation. There are no standard procedures, every client is different, and everyone has to be treated as an individual. So we have a team of individuals who rise to the challenge each time and give great service. By contrast, the routine work is a lot less interesting, yet sometimes very harrowing. The more junior staff who tend to take on the routine cases can sometimes feel themselves to be "second-class citizens". Many of them would like to get more experience with the complex high value work, but I can't take the risk of giving them that degree of responsibility, the work is too valuable. Also, frankly, the senior people who deal with the high value work don't want to give up their more glamorous work. I have been trying to make sure that everyone in my team who wants to has a mix of interesting and routine work over the year. It's the only way to develop them in the long term. You have to encourage them to exercise and develop their professional judgement. They are empowered to deal with any issues themselves or call on one of the more senior members of the team for advice if appropriate. It is important to give this kind of responsibility to them so that they see themselves as part of a team. But there are still tensions between senior and more junior staff. We are thinking about adopting an open-plan office arrangement centred around our specialist library of family case law, to try and encourage more cooperation.'

Litigation

Grace was less concerned about the litigation team, led by Hazel Lewis. 'The litigation team has been our best success story. The have grown far faster than any other part of the firm, and a lot of that is down to Hazel. She provides a key service for our commercial client base. Their primary work consists of handling bulk collections of debt. The group has 17 clients of which 5 provide 85% of total volume. They work closely with the accounts departments of the client companies and have developed a semi-automatic approach to debt collection. It's a great service that Hazel has largely automated.'

Hazel had led the litigation team since it had been set up four years ago. As well as being the partner in charge of litigation, unusually she and her assistant were the only qualified lawyers in the team. 'Our problems in the litigation team are not really because of any internal tensions or disputes. Broadly, our people are happy with what they do and how they are supervised. The issue is just that we are so different from the rest of the firm. Apart from myself and Raymond [her assistant] everyone else in the team are either technicians who look after and develop the systems that we use, or people who have worked in processing or call centres, before they came to us. And between us we have developed a smart operation here. Our staff input data received from their clients into the system, from that point everything progresses through a pre-defined process, letters are produced, queries responded to and eventually debts collected, ultimately through court proceedings if necessary. Work tends to come in batches from clients and varies according to the time of year and client sales activities. At the moment things are fairly steady; we had almost 900 new cases to deal with last week. The details of each case are sent over by the client; our people input the data onto our screens and set up a standard diary system for sending letters out. Some people respond quickly to the first letter and often the case is closed within a week or so, other people ignore letters and eventually we initiate court proceedings. We know exactly what is required for court dealings and have a pretty good process to make sure all the right documentation is available on the day. Our problem is that the rest of the firm does not see us as being "proper lawyers", and they are right, we're not. But it does get difficult for our people, being looked down upon all the time. Our salary structure is different, our bonus scheme is different, and how we measure performance is different. But there is a solution. Because we have expanded so much, we need more space than is available in this building. I think that we should think about moving the litigation team. There is a great location out by the airport that could be expanded in the future if needed. There is really no reason for us to be located with the other teams.'

Property

The 'property' team was one of the largest parts of the firm and was well established in the local market with an excellent reputation for being fast, friendly and giving value for money. Most of its work was 'domestic', acting for individuals buying or selling their home, or their second home. Each client was allocated to a solicitor who becomes his or her main point of contact. But, given that they can have up to a hundred domestic clients a week, most of the work was actually carried out by the rest of the team of 'paralegal' staff (staff with qualifications less than a fully qualified lawyer) behind the scenes.

Kate Hutchinson, who led the property team, was proud of the process she and her team had set up. 'There is a relatively standard process to domestic property sales and purchases and we think that we are pretty efficient at managing these standard jobs. Our process has four stages, one dealing with land registry searches, one liaising with banks who are providing the mortgage finance, one to make sure surveys are completed and one section that finalises the whole process to completion. We believe that this degree of specialisation can help us achieve the efficiencies that are becoming important, as the market gets more competitive. Our particular problem is that increasingly we are also getting more complex "special" jobs. These are things like "volume re-mortgage" arrangements and rather complex "one-off" jobs, where a mortgage lender transfers a complex set of loan assets to another lender. These "special" jobs are always more complex than the domestic work and they are not popular with our staff. They don't always fit easily into our standard process, and they disrupt the routine of working. For example, sometimes there are occasions when fast completion is particularly important and that can throw us a bit.'

Grace was more worried about the property team than Kate appeared to be. The firm had recently formed partnerships with two large speculative builders, which dealt in special 'plot sales' that would also be classed as non-standard 'specials' by Kate. Grace knew that all these 'specials' did involve a lot of work and could occupy several members of the team for a time. But they were an important source of revenue. Currently the team was dealing with up to 25 'specials' each week, and this would certainly increase. Grace suspected that Kate was mistaken to try and follow the same process with them as the normal domestic jobs. Maybe trying to do different things on the same process was the cause of the dissatisfaction in the team?

QUESTIONS

1 What are the problems amongt the staff of each of the three teams?

2 What are the individual 'services' offered by each of the three teams?

3 How would you describe each team's process in terms of jobs of its staff?

4 What do you think each team leader should be doing to try and overcome their teams' problems?

PROBLEMS AND APPLICATIONS

1 A hotel has two wings, an east wing and a west wing. Each wing has four 'room service maids' working seven-hour shifts to service the rooms each day. The east wing has 40 standard rooms, 12 deluxe rooms and 5 suites. The west wing has 50 standard rooms and 10 deluxe rooms. The standard times for servicing rooms are as follows: standard rooms 20 standard minutes, deluxe rooms 25 standard minutes, and suites 40 standard minutes. In addition, an allowance of 5 standard minutes per room is given for any miscellaneous jobs such as collecting extra items for the room or dealing with customer requests. What is the productivity of the maids in each wing of the hotel? What other factors might also influence the productivity of the maids?

2 In the problem above, one of the maids in the west wing wants to job-share with her partner, each working three hours per day. Her colleagues have agreed to support her and will guarantee to service all the rooms in the west wing to the same standard each day. If they succeed in doing this, how has it affected their productivity?

3 *Step 1* – Make a sandwich. Any type of sandwich, preferably one that you enjoy, and document the tasks you have to perform in order to complete the job. Make sure you include all the activities including the movement of materials (bread etc.) to and from the work surface. *Step 2* – So impressed were your friends with the general appearance of your sandwich that they have persuaded you to make one each for them every day. You have 10 friends so every morning you must make 10 identical sandwiches (to stop squabbling). How would you change the method by which you make the sandwiches to accommodate this higher volume?

Step 3 – The fame of your sandwiches had spread. You now decide to start a business making several different types of sandwich in high volume. Design the jobs of the two or three people who will help you in this venture. Assume that volumes run into at least 100 of three types of sandwich every day.

4 A little-known department of your local government authority has the responsibility for keeping the area's public lavatories clean. It employs 10 people who each have a number of public lavatories that they visit, clean and report any necessary repairs every day. Draw up a list of ideas for how you would keep this fine body of people motivated and committed to performing this unpleasant task.

5 Visit a supermarket and observe the people who staff the checkouts.
(a) What kind of skills do people who do this job need to have?
(b) How many customers per hour are they capable of 'processing'?
(c) What opportunities exist for job enrichment in this activity?
(d) How would you ensure motivation and commitment among the staff who do this job?

SELECTED FURTHER READING

Argyris, C. (1998) Empowerment: the emperor's new clothes, *Harvard Business Review*, May–June.

A critical but fascinating view of empowerment.

Bock, L. (2015) *Work Rules! Insights from Inside Google That Will Transform How You Live and Lead*, John Murray, London.

With an agenda far wider than this chapter, it is nevertheless an absorbing book that gives an insight into an absorbing firm.

Bond, F.W. and Bunce, D. (2001) Job control mediates change in a work reorganization intervention for stress reduction, *Journal of Occupational Health Psychology*, vol. 6, 290–302.

An academic paper that is interesting on stress issues.

Bridger, R. (2003) *Introduction to Ergonomics*, Taylor & Francis, London.

Exactly what it says in the title, an introduction (but a good one) to ergonomics.

Dul, J. and Weerdmeester, B. (2008) *Ergonomics for Beginners: A Quick Reference Guide*, 3rd edn, CRC Press, Boca Raton, FL.

Good, practical guidance on the removal from the workplace of physical and mental stresses caused by poor job or environmental design.

Hackman, R.J. and Oldham, G. (1980) *Work Redesign*, Addison-Wesley, Reading, MA.

Somewhat dated but, in its time, ground breaking and certainly hugely influential.

Herzberg, F. (1987) One more time: how do you motivate employees? (with retrospective commentary), *Harvard Business Review*, January.

An interesting look back by one of the most influential figures in the behavioural approach to job design school.

Lantz, A. and Brav, A. (2007) Job design for learning in work groups, *Journal of Workplace Learning*, vol. 19, issue 5, 269–285.

Another academic paper, but one that addresses the important issue of learning as a job design objective.

Supplement to Chapter 9
Work study

INTRODUCTION

A tale is told of Frank Gilbreth (the founder of method study) addressing a scientific conference with a paper entitled 'The best way to get dressed in a morning'. In his presentation, he rather bemused the scientific audience by analysing the 'best' way of buttoning up one's waistcoat in the morning. Among his conclusions was that waistcoats should always be buttoned from the bottom upwards. (To make it easier to straighten a tie in the same motion; buttoning from the top downwards requires the hands to be raised again). Think of this example if you want to understand scientific management and method study in particular. First of all, he is quite right. Method study and the other techniques of scientific management may often be without any intellectual or scientific validation, but by and large they work in their own terms. Second, Gilbreth reached his conclusion by a systematic and critical analysis of what motions were necessary to do the job. Again, these are characteristics of scientific management – detailed analysis and painstakingly systematic examination. Third (and possibly most important), the results are relatively trivial. A great deal of effort was put into reaching a conclusion that was unlikely to have any earth-shattering consequences. Indeed, one of the criticisms of scientific management, as developed in the early part of the twentieth century, is that it concentrated on relatively limited, and sometimes trivial, objectives.

The responsibility for its application, however, has moved away from specialist 'time and motion' staff to the employees who can use such principles to improve what they do and how they do it. Further, some of the methods and techniques of scientific management, as opposed to its philosophy (especially those which come under the general heading of 'method study'), can in practice prove useful in critically re-examining job designs. It is the practicality of these techniques which possibly explains why they are still influential in job design almost a century after their inception.

METHOD STUDY IN JOB DESIGN

Method study is a systematic approach to finding the best method. There are six steps:

1 Select the work to be studied.
2 Record all the relevant facts of the present method.
3 Examine those facts critically and in sequence.
4 Develop the most practical, economic and effective method.
5 Install the new method.
6 Maintain the method by periodically checking it in use.

Step 1 – Selecting the work to be studied

Most operations have many hundreds and possibly thousands of discrete jobs and activities which could be subjected to study. The first stage in method study is to select those jobs to be studied which will give the most return on the investment of the time spent studying them. This means it is unlikely that it will be worth studying activities which, for example, may soon be discontinued or are only performed occasionally. On the other hand, the types of jobs which should be studied as a matter of priority are those which, for example, seem to offer the greatest scope for improvement, or which are causing bottlenecks, delays or problems in the operation.

Step 2 – Recording the present method

There are many different recording techniques used in method study. Most of them:

- record the sequence of activities in the job;
- record the time interrelationship of the activities in the job; or
- record the path of movement of some part of the job.

Perhaps the most commonly used recording technique in method study is process mapping, which was discussed in Chapter 4. Note that we are here recording the present method of doing the job. It may seem strange to devote so much time and effort to recording what is currently happening when, after all, the objective of method study is to devise a better method. The rationale for this is, first of all, that recording the present method can give a far greater insight into the job itself, and this can lead to new ways of doing it. Second, recording the present method is a good starting point from which to evaluate it critically and therefore improve it. In this last point the assumption is that it is easier to improve the method by starting from the current method and then criticizing it in detail than by starting with a 'blank sheet of paper'.

Step 3 – Examining the facts

This is probably the most important stage in method study and the idea here is to examine the current method thoroughly and critically. This is often done by using the so-called 'questioning technique'. This technique attempts to detect weaknesses in the rationale for existing methods so that alternative methods can be developed (see Table S9.1).

Table S9.1 **The method study questioning technique**

Broad question	Detailed question
The purpose of each activity (questions the fundamental need for the element)	What is done? Why is it done? What else could be done? What should be done?
The place in which each element is done (may suggest a combination of certain activities or operations)	Where is it done? Why is it done there? Where else could it be done? Where should it be done?
The sequence in which the elements are done (may suggest a change in the sequence of the activity)	When is it done? Why is it done then? When should it be done?
The person who does the activity (may suggest a combination and/or change in responsibility or sequence)	Who does it? Why does that person do it? Who else could do it? Who should do it?
The means by which each activity is done (may suggest new methods)	How is it done? Why is it done in that way? How else could it be done? How should it be done?

The approach may appear somewhat detailed and tedious, yet it is fundamental to the method study philosophy – everything must be critically examined. Understanding the natural tendency to be less than rigorous at this stage, some organizations use pro forma questionnaires, asking each of these questions and leaving space for formal replies and/or justifications, which the job designer is required to complete.

Step 4 – Developing a new method

The previous critical examination of current methods has by this stage probably indicated some changes and improvements. This step involves taking these ideas further in an attempt to:

- eliminate parts of the activity altogether;
- combine elements together;
- change the sequence of events so as to improve the efficiency of the job; or
- simplify the activity to reduce the work content.

A useful aid during this process is a checklist such as the revised principles of motion economy. Table S9.2 illustrates these.

Steps 5 and 6 – Installing the new method and regularly maintaining it

The method study approach to the installation of new work practices concentrates largely on 'project managing' the installation process. It also emphasizes the need to monitor regularly the effectiveness of job designs after they have been installed.

Table S9.2 **The principles of motion economy**

Broad principle	How to do it
Use the human body the way it works best	Work should be arranged so that a natural rhythm can become automatic
	Motion of the body should be simultaneous and symmetrical if possible
	The full capabilities of the human body should be employed
	Arms and hands as weights are subject to the physical laws and energy should be conserved
	Tasks should be simplified
Arrange the workplace to assist performance	There should be a defined place for all equipment and materials
	Equipment, materials and controls should be located close to the point of use
	Equipment, materials and controls should be located to permit the best sequence and path of motions
	The workplace should be fitted both to the tasks and to human capabilities
Use technology to reduce human effort	Work should be presented precisely where needed
	Guides should assist in positioning the work without close operator attention
	Controls and foot-operated devices can relieve the hands of work
	Mechanical devices can multiply human abilities
	Mechanical systems should be fitted to human use

Source: Adapted from Barnes, Frank C. (1983) 'Principles of Motion Economy: Revisited, Reviewed, and Restored', *Proceedings of the Southern Management Association Annual Meeting* (Atlanta, GA 1983), p. 298.

WORK MEASUREMENT IN JOB DESIGN

Basic times

Terminology is important in work measurement. When a *qualified worker* is working on a *specified job* at *standard performance*, the time he or she takes to perform the job is called the basic time for the job. Basic times are useful because they are the 'building blocks' of time estimation. With the basic times for a range of different tasks, an operations manager can construct a time estimate for any longer activity which is made up of the tasks. The best-known technique for establishing basic times is probably time study.

Time study

Time study is 'a work measurement technique for recording the times and rate of working for the elements of a specified job, carried out under specified conditions, and for analysing the data so as to obtain the time necessary for the carrying out of the job at a defined level of performance'. The technique takes three steps to derive the basic times for the elements of the job:

- observing and measuring the time taken to perform each element of the job;
- adjusting, or 'normalizing', each observed time;
- averaging the adjusted times to derive the basic time for the element.

Step 1 – Observing, measuring and rating

A job is observed through several cycles. Each time an element is performed, it is timed using a stopwatch. Simultaneously with the observation of time, a rating of the perceived performance of the person doing the job is recorded. Rating is 'the process of assessing the worker's rate of working relative to the observer's concept of the rate corresponding to standard performance. The observer may take into account, separately or in combination, one or more factors necessary to carrying out the job, such as speed of movement, effort, dexterity, consistency, etc.' There are several ways of recording the observer's rating. The most common is on a scale which uses a rating of 100 to represent standard performance. If an observer rates a particular observation of the time to perform an element at 100, the time observed is the actual time which anyone working at standard performance would take.

Step 2 – Adjusting the observed times

The adjustment to normalize the observed time is:

$$\frac{\text{Observed rating}}{\text{Standard rating}}$$

where standard rating is 100 on the common rating scale we are using here. For example, if the observed time is 0.71 minutes and the observed rating is 90, then:

$$\text{Basic time} = \frac{0.71 \times 9}{100} = 0.64 \text{ min}$$

Step 3 – Averaging the basic times

In spite of the adjustments made to the observed times through the rating mechanism, each separately calculated basic time will not be the same. This is not necessarily a function of inaccurate rating, or even the vagueness of the rating procedure itself; it is a natural phenomenon of the time taken to perform tasks. Any human activity cannot be repeated in *exactly* the same time on every occasion.

Standard times

The standard time for a job is an extension of the basic time and has a different use. Whereas the basic time for a job is a piece of information which can be used as the first step in estimating the time to perform a job under a wide range of conditions, standard time refers to the time *allowed* for the job under specific circumstances. This is because standard time includes allowances which reflect the rest and relaxation allowed because of the conditions under which the job is performed. So the standard time for each element consists principally of two parts, the basic time (the time taken by a qualified worker, doing a specified job at standard performance) and an allowance (this is added to the basic time to allow for rest, relaxation and personal needs).

Allowances

Allowances are additions to the basic time intended to provide the worker with the opportunity to recover from the physiological and psychological effects of carrying out specified work under specified conditions and to allow for personal needs. The amount of the allowance will depend on the nature of the job. The way in which relaxation allowance is calculated, and the exact allowances given for each of the factors which determine the extent of the allowance, varies between different organizations. Table S9.3 illustrates the allowance table used by

Table S9.3 **An allowances table used by a domestic appliance manufacturer**

Allowance factors	Example	Allowance (%)
Energy needed		
Negligible	None	0
Very light	0–3 kg	3
Light	3–10 kg	5
Medium	10–20 kg	10
Heavy	20–30 kg	15
Very heavy	Above 30 kg	15–30
Posture required		
Normal	Sitting	0
Erect	Standing	2
Continuously erect	Standing for long periods	3
Lying	On side, face or back	4
Difficult	Crouching, etc.	4–10
Visual fatigue		
Nearly continuous attention		2
Continuous attention with varying focus		3
Continuous attention with fixed focus		5
Temperature		
Very low	Below 0°C	Over 10
Low	0–12°C	0–10
Normal	12–23°C	0
High	23–30°C	0–10
Very high	Above 30°C	Over 10
Atmospheric conditions		
Good	Well ventilated	0
Fair	Stuffy/smelly	2
Poor	Dusty/needs filter	2–7
Bad	Needs respirator	7–12

Element		Observation										Average basic time	Allowances	Element standard time
		1	2	3	4	5	6	7	8	9	10			
Make box	Observed time	0.71	0.71	0.71	0.69	0.75	0.68	0.70	0.72	0.70	0.68			
	Rating	90	90	90	90	80	90	90	90	90	90			
	Basic time	0.64	0.64	0.63	0.62	0.60	0.61	0.63	0.65	0.63	0.61	0.626	10%	0.689
Pack x 20	Observed time	1.30	1.32	1.25	1.33	1.33	1.28	1.32	1.32	1.30	1.30			
	Rating	90	90	100	90	90	90	90	90	90	90			
	Basic time	1.17	1.19	1.25	1.20	1.20	1.15	1.19	1.19	1.17	1.17	1.168	12%	1.308
Seal and secure	Observed time	0.53	0.55	0.55	0.56	0.53	0.53	0.60	0.55	0.49	0.51			
	Rating	90	90	90	90	90	90	85	90	100	100			
	Basic time	0.48	0.50	0.50	0.50	0.48	0.48	0.51	0.50	0.49	0.51	0.495	10%	0.545
Assemble outer,	Observed time	1.12	1.21	1.20	1.25	1.41	1.27	1.11	1.15	1.20	1.23			
fix and label	Rating	100	90	90	90	90	90	100	100	90	90			
	Basic time	1.12	1.09	1.08	1.13	1.27	1.14	1.11	1.15	1.08	1.21	1.138	12%	1.275

Job _Pack 20 x pt # 7312A_   Location _Packing Dept._   Observer _FWT_

Raw standard time		3.817
Allowances for total job	5%	0.191
Standard time for job		4.01 SM

Figure S9.1 Time study of a packing task – standard time for the whole task calculated

one company which manufactures domestic appliances. Every job has an allowance of 10 per cent; the table shows the further percentage allowances to be applied to each element of the job. In addition, other allowances may be applied for such things as unexpected contingencies, synchronization with other jobs, unusual working conditions, and so on.

Figure S9.1 shows how average basic times for each element in the job are combined with allowances (low in this example) for each element to build up the standard time for the whole job.

Worked example

Two work teams in the Monrovian Embassy have been allocated the task of processing visa applications. Team A processes applications from Europe, Africa and the Middle East. Team B processes applications from North and South America, Asia and Australasia. Team A has chosen to organize itself in such a way that each of its three team members processes an application from start to finish. The four members of Team B have chosen to split themselves into two sub-teams. Two open the letters and carry out the checks for a criminal record (no one who has been convicted of any crime other than a motoring offence can enter Monrovia), while the other two team members check for financial security (only people with more than Monrovian $1,000 may enter the country). The head of consular affairs is keen to find out if one of these methods of organizing the teams is more efficient than the other. The problem is that the mix of applications differs region by region. Team A typically processes around two business applications to every one tourist application. Team B processes around one business application to every two tourist applications.

A study revealed the following data:

Average standard time to process a business visa = 63 standard minutes

Average time to process a tourist visa = 55 standard minutes

Average weekly output from Team A is:
    85.2   Business visas
    39.5   Tourist visas

Average weekly output from Team B is:
    53.5   Business visas
    100.7   Tourist visas

All team members work a 40-hour week.

The efficiency of each team can be calculated by comparing the actual output in standard minutes and the time worked in minutes.

So Team A processes:

$$(85.2 \times 63) + (39.5 \times 55) = 7,540.1 \text{ standard minutes of work}$$

$$\text{in } 3 \times 40 \times 60 \text{ minutes} = 7,200 \text{ minutes}$$

$$\text{So its efficiency} = \frac{7,540.1}{7,200} \times 100 = 104.72\%$$

Team B processes:

$$(53.5 \times 63) + (100.7 \times 55) = 8,909 \text{ standard minutes of work}$$

$$\text{in } 4 \times 40 \times 60 \text{ minutes} = 9,600 \text{ minutes}$$

$$\text{So its efficiency} = \frac{8,909}{9,600} \times 100 = 92.8\%$$

The initial evidence therefore seems to suggest that the way Team A has organized itself is more efficient.

DELIVER – PLANNING AND CONTROLLING OPERATIONS

Part Three
DELIVER

All the activities involved in the design of an operation should have provided the nature and shape of the transforming resources that are capable of satisfying customers' demands. Products and services then have to be created and delivered to customers. This is done by planning and controlling the activities of the transforming resources on a day-to-day basis to ensure the appropriate supply of products and services to meet the requirements of the market. This part of the book will look at six different aspects of planning and controlling the delivery of products and services as they flow through processes, operations and supply networks.

The chapters in this part are:

- Chapter 10 Planning and control – This examines how operations organize the delivery of their products and services on an ongoing basis so that customers' demands are satisfied.
- Chapter 11 Capacity management – This explains how operations need to decide how to vary their capacity (if at all) as demand for their products and services fluctuates.

- Chapter 12 Supply chain management – This describes how operations relate to each other in the context of a wider network of suppliers and customers, and how these relationships can be managed.
- Chapter 13 Inventory management – This looks at how transformed resources accumulate as inventories as they flow through processes, operations or supply networks.
- Chapter 14 Planning and control systems – This describes how systems are needed to manage the very large amounts of information required to plan and control operations, and how enterprise resource planning (ERP) is used to do this.
- Chapter 15 Lean operations – This explains the concepts that underlie one of the most influential sets of ideas to impact operations management.

10

Planning and control

Key questions

❯ What is planning and control?

❯ What is the difference between planning and control?

❯ How do supply and demand affect planning and control?

❯ What are the activities of planning and control?

INTRODUCTION

The design of an operation determines the resources with which it creates its services and products, but then the operation has to deliver those services and products on an ongoing basis. And central to an operation's ability to deliver is the way it plans its activities and controls them so that customers' demands are satisfied. This chapter introduces and provides an overview of some of the principles and methods of planning and control. Later chapters in this part of the book develop some specific issues that are vital to an operation delivering its services and products. These issues start with managing capacity and moves through managing inventory, providing an overview of supply chain management and looking at how planning and control systems, particularly enterprise resources planning (ERP), manages the information that ensures effective delivery. We then examine how 'lean' philosophy has influenced operations practice. Figure 10.1 shows where this topic fits into the activities of operations management.

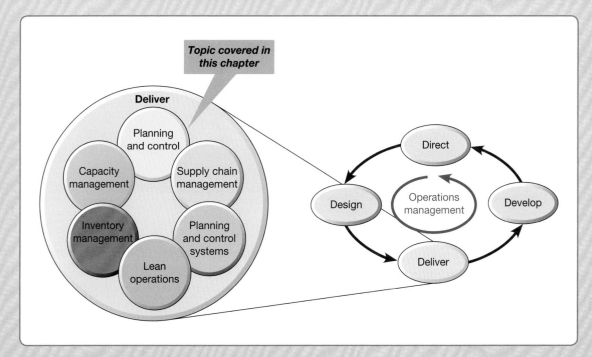

Figure 10.1 This chapter examines planning and control

WHAT IS PLANNING AND CONTROL?

Planning and control is concerned with the activities that attempt to reconcile the demands of the market and the ability of the operation's resources to deliver. It provides the systems, procedures and decisions which bring different aspects of supply and demand together. Consider, for example, the way in which routine surgery is organized in a hospital. When a patient arrives and is admitted to the hospital, much of the planning for the surgery will already have happened. The operating theatre will have been reserved, and the doctors and nurses who staff the operating theatre will have been provided with all the information regarding the patient's condition. Appropriate preoperative and postoperative care will have been organized. All this will involve staff and facilities in different parts of the hospital, all of whom must have been given the same information and their activities co-ordinated. Soon after the patient arrives, he or she will be checked to make sure that the condition is as expected (in much the same way as material is inspected on arrival in a factory). Blood, if required, will be cross-matched and reserved, and any medication will be made ready (in the same way that all the different materials are brought together in a factory). Any last-minute changes may require some degree of re-planning. For example, if the patient shows unexpected symptoms, observation may be necessary before the surgery can take place. Not only will this affect the patient's own treatment, but other patients' treatment may also have to be rescheduled (in the same way as machines will need rescheduling if a job is delayed in a factory). All these activities of scheduling, co-ordination and organization are concerned with the planning and control of the hospital.

> **✳ Operations principle**
>
> Customers' perceptions of an operation will partially be shaped by the customer interface of its planning and control system.

Joanne manages the schedule[1]

Joanne Cheung is the Senior Service Adviser at a premier BMW dealership. She and her team act as the interface between customers who want their cars serviced and repaired and the 16 technicians who carry out the work in their state-of-the-art workshop. *'There are three types of work that we have to organize'*, says Joanne. *'The first is performing repairs on customers' vehicles. They usually want this doing as soon as possible. The second type of job is routine servicing. It is usually not urgent so customers are generally willing to negotiate a time for this. The remainder of our work involves working on the pre-owned cars which our buyer has bought-in to sell on to customers. Before any of these cars can be sold they have to undergo extensive checks. To some extent we treat these categories of work slightly differently. We have to give good service to our internal car buyers, but there is some flexibility in planning these jobs. At the other extreme, emergency repair work for customers has to be fitted into our schedule as quickly as possible. If someone is desperate to have their car repaired at very short notice, we sometimes ask them to drop their car in as early as they can and pick it up as late as possible. This gives us the maximum amount of time to fit it into the schedule.*

Source: Shutterstock.com; Jordan Tan

'There are a number of service options open to customers. We can book short jobs in for a fixed time and do it while they wait. Most commonly, we ask the customer to leave the car with us and collect it later. To help customers we have ten loan cars which are booked out on a first-come first-served basis. Alternatively, the vehicle can be collected from the customer's home and delivered back there when it is ready. Our four drivers who do this are able to cope with up to twelve jobs a day.

'Most days we deal with fifty to eighty jobs, taking from half-an-hour up to a whole day. To enter a job

into our process all Service Advisers have access to the computer-based scheduling system. On-screen it shows the total capacity we have day-by-day, all the jobs that are booked in, the amount of free capacity still available, the number of loan cars available, and so on. We use this to see when we have the capacity to book a customer in, and then enter all the customer's details. BMW have issued "standard times" for all the major jobs. However, you have to modify these standard times a bit to take account of circumstances. That is where the Service Adviser's experience comes in.

'We keep all the most commonly used parts in stock, but if a repair needs a part which is not in stock, we can usually get it from the BMW parts distributors within a day. Every evening our planning system prints out the jobs to be done the next day and the parts which are likely to be needed for each job. This allows the parts staff to pick out the parts for each job so that the technicians can collect them first thing the next morning without any delay.

'Every day we have to cope with the unexpected. A technician may find that extra work is needed, customers may want extra work doing, and technicians are sometimes ill, which reduces our capacity. Occasionally parts may not be available so we have to arrange with the customer for the vehicle to be rebooked for a later time. Every day up to four or five customers just don't turn up. Usually they have just forgotten to bring their car in so we have to rebook them in at a later time. We can cope with most of these uncertainties because our technicians are flexible in terms of the skills they have and also are willing to work overtime when needed. Also, it is important to manage customer's expectations. If there is a chance that the vehicle may not be ready for them, it shouldn't come as a surprise when they try and collect it.'

WHAT IS THE DIFFERENCE BETWEEN PLANNING AND CONTROL?

Notice that we have chosen to treat 'planning and control' together. This is because the division between 'planning' and 'control' is not clear, either in theory or in practice. However, there are some general features that help to distinguish between the two. Planning is a formalization of what is intended to happen at some time in the future. But a plan does not guarantee that an event will actually happen. Rather it is a statement of intention. Although plans are based on expectations, during their implementation things do not always happen as expected. Customers change their minds about what they want and when they want it. Suppliers may not always deliver on time, process technology may fail, or staff may be absent through illness. Control is the process of coping with these types of change. It may mean that plans need to be redrawn in the short term. It may also mean that an 'intervention' will need to be made in the operation to bring it back 'on track' – for example, finding a new supplier who can deliver quickly, getting process technology up and running again, or moving staff from another part of the operation to cover for absentees. Control activities make the adjustments which allow the operation to achieve the objectives that the plan has set, even when the assumptions on which the plan was based do not hold true.

> ✳ **Operations principle**
>
> Planning and control are separate but closely related activities.

Long-, medium- and short-term planning and control

The nature of planning and control activities changes over time. In the very long term, operations managers make plans concerning what they intend to do, what resources they need, and what objectives they hope to achieve. The emphasis is on planning rather than control, because there is little to control as such. They will use forecasts of likely demand described in aggregated terms. For example, a hospital will make plans for '2,000 patients' without necessarily going into the details of the individual needs of those 2,000 patients. Similarly, the hospital might plan to have 100 nurses and 20 doctors, but again without deciding on the specific attributes of the staff. Operations managers will focus mainly on volume and financial targets.

Medium-term planning and control is more detailed. It looks ahead to assess the overall demand which the operation must meet in a partially disaggregated manner. By this time, for example, the hospital must distinguish between different types of demand. The number of patients coming as accident and emergency cases will need to be distinguished from those requiring routine operations. Similarly, different categories of staff will have been identified and broad staffing levels in each category set. Just as important, contingencies will have been put in place which allow for slight deviations from the plans. These contingencies will act as 'reserve' resources and make planning and control easier in the short term.

In short-term planning and control, many of the resources will have been set and it will be difficult to make large changes. However, short-term interventions are possible if things are not going to plan. By this time, demand will be assessed on a totally disaggregated basis, with all types of surgical procedures treated as individual activities. More importantly, individual patients will have been identified by name, and specific time slots booked for their treatment. In making short-term interventions and changes to the plan, operations managers will be attempting to balance the quality, speed, dependability, flexibility and costs of their operation dynamically on an ad hoc basis. It is unlikely that they will have the time to carry out detailed calculations of the effects of their short-term planning and control decisions on all these objectives, but a general understanding of priorities will form the background to their decision making. Figure 10.2 shows how the control aspects of planning and control increase in significance closer to the date of the event.

The volume–variety effect on planning and control

As we have found previously, the volume and variety characteristics of an operation will have an effect on its planning and control activities. Operations which produce a high variety of services or products in relatively low volume will have customers with different requirements

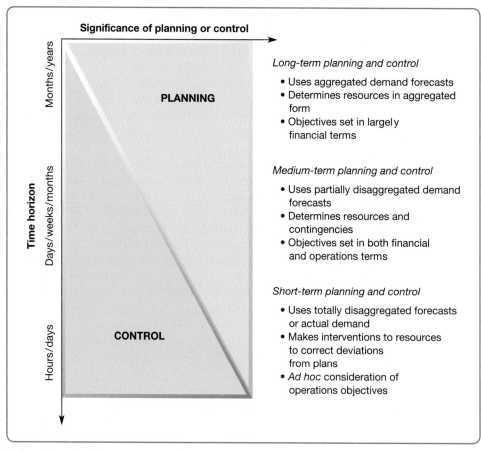

Figure 10.2 The balance between planning and control activities changes in the long, medium and short terms

Table 10.1 The volume–variety effects on planning and control

Volume	Variety	Customer responsiveness	Planning horizon	Major planning decision	Control decisions	Robustness
Low	High	Slow	Short	Timing	Detailed	High
↓	↓	↓	↓	↓	↓	↓
High	Low	Fast	Long	Volume	Aggregated	Low

and use different processes from operations which create standardized services or products in high volume (*see* Table 10.1).

Take two contrasting operations – an architects' practice and an electricity utility. The architects' high variety of customized services means they cannot produce designs in advance of customers requesting them. Because of this, the time it will take to deliver their services finally to customers will be relatively slow. Customers will understand this, but will expect to be consulted extensively as to their needs. The details and requirements of each job will emerge only as each individual building is designed to the client's requirements, so planning occurs on a relatively short-term basis. The individual decisions which are taken in the planning process will usually concern the timing of activities and events – for example, when a design is to be delivered, when building should start, when each individual architect will be needed to work on the design. Control decisions also will be at a relatively detailed level. A small delay in fixing one part of the design could have significant implications in many other parts of the job. For an architect, planning and control cannot be a totally routine matter; projects need managing on an individual basis. However, the robustness of the operation (that is, its vulnerability to serious disruption if one part of the operation fails) will be relatively high. There are probably plenty of other things to get on with if an architect is prevented from progressing one part of the job.

The electricity utility, on the other hand, is very different. Volume is high, production is continuous and variety is non-existent. Customers expect instant 'delivery' whenever they plug in an appliance. The planning horizon in electricity generation can be very long. Major decisions regarding the capacity of power stations are made years in advance. Even the fluctuations in demand over a typical day can be forecast in advance. Popular television programmes can affect minute-by-minute demand and these are scheduled weeks or months ahead. The weather, which also affects demand, is more uncertain, but can to some extent be predicted. Individual planning decisions made by the electricity utility are not concerned with the timing, but rather the volume of output. Control decisions will concern aggregated measures of output such as the total kilowatts of electricity generated, because the product is more or less homogeneous. However, the robustness of the operation is very low because, if a generator fails, the operation's capability of supplying electricity from that part of the operation also fails.

> **✳ Operations principle**
>
> The volume–variety characteristics of an operation will affect its planning and control activities.

HOW DO SUPPLY AND DEMAND AFFECT PLANNING AND CONTROL?

If planning and control is the process of reconciling demand with supply, then the nature of the decisions taken to plan and control an operation will depend on both the nature of demand and the nature of supply in that operation. In this section, we examine some differences in demand and supply which can affect the way in which operations managers plan and control their activities.

Operations control at Air France[2]

'In many ways a major airline can be viewed as one large planning problem which is usually approached as many independent, smaller (but still difficult) planning problems. The list of things which need planning seems endless: crews, reservation agents, luggage, flights, through trips, maintenance, gates, inventory, equipment purchases. Each planning problem has its own considerations, its own complexities, its own set of time horizons, its own objectives, but all are interrelated.'

Air France has 80 flight planners working 24-hour shifts in its flight planning office at Roissy, Charles de Gaulle. Their job is to establish the optimum flight routes, anticipate any problems such as weather changes and minimize fuel consumption. Overall the goals of the flight planning activity are first, and most important, safety, followed by economy and passenger comfort. Increasingly powerful computer programs process the mountain of data necessary to plan the flights, but in the end many decisions still rely on human judgement. Even the most sophisticated expert systems only serve as support for the flight planners. Planning Air France's schedule is a massive job. Just some of the considerations which need to be taken into account include the following:

Source: Shutterstock.com: Angelo

- *Frequency* – for each airport how many separate services should the airline provide?
- *Fleet assignment* – which type of aircraft should be used on each leg of a flight?
- *Banks* – at any airline hub where passengers arrive and may transfer to other flights to continue their journey, airlines like to organize flights into 'banks' of several plans which arrive close together, pause to let passengers change planes, and all depart close together. So, how many banks should there be and when should they occur?
- *Block times* – a block time is the elapsed time between an aircraft leaving the departure gate at an airport and arriving at its gate in the arrival airport.

The longer the allowed block time, the more likely an aircraft will keep to schedule even if it suffers minor delays. However, longer block times also mean fewer flights can be scheduled.

- *Planned maintenance* – any schedule must allow time for aircraft to have time at a maintenance base.
- *Crew planning* – pilot and cabin crew must be scheduled to allocate pilots to fly aircraft on which they are licensed and to keep within maximum 'on duty' times for all staff.
- *Gate plotting* – if many aircraft are on the ground at the same time there may be problems in loading and unloading them simultaneously.
- *Recovery* – many things can cause deviations from any plan in the airline industry. Allowances must be built in to allow for recovery.

For flights within and between Air France's 12 geographic zones, the planners construct a flight plan that will form the basis of the actual flight only a few hours later. All planning documents need to be ready for the flight crew who arrive two hours before the scheduled departure time. Being responsible for passenger safety and comfort, the captain always has the final say and, when satisfied, co-signs the flight plan together with the planning officer.

Uncertainty in supply and demand

Uncertainty is important in planning and control because it makes it more difficult. Sometimes the supply of inputs to an operation may be uncertain. Local village carnivals, for example, rarely work to plan. Events take longer than expected, some of the acts scheduled in the programme may be delayed en route and some traders may not even arrive. In other operations supply is relatively predictable, and the need for control is minimal. For example, cable TV services provide programmes to a schedule into subscribers' homes. It is rare to change the programme plan. Similarly demand may be unpredictable. A fast food outlet inside a shopping centre does not know how many people will arrive, when they will arrive and what they will order. It may be possible to predict certain patterns, such as an increase in demand over the lunch and teatime periods, but a sudden rainstorm that drives shoppers indoors into the centre could significantly and unpredictably increase demand in the very short term. Conversely, demand may be more predictable. In a school, for example, once classes are fixed and the term or semester has started, a teacher knows how many pupils are in the class. Both supply and demand uncertainty make planning and control more difficult, but a combination of supply *and* demand uncertainty is particularly difficult.

> ❋ **Operations principle**
>
> Planning and control systems should be able to cope with uncertainty in demand.

Dependent and independent demand

Some operations can predict demand with relative certainty because demand for their services or products is dependent upon some other factor which is known. This is known as dependent demand. For example, the demand for tyres in an automobile factory is not a totally random variable. The process of demand forecasting is relatively straightforward. It will consist of examining the manufacturing schedules in the car plant and deriving the demand for tyres from these. If 600 cars are to be manufactured on a particular day, then it is simple to calculate that 3,000 tyres will be demanded by the car plant (each car has five tyres) – demand is dependent on a known factor, the number of cars to be manufactured. Because of this, the tyres can be ordered from the tyre manufacturer to a delivery schedule which is closely related to the demand for tyres from the plant (as in Fig. 10.3). In fact, the demand for every part of the car plant will be derived from the assembly schedule for the finished cars. Other operations will act in a dependent demand manner because of the nature of the service or product which they provide. For example, a custom-made dressmaker will not buy fabric and make up dresses in many different sizes just in case someone comes along and

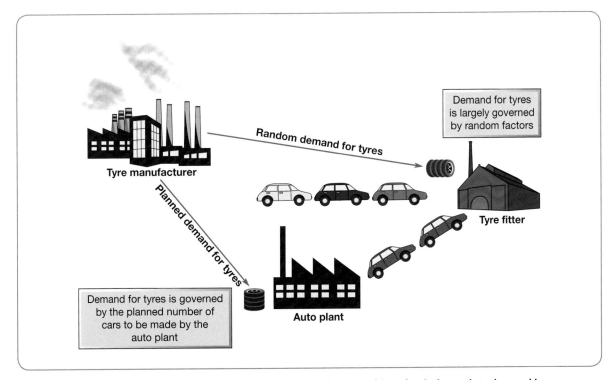

Figure 10.3 Dependent demand is derived from the demand for something else; independent demand is more random

wants to buy one. Nor will a high-class restaurant begin to cook food just in case a customer arrives and requests it. In both these cases, a combination of risk and the perishability of the product or service prevents the operation from starting to create the goods or services until it has a firm order. Planning and control in dependent demand situations is largely concerned with how the operation should respond when demand has occurred.

By contrast, some operations are subject to independent demand. They need to supply future demand without knowing exactly what that demand will be; or in the terminology of planning and control, they do not have firm 'forward visibility' of customer orders. For example, the tyre fitter, which operates a drive-in tyre replacement service, will need to manage a stock of tyres. In that sense it is exactly the same task that faced the manager of tyre stocks in the car plant. However, demand is very different for the tyre fitter. It cannot predict either the volume or the specific needs of customers. It must make decisions on how many and what type of tyres to stock, based on demand forecasts and in the light of the risks it is prepared to run of being out of stock. This is the nature of *independent demand planning and control*. It makes 'best guesses' concerning future demand, attempts to put the resources in place which can satisfy this demand, and attempts to respond quickly if actual demand does not match the forecast. Inventory planning and control, treated in Chapter 12, is typical of independent demand planning and control.

> ✳ **Operations principle**
>
> Planning and control systems should distinguish between dependent and independent demand.

Responding to demand

It is clear then that the nature of planning and control in any operation will depend on how it responds to demand, which is in turn related to the type of services or products it produces. For example, an advertising agency will only start the process of planning and controlling the creation of an advertising campaign when the customer (or client as the agency will refer to them) confirms the contract with the agency. The creative 'design' of the advertisements will be based on a 'brief' from the client. Only after the design is approved will the appropriate resources (director, scriptwriters, actors, production company, etc.) be contracted. The actual shooting of the advertisement and post-production (editing, putting in the special effects, etc.) then goes ahead after which the finished advertisements are 'delivered' through television slots. This is shown in Figure 10.4 as a 'Design, resource, create and deliver to order' operation.

Other operations might be sufficiently confident of the nature of demand, if not its exact details, to keep 'in stock' most of the resources the operation requires to satisfy its customers. Certainly it will keep its transforming resources, if not its transformed resources. However, it would still make the actual service or product only when it receives a firm customer order. For example, a website designer will have most of its resources (graphic designers, software developers, specialist development software, etc.) in place, but must still design, create and deliver the website after it understands its customer's requirements. (See the 'Operations in practice' case on Torchbox, in Chapter 1.) This is shown in Figure 10.4 as a 'Design, create and deliver to order' operation.

Some operations offer relatively standard services or products, but do not create them until the customer has chosen which particular service or product to have. So a house builder who has standard designs might choose to build each house only when a customer places a firm order. Because the design of the house is relatively standard, suppliers of materials will have been identified, even if the building operation does not keep the items in stock itself. This is shown in Figure 10.4 as a 'Create and deliver to order' operation. In manufacturing it would be called a 'Make to order' operation.

Some operations have services or products that are so predictable that they can start to 'create' them before specific customer orders arrive. Possibly the best known example of this is Dell Computers, where customers can 'specify' their computer by selecting between various components through the company's website. These components will have already been created (usually by suppliers) but assembled to a specific customer order. This is shown in Figure 10.4 as a 'Partially create and deliver to order' operation. In manufacturing it would be called an 'Assemble to order' operation.

When an operation's services or products are standardized, there is the potential to create them entirely before demand is known. Almost all domestic products for example are 'Created to stock', or 'Make to stock' (shown in Fig. 10.4) from which they are delivered to customers. Taking this evolving logic to its conclusion, some operations require their customers to collect their own services or products. This is the 'Choose/collect from stock' illustration in Figure 10.4. IKEA, and most high street retail operations, are like this.

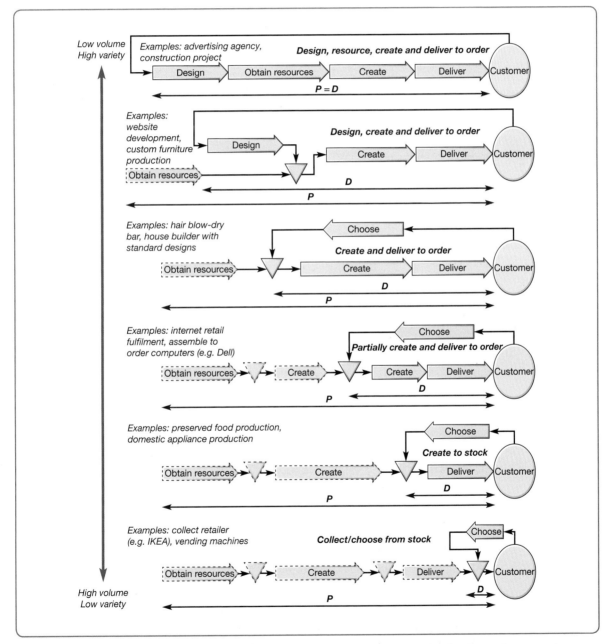

Figure 10.4 The *P:D* ratio of an operation indicates how long the customer has to wait for the service or product as compared with the total time to carry out all the activities to make the service or product available to the customer

One point to note in the operations illustrated in Figure 10.4 is that there is a relationship between how operations respond to demand and their volume–variety characteristics. It is easy to see that 'Design, resource, create and deliver to order' operation is intended for low-volume and high-variety businesses. By definition, designing different services or products will result in high variety, and performing each activity for each customer would be too cumbersome for a high-volume business. Conversely, 'Create for stock' or 'Choose/collect from stock' clearly rely on standardized services or products.

OPERATIONS IN PRACTICE — Uber[3]

Uber is a company that has gathered many opponents, namely conventional taxi drivers in several countries, some regulatory bodies around the world, its competitors (obviously) – and sometimes even its customers. Why? Well partly because the company, and especially its boss, Travis Kalanick, is so outspoken, but mainly because it has challenged the way that the business of ordering a taxi is managed. Now, the smartphone-based car service has succeeded in disrupting the taxi industry in many of its markets. It has done this because the key input to any planning and control system is information: that is, information on what customers have ordered, or are likely to order, information on what resources are available to meet customer orders, information on priorities, and so on. And this holds true when you order a taxi. The job of managing the constant flow of customer requests and matching them to taxi availability has traditionally been the responsibility of central 'despatching centres'. They are an information clearing-house, offering customers a central point of contact and offering busy drivers directions to the nearest prospective passenger. Taxi drivers pay these despatchers a fee to keep the jobs coming. But then the central despatching operations started to be threatened by location-enabled smartphones.

These offered the potential directly to connect customers with drivers, effectively cutting out the intermediary. It was an opportunity spotted by Travis Kalanick and his friend Garrett Camp one snowy night in Paris when they could not get a cab. The frustration led them to the idea of a simple app that could solve the problem. Why should it

Source: Getty Images: Bloomberg / Junko Kimura-Matsumoto

not be possible to 'push a button and get a car'? (It is ironic that the idea came to them in Paris, which became a centre of resistance to the company; Parisian taxi drivers have been known to slash the tyres of Uber cars and smash their windows.) The advantages to the customer were obvious. Instead of either calling the despatching centre or standing on the street until an available taxi happens to come along, then explaining where you want to go and having to find the cash (or fiddling with a credit card machine), using the app-based process is much simpler. Passengers summon a vehicle from a smartphone, whose location facility allows them to be told when the cab is outside. It enters the destination into the driver's navigation software and, because the cost is automatically charged to the customer's account, lets them walk out immediately upon arrival.

P:D ratios[4]

Another way of characterizing the graduation between 'Design, resource, create and deliver to order' and 'Choose/collect from stock' planning and control is by using a P:D ratio. This contrasts the total length of time customers have to wait between asking for the service or product and receiving it, called the demand time, D, and the total throughput time from start to finish, P. Throughput time is how long the operation takes to design the service or product (if it is customized), obtain the resources, create and deliver it.

P and *D* times depend on the operation

P and *D* are illustrated for each type of operation in Figure 10.4. Generally the ratio of *P* to *D* gets larger as operations move from 'Design, resource, create and deliver to order' to 'Choose/collect from stock'. In other words, as one moves down this spectrum towards the 'Create to stock' and 'Choose/collect from stock' end, the operation has anticipated customer demand and already created the services and products even though it has no guarantee that the anticipated demand will really happen. This is a particularly important point for the planning and control activity. The larger the *P:D* ratio, the more speculative the operation's planning and control activities will be. In its extreme form, the 'Choose/collect from stock' operation, such as a high street retailer, has taken a gamble by designing, resourcing, creating and delivering (or, more likely, paying someone else to do so) products to its shops before it has any certainty that any customers will want them. Contrast this with a 'Design, resource, create and deliver to order' operation as in the advertising agency mentioned earlier. Here, *D* is the same as *P* and speculation regarding the volume of demand in the short term is eliminated because everything happens in response to a firm order. So by reducing their *P:D* ratio operations reduce their degree of speculative activity and also reduce their dependence on forecasting (although bad forecasting will lead to other problems).

But do not assume that when the *P:D* ratio approaches 1, all uncertainty is eliminated. The volume of demand (in terms of the number of customer 'orders') may be known, but not the time taken to perform each 'order'. Take the advertising agency again: during each stage of the process, from design to delivery, it is common to have to seek the customer's approval and/or feedback many times during each stage. Moreover, there will almost certainly be some recycling back through stages as modifications are made. And, in a similar way to how simultaneous development works in new service and product design (see Chapter 5), a stage can be started before the previous one has been completed. So, for example, the video shoot director will have started prior to the artwork design being completed. This is illustrated in Figure 10.5. So here it is the timings that are uncertain.

> **✳ Operations principle**
>
> The *P:D* ratio of an operation contrasts how long customers have to wait for a service or product with its total throughput time.

WHAT ARE THE ACTIVITIES OF PLANNING AND CONTROL?

Planning and control requires the reconciliation of supply and demand in terms of volumes, timing and quality. In this chapter we will focus on an overview of the activities that plan and control volume and timing (most of this part of the book is concerned with these issues). There

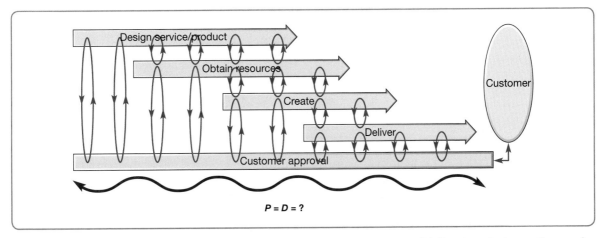

Figure 10.5 The relationship between stages in some 'Design, resource, create and deliver to order' operations such as an advertising agency, can be complex with frequent consultation and unpredictable recycling

are four overlapping activities: loading, sequencing, scheduling, and monitoring and control (*see* Fig. 10.6). Some caution is needed when using these terms. Different organizations may use them in different ways, and even textbooks in the area adopt different definitions. For example, some authorities term what we have called planning and control as 'operations scheduling'. However, the terminology of planning and control is less important than understanding the basic ideas described in the remainder of this chapter.

Loading

Loading is the amount of work that is allocated to a work centre. For example, a machine on the shop floor of a manufacturing business is available, in theory, 168 hours a week. However, this does not necessarily mean that 168 hours of work can be loaded onto that machine. Figure 10.7 shows what erodes this available time. For some periods the machine cannot be worked; for example, it may not be available on statutory holidays and weekends. Therefore, the load put onto the machine must take this into account. Of the time that the machine is available for work, other

losses further reduce the available time. For example, time may be lost while changing over from making one component to another. If the machine breaks down, it will not be available. If there is machine reliability data available, this must also be taken into account. Sometimes the machine may be waiting for parts to arrive or be 'idling' for some other reason. Other losses could include an allowance for the machine being run below its optimum speed (for example, because it has not been maintained properly) and an allowance for the 'quality losses' or defects which the machine may produce. Of course, many of these losses (shown in Fig. 10.6) should be small or non-existent in a well-managed operation. However, the valuable operating time available for productive working, even in the best operations, can be significantly below the maximum time available. This idea is taken further in Chapter 11 when we discuss the measurement of capacity.

Finite and infinite loading

Finite loading is an approach which only allocates work to a work centre (a person, a machine, or perhaps a group of people or machines) up to a set limit. This limit is the estimate of capacity for the work centre (based on the times available for loading). Work over and above this

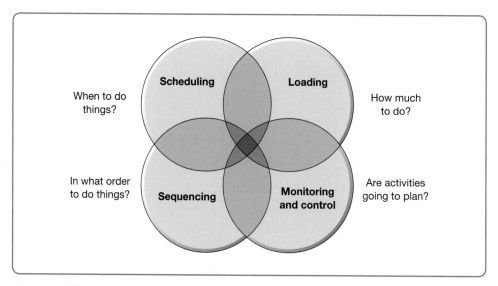

Figure 10.6 Planning and control activities

Figure 10.7 **The reduction in the time available for valuable operating time**

capacity is not accepted. Figure 10.8 first shows how the load on the work centres is not allowed to exceed the capacity limit. Finite loading is particularly relevant for operations where:

- *it is possible to limit the load* – for example, it is possible to run an appointment system for a general medical practice or a hairdresser;
- *it is necessary to limit the load* – for example, for safety reasons only a finite number of people and weight of luggage are allowed on aircraft;
- *the cost of limiting the load is not prohibitive* – for example, the cost of maintaining a finite order book at a specialist sports car manufacturer does not adversely affect demand, and may even enhance it.

Infinite loading is an approach to loading work which does not limit accepting work, but instead tries to cope with it. The second diagram in Figure 10.8 illustrates this loading pattern where capacity constraints have not been used to limit loading so the work is completed earlier. Infinite loading is relevant for operations where:

- *it is not possible to limit the load* – for example, an accident and emergency department in a hospital should not turn away arrivals needing attention;

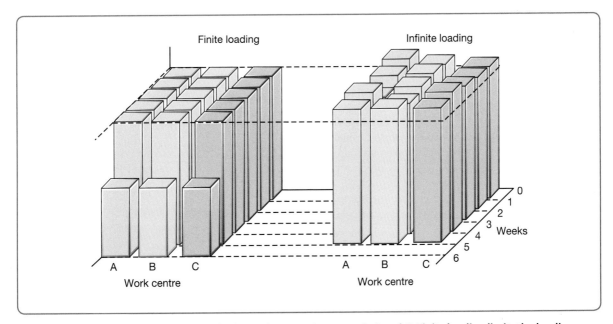

Figure 10.8 **Finite and infinite loading of jobs on three work centres A, B and C. Finite loading limits the loading on each centre to their capacities, even if it means that jobs will be late. Infinite loading allows the loading on each centre to exceed their capacities to ensure that jobs will not be late**

- *it is not necessary to limit the load* – for example, fast food outlets are designed to flex capacity up and down to cope with varying arrival rates of customers. During busy periods, customers accept that they must queue for some time before being served. Unless this is extreme, the customers might not go elsewhere;
- *the cost of limiting the load is prohibitive* – for example, if a retail bank turned away customers at the door because a set number were inside, customers would feel less than happy with the service.

In complex planning and control activities where there are multiple stages, each with different capacities and with a varying mix arriving at the facilities, such as a machine shop in an engineering company, the constraints imposed by finite loading make loading calculations complex and not worth the considerable computational power which would be needed.

Sequencing

Whether the approach to loading is finite or infinite, when work arrives, decisions must be taken on the order in which the work will be tackled. This activity is termed 'sequencing'. The priorities given to work in an operation are often determined by some predefined set of rules, some of which are relatively complex. Some of these are summarized below.

Physical constraints

The physical nature of the inputs being processed may determine the priority of work. For example, in an operation using paints or dyes, lighter shades will be sequenced before darker shades. On completion of each batch, the colour is slightly darkened for the next batch. This is because darkness of colour can only be added to and not removed from the colour mix. Sometimes the mix of work arriving at a part of an operation may determine the priority given to jobs. For example, when fabric is cut to a required size and shape in garment manufacture, the surplus fabric would be wasted if not used for another product. Therefore, jobs that physically fit together may be scheduled together to reduce waste. The sequencing issue described in the case on airline passengers is of this type.

OPERATIONS IN PRACTICE | **Can airline passengers be sequenced?[5]**

Source: Shutterstock.com: TravnikovStudio

Like many before him, Dr Jason Steffen, a professional astrophysicist from the world-famous Fermilab, was frustrated by the time it took to load him and his fellow passengers onto an aircraft. He decided to devise a way to make the experience a little less tedious. So, for a while, he neglected his usual work of examining extra-solar planets, dark matter and cosmology, and experimentally tested a faster method of boarding aircraft. He found that, by changing the sequence in which passengers are loaded onto the aircraft, airlines could potentially save both time and money. Using a computer simulation and the arithmetic techniques routinely used in his day-to-day job, he was able to find what seemed to be a superior sequencing method. In fact the most common way of boarding airliners proved to be the least efficient. This is called the 'block method' where blocks of seats are called for boarding, starting from the back.

Previously other experts in the airline industry had suggested boarding those in window seats first followed by middle and aisle seats. This is called the Wilma method.

But according to Dr Steffen's simulations, two things slow down the boarding process. The first is that passengers may be required to wait in the aisle while those ahead of them store their luggage before they can take their seat. The second is that passengers already seated in aisle or middle seats frequently have to rise and move into the aisle to let others take seats nearer the window. So Dr Steffen suggested a variant of the Wilma method that minimized the first type of disturbance and eliminated the second. He suggested boarding in alternate rows, progressing from the rear forward, window seats first. Using this approach (now called the Steffen method), first the window seats for every other row on one side of the aircraft are boarded. Next, alternate rows of window seats on the opposite side are boarded. Then, the window seats in the skipped rows are filled in on each side. The procedure then repeats with the middle seats and the aisles. *See* Figure 10.9.

Later, the effectiveness of the various approaches were tested using a mock-up of a Boeing 757 aircraft and 72 luggage-carrying volunteers. Five different scenarios were tested: 'block' boarding in groups of rows from back to front, one by one from back to front, the Wilma method, the Steffen method and completely random boarding. In all cases, parent–child pairs were allowed to board first. It was assumed that families were likely to want to stay together. As Dr Steffen had predicted, the conventional block approach came out as the slowest, with the strict back-to-front approach not much better. Completely random boarding (unallocated seating), which is used by several low-cost airlines, fared much better, most probably because it randomly avoids space conflicts. The times in minutes and seconds for fully boarding the 72 passengers using each method were as follows: block boarding, 6:54; back-to-front, 6:11; random boarding, 4:44; Wilma method, 4:13; Steffen method 3:36.

The big question is: 'would passengers really be prepared to be sequenced in this way as they queue to board the aircraft?' Some airlines argue that directing passengers onto an aircraft is a little like herding cats. But if they could adopt Dr Steffen's system it would save time for customers and very significant amounts of money for airlines.

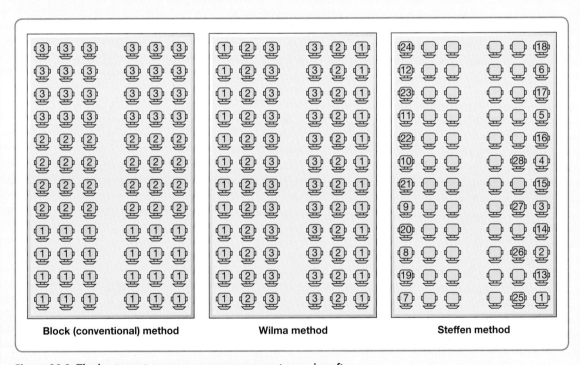

Figure 10.9 **The best way to sequence passengers onto an aircraft**

Customer priority

Operations will sometimes use customer priority sequencing, which allows an important or aggrieved customer, or item, to be 'processed' prior to others, irrespective of the order of arrival of the customer or item. This approach is typically used by operations whose customer

1	Immediate resuscitation	Patient in need of immediate treatment for preservation of life
2	Very urgent	Seriously ill or injured patients whose lives are not in immediate danger
3	Urgent	Patients with serious problems, but apparently stable conditions
4	Standard	Standard cases without immediate danger or distress
5	Non-urgent	Patients whose conditions are not true accidents or emergencies

Figure 10.10 A triage prioritization scale

base is skewed, containing a mass of small customers and a few large, very important customers. Some banks, for example, give priority to important customers. Similarly, in hotels, complaining customers will be treated as a priority because their complaint may have an adverse effect on the perceptions of other customers. More seriously, the emergency services often have to use their judgement in prioritizing the urgency of requests for service. For example, Figure 10.10 shows a typical triage system used in hospitals to prioritize patients (see the 'Operations in practice' case). However, customer priority sequencing, although giving a high level of service to some customers, may erode the service given to many other. This may lower the overall performance of the operation if work flows are disrupted to accommodate important customers.

Due date (DD)

Prioritizing by due date means that work is sequenced according to when it is 'due' for delivery, irrespective of the size of each job or the importance of each customer. For example, a support service, such as a printing unit, will often ask when copies are required, and then sequence the work according to that due date. Due date sequencing usually improves the delivery dependability and average delivery speed. However, it may not provide optimal productivity, as a more efficient sequencing of work may reduce total costs. However, it can be flexible when new, urgent work arrives at the work centre.

Last in, first out (LIFO)

Last in, first out (LIFO) is a method of sequencing usually selected for practical reasons. For example, unloading an elevator is more convenient on a LIFO basis, as there is only one entrance and exit. However, it is not an equitable approach. Patients at hospital clinics may be infuriated if they see newly arrived patients examined first.

First in, first out (FIFO)

Some operations serve customers in exactly the sequence they arrive in. This is called first in, first out (FIFO) sequencing, or sometimes 'first come, first served' (FCFS). For example, UK passport offices receive mail and sort it according to the day when it arrived. They work through the mail, opening it in sequence, and process the passport applications in order of arrival. Queues in theme parks may be designed so that one long queue snakes around the lobby area until the row of counters is reached. When customers reach the front of the queue, they are served at the next free counter.

One of the hospital environments that is most difficult to schedule is the accident and emergency department, where patients arrive at random, without any prior warning, throughout the day. It is up to the hospital's reception and the medical staff to devise very rapidly a schedule which meets most of the necessary criteria. In particular, patients who arrive having had very serious accidents, or presenting symptoms of a serious illness, need to be attended to urgently. Therefore, the hospital will schedule these cases first. Less urgent cases – perhaps patients who are in some discomfort, but whose injuries or illnesses are not life-threatening – will have to wait until the urgent cases are treated. Routine non-urgent cases will have the lowest priority of all. In many circumstances, these patients will have to wait for the longest time, which may be many hours, especially if the hospital is busy. Sometimes these non-urgent cases may even be turned away if the hospital is too busy with more important cases. In situations where hospitals expect

Source: Shutterstock.com: SV Luma

sudden influxes of patients, they have developed what is known as a triage system, whereby medical staff hurriedly sort through the patients who have arrived to determine which category of urgency each patient fits into. In this way a suitable schedule for the various treatments can be devised in a short period of time.

Longest operation time (LOT)

Operations may feel obliged to sequence their longest jobs first, called longest operation time sequencing. This has the advantage of occupying work centres for long periods. By contrast, relatively small jobs progressing through an operation will take up time at each work centre because of the need to change over from one job to the next. However, although longest operation time sequencing keeps utilization high, this rule does not take into account delivery speed, reliability or flexibility. Indeed, it may work directly against these performance objectives.

Shortest operation time (SOT) first

Most operations at some stage become cash constrained. In these situations, the sequencing rules may be adjusted to tackle short jobs first; this is called shortest operation time sequencing. These jobs can then be invoiced and payment received to ease cash-flow problems. Larger jobs that take more time will not enable the business to invoice as quickly. This has an effect of improving delivery performance, if the unit of measurement of delivery is jobs. However, it may adversely affect total productivity and can damage service to larger customers.

Judging sequencing rules

All five performance objectives, or some variant of them, could be used to judge the effectiveness of sequencing rules. However, the objectives of dependability, speed and cost are particularly important. So, for example, the following performance objectives are often used:

- Meeting 'due date' promised to customer (dependability).
- Minimizing the time the job spends in the process, also known as 'flow time' (speed).
- Minimizing work-in-progress inventory (an element of cost).
- Minimizing idle time of work centres (another element of cost).

Steve Smith is a website designer in a business school. On returning from his annual vacation (he finished all outstanding jobs before he left), he is given five design jobs upon arrival at work. He gives them the codes A to E. Steve has to decide in which sequence to undertake the jobs. He wants both to minimize the average time the jobs are tied up in his office and, if possible, to meet the deadlines (delivery times) allocated to each job.

His first thought is to do the jobs in the order they were given to him, that is first in, first out (FIFO):

Sequencing rule – first in, first out (FIFO)

Sequence of jobs	Process time (days)	Start time	Finish time	Due date	Lateness (days)
A	5	0	5	6	0
B	3	5	8	5	3
C	6	8	14	8	6
D	2	14	16	7	9
E	1	16	17	3	14

Total time in process			60	Total lateness	32
Average time in process (total/5)			12	Average lateness (total/5)	6.4

Alarmed by the average lateness, he tries the due date (DD) rule:

Sequence of jobs	Process time (days)	Start time	Finish time	Due date	Lateness (days)
E	1	0	1	3	0
B	3	1	4	5	0
A	5	4	9	6	3
D	2	9	11	7	4
C	6	11	17	8	9

Total time in process			42	Total lateness	16
Average time in process (total/5)			8.4	Average lateness (total/5)	3.2

Better! But Steve tries out the shortest operation time (SOT) rule:

Sequencing rule – shortest operation time (SOT)

Sequence of jobs	Process time (days)	Start time	Finish time	Due date	Lateness (days)
E	1	0	1	3	0
D	2	1	3	7	0
B	3	3	6	5	1
A	5	6	11	6	5
C	6	11	17	8	9

Total time in process			38	Total lateness	16
Average time in process (total/5)			7.6	Average lateness (total/5)	3.2

This gives the same degree of average lateness but with a lower average time in the process. Steve decides to use the SOT rule.

Table 10.2 Comparison of five sequencing decision rules

Rule	Average time in process (days)	Average lateness (days)
FIFO	12	6.4
DD	8.4	3.2
SOT	7.6	3.2
LIFO	8.4	3.8
LOT	12.8	7.4

Comparing the results from the three sequencing rules described in the worked example together with the two other sequencing rules described earlier, and applied to the same problem, gives the results summarized in Table 10.2. The SOT rule resulted in both the best average time in process and the best (or least bad) in terms of average lateness. Although different rules will perform differently depending on the circumstances of the sequencing problem, in practice the SOT rule generally performs well.

Scheduling

Having determined the sequence that work is to be tackled in, some operations require a detailed timetable showing at what time or date jobs should start and when they should end – this is scheduling. Schedules are familiar statements of volume and timing in many consumer environments. For example, a bus schedule shows that more buses are put on routes at more frequent intervals during rush-hour periods. The bus schedule shows the time each bus is due to arrive at each stage of the route. Schedules of work are used in operations where some planning is required to ensure that customer demand is met. Other operations, such as rapid-response service operations where customers arrive in an unplanned way, cannot schedule the operation in a short-term sense. They can only respond at the time demand is placed upon them.

The complexity of scheduling

The scheduling activity is one of the most complex tasks in operations management. First, schedulers must deal with several different types of resource simultaneously. Machines will have different capabilities and capacities; staff will have different skills. More importantly, the number of possible schedules increases rapidly as the number of activities and processes increases. For example, suppose one machine has five different jobs to process. Any of the five jobs could be processed first and, following that, any one of the remaining four jobs, and so on. This means that there are:

$$5 \times 4 \times 3 \times 2 = 120 \text{ different schedules possible}$$

In other words, for n jobs there are $n!$ (factorial n) different ways of scheduling the jobs through a single process. But when there are (say) two machines, there is no reason why the sequence on machine 1 would be the same as the sequence on machine 2. If we consider the two sequencing tasks to be independent of each other, for two machines there would be:

$$120 \times 120 = 14,400 \text{ possible schedules of the two machines and five jobs}$$

So a general formula can be devised to calculate the number of possible schedules in any given situation, as follows:

$$\text{Number of possible schedules} = (n!)^m$$

where n is the number of jobs and m is the number of machines.

Table 10.3 **The effects of forward and backward scheduling**

Task	Duration	Start time (backwards)	Start time (forwards)
Press	1 hour	3.00 pm	1.00 pm
Dry	2 hours	1.00 pm	11.00 am
Wash	3 hours	10.00 am	8.00 am

In practical terms, this means that there are often many millions of feasible schedules, even for relatively small scheduling tasks. This is why scheduling rarely attempts to provide an 'optimal' solution but rather satisfies itself with an 'acceptable' feasible one.

Forward and backward scheduling

Forward scheduling involves starting work as soon as it arrives. Backward scheduling involves starting jobs at the last possible moment to prevent them from being late. For example, assume that it takes six hours for a contract laundry to wash, dry and press a batch of overalls. If the work is collected at 8.00 am and is due to be picked up at 4.00 pm, there are more than six hours available to do it. Table 10.3 shows the different start times of each job, depending on whether they are forward or backward scheduled.

> ✱ **Operations principle**
>
> An operation's planning and control system should allow for the effects of alternative schedules to be assessed.

The choice of backward or forward scheduling depends largely upon the circumstances. Table 10.4 lists some advantages and disadvantages of the two approaches. In theory, both materials requirements planning (MRP, see Chapter 14) and lean, or just-in-time, planning (JIT, see Chapter 15) use backward scheduling, only starting work when it is required. In practice, however, users of MRP have tended to allow too long for each task to be completed, and therefore each task is not started at the latest possible time. In comparison, JIT is started, as the name suggests, just in time.

Gantt charts

One crude but simple method of scheduling is by use of the Gantt chart. This is a simple device which represents time as a bar, or channel, on a chart. The start and finish times for activities can be indicated on the chart and sometimes the actual progress of the job is also indicated. The advantages of Gantt charts are that they provide a simple visual representation both of what should be happening and of what actually is happening in the operation. Furthermore, they can be used to 'test out' alternative schedules. It is a relatively simple task to represent alternative schedules (even if it is a far from simple task to find a schedule which fits all the resources satisfactorily). Figure 10.11 illustrates a Gantt chart for a specialist software developer. It indicates the progress of several jobs as they are expected to progress through five stages of the process. Gantt charts are not an optimizing tool; they merely facilitate the development of alternative schedules by communicating them effectively.

Table 10.4 **Advantages of forward and backward scheduling**

Advantages of forward scheduling	Advantages of backward scheduling
High labour utilization – workers always start work to keep busy	Lower material costs – materials are not used until they have to be, therefore delaying added value until the last moment
Flexible – the time slack in the system allows unexpected work to be loaded	Less exposed to risk in case of schedule change by the customer
	Tends to focus the operation on customer due dates

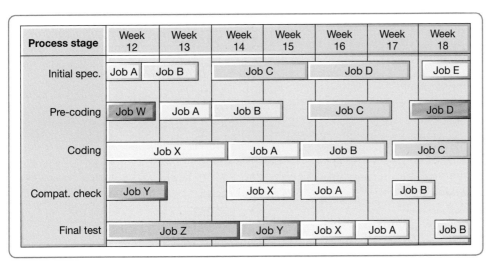

Process stage	Week 12	Week 13	Week 14	Week 15	Week 16	Week 17	Week 18
Initial spec.	Job A	Job B	Job C		Job D		Job E
Pre-coding	Job W	Job A	Job B		Job C		Job D
Coding		Job X		Job A	Job B		Job C
Compat. check	Job Y			Job X	Job A	Job B	
Final test		Job Z		Job Y	Job X	Job A	Job B

Figure 10.11 Gantt chart showing the schedule for jobs at each process stage

The life and times of a chicken salad sandwich – part one[6]

Pre-packed sandwiches are a growth product around the world as consumers put convenience and speed above relaxation and cost. But if you have recently consumed a pre-packed sandwich, think about the schedule of events which has gone into its making. For example, take a chicken salad sandwich. Less than five days ago, the chicken was on the farm, unaware that it would never see another weekend. The Gantt chart schedule shown in Figure 10.12 tells the story of the sandwich, and (posthumously) of the chicken.

From the forecast, orders for non-perishable items are placed for goods to arrive up to a week in advance of their use. Orders for perishable items will be placed daily, a day or two before the items are required. Tomatoes, cucumbers and lettuces have a three-day shelf life so may be received up to three days before production. Stock is held on a strict first in, first out (FIFO) basis. If today is (say) Wednesday, vegetables are processed that have been received during the last three days. This morning the bread arrived from a local bakery and the chicken arrived fresh, cooked and in strips ready to be placed directly in the sandwich during assembly. Yesterday (Tuesday) it had been killed, cooked, prepared and sent on its journey to the factory. By mid-day orders for tonight's production will have been received on the Internet. From 2.00 pm until 10.00 pm the production lines are closed down for maintenance and a very thorough cleaning. During this time the production planning team is busy planning the night's production run. Production for delivery to customers furthest away from the factory will have to be scheduled first. By 10 pm production is ready to start. Sandwiches are made on production lines. The bread is loaded onto a conveyor belt

Source: Shutterstock.com: Yeko Photo Studio

by hand and butter is spread automatically by a machine. Next the various fillings are applied at each stage according to the specified sandwich 'design', see Figure 10.13. After the filling has been assembled, the top slice of bread is placed on the sandwich and machine-chopped into two triangles, packed and sealed by machine. It is now early Thursday morning and by 2.00 am the first refrigerated lorries are already departing on their journeys to various customers. Production continues through until 2.00 pm on the Thursday, after which once again the maintenance and cleaning teams move in. The last sandwiches are despatched by 4.00 pm on the Thursday. There is no finished goods stock.

Part two of the life and times of a chicken salad sandwich is in Chapter 14.

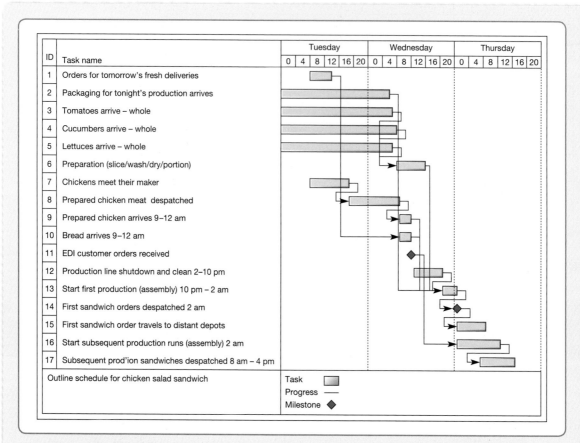

Figure 10.12 Simplified schedule for the manufacture and delivery of a chicken salad sandwich

Figure 10.13 Design for a chicken salad sandwich

Scheduling work patterns

Where the dominant resource in an operation is its staff, then the schedule of work times effectively determines the capacity of the operation itself. The main task of scheduling, therefore, is to make sure that sufficient numbers of people are working at any point in time to provide a capacity appropriate for the level of demand at that point in time. This is often called staff rostering. Operations such as call centres, postal delivery, policing, holiday couriers, retail shops and hospitals will all need to schedule the working hours of their staff with demand in mind. This is a direct consequence of these operations having relatively high 'visibility' (we introduced this idea in Chapter 1). Such operations cannot store their outputs in inventories and so must respond directly to customer demand. For example, Figure 10.14 shows the scheduling of shifts for a small technical 'hot line' support service for a small software company. It gives advice to customers on their technical problems. Its service times are 4:00 to 20:00 hours on Monday, 4:00 to 22:00 hours Tuesday to Friday, 6:00 to 22:00 hours on Saturday, and 10:00 to 20:00 hours on Sunday. Demand is heaviest Tuesday to Thursday, starts to decrease on Friday, is low over the weekend and starts to increase again on Monday.

The scheduling task for this kind of problem can be considered over different timescales, two of which are shown in Figure 10.14. During the day, working hours need to be agreed with individual staff members. During the week, days off need to be agreed. During the year, vacations, training periods, and other blocks of time where staff are unavailable need to be agreed. All this has to be scheduled such that:

- capacity matches demand;
- the length of each shift is neither excessively long nor too short to be attractive to staff;
- working at unsocial hours is minimized;
- days off match agreed staff conditions (in this example staff prefer two consecutive days off every week);
- vacation and other 'time-off' blocks are accommodated;
- sufficient flexibility is built into the schedule to cover for unexpected changes in supply (staff illness) and demand (surge in customer calls).

Scheduling staff times is one of the most complex of scheduling problems. In the relatively simple example shown in Figure 10.14 we have assumed that all staff have the same level and type of skill. In very large operations with many types of skill to schedule and uncertain demand (for example, a large hospital) the scheduling problem becomes extremely complex. Some mathematical techniques are available but most scheduling of this type is, in practice, solved using heuristics (rules of thumb), some of which are incorporated into commercially available software packages.

Monitoring and controlling the operation

Having created a plan for the operation through loading, sequencing and scheduling, each part of the operation has to be monitored to ensure that planned activities are indeed happening. Any deviation from the plans can then be rectified through some kind

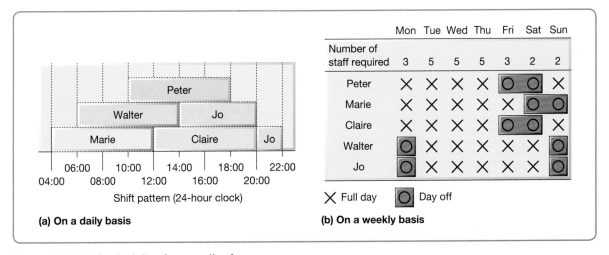

Figure 10.14 Shift scheduling for a small software company

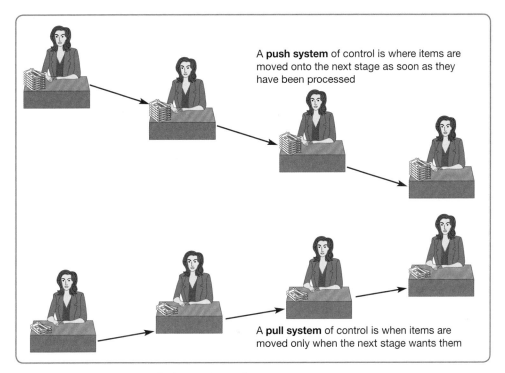

A **push system** of control is where items are moved onto the next stage as soon as they have been processed

A **pull system** of control is when items are moved only when the next stage wants them

Figure 10.16 Push versus pull: the gravity analogy

each stage of which is on a lower level than the previous stage. When items are processed by each stage, gravity pushes them down the slope to the next stage. Any delay or variability in processing time at that stage will result in the items accumulating as inventory. In the pull system, items cannot naturally flow uphill, so they can only progress if the next stage along deliberately pulls them forward. Under these circumstances, inventory cannot accumulate as easily.

Drum, buffer, rope

The drum, buffer, rope concept comes from the theory of constraints (TOC) and a concept called optimized production technology (OPT), originally described by Eli Goldratt in his novel *The Goal*.[7] (We will deal more with his ideas in Chapter 15.) It is an idea that helps to decide exactly *where* in a process control should occur. Most do not have the same amount of work loaded onto each separate work centre (that is, they are not perfectly balanced). This means there is likely to be a part of the process which is acting as a bottleneck on the work flowing through the process. Goldratt argued that the bottleneck in the process should be the control point of the whole process. It is called the *drum* because it sets the 'beat' for the rest of the process to follow. Because it does not have sufficient capacity, a bottleneck is (or should be) working all the time. Therefore, it is sensible to keep a *buffer* of inventory in front of it to make sure that it always has something to work on. Because it constrains the output of the whole process, any time lost at the bottleneck will affect the output

> **∗ Operations principle**
> The constraints of bottleneck processes and activities should be a major input to the planning and control activity.

from the whole process. So it is not worthwhile for the parts of the process before the bottleneck to work to their full capacity. All they would do is produce work which would accumulate further along in the process up to the point where the bottleneck is constraining the flow. Therefore, some form of communication between the bottleneck and the input to the process is needed to make sure that activities before the bottleneck do not overproduce. This is called the *rope* (*see* Fig. 10.17).

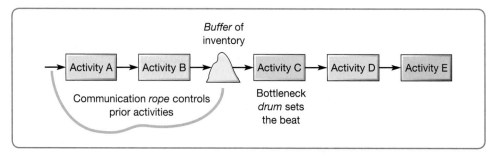

Figure 10.17 The drum, buffer, rope concept

Critical commentary

Most of the perspectives on control taken in this chapter are simplifications of a far more messy reality. They are based on models used to understand mechanical systems such as car engines. But anyone who has worked in real organizations knows that organizations are not machines. They are social systems, full of complex and ambiguous interactions. Simple models such as these assume that operations objectives are always clear and agreed, yet organizations are political entities where different and often conflicting objectives compete. Local government operations, for example, are overtly political. Furthermore, the outputs from operations are not always easily measured. A university may be able to measure the number and qualifications of its students, for example, but it cannot measure the full impact of its education on their future happiness. Also, even if it is possible to work out an appropriate intervention to bring an operation back into 'control', most operations cannot perfectly predict what effect the intervention will have. Even the largest of burger bar chains does not know *exactly* how a new shift allocation system will affect performance. Also, some operations never do the same thing more than once anyway. Most of the work done by construction operations are one-offs. If every output is different, how can 'controllers' ever know what is supposed to happen? Their plans themselves are mere speculation.

Controlling operations is not always routine

The simple monitoring control model in Figure 10.15 helps us to understand the basic functions of the monitoring and control activity. But, as the critical commentary box says, it is a simplification. Some simple routine processes may approximate to it, but many other operations do not. In fact, some of the specific criticisms cited in the critical commentary box provide a useful set of questions which can be used to assess the degree of difficulty associated with control of any operation, In particular:

- Is there consensus over what the operation's objectives should be?
- Are the effects of interventions into the operation predictable?
- Are the operation's activities largely repetitive?

Starting with the first question, are strategic objectives clear and unambiguous? It is not always possible (or necessarily desirable) to articulate every aspect of an operation's objectives in detail. Many operations are just too complex for that. Nor does every senior manager always agree on what the operation's objectives *should* be. Often the lack of a clear objective is because individual managers have different and conflicting interests. In social care organizations, for example, some managers are charged with protecting vulnerable members of society, others with ensuring that public money is not wasted, and yet others may be required to protect the independence of professional staff. At other times objectives are ambiguous because the strategy has to cope with unpredictable changes in the environment, making the original objectives redundant. A further assumption in the simplified control model is that there is some reasonable knowledge of how to bring about the desired outcome. That is, when a decision is made, one can predict its effects with a reasonable degree of confidence. In other words, operational control assumes that any interventions which are intended to bring a process back under control will indeed have the intended effect. Yet, this implies that the relationships between the intervention and the resulting consequence within the process are predictable, which in turn assumes that the degree of process knowledge is high. For example, if an organization decides to relocate in order to be more convenient for its customers, it may or may not prove to be correct. Customers may react in a manner that was not predicted. Even if customers seem initially to respond well to the new location, there may be a lag before negative reactions become evident. In fact many operations decisions are taken on activities about which the cause–effect relationship is only partly understood. The final assumption about control is that control interventions are made in a repetitive way and occur frequently (for example, checking on a process, hourly or daily). This means that the operation has the opportunity to learn how its interventions affect the process which considerably facilitates control. However, some control situations are non-repetitive: for example, those involving unique services or products. So because the intervention, or the deviation from plan that caused it, may not be repeated, there is little opportunity for learning.

Figure 10.18 illustrates how these questions can form a 'decision tree' type of model that indicates how the nature of operations control may be influenced.[8] Operational control is relatively straightforward: objectives are unambiguous, the effects of interventions are known, and activities are repetitive. This type of control can be done using predetermined conventions and rules. There are, however, still some challenges to successful routine control. It needs operational discipline to make sure that control procedures are systematically implemented. The main point, though, is that any divergence from the conditions necessary for routine control implies a different type of control.

> **❋ Operations principle**
>
> Planning and control is not always routine, especially when objectives are ambiguous, the effects of interventions into the operation are not predictable and activities are not repetitive.

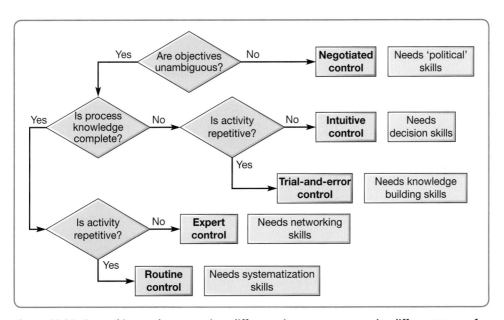

Figure 10.18 Control is not always routine; different circumstances require different types of control

Expert control

If objectives are unambiguous, yet the effects of interventions relatively well understood, but the activity is not repetitive (for example, installing or upgrading software or IT systems), control can be delegated to an 'expert' – someone for whom such activities are repetitive because they have built their knowledge on previous experience elsewhere. Making a success of expert control requires that such experts exist and can be 'acquired' by the firm. It also requires that the expert takes advantage of the control knowledge already present in the firm and integrates his or her 'expert' knowledge with the support that potentially exists internally. Both of these place a stress on the need to 'network', in terms of both acquiring expertise and then integrating that expertise into the organisation.

Trial-and-error control

If strategic objectives are relatively unambiguous, but effects of interventions not known, yet the activity is repetitive, the operation can gain knowledge of how to control successfully through its own failures. In other words, although simple prescriptions may not be available in the early stages of making control interventions, the organization can learn how to do it through experience. For example, if a fast food chain is opening new stores in new markets, it may not be sure how best to arrange the openings at first. But if the launch is the first of several, the objective must be not only to make a success of each launch, but equally (or more) important, to learn from each experience. It is these knowledge-building skills that will ultimately determine the effectiveness of trial-and-error control.

Intuitive control

If objectives are relatively unambiguous (so it is clear what the operation is trying to do), but effects of control interventions not known, and neither are they repetitive, learning by trial and error is not possible. Here control becomes more of an art than a science. And in these circumstances control must be based on the management team using its intuition to make control decisions. Many strategic operations processes fall into this category – for example, setting up a strategic supply partnership (see Chapter 13). Objectives are clear (jointly survive in the long term, make an acceptable return, and so on) but not only are control interventions not repetitive and their effects not fully understood, but also sometimes the supplier's interests may be in conflict with yours. Yet, simply stating that 'intuition' is needed in these circumstances is not particularly helpful. Instinct and feelings are, of course, valuable attributes in any management team, but they are the result, at least partly, of understanding how best to organize the team members' shared understanding, knowledge and decision-making skills. It requires thorough decision analysis, not to 'mechanistically' make the decision, but to frame it so that connections can be made, consequences understood and insights gained.

Negotiated control

The most difficult circumstance for strategic control is when objectives are ambiguous. This type of control involves reducing ambiguity in some way by making objectives less uncertain. Sometimes this is done simply by senior managers 'pronouncing' or arbitrarily deciding what objectives *should* be, irrespective of opposing views. For example, controlling the activities of a childcare service can involve very different views among the professional social workers making day-to-day decisions. Often a negotiated settlement may be sought which then can become an unambiguous objective. Alternatively, outside experts could be used, either to help with the negotiations or to remove control decisions from those with conflicting views. But, even within the framework of negotiation, there is almost always a political element when ambiguities in objectives exist. Negotiation processes will be, to some extent, dependent on power structures.

❯ What is planning and control?

- Planning and control is the reconciliation of the potential of the operation to supply products and services, and the demands of its customers on the operation. It is the set of day-to-day activities that run the operation on an ongoing basis.

❯ What is the difference between planning and control?

- A plan is a formalization of what is intended to happen at some time in the future. Control is the process of coping with changes to the plan and the operation to which it relates. Although planning and control are theoretically separable, they are usually treated together.
- The balance between planning and control changes over time. Planning dominates in the long term and is usually done on an aggregated basis. At the other extreme, in the short term, control usually operates within the resource constraints of the operation but makes interventions into the operation in order to cope with short-term changes in circumstances.

❯ How do supply and demand affect planning and control?

- The degree of uncertainty in demand affects the balance between planning and control. The greater the uncertainty, the more difficult it is to plan, and greater emphasis must be placed on control.
- This idea of uncertainty is linked with the concepts of dependent and independent demand. Dependent demand is relatively predictable because it is dependent on some known factor. Independent demand is less predictable because it depends on the chances of the market or customer behaviour.
- The different ways of responding to demand can be characterized by differences in the *P:D* ratio of the operation. The *P:D* ratio is the ratio of total throughput time of services or products to demand time.

❯ What are the activities of planning and control?

- In planning and controlling the volume and timing of activity in operations, four distinct activities are necessary:
  - loading, which dictates the amount of work that is allocated to each part of the operation;
  - sequencing, which decides the order in which work is tackled within the operation;
  - scheduling, which determines the detailed timetable of activities and when activities are started and finished;
  - monitoring and control, which involve detecting what is happening in the operation, re-planning if necessary, and intervening in order to impose new plans. Two important types are 'pull' and 'push' control. Pull control is a system whereby demand is triggered by requests from a work centre's (internal) customer. Push control is a centralized system whereby control (and sometimes planning) decisions are issued to work centres which are then required to perform the task and supply the next workstation. In manufacturing, 'pull' schedules generally have far lower inventory levels than 'push' schedules.
- The ease with which control can be maintained varies between operations.

subText **Studios Singapore**[9]

C.K. was clearly upset. Since he had founded *subText* in the fast-growing South-East Asian computer-generated imaging (CGI) market, three years ago, this was the first time that he had needed to apologize to his clients. In fact, it had been more than an apology; he had agreed to reduce his fee, though he knew that did not make up for the delay. He admitted that, up to that point, he had not fully realized just how much risk there was, both reputational and financial, in failing to meet schedule dates. It was not that either he or his team was unaware of the importance of reliability. On the contrary. 'Imagination', 'expertise' and 'reliability' all figured prominently in the studios' promotional literature, mission statements, and so on. It was just that the 'imagination' and 'expertise' parts had seemed to be the things that had been responsible for their success so far. Of course, it had been bad luck that, after more than a year of perfect reliability (not one late job), the two that had been late in the first quarter of this year had been particularly critical. *'They were both for new clients'*, said C.K., *'And neither of them indicated just how important the agreed delivery date was to them. We should have known, or found out, I admit. But it's always more difficult with new clients, because without a track record with them, you don't really like even to admit the possibility of being late.'*

The company

After studying computer science at the National University of Singapore, C.K. Ong had worked in CGI workshops in and around the Los Angeles area of California, after which he returned to Singapore to start *subText* Studios. At the heart of the company were the three 'core' departments that dealt sequentially with each job taken on. These three departments were 'Pre-production', 'Production' and 'Post-production'.

Pre-production was concerned with taking and refining the brief as specified by the client, checking with and liaising with the client to iron out any ambiguities in the brief, storyboarding the sequences, and obtaining outline approval of the brief from the client. In addition, pre-production also acted as account liaison with the client and was also responsible for estimating the resources and timing for each job. Pre-production also had nominal responsibility for monitoring the job through the remaining two stages, but generally it only did this if the client needed to be consulted during the production and post-production processes.

Production involved the creation of the imagery itself. This could be a complex and time-consuming process involving the use of state-of-the-art workstations and CGI software. Around 80 per cent of all production work was carried out in-house, but for some jobs other specialist

Source: Shutterstock.com: Haider Y. Abdulla

workshops were contracted. This was only done for work that *subText* either could not do, or would find difficult to do.

Post-production had two functions: the first was to integrate the visual image sequences produced by Production with other effects such as sound effects, music, voiceovers, etc.; the second was to cut, edit and generally produce the finished 'product' in the format required by the client.

Each of the three department employed teams of two people. Pre-production had two teams, Production three teams and Post-production two teams. For Pre-production and Post-production work, one team is always exclusively devoted to one job. *'We never allow either one team to be working on two jobs at the same time, or have both teams working on one job. It just doesn't work because of the confusion it creates. That doesn't apply to Production. Usually (but not always) the Production work can be parcelled up so that two or even all three of the teams could be working on different parts of it at the same time. Provided there is close coordination between the teams and provided that they are all committed to pulling it together at the end, there should be a more or less inverse relationship between the number of bodies working on the job and the length of time it takes. In fact, with the infamous "fifty-three slash F" job that's exactly what we had to do. However, not withstanding what I just said about shortening the time, we probably did lose some efficiency there by having all three teams working on it. Our teams generally work until the job is finished. That level of work is factored in to the time estimates we make for each stage of the process. And, although we can be a little inaccurate sometimes, it's because this type of thing is difficult to estimate.'* (C.K. Ong)

The fifty-three slash F job

The fifty-three slash F job, recently finished (late) and delivered to the client (dissatisfied), had been the source

Table 10.5 *subText* Studios Singapore – planning data for day 02 to day 58

Job (04)	Day in	Estimated total time	Actual total time	Due date	Actual delivery	Pre-prod		Prod		Post-prod	
						Est	Actual	Est	Actual	Est	Actual
06/A	–4	29	30	40	34	6	8	11	10	12	12
11/B	–4	22	24	42	31	4	5.5	7	7.5	11	11
04/C	2	31	30.5	43	40	9	9.5	12	13	10	9
54/D	5	28	34	55	58	10	12	12	17	6	5
31/E	15	34	25	68	57	10	11	12	14	12	–
53/F	18	32	49	50	53	6	10	18	28	8	11
24/G	25	26	20	70	–	9	11	9	9	8	–
22/H	29	32	26	70	–	10	12	14	14	8	–
22/I	33	30	11	75	–	10	11	12	–	8	–
09/J	41	36	14	81	–	12	14	14	–	10	–
20/K	49	40	–	89	–	12	–	14	–	14	–

of much chaos, confusion and recrimination over the last two or three weeks. Although the job was only three days late, it had caused the client to postpone a presentation to its own client. Worse, *subText* had given only five days' notice of late delivery, trying until the last minute to pull back onto schedule.

The full name of the job that had given *subText* so much trouble was 04/53/F. Table 10.5 shows the data for all the jobs started this year up to the current time (day 58; every working day was numbered throughout the year). Figure 10.19 shows the schedule for this period. The job had been accepted on day 18 and had seemed relatively

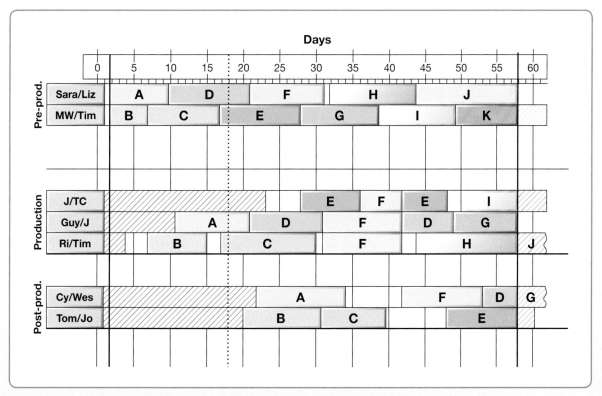

Figure 10.19 *subText* Studios Singapore – actual schedule for day 02 to 58

straightforward, although it was always clear that it would be a long production job. It was also clear that time was always going to be tight. There were 32 days in which to finish a job that was estimated to take 30 days.

'In hindsight we underestimated how much having three teams working on the production stage of this job at one point or other would increase its complexity. OK, it was not an easy piece of CGI to carry off, but we probably would have been OK if we had organized the CGI stage better. It was also real bad luck that, in our efforts to deliver the fifty-three slash F job on time, we also disrupted the fifty-four slash D job that turned out to be the only other new client we have had this year.' (C.K. Ong)

The job had proved difficult from the start. The pre-production stage took longer than estimated, mainly because the client's creative team changed just before the start of subText beginning the work. But it was the actual CGI itself that proved to be the major problem. Not only was the task intrinsically difficult, but it was also difficult to parcel it up into separate packages that could be co-ordinated for working on by the two teams allocated to the job. More seriously, it became apparent within two or three days of starting the production work that they would need the help of another studio for some of the effects. Although the other studio was a regular supplier at short notice, this time it was too busy with its own work to help out. Help eventually came from a specialist studio in Hong Kong. 'The subcontracting delay was clearly a problem, but it was only half way through the production phase that we first realized just how much difficulty the fifty-three slash F job was in. It was at that stage that we devoted all our production resources to finishing it. Unfortunately, even then, the job was late. The decision eventually to put all three teams on to the fifty-three slash F job was not easy because we knew that it would both disrupt other jobs and potentially cause more coordination problems.'

'No way will we be doing that again'

'No way will we be doing that again', said C.K. to the core teams when they met to pick over what had gone wrong. 'We are desperately in need of a more professional approach to keeping track of our activities. There is no point in me telling everyone how good we are if we then let them down. The problem is that I don't want to encourage a "command and control" culture in the studio. We depend on all staff feeling that they have the freedom to explore seemingly crazy options that may just lead to something real special. We aren't a factory. But we do need to get a grip on our estimating so that we have a better idea of how long each job really will take. After that each of the core departments can be responsible for their own planning.'

QUESTIONS

1 What went wrong with the fifty-three slash F job and how could the company avoid making the same mistakes again?

2 What would you suggest that subText do to tighten up its planning and control procedures?

PROBLEMS AND APPLICATIONS

1. Reread the 'Operations in practice' case on automobile service scheduling at the beginning of the chapter and also the case on Air France. What are the differences and what are the similarities between the planning and control task in these two operations?

2. A specialist sandwich retailer must order sandwiches at least eight hours before they are delivered. When they arrive in the shop, they are immediately displayed in a temperature-controlled cabinet. The average time that the sandwiches spend in the cabinet is six hours. What is the P:D ratio for this retail operation?

3. It is the start of the week and Marie, Willy and Silvie have three jobs to complete. The three of them can work on these jobs in any order. Job A requires 4 hours of Marie's time, 5 hours of Willy's time and 3 hours of Silvie's time. Job B requires 2 hours of Marie's time, 8 hours of Willy's time and 7 hours of Silvie's time. Job C requires 10 hours of Marie's time, 4 hours of Willy's time and 5 hours of Silvie's time. Devise a schedule for Marie, Willy and Sylvie that details when they will be working on each job. (Assume that they work seven hours per day.)

4. For the problem above, what is the loading on Marie, Willy and Silvie? If all the jobs have to be finished within two days, how much extra time must each of them work?

Step 1 – Make a list of all the jobs you have to do in the next week. Include in this list jobs relating to your work and/or study, jobs relating to your domestic life, in fact all the things you have to do.

Step 2 – Prioritize all these jobs on a 'most important' to 'least important' basis.

Step 3 – Draw up an outline schedule of exactly when you will do each of these jobs.

Step 4 – At the end of the week compare what your schedule said you *would* do with what you actually *have* done. If there is a discrepancy, why did it occur?

Step 5 – Draw up you own list of planning and control rules from your experience in this exercise in personal planning and control.

6   From your own experience of making appointments at your GP's surgery, or by visiting whoever provides you with primary medical care, reflect on how patients are scheduled to see a doctor or nurse.

(a)   What do you think planning and control objectives are for a GP's surgery?

(b)   How could your own medical practice be improved?

SELECTED FURTHER READING

Chapman, S.N. (2005) *Fundamentals of Production Planning and Control*, Pearson, Harlow.

A detailed textbook, intended for those studying the topic in depth.

Goldratt, E.Y. and Cox, J. (1984) *The Goal*, North River Press, Croton-on-Hudson, NY.

Do not read this if you like good novels, but do read this if you want an enjoyable way of understanding some of the complexities of scheduling. It particularly applies to the drum, buffer, rope concept described in this chapter and it also sets the scene for the discussion of OPT in Chapter 14.

Kehoe, D.F. and Boughton, N.J. (2001) New paradigms in planning and control across manufacturing supply chains – the utilization of Internet technologies, *International Journal of Operations & Production Management*, vol. 21, issue 5/6, 582–593.

An academic study of planning and control.

Vollmann, T.E., Berry, W.L., Whybark, D.C. and Jacobs, F.R. (2004) *Manufacturing Planning and Control Systems for Supply Chain Management: The Definitive Guide for Professionals*, McGraw-Hill Higher Education, New York.

The latest version of the 'bible' of manufacturing planning and control.

11

Capacity management

Key questions

> What is capacity management?

> How are demand and capacity measured?

> How should the operation's base capacity be set?

> What are the ways of coping with mismatches between demand and capacity?

> How can operations understand the consequences of their capacity decisions?

INTRODUCTION

Capacity management is the activity of understanding the nature of an operation's supply and demand, and of coping with any differences between them. It involves selecting supply-side responses (called capacity plans) and demand-side responses (called demand management and yield management). It aims to meet the needs of customers while maintaining the efficiency of the operation's resources. And to do this, operations managers must be able to understand and reconcile two competing requirements. On the one hand there is the importance of maintaining customer satisfaction by delivering products and services to customers reasonably quickly. On the other there is the need for operations (and their extended supply networks) to maintain efficiency by minimizing the costs of excess capacity. In this chapter, we look at these competing tensions at an aggregated level. At this level, managers do not discriminate between the different products and services that might be produced by the operation. Instead, they aim to ensure that the overall ability to supply is in line with the overall demand placed on the operation. Figure 11.1 shows where this chapter fits in the structure of the book. At the end of the chapter there is a supplement on queuing for those wishing to go into more detail on this important sub-topic of capacity management.

Figure 11.1 This chapter examines capacity management

WHAT IS CAPACITY MANAGEMENT?

The capacity of an operation is the *maximum level of value-added activity over a period of time* that the process can achieve under normal operating conditions. Critically, this definition reflects the scale of capacity but, more importantly, its *processing capabilities.* Suppose a pharmaceutical manufacturer invests in a new 1,000-litre capacity reactor or a property company purchases a 500-vehicle capacity car park. This information gives you a good sense of the *scale* of capacity but it is far from a useful measure of capacity for an operations manager. Instead, the pharmaceutical company will be concerned with the level of output (that is, the processing capability) that can be achieved from the 1,000-litre reactor vessel. If a batch of standard products can be produced every hour, the planned processing capacity could be as high as 24,000 litres per day. If the reaction takes four hours, and two hours are used for cleaning between batches, the vessel may only produce 4,000 litres per day. Similarly, the car park may be fully occupied by office workers during the working day, 'processing' only 500 cars per day. Alternatively, it may be used for shoppers staying on average only one hour, and theatre-goers occupying spaces for three hours, in the evening. The processing capability would then be up to 5,000 cars per day.

Capacity management is the activity of understanding the nature of demand for products and services, and effectively planning and controlling capacity in the short term, medium term and long term. All this must be done while reconciling the competing demands of customer satisfaction and resource efficiency. In Chapter 5, we examined how long-term changes in demand can be considered in the structure and scope of operations. These decisions, termed 'long-term capacity strategy', are concerned with introducing (or removing) major increments of capacity. In this chapter we focus more on the medium- and short-term aspects of capacity management, where decisions are being made largely within the constraints of the physical capacity set by the operation's long-term capacity strategy.

> ✳ **Operations principle**
>
> Capacity is the maximum level of value-added activity over a period of time that the process or operation can achieve under normal operating conditions.

Medium- and short-term capacity management

Having established long-term capacity, operations managers must decide how to adjust the capacity of the operation in the medium term. This usually involves an assessment of the demand forecasts over a period of 2–18 months ahead, during which time planned output can be varied, for example by changing the number of hours when resources are used. In practice, however, few forecasts are accurate, and most operations also need to respond to changes in demand that occur over an even shorter timescale – termed 'short-term capacity management'. Hotels and restaurants have unexpected and apparently random changes in demand from night to night, but also know from experience that certain days are on average busier than others. So operations managers also have to make short-term capacity adjustments, which enable them to flex output for a short period, either on a predicted basis (for example, bank checkouts are always busy at lunchtimes) or at short notice (for example, a warm sunny day at a theme park).

Aggregate demand and capacity

The important characteristic of capacity management, as we are treating it here, is that it is concerned with setting capacity levels over the medium and short terms in *aggregated* terms (in fact what we call capacity management here is sometimes called 'aggregate planning'). That is, it is making overall, broad capacity decisions, but is not concerned with all of the detail of the individual products and services offered. This is what 'aggregated' means – different products and services are bundled together in order to get a broad view of demand and capacity. This may mean some degree of approximation, especially if the mix of

Heathrow's capacity crises[1]

With over 469,000 flights and 72.3 million passengers arriving and departing each year, London Heathrow is one of the busiest international hubs in the world. Its size and location give it powerful 'network effects'. This means that it can match incoming passengers with outgoing flights to hundreds of different cities. And yet its attractiveness to the airlines is one of its main problems. On an average day, 60 per cent of arrivals, totalling over 55,000 customers, spend time in one of Heathrow's four 'holding stacks'. These delays range from 4 to 10 minutes, rising to 20 minutes in the late morning peak, when between 32 and 40 jets typically circle over London. The costs of these delays include £119,000 of wasted fuel per day, 600 tonnes of additional CO_2 emissions, and the frustration of many customers losing valuable work and leisure time. The key problem is operating capacity, which currently stands at 98 per cent compared with around 70 per cent at most other major airports. '[When] *you have* [one of] *the most utilised pieces of infrastructure in the world, then one of the results is that you have airborne holding*', says Jon Proudlove, Managing Director of the national air traffic service (NAS) at Heathrow. With no slack in capacity, the effect (as we have seen with the operations triangle in Chapter 6) is that any variations (such as poor weather or poor conditions on the ground) have an immediate impact on aircraft processing speeds. The effects of Heathrow's capacity management problem are starting to be felt, with several airlines seeking alternative capacity in the UK and Europe to expand their operations. Yet the solutions to the problem are far

Source: Alamy Images: Roger Bamber

less clear. Considering medium- and short-term capacity management, significant investments have been made to air traffic systems to try to increase existing capacity (that is, to expand the 'ability to serve'), and improvements to boarding processes have been trialled to ensure rapid plane turnaround. However, in the longer term the capacity question (within which medium- and short-term capacity management decisions are made) inevitably turns to runway expansion. Heathrow currently operates two runways, compared with the four or five of its major European competitors Schiphol, Madrid, Paris and Frankfurt. Yet building a new runway, while perhaps the obvious *capacity* solution, has recently been vetoed by UK politicians in the face of strong, largely environmental, opposition. So for the time being, Heathrow's operations managers must manage existing capacity as best they can.

products or services being created varies significantly (as we will see later in this chapter). Nevertheless, as a first step in capacity management, aggregation is necessary. For example, a hotel might think of demand and capacity in terms of 'room nights per month'; this ignores the number of guests in each room and their individual requirements, but it is a good first approximation. A woollen knitwear factory might measure demand and capacity in the number of units (garments) it is capable of making per month, ignoring size, colour or style variations. Aluminium producers could use tonnes per month, ignoring types of alloy, gauge and batch size variation. The ultimate aggregation measure is money. For example, retail stores, which sell an exceptionally wide variety of products, use revenue per month, ignoring variation in spend, number of items bought, the gross margin of each item and the number of items per customer transaction. If all this seems very approximate, remember that most operations have sufficient experience of dealing with aggregated data to find it useful.

Capacity constraints

Many organizations operate at below their maximum processing capacity, either because there is insufficient demand completely to 'fill' their capacity, or as a deliberate policy, so that the operation can respond quickly to every new order. Often, though, organizations find themselves with some parts of their operation operating below their

capacity while other parts are at their capacity 'ceiling'. It is the parts of the operation that are operating at their capacity 'ceiling' which are the *capacity constraint* for the whole operation. For example, a retail superstore might offer a gift-wrapping service that at normal times can cope with all requests for its services without delaying customers unduly. At Christmas, however, the demand for gift wrapping might increase proportionally far more than the overall increase in custom for the store as a whole. Unless extra resources are provided to increase the capacity of this micro operation, it could constrain the capacity of the whole store.

The objectives of capacity management

The decisions taken by operations managers in devising their capacity plans will affect several different aspects of performance:

- *Costs* will be affected by the balance between capacity and demand. Capacity levels in excess of demand could mean under-utilization of capacity and therefore high units cost.
- *Revenues* will also be affected by the balance between capacity and demand, but in the opposite way. Capacity levels equal to or higher than demand at any point in time will ensure that all demand is satisfied and no revenue lost.
- *Working capital* will be affected if an operation decides to build up finished goods inventory prior to demand. This might allow demand to be satisfied, but the organization will have to fund the inventory until it can be sold.
- *Quality* of goods or services might be affected by a capacity plan that involves large fluctuations in capacity levels, by hiring temporary staff, for example. The new staff and the disruption to the routine working of the operation could increase the probability of errors being made.
- *Speed* of response to customer demand could be enhanced either by the build-up of inventories (allowing customers to be satisfied directly from the inventory rather than having to wait for items to be manufactured) or by the deliberate provision of surplus capacity to avoid queuing.
- *Dependability* of supply will also be affected by how close demand levels are to capacity. The closer demand gets to the operation's capacity ceiling, the less able it is to cope with any unexpected disruptions and the less dependable its deliveries of goods and services could be.
- *Flexibility*, especially volume flexibility, will be enhanced by surplus capacity. If demand and capacity are in balance, the operation will not be able to respond to any unexpected increase in demand.

The process of managing capacity

The process of managing capacity is illustrated in Figure 11.2. Typically, operations managers are faced with a forecast of demand which is unlikely to be either certain or constant. They will also have some idea of their own ability to meet this demand. Nevertheless, before any further decisions are taken, they must have quantitative data on both capacity and demand. So the first step will be to *measure the aggregate demand and capacity* levels and *understand changes in these levels* for the planning period. The second step is to *determine the operation's base level of capacity* from which adjustments up or down will be made. This will largely be determined by the performance objectives of the operation, as well as the perishability of outputs, and degree of variability in both demand and supply. The third step is to *identify and select methods of coping with mismatches between demand and capacity*. Often operations managers will use a combination of 'pure' approaches – level capacity plan, chase demand

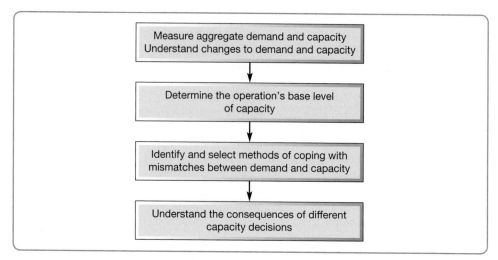

Figure 11.2 **The process of managing capacity**

plan and demand management. The fourth and final step is to *understand the consequences of different capacity decisions*. This often involves the use of cumulative representations, queuing principles and longer term outlooks.

HOW ARE DEMAND AND CAPACITY MEASURED?

Understanding demand for products and services

The first task of capacity management is to understand the nature of demand. Key questions include: What is the overall demand for a product or service over a period of time? How much does demand change? Are the total requirements and/or the changes in demand easy or difficult to predict? In any period of time, how much does demand change, and how accurate is forecast demand likely to be? Although demand forecasting is often the responsibility of the sales and/or marketing functions, it is a very important input into the capacity management decisions, and so is of interest to operations managers. After all, without an estimate of future demand it is not possible to plan effectively for future events, only to react to them. It is therefore important to understand the basis and rationale for these demand forecasts (see the supplement on forecasting after Chapter 5). As far as capacity management is concerned, there are three requirements from a demand forecast:

- It is expressed in terms that are useful for capacity management. If forecasts are expressed only in money terms and give no indication of the demands that will be placed on an operation's capacity, they will need to be translated into realistic expectations of demand, expressed in the same units as the capacity (for example, machine hours per year, operatives required, space, etc.).
- It is as accurate as possible. In capacity management, the accuracy of a forecast is important because, whereas demand can change instantaneously, there is usually a lag between deciding to change capacity and the change taking effect. Thus, many operations managers are faced with a dilemma. In order to attempt to meet demand, they must often decide output in advance, based on a forecast, which might change before the demand occurs or, worse, prove not to reflect actual demand at all.
- It gives an indication of relative uncertainty. Decisions to operate extra hours and recruit extra staff are usually based on forecast levels of demand, which could in practice differ considerably from actual demand, leading to unnecessary costs or unsatisfactory customer service. For example, a forecast of demand levels in a supermarket may show initially slow business that builds up to a lunchtime rush. After this, demand slows, only to build up again

for the early evening rush, and finally falls again at the end of trading. The supermarket manager can use this forecast to adjust (say) checkout capacity throughout the day. But although this may be an accurate average demand forecast, no single day will exactly conform to this pattern. Of equal importance is an estimate of how much actual demand could differ from the average. This can be found by examining demand statistics to build up a distribution of demand at each point in the day. The importance of this is that the manager now has an understanding of when it will be important to have reserve staff, perhaps filling shelves, but on call to staff the checkouts should demand warrant it. Generally, the advantage of probabilistic forecasts such as this is that it allows operations managers to make a judgement between possible plans that would virtually guarantee the operation's ability to meet actual demand and plans that minimize costs. Ideally, this judgement should be influenced by the nature of the way the business wins orders: price-sensitive markets may require a risk-avoiding cost minimization plan that does not always satisfy peak demand, whereas markets that value responsiveness and service quality may justify a more generous provision of operational capacity.

Understanding changes in demand

Most markets are influenced by some kind of seasonality. Sometimes the causes of seasonality are climatic (holidays), sometimes festive (gift purchases), sometimes financial (tax processing), or social, or political; in fact there are many factors that affect the volume of activity in everything from construction materials to clothing, from healthcare to hotels. Typically, the term 'seasonality' is used to describe changes to demand over a period of a year. Yet similar variations in demand can also occur for some products and services over a shorter cycle. The daily and weekly demand patterns of a supermarket will fluctuate, with some degree of predictability. Demand might be low in the morning, higher in the afternoon, with peaks at lunchtime and after work in the evening. Demand might be low on Monday and Tuesday, build up during the latter part of the week and reach a peak on Friday and Saturday. Banks, public offices, telephone sales organizations and electricity utilities all have weekly and daily, or even hourly, demand patterns which require capacity adjustment. The extent to which an operation will have to cope with very short-term demand fluctuations is partly determined by how long its customers are prepared to wait for their products or services. An operation whose customers are incapable of, or unwilling to, wait will have to plan for very short-term demand fluctuations. Emergency services, for example, will need to understand the hourly variation in the demand for their services and plan capacity accordingly.

Better forecasting or better operations responsiveness?

The degree of effort (and cost) to devote to forecasting is often a source of heated debate within organizations. This often comes down to two opposing arguments. One goes something like this. *'Of course it is important for forecasts to be as accurate as possible; we cannot plan operations capacity otherwise. This invariably means we finish up with too much capacity (thereby increasing costs), or too little capacity (thereby losing revenue and dissatisfying customers).'* The counter-argument is very different. *'Demand will always be uncertain, that is the nature of demand. Get used to it. The only way to satisfy customers is to make the operation sufficiently responsive to cope with demand, almost irrespective of what it is.'* Both these arguments have some merit, but both are extreme positions. In practice, operations must find some balance between having better forecasts and being able to cope without perfect forecasts.

Trying to get forecasts right has particular value where the operation finds it difficult or impossible to react to unexpected demand fluctuations in the short term. Internet-based retailers at some holiday times, for example, find it difficult to flex the quantity of goods they have in stock in the short term. Customers may

> ✳ **Operations principle**
>
> Capacity management requires combining attempts to increase market knowledge with attempts to increase operations flexibility.

Panettone: how Italy's bakers cope with seasonal demand[2]

Panettone has become a national symbol of the Italian Christmas. The light and fluffy, dome-shaped, confection is dotted with sultanas and candied citrus peel, and is *the* Italian Christmas cake. Traditionally made in Milan, about 40 million of them are consumed throughout Italy over the holiday period. Now, they are becoming popular around the world. Over a million are exported to the USA, while an endorsement from Delia Smith, a celebrity chef, caused a surge in demand in the UK with a well-publicized recipe for trifle made with panettone. This boost to production is good news for the big Italian manufacturers, but although volumes are higher, the product is still seasonal, which poses a problem for even the experienced Milanese confectioners. Smaller, 'artisan' producers simply squeeze a few batches of panettone into their normal baking schedules as Christmas approaches. But for the large industrial producers which need to make millions for the Christmas season it is not possible. And no panettone manufacturer is larger than the Bauli Group. It is one of the foremost manufacturers of confectionery in Europe. Founded over 70 years ago, and in spite of its mass production approach, it has a reputation for quality and technological improvement. The company's output of panettone accounts for 38 per cent of Italian sales. The key to its success, according to the company, is in having *'combined the skill of home-made recipes with high technology* [and] *quality guaranteed by high standards that are unattainable in craftsman production, but that can only be reached by selecting top quality raw materials, by thousands of tests and checks on the entire production line and the production process'*. In fact, the company says that its size is an advantage. *'High investment in research and technology allow us to manage natural fermentation and guarantee a uniform quality that artisanal bakeries find hard to achieve.'*

In fact, although Bauli has diversified into year-round products like croissants and biscuits, it has acquired a leadership role in the production of products for festive occasions. Seasonal cakes account for over 50 per cent of its turnover of around €420 million.

And so successful has it been in its chosen markets that in 2009 it bought Motta and Alemagna, the two big Milanese brands that pioneered the manufacture of panettone. So how does Bauli cope with such seasonality? Partly it is by hiring large numbers of temporary seasonal workers to staff its dedicated production lines. At peak times there can be 1,200 seasonal workers in the factory, more than its permanent staff of around 800. It also starts to build up inventories before demand begins to increase for the Christmas peak. Production of panettone lasts about four months, starting in September. *'Attention to ingredients and the use of new technologies in production give a shelf-life of five months without preservatives'*, says Michele Bauli, Deputy Chairman, who comes from the firm's founding family. Temporary workers are also hired to bake other seasonal cakes such as the *colomba*, a dove-shaped Easter treat, which keeps them occupied for a month and a half in the spring.

not be willing to wait. On the other hand, other types of operations working in intrinsically uncertain markets may develop fast and flexible processes to compensate for the difficulty in obtaining accurate forecasts. For example, fashion garment manufacturers try to overcome the uncertainty in their market by shortening their response time to new fashion ideas (catwalk to rack time) and the time taken to replenish stocks in the stores (replenishment time). Similarly, when the cost of not meeting demand is very high, processes also have to rely on their responsiveness rather than accurate forecasts. For example, accident and emergency departments in hospitals must be responsive even if it means under-utilized resources at times.

Christmas at Amazon[3]

Founded as an online bookseller by Jeff Bezos, Amazon, now the world's biggest online retailer, started business in Europe in 1998. Since then the Seattle-based firm has experienced remarkable growth, employing around 40,000 people around the world and dominating a fiercely competitive consumer market, where its success is unquestionably based partly on its keen pricing. But low prices are not the only thing supporting Amazon's success. Without fast, accurate and efficient delivery it could not have secured its 'top e-retailer' position.

This is why Amazon devotes so much investment and effort to its fulfilment centres, customer service centres and software development centres across Europe, North America, Latin America and Asia that organize the shipment of millions of individual items from bird tables to baby clothes. (Amazon says that the exact number of different items it sells is difficult to define, especially if you take the articles into account that are offered via the 'marketplace', and changes every day.) Typical of Amazon's shipment operations is its 46,000 m² warehouse in Milton Keynes, one of eight in the UK. In the warehouse products are stocked within its extensive shelving arrangement with the position of every item referenced using a portable satellite navigation system. Amazon says that it saves time when their staff retrieve items. *'The computer shows the shortest pick-path'*, said Arthur Valdez, vice-President of Amazon's UK operations. The item is then scanned and picked, after which it moves along a conveyor belt to be packed or gift wrapped and then labelled. At this point an email is automatically sent to the customer informing them that the product is on its way.

Mr Valdez manages a network of fast-moving operations that must always maintain a tight control of its activities, but no time is more testing than the run-up to Christmas. The gift-buying habits of Western consumers mean that up to 40 per cent of annual sales value can come in the final three months of the year, with half of the multibillion online Christmas sales taking place over the end of November and the first two weeks of December. The average number of articles being sold each day soars from 300,000 to, at its peak, 3.6 million being sold in one day. In the UK, this day – which it calls 'Cyber Monday' – is at the beginning of December, or, to be more precise, at 9 pm on that

Source: Shutterstock.com: Jezper

day, when shoppers, having normally been paid for the month and having spent the weekend browsing the high street, return from work to begin their Christmas shopping in earnest. It makes for a hectic time: *'A full truck is dispatched every three minutes and 24 seconds on our busiest trading day'*, says Mr Valdez. But careful forecasting can at least stop the Christmas peak being a surprise. And careful monitoring of customer behaviour has revealed a further trend: after 'Cyber Monday' comes 'Boomerang Thursday', when customers start to return their unwanted items. *'As the online retail sector continues to grow, so too has consumer demand and confidence to return items, often before Christmas'*, says Mark Lewis, Chief Executive of CollectPlus, which allows customers to return items to a local convenience store. *'This suits retailers. They want to get [items] back as soon as possible, so they can sell them on.'* Mark Lewis says that half of his customers return items at off-peak times. *'It peaks at 7 pm. It reflects how we live our lives these days.'*

However, some retail analysts believe that the advance of technology in the form of mobile phone transactions and broadband has also meant that the significance of 'Cyber Monday' and 'Boomerang Thursday' will diminish because such technology makes it easier to stagger transactions. But for Mr Valdez, it is continual vigilance that allows Amazon to keep up with demand trends. *'Every year it feels like [Christmas starts on] January 1. We are all-year-long focused on understanding the lessons learnt from the previous Christmas,'* he says.

Understanding capacity

The second task of capacity management is to understand the nature of capacity or supply. Measuring capacity may sound simple, but can in fact be relatively hard to define unambiguously unless the operation is standardized and repetitive. So if a television factory produces only one basic model, the weekly capacity could be described as 2,000 Model A televisions. A government office may have the capacity to print and post 500,000 tax forms per week. A fast ride at a theme park might be designed to process batches of 60 people every three minutes – a capacity to convey 1,200 people per hour. In each case, an *output capacity measure* is the most appropriate measure because the output from the operation does not vary in its nature. For many operations, however, the definition of capacity is not so obvious. When a much wider range of outputs places varying demands on the process, for instance, output measures of capacity are less useful. Here *input capacity measures* are frequently used to define capacity. Almost every type of operation could use a mixture of both input and output measures, but in practice most choose to use one or the other (*see* Table 11.1).

> **✳ Operations principle**
>
> Any measure of capacity should reflect the ability of an operation or process to supply demand.

Capacity depends on activity mix

How much an operation can do depends on what it is being required to do. For example, a hospital may have a problem in measuring its capacity because the nature of the products and service may vary significantly. If all its patients required relatively minor treatment with only short stays in hospital, it could treat many people per week. Alternatively, if most of its patients required long periods of observation or recuperation, it could treat far fewer. Output depends on the mix of activities in which the hospital is engaged and, because most hospitals perform many different types of activities, output is difficult (though not impossible!) to predict. Some of the problems caused by variation mix can be partially overcome by using aggregated capacity measures. (Remember that 'aggregated' means that different products and services are bundled together in order to get a broad view of demand and capacity.)

> **✳ Operations principle**
>
> Capacity is a function of service/product mix, duration, and product service specification.

Table 11.1 **Input and output capacity measures for different operations**

Operation	Input measure of capacity	Output measure of capacity
Air-conditioner plant	Machine hours available	**Number of units per week**
Hospital	**Beds available**	Number of patients treated per week
Theatre	**Number of seats**	Number of customers entertained per week
University	**Number of students**	Students graduated per year
Retail store	**Sales floor area**	Number of items sold per day
Airline	**Number of seats available on the sector**	Number of passengers per week
Electricity company	Generator size	**Megawatts of electricity generated**
Brewery	Volume of fermentation tanks	**Litres per week**

Note: The most commonly used measure is shown in bold.

Suppose an air-conditioner factory produces three different models of air-conditioner unit: the deluxe, the standard and the economy. The deluxe model can be assembled in 1.5 hours, the standard in 1 hour and the economy in 0.75 hours. The assembly area in the factory has 800 staff hours of assembly time available each week.

If demand for deluxe, standard and economy units is in the ratio 2:3:2, the time needed to assemble $2 + 3 + 2 = 7$ units is:

$$(2 \times 1.5) + (3 \times 1) + (2 \times 0.75) = 7.5 \text{ hours}$$

The number of units produced per week is:

$$\frac{800}{7.5} \times 7 = 746.7 \text{ units}$$

If demand changes to a ratio of deluxe, economy, standard units of 1:2:4, the time needed to assemble $1 + 2 + 4 = 7$ units is:

$$(1 \times 1.5) + (2 \times 1) + (4 \times 0.75) = 6.5 \text{ hours}$$

Now the number of units produced per week is:

$$\frac{800}{6.5} \times 7 = 861.5 \text{ units}$$

Capacity depends on the duration over which output is required

Capacity is the output that an operation can deliver *in a defined unit of time*. The level of activity and output that may be achievable over short periods of time is not the same as the capacity that is sustainable on a regular basis. For example, a tax return processing office, during its peak periods at the end (or beginning) of the financial year, may be capable of processing 120,000 applications a week. It does this by extending the working hours of its staff, discouraging its staff from taking vacations during this period, avoiding any potential disruption to its IT systems (not allowing upgrades during this period etc.), and maybe just by working hard and intensively. Nevertheless, staff do need vacations, nor can they work long hours continually, and eventually the information system will have to be upgraded. As such, when measuring capacity, operations managers should consider three different measures of capacity as shown in Figure 11.3:

> **❋ Operations principle**
>
> Useable capacity is rarely equal to theoretical or 'design' capacity.

- *Design capacity* – the theoretical capacity of an operation that one of its technical designers had in mind when they commissioned it. For example, a company coating photographic paper will have several coating lines which deposit thin layers of chemicals onto rolls of paper at high speed. Each line will be capable of running at a particular speed. Multiplying the maximum coating speed by the operating time of the plant gives the theoretical design capacity of the line.
- *Effective capacity* – the capacity of an operation after planned losses are accounted for. For example, in the case above, the line cannot realistically be run continuously at its maximum

Figure 11.3 Design capacity, effective capacity and actual output

rate. Different products will have different coating requirements, so the line will need to be stopped while it is changed over. Maintenance will need to be performed on the line, which will take out further productive time. Technical scheduling difficulties might mean further lost time. Not all of these losses are the operations manager's fault; they have occurred because of the market and technical demands on the operation.

- *Actual output* – the capacity of an operation after both planned and unplanned losses are accounted for. For example, quality problems, machine breakdowns, absenteeism and other avoidable problems all take their toll. This means that the *actual output* of the line will be even lower than the effective capacity. The ratio of the output actually achieved by an operation to its design capacity, and the ratio of output to effective capacity, are called, respectively, the utilization and the efficiency of an operation:

$$\text{Utilization} = \frac{\text{Actual output}}{\text{Design capacity}}$$

$$\text{Efficiency} = \frac{\text{Actual output}}{\text{Effective capacity}}$$

Worked example

Suppose the photographic paper manufacturer has a coating line with a design capacity of 200 m^2 per minute, and the line is operated on a basis of 24 hours a day, 7 days per week (168 hours per week).

Design capacity is $200 \times 60 \times 24 \times 7 = 2.016$ million m^2 per week. The records for a week's production show the following lost production time:

1	Product changeovers (set-ups)	20 hours
2	Regular preventative maintenance	16 hours
3	No work scheduled	8 hours
4	Quality sampling checks	8 hours
5	Shift change times	7 hours
6	Maintenance breakdown	18 hours
7	Quality failure investigation	20 hours
8	Coating material stockouts	8 hours
9	Labour shortages	6 hours
10	Waiting for paper rolls	6 hours

During this week the actual output was only 582,000 m^2.

The first five categories of lost production occur as a consequence of reasonably unavoidable, planned occurrences and amount to a total of 59 hours. The last five categories are unplanned, and avoidable, losses and amount to 58 hours.

Measured in hours of production:

$$\text{Design capacity} = 168 \text{ hours per week}$$
$$\text{Effective capacity} = 168 - 59 = 109 \text{ hrs}$$
$$\text{Actual output} = 168 - 59 - 58 = 51 \text{ hours}$$

Therefore:

$$\text{Utilization} = \frac{\text{Actual output}}{\text{Design capacity}} = \frac{51 \text{ hours}}{168 \text{ hours}} = 0.304 = 30\%$$

$$\text{Efficiency} = \frac{\text{Actual output}}{\text{Effective capacity}} = \frac{51 \text{ hours}}{109 \text{ hours}} = 0.468 = 47\%$$

For such an important topic, there is surprisingly little standardization in how capacity is measured. Not only is a reasonably accurate measure of capacity needed for operations planning and control, but it is also needed to decide whether it is worth investing in extra capacity. Yet not all practitioners would agree with the way in which design and effective capacity have been defined or measured in the previous worked example. For example, some would argue that the first five categories do *not* occur as a consequence of reasonably unavoidable, planned occurrences. Product changeover set-ups can be reduced, allocating work in a different manner between processes could reduce the amount of time when no work is scheduled, and re-examining preventative maintenance schedules could lead to a reduction in lost time. One school of thought is that whatever capacity efficiency measures are used, they should be useful as diagnostic measures which can highlight the root causes of inefficient use of capacity. The idea of overall equipment effectiveness (OEE), described in the 'capacity leakage' section, is often put forward as a useful way of measuring capacity efficiencies.

Capacity depends on the specification of output

Some operations can increase their output by changing the specification of the product or service (although this is more likely to apply to a service). For example, a postal service may effectively reduce its delivery dependability at peak times. So, during the busy Christmas period, the number of letters delivered the day after being posted may drop from 95 per cent to 85 per cent. Similarly, accounting firms may avoid long 'relationship-building' meetings with clients during busy periods. Important though these are, they can usually be deferred to less busy times. The important task is to distinguish between the 'must do' elements of the service that should not be sacrificed and the 'nice to do' parts of the service that can be omitted or delayed in order to increase capacity in the short term.

Capacity 'leakage'

Even after allowing for all the difficulties inherent in measuring capacity, the theoretical capacity of a process (the capacity that it was designed to have) is rarely achieved in practice. Some reasons for this are, to some extent, predictable. Different products or services may have different requirements, so people and machinery will have delays when switching between tasks. Maintenance will need to be performed on machines while training will be required for employees. Scheduling difficulties could mean further lost time. Not all of these losses are necessarily avoidable; they may occur because of the market and technical demands on the process. However, some of the reduction in capacity can be the result of less predictable events. For example, labour shortages, quality problems, delays in the delivery of bought-in products and services, and machine, or system, breakdown can all reduce capacity. This reduction in capacity is sometimes called 'capacity leakage' and one popular method of assessing this leakage is the overall equipment effectiveness (OEE) measure that is calculated as follows (*see* Fig. 11.4):

$$OEE = a \times p \times q$$

where a is the availability of a process, p is the performance or speed of a process, and q is the quality of product or services that the process creates. OEE works on the assumption that some capacity leakage occurs causing reduced availability. For example, availability can be lost through time losses such as set-up and changeover losses (when equipment, or people in a service context, are being prepared for the next activity) and breakdown failures (when the machine is being repaired or in a service context where employees are being trained/absent).

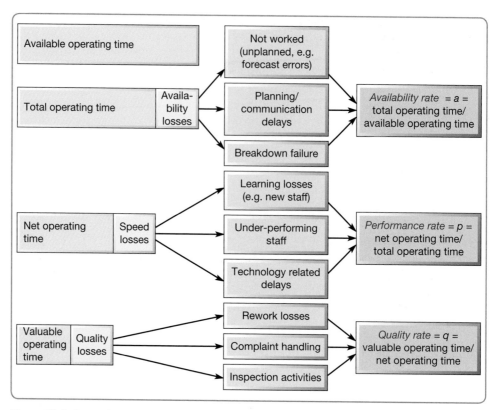

Figure 11.4 **Operating equipment effectiveness (OEE)**

Some capacity is lost through speed losses, such as when equipment is idling (for example, when it is temporarily waiting for work from another process) and when equipment is being run below its optimum work rate. In a service context, the same principle can be seen when individuals are not working at an optimum rate, for example mail order call centre employees in the quiet period after the winter holiday season. Finally, not everything processed by an operation will be error-free. So some capacity is lost through quality losses.

For processes to operate effectively, they need to achieve high levels of performance against all three dimensions – availability, performance (speed) and quality. Viewed in isolation, these individual metrics are important indicators of performance, but they do not give a complete picture of the process's *overall* effectiveness. And critically, all these losses in the calculation mean that OEE represents the valuable operating time as a percentage of the capacity something was designed to have.

Understanding changes in capacity

While many operations are most concerned with dealing with changes in demand, some operations also have to cope with variation in *capacity* (if it is defined as 'the ability to supply'). For example, Figure 11.5 shows the demand and capacity variation of two businesses. The first is a domestic appliance repair service. Both demand and capacity vary month on month. Capacity varies because the field service operatives in the business prefer to take their vacations at particular times of the year. Nevertheless, capacity is relatively stable throughout the year. Demand, by contrast, fluctuates more significantly. It would appear that there are two peaks of demand through the year, with peak demand being approximately twice the level of the low point in demand. The second business is a food manufacturer producing frozen spinach. The demand for this product is relatively constant throughout the year but the capacity of the business varies significantly. During the growing and harvesting season capacity to supply is high, but it falls off almost to zero for part of the year. Yet although the mismatch between demand and capacity is driven primarily by fluctuations in demand in the first case, and capacity in the second case, the essence of the capacity management activity is essentially similar for both.

Worked example

In a typical seven-day period, the planning department programmes a particular machine to work for 150 hours – its loading time. Changeovers and set-ups take an average of 10 hours and breakdown failures average 5 hours every seven days. The time when the machine cannot work because it is waiting for material to be delivered from other parts of the process is five hours on average and during the period when the machine is running, it averages 90 per cent of its rated speed. Of the parts processed by the machine, 3 per cent are subsequently found to be defective in some way.

$$\text{Maximum time available} = 7 \times 24 \text{ hours}$$
$$= 168 \text{ hours}$$
$$\text{Loading time} = 150 \text{ hours}$$
$$\text{Availability losses} = 10 \text{ hours (set-ups)} + 5 \text{ hours (breakdowns)}$$
$$= 15 \text{ hours}$$
$$\text{So, total operating time} = \text{Loading time} - \text{Availability}$$
$$= 150 - 15$$
$$= 135 \text{ hours}$$
$$\text{Speed losses} = 5 \text{ hours (idling)} + [(135 - 5) \times 0.1]$$
$$(10\% \text{ of remaining time})$$
$$= 18 \text{ hours}$$
$$\text{So, net operating time} = \text{Total operating time} - \text{Speed losses}$$
$$= 135 - 18$$
$$= 117 \text{ hours}$$
$$\text{Quality losses} = 117 \text{ (net operating time)} \times 0.03 \text{ (error rate)}$$
$$= 3.51 \text{ hours}$$
$$\text{So, valuable operating time} = \text{Net operating time} - \text{quality losses} = 117 - 3.51$$
$$= 113.49 \text{ hours}$$

$$\text{Therefore, availability rate, } a = \frac{\text{Total operating time}}{\text{Loading time}}$$
$$= \frac{117}{135} = 86.67\%$$

$$\text{performance rate, } p = \frac{\text{Net operating time}}{\text{Total operating time}}$$
$$= \frac{117}{135} = 86.67\%$$

$$\text{and quality rate, } q = \frac{\text{Valuable operating time}}{\text{Net operating time}}$$
$$= \frac{113.49}{117} = 97\%$$

$$\text{OEE } (a \times p \times q) = 75.6\%$$

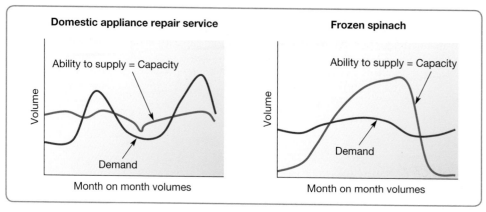

Figure 11.5 Volatility in demand versus volatility in capacity

HOW SHOULD THE OPERATION'S BASE CAPACITY BE SET?

The most common way of managing capacity is to decide the 'base level' of capacity and then adjust it periodically up or down to reflect fluctuations in demand. In fact, the concept of 'base' capacity is unusual because, although nominally it is the capacity level from which increases and decreases in capacity level are planned, in very unstable markets, where fluctuations are significant, it may never occur. Also, the two decisions of 'what should the base level of capacity be?' and 'how do we adjust capacity around that base to reflect demand?' are interrelated. An operation could set its base level of capacity at such a high level compared with demand that there is never a need to adjust capacity levels. However, this is clearly wasteful, which is why most operations will adjust their capacity level over time. Nevertheless, although the two decisions are interrelated it is usually worthwhile setting a nominal base level of capacity before going on to consider how it can be adjusted.

> **✳ Operations principle**
>
> The higher the base level of capacity, the less capacity fluctuation is needed to satisfy demand.

Setting base capacity

The base level of capacity in any operation is influenced by many factors, but should be related to three in particular:

- The relative importance of the operation's performance objectives.
- The perishability of the operation's outputs.
- The degree of variability in demand or supply.

Operation's performance objectives

Base levels of capacity should be set primarily to reflect an operation's performance objectives, *see* Figure 11.6. For example, setting the base level of capacity high compared with average demand will result in relatively high levels of under-utilization of capacity and therefore high costs. This is especially true when an operation's fixed costs are high and therefore the consequences of under-utilization are also high. Conversely, high base levels of capacity result in a capacity 'cushion' for much of the time, so the ability to flex output to give responsive customer service will be enhanced. When the output from the operation is capable of being stored, there may also be a trade-off between fixed capital and working capital where base capacity level is set. A high level of base capacity can require considerable investment while a lower base level would reduce the need for capital investment but may require inventory to

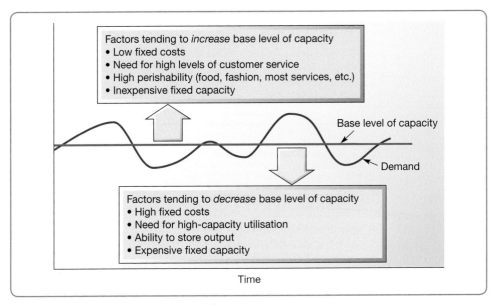

Figure 11.6 **The base level of capacity should reflect the relative importance of the operation's performance objectives**

be built up to satisfy future demand, thus increasing working capital. For some operations, building up inventory is risky either because products have a short shelf life (for example, perishable food, high-performance computers, or fashion items) or because the output cannot be stored at all (most services).

The perishability of the operation's outputs

When either supply or demand is perishable, base capacity will need to be set at a relatively high level because inputs to the operation or outputs from the operation cannot be stored for long periods. For example, a factory that produces frozen fruit will need sufficient freezing, packing and storage capacity to cope with the rate at which the fruit crop is being harvested during its harvesting season. Similarly, a hotel cannot store its accommodation services. If an individual hotel room remains unoccupied, the ability to sell for that night has 'perished'. In fact, unless a hotel is fully occupied every single night, its capacity is always going to be higher than the average demand for its services.

The degree of variability in demand or supply

Variability, either in demand or capacity, will reduce the ability of an operation to process its inputs. That is, it will reduce its effective capacity. This effect was explained in Chapter 6 when the consequences of variability in individual processes were discussed. As a reminder, the greater the variability in arrival time or activity time at a process, the more the process will suffer both high throughput times *and* reduced utilization. This principle holds true for whole operations, and because long throughput times mean that queues will build up in the operation, high variability also affects inventory levels. This is illustrated in Figure 11.7. The implication of this is that the greater the variability, the more extra capacity will need to be provided to compensate for the reduced utilization of available capacity. Therefore, operations with high levels of variability will tend to set their base level of capacity relatively high in order to provide this extra capacity. Of course, as we have seen earlier, not all operations have the option of simply increasing capacity! (See the 'Operations in practice' case on capacity constraints at Heathrow.)

Figure 11.7 **The effect of variability on the utilization of capacity**

WHAT ARE THE WAYS OF COPING WITH MISMATCHES BETWEEN DEMAND AND CAPACITY?

With an understanding of both demand and capacity, the next step is to consider the alternative methods of responding to any mismatches between them. For most organizations, this equates to understanding how demand might vary (although the same logic would apply to variation in capacity). In particular, the balance between predictable and unpredictable variation in demand affects the nature of capacity management. When demand is stable and predictable, the life of an operations manager is relatively easy! If demand is changeable, but this change is predictable, capacity adjustments may be needed, but at least they can be planned in advance. With unpredictable variation in demand, if an operation is to react to it at all, it must do so quickly; otherwise, the change in capacity will have little effect on the operation's ability to deliver products and services as needed by their customers. Figure 11.8 illustrates how the objective and tasks of capacity management vary depending on the balance between predictable and unpredictable variation.

There are three 'pure' options available for coping with such variation (illustrated in Fig. 11.9), though organizations do tend to use a combination of all of these in practice:

- **Level capacity plan** – Ignore demand fluctuations and keep nominal capacity levels constant.
- **Chase demand plan** – Adjust capacity to reflect the fluctuations in demand.
- **Demand management** – Attempt to change demand to align with capacity.

Level capacity plan

In a level capacity plan, the capacity is fixed throughout the planning period, regardless of the fluctuations in forecast demand. This means that the same number of staff operate the same processes and should therefore be capable of producing the same aggregate output in each period. Where non-perishable materials are processed, but not immediately sold, they can be transferred to finished goods inventory in anticipation of sales at a later time.

Level capacity plans of this type can achieve the objectives of stable employment patterns, high process utilization, and usually also high productivity with low unit costs.

		Unpredictable variation	
		Low	**High**
Predictable variation	**High**	*Objective* – Adjust planned capacity as efficiently as possible *Capacity management tasks* • Evaluate optimum mix of methods for capacity fluctuation • Work on how to reduce cost of putting plan into effect	*Objective* – Adjust planned capacity as efficiently as possible and enhance capability for further fast adjustments *Capacity management tasks* • Combination of those for predictable and unpredictable variation
	Low	*Objective* – Make sure the base capacity is appropriate *Capacity management tasks* • Seek ways of providing steady capacity effectively	*Objective* – Adjust capacity as fast as possible *Capacity management tasks* • Identify sources of extra capacity and/or uses for surplus capacity • Work on how to adjust capacity and/or uses of capacity quickly

Figure 11.8 The nature of capacity management depends on the mixture of predictable and unpredictable demand and capacity variation

(a) Level capacity plan – absorb fluctuations

(b) Chase demand plan – change capacity to reflect demand fluctuations

(c) Demand management plan – attempt to change demand to reduce fluctuations

Figure 11.9 Managing mismatches between demand and capacity: 'level capacity', 'chase demand' and 'demand management' plans

Unfortunately, they can also create considerable inventory which has to be financed and stored. Perhaps the biggest problem, however, is that decisions have to be taken as to what to produce for inventory rather than for immediate sale. Will green woollen sweaters knitted in July still be fashionable in October? Could a particular aluminium alloy in a specific sectional shape still be sold months after it has been produced? Most firms operating this plan, therefore, give priority to only creating inventory where future sales are relatively certain and unlikely to be affected by changes in fashion or design. Clearly, such plans are not suitable for 'perishable' products, such as foods and some pharmaceuticals, for products where fashion changes rapidly and unpredictably (for example, fashion garments), or for customized products.

A level capacity plan could also be used by a hotel and supermarket, although this would not be the usual approach of such organizations, because it usually results in a waste of staff resources, reflected in low productivity. Because service cannot be stored as inventory, a level capacity plan would involve running the operation at a uniformly high level of capacity availability. The hotel would employ sufficient staff to service all the rooms, to run a full restaurant and to staff the reception even in months when demand was expected to be well below capacity. Similarly, the supermarket would plan to staff all the checkouts, warehousing operations, and so on, even in quiet periods.

Low utilization can make level capacity plans prohibitively expensive in many service operations, but may be considered appropriate where the opportunity costs of individual lost sales are very high, for example in the high-margin retailing of jewellery and in (real) estate agents. It is also possible to set the capacity somewhat below the forecast peak demand level in order to reduce the degree of under-utilization. However, in the periods where demand is expected to exceed planned capacity, customer service may deteriorate. Customers may have to queue for long periods or may be 'processed' faster and less sensitively. While this is obviously far from ideal, the benefits to the organization of stability and productivity may outweigh the disadvantages of upsetting some customers.

Chase demand plan

The opposite of a level capacity plan is one which attempts to match capacity closely to the varying levels of forecast demand. This is much more difficult to achieve than a level capacity plan, as different numbers of staff, different working hours and even different amounts of equipment may be necessary in each period. For this reason, pure chase demand plans are unlikely to appeal to operations that manufacture standard, non-perishable products. Also, where manufacturing operations are particularly capital intensive, the chase demand policy would require a level of physical capacity, all of which would only be used occasionally. It is for this reason that such a plan is less likely to be appropriate for an aluminium producer than for a woollen garment manufacturer, for example. A pure chase demand plan is more usually adopted by operations that are not able to store their output, such as customer-processing operations or manufacturers of perishable products. It avoids the wasteful provision of excess staff that occurs with a level capacity plan, and yet should satisfy customer demand throughout the planned period. Where output can be stored, the chase demand policy might still be adopted in order to minimize or eliminate finished goods inventory, especially if the nature of future demand (in terms of volume or mix) is relatively unpredictable. There are a number of different methods for adjusting capacity, although they may not all be feasible for all types of operation. Some of these methods are shown in Table 11.2.

Demand management plan

The third pure capacity management approach is demand management. Here, the objective is to change the pattern of demand to bring it closer to available capacity, by either stimulating off-peak demand or by constraining peak demand. There are a number of methods for achieving this:

● *Constraining customer access* – customers may only be allowed access to the operation's products or services at particular times. For example, reservation and appointment systems in hospitals.
● *Price differentials* – adjusting price to reflect demand. That is, increasing prices during periods of high demand and reducing prices during periods of low demand. For example, skiing and camping holidays are cheapest at the beginning and end of the season and are particularly expensive during school vacations, while ice cream is on offer in many supermarkets during the winter.
● *Scheduling promotion* – varying the degree of market stimulation through promotion and advertising in order to encourage demand during normally low periods. For example, turkey growers in the UK and the USA make vigorous attempts to promote their products at times other than Christmas and Thanksgiving.

Table 11.2 **Methods of executing a chase demand plan**

Method of adjusting capacity	Advantages	Disadvantages
Overtime – staff working longer than their normal working times	Quickest and most convenient	Extra payment normally necessary and agreement of staff to work can reduce productivity over long periods
Annualized hours – staff contracting to work a set number of hours per year rather than a set number of hours per week	Without many of the costs associated with overtime the number of staff time available to an organization can be varied throughout the year to reflect demand	When very large and unexpected fluctuations in demand are possible, all the negotiated annual working time flexibility can be used before the end of the year
Staff scheduling – arranging working times (start and finish times) to vary the aggregate number of staff available for working at any time	Staffing levels can be adjusted to meet demand without changing job responsibilities or hiring new staff	Providing start and finish (shift) times that both satisfy staffs' need for reasonable working times and shift patterns as well as providing appropriate capacity can be difficult
Varying the size of the workforce – hiring extra staff during periods of high demand and laying them off as demand falls, or hire and fire	Reduces basic labour costs quickly	Hiring costs and possible low productivity while new staff go through the learning curve. Lay-offs may result in severance payments and possible loss of morale in the operation and loss of goodwill in the local labour market
Using part-time staff – recruit staff who work for less than the normal working day (at the busiest periods)	Good method of adjusting capacity to meet predictable short-term demand fluctuations	Expensive if the fixed costs of employment for each employee (irrespective of how long he or she works) are high
Skills flexibility – designing flexibility in job design and job demarcation so that staff can transfer across from less busy parts of the operation	Fast method of reacting to short-term demand fluctuations	Investment in skills training needed and may cause some internal disruption
Subcontracting/outsourcing – buying, renting or sharing capacity or output from other operations	No disruption to the operation	Can be very expensive because of subcontractor's margin and subcontractor may not be as motivated to give same service, or quality. Also a risk of leakage of knowledge
Change output rate – expecting staff (and equipment) to work faster than normal	No need to provide extra resources	Can only be used as a temporary measure, and even then can cause staff dissatisfaction, a reduction in the quality of work, or both

- *Service differentials* – allowing service levels to reflect demand (implicitly or explicitly), allowing service to deteriorate in periods of high demand and increase in periods of low demand. If this strategy is used explicitly, customers are being educated to expect varying levels of service and hopefully move to periods of lower demand.

A more radical approach attempts to create alternative products or services to fill capacity in quiet periods. It can be an effective demand management method but, ideally, new products or services should meet three criteria: (a) they can be produced on the same processes, (b) they have different demand patterns to existing offerings, and (c) they are sold through similar marketing channels. For example, most universities fill their accommodation and lecture theatres with conferences and company meetings during vacations. Ski resorts may provide organized mountain activity holidays in the summer, and garden tractor companies may make snow blowers in the autumn and winter. However, the apparent benefits of filling

Annualized hours at Lowaters[4]

Lowaters Nursery is a garden plant and horticulture specialist in the south of England employing around 25 people. Like any business that depends on seasonal weather conditions, it faces fluctuating demand for its services and products. It also prides itself on offering *'the best service in partnership with our customers, by communicating in a friendly professional manner and listening to our customers to provide the result required'*. (Lowaters mission statement). But to maintain its quality of service throughout the seasonal ups and down in workload means keeping your core team happy and employed throughout the year. This is why Lowaters introduced its annualized hours scheme, a method of fluctuating capacity as demand varies throughout the year without many of the costs associated with overtime or hiring temporary staff. It involves staff contracting to work a set number of hours per year rather than a set number of hours per week. The main advantage of this is that the amount of staff time available to an organization can be varied throughout the year to reflect the real state of demand. Annual hours plans can also be useful when supply varies throughout the year. Maria Fox, one of the management team at Lowaters, says that annualized hours give the company several advantages. *'It simplifies administration and gives us the flexibility we need to run the business while delivering some real advantages to the employees. They are all effectively on salary with fixed monthly payments. We can flex the hours worked over the year – when we are busy we work longer and when things are quiet, in the winter, they can take time off. Everyone other than directors is contracted to work 39 hours on average over 52 weeks of the year.'*

The company created a simple spreadsheet that sets out the actual hours worked and compares them with a target distribution of the annualized hours that

Source: Alistair Brandon-Jones

are expected to be worked over the year. This allows employees to see at a glance whether someone is over or under target. *'We email them a copy of their sheet at the beginning of the year so they can keep track of their own progress as they go'*, says Maria Fox. *'It also allows us to keep track of how many hours they do. If at the end of the year they come in plus or minus 50 hours we simply adjust it up or down for the next year. If there is a bigger discrepancy than that we'll look at the job structure.'*

However, not all experiments with annualized hours have been as successful as that at Lowaters. In cases where demand is very unpredictable, staff can be asked to come in to work at very short notice. This can cause considerable disruption to social and family life. For example, at one news broadcasting company, the scheme caused problems. Journalists and camera crew who went to cover a foreign crisis found that they had worked so many hours that they were asked to take the whole of one month off to compensate. Since they had no holiday plans, many would have preferred to work for additional income.

Critical commentary

To many, the idea of fluctuating the workforce to match demand, either by using part-time staff or by hiring and firing, is more than just controversial. It is regarded as unethical. It is any business's responsibility, they argue, to engage in a set of activities which are capable of sustaining employment at a steady level. Hiring and firing merely for seasonal fluctuations, which can be predicted in advance, is treating human beings in a totally unacceptable manner. Even hiring people on a short-term contract, in practice, leads to their being offered poorer conditions of service and leads to a state of permanent anxiety as to whether they will keep their jobs. On a more practical note, it is pointed out that, in an increasingly global business world where companies may have sites in different countries, those countries that allow hiring and firing are more likely to have their plants 'downsized' than those where legislation makes this difficult.

Demand management through gaming[5]

In service settings, queues will build up when demand exceeds capacity. Nowhere is this more evident than during the daily rush hour. But in California, USA, a novel gaming approach may just offer an innovative solution to this age-old problem. Balaji Prabhakat, a computer science professor, wanted to support Stanford's efforts to alleviate rush-hour traffic in the local Santa Clara County. First, he managed to persuade nearly half of the university's 8,000 parking permit holders to install tracking devices in their cars. Second, he created a simple system that awards points to a person each time they arrive or leave an hour before or after rush hour. Third, these points can then be used in an online game of chance with random cash rewards from $2 to $50. While the prizes are small, the idea has proved popular, with around 15 per cent of trips taken shifting out of the rush-hour periods. Students are tending to arrive at and leave university later, while faculty are arriving and leaving earlier! The scheme is unlike classic peak-load pricing schemes, where customers pay more to use capacity when there is naturally high demand for it. For example, Seattle's transit system charges a 75-cent excess to travel between 6.00 and 9.00 am. Rather, the gaming idea is that some participants will change their habits for little or no reward, while others gain a (relatively) much bigger reward. So, it is the randomness of the reward that makes this example a particularly interesting one. If the scheme can be rolled out to a wider population in the area, the effect of reducing load on stretched capacity by 15 per cent will be significant. The challenge, as with many improvement projects, is to retain the incentives for individuals to stick with the game even when they are not 'winning' and when their attention is on other things.

Source: Getty Images: Look / Hendrik Holler

capacity in this way must be weighed against the risks of damaging the core product or service, and the operation must be fully capable of serving both markets.

Yield management

In operations which have relatively fixed capacities, such as airlines and hotels, it is important to use the capacity of the operation for generating revenue to its full potential. One approach used by such operations is called yield management.[6] This is really a collection of methods, some of which we have already discussed, which can be used to ensure that an operation maximizes its potential to generate profit. Yield management is especially useful where capacity is relatively fixed; the market can be fairly clearly segmented; the service cannot be stored in any way; the service is sold in advance; and the marginal cost of making a sale is relatively low.

Airlines, for example, fit all these criteria. They adopt a collection of methods to try to maximize the yield (that is, profit) from their capacity. Over-booking capacity may be used to compensate for passengers who do not show up for the flight. However, if more passengers show up than they expect, the airlines will have a number of upset passengers. By studying past data on flight demand, airlines try to balance the risks of over-booking and under-booking. Operations may also use price discounting at quiet times, when demand is unlikely to fill capacity. For example, hotels will typically offer cheaper room rates outside of holiday periods to try and increase naturally lower demand. In addition, many larger chains will sell heavily discounted rooms to third parties who in turn take on the risk (and reward) of finding customers for these rooms.

Knowing when to watch a baseball game[7]

Baseball remains to this day one of the most popular sports in the USA and going to a match is a national pastime. Still, some games are a great deal more popular than others. For the New York Mets, a Saturday night game against their cross-town rivals, the New York Yankees, will have a great deal more natural demand than a mid-week game against a low-performing team from the other side of the country. And yet, for years, the price of a ticket at most baseball matches was based solely on the location of the ticket in the stadium rather than what the actual demand for the game was. However, this is changing across Major League Baseball and nowhere more so than at Wrigley Field, home of the Chicago Cubs. Here, yield management, often referred to as 'dynamic pricing', is being used to set ticket prices for games. So now, rather than having a 'face value' for a specific seat location within Wrigley Field, prices fluctuate daily based on 'changing market factors', as the team website states. So what are these factors? There are two that appear to dominate this approach to pricing – the day of the week and the opponent. First, prices of tickets rise steadily through the week, with a Monday game averaging just $27 in the bleachers (the section of the stadium where analysis has been carried out), while a Saturday game ticket averages around $76.

Source: Getty Images: Ron Vesely

On Sunday, the price falls back to $46. The opponent is also key to dynamic pricing too. Games against the Boston Red Sox and the Chicago White Sox fetch the highest average ticket prices, given the prestige of the former and the local rivalry of the latter. Conversely, tickets for (apologies to their fans!) games against the Atlanta Braves and the Milwaukee Brewers average just $19 and $16. So for those with limited resources, go to a mid-week game against lowly opposition; for those who cannot skip work, go to a Sunday game; and for those where money is no object, enjoy Saturday night against the mighty Boston Red Sox!

Mixed plans

Each of the three 'pure' plans is applied only where its advantages strongly outweigh its disadvantages. For many organizations, however, these 'pure' approaches do not match their required combination of competitive and operational objectives. Most operations managers are required simultaneously to reduce costs and inventory, to minimize capital investment, and yet to provide a responsive and customer-oriented approach at all times. For this reason, most organizations choose to follow a mixture of the three approaches. This can be illustrated by looking at a woollen knitwear company (*see* Fig. 11.10). Here some of the peak demand has been brought forward by the company offering discounts to selected retail customers (manage demand plan). Capacity has also been adjusted at two points in the year to reflect the broad changes in demand (chase demand plan). Yet the adjustment in capacity is not sufficient to avoid totally the build-up of inventories (level capacity plan).

Figure 11.10 A mixed capacity plan for a woollen knitwear factory

HOW CAN OPERATIONS UNDERSTAND THE CONSEQUENCES OF THEIR CAPACITY DECISIONS?

Before an operation adopts one or more of the three 'pure' capacity plans (level capacity, chase demand or demand management), it should examine the likely consequences. Three methods are particularly useful in helping to assess the consequences of adopting particular capacity plans:

- Consider capacity decisions using cumulative representations.
- Consider capacity decisions using queuing principles.
- Consider capacity decisions over time.

Considering capacity decisions using cumulative representations

Figure 11.11 shows the forecast aggregated demand for a chocolate factory that makes confectionery products. Demand for its products in the shops is greatest at Christmas. To meet this demand and allow time for the products to work their way through the distribution system, the factory must supply a demand that peaks in September, as shown. One method of assessing whether a particular level of capacity can satisfy the demand would be to calculate the degree of over-capacity below the graph which represents the capacity levels (areas A and C) and the degree of under-capacity above the graph (area B). If the total over-capacity is greater than the total under-capacity for a particular level of capacity, then that capacity could be regarded as adequate to satisfy demand fully, the assumption being that inventory has been accumulated in the periods of over-capacity. However, there are two problems with this approach. The first is that each month shown in Figure 11.11 may not have the same amount of productive time. Some months (August, for example) may contain vacation periods that reduce the availability of capacity. The second problem is that a capacity level that seems adequate may only be able to supply products *after* the demand for them has occurred. For example, if the period of under-capacity occurred at the beginning of the year, no inventory

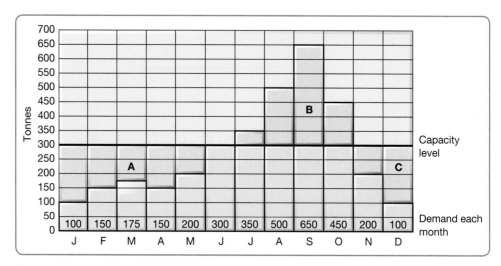

Figure 11.11 If the over-capacity areas (A + C) are greater than the under-capacity area (B), the capacity level seems adequate to meet demand. However, this may not necessarily be the case

could have accumulated to meet demand. A far superior way of assessing capacity plans is first to plot demand on a *cumulative* basis. This is shown as the heavier line in Figure 11.11.

The cumulative representation of demand immediately reveals more information. First, it shows that although total demand peaks in September, because of the restricted number of available productive days, the peak demand per productive day occurs a month earlier in August. Second, it shows that the fluctuation in demand over the year is even greater than it seemed. The ratio of monthly peak demand to monthly lowest demand is 6.5:1, but the ratio of peak to lowest demand per productive day is 10:1. Demand per productive day is more relevant to operations managers, because productive days represent the time element of capacity.

The most useful consequence of plotting demand on a cumulative basis is that, by plotting capacity on the same graph, the feasibility and consequences of a capacity plan can be assessed. Figure 11.12 also shows a level capacity plan which produces at a rate of 14.03 tonnes per productive day. This meets cumulative demand by the end of the year. It would also pass our earlier test of total over-capacity being the same as or greater than under-capacity.

However, if one of the aims of the plan is to supply demand when it occurs, the plan is inadequate. Up to around day 168, the line representing cumulative production is above that representing cumulative demand. This means that at any time during this period, the factory has produced more products than has been demanded from it. In fact the vertical distance between the two lines is the level of inventory at that point in time. So by day 80, 1,122 tonnes have been produced but only 575 tonnes have been demanded. The surplus of production above demand, or inventory, is therefore 547 tonnes. When the cumulative demand line lies above the cumulative production line, the reverse is true. The vertical distance between the two lines now indicates the shortage, or lack of supply. So by day 198, 3,025 tonnes have been demanded but only 2,778 tonnes produced. The shortage is therefore 247 tonnes.

Operations principle

For any capacity plan to meet demand as it occurs, its cumulative production line must always lie above its cumulative demand line.

For any capacity plan to meet demand as it occurs, its cumulative production line must always lie above the cumulative demand line. This makes it a straightforward task to judge the adequacy of a plan, simply by looking at its cumulative representation. An impression of the inventory implications can also be gained from a cumulative representation by judging the area between the cumulative production and demand curves. This represents the amount of inventory carried

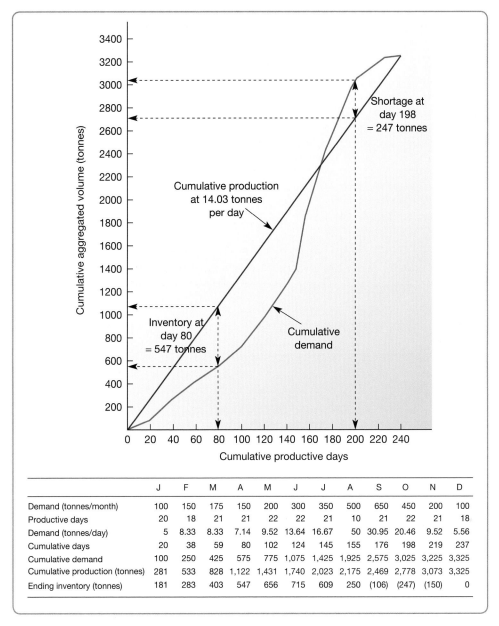

	J	F	M	A	M	J	J	A	S	O	N	D
Demand (tonnes/month)	100	150	175	150	200	300	350	500	650	450	200	100
Productive days	20	18	21	21	22	22	21	10	21	22	21	18
Demand (tonnes/day)	5	8.33	8.33	7.14	9.52	13.64	16.67	50	30.95	20.46	9.52	5.56
Cumulative days	20	38	59	80	102	124	145	155	176	198	219	237
Cumulative demand	100	250	425	575	775	1,075	1,425	1,925	2,575	3,025	3,225	3,325
Cumulative production (tonnes)	281	533	828	1,122	1,431	1,740	2,023	2,175	2,469	2,778	3,073	3,325
Ending inventory (tonnes)	181	283	403	547	656	715	609	250	(106)	(247)	(150)	0

Figure 11.12 A level capacity plan which produces shortages in spite of meeting demand at the end of the year

over the period. Figure 11.13 illustrates an adequate level capacity plan for the chocolate manufacturer, together with the costs of carrying inventory. It is assumed that inventory costs £2 per tonne per day to keep in storage. The average inventory each month is taken to be the average of the beginning- and end-of-month inventory levels, and the inventory carrying cost each month is the product of the average inventory, the inventory cost per day per tonne and the number of days in the month.

Comparing plans on a cumulative basis

Chase demand plans can also be illustrated on a cumulative representation. Rather than the cumulative production line having a constant gradient, it would have a varying gradient representing the production rate at any point in time. If a pure demand chase plan

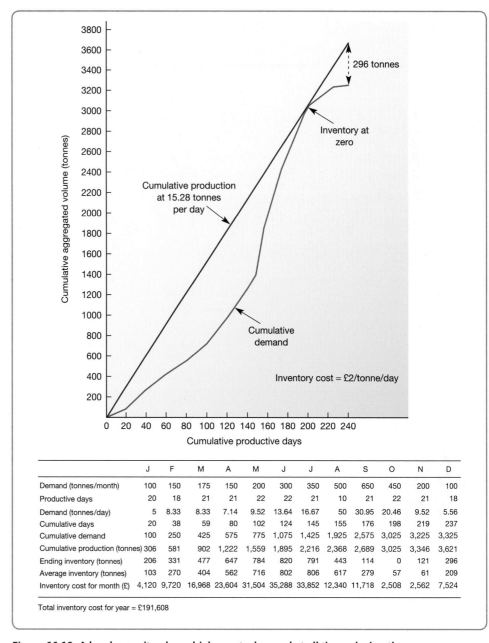

	J	F	M	A	M	J	J	A	S	O	N	D
Demand (tonnes/month)	100	150	175	150	200	300	350	500	650	450	200	100
Productive days	20	18	21	21	22	22	21	10	21	22	21	18
Demand (tonnes/day)	5	8.33	8.33	7.14	9.52	13.64	16.67	50	30.95	20.46	9.52	5.56
Cumulative days	20	38	59	80	102	124	145	155	176	198	219	237
Cumulative demand	100	250	425	575	775	1,075	1,425	1,925	2,575	3,025	3,225	3,325
Cumulative production (tonnes)	306	581	902	1,222	1,559	1,895	2,216	2,368	2,689	3,025	3,346	3,621
Ending inventory (tonnes)	206	331	477	647	784	820	791	443	114	0	121	296
Average inventory (tonnes)	103	270	404	562	716	802	806	617	279	57	61	209
Inventory cost for month (£)	4,120	9,720	16,968	23,604	31,504	35,288	33,852	12,340	11,718	2,508	2,562	7,524

Total inventory cost for year = £191,608

Figure 11.13 A level capacity plan which meets demand at all times during the year

were adopted, the cumulative production line would match the cumulative demand line. The gap between the two lines would be zero and hence inventory would be zero. Although this would eliminate inventory-carrying costs, as we discussed earlier, there would be costs associated with changing capacity levels. Usually, the marginal cost of making a capacity change increases with the size of the change. For example, if the chocolate manufacturer wishes to increase capacity by 5 per cent, this can be achieved by requesting its staff to work overtime – a simple, fast and relatively inexpensive option. If the change is 15 per cent, overtime cannot provide sufficient extra capacity and temporary staff will need to be employed – a more expensive solution which also would take more time. Increases in capacity of above 15 per cent might only be achieved by subcontracting some work out. This would be even more expensive. The point from which the change is being made, as well as the direction of the change, will also affect the cost of the change. Usually, it is less expensive to change capacity towards what is regarded as the 'normal' capacity level than away from it.

Worked example

Suppose the chocolate manufacturer, which has been operating the level capacity plan as shown in Figure 11.14, is unhappy with the inventory costs of this approach. It decides to explore two alternative plans, both involving some degree of demand chasing.

Plan 1
- Organize and staff the factory for a 'normal' capacity level of 8.7 tonnes per day.
- Produce at 8.7 tonnes per day for the first 124 days of the year, then increase capacity to 29 tonnes per day by heavy use of overtime, hiring temporary staff and some subcontracting.
- Produce at 29 tonnes per day until day 194, then reduce capacity back to 8.7 tonnes per day for the rest of the year.

The costs of changing capacity by such a large amount (the ratio of peak to normal capacity is 3.33:1) are calculated by the company as being:

Cost of changing from 8.7 tonnes/day to 29 tonnes/day = £10,000

Cost of changing from 29 tonnes/day to 8.7 tonnes/day = £60,000

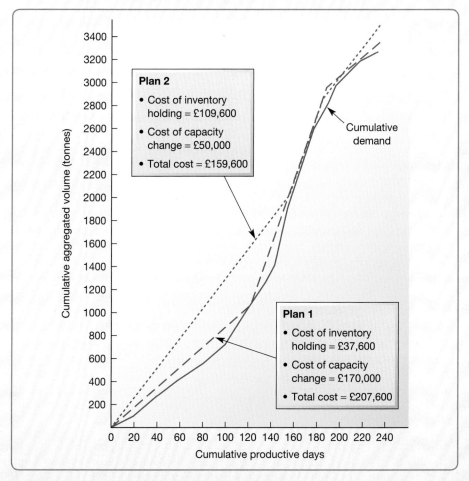

Figure 11.14 Comparing two alternative capacity plans

Considering capacity decisions using queuing principles

Cumulative representations of capacity plans are useful where the operation has the ability to store its finished goods as inventory. However, for operations where it is not possible to produce products and services *before* demand for them has occurred, a cumulative representation would tell us relatively little. The cumulative 'production' could never be above the cumulative demand line. At best, it could show when an operation failed to meet its demand. So the vertical gap between the cumulative demand and production lines would indicate the amount of demand unsatisfied. Some of this demand would look elsewhere to be satisfied, but some would wait. This is why, for operations which, by their nature, cannot store their output, such as most service operations, capacity planning and control is best considered using waiting or queuing theory.

When we were illustrating the use of cumulative representations for capacity management, our assumption was that, generally, any plan should aim to meet demand at any point in time (the cumulative production line must be above the cumulative demand line). Looking at the issue as a queuing problem (in many parts of the world queuing concepts are referred to as 'waiting line' concepts) accepts that, while sometimes demand may be satisfied instantly, at other times customers may have to wait. This is particularly true when the arrival of individual demands on an operation are difficult to predict, or the time to produce a product or service is uncertain, or both. These circumstances make providing adequate capacity at all points in time particularly difficult. Figure 11.15 shows the general form of this capacity issue. Customers arrive according to some probability distribution and wait to be processed (unless part of the operation is idle); when they have reached the front of the queue, they are processed by one of the *n* parallel 'servers' (their processing time also being described by a probability distribution), after which they leave the operation. There are many examples of this kind of system. Table 11.3 illustrates some of these. All of these examples can be described by a common set of elements that define their queuing behaviour:

- **The source of customers** – Sometimes called the calling population, this is the source of supply of customers. In queue management 'customers' are not always human. 'Customers' could for example be trucks arriving at a weighbridge, orders arriving to be processed, machines waiting to be serviced, etc. The source of customers for a

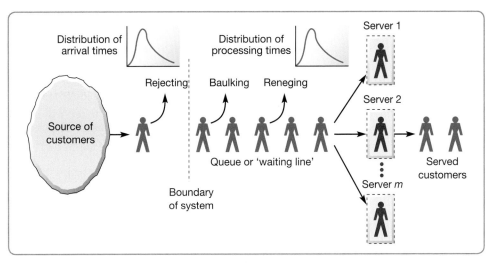

Figure 11.15 Capacity management as a queuing problem

Table 11.3 Examples of operations which have parallel processors

Operation	Arrivals	Processing capacity
Bank	Customers	Tellers
Supermarket	Shoppers	Checkouts
Hospital clinic	Patients	Doctors
Graphic artist	Commissions	Artists
Custom cake decorators	Orders	Cake decorators
Ambulance service	Emergencies	Ambulances with crews
Telephone switchboard	Calls	Telephonists
Maintenance department	Breakdowns	Maintenance staff

queuing system can be either *finite* or *infinite*. A finite source has a known number of possible customers. For example, if one maintenance person serves four assembly lines, the number of customers for the maintenance person is known, namely four. There will be a certain probability that one of the assembly lines will break down and need repairing. However, if one line really does break down, the probability of another line needing repair is reduced because there are now only three lines to break down. So, with a finite source of customers the probability of a customer arriving depends on the number of customers already being serviced. By contrast, infinite customer sources assume that there are a large number of potential customers so that it is always possible for another customer to arrive no matter how many are being serviced. Most queuing systems that deal with outside markets have infinite, or 'close-to-infinite', customer sources.

- **The arrival rate** – This is the rate at which customers needing to be served arrive at the server or servers. Rarely do customers arrive at a steady and predictable rate. Usually there is variability in their arrival rate. Because of this it is necessary to describe arrival rates in terms of probability distributions. The important issue here is that, in queuing systems, it is normal that at times no customers will arrive and at other times many will arrive relatively close together.
- **The queue** – Customers waiting to be served form the queue or waiting line itself. If there is relatively little limit on how many customers can queue at any time, we can assume that, for all practical purposes, an infinite queue is possible. Sometimes, however, there is a limit to how many customers can be in the queue at any one time.

- **Rejecting** – If the number of customers in a queue is already at the maximum number allowed, then the customer could be rejected by the system. For example, during periods of heavy demand some websites will not allow customers to access part of the site until the demand on its services has declined.
- **Baulking** – When a customer is a human being with free will (and the ability to get annoyed) he or she may refuse to join the queue and wait for service if it is judged to be too long. In queuing terms this is called baulking.
- **Reneging** – This is similar to baulking but here the customer has queued for a certain length of time and then (perhaps being dissatisfied with the rate of progress) leaves the queue and therefore the chance of being served.
- **Queue discipline** – This is the set of rules that determine the order in which customers waiting in the queue are served. Most simple queues, such as those in a shop, use a *first-come, first-served* queue discipline. The various sequencing rules described in Chapter 10 are examples of different queue disciplines.
- **Servers** – A server is the facility that processes the customers in the queue. In any queuing system there may be any number of servers configured in different ways. In Figure 11.15 servers are configured in parallel, but some may have servers in a series arrangement. For example, on entering a self-service restaurant you may queue to collect a tray and cutlery, move on to the serving area where you queue again to order and collect a meal, move on to a drinks area where you queue once more to order and collect and drink, and then finally queue to pay for the meal. In this case you have passed through four servers (even though the first one was not staffed) in a series arrangement. Of course, many queue systems are complex arrangements of series and parallel connections. There is also likely to be variation in how long it takes to process each customer. Even if customers do not have differing needs, human servers will vary in the time they take to perform repetitive serving tasks. Therefore processing time, like arrival time, is usually described by a probability distribution.

Balancing capacity and demand

The dilemma in managing the capacity of a queuing system is how many servers to have available at any point in time in order to avoid unacceptably long queuing times or unacceptably low utilization of the servers. Because of the probabilistic arrival and processing times, only rarely will the arrival of customers match the ability of the operation to cope with them. Sometimes, if several customers arrive in quick succession and require longer than average processing times, queues will build up in front of the operation. At other times, when customers arrive less frequently than average and also require shorter than average processing times, some of the servers in the system will be idle. So even when the average capacity (processing capability) of the operation matches the average demand (arrival rate) on the system, both queues and idle time will occur.

If the operation has too few servers (that is, capacity is set at too low a level), queues will build up to a level where customers become dissatisfied with the time they are having to wait, although the utilization level of the servers will be high. If too many servers are in place (that is, capacity is set at too high a level), the time which customers can expect to wait will not be long but the utilization of the servers will be low. This is why the capacity planning and control problem for this type of operation is often presented as a trade-off between customer waiting time and system utilization. What is certainly important in making capacity decisions is being able to predict both of these factors for a given queuing system. The supplement to this chapter details some of the more simple mathematical approaches to understanding queue behaviour.

Customer perceptions of queuing

Few of us like waiting. Yet queuing is something we all have to do. So if you have ever wondered if you are alone in particularly hating queuing, you are not – it is official. According to research involving 45,000 iPhone users who provided regular updates on their level of happiness via an app, it is one of the activities that most upsets us.[8] In fact, of all the things that make us feel unhappy, queuing is beaten only by being in bed sick. Yet, an important aspect of how people judge the service they receive from a queuing system is how they perceive the time spent queuing. It is well known that if you are told that you will be waiting in a queue for 20 minutes and you are actually serviced in 10 minutes, your perception of the queuing experience will be more positive than if you were told that you would be waiting 10 minutes but the queue actually took 20 minutes. Because of this, the management of queuing systems usually involves attempting to manage customers' perceptions and expectations in some way. Below is a set of 'principles' that can help in evaluating and improving queues (of course, in cases where the queue itself cannot be removed through process improvement):

> ✳ **Operations principle**
>
> Customer reactions to having to queue will be influenced by more factors than waiting time.

1. Unoccupied time feels longer than occupied time.
2. Pre-process waits feel longer than in-process waits.
3. Anxiety makes the wait seem longer.
4. Uncertain waits feel longer than known, finite waits.
5. Unexplained waits feel longer than explained waits.
6. Unfair waits feel longer than equitable waits.
7. The more valuable the service, the longer customers will 'happily' wait.
8. Solo waiting feels longer than group waiting.
9. Uncomfortable waits feel longer than comfortable waits.
10. New or infrequent users feel they wait longer than frequent users.

Considering capacity de.5cisions over time

Our emphasis so far has been on the planning aspects of capacity management. In practice, capacity management is a far more dynamic process, which involves controlling and reacting to *actual* demand and *actual* capacity as it occurs. The capacity control process can be seen as a sequence of partially reactive capacity decisions. At the beginning of each period, operations management considers its forecasts of demand, its understanding of current capacity and, if appropriate, how much inventory has been carried forward from the previous period. Based on all this information, it makes plans for the following period's capacity. During the next period, demand might or might not be as forecast and the actual capacity of the operation might or might not turn out as planned. But whatever the actual conditions during that period, at the beginning of the next period the same types of decisions must be made, in the light of the new circumstances.

> ✳ **Operations principle**
>
> The learning from managing capacity in practice should be captured and used to refine both demand forecasting and capacity planning.

The success of capacity management is generally measured by some combination of costs, revenue, working capital and customer satisfaction (which goes on to influence revenue). This is influenced by the actual capacity available to the operation in any period and the demand for that period. However, capacity management is essentially a forward-looking activity. Overriding other considerations of what capacity strategy to adopt is usually the difference between the long- and short-term outlook for the volume of demand. If the long-term outlook for demand is 'good' (in the sense that it is higher than current capacity can cope with) then it is unlikely that even 'poor' (demand less than capacity) short-term demand would cause an operation to make large, or difficult to reverse, cuts in capacity. Conversely if long-term outlook for demand is 'poor' (in the sense that it is lower than current capacity) then it is unlikely that even 'good' (demand more than capacity) short-term demand would cause an operation to take on large, or difficult to reverse, extra capacity. Figure 11.16 illustrates some appropriate capacity management strategies depending on the comparison of long- and short-term outlooks.

	Short-term outlook for volume		
	Decreasing below current capacity	Level with current capacity	Increasing above current capacity
Decreasing below current capacity	Reduce capacity (semi) permanently. For example, reduce staffing levels; reduce supply agreements.	Plan to reduce capacity (semi) permanently. For example, freeze recruitment; modify supply agreements.	Increase capacity temporarily. For example, increase working hours, and/or hire temporary staff; modify supply agreements.
Level with current capacity	Reduce capacity temporarily. For example, reduce staff working hours; modify supply agreements.	Maintain capacity at current level.	Increase capacity temporarily. For example, increase working hours, and/or hire temporary staff; modify supply agreements.
Increasing above current capacity	Reduce capacity temporarily. For example, reduce staff working hours, but plan to recruit; modify supply agreements.	Plan to increase capacity above current level; plan to increase supply agreements.	Increase capacity (semi) permanently. For example, hire staff; increase supply agreements.

Left axis label: **Long-term outlook for volume**

Figure 11.16 Capacity management strategies are partly dependent on the long- and short-term outlook for volumes

SUMMARY ANSWERS TO KEY QUESTIONS

❭ What is capacity management?

- The capacity of an operation is the *maximum level of value-added activity over a period of time* that the process can achieve under normal operating conditions.

- Capacity management is the activity of understanding the nature of demand for products and services, and effectively planning and controlling capacity in the short term, medium term and long term.

- Long-term capacity management (or strategy) focuses on introducing or deleting major increments of capacity (see Chapter 5). Medium- and short-term capacity management focuses on adjusting capacity and demand within the constraints imposed by long-term capacity decisions.

- The process of managing capacity involves (1) measuring and understanding changes in aggregate demand and capacity (supply); (2) determining the operation's base level of capacity; (3) identifying and selecting methods of coping with demand–supply mismatches; and (4) understanding the consequences of different capacity decisions.

〉 How are demand and capacity measured?

- Demand forecasts should be expressed in terms that are useful (for example, units per hour, operatives per month, etc.), be as accurate as possible and give an indication of uncertainty.
- Typically, the demand for products and services is not completely stable. Climatic, social, cultural, political and economic factors all act to influence both predictable and unpredictable volatility in demand.
- Capacity can be measured by the availability of its input resources or by the output that is created. Which of these measures is used partly depends on how stable is the mix of outputs. If it is difficult to aggregate the different types of output from an operation, input measures are usually preferred.
- It is managed either by the availability of its input resources or by the output which is produced. Which of these measures is used partly depends on how stable is the mix of outputs. If it is difficult to aggregate the different types of output from an operation, input measures are usually preferred.
- The usage of capacity is measured by the factors of 'utilization' and 'efficiency'. A useful measure of capacity leakage is overall operations effectiveness (OEE).

〉 How should the operation's base capacity be set?

- Capacity planning often involves setting a base level of capacity and then planning capacity fluctuations around it. The level at which base capacity is set depends on three main factors: the relative importance of the operation's performance objectives, the perishability of the operation's outputs, and the degree of variability in demand or supply.
- High service levels, high perishability of an operation's outputs and a high degree of variability, either in demand or supply, all indicate a relatively high level of base capacity.

〉 What are the ways of coping with mismatches between demand and capacity?

- Demand–capacity mismatches usually call for some degree of capacity adjustment over time. There are three pure methods of achieving this, although in practice a mixture of all three may be used:
  - 'Level capacity' plans involve no change in capacity and require that the operation absorb demand–capacity mismatches, usually through under- or over-utilization of its resources, or the use of inventory.
  - 'Chase demand' plans involve the changing of capacity through such methods as overtime, varying the size of the work force, subcontracting, etc.
  - 'Demand management' plans involve an attempt to change demand through pricing or promotion methods, or changing product or service mix to reduce fluctuations in activity levels. When outputs cannot be stored, yield management is a common method of coping with mismatches.

〉 How can operations understand the consequences of their capacity decisions?

- Presenting demand and output in the form of cumulative representations allows the feasibility of alternative capacity plans to be assessed.
- In many operations, especially service operations, a queuing approach can be used to explore the consequences of capacity strategies..
- Using long-term and short-term outlook for demand allows further evaluation of alternative capacity management decisions.

'Six years ago I had never heard of agri-tourism. As far as I was concerned, I had inherited the farm and I would be a farmer all my life.' (Jim Walker, Blackberry Hill Farm)

The 'agri-tourism' that Jim was referring to is 'a commercial enterprise at a working farm, or other agricultural centre, conducted for the enjoyment of visitors that generates supplemental income for the owner'. *'Farming has become a tough business'*, says Jim. *'Low world prices, a reduction in subsidies, and increasingly uncertain weather patterns have made it a far more risky business than when I first inherited the farm. Yet, because of our move into the tourist trade we are flourishing. Also ... I've never had so much fun in my life.'* But, Jim warns, agri-tourism is not for everyone. *'You have to think carefully. Do you really want to do it? What kind of life style do you want? How open-minded are you to new ideas? How business-minded are you? Are you willing to put a lot of effort into marketing your business? Above all, do you like working with people? If you had rather be around cows than people, it isn't the business for you.'*

Source: Shutterstock.com: Karel Gallas

History

Blackberry Hill Farm was a 200-hectare mixed farm in the south of England when Jim and Mandy Walker inherited it 15 years ago. It was primarily a cereal growing operation with a small dairy herd, some fruit and vegetable growing and mixed woodland that was protected by local preservation laws. Six years ago it had become evident to Jim and Mandy that they may have to rethink how the farm was being managed. *'We first started a pick-your-own (PYO) operation because our farm is close to several large centres of population. Also the quantities of fruit and vegetables that we were producing were not large enough to interest the commercial buyers. Entering the PYO market was a reasonable success and in spite of making some early mistakes, it turned our fruit and vegetable growing operation from making a small loss to making a small profit. Most importantly, it gave us some experience of how to deal with customers face-to-face and of how to cope with unpredictable demand. The biggest variable in PYO sales is weather. Most business occurs at the weekends between late spring and early autumn. If rain keeps customers away during part of those weekends, nearly all sales have to occur in just a few days.'*

Within a year of opening up the PYO operation Jim and Mandy had decided to reduce the area devoted to cereals and increase their fruit and vegetable growing capability. At the same time they organized a petting zoo that allowed children to mix with, feed and touch various animals.

'We already had our own cattle and poultry but we extended the area and brought in pigs and goats. Later we also introduced some rabbits, ponies and donkeys, and even

a small bee keeping operation.' At the same time the farm started building up its collection of 'farm heritage' exhibits. These were static displays of old farm implements and 'recreations' of farming processes together with information displays. This had always been a personal interest of Jim's and it allowed him to convert two existing farm outbuildings to create a 'Museum of Farming Heritage'.

The year after, they introduced tractor rides for visitors around the whole farm and extended the petting zoo and farming tradition exhibits further. But the most significant investment was in the 'preserving kitchen'. *'We had been looking for some way of using the surplus fruits and vegetable that we occasionally accumulated and also for some kind of products that we could sell in a farm shop. We started the Preserving Kitchen to make jams and fruit, vegetables and sauces preserved in jars. The venture was an immediate success. We started making just fifty kilogrammes of preserves a week, within three months that had grown to three hundred kilogrammes a week and we are now producing around a thousand kilogrammes a week, all under the "Blackberry Hill Farm" label.'* The following year the preserving kitchen was extended and a viewing area added. *'It was a great attraction from the beginning'*, says Mandy. *'We employed ladies from the local village to make the preserves. They are all extrovert characters, so when we asked them to dress up in traditional "farmers wives" type clothing they were happy to do it. The visitors love it, especially the good natured repartee with our ladies. The ladies also enjoy giving informal history lessons when we get school parties visiting us.'*

Table 11.4(a) Number of visitors last year

Month	Total visitors
January	1,006
February	971
March	2,874
April	6,622
May	8,905
June	12,304
July	14,484
August	15,023
September	12,938
October	6,687
November	2,505
December	3,777
Total	88,096
Average	7,341.33

Table 11.4(b) Farm opening times*

January–Mid-March	Wednesday–Sunday	10:00–16:00
Mid-March–May	Tuesday–Sunday	09:00–18:00
May–September	All week	08:30–19:00
October–November	Tuesday–Sunday	10:00–16:00
December	Tuesday–Sunday	09:00–18:00

*Special evening events Easter, summer weekends and Christmas.

Within the last two years the farm had further extended its preserving kitchen, farm shop, exhibits and petting zoo. It had also introduced a small adventure playground for the children, a café serving drinks and its own produce, a picnic area and a small bakery. The bakery was also open to view by customers and staffed by bakers in traditional dress. 'It's a nice little visitor attraction', says Mandy, 'and it gives us another opportunity to squeeze more value out of our own products.' Table 11.4(a) shows last year's visitor numbers, and Table 11.4(b) shows the farm's opening times..

Demand

The number of visitors to the farm was extremely seasonal. From a low point in January and February, when most people just visited the farm shop, the spring and summer months could be very busy, especially on public holidays. The previous year Mandy had tracked the number of visitors arriving at the farm each day. 'It is easy to record the number of people visiting the farm attractions, because they pay the entrance charge. What we had not done before is include the people who just visited the farm shop and bakery that can be accessed both from within the farm and from the car park. We estimate that the number of people visiting the shop but not the farm ranges from 74 per cent in February down to around 15 per cent in August.' Figure 11.17 shows the number of visitors in the previous year's August. 'What our figures do not include are those people who visit the shop but don't buy anything. This is unlikely to be a large number.' Figure 11.18 shows visitor arrivals on a public holiday in August and a Wednesday in February.

Mandy had also estimated the average stay at the farm and/or farm shop. She reckoned that in winter time the average stay was 45 minutes, but in August in climbed to 3.1 hours.

Current issues

Both Jim and Mandy agreed that their lives had fundamentally changed over the last few years. Income from visitors and from the Blackberry Hill brand of preserves now accounted for 70 per cent of the farm's revenue. More importantly, the whole enterprise was significantly

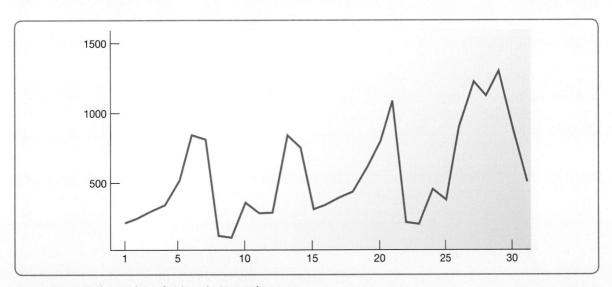

Figure 11.17 Daily number of visitors in August last year

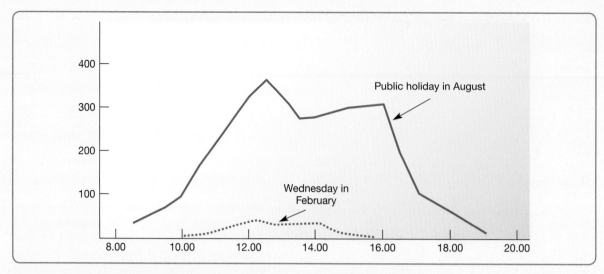

Figure 11.18 Visitor arrivals, public holiday in August and a Wednesday in February

more profitable than it had ever been. Nevertheless, the farm faced a number of issues.

The first was the balance between its different activities. Jim was particularly concerned that the business remained a genuine farm. *'When you look at the revenue per hectare, visitor and production activities bring in far more revenue than conventional agricultural activities. However, if we push the agri-tourism too far we become no better than a theme park. We represent something more than this to our visitors. They come to us partly because of what we represent as well as what we actually do. I am not sure that we would want to grow much more. Anyway, more visitors would mean that we have to extend the car park. That would be expensive, and although it would be necessary, it does not directly bring in any more revenue. There are already parking problems during peak periods and we have had complaints from the police that our visitors park inappropriately on local roads.*

'There is also the problem of complexity. Every time we introduce a new attraction, the whole business gets that little bit more complex to manage. Although we enjoy it tremendously, both Mandy and I are spreading ourselves thinly over an ever widening range of activities [Mandy was also concerned over this]. *I'm starting to feel that my time is being taken up in managing the day-to-day problems of the business. This does not leave time either for thinking about the overall direction in which we should be going, or spending time talking with the staff. That is why we both see this coming year as a time for consolidation and for smoothing out the day-to-day problems of managing the business, particularly the queuing, which is getting excessive at busy times. That is why this year we are limiting ourselves to just one new venture for the business.'*

Staff management was also a concern for Mandy. The business had grown to over 80 (almost all part-time and seasonal) employees. *'We have become a significant employer in the area. Most of our employees are still local people working part-time for extra income but we are also now employing 20 students during the summer period and, last year, 8 agricultural students from Eastern Europe. But now, labour is short in this part of the country and it is becoming more difficult to attract local people, especially to produce Blackberry Hill Farm Preserves. Half of the Preserving Kitchen staff work all year, with the other employed during the summer and autumn periods. But most of them would prefer guaranteed employment throughout the year'*

Table 11.5 gives more details of some of the issues of managing the facilities at the farm, and Table 11.6 shows the preserve demand and production for the previous year.

Where next?
By the 'consolidation' and improvement of 'day-to-day' activities Jim and Mandy meant that they wanted to increase their revenue, while at the same time reducing the occasional queues that they knew could irritate their visitors, preferably without any significant investment in extra capacity. They also were concerned to be able to offer more stable employment to the preserving kitchen 'ladies' throughout the year, who would produce at a near constant rate. However, they were not sure if this could be done without storing the products for so long that their shelf life would be seriously affected. There was no problem with the supply of produce to keep production level – less than 2 per cent of the fruit and vegetables that go into preserves are actually grown on the farm. The remainder were bought at wholesale markets, although this was not generally understood by customers.

Of the many ideas being discussed as candidates for the 'one new venture' for next year, two were emerging as particularly attractive. Jim liked the idea of developing a Maize Maze, a type of attraction that had become

Table 11.5 The farm's main facilities and some of the issues concerned with managing them

Facility	Issues
Car park	• 85 car parking spaces, 4 × 40-seater tour bus spaces
Fixed exhibits etc. Recreation of old farmhouse kitchen, recreation of barnyard, old-fashioned milking parlour, various small exhibits on farming past and present, adventure playground, ice cream and snack stands	• Most exhibits in, or adjacent to, the farm museum • At peak times have helpers dressed in period costume to entertain visitors • Feedback indicates customers find exhibits more interesting than they thought they would • Visitors free to look when they wish absorbs demand from busy facilities
Tractor rides One tractor towing decorated covered cart with maximum capacity of 30 people, tour takes around 20 minutes on average (including stops). Waits 10 minutes between tours except at peak times when tractor circulates continuously	• Tractor acts both as transport and entertainment, approximately 60% of visitors stay on for the whole tour, 40% use it as 'hop-on, hop-off' facility • Overloaded at peak times, long queues building • Feedback indicates it is popular, except for queuing • Jim reluctant to invest in further cart and tractor
Pick-your-own area Largest single facility on the farm. Use local press, dedicated telephone line (answering machine) and website to communicate availability of fruit and vegetables. Checkout and weighing area next to farm shop, also displays picked produce, preserves, etc., for sale	• Very seasonal and weather dependent, both for supply and demand • Farm plans for a surplus over visitor demand, uses surplus in preserves • Six weighing/paying stations at undercover checkout area • Queues develop at peak times. Feedback indicates some dissatisfaction with this • Can move staff from farm shop to help with checkout in busy periods, but farm shop also tends to be busy at the same time • Considering using packers at pay stations to speed up the process
Petting zoo Accommodation for smaller animals including sheep and pigs. Large animals (cattle, horses) brought to viewing area daily. Visitors can view all animals and handle/stroke most animals under supervision	• Approximately 50% of visitors view petting zoo • Number of staff in attendance varies between 0 (off-peak) and 5 (peak periods) • The area can get congested during peak periods • Staff need to be skilled at managing children
Preserving kitchen Boiling vats, mixing vats, jar sterilizing equipment, etc. Visitor viewing area can hold 15 people comfortably. Average length of stay 7 minutes in off-season, 14 minutes in peak season	• Capacity of kitchen is theoretically 4,500 kilograms per month on a 5-day week and 6,000 kilograms on a 7-day week • In practice, capacity varies with season because of interaction with visitors. Can be as low as 5,000 kilograms on a 7-day week in summer, or up to 5,000 kilograms on a 5-day week in winter • Shelf life of products is on average 12 months • Current storage area can hold 16,000 kilograms
Bakery Contains mixing and shaping equipment, commercial oven, cooling racks, display stand, etc. Just installed doughnut making machine. All pastries contain farm's preserved fruit	• Starting to become a bottleneck since doughnut making machine installed – visitors like watching it • Products also on sale at farm shop adjacent to bakery • Would be difficult to expand this area because of building constraints
Farm shop and café Started by selling farm's own products exclusively. Now sells a range of products from farms in the region and wider. Started selling frozen menu dishes (lasagne, goulash, etc.) produced off-peak in the preserving kitchen	• The most profitable part of the whole enterprise, Jim and Mandy would like to extend the retailing and café operation • Shop includes area for cooking displays, cake decoration, fruit dipping (in chocolate), etc. • Some congestion in shop at peak times but little visitor dissatisfaction • More significant queuing for café in peak periods • Considering allowing customers to place orders before they tour the farm's facilities and collect their purchases later • Retailing more profitable per square metre than café

Table 11.6 Preserve demand and production (previous year)

Month	Demand (kg)	Cumulative demand (kg)	Production (kg)	Cumulative product (kg)	Inventory (kg)
January	682	682	4,900	4,900	4,218
February	794	1,476	4,620	9,520	8,044
March	1,106	2,582	4,870	14,390	11,808
April	3,444	6.026	5,590	19,980	13,954
May	4,560	10,586	5,840	25,820	15,234
June	6,014	16,600	5,730	31,550	14,950
July	9,870	26,470	5,710	37,260	10,790
August	13,616	40,086	5,910	43,170	3,084
September	5,040	45,126	5,730	48,900	3,774
October	1,993	47,119	1,570*	50,470	3,351
November	2,652	49,771	2,770*	53,240	3,467
December	6,148	55,919	4,560	57,800	1,881
Average demand	4,660			Average inventory	7,880

*Technical problems reduced production level.

increasingly popular in Europe and North America in the last five years. It involved planting a field of maize (corn) and, once grown, cutting through a complex serious of paths in the form of a maze. Evidence from other farms indicated that a maze would be extremely attractive to visitors and Jim reckoned that it could account for up to an extra 10,000 visitors during the summer period. Designed as a separate activity with its own admission charge, it would require an investment of around £20,000, but generate more than twice that in admission charges as well as attracting more visitors to the farm itself.

Mandy favoured the alterative idea – that of building up their business in organized school visits. *'Last year we joined the National Association of Farms for Schools. Their advice is that we could easily become one of the top school attractions in this part of England. Educating visitors about farming tradition is already a major part of what we do. And many of our staff have developed the skills to communicate to children exactly what farm life used to be like. We would need to convert and extend one of our existing underused farm outbuildings to make a 'school room' and that would cost between and £30,000 and £35,000. And although we would need to discount our admission charge substantially, I think we could break even on the investment within around two years.'*

QUESTIONS

1 How could the farm's day-to-day operations be improved?

2 What advice would you give Jim and Mandy regarding this year's 'new venture'?

PROBLEMS AND APPLICATIONS

1 A local government office issues hunting licences. Demand for these licences is relatively slow in the first part of the year but then increases after the middle of the year before slowing down again towards the end of the year. The department works a 220-day year on a basis of 5 days a week. Between working days 0 and 100, demand is 25 per cent of demand during the peak period that lasts between day 100 and day 150. After day 150, demand reduces to about 12 per cent of the demand during the peak period. In total, the department processes 10,000 applications per year. The department has two permanent members of staff who are capable of processing 15 licence applications per day. If an untrained temporary member of

staff can only process 10 licences per day, how many temporary staff should the department recruit between days 100 and 150?

2 In the problem above, if a new computer system is installed that allows experienced staff to increase their work rate to 20 applications per day, and untrained staff to 15 applications per day, (a) does the department still need two permanent staff, and (b) how many temporary members of staff will be needed between days 100 and 150?

3 A field service organization repairs and maintains printing equipment for a large number of customers. It offers one level of service to all its customers and employs 30 staff. The operations marketing's vice-president has decided that in future the company will offer three standards of service: platinum, gold and silver. It is estimated that platinum service customers will require 50 per cent more time from the company's field service engineers than the current service. The current service is to be called 'the gold service'. The silver service is likely to require about 80 per cent of the time of the gold service. If future demand is estimated to be 20 per cent platinum, 70 per cent gold and 10 per cent silver service, how many staff will be needed to fulfil demand?

4 Look again at the principles that govern customers' perceptions of the queuing experience. For the following operations, apply the principles to minimize the perceived negative effects of queuing:
   (a) A cinema
   (b) A doctor's surgery
   (c) Waiting to board an aircraft.

5 Consider how airlines cope with balancing capacity and demand. In particular, consider the role of yield management. Do this by visiting the website of a low-cost airline, and for a number of flights price the fare that is being charged by the airline from tomorrow onwards. In other words, how much would it cost if you needed to fly tomorrow, how much if you needed to fly next week, how much if you needed to fly in 2 weeks, etc.? Plot the results for different flights and debate the findings.

6 Calculate the overall equipment efficiency (OEE) of the following facilities by investigating their use:
   (a) A lecture theatre
   (b) A cinema
   (c) A coffee machine.

   Discuss whether it is worth trying to increase the OEE of these facilities and, if it is, how you would go about it.

SELECTED FURTHER READING

Gunther, N.J. (2007) *Guerrilla Capacity Planning*, **Springer, New York.**

This book provides a tactical approach for planning capacity in both product-based and service-based contexts. Particularly interesting for those new to the ideas of capacity planning as it covers basic and more advanced demand forecasting techniques as well as 'classic' capacity responses.

Hansen, R.C. (2005) *Overall Equipment Effectiveness (OEE)*, **Industrial Press, South Norwalk, CT.**

If you want to know more about OEE, its origins and application, this is the place to start.

Van Mieghem, J. (2003) Capacity management, investment, and hedging: review and recent developments, *Manufacturing and Service Operations Management*, vol. 5, no. 4, 269–302.

An academic article reviewing the literature on strategic capacity management. It does a nice job of covering the different approaches to capacity management under conditions of stability versus volatility (demand change) and of certainty versus uncertainty (that is, the predictability of change).

Supplement to Chapter 11
Analytical queuing models

INTRODUCTION

In the main part of Chapter 11 we described how the queuing approach (in the USA it would be called the 'waiting line approach') can be useful in thinking about capacity, especially in service operations. It is useful because it deals with the issue of variability, both of the arrival of customers (or items) at a process and of how long each customer (or item) takes to process. And where variability is present in a process (as it is in most processes, but particularly in service processes) the capacity required by an operation cannot easily be based on averages but must include the effects of the variation. Unfortunately, many of the formulae that can be used to understand queuing are extremely complicated, especially for complex systems, and are beyond the scope of this book. In fact, computer programs are almost always now used to predict the behaviour of queuing systems. However, studying queuing formulae can illustrate some useful characteristics of the way queuing systems behave.

NOTATION

Unfortunately there are several different conventions for the notation used for different aspects of queuing system behaviour. It is always advisable to check the notation used by different authors before using their formulae. We will use the following notation:

t_a = average time between arrival

r_a = arrival rate (items per unit time) = $1/t_a$

c_a = coefficient of variation of arrival times

m = number of parallel servers at a station

t_e = mean processing time

r_e = processing rate (items per unit time) = m/t_e

c_e = coefficient of variation of process time

u = utilization of station = r_a/r_e = $(r_a t_e)/m$

WIP = average work-in-progress (number of items) in the queue

WIP_q = expected work-in-progress (number of times) in the queue

W_q = expected waiting time in the queue

W = expected waiting time in the system (queue time + processing time)

Some of these factors are explained later.

VARIABILITY

The concept of variability is central to understanding the behaviour of queues. If there were no variability there would be no need for queues to occur because the capacity of a process could be relatively easily adjusted to match demand. For example, suppose one member of staff (a server) serves customers at a bank counter who always arrive exactly every five minutes (that is, 12 per hour). Also suppose that every customer takes exactly five minutes to be served. Then because

(a) the arrival rate is less than or equal to the processing rate, and
(b) there is no variation

no customer need ever wait because the next customer will arrive when, or before, the previous customer leaves. That is, $WIP_q = 0$.

Also, in this case, the server is working all the time, again because exactly as one customer leaves the next one is arriving. That is, $u = 1$.

Even with more than one server, the same may apply. For example, if the arrival time at the counter is five minutes (12 per hour) and the processing time for each customer is now always exactly 10 minutes, the counter would need two servers, and because

(a) arrival rate is less than or equal to processing rate m, and
(b) there is no variation

again $WIP_q = 0$ and $u = 1$.

Of course, it is convenient (but unusual) if arrival rate/processing rate = a whole number. When this is not the case (for this simple example with no variation)

$$\text{Utilization} = \text{Processing rate}/(\text{Arrival rate} \times m)$$

For example:

$$\text{if arrival rate, } r_a = 5 \text{ minutes}$$
$$\text{processing rate, } r_e = 8 \text{ minutes}$$
$$\text{number of servers, } m = 2$$
$$\text{then utilization, } u = 8/(5 \times 2) = 0.8 \text{ or } 80\%$$

Incorporating variability

The previous examples were not realistic because the assumption of no variation in arrival or processing times very rarely occurs. We can calculate the average or mean arrival and process times but we also need to take into account the variation around these means. To do that we need to use a probability distribution. Figure S11.1 contrasts two processes with different arrival distributions. The units arriving are shown as people, but they could be jobs arriving at a machine, trucks needing servicing, or any other uncertain event. The upper example shows low variation in arrival time where customers arrive in a relatively predictable manner. The lower example has the same average number of customer arriving but this time they arrive unpredictably with sometimes long gaps between arrivals and at other times two or three customers arriving close together. Of course, we could do a similar analysis to describe processing times. Again, some would have low variation, some higher variation, and others somewhere in between.

In Figure S11.1 high arrival variation has a distribution with a wider spread (called 'dispersion') than the distribution describing lower variability. Statistically the usual measure

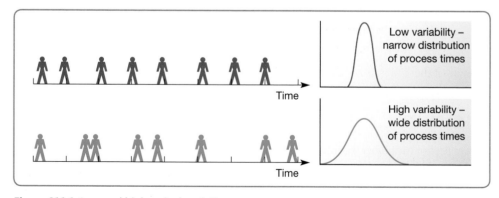

Figure S11.1 Low and high arrival variation

for indicating the spread of a distribution is its standard deviation, σ. But variation does not just depend on standard deviation. For example, a distribution of arrival times may have a standard deviation of 2 minutes. This could indicate very little variation when the average arrival time is 60 minutes. But it would mean a very high degree of variation when the average arrival time is 3 minutes. Therefore to normalize standard deviation, it is divided by the mean of its distribution. This measure is called the coefficient of variation of the distribution. So:

$$c_a = \text{coefficient of variation of arrival times} = \sigma_a/t_a$$
$$c_e = \text{coefficient of variation of processing times} = \sigma_e/t_e$$

INCORPORATING LITTLE'S LAW

In Chapter 6 we discussed one of the fundamental laws of processes that describes the relationship between the cycle time of a process (how often something emerges from the process), the work-in-progress in the process and the throughput time of the process (the total time it takes for an item to move through the whole process including waiting time). It was called Little's law and it was denoted by the following simple relationship:

$$\text{Throughput time} = \text{Throughout time/Cycle time}$$

Therefore:

$$\text{Work-in-progress} = \text{Throughout time/Cycle time}$$

or:

$$\text{WIP} = T/C$$

We can make use of Little's law to help understand queuing behaviour. Consider the queue in front of a station.

Work-in-progress in the queue = Arrival rate at the queue (equivalent to 1/cycle time) × Waiting time in the queue (equivalent to throughput time)

$$\text{WIP}_q = r_a \times W_q$$

and:

Waiting time in the whole system = Waiting time in the queue + Average process time at the station

$$W = W_q + t_e$$

We will use this relationship later to investigate queuing behaviour.

TYPES OF QUEUING SYSTEM

Conventionally queuing systems are characterized by four parameters:

A – the distribution of arrival times (or more properly inter-arrival times, the elapsed times between arrivals)

B – the distribution of process times

m – the number of servers at each station

b – the maximum number of items allowed in the system.

The most common distributions used to describe A or B are either:

(a) the exponential (or Markovian) distribution denoted by M; or
(b) the general (for example, normal) distribution denoted by G.

So, for example, an M/G/1/5 queuing system would indicate a system with exponentially distributed arrivals, process times described by a general distribution such as a normal distribution, with one server and a maximum number of items allowed in the system of five. This type of notation is called Kendall's notation.

Queuing theory can help us investigate any type of queuing system, but in order to simplify the mathematics, we will deal here only with the two most common situations. Namely,

M/M/m – the exponential arrival and processing times with m servers and no maximum limit to the queue.

G/G/m – the general arrival and processing distributions with m servers and no limit to the queue.

First we will start by looking at the simple case when $m = 1$.

For M/M/1 queuing systems

The formulae for this type of system are as follows:

$$WIP = \frac{u}{1-u}$$

Using Little's law:

$$WIP = \text{Cycle time} \times \text{Throughput time}$$
$$\text{Throughput time} = WIP/\text{Cycle time}$$

Then:

$$\text{Throughput time} = \frac{u}{1-u} \times \frac{1}{r_a} = \frac{t_e}{1-u}$$

and since:

$$\text{Throughput time in the queue} = \text{Total throughput time} - \text{Average processing time}$$

then:

$$W_q = W - t_e$$
$$= \frac{t_e}{1-u} - t_e$$
$$= \frac{t_e - t_e(1-u)}{1-u} = \frac{t_e - t_e - ut_e}{1-u}$$
$$= \frac{u}{(1-u)}t_e$$

Again, using Little's law:

$$WIP_q = r_a \times W_q = \frac{u}{(1-u)}t_e r_a$$

and since:

$$u = \frac{r_a}{r_e} = r_a t_e$$
$$r_a = \frac{u}{t_e}$$

then:

$$WIP_q = \frac{u}{(1-u)} \times t_e \times \frac{u}{t_e}$$
$$= \frac{u^2}{(1-u)}$$

For M/M/m systems

When there are m servers at a station the formula for waiting time in the queue (and therefore all other formulae) needs to be modified. Again, we will not derive these formulae but just state them:

$$W_q = \frac{u^{\sqrt{2(m+1)}-1}}{m(1-u)}t_e$$

From which the other formulae can be derived as before.

For G/G/1 systems

The assumption of exponential arrival and processing times is convenient as far as the mathematical derivation of various formulae are concerned. However, in practice, process times in particular are rarely truly exponential. This is why it is important to have some idea of how a G/G/1 and G/G/m queue behaves. However, exact mathematical relationships are not possible with such distributions. Therefore some kind of approximation is needed. The one here is in common use, and although it is not always accurate, it is for practical purposes. For G/G/1 systems the formula for waiting time in the queue is as follows:

$$W_q = \left(\frac{c_a^2 + c_e^2}{2} \right) \frac{u}{(1 - u)} t_e$$

There are two points to make about this equation. The first is that it is exactly the same as the equivalent equation for an M/M/1 system but with a factor to take account of the variability of the arrival and process times. The second is that this formula is sometimes known as the VUT formula because it describes the waiting time in a queue as a function of:

- V – the variability in the queuing system;
- U – the utilization of the queuing system (that is, demand versus capacity); and
- T – the processing times at the station.

In other words, we can reach the intuitive conclusion that queuing time will increase as variability, utilization or processing time increases.

For G/G/m systems

The same modification applies to queuing systems using general equations and m servers. The formula for waiting time in the queue is now as follows:

$$W_q = \left(\frac{c_a^2 + c_e^2}{2} \right) \left(\frac{u^{\sqrt{2(m+1)}-1}}{m(1 - u)} \right) t_e$$

Worked example 1

'I can't understand it. We have worked out our capacity figures and I am sure that one member of staff should be able to cope with the demand. We know that customers arrive at a rate of around 6 per hour and we also know that any trained member of staff can process them at a rate of 8 per hour. So why is the queue so large and the wait so long? Have at look at what is going on there please.'

Sarah knew that it was probably the variation, both in customers arriving and in how long it took each of them to be processed, that was causing the problem. Over a two-day period when she was told that demand was more or less normal, she timed the exact arrival times and processing times of every customer. Her results were as follows:

The coefficient of variation, c_a, of customer arrivals $= 1$

The coefficient of variation, c_e, of processing time $= 3.5$

The average arrival rate of customers, $r_a = 6$ per hour

therefore the average inter-arrival time $= 10$ minutes

The average processing rate, $r_e = 8$ per hour

therefore the average processing time $= 7.5$ minutes

Thus the utilization of the single server, $u = 6/8 = 0.75$

Using the waiting time formula for a G/G/1 queuing system:

$$W_q = \left(\frac{1 + 12.25}{2}\right)\left(\frac{0.75}{1 - 0.75}\right)7.5$$

$$= 6.625 \times 3 \times 7.5 = 149.06 \text{ minutes}$$

$$= 2.48 \text{ hours}$$

Also because:

$$WIP_q = \text{Cycle time} \times \text{Throughput time}$$

$$= 6 \times 2.48 = 14.68$$

So, Sarah had found out that the average wait that customers could expect was 2.48 hours and that there would be an average of 14.68 people in the queue.

> 'Ok, so I see that it's the very high variation in the processing time that is causing the queue to build up. How about investing in a new computer system that would standardize processing time to a greater degree? I have been talking with our technical people and they reckon that, if we invested in a new system, we could cut the coefficient of variation of processing time down to 1.5. What kind of a difference would this make?'

Under these conditions with $c_e = 1.5$:

$$W_q = \left(\frac{1 + 2.25}{2}\right)\left(\frac{0.75}{1 - 0.75}\right)7.5$$

$$= 1.625 \times 3 \times 7.5 = 36.56 \text{ minutes}$$

$$= 0.61 \text{ hours}$$

Therefore:

$$WIP_q = 6 \times 0.61 = 3.66$$

In other words, reducing the variation of the process time has reduced average queuing time from 2.48 hours down to 0.61 hours and has reduced the expected number of people in the queue from 14.68 down to 3.66.

Worked example 2

A bank wishes to decide how many staff to schedule during its lunch period. During this period customers arrive at a rate of nine per hour and the enquiries that customers have (such as opening new accounts, arranging loans, etc.) take on average 15 minutes to deal with. The bank manager feels that four staff should be on duty during this period but wants to make sure that the customers do not wait more than three minutes on average before they are served. The manager has been told by his small daughter that the distributions that describe both arrival and processing times are likely to be exponential. Therefore:

$$r_a = 9 \text{ per hour, therefore}$$
$$t_a = 6.67 \text{ minutes}$$
$$r_e = 4 \text{ per hour, therefore}$$
$$t_e = 15 \text{ minutes}$$

The proposed number of servers, $m = 4$.

Therefore the utilization of the system is:

$$u = 9/(4 \times 4) = 0.5625$$

From the formula for waiting time for a M/M/m system:

$$
\begin{aligned}
W_q &= \frac{u^{\sqrt{2(m+1)}-1}}{m(1-u)}t_e \\
&= \frac{0.5625^{\sqrt{10}-1}}{4(1-0.5625)} \times 0.25 \\
&= \frac{0.5625^{2.162}}{1.75} \times 0.25 \\
&= 0.042 \text{ hours} \\
&= 2.52 \text{ minutes}
\end{aligned}
$$

Therefore the average waiting time with four servers would be 2.52 minutes, that is well within the manager's acceptable waiting tolerance.

12

Supply chain management

Key questions

> **What is supply chain management?**

> **How should supply chains compete?**

> **How should relationships in supply chains be managed?**

> **How is the supply side managed?**

> **How is the demand side managed?**

> **What are the dynamics of supply chains?**

INTRODUCTION

How is it that businesses such as Apple, Toyota, Zara and Maersk achieve notable results in highly competitive markets? Partly, it is down to their products and services, but partly it is down to the way they mange their supply chains. This is what supply chain management is concerned with – the way operations managers have to look beyond a purely internal view to consider also the performance of suppliers, and suppliers' suppliers, as well as customers, and customers' customers. In addition, increasingly operations are outsourcing many of their activities, buying more of their services and materials from outside specialists. So the way they manage supplies to their operations becomes increasingly important, as does the integration of their distribution activities. In Chapter 5 we explored the structure and scope of operations; by contrast, this chapter is more concerned with how supply chains and networks are subsequently managed.

Figure 12.1 This chapter examines supply chain management

WHAT IS SUPPLY CHAIN MANAGEMENT?

Supply chain management (SCM) is the management of the relationships and flows between the 'string' of operations and processes that produce value in the form of products and services to the ultimate consumer. It is a holistic approach to managing across the boundaries of companies and of processes. Technically, supply *chains* are different to supply *networks*. A supply network is *all* the operations that are linked together so as to provide products and services through to end customers. In large supply networks there can be many hundreds of supply chains of linked operations passing through a single operation (*see* Figs 12.2 and 12.3). The same distinction holds within operations. For internal supply networks, and supply chains, management concerns flow between processes or departments. Confusingly, the terms 'supply network management' and 'supply chain management' are often (mistakenly) used interchangeably. It is also worth noting that the 'flows' in supply chains are not restricted to the downstream flow of products and services from suppliers through to customers. Although the most obvious failure in supply chain management occurs when the downstream flow of products and services fails to meet customer requirements, the root cause may be a failure in the upstream flow of information. Modern supply chain management is as much concerned with managing information flows (upstream and downstream) as it is with managing the flow of products and services.

> * **Operations principle**
>
> The supply chain concept applies to the internal relationships between processes as well as the external relationships between operations.

Internal and external supply chains

Although we often describe supply chains as an interconnection of 'organizations', this does not necessarily mean that these 'organizations' are distinctly separate entities belonging to and managed by different owners. Earlier in the book, we pointed out how the idea of networks can be applied, not just at the supply network level of

> * **Operations principle**
>
> The supply chain concept applies to the internal relationships between processes as well as the external relationships between operations.

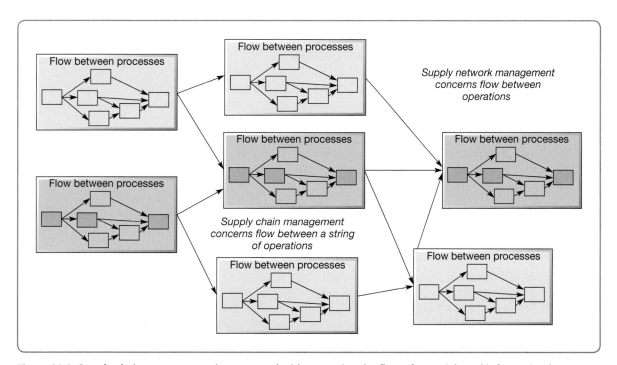

Figure 12.2 Supply chain management is concerned with managing the flow of materials and information between a string of operations that form the strands or 'chains' of a supply network

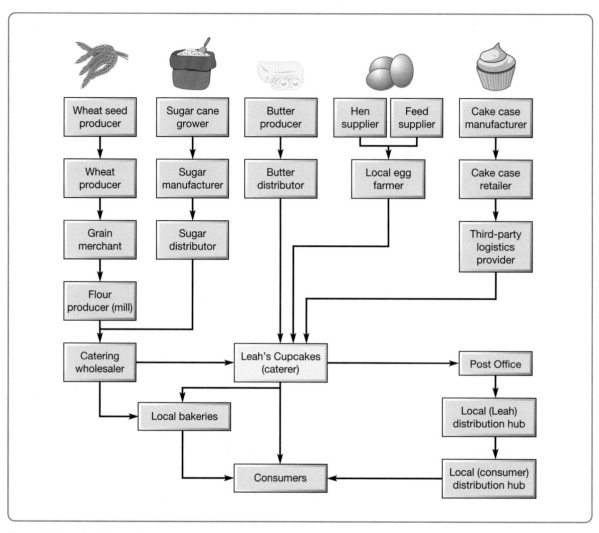

Figure 12.3 A simple supply network for a small catering company

Ocado[1]

The UK grocery market is tough. Giant retailers battle for increasingly cost-conscious customers who also demand quality and service. So, when Mark Richardson, the head of Ocado's technology operation, was promoted to the newly created role of Operations Director it was greeted as an announcement that reinforced the importance of Ocado's high-tech operations processes. It was also seen as reflecting the urgent need for Ocado to get its state-of-the-art distribution centre operating at full efficiency. The company's on-time delivery performance, although still better than its rivals, had been slipping in the months prior to the announcement. This had been an unusual experience for Ocado, which was the only dedicated

online supermarket in the UK and the largest dedicated online supermarket in the world. It had succeeded in reshaping the final 'business-to-consumer' configuration of the traditional food supply chain in its UK home market, and in the process had become one of the most successful online grocers in the world. Tim Steiner, the Chief Executive Officer of Ocado, said: 'For a business that didn't deliver to its first customer until 2002, I'm immensely proud of where Ocado has got to in a few years. To now have our achievements recognised globally is a great accolade for all of our 4,500-strong team.'

But it was not the first. Back in 1999 an Internet grocer called Webvan erupted onto the scene in California.

It gained considerable publicity and more than $1 billion from backers wanting to join in what promised to be the exciting new world of online retailing. However, it proved far more difficult than Webvan's management and investors thought to make a totally new form of supply chain work. Although its market value had been as high as $15 billion by February 2001, Webvan filed for bankruptcy protection with $830 million in accumulated losses. Yet Ocado has thrived. One of its first decisions was to enter into a branding and sourcing arrangement with Waitrose, a leading high-quality UK supermarket, from where the vast majority of Ocado's products are still sourced. But, just as important, it has developed a supply process that provides both relative efficiency and high levels of service (a typical Ocado delivery has a lower overall carbon footprint than walking to your local supermarket). Most online grocers fulfil web orders by gathering goods from the shelf of a local supermarket and then loading them on a truck for delivery. By contrast, from its distribution centre in Hatfield, 20 miles (32 km) north of London, Ocado offers 'doorstep' delivery of grocery products through its supply process to over 1.5 million registered customers' homes. The orders are centrally picked from a single, state-of-the-art, highly automated warehouse (the customer fulfilment centre or 'CFC'). This is a space the size of 10 football pitches; a 15 km system of conveyor belts handles upwards of 8,000 grocery containers an hour, which are then shipped to homes, mainly in the southern part of the UK. The largely automated picking process, which was developed by Ocado's own software engineers, allows the company to pick and prepare groceries for delivery up to seven times faster than its rivals. Making its deliveries of more than 21,000 different products from a central location means it can carry more items than smaller local stores which are more likely to run out of stock. Also, fresh or perishable items that are prepared centrally will have more 'shelf life'. Ocado's food waste, at 0.3 per cent of sales, is the lowest in the industry. The structural advantage of this supply arrangement means that 99 per cent of all orders are fulfilled accurately. Just as important as the physical distribution to the customer's door is the ease of use of the company's website (Ocado.com) and the convenience of booking a delivery slot. Ocado offers reliable one-hour, next-day timeslots in an industry where two-hour timeslots prevail. This is made possible due, again, to the centralized model and world-class processes, systems and controls. The company says that its website is designed to be simple to use and intuitive. Smart lists personalized to each customer offer prompts and ideas so that the absence of any in-store inspiration becomes irrelevant. For a pre-registered customer, a weekly shop can be completed in less than five minutes. The site also has an extensive range of recipes, including some on video, and ideas such as craft activities and lunchbox fillers. Ocado makes a conscious effort to recruit people with customer service skills and then train them as drivers rather than vice versa. Drivers, known as Customer Service Team Members, are paid well above the industry norm and are empowered to process refunds and deal with customer concerns on the doorstep. Yet although as many as 1 million separate items are picked for individual customer orders every day, there are fewer than 80 mistakes.

It was the decision to increase the capacity of this distribution centre that had proved problematic. When its construction started to run behind schedule a vital part of Ocado's supply network was affected. The automated systems had suffered from teething problems, capacity had been restricted, delivery performance adversely influenced, and hiring the extra staff to handle orders had affected profitability. Because Ocado operates what it calls its 'hub and spoke' supply system, with its central CFC (hub) serving regional (spoke) distribution points it is particularly vulnerable to disruption at its 'hubs'. In contrast with traditional 'bricks-and-mortar' supermarkets (Ocado has no 'physical' shops) it delivers direct to customers from its distribution centre rather than from stores. This has led some commentators to label Ocado 'the new Amazon'. 'Not so', say others. 'In some ways it's actually more complex than Amazon's operation. Amazon built a dominant brand in the US, the world's biggest market, by selling books and CDs, which essentially you just stick in an envelope and put a stamp on. That is not the same as having a highly automated warehouse with expensive machines and a huge fleet of delivery vans taking the goods to every house.'

'organization-to-organization' relationships, but also at the 'process-to-process' within-operation level and even at the 'resource-to-resource' within-process level. We also introduced the idea of internal customers and suppliers. Put these two related ideas together and one can understand how some of the issues that we will be discussing in the context of 'organization-to-organization' supply chains can also provide insight into internal 'process-to-process' supply chains.

Tangible and intangible supply chains

Almost all the books, blogs and articles on supply chain management deal with relationships between what we called 'material transformation' operations: that is, operations concerned

> **✳ Operations principle**
>
> The supply chain concept applies to non-physical flow between operations and processes as well as physical flows.

with the creation, movement, storage or sale of physical products. But, as we mentioned in Chapter 5, the idea of supply networks (and therefore, supply chains) applies equally to operations with largely or exclusively intangible inputs and outputs, such as financial services, retail shopping malls, insurance providers, healthcare operations, consultants, universities, and so on. All these operations have suppliers and customers, they all purchase services, they all have to choose how they get their services to consumers – in other words, they all have to manage their supply chains.

HOW SHOULD SUPPLY CHAINS COMPETE?

Supply chain management shares one common, and central, objective – to satisfy the end customer. All stages in the various chains that form the supply network must eventually include consideration of the final customer, no matter how far an individual operation is from the end customer. When a customer decides to make a purchase, he or she triggers action back along a whole series of supply chains in the network. All the businesses in the supply network pass on portions of that end customer's money to each other, each retaining a margin for the value it has added. Thus, each operation in each chain should be satisfying its own customer, but also making sure that eventually the end customer is also satisfied.

For a demonstration of how end customer perceptions of supply satisfaction can be very different from that of a single operation, examine the customer 'decision tree' in Figure 12.4. It charts the hypothetical progress of 100 customers requiring service (or products) from a business (for example, a printer requiring paper from an industrial paper stockist). Supply perfor-

> **✳ Operations principle**
>
> The performance of an operation in a supply chain does not necessarily reflect the performance of the whole supply chain.

mance, as seen by the core operation (the warehouse), is represented by the shaded part of the diagram. It has received 20 orders, 18 of which were 'produced' (shipped to customers) as promised (on time, and in full). However, originally 100 customers may have requested service, 20 of whom found the business did not have appropriate products (did not stock the right paper), 10 of whom could not be served because the products were not available (out of stock), 50 of whom were not satisfied with the price and/or delivery (of whom 10 placed

an order notwithstanding). Of the 20 orders received, 18 were produced as promised (shipped) but 2 were not received as promised (delayed or damaged in transport). So what seems a 90 per cent supply performance is in fact an 8 per cent performance from the customer's perspective.

This is just one operation in a whole network. Include the cumulative effect of similar reductions in performance for all the operations in a chain, and the probability that the end customer is adequately served could become remote. The point here is not that all supply chains have unsatisfactory supply performances (although most supply chains have considerable potential for improvement). Rather it is that the performance both of the supply chain as a whole and of its constituent operations should be judged in terms of how all end customer needs are satisfied.

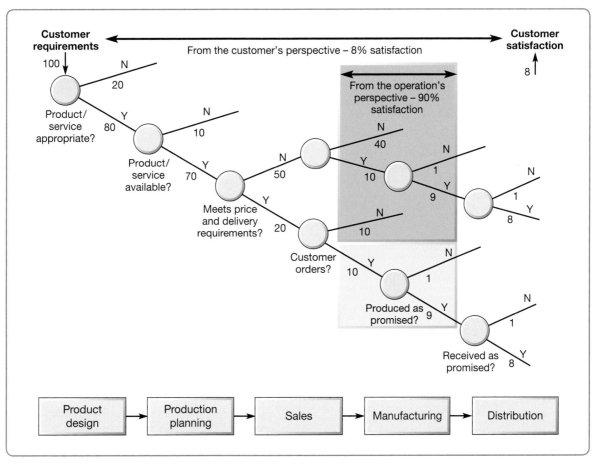

Figure 12.4 **Taking a customer perspective to supply chain performance can lead to very different conclusions**

North Face's sustainable purchasing[2]

Few outdoor clothing brands have had the impact of The North Face since it was founded over 40 years ago in San Francisco. Now, The North Face is part of the VF Corporation, a $9 billion giant that dominates the leisurewear garment market. According to the influential WebTogs blog, 'one of the brilliant things about The North Face jackets is that no matter whether you're off to battle with some sub-zero temperatures or just to chill out and take a load off there is always a North Face jacket to accompany you and keep you warm and snug'. Named for the coldest, most unforgiving side of northern hemisphere mountains, its range of high-performance outdoor apparel, equipment and footwear has developed a reputation for durability, fashionable styling and, increasingly, sustainable sourcing of its materials. VF Corporation's claim is that it 'responsibly manage[s] the industry's most efficient and complex supply chain, which spans multiple geographies, product categories and distribution channels'.

Source: Shutterstock.com: Cappi Thompson

In particular, The North Face is keen to promote sustainable purchasing in its supply chain management. The commitment to sustainability, it says, comes from a desire to protect the natural places associated with how and where its products are used and from its concern about the effects of climate change. As a sign of its determination to pursue sustainable purchasing, The North Face has partnered with the independent bluesign® standard, a Swiss-based organization that promotes '*maximum resource productivity with a view to environmental protection, health and safety represent an assurance for manufacturers and retailers that today's quality criteria are fulfilled in the best possible way and that applicable regulations and limits are complied with*'. The idea of bluesign® is to tackle sustainability at its roots and exclude substances and practices which are potentially hazardous to human health or the environment from all processes in the garment supply chain. So to be considered as a supplier to The North Face any factory must meet the rigorous, independent bluesign® standard which ensures that suppliers address harmful chemicals at the fabric level and meet demanding requirements for consumer and worker safety, efficient resource use and environmental protection. But it is not just the monitoring of suppliers that is important in meeting sustainability targets, says The North Face, product and process innovation is also vital: '*For example, our Venture jacket is a great illustration of innovation going hand-in-hand with environmental sustainability. We reduced the synthetic compounds in the membrane of our Venture product line by 50% by incorporating castor oil, a renewable resource. The castor bean plant, widely grown throughout the tropics, produces oil from its seeds that provides an effective substitute for half of the petroleum-derived materials in the waterproof membrane of our best-selling Venture product line.*'

Performance objectives for supply networks

The objective of any supply network is to meet the requirements of end customers by supplying appropriate products and services through its many supply chains when they are needed at a competitive cost. Doing this requires the supply network to achieve appropriate levels of the five operations performance objectives of quality, speed, dependability, flexibility and cost:

- **Quality** – The quality of a product or service when it reaches the customer is a function of the quality performance of every operation in the chain that supplied it. The implication of this is that errors in each stage of the chain can multiply in their effect on end customer service (if each of seven stages in a supply chain has a 1 per cent error rate, only 93.2 per cent of products or services will be of good quality on reaching the end customer, that is 0.99^7). This is why, only by every stage taking some responsibility for its own *and its suppliers'* performance, can a supply chain achieve high end customer quality.
- **Speed** – This has two meanings in a supply chain context. The first is how fast customers can be served (the elapsed time between a customer requesting a product or service and receiving it in full), an important element in any business's ability to compete. However, fast customer response can be achieved simply by over-resourcing or over-stocking within the supply chain. For example, very large stocks in a retail operation can reduce the chances of a stockout to almost zero, so reducing customer waiting time virtually to zero. Similarly, an accounting firm may be able to respond quickly to customer demand by having a very large number of accountants on standby waiting for demand that may (or may not) occur. An alternative perspective on speed is the time taken for goods and services to move through the chain. So, for example, products that move quickly down a supply chain from raw materials suppliers through to retailers will spend little time as inventory because, to achieve fast throughput time, materials cannot dwell for significant periods as inventory. This in turn reduces the working capital requirements and other inventory costs in the supply chain, so reducing the overall cost of delivering to the end customer. Achieving a balance between speed as responsiveness to customers' demands and speed as fast throughput (although they are not incompatible) will depend on how the supply chain is choosing to compete.
- **Dependability** – Dependability in a supply chain context is similar to speed in as much as one can almost guarantee 'on-time' delivery by keeping excessive resources, such as inventory, within the chain. However, dependability of throughput time is a much more

desirable aim because it reduces uncertainty within the chain. If the individual operations in a chain do not deliver on time as promised, there will be a tendency for customers to over-order, or order early, in order to provide some kind of insurance against late delivery. The same argument applies if there is uncertainty regarding the *quantity* of products or services delivered. This is why delivery dependability is often measured as 'on time, in full' in supply chains.

- **Flexibility** – In a supply chain context this is usually taken to mean the chain's ability to cope with changes and disturbances. Very often this is referred to as supply chain agility. The concept of agility includes previously discussed issues such as focusing on the end customer and ensuring fast throughput and responsiveness to customer needs. But, in addition, agile supply chains are sufficiently flexible to cope with changes, either in the nature of customer demand or in the supply capabilities of operations within the chain.

- **Cost** – In addition to the costs incurred within each operation to transform its inputs into outputs, the supply chain as a whole incurs additional costs that derive from each operation in a chain doing business with each other. These transaction costs may include such things as the costs of finding appropriate suppliers, setting up contractual agreements, monitoring supply performance, transporting products between operations, holding inventories, and so on. Many of the recent developments in supply chain management, such as partnership agreements or reducing the number of suppliers, are an attempt to minimize transaction costs.

OPERATIONS IN PRACTICE — Disaster at Rana Plaza[3]

Do not think that judging supply chain performance is only concerned with the more obvious 'operational' measures. An operations supply chain policies can have profound ethical and reputational consequences. There is no better (and tragic) illustration of this than the collapse of Rana Plaza, a garment factory near Dhaka in Bangladesh. On 24th April 2013 the factory collapsed, killing at least 1,100 people, leaving over 2500 injured and at least 800 children orphaned.. It was a disaster that grabbed the attention of the world. Many well known clothing brands were sourcing products, either directly or indirectly, from factory. It was claimed that local police and an industry association issued a warning that the building was unsafe, but the owners had responded by threatening to fire people who refused carry on working as usual. Understadably there was an immediate call for tighter regulation and oversight by the Bangladesh authorities and for the the predominantly Western retailers who sourced from the Rana Plaza, and similar unsafe factories to accept some of the responsibility for the disaster and change their buying policies. Campaigning organisations

Source: Corbis: Nur Photo / Zakir Hossain Chowdury

including 'Labour Behind the Label', 'War on Want' and 'Made in Europe' urged retailers to be more transparent about their supply chains. They also called for compensation to be paid. But a year after the tragedy the compensation initiative that intended to raise $30m had raised only $15m, despite being backed the UN's International Labour Organisation. Less than half the brands linked to clothes-making at the building had made donations. Benetton and Matalan said they

▶

prefered to support other funds that assissted victims, while the French retailer Auchan claimed that they had no official production taking place in the building when it collapsed so they do not need to contribute towards compensation. Other contributions were relatively small. Walmart, the largest retailer in the world, offered to contribute about $1m compared to more than $8m from the far smaller Primark. It would be 2015 before the fund finally reached its target after a significant anonymous donation. Ineke Zeldenrust of the Clean Clothes Campaign, which had been campaigning since the disaster, said: "This day has been long in coming. Now that all the families impacted by this disaster will finally receive all the money they are owed, they can finally focus on rebuilding their lives. The Bangladeshi authorities also came in for international criticism. For years they had made only relatively weak attempts to enforce national building regulations, especially if the landlords involved were politically well-connected. After the disaster, they promised to apply the laws more rigorously, but such promises had been made before.

So, what are the options for western retailers? One option is to carry on as before and simply source garments from wherever is cheapest. Doing so would obviously be ethically questionable, but would it also carry a reputational cost, or would consumers not enquire too deeply about where garments came from if they were cheap enough? Alternatively, retailers could quit sourcing from Bangladesh until they improve. But that may be difficult to enforce unless they took on the responsibility to police the whole supply chsain right back to the cotton growers. It would also damage all Bangladesh firms, even those who try to abide by safety rules. This in turn could also be damaging to the retailers' reputations. The third option is to stay and try to change how things are done in the country. Even before the Rana Plaza disaster retailers had met with some interested parties and governments to develop a strategy to improve safety in Bangladesh's 5,000 factories. Also some individual retailers had launched initiatives. Walmart had launched a fire-safety training academy and Gap had announced a plan to help factory owners upgrade their plants. However, individual initiatives are no substitute for properly coordinated safety improvements. And anyway, some claim, what right have western companies to impose their rules on another soveregn state?

Lean versus agile supply networks

A distinction is often drawn between supply networks that are managed to emphasize efficiency – *lean supply networks* – and those that emphasize responsiveness and flexibility – *agile supply networks*. These two modes of managing supply chains are reflected in an idea proposed by Professor Marshall Fisher[4] that supply networks serving different markets should be managed in different ways. Even companies that have seemingly similar products or services, in fact, may compete in different ways with different products. For example, shoe manufacturers may produce classics that change little over the years, as well as fashion shoes that last only one season. Chocolate manufacturers have stable lines that have been sold for 50 years, but also produce 'specials' associated with an event or film release, the latter selling only for a matter of months. Hospitals have routine 'standardized' surgical procedures such as cataract removal, but also have to provide emergency post-trauma surgery. Demand for the former products will be relatively stable and predictable, but demand for the latter will be far more uncertain. Also, the profit margin commanded by the innovative product will probably be higher than that of the more functional product. However, the price (and therefore the margin) of the innovative product may drop rapidly once it has become unfashionable in the market. Figure 12.5 illustrates key differences between what are typically described as 'functional' and 'innovative' products.

The supply chain policies that are seen to be appropriate for functional products and innovative products are termed efficient (or lean) and responsive (or agile) supply chain policies, respectively. Efficient supply chain policies include keeping inventories low, especially in the downstream parts of the network, so as to maintain fast throughput and reduce the amount of working capital tied up in the inventory. What inventory

> ✴ **Operations principle**
>
> Supply chains with different end objectives need managing differently.

FUNCTIONAL ⟵————————————————⟶ INNOVATIVE				
Product	**Bucket**	**Bread**	**Mobile phone**	**Fashion handbag**
Time between new product/ service introductions	10 yr+	1 yr–10 yr+	1yr–18 months	3–6 months
Profit margins	Tiny	Small	Very high	High
Volume and variety	High/very low	High/low	Moderate/ moderate	Moderate/ moderate
Demand volatility and uncertainty	Very low	Very low	Moderate	Moderate–high

Figure 12.5 'Functional' versus 'innovative' products

there is in the network is concentrated mainly in the manufacturing operation, where it can keep utilization high and therefore manufacturing costs low. Information must flow quickly up and down the chain from retail outlets back up to the manufacturer so that schedules can be given the maximum amount of time to adjust efficiently. The chain is then managed to make sure that products flow as quickly as possible down the chain to replenish what few stocks are kept downstream.

By contrast, responsive supply chain policy stresses high service levels and responsive supply to the end customer. The inventory in the network will be deployed as closely as possible to the customer. In this way, the chain can still supply even when dramatic changes occur in customer demand. Fast throughput from the upstream parts of the chain will still be needed to replenish downstream stocks, but those downstream stocks are needed to ensure high levels of availability to end customers. Figure 12.6 illustrates how the different supply chain policies match the different market requirements implied by functional and innovative products.

> ❋ **Operations principle**
>
> 'Functional' products and services require lean supply chain management; 'innovative' products and service require agile supply chain management.

HOW SHOULD RELATIONSHIPS IN SUPPLY CHAINS BE MANAGED?

The 'relationship' between operations in a supply chain is the basis on which the exchange of products, services, information and money is conducted. As such, managing supply chains is about managing relationships, because relationships influence the smooth flow between operations and processes. Different forms of relationship will be appropriate in different circumstances. Two dimensions are particularly important – *what* the company chooses to outsource and *who* it chooses to supply it. In terms of *what* is outsourced, key questions are 'how many activities are outsourced?' (from doing everything in-house at one extreme to outsourcing everything at the other extreme), and 'how important are the activities outsourced?' (from outsourcing only trivial activities at one extreme to outsourcing even core activities at the other extreme). We discussed these in detail in Chapter 5 when exploring the scope of supply networks.

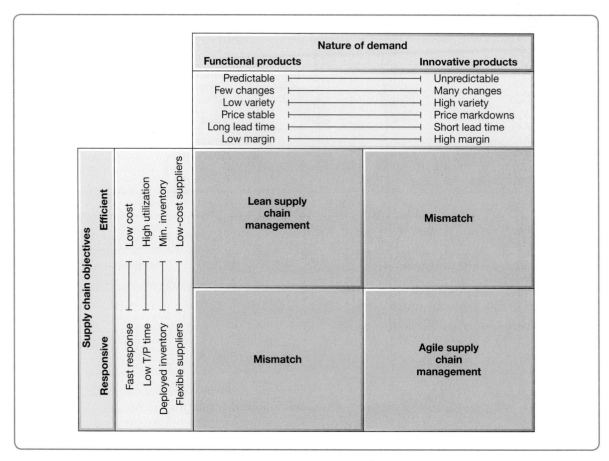

Figure 12.6 Matching the operations resources in the supply chain with market requirements

Source: Adapted from What is the right supply chain for your product?, *Harvard Business Review*, March-April, pp. 105-116 (Fisher, M.C. 1997), Reprinted by permission of Harvard Business Review. Copyright ©1997 by Harvard Business Publishing; all rights reserved.

When dealing with the question of *who* is chosen to supply products and services, again two questions are important: 'how many suppliers will be used by the operation?' (from using many suppliers to perform the same set of activities at one extreme to only one supplier for each activity at the other extreme), and 'how close are the relationships?' (from 'arm's length' relationships at one extreme to close and intimate relationships at the other extreme). Figure 12.7 illustrates this way of characterizing relationships.

Contracting and relationships

There are two basic ingredients of supply interactions that are connected to the horizontal axis of Figure 12.7, namely 'contracts' and 'relationships'. Whatever is the arrangement with its suppliers that a firm chooses to take, it can be described by the balance between contracts and relationships (*see* Fig. 12.8). They complement each other, but can cause major problems with suppliers if they are not balanced. The more a supply agreement is market based with purchases based on relatively short-term arrangements, the more the agreement is likely to be defined in a detailed contract. By contracts we mean explicit, usually written and formal documents that specify the legally binding obligations and roles of both parties in a relationship. The more a supply agreement is based on long-term, usually exclusive, agreements, the more a broad, trust-based, partnership agreement is appropriate. In any one operation a range of different approaches will be required. We will now examine contracts and relationships in more detail.

> **✳ Operations principle**
>
> All supply chain relationships can be described by the balance between their 'contractual' and 'partnership' elements.

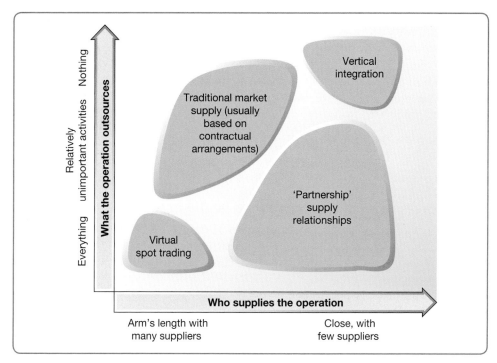

Figure 12.7 Types of supply network arrangement

Contract-based 'transactional' relationships

Contract-based transactional relationships involve purchasing goods and services in a 'pure' market fashion, often seeking the 'best' supplier every time it is necessary to make a purchase. Each transaction effectively becomes a separate decision and as such the orientation is short term. Often, price will dominate the decision-making process with minimal information sharing between the buyer and the supplier, and with no guarantee of further trading between the parties once the goods or services are delivered and payment is made. The *advantages* of contract-based transactional relationships are usually seen as follows:

● They maintain competition between alternative suppliers. This promotes a constant drive between suppliers to provide best value.
● A supplier specializing in a small number of products or services, but supplying them to many customers, can gain natural economies of scale, enabling the supplier to offer the

Figure 12.8 Supply arrangements are a balance between contracting and relationships

products and services at a lower price than if customers performed the activities themselves on a smaller scale.

- There is inherent flexibility in outsourced supplies. If demand changes, customers can simply change the number and type of suppliers – a faster and cheaper alternative to redirecting internal activities.
- Innovations can be exploited no matter where they originate. Specialist suppliers are more likely to come up with innovations that can be acquired faster and cheaper than developing them in-house.

There are, however, *disadvantages* of buying in a purely contractual manner:

- Suppliers owe little loyalty to customers. If supply is difficult, there is no guarantee of receiving supply.
- Choosing who to buy from takes time and effort. Gathering sufficient information and making decisions continually are, in themselves, activities that need to be resourced.
- Short-term contractual relationships of this type may be appropriate when new companies are being considered as more regular suppliers, or when purchases are one-off or very irregular (for example, the replacement of all the windows in a company's office block would typically involve this type of competitive-tendering market relationship).

Long-term 'partnership' relationships

Partnership relationships in supply chains are sometimes seen as a compromise between vertical integration on the one hand (owning the resources which supply you) and transactional relationships on the other. Partnership (or 'collaborative') relationships involve a longer term commitment between buyers and suppliers. These relationships emphasize co-operation, frequent interaction, information sharing and joint problem solving (*see* Fig. 12.9). At their core, partnerships are *close* and *trusting* relationships, the degree to which is influenced by a number of factors:

- *Sharing success* – both partners jointly benefit from the co-operation rather than manoeuvring to maximize their own individual contribution. This may sometimes involve formal profit-sharing arrangements.
- *Long-term expectations* – relatively long-term commitments, but not necessarily permanent ones.
- *Multiple points of contact* – communication not restricted to formal channels, but may take place between many individuals in both organizations.
- *Joint learning* – a relationship commitment to learn from each other's experience.
- *Few relationships* – a commitment on the part of both parties to limit the number of customers or suppliers with whom they do business.

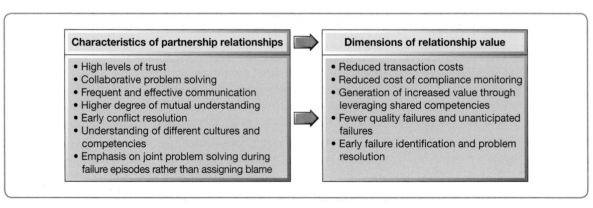

Figure 12.9 The value of partnership relationships

- *Joint co-ordination of activities* – fewer relationships allow joint co-ordination of activities such as the flow of materials or service, payment, and so on.
- *Information transparency* – confidence is built through information exchange between the partners.
- *Joint problem solving* – jointly approaching problems can increase closeness over time.
- *Trust* – probably the key element in partnership relationships. In this context, trust means the willingness of one party to relate to the other on the understanding that the relationship will be beneficial to both, even though that cannot be guaranteed. Trust is widely held to be both the key issue in successful partnerships and, by far, the most difficult element to develop and maintain.

Which type of relationship?

It is very unlikely that any business will find it sensible to engage exclusively in one type of relationship or another. Most businesses will have a portfolio of, possibly, widely differing relationships. Also, there are degrees to which any particular relationship can be managed on a transactional or partnership basis. The real question is: 'where, on the spectrum from transactional to partnership, should each relationship be positioned?' And, while there is no simple formula for choosing the 'ideal' form of relationship in each case, there are some important factors that can sway the decision. The most obvious issue will concern how a business intends to compete in its marketplace. If price is the main competitive factor then the relationship could be determined by which approach offers the highest potential savings. On the one hand, market-based contractual relationships could minimize the actual price paid for purchased products and services, while partnerships could minimize the transaction costs of doing business. If a business is competing primarily on product or service innovation, the type of relationship may depend on where innovation is likely to happen. If innovation depends on close collaboration between supplier and customer, partnership relationships are needed. On the other hand, if suppliers are busily competing to outdo each other in terms of their innovations, and especially if the market is turbulent and fast growing (as with many software and Internet-based industries), then it may be preferable to retain the freedom to change suppliers quickly using market mechanisms. However, if markets are very turbulent, partnership relationships may reduce the risks of being unable to secure supply.

> ✳ **Operations principle**
>
> All supply chain relationships can be described by the balance between their 'contractual' and 'partnership' elements.

The main differences between the two ends of this relationship spectrum concerns whether a customer sees advantage in long-term or short-term relationships. Contractual relationships can be either long or short term, but there is no guarantee of anything beyond the immediate contract. They are appropriate when short-term benefits are important. Many relationships and many businesses are best concentrating on the short term (especially if, without short-term success, there is no long term). Partnership relationships are by definition long term. There is a commitment to work together over time to gain mutual advantage. The concept of mutuality is important here. A supplier does not become a 'partner' merely by being called one. True partnership implies mutual benefit, and often mutual sacrifice. Partnership means giving up some freedom of action in order to gain something more beneficial over the long term. If it is not in the culture of a business to give up some freedom of action, it is very unlikely ever to make a success of partnerships. Opportunities to develop relationships can be limited by the structure of the market itself. If the number of potential suppliers is small, there may be few opportunities to use market mechanisms to gain any kind of supply advantage and it would probably be sensible to develop a close relationship with at least one supplier. On the other hand, if there are many potential suppliers, and especially if it is easy to judge the capabilities of the suppliers, contractual relationships are likely to be best.

> ✳ **Operations principle**
>
> True 'partnership' relationships involve mutual sacrifice as well as mutual benefit.

HOW IS THE SUPPLY SIDE MANAGED?

The ability of any process or operation to produce outputs is dependent on the inputs it receives. So good supply management is a necessary (but not sufficient) condition for effective operations management in general. Once a decision has been made to buy products or services (as opposed to make or do in-house), managers must decide on sourcing strategies for different products and services, select appropriate suppliers, manage ongoing supply and improve suppliers' capabilities over time. These activities are usually the responsibility of the purchasing or procurement function within the business. Purchasing should provide a vital link between the operation itself and its suppliers. They all should understand the requirements of all the processes within their own operation and also the capabilities of the suppliers who could potentially provide products and services for the operation.

Sourcing strategy

In Chapter 5, we outlined a number of issues concerning the configuration of a supply network. Changing the shape of the supply network may involve reducing the number of suppliers to the operation so as to develop closer relationships, and bypassing or disintermediating operations in the network. Here, we go a bit further by examining four key sourcing approaches: multiple sourcing, single sourcing, delegated sourcing and parallel sourcing.

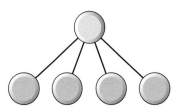

Multiple sourcing involves obtaining a product or service component from more than one supplier. It is commonly seen in competitive markets where switching costs are low and performance objectives are primarily focused on price and dependability. Multiple sourcing can help maintain competition in the supply market, reduce supply risk and increase flexibility in the face of supplier failure or changes in customer demand. In addition, some firms like to use multiple sourcing to prevent supplier dependence, thus allowing for changes in purchase volumes without the risk of supplier bankruptcy. However, the disadvantage of multiple sourcing is that it becomes hard to encourage supplier commitment and as such limits the opportunity to develop a partnership approach to supply management.

Single sourcing involves buying all of one product or service component from a single supplier. Often these components represent a high proportion of total spend or are of strategic importance. In other cases, however, firms simply prefer the simplicity (and reduced transaction costs) of single sourcing. Many single-source arrangements have a longer term focus than multiple-source arrangements and focus on a wider range of performance objectives. However, single-source arrangements can carry an increased risk of lock-in and a reduction in the firm's bargaining power.

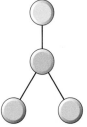

Delegated sourcing involves a tiered approach to managing supplier relationships. This means that one supplier is responsible for delivering an entire sub-assembly as opposed to a single part, or a package of services as opposed to an individual service. This has the advantage of reducing the number of tier 1 suppliers significantly while simultaneously allowing a focus on strategic partners. However, delegated sourcing can alter the dynamics of the supply market and risk creating 'mega-suppliers' with significant power in the network.

Parallel sourcing has the aim of providing the advantages of both multiple sourcing and single sourcing simultaneously. It involves having single-source relationships for components or services for different product models or service packages. If a supplier is deemed unsatisfactory, it is possible to switch to the alternative supplier who currently provides the same component but for a different model. The advantage of this sourcing approach is that it maintains competition and allows for switching. However, managing delegated sourcing arrangements is relatively complex.

Making the sourcing strategy decision

Given that each sourcing strategy has its advantages and disadvantages, a key challenge is to decide which is most suitable. Here, we can explore two key questions: what is the risk in the supply market, and what is the criticality of the product or service to the business? Considering risk, we can consider the number of alternative suppliers, how easy it is to switch from one supplier to another, exit barriers, and the cost of bringing operations back in-house. For criticality, mangers may consider a product or service component's importance in terms of volume purchased, percentage of total purchase cost, or the impact on business growth. By looking at these two dimensions, it is possible to position product or service components broadly in one of four key quadrants – leverage, strategic, non-critical or bottleneck[5] – and to select appropriate sourcing strategies. Figure 12.10 shows this for a high-end bicycle manufacturer:

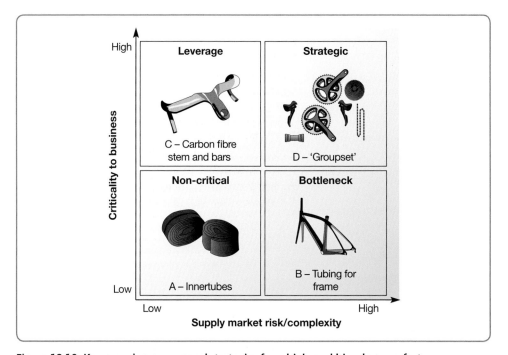

Figure 12.10 Key sourcing groups and strategies for a high-end bicycle manufacturer
Source: Adapted from Purchasing must become supply management, *Harvard Business Review*, September (Kraljic, Peter 1983), Reprinted by permission of Harvard Business Review. Copyright ©1983 by Harvard Business Publishing; all rights reserved.

- *Non-critical:* The innertubes (A) account for a relatively low proportion of the total cost of the product and, with the large number of alternative suppliers, the supply risk is low. For the non-critical purchase category, multiple-sourcing strategies tend to be most common.
- *Bottleneck:* The tubing (B) on the bike frame is a particular grade of carbon and is specially moulded for different types of model. While this component accounts for a relatively low proportion of the total cost of the product, the limited supply alternatives and high switching costs increase risk. For products and services in the bottleneck category, single sourcing is common because of a lack of choice in the supply market.
- *Leverage:* The carbon fibre stem and bars (C) account for a high proportion of the cost of this bicycle but are relatively easy to source as there are a relatively large number of available suppliers. For leverage products and services, bundling of requirements allows a shift towards delegated sourcing in many cases.
- *Strategic:* The 'groupset' (D) refers to the gearing systems on the bicycle. These are complex to source, and account for a high proportion of total spending. In addition, there are few suppliers capable of manufacturing these components to sufficient quality for high-end bikes and so the cost of switching is high. For strategic products and services, single-sourcing approaches remain popular. However, given the associated risks of single sourcing, many firms have moved to delegated or parallel approaches for this group of purchases.

Supplier selection

In conjunction with deciding on sourcing strategies for different products and services, organizations must select appropriate suppliers. Given the trends of outsourcing, supply base rationalization, supplier involvement in new product/service development, and longer term supplier relationships, the selection process is all the more important to the success of organizations. Figure 12.11 outlines the four key steps in supplier selection:

- *Initial qualification:* This is aimed at reducing possible suppliers to a manageable set for subsequent assessment. Pre-qualification criteria often include financial viability, accreditation (such as ISO 9000), location (for example, only considering suppliers located within a certain distance of a manufacturer) and scale.
- *Agree measurement criteria:* Determining the relative importance of key performance objectives (quality, speed, dependability, flexibility, cost, and others) is critical in the selection of suppliers. For key performance objectives, measurable criteria are then needed. For example, for cost a firm might consider unit price, pricing terms (for instance, volume discounts), exchange rate effects, and so on.
- *Obtain relevant information:* As firms narrow down to a smaller group of potential suppliers, further information can be gathered to inform the selection decision. This may include additional levels of detail in delivery options and cost structure, site visits, and tests (for example, test orders in small quantities) to assess competence prior to potential ramp-up of supply.
- *Make selection:* Having obtained a group of viable alternatives, selection may be supported using various multi-criteria decision-making models including the weighted score method

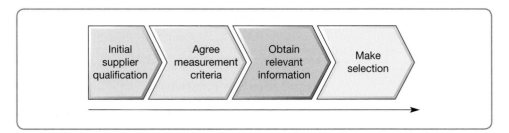

Figure 12.11 The supplier selection process

(see the worked example below) and analytical hierarchy process (AHP). These models aim to provide quantifiable information for key selection criteria and a weighting of their relative importance to allow for an objective assessment of different suppliers. Total cost of ownership (TCO) is an alternative approach that seeks to provide detailed information on all possible costs (rather than simply product or service price) associated with procurement to reach more 'rational' decisions during supplier selection.

Worked example

A hotel chain has decided to change its supplier of cleaning supplies because its current supplier has become unreliable in its delivery performance. The two alternative suppliers that the chain is considering have been evaluated, on a 1–10 scale, against the criteria shown in Table 12.1. The table also shows the relative importance of each criterion, also on a 1–10 scale. Based on this evaluation, Supplier B has the superior overall score.

Table 12.1 **Weighted supplier selection criteria for the hotel chain**

Factor	Weight	Supplier A score	Supplier B score
Cost performance	10	8 ($8 \times 10 = 80$)	5 ($5 \times 10 = 50$)
Quality record	10	7 ($7 \times 10 = 70$)	9 ($9 \times 10 = 90$)
Delivery speed promised	7	5 ($5 \times 7 = 35$)	5 ($5 \times 7 = 35$)
Delivery speed achieved	7	4 ($4 \times 7 = 28$)	8 ($8 \times 7 = 56$)
Dependability record	8	6 ($6 \times 8 = 48$)	8 ($8 \times 8 = 64$)
Range provided	5	8 ($8 \times 5 = 40$)	5 ($5 \times 5 = 25$)
Innovation capability	4	6 ($6 \times 4 = 24$)	9 ($9 \times 4 = 36$)
Total weighted score		325	356

Managing ongoing supply

Managing supply relationships is not just a matter of choosing the right suppliers and then leaving them to get on with day-to-day supply. It is also about ensuring that suppliers are given the right information and encouragement to maintain smooth supply, and that internal inconsistency does not negatively affect their ability to supply. A basic requirement is that some mechanism should be set up that ensures the two-way flow of information between customer and supplier. It is easy for both suppliers and customers simply to forget to inform each other of internal developments that could affect supply. Customers may see suppliers as having the responsibility for ensuring appropriate supply 'under any circumstances'. Suppliers themselves may be reluctant to inform customers of any potential problems with supply because they see it as risking the relationship. Yet, especially if customer and supplier see themselves as 'partners', the free flow of information, and a mutually supportive tolerance of occasional problems, is the best way to ensure smooth supply. Often day-to-day supplier relationships are damaged because of internal inconsistencies. For example, one part of a business may be asking a supplier for some special service beyond the strict nature of their agreement, while another part of the business is not paying suppliers on time.

The volcanic ash from Iceland that disrupted air transport across Europe provided a pre-view of how natural disasters could throw global supply chains into disarray, espe-cially those that had adopted the lean, low-inventory, just-in-time philosophy. That was in 2010. Yet the following year an even more severe disaster caused chaos in all supply chains with a Japanese connection, and that is a lot of supply chains. It was a quadruple disaster: an earthquake off Japan's east-ern coast, one of the largest ever recorded, caused a tsunami that killed thousands of people and caused a meltdown at a nearby nuclear power plant, which necessitated huge evacuations and nationwide power shortages. The effect on global supply net-works was immediate and drastic. Sony Corporation shut down some of its operations in Japan because of the ongoing power shortages and announced that it was giving its staff time off during the summer (when air-conditioning needs are high) to save energy. Japanese automobile companies' production was among the worst affected. Toyota suspended production at most of its Japanese plants, and reduced and then suspended out-put from its North American and European operations. Nissan said it would be suspending its UK production for three days at the end of the month due to a shortfall in parts from Japan. Honda announced that it was halving production at its factory in Swindon in the south-west of the UK. However, the disruption was not as severe as it might have been. Honda said that the vast majority of the parts used in Swindon are made in Europe, and added that its flexible working policy would allow it to make up for the lost production later in the year.

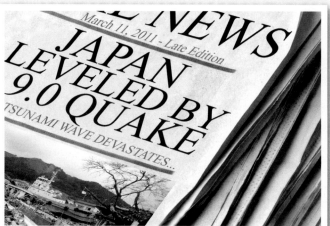

Source: Shutterstock.com; Justasc

In the longer term, the disruption caused a debate among practitioners about how supply chains could be made more robust. Hans-Paul Bürkner, Chief of the Boston Consulting Group, said, 'It is very important now to think the extreme. You have to have some buffers.' Some commenta-tors even drew parallels with financial meltdowns, claiming that just as some financial institutions proved 'too big to fail', some Japanese suppliers may be too crucial to do without. For example, at the time of the disruption, two companies, Mitsubishi Gas Chemical and Hitachi Chemical, controlled about 90 per cent of the market for a specialty resin used to make the microchips that go into smartphones and other devices. Both firms' plants were damaged and the effect was felt around the world. So maybe suppliers who have near monopolies on vital components should spread their production facilities geographically. Similarly, businesses that rely on single suppliers may be more willing to split their orders between two or more suppliers.

Service-level agreements

Some organizations bring a degree of formality into supplier relationships by encouraging (or requiring) all suppliers to agree service-level agreements (SLAs). SLAs are formal definitions of the dimensions of service and the relationship between operations: for example, between a sup-plier and its customer, or between an internal supplier of service and its internal customer. SLAs are also an important tool in quality management and are described more fully in Chapter 17.

Improving supplier capabilities

In any relationship other than pure market-based transactional relationships, it is in a custom-er's long-term interests to take some responsibility for developing supplier capabilities. Helping a supplier to improve not only enhances the service (and hopefully price) from the supplier, but may also lead to greater supplier loyalty and long-term commitment. This is why some particularly successful businesses invest in supplier development teams whose responsibility is to help suppliers to improve their own operations processes. Of course, committing the resources to help suppliers is only worthwhile if it improves the effectiveness of the supply chain as a whole. Nevertheless, the potential for such enlightened self-interest can be significant.

How customers and suppliers see each other[7]

One of the major barriers to supplier development is the mismatch between how customers and suppliers perceive both what is required and how the relationship is performing. Exploring potential mismatches is often a revealing exercise, both for customers and for suppliers. Figure 12.12 illustrates this. It shows that gaps may exist between four sets of ideas. As a customer you (presumably) have an idea about what you really want from a supplier. This may, or may not, be formalized in the form of an SLA. But no SLA can capture everything about what is required. There may be a gap between how you as a customer interpret what is required and how the supplier interprets it. This is the *requirements perception gap*. Similarly, as a customer, you (again presumably) have a view on how your supplier is performing in terms of fulfilling your requirements. That may not coincide with how your supplier believes it is performing. This is the *fulfilment perception gap*. Both these gaps are a function of the effectiveness of the communication between supplier and customer. But there are also two other gaps. The gap between what you want from your supplier and how it is performing indicates the type of development that, as a customer, you should be giving to your supplier. Similarly, the gap between your supplier's perceptions of your needs and its performance indicates how the supplier should initially see itself improving its own performance. Ultimately, of course, the supplier's responsibility for improvement should coincide with the customer's views of requirements and performance.

> **✷ Operations principle**
> Unsatisfactory supplier relationships can be caused by requirements and fulfilment perception gaps.

Global sourcing

One of the major supply chain developments of recent years has been the expansion in the proportion of products and (occasionally) services which businesses are willing to source from outside their home country; this is called global sourcing. It is the process of identifying,

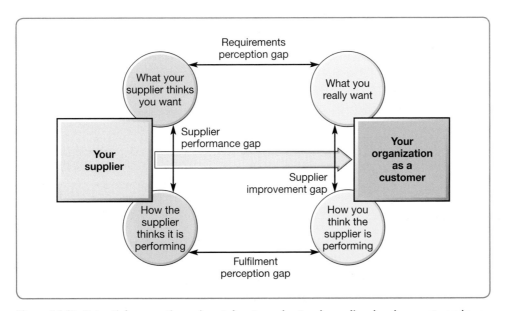

Figure 12.12 Potential perception mismatches to understand supplier development needs

evaluating, negotiating and configuring supply across multiple geographies. Traditionally, even companies which exported their goods and services all over the world (that is, they were international on their demand side) still sourced the majority of their supplies locally (that is, they were not international on their supply side). This has changed – companies are now increasingly willing to look further afield for their supplies, and for very good reasons. There can be significant cost savings by sourcing from low-cost-country suppliers.[8] And tougher world competition has forced companies to look to reducing their total costs. Given that in many industries bought-in items are the largest single part of operations costs, an obvious strategy is to source from wherever is cheapest. But it is not just cost that has driven the move towards global sourcing. Partly it is also because the barriers to sourcing outside one's own country have been lowered. The formation of trading blocs in different parts of the world has had the effect of lowering tariff barriers, at least within those blocs. Transportation infrastructures are considerably more sophisticated and cheaper than they once were. Super-efficient port operations in Rotterdam and Singapore, for example, integrated road–rail systems, jointly developed auto route systems, and cheaper air freight have all reduced some of the cost barriers to international trade.

There are of course problems with global sourcing. The risks of increased complexity and increased distance need managing carefully. Suppliers which are a significant distance away need to transport their products across long distances. The risks of delays and hold-ups can be far greater than when sourcing locally (see the 'Operations in practice' case on the problems that the tsunami effect raised). Also, negotiating with suppliers whose native language is different from one's own makes communication more difficult and can lead to misunderstandings over contract terms. Therefore, global sourcing decisions require businesses to balance cost, performance, service and risk factors, not all of which are obvious. These factors are important in global sourcing because of non-price or 'hidden' cost factors such as cross-border freight and handling fees, complex inventory stocking and handling requirements, and even more complex administrative, documentation and regulatory requirements.

Global sourcing and social responsibility

Although the responsibility of operations to ensure that they only deal with ethical suppliers has always been important, the expansion of global sourcing has brought the issue into sharper focus. Local suppliers can (to some extent) be monitored relatively easily. However, when suppliers are located around the world, often in countries with different traditions and ethical standards, monitoring becomes more difficult. Not only that, but also there may be genuinely different views of what is regarded as ethical practice. Social, cultural and religious differences can easily make for mutual incomprehension regarding each other's ethical perspective. This is why many companies are putting significant effort into articulating and clarifying their supplier selection policies. The 'Operations in practice' case on Levi Strauss's policy is typical of an enlightened organization's approach to global sourcing.

OPERATIONS IN PRACTICE — **Extracts from Levi Strauss's global sourcing policy[9]**

Our Global Sourcing and Operating Guidelines help us to select business partners who follow workplace standards and business practices that are consistent with our company's values. These requirements are applied to every contractor who manufactures or finishes products for Levi Strauss & Co. Trained inspectors closely audit and monitor compliance among approximately 600 cutting, sewing, and finishing contractors in more than 60 countries...The numerous countries where Levi Strauss & Co. has existing or future business interests present a variety of cultural, political, social and economic circumstances...The Country Assessment Guidelines help us assess any issue that might present concern in light of the ethical principles we have set for ourselves. Specifically, we assess how...the...Health and Safety Conditions, Human Rights Environment,

▶

the Legal System and the Political, Economic and Social Environment would protect the company's commercial interests and brand/corporate image. The company's employment standards state that they will only do business with partners who adhere to the following guidelines:

- *Child Labor*: Use of child labor is not permissible. Workers can be no less than 15 years of age and not younger than the compulsory age to be in school. We will not utilize partners who use child labor in any of their facilities.
- *Prison Labor/Forced Labor*: We will not utilize prison or forced labor in contracting relationships in the manufacture and finishing of our products. We will not utilize or purchase materials from a business partner utilizing prison or forced labor.
- *Disciplinary Practices*: We will not utilize business partners who use corporal punishment or other forms of mental or physical coercion.
- *Working Hours*: While permitting flexibility in scheduling, we will identify local legal limits on work hours and seek business partners who do not exceed them except for appropriately compensated overtime. Employees should be allowed at least one day off in seven.
- *Wages and Benefits*: We will only do business with partners who provide wages and benefits that comply with any applicable law and match the prevailing local manufacturing or finishing industry practices.
- *Freedom of Association*: We respect workers' rights to form and join organizations of their choice and

Source: Alamy Images: Helen Sessions

to bargain collectively. We expect our suppliers to respect the right to free association and the right to organize and bargain collectively without unlawful interference.
- *Discrimination*: While we recognize and respect cultural differences, we believe that workers should be employed on the basis of their ability to do the job, rather than on the basis of personal characteristics or beliefs. We will favor business partners who share this value.
- *Health & Safety*: We will only utilize business partners who provide workers with a safe and healthy work environment. Business partners who provide residential facilities for their workers must provide safe and healthy facilities.

HOW IS THE DEMAND SIDE MANAGED?

The management of demand-side relationships will depend partly on the nature of demand, in particular how uncertain it is. Knowing the exact demands that customers are going to require allows a supplier to plan its own internal processes in a systematic manner. As we outlined in Chapter 10, this type of demand is called 'dependent' demand; it is relatively predictable because it is dependent upon some factor that is itself predictable. For example, supplying tyres to the bicycle manufacturer described above involves examining the manufacturing schedules in its manufacturing plant and deriving the demand for tyres from these. If 200 bicycles are to be manufactured on a particular day, then it is simple to calculate that 400 tyres will be demanded by the plant (each bicycle has two tyres). Because of this, the tyres can be ordered from the tyre manufacturer to a delivery schedule which is closely in line with the demand for tyres from the plant. In fact, the demand for every part of the plant will be derived from the assembly schedule for the finished bicycles. Manufacturing instructions and purchasing requests will all be dependent upon this figure. Managing internal process networks when external demand is dependent is largely a matter of calculating, in as precise a way as possible, the internal consequences of demand. Materials requirements planning, treated in Chapter 14, is the best-known dependent demand approach.

But, again as we noted in Chapter 10, not all operations have such predictable demand. Some operations are subject to independent demand. There is a random element in demand which is virtually independent of any obvious factors. They, like their suppliers, are required to supply demand without having any firm forward visibility of customer orders. In Chapter 10 we used the example of a drive-in tyre replacement service. It cannot predict either the volume or the specific needs of customers. It must make decisions on how many and what type of tyres to stock, based on demand forecasts and in light of the risks it is prepared to take of running out of stock. Managing internal process networks when external demand is independent involves making 'best guesses' concerning future demand, attempting to put the resources in place to satisfy this demand, and attempting to respond quickly if actual demand does not match the forecast. Inventory management, which we treat in Chapter 13, is a typical approach to this situation.

Logistics services

Logistics means moving products to customers. Sometimes the term 'physical distribution management' or simply 'distribution' is used as being analogous to logistics. An important decision is how much of the logistical process of organizing the movement of goods to trust to outside service providers. The extent and integration of this type of service provision is often referred to as first-, second-, third- or fourth-party logistics (or 1PL, 2PL, 3PL, 4PL, for short). However, the distinction between the PL classifications can sometimes be blurred, with different firms using slightly different definitions:

- *First-party logistics (1PL)* – is when, rather than outsourcing the activity, the owner of whatever is being transported organizes and performs product movements itself. For example, a manufacturing firm will deliver directly, or a retailer such as a supermarket will collect products from a supplier. The logistics activity is an entirely internal process.
- *Second-party logistics (2PL)* – is when a firm decides to outsource or subcontract logistics services over a specific segment of a supply chain. It could involve a road, rail, air or maritime shipping company being hired to transport, and if necessary store, products from a specific collection point to a specific destination.
- *Third-party logistics (3PL)* – is when a firm contracts a logistics company to work with other transport companies to manage the firm's logistics operations. It is a broader concept than 2PL and can involve transportation, warehousing, inventory management and even packaging or repackaging products. Generally 3PL involves services that are scaled and customized to a customer's specific needs.
- *Fourth-party logistics (4PL)* – is a yet broader idea than 3PL. Accenture, the consulting group, originally used the term '4PL'. Accenture's definition of 4PL is: '*A 4PL is an integrator that assembles the resources, capabilities, and technology of its own organization and other organizations to design, build and run comprehensive supply chain solutions.*' 4PL service suppliers pool transport capabilities, processes, technology support and co-ordination activities to provide customized supply chain services for part or all of a client's supply chain. 4PL firms can manage all aspects of a client's supply chain. They may act as a single interface between the client and multiple logistics service providers, and are often separate organizational entities founded on a long-term basis or as a joint venture between a client and one or more partners.
- *5PL?* – you guessed it! Almost inevitably, some firms are selling themselves as fifth-party logistics providers, mainly by defining themselves as broadening the scope further to e-business.

Logistics management and the Internet

In fact, Internet-based communication has had a significant impact on physical distribution management. Information can be made available more readily along the distribution chain, so that transport companies, warehouses, suppliers and customers can share knowledge of where goods are in the chain (and sometimes where they are going next). This allows the operations within the chain to co-ordinate their activities more readily. It also gives the potential for some significant cost savings. For example, an important issue for transportation companies is back-loading. When the company is contracted to transport goods from A to B, its vehicles may have to return from B to A empty. Back-loading means finding a potential customer which wants its goods transported from B to A in the right time frame. With the increase in information availability through the Internet, the possibility of finding a back-load increases. Companies that can fill their vehicles on both the outward and return journeys will have significantly lower costs per distance travelled than those whose vehicles are empty for half the total journey. Similarly, Internet-based technology that allows customers visibility of the progress of distribution can be used to enhance the perception of customer service. 'Track-and-trace' technologies, for example, allow package distribution companies to inform and reassure customers that their service is being delivered as promised.

Perhaps the most significant recent development of Internet-based technologies on logistics is the 'Internet of Things' (or 'IoT'; *see* Chapter 8 for a full explanation). Its use of 'automatic identification technologies' such as radio frequency identification (RFID) to trace the progress of items through a supply chain means that during every stage of manufacturing and distribution, storage and sale of each product can be individually tracked and the information used to co-ordinate supply.

Customer relationship management (CRM)

There is a story (which may or may not be true) that is often quoted to demonstrate the importance of using information technology to analyse customer information. It goes like this. Wal-Mart, the huge US-based supermarket chain, did an analysis of customers' buying habits and found a statistically significant correlation between purchases of beer and purchases of diapers (nappies), especially on Friday evenings. The reason? Fathers were going to the supermarket to buy nappies for their babies, and because fatherhood restricted their ability to go out for a drink as often, they would also buy beer. Supposedly this led the supermarket to start locating nappies next to the beer in their stores, resulting in increased sales of both.

Whether this is true or not, it does illustrate the potential of analyzing data to understand customers. This is the basis of customer relationship management (CRM). It is a method of learning more about customers' needs and behaviours in order to develop stronger relationships with them. Although CRM usually depends on information technology, it is misleading to see it as a 'technology'. Rather it is a process that helps to understand customers' needs and develop ways of meeting those needs while maximizing profitability. CRM brings together all the disparate information about customers so as to gain insight into their behaviour and their value to the business. It helps to sell products and services more effectively and increase revenues by:

- providing services and products that are exactly what customers want;
- retaining existing customers and discovering new ones;
- offering better customer service;
- cross-selling products more effectively.

CRM tries to help organizations understand who their customers are and what their value is over a lifetime. It does this by building a number of steps into its customer interface processes. First, the business must determine the needs of its customers and how best to meet those needs. For example, banks may keep track of its customers' age and lifestyle so that it can offer appropriate products like mortgages or pensions to them when they fit their needs. Second, the business must examine all the different ways and parts of the organization where customer-related information is collected, stored and used. Businesses may interact with customers in different ways and through different people. For example, salespeople, call centres, technical staff, operations and distribution managers may all, at different times, have contact with customers. CRM systems should integrate this data. Third, all customer-related data must be analysed to obtain a holistic view of each customer and identify where service can be improved.

Critical commentary

Despite its name, some critics of CRM argue that the greatest shortcoming is that it is insufficiently concerned with directly helping customers. CRM systems are sold to executives as a way to increase efficiency, force standardized processes and gain better insight into the state of the business. But they rarely address the need to help organizations resolve customer problems, answer customer questions faster, or help them solve their own problems. This may explain the trend towards a shift in focus from automating internal front-office functions to streamlining processes such as online customer support.

Customer development

Earlier in the chapter, Figure 12.12 illustrated some of the gaps in perception and performance that can occur between customers and suppliers. The purpose then was to demonstrate the nature of supplier development. The same approach can be used to analyse the nature of requirements and performance with customers. In this case the imperative is to understand customer perceptions, both of their requirements and their view of your performance, and feed these into your own performance improvement plans. What is less common, but can be equally valuable, is to use these gaps (shown in Fig. 12.13) to examine the question of whether customer requirements and perceptions of performance are either accurate or reasonable. For example, customers may be placing demands on suppliers without fully considering their consequences. It may be that slight modifications in what is demanded would not inconvenience customers and yet would provide significant benefits to suppliers that could then be passed on to customers. Similarly, customers may be incompetent at measuring supplier performance, in which case the benefits of excellent supplier service will not be recognized. So, just as customers have a responsibility to help develop their own supplier's performance, in their own as well as their supplier's interests, suppliers have a responsibility to develop their customer's understanding of how supply should be managed.

> ✱ Operations principle
>
> Unsatisfactory customer relationships can be caused by requirement and fulfilment perception gaps.

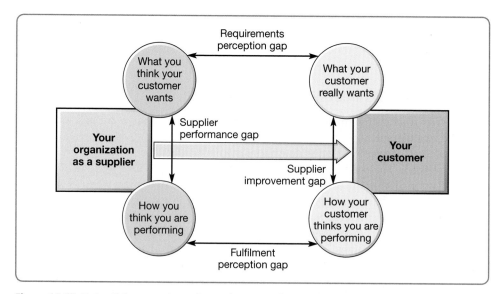

Figure 12.13 Potential perception mismatches to understand customer development needs

WHAT ARE THE DYNAMICS OF SUPPLY CHAINS?

There are dynamics that exist between firms in supply chains that cause errors, inaccuracies and volatility, and these increase for operations further upstream in the supply chain. This effect is known as the bullwhip effect,[10] so called because a small disturbance at one end of the chain causes increasingly large disturbances as it works its way towards the end. Its main cause is a perfectly understandable and rational desire by the different links in the supply chain to manage their levels of activity and inventory sensibly. To demonstrate this, examine the production rate and stock levels for the supply chain shown in Table 12.2. This is a four-stage supply chain where an original equipment manufacturer (OEM) is served by three tiers of suppliers. The demand from the OEM's market has been running at a rate of 100 items per period, but in period 2, demand reduces to 95 items per period. All stages in the supply chain work on the principle that they will keep in stock one period's demand. This is a simplification but not a gross one. Many operations gear their inventory levels to their demand rate. The column headed 'stock' for each level of supply shows the starting stock at the beginning of the period and the finish stock at the end of the period. At the beginning of period 2, the OEM has 100 units in stock (this being the rate of demand up to period 2). Demand in period 2 is 95 and so the OEM knows that it would need to produce sufficient items to finish up at the end of the period with 95 in stock (this being the new demand rate). To do this, it needs only manufacture 90 items; these, together with 5 items taken out of the starting stock, will supply demand and leave a finished stock of 95 items. The beginning of period 3 finds the OEM with 95 items in stock. Demand is also 95 items and therefore its production rate to maintain a stock level of 95 will be 95 items per period. The OEM now operates at a steady rate of

Table 12.2 Fluctuations of production levels along supply chain in response to small change in end customer demand (Starting stock (a) + Production (b) = Finishing stock (c) + Demand, that is production in previous tier down (d). See explanation in text. Note that all stages in the supply chain keep one period's inventory, c = d.)

Period	Third-tier supplier		Second-tier supplier		First-tier supplier		Original equipment mfr		Demand
	Prodn.	Stock	Prodn.	Stock	Prodn.	Stock	Prodn.	Stock	
1	100	100	100	100	100	100	100	100	100
		100		100		100		100	
2	20	100	60	100	80	100	90	100	95
		60		80		90		95	
3	180	60	120	80	100	90	95	95	95
		120		100		95		95	
4	60	120	90	100	95	95	95	95	95
		90		95		95		95	
5	100	90	95	95	95	95	95	95	95
		95		95		95		95	
6	95	95	95	95	95	95	95	95	95
		95		95		95		95	

producing 95 items per period. Note, however, that a change in demand of only 5 items has produced a fluctuation of 10 items in the OEM's production rate.

Carrying this same logic through to the first-tier supplier, at the beginning of period 2 the second-tier supplier has 100 items in stock. The demand which it has to supply in period 2 is derived from the production rate of the OEM. This has dropped down to 90 in period 2. The first-tier supplier therefore has to produce sufficient to supply the demand of 90 items (or the equivalent) and leave one month's demand (now 90 items) as its finish stock. A production rate of 80 items per month will achieve this. It will therefore start period 3 with an opening stock of 90 items, but the demand from the OEM has now risen to 95 items. It therefore has to produce sufficient to fulfil this demand of 95 items and leave 95 items in stock. To do this, it must produce 100 items in period 3. After period 3 the first-tier supplier then resumes a steady state, producing 95 items per month. Note again, however, that the fluctuation has been even greater than that in the OEM's production rate, decreasing to 80 items a period, increasing to 100 items a period, and then achieving a steady rate of 95 items a period. Extending the logic back to the third-tier supplier, it is clear that the further back up the supply chain an operation is placed, the more drastic are the fluctuations.

> ✳ **Operations principle**
>
> Demand fluctuations become progressively amplified as their effects work back up the supply chain.

This relatively simple demonstration ignores any time lag in material and information flow between stages. In practice there will be such a lag, and this will make the fluctuations even more marked. Figure 12.14 shows the net result of all these effects in a typical supply chain. Note the increasing volatility further back in the chain.

Controlling supply chain dynamics

The first step in improving supply chain performance involves attempting to reduce the bull-whip effect. This usually means co-ordinating the activities of the operations in the chain in several ways.[11]

E-enabling supply networks

One of the reasons for the fluctuations in output described in the example earlier was that each operation in the chain reacted to the orders placed by its immediate customer. None of the operations had an overview of what was happening throughout the chain. If information had been available and shared throughout the chain, it is unlikely that such wild fluctuations would have occurred. It is sensible therefore to try to transmit information throughout

Figure 12.14 Typical supply chain dynamics

the chain so that all the operations can monitor true demand, free of these distortions. An obvious improvement is to make information on end customer demand available to upstream operations. Electronic point-of-sale (EPOS) systems used by many retailers attempt to do this. Sales data from checkouts or cash registers is consolidated and transmitted to the warehouses, transportation companies and supplier manufacturing operations that form the supply chain. Similarly, electronic data interchange (EDI) helps to share information and can affect the economic order quantities shipped between operations in the supply chain.

OPERATIONS IN PRACTICE   Seven-Eleven Japan's agile supply chain[12]

Source: Shutterstock.com: Sean Pavone

Seven-Eleven Japan (SEJ) is that country's largest and most successful retailer. The average amount of stock in an SEJ store is between 7 and 8.4 days of demand, a remarkably fast stock turnover for any retailer. Industry analysts see SEJ's agile supply chain management as being the driving force behind its success. It is an agility that is supported by a fully integrated information system that provides visibility of the whole supply chain and ensures fast replenishment of goods in its stores, customized exactly to the needs of individual stores. As a customer comes to the checkout counter the assistant first keys in the customer's gender and approximate age and then scans the bar codes of the purchased goods. This sales data is transmitted to the SEJ headquarters through its own high-speed lines. Simultaneously, the store's own computer system records and analyses the information so that store managers and headquarters have immediate point-of-sale information. This allows both store managers and headquarters to analyse, hour by hour, sales trends, any stockouts, types of customer buying certain products, and so on. The headquarters' computer aggregates all this data by region, product and time so that all parts of the supply chain, from suppliers through to the stores, has the information by the next morning. Every Monday, the company chairman and top executives review all performance information for the previous week and develop plans for the upcoming week. These plans are presented on Tuesday morning to SEJ's 'operations field counsellors' each of whom is responsible for facilitating performance improvement in around eight stores. On Tuesday afternoon the field counsellors for each region meet to decide how they will implement the overall plans for their region. On Tuesday night the counsellors fly back to their regions and by next morning are visiting their stores to deliver the messages developed at headquarters which will help the stores implement the plans. SEJ's physical distribution is also organized on an agile basis. The distribution company maintains radio communications with all drivers and SEJ's headquarters keeps track of all delivery activities. Delivery times and routes are planned in great detail and published in the form of a delivery timetable. On average each delivery takes only 1.5 minutes at each store, and drivers are expected to make their deliveries within 10 minutes of scheduled time. If a delivery is late by more than 30 minutes the distribution company has to pay the store a fine equivalent to the gross profit on the goods being delivered. The agility of the whole supply system also allows SEJ headquarters and the distribution company to respond to disruptions. For example, on the day of the Kobe earthquake, SEJ used 7 helicopters and 125 motor cycles to rush through a delivery of 64,000 rice balls to earthquake victims.

Channel alignment in supply networks

Channel alignment means the adjustment of scheduling, materials movements, stock levels, pricing and other sales strategies so as to bring all the operations in the chain into line with each other. This goes beyond the provision of information. It means that the systems and methods of planning and control decision making are harmonized through the chain. For example, even when using the same information, differences in forecasting methods or purchasing practices can lead to fluctuations in orders between operations in the chain. One way of avoiding this is to allow an upstream supplier to manage the inventories of its downstream customer. This is known as vendor-managed inventory (VMI). So, for example, a packaging supplier could take responsibility for the stocks of packaging materials held by a food manufacturing customer. In turn, the food manufacturer takes responsibility for the stocks of its products that are held in its customer's, the supermarket's, warehouses.

Operational efficiency in supply networks

'Operational efficiency' in this context means the efforts that each operation in the chain makes to reduce its own complexity, the cost of doing business with other operations in the chain, and its throughput time. The cumulative effect of this is to simplify throughput in the whole chain. For example, imagine a chain of operations whose performance level is relatively poor: quality defects are frequent, the lead time to order products and services is long, delivery is unreliable, and so on. The behaviour of the chain would be a continual sequence of errors and effort wasted in re-planning to compensate for the errors. Poor quality would mean extra and unplanned orders being placed, and unreliable delivery and slow delivery lead times would mean high safety stocks. Just as important, most operations managers' time would be spent coping with the inefficiency. By contrast, a chain whose operations had high levels of operations performance would be more predictable and have faster throughput, both of which would help to minimize supply chain fluctuations.

Forecasting in supply networks

Improved forecast accuracy also helps to reduce the bullwhip effect. This effect is caused by demand patterns, lead times, forecasting mechanisms and the replenishment decisions used to order product from production facilities or suppliers. Improving the accuracy of forecasts directly reduces the inventory holding requirements that will achieve customer service-level targets. Reducing lead times means that one needs to forecast less far into the future and thus lead times have a large impact on bullwhip and inventory costs. The exact nature of how the bullwhip effect propagates in a supply chain is also dependent on the nature of the demand pattern. Negatively correlated demands require less inventory in the supply chain than positively correlated demand patterns, for example. But the bullwhip effect is not unavoidable. By using sophisticated replenishment policies, designed using control engineering principles, many businesses have been able to eliminate bullwhip effects. Sometimes this comes at a cost. Extra inventory may be required in parts of the chain, or customer service levels reduce. But more often, bullwhip avoidance creates a 'win–win' situation. It reduces inventory requirements and improves customer service.

SUMMARY ANSWERS TO KEY QUESTIONS

❯ What is supply chain management?

- Supply chain management is the management of relationships and flows between operations and processes. Technically, it is different from supply network management, which looks at all the operations or processes in a network, but the two terms are often used interchangeably.

- Many of the principles of managing external supply chains (flow between operations) are also applicable to internal supply chains (flow between processes and departments).

〉 How should supply chains compete?

- The central objective of supply chain management is to satisfy the needs of the end customer.
- So, each operation in the chain (and each chain in the supply network) should contribute to whatever mix of quality, speed, dependability, flexibility and cost that the end customer requires.
- Individual operations failure in any of these objectives can be multiplied throughout the chain. So, although each operation's performance may be adequate, the performance of the whole chain could be poor.
- An important distinction is between lean and agile supply chain performance. Broadly, lean (or efficient) supply chains are appropriate for stable 'functional' products and services, while agile (or responsive) supply chains are more appropriate for less predictable innovative products and services.

〉 How should relationships in supply chains be managed?

- Supply chain relationships can be described on a spectrum from market-based, contractual, 'arm's length' relationships to close and long-term partnership relationships.
- The types of relationships adopted may be dictated by the structure of the market itself.

〉 How is the supply side managed?

- Managing supply-side relationships involves determining sourcing strategy, selecting appropriate suppliers, managing ongoing supply activity and supplier development.
- Sourcing strategies include multiple sourcing, single sourcing, delegated sourcing and parallel sourcing. Their selection is influenced by the complexity and risk of the supply market and the criticality to the business.
- Supplier selection involves trading off different supplier attributes, often using scoring assessment methods.
- Managing ongoing supply involves clarifying supply expectations, often using service-level agreements to manage the supply relationships.
- Supplier development can benefit both suppliers and customers, especially in partnership relationships. Very often barriers are the mismatches in perception between customers and suppliers.

〉 How is the demand side managed?

- This will depend partly on whether demand is dependent on some known factor and therefore predictable, or independent of any known factor and therefore less predictable. Approaches such as materials requirements planning (MRP) are used in the former case, while approaches such as inventory management are used in the latter case.
- The increasing outsourcing of physical distribution and the use of new tracking technologies, such as RFID, have brought efficiencies to the movement of physical goods and customer service.

- Supply chains have a dynamic of their own that is often called the *bullwhip effect*. It means that relatively small changes at the demand end of the chain increasingly amplify into large disturbances as they move upstream.

- Four key methods can be used to reduce this effect. E-enabled supply chains can prevent over-reaction to immediate stimuli and give a better view of the whole chain. Channel alignment through standardized planning and control methods allows for easier co-ordination of the whole chain. Improving the operational efficiency of each part of the chain prevents local errors multiplying to affect the whole chain. Improved forecasts reduce the inventory holding requirements for supply chains while maintaining customer service levels.

CASE STUDY   Supplying fast fashion

Garment retailing has changed. No longer is there a standard look that all retailers adhere to for a whole season. Fashion is fast, complex and furious. Different trends overlap and fashion ideas that are not even on a store's radar screen can become 'must haves' within six months. Many retail businesses with their own brands, such as H&M and Zara, sell up-to-the-minute clothes at low prices, in stores that are clearly focused on one particular market. In the world of fast fashion catwalk designs speed their way into high street stores at prices anyone can afford. The quality of the garment means that it may only last one season, but fast fashion customers do not want yesterday's trends. As *Newsweek* puts it, '*being a "quicker picker-upper" is what made fashion retailers H&M and Zara successful. [They] thrive by practicing the new science of "fast fashion"; compressing product development cycles as much as six times.*' But the retail operations that customers see are only the end part of the supply chains that feeds them. And these have also changed.

At its simplest level, the fast-fashion supply chain has four stages. First, the garments are designed, after which they are manufactured; they are then distributed to the retail outlets where they are displayed and sold in retail operations designed to reflect the businesses' brand values. In this case study we examine two fast-fashion operations, Hennes and Mauritz (known as H&M) and Zara, together with United Colours of Benetton (UCB), a similar chain, but with a different market positioning.

Benetton. Almost 50 years ago, Luciano Benetton took the world of fashion by storm by selling the bright, casual sweaters designed by his sister across Europe (and later the rest of the world), promoted by controversial adver-

tising. The Benetton Group is present in over 20 countries throughout the world. Selling casual garments, mainly under its United Colours of Benetton (UCB) and its more fashion-oriented Sisley brands, it produces 110 million garments a year, over 90 per cent of them in Europe. Its retail network of over 6,000 stores produces revenue of around €1.6 billion. Benetton products are seen as less 'high fashion' but higher quality and durability, with higher prices, than H&M and Zara.

H&M. Established in Sweden in 1947, H&M now sells clothes and cosmetics in over 1,000 stores in 20 countries around the world. The business concept is 'fashion and quality at the best price'. With more than 40,000 employees, and revenues of around SKr60,000 million, its biggest market is Germany, followed by Sweden and the UK. H&M is seen by many as the originator of the fast-fashion concept. Certainly it has years of experience at driving down the price of up-to-the-minute fashions. 'We ensure the best price', it says, 'by having few middlemen, buying large volumes, having extensive experience of the clothing industry, having a great knowledge of which goods should be bought from which markets, having efficient distribution systems, and being cost-conscious at every stage.'

Zara. The first store opened almost by accident in 1975 when Amancio Ortega Gaona, a women's pyjama manufacturer, was left with a large cancelled order. The shop he opened was intended only as an outlet for cancelled orders. Inditex, the holding group that includes the Zara brand, currently has over 2,000 stores in over 100 countries and revenues of over €11.5 billion. The Zara brand accounts for over 75 per cent of the group's total retail sales, and it is still based in north-west Spain. The Inditex Group also has several other branded chains including Pull and Bear, and Massimo Dutti. In total it employs almost 40,000 people in a business that is known for a high degree of vertical integration compared with most fast-fashion companies. The company believes that it is its integration along the supply chain that allows it to respond to customer demand fast and flexibly while keeping stock to a minimum.

Design

All three businesses emphasize the importance of design in this market. Although not *haute couture*, capturing design trends is vital to success. Even the boundary between high and fast fashion is starting to blur. In 2004 H&M recruited high-fashion designer Karl Lagerfeld, previously noted for his work with more exclusive brands. For H&M his designs were priced for value rather than exclusivity. *'Why do I work for H&M? Because I believe in inexpensive clothes, not "cheap" clothes'*, said Lagerfeld. Yet most of H&M's products come from over 100 designers in Stockholm who work with a team of 50 pattern designers, around 100 buyers and a number of budget controllers. The department's task is to find the optimum balance between the three components comprising H&M's business concept: fashion, price and quality. Buying volumes and delivery dates are then decided.

Zara's design functions are organized in a different way to most similar companies. Conventionally, the design input comes from three *separate* functions: the designers themselves, market specialists, and buyers who place orders with suppliers. At Zara the design stage is split into three product areas: women's, men's and children's garments. In each area, designers, market specialists and buyers are co-located in design halls that also contain small workshops for trying out prototype designs. The market specialists in all three design halls are in regular contact with Zara retail stores, discussing customer reaction to new designs. In this way, the retail stores are not the end of the whole supply chain, but the beginning of the design stage of the chain. Zara's 300 or so designers,

whose average age is 26, produce approximately 40,000 items per year, of which about 10,000 go into production.

Benetton also has around 300 designers, who not only design for all their brands, but also are engaged in researching new materials and clothing concepts. Since 2000 the company has moved to standardize its range globally. At one time more than 20 per cent of its ranges were customized to the specific needs of each country, but now only between 5 and 10 per cent of garments are customized. This reduced the number of individual designs offered globally by over 30 per cent, strengthening the global brand image and reducing production costs.

Both H&M and Zara have moved away from the traditional industry practice of offering two 'collections' a year, for spring/summer and autumn/winter. Their 'seasonless cycle' involves the continual introduction of new products on a rolling basis throughout the year. This allows designers to learn from customers' reactions to their new products and incorporate them quickly into more new products. The most extreme version of this idea is practised by Zara. A garment will be designed, then a batch manufactured and 'pulsed' through the supply chain. Often the design is never repeated; it may be modified and another batch produced, but there are no 'continuing' designs as such. Even Benetton has increased the proportion of what it calls 'flash' collections, small collections that are put into its stores during the season.

Manufacturing

At one time Benetton focused its production on its Italian plants. Then it significantly increased its production outside Italy to take advantage of lower labour costs. Non-Italian operations include factories in North Africa, Eastern Europe and Asia. Yet each location operates in a very similar manner. A central, Benetton-owned, operation performs some manufacturing operations (especially those requiring expensive technology) and co-ordinates the more labour-intensive production activities that are performed by a network of smaller contractors (often owned and managed by ex-Benetton employees). These contractors may in turn subcontract some of their activities. The company's central facility in Italy allocates production to each of the non-Italian networks, deciding what and how much each is to produce. There is some specialization, for example jackets are made in Eastern Europe while T-shirts are made in Spain. Benetton also has a controlling share in its main supplier of raw materials, to ensure fast supply to its factories. Benetton is also known for the practice of dyeing garments after assembly rather than using dyed thread or fabric. This postpones decisions about colours until late in the supply process so that there is a greater chance of producing what is needed by the market.

H&M does not have any factories of its own, but instead works with around 750 suppliers. Around half of production takes place in Europe and the rest mainly in Asia. It has 21 production offices around the world that between them are responsible for co-ordinating the suppliers who produce over half a billion items a year for H&M. The relationship between production offices and suppliers is vital, because it allows fabrics to be bought in early. The actual dyeing and cutting of the garments can then be decided at a later stage in the production. The later an order can be placed with suppliers, the less the risk of buying the wrong thing. Average supply lead times vary from three weeks up to six months, depending on the nature of the goods. However, 'The most important thing', H&M says, 'is to find the optimal time to order each item. Short lead times are not always best. [For] some high-volume fashion basics, it is to our advantage to place orders far in advance. Trendier garments require considerably shorter lead times.'

Zara's lead times are said to be the fastest in the industry, with a 'catwalk to rack' time as little as 15 days. According to one analyst, this is because it 'owned most of the manufacturing capability used to make their products, which they use as a means of exciting and stimulating customer demand'. About half of Zara's products are produced in its network of 20 Spanish factories, which, like Benetton, tended to concentrate on the more capital-intensive operations such as cutting and dyeing. Subcontractors are used for most labour-intensive operations like sewing. Zara buys around 40 per cent of its fabric from its own wholly owned subsidiary, most of which is in undyed form for dyeing after assembly. Most Zara factories and their subcontractors work on a single shift system to retain some volume flexibility.

Distribution

Both Benetton and Zara have invested in highly automated warehouses, close to their main production centres that store, pack and assemble individual orders for their retail networks. These automated warehouses represent a major investment for both companies. In 2001, Zara caused some press comment by announcing that it would open a second automated warehouse even though, by its own calculations, it was only using about half its existing warehouse capacity. More recently, Benetton caused some controversy by announcing that it was exploring the use of RFID tags to track its garments.

At H&M, while stock management is primarily handled internally, physical distribution is subcontracted. A large part of the flow of goods is routed from the production site to the retail country via H&M's transit terminal in Hamburg. Upon arrival the goods are inspected and allocated to the stores or to the centralized store stockroom. This centralized store stockroom, within H&M referred to as the 'Call-Off warehouse', replenishes stores on item level according to what is selling.

Retail

All H&M stores (average size 1,300 m^2) are owned and solely run by H&M. The aim is to 'create a comfortable and inspiring atmosphere in the store that makes it simple for customers to find what they want and to feel at home'. This is similar to Zara stores, although they tend to be smaller (average size, 800 m^2). Perhaps the most remarkable characteristic of Zara stores is that garments rarely stay in the store for longer than two weeks. Because product designs are often not repeated and produced in relatively small batches, the range of garments displayed in the store can change radically every two or three weeks. This encourages customers both to avoid delaying a purchase and to revisit the store frequently.

Since 2000 Benetton has been reshaping its retail operations. At one time the vast majority of Benetton retail outlets were small shops run by third parties. Now these small stores have been joined by several, Benetton owned and operated, larger stores (1,500 to 3,000 m^2). These megastores can display the whole range of Benetton products and reinforce the Benetton shopping experience.

QUESTION

1 **Compare and contrast the approaches taken by H&M, Benetton and Zara to managing their supply networks.**

PROBLEMS AND APPLICATIONS

1 If you were the owner of a small local retail shop, what criteria would you use to select suppliers for the goods that you wish to stock in your shop?

2 Visit three shops that are local to you and ask the owners how they select their suppliers. In what way were their answers different from what you thought they might be?

3 Visit a C2C (consumer-to-consumer) auction site (for example, eBay) and analyse the function of the site in terms of the way it facilitates transactions. What does such a site have to get right to be successful?

4 The example of the bullwhip effect shown in Table 12.2 shows how a simple 5 per cent reduction in demand at the end of the supply chain causes fluctuations that increase in severity the further back an operation is placed in the chain.

    (a) Using the same logic and the same rules (that is, all operations keep one period's inventory), what would the effect on the chain be if demand fluctuated period by period between 100 and 95? That is, period 1 has a demand of 100, period 2 has a demand of 95, period 3 a demand of 100, period 4 a demand of 95, and so on?

    (b) What happens if all operations in the supply chain decide to keep only half of the period's demand as inventory?

    (c) Find examples of how supply chains try to reduce this bullwhip effect.

5 Visit the websites of some distribution and logistics companies. For example, you might start with some of the following: www.eddiestobart.co.uk, www.norbert-dentressangle.com, www.accenture.com (under 'services' look for supply chain management), www.logisticsonline.com:

- What do you think are the market promises that these companies make to their clients and potential clients?
- What are the operations capabilities they need to carry out these promises successfully?

SELECTED FURTHER READING

Akkermans, H. and Voss, C. (2013) The service bullwhip effect, *International Journal of Operations & Production Management*, **vol. 33, no. 6, 765–788.**

An academic paper that deals with the important issue of service supply.

Chopra, S. and Meindl, P. (2015) *Supply Chain Management*, **5th edn, Pearson, Upper Saddle River, NJ.**

One of the best of the specialist texts.

Christopher, M. (2011) *Logistics and Supply Chain Management: Creating Value-Adding Networks*, **Financial Times Prentice Hall, Harlow.**

Updated version of a classic that gives a comprehensive treatment on supply chain management from a distribution perspective by one of the gurus of supply chain management.

Johnsen, T., Howard, M. and Miemczyk, J. (2014) *Purchasing and Supply Chain Management: A Sustainability Perspective*, **Routledge, Milton.**

Focuses on the important topic of the longer-term implications of global sourcing and sustainability.

13

Inventory management

Key questions

> What is inventory?

> Why should there be any inventory?

> How much to order? The volume decision

> When to place an order? The timing decision

> How can inventory be controlled?

INTRODUCTION

Operations managers often have an ambivalent attitude towards inventories. On the one hand, they are costly, sometimes tying up considerable amounts of working capital. They are also risky because items held in stock could deteriorate, become obsolete or just get lost, and, furthermore, they take up valuable space in the operation. On the other hand, they provide some security in an uncertain environment that one can deliver items in stock, should customers demand them. This is the dilemma of inventory management: in spite of the cost and the other disadvantages associated with holding stocks, they do facilitate the smoothing of supply and demand. In fact they only exist because supply and demand are not exactly in harmony with each other (see Fig. 13.1).

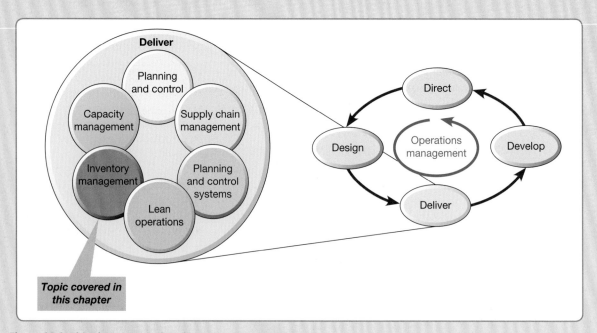

Figure 13.1 This chapter examines inventory management

The blood bank's 'perfect storm'[1]

Inventory depends on both supply and demand, so when both are uncertain, inventory management poses particular challenges. And when, in addition, the consequences of running out of stock can affect people's health, then inventory management becomes a particularly vital task. Welcome to the world of the Blood Stocks Management Scheme of the National Health Service Blood and Transplant (NHSBT) that manages blood stocks across the blood supply chain in the UK. NHSBT is responsible for the collection, processing, testing and issuing of blood across England and North Wales. Each year approximately 2 million blood donations are collected from 1.4 million donors to supply hospitals with all the blood needed for accident and emergency situations and regular medical treatment. Many people owe their lives to transfusions that were made possible by the efficient management of blood, stocked in a supply network that stretches from donation centres through to hospital blood banks. The blood supply chain has three main stages:

Source: Alamy Images: David J. Green

- *Collection*, which involves recruiting and retaining blood donors, encouraging them to attend donor sessions and transporting the donated blood.
- *Processing*, which breaks blood down into its constituent parts.
- *Distribution*, which transports blood from blood centres to hospitals in response to both routine and emergency requests.

Inventory accumulates at all three stages, as well as in individual hospitals' blood banks. Within the supply chain some, less than 10 per cent, of donated red blood cells are lost. Much of this is due to losses in processing, but around 5 per cent is not used because it has 'become unavailable', mainly because it has been stored for too long. Part of the inventory management task is to keep this 'time expired' loss to a minimum. In fact most blood is lost when it is stored in hospital blood banks that are outside the service's direct control. Also, blood components will deteriorate over time. Platelets have a shelf life of only five days and demand can fluctuate significantly, which makes stock control particularly difficult. Even red blood cells that have a shelf life of 35 days may not be acceptable to hospitals if they are close to their 'use by date'. Stock accuracy is crucial. Giving a patient the wrong type of blood can be fatal.

At a local level demand can be affected significantly by accidents. One serious accident involving a cyclist used 750 units of blood, which completely exhausted the available supply (miraculously, he survived). Large-scale accidents usually generate a surge of offers from donors wishing to make immediate donations. There is also a more predictable seasonality to the donating of blood, however, with a low period during the summer vacation. During public holidays and sporting events blood donations drop. For example, on one day when the football World Cup quarter final and Andy Murray's (a British tennis player) Wimbledon semi-final coincided, there was a 12 per cent drop in donations compared with the previous year. Similarly, one summer when public holidays coincided with the Queen's Jubilee, European football events, the London Olympic Games and the Paralympic Games proved particularly difficult. Not only did these events reduce donations (supply), but also the increased number of visitors to London also increased demand. Before the period NHSBT said that the number of major events would create a 'perfect storm' and dramatically impact the number of blood donations coming in.

WHAT IS INVENTORY?

Inventory is a term used to describe the accumulations of materials, customers or information as they flow through processes or networks. Occasionally the term is also used to describe transforming resources, such as rooms in hotels or automobiles in a vehicle hire firm, but here we use the term for the accumulation of the transformed resources that flow through processes, operations or supply networks. Physical inventory (sometimes called 'stock') is the accumulation of physical materials such as components, parts, finished goods or physical (paper) information records. Queues are accumulations of customers, physical as in a queuing line or people in an airport departure lounge, or waiting for service at the end of phone lines. Databases are stores for accumulations of digital information, such as medical records or insurance details. Managing these accumulations is what we call 'inventory management'. And it is important. Material inventories in a factory can represent a substantial proportion of cash tied up in working capital. Minimizing them can release large quantities of cash. However, reducing them too far can lead to customers' orders not being fulfilled. Customers held up in queues for too long can get irritated, angry and possibly leave, so reducing revenue. Databases are critical for storing digital information and while storage may be inexpensive, maintaining databases may not be.

All processes, operations and supply networks have inventories

Most things that flow do so in an uneven way. Rivers flow faster down steep sections or where they are squeezed into a ravine. Over relatively level ground they flow slowly, and form pools or even large lakes where there are natural or artificial barriers blocking their path. It is the same in operations. Passengers in an airport flow from public transport or their vehicles and then have to queue at several points including check-in, security screening and immigration. They then have to wait (a queue even if they are sitting) again in the departure lounge as they are joined (batched) with other passengers to form a group of several hundred people who are ready to board the aircraft. They are then squeezed down the air bridge as they file in one at a time to board the aircraft. Likewise in a tractor assembly plant, stocks of components such as gearboxes, wheels, lighting circuits, etc., are brought into the factory in their tens or hundreds and are then stored next to the assembly line ready for use. Finished tractors will also be stored until the transporter comes to take them away in ones or tens to the dealers or directly to the end customer. Similarly, a government tax department collects information about us and our finances from various sources, including our employers, our tax forms, information from banks or other investment companies, and stores this in databases until it is checked, sometimes by people, sometimes automatically, to create our tax codes and/or tax bills. In fact, because most operations involve flows of materials, customers and/or information, at some points they are likely to have material and information inventories and queues of customers waiting for goods or services, *see* Table 13.1.

Inventories are often the result of uneven flows. If there is a difference between the timing or the rate of supply and demand at any point in a process or network then accumulations will occur. A common analogy is the water tank shown in Figure 13.2. If, over time, the rate of supply of water to the tank differs from the rate at which it is demanded, a tank of water (inventory) will be needed to maintain supply. When the rate of supply exceeds the rate of demand, inventory increases; when the rate of demand exceeds the rate of supply, inventory decreases. So if an operation or process can match supply and demand rates, it will also succeed in reducing its inventory levels. But most organizations must cope with unequal supply and demand, at least at some points in their supply chain. Both the following organizations depend on the ability to manage supply and demand inequality through their inventory management.

There is a complication when using this 'water flow' analogy to represent flows and accumulations (inventories) of information. Inventories of information can either be stored

Table 13.1 Examples of inventory held in processes, operations or supply networks

Process, operation or supply network	'Inventories'		
	Physical inventories	Queues of customers	Information in databases
Hotel	Food items, drinks, toilet items	At check-in and checkout	Customer details, loyalty card holders, catering suppliers
Hospital	Dressings, disposable instruments, blood	Patients on a waiting list, patients in bed waiting for surgery, patients in recovery wards	Patient medical records
Credit card application process	Blank cards, form letters	Customers waiting on the phone	Customer's credit and personal information
Computer manufacturer	Components for assembly, packaging materials, finished computers ready for sale	Customers waiting for delivery of their computer	Customers' details, supplier information

Figure 13.2 Inventory is created to compensate for the differences in timing between supply and demand

because of uneven flow, in the same way as materials and people, or be stored because the operation needs to use the information to process something in the future. For example, an Internet retail operation will process each order it receives, and inventories of information may accumulate because of uneven flows as we have described. But, in addition, during order processing customer details could be permanently stored in a database. This information will then be used, not only for future orders from the same customer, but also for other processes, such as targeting promotional activities. In this case the inventory of information has turned from a transformed resource into a transforming resource, because it is being used to transform other information rather than being transformed itself. So, whereas managing physical material concerns ordering and holding the right amounts of goods or materials to deal with the variations in flow, and managing queues is about the level of resources to deal with demand, a database is the accumulation of information but may not cause an interruption to the flow. Managing databases is about the organization of the data, its storage, security and retrieval (access and search).

An inventory of energy?[2]

Inventory exists to smooth out the differences over time between supply and demand. And the bigger the gap between supply and demand, the more useful inventory is. But for some industries there is a big problem – they deal in things that cannot be stored very easily. And probably the best illustration of this is the business of generating and supplying energy. First, demand can fluctuate wildly, especially in countries that use large amounts of energy for cooling or heating. Nor can generating capacity be planned purely on the basis of average demand. In electricity generation, aggregated demand and average usage do not count for much when demand can spike with little warning. Second, supply, especially of the most convenient or cleaner forms of energy, is not always available at the right time. For example, wind does not blow all the time. Worse than that, it tends to be at its strongest at night, when demand is low. Third, in most countries regulators require energy firms to preserve a safety margin over total estimated demand to safeguard a reliable supply to citizens. Finally, energy is not easy to store. If only it were easier for energy firms to store excess energy, such as that produced by wind turbines at night, for later use at peak times, this so-called 'time shifting' would counteract the irregular supply from 'green' sources such as wind and solar power, which would make them simpler to integrate into the grid. If energy could be stored it would also permit what energy companies call 'peak shaving', that is using stored energy instead of having to buy more expensive energy on the spot (short-term) market.

So how can energy be stored? On a small scale batteries can deliver power for short periods, but they cannot store (or discharge) energy at the high rates (hundreds of megawatts) or the huge quantities (thousands of megawatt hours) to realistically supply a distribution grid. The most practical method of energy storage, and the most widely used, is pumped-storage hydropower (PSH). This method harnesses water and gravity to 'store' off-peak power and release it during periods of high demand by using off-peak electricity to pump water from one reservoir up to another higher one. The water is then released back down to the lower reservoir, when power is needed, through a turbine that produces electricity. The drawback to traditional PSH is that it requires two reservoirs at different heights. Which is why, if greener energy is to be stored, new methods need to be developed. Ideas include using wind turbines to pump water from a deep central reservoir out to sea, which is allowed to flow back into the reservoir through turbines that produce electricity; pumping water to raise a piston that sinks back down through a generator; using modified railway cars on a specially built track that utilize off-peak electricity to get to the top of a hill, and releasing the cars to run back down the track so that their motion can drive a generator. Other ideas include using compressed air to store the energy; using argon gas to transfer heat between two vast tanks filled with gravel; and storing energy in molten salt. And these are just a few of the different approaches being explored. But for whichever method proves the most effective at creating energy inventories, there will be rewards, both in terms of the potential market and in enabling the better use of sustainable energy.

Source: Shutterstock.com: Arina P Habich

WHY SHOULD THERE BE ANY INVENTORY?

There are plenty of reasons to avoid accumulating inventory where possible. Table 13.2 identifies some of these, particularly those concerned with cost, space, quality and operational/organizational issues.

So why have inventory?

On the face of it, it may seem sensible to have a smooth and even flow of materials, customers and information through operational processes and networks and thus not have any accumulations. In fact, inventories provide many advantages for both operations and their customers. If a customer has to go to a competitor because a part is out of stock, or because there is too long a wait, or because the company insists on collecting personal details each time the customer calls, the value of inventories seems indisputable. The task of operations management is to allow inventory to accumulate only when its benefits outweigh its disadvantages. The following are some of the benefits of inventory:

- **Physical inventory is an insurance against uncertainty** – Inventory can act as a buffer against unexpected fluctuations in supply and demand. For example, a retail operation can never forecast demand perfectly over the lead time. It will order goods from its suppliers such that there is always a minimum level of inventory to cover against the possibility that demand will be greater than expected during the time taken to deliver the goods. This is buffer, or safety, inventory. It can also compensate for the uncertainties in the process of the supply of goods into the store.

> ✳ **Operations principle**
> Inventory should only accumulate when the advantages of having it outweigh its disadvantages.

  The same applies with the output inventories, which is why hospitals always have a supply of blood, sutures and bandages for immediate response to accident and emergency patients. Similarly, auto servicing services, factories and airlines may hold selected critical spare parts inventories so that maintenance staff can repair the most common faults without delay. Again, inventory is being used as 'insurance' against unpredictable events.
- **Physical inventory can counteract a lack of flexibility** – Where a wide range of customer options is offered, unless the operation is perfectly flexible, stock will be needed to ensure

Table 13.2 **Some reasons to avoid inventories**

	'Inventories'		
	Physical inventories	Queues of customers	Digital information in databases
Cost	Ties up working capital and there could be high administrative and insurance costs	Primarily time cost to the customer, i.e. wastes customer's time	Cost of set-up, access, update and maintenance
Space	Requires storage space	Requires areas for waiting or phone lines for held calls	Requires memory capacity. May require secure and/or special environment
Quality	May deteriorate over time, become damaged or obsolete	May upset customers if they have to wait too long. May lose customers	Data may be corrupted or lost or become obsolete
Operational/organizational	May hide problems (see the chapter on 'lean' – Chapter 15)	May put undue pressure on the staff and so quality is compromised for throughput	Databases need constant management; access control, updating and security

supply when it is engaged on other activities. This is sometimes called cycle inventory. For example, Figure 13.3 shows the inventory profile of a baker who makes three types of bread. Because of the nature of the mixing and baking process, only one kind of bread can be produced at any time. The baker will have to produce each type of bread in batches large enough to satisfy the demand for each kind of bread between the times when each batch is ready for sale. So, even when demand is steady and predictable, there will always be some inventory to compensate for the intermittent supply of each type of bread.

- **Physical inventory allows operations to take advantage of short-term opportunities** – Sometimes opportunities arise that necessitate accumulating inventory, even when there is no immediate demand for it. For example, a supplier may be offering a particularly good deal on selected items for a limited time period, perhaps because it wants to reduce its own finished goods inventories. Under these circumstances a purchasing department may opportunistically take advantage of the short-term price advantage.

- **Physical inventory can be used to anticipate future demands** – Medium-term capacity management (see Chapter 11) may use inventory to cope with demand. Rather than trying to make a product (such as chocolate) only when it is needed, it is produced throughout the year ahead of demand and put into inventory until it is needed. This type of inventory is called anticipation inventory and is most commonly used when demand fluctuations are large but relatively predictable.

- **Physical inventory can reduce overall costs** – Holding relatively large inventories may bring savings that are greater than the cost of holding the inventory. This may be when bulk buying gets the lowest possible cost of inputs, or when large order quantities reduce both the number of orders placed and the associated costs of administration and material handling. This is the basis of the 'economic order quantity' (EOQ) approach that will be treated later in this chapter.

- **Physical inventory can increase in value** – Sometimes the items held as inventory can increase in value and so become an investment. For example, dealers in fine wines are less reluctant to hold inventory than dealers in wine that does not get better with age. (However, it can be argued that keeping fine wines until they are at their peak is really part of the overall process rather than inventory as such.) A more obvious example is inventories of money. The many financial processes within most organizations will try to maximize the inventory of cash they hold because it is earning them interest.

- **Physical inventory fills the processing 'pipeline'** – 'Pipeline' inventory exists because transformed resources cannot be moved instantaneously between the point of supply and the point of demand. When a retail store places an order, its supplier will 'allocate' the stock to the retail store in its own warehouse, pack it, load it onto its truck, transport it to its destination and unload it into the retailer's inventory. From the time that stock is allocated (and therefore it is unavailable to any other customer) to the time it becomes available for the retail store, it is pipeline inventory. Especially in geographically dispersed supply networks, pipeline inventory can be substantial.

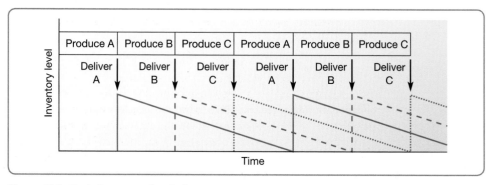

Figure 13.3 Cycle inventory in a bakery

- **Queues of customers help balance capacity and demand** – This is especially useful if the main service resource is expensive, for example doctors, consultants, lawyers or expensive equipment such as CAT scans. By waiting a short time after their arrival, and creating a queue of customers, the service always has customers to process. This is also helpful where arrival times are less predictable, for example where an appointment system is not used or not possible.
- **Queues of customers enable prioritization** – In cases where resources are fixed and customers are entering the system with different levels of priority, the formation of a queue allows the organization to serve urgent customers while keeping other less urgent ones waiting. In some circumstances it is not usual to have to wait 3–4 hours for treatment in an accident and emergency ward, with more urgent cases taking priority.
- **Queuing gives customers time to chose** – Time spent in a queue gives customers time to decide what products/services they require; for example, customers waiting in a fast food restaurant have time to look at the menu so that when they get to the counter they are ready to make their order without holding up the server.
- **Queues enable efficient use of resources** – By allowing queues to form, customers can be batched together to make efficient use of operational resources. For example, a queue for an elevator makes better use of its capacity; in an airport, by calling customers to the gate staff can load the aircraft more efficiently and quickly.
- **Databases provide efficient multi-level access** – Databases are relatively cheap ways of storing information and providing many people with access, although there may be restrictions or different levels of access. The doctor's receptionist will be able to call up a patient's records to check name and address and make an appointment, the doctor will then be able to call up the appointment and the patient's records, the pharmacist will be able to call up the patient's name and prescriptions and cross-check for other prescriptions, known allergies, etc.
- **Databases of information allow single data capture** – There is no need to capture data at every transaction with a customer or supplier, though checks may be required.
- **Databases of information speed the process** – Amazon, for example, stores, if you agree, your delivery address and credit card information so that purchases can be made with a single click, making it fast and easy for the customer.

Reducing physical inventory

For the remainder of this chapter we will focus on physical inventory largely because this is what most operations managers assume is meant by the term 'inventory'. Moreover, we assume that the objective of those who manage physical inventories is to reduce the overall level (and/or cost) of inventory while maintaining an acceptable level of customer service. Table 13.3 identifies some of the ways in which physical inventory may be reduced.

The effect of inventory on return on assets

One can summarize the effects on the financial performance of an operation by looking at how some of the factors of inventory management impact 'return on assets', a key financial performance measure. Figure 13.4 shows some of these factors:

- Inventory governs the operation's ability to supply its customers. The absence of inventory means that customers are not satisfied with the possibility of reduced revenue.
- Inventory may become obsolete as alternatives become available, or could be damaged, deteriorate or simply get lost. This increases costs (because resources have been wasted) and reduces revenue (because the obsolete, damaged or lost items cannot be sold).
- Inventory incurs storage costs (leasing space, maintaining appropriate conditions, etc.). This could be high if items are hazardous to store (for example, flammable solvents, explosives, chemicals) or difficult to store and require special facilities (for example, frozen food).

Table 13.3 Some ways in which physical inventory may be reduced

Reason for holding inventory	Example	How inventory could be reduced
As an insurance against uncertainty	Safety stocks for when demand or supply is not perfectly predictable	• Improve demand forecasting • Tighten supply, e.g. through service level penalties
To counteract a lack of flexibility	Cycle stock to maintain supply when other products are being made	• Increase flexibility of processes, e.g. by reducing changeover times (*see* Chapter 15) • Using parallel processes producing output simultaneously (*see* Chapter 6)
To take advantage of relatively short-term opportunities	Suppliers offer 'time-limited' special low-cost offers	• Persuade suppliers to adopt 'everyday low prices' (*see* Chapter 12)
To anticipate future demands	Build up stocks in low-demand periods for use in high-demand periods	• Increase volume flexibility by moving towards a 'chase demand' plan (*see* Chapter 11)
To reduce overall costs	Purchasing a batch of products in order to save delivery and administration costs	• Reduce administration costs through purchasing process efficiency gains • Investigate alternative delivery channel that reduce transport costs
To fill the processing 'pipeline'	Items being delivered to customer	• Reduce process time between customer request and dispatch of items • Reduce throughput time in the downstream supply chain (*see* Chapter 12)

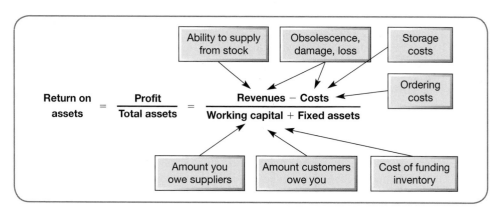

Figure 13.4 Inventory management has a significant effect on return on assets

- Inventory involves administrative and insurance costs. Every time a delivery is ordered, time and costs are incurred.
- Inventory ties up money, in the form of working capital, which is therefore unavailable for other uses, such as reducing borrowings or making investments in productive fixed assets (we will expand on the idea of working capital later).

> ✳ **Operations principle**
>
> Inventory management can have a significant effect on return on assets.

- Inventory contracts with suppliers can dictate the timing of when suppliers need to be paid. If they require paying before the operation receives payment from its customers (as is normal), the difference between the amount the operation owes suppliers and the amount suppliers owe the operation adds to working capital requirements.

Treasury Wine's hangover[3]

Not all wine improves with age, as Treasury Wine Estates found out when its forecast for the US market proved to be disastrously wrong. It had to pour over £20 million of its wine down the drain because it had spent too much time in storage and had become 'too old', was 'deteriorating' and was in danger of 'damaging its brands'. Faced with demand that was less than it had predicted, the group decided to destroy its old and aged commercial stock, to make sure that only the freshest and highest quality wines were made available for brand-conscious US consumers. The scrapping of the wine was a blow to Treasury Wine Estates, a largely successful group that was founded in 1843 with the establishment of Lindeman's Vineyard in the Hunter Valley in New South Wales. Today, it operates on three continents and has more than 50 brands and 11,000 hectares of vineyards around the world, as well as owning some of Australasia's premium wine brands, including Penfolds, Beringer, Lindemans and Wynns. David Dearie, Treasury's Chief Executive, said that the USA was the world's largest wine-consuming nation and a growing market, particularly at the upper (more expensive) end. He had taken the difficult decision to destroy the wine, he said, because it was a *'one-off rebasing of its inventory levels'*. Part of the problem is that Australia's commercial wine is intended to be consumed at a younger age than some other types of wine, so keeping the wine as inventory reduces its attractiveness. This means it has to be sold relatively quickly – which contributed to the total write-down caused by the poor forecasting, close to A$160 million (£96.2 million). Much of the extra cost was due to the discounts and rebates to its key US distributors to speed up the sale of current vintage wines.

Source: Shutterstock.com: Anna Bogush

Day-to-day inventory decisions

Wherever inventory accumulates, operations need to manage the day-to-day tasks of managing inventory. Orders will be received from internal or external customers; these will be despatched and demand will gradually deplete the inventory. Orders will need to be placed for replenishment of the stocks; deliveries will arrive and require storing. In managing the system, operations managers are involved in three major types of decision:

- **How much to order** – Every time a replenishment order is placed, how big should it be (sometimes called the *volume decision*)?
- **When to order** – At what point in time, or at what level of stock, should the replenishment order be placed (sometimes called the *timing decision*)?
- **How to control the system** – What procedures and routines should be installed to help make these decisions? Should different priorities be allocated to different stock items? How should stock information be stored?

HOW MUCH TO ORDER? THE VOLUME DECISION

To illustrate this decision, consider the example of the food and drinks we keep at our home. In managing this inventory we implicitly make decisions on *order quantity*, which is how much to purchase at one time. In making this decision we are balancing two sets of costs: the costs associated with going out to purchase the food items and the costs associated with holding the stocks. The option of holding very little or no inventory of food and purchasing each item only when it is needed has the advantage that it requires little money since purchases are made only when needed. However, it would involve purchasing provisions several times a day, which is inconvenient. At the very opposite extreme, making one journey to the local superstore every few months and purchasing all the provisions we would need until our next visit reduces the time and costs incurred in making the purchase but requires a very large amount of money each time the trip is made – money which could otherwise be in the bank and earning interest. We might also have to invest in extra cupboard units and a very large freezer. Somewhere between these extremes there will lie an ordering strategy which will minimize the total costs and effort involved in the purchase of food.

Inventory costs

The same principles apply in commercial order-quantity decisions as in the domestic situation. In making a decision on how much to purchase, operations managers must try to identify the costs which will be affected by their decision. Earlier we examined how inventory decisions affect some of the important components of return on assets. Here we take a cost perspective and re-examine these components in order to determine which costs go up and which go down as the order quantity increases. In the following list, the first three costs will decrease as order size is increased, whereas the next four generally increase as order size is increased:

1 *Cost of placing the order*. Every time that an order is placed to replenish stock, a number of transactions are needed which incur costs to the company. These include preparing the order, communicating with suppliers, arranging for delivery, making payment and maintaining internal records of the transaction. Even if we are placing an 'internal order' on part of our own operation, there are still likely to be the same types of transaction concerned with internal administration.

2 *Price discount costs*. Often suppliers offer discounts for large quantities and cost penalties for small orders.

3 *Stockout costs*. If we misjudge the order-quantity decision and our inventory runs out of stock, there will be lost revenue (opportunity costs) of failing to supply customers. External customers may take their business elsewhere, internal customers will suffer process inefficiencies.

4 *Working capital costs*. After receiving a replenishment order, the supplier will demand payment. Of course, eventually, after we supply our own customers, we in turn will receive payment. However, there will probably be a lag between paying our suppliers and receiving payment from our customers. During this time we will have to fund the costs of inventory. This is called the working capital of inventory. The costs associated with it are the interest we pay the bank for borrowing it, or the opportunity costs of not investing it elsewhere.

5 *Storage costs*. These are the costs associated with physically storing the goods. Renting, heating and lighting the warehouse, as well as insuring the inventory, can be expensive, especially when special conditions are required such as low temperatures or high security.

6 *Obsolescence costs*. When we order large quantities, this usually results in stocked items spending a long time stored in inventory. This increases the risk that the items might either become obsolete (in the case of a change in fashion, for example) or deteriorate with age (in the case of most foodstuffs, for example).

7 *Operating inefficiency costs*. According to just-in-time philosophies, high inventory levels prevent us seeing the full extent of problems within the operation. This argument is fully explored in Chapter 15.

Mountains of grit[4]

Students of operations management from Singapore to Saudi Arabia will perhaps not have a full appreciation of how important this decision is in the colder parts of the world, but, believe it or not, road gritting is big news every winter where snow and ice can cause huge disruption to everyday life. But not every time it snows and, more interestingly, not everywhere it snows. The local government authorities around northern Europe and America differ significantly in how well they cope with freezing weather, usually by spreading grit (actually rock salt, a mixture of salt and grit) on the roads. So how do the authorities decide how much grit to stock up

Source: Digital Vision

in preparation for winter, and when to spread it on the roads? For example, in the UK, when snow is forecast, potential trouble spots are identified by networks of sensors embedded in the road surface to measure climatic conditions. Each sensor is connected by cable or mobile phone technology to an automatic weather station by the roadside. The siting of the sensors is important. They must be sited either on a representative stretch of road (no nearby trees, buildings or bridges, which offer some protection from the cold), or in traditional cold spots. The weather stations then beam back data about air and road temperatures, wind speed and direction, and the wetness of roads. Salt levels are also measured to ensure that grit already spread has not been blown away by wind or washed away by rain. It has been known for cold weather to be forecast and the gritting trucks to be despatched, only for the weather to change, with snow turning to rain, which washed away the grit. Then when temperatures suddenly drop again, the rain freezes on the road. But forecasting how much grit will be needed is even more difficult. Long-range weather forecasts are notoriously inaccurate, so no one knows just how bad a coming winter will be. To make matters worse, the need for road grit depends on more than just the total volume of snow. Local authorities can use the same amount of salt on one 30 cm snowfall as one 5 cm snowfall. Furthermore, the number of snowy days is important in

determining how much grit will be needed. In the skiing areas of Central Europe, most winter days will have snow predictably, while parts of the UK could have little or no snow one winter and many weeks of snow the next.

Supplies of road grit can also vary, as can its price. There are many reasons for this. Mainly of course, if a bad winter is forecast, all authorities in an area will want to buy the same grit, which will reduce supply and put prices up. Also salt mines can flood, especially in winter. Nor is it cheap to transport grit from one area to another; grit is a low-value but heavy material. As a consequence some authorities organize purchasing groups to get better prices before the season starts. Getting more salt during the season may be possible but prices are higher and supply is not guaranteed. In addition, an authority has to decide how fast to use up its inventory of grit. At the start of the winter period, authorities may be cautious about gritting because, once used, the grit cannot be used again, and who knows what the weather will be like later in the season? But in the final analysis the decision of how large an inventory of grit to buy and how to use it is a balance between risks and consequences. Build up too big an inventory of grit and it may not all be used, with the cost of carrying it over to next year being borne by local taxpayers. Build up too small an inventory and incur the wrath of local voters when the roads are difficult to negotiate. Of course a perfect weather forecast would help!

It is worth noting that it may not be the same organization that incurs the costs. For example, sometimes suppliers agree to hold consignment stock. This means that they deliver large quantities of inventory to their customers to store but will only charge for the goods as and when they are used. In the meantime they remain the supplier's property so do not have to be financed by the customer, who does, however, provide storage facilities.

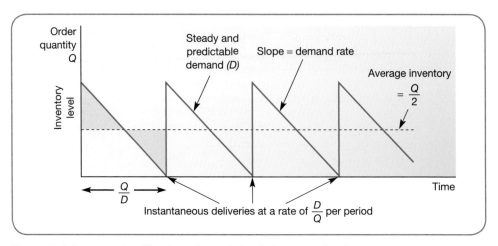

Figure 13.5 Inventory profiles chart the variation in inventory level

Inventory profiles

An inventory profile is a visual representation of the inventory level over time. Figure 13.5 shows a simplified inventory profile for one particular stock item in a retail operation. Every time an order is placed, Q items are ordered. The replenishment order arrives in one batch instantaneously. Demand for the item is then steady and perfectly predictable at a rate of D units per month. When demand has depleted the stock of the items entirely, another order of Q items instantaneously arrives, and so on. Under these circumstances:

The average inventory $= \dfrac{Q}{2}$ (because the two shaded areas in Fig. 13.5 are equal)

The time interval between deliveries $= \dfrac{Q}{D}$

The frequency of deliveries $=$ the reciprocal of the time interval $= \dfrac{D}{Q}$

The economic order quantity (EOQ) formula

The most common approach to deciding how much of any particular item to order when stock needs replenishing is called the economic order quantity (EOQ) approach. This approach attempts to find the best balance between the advantages and disadvantages of holding stock. For example, Figure 13.6 shows two alternative order-quantity policies for an item. Plan A, represented by the solid line, involves ordering in quantities of 400 at a time. Demand in this case is running at 1,000 units per year. Plan B, represented by the dashed line, uses smaller but more frequent replenishment orders. This time only 100 are ordered at a time, with orders being placed four times as often. However, the average inventory for plan B is one-quarter of that for plan A.

To find out whether either of these plans, or some other plan, minimizes the total cost of stocking the item, we need some further information, namely the total cost of holding one unit in stock for a period of time (C_h) and the total costs of placing an order (C_o). Generally, holding costs are taken into account by including:

● working capital costs
● storage costs
● obsolescence risk costs.

Order costs are calculated by taking into account:

● cost of placing the order (including transportation of items from suppliers if relevant);
● price discount costs.

Figure 13.6 Two alternative inventory plans with different order quantities (Q)

In this case the cost of holding stocks is calculated at £1 per item per year and the cost of placing an order is calculated at £20 per order.

We can now calculate total holding costs and ordering costs for any particular ordering plan as follows:

$$\text{Holding costs} = \text{Holding cost/unit} \times \text{Average inventory}$$

$$= C_h \times \frac{Q}{2}$$

$$\text{Ordering costs} = \text{Ordering cost} \times \text{number of orders per period}$$

$$= C_o \times \frac{D}{Q}$$

So, total cost is:

$$C_t = \frac{C_h Q}{2} + \frac{C_o D}{Q}$$

We can now calculate the costs of adopting plans with different order quantities. These are illustrated in Table 13.4. As we would expect with low values of Q, holding costs are low but the costs of placing orders are high because orders have to be placed very frequently. As Q increases, the holding costs increase but the costs of placing orders decrease. Initially the decrease in ordering costs is greater than the increase in holding costs and the total cost falls. After a point, however, the decrease in ordering costs slows, whereas the increase in holding costs remains constant and the total cost starts to increase. In this case the order quantity, Q, which minimizes the sum of holding and order costs, is 200. This 'optimum' order quantity is called the *economic order quantity (EOQ)*. This is illustrated graphically in Figure 13.7.

A more elegant method of finding the EOQ is to derive its general expression. This can be done using simple differential calculus as follows. From before:

$$\text{Total cost} = \text{Holding cost} + \text{Order cost}$$

$$C_t = \frac{C_h Q}{2} + \frac{C_o D}{Q}$$

The rate of change of total cost is given by the first differential of C_t with respect to Q:

$$\frac{dC_t}{dQ} = \frac{C_h}{2} - \frac{C_o D}{Q^2}$$

The lowest cost will occur when $\dfrac{dC_t}{dQ} = 0$, that is:

$$0 = \frac{C_h}{2} - \frac{C_o D}{Q_o^2}$$

where Q_o is the EOQ. Rearranging this expression gives:

$$Q_o = \text{EOQ} = \sqrt{\frac{2C_o D}{C_h}}$$

Table 13.4 **Costs of adoption of plans with different order quantities**

Demand (D) = 1,000 units per year Order costs (C_o) = £20 per order			Holding costs (C_h) = £1 per item per year		
Order quantity (Q)	Holding costs ($0.5Q \times C_h$)	+	Order costs ($(D/Q) \times C_o$)	=	Total costs
50	25		$20 \times 20 = 400$		425
100	50		$10 \times 20 = 200$		250
150	75		$6.7 \times 20 = 134$		209
200	100		$5 \times 20 = 100$		200*
250	125		$4 \times 20 = 80$		205
300	150		$3.3 \times 20 = 66$		216
350	175		$2.9 \times 20 = 58$		233
400	200		$2.5 \times 20 = 50$		250

*Minimum total cost.

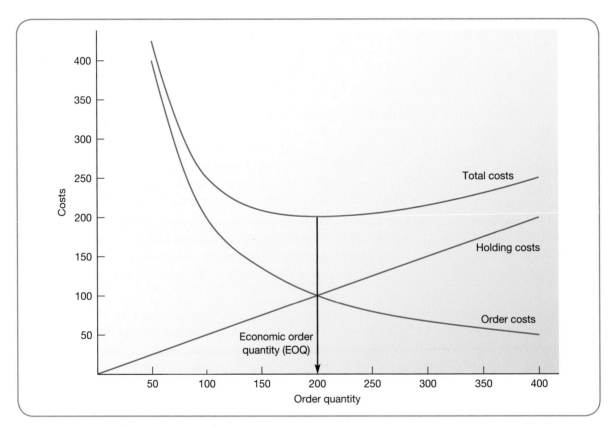

Figure 13.7 **Graphical representation of the economic order quantity**

When using the EOQ:

$$\text{Time between orders} = \frac{\text{EOQ}}{D}$$

$$\text{Order frequency} = \frac{D}{\text{EOQ}} \text{ per period}$$

Sensitivity of the EOQ

Examination of the graphical representation of the total cost curve in Figure 13.7 shows that, although there is a single value of Q which minimizes total costs, any relatively small deviation from the EOQ will not increase total costs significantly. In other words, costs will be near optimum provided a value of Q is chosen that is reasonably close to the EOQ. Put another way, small errors in estimating either holding costs or order costs will not result in a significant deviation from the EOQ. This is a particularly convenient phenomenon because, in practice, both holding and order costs are not easy to estimate accurately.

Worked example

A building materials supplier obtains its bagged cement from a single supplier. Demand is reasonably constant throughout the year, and last year the company sold 2,000 tonnes of this product. It estimates the costs of placing an order at around £25 each time an order is placed, and calculates that the annual cost of holding inventory is 20 per cent of purchase cost. The company purchases the cement at £60 per tonne. How much should the company order at a time?

$$\text{EOQ for cement} = \sqrt{\frac{2C_oD}{C_h}}$$

$$= \sqrt{\frac{2 \times 25 \times 2,000}{0.2 \times 60}}$$

$$= \sqrt{\frac{100,000}{12}}$$

$$= 91.287 \text{ tonnes}$$

After calculating the EOQ the operations manager feels that placing an order for 91.287 tonnes *exactly* seems somewhat over-precise. Why not order a convenient 100 tonnes?

Total cost of ordering plan for Q = 91.287 is:

$$= \frac{C_hQ}{2} + \frac{C_oD}{Q}$$

$$= \frac{(0.2 \times 60) \times 91.287}{2} + \frac{25 \times 2,000}{91.287}$$

$$= £1,095.454$$

Total cost of ordering plan for Q = 100 is:

$$= \frac{(0.2 \times 60) \times 100}{2} + \frac{25 \times 2,000}{100}$$

$$= £1,100$$

The extra cost of ordering 100 tonnes at a time is £1,100 − £1,095.45 = £4.55. The operations manager therefore should feel confident in using the more convenient order quantity.

Gradual replacement – the economic batch quantity (EBQ) model

Although the simple inventory profile shown in Figure 13.5 made some simplifying assumptions, it is broadly applicable in most situations where each complete replacement order arrives at one point in time. In many cases, however, replenishment occurs over a time period rather than in one lot. A typical example of this is where an internal order is placed for a batch of parts to be produced on a machine. The machine will start to produce the parts and ship them in a more or less continuous stream into inventory, but at the same time demand

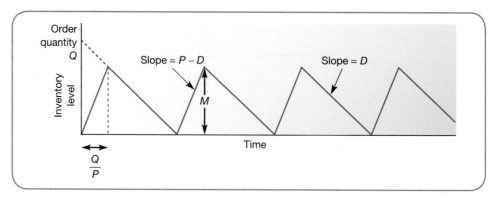

Figure 13.8 Inventory profile for gradual replacement of inventory

is continuing to remove parts from the inventory. Provided the rate at which parts are being made and put into the inventory (P) is higher than the rate at which demand is depleting the inventory (D) then the size of the inventory will increase. After the batch has been completed the machine will be reset (to produce some other part), and demand will continue to deplete the inventory level until production of the next batch begins. The resulting profile is shown in Figure 13.8. Such a profile is typical for cycle inventories supplied by batch processes, where items are produced internally and intermittently. For this reason the minimum cost batch quantity for this profile is called the economic batch quantity (EBQ). It is also sometimes known as the economic manufacturing quantity (EMQ), or the production order quantity (POQ). It is derived as follows:

$$\text{Maximum stock level} = M$$
$$\text{Slope of inventory build-up} = P - D$$

Also, as is clear from Figure 13.8:

$$\text{Slope of inventory build-up} = M \div \frac{Q}{P}$$
$$= \frac{MP}{Q}$$

So:

$$\frac{MP}{Q} = P - D$$
$$M = \frac{Q(P - D)}{P}$$
$$\text{Average inventory level} = \frac{M}{2}$$
$$= \frac{Q(P - D)}{2P}$$

As before:

$$\text{Total cost} = \text{Holding cost} + \text{Order cost}$$
$$C_t = \frac{C_h Q(P - D)}{2P} + \frac{C_o D}{Q}$$
$$\frac{dC_t}{dQ} = \frac{C_h(P - D)}{2P} - \frac{C_o D}{Q^2}$$

Again, equating to zero and solving Q gives the minimum cost order quantity EBQ:

$$\text{EBQ} = \sqrt{\frac{2C_o D}{C_h(1 - (D/P))}}$$

The manager of a bottle-filling plant which bottles soft drinks needs to decide how long a 'run' of each type of drink to process. Demand for each type of drink is reasonably constant at 80,000 per month (a month has 160 production hours). The bottling lines fill at a rate of 3,000 bottles per hour, but take an hour to clean and reset between different drinks. The cost (of labour and lost production capacity) of each of these changeovers has been calculated at £100 per hour. Stock-holding costs are counted at £0.1 per bottle per month.

$$D = 80,000 \text{ per month}$$
$$= 500 \text{ per hour}$$

$$EBQ = \sqrt{\frac{2\,C_o D}{C_h(1 - (D/P))}}$$

$$= \sqrt{\frac{2 \times 100 \times 80,000}{0.1(1 - (500/3,000))}}$$

$$= 13.856$$

The staff who operate the lines have devised a method of reducing the changeover time from 1 hour to 30 minutes. How would that change the EBQ?

$$\text{New } C_o = £50$$

$$\text{New EBQ} = \sqrt{\frac{2 \times 50 \times 80,000}{0.1(1(500/3,000))}}$$

$$= 9,798$$

The approach to determining order quantity which involves optimizing costs of holding stock against costs of ordering stock, typified by the EOQ and EBQ models, has always been subject to criticisms. Originally these concerned the validity of some of the assumptions of the model; more recently they have involved the underlying rationale of the approach itself. The criticisms fall into four broad categories, all of which we will examine further:

- The assumptions included in the EOQ models are simplistic.
- The real costs of stock in operations are not as assumed in EOQ models.
- The models are really descriptive, and should not be used as prescriptive devices.
- Cost minimization is not an appropriate objective for inventory management.

Responding to the criticisms of EOQ

In order to keep EOQ-type models relatively straightforward, it was necessary to make assumptions. These concerned such things as the stability of demand, the existence of a fixed and identifiable ordering cost, that the cost of stock holding can be expressed by a linear function, shortage costs which were identifiable, and so on. While these assumptions are rarely strictly true, most of them can approximate to reality. Furthermore, the shape of the total cost curve has a relatively flat optimum point, which means that small errors will not significantly affect the total cost of a near-optimum order quantity. However, at times the assumptions do pose severe limitations to the models. For example, the assumption of steady demand (or even demand which conforms to some known probability distribution) is untrue for a wide range of the operation's inventory problems. For example, a bookseller might be very happy to adopt an EOQ-type ordering policy for some of its most regular and stable products such as dictionaries and popular reference books. However, the demand patterns for many other books could be highly erratic, dependent on critics' reviews and word-of-mouth recommendations. In such circumstances it is simply inappropriate to use EOQ models.

Cost of stock

Other questions surround some of the assumptions made concerning the nature of stock-related costs. For example, placing an order with a supplier as part of a regular and multi-item order might be relatively inexpensive, whereas asking for a special one-off delivery of an item could prove far more costly. Similarly with stock-holding costs – although many companies make a standard percentage charge on the purchase price of stock items, this might not be appropriate over a wide range of stock-holding levels. The marginal costs of increasing stock-holding levels might be merely the cost of the working capital involved. On the other hand, it might necessitate the construction or lease of a whole new stock-holding facility such as a warehouse. Operations managers using an EOQ-type approach must check that the decisions implied by the use of the formulae do not exceed the boundaries within which the cost assumptions apply. In Chapter 15 we explore the 'lean' approach that sees inventory as being largely negative. However, it is useful at this stage to examine the effect on an EOQ approach of regarding inventory as being more costly than previously believed. Increasing the slope of the holding cost line increases the level of total costs of *any* order quantity, but, more significantly, shifts the minimum cost point substantially to the left, in favour of a lower EOQ. In other words, the less willing an operation is to hold stock on the grounds of cost, the more it should move towards smaller, more frequent ordering.

Using EOQ models as prescriptions

Perhaps the most fundamental criticism of the EOQ approach again comes from the Japanese-inspired 'lean' and JIT philosophies. The EOQ tries to optimize order decisions. Implicitly the costs involved are taken as fixed, in the sense that the task of operations managers is to find out what are the true costs rather than to change them in any way. EOQ is essentially a reactive approach. Some critics would argue that it fails to ask the right question. Rather than asking the EOQ question of 'What is the optimum order quantity?' operations managers should really be asking, 'How can I change the operation in some way so as to reduce the overall level of inventory I need to hold?' The EOQ approach may be a reasonable description of stock-holding costs but should not necessarily be taken as a strict prescription over what decisions to take. For example, many organizations have made considerable efforts to reduce the effective cost of placing an order. Often they have done this by working to reduce changeover times on machines. This means that less time is taken changing over from one product to the other, and therefore less operating capacity is lost, which in turn reduces the cost of the changeover. Under these circumstances, the order cost curve in the EOQ formula reduces and, in turn, reduces the effective EOQ. Figure 13.9 shows the EOQ formula represented graphically with increased holding costs (see the previous discussion) and reduced order costs. The net effect of this is to reduce significantly the value of the EOQ.

Should the cost of inventory be minimized?

Many organizations (such as supermarkets and wholesalers) make most of their revenue and profits simply by holding and supplying inventory. Because their main investments is in the inventory it is critical that they make a good return on this capital, by ensuring that it has the highest possible 'stock turn' (defined later in this chapter) and/or gross profit margin. Alternatively, they may also be concerned to maximize the use of space by seeking to maximize the profit earned per square metre. The EOQ model does not address these objectives. Similarly for products that deteriorate or go out of fashion, the EOQ model can result in excess inventory of slower moving items. In fact the EOQ model is rarely used in such organizations,

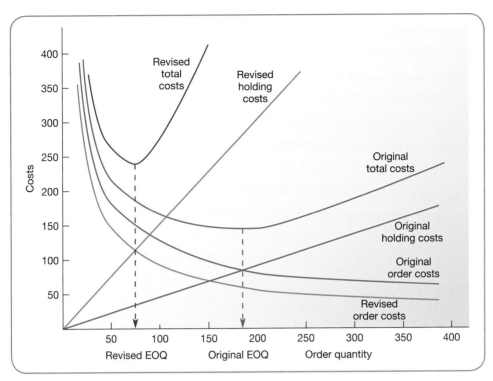

Figure 13.9 If the true costs of stock holding are taken into account, and if the cost of ordering (or changeover) is reduced, the economic order quantity (EOQ) is much smaller

Inventory management at Flame Electrical

Inventory management in some operations is more than just a part of their responsibility; it is their very reason for being in business. Flame Electrical was South Africa's largest independent supplier and distributor of lamps. It stocked almost 3,000 different types of lamps, which were sourced from 14 countries and distributed to customers throughout the country. '*In effect our customers are using us to manage their stocks of lighting sources for them*', said Jeff Schaffer, the Managing Director of Flame Electrical. '*They could, if they wanted to, hold their own stock but might not want to devote the time, space, money or effort to doing so. Using us they get the widest range of products to choose from, and an accurate, fast and dependable service.*'

Orders for the replenishment of stocks in the warehouse were triggered by a re-order point system. The re-order point for each stocked item took into account

the likely demand for the product during the order lead time (forecast from the equivalent period's orders the previous year), the order lead time for the item (which varies from 24 hours to four months) and the variability of the lead time (from previous experience). Flame preferred most orders to its suppliers to be for a whole number of container loads (the shipping costs for part-container loads being more expensive). However, lower order quantities of small or expensive lamps may be used. The order quantity for each lamp was based on its demand, its value and the cost of transportation from the suppliers. However, all this could be overridden in an emergency. If a customer, such as a hospital, urgently needed a particular lamp which was not in stock, the company would even use a fast courier to fly the item in from overseas – all for the sake of maintaining its reputation for high service levels.

'We have to get the balance right', says Jeff Schaffer. 'Excellent service is the foundation of our success. But we could not survive if we did not control stocks tightly. After all we are carrying the cost of every lamp in our warehouse until the customer eventually pays for it. If stock levels were too high we just could not operate profitably. It is for that reason that we go as far as to pay incentives to the relevant staff based on how well they keep our working capital and stocks under control.'

and there is more likely to be a system of periodic review (described later) for regular ordering of replenishment inventory. For example, a typical builders' supply merchant might carry around 50,000 different items of stock (SKUs). However, most of these cluster into larger families of items such as paints, sanitary ware or metal fixings. Single orders are placed at regular intervals for all the required replenishments in the supplier's range, and these are then delivered together at one time. For example, if such deliveries were made weekly, then, on average, the individual item order quantities will be for only one week's usage. Less popular items, or ones with erratic demand patterns, can be individually ordered at the same time, or (when urgent) can be delivered the next day by carrier.

WHEN TO PLACE AN ORDER? THE TIMING DECISION

When we assumed that orders arrived instantaneously and demand was steady and predictable, the decision of when to place a replenishment order was self-evident. An order would be placed as soon as the stock level reached zero. This would arrive instantaneously and prevent any stockout occurring. If replenishment orders do not arrive instantaneously, but have a lag between the order being placed and arriving in the inventory, we can calculate the timing of a replacement order as shown in Figure 13.10. The lead time for an order to arrive is in this case two weeks, so the re-order point (ROP) is the point at which stock will fall to zero minus the order lead time. Alternatively, we can define the point in terms of the level which the inventory will have reached when a replenishment order needs to be placed. In this case this occurs at a re-order level (ROL) of 200 items.

However, this assumes that both the demand and the order lead time are perfectly predictable. In most cases, of course, this is not so. Both demand and the order lead time are likely to vary to produce a profile which looks something like that in Figure 13.11. In these circumstances it is necessary to make the replenishment order somewhat earlier than would be the case in a purely deterministic situation. This will result in, on average, some stock still being in the inventory when the replenishment order arrives. This is buffer (safety) stock. The earlier the replenishment order is placed, the higher will be the expected level of safety stock (s) when the replenishment order arrives. But because of the variability of both lead time (t) and demand rate (d), there will sometimes be a higher than average level of safety stock and sometimes lower. The main consideration in setting safety stock is not so much the average level of stock when a replenishment order arrives, but rather the probability that the stock will not have run out before the replenishment order arrives.

The key statistic in calculating how much safety stock to allow is the probability distribution which shows the lead-time usage. This lead-time usage distribution is a combination of the distributions which describe lead-time variation and the demand rate during the lead time. If safety stock is set below the lower limit of this distribution, then there will be shortages every single replenishment cycle. If safety stock is set above the upper limit of the

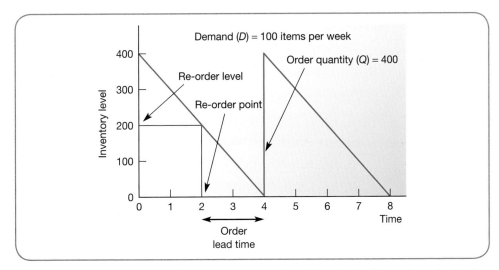

Figure 13.10 Re-order level (ROL) and re-order point (ROP) are derived from the order lead time and demand rate

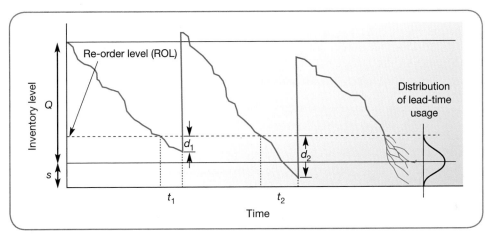

Figure 13.11 Safety stock (*s*) helps to avoid stockouts when demand and/or order lead time are uncertain

distribution, there is no chance of stockouts occurring. Usually, safety stock is set to give a predetermined likelihood that stockouts will not occur. Figure 13.11 shows that, in this case, the first replenishment order arrived after t_1, resulting in a lead-time usage of d_1. The second replenishment order took longer, t_2, and demand rate was also higher, resulting in a lead-time usage of d_2. The third order cycle shows several possible inventory profiles for different conditions of lead-time usage and demand rate.

> ✳ **Operations principle**
>
> For any stock replenishment activity, the timing of replenishment should reflect the effects of uncertain lead time and uncertain demand during that lead time.

Worked example

A company which imports running shoes for sale in its sports shops can never be certain of how long, after placing an order, the delivery will take. Examination of previous orders reveals that, out of 10 orders, one took one week, two took two weeks, four took three weeks, two took four weeks and one took five weeks. The rate of demand for the shoes also varies between 110 and 140 pairs per week. There is a 0.2 probability of the demand rate being

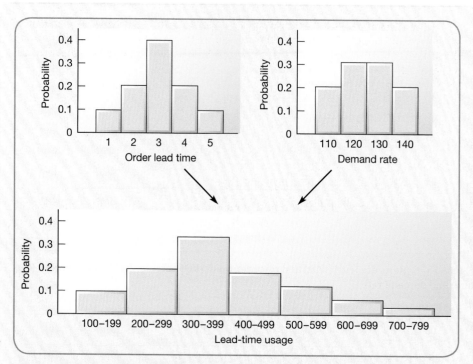

Figure 13.12 The probability distributions for order lead time and demand rate combine to give the lead-time usage distribution

either 110 or 140 pairs per week, and a 0.3 chance of demand being either 120 or 130 pairs per week. The company needs to decide when it should place replenishment orders if the probability of a stockout is to be less than 10 per cent.

Both lead time and the demand rate during the lead time will contribute to the lead-time usage. So the distributions which describe each will need to be combined. Figure 13.12 and Table 13.5 show how this can be done. Taking lead time to be one, two, three, four or five weeks, and demand rate to be 110, 120, 130 or 140 pairs per week, and also assuming the two variables to be independent, the distributions can be combined as shown in Table 13.5. Each element in the matrix shows a possible lead-time usage with the probability of its occurrence. So if the lead time is one week and the demand rate is 110 pairs per week, the actual lead-time usage will be 1 × 110 = 110 pairs. Since there is a 0.1 chance of the lead time being one week, and a 0.2 chance of demand rate being 110 pairs per week, the probability of both these events occurring is 0.1 × 0.2 = 0.02.

Table 13.5 Matrix of lead-time and demand-rate probabilities

			Lead-time probabilities				
			1 0.1	2 0.2	3 0.4	4 0.2	5 0.1
	110	0.2	110 (0.02)	220 (0.04)	330 (0.08)	440 (0.04)	550 (0.02)
Demand-rate	120	0.3	120 (0.03)	240 (0.06)	360 (0.12)	480 (0.06)	600 (0.03)
probabilities	130	0.3	130 (0.03)	260 (0.06)	390 (0.12)	520 (0.06)	650 (0.03)
	140	0.2	140 (0.02)	280 (0.04)	420 (0.08)	560 (0.04)	700 (0.02)

We can now classify the possible lead-time usages into histogram form. For example, summing the probabilities of all the lead-time usages which fall within the range 100–199 (all the first column) gives a combined probability of 0.1. Repeating this for subsequent intervals results in Table 13.6.

Table 13.6 **Combined probabilities**

Lead-time usage	100–199	200–299	300–399	400–499	500–599	600–699	700–799
Probability	0.1	0.2	0.32	0.18	0.12	0.06	0.02

This shows the probability of each possible range of lead-time usage occurring, but it is the cumulative probabilities that are needed to predict the likelihood of stockout (*see* Table 13.7).

Table 13.7 **Combined probabilities**

Lead-time usage X	100	200	300	400	500	600	700	800
Probability of usage being greater than X	1.0	0.9	0.7	0.38	0.2	0.08	0.02	0

Setting the re-order level at 600 would mean that there is only a 0.08 chance of usage being greater than available inventory during the lead time; that is, there is a less than 10 per cent chance of a stockout occurring.

Continuous and periodic review

The approach we have described to making the replenishment timing decision is often called the continuous review approach. This is because, to make the decision in this way, there must be a process to review the stock level of each item continuously and then place an order when the stock level reaches its re-order level. The virtue of this approach is that, although the timing of orders may be irregular (depending on the variation in demand rate), the order size (Q) is constant and can be set at the optimum EOQ. Such continual checking on inventory levels can be time consuming, especially when there are many stock withdrawals compared with the average level of stock, but in an environment where all inventory records are computerized, this should not be a problem unless the records are inaccurate.

An alternative and far simpler approach, but one which sacrifices the use of a fixed (and therefore possibly optimum) order quantity, is called the periodic review approach. Here, rather than ordering at a predetermined re-order level, the periodic approach orders at a fixed and regular time interval. So the stock level of an item could be found, for example, at the end of every month and a replenishment order placed to bring the stock up to a predetermined level. This level is calculated to cover demand between the replenishment order being placed and the following replenishment order arriving. Figure 13.13 illustrates the parameters for the periodic review approach.

At time T_1 in Figure 13.13 the inventory manager would examine the stock level and order sufficient to bring it up to some maximum, Q_m. However, that order of Q_1 items will not arrive until a further time of t_1 has passed, during which demand continues to deplete the stocks. Again, both demand and lead time are uncertain. The Q_1 items will arrive and bring the stock up to some level lower than Q_m (unless there has been no demand during t_1). Demand then continues until T_2, when again an order Q_2 is placed which is the difference between the current stock at T_2 and Q_m. This order arrives after t_2, by which time demand has depleted the stocks further. Thus the replenishment order placed at T_1 must be able to cover for the

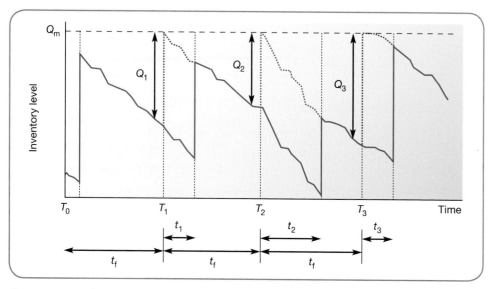

Figure 13.13 A periodic review approach to order timing with probabilistic demand and lead time

demand which occurs until T_2 and t_2. Safety stocks will need to be calculated, in a similar manner as before, based on the distribution of usage over this period.

The time interval

The interval between placing orders, t_1, is usually calculated on a deterministic basis, and derived from the EOQ. So, for example, if the demand for an item is 2,000 per year, the cost of placing an order £25, and the cost of holding stock £0.5 per item per year:

$$\text{EOQ} = \sqrt{\frac{2C_oD}{C_h}} = \sqrt{\frac{2 \times 2,000 \times 25}{0.5}} = 447$$

The optimum time interval between orders, t_f, is therefore:

$$t_f = \frac{\text{EOQ}}{D} = \frac{447}{2,000}\text{ years}$$

$$= 2.68 \text{ months}$$

It may seem paradoxical to calculate the time interval assuming constant demand when demand is, in fact, uncertain. However, uncertainties in both demand and lead time can be allowed for by setting Q_m to allow for the desired probability of stockout based on usage during the period t_f + lead time.

Two-bin and three-bin systems

Keeping track of inventory levels is especially important in continuous review approaches to re-ordering. A simple and obvious method of indicating when the re-order point has been reached is necessary, especially if there are a large number of items to be monitored. The two- and three-bin systems illustrated in Figure 13.14 are such methods. The simple two-bin system involves storing the re-order point quantity plus the safety inventory quantity in the second bin and using parts from the first bin. When the first bin empties, that is the signal to order the next re-order quantity. Sometimes the safety inventory is stored in a third bin (the three-bin system), so it is clear when demand is exceeding that which was expected. Different 'bins' are not always necessary to operate this type of system. For example, a common practice in retail operations is to store the second 'bin' quantity upside down behind or under the first 'bin' quantity. Orders are then placed when the upside-down items are reached.

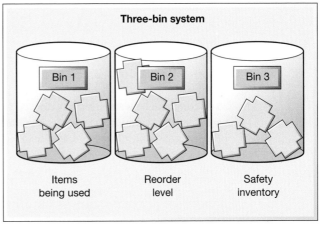

Figure 13.14 The two-bin and three-bin systems of re-ordering

Amazon's 'anticipatory shipping'[5]

Forecast accuracy and time to deliver are related. Poor forecasts mean that the wrong items will be stored, which in turn means that delivery will be delayed until the right items are received. But what if a supplier could know what its customers were going to order, even before they do? That is the ambition of Amazon's online retail operation. It filed a patent to protect its system for the technology that hopes to predict what its customers will buy, even before they have clicked the 'order' button. The company, which is the world's largest online retailer, calls its new system 'anticipatory shipping' and perceives it as a way to speed up its delivery times. Amazon's patent application reveals the thinking behind the system. Its application says that: 'One substantial disadvantage to the virtual storefront model is that in many instances, customers cannot receive their merchandise immediately upon purchase, but must instead wait for product to be shipped to them. The availability of expedited shipping methods from various common carriers may mitigate the delay in shipment, but often at substantial additional cost that may rival the price paid for the merchandise. Such delays may dissuade customers from buying items from online

Source: Alamy Images: David J. Green

merchants, particularly if those items are more readily available locally.' The approach is reported as using several elements to predict what purchases a person may make. Factors to be taken into account could include age, income, previously purchased items, searched for items, 'wish lists' and maybe even the time a user's cursor lingers over a product. Armed with this information, Amazon could ship items that are likely to be ordered to the inventory 'hub' nearest to the customer. So, when a customer really does order, the item can be delivered far faster.

HOW CAN INVENTORY BE CONTROLLED?

The models we have described, even the ones which take a probabilistic view of demand and lead time, are still simplified compared with the complexity of real stock management. Coping with many thousands of stocked items, supplied by many hundreds of different suppliers, with possibly tens of thousands of individual customers, makes for a complex and dynamic operations task. In order to control such complexity, operations managers have to do two things. First, they have to discriminate between different stocked items, so that they can apply a degree of control to each item which is appropriate to its importance. Second, they need to invest in an information-processing system which can cope with their particular set of inventory control circumstances.

Inventory priorities – the ABC system

In any inventory which contains more than one stocked item, some items will be more important to the organization than others. Some, for example, might have a very high usage rate, so if they ran out many customers would be disappointed. Other items might be of particularly high value, so excessively high inventory levels would be particularly expensive. One common way of discriminating between different stock items is to rank them by their usage value (their usage rate multiplied by their individual value). Items with a particularly high usage value are deemed to warrant the most careful control, whereas those with low usage values need not be controlled quite so rigorously. Generally, a relatively small proportion of the total range of items contained in an inventory will account for a large proportion of the total usage value. This phenomenon is known as the Pareto law (after the person who described it), sometimes referred to as the 80/20 rule. It is called this because, typically, 80 per cent of an operation's sales are accounted for by only 20 per cent of all stocked item types. The Pareto law is also used elsewhere in operations management (see, for example, Chapter 16). Here the relationship can be used to classify the different types of items kept in an inventory by their usage value. ABC inventory control allows inventory managers to concentrate their efforts on controlling the more significant items of stock:

- *Class A items* are those 20 per cent or so of high usage value which account for around 80 per cent of the total usage value.

- *Class B items* are those of medium usage value, usually the next 30 per cent of items which often account for around 10 per cent of the total usage value.
- *Class C items* are those of low usage value which, although comprising around 50 per cent of the total types of items stocked, probably only account for around 10 per cent of the total usage value of the operation.

> ✳ **Operations principle**
> Different inventory management decision rules are needed for different classes of inventory.

Worked example

Table 13.8 shows all the parts stored by an electrical wholesaler. The 20 different items stored vary in terms of both their usage per year and cost per item as shown. However, the wholesaler has ranked the stock items by their usage value per year. The total usage value per year is £5,569,000. From this it is possible to calculate the usage value per year of each item as a percentage of the total usage value, and from that a running cumulative total of the usage value as shown. The wholesaler can then plot the cumulative percentage of all stocked items against the cumulative percentage of their value. So, for example, the part with stock number A/703 is the highest value part and accounts for 25.14 per cent of the total inventory value. As a part, however, it is only 1/20th or 5 per cent of the total number of items stocked. This item together with the next highest value item (D/012) account for only 10 per cent of the total number of items stocked, yet account for 47.37 per cent of the value of the stock, and so on.

▶

Table 13.8 Warehouse items ranked by usage value

Stock no.	Usage (items/year)	Cost (£/item)	Usage value (£000/year)	% of total value	Cumulative % of total value
A/703	700	20.00	14,000	77.1%	77.1%
D/102	450	2.75	1,238	6.8%	83.9%
A/135	1,000	0.90	900	5.0%	88.8%
C/732	95	8.50	808	4.4%	93.3%
C/375	520	0.54	281	1.5%	94.8%
A/500	73	2.30	168	0.9%	95.7%
D/111	520	0.22	114	0.6%	96.4%
D/231	170	0.65	111	0.6%	97.0%
E/781	250	0.34	85	0.5%	97.4%
A/138	250	0.30	75	0.4%	97.9%
D/175	400	0.14	56	0.3%	98.2%
E/001	80	0.63	50	0.3%	98.4%
C/150	230	0.21	48	0.3%	98.7%
F/030	400	0.12	48	0.3%	99.0%
D/703	500	0.09	45	0.2%	99.2%
D/535	50	0.88	44	0.2%	99.5%
C/541	70	0.57	40	0.2%	99.7%
A/260	50	0.64	32	0.2%	99.9%
B/141	50	0.32	16	0.1%	99.9%
D/021	20	0.50	10	0.1%	100.0%
Total			18,169	100.0%	

This is shown graphically in Figure 13.15. Here the wholesaler has classified the first four part numbers (20 per cent of the range) as Class A items and will monitor the usage and ordering of these items very closely and frequently. A few improvements in order quantities or safety stocks for these items could bring significant savings. The six next part numbers, C/375 to A/138 (30 per cent of the range), are to be treated as Class B items with slightly less effort devoted to their control. All other items are classed as Class C items, whose stocking policy is reviewed only occasionally.

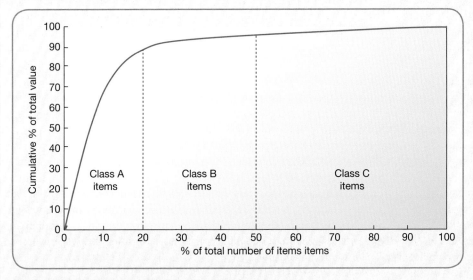

Figure 13.15 Pareto curve for items in a warehouse

Although annual usage and value are the two criteria most commonly used to determine a stock classification system, other criteria might also contribute towards the (higher) classification of an item:

- *Consequence of stockout*. High priority might be given to those items which would seriously delay or disrupt other operations, or the customers, if they were not in stock.
- *Uncertainty of supply*. Some items, although of low value, might warrant more attention if their supply is erratic or uncertain.
- *High obsolescence or deterioration risk*. Items which could lose their value through obsolescence or deterioration might need extra attention and monitoring.

Some more complex stock classification systems might include these criteria by classifying on an A, B, C basis for each. For example, a part might be classed as A/B/A, meaning it is an A category item by value, a class B item by consequence of stockout and a class A item by obsolescence risk.

Critical commentary

This approach to inventory classification can sometimes be misleading. Many professional inventory managers point out that the Pareto law is often misquoted. It does not say that 80 per cent of the SKUs (Stock Keeping Units) account for only 20 per cent inventory value. It accounts for 80 per cent of inventory 'usage' or throughput value: in other words, sales value. In fact it is the slow-moving items (the C category items) that often pose the greatest challenge in inventory management. Often these slow-moving items, although only accounting for 20 per cent of sales, require a large part (typically between one-half and two-thirds) of the total investment in stock. This is why slow-moving items are a real problem. Moreover, if errors in forecasting or ordering result in excess stock in 'A class' fast-moving items, it is relatively unimportant in the sense that excess stock can be sold quickly. However, excess stock in slow-moving C items will be there a long time. According to some inventory managers, it is the A items that can be left to look after themselves; it is the B and even more the C items that need controlling.

Measuring inventory

In our example of ABC classifications we used the monetary value of the annual usage of each item as a measure of inventory usage. Monetary value can also be used to measure the absolute level of inventory at any point in time. This would involve taking the number of each item in stock, multiplying it by its value (usually the cost of purchasing the item) and summing the value of all the individual items stored. This is a useful measure of the investment that an operation has in its inventories but gives no indication of how large that investment is relative to the total throughput of the operation. To do this we must compare the total number of items in stock against their rate of usage. There are two ways of doing this. The first is to calculate the amount of time the inventory would last, subject to normal demand, if it were not replenished. This is sometimes called the number of weeks' (or days', months', years', etc.) *cover* of the stock. The second method is to calculate how often the stock is used up in a period, usually one year. This is called the stock turn or turnover of stock and is the reciprocal of the stock-cover figure mentioned earlier.

A small specialist wine importer holds stocks of three types of wine, Chateau A, Chateau B and Chateau C. Current stock levels are 500 cases of Chateau A, 300 cases of Chateau B and 200 cases of Chateau C. Table 13.9 shows the number of each held in stock, their cost per item and the demand per year for each.

Table 13.9 **Stock, cost and demand for three stocked items**

Item	Average no. in stock	Cost per item (£)	Annual demand
Chateau A	500	3.00	2,000
Chateau B	300	4.00	1,500
Chateau C	200	5.00	1,000

$$\text{The total value of stock} = \sum(\text{average stock level} \times \text{cost per item})$$

$$= (500 \times 3) + (300 \times 4) + (200 \times 5)$$

$$= 3,700$$

The amount of *stock cover* provided by each item stocked is as follows (assuming 50 sales weeks per year):

$$\text{Chateau A, stock cover} = \frac{\text{Stock}}{\text{Demand}} = \frac{500}{2,000} \times 50 = 12.5 \text{ weeks}$$

$$\text{Chateau B, stock cover} = \frac{\text{Stock}}{\text{Demand}} = \frac{300}{1,500} \times 50 = 10 \text{ weeks}$$

$$\text{Chateau C, stock cover} = \frac{\text{Stock}}{\text{Demand}} = \frac{200}{1,000} \times 50 = 10 \text{ weeks}$$

The *stock turn* for each item is calculated as follows:

$$\text{Chateau A, stock turn} = \frac{\text{Demand}}{\text{Stock}} = \frac{2,000}{500} = 4 \text{ times/year}$$

$$\text{Chateau B, stock turn} = \frac{\text{Demand}}{\text{Stock}} = \frac{1,500}{300} = 5 \text{ times/year}$$

$$\text{Chateau C, stock turn} = \frac{\text{Demand}}{\text{Stock}} = \frac{1,000}{200} = 5 \text{ times/year}$$

To find the average stock cover or stock turn for the total items in the inventory, the individual item measures can be weighted by their demand levels as a proportion of total demand (4,500). Thus:

$$\text{Average stock cover} = \left(12.5 \times \frac{2,000}{4,500}\right) + \left(10 \times \frac{1,500}{4,500}\right) + \left(10 \times \frac{1,000}{4,500}\right)$$

$$= 11.11$$

$$\text{Average stock turn} = \left(4 \times \frac{2,000}{4,500}\right) + \left(50 \times \frac{1,500}{4,500}\right) + \left(50 \times \frac{1,000}{4,500}\right)$$

$$= 4.5$$

Inventory information systems

Most inventories of any significant size are managed by computerized systems. The many relatively routine calculations involved in stock control lend themselves to computerized support. This is especially so since data capture has been made more convenient through the use of bar-code readers and the point-of-sale recording of sales transactions. Many commercial systems of stock control are available, although they tend to share certain common functions.

Updating stock records

Every time a transaction takes place (such as the sale of an item, the movement of an item from a warehouse into a truck, or the delivery of an item into a warehouse) the position, status and possibly value of the stock will have changed. This information must be recorded so that operations managers can determine their current inventory status at any time.

Generating orders

The two major decisions we have described previously, namely how much to order and when to order, can both be made by a computerized stock control system. The first decision, setting the value of how much to order (Q), is likely to be taken only at relatively infrequent intervals. Originally almost all computer systems automatically calculated order quantities by using the EOQ formulae covered earlier. Now more sophisticated algorithms are used, often using probabilistic data and based on examining the marginal return on investing in stock. The system will hold all the information which goes into the ordering algorithm but might periodically check to see if demand or order lead times, or any of the other parameters, have changed significantly and recalculate Q accordingly. The decision on when to order, on the other hand, is a far more routine affair which computer systems make according to whatever decision rules operations managers have chosen to adopt: either continuous review or periodic review. Furthermore, the systems can automatically generate whatever documentation is required, or even transmit the re-ordering information electronically through an electronic data interchange (EDI) system.

Generating inventory reports

Inventory control systems can generate regular reports of stock value for the different items stored, which can help management monitor its inventory control performance. Similarly, customer service performance, such as the number of stockouts or the number of incomplete orders, can be regularly monitored. Some reports may be generated on an exception basis. That is, the report is only generated if some performance measure deviates from acceptable limits.

Forecasting

Inventory replenishment decisions should ideally be made with a clear understanding of forecast future demand. The inventory control system can compare actual demand against forecast and adjust the forecast in the light of actual levels of demand. Control systems of this type are treated in more detail in Chapter 14.

Common problems with inventory systems

Our description of inventory systems has been based on the assumption that operations (a) have a reasonably accurate idea of costs such as holding cost, or order cost, and (b) have accurate information that really does indicate the actual level of stock and sales. But data inaccuracy often poses one of the most significant problems for inventory managers. This is because most computer-based inventory management systems are based on what is called the perpetual inventory principle. This is the simple idea that stock records are (or should be) automatically updated every time that items are recorded as having been received into an inventory or taken out of the inventory. So:

$$\text{Opening stock level} + \text{Receipts in} - \text{Despatches out} = \text{New stock level}$$

Any errors in recording these transactions, and/or in handling the physical inventory, can lead to discrepancies between the recorded and actual inventory, and these errors are perpetuated until physical stock checks are made (usually quite infrequently). In practice there are many opportunities for errors to occur, if only because inventory transactions are numerous. This means that it is surprisingly common for the majority of inventory records to be inaccurate. The underlying causes of errors include:

> *** Operations principle**
>
> The maintenance of data accuracy is vital for the day-to-day effectiveness of inventory management systems.

- keying errors – entering the wrong product code;
- quantity errors – a mis-count of items put into or taken from stock;
- damaged or deteriorated inventory not recorded as such, or not correctly deleted from the records when it is destroyed;
- the wrong items being taken out of stock, but the records not being corrected when they are returned to stock;
- delays between the transactions being made and the records being updated;
- items stolen from inventory (common in retail environments, but also not unusual in industrial and commercial inventories).

SUMMARY ANSWERS TO KEY QUESTIONS

❯ What is inventory?

- Inventory, or stock, is the stored accumulation of the transformed resources in an operation. Sometimes the words 'stock' and 'inventory' are also used to describe transforming resources, but the terms 'stock control' and 'inventory control' are nearly always used in connection with transformed resources.
- Almost all operations keep some kind of inventory, most usually of materials but also of information and customers (customer inventories are normally called queues).

❯ Why should there be any inventory?

- Inventory occurs in operations because the timing of supply and the timing of demand do not always match. Inventories are needed, therefore, to smooth the differences between supply and demand.
- There are five main reasons for keeping physical inventory:
  - to cope with random or unexpected interruptions in supply or demand (buffer inventory);
  - to cope with an operation's inability to make all products simultaneously (cycle inventory);
  - to allow different stages of processing to operate at different speeds and with different schedules (de-coupling inventory);
  - to cope with planned fluctuations in supply or demand (anticipation inventory);
  - to cope with transportation delays in the supply network (pipeline inventory).
- Inventory is often a major part of working capital, tying up money which could be used more productively elsewhere.

- If inventory is not used quickly, there is an increasing risk of damage, loss, deterioration or obsolescence.
- Inventory invariably takes up space (for example, in a warehouse) and has to be managed, stored in appropriate conditions, insured and physically handled when transactions occur. It therefore contributes to overhead costs.

❯ How much to order? The volume decision

- This depends on balancing the costs associated with holding stocks against the costs associated with placing an order. The main stock-holding costs are usually related to working capital, whereas the main order costs are usually associated with the transactions necessary to generate the information to place an order.
- The best-known approach to determining the amount of inventory to order is the economic order quantity (EOQ) formula. The EOQ formula can be adapted to different types of inventory profile using different stock behaviour assumptions.
- The EOQ approach, however, has been subject to a number of criticisms regarding the true cost of holding stock, the real cost of placing an order, and the use of EOQ models as prescriptive devices.

❯ When to place an order? The timing decision

- Partly this depends on the uncertainty of demand. Orders are usually timed to leave a certain level of average safety stock when the order arrives. The level of safety stock is influenced by the variability of both demand and the lead time of supply. These two variables are usually combined into a lead-time usage distribution.
- Using re-order level as a trigger for placing replenishment orders necessitates the continual review of inventory levels. This can be time consuming and expensive. An alternative approach is to make replenishment orders of varying size but at fixed time periods.

❯ How can inventory be controlled?

- The key issue here is how managers discriminate between the levels of control they apply to different stock items. The most common way of doing this is by what is known as the ABC classification of stock. This uses the Pareto principle to distinguish between the different values of, or significance placed on, types of stock.
- Inventory is usually managed through sophisticated computer-based information systems which have a number of functions: the updating of stock records, the generation of orders, the generation of inventory status reports and demand forecasts. These systems critically depend on maintaining accurate inventory records.

supplies4medics.com

Founded almost 20 years ago, supplies4medics.com has become one of Europe's most successful direct mail suppliers of medical hardware and consumables to hospitals, doctors' and dentists' surgeries, clinics, nursing homes and other medical-related organizations. Its physical and online catalogues list just over 4,000 items, categorized by broad applications such as 'hygiene consumables' and 'surgeons' instruments'. Quoting its website:

'We are the pan-European distributors of wholesale medical and safety supplies...We aim to carry everything you might ever need; from nurses' scrubs to medical kits, consumables for operations, first aid kits, safety products, chemicals, fire-fighting equipment, nurse and physicians' supplies, etc. Everything is at affordable prices – and backed by our very superior customer service and support – supplies4medics is your ideal source for all medical supplies. Orders are normally despatched same-day, via our European distribution partner, the Brussels Hub of DHL. You should therefore receive your complete order within one week, but you can request next day delivery if required, for a small extra charge. You can order our printed catalogue on the link at the bottom of this page, or shop on our easy-to-use on-line store.'

Last year turnover grew by over 25 per cent to about €120 million, a cause for considerable satisfaction in the company. However, profit growth was less spectacular; and market research suggested that customer satisfaction, although generally good, was slowly declining. Most worrying, inventory levels had grown faster than sales revenue, in percentage terms. This was putting a strain on cash flow, requiring the company to borrow more cash to fund the rapid growth planned for the next year. Inventory holding is estimated to be costing around 15 per cent per annum, taking account of the cost of borrowing, insurance and all warehousing overheads.

Pierre Lamouche, The Head of Operations, summarized the situation faced by his department: 'As a matter of urgency, we are reviewing our purchasing and inventory management systems! Most of our existing re-order levels (ROLs) and re-order quantities (ROQs) were set several years ago, and have never been recalculated. Our focus has been on rapid growth through the introduction of new product lines. For more recently introduced items, the ROQs were based only on forecast sales, which actually can be quite misleading. We estimate that it costs us, on average, 50 euros to place and administer every purchase order, since most suppliers are still not able to take orders over the internet or by EDI. In the meantime, sales of some products have grown fast, whilst others have declined. Our average inventory (stock) cover is

Source: Imagemore Co., Ltd

about 10 weeks, but...amazingly...we still run out of critical items! In fact, on average, we are currently out of stock of about 500 SKUs (Stock Keeping Units) at any time. As you can imagine, our service level is not always satisfactory with this situation. We really need help to conduct a review of our system, so have employed a mature intern from the local business school to review our system. He has first asked my team to provide information on a random, representative sample of twenty items from the full catalogue range, which is copied below. [See Table 13.10.]'

QUESTIONS

1 Prepare a spreadsheet-based ABC analysis of usage value. Classify as follows:

   A-items: top 20 per cent of usage value
   B-items: next 30 per cent of usage value
   C-items: remaining 50 per cent of usage value

2 Calculate the inventory weeks for each item, for each classification and for all the items in total. Does this suggest that the Head of Operations' estimate of inventory weeks is correct?

3 If so, what is your estimate of the overall inventory at the end of the base year, and how much might that have increased during the year?

4 Based on the sample, analyse the underlying causes of the availability problem described in the text.

5 Calculate the EOQs for the A-items.

6 What recommendations would you give to the company?

Table 13.10 Representative sample of 20 catalogue items

Sample number	Catalogue reference number*	Sales unit description**	Sales unit cost (euros)	Last 12 months' sales (units)	Inventory as at last year end (units)	Re-order quantity (units)
1	11036	Disposable Aprons (10pk)	2.40	100	0	10
2	11456	Ear-loop Masks (Box)	3.60	6,000	120	1,000
3	11563	Drill Type 164	1.10	220	420	250
4	12054	Incontinence Pads Large	3.50	35,400	8,500	10,000
5	12372	150ml Syringe	11.30	430	120	100
6	12774	Rectal Speculum 3 Prong	17.40	65	20	20
7	12979	Pocket Organiser Blue	7.00	120	160	500
8	13063	Oxygen Trauma Kit	187.00	40	2	10
9	13236	Zinc Oxide Tape	1.50	1260	0	50
10	13454	Dual Head Stethoscope	6.25	10	16	25
11	13597	Disp. Latex Catheter	0.60	3,560	12	20
12	13999	Roll-up Wheelchair Ramp	152.50	12	44	50
13	14068	WashClene Tube	1.40	22,500	10,500	8,000
14	14242	Cervical Collar	12.00	140	24	20
15	14310	Head Wedge	89.00	44	2	10
16	14405	Three-Wheel Scooter	755.00	14	5	5
17	14456	Neonatal Trach. Tube	80.40	268	6	100
18	14675	Mouldable Strip Paste	10.20	1,250	172	100
19	14854	Sequential Comp. Pump	430.00	430	40	50
20	24943	Toilet Safety Frame	25.60	560	18	20

*Reference numbers are allocated sequentially as new items are added to catalogue.
**All quantities are in sales units (for example, item, box, case, pack).

PROBLEMS AND APPLICATIONS

1 An electronics circuit supplier buys microchips from a large manufacturer. Last year the company supplied 2,000 specialist D/35 chips to customers. The cost of placing an order is $50 and the annual holding cost is estimated to be $2.4 per chip per year. How much should the company order at a time, and what is the total cost of carrying inventory of this product?

2 Jollyfrighteningmasks.com is an Internet supplier of uncannily realistic masks. One of its most profitable lines is the 'Zombie'. Demand for this product is 15,000 per year, the cost of holding the product is estimated to be €25 per year and the cost of placing an order €75. How many 'Zombie' masks should the company order at a time?

3 Jollyfrighteningmasks.com works a 44-week year. If the lead time between placing an order for 'Zombie' masks and receiving them is two weeks, what is the re-order point for the 'Zombie' mask?

4 The Super Pea Canning Company produces canned peas. It uses 10,000 litres of green dye per month. Because of the hazardous nature of this product it needs special transport; therefore the cost of placing an order is €2,000. If the storage costs of holding the dye are €5 per litre per month, how much dye should be ordered at a time?

5 Estimate the annual usage value and average inventory level (or value) and space occupied by 20 representative items of food used within your household, or that of your family. Using Pareto analysis, categorize this into usage value groups (for example, A, B, C), and calculate the average stock turn for each group. Does this analysis indicate a sensible use of capital and space, and, if not, what changes might you make to the household's shopping strategy?

6 Obtain the last few years' annual report and accounts (you can usually download these from the company's website) for two materials-processing operations (as opposed to customer- or information-processing operations) within one industrial sector. Calculate each operation's stock–turnover ratio and the proportion of inventory to current assets over the last few years. Try to explain what you think are the reasons for any differences and trends you can identify and discuss the likely advantages and disadvantages for the organizations concerned.

SELECTED FURTHER READING

Axsäter S. (2015) *Inventory Control*, **3rd edn, Springer, New York.**

A traditional, but comprehensive textbook that takes an 'operational research' quantitative approach.

Emmett, S. and Granville, D. (2007) *Excellence in Inventory Management: How to Minimise Costs and Maximise Service*, **Cambridge Academic, Cambridge.**

A practical guide.

Muller, M. (2011) *Essentials of Inventory Management*, **2nd edn, Amacom, New York.**

Straightforward treatment.

Relph, G. and Milner, C. (2015) *Inventory Management: Advanced Methods for Managing Inventory within Business Systems*, **Kogan Page, London.**

An advanced book that covers most topics in the subject, including the 'k-curve', which is not included in this chapter.

Waters, D. (2003) *Inventory Control and Management*, **Wiley, Chichester.**

Conventional but useful coverage of the topic.

Wild, T. (2002) *Best Practice in Inventory Management*, **Butterworth–Heinemann, Oxford.**

A straightforward and readable practice-based approach to the subject.

Planning and control systems

Key questions

> What are planning and control systems?

> What is enterprise resource planning and how did it develop into the most common planning and control system?

> How should planning and control systems be implemented?

INTRODUCTION

One of the most important issues in planning and controlling operations is managing the sometimes vast amounts of information generated by the activity. It is not just the operations function that is the author and recipient of this information; almost every other function of a business will be involved. So, it is important that all relevant information that is spread throughout the organization is brought together, and that, based on this information, appropriate decisions are taken. This is the function of planning and control systems. They bring information together, help to make decisions (with or without human intervention), then inform the relevant parts of the operation about decisions such as when activities should take place, where they should happen, who should be doing them, how much capacity will be needed, and so on. In this chapter we will also look at what has become the dominant form of planning and control system – enterprise resource planning (ERP). It grew out of a set of calculations known as materials requirements planning (MRP), which is described in the supplement to this chapter. Figure 14.1 shows where this topic fits in our overall model of operations activities.

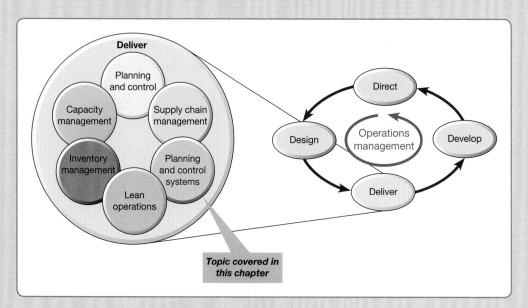

Figure 14.1 This chapter examines planning and control systems

WHAT ARE PLANNING AND CONTROL SYSTEMS?

Before treating this question, it is worth reminding ourselves what planning and control is by looking again at what we covered in Chapter 10. The activity of planning and control is concerned with managing the ongoing allocation of resources and activities to ensure that the operation's processes are both efficient and reflect customer demand for products and services. Planning and control activities are distinct but often overlap. Formally, planning determines what is *intended* to happen at some time in the future, while control is the process of *coping* when things do not happen as intended. Control makes the adjustments that help the operation to achieve the objectives that the plan has set, even when the assumptions on which the plan was based do not hold true.

Planning and control systems

Planning and control systems are the information-processing, decision support and execution mechanisms that support the operations planning and control activity. Although planning and control systems can differ, they tend to have a number of common elements. These are: a customer (demand) interface that forms a two-way information link between the operation's activities and its customers; a supply interface that does the same thing for the operation's suppliers; a set of overlapping 'core' mechanisms that perform basic tasks such as loading, sequencing, scheduling, and monitoring and control; a decision mechanism involving both operations staff and information systems that makes or confirms planning and control decisions. It is important that all these elements are effective in their own right and work together. Figure 14.2 illustrates the elements that should be present in all planning and control systems. In more sophisticated systems they may even be extended to include the integration of this core operations resource planning and control task with other functional areas of the firm such as finance, marketing and personnel. We deal with this cross-functional perspective when we discuss enterprise resource planning (ERP) later.

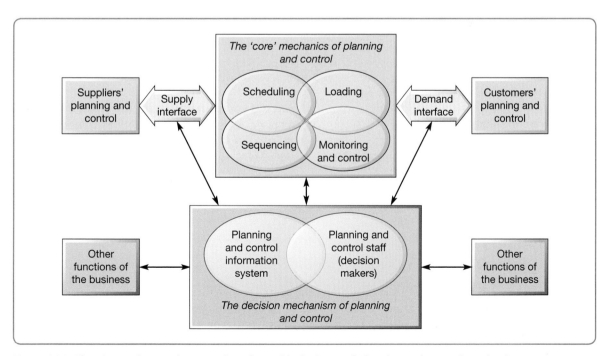

Figure 14.2 **Planning and control systems interface with the internal planning and control mechanisms, customers, suppliers and the other functions of the business**

Butcher's Pet Care co-ordinates its ERP[1]

It may not be a glamorous business, but pet food is certainly big business. It is also competitive, with smaller suppliers battling against giants like Nestlé. One of the most successful of the smaller European producers of dog food is Butcher's Pet Care, located in the Midlands of the UK, which takes a positive moral and ethical approach towards the dog food it produces. It also needs to be super-efficient at co-ordinating its production and distribution if it is to compete with larger rivals. Listen to how Butchers' IT Manager, Malcolm Burrows, explains his vision of how its planning and control system helps it do this.

Why implement a new planning and control system?

'There were specific goals that needed to be achieved, as the legacy systems created long processes, and it was an issue to find out what was in the warehouse, etc. A lot of manual planning tasks took place outside of the system, whereas now the planning, the enterprise resource planning (ERP), and the scheduling of material coming in is a lot better.'

What were the benefits of the new system?

'We're definitely getting a better view of what stock we're holding, and a much quicker response in being able to change product fore-ordering. As you can probably guess, within an environment whereby we are supplying to supermarkets and supply chains, there are regularly promotions that affect the manufacturing we produce to, and it's a fairly quick turnaround. So from that point of view, the system does have a core value in that we can respond and meet requirements much quicker and easier.'

What were the challenges in implementing the system?

'It was a very big cultural change for the staff…As with any ERP [planning and control, see later] system, business and process mapping is crucial. The interesting challenges were working-out how we needed to change to get the

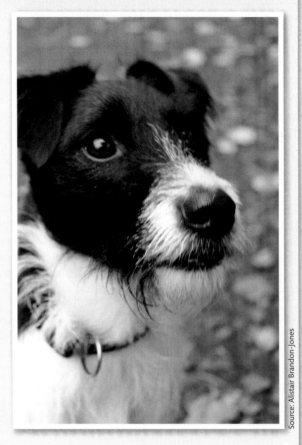

Source: Alistair Brandon-Jones

best out of the system, and that we had agreed a timeline for its implementation.'

How did you train staff to use the system?

'We had a core project team, and they were the "champions" who had to go out and then work within their areas. [The] IT [department] really cannot dictate that; [users] need to be able to have that autonomy to say "this is how we want to operate it". We will get involved if there are technical queries, but otherwise the "champions" [are in charge].'

How does the system interface with customers?

The part of the resource planning and control system that manages the way customers' interact with the business on a day-to-day basis is called the 'customer interface' or sometimes 'demand management'. This is a set of activities that interface with both individual customers and the market more broadly. Depending on the business, these activities may include customer negotiation, order entry, demand forecasting, order promising, updating customers, keeping customer histories, post-delivery customer service and physical distribution.

Customer interface defines the customer experience

The customer interface is important because it defines the nature of the customer experience. It is the public face of the operation (the 'line of visibility' as it was called in Chapter 6). Therefore, it needs to be managed like any other 'customer-processing' process, where the quality of the service, as the customer sees it, is defined by the gap between customers' expectations and their perceptions of the service they receive. Figure 14.3 illustrates a typical customer experience of interacting with a planning and control customer interface. The experience itself will start before any customer contact is initiated. Customer expectations will have been influenced by the way the business presents itself through promotional activities, the ease with which channels of communication can be used (for example, design of the website), and so on. The question is 'Does the communication channel give any indication of the kind of service response (for example, how long will we have to wait?) that the customer can expect?' At the first point of contact when an individual customer requests services or products, this request must be understood, delivery possibly negotiated and a delivery promise made. Prior to the delivery of the service or product, customers may or may not change their mind, which in turn may or may not involve renegotiated delivery promises. Similarly, customers may require or value feedback on the progress of their request. At the point of delivery, not only are the products and services handed over to the customer, but there may also be an opportunity to explain the nature of the delivery and gauge customers' reactions. Following completion of the delivery there may also be some sort of post-delivery action, such as a phone call to confirm that all is well.

> *** Operations principle**
>
> Customers' perceptions of an operation will partially be shaped by the customer interface of its planning and control system.

As is usual with such customer experiences, the managing of customer expectations is particularly important in the early stages of the experience. For example, if there is a possibility that a delivery may be late (perhaps because of the nature of the service being requested) then that possibility is established as an element in the customer's expectations. As the experience continues, various interactions with the customer interface service build up customer perceptions of the level of support and care exhibited by the operation. (We will deal with this idea of customer perceptions and expectations further in Chapter 17.)

Figure 14.3 The customer interface as a 'customer experience'

The customer interface should reflect the operation's objectives

In managing a customer's experience, the customer interface element of the planning and control system is, in effect, operationalizing the business's operations objectives. It may have to prioritize one type of customer over another. It may have to encourage some types of customer to transact business more than other (possibly less profitable) types of customer. It will almost certainly have to trade off elements of customer service against the efficiency and utilization of the operations resources. No matter how sophisticated the customer interface technology, or how skilled the customer interface staff, this part of the planning and control system cannot operate effectively without clear priorities derived from the operation's strategic objectives.

The customer interface acts as a trigger function

Acceptance of an order should prompt the customer interface to trigger the operation's processes. Exactly what is triggered will depend on the nature of the business. For example, some building and construction companies, because they are willing to build almost any kind of construction, will keep relatively few of their own resources within the business, but rather hire them in when the nature of the job becomes evident. This is a 'resource-to-order' operation where the customer interface triggers the task of hiring in the relevant equipment (and possibly labour) and purchasing the appropriate materials. If the construction company confined itself to a narrower range of construction tasks, thereby making the nature of demand slightly more predictable, it would be likely to have its own equipment and labour permanently within the operation. Here, accepting a job would only need to trigger the purchase of the materials to be used in the construction, and the business is a 'produce-to-order' operation. Some construction companies will construct pre-designed standard houses or apartments ahead of any firm demand for them. If demand is high, customers may place requests for houses before they are started or during their construction. In this case, the customers will form a backlog of demand and must wait. However, the company is also taking the risk of holding a stock of unsold houses. Operations of this type are 'produce-ahead-of-order' operations.

How does the system interface with suppliers?

The supplier interface provides the link between the activities of the operation itself and those of its suppliers. The timing and level of activities within the operation or process will have implications for the supply of products and services to the operation. Suppliers need to be informed so that they can make products and services available when needed. In effect this is the mirror image of the customer interface. As such, the supplier interface is concerned with managing the supplier experience to ensure appropriate supply. Because the customer is not directly involved in this does not make it any less important. Ultimately, customer satisfaction will be influenced by supply effectiveness because that in turn influences delivery to customers. Using the expectations–perception gap to judge the quality of the supplier interface function may at first seem strange. After all, suppliers are not customers as such. Yet, it is important to be a 'quality customer' to suppliers because this increases the chances of receiving high-quality service from them. This means that suppliers fully understand expectations because they have been made clear and unambiguous.

> ✻ **Operations principle**
>
> An operation's planning and control system can enhance or inhibit the ability of its suppliers to support delivery effectiveness.

The supplier interface has both a long- and short-term function. It must be able to cope with different types of long-term supplier relationship and also handle individual transactions with suppliers. To do the former it must understand the requirements of all the processes within the operation and also the capabilities of the suppliers (in large operations, there could be thousands of suppliers). Figure 14.4 shows a simplified sequence of events in the management of a typical supplier–operation interaction that the supplier interface must facilitate. When the planning and control activity requests supply, the supplier interface must

Figure 14.4 The supplier interface as a 'customer' experience

have identified potential suppliers and might also be able to suggest alternative materials or services if necessary. Formal requests for quotations may be sent to potential suppliers if no supply agreement exists. These requests might be sent to several suppliers or a smaller group, who may be 'preferred' suppliers. Just as it was important to manage customer expectations, it is important to manage supplier expectations, often prior to any formal supply of products or services. This issue was discussed in Chapter 12 as supplier development. To handle individual transactions, the supplier interface will need to issue formal purchase orders. These may be stand-alone documents or, more likely, electronic orders. Whatever the mechanisms, it is an important activity because it often forms the legal basis of the contractual relationship between the operation and its supplier. Delivery promises will need to be formally confirmed. While waiting for delivery, it may be necessary to negotiate changes in supply and track progress to get early warning of potential changes to delivery. Also, delivery supplier performance needs to be established and communicated with follow-up as necessary.

Hierarchical planning and control[2]

The activity of operations planning and control is a complicated process. Demand for products and services is usually uncertain, supply can be problematic, the composition of products and services are often complex with many components and sub-components. And to add to the difficulty, the cumulative lead times for sourcing components and for production itself are usually longer than customers are prepared to wait (see Chapter 10).

The 'hierarchical approach' to operations planning recognizes these difficulties and tries to bring some order to the complexity by dividing up the many interrelated planning and control decisions into sub-problems to reflect the organizational hierarchy. So decisions at a high level link with decisions at lower levels in an effective manner. Decisions that are made at the higher level will of course impose some constraints on the lower level decisions. And the execution of detailed decisions at the lower level will provide the

> **✳ Operations principle**
>
> Hierarchical planning and control systems separate different kinds of decisions at different levels in the organization and over different time periods.

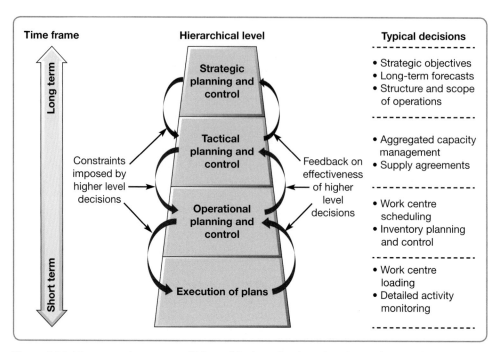

Figure 14.5 The general structure of hierarchical production planning and control

necessary feedback so that the quality of higher level decision making can be judged. In this way the hierarchical approach separates different kinds of decisions at different levels in the organization and over different time periods. It allows a degree of stability in the planning process so that relatively complex operations are, to some extent, protected against too many short-term changes. In addition it gives a certain amount of independence to the planners at different levels. Figure 14.5 illustrates this hierarchical approach. This shows a general structure of the approach. In practice different operations will interpret this structure in different ways, probably using different terms, incorporating different decisions and having different numbers of levels. How well the hierarchical approach works will depend largely on how effective and consistent the boundaries between the levels of the hierarchy are managed. Each hierarchical level is likely to have its own set of decision rules and methods with different planning horizons, levels of detail of information and forecasts, scope of the planning activity and managerial authority – all of which can lead to problems in translating the decisions at one level to another. This hierarchical approach is closely associated with ERP, which we will deal with later in this chapter.

Critical commentary[3]

Hierarchical planning and control looks to be both rational and straightforward; however, making it work in practice can be problematic. Several questions need to be addressed: How many levels are needed? What should constrain what, and how tightly? What should one plan in advance? Does a hierarchical approach reduce the speed of decision making by requiring continual upward referral? How much autonomy and local control should be devolved to lower levels or to distributed production facilities? Is stability achieved by rigidity and at the expense of speed and responsiveness? In addition, data must be accurate, timely and in a common format. Effective transition between the levels also requires a significant degree of managerial discipline.

Does the system integrate human with 'automated' decision making?

Although computer-based resource planning and control systems are now widespread in many industries, much of the decision making is still carried out partially by people. This is always likely to be the case because some elements of the task, such as negotiating with customers and suppliers, are difficult to automate. Yet the benefits of computer-aided decision making are difficult to ignore. Unlike humans, computer-based planning and control can cope with immense complexity, both in terms of being able to model the interrelationship between decisions and in terms of being able to store large quantities of information. However, humans are generally better at many of the 'soft' qualitative tasks that can be important in planning and control. In particular, humans are good at the following:

- *Flexibility, adaptability and learning*. Humans can cope with ambiguous, incomplete, inconsistent and redundant goals and constraints. In particular they can deal with the fact that planning and control objectives and constraints may not be stable for more than a few hours.
- *Communication and negotiation*. Humans are able to understand and sometimes influence the variability inherent in an operation. They can influence job priorities and sometimes processing times. They can negotiate between internal processes and communicate with customers and suppliers in a way that could minimize misunderstanding.
- *Intuition*. Humans can fill in the blanks of missing information that is required to plan and control. They can accumulate the tacit knowledge about what is, and what may be, really happening with the operation's processes.

These strengths of human decision making versus computer decision making provide a clue as to what should be the appropriate degree of automation built into decision making in this area. When planning and controlling stable and relatively straightforward processes that are well understood, decision making can be automated to a greater degree than processes that are complex, unstable and poorly understood.

WHAT IS ENTERPRISE RESOURCE PLANNING AND HOW DID IT DEVELOP INTO THE MOST COMMON PLANNING AND CONTROL SYSTEM?

An easy way of thinking about enterprise resource planning (ERP) is to imagine that you have decided to hold a party in two weeks' time and expect about 40 people to attend. As well as drinks, you decide to provide sandwiches and snacks. You will probably do some simple calculations, estimating guests' preferences and how much people are likely to eat and drink. You may already have some food and drink in the house that you will use, so you will take this into account when making your shopping list. If any of the food is to be cooked from a recipe, you may have to multiply up the ingredients to cater for 40 people. Also, you may also wish to take into account the fact that you will prepare some of the food the week before and freeze it, while leaving the rest to either the day before or the day of the party. So, you will need to decide when each item is required so that you can shop in time. In fact planning a party requires a series of interrelated decisions about the volume (quantity) and timing of the *materials* needed. This is the basis of the foundation concept for ERP called materials requirements planning (MRP). It is a process that helps companies make volume and timing calculations (similar to those for the party, but on a much larger scale, and with a greater degree of complexity). But your planning may extend beyond 'materials'. You may want to hire in a sound system from a local supplier – you will have to plan for this. The party also has financial implications. You may have to agree a temporary increase to your credit card limit. Again, this requires some forward planning and calculations of how much it is going to cost, and how much extra credit you require. Both the equipment and financial implications may vary if you increase the number of guests. But, if you postpone the party for a month, these arrangements will change. Also, there are other implications of organizing the party. You will need to give friends, who are helping with its organization, an idea of when they should come and for how long. This will depend on the timing of the various tasks to be done (making sandwiches etc.).

So, even for this relatively simple activity, the key to successful planning is how we generate, integrate and organize all the information on which planning and control depends. Of course in business operations it is more complex than this. Companies usually sell many different products to many hundreds of customers who are likely to vary their demand for the products. This is a bit like organizing 200 parties one week, 250 the next and 225 the following week, all for different groups of guests with different requirements who keep changing their minds about what they want to eat and drink. This is what an ERP system does; it automates and integrates core business processes such as customer demand, scheduling operations, ordering items, keeping inventory records and updating financial data. It helps companies to 'forward-plan' these types of decisions and understand all the implications of any changes to the plan.

How did ERP develop?

ERP is the latest, and the most significant, development of the original MRP philosophy. The (now) large companies which have grown almost exclusively on the basis of providing ERP systems include SAP and Oracle. Yet to understand ERP, it is important to understand the various stages in its development, summarized in Figure 14.6. The original MRP became popular during the 1970s, although the planning and control logic that underlies it had, by then, been known for some time. What popularized MRP was the availability of computer power to drive the basic planning and control mathematics. We will deal with MRP in detail in the supplement to this chapter. MRP uses product information in the form of a bill of materials (BOM) that is similar to the 'component structure' that was discussed in Chapter 4, together with demand information in the form of a master production schedule (MPS).

Manufacturing resource planning (MRP II) expanded out of MRP during the 1980s. Again, it was a technology innovation that allowed the development. Connected networks together with increasingly powerful desktop computers allowed a much higher degree of processing power and communication between different parts of a business. Also MRP II's extra sophistication allowed the forward modelling of 'what-if' scenarios. The strength of MRP and MRP II lay always in the fact that they could explore the *consequences* of any changes to what an operation was required to do. So, if demand changed, the MRP system would calculate all the

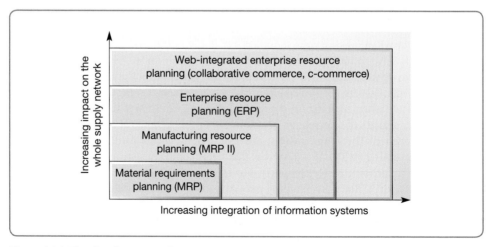

Figure 14.6 The development of ERP

'knock-on' effects and issue instructions accordingly. This same principle also applies to ERP, but on a much wider basis. ERP has been defined as:

'a complete enterprise wide business solution. The ERP system consists of software support modules such as: marketing and sales, field service, product design and development, production and inventory control, procurement, distribution, industrial facilities management, process design and development, manufacturing, quality, human resources, finance and accounting, and information services. Integration between the modules is stressed without the duplication of information.'[4]

Some authorities caution against taking a naive view of ERP. Look at this view:

'Enterprise resource planning software, or ERP, doesn't live up to its acronym. Forget about planning – it doesn't do much of that – and forget about resource, [it is] a throwaway term. But remember the enterprise part. This is ERP's true ambition. It attempts to integrate all departments and functions across a company onto a single computer system that can serve all those different departments' particular needs.'[5]

So ERP systems allow decisions and databases from all parts of the organization to be integrated so that the consequences of decisions in one part of the organization are reflected in the planning and control systems of the rest of the organization (*see* Fig. 14.7). ERP is the equivalent of the organization's central nervous system, sensing information about the condition of different parts of the business and relaying the information to other parts of the business that need it. The information is updated in real time by those who use it and yet is always available to everyone connected to the ERP system.

Also, the potential of Internet-based communication has provided a further boost to ERP development. Many companies have suppliers, customers and other businesses with whom they collaborate who themselves have ERP-type systems. An obvious development is to allow these systems to communicate. However, the technical, as well as the organizational and strategic, consequences of this can be formidable. Nevertheless, many authorities believe that the true value of ERP systems is only fully exploited when such web-integrated ERP (known by some people as 'collaborative commerce', or c-commerce) becomes widely implemented.

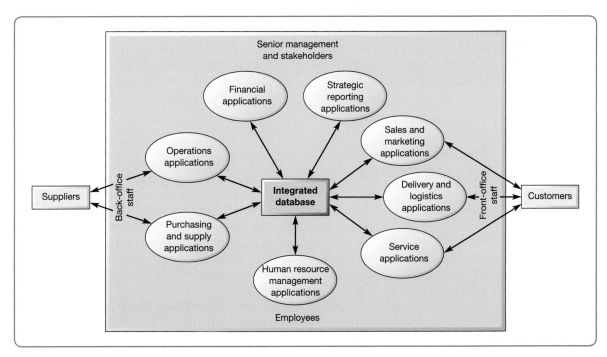

Figure 14.7 ERP integrates information from all parts of the organization

SAP and its partners[6]

The growth of SAP, the largest European software company, based in Walldorf, Germany, over the years has matched the popularity of the ERP systems that are still the foundation of its success. Founded by five former IBM engineers in 1972, SAP launched its ground-breaking SAP R/1 system one year later. This was followed by SAP R/2 in 1979 and R/3 in 1992. Now its SAP S/4HANA Business Suite products offer cloud, on-premise and hybrid deployment options to provide, it says, more choice to customers.

With almost 300,000 customers in more than 130 countries, a wide variety of businesses run SAP 'business software' applications. These range, as the company phrases it, from distinct solutions addressing the needs of small businesses and midsize companies to suite offerings for global organizations. SAP defines 'business software' as comprising enterprise resource planning and related applications such as supply chain management, customer relationship management, product life cycle management, and supplier relationship management.

Source: Shutterstock.com: Monkey Business Images

SAP is well known for developing a network of 'business partners' to develop new products, sell its 'solutions', implement them into customers' operations, provide service, educate end users, and several other activities. There are various categories of partnerships:

- *Global Alliances*. SAP global alliance partners are themselves global leaders and are therefore strategic partners with significant global presence. Membership is by invitation only.

- *Original Equipment Manufacturers (OEM)*. This is for independent software vendors who integrate SAP technologies with their own products. OEM partners may add on, bundle, host or embed SAP software.
- *Solution Providers*. These partners offer customized solutions (a combination of business, technical or application expertise) that include SAP software.
- *Complementary Technology Partners*. These partners provide complete, technically verified turnkey (out-of-the-box) software solutions that extend and add value to SAP solutions.
- *Volume Resellers*. These partners resell all or part of the SAP software portfolio and derive their primary revenue from licence sales.
- *Authorized Education*. Partners are authorized by SAP to provide official training and education services to ensure that customers' employees gain optimal training.

The benefits of ERP

ERP is generally seen as having the potential to improve very significantly the performance of many companies in many different sectors. This is partly because of the very much enhanced visibility that information integration gives, but it is also a function of the discipline that ERP demands. Yet this discipline is itself a 'double-edged' sword. On the one hand, it 'sharpens up' the management of every process within an organization, allowing best practice (or at least common practice) to be implemented uniformly through the business. No longer will individual idiosyncratic behaviour by one part of a company's operations cause disruption to all other processes. On the other hand, it is the rigidity of this discipline that is both difficult to achieve and (arguably) inappropriate for all parts of the business. Nevertheless, the generally accepted benefits of ERP are usually held to be the following:

- Because software communicates across all functions, there is absolute visibility of what is happening in all parts of the business.

- The discipline of forcing business-process-based changes is an effective mechanism for making all parts of the business more efficient.
- There is better 'sense of control' of operations that will form the basis for continuous improvement (albeit within the confines of the common process structures).
- It enables far more sophisticated communication with customers, suppliers and other business partners, often giving more accurate and timely information.
- It is capable of integrating whole supply chains including suppliers' suppliers and customers' customers.

In fact, although the integration of several databases lies at the heart of ERP's power, it is nonetheless difficult to achieve in practice. This is why ERP installation can be particularly expensive. Attempting to get new systems and databases to talk to old (sometimes called *legacy*) systems can be very problematic. Not surprisingly, many companies choose to replace most, if not all, of their existing systems simultaneously. Common systems and relational databases help to ensure the smooth transfer of data between different parts of the organization. In addition to the integration of systems, ERP usually includes other features that make it a powerful planning and control tool.

OPERATIONS IN PRACTICE

The life and times of a chicken salad sandwich – part two[7]

In Chapter 10 we looked at the schedule for the manufacture of a chicken salad sandwich. This concentrated on the lead times for the ordering of the ingredients and the manufacturing schedule for producing the sandwiches during the afternoon and night-time of each day for delivery during the evening and the night-time, and the morning of the following day. But that is only half the story, the half that is concerned with planning and controlling the timing of events. The other half concerns how the sandwich company manages the *quantity* of ingredients to order, the quantity of sandwiches to be made, and the whole chain of implications for the whole company. In fact, this sandwich company uses an ERP system that has at its core an MRP II package. This MRP II system has the two normal basic drivers of, first, a continually updated sales forecast and, second, a product structure database. In this case the product structure and/or bill of materials is the 'recipe' for the sandwich; within the company this database is called the 'Recipe Management System'. The 'recipe' for the chicken sandwich (its bill of materials) is shown in Table 14.1.

Figure 14.8 shows the ERP system used by this sandwich company. Orders are received from customers electronically through the ordering system. These orders are then checked through what the company calls a 'Validation System' that checks the order against current product codes and expected quantities to make sure that the customer has not made any mistakes, such as forgetting to order some products (this happens surprisingly often). After validation the orders are transferred through the central database to the MRP II system that performs the main requirements breakdown. Based on these requirements and forecasted requirements for the next few days, orders are placed with the company's suppliers for raw materials and packaging. Simultaneously, confirmation is sent to customers, accounts are updated, staffing schedules are finalized for the next two weeks (on a rolling basis), customers are invoiced, and all this information is made available both to the customers' own ERP systems and to the transportation company's planning system.

Interestingly, the company, like many others, found it difficult to implement its ERP system. *'It was a far bigger job than we thought'*, according to the company's operations director. *'We had to change the way we organized our processes so that they would fit in with the ERP system that we bought. But that was relatively easy compared to making sure that the system integrated with our customers', suppliers' and distributors' systems. Because some of these companies were also implementing new systems at the time, it was like trying to hit a moving target.'* However, three years after the start of implementation, the whole process was working relatively smoothly.

Table 14.1 Bill of materials for a chicken salad sandwich

FUNCTION: MBIL		MULTI-LEVEL BILL INQUIRY						
PARENT: BTE80058 RV: PLNR: LOU		UM:EA	DESC: RUNLT: PLN POL: N			HE CHICKEN SALAD TRY 0 FIXED LT: 0 DRWG: WA1882		LA
LEVEL 1...5 ...10	PT USE	SEQN	COMPONENT	C T	PARTIAL DESCRIPTION		QTY	UM
1	PACK	010	FTE80045	P	H.E. CHICKENS		9	EA
2	ASSY	010	MBR-0032	P	BREAD HARVESTE		2	SL
3	HRPR	010	RBR-0023	N	BREAD HARVESTE		.4545455	EA
2	ASSY	020	RDY-0001	N	SPREAD BUTTER		.006	KG
2	ASSY	030	RMA-0028	N	MAYONNAISE MYB		.01	KG
2	ASSY	040	MFP-0016	P	CHICKEN FRESH		.045	KG
3	HRPR	010	RFP-0008	N	CHICKEN FRESH		1	KG
	ASSY	050	MVF-0063	P	TOMATO SLICE 4		3	SL
3	ALTI	010	RVF-0026	P	TOMATOES PRE-S		.007	KG
4	HRPR	010	RVF-0018	N	TOMATOES		1	KG
2	ASSY	060	MVF-0059	P	CUCUMBER SLICE		2	SL
3	ALTI	010	RVF-0027	P	CUCUMBER SLICE		.004	KG
4	TRAN	010	RVF-0017	N	CUCUMBER		1	KG
2	ASSY	070	MVF-0073	P	LETTUCE COS SL		.02	KG
3	HRPR	010	RVF-0015	N	LETTUCE COS		1	KG
2	ASSY	080	RPA-0070	N	WEBB BASE GREY		.00744	KG
2	ASSY	090	RPA-0071	N	WEBB TOP WHITE		.0116	KG
2	ASSY	100	RLA-0194	N	LABEL SW H		1	EA
2	ASSY	110	RLA-0110	N	STICKER NE		1	EA
1	PACK	010	RPA-0259	N	SOT LABELL		1	EA
1	PACK	030	RPA-0170	N	TRAY GREEN		1	EA

Figure 14.8 The ERP structure for the sandwich company

ERP changes the way companies do business

Arguably the most significant issue in many company's decision to buy an off-the-shelf ERP system is that of its compatibility with the company's current business processes and practices. The advice that is emerging from the companies that have adopted ERP (either successfully or unsuccessfully) is that it is extremely important to make sure that their current way of doing business will fit (or can be changed to fit) with a standard ERP package. In fact, one of the most common reasons for companies deciding not to install ERP is that they cannot reconcile the assumptions in the software of the ERP system with their core business processes. If, as most businesses find, their current processes do not fit, they can do one of two things. They could change their processes to fit the ERP package. Alternatively, they could modify the software within the ERP package to fit their processes. Both of these options involve costs and risks. Changing business practices that are working well will involve reorganization costs as well introducing the potential for errors to creep into the processes. Adapting the software will both slow down the project and introduce potentially dangerous software 'bugs' into the system. It would also make it difficult to upgrade the software later on.

> **❋ Operations principle**
>
> ERP systems are only fully effective if the way a business organizes its processes is aligned with the underlying assumptions of its ERP system.

Why do companies invest in ERP?

If one accepts only some of the criticisms of ERP outlined in the critical commentary box here, it does pose the question as to why companies have invested such large amounts of money in ERP. Partly it was the attraction of turning the company's information systems into a 'smooth-running and integrated machine'. The prospect of such organizational efficiency is attractive to most managers, even if it does presuppose a very simplistic model of how organizations work in practice. After a while, although organizations could now see the formidable problems in ERP implementation, the investments were justified on the basis that, *'even if we gain no significant advantage by investing in ERP, we will be placed at a disadvantage by not investing in it because all our competitors are doing so'*. There is probably some truth in this; sometimes businesses have to invest just to stand still.

Web-integrated ERP

Perhaps the most important justification for embarking on ERP is the potential it gives the organization to link up with the outside world. For example, it is much easier for an operation to move into Internet-based trading if it can integrate its external Internet systems into its

Far from being the magic ingredient that allows operations to integrate fully all their information, ERP is regarded by some as one of the most expensive ways of getting zero or even negative return on investment. For example, the US chemicals giant, Dow Chemical, spent almost half a billion dollars and seven years implementing an ERP system which became outdated almost as soon as it was implemented. One company, FoxMeyer Drug, claimed that the expense and problems that it encountered in implementing ERP eventually drove it into bankruptcy. One problem is that ERP implementation is expensive. This is partly because of the need to customize the system, understand its implications on the organization, and train staff to use it. Spending on what some call the *ERP ecosystem* (consulting, hardware, networking and complementary applications) has been estimated as being twice the spending on the software itself. But it is not just the expense that has disillusioned many companies; it is also the returns they have had for their investment. Some studies show that the vast majority of companies implementing ERP are disappointed with the effect it has had on their businesses. Certainly many companies find that they have to change (sometimes fundamentally) the way they organize their operations in order to fit in with ERP systems. This organizational impact of ERP (which has been described as the corporate equivalent of root-canal work) can have a significantly disruptive effect on the organization's operations.

internal ERP systems. However, as has been pointed out by some critics of the ERP software companies, ERP vendors were not prepared for the impact of e-commerce and had not made sufficient allowance in their products for the need to interface with Internet-based communication channels. The result of this has been that, whereas the internal complexity of ERP systems was designed only to be intelligible to systems experts, the Internet has led customers and suppliers (who are non-experts) to demand access to the same information. So, important pieces of information, such as the status or orders, whether products are in stock, the progress of invoicing, etc., need to be available, via the ERP system, on a company's website.

One problem is that different types of external company often need different types of information. Customers need to check the progress of their orders and invoicing, whereas suppliers and other partners want access to the details of operations planning and control. Not only that, but they also want access all the time. The Internet is always there, but web-integrated ERP systems are often complex and need periodic maintenance. This can mean that every time the ERP system is taken offline for routine maintenance or other changes, the website also goes offline. To combat this some companies configure their ERP and e-commerce links in such a way that they can be decoupled so that ERP can be periodically shut down without affecting the company's web presence.

Supply chain ERP

The step beyond integrating internal ERP systems with immediate customers and suppliers is to integrate all the ERP and similar systems along a supply chain. Of course, this can never be straightforward and is often exceptionally complicated. Not only do different ERP systems have to communicate together, but also they have to integrate with other types of system. For example, sales and marketing functions often use systems such as customer relationship management (CRM) that manage the complexities of customer requirements, promises and transactions. Getting ERP and CRM systems to work together is itself often difficult. Sometimes the information from ERP systems has to be translated into a form that CRM and other e-commerce applications are able to understand. Nevertheless, such web-integrated

ERP, or c-commerce (collaborative commerce), applications are emerging and starting to have an impact on the way companies do business. Although a formidable task, the benefits are potentially great. The costs of communicating between supply chain partners could be dramatically reduced and the potential for avoiding errors as information and products move between partners in the supply chain is significant. Yet as a final warning note, it is well to remember that although integration can bring all the benefits of increased transparency in a supply chain, it may also transmit systems failure. If the ERP system of one operation within a supply chain fails for some reason, it may block the effective operation of the whole integrated information system throughout the chain.

> ✳ **Operations principle**
> The effectiveness of ERP systems depends partly on suppliers' and customers' ERP systems.

HOW SHOULD PLANNING AND CONTROL SYSTEMS BE IMPLEMENTED?

By their nature, planning and control systems are designed to address problems of information having to be obtained from different parts of a business. Not surprising then that any planning and control system will be complex and difficult to get right. Implementing this type of system will necessarily involve crossing organizational boundaries and integrating internal processes that cover many, if not all, functional areas of a business. Building a single system that simultaneously satisfies the requirements of operations managers, marketing and sales managers, finance managers and everyone else in the organization is never going to be easy. It is likely that each function will have its own set of processes and well-understood system that has been designed for its specific needs. Moving everyone onto a single, integrated system that runs off a single database is going to be potentially very unpopular. Furthermore, few people like to change, and planning and control systems, particularly ERP, ask almost everyone to change how they do their jobs. If planning and control system implementation were not difficult there would not be so many reports of the failure of ERP implementations, or even the complete abandonment of systems.

The particular challenges of IT implementation

Surprisingly, given the ubiquity of IT systems, such as planning and control systems, the cost-effectiveness of investment in IT is not altogether straightforward. Generally research recognizes a plain and positive connection between investment in IT and increased operations effectiveness, even if the benefits can vary widely. As one authority put it, 'there's no bank where companies can deposit IT investment and withdraw an "average" return...[A] strategy of blindly investing in IT and expecting productivity to automatically rise is sure to fail.'[8] Moreover, there is a high failure rate for IT projects (often cited as between 35 and 75 per cent, although the definition of 'failure' is debated). Yet there is extensive agreement that the most common reasons for failure are connected in some way with managerial, implementation or organizational factors. And of these managerial, implementation or organizational factors, one of the main issues was the degree of alignment and integration between a firm's overall IT strategy and the general strategy of the firm. This is a particularly important point for operations strategy. It reinforces the idea that IT strategy must be regarded as an integral part of overall operations strategy.

Of course, different kinds of IT pose different kinds of challenge. The impact of some IT is limited to a defined and (relatively) limited part of the operation. This type of IT is sometimes called 'function IT' because it facilitates a single function or task.[9] Examples include computer-aided design (CAD), spreadsheets and simple decision support systems. The organizational challenges for this type of technology can usually be treated separately from the technology itself. Put another way, function IT can be adopted with or without any changes to other organizational structures. Yet this does not mean that no organizational, cultural or development challenges will be faced. Often the effectiveness of the technology can be enhanced by appropriate changes to other aspects of the operation. By contrast, 'enterprise IT' extends across much of or even the entire organization. Because of this, enterprise IT will need potentially extensive changes to the organization. And the most common (and problematic) enterprise IT systems are ERP systems. The third IT category is 'network IT'. Network IT facilitates exchanges between people and groups inside and/or outside the organization. However, it does not necessarily predefine how these exchanges should work. For example, simple email is a network IT. It has brought significant changes to how operations and supply networks function, but the changes are not imposed by the technology itself; rather they emerge over time as people gain experience of using the technology. The challenge with this type of technology is to learn how to exploit its emergent potential. This is the challenge for many operations as they extend their ERP systems to encompass the whole, or even a part, of their supply chain.

Implementation critical success factors

One of the key issues in ERP implementation is what critical success factors (CSFs) should be managed to increase the chances of a successful implementation. In this case, CSFs are those things that the organization must 'get right' in order for the ERP system to work effectively. Much of the research in this area has been summarized by Finney and Corbett[10] who distinguish between the broad, organization-wide, or strategic, factors, and the more project-specific, or tactical, factors. These are shown in Table 14.2.

What a waste[11]

Not only can ERP implementation go wrong, even when undertaken by experienced professionals, but also sometimes it can end up in the law courts. Waste Management, Inc. is the leading provider of waste and environmental services in North America. So when it announced that it was suing SAP (see the earlier 'Operations in practice' case) over the failure of an ERP implementation, planning and control systems practitioners took notice. Waste Management said that it was seeking the recovery of more than $100 million in project expenses as well as *'the savings and benefits that the SAP software was promised to deliver to Waste Management'*. It said that SAP promised that the software could be fully implemented throughout all of Waste Management within 18 months, and that its software was an 'out-of-the-box' solution that would meet Waste Management's needs without any customization or enhancements.

Waste Management signed a sales pact with SAP in October 2005, but, according to Waste Management, *'Almost immediately following execution of the agreements, the SAP implementation team discovered significant "gaps" between the software's functionality and Waste Management's business requirements. Waste*

Source: PhotoDisc

Management has discovered that these gaps were already known to the product development team in Germany even before the SLA (service level agreement) was signed.' But members of SAP's implementation team had reportedly blamed Waste Management for the functional gaps and had submitted change orders requiring that Waste Management pay for fixing them. Five years later, the dispute was settled when SAP made a one-time cash payment to Waste Management.

Table 14.2 Strategic and tactical critical success factors (CSFs) related to successful ERP implementation

Strategic CSFs	Tactical CSFs
● Top management commitment and support – strong and committed leadership at the top management level is essential to the success of an ERP implementation ● Visioning and planning – articulating a business vision to the organization, identifying clear goals and objectives, and providing a clear link between business goals and systems strategy ● Project champion – the individual should possess strong leadership skills as well as business, technical and personal managerial competences ● Implementation strategy and time frame – implement the ERP under a time-phased approach ● Project management – the ongoing management of the implementation plan ● Change management – this concept refers to the need for the implementation team to prepare formally a change management programme and be conscious of the need to consider the implications of such a project. One key task is to build user acceptance of the project and a positive employee attitude. This might be accomplished through education about the benefits and need for an ERP system. Part of this building of user acceptance should also involve securing the support of opinion leaders throughout the organization. There is also a need for the team leader to negotiate effectively between various political turfs. Some authorities also stress that, in planning the ERP project, it must be looked upon as a change management initiative, not an IT initiative	● Balanced team – the need for an implementation team that spans the organization, as well as one that possesses a balance of business and IT skills ● Project team – there is a critical need to put in place a solid, core implementation team that is composed of the organization's 'best and brightest' individuals. These individuals should have a proven reputation and there should be a commitment to 'release' these individuals to the project on a full-time basis ● Communication plan – planned communication among various functions and organizational levels (specifically between business and IT personnel) is important to ensure that open communication occurs within the entire organization, as well as with suppliers and customers ● Project cost planning and management – it is important to know up front exactly what the implementation costs will be and dedicate the necessary budget ● IT infrastructure – it is critical to assess the IT readiness of the organization, including the architecture and skills. If necessary, infrastructure might need to be upgraded or revamped ● Selection of ERP – the selection of an appropriate ERP package that matches the businesses processes ● Consultant selection and relationship – some authorities advocate the need to include an ERP consultant as part of the implementation team ● Training and job redesign – training is a critical aspect of an implementation. It is also necessary to consider the impact of the change on the nature of work and the specific job descriptions ● Troubleshooting/crises management – it is important to be flexible in ERP implementations and to learn from unforeseen circumstances, as well as be prepared to handle unexpected crises situations. The need for troubleshooting skills will be an ongoing requirement of the implementation process

Source: Based on Sherry Finney and Martin Corbett (2007) ERP implementation: a compilation and analysis of critical success factors, *Business Process Management Journal*, vol. 13, no. 3, 329–347.

Of course, some of these CSFs could be appropriate for any kind of complex implementation, whether of an ERP system, or some other major change to an operation. But that is the point. ERP implementation certainly has some specific technical requirements, but good ERP implementation practice is very similar to other complicated and sensitive implementation. Again, what is different about ERP is that it is enterprise-wide, so implementation should always be considered on an enterprise-wide level. Therefore there will at all times be many different stakeholders to consider, each with their own concerns. That is why implementing an ERP system is always going to be an exercise in change management. Only if the anxieties of all relevant groups are addressed effectively will the prospect of achieving superior system performance be high.

At a purely practical level, many consultants who have had to live through the difficulties of implementing ERP have summarized their experiences. The following list of likely problems with an ERP implementation is typical (and really does reflect reality):[12]

● The total cost is likely to be underestimated.
● The time and effort to implement it are likely to be underestimated.

- The resourcing from both the business and the IT function is likely to be higher than anticipated.
- The level of outside expertise required will be more than anticipated.
- The changes required to business processes will be greater than expected.
- Controlling the scope of the project will be more difficult than expected.
- There will never be enough training.
- The need for change management is not likely to be recognized until it is too late, and the changes required to corporate culture are likely to be grossly underestimated. (This is the single biggest failure point for ERP implementations.)

SUMMARY ANSWERS TO KEY QUESTIONS

❯ What are planning and control systems?

- Planning and control systems are the information-processing, decision support and execution mechanisms that support the operations planning and control activity.
- Planning and control systems can take various forms, but usually have some common elements such as customer and supplier interfaces, an information system, a set of decision rules and functions to schedule, sequence, load and monitor operations activities.
- Hierarchical planning and control systems separate different kinds of decisions at different levels in the organization and over different time periods.

❯ What is enterprise resource planning and how did it develop into the most common planning and control system?

- ERP is an enterprise-wide information system that integrates all the information from many functions needed for planning and controlling operations activities. This integration around a common database allows for transparency.
- ERP often requires very considerable investment in the software itself, as well as its implementation. More significantly, it often requires a company's processes to be changed to bring them in line with the assumptions built into the ERP software.
- ERP can be seen as the latest development from the original planning and control approach known as materials requirements planning (MRP).
- Although ERP is becoming increasingly competent at the integration of internal systems and databases, there is the even more significant potential of integration with other organizations' ERP (and equivalent) systems.
- In particular, the use of Internet-based communication between customers, suppliers and other partners in the supply chain has opened up the possibility of wider integration.

❯ How should planning and control systems be implemented?

- Because planning and control systems are designed to address problems of information fragmentation, implementation will be complex, crossing organizational boundaries.
- There are a number of critical success factors (CSFs) that the organization must 'get right' in order for the ERP system to work effectively. Some of these are broad, organization-wide, or strategic, factors. Others are more project-specific, or tactical, factors.

Peter Townsend knew that he would have to make some decisions pretty soon. His sports goods manufacturing business, Psycho Sports, had grown so rapidly over the last two years that he would soon have to install some systematic procedures and routines to manage the business. His biggest problem was in manufacturing control. He had started making specialist high-quality table tennis bats but now made a wide range of sports products, including tennis balls, darts and protective equipment for various games. Furthermore, his customers, once limited to specialist sports shops, now included some of the major sports retail chains. 'We really do have to get control of our manufacturing. I keep getting told that we need what seems to be called an MRP system. I wasn't sure what this meant and so I have bought a specialist production control book from our local bookshop and read all about MRP principles. I must admit, these academics seem to delight in making simple things complicated. And there is so much jargon associated with the technique, I feel more confused now than I did before.

'Perhaps the best way forward is for me to take a very simple example from my own production unit and see whether I can work things out manually. If I can follow the process through on paper then I will be far better equipped to decide what kind of computer-based system we should get, if any!'

Peter decided to take as his example one of his new products: a table tennis bat marketed under the name of the 'high-resolution' bat, but known within the manufacturing unit more prosaically as Part Number 5654. Figure 14.9 shows the product structure for this table tennis bat, showing the bat made up of two main assemblies: a handle assembly

Source: Shutterstock.com: Chen WS

and a face assembly. In order to bring the two main assemblies together to form the finished bat, various fixings are required, such as nails, connectors, etc.

The gross requirements for this particular bat are shown below. The bat is not due to be launched until Week 13 (it is now Week 1), and sales forecasts have been made for the first 23 weeks of sales:

Weeks 13–21 inclusive, 100 per week
Weeks 22–29 inclusive, 150 per week
Weeks 30–35 inclusive, 200 per week

Peter also managed to obtain information on the current inventory levels of each of the parts which made up the finished bat, together with cost data and lead times. He was surprised, however, how long it took him to obtain this

Figure 14.9 Product structure for bat 5654

Table 14.3 Inventory, cost and lead-time information for parts

Part no.	Description	Inventory	EQ	LT	Std cost
5645	Bat	0	500	2	12.00
0499	Handle assy	0	400	3	4.00
7754	Shaft	15	1,000	5	1.00
0955	Connector	350	5,000	4	0.02
9110	Nail	120	5,000	4	0.01
8744	Rivet	3,540	5,000	4	0.01
0772	Face assy	0	250	4	5.00
1821	Handle	0	500	4	2.00
6511	Rubber face	0	2,000	10	0.50
2547	Wooden inner	10	300	7	1.50
8561	Foam panel	0	1,000	8	0.50

EQ = economic quantity for ordering; LT = lead time for ordering (in weeks);
Std cost = standard cost in £.

information. 'It has taken me nearly two days to get hold of all the information I need. Different people held it, nowhere was it conveniently put together, and sometimes it was not even written down. To get the inventory data, I actually had to go down to the stores and count how many parts were in the boxes.'

The data Peter collected was as shown in Table 14.3.

Peter set himself six exercises which he knew he would have to master if he was to understand fully the basics of MRP.

Exercise 1

Draw up:

(a) the single-level bill of materials for each level of assembly;
(b) a complete indented bill of materials for all levels of assembly.

Exercise 2

(a) Create the materials requirements planning records for each part and sub-assembly in the bat.
(b) List any problems that the completed MRP records identify.
(c) What alternatives are there that the company could take to solve any problems? What are their relative merits?

Exercise 3

Based on the first two exercises, create another set of MRP records, this time allowing one week's safety lead time for each item: that is, ensuring the items are in stock the week prior to when they are required.

Exercise 4

Over the time period of the exercise, what effect would the imposition of a safety lead time have on average inventory value?

Exercise 5

If we decided that our first task was to reduce inventory costs by 15 per cent, what action would we recommend? What are the implications of our action?

Exercise 6

How might production in our business be smoothed?

QUESTIONS

1 Why did Peter have such problems getting to the relevant information?

2 Perform all the exercises which Peter set for himself. Do you think he should now fully understand MRP?

PROBLEMS AND APPLICATIONS

1   Your company has developed a simple, but amazingly effective mango peeler. It is constructed from a blade and a supergrip handle that has a top piece and a bottom piece. The assembled mango peeler is packed in a simple recycled card pack. All the parts simply clip together and are bought in from suppliers, who can deliver the parts within one week of orders being placed. Given enough parts, your company can produce products within a day of firm orders being placed. Initial forecasts indicate that demand will be around 500 items per week.
   (a)   Draw a component structure and bill of materials for the mango peeler.
   (b)   Develop a master production schedule for the product.
   (c)   Develop a schedule indicating when and how many of each component should be ordered (your scheduler tells you that the economic order quantity, EOQ, for all parts is 2,500).

2   The mango peeler described above was a huge success. Demand is now level at 800 items per week. You now have also developed two further products, a melon baller and a passion fruit pulper. Both new products use the same handle, but have their own specially designed handle and pack. Demand for the new products is expected to be 400 items per week. Also your suppliers have indicated that, because of the extra demand, they will need two weeks to deliver orders. Similarly, your own assembly department is now taking a week to assemble the products.
   (a)   Draw new component structures and bills of material for the new products.
   (b)   Develop a master production schedule for all the products.
   (c)   Develop a schedule indicating when and how many of each component should be ordered.

3   Using a cookery book, choose three similar, fairly complex, recipe items such as layered and decorated gateaux (cakes) or desserts. For each, construct the indented bill of materials and identify all the different materials, sub-assemblies and final products with one set of part numbers (that is, no duplication). Using the times given in the recipes (or your own estimates), construct a table of lead times (for example, in minutes or hours) for each stage of production and for procurement of the ingredients. Using these examples (and a bit of your own imagination!), show how this information could be used with an MRP system to plan and control the batch production processes within a small cake or dessert factory making thousands of each product every week. Show part of the MRP records and calculations that would be involved.

4   **(Advanced)** Working in a small study group, construct a model of the information systems that you think would be needed to plan and control the most important day-to-day operations and finances of a large university or college. In particular, identify and include at least three processes that cross departmental and functional boundaries, and show how ERP might be used to improve the quality, speed, dependability, flexibility and/or costs of such processes. Then discuss:
   (a)   If ERP is not already in use at your chosen organization, should it be introduced, and if so why? What would the difficulties be in doing this, and how could they be overcome?
   (b)   If ERP is already in use, what advantages and disadvantages are already apparent to the staff (for example, ask a lecturer, an administrator and a support services manager, such as someone who runs cleaning or catering services).

SELECTED FURTHER READING

Atkinson, R. (2013) *Enterprise Resource Planning (ERP) The Great Gamble: An Executive's Guide to Understanding an ERP Project*, Xlibris, Bloomington, IN.

A basic book. Don't look for great depth, but it is a good introduction.

Bradford, M. (2010) **Modern ERP: Select, implement & use today's advanced business systems, lulu.com**

A good, solid class text.

Davenport, T.H. (1998) **Putting the enterprise into the enterprise system**, *Harvard Business Review*, July–August.

Covers some of the more managerial and strategic aspects of ERP.

Koch, C. and Wailgum, T. (2007) **ERP definition and solutions, www.cio.com**

CIO.com has some really useful articles; this is one of the most thought provoking.

MacCarthy, B.L. (2006) **Organizational, systems and human issues in production planning, scheduling and control, in Hermann, J. (ed.)** *Handbook of Production Scheduling*, **International Series in Operations Research and Management Science, Springer, New York.**

This is an academic paper, but do not be put off – it is a good and sensible overview of the topic by one of the best authorities in the area.

Srivastava, D. and Batra, A. (2010) *ERP Systems*, I K International Publishing House, New Delhi.

An in-depth study of ERP systems and its benefits including implementation.

Turbit, N. (2005) **ERP implementation – the traps, The Project Perfect White Paper Collection, www.projectperfect.com.au**

Practical (and true).

Vollmann,T., Berry, W., Whybark, D.C. and Jacobs, F.R. (2004) *Manufacturing Planning and Control Systems for Supply Chain Management: The Definitive Guide for Professionals*, McGraw-Hill Higher Education, New York.

The latest version of the 'bible' of manufacturing planning and control. Explains the 'workings' of MRP and ERP in detail.

Supplement to Chapter 14
Materials requirements planning (MRP)

INTRODUCTION

Materials requirements planning (MRP) is an approach to calculating how many parts or materials of particular types are required and what times they are required. This requires data files which, when the MRP program is run, can be checked and updated. Figure S14.1 shows how these files relate to each other. The first inputs to MRP are customer orders and forecast demand. MRP performs its calculations based on the combination of these two parts of future demand. All other requirements are derived from, and dependent on, this demand information.

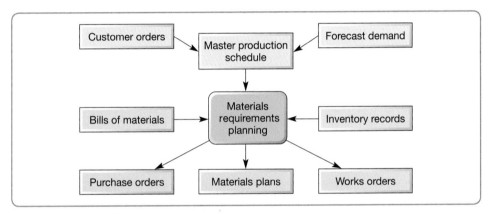

Figure S14.1 **Materials requirements planning (MRP) schematic**

MASTER PRODUCTION SCHEDULE

The master production schedule (MPS) forms the main input to MRP and contains a statement of the volume and timing of the end products to be made. It drives all the production and supply activities that eventually will come together to form the end products. It is the basis for the planning and utilization of labour and equipment, and it determines the provisioning of materials and cash. The MPS should include all sources of demand, such as spare parts, internal production promises, etc. For example, if a manufacturer of earth excavators plans an exhibition of its products and allows a project team to raid the stores so that it can build two pristine examples to be exhibited, this is likely to leave the factory short of parts. MPSs can also be used in service organizations. For example, in a hospital theatre there is a master schedule that contains a statement of which operations are planned and when. This can be used to provision materials for the operations, such as the sterile instruments, blood and dressings. It may also govern the scheduling of staff for operations.

The MPS record

MPSs are time-phased records of each end product, which contain a statement of demand and currently available stock of each finished item. Using this information, the available inventory is projected ahead in time. When there is insufficient inventory to satisfy forward demand, order

Table S14.1 **Example of an MPS**

| | \multicolumn{9}{c}{Week number} | | | | | | | | |
	1	2	3	4	5	6	7	8	9
Demand	10	10	10	10	15	15	15	20	20
Available	20	10	0	0	0	0	0	0	0
MPS	0	0	10	10	15	15	15	20	20
On hand	30								

quantities are entered on the master schedule line. Table S14.1 is a simplified example of part of an MPS for one item. In the first row the known sales orders and any forecasts are combined to form 'Demand'. The second row, 'Available', shows how much inventory of this item is expected to be in stock at the end of each weekly period. The opening inventory balance, 'On hand', is shown separately at the bottom of the record. The third row is the MPS; this shows how many finished items need to be completed and available in each week to satisfy demand.

Chase or level MPSs

In the example in Table S14.1, the MPS increases as demand increases and aims to keep available inventory at zero. The MPS is 'chasing' demand (see Chapter 11) and so adjusting the provision of resources. An alternative 'levelled' MPS for this situation is shown in Table S14.2. Level scheduling involves averaging the amount required to be completed to smooth out peaks and troughs; it generates more inventory than the previous MPS.

Available to promise (ATP)

The MPS provides information to the sales function on what can be promised to customers and when delivery can be promised. The sales function can load known sales orders against the MPS and keep track of what is available to promise (ATP) (*see* Table S14.3). The ATP line in the MPS shows the maximum that is still available in any one week, against which sales orders can be loaded.

THE BILL OF MATERIALS (BOM)

From the master schedule, MRP calculates the required volume and timing of assemblies, sub-assemblies and materials. To do this it needs information on what parts are required for each product. This is called the 'bill of materials'. Initially it is simplest to think

Table S14.2 **Example of a 'level' MPS**

| | \multicolumn{9}{c}{Week number} | | | | | | | | |
	1	2	3	4	5	6	7	8	9
Demand	10	10	10	10	15	15	15	20	20
Available	31	32	33	34	30	26	22	13	4
MPS	11	11	11	11	11	11	11	11	11
On hand	30								

Table S14.3 Example of a level MPS including ATP

	Week number								
	1	2	3	4	5	6	7	8	9
Demand	10	10	10	10	15	15	15	20	20
Sales orders	10	10	10	8	4				
Available	31	32	33	34	30	26	22	13	4
ATP	31	1	1	3	7	11	11	11	11
MPS	11	11	11	11	11	11	11	11	11
On hand	30								

about these as a product structure. The product structure in Figure S14.2 is a simplified structure showing the parts required to make a simple board game. Different 'levels of assembly' are shown with the finished product (the boxed game) at level 0, the parts and sub-assemblies that go into the boxed game at level 1, the parts that go into the sub-assemblies at level 2, and so on.

A more convenient form of the product structure is the 'indented bill of materials'. Table S14.4 shows the whole indented bill of materials for the board game. The term 'indented' refers to the indentation of the level of assembly, shown in the left-hand column. Multiples of some parts are required; this means that MRP has to know the required number of each part to be able to multiply up the requirements. Also, the same part (for example, the TV label, part number 10062) may be used in different parts of the product

Figure S14.2 Product structure for the Treasure Hunt game

Table S14.4 Indented bill of materials for board game

Part number: 00289

Description: Board game

Level: 0

Level	Part number	Description	Quantity
0	00289	Board game	1
.1	10077	Box lid	1
.1	10089	Box base assy	1
..2	20467	Box base	1
..2	10062	TV label	1
..2	23988	Inner tray	1
.1	10023	Quest cards set	1
.1	10045	Character set	1
.1	10067	Die	2
.1	10062	TV label	1
.1	10033	Game board	1
.1	10056	Rules booklet	1

structure. This means that MRP has to cope with this commonality of parts and, at some stage, aggregate the requirements to check how many labels in total are required.

INVENTORY RECORDS

MRP calculations need to recognize that some required items may already be in stock. So, it is necessary, starting at level 0 of each bill, to check how much inventory is available of each finished product, sub-assembly and component, and then to calculate what is termed the 'net' requirements, that is the extra requirements needed to supplement the inventory so that demand can be met. This requires that three main inventory records are kept: the item master file, which contains the unique standard identification code for each part or component; the transaction file, which keeps a record of receipts into stock, issues from stock and a running balance; and the location file, which identifies where inventory is located.

THE MRP NETTING PROCESS

The information needs of MRP are important, but it is not the 'heart' of the MRP procedure. At its core, MRP is a systematic process of taking this planning information and calculating the volume and timing requirements which will satisfy demand. The most important element of this is the MRP netting process. Figure S14.3 illustrates the process that MRP performs to calculate the volumes of materials required. The MPS is 'exploded', examining the implications of the schedule through the bill of materials, checking how many sub-assemblies and parts are required. Before moving down the bill of materials to the next level, MRP checks how

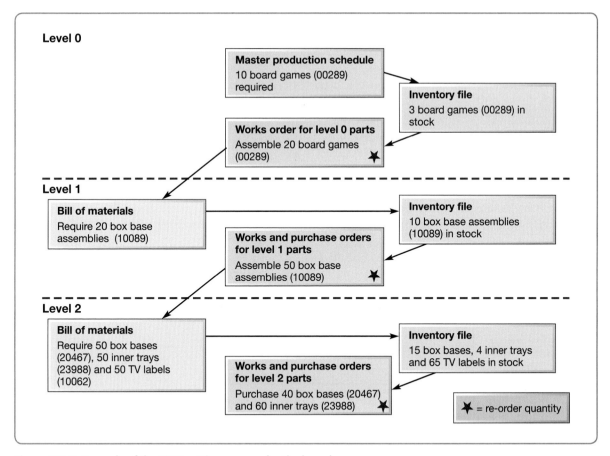

Figure S14.3 Example of the MRP netting process for the board game

many of the required parts are already available in stock. It then generates 'works orders', or requests, for the net requirements of items. These form the schedule which is again exploded through the bill of materials at the next level down. This process continues until the bottom level of the bill of materials is reached.

Table S14.5 **Back-scheduling of requirements in MRP**

Part no.	Description	Inventory on hand day 0	Lead time (days)	Re-order quantity
00289	Board game	3	2	20
10077	Box lid	4	8	25
10089	Box base assy	10	4	50
20467	Box base	15	12	40
23988	Inner tray	4	14	60
10062	TV label	65	8	100
10023	Quest cards set	4	3	50
10045	Character set	46	3	50
10067	Die	22	5	80
10033	Game board	8	15	50
10056	Rules booklet	0	3	80

00289: Treasure Hunt game Assembly lead time = 2 Re-order quantity = 20

Day Number:	0	1	2	3	4	5	6	7	8	9	10	11	12	13	14	15	16	17	18	19	20
Requirements Gross																					10
Scheduled Receipts																					
On hand Inventory	3	3	3	3	3	3	3	3	3	3	3	3	3	3	3	3	3	3	3	3	13
Planned Order Release																			20		

10077: Box lid Purchase lead time = 8 Re-order quantity = 25

Day Number:	0	1	2	3	4	5	6	7	8	9	10	11	12	13	14	15	16	17	18	19	20
Requirements Gross																			20		
Scheduled Receipts																					
On hand Inventory	4	4	4	4	4	4	4	4	4	4	4	4	4	4	4	4	4	4	9	9	9
Planned Order Release											25										

10089: Box base assembly Assembly lead time = 4 Re-order quantity = 50

Day Number:	0	1	2	3	4	5	6	7	8	9	10	11	12	13	14	15	16	17	18	19	20
Requirements Gross																			20		
Scheduled Receipts																					
On hand Inventory	10	10	10	10	10	10	10	10	10	10	10	10	10	10	10	10	10	10	40	40	40
Planned Order Release														50							

20467: Box base Purchase lead time = 12 Re-order quantity = 40

Day Number:	0	1	2	3	4	5	6	7	8	9	10	11	12	13	14	15	16	17	18	19	20
Requirements Gross														50							
Scheduled Receipts																					
On hand Inventory	15	15	15	15	15	15	15	15	15	15	15	15	15	15	5	5	5	5	5	5	5
Planned Order Release		40																			

23988: Inner tray Purchase lead time = 14 Re-order quantity = 60

Day Number:	0	1	2	3	4	5	6	7	8	9	10	11	12	13	14	15	16	17	18	19	20
Requirements Gross															50						
Scheduled Receipts																					
On hand Inventory	4	4	4	4	4	4	4	4	4	4	4	4	4	4	14	14	14	14	14	14	14
Planned Order Release	60																				

10062: TV label Purchase lead time = 8 Re-order quantity = 100

Day Number:	0	1	2	3	4	5	6	7	8	9	10	11	12	13	14	15	16	17	18	19	20
Requirements Gross															50				20		
Scheduled Receipts																					
On hand Inventory	65	65	65	65	65	65	65	65	65	65	65	65	65	65	15	15	15	15	95	95	95
Planned Order Release											100										

10023: Quest card set Purchase lead time = 3 Re-order quantity = 50

Day Number:	0	1	2	3	4	5	6	7	8	9	10	11	12	13	14	15	16	17	18	19	20
Requirements Gross																			20		
Scheduled Receipts																					
On hand Inventory	4	4	4	4	4	4	4	4	4	4	4	4	4	4	4	4	4	4	34	34	34
Planned Order Release															50						

10045: Character set Purchase lead time = 3 Re-order quantity = 50

Day Number:	0	1	2	3	4	5	6	7	8	9	10	11	12	13	14	15	16	17	18	19	20
Requirements Gross																			20		
Scheduled Receipts																					
On hand Inventory	46	46	46	46	46	46	46	46	46	46	46	46	46	46	46	46	46	46	26	26	26
Planned Order Release																					

10067: Die Purchase lead time = 5 Re-order quantity = 80

Day Number:	0	1	2	3	4	5	6	7	8	9	10	11	12	13	14	15	16	17	18	19	20
Requirements Gross																			40		
Scheduled Receipts																					
On hand Inventory	3	3	3	3	3	3	3	3	3	3	3	3	3	3	3	3	3	3	3	3	13
Planned Order Release														80							

10033: Game board Purchase lead time = 15 Re-order quantity = 50

Day Number:	0	1	2	3	4	5	6	7	8	9	10	11	12	13	14	15	16	17	18	19	20
Requirements Gross																			20		
Scheduled Receipts																					
On hand Inventory	8	8	8	8	8	8	8	8	8	8	8	8	8	8	8	8	8	8	38	38	38
Planned Order Release			50																		

10056: Rules booklet Purchase lead time = 3 Re-order quantity = 80

Day Number:	0	1	2	3	4	5	6	7	8	9	10	11	12	13	14	15	16	17	18	19	20
Requirements Gross																			20		
Scheduled Receipts																					
On hand Inventory	0	0	0	0	0	0	0	0	0	0	0	0	0	0	0	0	0	0	60	60	60
Planned Order Release																80					

Figure S14.4 Extract of the MRP records for the board game

Back-scheduling

In addition to calculating the volume of materials required, MRP also considers when each of these parts is required, that is the timing and scheduling of materials. It does this by a process called back-scheduling, which takes into account the lead time (the time allowed for completion of each stage of the process) at every level of assembly. Again using the example of the board game, assume that 10 board games are required to be finished by a notional planning day which we will term day 20. To determine when we need to start work on all the parts that make up the game, we need to know all the lead times that are stored in MRP files for each part (*see* Table S14.5).

Using the lead-time information, the programme is worked backwards to determine the tasks that have to be performed and the purchase orders that have to be placed. Given the lead times and inventory levels shown in Table S14.5, the MRP records shown in Figure S14.4 can be derived.

MRP CAPACITY CHECKS

The MRP process needs a feedback loop to check whether a plan was achievable and whether it has actually been achieved. Closing this planning loop in MRP systems involves checking production plans against available capacity and, if the proposed plans are not achievable at any level, revising them. All but the simplest MRP systems are now closed-loop systems. They use three planning routines to check production plans against the operation's resources at three levels:

- Resource requirements plans (RRPs) involve looking forward in the long term to predict the requirements for large structural parts of the operation, such as the numbers, locations and sizes of new plants.
- Rough-cut capacity plans (RCCPs) are used in the medium to short term, to check the MPSs against known capacity bottlenecks, in case capacity constraints are broken. The feedback loop at this level checks the MPS and key resources only.
- Capacity requirements plans (CRPs) look at the day-to-day effect of the works orders issued from the MRP on the loading individual process stages.

SUMMARY

> MRP stands for materials requirements planning, which is a dependent demand system that calculates materials requirements and production plans to satisfy known and forecast sales orders. It helps to make volume and timing calculations based on an idea of what will be necessary to supply demand in the future.

> MRP works from a master production schedule (MPS), which summarizes the volume and timing of end products or services. Using the logic of the bill of materials (BOM) and inventory records, the production schedule is 'exploded' (called the MRP netting process) to determine how many sub-assemblies and parts are required, and when they are required.

> Closed-loop MRP systems contain feedback loops which ensure that checks are made against capacity to see if plans are feasible.

> MRP II systems are a development of MRP. They integrate many processes that are related to MRP, but which are located outside the operation's function.

15

Lean operations

Key questions

> What is lean?

> How does lean eliminate waste?

> How does lean apply throughout the supply network?

> How does lean compare with other approaches?

INTRODUCTION

This chapter examines an approach to managing operations and the supply chain that is typically referred to as 'lean'. It is, at the same time, a philosophy, a method of operations planning and control, and an approach to improvement. Lean aims to meet demand instantaneously, with perfect quality, no waste and at low cost. This involves supplying products and services in perfect synchronization with the demand for them. These principles were once a radical departure from traditional operations practice, but have now become orthodox in promoting the synchronization of flow through processes, operations and supply networks. And although the topic was once narrowly treated as a manufacturing phenomenon (perhaps unsurprisingly given the pioneering role of Toyota in lean management), lean principles are applied across all sectors, including finance, healthcare, IT, retailing, construction, agriculture and the public sector. Figure 15.1 places lean in the overall model of operations management.

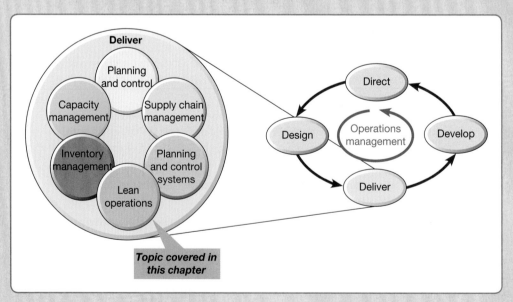

Figure 15.1 This chapter examines lean operations

WHAT IS LEAN?

The focus of lean is to achieve a flow of materials, information or customers that delivers exactly what customers want (perfect quality), in exact quantities (neither too much nor too little), exactly when needed (not too early nor too late), exactly where required (in the right location) and at the lowest possible cost. It is a concept that is almost synonymous with terms such as 'just-in-time' (JIT), the 'Toyota Production System' (TPS), 'stockless production' and 'lean synchronization'. It results in items flowing rapidly and smoothly through processes, operations and supply networks.

In this chapter, we provide examples of organizations in a wide range of sectors that apply aspects of lean to their operations and supply networks. Many of the examples of lean philosophy and lean techniques in service industries are directly analogous to those found in manufacturing because physical items are being moved or processed in some way. For example, supermarkets usually replenish their shelves only when customers have taken sufficient products off the shelf. The movement of goods from the 'back-office' store to the shelf is triggered only by the 'empty-shelf' demand signal. Construction companies increasingly make a rule of only calling for material deliveries to their sites the day before the materials are needed. This reduces clutter and the chances of theft. Both are examples of the application of *pull control* principles. Other examples of lean concepts and methods apply even when most of the service elements are intangible. For example, new publishing technologies allow professors to assemble printed and e-learning course material customized to the needs of individual courses or even individual students. Here, we see the lean principles of flexibility and small batch sizes allowing customization and rapid delivery.

OPERATIONS IN PRACTICE — Jamie's 'lean' meals[1]

Source: Getty Images: Paul Zimmerman

Most people do not have the time to devote long hours to cooking – which is possibly why the celebrity chef Jamie Oliver has written a book *Jamie's 30-minute meals*, whose philosophy is that cooking a delicious dinner should be as quick as and cheaper than buying and heating a take-away. The book presents 50 ready-made menus with three to four courses per menu designed to take no more than 30 minutes to prepare. To achieve this performance Jamie has, perhaps inadvertently, applied the principles and methods of lean synchronization to the everyday activity of cooking.

Let us imagine that your family is coming over for dinner and you want to surprise them with a new Indian multi-course meal with chicken, rice, salad on the side and of course a dessert. Traditionally, you would search and look up four different recipes, one for each dish. Because all recipes come from different places, you need to figure out the quantity of food to buy, doing the maths in case of shared ingredients across the dishes, how to allocate pots, pans and other equipment to the different ingredients and, most importantly, you need to figure out in what order to prepare things, especially if you want all your dishes ready at the same time. Jamie's approach significantly reduces this complexity by ensuring dishes are prepared right when the next step in the process needs them, regardless of which dish it is. In other words, dishes are not cooked in sequence, one after another, but they are prepared and completed simultaneously.

If we identify all the tasks related to preparing the salad (for example, chopping the vegetables) with the letter A, cooking the rice (for example, blending) with letter B, cooking the chicken with letter C, and finally making the dessert with the letter D, then in the traditional way of cooking our task scheduling would look something like AAAA BBBBBBB CCCCCCC DDDD. This results in batching, waiting time and causing dishes to be ready before the dinner is supposed to be served. Conversely, Jamie Oliver's 30-minute cooking involves scheduling tasks in a sequence like ABCDACBADCBABDC, where single tasks related to different dishes follow smoothly, as the chef chops a salad ingredient, then blends the rice, then chops some more salad ingredients while the chicken is being roasted in the oven and a part of the desert is being prepared. This way, all dishes are ready at the same time, just in time and nothing is prepared before it has to be, avoiding any form of waste. Such a levelled approach to scheduling is called *heijunka* (mixed modelling) in the lean approach.

In addition, Jamie's lean cooking builds on reduced set-up times. At the beginning of each recipe, the equipment needed to prepare the menu is presented under the headline 'To Start'. Other necessary preparations, such as heating the oven, are also specified. Having all equipment ready from the start saves time in the process, and is, according to Jamie, a prerequisite for getting done in 30 minutes. The use of simple equipment that is suitable for many different purposes also makes the process quicker as changeovers are minimized. The rationale is to make the most out of the time available, eliminating the 'faffing around' in cooking (non-value-added activity in OM language) and leaving only what is strictly 'good, fast cooking', without compromising on quality.

Three perspectives of lean

Defining lean is not entirely straightforward! In many ways lean can be viewed as three related, but distinct things: a philosophy, a method of planning and control with useful prescriptions of how to manage day-to-day operations, and a set of improvement tools.

- **Lean is a philosophy of how to run operations** – It is a coherent set of principles that are founded on smoothing flow through processes by doing all the simple things well, on gradually doing them better, on meeting customer needs exactly and (above all) on squeezing out waste every step of the way. Three key issues define the lean philosophy: the involvement of staff in the operation, the drive for continuous improvement, and the elimination of waste. Other chapters look at the first two issues, so we devote much of this chapter to the central idea of waste elimination.
- **Lean is a method of planning and controlling operations** – Many lean ideas are concerned with how items (materials, information, customers) flow through operations and, more specifically, how operations managers can manage this flow. For this reason lean can be viewed as a method of planning and control. Yet it is planning and control in pursuit of lean's philosophical aims. Uncoordinated flow causes unpredictability, and unpredictability causes waste because people hold inventory, capacity or time, to protect themselves against it. So lean planning and control uses several methods to achieve synchronized flow and reduce waste. Above all it uses 'pull' control that was described in Chapter 10 (in contrast to MRP, described in Chapter 14, which relies on 'push' control). This is usually achieved using some sort of kanban system (described later). In addition the other lean planning and control methods which promote smooth flow include levelled scheduling and delivery, and mixed modelling (again described later in this chapter).
- **Lean is a set of tools that improve operations performance** – The 'engine room' of the lean philosophy is a collection of improvement tools and techniques that are the means for cutting out waste. There are many techniques that could be termed 'lean techniques' and, again, many of them follow on naturally and logically from the overall lean philosophy. What is just as important to understand is how the introduction of lean as a philosophy helped to shift the focus of operations management generally towards viewing improvement as its main purpose. In addition, the rise of lean ideas gave birth to techniques that have now become mainstream in operations management. Some of these tools and techniques are well known outside the lean sphere and are covered in other chapters of this book.

> **✳ Operations principle**
>
> Lean can be viewed as a philosophy of how to run operations, a method of planning and controlling operations, and a set of tools that improve operations performance.

It seems that lean principles (or some lean principles) can be applied even to the most unlikely of processes. None less likely than Pixar Animation Studios, the Academy-Award-winning computer animation studio and makers of feature films that have resulted in an unprecedented streak of both critical and box office success including *Toy Story* (1, 2 and 3), *A Bug's Life, Monsters, Inc., Finding Nemo, The Incredibles, Ratatouille, WALL-E* and *Up*. Since its incorporation, Pixar has been responsible for many important breakthroughs in the application of computer graphics (CG) for film making. So, the company has attracted some of the world's finest technical, creative and production talent in the area. And such 'knowledge-based' talent is notoriously difficult to manage – certainly not the types of processes that are generally seen as being appropriate for lean synchronization. Managing creativity involves a difficult trade-off between encouraging the freedom to produce novel ideas and making sure that they work within an effective overall structure.

Nevertheless, Pixar did get the inspiration from Toyota and the way it uses lean production – in particular, the way Toyota has encouraged continuous advice and criticism from its production line workers to improve its performance. Pixar realized that it could do the same with

Source: Alamy Images: AF Archive

producing cartoon characters. Adopting constant feedback surfaces problems before they become crises, and provides creative teams with inspiration and challenge. Pixar also puts a great deal of effort into persuading its creative staff to work together. In similar companies, people may collaborate on specific projects, but are less good at focusing on what is going on elsewhere in the business. Pixar, however, tries to cultivate a sense of collective responsibility. Staff even show unfinished work to one another in daily meetings, so get used to giving and receiving constructive criticism.

How lean operations consider flow

The best way to understand how lean differs from more traditional approaches to managing flow is to contrast the two simple processes in Figure 15.2. The traditional approach assumes that each stage in the process will place its output in an inventory that 'buffers' that stage from the next one downstream in the process. The next stage down will then (eventually) take outputs from the inventory, process them and pass them through to the next buffer inventory. These buffers are there to 'insulate' each stage from its neighbours making each stage relatively independent so that if, for example, stage A stops operating for some reason, stage B can continue, at least for a time. The larger the buffer inventory, the greater the degree of insulation between the stages. This insulation has to be paid for in terms of inventory or queues and slow throughput times because products, customers or information will spend time waiting between stages in the process.

But the main argument against this traditional approach lies in the very conditions it seeks to promote, namely the insulation of the stages from one another. When a problem occurs at one stage, the problem will not immediately be apparent elsewhere in the system. The responsibility for solving the problem will be centred largely on the people within that stage, and the consequences of the problem will be prevented from spreading to the whole system. However, contrast this with the pure lean process illustrated in Figure 15.2. Here, products, customers or information are processed and then passed directly to the next stage in a synchronized manner 'just-in-time' for them to be processed further. Problems at any stage have a very different effect in such a system. Now if stage A stops processing, stage B will notice immediately

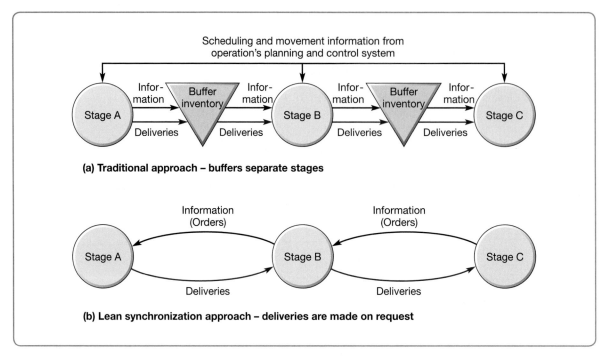

Figure 15.2 (a) Traditional and (b) lean synchronized flow between stages

and stage C very soon after. Stage A's problem is now quickly exposed to the whole process, which is immediately affected by the problem. This means that the responsibility for solving the problem is no longer confined to the staff at stage A. It is now shared by everyone, considerably improving the chances of the problem being solved, if only because it is now too important to be ignored. In other words, by preventing items accumulating between stages, the operation has increased the chances of the intrinsic efficiency of the plant being improved. Non-synchronized approaches seek to encourage efficiency by protecting each part of the process from disruption. The lean approach takes the opposite view. Exposure of the system (although not suddenly, as in our simplified example) to problems can both make them more evident and change the 'motivation structure' of the whole system towards solving the problems. Lean sees accumulations of inventory, be they product, customer or information inventories, as a 'blanket of obscurity' that lies over the system and prevents problems being noticed.

Now think of the logic behind the explanation above. There are four interrelated ideas that 'mesh' with each other to form a logical chain. First, between each stage, it is the downstream 'customer' stage that signals the need for action. It is the customer who, in effect, 'pulls' items through the process. The starting point of the lean philosophy is a customer focus. Second, this customer 'pull' encourages items to flow through the process in a synchronized manner (rather than dwelling in inventory). Third, the smooth synchronized flow and resulting reduction in inventory affect the motivation to improve because stages are no longer decoupled. Fourth, the increased motivation to improve exposes waste and encourages its elimination. These four related ideas are illustrated in Figure 15.3, and we will discuss them further in the rest of this chapter.

How lean operations consider inventory

The idea of obscuring effects of inventory is often illustrated diagrammatically, as in Figure 15.4. The many problems of the operation are shown as rocks in a river bed that cannot be seen because of the depth of the water. The water in this analogy represents

Figure 15.3 The four elements of lean

the inventory in the operation. Yet, even though the rocks cannot be seen, they slow the progress of the river's flow and cause turbulence. Gradually reducing the depth of the water (inventory) exposes the worst of the problems that can be resolved, after which the water is lowered further, exposing more problems, and so on. The same argument will also apply for the flow between whole processes, or whole operations. For example, stages A, B and C in Figure 15.2 could be a supplier operation, a manufacturer and a customer's operation, respectively.

How lean operations consider capacity utilization

Lean has many benefits but these come at the cost of capacity utilization. Return to the process shown in Figure 15.2. When stoppages occur in the traditional system, the buffers allow each stage to continue working and thus achieve high capacity utilization. However, the high utilization does not necessarily make the process as a whole produce more. Often extra

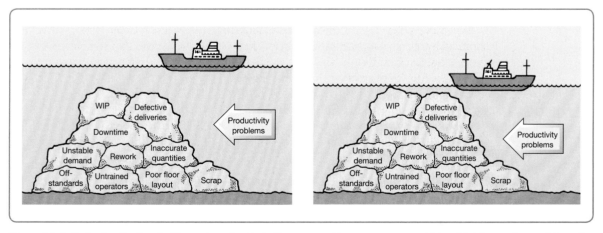

Figure 15.4 Reducing the level of inventory (water) allows operations management (the ship) to see the problems in the operation (the rocks) and work to reduce them

'production' goes into buffer inventories or queues of customers. In a lean process, any stoppage will affect the whole process. This will necessarily lead to lower capacity utilization, at least in the short term. In organizations that place a high value on the utilization of capacity this can prove particularly difficult to accept. However, there is no point in producing output just for its own sake. In fact, producing just to keep utilization high is not only pointless, but also counter-productive, because the extra inventory produced merely serves to make improvements less likely. Figure 15.5 illustrates the two approaches to capacity utilization.

How lean operations consider the role of people

Lean proponents frequently stress the importance of involving all staff in the lean approach. In this way it is similar to other improvement-based concepts such as 'total quality' which is discussed in detail in Chapter 17. However, the lean approach to people management is very much influenced by its Japanese origins, which is evident from both the terminology and the concepts themselves. So, for example, the original lean advocates called their approach the 'respect-for-humans' system. It encourages (and often requires) team-based problem solving, job enrichment (by including maintenance and set-up tasks in operators' jobs), job rotation and multi-skilling. The intention is to encourage a high degree of personal responsibility, engagement and 'ownership' of the job. Similarly, what are called 'basic working practices' are sometimes used to implement the 'involvement of everyone' principle. These include the following:

- **Discipline** – Work standards that are critical for the safety of staff, the environment and quality must be followed by everyone all the time.
- **Flexibility** – It should be possible to expand responsibilities to the extent of people's capabilities. This applies as equally to managers as it does to shop-floor personnel. Barriers to flexibility, such as grading structures and restrictive practices, should be removed.
- **Equality** – Unfair and divisive personnel policies should be discarded. Many companies implement the egalitarian message through to company uniforms, consistent pay structures which do not differentiate between full-time staff and hourly rated staff, and open-plan offices.
- **Autonomy** – Delegate responsibility to people involved in direct activities so that management's task becomes one of supporting processes. Delegation includes giving staff the

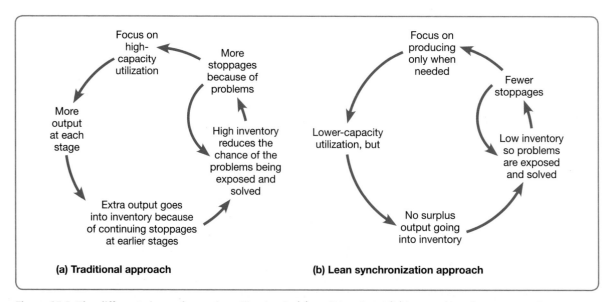

Figure 15.5 The different views of capacity utilization in (a) traditional and (b) lean approaches to operations

responsibility for stopping processes in the event of problems, scheduling work, gathering performance monitoring data and general problem solving.

- **Development of personnel** – Over time, the aim is to create more company members who can support the rigours of being competitive.
- **Quality of working life (QWL)** – This may include, for example, involvement in decision making, security of employment, enjoyment and working area facilities.
- **Creativity** – This is one of the indispensable elements of motivation. Creativity in this context means not just doing a job, but also improving how it is done, and building the improvement into the process.
- **Total people involvement** – Staff take on more responsibility to use their abilities to the benefit of the company as a whole. They are expected to participate in activities such as the selection of new recruits, dealing directly with suppliers and customers over schedules, quality issues, delivery information, spending improvement budgets, and planning and reviewing work done each day through communication meetings.

OPERATIONS IN PRACTICE — Toyota's lean DNA

Seen as the leading practitioner and the main originator of the lean approach, the Toyota Motor Company has progressively synchronized all its processes simultaneously to give high quality, fast throughput and exceptional productivity. It has done this by developing a set of practices that has largely shaped what we now call 'lean' or 'just-in-time' but which Toyota calls the Toyota Production System (TPS). The TPS has two themes, 'just-in-time' and 'jidoka'. Just-in-time is defined as the rapid and co-ordinated movement of parts throughout the production system and supply network to meet customer demand. It is operationalized by means of *heijunka* (levelling and smoothing the flow of items), *kanban* (signalling to the preceding process that more parts are needed) and *nagare* (laying out processes to achieve smoother flow of parts throughout the production process). *Jidoka* is described as 'humanizing the interface between operator and machine'. Toyota's philosophy is that the machine is there to serve the operator's purpose. The operator should be left free to exercise his or her judgement. *Jidoka* is operationalized by means of fail-safeing (or machine jidoka), line-stop authority (or human jidoka) and visual control (at-a-glance status of production processes and visibility of process standards).

Toyota believe that both just-in-time and jidoka should be applied ruthlessly to the elimination of waste, where waste is defined as 'anything other than the minimum amount of equipment, items, part and workers that are absolutely essential to production'. Fujio Cho of Toyota identified seven types of waste that must be eliminated from all operations processes. They are: waste from overproduction, waste from waiting time, transportation waste, inventory waste, processing waste,

Source: Shutterstock.com: Creations

waste of motion and waste from product defects. Beyond this, authorities on Toyota claim that its strength lies in understanding the differences between the tools and practices used with Toyota operations and the overall philosophy of its approach to lean synchronization. This is what some have called the apparent paradox of the TPS, 'namely, that activities, connections and production flows in a Toyota factory are rigidly scripted, yet at the same time Toyota's operations are enormously flexible and adaptable. Activities and processes are constantly being challenged and pushed to a higher level of performance, enabling the company to continually innovate and improve.' While some adopters of lean principles may think they have 'done lean', Toyota simply changes the goal constantly to challenge improvement. As such, we see a key distinction between those that see lean as a specific end point to be achieved through the application of a series of improvement tools and those such as Toyota who treat lean as a philosophy that defines a way of conducting business.

How lean operations consider improvement

Lean objectives are often expressed as ideals, such as our definition: 'to meet demand instantaneously with perfect quality and no waste'. While any operation's current performance may be far removed from such ideals, a fundamental lean belief is that it is possible to get closer to them over time. Without such beliefs to drive progress, lean proponents argue that improvement is more likely to be transitory than continuous. This is why the concept of continuous improvement is such an important part of the lean philosophy. If its aims are set in terms of ideals which individual organizations may never fully achieve, then the emphasis must be on the way in which an organization moves closer to the ideal state. The Japanese word for continuous improvement is *kaizen*, and it is a key part of the lean philosophy. It is explained fully in Chapter 17.

HOW DOES LEAN ELIMINATE WASTE?

Arguably the most significant part of the lean philosophy is its focus on the elimination of all forms of waste. Waste can be defined as any activity that does not add value. For example, studies often show that as little as 5 per cent of total throughput time is actually spent directly adding value. This means that for 95 per cent of its time, an operation is adding cost to the service or product, not adding value. Such calculations can alert even relatively efficient operations to the enormous waste which is dormant within all operations. This same phenomenon applies as much to service processes as it does to manufacturing ones. Relatively simple requests, such as applying for a driving licence, may only take a few minutes actually to process, yet take days (or weeks) to be returned.

✲ **Operations principle**

Simple, transparent flow exposes sources of waste.

Causes of waste – muda, mura, muri

As so often in lean philosophy, Japanese terms are often used to describe core ideas. And waste elimination is certainly a core lean idea. The terms *muda*, *mura* and *muri* are Japanese words conveying three causes of waste that should be reduced or eliminated:

● *Muda* – are activities in a process that are wasteful because they do not add value to the operation or the customer. The main causes of these wasteful activities are likely to be poorly communicated objectives (including not understanding the customer's requirements), or the inefficient use of resources. The implication of this is that, for an activity to be effective, it must be properly recorded and communicated to whoever is performing it.

- *Mura* – means 'lack of consistency' or unevenness that results in periodic overloading of staff or equipment. So, for example, if activities are not properly documented so that different people at different times perform a task differently, then not surprisingly the result of the activity may be different. The negative effects of this are similar to a lack of dependability (see Chapter 2).
- *Muri* – means absurd or unreasonable. It is based on the idea that unnecessary or unreasonable requirements put on a process will result in poor outcomes. The implication of this is that appropriate skills, effective planning, accurate estimation of times and schedules will avoid this 'muri' overloading waste. In other words, waste can be caused by failing to carry out basic operations planning tasks such as prioritizing activities (sequencing), understanding the necessary time (scheduling) and resources (loading) to perform activities. All these issues are discussed in Chapter 10.

These three causes of waste are obviously related. When a process is inconsistent (mura), it can lead to the overburdening of equipment and people (muri) which, in turn, will cause all kinds of non-value-adding activities (muda).

Types of waste

Muda, mura and muri are three *causes* of waste. Now we turn to *types* of waste, which apply in many different types of operations – both service and production – and which form the core of lean philosophy. Here we consolidate these into four broad categories.

Waste from irregular flow

Perfect synchronization means smooth and even flow through processes, operations and supply networks. Barriers that prevent streamlined flow include the following:

- *Waiting time* – machine efficiency and labour efficiency are two popular measures that are widely used to measure machine and labour waiting time, respectively. Less obvious is the time when products, customers or information wait as inventory or queues, there simply to keep operators busy.
- *Transport* – moving items or customers around the operation, together with double and triple handling, does not add value. Layout changes that bring processes closer together, improvements in transport methods and workplace organization can all reduce waste.
- *Process inefficiencies* – the process itself may be a source of waste. Some operations may only exist because of poor component design, or poor maintenance, and so could be eliminated.
- *Inventory* – regardless of type (product, customer, information) all inventories should become a target for elimination. However, it is only by tackling the causes of inventory or queues, such as irregular flow, that it can be reduced.
- *Wasted motion* – an operator may look busy but sometimes no value is being added by the work. Simplification of work is a rich source of reduction in the waste of motion.

Waste from inexact supply

Perfect synchronization also means supplying exactly what is wanted, exactly when it is needed. Any under- or over-supply and any early or late delivery will result in waste, something we have already explored in the capacity management chapter in particular. Barriers to achieving an exact match between supply and demand include the following:

- *Over-production or under-production* – supplying more than, or less than, is immediately needed by the next stage, process or operation. (This is the greatest source of waste according to Toyota.)
- *Early or late delivery* – items should only arrive exactly when they are needed. Early delivery is as wasteful as late delivery.
- *Inventory* – again, all inventories should become a target for elimination. However, it is only by tackling the causes of inventory, such as inexact supply, that it can be reduced.

Waste from inflexible response

Customer needs can vary, in terms of what they want, how much they want and when they want it. However, processes usually find it more convenient to change what they do relatively infrequently, because every change implies some kind of cost. That is why hospitals schedule specialist clinics only at particular times, and why machines often make a batch of similar products together. Yet responding to customer demands exactly and instantaneously requires a high degree of process flexibility. Symptoms of inadequate flexibility include the following:

- *Large batches* – sending batches of items through a process inevitably increases inventory as the batch moves through the whole process.
- *Delays between activities* – the longer the time (and the cost) of changing over from one activity to another, the more difficult it is to synchronize flow to match customer demand instantaneously.
- *More variation in activity mix than in customer demand* – if the mix of activities in different time periods varies more than customer demand varies, then some 'batching' of activities must be taking place.

Waste from variability

Synchronization implies exact levels of quality. If there is variability in quality levels then customers will not consider themselves as being adequately supplied. Variability therefore is an important barrier to achieving synchronized supply. Symptoms of poor variability include the following:

- *Poor reliability of equipment* – unreliable equipment usually indicates a lack of conformance in quality levels. It also means that there will be irregularity in supplying customers. Either way, it prevents synchronization of supply.
- *Defective products or services* – waste caused by poor quality is significant in most operations. Service or product errors cause both customers and processes to waste time until they are corrected.

Looking for waste (and kaizen opportunities) – the 'Gemba walk'

Gemba (also sometimes called 'ganba'), when roughly translated from the Japanese, means 'the actual place' where something happens. It is a term often used in lean philosophy or in improvement generally, to convey the idea that, if you really want to understand something, you go to where it actually takes place. Only then can a true appreciation of the realities of improvement opportunities be gained. Lean improvement advocates often use the idea of 'the gemba walk' to make problems visible. By this they mean that managers should regularly visit the place where the job is done to seek out waste. (The Western idea of 'Management By Walking Around' is similar.) The concept of gemba is also used in new service or product development to mean that designers should go to where the service happens, or where the product is used, to develop their ideas.

> **✳ Operations principle**
> There is no substitute for seeing the way processes actually operate in practice.

Eliminating waste through streamlined flow

The smooth flow of materials, information and people in the operation is a central idea of lean synchronization. Long process routes provide opportunities for delay and inventory build-up, add no value and slow down throughput time. So, the first contribution any operation can make to streamline flow is to reconsider the basic layout of its processes. Primarily, reconfiguring the layout of a process to aid lean synchronization involves moving it down the 'natural diagonal' of process design that was discussed in Chapter 6. Broadly speaking, this means moving from functional layouts towards cell-based layouts, or from cell-based layouts towards line layouts. Either way, it is necessary to move towards a layout that brings more systematization and control to the process flow. At a more detailed level, typical layout techniques include placing workstations close together so that inventory physically just cannot build up because there is no space for it to do so, and arranging workstations in such a way that all those who contribute to a common activity are in sight of each other and can provide mutual help. For example, at the Virginia Mason Medical Center, Seattle, USA, a leading proponent of lean synchronization in healthcare, many of the waiting rooms have been significantly reduced in their capacity or removed entirely. This forces a focus on the flow of the whole process because patients have literately nowhere to be stored.

Examining all elements of throughput time

Throughput time is often taken as a surrogate measure for waste in a process. The longer that items being processed are held in inventory, moved, checked, or subject to anything else that does not add value, the longer they take to progress through the process. So, looking at exactly what happens to items within a process is an excellent method of identifying sources of waste.

Value stream mapping (also known as 'end-to-end' system mapping) is a simple but effective approach to understanding the flow of material and information as a product or service has value added as it progresses through a process, operation or supply chain. It visually maps a product or services 'production' path from start to finish. In doing so it records not only the direct activities of creating products and services, but also the 'indirect' information systems that support the direct process. It is called 'value stream' mapping because it focuses on value-adding activities and distinguishes between value-adding and non-value-adding activities. It is similar to process mapping (see Chapter 6) but different in four ways:

- It uses a broader range of information than most process maps.
- It is usually at a higher level (5–10 activities) than most process maps.
- It often has a wider scope, frequently spanning the whole supply chain.
- It can be used to identify where to focus future improvement activities.

A value stream perspective involves working on (and improving) the 'big picture', rather than just optimizing individual processes. Value stream mapping is seen by many practitioners as a starting point to help recognize waste and identify its causes. It is a four-step technique that identifies waste and suggests ways in which activities can be streamlined. First, it involves identifying the value stream (the process, operation or supply chain) to map. Second, it involves physically mapping a process, then, above it, mapping the information flow that enables the process to occur. This is the so-called 'current state' map. Third, problems are diagnosed and changes suggested making a future state map that represents the improved process, operation or supply chain. Finally, the changes are implemented. Figure 15.6 shows a value stream map for an industrial air-conditioning installation service. The service process itself is broken down into five relatively large stages, and various items of data for each stage are marked on the chart. The type of data collected here does vary, but all types of value stream map compare the total throughput time with the amount of value-added time within the larger process. In this case, only 8 of the 258 hours of the process are value adding.

Adopting visual management

Visual management is one of the lean techniques designed to make the current and planned state of the operation or process transparent to everyone, so that anyone (whether working in the process or not) can very quickly see what is going on. It usually employs some kind of visual sign, such as a noticeboard, computer screen, or simply lights or other signals which convey what is happening. Although a seemingly trivial and usually simple device, visual management has several benefits. It can:

- act as a common focus for team meetings;
- demonstrate methods for safe and effective working practices;
- communicate to everyone how performance is being judged;

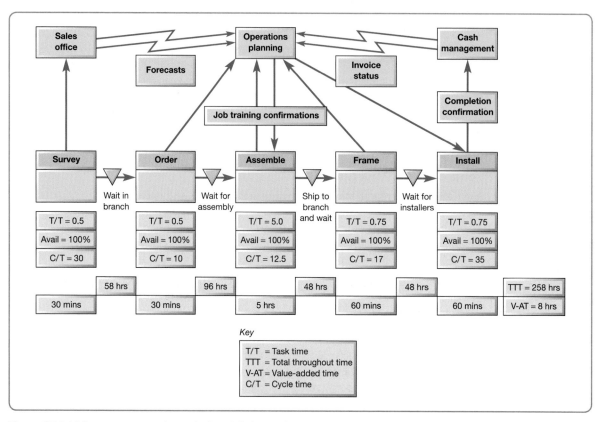

Figure 15.6 Value stream map for an industrial air-conditioning installation service

Waste reduction in airline maintenance[2]

Aircraft maintenance is important. Aircraft have a distressing tendency to fall out of the sky unless they are checked, repaired and generally maintained regularly! So the overriding objective of the operations that maintain aircraft must be the quality of maintenance activities. But it is not the only objective. Improving maintenance turnaround time can reduce the number of aircraft an airline needs to own, because they are not out of action for as long. Also, the more efficient the maintenance process, the more profitable is the activity and the more likely a major airline with established maintenance operations can create additional revenue streams by doing maintenance for other airlines. Figure 15.7 shows how one airline maintenance operation applied lean principles to achieve all these objectives. The objectives of the lean analysis were to preserve, or even improve, quality levels while at the same time improving the cost of maintaining airframes and increasing the availability of airframes by reducing turnaround time.

Source: Corbis: Monty Rakusen

The lean analysis focused on identifying waste in the maintenance process. Two findings emerged from this. First, the sequence of activities on the airframe itself was being set by the tasks identified in the technical

Before:
- Maintenance staff follow the steps as detailed in the technical documentation.
- The overall sequence of tasks is not optimized.
- Preparation work and set-ups included as part of the task.

After:
- The overall sequence of tasks is defined and allocated to minimize non-value-added.
- Preparation work and set-ups may be done ahead of time to minimize aircraft contact time.
- Increased productivity and reduced aircraft waiting time.

Figure 15.7 Aircraft maintenance procedures subject to waste reduction analysis

manuals supplied by the engine, body, control system and other suppliers. No one had considered all the individual activities together to work out a sequence that would save maintenance staff time and effort. The overall sequence of activities was defined and allocated with structured work preparation of tools, materials and equipment. Figure 15.7 shows the path taken by maintenance staff before and after the lean analysis. Second, maintenance staff would often be waiting until the airframe became available. Yet some of the preparatory work and set-ups did not need to be done while the airframe was present. Therefore why not get maintenance staff to do these tasks when they would otherwise be waiting before the airframe became available? The result of these changes was a substantial improvement in cost and availability. In addition work preparation was conducted in a more rigorous and routine manner and maintenance staff were more motivated because many minor frustrations and barriers to their efficient working were removed.

- assess at a glance the current status of the operation;
- understand tasks and work priorities;
- judge your and others' performance;
- identify the flow of work, namely what has been and is being done;
- identify when something is not going to plan;
- show what agreed standards should be;
- provide real-time feedback on performance to everyone involved;
- reduce the reliance on formal meetings.

As an example of how visual management works, a finance office in a web-based retailer was having problems. Service levels were low, and complaints high, as the office attempted to deal with payments from customers, invoices from suppliers, requests for information from its distribution centre – all while demand was increasing. It was agreed that the office's processes were chaotic and poorly managed, with little understanding of priorities or how each member of staff was contributing. To remedy this state of affairs, first the manager responsible for the office tried to bring clarity to the process, defined individual and team roles, and started establishing visual management. Collectively the staff mapped processes and set performance objectives. These objectives were shown on a large board placed so everyone in the office could see it. At the end of each day, process supervisors updated the board with each process's performance for the day. Also indicated on the board were visual representations of various improvement projects being carried out by the teams. Every morning, staff gathered in what was called 'the morning huddle' to discuss the previous day's performance, identify how it could be improved, review the progress of ongoing improvement projects and plan for the upcoming day's work.

The above example illustrates the three main functions of visual management:

- To act as a communication mechanism.
- To encourage commitment to agreed goals.
- To facilitate co-operation between team members.

An important technique used to ensure flow visibility is the use of simple, but highly visual signals to indicate that a problem has occurred, together with operational authority to stop the process. For example, on an assembly line, if an employee detects some kind of quality problem, he or she could activate a signal that illuminates a light (called an 'andon' light) above the workstation and stops the line. Although this may seem to reduce the efficiency of the line, the idea is that this loss of efficiency in the short term is less than the accumulated losses of allowing defects to continue on in the process. Unless problems are tackled immediately, they may never be corrected.

OPERATIONS IN PRACTICE   Andons in Amazon[3]

Source: Alamy Images: Zoonar GmbH

The principles of an andon cord or light have been applied in Amazon. Every day, service agents at Amazon receive calls from customers who are unhappy with some aspect of the product delivered to them. Customer agents dealing with these complaints are now empowered to make judgements on the extent to which such complaints may be systemic. In cases where they suspect it is a repetitive defect, service agents can 'stop the line' for a particular product. This involves taking the product off the website while the problem is fully investigated. According to Amazon, the improved visibility of the system has eliminated tens of thousands of defects a year and has also given service agents a strong sense of being able to deal effectively with customer complaints. Now an agent can not only refund the individual customer, but also tell the customer that others will not receive products until the problem has been properly investigated. The firm also claims that around 98 per cent of the times when the andon cord is pulled, there really is a systemic problem, highlighting the value of trusting in the service agents to make sensible decisions as to when and when not to stop the line.

Using small-scale simple process technology

There may also be possibilities to encourage smooth streamlined flow through the use of small-scale technologies. That is, using several small units of process technology (for example, machines) rather than one large unit. Small machines have several advantages over large ones. First, they can process different products and services simultaneously. For example, in Figure 15.8 one large machine produces a batch of A, followed by a batch of B and then by a batch of C. However, if three smaller machines are used they can each produce A, B or C simultaneously. The system is also more robust. If one large machine breaks down, the whole system ceases to operate. If one of the three smaller machines breaks down, the system is still operating at two-thirds effectiveness. Small machines are also easily moved, so that layout flexibility is enhanced, and the risks of making errors in investment decisions are reduced. However, investment in capacity may increase in total because parallel facilities are needed, so utilization may be lower (see the earlier arguments).

Eliminating waste through matching supply and demand exactly

The value of the supply of services or products is always time dependent. Something that is delivered early or late often has less value than something that is delivered exactly when it is needed. For example, parcel delivery companies charge more for guaranteed faster delivery. This is because our real need for the delivery is often for it to be as fast as possible. The closer to instantaneous delivery we can get, the more value the delivery has for us and the more we are willing to pay for it. In fact delivery of information earlier than it is required can be even more harmful than late delivery because it results in information inventories that serve to confuse flow through the process.

> **✳ Operations principle**
>
> Delivering only and exactly what is needed, and when it is needed, smooths flow and exposes waste.

Using pull control

The exact matching of supply and demand is often best served by using 'pull control' wherever possible (see Chapter 10). At its simplest, consider how some fast food restaurants cook and assemble food and place it in the warm area only when the customer-facing server has sold an item. Production is being triggered only by real customer demand. In another example, an Australian tax office used to receive applications by mail, open the mail and send it through to the relevant department who, after processing it, sent it to the next department. This led to piles of unprocessed applications building up within its processes causing problems in tracing applications, and losing them, sorting through and prioritizing applications,

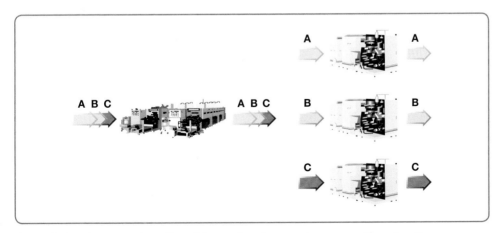

Figure 15.8 Using several small machines rather than one large one allows simultaneous processing, is more robust and is more flexible

and worst of all, long throughput times. Now they only open mail when the stages in front can process it. Each department requests more work only when they have processed previous work. The essence of pull control is to let the downstream stage in a process, operation or supply network pull items (product, customers or information) through the system rather than have them 'pushed' to them by the supplying stage.

Using kanbans

The use of kanbans is one method of operationalizing pull control. *Kanban* is the Japanese for card or signal. It is sometimes called the 'invisible conveyor' that controls the transfer of items between the stages of an operation. In its simplest form, it is a card used by a customer stage to instruct its supplier stage to send more items. Kanbans can also take other forms. In some Japanese companies, they are solid plastic markers or even coloured ping-pong balls. Whichever kind of kanban is being used, the principle is always the same: the receipt of a kanban triggers the movement, production or supply of one unit or a standard container of units. If two kanbans are received, this triggers the movement, production or supply of two units or standard containers of units, and so on. Kanbans are the only means by which movement, production or supply can be authorized. Some companies use 'kanban squares'. These are marked spaces on the shop floor or bench that are drawn to fit one or more work pieces or containers. Only the existence of an empty square triggers production at the stage that supplies the square. Likewise, 'kanban' whiteboards are increasingly used to 'pull' activity through service process (see the Torchbox 'Operations in practice' case). The kanban is seen as serving three purposes:

- It is an instruction for the preceding process to send more.
- It is a visual control tool to show up areas of overproduction and lack of synchronization.
- It is a tool for kaizen (continuous improvement). Toyota's rules state that 'the number of kanbans should be reduced over time'.

OPERATIONS IN PRACTICE

Kanban control at Torchbox web designers[4]

Torchbox is an independently owned web design and development company based in Oxfordshire (see the case in Chapter 1, 'Torchbox: award-winning web designers' for more details). It provides high-quality, cost-effective and ethical solutions for its clients. And because it is a company that relies on its staff's creative capabilities, this does not mean that lean techniques have no place in its operations. On the contrary, it makes full use of the 'kanban' approach to controlling its work as it progresses through the web design process. *'We know that kanban control originated from car manufacturers like Toyota, but our development teams can also benefit from its basic principles'*, says Edward Kay, the Head of Production at Torchbox. *'It is a way of scheduling work based on what needs to be produced and what resources*

Source: Shutterstock.com: Alphaspirit

are available to produce it with. At Torchbox we use a large magnetic whiteboard (called the "kanban board") to track completed features through each stage of the design process; from discovery through development, design, demo, deployment and on to the finish of the design (called the "done" stage). Each feature has its own paper slip which physically moves across the board, held in place with a magnet. You can't have more features in progress than the number of magnets you have to hold them in place, so the principle is enforced with a physical limitation. When one feature enters the "done" column, another one can be pulled through into discovery. There's a pulling process, where completing work allows you to start on something new.'

At the start of every day, the team has a stand-up meeting at the kanban board where each member quickly runs through what they did the day before, and what they will do in the coming day. Each developer has a few tokens which they place on the features they are working on. This helps link up the 'big picture' of how a design's features are developing with the 'little picture' of what each developer is working on each day, and helps teams to make sure that all work being done is being tracked across the board.

'One of the big benefits of using kanban', says Edward Kay, 'is that because we're visualising the steps a feature goes through to be completed, we're able to see where the bottlenecks are that work gets held up on. Because we can see where work is being held up, we're then able to continually improve our processes to make sure we're working as efficiently as possible. If we're finding that a project's features keep getting held up in the design stage, we can bring more designers onto the project to widen the bottleneck. Using kanban with feature-driven development helps us constantly deliver value to our clients. This more measured and controlled approach to handling and controlling incoming work helps ensure that every hour we work produces an hour's worth of value. Ultimately, it's all about delivering great products on time and to budget, and kanban is a great tool to help achieve this.'

Eliminating waste through flexible processes

Responding exactly and instantaneously to customer demand implies that operations resources need to be sufficiently flexible to change both what they do and how much they do of it without incurring high cost or long delays. In fact, flexible processes (often with flexible technologies) can significantly enhance smooth and synchronized flow. For example, a firm of lawyers used to take 10 days to prepare its bills for customers. This meant that customers were not asked to pay until 10 days after the work had been done. Now they use a system that, every day, updates each customer's account. So, when a bill is sent it includes all work up to the day before the billing date. The principle here is that process inflexibility also delays cash flow.

Reducing changeover times[5]

For many processes, increasing flexibility means reducing the time taken to change over the process from one activity to the next. And changeover time can usually be reduced, sometimes radically. For example, compare the time it takes you to change the tyre on your car with the time taken by a Formula One team. Changeover time reduction can be achieved by a variety of methods such as the following:

> ✳ **Operations principle**
> Changeover flexibility reduces waste and smooths flow.

- *Measure and analyse changeover activities* – Sometimes simply measuring the current changeover times, recording them and analysing exactly what activities are performed can help to improve changeover times.
- *Separate external and internal activities* – 'External' activities are simply the activities that can be carried out while the process is continuing. For example, processes could be getting ready for the next customer or job while waiting for the next one (see the example of aircraft maintenance described earlier). 'Internal' activities are those which cannot be carried out while the process is going on (for example, interviewing the customer while completing a service request for the previous customer). By identifying and separating internal and external activities, the intention is to do as much as possible while the step/process is continuing.
- *Convert internal to external activities* – The other common approach to changeover time reduction is to convert work which was previously performed during the changeover to

work that is performed outside the changeover period. There are three major methods of achieving the transfer of internal set-up work to external work:

- Pre-prepare activities or equipment instead of having to do it during changeover periods.
- Make the changeover process intrinsically flexible and capable of performing all required activities without any delay.
- Speed up any required changes of equipment, information or staff, for example by using simple devices.

- *Practise changeover routines* – Not surprisingly, the constant practice of changeover routines and the associated learning curve effect tends to reduce changeover times.

Fast changeovers are particularly important for airlines because they cannot make money from aircraft that are sitting idle on the ground. It is called 'running the aircraft hot' in the industry. For many smaller airlines, the biggest barrier to running hot is that their markets are not large enough to justify passenger flights during the day and night. So, in order to avoid aircraft being idle over night, they must be used in some other way. That was the motive behind Boeing's 737 'Quick Change' (QC) aircraft. With it, airlines have the flexibility to use it for passenger flights during the day and, with less than a one-hour changeover (set-up) time, use it as a cargo aircraft throughout the night. Boeing engineers designed frames that hold entire rows of seats that could smoothly glide on and off the aircraft, allowing 12 seats to be rolled into place at once. When used for cargo, the seats are simply rolled out and replaced by special cargo containers designed to fit the curve of the fuselage and prevent damage to the interior. Before reinstalling the seats the sidewalls are thoroughly cleaned so that, once the seats are in place, passengers cannot tell the difference between a QC aircraft and a normal 737. Some airlines particularly value the aircraft's flexibility. It allows them to provide frequent reliable services in both passenger and cargo markets. So the aircraft that has been carrying passengers during the day can be used to ship freight during the night.

Eliminating waste through minimizing variability

One of the biggest causes of the variability that will disrupt flow and prevent lean synchronization is variation in the quality of items. This is why a discussion of lean synchronization should always include an evaluation of how quality conformance is ensured within processes, what was referred to as 'mura' earlier. In particular, the principles of statistical process control (SPC) can be used to understand quality variability. Chapter 17 and its supplement on SPC examine this subject, so in this section we will focus on other causes of variability. The first of these is variability in the mix of items moving through processes, operations or supply networks.

Levelling product or service schedules

Levelled scheduling (or heijunka) means keeping the mix and volume of flow between stages at an even rate over time. For example, instead of producing 500 items in one batch, which would cover the needs for the next three months, levelled scheduling would require the process to produce items on a regular basis that satisfied demand. Thus, the principle of levelled scheduling is very straightforward; however, the requirements to put it into practice are quite severe, although the benefits resulting from it can be substantial. The move from conventional to levelled scheduling is illustrated in Figure 15.9. Conventionally, if a mix of items were required in a time period (usually a month), a batch size would be calculated for each item and the batches produced in some sequence. Figure 15.9(a) shows three items that are produced in a 20-day time period in an operation:

Quantity of item A required = 3,000
Quantity of item B required = 1,000
Quantity of item C required = 1,000

Batch size of item A = 600
Batch size of item B = 200
Batch size of item C = 200

(a) Scheduling in large batches

(b) Levelled scheduling

Figure 15.9 Levelled scheduling equalizes the mix of items made each day

Starting at day 1, the unit commences producing item A. During day 3, the batch of 600 As is finished and despatched to the next stage. The batch of Bs is started but is not finished until day 4. The remainder of day 4 is spent making the batch of Cs and both batches are despatched at the end of that day. The cycle then repeats itself. The consequence of using large batches is, first, that relatively large amounts of inventory accumulate within and between the units, and, second, that most days are different from one another in terms of what they are expected to produce (in more complex circumstances, no two days would be the same).

Now suppose that the flexibility of the unit could be increased to the point where the batch sizes for the items were reduced to a quarter of their previous levels without loss of capacity (see Fig. 15.9(b)):

$$\text{Batch size of item A} = 150$$
$$\text{Batch size of item B} = 50$$
$$\text{Batch size of item C} = 50$$

A batch of each item can now be completed in a single day, at the end of which the three batches are despatched to their next stage. Smaller batches of inventory are moving between each stage, which will reduce the overall level of work-in-progress in the operation. Just as significant, however, is the effect on the regularity and rhythm of production at the unit. Now, every day in the month is the same in terms of what needs to be processed. This makes planning and control of each stage in the operation much easier. For example, if on day 1 of the month the daily batch of As was finished by 11.00 am, and all the batches were successfully completed in the day, then the following day the unit will know that, if it again completes all the As by 11.00 am, it is on schedule. When every day is different, the

> **❋ Operations principle**
>
> Variability, in product/service quality, or quantity or timing, acts against smooth flow and waste elimination.

simple question 'Are we on schedule to complete our processing today?' requires some investigation before it can be answered. However, when every day is the same, everyone in the unit can tell whether production is on target by looking at the clock. Control becomes visible and transparent to all, and the advantages of regular, daily schedules can be passed to upstream suppliers.

Levelling delivery schedules

A similar concept to levelled scheduling can be applied to many transportation processes. For example, a chain of convenience stores may need to make deliveries of all the different types of products it sells every week. Traditionally it may have despatched a truck loaded with one particular product around all its stores so that each store received the appropriate amount of the product that would last them for one week. This is equivalent to the large batches discussed in the previous example. An alternative would be to despatch smaller quantities of all products in a single truck more frequently. Then, each store would receive smaller deliveries more frequently, inventory levels would be lower and the system could respond to trends in demand more readily because more deliveries means more opportunity to change the quantity delivered to a store. This is illustrated in Figure 15.10.

Adopting mixed modelling

The principle of levelled scheduling can be taken further to give a repeated mix of outputs – what is known as mixed modelling. Suppose that processes can be made so flexible that they achieve the ideal of a 'batch' size of one. The sequence of individual items emerging from the process could be reduced progressively as illustrated in Figure 15.11. This would produce a steady stream of each item flowing continuously from the process. However, the sequence of items does not always fall as conveniently as in Figure 15.11. The unit processing times for each item are not usually identical and the ratios of required volumes are less convenient. For example, if a process is required to process items A, B and C in the ratio 8:5:4, it could produce 800 of A, followed by 500 of B, followed by 400 of A, or 80A, 50B and 40C. But ideally, to sequence the items as smoothly as possible, it would produce in the order BACABACABACABACAB…repeated…repeated…, etc. Doing this achieves relatively smooth flow (but does rely on significant process flexibility).

Keeping things simple – the 5Ss

The 5S terminology[6] comes originally from Japan, and although the translation into English is approximate, the 5Ss are generally taken to represent the following.

1 **Sort** (*seiri*). Eliminate what is not needed and keep what is needed.
2 **Straighten** (*seiton*) Position things in such a way that they can be easily reached whenever they are needed.
3 **Shine** (*seiso*). Keep things clean and tidy; no refuse or dirt in the work area.
4 **Standardize** (*seiketsu*) Maintain cleanliness and order – perpetual neatness.
5 **Sustain** (*shitsuke*) Develop a commitment and pride in keeping to standards.

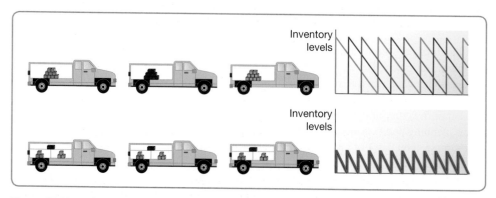

Figure 15.10 Delivering smaller quantities more often can reduce inventory levels

Figure 15.11 Levelled scheduling and mixed modelling: mixed modelling becomes possible as the batch size approaches one

The 5Ss can be thought of as a simple housekeeping methodology to organize work areas that focuses on visual order, organization, cleanliness and standardization. It helps to eliminate all types of waste relating to uncertainty, waiting, searching for relevant information, creating variation, and so on. By eliminating what is unnecessary, and making everything clear and predictable, clutter is reduced, needed items are always in the same place and work is made easier and faster.

Adopting total productive maintenance (TPM)

Total productive maintenance aims to eliminate the variability in operations processes caused by the effect of breakdowns. TPM is discussed in the risk and recovery chapter (see Chapter 18).

HOW DOES LEAN APPLY THROUGHOUT THE SUPPLY NETWORK?

Although most of the concepts and techniques discussed in this chapter are devoted to the management of stages *within* processes and processes *within* an operation, the same principles can apply to the whole supply chain. In this context, the stages in a process are the whole businesses, operations or processes between which products flow. And as any business starts to approach lean it will eventually come up against the constraints imposed by the lack of synchronization of the other operations in its supply chain. So, achieving further gains must involve trying to spread lean practice outwards to its partners in the chain. Ensuring the entire supply networks are lean is clearly a far more demanding task than doing the same within a single process. The nature of the interaction between whole operations is far more complex than between individual stages within a process. A far more complex mix of products and services is likely to be provided and the whole network is likely to be subject to a less predictable set of potentially disruptive events. To make a supply chain lean means more than making each operation in the chain lean. A collection of localized lean operations rarely leads to an overall lean chain. Rather one needs to apply the lean philosophy to the supply chain as a whole. Yet the advantages from truly lean chains can be significant.

Essentially the principles of lean are the same for a supply chain as they are for a process. Fast throughput throughout the whole supply network is still valuable and will save cost throughout the supply network. Lower levels of inventory will still make it easier to achieve lean. Waste is just as evident (and even larger) at the level of the supply network and reducing waste is still a worthwhile task. Streamline flow, exact matching of supply and demand,

* Operations principle

The advantages of lean synchronization apply at the level of the process, the operation and the supply network.

enhanced flexibility and minimizing variability are all still tasks that will benefit the whole network. The principles of pull control can work between whole operations in the same way as they can between stages within a single process. In fact, the principles and the techniques of lean synchronization are essentially the same no matter what level of analysis is being used. And because lean is being implemented on a larger scale, the benefits will also be proportionally greater.

One of the weaknesses of lean principles is that it is difficult to achieve when conditions are subject to unexpected disturbance. This is especially a problem with applying lean synchronization principles in the context of the whole supply network. Whereas unexpected fluctuations and disturbances do occur within operations, local management has a reasonable degree of control that they can exert in order to reduce them. Outside the operation, within the supply network, it is far more difficult. Nevertheless, it is generally held that, although the task is more difficult and although it may take longer to achieve, the aim of lean is just as valuable for the supply network as a whole as it is for an individual operation.

Lean supply chains are like air traffic control systems

The concept of the lean supply chain has been likened to an air traffic control system, in that it attempts to provide continuous, 'real-time visibility and control' to all elements in the chain. This is the secret of how the world's busiest airports handle thousands of departures and arrivals daily. All aircraft are given an identification number that shows up on a radar map. Aircraft approaching an airport are detected by radar and contacted using radio. The control tower precisely positions the aircraft in an approach pattern which it co-ordinates. The radar detects any small adjustments that are necessary, which are communicated to the aircraft. This real-time visibility and control can optimize airport throughput while maintaining extremely high safety and reliability.

Contrast this to how most supply chains are co-ordinated. Information is captured only periodically, probably once a day, and any adjustments to logistics and output levels at the various operations in the supply chain are adjusted, and plans rearranged. But imagine what would happen if this was how the airport operated, with only a 'radar snapshot' once a day. Co-ordinating aircraft with sufficient tolerance to arrange take-offs and landings every two minutes would be out of the question. Aircraft would be jeopardized, or, alternatively, if aircraft were spaced further apart to maintain safety, throughput would be drastically reduced. Yet this is how most supply chains have traditionally operated. They use a daily 'snapshot' from their ERP systems (see Chapter 14). This limited visibility means that operations must either space their work out to avoid 'collisions' (that is, missed customer orders), thereby reducing output, or they must 'fly blind', thereby jeopardizing reliability.

Critical commentary

Recall the section on supply chain vulnerability in Chapter 13 where it was argued that lean principles can be taken to an extreme. When just-in-time ideas first started to have an impact on operations practice in the West, some authorities advocated the reduction of between-process inventories to zero. While in the long term this provides the ultimate in motivation for operations managers to ensure the efficiency and reliability of each process stage, it does not admit the possibility of some processes always being intrinsically less than totally reliable. An alternative view is to allow inventories (albeit small ones) around process stages with higher than average uncertainty. This at least allows some protection for the rest of the system. The same ideas apply to just-in-time delivery between factories. Severe disruption to supply chains, as from the effects of the Japanese tsunami, caused many overseas Japanese factories to close down for a time because of a shortage of key parts.

HOW DOES LEAN COMPARE WITH OTHER APPROACHES?

Either as a broad philosophy or as a practical method of operations planning and control, lean is not the only approach that is used in practice. There are other approaches that can be used to underpin operations improvement and operations planning and control. We will describe how lean compares with other improvement approaches in Chapter 16. In this chapter we look briefly at two alternatives to lean synchronization as a planning and control method: the theory of constraints (TOC) and materials requirements planning (MRP) that we examined in the supplement to Chapter 14.

Lean and the theory of constraints

A central idea of lean is the smooth flow of items through processes, operations and supply networks. Any bottleneck will disrupt this smooth progress. Therefore, it is important to recognize the significance of capacity constraints to the planning and control process. This is the idea behind the theory of constraints (TOC) which has been developed to focus attention on the capacity constraints or bottleneck parts of the operation. By identifying the location of constraints, working to remove them, then looking for the next constraint, an operation is always focusing on the part that critically determines the pace of output. The approach which uses this idea is called optimized production technology (OPT). Its development and the marketing of it as a proprietary software product were originated by Eliyahu Goldratt.[7] OPT is a computer-based technique and tool which helps to schedule production systems to the pace dictated by the most heavily loaded resources, that is, bottlenecks. If the rate of activity in any part of the system exceeds that of the bottleneck, then items are being produced that cannot be used. If the rate of working falls below the pace at the bottleneck, then the entire system is under-utilized. There are principles underlying OPT which demonstrate this focus on bottlenecks:

1 Balance flow, not capacity. It is more important to reduce throughput time rather than achieving a notional capacity balance between stages or processes.
2 The level of utilization of a non-bottleneck is determined by some other constraint in the system, not by its own capacity. This applies to stages in a process, processes in an operation, and operations in a supply network.
3 Utilization and activation of a resource are not the same. According to the TOC, a resource is being utilized only if it contributes to the entire process or operation creating more output. A process or stage can be activated in the sense that it is working, but it may only be creating stock or performing other non-value-added activity.
4 An hour lost (not used) at a bottleneck is an hour lost for ever out of the entire system. The bottleneck limits the output from the entire process or operation, therefore the under-utilization of a bottleneck affects the entire process or operation.
5 An hour saved at a non-bottleneck is a mirage. Non-bottlenecks have spare capacity anyway. Why bother making them even less utilized?
6 Bottlenecks govern both throughput and inventory in the system. If bottlenecks govern flow, then they govern throughput time, which in turn governs inventory.
7 You do not have to transfer batches in the same quantities as you produce them. Flow will probably be improved by dividing large production batches into smaller ones for moving through a process.
8 The size of the process batch should be variable, not fixed. Again, from the EBQ model, the circumstances that control batch size may vary between different products.
9 Fluctuations in connected and sequence-dependent processes add to each other rather than averaging out. So, if two parallel processes or stages are capable of a particular average output rate, in parallel, they will never be able to achieve the same average output rate.
10 Schedules should be established by looking at all constraints simultaneously. Because of bottlenecks and constraints within complex systems, it is difficult to work out schedules according to a simple system of rules. Rather, all constraints need to be considered together.

OPT uses the terminology of 'drum, buffer, rope' to explain its planning and control approach. We explained this idea in Chapter 10. The bottleneck work centre becomes a 'drum', beating the pace for the rest of the factory. This 'drum beat' determines the schedules in non-bottleneck areas, pulling through work (the rope) in line with the bottleneck capacity, not the capacity of the work centre. A bottleneck should never be allowed to be working at less than full capacity; therefore, inventory buffers should be placed before it to ensure that it never runs out of work.

The five steps of the TOC

As a practical method of synchronizing flow, TOC emphasizes the following five steps:[8]

1 *Identify the system constraint* – the part of a system that constitutes its weakest link; it could be a physical constraint or even a decision-making or policy constraint.
2 *Decide how to exploit the constraint* – obtain as much capability as possible from the constraint, preferably without expensive changes. For example, reduce or eliminate any non-productive time at the bottleneck.
3 *Subordinate everything to the constraint* – the non-constraint elements of the process are adjusted to a level where the constraint can operate at maximum effectiveness. After this, the overall process is evaluated to determine if the constraint has shifted elsewhere in the process. If the constraint has been eliminated, go to step 5.
4 *Elevate the constraint* – 'elevating' the constraint means eliminating it. This step is only considered if steps 2 and 3 have not been successful. Major changes to the existing system are considered at this step.
5 Start again from step 1.

Table 15.1 shows some of the differences between the TOC and lean synchronization. Arguably, the main contribution of TOC to smooth, synchronized flow is its inclusion of the idea that the effects of bottleneck constraints (a) must be prioritized, and (b) can 'excuse' inventory, if it means maximizing the utilization of the bottleneck. Nor (unlike ERP/MRP, for example) does it necessarily require large investment in new IT. Further, because it attempts to improve the flow of items through a process, it can release inventory that in turn releases invested capital. Claims of the financial payback from OPT are often based on this release of capital and fast throughput.

Lean and MRP

The operating philosophies of lean synchronization and MRP do seem to be fundamentally opposed. Lean synchronization encourages a 'pull' system of planning and control, whereas MRP is a 'push' system. Lean has aims which are wider than the operations planning and control activity, whereas MRP is essentially a planning and control 'calculation mechanism'. Yet the two approaches can reinforce each other in the same operation, provided their

Table 15.1 **Theory of constraints compared with lean synchronization**[9]

	Theory of constraints	Lean synchronization
Overall objectives	To increase profit by increasing the throughput of a process or operation	To increase profit by adding value from the customers' perspective
Measures of effectiveness	• Throughput • Inventory • Operating expense	• Cost • Throughput time • Value-added efficiency
Achieve improvement by...	Focusing on the constraints (the 'weakest links') in the process	Eliminating waste and adding value by considering the entire process, operation or supply network
How to implement	A five-step, continuous process (see above) emphasizing acting locally	Continuous improvement emphasizing the whole supply network

respective advantages are preserved. The irony is that lean and MRP have similar objectives. JIT scheduling aims to connect the new network of internal and external supply processes by means of invisible conveyors so that parts only move in response to co-ordinated and synchronized signals derived from end customer demand. MRP seeks to meet projected customer demand by directing that items are only produced as needed to meet that demand. However, there are differences. MRP is driven by the master production schedule, which identifies future end item demand. It models a fixed lead-time environment, using the power of the computer to calculate how many of, and when, each part should be made. Its output is in the form of time-phased requirements plans that are centrally calculated and co-ordinated. Parts are made in response to central instructions. Day-to-day disturbances, such as inaccurate stock records, undermine MRP authority and can make the plans unworkable. While MRP is excellent at planning, it is weak at control. On the other hand, lean scheduling aims to meet demand instantaneously through simple control systems based on kanban. If the total throughput time (P) is less than the demand lead time (D), then lean synchronization systems should be capable of meeting that demand. But if the $P{:}D$ ratio is greater than 1, some speculative production will be needed. And if demand is suddenly far greater than expected for certain products, the JIT system may be unable to cope. Pull scheduling is a reactive concept that works best when independent demand has been levelled and dependent demand synchronized. While lean synchronization may be good at control, it is weak on planning.

MRP is also better at dealing with complexity, as measured by numbers of items being processed. It can handle detailed requirements even for 'strangers'. Lean synchronization pull scheduling is less capable of responding instantaneously to changes in demand as the part count, options and colours increase. Therefore, lean synchronization production systems favour designs based on simpler product structures with high commonality of parts. Such disciplines challenge needless complexity, so that more parts may be brought under pull-scheduling control.

When to use lean, MRP and combined systems

Figure 15.12 distinguishes between the complexity of product structures and the complexity of the flow-path routings through which they must pass.[10] Simple product structures which have routings with high repeatability are prime candidates for pull control. Lean can easily cope with their relatively straightforward requirements. As structures and routings become more complex, so the power of the computer is needed in order to break down product structures and so assign orders to suppliers. In many environments, it is possible to use pull scheduling

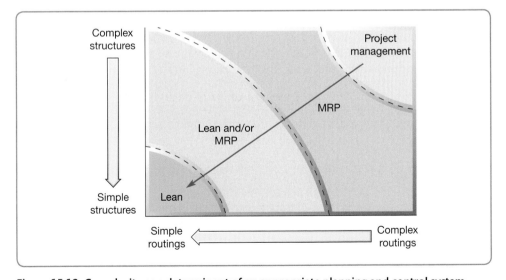

Figure 15.12 Complexity as a determinant of an appropriate planning and control system

Source: Adapted from Voss, C.A. and Harrison, A. (1987) Strategies for Implementing JIT, in Voss, C.A. (ed.) *Just-in-Time Manufacture,* IFS/Springer-Verlag.

for the control of most internal materials. Again, prime candidates for pull control are materials which are used regularly each week or each month. Their number can be increased by design standardization, as indicated by the direction of the arrow in Figure 15.12. As structures and routings become even more complex, and usages of parts become more irregular, so the opportunities for using pull scheduling decrease. Very complex structures require network planning methods (see Chapter 19) for planning and control.

SUMMARY ANSWERS TO KEY QUESTIONS

〉 What is lean?

- Lean is an approach to operations which tries to meet demand instantaneously with perfect quality and no waste. It is an approach which differs from traditional operations practices in as much as it stresses waste elimination and fast throughput, both of which contribute to low inventories.
- The ability to deliver just in time not only saves working capital (through reducing inventory levels), but also has a significant impact on the ability of an operation to improve its intrinsic efficiency.
- The lean philosophy can be summarized as concerning three overlapping elements: (a) the elimination of waste in all its forms, (b) the inclusion of all staff of the operation in its improvement, and (c) the idea that all improvement should be on a continuous basis.
- Most of the ideas of lean synchronization are directly applicable to service operations.

〉 How does lean eliminate waste?

- The most significant part of the lean philosophy is its focus on the elimination of all forms of waste, defined as any activity that does not add value.
- Lean identifies seven types of waste that, together, form four barriers to achieving lean synchronization. They are: waste from irregular (non-streamlined) flow, waste from inexact supply, waste from inflexible response, and waste from variability.

〉 How does lean apply throughout the supply network?

- Most of the concepts and techniques of lean synchronization, although usually described as applying to individual processes and operations, also apply to the whole supply networks.
- The concept of the lean supply chain has been likened to an air traffic control system, in that it attempts to provide continuous, 'real-time visibility and control' to all elements in the chain.

〉 How does lean compare with other approaches?

- There are other approaches that attempt to perform the same function as lean. Two alternatives to lean synchronization as a planning and control method are the theory of constraints (TOC) and materials requirements planning (MRP).
- Although both TOC and MRP may seem to be different approaches, they can be combined.
- The way in which they can be combined depends on the complexity of product structures, the complexity of product routing, the volume–variety characteristics of the operation and the level of control required.

Saint Bridget's Hospital[11]

When Denize Ahlgren arrived at St Bridget's, one of the main hospitals in the Götenborg area, she knew that it had gained a reputation for fresh thinking on how healthcare could be organized to give superior levels of public care at lower cost to the taxpayer. In fact, that was one of the reasons she had taken the job of its Chief of Administration (COA). In particular Denize had been reading about St Bridget's 'Quality Care' (QC) initiative. 'Yes, QC is obviously important', explained Dr Pär Solberg who, in addition to his clinical duties, also headed the QC initiative, 'but don't think that it is only about "quality". We don't just throw money at improving the quality of care; we also want to improve efficiency. Any money saved by improving efficiency can then be invested in improving clinical outcomes.'

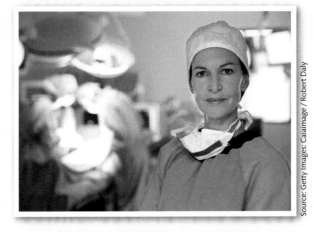

Source: Getty Images: Caiaimage / Robert Daly

'It all started with quality'

Although run by a private company, St Bridget's is little different from any other Swedish hospital. To its patients, treatment is free, after a minimal charge that is universal in Sweden. St Bridget's gets virtually all its revenue from the government. However, in terms of how it organizes itself, it is at the forefront of implementing ideas that are more common in private business. 'It all started with our efforts a few years ago to be systematic in how we measured quality', said Pär Solberg. 'We felt that quality must be reported on a systematic and logical basis if it is going to be meaningful. It should also be multi-faceted, and not just focus on one aspect of quality. We measure three aspects, "reported patient experience" (RPE), what the patient thinks about the total experience of receiving treatment, "reported patient outcome" (RPO), how the patient views the effectiveness of the treatment received, and most importantly "reported clinical outcome" (RCO), how the clinicians view the effectiveness of the treatment. Of course these three measures are interconnected. So, RPO eventually depends on the medical outcome (RCO) and how much discomfort and pain the treatment triggers. But it is also influenced by the patient's experience (RPE), for example how well we keep the patient informed, how empathetic our staff are, and so on.'

'Measuring quality led naturally to continuous improvement'

The hospital's quality measurement processes soon developed into a broader approach to improvement in general. In particular the idea of continuous improvement began to be discussed. 'Measuring quality led naturally to continuous improvement', explained Pär Solberg. 'Once we had measurable indicators of quality, we could establish targets, and most importantly we could start to think about what was preventing us improving quality. This, in turn, led to an understanding of all the processes that affected quality indicators. It was a shift to seeing the hospital as a whole set of processes that governed a set of flows – flows of patients through their treatment stages, flows of clinical staff, flows of information, flows of pharmaceuticals, flows of equipment, and so on. It was a revolution in our thinking. We started examining these flows and looking at how they impacted on our performance and how we could improve the working methods that we considered significant for the quality indicators that we wanted to influence. That was when we discovered the concept of "lean".'

'Continuous improvement introduced us to lean'

It was at an 'Improving European Healthcare' conference that was attended by Pär and another colleague that first introduced St Bridget's to the idea of 'lean'. 'We were talking to some representatives from the UK's National Health Service Institute, who had been involved in introducing lean principles in UK hospitals. They explained that lean was an improvement approach that improved flow and eliminated waste that had been used successfully in some hospitals to build on continuous improvement. Lean, they said, as developed by Toyota was about getting the right things to the right place, at the right time, in the right quantities, while minimising waste and being flexible and open to change. It sounded worth following up. However, they admitted that not every attempt to introduce lean principles had met with success.'

'It can easily all get political'

Intrigued by the conversation, Pär contacted one of the hospitals in the UK that had been mentioned, and talked to Marie Watson, who had been the 'Head of Lean' and had initiated several lean projects. She said that one of the problems she had faced was her chief executive's insistence on bringing in several firms of consultants to implement lean ideas. To make matters more confusing, when a new chief executive was appointed, he brought in his own preferred consultants in addition to those already operating in the hospital. Marie had not been happy with the change. *'Before the change of executives we had a very clear way of how we were going to move forward and spread lean throughout the organisation, then we became far less clear. The emphasis shifted to get some quick results. But that wasn't why we were set up. Originally it was about having a positive impact, getting people involved in lean, engaging and empowering them towards continuous improvement, there were things that were measurable but then it changed to "show us some quick results". People were forgetting the cultural side of it. Also it can easily all get "political". The different consultancy teams and the internal lean initiatives all had their own territories. For example, we [Marie's internal team] were about to start a study of A&E activities, when they were told to keep away from A&E so as not to "step on the toes" of the firm of consultants working there.'*

'We're not making cars, people are different'

Pär was determined not to make the same mistakes that Marie's hospital had, and consulted widely before attempting any lean improvements with his colleagues. Some were sceptical: *'we're not making cars, people are different and the processes that we put people through repeatedly are more complicated than the processes that you go through to make a car'*. Also, some senior staff were dubious about changes that they perceived to threaten their professional status. Instead of doctors and nurses maintaining separate and defined roles that focused solely on their field of medical expertise, they were encouraged to work (and sit) together in teams. The teams were also made responsible for suggesting process improvements. But most could be converted. One senior clinician, at first, claimed that *'this is all a load of rubbish. There's no point in mapping this process, we all know what happens: the patient goes from there to there and this is the solution and that's what we need to do.'* Yet only a few days later he was saying *'I never realized this is what really happens, that won't work now will it, actually this has been great because I never understood, I only saw my bit of it, now I understand all of the process'.*

'It works, it makes things better for the patients'

Over time, most (although not quite all) scepticism was overcome, mainly because, in the words of one doctor, *'It works, it makes things better for the patients.'* As more parts of the hospital became convinced of the effectiveness of the lean approach, the improvements to patient flow and quality started to accumulate. Some of the first improvements were relatively simple, such as a change of signage (to stop patients getting lost). Another simply involved a roll of yellow tape. Rather than staff wasting precious time looking for equipment such as defibrillators, the yellow tape was used to mark a spot on the floor where the machines were always kept. Another involved using magnetic dots on a progress chart to follow each patient's progress and indicate which beds were free. Some were even simpler, for example discharging patients throughout the day rather than all at the same time, so that they can easily find a taxi. Other improvements involved more analysis, such as reducing the levels of stock being held (for example, 25,000 pairs of surgical gloves from 500 different suppliers). Some involved a complete change in assumptions, such as the effectiveness of the medical records department. *'It was amazing. We just exploded the myth that when you didn't get case notes in a clinical area it was medical records' fault. But it never was. Medics had notes in their cars, they had them at home, we had a thousand notes in the secretaries' offices, there were notes in wards, drawers and cupboards, they were all over the place. And we wondered why we couldn't get case notes! Two people walked 7 miles a day to go and find case notes!'* (Pär Solberg)

'We need to go to the next level'

Denize Ahlgren was understandably impressed by the improvements that Pär had outlined to her; however, Pär was surprisingly downbeat about the future. *'OK, I admit that we have had some impressive gains from continuous improvement and latterly from the adoption of lean principles. I am especially impressed with Toyota's concept of the seven types of waste* [see details in this chapter]. *It is both a conceptually powerful and a very practical idea for identifying where we could improve. Also the staff like it. But it's all getting like a box-ticking exercise. Looking for waste is not exactly an exciting or radical idea. The more that I study how lean got going in Toyota and other manufacturing plants, the more I see that we haven't really embraced the whole philosophy. Yet, at the same time, I'm not totally convinced that we can. Perhaps some of the doubters were right, a hospital isn't a car plant, and we can apply only some lean ideas.'*

Ironically, as Pär was having doubts, some of his colleagues were straining to do more. One clinician in particular, Fredrik Olsen, Chief Physician at St Bridget's Lower Back Pain Clinic, thought that his clinic could benefit from a more radical approach. *'We need to go to the next level. The whole of Toyota's philosophy is concerned with smooth synchronous flow, yet we haven't fully got our heads round that here. I know that we are reluctant to talk about "inventories" of patients, but that is exactly what waiting rooms are. They are "stocks" of people, and we use them in exactly the same way as pre-lean manufacturers did – to buffer against short-term mismatches between supply and demand. What we should be doing is tackling the root causes of the mismatch. Waiting rooms are stopping us from moving towards smooth, value-added, flow for our patients.'*

Fredrik went on to make what Denize thought was an interesting, but radical, proposal. He proposed scrapping the current waiting room for the Lower Back Pain Clinic and replacing it with two extra consulting rooms to add to the two existing consulting rooms. Patients would be given appointments for specific times rather than being asked to arrive 'on the hour' (effectively in batches) as at present. A nurse would take the patients' details and perform some preliminary tests, after which they would call in the specialist physician. Staffing levels during clinic times would be controlled by nurses who would also monitor patients' arrival, direct them to consulting rooms and arrange any follow-up appointments (for MRI scans, for example).

Denize was not sure about Fredrik's proposal. *'It seems as though it might be a step too far. Patients expect to wait until a doctor can see them, so I'm not sure what benefits would result from the proposal. And what is the point of equipping two new consulting rooms if they are not going to be fully utilised?'*

QUESTIONS

1 What benefits did St Bridget's get from adopting first a continuous improvement, then a lean, approach?

2 Do you think that Pär Solberg is right in thinking that there is a limit to how far a hospital can go in adopting lean ideas?

3 On the St Bridget's website there are several references to its 'Quality Care' programme, but none to its lean initiatives, even though lean is regarded as important by most clinicians and administrators in the hospital. Why do you think this might be?

4 Denize cannot see the benefits of Fredrik's proposal. What do you think they might be?

5 Are any benefits of scrapping the waiting room in the clinic worth the under-utilization of the four consulting rooms that Fredrik envisages?

PROBLEMS AND APPLICATIONS

1 Think about the last time that you travelled by air. Analyse the journey in terms of value-added time (actually going somewhere) and non-value-added time (the time spent queuing etc.) from the time you left home to the exact time you arrived at your ultimate destination. Calculate the value-added time for the journey.

2 A simple process has four stages: A, B, C and D. The average amount of work needed to process items passing through these stages is as follows: Stage A = 68 minutes, Stage B = 55 minutes, Stage C = 72 minutes and Stage D = 60 minutes. A spot check on the work-in-progress between each stage reveals the following: between Stages A and B there are 82 items, between Stages B and C there are 190 items, and between Stages C and D there are 89 items.
   (a) Using Little's law (see Chapter 6), calculate the throughput time of the process.
   (b) What is the throughput efficiency of the process?

3 In the problem above, the operations manager in charge of the process reallocates the work at each stage to improve the 'balance' of the process. Now each stage has an average of 64 minutes of work. Also, the work-in-progress in front of Stages B, C and D is 75, 80 and 82 units respectively. How has this changed the throughput efficiency of the process?

4 A production process is required to produce 1,400 of product X, 840 of product Y and 420 of product Z in a four-week period. If the process works seven hours per day and five days per week, devise a mixed model schedule in terms of the number of each product required to be produced every hour that would satisfy demand.

5 Revisit the 'Operations in practice' case in the chapter (and any other source of information about the Toyota Production System) and (a) list all the different techniques and practices which Toyota adopts, and (b) state how the operations objectives (quality, speed, dependability, flexibility, cost) are influenced by the practices which Toyota adopts.

6 Consider how set-up reduction principles can be used on the following:
  (a) Changing a tyre at the side of the road (following a puncture).
  (b) Cleaning out an aircraft and preparing it for the next flight between its inbound flight landing and disembarking its passengers, and the same aircraft being ready to take off on its outbound flight.
  (c) The time between the end of one surgical procedure in a hospital operating theatre and the start of the next one.
  (d) The 'pit stop' activities during a Formula One race (how does this compare with (a) above?).

SELECTED FURTHER READING

Bicheno, J. and Holweg, M. (2010) *The Lean Toolbox: The Essential Guide to Lean Transformation*, 4th edn, PICSIE Books, Buckingham.

A practical guide from two of the European authorities on all matters lean.

Holweg, M. (2007) The genealogy of lean production, *Journal of Operations Management*, vol. 25, 420–437.

An excellent overview of how lean ideas developed.

Humble, J., Molesky, J. and O'Reilly, B. (2015) *Lean Enterprise: How High Performance Organizations Innovate at Scale*, O'Reilly Media, Sebastopol, CA.

An interesting example of how (some) lean ideas have spread outside the conventional operations management area.

Mann, D. (2010) *Creating a Lean Culture*, 2nd edn, Productivity Press, New York.

Treats the soft side of lean.

Modig, N. and Ahlstrom, P. (2012) *This is Lean: Resolving the Efficiency Paradox*, Rheologica Publishing, Stockholm.

A practical and easy-to-read, yet intellectually coherent treatment.

Womack, J.P. and Jones, D.T. (1996) *Lean Thinking: Banish Waste and Create Wealth in Your Corporation*, Simon & Schuster, New York.

Some of the lessons from The Machine that Changed the World (below) but applied in a broader context.

Womack, J.P., Jones, D.T. and Roos, D. (1990) *The Machine that Changed the World*, Rawson Associates, New York.

Arguably the most influential book on operations management practice of the last 50 years. Firmly rooted in the automotive sector but did much to establish lean.

IMPROVEMENT

Part Four
DEVELOPMENT

Even when an operation's direction is set, its design finalized and its deliveries planned and controlled, the operations manager's task is not finished. Even the best operation will need to improve and develop, partly because customers' expectations are likely to be rising, and partly because the operation's competitors will also be improving. This part of the book looks at four key issues for operations development.

The chapters in this part are:

- Chapter 16 Operations improvement – This examines how managers can make their operation perform better through the use of the many elements of new (and not so new) improvement approaches.
- Chapter 17 Quality management – This identifies some of the ideas of quality management and how they can be used to facilitate improvement.
- Chapter 18 Managing risk and recovery – This examines how operations managers can reduce the risk of things going wrong and how they can recover when they do.
- Chapter 19 Project management – This looks at how managers can project manage (among other things) improvement activities to organize the changes that improvement inevitably requires.

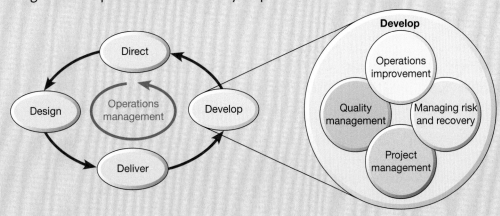

16

Operations improvement

INTRODUCTION

Improvement means to make something better. And all operations, no matter how well managed, are capable of being better. Of course, in one sense, all of operations management is concerned with being better, but there are some issues that relate specifically to the activity of improvement itself. Yet at one time improvement was not central to operations managers, who were expected simply to 'run the operation', 'keep the show on the road' and 'maintain current performance'. No longer. In fact in recent years the emphasis has shifted markedly towards making improvement one of the main responsibilities of operations managers. Moreover, the study of improvement as a specific activity has attracted significant attention from both academics and practitioners. Some of this attention focuses on specific techniques and prescriptions while some looks at the underlying philosophy of improvement. Both aspects are covered in this chapter, because both aspects of improvement have their place in effective improvement. Figure 16.1 shows where this topic fits into our overall model of operations management.

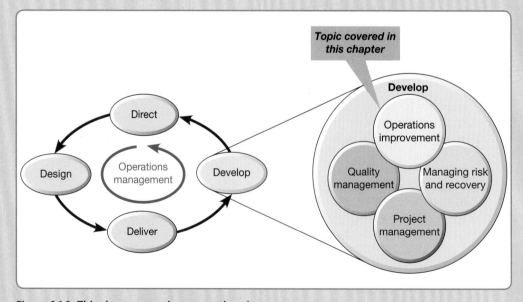

Figure 16.1 This chapter examines operations improvement

WHY IS IMPROVEMENT SO IMPORTANT IN OPERATIONS MANAGEMENT?

Why is operations improvement so important? Well, who does not want to get better? And businesses are (or should be) just the same as people – they generally want to get better. Not just for the sake of their own excellence, although that may be one factor, but mainly because improving operations performance has such an impact on what any organization is there to do. Emergency services want to reach distressed people faster and treat them better because by doing so they are fulfilling their role more effectively. Package delivery businesses want to deliver more reliably, at lower cost and reduce emissions, because it means happier customers, higher profits and less pollution. Development charities want to target their aid and campaign for improvement in human conditions as wisely and efficiently as possible because more money will find its way to beneficiaries rather than be wasted or consumed in administration. Not surprising then that the whole emphasis of operations management has shifted towards emphasizing improvement. Operations managers are judged not only on how they meet their ongoing responsibilities of producing products and services to acceptable levels of quality, speed, dependability, flexibility and cost, but also on how they improve the performance of the operations function overall.

> ✳ **Operations principle**
>
> Performance improvement is the ultimate objective of operations and process management.

Why the focus on improvement?

Various reasons have been suggested to explain the shift towards a focus on improvement in professional operations managers' activities:

- There is a perceived increase in the intensity of competitive pressures (or 'value for money' in not-for-profit or public sector operations). In fact economists argue about whether markets are really getting more competitive. As far as improvement is concerned it does not matter; there is a *perception* of increased competitive pressure, and certainly the owners of operations (shareholders or governments) are less likely to tolerate poor returns or value for money.
- The nature of world trade is changing. Economies such as China, India and Brazil are emerging as both producers and consumers of products and services. This has had a number of effects that have impacted more developed economies. It has introduced cost pressures in countries with relatively expensive labour and infrastructure costs; it has introduced new challenges for global companies, such as managing complex supply chains; and it has accelerated demand for resources (materials, food, energy), pushing up (or destabilizing) prices for these commodities.
- New technology has both introduced opportunities to improve operations practice and disrupted existing markets. Look at how operations in the music business have had to adapt their working practices to downloading and music streaming.
- The interest in operations improvement has resulted in the development of many new ideas and approaches to improving operations which have, in turn, focused attention on improvement. The more ways there are to improve operations, the more operations will be improved.
- The scope of operations management has widened from a subject associated largely with manufacturing to one that embraces all types of enterprise and processes in all functions of the enterprise. Because of this extended scope, operations managers have seen how they can learn from each other, even if their operations and processes seem, at first glance, different.

The Red Queen effect

The scientist Leigh Van Valen was looking to describe a discovery that he had made while studying marine fossils. He had established that, no matter how long a family of animals had already existed, the probability that the family will become extinct is unaffected. In other

Improving Sonae Corporation's retail operations

The retail industry may not seem to be the most likely setting for the use of improvement approaches more usually associated with manufacturing, but in Sonae Corporation's Continente supermarkets, 22,500 employees in its 170 stores and two distribution centres have demonstrated that any type of business can benefit. The operations improvement programme was originally a response to Portuguese labour laws requiring a minimum of 35 hours of training per year, per worker. Jaime Maia, Sonae's Human Resource Director, was keen that the training should be 'on-the-job' and asked a consulting firm, The Kaizen Institute (KI), to help, first by observing daily operations at several retail stores. The results were surprising. KI uncovered a significant amount of waste (or 'muda' in lean terminology, see Chapter 15). However, when Jaime Maia and KI presented their ideas to the chief operations officer (COO), their photographs showing examples of waste caused some discomfort; after all, Sonae was the most successful retailer in Portugal. Yet the programme went ahead, despite several managers arguing that lean principles would not work in retail.

Source: Shutterstock.com: Stokkete

Within a store, 'back-office' processes include unloading trucks, routing goods to sales areas or the warehouses, cleaning, shelf replenishment and store decoration. 'Front-office' processes include sales areas and their supporting checkout and customer service areas. Key operational goals include the efficient use of space, increasing sales per square metre of store space and customer satisfaction. The first stage of the programme focused on 'goods reception' and 'shelf replenishment'. Simple lean tools such as the 5Ss and visual management (see Chapter 15) were used, as was the idea of 'Gemba', or working out improvements in the workplace. After a seminar, store managers returned to work with their teams to develop training based on a 'lean manual', define an action plan, identify problem areas and select the lean tools to be applied. As Jaime Maia explained, *'Improvements were suggested by Store Managers, top down. But those ideas were immediately enriched and put into action by the teams in the stores, bringing about further improvements in a continuous fashion.'*

After just one year there had been an 'explosion of creativity' in the stores. Productivity had increased, inventory and stockouts were reduced, and customer satisfaction increased. As Jaime Maia put it, '[continuous improvement] *stimulates a good attitude and a constant sense of critique'.* A typical improvement project concerned the company's shelf-replenishing policy. Initially, stock was continuously replenished as sales took place during the day. However, this meant that product movements were constrained by customer flows and the need to keep the store clean and tidy. So a new method was tested. *'The store is fully loaded before the morning opening. From then on, we just need to perform minimal stock maintenance during the day. There is a time of the day at which a shelf may appear to be quite empty. However, typically, there is no need to replenish the shelf, but simply bring the products from the back to the front of the shelf, or from the upper shelves to the eye level shelves',* explained Nuno Almeida, Regional Operations Manager. Only a few fast-moving goods needed to be replenished during the day with the store open.

With the success of the programme it was expanded by involving all employees in it. A formal steering group was created with monthly general meetings and a video-conference meeting every two weeks to assess progress. Substantial improvements in performance continued, but progress was not uniform. Stores ranged from 87 per cent implementation, down to 37 per cent implementation. So, the steering group decided to place more emphasis on benchmarking and learning.

And the future? *'One challenge',* said Jaime Maia, *'is to sustain the motivation for the programme across the organization, after years of continuous successes.'* He also felt the programme was reaching a new turning point and needed to be reinvented. Until now, lean principles had been applied mainly to materials flows and workplace organization. Could lean principles be extended to customer flows?

Adapted, with permission, from an original case by Professors Rui Soucasaux Sousa and Sofia Salgado Pinto, Católica Porto Business School, Portugal.

words, the struggle for survival never gets easier. However well a species fits with its environment, it can never relax. The analogy that Van Valen drew came from *Through the Looking Glass*, by Lewis Carroll. In the book, Alice had encountered living chess pieces and, in particular, the 'Red Queen'. '*Well, in our country*', said Alice, still panting a little, '*you'd generally get to somewhere else – if you ran very fast for a long time, as we've been doing.*' '*A slow sort of country!*', said the Queen. '*Now, here, you see, it takes all the running you can do, to keep in the same place. If you want to get somewhere else, you must run at least twice as fast as that!*'[1]

In many respects this is like business. Improvements and innovations may be imitated or countered by competitors. For example, in the automotive sector, the quality of most firms' products is very significantly better than it was two decades ago. This reflects the improvement in those firm's operations processes. Yet their relative competitive position has in many cases not changed. Those firms that have improved their competitive position have improved their operations performance *more than* that of their competitors. Where improvement has simply matched that of competitors, survival has been the main benefit. The implications for operations improvement are clear. It is even more important, especially when competitors are actively improving their operations.

An important distinction in the approach taken by individual operations is that between radical or 'breakthrough' improvement, on the one hand, and continuous or 'incremental' improvement, on the other.

Radical or breakthrough change

Radical breakthrough improvement (or 'innovation'-based improvement as it is sometimes called) is a philosophy that assumes that the main vehicle of improvement is major and dramatic change in the way the operation works. The introduction of a new, more efficient machine in a factory, the total redesign of a computer-based hotel reservation system, and the introduction of an improved degree programme at a university are all examples of breakthrough improvement. The impact of these improvements is relatively sudden, abrupt and represents a step change in practice (and hopefully performance). Such improvements are rarely inexpensive, usually calling for high investment of capital, often disrupting the ongoing workings of the operation, and frequently involving changes in the product/service or process technology. The solid line in Figure 16.2(a) illustrates the pattern of performance with several breakthrough improvements. The improvement pattern illustrated by the dashed line in Figure 16.2(a) is regarded by some as being more representative of what really occurs when operations rely on pure breakthrough improvement. Breakthrough improvement places a high value on creative solutions. It encourages free thinking and individualism. It is a radical philosophy in as much as it fosters an approach to improvement which does not accept many constraints on what is possible. 'Starting with a clean sheet of paper', 'going back to first principles' and 'completely rethinking the system' are all typical breakthrough improvement principles.

> **✳ Operations principle**
> Performance improvement sometimes requires radical change.

Continuous or incremental improvement

Continuous improvement, as the name implies, adopts an approach to improving performance which assumes many small incremental improvement steps. For example, modifying the way a product is fixed to a machine to reduce changeover time, simplifying the question sequence when taking a hotel reservation, and rescheduling the assignment completion dates on a university course so as to smooth the students' workload are all examples of incremental improvements. While there is no guarantee that such small steps towards better performance will be followed by other steps, the whole philosophy of continuous improvement attempts to ensure that they will be. Continuous improvement is not concerned with promoting small improvements per se. It does view small improvements, however, as having one significant advantage over large ones – they can be followed relatively painlessly by other small improvements

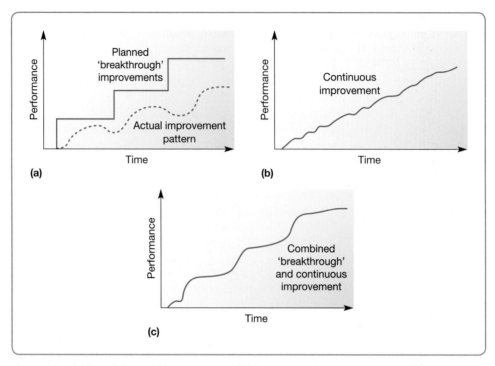

Figure 16.2 (a) 'Breakthrough' improvement, (b) 'continuous' improvement and (c) combined improvement patterns

(*see* Fig. 16.2(b)). Continuous improvement is also known as kaizen. Kaizen is a Japanese word, the definition of which is given by Masaaki Imai[2] (who has been one of the main proponents of continuous improvement) as follows: '*Kaizen means improvement. Moreover, it means improvement in personal life, home life, social life and work life. When applied to the work place, kaizen means continuing improvement involving everyone – managers and workers alike.*'

> ✳ **Operations principle**
>
> Performance improvement almost always benefits from continuous improvement.

In continuous improvement it is not the *rate* of improvement that is important; it is the *momentum* of improvement. It does not matter if successive improvements are small; what does matter is that every month (or week, or quarter, or whatever period is appropriate) some kind of improvement has actually taken place.

OPERATIONS IN PRACTICE   **The Checklist Manifesto**[3]

Improvement methodologies are often associated with repetitive operations. Performing the same task repeatedly means that there are plenty of opportunities to 'get it right'. The whole idea behind continuous improvement derives for this simple idea. By contrast, operations that have to perform more difficult activities, especially those that call for expert judgement and diagnostic ability, must call for equally complex improvement approaches, right? Well no, according to Atul Gawande, a physician at the prestigious Johns Hopkins Hospital. Mr Gawande thinks that the very opposite is true. Although medicine is advancing at an astounding rate and medical journals produce learned papers adding the results of advanced research to an ever-expanding pool of knowledge, medics are less good at the basics. Surgeons carry out over 200 major operations a year, unfortunately not all of them successfully, but the medical profession overall does not always have a reliable method for learning from its mistakes. Atul Gawande's idea is that his, and similar 'knowledge-based', professions are in danger of sinking under the weight of facts. Scientists are accumulating more and more information, and professions are fragmenting into ever-narrower specialisms. Mr Gawande tells the story of Peter Pronovost, a specialist in critical care at Johns Hopkins Hospital, who in 2001 tried to reduce the number of patients who were becoming infected on account of the use of intravenous central lines. There are five steps that medical teams can take to reduce the chances of contracting such infections. Initially Pronovost simply asked nurses to observe whether doctors took the five steps. What they found was that, at least a third of the time, they missed one or more of the steps. So nurses were authorized to stop doctors who had missed out any of the steps and, as a matter of course, ask whether existing intravenous central lines should be reviewed. As a result of applying these simple checklist-style rules, the 10-day line-infection rates went down from 11 per cent to zero. In one hospital, it was calculated that, over a year, this simple method had prevented 43 infections, eight deaths and saved about $2 million. Using the same checklist approach the hospital identified and applied the method to other activities. For example, a check in which nurses asked patients about their pain levels led to untreated pain reducing from 41 to 3 per cent. Similarly, the simple checklist method helped the average length of patient stay in intensive care to fall by half. When Pronovost's approach was adopted by other hospitals, within 18 months, 1,500 lives and $175 million had been saved.

Mr Gawande describes checklists, used in this way, as a 'cognitive net' – a mechanism that can help prevent experienced people from making errors due to flawed memory and attention, and ensure that teams work together. Simple checklists are common in other professions. Civil engineers use them to make certain that complicated structures are assembled on schedule. Chefs use them to make sure that food is prepared exactly to the customers' taste. Airlines use them to make sure that pilots take off safely and also to learn from, now relatively rare, crashes. Indeed, Mr Gawande is happy to acknowledge that checklists are not a new idea. He tells the story of the prototype of the Boeing B17 Flying Fortress that crashed after take-off on its trial flight in 1935. Most experts said that the bomber was 'too complex to fly'. Facing bankruptcy, Boeing investigated and discovered that, confronted with four engines rather than two, the pilot forgot to release a vital locking mechanism. But Boeing created a pilot's checklist, in which the fundamental actions for the stages of flying were made a mandated part of the pilot's job. In the following years, B17s flew almost 2 million miles (3.2 million km) without a single accident. Even for pilots, many of whom are rugged individualists, says Mr Gawande, it is usually the application of routine procedures that saves aircraft when things go wrong, rather than 'hero-pilotry' so feted by the media. It is discipline rather than brilliance that preserves life. In fact it is discipline that leaves room for brilliance to flourish.

Exploitation or exploration

A closely related distinction to that between continuous and breakthrough improvement is the one that management theorists draw between what they call 'exploitation' and 'exploration'. Exploitation is the activity of enhancing processes (and products) that already exist within a firm. The focus of exploitation is on creating efficiencies rather than radically changing resources or processes. Its emphasis is on tight control of the improvement process, standardizing processes, clear organizational structures and organizational stability. The benefits from exploitation tend to be relatively immediate, incremental and predictable. They also are likely to be better understood by the firm and fit into its existing strategic framework. Exploration, by contrast, is concerned with the exploration of new possibilities. It is associated with searching for and recognizing new mindsets and ways of doing things. It involves experimentation, taking risks, simulation of possible consequences, flexibility and innovation. The benefits from exploration are principally long term but can be relatively difficult to predict. Moreover, any benefits or discoveries that might come may be so different from what the firm is familiar with that it may not find it easy to take advantage of them.

Organizational 'ambidexterity'

It is clear that the organizational skills and capabilities to be successful at exploitation are likely to be very different from those that are needed for the radical exploration of new ideas. Indeed, the two views of improvement may actively conflict. A focus on thoroughly exploring for totally novel choices may consume managerial time and effort and the financial resources that would otherwise be used for refining existing ways of doing things, reducing the effectiveness of improving existing processes. Conversely, if existing processes are improved over time, there may be less motivation to experiment with new ideas. So, although both exploitation and exploration can be beneficial, they may compete both for resources and for management attention. This is where the concept of 'organizational ambidexterity' becomes important. Organizational ambidexterity means the ability of a firm both to exploit and explore as it seeks to improve; to be able to compete in mature markets where efficiency is important, by improving existing resources and processes, while also competing in new technologies and/or markets where novelty, innovation and experimentation are required.

> ✳ **Operations principle**
>
> Organizational ambidexterity is the ability both to exploit existing capabilities and to explore new ones as they seek to improve.

The structure of improvement ideas

There have been hundreds of ideas relating to operations improvement that have been proposed over the last few decades. To understand how these ideas relate to each other it is important to distinguish between four aspects of improvement:

- The *elements* contained within improvement approaches – these are the fundamental ideas of what improves operations. They are the 'building blocks' of improvement.
- The broad *approaches* to improvement – these are the underlying sets of beliefs that form a coherent philosophy and shape how improvement should be accomplished. Some improvement approaches have been used for over a century (for example, some work study approaches, see Chapter 9), others are relatively recent (for example, Six Sigma, explained later). But do not think that approaches to improvement are different in all respects; there are many elements that are common to several approaches.
- The improvement *techniques* – there are many 'step-by-step' techniques, methods and tools that can be used to help find improved ways of doing things, some of which use quantitative modelling and others are more qualitative.
- The *management* of improvement – how the process of improvement is managed is as important, if not more important, than understanding the elements and approaches to improvement. The improvement activity must be organized, resourced and generally controlled for it to be effective at actually achieving demonstrable improvement.

The rest of this chapter will treat each of these aspects of improvement. The best way to understand improvement is to deal with the elements contained within improvement approaches first, then see how they come together to form broad approaches to improvement, and then examine some typical improvement techniques, before looking briefly at how operations improvement can be managed. Figure 16.3 illustrates the structure of the four aspects of improvement.

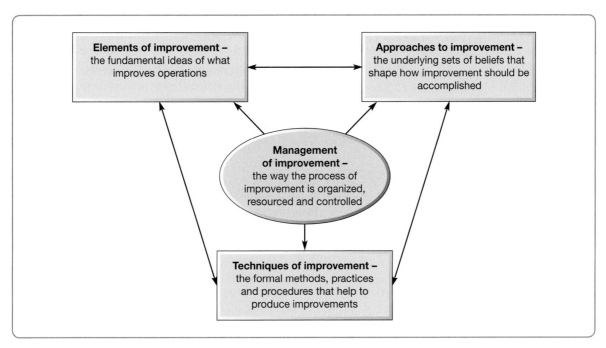

Figure 16.3 The structure of improvement ideas

Anarchy at 6Wunderkinder[4]

It is a problem every creative firm faces – how do you organize yourself so you can keep some kind of control over what is happening in the firm while not inhibiting the creativity of the people that you are paying to be creative? When 6Wunderkinder, a Berlin-based developer of 'Wunderlist', the task management tool, was founded in 2010 with only six people, it was relatively easy to foster a creative and innovative atmosphere. But by the time the company had grown tenfold, it was more difficult to preserve the 'start-up spirit'. Chad Fowler, the company's Chief Technology Officer, understands the importance of keeping the innovative culture: '*Probably every single company wants to maintain the feeling of being in a start-up, no matter how big they get.*' As the company grew it used several mechanisms to preserve the 'start-up spirit' such as the yearly 'Wundercamp', when all staff spend a week away in Bavarian forest cabins or on the Baltic coast, and 'Sexy Friday' when developers get a day a week to pursue their own passions, the aim being to challenge established patterns of working and encourage novel thinking. Christian Reber, the German Chief Executive and co-founder, says: '*On an assembly line you always get the work you expect. People do the stuff you tell them to do. What we, here, try to achieve is that we regularly get the "wow" factor...if*

Source: Alamy Images: 360b

everyone acts like a CEO, they make the decisions, [if] they are responsible for their own projects, then it completely changes [the] dynamics.' The relatively flat hierarchy is also an advantage in retaining skilled staff in a sector where the competition for the best developers can be fierce. '*The talent pool is extremely limited, people choose the workplace, especially developers, based more on the working atmosphere – the culture, rather than the salary*', says Christian Reber.

WHAT ARE THE KEY ELEMENTS OF OPERATIONS IMPROVEMENT?

The elements of improvement are the individual fundamental ideas of improvement. Think of these elements of improvement as the building blocks of the various improvement approaches that we will look at later. Here we explain some, but not all (there are lots), of the more common elements in use today.

Improvement cycles

An important element within some improvement approaches is the use of a literally never-ending process of repeatedly questioning and re-questioning the detailed working of a process or activity. This repeated and cyclical questioning is usually summarized by the idea of the improvement cycle, of which there are many, but two are widely used models – the PDCA cycle (sometimes called the Deming cycle, named after the famous quality 'guru', W.E. Deming) and the DMAIC (pronounced 'De-Make') cycle, made popular by the Six Sigma approach (see later). The PDCA cycle model is shown in Figure 16.4(a). It starts with the P (for plan) stage, which involves an examination of the current method or the problem area being studied. This involves collecting and analysing data so as to formulate a plan of action which is intended to improve performance. Once a plan for improvement has been agreed, the next step is the D (for do) stage. This is the implementation stage during which the plan is tried out in the operation. This stage may itself involve a mini-PDCA cycle as the problems of implementation are resolved. Next comes the C (for check) stage where the new implemented solution is evaluated to see whether it has resulted in the expected performance improvement. Finally, at least for this cycle, comes the A (for act) stage. During this stage the change is consolidated or standardized if it has been successful. Alternatively, if the change has not been successful, the lessons learned from the 'trial' are formalized before the cycle starts again.

The DMAIC cycle is in some ways more intuitively obvious than the PDCA cycle in as much as it follows a more 'experimental' approach (Fig. 16.4(b)). The DMAIC cycle starts with (D) defining the problem or problems, partly to understand the scope of what needs to be done and partly to define exactly the requirements of the process improvement. Often at this stage a formal goal or target for the improvement is set. After definition comes (M) the measurement stage. This stage involves validating the problem to make sure that it really is a problem worth solving, using data to refine the problem and measuring exactly what is happening. Once these measurements have been established, they can be (A) analysed.

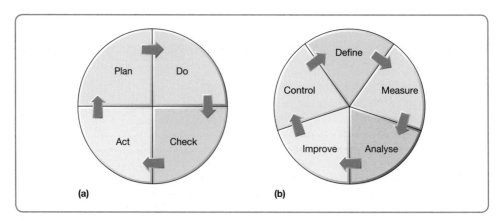

Figure 16.4 (a) The plan–do–check–act, or 'Deming', improvement cycle; and (b) the define–measure–analyse–improve–control, or DMAIC, Six Sigma improvement cycle

The analysis stage is sometimes seen as an opportunity to develop hypotheses as to what the root causes of the problem really are. Such hypotheses are validated (or not) by the analysis and the main root causes of the problem identified. Once the causes of the problem are identified, work can begin on (I) improving the process. Ideas are developed to remove the root causes of problems, solutions are tested and those solutions that seem to work are implemented, formalized and results measured. The improved process needs then to be continually monitored and (C) controlled to check that the improved level of performance is sustaining. After this point the cycle starts again and defines the problems which are preventing further improvement. Remember, though: it is the last point about both cycles that is the most important – the cycle starts again. It is only by accepting that in a continuous improvement philosophy these cycles quite literally never stop that improvement becomes part of every person's job.

A process perspective

Even if some improvement approaches do not explicitly or formally include the idea that taking a process perspective should be central to operations improvement, almost all do so implicitly. This has two major advantages. First, it means that improvement can be focused on what actually happens rather than which part of the organization has responsibility for what happens. In other words, if improvement is not reflected in the process of creating products and services, then it is not really improvement as such. Second, as we have mentioned before, all parts of the business manage processes. This is what we call operations as activity rather than operations as a function. So, if improvement is described in terms of how processes can be made more effective, those messages will have relevance for all the other functions of the business in addition to the operations function.

End-to-end processes

Some improvement approaches take the process perspective further and prescribe exactly how processes should be organized. One of the more radical prescriptions of business process re-engineering (BPR, see later), for example, is the idea that operations should be organized around the total process which adds value for customers, rather than the functions or activities which perform the various stages of the value-adding activity. We have already pointed out the difference between conventional processes within a specialist function and an end-to-end business process (see Chapter 1). Identified customer needs are entirely fulfilled by an 'end-to-end' business process. In fact the processes are designed specifically to do this, which is why they will often cut across conventional organizational boundaries. Figure 16.5 illustrates this idea.

Evidence-based problem solving

In recent years there has been a resurgence of the use of quantitative techniques in improvement approaches. Six Sigma (see later) in particular promotes systematic use of (preferably quantitative) evidence. Yet Six Sigma is not the first of the improvement approaches to use quantitative methods (some of the TQM gurus promoted statistical process control, for example) although it has done a lot to emphasize the use of quantitative evidence. In fact much of the considerable training required by Six Sigma consultants is devoted to mastering quantitative analytical techniques. However, the statistical methods used in improvement activities do not always reflect conventional academic statistical knowledge as such. They emphasize observational methods of collecting data and the use of experimentation to examine hypotheses. Techniques include graphical methods, analysis of variance and two-level factorial experiment design. Underlying the use of these techniques is an emphasis on the scientific method, responding only to hard evidence, and using statistical software to facilitate analysis.

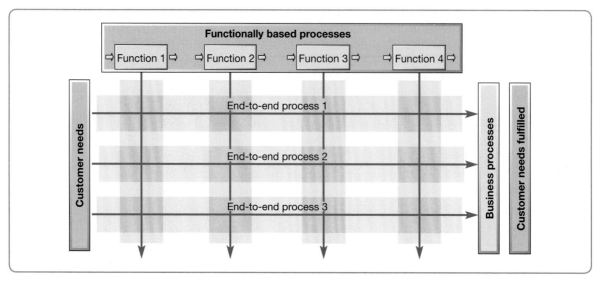

Figure 16.5 BPR advocates reorganizing (re-engineering) micro operations to reflect the natural customer-focused business processes

Customer centricity

There is little point in improvement unless it meets the requirements of the customers. However, in most improvement approaches, meeting the expectations of customers means more than this. It involves the whole organization in understanding the central importance of customers to its success and even to its survival. Customers are seen not as being external to the organization but as the most important part of it. However, the idea of being customer-centric does not mean that customers must be provided with everything that they want. Although 'What's good for customers' may frequently be the same as 'What's good for the business', it is not always. Operations managers are always having to strike a balance between what customers would like and what the operation can afford (or wants) to do.

Voice of the customer (VOC)

The 'voice of the customer' (VOC) is an idea that is closely related to the idea of customer centricity. The term means capturing a customer's requirements, expectations, perceptions and preferences in some depth. Sometimes a VOC exercise is done as part of new service and product development as part of quality function deployment (QFD) which was explained in Chapter 4. Sometimes it is part of a more general improvement activity. There are several ways to do this, but it usually involves using market research to derive a comprehensive set of customer requirements, which is ordered into a hierarchical structure, often prioritized to indicate the relative importance of different aspects of operations performance.

Systems and procedures

Improvement is not something that happens simply by getting everyone to 'think improvement'. Some type of system that supports the improvement effort may be needed. An improvement system (sometimes called a 'quality system') is defined as: *'the organizational structure, responsibilities, procedures, processes and resources for implementing quality management.'*[5] It should *'define and cover all facets of an organization's operation, from identifying and meeting the needs and requirements of customers, design, planning, purchasing, manufacturing, packaging, storage, delivery and service, together with all relevant activities carried out within these functions. It deals with organization, responsibilities, procedures and processes. Put simply [it] is good management practice.'*[6]

Reduce process variation

Processes change over time, as does their performance. Some aspect of process performance (usually an important one) is measured periodically (either as a single measurement or as a small sample of measurements). These are then plotted on a simple timescale. This has a number of advantages. The first is to check that the performance of the process is, in itself, acceptable (capable). They can also be used to check if process performance is changing over time, and to check on the extent of the variation in process performance. In Chapter 17 we illustrate how random variation in the performance of any process can obscure what was really happening within the process. So a potentially useful method of identifying improvement opportunities is to try and identify the sources of random variation in process performance.

OPERATIONS IN PRACTICE

Improvement at Heineken[7]

Heineken International produces and sells beer around the world with growing sales, especially in its Heineken and Amstel brands. However, sales growth can put pressure on any company's operations. For example, Heineken's Zoeterwoude facility, a packaging plant that fills bottles and cans in The Netherlands, had to increase its volume by between 8 and 10 per cent per year on a regular basis. The company faced two challenges. First, it needed to improve its operations processes to reduce its costs. Second, because it would have taken a year to build a new packaging line, it needed to improve the efficiency of its existing lines in order to increase its capacity. So, improving line efficiency was vital if the plant was to cut its costs and create the extra capacity it needed to delay investment in a new packaging line.

The objective of the improvement project was to improve the equipment efficiency of the operation. Setting a target of 20 per cent improvement was seen as important because it was challenging yet achievable as well as meeting cost and capacity objectives. It was also decided to focus the improvement project around two themes. First, obtaining accurate operational data that could be converted into useful business information on which improvement decisions could be based. Second, changing the culture of the operation to promote fast and effective decision making. Having access to accurate and up-to-date information would help people at all levels in the plant, as well as encouraging staff to focus on the *improvement* of how they do their job rather than just 'doing the job'. Before the improvement, project staff at the Zoeterwoude plant had approached problem solving as an ad hoc activity, only to be done when circumstances made it unavoidable. The improvement initiative taught the staff to use various problem-solving techniques such as cause–effect and Pareto diagrams (discussed later in this chapter). Other techniques included the analysis of improved

Source: Shutterstock.com: Valentyn Volkov

equipment maintenance and failure mode and effective analysis (FMEA). (Both discussed in Chapter 18.) *'Until we started using these techniques'*, says Wilbert Raaijmakers, Heineken Netherlands Brewery Director, *'there was little consent regarding what was causing any problems. There was poor communication between the various departments and job grades. For example, maintenance staff believed that production stops were caused by operating errors, while operators were of the opinion that poor maintenance was the cause.'* The use of better information, analysis and improvement techniques helped the staff to identify and treat the root causes of problems. With many potential improvements to make, staff teams were encouraged to set priorities that would reflect the overall improvement target. There was also widespread use of benchmarking performance against targets periodically so that progress could be reviewed.

At the end of 12 months the improvement project had achieved its objectives of a 20 per cent improvement in all the plant's packaging lines. This allowed it to increase the volume of its exports and cut its costs significantly. Not only that, but also other aspects of the plant's performance improved. Up to that point, the plant had gained a reputation for poor delivery dependability. After the project it was seen by the other operations in its supply chain as a much more reliable partner.

Yet Wilbert Raaijmakers still sees room for improvement: *'The optimization of an organization is a never-ending process. If you sit back and do the same thing tomorrow as you did today, you'll never make it. We must remain alert to the latest developments and stress the resulting information to its full potential.'*

Synchronized flow

This is another idea that we have seen before – in Chapter 15, as part of the lean philosophy. Synchronized flow means that items in a process, operation or supply network flow smoothly and with even velocity from start to finish. This is a function of how inventory accumulates within the operation. Whether inventory is accumulated in order to smooth differences between demand and supply, or as a contingency against unexpected delays, or simply to batch for purposes of processing or movement, it all means that flow becomes asynchronous. It waits as inventory rather than progressing smoothly on. Once this state of perfect synchronization of flow has been achieved, it becomes easier to expose any irregularities of flow which may be the symptoms of more deep-rooted underlying problems.

Emphasize education/training

Several improvement approaches stress the idea that structured training and organization of improvement should be central to improvement. Not only should the techniques of improvement be fully understood by everyone engaged in the improvement process, but the business and organizational context of improvement should also be understood. After all, how can one improve without knowing what kind of improvement would best benefit the organization and its customers? Furthermore, education and training have an important part to play in motivating all staff towards seeing improvement as a worthwhile activity. Some improvement approaches in particular place great emphasis on formal education. Six Sigma for example (see later) and its proponents often mandate a minimum level of training (measured in hours) that they deem necessary before improvement projects should be undertaken.

Perfection is the goal

Almost all organization-wide improvement programmes will have some kind of goal or target that the improvement effort should achieve. And while targets can be set in many different ways, some improvement authorities hold that measuring process performance against some kind of absolute target does most for encouraging improvement. By an 'absolute target' one literally means the theoretical level of perfection, for example zero errors, instant delivery, delivery absolutely when promised, infinite flexibility, zero waste, etc. Of course, in reality such perfection may never be achievable. That is not the point. What is important is that current performance can be calibrated against this target of perfection in order to indicate how much more improvement is possible. Improving (for example) delivery accuracy by 5 per cent may seem good until it is realized that only an improvement of 30 per cent would eliminate all late deliveries.

Waste identification

All improvement approaches aspire to eliminate waste. In fact any improvement implies that some waste has been eliminated, where waste is any activity that does not add value. But the identification and elimination of waste is sometimes a central feature. For example, as we discussed in Chapter 15, it is arguably the most significant part of the lean philosophy.

Include everybody

Harnessing the skills and enthusiasm of every person and all parts of the organization seems an obvious principle of improvement. The phrase 'quality at source' is sometimes used, stressing the impact that each individual has on improvement. The contribution of all individuals in the organization may go beyond understanding their contribution to 'not make mistakes'. Individuals are expected to bring something positive to improving the way they perform their jobs. The principles of 'empowerment' are frequently cited as supporting this aspect of improvement. When Japanese improvement practices first began to migrate in the late 1970s, this idea seemed even more radical. Yet now it is generally accepted that individual creativity and effort from all staff represent a valuable source of development. However, not all improvement approaches have adopted this idea. Some authorities believe that a small number of internal improvement consultants or specialists offer a better method of organizing improvement. However, these two ideas are not incompatible. Even with improvement specialists used to leading improvement efforts, the staff who actually operate the process can still be used as a valuable source of information and improvement ideas.

Develop internal customer–supplier relationships

One of the best ways to ensure that external customers are satisfied is to establish the idea that every part of the organization contributes to external customer satisfaction by satisfying its own internal customers. This idea was introduced in Chapter 15, as was the related concept of service-level agreements (SLAs). It means stressing that each process in an operation has a responsibility to manage these internal customer–supplier relationships. This is done primarily by defining as clearly as possible what their own and their customers' *requirements* are. In effect this means defining what constitutes 'error-free' service – the quality, speed, dependability and flexibility required by internal customers.

WHAT ARE THE BROAD APPROACHES TO IMPROVEMENT?

By the broad approaches to improvement we mean the underlying sets of beliefs that form a coherent philosophy and shape how improvement should be accomplished. But do not think that approaches to improvement are different in all respects; there are many elements that are common to several approaches. Some of these approaches have been, or will be, described in other chapters. For example, both lean operations (Chapter 15) and TQM (in Chapter 17) are discussed in some detail. So, in this section we will only briefly examine TQM and lean operations, specifically from an improvement perspective, and also add two further approaches – business process re-engineering (BPR) and Six Sigma.

> **✴ Operations principle**
> There is no one universal approach to improvement.

Total quality management as an improvement approach

Total quality management (TQM) was one of the earliest management 'fashions'. Its peak of popularity was in the late 1980s and early 1990s. As such it has suffered from something of a backlash in recent years. Yet the general precepts and principles that constitute TQM are still hugely influential. Few, if any, managers have not heard of TQM and its impact on improvement. Indeed, TQM has come to be seen as an approach to the way operations and processes should be managed and improved, generally. Even if TQM is not the label given to an improvement initiative, many of its elements will almost certainly have become routine. It is best thought of as a philosophy of how to approach improvement. This philosophy, above everything, stresses the 'total' of TQM. It is an approach that puts quality (and indeed improvement generally) at the heart of everything that is done by an operation. This totality can be summarized by the way TQM lays particular stress on the following elements (see Chapter 17):

- Meeting the needs and expectations of customers.
- Improvement covers all parts of the organization (and should be group based).
- Improvement includes every person in the organization (and success is recognized).
- Including all costs of quality.
- Getting things 'right first time', that is designing in quality rather than inspecting it in.
- Developing the systems and procedures which support improvement.

Lean as an improvement approach

The idea of 'lean' spread beyond its Japanese roots and became fashionable in the West at about the same time as TQM. And although its popularity has not declined to the same extent as TQM, over 25 years of experience have diminished the excitement once associated with the approach. But, unlike TQM, it was seen initially as an approach to be used exclusively in manufacturing. Now, lean has become fashionable as an approach that can be applied in service operations. As a reminder (see Chapter 15), the lean approach aims to meet demand instantaneously, with perfect quality and no waste. The key elements of lean when used as an improvement approach are as follows:

- Customer-centricity.
- Internal customer–supplier relationships.
- Perfection is the goal.
- Synchronized flow.
- Reduce variation.
- Include all people.
- Waste elimination.

Some organizations, especially now that lean is being applied more widely in service operations, view waste elimination as the most important of all the elements of the lean approach. In fact, they sometimes see the lean approach as consisting almost exclusively of waste elimination. What they fail to realize is that effective waste elimination is best achieved through changes in behaviour. It is the behavioural change brought about through synchronized flow and customer triggering that provides the window onto exposing and eliminating waste.

Business process re-engineering (BPR)

The idea of BPR originated in the early 1990s when Michael Hammer proposed that, rather than using technology to automate work, it would be better applied to doing away with the need for the work in the first place ('don't automate, obliterate'). In doing this he was warning against establishing non-value-added work within an IT system where it would be even more difficult to identify and eliminate. All work, he said, should be examined for whether it adds value for the customer and, if not, processes should be redesigned to eliminate it. In doing this BPR was echoing similar objectives in both scientific management and more recently lean approaches. But BPR, unlike those two earlier approaches, advocated radical changes rather than incremental changes to processes. Shortly after Hammer's article, other authors developed the ideas, again the majority of them stressing the importance of a radical approach to elimination of non-value-added work.

BPR has been defined as:[8] '*the fundamental rethinking and radical redesign of business processes to achieve dramatic improvements in critical, contemporary measures of performance, such as cost, quality, service and speed*'. But there is far more to it than that. In fact, BPR was a blend of a number of ideas which had been current in operations management for some time. Lean concepts, process flow charting, critical examination in method study, operations network management and customer-focused operations all contribute to the BPR concept. It was the potential of ITs to enable the fundamental redesign of processes, however, which acted as the catalyst in bringing these ideas together. It was the IT that allowed radical process redesign even if many of the methods used to achieve the redesign had been explored before. The main principles of BPR can be summarized in the following points:

- Rethink business processes in a cross-functional manner which organizes work around the natural flow of information (or materials or customers).
- Strive for dramatic improvements in performance by radically rethinking and redesigning the process.
- Have those who use the output from a process perform the process. Check to see if all internal customers can be their own supplier rather than depending on another function in the business to supply them (which takes longer and separates out the stages in the process).
- Put decision points where the work is performed. Do not separate those who do the work from those who control and manage the work.

Example[9]

We can illustrate this idea of reorganizing (or re-engineering) around business processes through the following simple example. Figure 16.6(a) shows the traditional organization of a trading company which purchases consumer goods from several suppliers, stores them and sells them on to retail outlets. At the heart of the operation is the warehouse which receives the goods, stores them, and packs and despatches them when they are required by customers. Orders for more stock are placed by Purchasing, which also takes charge of materials planning and stock control. Purchasing buys the goods based on a forecast which is prepared by Marketing, which takes advice from Sales, which is processing customers' orders. When a customer does place an order, it is Sales' job to instruct the warehouse to pack and despatch the order and tell Finance to invoice the customer for the goods. So, traditionally, five departments (each a micro-operation) have between them organized the flow of materials and information within the total operation. But at each interface between the departments there is the possibility of errors and miscommunication arising. Furthermore, *who is responsible for looking after the customer's needs?* Currently, three separate departments all have dealings with the customer. Similarly, *who is responsible for liaising with suppliers?* This time two departments have contact with suppliers.

Eventually the company reorganized around two essential business processes. The first process (called purchasing operations) dealt with everything concerning relationships with suppliers. It was this process's focused and unambiguous responsibility to develop good working relationships with suppliers. The other business process (called customer service operations) had total responsibility for satisfying customers' needs. This included speaking 'with one voice' to the customer.

Critical commentary

BPR has aroused considerable controversy, mainly because BPR sometimes looks only at work activities rather than at the people who perform the work. Because of this, people become 'cogs in a machine'. Many of these critics equate BPR with the much earlier principles of scientific management, pejoratively known as 'Taylorism'. Generally these critics mean that BPR is overly harsh in the way it views human resources. Certainly there is evidence that BPR is often accompanied by a significant reduction in staff. Studies at the time when BPR was at its peak often revealed that the majority of BPR projects could reduce staff levels by over 20 per cent. Often BPR was viewed as merely an excuse for getting rid of staff. Companies that wished to 'downsize' were using BPR as the pretext, putting the short-term interests of the shareholders of the company above either their longer term interests or the interests of the company's employees. Moreover, a combination of radical redesign together with downsizing could mean that the essential core of experience was lost from the operation. This leaves it vulnerable to any marked turbulence since it no longer possessed the knowledge and experience of how to cope with unexpected changes.

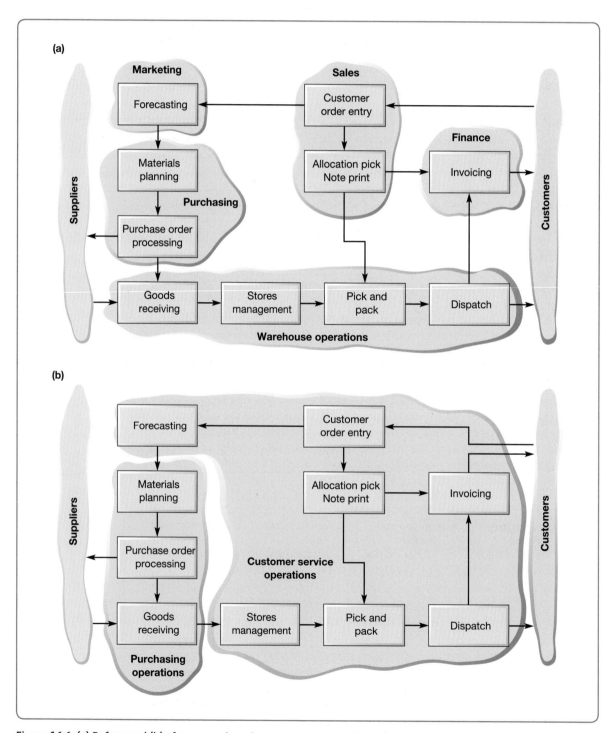

Figure 16.6 (a) Before and (b) after re-engineering a consumer goods trading company

Six Sigma

The Six Sigma approach was first popularized by Motorola, the electronics and communications systems company. When it set its quality objective as 'total customer satisfaction' in the 1980s, it started to explore what the slogan would mean to its operations processes. It decided that true customer satisfaction would only be achieved when its products were delivered when promised, with no defects, with no early-life failures and when the product did not fail excessively in service. To achieve this, Motorola initially focused on removing manufacturing defects. However, it soon came to realize that many problems were caused by latent defects, hidden within the design of its products. These may not show initially but eventually could cause failure in the field. The only way to eliminate these defects was to make sure that design specifications were tight (that is, narrow tolerances) and its processes very capable.

Motorola's Six Sigma quality concept was so named because it required that the natural variation of processes (± 3 standard deviations) should be half their specification range. In other words, the specification range of any part of a product or service should be ± 6 the standard deviation of the process (see Chapter 17). The Greek letter sigma (σ) is often used to indicate the standard deviation of a process, hence the Six Sigma label. Figure 16.7 illustrates the effect of progressively narrowing process variation on the number of defects produced by the process, in terms of defects per million. The defects per million measure is used within the Six Sigma approach to emphasize the drive towards a virtually zero defect objective.[10] Now the definition of Six Sigma has widened to well beyond this rather narrow statistical perspective. General Electric (GE), which was probably the best known of the early adopters of Six Sigma, defined it as: *'A disciplined methodology of defining, measuring, analyzing, improving, and controlling the quality in every one of the company's products, processes, and transactions – with the ultimate goal of virtually eliminating all defects.'* So, now Six Sigma should be seen as a broad improvement concept rather than a simple examination of process variation, even though this is still an important part of process control, learning and improvement.

Measuring performance

The Six Sigma approach uses a number of related measures to assess the performance of operations processes:

- **A defect** – is a failure to meet customer-required performance (defining performance measures from a customer's perspective is an important part of the Six Sigma approach).
- **A defect unit or item** – is any unit of output that contains a defect (that is, only units of output with no defects are not defective; defective units will have one or more than one defect).

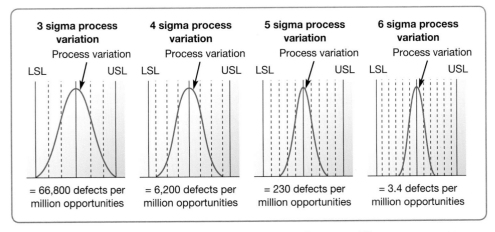

Figure 16.7 Process variation and its impact on process defects per million

- **A defect opportunity** – is the number of different ways a unit of output can fail to meet customer requirements (simple products or services will have few defect opportunities, but very complex products or services may have hundreds of different ways of being defective).
- **Proportion defective** – is the percentage or fraction of units that have one or more defect.
- **Process yield** – is the percentage or fraction of total units produced by a process that are defect-free (that is, 1 − proportion defective).
- **Defect per unit (DPU)** - is the average number of defects on a unit of output (the number of defects divided by the number of items produced).
- **Defects per opportunity** – is the proportion or percentage of defects divided by the total number of defect opportunities (the number of defects divided by (the number of items produced × the number of opportunities per item)).
- **Defects per million opportunities (DPMO)** – is exactly what it says, the number of defects which the process will produce if there were 1 million opportunities to do so.
- **The Sigma measurement**[11] is derived from the DPMO and is the number of standard deviations of the process variability that will fit within the customer specification limits.

Worked example

An insurance process checks details of insurance claims and arranges for customers to be paid. It samples 300 claims at random at the end of the process. It finds that 51 claims had one or more defects and there were 74 defects in total. Four types of error were observed: coding errors, policy conditions errors, liability errors and notification errors.

$$\text{Proportion defective} = \frac{\text{Number of defects}}{\text{Number of units processed}}$$

$$= \frac{51}{300} = 0.17 \ (17\% \text{ defective})$$

$$\text{Yield} = 1 - \text{proportion of defectives}$$
$$= 1 - 0.17 = 0.83 \text{ or } (83\% \text{ yield})$$

$$\text{Defects per unit} = \frac{\text{Number of defects}}{\text{Number of units processed}}$$

$$= \frac{74}{300} = 0.247 \ (\text{or } 24.7) \text{ DPO}$$

$$\text{Defects per opportunity} = \frac{\text{Number of defects}}{\text{Number of units processed} \times \text{Number of opportunities}}$$

$$= \frac{74}{300 \times 4} = 0.062 \text{ DPO}$$

$$\text{Defects per million opportunities} = \text{DPO} \times 10^6$$
$$= 62,000 \text{ DPMO}$$

Although the scope of Six Sigma is disputed, among elements frequently associated with Six Sigma are the following

- **Customer-driven objectives** – Six Sigma is sometimes defined as 'the process of comparing process outputs against customer requirements'. It uses a number of measures to assess the performance of operations processes. In particular it expresses performance in terms of defects per million opportunities (DPMO).
- **Use of evidence** – Although Six Sigma is not the first of the new approaches to operations to use statistical methods, it has done a lot to emphasize the use of quantitative evidence.

- **Structured improvement cycle** – The structured improvement cycle used in Six Sigma is the DMAIC cycle.
- **Process capability and control** – Not surprisingly, given its origins, process capability and control is important within the Six Sigma approach.
- **Process design** – Latterly Six Sigma proponents also include process design in the collection of elements that define the Six Sigma approach.
- **Structured training and organization of improvement** – The Six Sigma approach holds that improvement initiatives can only be successful if significant resources and training are devoted to their management.

The 'marshal arts' analogy

The terms that have become associated with Six Sigma experts (and denote their level of expertise) are Master Black Belt, Black Belt and Green Belt. Master Black Belts are experts in the use of Six Sigma tools and techniques as well as how such techniques can be used and implemented. Primarily Master Black Belts are seen as teachers who can not only guide improvement projects, but also coach and mentor Black Belts and Green Belts who are closer to the day-to-day improvement activity. They are expected to have the quantitative analytical skills to help with Six Sigma techniques and also the organizational and interpersonal skills to teach and mentor. Given their responsibilities, it is expected that Master Black Belts are employed full-time on their improvement activities. Black Belts can take a direct hand in organizing improvement teams. Like Master Black Belts, Black Belts are expected to develop their quantitative analytical skills and also act as coaches for Green Belts. Black Belts are dedicated full-time to improvement, and although opinions vary on how many Black Belts should be employed in an operation, some organizations recommend one Black Belt for every hundred employees. Green Belts work within improvement teams, possibly as team leaders. They have significant amounts of training, although less than Black Belts. Green Belts are not full-time positions; they have normal day-to-day process responsibilities but are expected to spend at least 20 per cent of their time on improvement projects.

OPERATIONS IN PRACTICE **Six sigma at Wipro[12]**

There are many companies that have benefited from Six-Sigma-based improvement, but few have gone on to be able to sell to others the expertise that they gathered from applying it to themselves. Wipro is one of these. Wipro is a global IT, consulting and outsourcing company with 145,000 employees serving over 900 clients in 60 countries. It provides a range of business services from 'business process outsourcing' (doing processing for other firms) to 'software development', and from 'information technology consulting' to 'cloud computing'. (Surprisingly for a global IT services giant, Wipro was actually started in 1945 in India as a vegetable oil company.) Wipro also has one of the most developed Six Sigma programmes in the IT and consulting industries, especially in its software development activities where key challenges involved included reducing the data transfer time within the process, reducing the risk of failures and errors, and avoiding interruption due to network downtime. For Wipro, Six

Source: Shutterstock.com: Stuart Jenner

Sigma simply means a measure of quality that strives for near perfection. It means:

- Having products and services that meet global standards.
- Ensuring robust processes within the organization.

- Consistently meeting and exceeding customer expectations.
- Establishing a quality culture throughout the business.

Individual Six Sigma projects were selected on the basis of their probability of success and were completed relatively quickly. This gave Wipro the opportunity to assess the success and learn from any problems that had occurred. Projects were identified on the basis of the problem areas under each of the critical business processes that could adversely impact business performance. Because Wipro took a customer-focused definition of quality, Six Sigma implementation was measured in terms of progress towards what the customer finds important (and what the customer pays for). This involved improving performance through a precise quantitative understanding of the customer's requirements. Wipro says that its adoption of Six Sigma has been an unquestionable success, whether in terms of customer satisfaction, improvement in internal performance, or in the improvement of shareowner value.

However, as the pioneers of Six Sigma in India, Wipro's implementation of Six Sigma was not without difficulties – and, Wipro stresses, opportunities for learning from them. To begin with, it took time to build the required support from the higher level managers, and to restructure the organization to provide the infrastructure, and training to establish confidence in the process. In particular, the first year of deployment was extremely difficult. Resourcing the stream of Six Sigma projects was problematic, partly because each project required different levels and types of resource. Also, the company learned not to underestimate the amount of training that would be required. To build a team of professionals and train them for various stages of Six Sigma was a difficult job. (In fact this motivated Wipro to start its own consultancy that could train its own people.) Nevertheless, regular and timely reviews of each project proved particularly important in ensuring the success of a project and Wipro had to develop a team of experts for this purpose.

Critical commentary

One common criticism of Six Sigma is that it does not offer anything that was not available before. Its emphasis on improvement cycles comes from TQM, its emphasis on reducing variability comes from statistical process control, its use of experimentation and data analysis is simply good quantitative analysis. The only contribution that Six Sigma has made, argue its critics, is using the rather gimmicky martial arts analogy of Black Belt etc. to indicate a level of expertise in Six Sigma methods. All Six Sigma has done is package pre-existing elements together in order for consultants to be able to sell it to gullible chief executives. In fact it is difficult to deny some of these points. Maybe the real issue is whether it is really a criticism. If bringing these elements together really does form an effective problem-solving approach, why is this is a problem? Six Sigma is also accused of being too hierarchical in the way it structures its various levels of involvement in the improvement activity (as well as the dubious use of martial-arts-derived names such as Black Belt). It is also expensive. Devoting such large amounts of training and time to improvement is a significant investment, especially for small companies. Nevertheless, Six Sigma proponents argue that the improvement activity is generally neglected in most operations and if it is to be taken seriously, it deserves the significant investment implied by the Six Sigma approach. Furthermore, they argue, if operated well, Six Sigma improvement projects run by experienced practitioners can save far more than their cost. There are also technical criticisms of Six Sigma. Most notably, that in purely statistical terms the normal distribution which is used extensively in Six Sigma analysis does not actually represent most process behaviour. Other technical criticisms (that are not really the subject of this book) imply that aiming for the very low levels of defects per million opportunities, as recommended by Six Sigma proponents, is far too onerous.

Differences and similarities

In this chapter we have chosen to explain very briefly four improvement approaches. It could have been more. Enterprise resource planning (ERP, see Chapter 14), total preventive maintenance (TPM, see Chapter 18), Lean Sigma (a combination of lean and Six Sigma) and others could have been added. But these four constitute a representative sample of the most commonly used approaches. Nor do we have the space to describe them fully. But there are clearly some common elements between some of these approaches that we have described. Yet there are also differences between them in that each approach includes a different set of elements and therefore a different emphasis, and these differences need to be understood. For example, one important difference relates to whether the approaches emphasize a gradual, continuous approach to change, or whether they recommend a more radical 'breakthrough' change. Another difference concerns the aim of the approach. What is the balance between whether the approach emphasizes *what* changes should be made or *how* changes should be made? Some approaches

> **✳ Operations principle**
>
> There is significant overlap between the various approaches to improvement in terms of the improvement elements they contain.

have a firm view of what is the best way to organize the operation's processes and resources. Other approaches hold no particular view on what an operation should do, but rather concentrate on how the management of an operation should decide what to do. Indeed we can position each of the elements and the approaches that include them. This is illustrated in Figure 16.8. The approaches differ in the extent that they prescribe appropriate operations practice. BPR for example is very clear in what it is recommending. Namely, that all processes should be organized on a end-to-end basis. Its focus is *what* should happen rather than *how* it should happen. To a slightly lesser extent, lean is the same. It has a definite list of things that processes should or should not be – waste should be eliminated, inventory should be reduced, technology should be flexible, and so on. Contrast this with both Six Sigma and TQM that focus to a far greater extent on *how* operations should be improved. Six Sigma in particular has relatively little to say about what is good or bad in the way operations resources are organized (with the possible

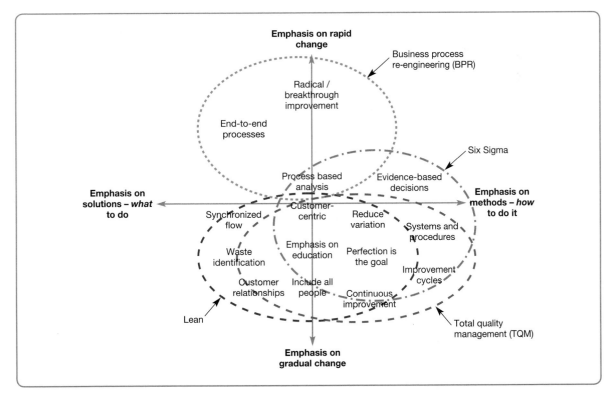

Figure 16.8 The four approaches on the two dimensions of improvement

exception of its emphasizing the negative effects of process variation). Its concern is largely the way improvements should be made: using evidence, using quantitative analysis, using the DMAIC cycle, and so on. The approaches also differ in terms of whether they emphasize gradual or rapid change. BPR is explicit in its radical nature. By contrast, TQM and lean both incorporate ideas of continuous improvement. Six Sigma is relatively neutral on this issue and can be used for small or very large changes.

Lean Sigma[13]

As if to emphasize the shared elements of the various approaches to operations improvement, some organizations are blending two or more approaches to form hybrids that try and combine their best characteristics. The best known of these is Lean Sigma (also called Lean Six Sigma or Six Sigma Lean). As its name suggests, Lean Six Sigma is a combination of lean methods and Six Sigma concepts. It attempts to build on the experience, methods and tools that have emerged from the several decades of operational improvement and implementation using lean and Six Sigma approaches separately. Lean Sigma includes the waste reduction, fast throughput time and impact of lean with the data-driven, rigour and variation control of Six Sigma. Some organizations also include other elements from other approaches. For example, the continuous improvement and error-free quality orientation of TQM is frequently included in the concept.

WHAT TECHNIQUES CAN BE USED FOR IMPROVEMENT?

Improvement techniques are the 'step-by-step' methods and tools that can be used to help find improved ways of doing things; some of these use quantitative modelling and others are more qualitative. All the techniques described in this book and its supplements can be regarded as 'improvement' techniques. However, some techniques are particularly useful for improving operations and processes generally. Here we select some techniques which either have not been described elsewhere or need to be reintroduced in their role of helping operations improvement particularly.

> ✳ **Operations principle**
> Improvement is facilitated by relatively simple analytical techniques.

Scatter diagrams

Scatter diagrams provide a quick and simple method of identifying whether there is evidence of a connection between two sets of data: for example, the time at which you set off for work every morning and how long the journey to work takes. Plotting each journey on a graph which has departure time on one axis and journey time on the other could give an indication of whether departure time and journey time are related, and if so how. Scatter diagrams can be treated in a far more sophisticated manner by quantifying how strong the relationship is between the sets of data. But however sophisticated the approach, this type of graph only identifies the existence of a relationship, not necessarily the existence of a cause–effect relationship. If the scatter diagram shows a very strong connection between the sets of data, it is important evidence of a cause–effect relationship, but not proof positive. It could be coincidence!

Example: Kaston Pyral Services Ltd (A)

Kaston Pyral Services Ltd (KPS) installs and maintains environmental control, heating and air-conditioning systems. It has set up an improvement team to suggest ways in which it might improve its levels of customer service. The improvement team had completed its first customer satisfaction survey. The survey asked customers to score the service they received from KPS in several ways. For example, it asked customers to score services on a scale of 1 to 10 on promptness, friendliness, level of advice, etc. Scores were then summed to give a 'total satisfaction score' for each customer – the higher the score, the greater the satisfaction. The spread of satisfaction scores puzzled the team and it considered what factors might be causing such differences in the way customers viewed service. Two factors were put forward to explain the differences:

(a) the number of times in the past year the customer had received a preventive maintenance visit;

(b) the number of times the customer had called for emergency service.

All this data was collected and plotted on scatter diagrams as shown in Figure 16.9. It shows that there seems to be a clear relationship between a customer's satisfaction score and the number of times the customer was visited for regular servicing. The scatter diagram in Figure 16.9(b) is less clear. Although all customers who had very high satisfaction scores had made very few emergency calls, so had some customers with low satisfaction scores. As a result of this analysis, the team decided to survey customers' views on its emergency service.

Process maps (flow charts)

Process maps (sometimes called flow charts in this context) can be used to give a detailed understanding prior to improvement. They were described in Chapter 6 and are widely used in improvement activities. The act of recording each stage in the process quickly shows up poorly organized flows. Process maps can also clarify improvement opportunities and shed further light on the internal mechanics or workings of an operation. Finally, and probably most importantly, they highlight problem areas where no procedure exists to cope with a particular set of circumstances.

Example: Kaston Pyral Services Ltd (B)

As part of its improvement programme the team at KPS is concerned that customers are not being served well when they phone in with minor queries over the operation of their heating systems. These queries are not usually concerned with serious problems, but often concern minor irritations which can be equally damaging to the customers' perception of KPS's service. Figure 16.10 shows the process map for this type of customer query. The team found the map illuminating. The procedure had never been formally laid out in this way before, and it showed up three areas where information was not being recorded. These are the three points marked with question marks on the process map in Figure 16.10. As a result of this investigation, it was decided to log all customer queries so that analysis could reveal further information on the nature of customer problems.

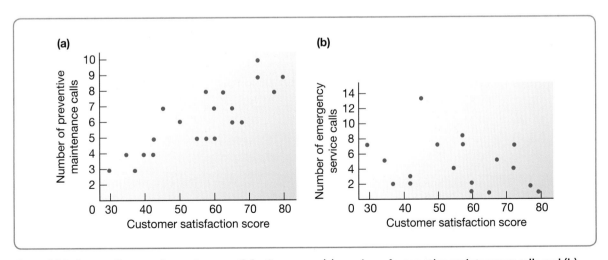

Figure 16.9 Scatter diagrams for customer satisfaction versus (a) number of preventive maintenance calls and (b) number of emergency service calls

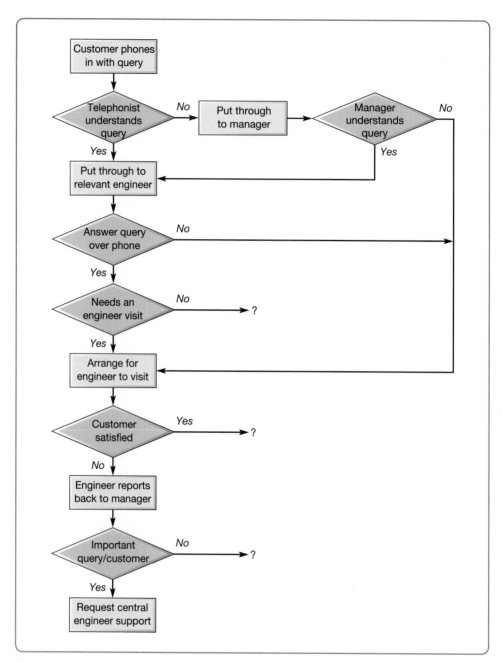

Figure 16.10 Process map for customer query

Cause–effect diagrams

Cause–effect diagrams are a particularly effective method of helping to search for the root causes of problems. They do this by asking what, when, where, how and why questions, but also add some possible 'answers' in an explicit way. They can also be used to identify areas where further data is needed. Cause–effect diagrams (which are also known as Ishikawa diagrams) have become extensively used in improvement programmes. This is because they provide a way of structuring group brainstorming sessions. Often the structure involves identifying possible causes under the (rather old-fashioned) headings of: machinery, manpower, materials, methods and money. Yet, in practice, any categorization that comprehensively covers all relevant possible causes could be used.

Example: Kaston Pyral Services Ltd (C)

The improvement team at KPS was working on a particular area which was proving a problem. Whenever service engineers were called out to perform emergency servicing for a customer, they took with them the spares and equipment which they thought would be necessary to repair the system. Although engineers could never be sure exactly what materials and equipment they would need for a job, they could guess what was likely to be needed and take a range of spares and equipment which would cover most eventualities. Too often, however, the engineers would find that they needed a spare that they had not brought with them. The cause–effect diagram for this particular problem, as drawn by the team, is shown in Figure 16.11.

Pareto diagrams

In any improvement process, it is worthwhile distinguishing what is important and what is less so. The purpose of the Pareto diagram (first introduced in Chapter 13) is to distinguish between the 'vital few' issues and the 'trivial many'. It is a relatively straightforward technique which involves arranging items of information on the types of problem or causes of problem into their order of importance (usually measured by 'frequency of occurrence'). This can be used to highlight areas where further decision making will be useful. Pareto analysis is based on the phenomenon of relatively few causes explaining the majority of effects. For example, most revenue for any company is likely to come from relatively few of the company's customers. Similarly, relatively few of a doctor's patients will probably occupy most of his or her time.

Example: Kaston Pyral Services Ltd (D)

The KPS improvement team which was investigating unscheduled returns from emergency servicing (the issue which was described in the cause–effect diagram in Figure 16.12) examined all occasions over the previous 12 months on which an unscheduled return had been made. The team categorized the reasons for unscheduled returns as follows:

1 The wrong part had been taken to a job because, although the information which the engineer received was sound, he or she had incorrectly predicted the nature of the fault.
2 The wrong part had been taken to the job because there was insufficient information given when the call was taken.

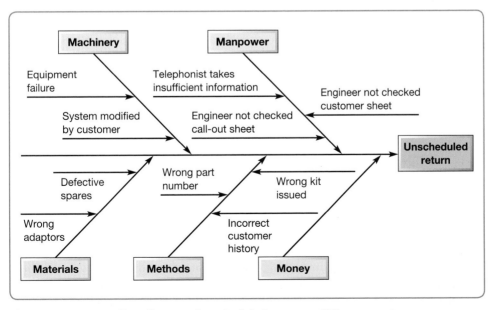

Figure 16.11 Cause-effect diagram of unscheduled returns at KPS

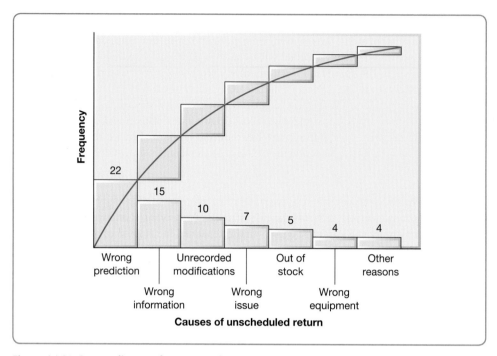

Figure 16.12 Pareto diagram for causes of unscheduled returns

3 The wrong part had been taken to the job because the system had been modified in some way not recorded on KPS's records.

4 The wrong part had been taken to the job because the part had been incorrectly issued to the engineer by stores.

5 No part had been taken because the relevant part was out of stock.

6 The wrong equipment had been taken for whatever reason.

7 Any other reason.

The relative frequency of occurrence of these causes is shown in Figure 16.12. About a third of all unscheduled returns were due to the first category, and more than half the returns were accounted for by the first and second categories together. It was decided that the problem could best be tackled by concentrating on how to get more information to the engineers which would enable them to predict the causes of failure accurately.

Why–why analysis

Why–why analysis starts by stating the problem and asking *why* that problem has occurred. Once the reasons for the problem occurring have been identified, each of the reasons is taken in turn and again the question is asked *why* those reasons have occurred, and so on. This procedure is continued until either a cause seems sufficiently self-contained to be addressed by itself or no more answers to the question 'Why?' can be generated.

Example: Kaston Pyral Services Ltd (E)

The major cause of unscheduled returns at KPS was the incorrect prediction of reasons for the customer's system failure. This is stated as the 'problem' in the why–why analysis in Figure 16.13. The question is then asked: 'why was the failure wrongly predicted?' Three answers are proposed: first, that the engineers were not trained correctly; second, that they had insufficient knowledge of the particular product installed in the customer's location; and third, that they had insufficient knowledge of the customer's particular system with its

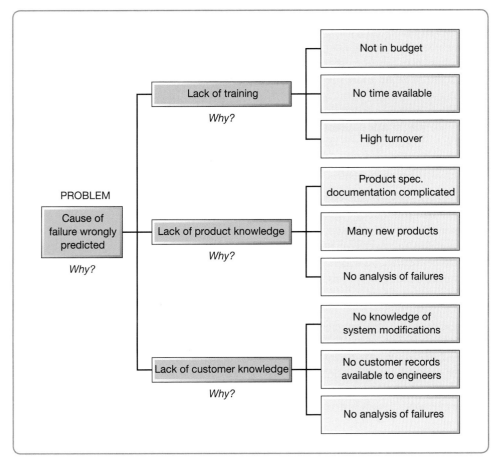

Figure 16.13 Why–why analysis for 'failure wrongly predicted'

modifications. Each of these three reasons is taken in turn, and the questions are asked: 'why is there a lack of training, why is there a lack of product knowledge, and why is there a lack of customer knowledge?' And so on.

HOW CAN THE IMPROVEMENT PROCESS BE MANAGED?

In the final part of this chapter we examine some of the managerial issues associated with how improvement can be organized. Not all the issues concerned with managing the improvement process are easily defined, and many are outside the traditional scope of an operations management text, but they are important. Many of the issues could be described as the 'soft' side of improvement. But do not dismiss this as in any way less important. In practice it is often the 'soft' stuff that determines the success or failure of improvement efforts. Moreover, the 'soft' stuff can be more difficult to get right than the 'hard', more technique-based, aspects of improvement. The 'hard' stuff is hard, but the 'soft' stuff is harder!

Why does the improvement effort need organizing?

Improvement does not just happen. It needs organizing and it needs implementing. It also needs a purpose that is well thought through and clearly articulated. Although much operations improvement will take place at an operational level, it may be small scale and incremental. Nevertheless, it must be placed in some kind of context. That is, it should be clear *why* improvement is happening as well as what it consists of. This means linking the improvement to the overall strategic objectives of the organization.

Remember also that the issue of how improvement should be organized is not a new concern. It has been a concern of management writers for decades. For example, W.E. Deming (considered in Japan to be the father of quality control) asserted that quality starts with top management and is a strategic activity.[14] It is claimed that much of the success in terms of quality in Japanese industry was the result of his lectures to Japanese companies in the 1950s.[15] Deming's basic philosophy is that quality and productivity increase as 'process variability' (the unpredictability of the process) decreases. In his *14 points for quality improvement*, he emphasizes the need for statistical control methods, participation, education, openness and purposeful improvement:

1 Create constancy of purpose.
2 Adopt new philosophy.
3 Cease dependence on inspection.
4 End awarding business on price.
5 Improve constantly the system of production and service.
6 Institute training on the job.
7 Institute leadership.
8 Drive out fear.
9 Break down barriers between departments.
10 Eliminate slogans and exhortations.
11 Eliminate quotas or work standards.
12 Give people pride in their job.
13 Institute education and a self-improvement programme.
14 Put everyone to work to accomplish it.

How can organizational culture affect improvement?

Almost all of Deming's points above are concerned with an organization's 'culture', and it is generally held by most organizational theorists that the ability to improve its operations performance depends to a large extent on its 'culture'. We discussed what is meant by culture in Chapter 9. It is 'the way we do things around here' or 'the organization's climate'.[16] So, organizational culture and improvement are clearly related. A receptive organizational culture that encourages a constant search for improved ways to do things nurtures improvement. At the same time the organization's view of improvement is an important indication of its culture. But what is meant by 'an improvement culture'? One view of the various elements that make up an improvement culture comes from Bessant and Caffyn,[17] who distinguish between what they call 'organizational abilities' (the capacity or aptitude to adopt a particular approach to improvement), 'constituent behaviours' (the routines of behaviour which staff adopt and which reinforce the approach to improvement) and 'enablers' (the procedural devices or techniques used to progress the improvement effort). They identify six generic organizational abilities, each with its own set of constituent behaviours. The authors write specifically about continuous improvement (CI), but their points apply more generally. These are identified in Table 16.1.

Sourcing improvement ideas

When we examined the elements of, and approaches to, improvement, earlier, they focused on generating improvement ideas that originated within the organization. Yet to ignore the improvements that other companies are deploying is to ignore a potentially huge source of innovation. Whether they are competitors, suppliers, customers, or simply other firms with similar challenges, external firms can provide solutions to internal problems. But some commentators argue that (legally) 'copying' from outsiders can be an effective, if underused,

Table 16.1 Continuous improvement (CI) abilities and some associated behaviours

Organizational ability	Constituent behaviours
Getting the CI habit	People use formal problem-finding and solving cycle
Developing the ability to generate sustained involvement in CI	People use simple tools and techniques People use simple measurement to shape the improvement process Individuals and/or groups initiate and carry through CI activities – they participate in the process Ideas are responded to in a timely fashion – either implemented or otherwise dealt with Managers support the CI process through allocation of resources Managers recognize in formal ways the contribution of employees to CI Managers lead by example, becoming actively involved in design and implementation of CI Managers support experiment by not punishing mistakes, but instead encouraging learning from them
Focusing on CI	Individuals and groups use the organization's strategic objectives to prioritize improvements
Generating and sustaining the ability to link CI activities to the strategic goals of the company	Everyone is able to explain what the operation's strategy and objectives are Individuals and groups assess their proposed changes against the operation's objectives Individuals and groups monitor/measure the results of their improvement activity CI activities are an integral part of the individual's or group's work, not a parallel activity
Spreading the word	People co-operate in cross-functional groups
Generating the ability to move CI activity across organizational boundaries	People understand and share an holistic view (process understanding and ownership) People are oriented towards internal and external customers in their CI activity Specific CI projects with outside agencies (customers, suppliers, etc.) take place Relevant CI activities involve representatives from different organizational levels
CI on the CI system	The CI system is continually monitored and developed
Generating the ability to manage strategically the development of the CI	There is a cyclical planning process whereby the CI system is regularly reviewed and amended There is periodic review of the CI system in relation to the organization as a whole Senior management make available sufficient resources (time, money, personnel) to support the continuing development of the CI system The CI system itself is designed to fit within the current structure and infrastructure When a major organizational change is planned, its potential impact on the CI system is assessed
Walking the talk	The 'management style' reflects commitment to CI values
Generating the ability to articulate and demonstrate CI's values	When something goes wrong, people at all levels look for reasons why, rather than blame individuals People at all levels demonstrate a shared belief in the value of small steps and that everyone can contribute, by themselves being actively involved in making and recognizing incremental improvements
Building the learning	Everyone learns from their experiences, both good and bad
Organization Generating the ability to learn through CI activity	Individuals seeks out opportunities for learning/personal development Individuals and groups at all levels share their learning The organization captures and shares the learning of individuals and groups Managers accept and act on all the learning that takes place Organizational mechanisms are used to deploy what has been learned across the organization

approach to improvement. Oded Shenkar, an authority on international management, claims that although to argue '*imitation can be strategic seems almost blasphemous in the current scholarly climate*', it can '*be strategic and should be part of the strategic repertoire of any agile firm*'.[18] In fact, '*imitation can be a differentiating factor and has the potential to deliver unique value*'. He identifies three 'strategic types' of imitators:

- *The pioneer importer* – is an imitator that is the pioneer in another place (another country, industry, or product market). This is what Ryanair did in Europe when it imported the Southwest model.
- *The fast second* – is a rapid mover arriving quickly after an innovator or pioneer, but before they have had an opportunity to establish an unassailable lead, and before other potentially rival imitators take a large share of the market.
- *The come from behind* – is a late entrant or adopter that has deliberately delayed adopting a new idea. Samsung did this with its chip-making business, by using its manufacturing capability and knowledge to halve the time it takes to build a semiconductor plant. Then Samsung established a lead over competitors by exploiting its strength in key technical, production and quality skills.

> ❋ **Operations principle**
>
> Many improvement ideas can originate from outside an organization.

Benchmarking

Benchmarking is clearly related to the idea of finding inspiration from outside the organization. It is 'the process of learning from others' and involves comparing one's own performance or methods against other comparable operations. It is a broader issue than setting performance targets, and includes investigating other organizations' operations practice in order to derive ideas that could contribute to performance improvement. Its rationale is based on the idea that (a) problems in managing processes are almost certainly shared by processes elsewhere, and (b) there is probably another operation somewhere that has developed a better way of doing things. For example, a bank might learn some things from a supermarket about how it could cope with demand fluctuations during the day. Benchmarking is essentially about stimulating creativity in improvement practice.

> ❋ **Operations principle**
>
> Improvement is aided by contextualizing processes and operations performance through some kind of benchmarking.

Types of benchmarking

There are many different types of benchmarking (which are not necessarily mutually exclusive), some of which are listed below:

- *Internal benchmarking* is a comparison between operations or parts of operations which are within the same total organization.
- *External benchmarking* is a comparison between an operation and other operations which are part of a different organization.
- *Non-competitive benchmarking* is benchmarking against external organizations which do not compete directly in the same markets.
- *Competitive benchmarking* is a comparison directly between competitors in the same, or similar, markets.
- *Performance benchmarking* is a comparison between the levels of achieved performance in different operations.
- *Practice benchmarking* is a comparison between an organization's operations practices, or way of doing things, and those adopted by another operation.

Benchmarking as an improvement tool

Although benchmarking has become popular, some businesses have failed to derive maximum benefit from it. Partly this may be because there are some misunderstandings as to what benchmarking actually entails. First, it is not a 'one-off' project. It is best practised as a continuous process of comparison. Second, it does not provide 'solutions'. Rather, it provides ideas and information that can lead to solutions. Third, it does not involve simply copying or imitating other operations. It is a process of learning and adapting in a pragmatic manner. Fourth, it means devoting resources to the activity. Benchmarking cannot be done without some investment, but this does not necessarily mean allocating exclusive responsibility to a set of highly paid managers. In fact, there can be advantages in organizing staff at all levels to investigate and collate information from benchmarking targets.

Critical commentary

It can be argued that there is a fundamental flaw in the whole concept of benchmarking. Operations that rely on others to stimulate their creativity, especially those that are in search of 'best practice', are always limiting themselves to currently accepted methods of operating or currently accepted limits to performance. In other words, benchmarking leads companies only as far as others have gone. 'Best practice' is not 'best' in the sense that it cannot be bettered; it is only 'best' in the sense that it is the best one can currently find. Indeed, accepting what is currently defined as 'best' may prevent operations from ever making the radical breakthrough or improvement that takes the concept of 'best' to a new and fundamentally improved level. This argument is closely related to the concept of breakthrough improvement discussed later in this chapter. Furthermore, methods or performance levels that are appropriate in one operation may not be in another. Because one operation has a set of successful practices in the way it manages its processes does not mean that adopting those same practices in another context will prove equally successful. It is possible that subtle differences in the resources within a process (such as staff skills or technical capabilities) or the strategic context of an operation (for example, the relative priorities of performance objectives) will be sufficiently different to make the adoption of seemingly successful practices inappropriate.

Improvement as learning

Note that many of the abilities and behaviours described in Table 16.1 are directly or indirectly related to learning in some way. This is not surprising given that operations improvement implies some kind of intervention or change to the operation, and change will be evaluated in terms of whatever improvement occurs. This evaluation adds to our knowledge of how the operation really works, which in turn increases the chances that future interventions will also result in improvement. This idea of an improvement cycle was discussed earlier. What is important is to realize that it is a learning process, and it is crucial that improvement is organized so that it encourages, facilitates and exploits the learning that occurs during improvement. This requires us to recognize that there is a distinction between single- and double-loop learning.[19]

> ✳ **Operations principle**
> There can be no intentional improvement without learning.

Single- and double-loop learning

Single-loop learning occurs when there is a repetitive and predictable link between cause and effect. This is similar to the idea of 'routine control' that we discussed in Chapter 10. Some kind of output characteristic from a process is measured and associated with the input conditions that caused it. Every time an operational error or problem is detected, it is corrected and, in doing so, more is learned about the process. However, this happens without questioning or altering the underlying values and objectives of the process, which may, over

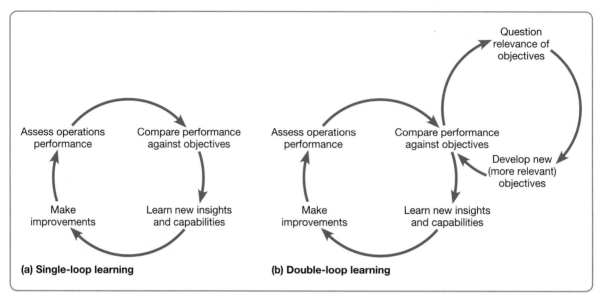

Figure 16.14 Single- and double-loop learning

time, create an unquestioning inertia that prevents its adapting to a changing environment. Double-loop learning, by contrast, questions the fundamental objectives, service or even the underlying culture of the operation. This kind of learning implies an ability to challenge existing operating assumptions in a fundamental way. It seeks to reframe competitive assumptions and remain open to any changes in the competitive environment. But being receptive to new opportunities sometimes requires abandoning existing operating routines, which may be difficult to achieve in practice, especially as many operations reward experience and past achievement (rather than potential) at both an individual and group level. Figure 16.14 illustrates single- and double-loop learning.

OPERATIONS IN PRACTICE   Learning from Formula One[20]

As driving jobs go, there could be no bigger difference than between Formula One racing drivers weaving their way through some of the fastest competitors in the world and a supermarket truck driver quietly delivering beans, beer and bacon to distribution centres and stores. But they have more in common than one would suspect. Both Formula One and truck drivers want to save fuel, either to reduce pit stops (Formula One) or keep delivery costs down (Heavy Goods Vehicles). And although grocery deliveries in the suburbs do not seem as thrilling as racing round the track at Monza, the computer-assisted simulation programs

Source: Shutterstock.com: Natursports

developed by the Williams Formula One team are being deployed to help Sainsbury's (a UK supermarket group) drivers develop the driving skills that could potentially cut its fuel bill by up to 30 per cent. The simulator technology, which allows realistic advanced training to be conducted in a controlled environment, was developed originally for the advanced training of Formula One drivers and was developed and extended at the Williams Technology Centre in Qatar. It can now train drivers to a high level of professional driving skills and road safety applications.

Williams F1's Chief Executive, Alex Burns, commented, 'Formula One is well recognised as an excellent technology incubator. It makes perfect sense to embrace some of the new and emerging technologies that the Williams Technology Centre in Qatar is developing from this incubator to help Sainsbury's mission to reduce its energy consumption and enhance the skills and safety of those supporting its crucial logistics operation.' Sainsbury's energy-related improvement programmes tackle energy supply (for example, wind, solar and geothermal energy) as well as energy consumption (for example, switching to LED lighting, CO_2 refrigeration, etc.). Learning from Formula One will help Sainsbury's to improve further in the field of energy efficiency. Roger Burnley, Sainsbury's Retail and Logistics Director, said, 'We are committed to reducing our environmental impact and as a result, we are often at the very forefront of technological innovation. By partnering with Williams F1, we can take advantage of some of the world's most advanced automotive technology, making our operations even more efficient and taking us a step closer to meeting our CO_2 reduction targets.'

Some key implementation issues?

Not all of the improvement initiatives which are launched by organizations, often with high expectations, will go on to fulfil their potential of having a major impact on performance. Estimates of the failure of improvement efforts range from 50 to 80 per cent. Yet, although there are many examples of improvement efforts that have failed, there are also examples of successful implementations. So why do some improvement efforts disappoint? Some reasons we have already identified – an organizational culture that discourages any change, for example. But there are some more tangible causes of implementation failure.

Top-management support

The importance of top-management support goes far beyond the allocation of resources to the programme: it sets the priorities for the whole organization. If the organization's senior managers do not understand and show commitment to the programme, it is only understandable that others will ask why they should do so. Usually this is taken to mean that top management must:

- understand and believe in the benefits of the improvement approach;
- communicate the principles and techniques of improvement;
- participate in the improvement process;
- formulate and maintain a clear 'improvement strategy'.

This last point is particularly important. Without thinking through the overall purpose and long-term goals of improvement it is difficult for any organization to know where it is going. An improvement strategy is necessary to provide the goals and guidelines which help to keep improvement efforts in line with strategic aims. Specifically, the improvement strategy should have something to say about the competitive priorities of the organization, the roles and improvement responsibilities of all parts of the organization, the resources available for improvement, and its overall improvement philosophy.

Senior managers may not fully understanding the improvement approach

Each of the improvement approaches that we described earlier in this chapter have been the subject of several books that describe them in great detail. There is no shortage of advice from consultants and academics as to how they should be used. Yet it is not difficult to find examples of where senior management have used one or more of these approaches without fully understanding them. The details of Six Sigma or lean, for example, are not simply technical matters. They are fundamental to how appropriate the approach could be in different contexts. Not every approach fits every set of circumstances. So understanding in detail what each approach means must be the first step in deciding whether it is appropriate.

Avoid excessive 'hype'

Operations improvement has, to some extent, become a fashion industry with new ideas and concepts continually being introduced as offering a novel way to improve business performance. There is nothing intrinsically wrong with this. Fashion stimulates and refreshes, through introducing novel ideas. Without it, things would stagnate. The problem lies not with new improvement ideas, but rather with some managers becoming a victim of the process, where some new idea will entirely displace whatever went before. Most new ideas have something to say, but jumping from one fad to another will not only generate a backlash against any new idea, but also destroy the ability to accumulate the experience that comes from experimenting with each one. Avoiding becoming an improvement fashion victim is not easy.

SUMMARY ANSWERS TO KEY QUESTIONS

❯ Why is improvement so important in operations management?

- Improvement is now seen as the prime responsibility of operations management. Furthermore, all operations management activities are really concerned with improvement in the long term. Also, companies in many industries are having to improve simply to retain their position relative to their competitors. This is sometimes called the 'Red Queen' effect.
- A common distinction is between radical or breakthrough improvement, on the one hand, and continuous or incremental improvement, on the other.
- This distinction is closely associated with the distinction between the exploitation of existing capabilities versus the exploration of new ones. The ability to do both is called 'organizational ambiguity'.

❯ What are the key elements of operations improvement?

- There are many 'elements' that are the building blocks of improvement approaches. The ones described in this chapter are:
  - improvement cycles;
  - a process perspective;
  - end-to-end processes;
  - radical change;
  - evidence-based problem solving;
  - customer centricity;
  - systems and procedures;
  - reduce process variation;
  - synchronized flow;
  - emphasize education/training;
  - perfection is the goal;
  - waste identification;
  - include everybody;
  - develop internal customer–supplier relationships.

> ### What are the broad approaches to improvement?

- What we have called 'the broad approaches to improvement' are relatively coherent collections of some of the 'elements' of improvement. The four most common are total quality management (TQM), lean, business process re-engineering (BPR) and Six Sigma.

- Total quality management was one of the earliest management 'fashions' and has suffered from a backlash, but the general precepts and principles of TQM are still influential.

- Lean was seen initially as an approach to be used exclusively in manufacturing, but has become seen as an approach that can be applied in service operations. Also, lean, when first introduced, was radical and counter-intuitive.

- BPR is a typical example of the radical approach to improvement. It attempts to redesign operations along customer-focused processes rather than on the traditional functional basis.

- Six Sigma is: 'A disciplined methodology of defining, measuring, analysing, improving, and controlling the quality in every one of the company's products, processes, and transactions – with the ultimate goal of virtually eliminating all defects.'

- There are differences between these improvement approaches. Each includes a different set of elements and therefore a different emphasis. They can be positioned on two dimensions. The first is whether the approaches emphasize a gradual, continuous approach to change or a more radical 'breakthrough' change. The second is whether the approach emphasizes *what* changes should be made or *how* changes should be made.

> ### What techniques can be used for improvement?

- Many of the techniques described throughout this book could be considered improvement techniques, for example statistical process control (SPC).

- Techniques often seen as 'improvement techniques' include: scatter diagrams, flow charts, cause–effect diagrams, Pareto diagrams, and why–why analysis.

> ### How can the improvement process be managed?

- Improvement does not just happen by itself. It needs organizing, information must be gathered so that improvement is treating the most appropriate issues, responsibility for looking after the improvement effort must be allocated, and resources must be allocated. It must also be linked to the organization's overall strategy.

- The process of benchmarking is often used as a means of obtaining competitor performance standards.

- An organization's ability to improve its operations performance depends to a large extent on its 'culture', that is 'the pattern of shared basic assumptions...that have worked well enough to be considered valid'. A receptive organizational culture that encourages a constant search for improved ways to do things can encourage improvement.

- According to Bessant and Caffyn, there are specific abilities, behaviours and actions which need to be consciously developed if improvement is to sustain over the long term.

- Many of the abilities and behaviours related to an improvement culture relate to learning in some way. This involves two types of learning: single- and double-loop learning.

- Improvement efforts often fail (estimates range from 50 to 80 per cent of programmes failing). Included in the reasons for this are the following:
  - Top-management support may be lacking.
  - Senior managers may not fully understanding the improvement approach.
  - The improvement may be 'hyped up' excessively, leading to unrealistic (and therefore unrealized) expectations.

By Professors Robert Johnston (Warwick Business School), Chai Kah Hin and Jochen Wirtz (National University of Singapore) and Christopher Lovelock (Yale University)

The National Library Board (NLB) in Singapore oversees the management of the national, reference, regional, community and children's libraries, as well as over 30 libraries belonging to government agencies, schools and private institutions. Over the last 15 years the NLB has completely changed the nature of libraries in Singapore and its work has been used as a blueprint for many other libraries across the world. Yet it was not always like this. In 1995 libraries in Singapore were traditional, quiet places full of old books where you went to study or borrow books if you could not afford to buy them. There were long queues to have books stamped or returned and the staff seemed unhelpful and unfriendly. But today, things are very different. There are cafés in libraries to encourage people to come in, browse and sit down with a book, and libraries in community centres (putting libraries where the people are). The NLB has developed specialist libraries aimed at children, and libraries in shopping malls aimed at attracting busy 18–35 year olds into the library while they are shopping. There are libraries dedicated to teenagers, one of the most difficult groups to entice into the library. These have even been designed by the teenagers themselves so they include drinks machines, cushions and music systems. The library also hosts a wide range of events from mother and baby reading sessions to rock concerts to encourage a wide range of people into the library.

'We started this journey back in 1995 when Dr Christopher Chia was appointed as Chief Executive. Looking back, we were a very traditional public service. Our customers used words like "cold" and "unfriendly", though, in fairness, our staff were working under great pressure to deal with the long queues for books and to answer enquiries on library materials posed by our customers. Christopher Chia and his team made a study of the problems, undertook surveys and ran focus groups. They then began to address the challenges with vision and imagination through the application of the project management methodology and the innovative use of technology. Staff involvement and contribution was key to the success of the transformation. We knew where we wanted to go, and were committed to the cause.' (Ms Ngian Lek Choh, the Deputy Chief Executive and Director of the National Library)

Underpinning many of the changes was the NLB's innovative use of technology. It was the first public library in the world to prototype radio frequency

Source: Shutterstock.com: VectorLifestylepic

identification (RFID) to create its Electronic Library Management System (ELiMS). RFID is an electronic system for automatically identifying items. It uses RFID tags, or transponders, which are contained in smart labels consisting of a silicon chip and coiled antenna. They receive and respond to radio frequency queries from an RFID transceiver, which enables the remote and automatic retrieval, storing and sharing of information (see Chapter 8). RFID tags are installed in its 10 million books making it one of the largest users of the technology in the world. Customers spend very little time queuing, with book issuing and returns automated. Indeed books can be returned to any of the NLB's 24-hour book drops (which look a bit like ATM machines) where RFID enables not only fast and easy returns, but also fast and easy sorting. The NLB has also launched a mobile service via SMS (text messaging). This allows users to manage their library accounts anytime and anywhere through their mobile phones. They can check their loan records, renew their books, pay library payments, and get reminder alerts to return library items before the due date.

Improving its services meant fully understanding the library's customers. Customers were studied using surveys and focus groups to understand how the library added value for customers, how customers could be segmented, the main learning and reading motivators, and people's general reading habits. And feedback from customers, both formal and informal, is an important source of design innovation – as are ideas from staff. Everyone in the NLB, from the chief executive to the library assistant, is expected to contribute to work improvement and innovations. So much so that innovation has become an integral part of the NLB's culture leading to a steady stream of both large and small innovations. In order to facilitate this, the chief executive holds 'express-o' sessions in discussions with staff. He also has a strategy called 'ask stupid questions' (ASQ) which encourages staff to challenge what is normally accepted. Dr Varaprasad, the Chief Executive, commented, 'In my view there are no stupid questions, there are only stupid answers! What we try to do is engage the staff by letting them feel they can ask stupid questions and that they are entitled to an answer.'

The NLB also makes use of small improvement teams to brainstorm ideas and test them out with colleagues from other libraries across the island. Good ideas attract financial rewards from S$5 to 1,000. One such idea was using a simple system of coloured bands on the spines of books (representing the identification number of each book) which make it much easier to shelve the books in the right places and also spot books that have been misplaced by customers. Staff are also encouraged to travel overseas to visit other libraries to learn about how they use their space, their programmes and collections, attend and speak at conventions and also visit very different organizations to get new ideas. The automatic book return for example was an idea borrowed and modified from the Mass Rapid Transport stations in Hong Kong where, with the flash of a card, the user is identified and given access across the system. The NLB applied a similar line of thought for seamless check-in and check-out of books and a return-anywhere concept. The NLB harvests ideas from many different industries including logistics, manufacturing, IT and supermarkets. However, some elements of the NLB's improvement process have changed. In the early days its approach to implementing ideas was informal and intuitive. It is now much more structured. Now, each good idea that comes forward is managed as a project, starting with a 'proof of concept' stage which involves selling the idea to management and checking with a range of people that the idea seems feasible. Then the services or processes are re-engineered, often involving customers or users. The new concepts are then prototyped and piloted allowing managers to gather customer feedback to enable them to assess, refine and, if appropriate, develop them for other sites.

QUESTIONS

1 How would the culture of the NLB have changed in order for it to make such improvements?

2 Where did the ideas for improvement originate? And how did the NLB encourage improvement ideas?

3 Why, do you think, has the improvement process become more systematic over the years?

4 What could be the biggest challenges to the NLB's improvement activities in the future?

PROBLEMS AND APPLICATIONS

1 Sophie was sick of her daily commute. 'Why', she thought, 'should I have to spend so much time in a morning stuck in traffic listening to some babbling halfwit on the radio? We can work flexi-time after all. Perhaps I should leave the apartment at some other time?' So resolved, Sophie deliberately varied her time of departure from her usual 8.30. Also, being an organized soul, she recorded her time of departure each day and her journey time. Her records are shown in Table 16.2.

(a) Draw a scatter diagram that will help Sophie decide on the best time to leave her apartment.

(b) How much time per (five-day) week should she expect to be saved from having to listen to a babbling halfwit?

Table 16.2 Sophie's journey times (in minutes)

Day	Leaving time	Journey time	Day	Leaving time	Journey time	Day	Leaving time	Journey time
1	7.15	19	6	8.45	40	11	8.35	46
2	8.15	40	7	8.55	32	12	8.40	45
3	7.30	25	8	7.55	31	13	8.20	47
4	7.20	19	9	7.40	22	14	8.00	34
5	8.40	46	10	8.30	49	15	7.45	27

2 The Printospeed laser printer company was proud of its reputation for high-quality products and services. Because of this it was especially concerned with the problems that it was having with its customers returning defective toner cartridges. About 2,000 of these were being returned every month. Its European service team suspected that not all the returns were actually the result of a faulty product, which is why the team decided to investigate the problem. Three major problems were identified. First, some users were not as familiar as they should have been with the correct method of loading the cartridge into the printer, or in being able to solve their own minor printing problems. Second, some of the dealers were also unaware of how to sort out minor problems. Third, there was clearly some abuse of Printospeed's 'no-questions-asked' returns policy. Empty toner cartridges were being sent to unauthorized refilling companies who would sell the refilled cartridges at reduced prices. Some cartridges were being refilled up to five times and were understandably wearing out. Furthermore, the toner in the refilled cartridges was often not up to Printospeed's high-quality standards.

(a) Draw a cause–effect diagram that includes both the possible causes mentioned, and any other possible causes that you think worth investigating.

(b) What is your opinion of the alleged abuse of the 'no-questions-asked' returns policy adopted by Printospeed?

3 Think back to the last product or service failure that caused you some degree of inconvenience. Draw a cause–effect diagram that identifies all the main causes of why the failure could have occurred. Try and identify the frequency with which such causes happen. This could be done by talking with the staff of the operation that provided the service. Draw a Pareto diagram that indicates the relatively frequency of each cause of failure. Suggest ways in which the operation could reduce the chances of failure.

4 Ruggo Carpets encourages continuous improvement based around the 'drive for customer focus'. The company's total quality process has graduated from 'total customer satisfaction' to 'total customer delight', to its present form – 'bridging the gap', which is effectively a 'where we are' and 'where we should be' yardstick for the company. Developments in the warehouse are typical. The supervisor has been replaced by a group leader who acts as a 'facilitator', working within the team. They are also trained to carry out their own jobs plus five others. Fixed hours are a thing of the past, as is overtime. At peak times the team works the required hours to despatch orders, and at off-peak times, when work is completed, the team can leave. Despatch labels and address labels are computer generated and the carpets are bar coded to reduce human error. Each process within the warehouse has been analysed and re-engineered. What is implied by the progression of the company's three initiatives from 'total customer satisfaction' to 'total customer delight' to 'bridging the gap'?

SELECTED FURTHER READING

Ahlstrom, J. (2015) *How to Succeed with Continuous Improvement: A Primer for Becoming the Best in the World*, McGraw-Hill Professional, New York.

This is very much a practical guide. Slightly evangelical, but it gets the message over.

George, M.L., Rowlands, D. and Kastle, B. (2003) *What Is Lean Six Sigma?*, McGraw-Hill, New York.

Very much a quick introduction on what Lean Six Sigma is and how to use it.

Goldratt, E.M. and Cox, J. (2004) *The Goal: A Process of Ongoing Improvement*, Gower, Aldershot.

Updated version of a classic.

Hendry, L. and Nonthaleerak, P. (2004) Six sigma: literature review and key future research areas, Lancaster University Management School, Working Paper 2005/044.

Good overview of the literature on Six Sigma.

Hindo, B. (2007) At 3M, a struggle between efficiency and creativity: how CEO George Buckley is managing the yin and yang of discipline and imagination, *Business Week*, **11 June.**

Readable article from the popular business press.

Pande, P.S., Neuman, R.P. and Cavanagh, R. (2002) *Six Sigma Way Team Field Book: An implementation guide for project improvement teams*, **McGraw-Hill, New York.**

Obviously based on the Six Sigma principle and related to the book by the same author team recommended in Chapter 17, this is an unashamedly practical guide to the Six Sigma approach.

Xingxing Zu, Fredendall, L.D. and Douglas, T.J. (2008) The evolving theory of quality management: the role of Six Sigma, *Journal of Operations Management*, **vol. 26, 630–650.**

As it says…

Quality management

INTRODUCTION

Quality management has always been an important part of operations management, but its position and role within the subject have changed. At one time it was seen largely as an essential, but 'routine,' activity that prevented errors having an impact on customers (and would have been located unambiguously in the 'Deliver' section of this book). And that function is still there. But increasingly quality management is viewed as also having a part to play in how operations improve. Quality management can contribute to improvement by making the changes to operations processes that lead to better outcomes for customers. In fact, in most organizations, quality management is one of the main drivers of improvement. It is also the only one of the five 'operations performance objectives' to have its own dedicated chapter in this book. Partly this is because of this central role of 'quality' in improvement. Some operations managers believe that, in the long run, quality is the most important single factor affecting an organization's performance relative to its competitors. But it is also because, in many organizations, a separate function is devoted exclusively to the management of quality. Figure 17.1 shows where quality management fits into the model of operations activities.

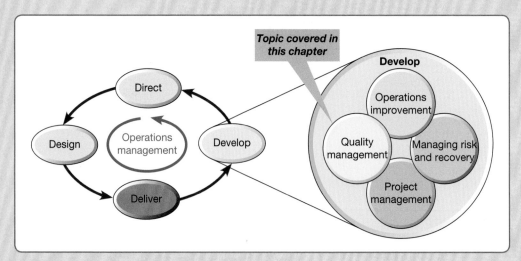

Figure 17.1 This chapter examines quality management

WHAT IS QUALITY AND WHY IS IT SO IMPORTANT?

It is worth revisiting some of the arguments which were presented in Chapter 2 regarding the benefits of high levels of quality. It will help to explain why quality is seen as being so important by most operations. Figure 17.2 illustrates the various ways in which quality improvements can affect other aspects of operations performance. Revenues can be increased by better sales and enhanced prices in the market. At the same time, costs can be brought down by improved efficiencies, productivity and the use of capital. So, a key task of the operations function must be to ensure that it provides quality goods and services, to both its internal and external customers.

The operation's view of quality

There are many definitions of quality. Here we define it as *consistent conformance to customers' expectations.*

The use of the word 'conformance' implies that there is a need to meet a clear specification. Ensuring a service or product conforms to specification is a key operations task. 'Consistent' implies that conformance to specification is not an ad hoc event but that the service or product meets the specification because quality requirements are used to design and run the processes that produce services or products. The use of 'customers' expectations' recognizes that the service or product must take the views of customers into account, which may be influenced by price. Also note the use of the word 'expectations' in this definition, rather than needs or wants.

Customers' view of quality

Past experiences, individual knowledge and history will all shape customers' expectations. Furthermore, customers may each *perceive* a service or product in different ways. One person may perceive a long-haul flight as an exciting part of a holiday; the person on the next seat

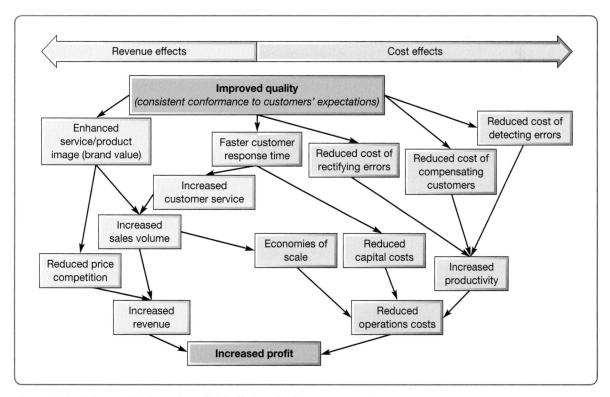

Figure 17.2 Higher quality has a beneficial effect on both revenues and costs

＊ **Operations principle**

Quality is multi-faceted; its individual elements differ for different operations.

may see it as a necessary chore to get to a business meeting. So quality needs to be understood from a customer's point of view because, to the customer, the quality of a particular service or product is whatever he or she perceives it to be. If the passengers on a skiing charter flight perceive it to be of good quality, despite long queues at check-in or cramped seating and poor meals, then the flight really is of good perceived quality.[1] Also customers may be unable to judge the 'technical' specification of the service or product and so use surrogate measures as a basis for their perception of quality. For example, a customer may find it difficult to judge the technical quality of dental treatment, except insofar as it does not give any more trouble. The customer may therefore perceive quality in terms of the demeanour of the dentist and technician and how he or she was treated.

OPERATIONS IN PRACTICE

Quality at three different operations: TNT Express, Victorinox and Four Seasons

Delivering customer service at TNT[2]

TNT is a global package delivery service, operating in over 200 countries and the market leader in business-to-business (B2B) express delivery services. Its 80,000 employees deliver around 150 million items per year. Headquartered in the Netherlands, it operates air and road networks around the world. And it is a highly competitive business, so service quality is not an option; it is a necessity if you are going to survive. Customers tend to be less than understanding if their package is late or, worse, does not arrive at all. Setting up a global network of hubs and routes takes immense amounts of capital, and because global networks are expensive to maintain, demand has to be kept high just to break even. In addition, increasingly society expects such companies to reduce their carbon emissions. So it is a 'no brainer': delivery operations must continually be improving levels of service and deploying resources in a manner as close to optimum as possible.

TNT knows that its reputation is very much influenced by how its customers perceive its services. High-quality service retains existing customers and brings new ones. Poor-quality service loses once-loyal customers and puts off potential new ones. But exactly how do customers judge TNT's quality? An obvious aspect of quality of service is on-time delivery. TNT aims to deliver all items to its customers 'as promised' through its door-to-door integrated air and road network. It also keeps its customers informed through its sophisticated online tracking technology that allows customers to track where their packages are at any time. Customized service can also be important for some customers. TNT can provide special or adapted services, for example for unusual or fragile items. TNT's motto of 'Sure we can' emphasizes what it sees as its 'can-do' attitude and positive mindset in dealing with customers' requirements. But high-quality, dependable and flexible delivery is no use if customers cannot access it easily. So

designing services that are easy to use and access as well as educating customers so they know how to get the best from the service are also important. TNT's own research showed that customer satisfaction depends not just on the process of delivering the service, but also on how the service is carried out. This resulted in TNT focusing on the quality of 'the customer experience' by developing a two-year programme to implement and communicate its 'Customer Promise' to both employees and customers. This tries to make sure that a high-quality experience starts from customers' initial contact through to after-sales care.

Victorinox and the Swiss Army Knife[3]

The famous Swiss Army Knife is made by the Victorinox Company in its factory in the Swiss town of Ibach. The company has numerous letters from its customers testifying to their product's quality and durability. For example, '*I was installing a new piece of equipment in a sewage treatment plant...The knife slipped out of my hand and fell into the aeration tank...that is extremely corrosive to metals. Four years later, I received a small parcel with a note from the supervisor of the plant. They had emptied the aeration tank and found my knife...that was in astonishingly good condition.. I can assure you that very few products could have survived treatment like this, the components would have dissolved or simply disappeared.'*

Today, the Victorinox factory assembles 27,000 knives a day (plus nearly 100,000 other items). More than 450 steps are required in their manufacture. But a major threat to sales that has been growing is the appearance on the market of fake 'Swiss Army' knives, made mostly in China. Many of them look similar to the original; they even have the familiar Swiss cross on the handle. So what is the company's defence against these fakes? *'Quality'*, says CEO Carl Elsener. *'We have exhausted all legal means for the brand protection of our popular products. Our best means of protection is quality which remains unsurpassed and speaks louder than words.'* It is the 'Victorinox quality control system' that is at the heart of this defence.

First, receiving inspection ensures that incoming materials conform to quality specifications. This includes precisely measuring all aspects of incoming quality. The Victorinox laboratory conforms to the latest standard of engineering and guarantees that only steel and plastic that comply with its rigorous quality standards are used in the manufacturing of the products. The steel consists of special alloys, which possess those material characteristics that are most important for the respective field of application. All alloys are tested for composition by means of spectrum analysis, which uses an electric arc on the material under protective gas, so that parts of its surface melt and evaporate. From the spectrometric analysis of the arc, the alloy composition of the various metals can be calculated. Metallurgical inspection is also used by polishing samples, casting them in plastic and etching with an acid. This allows faults in materials to be easily detected. The laboratory also has an 'edge retention test' using special equipment to test the ability of material to retain its edge during a series of cutting tests. During the production of the knives, process control is employed at all stages of the production process and is the responsibility of the company's employees, who use it to maintain, implement and improve the quality of the products. They are also responsible for following the company's quality procedures and for continuous, measurable improvement. At the end of the production process, the 'Final Inspection Department' employs 50–60 people who are responsible for ensuring that all products conform to requirements. Any non-conforming products are isolated and identified. Non-conforming parts are repaired or replaced at the repair department.

Four Seasons Canary Wharf[4]

The first Four Seasons Hotel opened over 50 years ago and has grown to 100 properties all over the world. Famed for its quality of service, the hotel group has won countless awards for the quality of its service. From its

inception the group has had the same guiding principle: 'to make the quality of our service our competitive advantage'. The company has what it calls its golden rule: 'Do to others (guests and staff) as you would wish others to do to you.' It is a simple rule, but it guides the whole organization's approach to quality. *'Quality service is our distinguishing edge and the company continues to evolve in that direction. We are always looking for better, more creative and innovative ways of serving our guests'*, says Michael Purtill, the General Manager of the Four Seasons Hotel Canary Wharf in London. *'We have recently refined all of our operating standards across the company enabling us to further enhance the personalised, intuitive service that all our guests receive. All employees are empowered to use their creativity and judgement in delivering exceptional service and making their own decisions to enhance our guests' stay. For example, one morning an employee noticed that a guest had a flat tyre on their car and decided on his own accord to change it for them, which was very much appreciated by the guest.'*

'The golden rule means that we treat our employees with dignity, respect and appreciation. This approach encourages them to be equally sensitive to our guests' needs and offer sincere and genuine service that exceeds expectations. Just recently one of our employees accompanied a guest to the hospital and stayed there with him for the entire afternoon. He wanted to ensure that the guest wasn't alone and was given the medical attention he needed. The following day that same employee took the initiative to return to the hospital (even though it was his day off) to visit and made sure that that guest's family in America was kept informed about his progress. We ensure that we have an on-going focus on recognising these successes and publicly praise and celebrate all individuals who deliver these warm, spontaneous, thoughtful touches.

'At Four Seasons we believe that our greatest asset and strength are our people. We pay a great deal of attention to selecting the right people with an attitude that takes great pride in delivering exceptional service. We know that motivated and happy employees are essential to our service culture and are committed to developing our employees to their highest potential. Our extensive training programmes and career development plans are designed with care and attention to support the individual needs of our employees as well as operational and business demands. In conjunction to traditional classroom based learning, we offer tailor-made web-based learning featuring exceptional quality courses for all levels of employee. Career wise, the sky is the limit and our goal is to build lifelong, international careers with Four Seasons.

Our objective is to exceed guest expectations and feedback from our guests and our employees is an invaluable barometer of our performance. We have created an in-house database that is used to record all guest feedback (whether positive or negative). We also use an on line guest survey and guest comment cards which are all personally responded to and analysed to identify any potential service gaps.

We continue to focus on delivering individual personalised experiences and our Guest History database remains vital in helping us to achieve this. All preferences and specific comments about service experience are logged on the database. Every comment and every preference is discussed and planned for, for every guest, for every visit. It is our culture that sets Four Seasons apart; the drive to deliver the best service in the industry that keeps their guests returning again and again.'

Reconciling the operation's and the customer's views of quality

The operation's view of quality is concerned with trying to meet customer expectations. The customer's view of quality is what he or she *perceives* the service or product to be. To create a unified view, quality can be defined as the degree of fit between customers' expectations and customer perception of the service or product.[5] Using this idea allows us to see the customers' view of quality of (and, therefore, satisfaction with) the service or product as the result of comparing their expectations of the service or product with their perception of how it performs. If the service or product experience was better than expected then the customer is satisfied and quality is perceived to be high. If the service or product was less than his or her expectations then quality is low and the customer may be dissatisfied. If the service or product matches expectations then the perceived quality of the service or product is seen to be acceptable. These relationships are summarized in Figure 17.3.

Both customers' expectations and perceptions are influenced by a number of factors, some of which cannot be controlled by the operation and some of which, to a certain extent, can be managed. Figure 17.4 shows some of the factors that will influence the gap between expectations and perceptions. This model of customer-perceived quality can help us understand how operations can manage quality and identify some of the problems in so doing. The bottom part of the diagram represents the operation's 'domain' of quality and the top part the customer's 'domain'. These two domains meet in the actual service or product, which is provided by the organization and experienced by the customer. Within the operation's domain, management are responsible for designing the service or product and providing a specification of the quality to which the service or product has to be created. Within the customer's domain, his or her expectations are shaped by such factors as previous experiences with the particular service or product, the marketing image provided by the organization and word-of-mouth information from other users. These expectations are internalized as a set of quality characteristics.

> ✳ **Operations principle**
>
> Perceived quality is governed by the magnitude and direction of the gap between customers' expectations and their perceptions of a product or service.

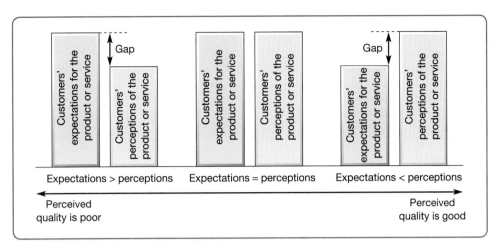

Figure 17.3 Perceived quality is governed by the magnitude and direction of the gap between customers' expectations and their perceptions of the service or product

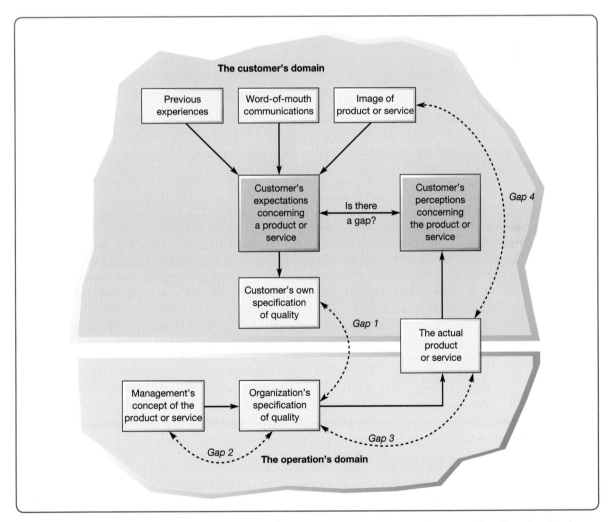

Figure 17.4 The customer's domain and the operations domain in determining the perceived quality, showing how the gap between customers' expectations and their perception of a service or product could be explained by one or more gaps elsewhere in the model

Source: Adapted from Parasuraman, A. et al. (1985) A conceptual model of service quality and implications for future research, *Journal of Marketing,* vol. 49, Fall.

Quality at Magic Moments

Magic Moments is a small, but successful wedding photography business. Its owner, Richard Webber, has seen plenty of changes over the last 20 years. *'In the past, my job involved taking a few photos during the wedding ceremony and then formal group shots outside. I was rarely at a wedding for more than two hours. Clients would select around 30 photos to go in a standard wedding album. It was important to get the photos right, because that was really the only thing I was judged on. Now it's different. I usually spend all day at a wedding, and sometimes late into the evening as well. This creates a very different dynamic with the wedding party, as you're almost like another guest. Whilst the bride and groom are still my primary concern, other guests at the wedding are also important. The challenge is to find the right balance between getting the best photos possible whilst being as discreet as possible. I could spend hours getting the perfect picture, but annoy everyone in the process. It's difficult, because clients judge you on both the technical quality of your work and the way you interact with everyone on the day. The product has changed too. Clients receive a CD or memory stick with around 500 photos taken during the day. Also I can give them a choice of 10 albums in different sizes, ranging from 30–100 photos. This year, I have started offering photo books which allow a much greater level of customization and have proved popular for younger couples. For the future, I'm considering offering albums with wedding items such as invitations, confetti, and menus; and individual paintings created from photographs. Obviously I would have to outsource the paintings. I'm also going to upgrade our website, so wedding guests can order photos and related products online. This will generate revenue and act as a good marketing tool. My anxiety is that advertising this additional service at the wedding will be seen as being too commercial, even if it's actually of benefit to guests.*

'One of the biggest problems for the business is the high level of demand in the summer months. Weekends in June, July and August are often booked up two years in advance. One option is to take on additional photographers during busy periods. However, the best ones are busy themselves. The concern is that the quality of the service I offer would deteriorate. A large part of the business is about how one relates to clients and that's hard to replicate. Having been to so many weddings, I often offer clients advice on various aspects of their wedding, such as locations, bands, caterers, and florists. However, with development, wedding planning is clearly an area that could be profitable to the business. Of course, another option is to move beyond weddings into other areas, such as school photos, birthdays, celebrations, or studio work.'*

How can quality problems be diagnosed?[6]

Figure 17.4 also shows how quality problems can be diagnosed. If the perceived quality gap is such that customers' perceptions of the service or product fail to match their expectations of it, then the reason (or reasons) must lie in other gaps elsewhere in the model as follows:

Gap 1: The customer's specification–operation's specification gap. Perceived quality could be poor because there may be a mismatch between the organization's own internal quality specification and the specification which is expected by the customer. For example, a car may be designed to need servicing every 10,000 kilometres but the customer may expect 15,000 kilometre service intervals.

Gap 2: The concept–specification gap. Perceived quality could be poor because there is a mismatch between the service or product concept (see Chapter 5) and the way the organization has specified quality internally. For example, the concept of a car might have been for an inexpensive, energy-efficient means of transportation, but the inclusion of a climate control system may have both added to its cost and made it less energy efficient.

Gap 3: The quality specification–actual quality gap. Perceived quality could be poor because there is a mismatch between actual quality and the internal quality specification (often called 'conformance to specification'). For example, the internal quality specification for a car may be that the gap between its doors and body, when closed, must not exceed 7 mm. However, because of inadequate equipment, the gap in reality is 9 mm.

Gap 4: The actual quality–communicated image gap. Perceived quality could be poor because there is a gap between the organization's external communications or market image and the actual quality delivered to the customer. This may be because the marketing function has set unachievable expectations, or operations are not capable of the level of quality expected by the customer. For example, an advertising campaign for an airline might show a cabin attendant offering to replace a customer's shirt on which food or drink has been spilt, whereas such a service may not in fact be available should this happen.

The sandcone theory

An endorsement of the importance of quality as a driver of improvement generally comes from what is known as the 'sandcone theory'.[7] It comes from the idea that there is a generic 'best' sequence of improvement. It is called the sandcone theory because the sand is analogous to management effort and resources. Building a stable sandcone needs a stable foundation of quality, claims the theory, upon which one can build layers of dependability, speed, flexibility and cost, *see* Figure 17.5. Building up improvement is thus a cumulative process, not a sequential one. Moving on to the second priority for improvement does not mean dropping the first, and so on. According to the sandcone theory, the first priority should be *quality*, since this is a precondition to all lasting improvement. Only when the operation has reached a minimally acceptable level in quality should it then tackle the next issue, that of internal *dependability*. Importantly though, moving on to include dependability in the improvement

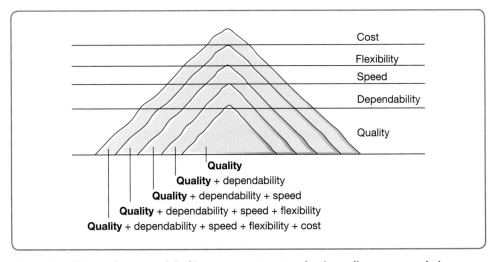

Figure 17.5 The sandcone model of improvement: cost reduction relies on a cumulative foundation of improvement in the other performance objectives

process will actually require further improvement in quality. Once a critical level of dependability is reached, enough to provide some stability to the operation, the next stage is to improve the *speed* of internal throughput. But again only while continuing to improve quality and dependability further. Soon it will become evident that the most effective way to improve speed is through improvements in response *flexibility*, which means changing things within the operation faster. Again, including flexibility in the improvement process should not divert attention from continuing to work further on quality, dependability and speed. Only then, according to the sandcone theory, should *cost* be tackled head on.

Conformance to specification

Conformance to specification means providing a service or producing a product to its design specification. It is usually seen as the most important contribution that operations management can make to the customer's perception of quality. We will examine how it can be achieved in the remainder of this chapter by describing quality management as six sequential steps.

WHAT STEPS LEAD TOWARDS CONFORMANCE TO SPECIFICATION?

Achieving conformance to specification requires the following steps:

Step 1 Define the quality characteristics of the service or product.

Step 2 Decide how to measure each quality characteristic.

Step 3 Set quality standards for each quality characteristic.

Step 4 Control quality against those standards.

Step 5 Find and correct causes of poor quality.

Step 6 Continue to make improvements.

Step 1 – Define the quality characteristics

Much of the 'quality' of a service or product will have been specified in its design and can be summarized by a set of quality characteristics. Table 17.1 shows a list of the quality characteristics which are generally useful. Also, many services have several elements, each with their own quality characteristics, and to understand the quality characteristics of the whole service it is necessary to understand the individual characteristics within and between each element of the whole service. For example, Figure 17.6 shows some of the quality characteristics for a web-based online grocery shopping service.

Step 2 – Decide how to measure each characteristic

These characteristics must be defined in such a way as to enable them to be measured and then controlled. This involves taking a very general quality characteristic such as 'appearance' and breaking it down, as far as one can, into its constituent elements. 'Appearance' is difficult to measure as such, but 'colour match', 'surface finish' and 'number of visible scratches' are all capable of being described in a more objective manner. They may even be quantifiable. Other quality characteristics pose more difficulty. The 'courtesy' of airline staff, for example, has no objective quantified measure. Yet operations with high customer contact, such as airlines, place a great deal of importance on the need to ensure courtesy in their staff. In cases like this, the operation will have to attempt to measure customer *perceptions* of courtesy.

Variables and attributes

The measures used by operations to describe quality characteristics are of two types: variables and attributes. Variable measures are those that can be measured on a continuously variable scale (for example, length, diameter, weight or time). Attributes are those which

Table 17.1 Quality characteristics for an automobile, bank loan and an air journey

Quality characteristic	Automobile (material transformation process)	Bank loan (information transformation process)	Air journey (customer transformation process)
Functionality – how well the service or product does its job	Speed, acceleration, fuel consumption, ride quality, road-holding, etc.	Interest rate, terms and conditions	Safety and duration of journey, onboard meals and drinks, car and hotel booking services
Appearance – the sensory characteristics of the service or product: its aesthetic appeal, look, feel, etc.	Aesthetics, shape, finish, door gaps, etc.	Aesthetics of information, website, etc.	Decor and cleanliness of aircraft, lounges and crew
Reliability – the consistency of the product's or service's performance over time	Mean time to failure	Keeping promises (implicit and explicit)	Keeping to the published flight times
Durability – the total useful life of the service or product	Useful life (with repair)	Stability of terms and conditions	Keeping up with trends in the industry
Recovery – the ease with which problems with the service or product can be resolved	Ease of repair	Resolution of service failures	Resolution of service failures
Contact – the nature of the person-to-person contact which might take place	Knowledge and courtesy of sales staff	Knowledge and courtesy of branch and call centre staff	Knowledge, courtesy and sensitivity of airline staff

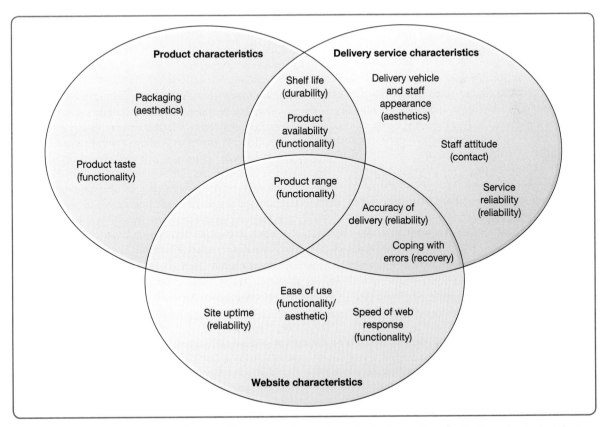

Figure 17.6 Quality characteristics for an online grocery shopping service including its website through which orders are placed, the products that are sold through the site and the delivery service that transports purchases to the customer

are assessed by judgment and are dichotomous, that is they have two states (for example, right or wrong, works or does not work, looks OK or not OK). Table 17.2 categorizes some of the measures which might be used for the quality characteristics of the automobile and the airline journey.

OPERATIONS IN PRACTICE

Ryanair reforms its view of service quality[8]

Ryanair is arguably the best-known budget airline in Europe, but it was not the first to focus its operations strategy on very low operating costs. The idea was born when Southwest Airlines in the USA organized its airline operations ruthlessly around providing a low-cost 'no-frills' service; it could both grow its customer base and do so profitably. In other ways these companies attempted to overcome trade-offs by focusing their operations. So Ryanair, like Southwest, focused on a standardized fleet of aircraft (keeping maintenance costs down), reducing aircraft turnaround time at the airports, keeping key processes (such as passenger handling) in-house while outsourcing more peripheral processes and selling direct to customers, often pioneering low-cost channels such as the Internet. To some extent the strategy included trading off quality of service for reduced costs. Complimentary in-flight services were kept to a minimum, secondary and sometimes less convenient airports were used, and one standard class of travel was offered. But some critics said that Ryanair went too far in its attitude towards service quality. The boss of the airline, Michael O'Leary, had a clear policy on customer service. 'Our customer service', he says, 'is about the most well defined in the world. We guarantee to give you the lowest air fare. You get a safe flight. You get a normally on-time flight. That's the package. We don't, and won't, give you anything more. Are we going to say sorry for our lack of customer service? Absolutely not. If a plane is cancelled, will we put you up in a hotel overnight? Absolutely not. If a plane is delayed, will we give you a voucher for a restaurant? Absolutely not.'

One attempt by Ryanair to cut costs prompted a backlash when it was accused of being 'puerile and childish' by the UK's Office of Fair Trading (OFT). John Fingleton, the OFT's boss, criticized the company for adding extra fees when customers use any but a MasterCard prepaid card to pay for flights, using, he said, a legal loophole to justify charging the extra fee. Mr Fingleton was reported as saying that 'Ryanair has this funny game where they have found some very low frequency payment mechanism and say: "Well because you can pay with that". It's almost like taunting consumers

Source: Alamy Images: Peter Treanor

and pointing out: "Oh well, we know this is completely outside the spirit of the law, but we think it's within the narrow letter of the law".' Stephen McNamara, Ryanair's Head of Communications, retorted that 'Ryanair is not for the overpaid John Fingletons of this world but for the everyday Joe Bloggs who opt for Ryanair's guaranteed lowest fares. What the OFT must realise is that passengers prefer Ryanair's model as it allows them to avoid costs, such as baggage charges, which are still included in the high fares of high cost, fuel surcharging...airlines.' But the backlash against Ryanair's policy continued, perhaps encouraged by the airline's reluctance to apologise, or sometimes even comment. Ryanair was even voted the worst of the UK's 100 biggest brands by readers of the consumer magazine Which?. Then, after a drop in its hitherto rapid profit growth and amid shareholder concern, Ryanair announced that it was to reform its 'abrupt culture, and try to eliminate things that unnecessarily annoy customers'. Included in these annoying practices were fines for small luggage size transgressions and an unpopular €70 fee for issuing boarding passes at the airport rather than printing them out at home (it was lowered to €10). Yet Ryanair insisted that such charges were not money-spinning schemes, but were designed to encourage operational efficiency that kept fares low – in fact fewer than 10 passengers a day had to pay for forgotten boarding passes.

Step 3 – Set quality standards

When operations managers have identified how any quality characteristic can be measured, they need a quality standard against which it can be checked; otherwise, they will not know whether it indicates good or bad performance. The quality standard is that level of quality which defines the boundary between acceptable and unacceptable. Such standards may well be constrained by operational factors such as the state of technology in the factory, and the cost limits of making the product. At the same time, however, they need to be appropriate to the expectations of customers. But quality judgements can be difficult. If one airline passenger out of every 10,000 complains about the food, is that good because 9,999 passengers out of 10,000 are satisfied? Or is it bad because, if one passenger complains, there must be others who, although dissatisfied, did not bother to complain? And if that level of complaint is similar to other airlines, should the airline regard its quality as satisfactory?

Step 4 – Control quality against those standards

After setting up appropriate standards the operation will then need to check that the products or services conform to those standards, doing things right, first time, every time. This involves three decisions:

1 Where in the operation should it check that it is conforming to standards?
2 Should it check every service or product or take a sample?
3 How should the checks be performed?

Where should the checks take place?

At the start of the process incoming resources may be inspected to make sure that they are to the correct specification. For example, a car manufacturer will check that components are of the right specification. A university will screen applicants to try to ensure that they have a high chance of getting through the course. During the process checks may take place

Table 17.2 **Variable and attribute measures for quality characteristics**

Quality characteristic	Automobile		Airline journey	
	Variable	Attribute	Variable	Attribute
Functionality	Acceleration and braking characteristics from test bed	Is the ride quality satisfactory?	Number of journeys which actually arrived at the destination (i.e. did not crash!)	Was the food acceptable?
Appearance	Number of blemishes visible on car	Is the colour to specification?	Number of seats not cleaned satisfactorily	Is the crew dressed smartly?
Reliability	Average time between faults	Is the reliability satisfactory?	Proportion of journeys which arrived on time	Were there any complaints?
Durability	Life of the car	Is the useful life as predicted?	Number of times service innovations lagged competitors'	Generally, is the airline updating its services in a satisfactory manner?
Recovery	Time from fault discovered to fault repaired	Is the serviceability of the car acceptable?	Proportion of service failures resolved satisfactorily	Do customers feel that staff deal satisfactorily with complaints?
Contact	Level of help provided by sales staff (1 to 5 scale)	Did customers feel well served (yes or no)?	The extent to which customers feel well treated by staff (1 to 5 scale)	Did customers feel that the staff were helpful (yes or no)?

before a particularly costly process, prior to 'difficult to check', immediately after a process with a high defective rate, before potential damage or distress might be caused, and so on. Checks may also take place after the process itself to ensure that customers do not experience non-conformance.

Check every product and service or take a sample?

While it might seem ideal to check every single service or product, a sample may be more practical for a number of reasons:

- It might be dangerous to inspect everything. A doctor, for example, checks just a small sample of blood rather than taking all of a patient's blood! The characteristics of this sample are taken to represent those of the rest of the patient's blood.
- Checking everything might destroy the product or interfere with the service. Not every light bulb is checked for how long it lasts – it would destroy every bulb. Waiters do not check that customers are enjoying the meal every 30 seconds.
- Checking everything can be time consuming and costly. It may not be feasible to check all output from a high-volume machine or to check the feelings of every bus commuter every day.

Also 100 per cent checking may not guarantee that all defects will be identified. Sometimes it is intrinsically difficult. For example, although a physician may undertake the correct testing procedure, he or she may not necessarily diagnose a (real) disease. Nor is it easy to notice everything. For example, try counting the number of 'e's on this page. Count them again and see if you get the same score.

Testing cars (close) to destruction[9]

Away from the public eye, at Millbrook Proving Ground, one of Europe's leading independent technology centres for the design, engineering, test and development of automotive and propulsion systems, the centre treats cars really badly. But all in a good cause. It is where auto manufacturers send their new vehicles to be tested, so that any glitches, from irritating rattles to more serious safety problems, can be exposed and corrected before the product reaches the market. The site, in Bedfordshire in the UK, is hidden away behind security fences and high embankments to discourage automobile paparazzi taking pictures of new models as they are put through their paces. Auto manufacturers also test their new models out on public roads, usually with stick-on panels to disguise them, but for repeatable, carefully measured conditions, a facility like the Millbrook Proving Ground is needed. The site has been called 'an automotive time machine', where a gleaming new model drives in, and about 20 weeks later it drives out (if it can), having been exposed to the equivalent of 10 years of severe weather and wear-and-tear comparable with being driven about 160,000 miles. During

Source: Alamy Images: David Burton

this time it will have been driven on straight and twisty roads, up and down hills, slowly and very fast, through saltwater baths (to accelerate rusting) and along gravel roads that damage its paintwork. But that is not all. It will be roasted at high temperatures, frozen down to arctic conditions, and drenched in water to expose any leaks. Also, it will be subjected to the infamous 'Belgian Pavé'. This is a mile-long track made from blocks of paving with rough sections and random depressions. The suspension takes such a beating that after five laps on the track vehicles need to be dowsed in a water trough to cool down their dampers. And during all this wrecking treatment engineers are periodically examining the vehicles for the signs of the wear or damage that allow carmakers to fine-tune their designs or manufacturing processes to avoid the failures which would be expensive and reputationally damaging if they occurred after product launch.

Type I and Type II errors

Although it reduces checking time, using a sample to make a decision about quality does have its own inherent problems. Like any decision activity, we may get the decision wrong. Take the example of a pedestrian waiting to cross a street. He or she has two main decisions: whether to continue waiting or to cross. If there is a satisfactory break in the traffic and the pedestrian crosses then a correct decision has been made. Similarly, if that person continues to wait because the traffic is too dense then he or she has again made a correct decision. There are two types of incorrect decisions or errors, however. One incorrect decision would be if the pedestrian decides to cross when there is not an adequate break in the traffic, resulting in an accident – this is referred to as a Type I error. Another incorrect decision would occur if the pedestrian decides not to cross even though there is an adequate gap in the traffic – this is called a Type II error. In crossing the road, therefore, there are four outcomes, which are summarized in Table 17.3.

Type I errors are those which occur when a decision was made to do something and the situation did not warrant it. Type II errors are those which occur when nothing was done, yet a decision to do something should have been taken as the situation did indeed warrant it. For example, if a school's inspector checks the work of a sample of 20 out of 1,000 pupils and all 20 of the pupils in the sample have failed, the inspector might draw the conclusion that all the pupils have failed. In fact, the sample just happened to contain 20 out of the 50 students who had failed the course. The inspector, by assuming a high fail rate, would be making a Type I error. Alternatively, if the inspector checked 20 pieces of work all of which were of a high standard, he or she might conclude that all the pupils' work was good despite having been given, or having chosen, the only pieces of good work in the whole school. This would be a Type II error. Although these situations are not likely, they are possible. Therefore any sampling procedure has to be aware of these risks.

How should the checks be performed?

In practice most operations will use some form of sampling to check the quality of their services or products. The most common approach for checking the quality of a sample service or product so as to make inferences about all the output from an operation is called statistical process control (SPC). SPC is concerned with sampling the process during the production of the goods or the delivery of service. Based on this sample, decisions are made as to whether the process is 'in control': that is, operating as it should be. A key aspect of SPC is that it looks at the variability in the performance of processes to check whether the process is operating as it should do (known as the process being 'in control'). In fact variability (or more specifically,

Table 17.3 **Type I and Type II errors for a pedestrian crossing the road**

Decision	Road conditions	
	Unsafe	Safe
Cross	Type I error	Correct decision
Wait	Correct decision	Type II error

reducing variability) is one of the most important objectives of quality improvement. For an illustration of this see the 'Operations in practice' case 'What a giveaway'. SPC is explained in detail in the supplement to this chapter.

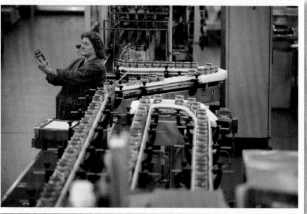

Source: Alamy Images: Mark Waugh

Go round any supermarket and look at all the products that are packaged, bottled, or otherwise 'filled' into their containers. Bottled drinks, detergent, bags of vegetables, cans of paint – they are all put in their containers in the manufacturing operations that produce them. And this filling or packing process is, in most countries, governed by strict government regulations. When a package claims to have a certain amount of product, customers have a right to expect that it really does include that amount; otherwise, they are paying for something that they are not getting. On any product sold that has an 'e' after its claimed weight printed on the container, the law states that the average weight must be greater than the declared weight on the container, with the average weight being determined by sampling. The problem is that the technology used to fill packages is not always totally consistent. There is always some degree of variation in the amount 'dispensed'. So, if packers or fillers want to conform to legal weights and measures stipulations on minimum fill levels, they must build in a margin of safety into filling levels in order to overcome the variation of the filling technology. This margin of safety is known as 'giveaway' or 'over-fill'. Experts in this technology estimate that this kind of routine over-filling can mean that 3 per cent

of an operation's output can literally be given away in this manner. This idea is illustrated in Figure 17.7.

Typical of the type of operation that has benefited from reducing the amount of variation in its processes, and therefore the amount of giveaway, is the food producer Quick Food Products. Founded in 1988 by immigrants from the Caribbean, it specializes in producing Jamaican patties with a range of meat, vegetable and fish fillings. Now it has expanded its range to include producing patties for the UK-based Nigerian community, as well as patties certified to carry the halal label,

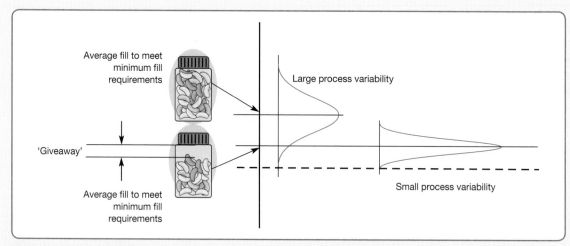

Figure 17.7 Average fill to meet minimum fill requirements has to be larger when process variability is large, resulting in 'giveaway'

indicating compliance with Muslim religious requirements. However, the firm had a problem – it needed extra capacity to manufacture and fill the new patties, but it was reluctant to spend the large sums that would be necessary to install new filling lines. To help it solve the problem, Quick Food Products called in operations improvement consultants. The consultants soon realized that there was too much variation in the weight of filling in the patties, and that reducing the variation in filling quantities could make significant savings – both in terms of reducing cost and in freeing up capacity. Maxine Chapman, one of the consultants, says, '*It wasn't a big technical problem, but more a question of agreeing best operating-practices, and then using them.*' And the improvement at Quick Foods is not a one-off: '*Time and again*', she says, '*significant improvements in the performance of filling and packing lines can be achieved by applying simple tools consistently, and through a better understanding of the parameters of the equipment that you're dealing with.*'

Step 5 and 6 – Find and correct causes of poor quality and continue to make improvements

The final two steps in our list of quality management activities are, in some ways, the most important yet also the most difficult. They also blend into the general area of operations improvement. The material that we covered in Chapter 16 has contributed to these two steps. Nevertheless, there is an aspect of quality management that has been particularly important in shaping how quality is improved and the improvement activity made self-sustaining. This is total quality management (TQM). The remainder of the main body of this chapter is devoted to TQM.

WHAT IS TOTAL QUALITY MANAGEMENT (TQM)?

TQM was one of the earliest of the current wave of management 'fashions'. Its peak of popularity was in the late 80s and early 90s. As such it has suffered from something of a backlash in recent years and there is little doubt that many companies adopted TQM in the simplistic belief that it would transform their operations performance overnight. Yet the general precepts and principles that constitute TQM are still the dominant mode of organizing operations improvement. The approach we take here is to stress the importance of the 'total' in total quality management and how it can guide the agenda for improvement.

TQM as an extension of previous practice

TQM can be viewed as a logical extension of the way in which quality-related practice has progressed (*see* Fig. 17.8). Originally quality was achieved by inspection – screening out defects before they were noticed by customers. The quality control (QC) concept developed a more systematic approach to not only detecting, but also treating quality problems. Quality assurance (QA) widened the responsibility for quality to include functions other than direct operations. It also made increasing use of more sophisticated statistical quality techniques. TQM included much of what went before but developed its own distinctive themes to make quality both more strategic and more widespread in the organization. We will use some of these themes to describe how TQM represents a clear shift from traditional approaches to quality.

What is TQM?

TQM is 'an effective system for integrating the quality development, quality maintenance and quality improvement efforts of the various groups in an organization so as to enable production and service at the most economical levels which allow for full customer satisfaction'.[11]

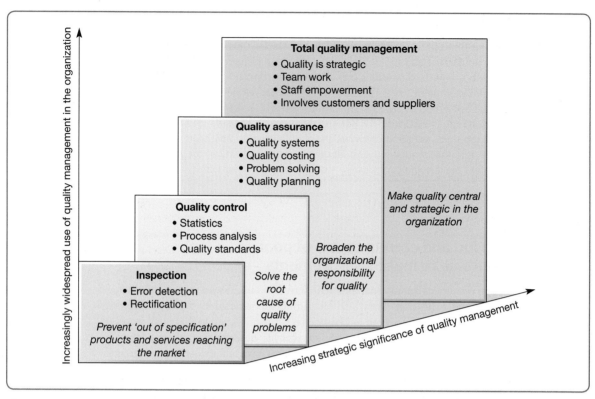

Figure 17.8 TQM as an extension of previous views of quality

However, it was the Japanese who first made the concept work on a wide scale and subsequently popularized the approach and the term 'TQM'. It was then developed further by several, so-called, 'quality gurus'. Each 'guru' stressed a different set of issues, from which emerged the TQM approach. It is best thought of as a philosophy of how to approach quality improvement. This philosophy, above everything, stresses the 'total' of TQM. It is an approach that puts quality at the heart of everything that is done by an operation and including all activities within an operation. This totality can be summarized by the way TQM lays particular stress on the following:

- meeting the needs and expectations of customers;
- covering all parts of the organization;
- including every person in the organization;
- examining all costs which are related to quality, especially failure costs and getting things 'right first time';
- developing the systems and procedures which support quality and improvement;
- developing a continuous process of improvement (this was treated in Chapter 16).

Not surprisingly, several researchers have tried to establish how much of a relationship there is between adopting TQM and the performance of the organization. One of the best-known studies[12] found that there was a positive relationship between the extent to which companies implement TQM and its overall performance. It found that TQM practices did indeed have a direct effect on operating performance but managers should implement TQM as a whole set of ideas rather than simply picking a few techniques to implement. The same study also suggests that where TQM does not prove successful in improving performance, the problems could be the result of poor implementation rather than in the TQM practices themselves and that a serious commitment on the part of top management to TQM is a prerequisite for success.

TQM means meeting the needs and expectations of customers

Earlier in this chapter we defined quality as 'consistent conformance to customers' expectations'. Therefore any approach to quality management must necessarily include the customer perspective. In TQM this customer perspective is particularly important. It may be referred to as 'customer centricity' (discussed briefly in Chapter 16) or the 'voice of the customer'. However it is called, TQM stresses the importance of starting with an insight into customer needs, wants, perceptions and preferences. This can then be translated into quality objectives and used to drive quality improvement.

TQM means covering all parts of the organization

For an organization to be truly effective, every single part of it – each department, each activity, and each person and each level – must work properly together, because every person and every activity affect and in turn are affected by others. One of the most powerful concepts that has emerged from various improvement approaches is the concept of the internal customer/supplier. This is recognition that everyone is a customer within the organization and consumes goods or services provided by other internal suppliers, and everyone is also an internal supplier of goods and services for other internal customers. The implication of this is that errors in the service provided within an organization will eventually affect the service or product which reaches the external customer.

Service-level agreements

Some organizations bring a degree of formality to the internal customer concept by encouraging (or requiring) different parts of the operation to agree service-level agreements (SLAs) with each other. SLAs are formal definitions of the dimensions of service and the relationship between two parts of an organization. The type of issues which would be covered by such an agreement could include response times, the range of services, dependability of service supply, and so on. Boundaries of responsibility and appropriate performance measures could also be agreed. For example, an SLA between an information systems support unit and a research unit in the laboratories of a large company could define such performance measures as:

> ✳ **Operations principle**
>
> An appreciation of, involvement in, and commitment to quality should permeate the entire organization.

- the types of information network services which may be provided as 'standard';
- the range of special information services which may be available at different periods of the day;
- the minimum 'uptime', that is the proportion of time the system will be available at different periods of the day;
- the maximum response time and average response time to get the system fully operational should it fail;
- the maximum response time to provide 'special' services, and so on.

Critical commentary

While some see the strength of SLAs as the degree of formality they bring to customer–supplier relationships, there also some clear drawbacks. The first is that the 'pseudo-contractual' nature of the formal relationship can work against building partnerships (see Chapter 12). This is especially true if the SLA includes penalties for deviation from service standards. Indeed, the effect can sometimes be to inhibit rather than encourage

▶

joint improvement. The second, and related, problem is that SLAs, again because of their formal documented nature, tend to emphasize the 'hard' and measurable aspects of performance rather than the 'softer' but often more important aspects. So a telephone may be answered within four rings, but how the caller is treated, in terms of 'friendliness', may be far more important.

TQM means including every person in the organization

Every person in the organization has the potential to contribute to quality, and TQM was among the first approaches to stress the centrality of harnessing everyone's potential contribution to quality. There is scope for creativity and innovation even in relatively routine activities, claim TQM proponents. The shift in attitude which is needed to view employees as the most valuable intellectual and creative resource which the organization possesses can still prove difficult for some organizations. Yet most advanced organizations do recognize that quality problems are almost always the results of human error.

<table>
<tr><td>OPERATIONS IN PRACTICE</td><td>Fat finger syndrome[13]</td></tr>
</table>

Feeling sleepy one day, a German bank worker briefly fell asleep on his keyboard when processing a €64 debit (withdrawal) from a pensioner's account, repeatedly pressing the number 2. The result was that the pensioner's account had €222 million withdrawn from it instead of the intended €64. Fortunately the bank spotted the error before too much damage was done (and before the account holder noticed). More seriously, the supervisor who should have checked his junior colleague's work was sacked for failing to notice the blunder (unfairly, a German labour tribunal later ruled). It is known as 'fat finger syndrome' – a term used to describe a person who makes keyboard errors when chatting, tired or overstressed. And for some people, like traders working in fast-moving electronic financial markets, if they press the wrong button on their keyboard, it means a potential fortune could be lost.

Fat finger trading mistakes are not uncommon. In 2009, Swiss bank UBS mistakenly ordered 3 trillion yen (instead of 30 million yen) of bonds in a Japanese video games firm. In 2005 a Japanese trader tried to sell one share of a recruitment company at 610,000 yen per share. But he accidentally sold 610,000 shares at 1 yen each, despite this being 41 times the number of shares available. Unlike the German example, the error was not noticed and the Tokyo Stock Exchange processed the order. It resulted in Mizuho Securities losing

Source: Shutterstock.com: Robert Kneschke

27 billion yen. The head of the Exchange later resigned. But what is believed to be the biggest fat finger error on record occurred in 2014, when share trades worth more than the size of Sweden's economy had to be cancelled in Tokyo. The error briefly sparked panic after a trader accidentally entered a trade worth nearly 68 trillion yen in several of the Asian country's largest blue-chip companies. The Japan Securities Dealers Association said the trader had in error put together the volume and price of a series of transactions instead of the volume alone. However, the transactions were cancelled 17 minutes after they were made and no permanent (financial) damage was done.

TQM means all costs of quality are considered

The costs of controlling quality may not be small, whether the responsibility lies with each individual or a dedicated quality control department. It is therefore necessary to examine all the costs and benefits associated with quality (in fact 'cost of quality' is usually taken to refer to both costs and benefits of quality). These costs of quality are usually categorized as *prevention costs*, *appraisal costs*, *internal failure costs* and *external failure costs*.

- **Prevention costs** are those costs incurred in trying to prevent problems, failures and errors from occurring in the first place. They include such things as:
  - identifying potential problems and putting the process right before poor quality occurs;
  - designing and improving the design of products and services and processes to reduce quality problems;
  - training and development of personnel in the best way to perform their jobs;
  - process control through SPC.
- **Appraisal costs** are those costs associated with controlling quality to check to see if problems or errors have occurred during and after the creation of the service or product. They might include such things as:
  - the setting up of statistical acceptance sampling plans;
  - the time and effort required to inspect inputs, processes and outputs;
  - obtaining processing inspection and test data;
  - investigating quality problems and providing quality reports;
  - conducting customer surveys and quality audits.
- **Internal failure costs** are failure costs associated with errors which are dealt with inside the operation. These costs might include such things as:
  - the cost of scrapped parts and material;
  - reworked parts and materials;
  - the lost production time as a result of coping with errors;
  - lack of concentration due to time spent troubleshooting rather than on improvement.
- **External failure costs** are those which are associated with an error going out of the operation to a customer. These costs include such things as:
  - loss of customer goodwill affecting future business;
  - aggrieved customers who may take up time;
  - litigation (or payments to avoid litigation);
  - guarantee and warranty costs;
  - the cost to the company of providing excessive capability (too much coffee in the pack or too much information to a client).

The relationship between quality costs

In traditional quality management it was assumed that failure costs reduce as the money spent on appraisal and prevention increases. Furthermore, it was assumed that there is an *optimum* amount of quality effort to be applied in any situation, which minimizes the total costs of quality. The argument is that there must be a point beyond which diminishing returns set in – that is, the cost of improving quality gets larger than the benefits which it brings. Figure 17.9(a) sums up this idea. As quality effort is increased, the cost of providing the effort – through extra quality controllers, inspection procedures, and so on – increases proportionally. At the same time, however, the cost of errors, faulty products, and so on, decreases because there are fewer of them. However, TQM proponents believe that this logic is flawed. First, it implies that failure and poor quality are acceptable. Why, TQM proponents argue, should any operation accept the *inevitability* of errors? Some occupations seem to be able to accept a zero-defect standard. No one accepts that pilots are allowed to crash a certain proportion of their aircraft, or that nurses will drop a certain proportion of the babies they deliver. Second, it assumes that costs are known and measurable. In fact putting realistic figures to the cost of quality is not a straightforward matter. Third, it is argued that

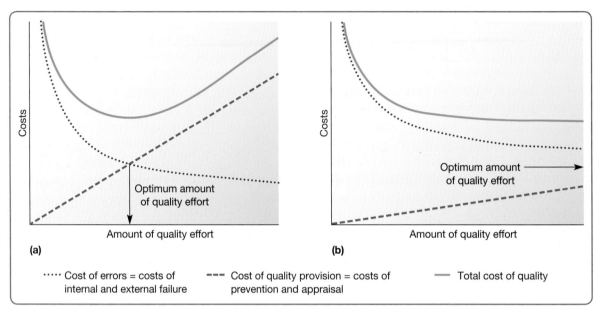

Figure 17.9 (a) The traditional cost of quality model, and (b) the traditional cost of quality model with adjustments to reflect TQM criticisms

failure costs in the traditional model are greatly underestimated. In particular, all the management time wasted by failures and the loss of concentration it causes are rarely accounted for. Fourth, it implies that prevention costs are inevitably high because they involve expensive inspection. But why should quality not be an integral part of everyone's work rather than employing extra people to inspect it? Finally, the 'optimum-quality level' approach, by accepting compromise, does little to challenge operations managers and staff to find ways of improving quality. Put these corrections into the optimum-quality effort calculation and the picture looks very different (*see* Fig. 17.9(b)). If there is an 'optimum', it is a lot further to the right, in the direction of putting more effort (but not necessarily cost) into quality.

The TQM quality cost model

TQM rejects the optimum-quality level concept and strives to reduce all known and unknown failure costs by preventing errors and failure taking place. Rather than looking for 'optimum' levels of quality effort, TQM stresses the relative balance between different types of quality cost. Of the four cost categories, two (costs of prevention and costs of appraisal) are open to managerial influence, while the other two (internal costs of failure and external costs of failure) show the consequences of changes in the first two. So, rather than placing most emphasis on appraisal (so that 'bad products and service do not get through to the customer') TQM emphasizes prevention (to stop errors happening in the first place). That is because the more effort that is put into error prevention, the more internal and external failure costs are reduced. Then, once confidence has been firmly established, appraisal costs can be reduced. Eventually even prevention costs can be stepped down in absolute terms, though prevention remains a significant cost in relative terms. Figure 17.10 illustrates this idea. Initially total quality costs may rise as investment in some aspects of prevention – mainly training – is increased. However, a reduction in total costs can quickly follow.

Getting things 'right first time'

Accepting the relationships between categories of quality cost as illustrated in Figure 17. 10 has a particularly important implication for how quality is managed. It shifts the emphasis from *reactive* (waiting for something to happen) to *proactive* (doing something before

Deliberate defectives

A story which illustrates the difference in attitude between a TQM and a non-TQM company has become almost a legend among TQM proponents. It concerns a plant in Ontario, Canada, of IBM, the computer company. It ordered a batch of components from a Japanese manufacturer and specified that the batch should have an acceptable quality level (AQL) of three defective parts per thousand. When the parts arrived in Ontario they were accompanied by a letter which expressed the supplier's bewilderment at being asked to supply defective parts as well as good ones. The letter also explained that the supplier had found it difficult to make parts which were defective, but had indeed managed it. These three defective parts per thousand had been included and were wrapped separately for the convenience of the customer.

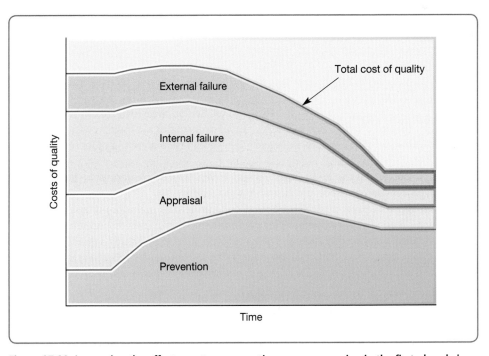

Figure 17.10 Increasing the effort spent on preventing errors occurring in the first place brings a more than equivalent reduction in other cost categories

anything happens). This change in the view of quality costs has come about with a movement from an inspect-in (appraisal-driven) approach to a design-in (getting it right first time) approach.

TQM means developing the systems and procedures which support quality and improvement

The emphasis on highly formalized systems and procedures to support TQM has declined in recent years, yet one aspect is still active for many companies. This is the adoption of the ISO 9000 standard. And although ISO 9000 can be regarded as a stand-alone issue, it is very closely associated with TQM.

The ISO 9000 approach

The ISO 9000 series is a family of standards compiled by the International Organization for Standardization (ISO), which is the world's largest developer and publisher of international standards, based in Geneva, Switzerland. According to the ISO, *'the standards represent an international consensus on good quality management practices. It consists of standards and guidelines relating to quality management systems and related supporting standards.'* To be precise, it is the 'ISO 9001:2008' standard that provides the set of standardized requirements for a quality management system which should apply to any organization, regardless of size, or whether it is in the private or public sector. It is the only standard in the family against which organizations can be certified – although certification is not a compulsory requirement of the standard. Its purpose when it was first framed was to provide an assurance to the purchasers of products or services that they have been produced in such a way that they meet their requirements. The best way to do this, it was argued, was to define the procedures, standards and characteristics of the management control system which governs the operation. Such a system would help to ensure that quality was 'built into' the operation's transformation processes. Rather than using different standards for different functions within a business, it takes a 'process' approach that focused on outputs from any operation's process rather than detailed procedures. This process orientation requires operations to define and record core processes and sub-processes (in a manner very similar to the 'hierarchy of processes' principle that was outline in Chapter 1). In addition, processes are documented using the process mapping approach that was described in Chapter 4. It also stresses four other principles:

- Quality management should be customer focused. Customer satisfaction should be measured through surveys and focus groups and improvement against customer standards should be documented.
- Quality performance should be measured. In particular, measures should relate both to processes that create products and services and to customer satisfaction with those products and services. Furthermore, measured data should be analysed in order to understand processes.
- Quality management should be improvement driven. Improvement must be demonstrated in both process performance and customer satisfaction.
- Top management must demonstrate their commitment to maintaining and continually improving management systems. This commitment should include communicating the importance of meeting customer and other requirements, establishing a quality policy and quality objectives, conducting management reviews to ensure the adherence to quality policies, and ensuring the availability of the necessary resources to maintain quality systems.

The ISO illustrates the benefits of the standard as follows: *'Without satisfied customers, an organization is in peril! To keep customers satisfied, the organization needs to meet their requirements. The ISO 9001:2008 standard provides a tried and tested framework for taking a systematic approach to managing the organization's processes so that they consistently turn out product that satisfies customers' expectations.'*[14] In addition it is also seen as providing benefits both to the organizations adopting it (because it gives them detailed guidance on how to design their control procedures) and especially to customers (who have the assurance of knowing that the products and services they purchase are produced by an operation working to a defined standard). Further, it may also provide a useful discipline to stick to 'sensible' process-oriented procedures which lead to error reduction, reduced customer complaints and reduced costs of quality, and may even identify existing procedures which are not necessary and can be eliminated. Moreover, gaining the certificate demonstrates that the company takes quality seriously; it therefore has a marketing benefit.

Critical commentary

Notwithstanding its widespread adoption (and its revision to take into account some of its perceived failing), ISO 9000 is not seen as beneficial by all authorities, and is still subject to some specific criticisms. These include the following:

- The continued use of standards and procedures encourages 'management by manual' and over-systematized decision making.
- The whole process of documenting processes, writing procedures, training staff and conducting internal audits is expensive and time consuming.
- Similarly, the time and cost of achieving and maintaining ISO 9000 registration are excessive.
- It is too formulaic. It encourages operations to substitute a 'recipe' for a more customized and creative approach to managing operations improvement.

Quality awards

Various bodies have sought to stimulate improvement through establishing 'quality' awards. The three best-known awards are the Deming Prize, the Malcolm Baldrige National Quality Award and the European Quality Award.

The Deming Prize

The Deming Prize was instituted by the Union of Japanese Scientists and Engineers in 1951 and is awarded to those companies, initially in Japan, but more recently opened to overseas companies, which have successfully applied 'company-wide quality control' based upon statistical quality control. There are 10 major assessment categories: policy and objectives, organization and its operation, education and its extension, assembling and disseminating of information, analysis, standardization, control, quality assurance, effects and future plans. The applicants are required to submit a detailed description of quality practices. This is a significant activity in itself and some companies claim a great deal of benefit from having done so.

The Malcolm Baldrige National Quality Award

In the early 1980s the American Productivity and Quality Center recommended that an annual prize, similar to the Deming Prize, should be awarded in the USA. The purpose of the awards was to stimulate US companies to improve quality and productivity, to recognize achievements, to establish criteria for a wider quality effort and to provide guidance on quality improvement. The main examination categories are: leadership, information and analysis, strategic quality planning, human resource utilization, quality assurance of products and services, quality results and customer satisfaction. The process, like that of the Deming Prize, includes a detailed application and site visits.

The EFQM Excellence Model

In 1988, 14 leading Western European companies formed the European Foundation for Quality Management (EFQM). An important objective of the EFQM is to recognize quality achievement. Because of this, it launched the European Quality Award (EQA), awarded to the most successful exponent of TQM in Europe each year. To receive a prize, companies must demonstrate that their approach to TQM has contributed significantly to satisfying the expectations of customers, employees and others with an interest in the company for the past few years. In 1999, the model on which the European Quality Award was based was modified and renamed the EFQM Excellence Model or Business Excellence Model. The changes made were not fundamental but did attempt to reflect some new areas of management and quality thinking (for example, partnerships and innovation) and placed more emphasis on customer and market focus. It is based on the idea that the outcomes of quality management in terms of what it calls 'people results', 'customer results', 'society results' and 'key performance results' are achieved through a number of 'enablers'. These enablers are leadership and constancy of purpose, policy and strategy, how the organization develops its people, partnerships and resources, and the way it organizes its processes. These ideas are incorporated in the EFQM Excellence Model as shown in Figure 17.11. The five enablers are concerned with how results are being achieved, while the four 'results' are concerned with what the company has achieved and is achieving.

Self-assessment

The EFQM defines self-assessment as 'a comprehensive, systematic, and regular review of an organization's activities and results referenced against a model of business excellence', in its case the model shown in Figure 17.11. The main advantage of using such models for self-assessment seems to be that companies find it easier to understand some of the more philosophical concepts of TQM when they are translated into specific areas, questions and percentages. Self-assessment also allows organizations to measure their progress in changing their organization and in achieving the benefits of TQM. An important aspect of self-assessment is an organization's ability to judge the relative importance of the assessment categories to its own circumstances. The EFQM Excellence Model originally placed emphasis on a generic set of weightings for each of its nine categories. With the increasing importance of self-assessment, the EFQM moved to encourage organizations using its model to allocate their own weightings in a rational and systematic manner.

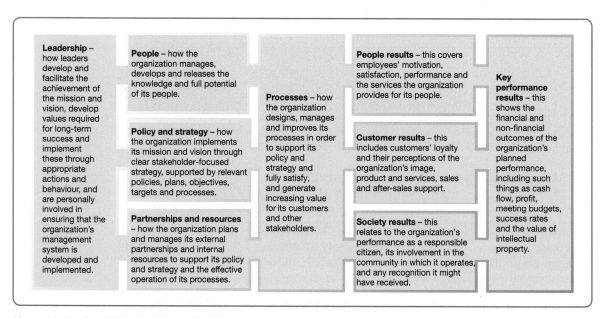

Figure 17.11 The EFQM Excellence Model

Green reporting and ISO 14000[15]

Until recently, relatively few companies around the world provided information on their environmental practices and performance. Now environmental reporting is increasingly common. Another emerging issue has been the introduction of the ISO 14000 standard. It has a three-section environmental management system which covers initial planning, implementation and objective assessment. Although it has had some impact, it is largely limited to Europe.

ISO 14000 makes a number of specific requirements, including the following:

- a commitment by top-level management to environmental management;
- the development and communication of an environmental policy;
- the establishment of relevant and legal and regulatory requirements;
- the setting of environmental objectives and targets;
- the establishment and updating of a specific environmental programme, or programmes, geared to achieving the objectives and targets;
- the implementation of supporting systems such as training, operational control and emergency planning;
- regular monitoring and measurement of all operational activities;
- a full audit procedure to review the working and suitability of the system.

Critical commentary

The similarity of ISO 14000 to the quality procedures of ISO 9000 is a bit of a giveaway. ISO 14000 can contain all the problems of ISO 9000 (management by manual, obsession with procedures rather than results, a major expense to implement it, and, at its worst, the formalization of what was bad practice in the first place). But ISO 14000 also has some further problems. The main one is that it can become a 'badge for the smug'. It can be seen as 'all there is to do to be a good environmentally sensitive company'. At least with quality standards like ISO 9000 there are real customers continually reminding the business that quality does matter. Pressures to improve environmental standards are far more diffuse. Customers are not likely to be as energetic in forcing good environmental standards on suppliers as they are in forcing the good-quality standards from which they benefit directly. Instead of this type of procedure-based system, surely the only way to influence a practice that has an effect on a societal level is through society's normal mechanism – legal regulation. If quality suffers, individuals suffer and have the sanction of not purchasing goods and services again from the offending company. With bad environmental management, we all suffer. Because of this, the only workable way to ensure environmentally sensitive business policies is by insisting that our governments protect us. Legislation, therefore, is the only safe way forward.

SUMMARY ANSWERS TO KEY QUESTIONS

❯ What is quality and why is it so important?

- The definition of quality used in this book defines quality as 'consistent conformance to customers' expectations'. It is important because it has a significant impact on profitability.

- At a broad level, quality is best modelled as the gap between customers' expectations concerning the service or product and their perceptions concerning the service or product.
- Modelling quality this way will allow the development of a diagnostic tool that is based around the perception–expectation gap. Such a gap may be explained by four other gaps:
  - the gap between a customer's specification and the operation's specification;
  - the gap between the service or product concept and the way the organization has specified it;
  - the gap between the way quality has been specified and the actual delivered quality;
  - the gap between the actual delivered quality and the way the service or product has been described to the customer.
- The 'sandcone' theory of improvement holds that it is generally better to start with improving quality rather than other performance objectives, but then keep improving quality even as other performance objectives are pursued.

❭ What steps lead towards conformance to specification?

- There are six steps:
  - define quality characteristics;
  - decide how to measure each of the quality characteristics;
  - set quality standards for each characteristic;
  - control quality against these standards;
  - find and correct the causes of poor quality;
  - continue to make improvements.
- Most quality planning and control involves sampling the operations performance in some way. Sampling can give rise to erroneous judgements which are classed as either Type I or Type II errors. Type I errors involve making corrections where none are needed. Type II errors involve not making corrections where they are in fact needed.

❭ What is total quality management (TQM)?

- TQM is 'an effective system for integrating the quality development, quality maintenance and quality improvement efforts of the various groups in an organization so as to enable production and service at the most economical levels which allow for full customer satisfaction'.
- It is best thought of as a philosophy that stresses the 'total' of TQM and puts quality at the heart of everything that is done by an operation.
- Total in TQM means the following:
  - meeting the needs and expectations of customers;
  - covering all parts of the organization;
  - including every person in the organization;
  - examining all costs which are related to quality, and getting things 'right first time';
  - developing the systems and procedures which support quality and improvement, potentially including 'quality awards'.

Turnaround at the Preston plant[16]

Introduction

'Before the crisis, production monitoring was done to please the client, not for problem solving. Data readouts were brought to Production meetings, we would all look at it, but none of us were looking behind it.' (Chief operating officer (COO), Preston Plant).

The Preston plant was located in Preston, Vancouver. Precision-coated papers for specialist printing uses accounted for the majority of the plant's output. The plant used state-of-the-art coating machines that allowed very precise coatings to be applied to bought-in rolls of paper. After coating, the coated rolls were cut into standard sizes.

The curl problem

In the spring of 2008 Hewlett Packard (the plant's main customer) informed the plant of problems it had encountered with paper curling under conditions of low humidity. There had been no customer complaints. HP's own personnel had noticed the problem, but they took the problem seriously. Over the next eight months the plant's production staff worked to isolate the cause of the problem and improve systems that monitored processing metrics. By January 2009 the process was producing acceptable product, yet it had not been a good year for the plant. Although volumes were buoyant the plant was making a loss of around C$10 million a year. In October 2008, Tom Branton was appointed as COO.

Slipping out of control

Although the curl project was solved, productivity, scrap and rework levels were poor. In response to this, operations managers increased the speed of the line in order to raise productivity. *'Looking back, changes were made without any proper discipline, there was no real concept of control and the process was allowed to drift. Our culture said, "If it's within specification then it's OK", and we were very diligent in making sure that the product which was shipped was in specification. However, Hewlett Packard gets "process data" which enables them to see exactly what is happening right inside your operation. We were also getting all the data but none of it was being internalized. By contrast, HP has a "capability mentality". They say, "You might be capable of making this product but we are thinking two or three product generations forward and asking ourselves, do we want to invest in this relationship for the future?"* (Tom Branton)

The spring of 2009 was eventful. First, HP asked the plant to carry out preliminary work for a new paper to supply its next generation of printers, known as the Viper project. Second, the plant was acquired by the Rendall Group, which was not impressed by what it found. The plant had

been making a loss for two years and had incurred HP's disapproval over the curl issue. The group made it clear that, if the plant did not get the Viper contract, its future looked bleak. Meanwhile, in the plant, the chief concern was plant productivity, but also HP was starting to make complaints about quality levels. Yet HP's attitude caused bewilderment in the production team. *'When HP asked questions about our process the operations guys would say, "Look we're making roll after roll of paper, it's within specification and we've got 97 per cent up-time. What's the problem?"'* (COO, Preston Plant). But it was not until summer that the full extent of HP's disquiet was made clear. *'I will never forget that day in June of 2009. I was with HP in Chicago and during the meeting one of their engineers handed me some of the process data that we had to supply with every batch of product, and said "Here's your latest data. We think you're out of control and you don't know that you're out of control and we think that HP is looking at this data more than you are." He was absolutely right.'* (Tom Branton)

The crisis

Tom immediately set about the task of bringing the plant back under control. The plant first of all decided to go back to the conditions which the monitoring system indicated had prevailed in January, when the curl problem had been solved and before productivity pressures had caused the process to be adjusted. At the same time, Production worked on ways of implementing unambiguous 'shut-down rules' which would indicate to operators when a line should be halted if they were in doubt about operating quality. '*At one point in May of 2009 we had to throw away 64 jumbo rolls of out-of-specification product. That's over $400,000 of product scrapped in one run. That was because operators had been afraid to shut the line down. Either that or they had tried to tweak the line while it was running to get rid of the defect. The shut-down system says, "We are not going to operate when we are not in a state of control." Prior to that, our operators just couldn't win. If they failed to keep the process running we would say, "You've got to keep productivity up." If they kept the machines running but had quality problems as a result, we criticized them for making garbage. Now you get into far more trouble for violating process procedures than for not meeting productivity targets. We did two further things. First each production team started holding daily reviews of processing data and some "first pass" analysis of the data. Second, one day a month we brought all three shifts together, looked at the processing data and debated the implications of production data. Some people got nervous because we were not producing anything. But for the first time you got operators from the three shifts, together with the Production team talking about operating issues. We also invited HP up to attend these meetings. Remember these weren't staged meetings, it was the first time these guys had met together and there was plenty of heated discussion, all of which the Hewlett Packard representatives witnessed.*' (Engineer, Preston Plant)

In spite of the changes, morale on the shop floor was good. At last something positive was happening. By September 2009 the process was coming under control, the efficiency of the plant was improving, as was its outgoing quality level, its on-time delivery, its responsiveness to customer orders and its inventory levels. Yet the Preston team did not have time to enjoy its emerging success. In September of 2009 HP announced that the plant would not get the Viper project because of its discomfort about quality levels, and Rendall formally made the decision on the future of the plant. '*We lost ten million dollars in 2009. We had also lost the Viper project. It was no surprise when they made the decision to shut the plant down. I told the senior management team that we would announce it, in April of 2010. The irony was that we knew that we had already turned the corner. It would take perhaps three or four months, but we were convinced that we would become profitable.*' (Tom Branton)

Convincing the rest of the world

Notwithstanding the closure decision, the management team in Preston set about the task of convincing both HP and Rendall that the plant could be viable. The team figured it would take three things. First, it was vital that the plant continue to improve quality. Second, costs had to be brought down further. Third, the plant had to create a portfolio of new product ideas.

Improving quality further involved establishing full statistical process analysis in the process monitoring system.

It also meant establishing quality-consciousness and problem-solving tools throughout the plant. '*We had people out there, technologists and managers, who saw themselves as concerned with investment projects rather than the processes that were affected. But taking time out and discussing process performance and improvement, we got used to discussing the basic capabilities that we needed to improve.*' (Tom Branton)

Working on cost reduction was inevitably going to be painful. The first task was to get an understanding of what should be an appropriate level of operating costs. '*We went through a zero-based assessment to decide what ideal processes would look like. By the way, in hindsight, cutting numbers had a greater impact on cost than the payroll saving figures seems to suggest. If you really understand your process, when you cut people it cuts complexity and makes things clearer to understand. Although most staff had not been told about the closure decision, they were left in no doubt that the plant had its back to the wall. We were careful to be very transparent. We made sure that everyone knew whether they would be affected or not. I did lots of walking around explaining the company's position. There were tensions and some negative reactions from the people who had to leave. Yet most accepted the business logic of what we were doing.*' (Tom Branton)

By December of 2009 there were 40 per cent fewer people in the plant than two months earlier. All departments were affected. Surprisingly the quality department shrank more than most, moving from 22 people down to 9. '*When the plant was considering down-sizing they asked me, "How can we run a lab with six technicians?" Remember that at this time we had 22 technicians. I said, "Easy. We get production to make good product in the first place, and then we don't have to control all the garbage.*' (Quality Manager, Preston Plant)

Several new product ideas were investigated, including some that were only possible because of the plant's enhanced capability. The most important of these became known as 'Ecowrap', a recyclable protective wrap, aimed at the Japanese market. It was technically difficult, but the plant's new capabilities allowed it to develop appropriate coatings at a cost that made the product attractive.

Out of the crisis

In spite of the trauma in the fall, the plant's management team faced Christmas of 2009 with increasing satisfaction, if not optimism for the plant's future. In December it made an operational profit for the first time for over two years. By spring of 2010 even HP, at a corporate level, was starting to look more favourably on the Preston plant. More significantly, HP had asked the plant to start work on trials for a new product – 'heavyweight' paper. April 2010 was a good month for the plant. It had chalked up three months of profitability and HP formally gave the heavyweight inkjet paper contract to Preston, and was generally more upbeat about the future. At the end of April, Rendall reversed its decision to close the plant.

The future

The year of 2010 was a profitable year for the plant, by the end of which it had captured 75 per cent of HP's US printing paper business and was being asked to work on several other large projects. 'Hewlett Packard now seems very keen to work with us. It has helped us with our own suppliers also. We have already given considerable assistance to our main paper supplier to improve their own internal process control procedures. Recently we were in a meeting with people from all different parts of HP. There were all kinds of confidential information going around. But you could never tell that there was an outsider (us) in the room. They were having arguments amongst themselves about certain issues and no one could have been there without feeling that basically we were a part of that company. In the past they've always been very close with some information. Basically the change is all down to their new found trust in our capabilities.' (Tom Branton)

QUESTIONS

1 What are the most significant events in the story of how the plant survived because of its adoption of quality-based principles?

2 The plant's processes eventually were brought under control. What were the main benefits of this?

3 SPC is an operational-level technique of ensuring quality conformance. How many of the benefits of bringing the plant under control would you class as strategic?

PROBLEMS AND APPLICATIONS

(Read the supplement on statistical process control, before attempting problems 3, 4, 5 and 6.)

1 Reread the 'Operations in practice' case towards the beginning of the chapter that describes TNT, Victorinox and the Four Seasons Hotel. For each organization:
(a) describe how quality is defined;
(b) identify why quality is so important for them;
(c) describe the main activities that have an impact on the quality of their products/services.

2 What could be done to minimize the chances of the kind of errors described in the 'Operations in practice' case on 'fat finger syndrome'?

3 A call centre for a bank answers customers' queries about their loan arrangements. All calls are automatically timed by the call centre's information system and the mean and standard deviation of call lengths are monitored periodically. The bank has decided that only on very rare occasions should calls be less than 0.5 minutes because customers would think this was impolite even if the query was so simple that it could be answered in this time. Also, the bank reckoned that it was unlikely that any query should ever take more than 7 minutes to answer satisfactorily. The figures for last week's calls show that the mean of all call lengths was 3.02 minutes and the standard deviation was 1.58 minutes. Calculate the C_p and the C_{pk} for the call centre process.

4 In the above call centre, if the mean call length changes to 3.2 minutes and the standard deviation to 0.9 minutes, how does this affect the C_p and C_{pk}? Do you think this is an appropriate way for the bank to monitor its call centre performance?

5 A vaccine production company has invested in an automatic tester to monitor the impurity levels in its vaccines. Previously all testing was done by hand on a sample of batches of serum. According to the company's specifications, all vaccine must have impurity levels of less than 0.03 milligrams per 1,000 litres. In order to test the effectiveness of its new automatic sampling equipment, the company runs a number of batches through the process with known levels of impurity. The table below shows the level of impurity of each batch and whether the new process accepted or rejected the batch. From this data, estimate the Type I and Type II error levels for the process.

0.035 (rejected)	0.028 (accepted)	0.031 (accepted)	0.029 (accepted)	0.028 (accepted)	0.034 (accepted)	0.031 (accepted)
0.040 (rejected)	0.011 (accepted)	0.028 (rejected)	0.025 (accepted)	0.019 (accepted)	0.018 (accepted)	0.033 (rejected)
0.022 (accepted)	0.029 (rejected)	0.012 (accepted)	0.034 (accepted)	0.027 (accepted)	0.017 (accepted)	0.021 (accepted)
0.031 (rejected)	0.015 (accepted)	0.037 (rejected)	0.030 (accepted)	0.025 (accepted)	0.034 (rejected)	0.020 (accepted)

6   A utility has a department which does nothing but change the addresses of customers on the company's information systems when customers move house. The process is deemed to be in control at the moment and a random sample of 2,000 transactions shows that 2.5 per cent of these transactions had some type of error. If the company is to use statistical process control to monitor error levels, calculate the mean, upper control level (UCL) and lower control level (LCL) for its SPC chart.

7   Find two products, one a manufactured food item (for example, a pack of breakfast cereals, packet of biscuits, etc.) and the other a domestic electrical item (for example, electric toaster, coffee maker, etc.):
   (a)   Identify the important quality characteristics for these two products.
   (b)   How could each of these quality characteristics be specified?
   (c)   How could each of these quality characteristics be measured?

8   Many organizations check up on their own level of quality by using 'mystery shoppers'. This involves an employee of the company acting out the role of a customer and recording how the employee is treated by the operation. Choose two or three high-visibility operations (for example, a cinema, a department store, the branch of a retail bank, etc.) and discuss how you would put together a mystery shopper approach to testing their quality. This may involve your determining the types of characteristics you would wish to observe, the way in which you would measure these characteristics, an appropriate sampling rate, and so on. Try out your mystery shopper plan by visiting these operations.

SELECTED FURTHER READING

ASQ Quality Press (2010) *Seven Basic Quality Tools*, ASQ Quality Press, Milwaukee, WI.

Very much a 'how to do it' handbook.

Dale, B.G., van der Wiele, T. and van Iwaarden, J. (2007) *Managing Quality*, 5th edn, Wiley-Blackwell, Oxford.

This is the latest version of a long-established, comprehensive and authoritative text.

Garvin, D.A. (1988) *Managing Quality*, Free Press, New York.

Somewhat dated now but relates to our discussion at the beginning of this chapter.

Oakland, J.S. (2014) *Total Quality Management and Operational Excellence: Text with Cases*, 4th edn, Routledge, Milton.

A classic text from one of the founders of TQM in Europe.

Webber, L. (2007) *Quality Control For Dummies*, Wiley, Hoboken, NJ.

Not just for dummies (though they might like it too).

Supplement to Chapter 17
Statistical process control

INTRODUCTION

Statistical process control (SPC) is concerned with checking a service or product during its creation. If there is reason to believe that there is a problem with the process, then it can be stopped and the problem can be identified and rectified. For example, an international airport may regularly ask a sample of customers if the cleanliness of its restaurants is satisfactory. If an unacceptable number of customers in one sample are found to be unhappy, airport managers may have to consider improving its procedures. Similarly, an automobile manufacturer will periodically check whether a sample of door panels conforms to its standards so it knows whether the machinery which produces them is performing correctly.

CONTROL CHARTS

The value of SPC is not just to make checks of a single sample but to monitor the quality over a period of time. It does this by using control charts, to see if the process seems to be performing as it should, or alternatively if it is 'out of control'. If the process does seem to be going out of control, then steps can be taken *before* there is a problem. Actually, most operations chart their quality performance in some way. Figure S17.1, or something like it, could be found in almost any operation. The chart could, for example, represent the percentage of customers in a sample of 1,000 who, each month, were dissatisfied with the restaurant's cleanliness.

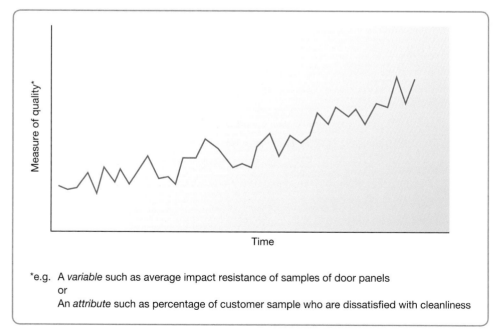

*e.g. A *variable* such as average impact resistance of samples of door panels
or
An *attribute* such as percentage of customer sample who are dissatisfied with cleanliness

Figure S17.1 **Charting trends in quality measures**

While the amount of dissatisfaction may be acceptably small, management should be concerned that it has been steadily increasing over time and may wish to investigate why this is so. In this case, the control chart is plotting an attribute measure of quality (satisfied or not). Looking for trends is an important use of control charts. If the trend suggests the process is getting steadily worse, then it will be worth investigating the process. If the trend is steadily improving, it may still be worthy of investigation to try to identify what is happening that is making the process better. This information might then be shared with other parts of the organization, or, on the other hand, the process might be stopped as the cause could be adding unnecessary expense to the operation.

VARIATION IN PROCESS QUALITY

Common causes

The processes charted in Figure S17.1 showed an upward trend. But the trend was neither steady nor smooth; it varied, sometimes up, sometimes down. All processes vary to some extent. No machine will give precisely the same result each time it is used. People perform tasks slightly differently each time. Given this, it is not surprising that the measure of quality will also vary. Variations which derive from these *common causes* can never be entirely eliminated (although they can be reduced). For example, if a machine is filling boxes with rice, it will not place *exactly* the same weight of rice in every box it fills. When the filling machine is in a stable condition (that is, no exceptional factors are influencing its behaviour) each box could be weighed and a histogram of the weights could be built up. Figure S17.2 shows how the histogram might develop. The first boxes weighed could lie anywhere within the natural variation of the process but are more likely to be close to the average weight (*see* Fig. S17.2(a)). As more boxes are weighed they clearly show the tendency to be close to the process average (*see* Fig. S17.2(b) and (c)). After many boxes have been weighed they form a smoother distribution (Fig. S17.2(d)), which can be drawn as a histogram (Fig. S17.2(e)), which will approximate to the underlying process variation distribution (Fig. S17.2(f)).

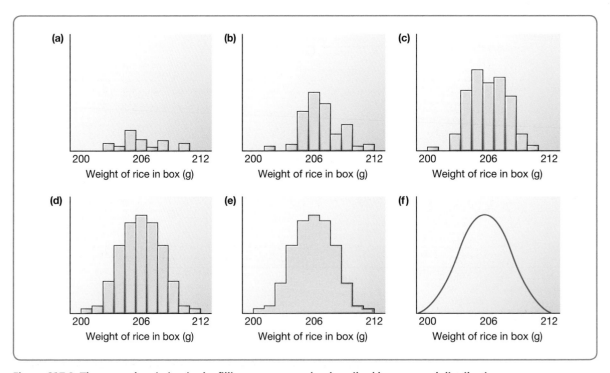

Figure S17.2 The natural variation in the filling process can be described by a normal distribution

Usually this type of variation can be described by a normal distribution with 99.7 per cent of the variation lying within ±3 standard deviations. In this case the weight of rice in the boxes is described by a distribution with a mean of 206 grams and a standard deviation of 2 grams. The obvious question for any operations manager would be: 'Is this variation in the process performance acceptable?' The answer will depend on the acceptable range of weights which can be tolerated by the operation. This range is called the *specification range*. If the weight of rice in the box is too small then the organization might infringe labelling regulations; if it is too large, the organization is 'giving away' too much of its product for free.

Process capability

Process capability is a measure of the acceptability of the variation of the process. The simplest measure of capability (C_p) is given by the ratio of the specification range to the 'natural' variation of the process (that is, ±3 standard deviations):

$$C_p = \frac{UTL - LTL}{6s}$$

where:

UTL = the upper tolerance limit
LTL = the lower tolerance limit
s = the standard deviation of the process variability

Generally, if the C_p of a process is greater than 1, it is taken to indicate that the process is 'capable', and a C_p of less than 1 indicates that the process is not 'capable', assuming that the distribution is normal (*see* Fig. S17.3(a–c)).

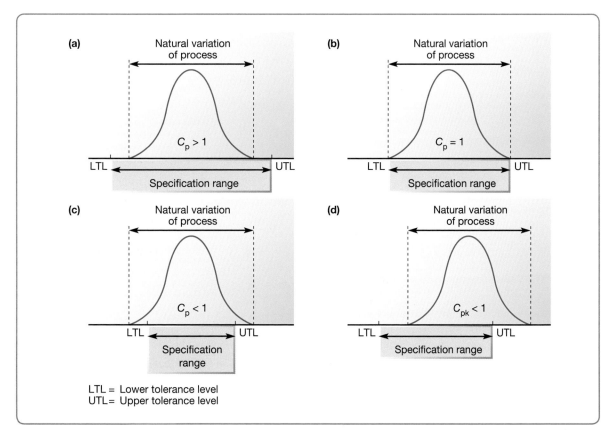

Figure S17.3 Process capability compares the natural variation of the process with the specification range which is required

The simple C_p measure assumes that the average of the process variation is at the mid-point of the specification range. Often the process average is offset from the specification range, however (*see* Fig. S17.3(d)). In such cases, *one-sided* capability indices are required to understand the capability of the process:

$$\text{Upper one-sided index } C_{pu} = \frac{\text{UTL} - X}{3s}$$

$$\text{Lower one-sided index } C_{pl} = \frac{X - \text{LTL}}{3s}$$

where X = the process average.

Sometimes only the lower of the two one-sided indices for a process is used to indicate its capability (C_{pk}):

$$C_{pk} = \min(C_{pu}, C_{pl})$$

Worked example

In the case of the process filling boxes of rice, described previously, process capability can be calculated as follows:

$$\text{Specification range} = 214 - 198 = 16 \text{ g}$$
$$\text{Natural variation of process} = 6 \times \text{standard deviation}$$
$$= 6 \times 2 = 12 \text{ g}$$
$$C_p = \text{process capability}$$
$$= \frac{\text{UTL} - \text{LTL}}{6s}$$
$$= \frac{214 - 198}{6 \times 2} = \frac{16}{12}$$
$$= 1.333$$

If the natural variation of the filling process changed to have a process average of 210 grams but the standard deviation of the process remained at 2 grams, then:

$$C_{pu} = \frac{214 - 210}{3 \times 2} = \frac{4}{6} = 0.666$$
$$C_{pl} = \frac{210 - 198}{3 \times 2} = \frac{12}{6} = 2.0$$
$$C_{pk} = \min(0.666, 2.0)$$
$$= 0.666$$

Assignable causes of variation

Not all variation in processes is the result of common causes. There may be something wrong with the process which is assignable to a particular and preventable cause. Machinery may have worn or been set up badly. An untrained person may not be following prescribed procedures. The causes of such variation are called *assignable causes*. The question is whether the results from any particular sample, when plotted on the control chart, simply represent the variation due to common causes or are due to some specific and correctable, *assignable* cause. Figure S17.4, for example, shows the control chart for the average impact resistance of samples of door panels taken over time. Like any process the results vary, but the last three points seem to be lower than usual. So, is this natural (common-cause) variation, or the symptom of some more serious (assignable) cause?

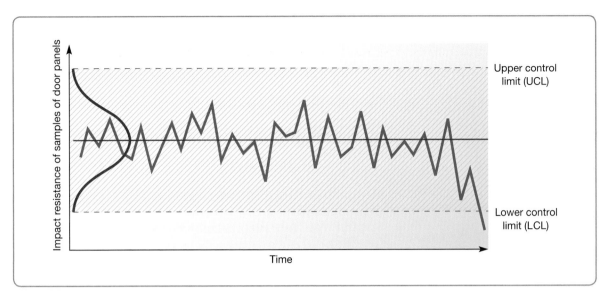

Figure S17.4 Control chart for the impact resistance of door panels, together with control limits

To help make this decision, control limits can be added to the control chart (the red dashed lines) which indicates the expected extent of 'common-cause' variation. If any points lie outside these control limits (the shaded zone) then the process can be deemed out of control in the sense that variation is likely to be due to assignable causes. These control limits could be set intuitively by examining past variation during a period when the process was thought to be free of any variation which could be due to assignable causes. But control limits can also be set in a more statistically revealing manner. For example, if the process which tests door panels had been measured to determine the normal distribution which represents its common-cause variation, then control limits can be based on this distribution. Figure S17.4 also shows how control limits can be added – here put at ± 3 standard deviations (of the population of sample means) away from the mean of sample averages. It shows that the probability of the final point on the chart being influenced by an assignable cause is very high indeed. When the process is exhibiting behaviour which is outside its normal 'common-cause' range, it is said to be 'out of control'. Yet there is a small but finite chance that the (seemingly out of limits) point is just one of the rare but natural results at the tail of the distribution which describes perfectly normal behaviour. Stopping the process under these circumstances would represent a Type I error because the process is actually in control. Alternatively, ignoring a result which in reality is due to an assignable cause is a Type II error (*see* Table S17.1).

Control limits are usually set at three standard deviations either side of the population mean. This would mean that there is only a 0.3 per cent chance of any sample mean falling outside these limits by chance causes (that is, a chance of a Type I error of 0.3 per cent). The control limits may be set at any distance from the population mean, but the closer the limits are to the population mean, the higher the likelihood of investigating and trying to rectify a process which is actually problem-free. If the control limits are set at two standard deviations,

Table S17.1 Type I and Type II errors in SPC

Decision	Actual process state	
	In control	**Out of control**
Stop process	Type I error	Correct decision
Leave alone	Correct decision	Type II error

the chance of a Type I error increases to about 5 per cent. If the limits are set at one standard deviation then the chance of a Type I error increases to 32 per cent. When the control limits are placed at ±3 standard deviations away from the mean of the distribution which describes 'normal' variation in the process, they are called the *upper control limit* (UCL) and *lower control limit* (LCL).

Critical commentary

When its originators first described SPC more than half a century ago, the key issue was only to decide whether a process was 'in control' or not. Now, we expect SPC to reflect common sense as well as statistical elegance and promote continuous operations improvement. This is why two (related) criticisms have been levelled at the traditional approach to SPC. The first is that SPC seems to assume that any values of process performance which lie within the control limits are equally acceptable, while any values outside the limits are not. However, surely a value close to the process average or 'target' value will be more acceptable than one only just within the control limits. For example, a service engineer arriving only 1 minute late is a far better 'performance' than one arriving 59 minutes late, even if the control limits are 'quoted time ± one hour'. Also, arriving 59 minutes late would be almost as bad as 61 minutes late! Second, a process always within its control limits may not be deteriorating, but is it improving? So rather than seeing control limits as fixed, it would be better to view them as a reflection of how the process is being improved. We should expect any improving process to have progressively narrowing control limits.

Why variability is a bad thing

Assignable variation is a signal that something has changed in the process, which therefore must be investigated. But normal variation is itself a problem because it masks any changes in process behaviour. Figure S17.5 shows the performance of two processes both of which are subjected to a change in their process behaviour at the same time. The process on the left has such a wide natural variation that it is not immediately apparent that any change has taken place. Eventually it will become apparent because the likelihood of process performance violating the lower (in this case) control limit has increased, but this may take some time. By contrast, the process on the right has a far narrower band of natural variation. Because of this, the same change in average performance is more easily noticed (both visually and statistically). So, the narrower the natural variation of a process, the more obvious are changes in the behaviour of that process. And the more obvious are the process changes, the easier it is to understand how and why the process is behaving in a particular way. Accepting any variation in any process is, to some degree, admitting to ignorance of how that process works.

> ✳ **Operations principle**
>
> High levels of variation reduce the ability to detect changes in process performance.

CONTROL CHARTS FOR ATTRIBUTES

Attributes have only two states – 'right' or 'wrong', for example – so the statistic calculated is the proportion of wrongs (p) in a sample. (This statistic follows a binomial distribution.) Control charts using p are called 'p-charts'. In calculating the limits, the population mean ($\bar{p}$) – the actual, normal or expected proportion of 'defectives' or wrongs to rights – may not be known. Who knows, for example, the actual number of city commuters who are dissatisfied with their journey

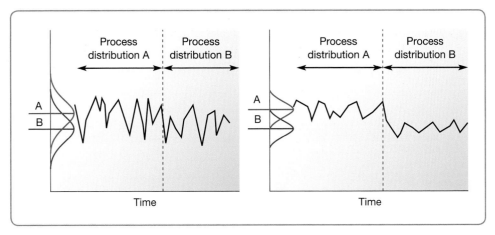

Figure S17.5 Low process variation allows changes in process performance to be readily detected

time? In such cases the population mean can be estimated from the average of the proportion of 'defectives' ($\bar{p}$), from m samples each of n items, where m should be at least 30 and n should be at least 100:

$$\bar{p} = \frac{p_1 + p_2 + p_3 + \cdots + p_n}{m}$$

One standard deviation can then be estimated from:

$$\sqrt{\frac{\bar{p}(1 - p^n)}{n}}$$

The upper and lower control limits can then be set as:

$$\text{UCL} = \bar{p} + 3 \text{ standard deviations}$$
$$\text{LCL} = \bar{p} - 3 \text{ standard deviations}$$

Of course, the LCL cannot be negative, so when it is calculated to be so it should be rounded up to zero.

Worked example

A credit card company deals with many hundreds of thousands of transactions every week. One of its measures of the quality of service it gives its customers is the dependability with which it mails customers' monthly accounts. The quality standard it sets itself is that accounts should be mailed within two days of the 'nominal post date' which is specified to the customer. Every week the company samples 1,000 customer accounts and records the percentage which was not mailed within the standard time. When the process is working normally, only 2 per cent of accounts are mailed outside the specified period, that is 2 per cent are 'defective'.

Control limits for the process can be calculated as follows:

$$\text{Mean proportion defective, } \bar{p} = 0.02$$
$$\text{Sample size } n = 1,000$$

$$\text{Standard deviation } s = \sqrt{\frac{\bar{p}(1 - p^n)}{n}}$$
$$= \sqrt{\frac{0.02(0.98)}{1,000}}$$
$$= 0.0044$$

With the control limits at $\bar{p} \pm 3s$:

$$\text{Upper control limit (UCL)} = 0.02 + 3(0.0044) = 0.0332 = 3.32\%$$
$$\text{Lower control limit (LCL)} = 0.02 - 3(0.0044) = 0.0068 = 0.68\%$$

Figure S17.6 shows the company's control chart for this measure of quality over the last few weeks, together with the calculated control limits. It also shows that the process is in control. Sometimes it is more convenient to plot the actual number of defects (c) rather than the proportion (or percentage) of defectives, on what is known as a c-chart. This is very similar to the p-chart but the sample size must be constant and the process mean and control limits are calculated using the following formulae:

$$\text{Process mean } \bar{c} = \frac{c_1 + c_2 + c_3 + \ldots + c_m}{m}$$

$$\text{Control limits} = \bar{c} \pm 3\sqrt{c}$$

where:

$$c = \text{number of defects}$$
$$m = \text{number of samples}$$

Figure S17.6 Control chart for the percentage of customer accounts which are mailed outside their two-day period

CONTROL CHART FOR VARIABLES

The most commonly used type of control chart employed to control variables is the $\bar{X}$–R chart. In fact this is really two charts in one. One chart is used to control the sample average or mean ($\bar{X}$). The other is used to control the variation within the sample by measuring the range (R). The range is used because it is simpler to calculate than the standard deviation of the sample.

The means ($\bar{X}$) chart can pick up changes in the average output from the process being charted. Changes in the means chart would suggest that the process is drifting generally away from its supposed process average, although the variability inherent in the process may not have changed (*see* Fig. S17.7).

The range (R) chart plots the range of each sample, that is the difference between the largest and the smallest measurement in the samples. Monitoring sample range gives an indication of whether the variability of the process is changing, even when the process average remains constant (*see* Fig. S17.7).

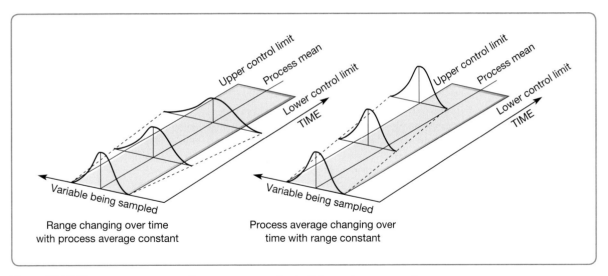

Figure S17.7 **The process mean or the process range (or both) can change over time**

Control limits for variables control chart

As with attributes control charts, a statistical description of how the process operates under normal conditions (when there are no assignable causes) can be used to calculate control limits. The first task in calculating the control limits is to estimate the grand average or population mean ($\overline{\overline{X}}$) and average range ($\overline{R}$) using m samples each of sample size n.

The population mean is estimated from the average of a large number (m) of sample means:

$$\overline{\overline{X}} = \frac{\overline{X}_1 + \overline{X}_2 + \ldots + \overline{X}_m}{m}$$

The average range is estimated from the ranges of the large number of samples:

$$\overline{R} = \frac{R_1 + R_2 + \ldots + R_m}{m}$$

The control limits for the sample means chart are:

$$\text{Upper control limit (UCL)} = \overline{\overline{X}} + A_2\overline{R}$$
$$\text{Lower control limit (LCL)} = \overline{\overline{X}} - A_2\overline{R}$$

The control limits for the range charts are:

$$\text{Upper control limit (UCL)} = D_4\overline{R}$$
$$\text{Lower control limit (LCL)} = D_3\overline{R}$$

The factors A_2, D_3 and D_4 vary with sample size and are shown in Table S17.2.

The LCL for the means chart may be negative (for example, temperature or profit may be less than zero) but it may not be negative for a range chart (or the smallest measurement in the sample would be larger than the largest). If the calculation indicates a negative LCL for a range chart then the LCL should be set to zero.

Interpreting control charts

Plots on a control chart which fall outside control limits are an obvious reason for believing that the process might be out of control, and therefore for investigating the process. This is not the only clue which could be revealed by a control chart, however. Figure S17.9 shows some other patterns which could be interpreted as behaviour sufficiently unusual to warrant investigation.

Table S17.2 **Factors for the calculation of control limits**

Sample size n	A_2	D_3	D_4
2	1.880	0	3.267
3	1.023	0	2.575
4	0.729	0	2.282
5	0.577	0	2.115
6	0.483	0	2.004
7	0.419	0.076	1.924
8	0.373	0.136	1.864
9	0.337	0.184	1.816
10	0.308	0.223	1.777
12	0.266	0.284	1.716
14	0.235	0.329	1.671
16	0.212	0.364	1.636
18	0.194	0.392	1.608
20	0.180	0.414	1.586
22	0.167	0.434	1.566
24	0.157	0.452	1.548

Worked example

GAM (Groupe As Maquillage) is a contract cosmetics company, based in France but with plants around Europe, which manufactures and packs cosmetics and perfumes for other companies. One of its plants, in Ireland, operates a filling line which automatically fills plastic bottles with skin cream and seals the bottles with a screw-top cap. The tightness with which the screw-top cap is fixed is an important part of the quality of the filling line process. If the cap is screwed on too tightly, there is a danger that it will crack; if screwed on too loosely it might come loose when packed. Either outcome could cause leakage of the product during its journey between the factory and the customer. The Irish plant had received some complaints of product leakage which it suspected was caused by inconsistent fixing of the screw-top caps on its filling line. The 'tightness' of the screw tops could be measured by a simple test device which recorded the amount of turning force (torque) that was required to unfasten the tops. The company decided to take samples of the bottles coming out of the filling-line process, test them for their unfastening torque and plot the results on a control chart. Several samples of four bottles were taken during a period when the process was regarded as being in control. The following data was calculated from this exercise:

The grand average of all samples $\overline{\overline{X}} = 812$ g/cm^3
The average range of the sample $\overline{R} = 6$ g/cm^3

Control limits for the means $(\overline{X})$ chart were calculated as follows:

$$UCL = \overline{\overline{X}} + A_2\overline{R}$$
$$= 812 + (A_2 \times 6)$$

From Table S17.2, we know, for a sample size of four, $A_2 = 0.729$. Thus:

$$UCL = 812 + (0.729 \times 6)$$
$$= 816.37$$

$$LCL = \overline{\overline{X}} - A_2 \overline{R}$$
$$= 812 - (0.729 \times 6)$$
$$= 807.63$$

Control limits for the range chart (R) were calculated as follows:

$$UCL = D_4 \times \overline{R}$$
$$= 2.282 \times 6$$
$$= 13.69$$

$$LCL = D_3 \overline{R}$$
$$= 0 \times 6$$
$$= 0$$

After calculating these averages and limits for the control chart, the company regularly took samples of four bottles during production, recorded the measurements and plotted them as shown in Figure S17.8. The control chart revealed that only with difficulty could the process average be kept in control. Occasional operator interventions were required. Also the process range was moving towards (and once breaking) the upper control limit. The process seemed to be becoming more variable. After investigation it was discovered that, because of faulty maintenance of the line, skin cream was occasionally contaminating the torque head (the part of the line which fitted the cap). This resulted in erratic tightening of the caps.

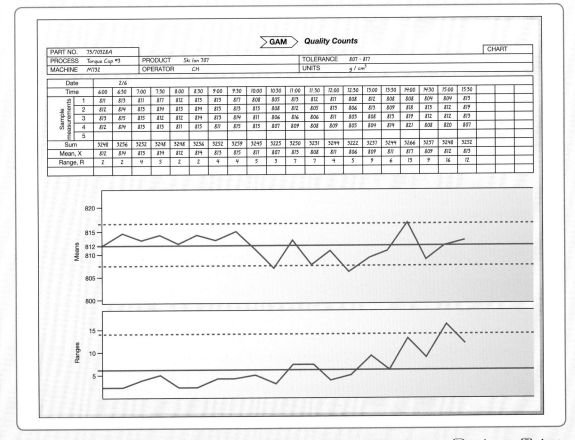

Figure S17.8 The completed control form for GAM's torque machine showing the mean $(\overline{X})$ and range (R) charts

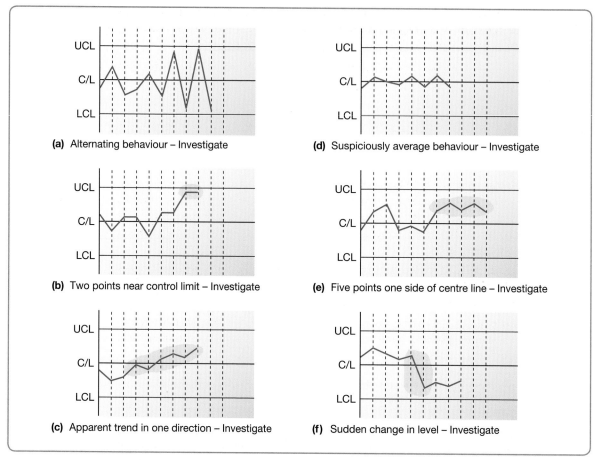

Figure S17.9 In addition to points falling outside the control limits, other unlikely sequences of points should be investigated

Process control, learning and knowledge

In recent years the role of process control, and SPC in particular, has changed. Increasingly, it is seen not just as a convenient method of keeping processes in control, but also as an activity which is fundamental to the acquisition of competitive advantage. This is a remarkable shift in the status of SPC. Traditionally it was seen as one of the most *operational*, immediate and 'hands-on' operations management techniques. Yet it is now being connected with an operation's *strategic* capabilities. This is how the logic of the argument goes:

1 SPC is based on the idea that process variability indicates whether a process is in control or not.
2 Processes are brought into *control* and improved by progressively reducing process variability. This involves eliminating the assignable causes of variation.
3 One cannot eliminate assignable causes of variation without gaining a better understanding of how the process operates. This involves *learning* about the process, where its nature is revealed at an increasingly detailed level.
4 This learning means that *process knowledge* is enhanced, which in turn means that operations managers are able to predict how the process will perform under different circumstances. It also means that the process has a greater capability to carry out its tasks at a higher level of performance.

5 This increased *process capability* is particularly difficult for competitors to copy. It cannot be bought 'off the shelf'. It only comes from time and effort being invested in controlling operations processes. Therefore, process capability leads to strategic advantage.

In this way, process control leads to learning which enhances process knowledge and builds difficult-to-imitate process capability.

SUMMARY OF SUPPLEMENT

❯ Statistical process control (SPC) involves using control charts to track the performance of one or more quality characteristics in the operation. The power of control charting lies in its ability to set control limits derived from the statistics of the natural variation of processes. These control limits are often set at ± 3 standard deviations of the natural variation of the process samples.

❯ Control charts can be used for either attributes or variables. An attribute is a quality characteristic which has two states (for example, right or wrong). A variable is one which can be measured on a continuously variable scale.

❯ Process control charts allow operations managers to distinguish between the 'normal' variation inherent in any process and the variations which could be caused by the process going out of control.

SELECTED FURTHER READING

Woodall, W.H. (2000) Controversies and contradictions in statistical process control, Paper presented at the Journal of Quality Technology Session at the 44th Annual Fall Technical Conference of the Chemical and Process Industries Division and Statistics Division of the American Society for Quality and the Section on Physical & Engineering Sciences of the American Statistical Association in Minneapolis, Minnesota, 12–13 October 2000.

Academic but interesting.

18 Managing risk and recovery

Key questions

> What is risk management?

> How can operations assess the potential causes and consequences of failure?

> How can failures be prevented?

> How can operations mitigate the effects of failure?

> How can operations recover from the effects of failure?

INTRODUCTION

No matter how much effort is put into improvement, all operations will face risk and occasionally experience failures. Some risks emerge from within the operation, sometimes through poor operations management practice, such as poor quality control. Some risks come from the operation's supply network, for example relying on over-powerful or unreliable suppliers. Other risks come from broader environmental (also called institutional) forces, such as political unrest, and environmental disasters. In the face of such risks, a 'resilient' operation is one that can identify likely sources of risk, prevent failures occurring, minimize their effects and learn how to recover from them. In a world where the sources of risk and the consequences of failure are becoming increasingly difficult to handle, managing risk is a vital task. From sudden changes in demand to the bankruptcy of a key supplier, from terrorist attacks to cybercrime, the threats to the normal smooth running of operations are rising. And the consequences of such events are becoming more serious. Paring down costs, cutting inventories and striving for higher levels of capacity utilization can all result in higher vulnerability. At the same time, more regulation, and attentive media, can make operations failure more damaging. In this chapter we examine both the dramatic and the more routine risks that can prevent operations working as they should. Figure 18.1 shows how this chapter fits into the operation's improvement activities.

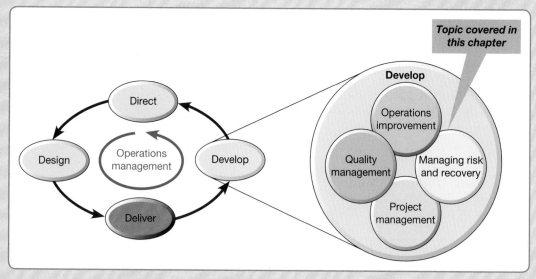

Figure 18.1 This chapter examines managing risk and recovery

Tesco, Findus and the horsemeat scandal[1]

On 15 January 2013, several news organizations reported that horse DNA had been discovered in frozen beefburgers that were widely available for sale in British and Irish supermarkets. Despite the fact that horsemeat is not harmful to health (it is eaten in many countries), consumers in the UK and Ireland do not generally view it as acceptable. Further European-wide investigations revealed high levels of horsemeat in 'beef' products, and in some cases pig DNA, a taboo food for people in the Muslim and Jewish communities. In the UK, two companies were the subject of much press attention: Tesco, the UK's largest supermarket chain, which had sold some of the offending products; and Findus, a frozen food brand that had produced 'beef' lasagne product found by the UK's Food Standards Agency to contain 100 per cent horsemeat. A subsequent investigation by Media Perception Insight (MPI), a consultancy, used a panel of trade journalists to research the comparative impact of Tesco's and Findus' reputation. The investigation revealed that both Tesco and Findus has suffered in terms of their reputation for corporate social responsibility, yet there was a significant difference in how the two companies' response to the crisis has affected their branding and marketing.

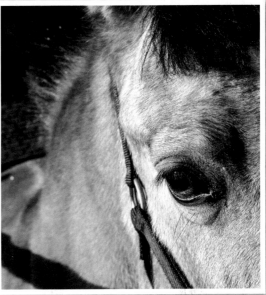

Source: Shutterstock.com: Anna Baburkina

The journalist panel judged Tesco's response as particularly successful, with a 'brand protection' score of 77.6 per cent. By contrast, Findus only scored 46.6 per cent. George Robinson, the Chairman of MPI, commented that, despite the negative publicity, Tesco's proactive approach to communications allowed it to preserve its positioning among the key trade media audience. *'While many experts commented that Findus tended to keep quiet as the scandal unfolded, Tesco was praised for facing the crisis head-on in the media – and this has been clearly reflected in the survey results. We can see the impact of Tesco's marketing strategy on its reputation, even at times where its responsibility to the public is being questioned.'* In particular, it was Tesco's speed of response, direct and clear messaging, and its willingness to take ownership of the problem that protected its reputation. Another risk authority commented that *'adopting the "active" approach enables large companies to respond to a crisis quickly by instilling the values of clarity, simplicity and humanity. Brands need to be defined in clear and simple terms that everyone within an organisation can remember and act upon. This enables a PR team to adopt a position that is readily identifiable as a meaningful and decisive response, not an evasion or quibbling over responsibilities that can be interpreted as 'playing for time.'*

WHAT IS RISK MANAGEMENT?

Risk management is about identifying things that could go wrong, stopping them going wrong, reducing the consequences when things do go wrong, and recovering after things have gone wrong. Things happen in operations, or to operations, that have negative consequences – this is failure. But accepting that failure occurs is not the same thing as tolerating or ignoring it. Though operations managers do generally attempt to minimize both the likelihood of failure and the effect it will have, the methods of coping with failure will depend on how serious its consequences are, and how likely it is to occur. At the lower end of the scale, the whole area of quality management is concerned with identifying and reducing every small error in the creation and delivery of products and services. Other failures will have more impact on the operation, even if they do not occur very frequently. For example, a server failure can seriously affect service and therefore customers, which is why system reliability is such as important measure of performance for IT service providers. Some failures, while much less likely, are so serious in terms of negative consequences that we class them as disasters. Examples may include major floods, earthquakes, hurricanes, wars and acts of terrorism, and financial collapses such as a stock market crash.

> **❋ Operations principle**
>
> Failure will always occur in operations; recognizing this does not imply accepting or ignoring it.

This chapter is concerned with all types of failure other than those with relatively minor consequences. This is illustrated in Figure 18.2. Some of these failures are irritating but relatively unimportant, especially those close to the bottom left-hand corner of the matrix in Figure 18.2. Other failures, especially those close to the top right-hand corner of the matrix, are normally avoided by all businesses because embracing such risks would be clearly foolish. In between these two extremes is where most operations-related risks occur. In this chapter will shall be treating various aspects of these types of failure, and in particular how they can be moved in the direction of arrows in Figure 18.2.

Obviously, some operations have to work in a more risky environment than others. Those operations with a high likelihood of failure and/or serious consequences deriving from that failure will need to give it more attention. But managing risk and recovery

> **❋ Operations principle**
>
> Resilience is governed by the effectiveness of failure prevention, mitigation and recovery.

is relevant to all organizations and generally involves four sets of activities. The first is concerned with understanding what failures could potentially occur in the operation and assessing their seriousness. The second task is to examine ways of preventing failures occurring. The third is to minimize the negative consequences of failure – called failure or risk 'mitigation'. The final task is to devise plans and procedures that will help the operation to recover from failures when they do occur. The remainder of this chapter deals with these four tasks, *see* Figure 18.3.

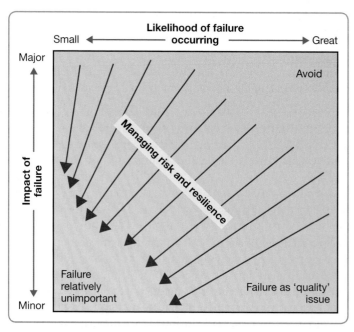

Figure 18.2 How failure is managed depends on its likelihood of occurrence and the negative consequences of failure

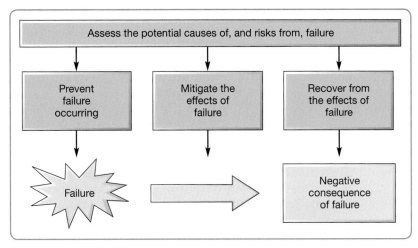

Figure 18.3 Risk management involves failure prevention, mitigating the negative consequences of failure, and failure recovery

HOW CAN OPERATIONS ASSESS THE POTENTIAL CAUSES AND CONSEQUENCES OF FAILURE?

The first stage of risk management is to understand the potential sources of risk. This means assessing where failure might occur and what the consequences of failure might be. Often it is a 'failure to understand failure' that results in unacceptable risk. Each potential cause of failure needs to be assessed in terms of how likely it is to occur and the impact it may have. Only then can measures be taken to prevent or minimize the effect of the more important potential failures. The classic approach to assessing potential failures is to inspect and audit operations activities. Unfortunately, inspection and audit cannot, on their own, provide complete assurance that undesirable events will be avoided. The content of any audit has to be appropriate, the checking process has to be sufficiently frequent and comprehensive, and the inspectors have to have sufficient knowledge and experience. But whatever approach to risk is taken, it can only be effective if the organizational culture that it is set in fully supports a 'risk-aware' attitude.

Identify the potential causes of failure

The causes of some failures are purely random, like lightning strikes, and are difficult, if not impossible, to predict. However, the vast majority of failures are caused by something that could have been avoided. So, as a minimum starting point, a simple checklist of failure causes is useful. Figure 18.4 illustrates how this might be done. Here, failure sources are classified as (1) failures of supply; (2) internal failures such as those deriving from human, organizational and technological sources; (3) failures deriving from the design of products and services; (4) failures deriving from customer failures; and (5) general environmental (or institutional) failures.

> ✳ **Operations principle**
> A 'failure to understand failure' can be the root cause of a lack of resilience.

Supply failure

Supply failure is any failure in the timing or quality of goods and services delivered into an operation – for example, suppliers delivering the wrong or faulty components, outsourced call centres suffering a telecoms failure, disruption to power supplies, and so on. It can be an important source of failure because of increasing dependence on outsourced activities in most industries. The more an operation relies on suppliers for materials or services, the more

Figure 18.4 The sources of potential failure in operations

it is at risk from failure caused by missing or substandard inputs. It is an important source of failure because of the increasing dependence on outsourced activities in many industries, and the emphasis on keeping supply chains 'lean' in order to cut costs. Other factors have also increased exposure to supply failure in recent years. For example, the rise of global sourcing usually means that parts are shipped around the world on their journey through the supply chain. Microchips manufactured in Taiwan could be assembled to printed circuit boards in Shanghai that are then assembled into a computer in Ireland and sold in the USA. At the same time, many industries are suffering increased volatility and uncertainty in demand. This may be as a result of market fragmentation, where small customer segments have to be accommodated. Or it may be as a result of faster changes in products, services or the supply base. But the result is to make demand forecasting extremely challenging. Perhaps most significantly there tends to be far less inventory in supply chains that could buffer interruptions to supply. According to one authority on supply chain management, *'Potentially the risk of disruption has increased dramatically as the result of a too-narrow focus on supply chain efficiency at the expense of effectiveness.'*[2]

Human failures

There are two broad types of human failure. The first is where key personnel leave, become ill, die, or in some way cannot fulfil their role. The second is where people are doing their job but are making mistakes. Understanding risk in the first type of failure involves identifying the key people without whom operations would struggle to operate effectively. These are not always the most senior individuals, but rather those fulfilling crucial roles that require special skills or tacit knowledge. Human failure through 'mistakes' also comes in two types: errors and violations. 'Errors' are mistakes in judgement, where a person should have done something different – for example, if the manager of a sports stadium fails to anticipate dangerous crowding during a championship event. 'Violations' are acts that are clearly contrary to defined operating procedure. For example, if a maintenance engineer fails to clean a filter in the prescribed manner, it is eventually likely to cause failure. Catastrophic failures are often caused by a combination of errors and violations, For example, one kind of accident, where an aircraft appears to be under control and yet still flies into the ground, is very rare (once in 2 million flights). For this type of failure to occur, first, the pilot has to be flying at the wrong altitude (error). Second, the co-pilot would have to fail to cross-check the altitude (violation). Third, air traffic controllers would have to miss the fact that the aircraft was at the wrong altitude (error). Finally, the pilot would have to ignore the ground-proximity warning alarm in the aircraft, which can be prone to give false alarms (violation).

Organizational failure

Organizational failure is usually taken to mean failures of procedures and processes, and failures that derive from a business's organizational structure and culture. This is a huge potential source of failure and includes almost all operations and process management. In particular, failure in the design of processes (such as bottlenecks causing system overloading) and failures in the resourcing of processes (such as insufficient capacity being provided at peak times) need to be investigated. But there are also many other procedures and processes within an organization that can make failure more likely. For example, remuneration policy may motivate staff to work in a way that, although increasing the financial performance of the organization, also increases the risk of failure. Examples of this can range from sales-people being so incentivized that they make promises to customers that cannot be fulfilled, through to investment bankers being more concerned with profit than the risks of financial overexposure. This type of risk can derive from an organizational culture that minimizes consideration of risk, or it may come from a lack of clarity in reporting relationships.

OPERATIONS IN PRACTICE

An Olympic security fiasco[3]

On 21 May 2013, Nick Buckles announced that he would be stepping down as Chief Executive of G4S, a leading global security company. Despite share growth and expansion of operations, for many, Mr Buckles' leadership will always be remembered for the failure to fulfil its obligations to provide security to the 2012 London Olympic Games. A year earlier, G4S was given the contract for security provision to provide training and management of the 10,000 security personnel that would be required for the games. By December of the same year the Olympic organizers announced that the number of security staff that would be needed for the Olympics was to be increased dramatically to 23,700, with G4S's initial 2,000 security staff rising to 10,400. The fee for this increased service rose too – from £7.3 million to around £60 million. However, although a large portion of the increased funds (£34 million) went towards the G4S 'programme management office' overseeing the security operation, only £2.8 million was added to the firm's recruitment spending.

By July 2012, media reports suggested that G4S was struggling to recruit and train staff. Worse still, a 'whistle-blower' claimed that security-vetting procedures were being overlooked and some employees were 'self-certifying'. Though initially denying these allegations, G4S was eventually forced to admit that it would not be able to deliver the number of security personnel that it had promised. The delays in admitting that there was a problem only went to fuel media claims of a cover-up and the firm's share price plummeted (more embarrassingly, it later emerged that the problem had been flagged up internally months earlier).

When the scale of the problem did become clear the UK government announced that it would have to call upon an extra 3,500 troops, who would be used for security duties. After the Olympics (which were both successful and security incident free), Mr Buckles was called to testify before a House of Commons (Government) Committee. His performance made for uncomfortable viewing and was widely derided. One media commentator said, 'The performance made me squirm. It showed little preparation and the company's approach was fundamentally wrong. [Any firm's] crisis management team must be senior, tightly managed and empowered to make serious strategic decisions; events can develop too quickly to allow decisions by committee. With G4S, like many companies, it appeared that too few hours had been spent considering the reputational risk of winning an Olympic contract. However, that planning could have been invaluable and should be a lesson for any chief executive.'

Later in the same year, G4S ruled out bidding for security contracts at the 2016 Olympics in Brazil because of 'the reputational damage that would be done to the company if the fiasco of the London contract was repeated'. Later in 2012, the company accepted the resignations of its UK boss and its managing director of global events. By February 2013, G4S had announced that its losses would be even bigger than expected, standing at £70 million.

Technology/facilities failures

By 'technology and facilities' we mean all the IT systems, machines, equipment and buildings of an operation. All are liable to failure, or breakdown. The failure may be only partial, for example a machine that has an intermittent fault. Alternatively, it can be what we normally regard as a 'breakdown' – a total and sudden cessation of operation. Either way, its effects could bring a large part of the operation to a halt. For example, a computer failure in a supermarket chain could paralyse several large stores until it is fixed. Such IT failures have occurred for several leading banks over recent years. The root cause of these failures can often be traced back to inadequate maintenance of exceptionally complex information systems. In other cases, cyber attacks on corporate information systems create a new, or at least increased, threat to operations.

Product/service design failures

In its design stage, a product or service might look fine on paper; only when it has to cope with real circumstances might inadequacies become evident. A recent example of this is Heathrow's Terminal 5, which reported that it had not been able to replace a single light bulb in five years since its opening. The reason? When designing this iconic structure, no one thought to examine how its many light fittings would be maintained when they reached the end of their life. After several failed attempts at finding a solution, Heathrow Airport Holdings announced they would be hiring the services of a specialist high-level rope-work company to carry out the work – they declined to state what the cost of such skilled operators would be! One could reasonably argue that during the design process, this potential risk of failure should have been identified and 'designed out'. But one only has to look at the number of 'product recalls' or service failures to understand that design failures are far from uncommon. Sometimes this is the result of a trade-off between fast time-to-market performance and the risk of the product or service failing in operation. And while no reputable business would deliberately market flawed products or services, equally most businesses cannot delay a product or service launch indefinitely to eliminate every single small risk of failure.

Customer failures

Not all failures are (directly) caused by the operation or by its suppliers. Customers may 'fail' in that they misuse products and services. For example, an IT system might have been well designed, yet the user could treat it in a way that causes it to fail. Customers are not 'always right'; they can be inattentive and incompetent. However, merely complaining about customers is unlikely to reduce the chances of this type of failure occurring. Most organizations will accept that they have a responsibility to educate and train customers, and to design their products and services so as to minimize the chances of failure.

Environmental disruption

Environmental disruption includes all the causes of failure that lie outside of an operation's direct influence. These include major political upheaval, hurricanes, floods, earthquakes, temperature extremes, fire, corporate crime, theft, fraud, sabotage, terrorism, other security attacks, and the contamination of products or processes. This source of potential failure has risen to near the top of many firms' agenda due to a series of major events over recent years. As operations become increasingly integrated (and increasingly dependent on integrated technologies such as information technologies), businesses are more aware of the critical events and malfunctions that have the potential to interrupt normal business activity and even stop the entire company.

E-security[4]

Any advance in processes or technology creates risks. No real advance comes without risk, threats and even danger. This applies particularly to e-business. In almost all businesses information has become critical. So, information security management has become a particularly high priority. But herein lies the problem. The Internet, which is the primary medium for conducting e-business, is by design an open, non-secure medium. Since the original purpose of the Internet was not for commercial purposes, it is not designed to handle secure transactions. So there is a trade-off between providing wider access through the Internet and the security concerns it generates. Three developments have amplified e-security concerns. First, increased connectivity (who does not rely on Internet-based systems?) means that everyone has at least the potential to 'see' everyone else. Organizations want to make enterprise systems and information more available to internal employees, business partners and customers (*see* Chapter 14 on planning and control systems). Second, there has been a loss of 'perimeter' security as more people work from home or through mobile communications. For example, some banks have been targeted by criminals who seek to exploit home working as a means to breach corporate security firewalls. Hackers had hoped to exploit lower levels of security in home computers to burrow into corporate networks. Third, for some new, sometimes unregulated technologies, such as some mobile networks, it takes time to discover all possible sources of risk. The Internet, after all, is an open system and the rapid rate of development of new software and systems often means that users do not have an adequate knowledge about software and systems architecture. This makes users oblivious to potential vulnerabilities that can lead to serious security breaches.

Post-failure analysis

While sources of failure can often be identified in advance of their occurrence, it is also valuable to use previous failures to learn about sources of potential risk. This activity is called post-failure analysis. It is used to uncover the root cause of failures. This includes such activities as the following:

- **Accident investigation** – where large-scale national disasters like oil tanker spillages and aircraft accidents are investigated using specifically trained staff. In many senses, the reason so much attention goes into examining these kinds of failures after the event is not only because of the damaging consequences of failure, but also because their infrequency makes it relatively hard to identify new sources of risks in advance of an event.
- **Failure traceability** – where some businesses (either by choice or because of a legal requirement) adopt traceability procedures to ensure that all their failures (such as contaminated food products) are traceable. Any failures can be traced back to the process which produced them, the components from which they were produced, or the suppliers who provided them. Bio-tagging in pharmaceuticals is one example of this approach. If a medical product is found or suspected to have a problem, all other products in the batch can be recalled.
- **Complaint analysis** – where complaints are used as a valuable source for detecting the root causes of failures of customer service. The prime function of complaint analysis involves analysing the number and 'content' of complaints over time to understand better the nature of the failure, as the customer perceives it. Two key advantages of complaints are that they come unsolicited and they are often very timely pieces of information that can pinpoint problems quickly. However, managers should be aware that for every customer who does complain, there might be many who do not!
- **Fault-tree analysis** – where a logical procedure starts with a failure or a potential failure and works backwards to identify all the possible causes and therefore the origins of that

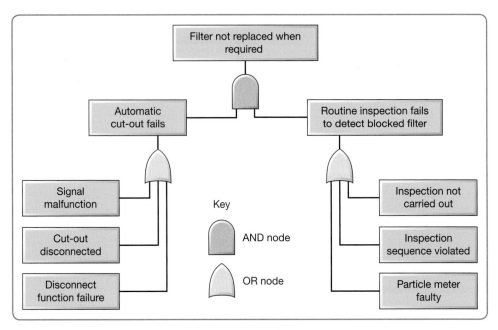

Figure 18.5 Fault-tree analysis for failure to replace filter when required

failure. Fault-tree analysis is made up of branches connected by two types of nodes: AND nodes and OR nodes. The branches below an AND node all need to occur for the event above the node to occur. Only one of the branches below an OR node needs to occur for the event above the node to occur. Figure 18.5 shows a simple tree identifying the possible reasons for a filter in a heating system not being replaced when it should have been.

Likelihood of failure

The difficulty of estimating the chance of a failure occurring varies greatly. Some failures are well understood through a combination of rational causal analysis and historical performance. For example, a mechanical component may fail between 10 and 17 months of its installation in 99 per cent of cases. Other types of failure are far more difficult to predict. The chances of a fire in a supplier's plant are (hopefully) low, but how low? There will be some data concerning fire hazards in this type of plant, but the estimated probability of failure will be subjective.

'Objective' estimates

Estimates of failure based on historical performance can be measured in three main ways:

- **failure rates** – how often a failure occurs;
- **reliability** – the chances of a failure occurring;
- **availability** – the amount of available useful operating time.

Failure rate Failure rate (FR) is calculated as the number of failures over a period of time. For example, the security of an airport can be measured by the number of security breaches per year, and the failure rate of an engine can be measured in terms of the number of failures divided by its operating time. It can be measured either as a percentage of the total number of products tested or as the number of failures over time:

$$FR = \frac{\text{Number of failures}}{\text{Total number of products tested}} \times 100$$

or:

$$FR = \frac{\text{Number of failures}}{\text{Operating time}}$$

> ## Worked example
>
> A batch of 50 electronic components is tested for 2,000 hours. Four of the components fail during the test as follows:
>
> Failure 1 occurred at 12:00 hours
>
> Failure 2 occurred at 14:50 hours
>
> Failure 3 occurred at 17:20 hours
>
> Failure 4 occurred at 19:05 hours
>
> $$\text{Failure rate as a percentage} = \frac{\text{Number of failures}}{\text{Number tested}} \times 100 = \frac{4}{50} \times 10 = 8\%$$
>
> The total time of the test $= 50 \times 2,000 = 100,000$ component hours
>
> But:
>
> one component was not operating $2,000 - 1,200 = 800$ hours
>
> one component was not operating $2,000 - 1,450 = 550$ hours
>
> one component was not operating $2,000 - 1,720 = 280$ hours
>
> one component was not operating $2,000 - 1,905 = 95$ hours
>
> Thus:
>
> $$\text{Total non-operating time} = 1,725 \text{ hours}$$
> $$\text{Operating time} = \text{Total time} - \text{Non-operating time}$$
> $$= 100,000 - 1,725 = 98,275 \text{ hours}$$
> $$\text{Failure rate (in time)} = \frac{\text{Number of failures}}{\text{Operating time}} = \frac{4}{98,275}$$
> $$= 0.000041$$

Bath-tub curves Sometimes failure is a function of time. For example, the probability of an electric lamp failing is relatively high when it is first used, but if it survives this initial stage, it could still fail at any point, and the longer it survives, the more likely its failure becomes. The curve that describes failure probability of this type is called the bath-tub curve. It comprises three distinct stages: the 'infant-mortality' or 'early-life' stage where early failures occur caused by defective parts or improper use; the 'normal-life' stage when the failure rate is usually low and reasonably constant, and caused by normal random factors; and the 'wear-out' stage when the failure rate increases as the part approaches the end of its working life and failure is caused by the ageing and deterioration of parts. Figure 18.6 illustrates three bath-tub curves with slightly different characteristics. Curve A shows a part of the operation which has a high initial infant-mortality failure but then a long, low-failure, normal life followed by the gradually increasing likelihood of failure as it approaches wear-out. Curve B is far less predictable. The distinction between the three stages is less clear, with infant-mortality failure subsiding only slowly and a gradually increasing chance of wear-out failure. Failure of the type shown in curve B is far more difficult to manage in a planned manner. The failure of operations that rely more on human resources than on technology, such as some services, can be closer to curve C. They may be less susceptible to component wear-out but more so to staff complacency as the service becomes tedious and repetitive.

Reliability Reliability measures the ability to perform as expected over time. Usually the importance of any particular failure is determined partly by how interdependent the other

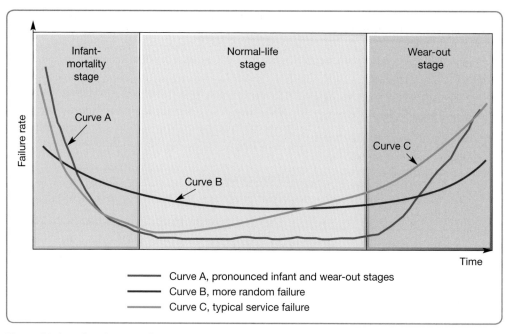

Figure 18.6 Bath-tub curves for three types of process

parts of the system are. With interdependence, a failure in one component will cause the whole system to fail. So, if an interdependent system has n components each with their own reliability, $R_1, R_2, ..., R_n$, the reliability of the whole system, R_s, is given by:

$$R_s = R_1 \times R_2 \times R_3 \times ... \times R_n$$

where:

R_1 = reliability of component 1

R_2 = reliability of component 2

etc.

Worked example

An automated pizza-making machine in a food manufacturer's factory has five major components, with individual reliabilities (the probability of the component not failing) as follows:

Dough mixer	Reliability = 0.95
Dough roller and cutter	Reliability = 0.99
Tomato paste applicator	Reliability = 0.97
Cheese applicator	Reliability = 0.90
Oven	Reliability = 0.98

If one of these parts of the production system fails, the whole system will stop working. Thus the reliability of the whole system is:

$$R_s = 0.95 \times 0.99 \times 0.97 \times 0.90 \times 0.98$$
$$= 0.805$$

The number of components In the example, the reliability of the whole system was only 0.8, even though the reliability of the individual components was significantly higher. If the system had been made up of more components, then its reliability would have been even lower. The more interdependent components an operations or process has, the lower its reliability will be. For one composed of components which each have an individual reliability of 0.99, with 10 components the system reliability will shrink to 0.9, with 50 components it is below 0.8, with 100 components it is below 0.4, and with 400 components it is down below 0.05. In other words, with a process of 400 components (not unusual in a large automated operation), even if the reliability of each individual component is 99 per cent, the whole system will be working for less than 5 per cent of its time.

Mean time between failures An alternative (and common) measure of failure is the mean time between failures (MTBF) of a component or system. MTBF is the reciprocal of failure rate (in time). Thus:

$$\text{MTBF} = \frac{\text{Operating hours}}{\text{Number of failures}}$$

Worked example

In the previous worked example which was concerned with electronic components, the failure rate (in time) of the electronic components was 0.000041. For that component:

$$\text{MTBF} = \frac{1}{0.000041} = 24{,}390.24 \text{ hours}$$

That is, a failure can be expected once every 24,390.24 hours on average.

Availability Availability is the degree to which the operation is ready to work. An operation is not available if it has either failed or is being repaired following failure. There are several different ways of measuring it depending on how many of the reasons for not operating are included. Lack of availability because of planned maintenance or changeovers could be included, for example. However, when 'availability' is being used to indicate the operating time excluding the consequence of failure, it is calculated as follows:

$$\text{Availability } (A) = \frac{\text{MTBF}}{\text{MTBF} + \text{MTTR}}$$

Where:

  MTBF = the mean time between failures of the operation

  MTTR = the mean time to repair, which is the average time taken to repair the operation, from the time it fails to the time it is operational again

Worked example

A company which designs and produces display posters for exhibitions and sales promotion events competes largely on the basis of its speedy delivery. One particular piece of equipment which the company uses is causing some problems. This is its large-platform colour laser printer. Currently, the mean time between failures of the printer is 70 hours and its mean time to repair is six hours. Thus:

$$\text{Availability} = \frac{70}{70 + 6} = 0.92$$

The company has discussed its problem with the supplier of the printer, who has offered two alternative service deals. One option would be to buy some preventive maintenance (see later for a full description of preventive maintenance) which would be carried out each week-end. This would raise the MTBF of the printer to 90 hours. The other option would be to sub-scribe to a faster repair service which would reduce the MTTR to 4 hours. Both options would cost the same amount. Which would give the company the higher availability?

With MTBF increased to 90 hours:

$$\text{Availability} = \frac{90}{90 + 6} = 0.938$$

With MTTR reduced to 4 hours:

$$\text{Availability} = \frac{70}{70 + 4} = 0.946$$

Availability would be greater if the company took the deal which offered the faster repair time.

The rise of the MicroMort[5]

Source: 123RF.com: Andrew Mayovskyy

Calculating risk is far from easy. However, two authorities on risk, Michael Blastand and David Spiegelhalter, try to untangle the nature of risk and probability through the concept of the 'MicroMort'. The MicroMort is defined as a one-in-a-million chance of death and its use allows for some interesting comparisons to be made. For example, the chance of dying on a return motorbike trip from Edinburgh to London in the UK is around 120 MicroMorts (that is, a 120-in-a-million chance). This is com-parable with the risk faced by mothers giving birth in the UK or a soldier spend-ing 2.5 days in the most dangerous period of the Afghanistan conflict. The concept also allows us to examine how risks have changed over time. For example, aircrews involved in bombing raids during the Second World War were 'exposed' to 25,000 MicroMorts – a depressing 2.5 per cent chance of death – per mission. Soldiers in Afghanistan in the recent conflict faced (just) 47 Micromorts – or 0.0047 per cent chance of death – per day on the ground. What is perhaps most interesting about the work is that it explores just how irrational humans are when attempting to cal-culate risk. Typically high-impact/low-probability risk is over-emphasized, while low-impact/high-probability risk is under-emphasized. For organizations, appreciat-ing the innate irrationality and cognition biases of most of its managers and employees can be a important step towards developing better assessments of various poten-tial sources of failure.

'Subjective' estimates Failure assessment, even for subjective risks, is increasingly a formal exercise that is carried out using standard frameworks, often prompted by health and safety, environmental or other regulatory reasons. These frameworks are similar to the formal quality inspection methods associated with quality standards like ISO 9000 (see Chapter 17) that often implicitly assume unbiased objectivity. However, individual attitudes to risk are complex and subject to a wide variety of influences. In fact many studies have demonstrated that people are generally very poor at making risk-related judgements. Consider the success of state and national lotteries. The chances of winning, in nearly every case, are so low as to make the financial value of the investment entirely negative. If players have to drive their car in order to purchase a ticket, they may be more likely to be killed or seriously injured than they are to win the top prize. But although people do not always make rational decisions concerning the chances of failure, this does not mean abandoning the attempt. But it does mean that one must understand the limits to overly rational approaches to failure estimation, for example how people tend to pay too much attention to dramatic low-probability events and overlook routine events. Even when 'objective' evaluations of risks are used, they may still cause negative consequences. For example, when the oil giant Royal Dutch Shell took the decision to employ deep-water disposal in the North Sea for its Brent Spar oil platform, the company felt that it was making a rational operational decision based upon the best available scientific evidence concerning environmental risk. Unfortunately Greenpeace disagreed and put forward an alternative 'objective analysis' showing significant risk from deep-water disposal. Eventually Greenpeace admitted its evidence was flawed but by that time Shell had lost the public relations battle and had altered its plans.

> ✱ **Operations principle**
> Subjective estimates of failure probability are better than no estimates at all.

Non-evident failure estimation Not all failures are immediately evident. Small failures may be accumulating for a while before they become evident, making objective and subjective estimation challenging. For example, purchasing managers who encounter difficulties in using an e-procurement system may simply circumvent the system and the failure points may only become evident when levels of non-compliance reach sufficient levels for senior management to notice. Likewise, within an automated production line, debris can accumulate. This may not cause an immediate failure, but could eventually lead to sudden and dramatic failure. Even when such failures are detected, they may not always receive the appropriate attention, either because there are inadequate failure identification systems, or because there is insufficient managerial support or interest in making improvements. The mechanisms available to seek out failures in a proactive way include machine diagnostic checks, in-process checks, point-of-departure and phone interviews, and customer focus groups.

Critical commentary

The idea that failure can be detected through in-process inspection is increasingly seen as only partially true. Although inspecting for failures is an obvious first step in detecting them, it is not even close to being 100 per cent reliable. Accumulated evidence from research and practical examples consistently indicates that people, even when assisted by technology, are not good at detecting failure and errors. This applies even when special attention is being given to inspection. For example, airport security was significantly strengthened after 11 September 2001, yet one in ten lethal weapons that were entered into airports' security systems (in order to test them) were not detected. *'There is no such thing as one hundred per cent security, we are all human beings'*, says Ian Hutcheson, the Director of Security at airport operator BAA. No one is advocating abandoning inspection as a failure detection mechanisms. Rather it is seen as one of a range of methods of preventing failure.

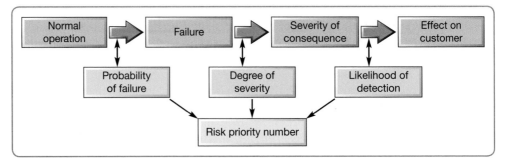

Figure 18.7 Procedure for failure mode and effect analysis (FMEA)

Failure mode and effect analysis

Having identified potential sources of failure (either in advance of an event or through post-failure analysis) and having then examined the likelihood of these failures occurring through some combination of objective and subjective analysis, managers can move to assigning relative priorities to risk. The most well-known approach for doing this is failure mode and effect analysis (FMEA). Its objective is to identify the factors that are critical to various types of failure as a means of identifying failures before they happen. It does this by providing a 'checklist' procedure built around three key questions for each possible cause of failure:

● What is the likelihood that failure will occur?
● What would the consequence of the failure be?
● How likely is such a failure to be detected before it affects the customer?

Based on a quantitative evaluation of these three questions, a risk priority number (RPN) is calculated for each potential cause of failure. Corrective actions, aimed at preventing failure, are then applied to those causes whose RPN indicates that they warrant priority, *see* Figure 18.7.

Worked example

Part of an FMEA exercise at a transportation company has identified three failure modes associated with the failure of 'goods arriving damaged' at the point of delivery:

● Goods not secured (failure mode 1)
● Goods incorrectly secured (failure mode 2)
● Goods incorrectly loaded (failure mode 3).

The improvement group which is investigating the failures allocates scores for the probability of the failure mode occurring, the severity of each failure mode, and the likelihood that they will be detected using the rating scales shown in Table 18.1, as follows:

Probability of occurrence
Failure mode 1	5
Failure mode 2	8
Failure mode 3	7

Severity of failure
Failure mode 1	6
Failure mode 2	4
Failure mode 3	4

Table 18.1 Rating scales for FMEA

A. Occurrence of failure Description	Rating	Possible failure occurrence
Remote probability of occurrence It would be unreasonable to expect failure to occur	1	0
Low probability of occurrence Generally associated with activities similar to previous ones with a relatively low number of failures	2 3	1:20,000 1:10,000
Moderate probability of occurrence Generally associated with activities similar to previous ones which have resulted in occasional failures	4 5 6	1:2,000 1:1,000 1:200
High probability of occurrence Generally associated with activities similar to ones which have traditionally caused problems	7 8	1:100 1:20
Very high probability of occurrence Near certainty that major failures will occur	9 10	1:10 1:2

B. Severity of failure Description	Rating
Minor severity A very minor failure which would have no noticeable effect on system performance	1
Low severity A minor failure causing only slight customer annoyance	2 3
Moderate severity A failure which would cause some customer dissatisfaction, discomfort or annoyance, or would cause noticeable deterioration in performance	4 5 6
High severity A failure which would engender a high degree of customer dissatisfaction	7 8
Very high severity A failure which would affect safety	9
Catastrophic A failure which may cause damage to property, serious injury or death	10

C. Detection of failure Description	Rating	Probability of detection
Remote probability that the defect will reach the customer (It is unlikely that such a defect would pass through inspection, test or assembly)	1 2	0 to 5% 6 to 15%
Low probability that the defect will reach the customer	3 4	16 to 25% 26 to 35%
Moderate probability that the defect will reach the customer	5 6 7	36 to 45% 46 to 55% 56 to 65%
High probability that the defect will reach the customer	8 9	66 to 75% 76 to 85%
Very high probability that the defect will reach the customer	10	86 to 100%

Probability of detection

Failure mode 1	2
Failure mode 2	6
Failure mode 3	7

The RPN of each failure mode is calculated:

Failure mode 1 (goods not secured)	$5 \times 6 \times 2 = 60$
Failure mode 2 (goods incorrectly secured)	$8 \times 4 \times 5 = 160$
Failure mode 3 (goods incorrectly loaded)	$7 \times 4 \times 7 = 196$

Priority is therefore given to failure mode 3 (goods incorrectly loaded) when attempting to eliminate the failure.

HOW CAN FAILURES BE PREVENTED?

'Prevention', it is said, is better than 'cure', which is why failure prevention is such an important responsibility for operations managers. The obvious way to do this is to examine systematically any processes involved and 'design out' any failure points. Many of the approaches used in Chapter 4 on product/service innovation, Chapter 6 on process design and Chapter 17 on quality management can be used to do this. In this section, we will look at three further approaches to reducing risk by trying to prevent failure: building redundancy into a process in case of failure, 'fail-safeing' some of the activities in the process, and maintaining the physical facilities in the process.

Redundancy

Building redundancy into an operation means having back-up systems or components in case of failure. It can be expensive and is generally used when the breakdown could have a critical impact. Redundancy means doubling or even tripling some parts of a process or system in case one component fails. Nuclear power stations, spacecraft and hospitals all have auxiliary systems in case of an emergency. Some organizations also have 'back-up' staff held in reserve in case someone does not turn up for work. Spacecraft have several back-up computers on board that will not only monitor the main computer, but also act as a back-up in case of failure.

One response to the threat of large failures, such as terrorist activity, has been a rise in the number of companies (known as 'business continuity' providers) offering 'replacement office' operations, fully equipped with normal Internet and telephone communications links, and often with access to a company's current management information. Should a customer's main operation be affected by a disaster, business can continue in the replacement facility within days or even hours.

The effect of redundancy can be calculated by the sum of the reliability of the original process component and the likelihood that the back-up component will both be needed and be working:

$$R_{a+b} = R_a + (R_b \times P(\text{failure}))$$

Where:

R_{a+b} = reliability of component a with its back-up component b

R_a = reliability of a alone

R_b = reliability of back-up component b

$P(\text{failure})$ = the probability that component a will fail and therefore component b will be needed

An e-auction provider has two servers, one of which will come online if the first server fails. If each server has a reliability of 90%, the two working together will have a reliability of:

$$0.9 + [0.9 \times (1 - 0.09)] = 0.99$$

Redundancy is often used for servers, where system availability is particularly important. In this context, the industry used three main types of redundancy:

- **Hot standby** – where both primary and secondary (back-up) systems run simultaneously. The data is copied to the secondary server in real time so that both systems contain identical information.
- **Warm standby** – where the secondary system runs in the background to the primary system. Data is copied to the secondary server at regular intervals, so there are times when both servers do not contain exactly the same data.
- **Cold standby** – where the secondary system is only called upon when the primary system fails. The secondary system receives scheduled data back-ups, but less frequently than a warm standby, so cold standby is mainly used for non-critical applications.

Fail-safeing

The concept of fail-safeing has emerged since the introduction of Japanese methods of operations improvement. Called poka-yoke in Japan (from *yokeru* (to prevent) and *poka* (inadvertent errors)), the idea is based on the principle that human mistakes are to some extent inevitable. What is important is to prevent them becoming defects. Poka-yokes are simple (preferably inexpensive) devices or systems that are incorporated into a process to prevent inadvertent mistakes by those providing a service as well as customers receiving a service. Examples of poka-yokes include:

> ✳ **Operations principle**
> Simple methods of fail-safeing can often be the most cost-effective.

- trays used in hospitals with indentations shaped to each item needed for a surgical procedure – any item not back in place at the end of the procedure might have been left in the patient;
- checklists which have to be filled in, either in preparation for, or on completion of, an activity, such as a maintenance checklist for an aircraft during turnaround;
- gauges placed on machines through which a part has to pass in order to be loaded onto, or taken off, the machine – an incorrect size or orientation stops the process;
- the locks on aircraft lavatory doors, which must be turned to switch the light on;
- Beepers on ATMs to ensure that customers remove their cards or in cars to remind drivers to take their keys with them;
- limit switches on machines which allow the machine to operate only if the part is positioned correctly;
- height bars on amusement rides to ensure that customers do not exceed size limitations.

OPERATIONS IN PRACTICE

Is failure designed-*in* to airline operations?[6]

Within the airline industry, it is common practice to overbook seats on airliners – whereby more seats are reserved for customers than technically exist on a given flight. Yield management, something that we examined in Chapter 11, helps to explain this approach to managing capacity. The thinking is that often some passengers will not turn up for the flight and, as such, overbooking helps to maximize finite (and non-reusable) capacity on airliners. So from a utilization perspective, overbooking makes a lot of sense. However, are the airlines guilty of designing-*in* failure rather than deigning-*out* failure by taking this approach? Here is what a recent customer flying through Schiphol, Europe's fourth busiest airports, had to say: '*I was recently in Amsterdam attending a conference for work. Tired after 3 days of intensive presentations and discussions, I arrived in plenty of time only to be told by the automated machine that my husband and I had been put on standby and wouldn't necessarily be able to have a seat on our flight. At the check-in desk, we were told that it was a random system that we could not have avoided, and that we would only know if we were flying once we were at the gate. This gave us over an hour of uncertainty. I was furious! As it turned out, we were able to board the flight, but this in no way made us feel satisfied. Although the staff had dealt with us well, it did not change the fact that we had felt stressed and anxious whilst we did not know what was happening. We also felt cheated – we had paid for a ticket, so why should an airline be allowed to not give us a seat?*'

This raises a number of important questions. Do customers have a *right* to a seat on an airliner? If overbooking is adopted, what is the best way to implement it – randomly assigning passengers for potential 'bumping' or excluding the last person to arrive, 'bumping' single passengers versus groups, looking at the importance of different passengers to the airline, or some other method? What are the effects on employees of having to deal with irate customers who are informed of (potentially) being 'bumped' off a flight that they have booked? And does ultimately the upside risk of overbooking outweigh the downside risk?

Source: 123RF.com: Igor Zakharevich

Maintenance

While managers can try to design out failures and use fail-safe (poka-yoke) mechanisms to reduce the likelihood of failures, operations also need maintaining. Maintenance is how organizations try to avoid failure by taking care of their physical facilities. It is an important part of most operations' activities, particularly in operations dominated by their physical facilities such as power stations, hotels, airlines and petrochemical refineries. The benefits of effective maintenance include enhanced safety, increased reliability, higher quality (badly maintained equipment is more likely to cause errors), lower operating costs (because regularly serviced process technology is more efficient), a longer life span for process technology, and higher 'end value' (because well-maintained facilities are generally easier to dispose of into the second-hand market).

The three basic approaches to maintenance

In practice an organization's maintenance activities will consist of some combination of the three basic approaches to the care of its physical facilities. These are run to breakdown (RTB), preventive maintenance (PM) and condition-based maintenance (CBM).

- **Run to breakdown maintenance (RTB)** – As its name implies, this involves allowing the facilities to continue operating until they fail. Maintenance work is performed only after failure has taken place. For example, the televisions, bathroom equipment and telephones in a hotel's guest rooms will probably only be repaired when they fail. The hotel will keep some spare parts and the staff available to make any repairs when needed. Failure in these circumstances is neither catastrophic (although perhaps irritating to the guest) nor so frequent as to make regular checking of the facilities appropriate.

- **Preventive maintenance (PM)** – This attempts to eliminate or reduce the chances of failure by servicing (cleaning, lubricating, replacing and checking) the facilities at pre-planned intervals. For example, the engines of passenger aircraft are checked, cleaned and calibrated according to a regular schedule after a set number of flying hours. Taking aircraft away from their regular duties for preventive maintenance is clearly an expensive option for any airline. The consequences of failure while in service are considerably more serious, however. The principle is also applied to facilities with less catastrophic consequences of failure. The regular cleaning and lubricating of machines, even the periodic painting of a building, could be considered preventive maintenance.
- **Condition-based maintenance (CBM)** – This attempts to perform maintenance only when the facilities require it. For example, continuous process equipment, such as that used in coating photographic paper, is run for long periods in order to achieve the high utilization necessary for cost-effective production. Stopping the machine to change, say, a bearing when it is not strictly necessary to do so would take the machine out of action for long periods and reduce its utilization. Here condition-based maintenance might involve continuously monitoring the vibrations, for example, or some other characteristic of the line.

How much maintenance?

The balance between preventive and breakdown maintenance is usually set to minimize the total cost of breakdown. Infrequent preventive maintenance will cost little to provide but will result in a high likelihood (and therefore cost) of breakdown maintenance. Conversely, very frequent preventive maintenance will be expensive to provide but will reduce the cost of having to provide breakdown maintenance (*see* Fig. 18.8(a)). The total cost of maintenance appears to minimize at an 'optimum' level of preventive maintenance. However, the cost of providing preventive maintenance may not increase quite so steeply as indicated in Figure 18.8(a). The curve assumes that it is carried out by a separate set of people (skilled maintenance staff) from the 'operators' of the facilities. Furthermore, every time preventive maintenance takes place, the facilities cannot be used productively. This is why the slope of the curve increases, because the maintenance episodes start to interfere with the

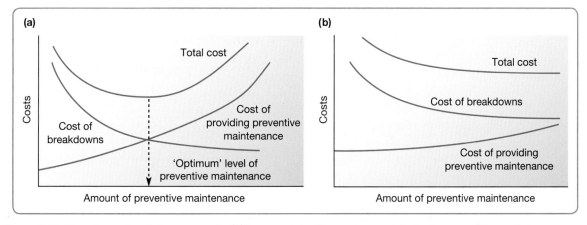

Figure 18.8 Two views of maintenance costs. (a) One model of the costs associated with preventive maintenance shows an optimum level of maintenance effort. (b) If routine preventive maintenance tasks are carried out by operators and if the real cost of breakdowns is considered, the 'optimum' level of preventive maintenance shifts towards higher levels

normal working of the operation. But in many operations some preventive maintenance can be performed by the operators themselves (which reduces the cost of providing it) and at times which are convenient for the operation (which minimizes the disruption to the operation). The cost of breakdowns could also be higher than is indicated in Figure 18.8(a). Unplanned breakdowns may do more than necessitate a repair and stop the operation – they can take away stability from the operation, which prevents it being able to improve itself. Put these two ideas together and the minimizing total curve and maintenance cost curve look more like Figure 18.8(b). The emphasis is shifted more towards the use of preventive maintenance than run-to-breakdown maintenance.

Total productive maintenance

Total productive maintenance (TPM) is 'the productive maintenance carried out by all employees through small-group activities', where productive maintenance is, 'maintenance management which recognizes the importance of reliability, maintenance and economic efficiency in plant design'.[7] In Japan, where TPM originated, it is seen as a natural extension in the evolution from run-to-breakdown to preventive maintenance. TPM adopts some of the team-working and empowerment principles discussed in Chapter 9, as well as a continuous improvement approach to failure prevention as discussed in Chapter 16. It also sees maintenance as an organization-wide issue, to which staff can contribute in some way. It is analogous to the total quality management approach discussed in Chapter 17.

The five goals of TPM

TPM aims to establish good maintenance practice in operations through the pursuit of 'the five goals of TPM':

1 Improve equipment effectiveness by examining all the losses which occur.
2 Achieve autonomous maintenance by allowing staff to take responsibility for some of the maintenance tasks and for the improvement of maintenance performance.
3 Plan maintenance with a fully worked-out approach to all maintenance activities.
4 Train all staff in relevant maintenance skills so that both maintenance and operating staff have all the skills to carry out their roles.
5 Achieve early equipment management by 'maintenance prevention' (MP), which involves considering failure causes and the maintainability of equipment during its design, manufacture, installation and commissioning.

Critical commentary

Much of the previous discussion surrounding the prevention of failure has assumed a 'rational' approach. In other words, it is assumed that operations managers and customers alike will put more effort into preventing failures that are either more likely to occur or more serious in their consequences. Yet this assumption is based on a rational response to risk. In fact, being human, managers often respond to the perception of risk rather than its reality. For example, Table 18.2 shows the cost of each life saved by investment in various road and rail transportation safety (in other words, failure prevention) investments. The table shows that investing in improving road safety is very much more effective than investing in rail safety. And while no one is arguing for abandoning efforts on rail safety, it is noted by some transportation authorities that actual investment reflects more the public perception of rail deaths (low) compared with road deaths (very high).

Table 18.2 **The cost per life saved of various safety (failure prevention) investments**

Safety investment	Cost per life (€m)
Advanced train protection system	30
Train protection warning systems	7.5
Implementing recommended guidelines on rail safety	4.7
Implementing recommended guidelines on road safety	1.6
Local authority spending on road safety	0.15

HOW CAN OPERATIONS MITIGATE THE EFFECTS OF FAILURE?

Even when a failure has occurred, its impact on the customer can, in many cases, be minimized through mitigation actions. Failure (or risk) mitigation means isolating a failure from its negative consequences. It is an admission that not all failures can be avoided. However, in some areas of operations management relying on mitigation, rather than prevention, is unfashionable. For example, 'inspection' practices in quality management were based on the assumption that failures were inevitable and they needed to be detected before they could cause harm. Modern total quality management places much more emphasis on prevention. Yet, to manage operations and supply networks effectively, mitigation can be vital when used in conjunction with prevention to reduce overall risk. One way of thinking about mitigation is as a series of decisions under conditions of uncertainty. Doing so enables the use of formal decision analysis techniques such as decision trees, for example the one illustrated in Figure 18.9. Here, an anomaly of some kind, which may or may not indicate that a failure has occurred, is detected. The first decision is whether to act to try and mitigate the supposed failure or, alternatively, wait until more information can be obtained. Even if mitigation is tried, it may or may not contain the failure. If not, then further action will be needed, which may or may not contain the failure, and so on. If more information is obtained prior to enacting mitigation, then the failure may or may not be confirmed. If mitigation is then tried, it may or may not work, and so on. Although the details of the specific mitigation actions will depend

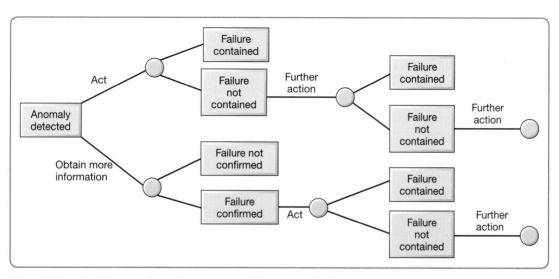

Figure 18.9 **A decision tree for mitigation when failure is not immediately obvious**

on circumstances, what is important in practical terms is that for all significant failures some kind of decision rules and mitigation planning has been established.

Failure mitigation actions

The nature of the action taken to mitigate failure will obviously depend on the nature of the risk. In most industries technical experts have established a classification of failure mitigation actions that are appropriate for the types of failure likely to be suffered. So, for example, in agriculture, government agencies and industry bodies have published mitigation strategies for such risks as the outbreak of crop disease, contagious animal infections, and so on. Likewise, governments have different contingency plans in place to deal with the spread of major health risks such as the H1N1 and H7Np influenza viruses or an Ebola outbreak in West Africa. Such documents will outline the various mitigation actions that can be taken under different circumstances and detail exactly who is responsible for each action. Although these classifications tend to be industry specific, the following generic categorization gives a flavour of the types of mitigation actions that may be generally applicable:

- **Mitigation planning** – This is the activity of ensuring that all possible failure circumstances have been identified and the appropriate mitigation actions identified. It is the overarching activity that encompasses all subsequent mitigation actions, and may be described in the form of a decision tree or guide rules. It is worth noting that mitigation planning, as well as an overarching action, also provides mitigation action in its own right. For example, if mitigation planning has identified appropriate training, job design, emergency procedures, and so on, then the financial liability of a business for any losses should a failure occur will be reduced. Certainly businesses that have not planned adequately for failures will be more liable in law for any subsequent losses.
- **Economic mitigation** – This includes actions such as insurance against losses from failure, spreading the financial consequences of failure, and 'hedging' against failure. Insurance is the best known of these actions and is widely adopted, although ensuring appropriate insurance and effective claims management is a specialized skill in itself. Hedging often takes the form of financial instruments, for example a business may purchase a financial 'hedge' against the price risk of a vital raw material deviating significantly from a set price.
- **Containment (spatial)** – This means stopping the failure physically spreading to affect other parts of an internal or external supply network. Preventing contaminated food from spreading through the supply chain, for example, will depend on real-time information systems that provide traceability data.
- **Containment (temporal)** – This means containing the spread of a failure over time. It particularly applies when information about a failure or potential failure needs to be transmitted without undue delay. For example, systems that give advanced warning of hazardous weather such as snowstorms must transmit such information to local agencies such as the police and road-clearing organizations in time for them to stop the problem causing excessive disruption.
- **Loss reduction** – This covers any action that reduces the catastrophic consequences of failure by removing the resources that are likely to suffer those consequences. For example, the road signs that indicate evacuation routes in the event of severe weather, or the fire drills that train employees in how to escape in the event of an emergency, may not reduce all the consequences of failure, but can help in reducing loss of life or injury.
- **Substitution** – This means compensating for failure by providing other resources that can substitute for those rendered less effective by the failure. It is a little like the concept of redundancy that was described earlier, but does not always imply excess resources if a failure has not occurred. For example, in a construction project, the risk of encountering unexpected geological problems may be mitigated by the existence of a separate work plan and that is invoked only if such problems are found.

Tiny and not so tiny recalls for General Motors[8]

Source: Corbis: Michael Spooneybarger

According to the data analytics company Teradata Corp., car recalls cost the automotive industry somewhere between $45 and $50 billion per annum. Which is why automotive giants including General Motors, Nissan and Toyota have looked to build sophisticated data-mining operations so they can move towards what industry insiders call 'tiny recalls'. When faced with an emerging potential mechanical problem, car manufacturers have traditionally had two choices. The first option is to issue a general recall for the model in question. But there is a major financial and reputational cost to this, as well as significant inconvenience for customers, many of who will not actually have a fault in their car. The second option is to ignore the fault and in doing so accept the risk that a very small number of customers may have problems (even serious accidents). While this may be justified in short-term financial (if not ethical) terms, the longer term consequences could be disastrous, especially if the media expose the fact. Now, there is a third option available. The rise of bar coding, radio frequency identification (RFID) and more advanced information systems has allowed automakers to track components in far greater detail. The result is that faults can often be isolated not only to a model range, but to a specific set of components, made in particular periods of time, even by a particular shift at the factory. This then enables a far more focused recall of only the cars that are most likely to have a defect. For example, when a braking fault was identified on the Chevrolet Volt, General Motors (GM) was able to identify all 'at-risk' cars through its advanced parts tracking, and issue a 'tiny recall' (in this case, just four cars in the whole of the USA). However, prevention is better than cure. Many auto manufacturers, while seeking to target recalls, still face large recalls brought about by quality problems. For example, during 2014, GM announced the recall of a staggering 29 million cars and vans in North America, a number greater than its total US sales between 2005 and 2013. One of the largest recalls was for ignition switch defects, which included models as old as 1997.

HOW CAN OPERATIONS RECOVER FROM THE EFFECTS OF FAILURE?

Failure recovery is the set of actions that are taken to reduce the impact of failure once the customer has experienced its negative effects. Recovery needs to be planned and procedures put in place that can discover when failures have occurred, guide appropriate action to keep everyone informed, capture the lessons learnt from the failure, and plan to absorb lessons into any future recovery. All types of operation can benefit from well-planned recovery. For example, a construction company whose mechanical digger breaks down can have plans in place to arrange a replacement from a hire company. The breakdown might be disruptive, but not as much as it might have been if the operations manager had not worked out what to do. Recovery procedures will also shape customers' perceptions of failure.

Even where the customer sees a failure, it may not necessarily lead to dissatisfaction. Indeed, in many situations, customers may well accept that things do go wrong. If there is a metre of snow on the train lines, or if the restaurant is particularly popular, we may accept that the product or service does not work. It is not necessarily the failure itself that leads to dissatisfaction but often the organization's response to the breakdown. While mistakes may be inevitable, dissatisfied customers are not. A failure may even be turned into a positive experience. A good recovery can turn angry, frustrated customers into loyal ones.

The complaint value chain

The complaint value chain, shown in Figure 18.10, helps us to visualize the potential value of good recovery at different stages. In Figure 18.10(a) an operation provides service to 5,000 customers, but 20 per cent of them experience some form of failure. Of these 1,000 customers, 40 per cent decide not to complain, perhaps because the complaint processes are too convoluted. Evidence suggests that around 80 per cent of these non-complainers will switch to an alternative service provider (of course the precise switching percentage will depend on the number of alternatives in the market and the ease of switching). Another group of the 1,000 customers who experienced a failure do decide to complain, in this case 60 per cent. Some will be satisfied (in this case, 75 per cent) and others will not be (in this case, 25 per cent). Dissatisfied complainers will generally leave the organizations (in this case, 80 per cent) while satisfied complainers will tend to remain loyal (in this case, 80 per cent). So assuming these percentages are correct, for every 5,000 customers processed by this particular service operation, 530 will switch.

Now let us assume that the operations manager decides to invest in small improvements to all stages in the complaint value chain In Figure 18.10(b) the company has reduced its failures from 20 to 18 per cent (still very poor of course!) and has encouraged more customers who experienced a failure to come forward and complain. So the percentage complaining has risen from 60 to 70 per cent. It has also made sure that a higher proportion (in this case, from 75 to 83 per cent) of those who do make the effort to complain are satisfied. The end result is that the number of lost customers falls from 530 to 406. Assuming that the extra 124 customers retained have a value that is equal, or more than, the costs of improvements, the organization is making a good investment in its recovery and prevention efforts. What is important to understand here is how a relatively small improvement across the failure and complaint process can have such a significant impact on customer loyalty and switching.

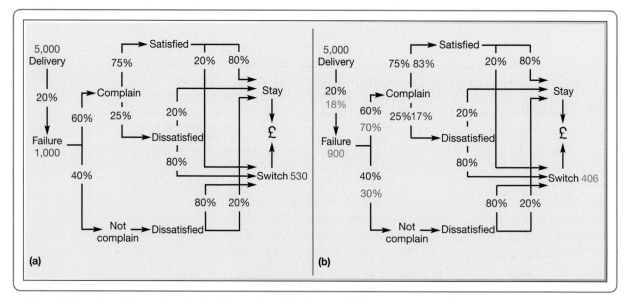

Figure 18.10 Complaint value chain: (a) initial value chain and (b) with small improvements to each step

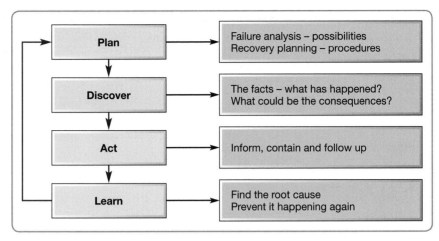

Figure 18.11 Recovery sequence for minimizing the impact from failure

Failure planning

Organizations need to design appropriate responses to failure that are suitably aligned with the cost and the inconvenience caused by the failure to their customers. Such recovery processes need to be carried out either by empowered front line staff or by trained personnel who are available to deal with recovery in a way which does not interfere with day-to-day service activities. Figure 18.11 illustrates a typical recovery sequence. We will follow it through from the point where failure is recognized:

- **Discover** – The first thing any manager needs to do when faced with a failure is to discover its exact nature. Three important pieces of information are needed: first of all, what exactly has happened; second, who will be affected by the failure; and, third, why did the failure occur? This last point is not intended to be a detailed inquest into the causes of failure (that comes later) but it is often necessary to know something of the causes of failure in case it is necessary to determine what action to take.

- **Act** – The discover stage might only take minutes or even seconds, depending on the severity of the failure. If the failure is a severe one with important consequences, we need to move on to doing something about it quickly. This means carrying out three actions, the first two of which could be carried out in reverse order, depending on the urgency of the situation. First, tell the significant people involved what you are proposing to do about the failure. In service operations this is especially important where customers need to be kept informed, both for their peace of mind and to demonstrate that something is being done. Second, the effects of the failure need to be contained in order to stop the consequences spreading and causing further failures. The precise containment actions will depend on the nature of the failure. Third, there needs to be some kind of follow-up to make sure that the containment actions really have contained the failure.

- **Learn** – As discussed earlier in this chapter, the benefits of failure in providing learning opportunities should not be underestimated. In failure planning, learning involves revisiting the failure to find out its root cause and then engineering out the causes of the failure so that it will not happen again. This is the key stage for much failure planning.

- **Plan** – Learning the lessons from a failure is not the end of the procedure. Operations managers need formally to incorporate the lessons into their future reactions to failures. This is often done by working through 'in theory' how they would react to failures in the future. Specifically, this involves first identifying all the possible failures which might occur (in a similar way to the FMEA approach). Second, it means formally defining the procedures which the organization should follow in the case of each type of identified failure.

❯ What is risk management?

- Risk management is about things going wrong and what operations can do to stop things going wrong. Or, more formally, 'the process which aims to help organizations understand, evaluate and take action on all their risks with a view to increasing the probability of their success and reducing the likelihood of failure'.

- It consists of four broad activities:

  - Understanding what failures could occur.

  - Preventing failures occurring.

  - Minimizing the negative consequences of failure (called risk 'mitigation').

  - Recovering from failures when they do occur.

❯ How can operations assess the potential causes and consequences of failure?

- There are several causes of failure, including design failures, facilities failure, staff failure, supplier failure, customer failure and environmental disruption.

- There are three ways of measuring failure. 'Failure rates' indicate how often a failure is likely to occur. 'Reliability' measures the chances of a failure occurring. 'Availability' is the amount of available and useful operating time left after taking account of failures.

- Failure over time is often represented as a failure curve. The most common form of this is the so-called 'bath-tub curve', which shows the chances of failure being greater at the beginning and end of the life of a system or part of a system.

- Failure analysis mechanisms include accident investigation, product liability, complaint analysis, critical incident analysis, and failure mode and effect analysis (FMEA).

❯ How can failures be prevented?

- There are four major methods of improving reliability: designing out the fail points in the operation, building redundancy into the operation, 'fail-safeing' some of the activities of the operation, and maintenance of the physical facilities in the operation.

- Maintenance is the most common way operations attempt to improve their reliability, with three broad approaches. The first is running all facilities until they break down and then repairing them, the second is regularly maintaining the facilities even if they have not broken down, and the third is to monitor facilities closely to try to predict when breakdown might occur.

- Total productive maintenance, where all employees carry out maintenance in small groups, is a particularly useful approach to managing maintenance.

❯ How can operations mitigate the effects of failure?

- Risk, or failure, mitigation means isolating a failure from its negative consequences.

- Risk mitigation actions include:
  - Mitigation planning
  - Economic mitigation
  - Containment (spatial and temporal)
  - Loss reduction
  - Substitution.

〉 How can operations recover from the effects of failure?

- Recovery can be enhanced by a systematic approach to discovering what has happened to cause failure, acting to inform, contain and follow up the consequences of failure, learning to find the root cause of the failure and preventing it from taking place again, and planning to avoid the failure occurring in the future.

CASE STUDY   Slagelse Industrial Services (SIS)

Slagelse Industrial Services (SIS) had become one of Europe's most respected die casters of zinc, aluminium and magnesium parts and a supplier for hundreds of companies in many industries, especially automotive and defence. The company cast and engineered precision components by combining the most modern production technologies with precise tooling and craftsmanship. Slagelse Industrial Services (SIS) began life as a classic family firm by Erik Paulsen, Anders' father, who opened a small manufacturing and die-casting business in his hometown of Slagelse, a town in east Denmark, about 100 km south-west of Copenhagen. He had successfully leveraged his skills and passion for craftsmanship over many years while serving a variety of different industrial and agricultural customers. His son, Anders, had spent nearly 10 years working as a production engineer for a large automotive parts supplier in the UK, but eventually returned to Slagelse to take over the family firm. Exploiting his experience in mass manufacturing, Anders spent years building the firm into a larger scale industrial component manufacturer but retained his father's commitment to quality and customer service. After 20 years he sold the firm to a UK-owned industrial conglomerate and within 10 years it had doubled in size again and now employed in the region of 600 people and had a turnover approaching £200 million. Throughout this period the firm had continued to target its products into niche industrial markets where its emphasis upon product quality and dependability meant it was less vulnerable to price and cost pressures. However, in 2009, in the midst of difficult economic times and widespread industrial restructuring,

the firm had been encouraged to bid for higher volume, lower margin work. This process was not very successful but eventually culminated in a tender for the design and production of a core metallic element of a child's toy (a 'transforming' robot).

Interestingly the client firm, Alden Toys, was also a major customer for other businesses owned by SIS's corporate parent. Alden Toys was adopting a preferred supplier policy and intended to have only one or two purchase points for specific elements in their global toy business. They had a high degree of trust in the parent organization and on visiting the SIS site were impressed by the firm's depth of experience and commitment to quality. In 2010, they selected SIS to complete the design and begin trial production.

'Some of us were really excited by the prospect...but you have to be a little worried when volumes are much greater than anything you've done before. I guess the risk seemed okay because in the basic process steps, in the type of product if you like, we were making something that felt very similar to what we'd been doing for many years.' (SIS Operations Manager)

'Well obviously we didn't know anything about the toy market but then again we didn't really know all that much about the auto industry or the defence sector or any of our traditional customers before we started serving them. Our key competitive advantage, our capabilities, call it what you will, they are all about keeping the customer happy, about meeting and sometimes exceeding specification.' (SIS Marketing Director)

The designers had received an outline product specification from Alden Toys during the bid process and some further technical detail afterwards. Upon receipt of this final brief, a team of engineers and managers confirmed that the product could and would be manufactured using an up-scaled version of current production processes. The key operational challenge appeared to be accessing sufficient (but not too much) capacity. Fortunately, for a variety of reasons, the parent company was very supportive of the project and promised to underwrite any sensible capital expenditure plans. Although this opinion of the nature of the production challenge was widely accepted throughout the firm (and shared by Alden Toys and SIS's parent group) it was left to one specific senior engineer to actually sign both the final bid and technical completion documentation. By early 2011, the firm had begun a trial period of full-volume production. Unfortunately, as would become clear later, during this design validation process SIS had effectively sanctioned a production method that would prove to be entirely inappropriate for the toy market, but it was not until 12 months later that any indication of problems began to emerge.

Throughout both North America and Europe, individual customers began to claim that their children had been 'poisoned' while playing with the end product. The threat of litigation was quickly levelled at Alden Toys and the whole issue rapidly became a 'full-blown' child health scare. A range of pressure groups and legal damage specialists supported and acted to aggregate the individual claims. Although similar accusations had been made before, the litigants and their supporters focused on the recent changes made to the production process at SIS and in particular the role of Alden Toys in managing its suppliers. '[I]t's all very well claiming that you trust your suppliers but you simply cannot have the same level of control over another firm in another country. I am afraid that this all comes down to simple economics, that Alden Toys put its profits before children's health. Talk about trust...parents trusted this firm to look out for them and their families and have every right to be angry that boardroom greed was more important!' (Legal spokesperson for US litigants when being interviewed on UK TV consumer rights show).

Under intense media pressure, Alden Toys rapidly convened a high-profile investigation into the source of the contamination. It quickly revealed that an 'unauthorized' chemical had been employed in an apparently trivial metal cleaning and preparation element of the SIS production process. Although when interviewed by the US media, the parent firm's legal director emphasized there was 'no causal link established or any admission of liability by either party', Alden Toys immediately withdrew its order and began to signal an intent to bring legal action against SIS and its parent. This action brought an immediate end to production in this part of the operation, and the inspection (and subsequent official and legal visits) had a crippling impact upon the productivity of the whole site. The competitive impact of the failure was extremely significant. After over a year of production, the new product accounted for more than a third (39 per cent) of the factory's output. In addition to major cash-flow implications, the various investigations took up lots of managerial time and the reputation of the firm was seriously affected. As the site operations manager explained, even their traditional customers expressed concerns: 'It's amazing but people we had been supplying for thirty or forty years were calling me up and asking "[Manager's name] what's going on?" and that they were worried about what all this might mean for them...these are completely different markets!'

QUESTIONS

1 What operational risks did SIS face when deciding to become a strategic supplier for Alden Toys?

2 What control problems did SIS encounter in implementing this strategy (pre and post investigation)?

PROBLEMS AND APPLICATIONS

1 Conduct a survey amongst colleagues, friends and acquaintances of how they cope with the possibility that their computers might 'fail', either in terms of ceasing to operate effectively, or in losing data. Discuss how the concept of redundancy applies in such failure.

2 '*We have a test bank where we test batches of 100 of our products continuously for 7 days and nights. This week only 3 failed, the first after 10 hours, the second after 72 hours, and the third after 1,020 hours.*' What is the failure rate in percentage terms and in time terms for this product?

3 An automatic testing process takes samples of ore from mining companies and subjects them to four sequential tests. The reliability of the four different test machines that perform the tasks is different. The first test machine has a reliability of 0.99, the second has a reliability of 0.92, the third has a reliability of 0.98, and the fourth a reliability of 0.95. If one of the machines stops working, the total process will stop. What is the reliability of the total process?

4 For the product-testing example in Problem 2, what is the mean time between failures (MTBF) for the products?

5 In terms of its effectiveness at managing the learning process, how does a university detect failures? What could it do to improve its failure detection processes?

6 Review your own (and your friends') approach to protecting against malicious data theft. What is the biggest risk that you/they face?

SELECTED FURTHER READING

Breakwell, G.M. (2014) *The psychology of risk*, Cambridge University Press, Cambridge.

An interesting book focused on the broader psychological aspects of risk.

Melnyk, S., Closs, D., Griffis, S., Zobel, C. and Macdonald, J. (2014) Understanding supply chain resilience, *Supply Chain Management Review*, January/February, 34–41.

A nice article outlining the key aspects of failure, prevention and resilience in operations and supply networks.

Regester, M. and Larkin, J. (2008) *Risk Issues and Crisis Management: A Casebook of Best Practice*, Kogan Page, London.

Aimed at practising managers with lots of advice. Good for getting the flavour of how it is in practice.

Simchi-Levi, D., Schmidt, W. and Wei, Y. (2014) From superstorms to factory fires: managing unpredictable supply-chain disruptions, *Harvard Business Review*, vol. 92, no. 1–2, 97–101.

Another practitioner-focused article looking at the low-probability, high-impact end of the failure continuum.

19

Project management

Key questions

> **What is project management?**

> **How are projects planned?**

> **How are projects controlled?**

INTRODUCTION

In this chapter, we are concerned with the management of 'projects'. Projects occupy the low-volume–high-variety end of the continuum of processes that we introduced in Chapter 6. So they are typical of the kind of improvement initiatives that often are a part of an operation's development activities. These 'project' processes come in all shapes and sizes, with differences in scale, uncertainty, complexity, novelty, technology and pace. Yet, in many respects, projects share key characteristics that make their management tasks broadly universal. First, managers must understand the fundamental characteristics of a project and the likely implications of these characteristics for management. Second, they must be able to understand the project environment and manage key project stakeholders. Third, they must be able to define, plan and control projects through their life cycle, while balancing competing performance objectives and competing (internal and external) stakeholder requirements. Figure 19.1 shows where this chapter fits in the overall activities of operations management. We have placed the topic within the 'develop' activity because it is a vital part of how operations are changed and (hopefully) improved.

Figure 19.1 This chapter examines managing projects

Imagineering projects at Disney[1]

Ever since the creation of famous characters such as Mickey Mouse and Snow White, the Disney Corporation has been synonymous with innovative quality entertainment. At the Walt Disney Studios and Parks, persuasive stories come alive and technology and artistry together delight visitors and audiences alike. Nowhere is this truer than Walt Disney's 'Imagineering' operation ('Imagineering' is a word that combines 'imagination' and 'engineering'), which, in effect, is the research and development arm of Walt Disney Parks and Resorts. It is responsible for creating many of the more significant attractions, shows, firework displays and parades at the Disney theme parks. Their complex and often innovative attractions will be closely scrutinized by thousands or millions of Disney's 'guests', so it is vital to pay attention to details. A famous Walt Disney saying is that a guest may not notice a specific (sometimes tiny) detail, but he or she will notice when the detail is not there. This means that the attractions need to be created with skill, creativity and, equally importantly, professional project management. Walt Disney World's Imagineering Department's project managers work with interactive technologies, the park staff, special-effects wizards, digital designers and others to create an interactive experience for the guests. Although many of the projects are technical in nature, project managers work with a wide range of different disciplines from construction to marketing.

Source: Shutterstock.com: Shadow216

David Van Wyk is the Vice-President of Project Management for Walt Disney Imagineering and he fully understands the importance of effective project management. 'Without it,' he says, 'how can we be as relevant tomorrow as we are today? How can we meet and exceed guest expectations in a changing world? We have somewhere between 140 and 150 different skill sets in Imagineering, including engineers, creative staff, artists, architects, accountants, writers, theme and new media specialists, and more. A culture of interdisciplinary coordination with diverse stakeholders aims to interact and socialize to understand issues and problems. We have developed and keep working on a culture of collaboration. We do not have an NIH (not invented here) culture.' The Imagineering group is very much aware of the implications of the MacLeamy curve (see later) that highlights the idea that cost increases while the ability to change decreases over the life of the project. So it is important to solve issues earlier in the design process, when it is more economical to make changes, especially those involving equipment. Which is why, says David Van Wyk, 'that we seek to incorporate more peer review earlier in the engineering-design process. We also look for on-time delivery, getting it right before it gets to the field, with a strong start, strong finish, and careful resource allocation.' All of which makes it important to develop excellent relationships with partners and make sure that they, and all stakeholders, fully subscribe to the objectives of predictability, collaboration, impeccable co-ordination, prompt decision making, collective quality and just-in-time delivery.

WHAT IS PROJECT MANAGEMENT?

First, what is a project? A project is a set of activities with a defined start point and a defined end state, which pursues a defined goal and uses a defined set of resources. Technically many small-scale operations management endeavours, taking minutes or hours, conform to this definition of a project. However, in this chapter we will also be examining the management of relatively larger scale projects, often taking days, months or years. Although all projects have a defined goal, some of these will be part of a larger purpose. So most operations improvement (even continuous improvement) can be seen as a series of overlapping 'mini-projects' that cumulatively contribute to a never-ending development effort. Likewise, organizational change projects often are contributing to a larger purpose. Research and development projects sometimes have a specific application or product in mind, but often, if the research is more 'blue sky', it will not. Capital goods and infrastructure projects, such as new buildings, railways, sports stadia and airports, do contribute to a larger social purpose (such as 'improving communications') but can be so large that they seem to stand alone. By contrast, some projects are relatively stand-alone in the sense that they are a 'one-off' end in themselves. These are often projects that are focused on delivering a specific event, such as the Olympics or a soccer world cup. Naturally, these types of projects draw on other projects, such as capital goods and infrastructure, and organizational change.

What do projects have in common?

While projects vary a great deal, they share a number of common features. All projects are mission focused – that is, they are dedicated to achieving a specific goal that should be delivered within a set time frame, to certain specifications, using a defined group of resources. The result is that project outcomes are unique or at least highly customized, involve many non-routine and complex tasks, and therefore face relatively high levels of risk and uncertainty when contrasted with higher volume and lower variety operations. And it is these features that perhaps explain why so many projects fail in some way, with changed specifications (quality), severe delays (time), cost escalation (cost) and major disputes between key stakeholders commonplace. However, it is not only the innate complexity of projects that leads to many failing, but also the lack of effective project management.

OPERATIONS IN PRACTICE | *Vasa's first voyage*[2]

Source: Bridgeman Art Library Ltd: Look and Learn

Do not think that projects going wrong are a recent phenomenon! Project specification changes, bad communication, schedule delays and simple bad luck are nothing new and have always been able to bring down even the most high-profile projects. In 1628, the *Vasa*, the most magnificent warship ever built for the Royal Swedish Navy, was launched in front of an excited crowd. It had sailed less than a few thousand metres during its maiden voyage in the waters of Stockholm harbour when, suddenly, after a gun salute was shot in celebration, the *Vasa* heeled over and, as water gushed in through the gun ports, it vanished beneath the surface killing 53 of the 150 passengers on board. Shocked officials were left questioning how such a disaster could happen.

Yet, as a project, the story of the *Vasa* displayed many of the signs of potential failure. When construction began in 1625, the *Vasa* was designed as a small traditional warship, similar to many others previously built by the experienced shipbuilder Henrik Hybertsson. Soon after, the Swedish King Gustav II Adolphus, at that time fighting the Polish Navy in the Baltic Sea, started ordering a series of changes to the shape and the size of the warship, making its design much longer and bigger than originally envisaged. Also his spies informed him that the Danes had started building warships with two gun decks, instead of the customary one. This would give the Danes a great advantage in terms of superior firepower from a longer distance. From the battlefront the king mailed his order to add a second gun deck to the *Vasa*. The message caused consternation when it reached the shipbuilder several months later, but he attempted to comply with the change even though it caused wasteful reworking and complex patching up, as no one had ever seen or built such a revolutionary design before. Yet more pressure was put on the project when a catastrophic storm in the Baltic Sea destroyed 10 of the king's ships, making the commissioning of the *Vasa* even more urgent. Then, as a final piece of bad luck (especially for him) the shipbuilder, Hybertsson, died. Nevertheless, just before the ship's completion, a navy representative, Admiral Fleming, conducted a stability test to assess the seaworthiness of the ship. Notwithstanding the strong signals of instability during the test, the *Vasa* was launched on its maiden voyage – with disastrous results for the king, for the Swedish Navy and for the passengers.

What is project management?

Project management is the activity of defining, planning and controlling, and learning from projects of any type. Going beyond this life cycle perspective, project management is also concerned with effectively balancing quality/deliverables, time and cost objectives within the so-called 'iron triangle'. Finally, from an organizational perspective, project management involves managing these life cycles and performance objectives across multiple functions within an organization. The activity of project management is very broad in as much as it could encompass almost all the operations management tasks described in this book. Partly because of this, it could have been treated almost anywhere within its direct, design, deliver, develop structure. We have chosen to place it in the context of operations development because the majority of projects that managers will be engaged in are essentially improvement projects. Of course, many projects are vast enterprises with very high levels of resourcing, complexity and uncertainty that will extend over many years. Look around you at the civil engineering, social, political and environmental successes (and failures) to see the evidence of major projects. Such projects require professional project management involving high-level technical expertise and management skills. But so do the smaller, yet important, projects that implement the many and continuous improvements that will determine the strategic impact of operations development. This is why it is equally important to take a rigorous and systematic approach to managing projects regardless of their size and type.

At this point it is also worth pointing out the distinction between 'projects' and 'programmes'. A programme, such as a continuous improvement programme, has no defined end point. Rather, it is an ongoing process of change. Individual projects may be individual subsections of an overall programme, but 'programme management' will overlay and integrate the individual projects. Generally, it is a more difficult task in the sense that it requires resource co-ordination, particularly when multiple projects share common resources.

In order to co-ordinate the efforts of many people in different parts of the organization (and often outside it as well), all projects need a project manager. Many of a project manager's activities are concerned with managing human resources. The people working in the project team need a clear understanding of their roles in the (usually temporary) organization. Controlling an uncertain project environment requires the rapid exchange of relevant information with the project stakeholders, both within and outside the organization. People, equipment and other resources must be identified and allocated to the various tasks. Undertaking these tasks successfully makes the management of a project a particularly challenging operations activity. Over the last decade, there have been significant moves towards professionalizing project management. More of those who lead projects hold professional qualifications and many organizations now treat the activity as a critical function for success.

Halting the growth of malaria[3]

In 2000 the World Health Organization (WHO) set a challenging objective – to halt the growth of malaria. At the time, there were an estimated 300–500 million cases of malaria each year, with between 1.1 and 2.7 million deaths, the largest proportion of these being children under 5 years old. The WHO faced a hugely complex project management climate, with major political, economic, climatic and cultural impediments to success. And yet, by 2013 the reported number of malaria cases was down to 198 million and the number of deaths down to 580,000. At the heart of its success was a clear overriding vision that gained buy-in from the project's diverse set of stakeholders. Building on this, the WHO spent significant time understanding the project environment – the internal and external factors that might influence the success or failure of its various malaria projects worldwide. It also committed significant resources to objective setting, scoping and planning of its projects. Finally, in technically executing different malaria-related projects, focused both on preventing incidence of malaria and on curing those infected, the WHO and its partners relied heavily on careful project monitoring, milestones and continuing stakeholder engagement to ensure that it was on track. The fight against malaria is far from over, but at least this preventable and curable disease is in decline.

Source: Shutterstock.com: Natursports

Differentiating between projects

The management of any project should begin by understanding its broad characteristics. So far, we have shown what projects have in *common* – temporary activities, with specific and highly customized goals, within time, cost and quality requirements, involving many non-routine and complex tasks. However, it is also critical to understand *differences* between projects. Key things for a project manager to consider are volume and variety characteristics, its scale, its complexity, the degree of uncertainty in the project, how much novelty is involved, the nature of technology (if any) and the 'pace' of the project.

Differentiating by projects' volume and variety characteristics

At a simple level, we can use the 'product–process' matrix, already explored in Chapter 6 of this book, to distinguish between projects based on their volume and variety characteristics. This is shown in Figure 19.2. Of course, all project processes are, by definition, in the top left corner of the matrix. But within that end of the 'natural diagonal' projects do vary. At the very top left-hand part of the matrix are projects that are genuinely 'first timers' with a very high degree of uniqueness, a volume of one and infinite variety. With less uniqueness, higher volume and less variety, '*as before, but…*' projects may in many ways share some of the attributes of previous projects, but may have new features where project managers have little or no previous experience to help guide them. With higher volume (therefore a greater degree of

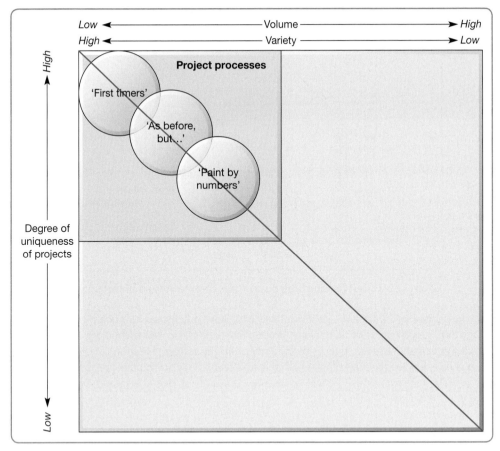

Figure 19.2 Differentiating projects using their volume and variety characteristics

repetition) and lower variety, so-called *'paint by numbers'* projects are relatively routine and predictable, and therefore (generally) more straightforward to manage.

Differentiating by projects' scale, complexity and uncertainty characteristics

An alternative approach to distinguishing between projects is by considering their scale, complexity and uncertainty. This is shown in Figure 19.3. For example, a wedding planning project has (relatively) low levels of scale, complexity and uncertainty. The effect is that the management challenges of such a project are significantly different to, for example developing the Airbus A380, which exhibits much higher levels of all three dimensions. The scale, complexity and uncertainty of such 'ground-breaking' projects demand far more sophisticated planning, greater and more flexible resources, and careful control if they are to be successful.

> **❊ Operations principle**
>
> The difficulty of managing a project is a function of its scale, complexity and uncertainty.

Differentiating using novelty, technology, complexity and pace – the 'diamond' model

Yet another alternative (and very useful) way to distinguish between projects is to consider their relative novelty, technology, complexity and pace. Based on the work of Aaron Shenhar and Dov Dvir,[4] Figure 19.4 illustrates the shape of the 'diamond', in this case for the development of the Airbus A380 project.

- *The novelty dimension* – is concerned with how new the outcome of the project is to the customers or users (that is, the market). Table 19.1 shows the three levels of novelty – derivative, platform and breakthrough – with examples of each type.

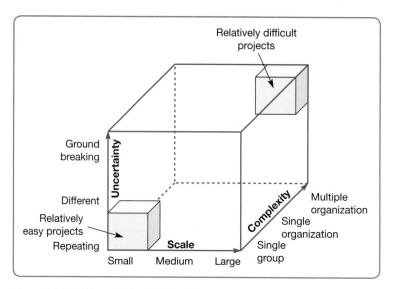

Figure 19.3 Differentiating projects by scale, complexity and uncertainty

- *The technology dimension* – is concerned with how much new technology is being used within the project. Low-technology projects have almost no new technology integrated, so designs can be 'frozen' (that is, fixed) early on in the project. Medium-technology projects typically involve the integration of a single new technology, for example the improvement of

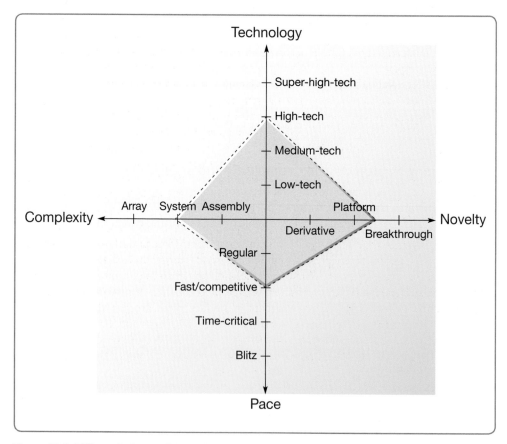

Figure 19.4 Differentiating projects using the 'diamond' model

Source: From *Reinventing Project Management: The Diamond Approach to Successful Growth and Innovation*, Harvard Business School Press (Shenhar, A.J. and Dvir, D. 2007) Reprinted by permission of Harvard Business Review Press. Copyright © 2007 by the Harvard Business Publishing Corporation; all rights reserved.

Table 19.1 Three levels of project novelty

Level of project novelty	Definition	Examples
Derivative project	Extending or improving existing products or services	Developing a new version of a laptop Upgrading a production line
Platform project	Developing and producing new generations of existing products or new types of services to existing markets	Building a new generation of car Creating a new generation of mobile systems
Breakthrough project	Introducing a new product, new idea or new use of a product that customers have never seen before	First photocopying machine First iPod First Moon landing

an existing product. This allows early design-freezes, but some testing, evaluation and corrections may be required as the project progresses. High-technology projects involve the integration of several new technologies and therefore must be flexible for a longer period of time to allow for integration and optimization. Finally, super-high-technology projects involve the integration of several non-existing technologies. This takes extended periods to develop and prove new technologies, so design-freeze typically occurs very late in the project.

- *The complexity dimension* – is concerned with how complex the system and its subsystems are. At the lowest level there are 'assembly' projects, with self-contained components that perform a function within a larger system. Examples may include developing a new iPod, creating a new undergraduate operations and process management module, or putting on a new play in a theatre. 'System' projects involve a collection of interactive elements and sub-elements. Examples include developing a new aircraft, constructing a new R&D facility, or developing a new portfolio of post-experience education within a university. While the sub-elements of the project have a common goal, the added complexity creates significantly higher co-ordination and integration problems. Finally, 'array' projects are 'systems of systems' – with each system having an independent function, but each with a common goal. Heathrow's Terminal 5 project, with its 16 major projects and 147 sub-projects, is a good example of an array project. Another is the South-to-North water diversion project in China, a multi-decade infrastructural mega-project expected to be completed in 2050 at a cost of $62 billion.

- *The pace dimension* – is concerned with how critical the time frame of the project is. Pace is not simply about speed – some projects have urgency but last for many years, others are not urgent but last a few weeks. For example, in May 1961, President John F. Kennedy delivered a speech to the US Congress in which he stated, '*I believe that this nation should commit itself to achieving the goal, before this decade is out, of landing a man on the moon and returning him safely to the earth.*' In doing so, the president set a time frame that was to be critical to the ambitions of the Moon-landing project. Some projects are regular pace in that they are not time critical. Many public works and internal projects fall into this category. Others are fast/competitive in that completion on time is important for competitive advantage and leadership. Many business-related projects, such as new product/service introductions and new capacity development in the face of market growth, fall into this category. Time-critical projects have a specific window of opportunity and delays mean project failure. The space launch or the Olympics are examples of this kind of project. Finally, blitz projects have the utmost urgency and often occur through crises such as war, response to natural disasters, and fast response to business surprises.

HOW ARE PROJECTS PLANNED?

Figure 19.5 shows the stages in project management:

Stage 1 Understanding the project environment – internal and external factors which may influence the project.

Stage 2 Defining the project – setting the objectives, scope and strategy for the project.

Stage 3 Project planning – deciding how the project will be executed.

Stage 4 Technical execution – performing the technical aspects of the project.

Stage 5 Project control – ensuring that the project is carried out according to plan.

We will examine the first three stages in this section as they broadly relate to activities that managers carry out in advance of the project. Stage 4, the technical execution of the project, is determined by the specific technicalities of individual projects, so we do not examine it in this book. Stage 5 focuses on the ongoing control of projects once they are underway, so we deal with this in the subsequent section to this. However, it is important to understand that the stages are not a simple sequential chain of steps. Project management is essentially an *iterative* process. Problems or changes that become evident in the control stage may require re-planning and may even cause modifications to the original project definition.

Stage 1 – Understanding the project environment

The project environment comprises all the factors that may affect the project during its life. It is the context and circumstances in which the project takes place. Understanding the project environment is important because the environment affects the way in which a project will need to be managed and (just as important) the possible dangers that may cause the project to fail. Environmental factors can be considered under the following four headings:

- Geo-social environment – geographical, climatic and cultural factors that may affect the project.
- Econo-political environment – the economic, governmental and regulatory factors in which the project takes place.
- The business environment – industrial, competitive, supply network and customer expectation factors that shape the likely objectives of the project.
- The internal environment – the individual company's or group's strategy and culture, the resources available, and the interaction with other projects that will influence the project.

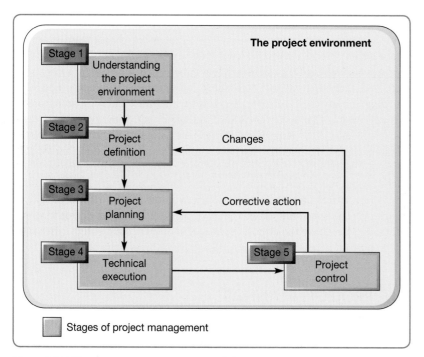

Figure 19.5 The project management model

The role of stakeholders in projects

One way of operationalizing the importance of understanding a project's environment is to consider the various 'stakeholders' (also called 'agents') who have some kind of interest in the project. Project stakeholders are those individuals, groups or entities that have an interest in the project process or outcome. In other words, they affect, or are affected by, the project. Internal stakeholders include the client, the project sponsor, the project team, functional managers, contractors and project support. External stakeholders (that is, those outside of the core project, rather than outside of the organization) include end users, suppliers, competitors, lobby groups, shareholders, government agencies, and employees.

All projects will have stakeholders – complex projects will have many stakeholders. They are likely to have different views on a project's objectives that may conflict with other stakeholders'. At the very least, different stakeholders are likely to stress different aspects of a project. So, as well an ethical imperative to include as many people as possible in a project from an early stage, it is often useful in preventing objections and problems later in the project. Moreover, there can be significant direct benefits from using a stakeholder-based approach. Project managers can use the opinions of powerful stakeholders to shape the project at an early stage. This makes it more likely that they will support the project, and also can improve its quality. Communicating with stakeholders early and frequently can ensure that they fully understand the project and understand potential benefits. Stakeholder support may even help to win more resources, making it more likely that projects will be successful. Perhaps most important, one can anticipate stakeholder reaction to various aspects of the project, and plan the actions that could prevent opposition, or build support.

> *** Operations principle**
> All projects have stakeholders with different interests and priorities.

Some (even relatively experienced) project managers are reluctant to include stakeholders in the project management process, preferring to 'manage them at a distance' rather than allow them to interfere with the project. Others argue that the benefits of stakeholder management are too great to ignore. Emphasizing the responsibilities as well as the rights of project stakeholders can moderate many of the risks of stakeholder involvement. For example, one IT company formally identifies the rights and responsibilities of project stakeholders as shown in Table 19.2.

> *** Operations principle**
> Project stakeholders have responsibilities as well as rights.

Table 19.2 The rights and responsibilities of stakeholders in one IT company

The rights of stakeholders	The responsibilities of project stakeholders
1 To expect developers to learn and speak their language	1 Provide resources (time, money, ...) to the project team
2 To expect developers to identify and understand their requirements	2 Educate developers about their business
3 To receive explanations of artefacts that developers use as part of working with project stakeholders, such as models they create with them (e.g. user stories or essential UI prototypes), or artefacts that they present to them (e.g. UML deployment diagrams)	3 Spend the time to provide and clarify requirements
	4 Be specific and precise about requirements
	5 Make timely decisions
	6 Respect a developer's assessment of cost and feasibility
	7 Set requirement priorities
4 To expect developers to treat them with respect	8 Review and provide timely feedback regarding relevant work artefacts of developers
5 To hear ideas and alternatives for requirements	9 Promptly communicate changes to requirements
6 To describe characteristics that make the product easy to use	10 Own their organization's software processes: both to follow them and actively to help fix them when needed
7 To be presented with opportunities to adjust requirements to permit reuse, reduce development time or to reduce development costs	
8 To be given good-faith estimates	
9 To receive a system that meets their functional and quality needs	

Managing stakeholders

Managing stakeholders can be a subtle and delicate task, requiring significant social and, sometimes, political skills. But it is based on three basic activities: identifying stakeholders; determining the nature of different stakeholders; and prioritizing and managing stakeholders.

Identifying stakeholders Think of all the people who are affected by your work, who have influence or power over it, or have an interest in its successful or unsuccessful conclusion. Although stakeholders may be both organizations and people, ultimately you must communicate with people, so look to identify key individuals within a stakeholder organization. In addition, even if one decides not to attempt to manage every identified stakeholder, the process of stakeholder mapping is still useful because it gets those working on a project to see the variety of competing forces at play in many complex projects.

Determining the nature of different stakeholders Once all stakeholders have been identified, it is important to understand how they are likely to feel about and react to the project, and how best to communicate with them. One method is to position key stakeholders in relation to their positive and negative 'energy' towards a project (also called the level of synergy and antagonism), in order to understand likely attitudes and behaviours towards projects. Figure 19.6 illustrates this 'socio-dynamic' perspective, pioneered by Jean-Christian Fauvet.[5] *Zealots* have high levels of positive energy towards the project and are almost always in agreement with the project leader. They often fail to understand a lack of commitment in others and so may find it hard to compromise. *Golden Triangles* also have relatively high levels of positive energy towards the project, but their slight antagonism (or negative energy) can be useful in providing a critical perspective on a project and makes it easier for such stakeholders to understand any

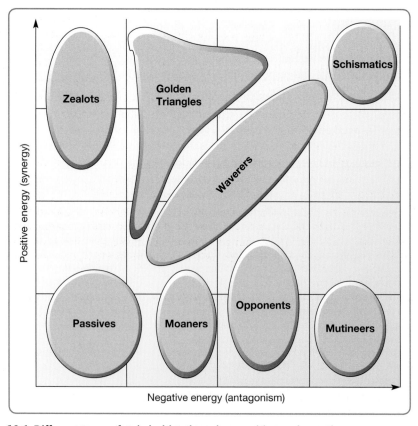

Figure 19.6 Different types of stakeholders based on positive and negative energy

Source: Adapted from D'Herbemont, O. and César, B. (1998) *Managing sensitive projects: A lateral approach*, English version by Cutrin, T. and Etcheber, P. Routledge, New York.

opposition to some or all of the project components. *Waverers* are stakeholders who have a balance of positive and negative energy towards a project. While they are sometimes considered to be time-wasters or ditherers, their doubts often reflect the 'passive majority', and they may be important in influencing other stakeholders. *Passive* stakeholders are those that do not hold strong positive or negative attitudes towards the project, but like to be kept informed and to ratify change. Zealot stakeholders will often dislike passive stakeholders because of their lack of any 'energy', either positive or negative! *Moaners* hold low levels of positive energy towards a project, but are more negative than passive stakeholders. These stakeholders are typically more active and can often act as an early warning of the views of *opponent* stakeholders. *Opponents*, as one might expect, are strongly opposed to the project and will look to ensure it fails. Unlike stakeholders with either higher levels of positive energy (for example, waverers) or lower levels of negative energy (for example, passives or moaners), the minds of opponent stakeholders are very hard to change and so methods of overcoming opposition are critical. *Mutineers* are stakeholders who are fervently opposed to the project. They represent a very small minority of all stakeholders but are extremely active in their opposition. Finally, *schismatic* stakeholders are rare in that they have very high levels of both positive *and* negative energy towards a project. An example might be an entrepreneur who has built up a business but is now retired and is on the board of directors. He or she may be strongly in favour of the organization and its overall project objectives, but feel that the decisions being made are completely wrong (academics are often considered to be schismatic stakeholders in universities).

Prioritizing and managing stakeholders Once the nature of key stakeholders, in terms of their positive and negative energy towards a project, has been determined, managers must prioritize different stakeholders and identify suitable methods of stakeholder engagement. One approach to discriminating between different stakeholders, and, more important, how they should be managed, is to distinguish between their power to influence the project and their interest in doing so. Stakeholders who have the power to exercise a major influence over the project should never be ignored. At the very least, the nature of their interest, and their motivation, should be well understood. But not all stakeholders who have the power to exercise influence over a project will be interested in doing so, and not everyone who is interested in the project has the power to influence it. The power–interest grid, shown in Figure 19.7, classifies stakeholders simply in terms of these two dimensions. Although there will be graduations between them, the two dimensions are useful in providing an indication of how stakeholders can be managed in terms of four categories.

High-power, interested groups must be fully engaged, with the greatest efforts made to satisfy them. High-power, less interested groups require enough effort to keep them satisfied, but not so much that they become bored or irritated with the message. Low-power, interested groups need to be kept adequately informed, with checks to ensure that no major issues are arising. These groups may be very helpful with the detail of the project. Low-power, less interested groups need monitoring, though without excessive communication. Some key questions that can help to understand high-priority stakeholders include the following:

> **✳ Operations principle**
> Different stakeholder groups will need managing differently.

- What financial or emotional interest do they have in the outcome of the project? Is it positive or negative?
- What motivates them most of all?
- What information do they need?
- What is the best way of communicating with them?
- What is their current opinion of the project?
- Who influences their opinions? Do some of these influencers therefore become important stakeholders in their own right?
- If they are not likely to be positive, what will win them around to support the project?
- If you do not think you will be able to win them around, how will you manage their opposition?

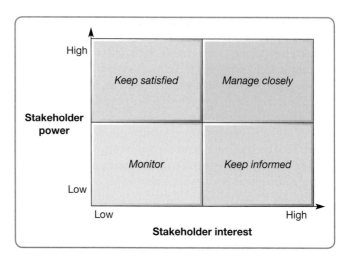

Figure 19.7 The stakeholder power–interest grid

Stage 2 – Project definition

Before starting the complex task of planning and executing a project, it is necessary to be clear about exactly what the project is – its definition. This is not always straightforward, especially in projects with many stakeholders. Three different elements define a project:

- its objectives: the end state that project management is trying to achieve;
- its scope: the exact range of the responsibilities taken on by project management;
- its strategy: how project management is going to meet its objectives.

Project objectives

Objectives help to provide a definition of the end point which can be used to monitor progress and identify when success has been achieved. They can be judged in terms of the five performance objectives – quality, speed, dependability, flexibility and cost. However, flexibility is regarded as a 'given' in most projects which, by definition, are to some extent one-offs, and speed and dependability are typically compressed to one composite objective – 'time'. This results in what is known as the 'iron triangle of project management' – cost, time and quality. Figure 19.8 shows the 'project objectives triangle' with three types of project marked.

The relative importance of each objective will differ for different projects. Some aerospace projects, such as the development of a new aircraft, which impact passenger safety, will place a very high emphasis on quality objectives. With other projects, for example a research project

> **✱ Operations principle**
>
> Different projects will place different levels of emphasis on cost, time and quality objectives.

that is being funded by a fixed government grant, cost might predominate. Other projects emphasize time: for example, the organization of an open-air music festival has to happen on a particular date if the project is to meet its objectives. In each of these projects, although one objective might be particularly important, the other objectives can never be totally forgotten.

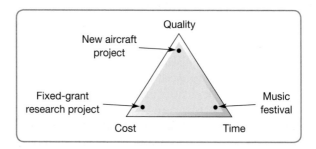

Figure 19.8 The iron triangle of project management

Good objectives are those which are clear, measurable and, preferably, quantifiable. Clarifying objectives involves breaking down project objectives into three categories – the purpose, the end results and the success criteria. For example, a project that is expressed in general terms as 'improve the budgeting process' could be broken down into:

- *Purpose* – to allow budgets to be agreed and confirmed prior the annual financial meeting.
- *End result* – a report that identifies the causes of budget delay, and which recommends new budgeting processes and systems.
- *Success criteria* – the report should be completed by 30 June, meet all departments' needs and enable integrated and dependable delivery of agreed budget statements. Cost of the recommendations should not exceed $200,000.

Project scope

The scope of a project identifies its work content and its products or outcomes. It is a boundary-setting exercise that attempts to define the dividing line between what each part of the project will do and what it will not do. Project scoping is critical and failure to scope appropriately or constantly changing scopes are one of the key reasons projects fail. Defining scope is particularly important when part of a project is being outsourced. A supplier's scope of supply will identify the legal boundaries within which the work must be done. Sometimes the scope of the project is articulated in a formal 'project specification'. This is the written, pictorial and graphical information used to define the output and the accompanying terms and conditions. The project scope will also outline limits or exclusions to the project. This is critical, because perceptions of project success or failure often originate from the extent to which deliverables, limits and exclusions have been clearly stated and understood by all parties during the scoping phase.

Project strategy

The third part of a project's definition is the project strategy, which defines, in a general rather than a specific way, how the project is going to meets its objectives. It does this in two ways: by defining the phases of the project, and by setting milestones and/or 'stagegates'. Milestones are important events during the project's life. Stagegates are the decision points that allow the project to move on to its next phase. A stagegate often launches further activities and therefore commits the project to additional costs etc. 'Milestone' is a more passive term, which may herald the review of a part-complete project or mark the completion of a stage, but does not necessarily have more significance than a measure of achievement or completeness. At this stage the actual dates for each milestone are not necessarily determined. It is useful, however, to identify at leas the significant milestones and stagegates, either to define the boundary between phases or to help in discussions with the project's customer.

Stage 3 – Project planning

All projects, even the smallest, need some degree of planning. The planning process fulfils four distinct purposes:

- It determines the cost and duration of the project. This enables major decisions to be made – such as the decision whether to go ahead with the project at the start.
- It determines the level of resources that will be needed.
- It helps to allocate work and to monitor progress. Planning must include the identification of who is responsible for what.
- It helps to assess the impact of any changes to the project.

Planning is not a one-off process. It may be repeated several times during the project's life as circumstances change; nor is re-planning a sign of project failure or mismanagement. As discussed earlier, projects can and should be differentiated based on their characteristics – in our case, we examined three alternative approaches of volume–

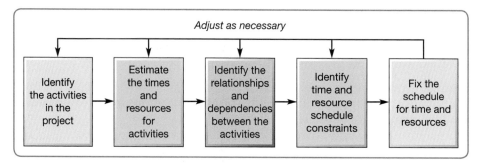

Figure 19.9 **Stages in the planning process**

variety, uncertainty–complexity–scale, and novelty–technology–complexity–pace. And when managing particularly difficult projects, it is a normal occurrence to repeat planning throughout the project's life. The process of project planning involves five steps (*see* Fig. 19.9).

Identify activities – the work breakdown structure

Most projects are too complex to be planned and controlled effectively unless they are first broken down into manageable portions. This is achieved by structuring the project into a 'family tree' that specifies major tasks or sub-projects. These in turn are divided up into smaller tasks until a defined, manageable series of tasks, called a *work package*, is arrived at. Each work package can be allocated its own objectives in terms of time, cost and quality. Typically, work packages do not exceed 10 days, should be independent from each other, should belong to one sub-deliverable, and should constantly be monitored. The output from this is called the work breakdown structure (WBS). The WBS brings clarity and definition to the project planning process. It shows 'how the jigsaw fits together'. It also provides a framework for building up information for reporting purposes.

Example project As a simple example to illustrate the application of each stage of the planning process, let us examine the following domestic project. The project definition is:

- *purpose:* to make breakfast in bed;
- *end result:* breakfast in bed of boiled egg, toast and orange juice;
- *success criteria:* plan uses minimum staff resources and time, and product is high quality (egg freshly boiled, warm toast, etc.);
- *scope:* project starts in kitchen at 6.00 am, and finishes in bedroom; needs one operator and normal kitchen equipment.

The WBS is based on the above definition and can be constructed as shown in Figure 19.10

Estimate times and resources

The second stage in project planning is to identify the time and resource requirements of the work packages. Without some idea of how long each part of a project will take and how many resources it will need, it is impossible to define what should be happening at any time during the execution of the project. Estimates are just that, however – a systematic best guess, not a perfect forecast of reality. Estimates may never be perfect but they can be made with some idea of how accurate they might be.

Example project Returning to our very simple example 'breakfast-in-bed' project, the activities were identified and times estimated as in Table 19.3. While some of the estimates may appear generous, they take into account the time of day and the state of the operator.

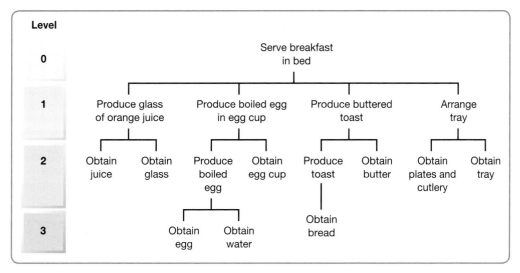

Figure 19.10 A work breakdown structure (WBS) for a simple domestic project

Probabilistic estimates The amount of uncertainty in a project has a major bearing on the level of confidence that can be placed on an estimate. The impact of uncertainty on estimating times leads some project managers to use a probability curve to describe the estimate. In practice, this is usually a positively skewed distribution, as in Figure 19.11. The greater is the risk, the greater is the range of the distribution. The natural tendency of some people is to produce *optimistic* estimates, but these will have a relatively low probability of being correct because they represent the time that would be taken if *everything* went well. *Most likely* estimates have the highest probability of proving correct. Finally, *pessimistic* estimates assume that almost everything that could go wrong does go wrong. Because of the skewed nature of the distribution, the expected time for the activity will not be the same as the most likely time.

> **✳ Operations principle**
>
> Probabilistic activity time estimates facilitate the assessment of a project being completed on time.

Table 19.3 Time and resources estimates for a 'breakfast-in-bed' project

Activity	Effort (person-min)	Duration (min)
Butter toast	1	1
Pour orange juice	1	1
Boil egg	0	4
Slice bread	1	1
Fill pan with water	1	1
Bring water to boil	0	3
Toast bread	0	2
Take loaded tray to bedroom	1	1
Fetch tray, plates, cutlery	1	1

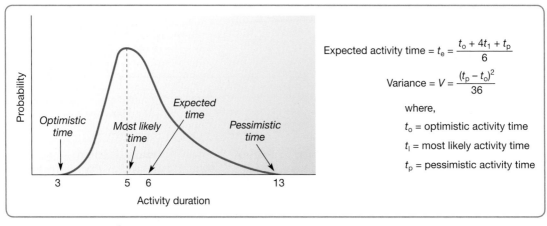

Figure 19.11 Probability distribution of time estimates

$$\text{Expected activity time} = t_e = \frac{t_o + 4t_1 + t_p}{6}$$

$$\text{Variance} = V = \frac{(t_p - t_o)^2}{36}$$

where,

t_o = optimistic activity time

t_l = most likely activity time

t_p = pessimistic activity time

Critical commentary

When project managers talk of 'time estimates', they are really talking about guessing. By definition, planning a project happens in advance of the project itself. Therefore, no one really knows how long each activity will take. Of course, some kind of guess is needed for planning purposes. However, some project managers believe that too much faith is put in time estimates. The really important question, they claim, is not how long *will* something take, but how long *could* something take without delaying the whole project. (We deal with this issue partially when we discuss the concept of float later in the chapter.) Also, if a single most likely time estimate is difficult to estimate, then using three, as one does for probabilistic estimates, is merely over-analysing what is highly dubious data in the first place.

OPERATION IN PRACTICE   The Scottish Parliament Building[6]

The Scottish Parliament Building, opened in 2004, divides opinions like few other projects in the world. To some, it is an architectural masterstroke that is without parallel in 100 years, described by one critic as '*A Celtic-Spanish cocktail to blow both minds and budgets [...] energetically mining a new seam of National Romanticism refined and reinterpreted for the twenty-first century.*' To others, it is an example of appalling cost estimation and lack of control. The project timeline makes for interesting reading:

- July 1997: A budget range of £10–40m was set.
- Sept. 1997: Indicative estimates were between £54 and £71m.
- June 1998: Five designers submit bids ranging from £58 to £90m.

- July 1998: The bid of Enric Miralles, the Spanish architect, is chosen with a cost in the range of £50 to £55m, not including VAT or site acquisition costs.
- June 1999: Provisional cost estimated at £109m including consultancy fees, site costs, demolition, VAT, archaeology work, risk and contingencies.
- Nov. 2001: Cost estimate rises to £241m due to increase in space and major design change.
- Dec. 2002: Cost estimate rises to £295m due to increased security needs and 'hidden extras' in the construction process.
- June 2003: Cost estimate rises to £374m due to higher than expected consultancy fees which now top £50m.
- Feb. 2004: Cost estimate rises to £430m due to construction problems.

At one level, the Scottish Parliament is still a success story, with around 400,000 visitors every year coming to a building that pushed the boundaries of architecture. Yet, from a project management perspective, it should be viewed as a failure. Ultimately, the project was delivered at cost of £414.6 million, 10–40 times the original budget of £10–£40 million, and instead of launching in 2001, it was not opened until 2004. Several causes have been identified for the failure of the project, including: the approved design being more complex than envisaged at the feasibility stage; increases in construction cost estimates, almost half of which was attributable to a 47 per cent increase in the total area of the building; additional costs for landscaping and road realignment work; poor cost reporting; and inadequate risk allowance. Yet, the Scottish Parliament project is not alone in failing to accurately predict or effectively manage its costs. The Wembley Stadium Project cost £900 million compared with the original forecast of £757 million and was delivered a year late, while the 2014 Brazil World Cup was originally estimated at $2.05 billion and had a final approximate cost of $4.25 billion.

Source: Alamy Images: Arcaid Images

Identify relationships and dependencies

The third stage of planning is to understand the interactions between different project work packages. All the work packages (or activities) that are identified will have some relationship with one another that will depend on the logic of the project. Some activities will, by necessity, need to be executed in a particular order. For example, in the construction of a house, the foundations must be prepared before the walls are built, which in turn must be completed before the roof is put in place. These activities have a *dependent* or *series* relationship. Other activities do not have any such dependence on each other. The rear garden of the house could probably be prepared totally independently of the garage being built. These two activities have an *independent* or *parallel* relationship.

Project planning is greatly aided by the use of techniques that help to handle time, resource and relationship complexity. The simplest of these techniques is the Gantt chart (or bar chart), which we introduced in Chapter 10. Gantt charts are the simplest way to exhibit an overall project plan, because they have excellent visual impact and are easy to understand. They are also useful for communicating project plans and status to senior managers as well as for day-to-day project control.

Example project Table 19.3 identified the activities for the breakfast preparation project. The list shows that some of the activities must necessarily follow others. For example, 'boil egg' cannot be carried out until 'fill pan with water' and 'bring water to boil' have been completed. Further logical analysis of the activities in the list shows that there are two major 'chains', where activities must be carried out in a definite sequence:

Slice bread – Toast bread – Butter toast

Fill pan with water – Bring water to boil – Boil egg

Both of these sequences must be completed before the activity 'take loaded tray to bedroom'. The remaining activities ('pour orange juice' and 'fetch tray, plates, cutlery') can be done at any time provided that they are completed before 'take loaded tray to bedroom'. An initial project plan might be as shown in Figure 19.12. Here, the activities have been represented as blocks of time in proportion to their estimated durations. From this, we can see that the 'project' can be completed in nine minutes. Some of the activities have spare time (called float). The sequence 'Fill pan – Boil water – Boil egg – Bedroom' has no float, and is called the *critical path* of the project. By implication, any activity that runs late in this sequence would cause the whole project to be delayed accordingly.

Identify schedule constraints

Once estimates have been made of the time and effort involved in each activity, and their dependencies identified, it is possible to compare project requirements with the available resources. The finite nature of critical resources – such as special skills – means that they should be taken into account in the planning process. This often has the effect of highlighting the need for more detailed re-planning. There are essentially two fundamental approaches:

● *Resource-constrained.* Only the available resource levels are used in resource scheduling, and are never exceeded. As a result, project completion may slip. Resource-limited scheduling is used, for example, when a project company has its own highly specialized assembly and test facilities.

● *Time-constrained.* The overriding priority is to complete the project within a given time. Once normally available resources have been used up, alternative ('threshold') resources are scheduled.

Example project Returning to the breakfast-in-bed project, we can now consider the resource implications of the plan in Figure 19.13. Each of the four activities scheduled at the start ('pour orange', 'cut bread', 'fill pan', 'fetch tray') consumes staff resources. There is clearly a resource-loading problem, because the project definition states that only one person is available. This is not an insuperable difficulty, however, because there is sufficient float to move some

Figure 19.12 Initial project plan for a simple project, with resources

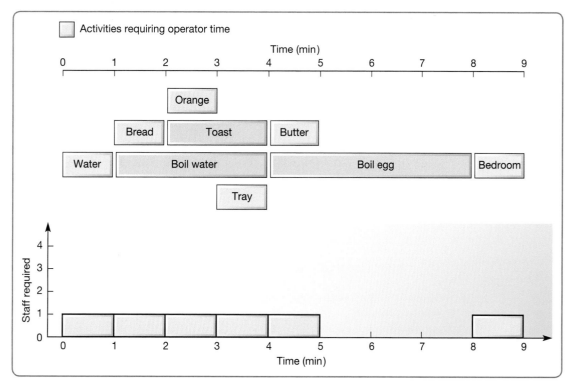

Figure 19.13 Revised plan with levelled resources

of the activities. A plan with levelled resources can be produced, as shown in Figure 19.13. All that has been necessary is to delay the toast preparation by one minute, and to use the elapsed time during the toasting and water-boiling processes to pour orange and fetch the tray.

Fix the schedule

Project planners should ideally have a number of alternatives to choose from. The one which best fits project objectives can then be chosen or developed. While it can be challenging to examine several alternative schedules, especially in very large or very uncertain projects, computer-based software packages such as Bitrix24, Trello, 2-Plan PMS, Asana, MS project and Producteev make critical path optimization more feasible.

> **❉ Operations principle**
>
> A prerequisite for project planning is some knowledge of times, resources and relationships between activities.

Example project A further improvement to the plan can be made. Looking again at the project definition, the success criteria state that the product should be 'high quality'. In the plan shown in Figure 19.13, although the egg is freshly boiled, the toast might be cold. An 'optimized' plan which would provide hot toast would be to prepare the toast during the 'boil egg' activity. This plan is shown in Figure 19.14.

Network analysis

As project complexity increases, it becomes more necessary to identify clearly the relationships between activities, and show the logical sequence in which activities must take place. This is typically done using the *critical path method* (CPM) to clarify the relationships between activities diagrammatically. Though there are alternative methods of carrying out critical path analysis, by far the most common, and also the one used in most project management software packages, is the 'activity on node' (AoN) method. For example, Table 19.4 shows the activities, time estimates, precedence relationships and resources needed (in terms of the

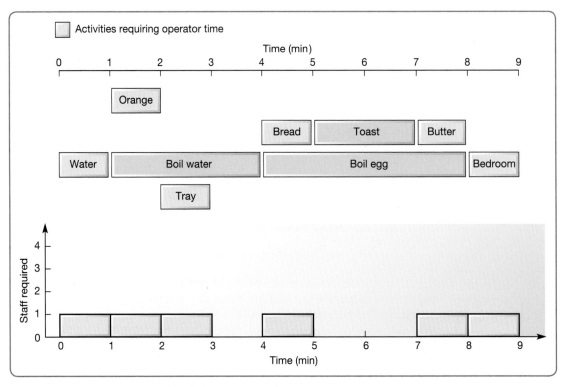

Figure 19.14 **Revised plan with levelled resources and warm toast**

number of IT developers) for one phase of a new sales knowledge management system that is being installed in an insurance company. The project is a co-operation between the company's IT systems department and its sales organization.

Figure 19.15 shows the critical path analysis for the new sales knowledge management system. Some of the conventions of the AoN representation of project network need explaining. Activities are drawn as boxes, and arrows are used to define the relationships between them. In the centre of each box is the description of the activity (in this case, 'Activity a', 'Activity b', and so on). Above the description is the duration (D) of the activity (or work package), the earliest start time (EST) and earliest finish time (EFT). Below the description is the latest start time (LST), the latest finish time (LFT) and the 'float' (F) (the number of extra days that the activity could take without slowing down the overall project). The diagram shows that there are a number of chains of events that must be completed before the project can be considered as finished (event 5). In this case, activity chains a–c–f, a–d–e–f and b–e–f must all be completed before the project can be considered as finished. The longest (in duration) of these

Table 19.4 **Time, resource and relationships for the sales system interface design project**

Code	Activity	Immediate predecessor(s)	Duration (days)	Resources (developers)
a	Form and train user group	None	10	3
b	Install systems	None	17	5
c	Specify sales training	a	5	2
d	Design initial screen interface	a	5	3
e	Test interface in pilot area	b, d	25	2
f	Modify interface	c, e	15	3

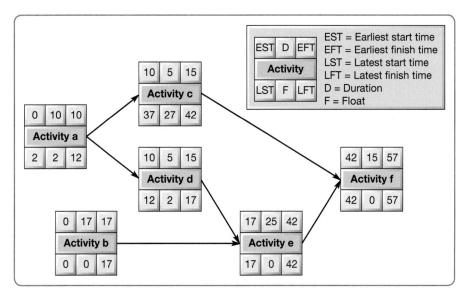

Figure 19.15 Critical path analysis (AoN method) for the project to design an information interface for a new sales knowledge management system in an insurance company

chains of activities is called the 'critical path' because it represents the shortest time in which the project can be finished, and therefore dictates the project timing. In this case b–e–f is the longest path and the earliest the project can finish is after 57 days.

Activities that lie on the critical path will have the same earliest and latest start times and earliest and latest finish times. That is why these activities are critical. Non-critical activities, however, have some flexibility as to when to start and finish. This flexibility is quantified into a figure that is known either as 'float' or 'slack'. So activity c, for example, is only of 5 days' duration and it can start any time after day 10 (when activity a is completed) and must finish any time before day 42 (when activities a, b, c and d are completed). Its 'float' is therefore $(42 - 10) - 5 = 27$ days (that is, latest finish time minus earliest start time minus activity duration). Obviously, activities on the critical path have no float; any change or delay in these activities would immediately affect the whole project.

The rather tedious computation necessary in network planning can be relatively easily performed by project planning models. All they need are the basic relationships between activities together with the timing and resource requirements for each activity. Earliest and latest event times, float and other characteristics of a network can be presented, often in the form of a Gantt chart (see Chapter 10). More significantly, the speed of computation allows for frequent updates to project plans. Similarly, if updated information is both accurate and frequent, such computer-based systems can also provide effective project control data.

Critical commentary

The idea that all project activities can be identified as entities with a clear beginning and a clear end point and that these entities can be described in terms of their relationship with each other is an obvious simplification. Some activities are more or less continuous and evolve over time. For example, take a simple project such as digging a trench and laying a communications cable in it. The activity 'dig trench' does not have to be completed before the activity 'lay cable' is started. Only 2 or 3 metres of the trench needs to be dug before cable laying can commence – a simple relationship, but one that is difficult to illustrate on a network diagram. Also, if the trench is being dug in difficult terrain, the time taken to complete the activity, or even the activity itself, may change, to include rock drilling activities, for example. However, if the trench cannot be dug because of rock formations, it may be possible to dig more of the trench elsewhere, a contingency not allowed for in the original plan. So, even for this simple project, the original network diagram may reflect neither what *will* happen nor *could* happen.

Program evaluation and review technique (PERT)

The program evaluation and review technique, or PERT as it is universally known, is a technique that recognizes that activity durations and costs in project management cannot be forecast perfectly, so probability theory should be used. In this type of network the duration of each activity is estimated on an optimistic, a most likely and a pessimistic basis, as shown in Figure 19.16. If it is assumed that these time estimates are consistent with a beta probability distribution, the mean and variance of the distribution can be estimated as follows:

$$t_e = \frac{t_o + 4t_1 + t_p}{6}$$

where:

t_e = the expected time for the activity

t_o = the optimistic time for the activity

t_1 = the most likely time for the activity

t_p = the pessimistic time for the activity

The variance of the distribution (V) can be calculated as follows:

$$V = \frac{(t_p - t_o)^2}{6^2} = \frac{(t_p - t_o)^2}{36}$$

The time distribution of any path through a network will have a mean which is the sum of the means of the activities that make up the path, and a variance which is a sum of their variances. In Figure 19.16:

$$\text{The mean of the first activity (a)} = \frac{2 + (4 \times 3) + 5}{6} = 3.17$$

$$\text{The variance of the first activity (a)} = \frac{(5 - 2)^2}{36} = 0.25$$

$$\text{The mean of the second activity (b)} = \frac{3 + (4 \times 4) + 7}{6} = 4.33$$

$$\text{The variance of the second activity (b)} = \frac{(7 - 3)^2}{36} = 0.44$$

The mean of the network distribution = 3.17 + 4.33 = 7.5

The variance of the network distribution = 0.25 + 0.44 = 0.69

It is generally assumed that the whole path will be normally distributed. The advantage of this extra information is that we can examine the 'riskiness' of each path through a network as well as its duration. Given the increased attention on risk management within project

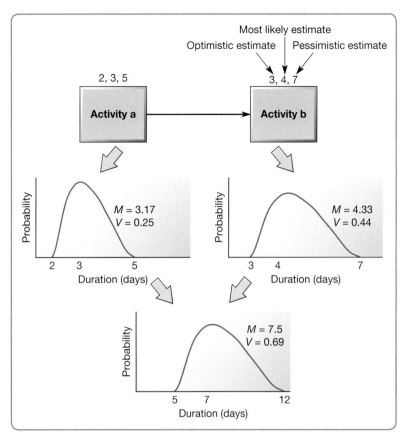

Figure 19.16 Probabilistic time estimates can be summed to give a probabilistic estimate for the whole project

management over recent years, this is essential. For example, Figure 19.17 shows a simple two-path network. The top path is the critical one; the distribution of its duration has a mean of 14.5 with a variance of 0.22. The distribution of the non-critical path has a lower mean of 12.66 but a far higher variance of 2.11. The implication of this is that there is a chance that the non-critical path could in reality be critical. Although we will not discuss the probability calculations here, it is possible to determine the probability of any sub-critical path turning out to be critical when the project actually takes place. However, on a practical level, even if the probability calculations are judged not to be worth the effort involved, it is useful to be able to make an approximate assessment of the riskiness of each part of a network.

HOW ARE PROJECTS CONTROLLED?

Understanding the project environment, project definition and project planning stages of project management largely takes place before the actual project begins. Project control, on the other hand, deals with the management activities that take place during execution of the project. As such, project control is the essential link between planning and doing. It involves four key challenges:

- how to *monitor* the project in order to check on its progress;
- how to *assess the performance* of the project by comparing monitored observations of the project with the project plan;
- how to *intervene* in the project in order to make the changes that will bring it back to plan;
- how to *manage matrix tensions* in the project in order to reconcile the interests of both the project and the different organizational functions.

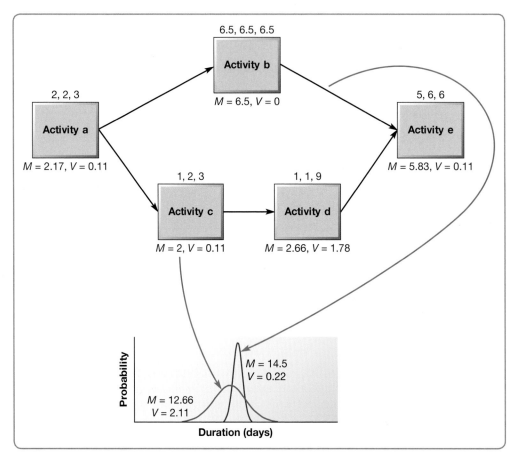

Figure 19.17 One path in the network can have the longest expected duration while another path has the greater variance

Project monitoring

Project managers have first to decide what they should be looking for as the project progresses. Usually a variety of measures are monitored. To some extent, the measures used will depend on the nature of the project. However, common measures include current expenditure to date, supplier price changes, amount of overtime authorized, technical changes to project, inspection failures, number and length of delays, activities not started on time, missed milestone, etc. Some of these monitored measures affect mainly cost, some mainly time. However, when something affects the quality of the project, there are also time and cost implications. This is because quality problems in project planning and control usually have to be solved in a limited amount of time.

Assessing project performance

The monitored measures of project performance at any point in time need to be assessed so that project management can make a judgement concerning overall performance. A typical planned cost profile of a project through its life is shown in Figure 19.18. At the beginning of a project some activities can be started, but most activities will be dependent on finishing. Eventually, only a few activities will remain to be completed. This pattern of a slow start followed by a faster pace with an eventual tail-off of activity holds true for almost all projects, which is why the rate of total expenditure follows an S-shaped pattern, even when the cost curves for the individual activities are linear. It is against this curve that actual costs can be

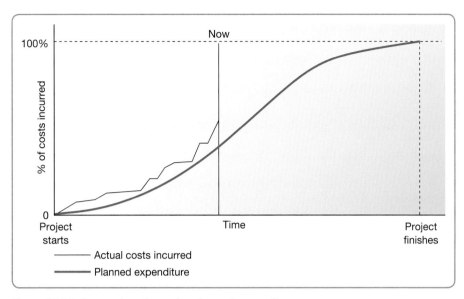

Figure 19.18 **Comparing planned and actual expenditure**

compared in order to check whether the project's costs are being incurred to plan. Figure 19.18 shows the planned and actual cost figures compared in this way. It shows that the project is incurring costs, on a cumulative basis, ahead of what was planned.

Intervening to change the project

If the project is obviously out of control in the sense that its costs, quality levels or times are significantly different from those planned, then some kind of intervention is almost certainly likely to be required. The exact nature of the intervention will depend on the technical characteristics of the project, but it is likely to need the advice of all the people who would be affected. Given the interconnected nature of projects – a change to one part of the project will have knock-on effects elsewhere – this means that interventions often require wide consultation. Sometimes intervention is needed even if the project looks to be proceeding according to plan. For example, the schedule and cost for a project may seem to be 'to plan', but when the project managers project activities and cost into the future, they see that problems are very likely to arise. In this case it is the *trend* of performance which is being used to trigger intervention.

The MacLeamy curve[7]

It has been accepted for many years by professional project managers that a project becomes more difficult to change as it progresses. The more developed it becomes, the more a project develops internal connections and complexities, therefore changing one part of the project is more likely to have implications in other parts of the project. Patrick MacLeamy, the boss of the architecture firm HOK, drew a set of curves based on this observation (although previous authors had also proposed similar curves). The idea is that, as the project moves forward, the cost of making changes to the original project plan increases, but the ability of project managers to influence the project goes down. The key point made by MacLeamy is that project managers focus their effort too late, during the time when design changes are relatively costly. Instead, they should move their efforts forward in the project, frontloading it, in order to reduce the cost of any changes to the project specification (*see* Fig. 19.19).

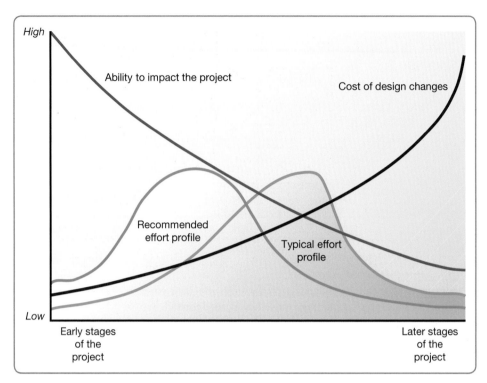

High

Ability to impact the project

Cost of design changes

Recommended
effort profile

Typical effort
profile

Low

Early stages
of the
project

Later stages
of the
project

Figure 19.19 The MacLeamy curve

Crashing or accelerating activities

Crashing (accelerating) activities in networks is the process of reducing time spans on critical path activities so that the project is completed in less time. Usually, crashing activities incur extra cost. This can be as a result of such actions as overtime working, acquiring additional resources, such as staff, or using subcontractors. Figure 19.20 shows an example of crashing a simple network. For each activity the duration and normal cost are specified, together with the (reduced) duration and (increased) cost of crashing them. Not all activities are capable of being crashed; here activity e cannot be crashed. The critical path is the sequence of activities a, b, c, e. If the total project time is to be reduced, one of the activities on the critical path must be crashed. In order to decide which activity to crash, the 'cost slope' of each is calculated. This is the cost per time period of reducing durations. The most cost-effective way of shortening the whole project then is to crash the activity on the critical path which has the lowest cost slope. This is activity a, the crashing of which will cost an extra €2,000 and will shorten the project by one week. After this, activity c can be crashed, saving a further two weeks and costing an extra €5,000. At this point all the activities have become critical and further time savings can only be achieved by crashing two activities in parallel.

The shape of the time–cost curve in Figure 19.20 is entirely typical. Initial savings come relatively inexpensively if the activities with the lowest cost slope are chosen. Later in the crashing sequence the more expensive activities need to be crashed and eventually two or more paths become jointly critical. Inevitably by that point, savings in time can only come from crashing two or more activities on parallel paths.

Managing matrix tensions

In all but the simplest project, project managers usually need to reconcile the interests of both the project itself and the departments contributing resources to the project. When calling on a variety of resources from various departments, projects are operating in a 'matrix

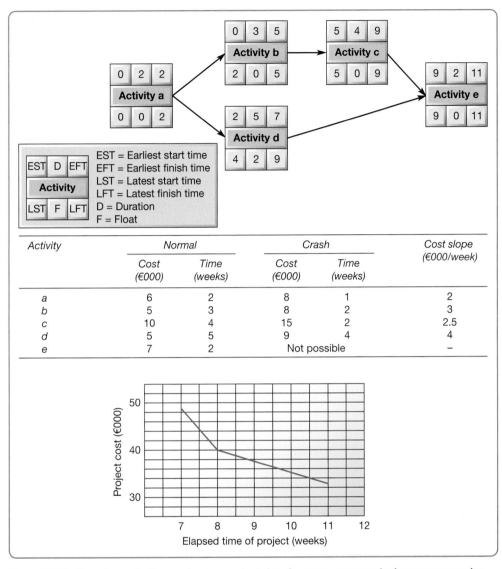

Figure 19.20 Crashing activities to shorten project time becomes progressively more expensive

management' environment, where projects cut across organizational boundaries and involve staff that are required to report to their own line manager as well as to the project manager. Figure 19.21 illustrates the type of reporting relationship that usually occurs in matrix management structures running multiple projects. A person in Department 1, assigned part-time to projects A and B, will be reporting to three different managers all of whom will have some degree of authority over their activities. This is why matrix management requires a high degree of co-operation and communication between all individuals and departments. Although decision-making authority will formally rest with either the project or departmental manager, most major decisions will need some degree of consensus. Arrangements need to be made that reconcile potential differences between project managers and departmental managers. To function effectively, matrix management structures should have the following characteristics:

● There should be effective channels of communication between all managers involved, with relevant departmental managers contributing to project planning and resourcing decisions.

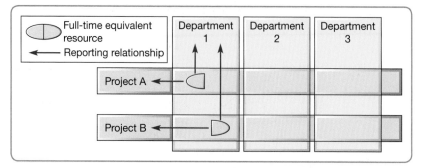

Figure 19.21 Matrix management structures often result in staff reporting to more than one project manager as well as their own department

- There should be formal procedures in place for resolving the management conflicts that do arise.
- Project staff should be encouraged to feel committed to their projects as well as to their own department.
- Project management should be seen as the central co-ordinating role, with sufficient time devoted to planning the project, securing the agreement of the line managers to deliver on time and within budget.

SUMMARY ANSWERS TO KEY QUESTIONS

❯ What is project management?

- A project is a set of activities with a defined start point and a defined end state, which pursues a defined goal and uses a defined set of resources.
- While projects share similarities, they can also be differentiated by volume and variety characteristics, their scale, complexity, the degree of uncertainty in the project, how much novelty is involved, the nature of technology (if any) and the 'pace' of the project.
- Project management is the activity of defining, planning and controlling, and learning from projects of any type.

❯ How are projects planned?

- Project planning involves three key activities: understanding the project environments, defining the project, and planning the project. It is important to understand the environment in which a project takes place for two reasons. First, the environment influences the way a project is carried out, often through stakeholder activity. Second, the nature of the environment in which a project takes place is the main determinant of the uncertainty surrounding it.
- Project definition involves (1) determining objectives (the end state which project management is trying to achieve), (2) scoping (the exact range of the responsibilities taken on by project management) and strategy (how project management is going to meet the project objectives).
- Project planning involves five stages:
  - identifying the activities within a project;
  - estimating times and resources for the activities;

- identifying the relationship and dependencies between the activities;
- identifying the schedule constraints;
- fixing the schedule.

- Gantt charts and network planning are the most common project planning techniques. Network planning, typically using the 'activity on node', is a useful method to assess the total duration of a project and the degree of flexibility or float of the individual activities within the project.

❯ How are projects controlled?

- Project control deals with the management activities that take place during the execution of the project and involves four key challenges:
  - how to *monitor* the project in order to check on its progress;
  - how to *assess the performance* of the project by comparing monitored observations of the project with the project plan;
  - how to *intervene* in the project in order to make the changes that will bring it back to plan, including crashing or accelerating activities;
  - how to *manage matrix tensions* in the project in order to reconcile the interests of both the project and the different organizational functions.

CASE STUDY   United Photonics Malaysia Sdn Bhd

Introduction

Anuar Kamaruddin, COO of United Photonics Malaysia (UPM), was conscious that the project in front of him was one of the most important he had handled for many years. The number and variety of the development projects underway within the company had risen sharply in the last few years, and although they had all seemed important at the time, this one – the 'Laz-skan' project – clearly justified the description given it by the President of United Photonics Corporation, the US parent of UPM, *'the make or break opportunity to ensure the division's long term position in the global instrumentation industry'.*

The United Photonics Group

United Photonics Corporation had been founded over 70 years ago (as the Detroit Gauge Company), a general instrument and gauge manufacturer for the engineering industry. By expanding its range into optical instruments, it eventually moved also into the manufacture of high-precision and speciality lenses, mainly for the photographic industry. Its reputation as a specialist lens manufacturer led to such a growth in sales that soon the optical side of the company accounted for about 60 per cent of

total business and it ranked one of the top two or three optics companies of its type in the world. Although its reputation for skilled lens making had not diminished since then, the instrument side of the company came to dominate sales as the market for microchip-making equipment expanded.

UPM product range

UPM's product range on the optical side included lenses for inspection systems that were used mainly in the manufacture of microchips. These lenses were sold both to the inspection system manufacturers and to the chip manufacturers themselves. They were very high-precision lenses; however, most of the company's optical products were specialist photographic and cinema lenses. In addition about 15 per cent of the company's optical work was concerned with the development and manufacture of 'one- or two-off' extremely high-precision lenses for defence contracts, specialist scientific instrumentation and other optical companies. The group's instrument product range consisted largely of electromechanical assemblies with an increasing emphasis on software-based recording, display and diagnostic abilities. This move towards

Source: Shutterstock.com: Aaron Amat

more software-based products had led the instrument side of the business towards accepting some customized orders. The growth of this part of the instrumentation had resulted in a special development unit being set up, namely the Customer Services Unit (CSU), which modified, customized or adapted products for those customers who required an unusual application. Often CSU's work involved incorporating the company's products into larger systems for a customer.

Some years earlier United Photonics Corporation had set up its first non-North-American facility just outside Kuala Lumpur in Malaysia. United Photonics Malaysia Sdn Bhd (UPM) had started by manufacturing sub-assemblies for photonics instrumentation products, but soon had developed into a laboratory for the modification of UPM products for customers throughout the Asian region. This part of the Malaysian business was headed by T.S. Lim, a Malaysian engineer who had taken his postgraduate qualifications at Stanford and three years ago moved back to his native Kuala Lumpur to head up the Malaysian outpost of the CSU, reporting directly to Bob Brierly, the Vice-President of Development, who ran the main CSU in Detroit. Over the last three years, T.S. Lim and his small team of engineers had gained quite a reputation for innovative development. Bob Brierly was delighted with their enthusiasm. *'Those guys really do know how to make things happen. They are giving us all a run for our money.'*

The Laz-skan project

The idea for Laz-skan had come out of a project which T.S. Lim's CSU had been involved with. The CSU had successfully installed a high-precision photonics lens into a character recognition system for a large clearing bank. The enhanced capability that the lens and software modifications had given had enabled the bank to scan documents even when they were not correctly aligned. This had led to the CSU proposing the development of a 'vision metrology' device that could optically scan a product at some point in the manufacturing process, and check the accuracy of up to 20 individual dimensions. The

geometry of the product to be scanned, the dimensions to be gauged, and the tolerances to be allowed, could all be programmed into the control logic of the device. The T.S. Lim team was convinced that the idea could have considerable potential. The proposal, which the CSU team had called the Laz-skan project, was put forward to Bob Brierly, who both saw the potential value of the idea and was again impressed by the CSU team's enthusiasm. *'To be frank, it was their evident enthusiasm that influenced me as much as anything. Remember that the Malaysian CSU had only been existence for two years at this time – they were a group of keen but relatively young engineers. Yet their proposal was well thought out and, on reflection, seemed to have considerable potential.'*

In the November following their proposal to Brierly, Lim and his team were allocated funds (outside the normal budget cycle) to investigate the feasibility of the Laz-skan idea. Lim was given one further engineer and a technician, and a three-month deadline to report to the board. In this time he was expected to overcome any fundamental technical problems, assess the feasibility of successfully developing the concept into a working prototype, and plan the development task that would lead to the prototype stage.

The Lim investigation

Lim, even at the start of his investigation, had some firm views as to the appropriate 'architecture' for the Laz-skan project. By 'architecture' he meant the major elements of the system, their functions and how they related to each other. The Laz-skan system architecture would consider five major subsystems: the lens and lens mounting, the vision support system, the display system, the control logic software and the documentation.

Lim's first task, once the system's overall architecture was set, was to decide whether the various components in the major subsystems would be developed in-house, developed by outside specialist companies from UPM's specifications, or bought in as standard units and if necessary modified in-house. Lim and his colleagues made these decisions themselves, while recognizing that a more consultative process might have been preferable. *'I am fully aware that ideally we should have made more use of the expertise within the company to decide how units were to be developed. But within the time available we just did not have the time to explain the product concept, explain the choices, and wait for already busy people to come up with a recommendation. Also there was the security aspect to think of. I'm sure our employees are to be trusted but the more people who know about the project, the more chance there is for leaks. Anyway, we did not see our decisions as final. For example, if we decided that a component was to be bought in and modified for the prototype building stage it does not mean that we can't change our minds and develop a better component in-house at a later stage.'* By February, Lim's small team had satisfied itself that the system could be built to achieve the original technical performance targets. The team's final task before reporting to Brierly would be to devise a feasible development plan.

Planning the Laz-skan development

As a planning aid the team drew up a network diagram for all the major activities within the project from its start through to completion, when the project would be handed over to Manufacturing Operations. A simplified activity on node (AoN) network is shown in Figure 19.22 and a complete list of all events in the diagram is given in Table 19.5. The duration of all the activities in the project were estimated either by Lim or (more often) by his consulting a more experienced engineer back in Detroit. While he was reasonably confident in the estimates, Lim was keen to stress that they were just that – estimates.

1 The lens

The lens was particularly critical since the shape was complex and precision was vital if the system was to perform up to its intended design specification. Lim was relying heavily upon the skill of the group's expert optics group in Pittsburgh to produce the lens to the required high tolerance. Since what in effect was a trial and error approach was involved in their manufacture, the exact time to manufacture would be uncertain. Lim realized this. 'The lens is going to be a real problem. We just don't know how easy

it will be to make the particular geometry and precision we need. The optics people won't commit themselves even though they are regarded as some of the best optics technicians in the World. If the development goes wrong it could overrun substantially. It is a relief that lens development is not amongst the "critical path" activities.'

2 Vision support system

The vision support system included many components that were commercially available, but considerable engineering effort would be required to modify them. Although the development design and resting of the vision support system was complicated, there was no great uncertainty in the individual activities, or therefore the schedule of completion. If more funds were allocated to their development, some tasks might even be completed ahead of time.

3 The control software

The control software represented the most complex task, and the most difficult to plan and estimate. In fact, the software development unit had little experience of this type of work but (partly in anticipation of this type of development) had recently recruited a young software engineer with some experience of the type of work that would be needed for Laz-skan. He was confident that any technical problems could be solved even though the system needs

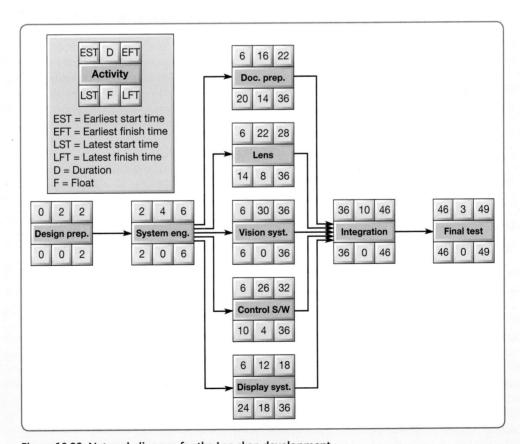

Figure 19.22 Network diagram for the Laz-skan development

Table 19.5 Event listing for the Laz-skan project

Event number	Event description
1	Start systems engineering
2	Complete interface transient tests
3	Complete compatibility testing
4	Complete overall architecture block and simulation
5	Complete costing and purchasing tender planning
6	End alignment system design
7	Receive S/T/G, start synch mods
8	Receive Triscan/G, start synch mods
9	Complete B/A mods
10	Complete S/T/G mods
11	Complete Triscan/G mods
12	Start laser subsystem compatibility tests
13	Complete optic design and specification, start lens manufacture
14	Complete lens manufacture, start lens housing S/A
15	Lens S/A complete, start tests
16	Start technical specifications
17	Start help routine design
18	Update engineering mods
19	Complete doc sequence
20	Start vision routines
21	Start interface (trinsic) tests
22	Start system integration compatibility routines
23	Co-ordinate trinsic tests
24	End interface development
25	Complete alignment integration routine
26	Final alignment integration data consolidation
27	Start interface (trinsic) programming
28	Complete alignment system routines
29	Start trinsic comparator routines
30	Complete (interface) trinsic coding
31	Begin all logic system tests
32	Start cycle tests
33	Lens S/A complete
34	Start assembly of total system
35	Complete total system assembly
36	Complete final tests and dispatch

were novel, but completion times would be difficult to predict with confidence.

4 Documentation

A relatively simple subsystem, 'documentation' included specifying and writing the technical manuals, maintenance routines, online diagnostics and 'help desk' information. It was a relatively predictable activity, part of which was subcontracted to technical writers and translation companies in Kuala Lumpur.

5 Display system

The simplest of the subsystems to plan, the display system would need to be manufactured entirely out of the company and tested and calibrated on receipt.

Market prospects

In parallel with Lim's technical investigation, Sales and Marketing had been asked to estimate the market potential of Laz-skan. In a very short time, the Laz-skan project had aroused considerable enthusiasm within the function, to the extent that Halim Ramli, the Asian Marketing Vice-President, had taken personal charge of the market study. The major conclusions from this investigation were:

(a) The global market for Laz-skan-type systems was unlikely to be less than 50 systems per year in two years' time, climbing to more than 200 per year after five years.

(b) The volume of the market in financial terms was more difficult to predict, but each system sold was likely to represent around US$300,000 of turnover.

(c) Some customization of the system would be needed for most customers. This would mean greater emphasis on commissioning and post-installation service than was necessary for UPM's existing products.

(d) Timing the launch of Laz-skan would be important. Two 'windows of opportunity' were critical. The first and most important was the major world trade show in Geneva in almost exactly a year's time (the following April). This show, held every two years, was the most prominent showcase for new products such as Laz-skan. The second related to the development cycles of the original equipment manufacturers that would be the major customers for Laz-skan. Critical decisions were generally taken in the fall. If Laz-skan was to be incorporated into these companies' products it would have to be available within 18 months (the September of the following year).

The Laz-skan go-ahead

At the end of February UPM considered both the Lim and the Ramli reports. In addition estimates of Laz-skan's manufacturing costs had been sought from George Hudson, the Head of Instrument Development. His estimates indicated that Laz-skan's operating contribution would be far higher than the company's existing products. The board approved the immediate commencement of the Laz-skan development through to prototype stage, with an initial development budget of US$4.5m. The objective of the project was to 'build three prototype Laz-skan systems to be "up and running" for April 2006'.

The decision to go ahead was unanimous. Exactly how the project was to be managed provoked far more discussion. The Laz-skan project posed several problems. First, engineers had little experience of working on such a major project. Second, the crucial deadline for the first batch of prototypes meant that some activities might have to be accelerated, an expensive process that would need careful judgement. A very brief investigation into which

Table 19.6 **Acceleration opportunities for Laz-skan**

Activity	Acceleration cost (US$/week)	Likely maximum activity time, with acceleration (weeks)	Normal most likely time (weeks)
5–6	23,400	3	6
5–9	10,500	2	5
5–13	25,000	8	10
20–24	5,000	2	3
24–28	11,700	3	5
33–34	19,500	1	2

activities could be accelerated had identified those where acceleration definitely would be possible and the likely cost of acceleration (Table 19.6). Finally, no one could agree whether there should be a single project leader, which function he or she should come from, or how senior the project leader should be. Anuar Kamaruddin knew that these decisions could affect the success of the project, and possible the company, for years to come.

QUESTIONS

1 **Who do you think should manage the Laz-skan development project?**

2 **What are the major dangers and difficulties that will be faced by the development team as it manages the projects towards its completion?**

3 **What can the team do about these dangers and difficulties?**

PROBLEMS AND APPLICATIONS

1 The activities, their durations and precedences for designing, writing and installing a bespoke computer database are shown in Table 19.7. Draw a Gantt chart and a network diagram for the project and calculate the fastest time in which the operation might be completed.

2 A business is launching a new product. The launch will require a number of related activities as follows – hire a sales manager (5 weeks), require the sales manager to recruit salespeople (4 weeks), train the salespeople (7 weeks), select an advertising agency (2 weeks), plan an advertising campaign with the agency (4 weeks), conduct the advertising campaign (10 weeks), design the packaging of the product (4 weeks), set up packing operation (12 weeks), pack enough products for the launch stock (8 weeks), order the launch quantity of products from the manufacturer (13 weeks), select distributors for the product (9 weeks), take initial orders from the distributors (3 weeks), despatch the initial orders to the distributors (2 weeks).

(a) What is the earliest time that the new product can be introduced to the market?

(b) If the company hire trained salespeople who do not need further training, could the product be introduced 7 weeks earlier?

(c) How long could one delay selecting the advertising agency?

3 In the problem above, if the sales manager cannot be hired for 3 weeks, how will that affect the total project?

4 In the previous problem, if the whole project launch operation is to be completed as rapidly as possible, what activities must be completed by the end of week 16?

5 Identify a project of which you have been part (for example, moving apartments, a holiday, dramatic production, revision for an examination, etc.).

(a) Who were the stakeholders in this project?

(b) What was the overall project objective (especially in terms of the relative importance of cost, quality and time)?

(c) Were there any resource constraints?

(d) Looking back, how could you have managed the project better?

Table 19.7 **Bespoke computer database activities**

Activity		Duration (weeks)	Activities that must be completed before it can start
1	Contract negotiation	1	–
2	Discussions with main users	2	1
3	Review of current documentation	5	1
4	Review of current systems	6	2
5	Systems analysis (a)	4	3, 4
6	Systems analysis (b)	7	5
7	Programming	12	5
8	Testing (prelim.)	2	7
9	Existing system review report	1	3, 4
10	System proposal report	2	5, 9
11	Documentation preparation	19	5, 8
12	Implementation	7	7, 11
13	System test	3	12
14	Debugging	4	12
15	Manual preparation	5	11

6   Identify your favourite sporting team (or if you are not a sporting person, choose any team you have heard of). What kind of projects do you think they need to manage? For example, merchandising, sponsorship, etc. What do you think are the key issues in making a success of managing each of these different types of project?

SELECTED FURTHER READING

There are hundreds of books on project management. They range from the introductory to the very detailed and from the managerial to the highly mathematical. Here are four general (as opposed to mathematical) books which are worth a look.

Maylor, H. (2010) *Project Management*, 4th edn, Financial Times Prentice Hall, Harlow.

Meredith, J.R. and Mantel, S. (2009) *Project Management: A Managerial Approach*, Wiley, Hoboken, NJ.

Pinto, J.K. (2015) *Project Management: Achieving Competitive Advantage*, 4th edn, Pearson, Harlow.

Long-running text with comprehensive coverage.

Shenhar, A.J. and Dvir, D. (2007) *Reinventing Project Management: The Diamond Approach to Successful Growth and Innovation*, Harvard Business School Press Boston, MA.

Notes on chapters

Chapter 1

1. Sources include: Trangbæk, R.R. (2015) Lego group among five most reputable companies in the world, LEGO Group Press Office, 21 April; Diaz, J. (2014) Exclusive look inside the Lego factory, Gizmodo.com, http://lego.gizmodo.com/exclusive-look-inside-the-lego-factory-5022769; Terdiman, D. (2011) Watching Lego make its world-famous bricks, CNET, http://www.cnet.com/uk/news/watching-lego-make-its-world-famous-bricks/, 15 June; The Economist (2014) Unpacking Lego – how the Danish firm became the world's hottest toy company, *The Economist*, 8 March.

2. Sources include discussions with Tom Dyson and Olly Willans of Torchbox, to whom we are grateful for their advice and assistance.

3. Sources include: MSF website (2015), http://www.msf.org.uk; Beaumont, P. (2011) Médecins sans Frontières book reveals aid agencies' ugly compromises, *Guardian*, 20 November.

4. Sources include: Goodman, M. (2011) Pret Smile, it will pay for everyone, *Sunday Times*, 6 March; Pret a manger website, http://www.pret.com/

5. Sources include: HP website (2015), http://www8.hp.com/us/en/hp-information/environment/product-recycling.html

6. Sources include: Johnston, R. and Staughton, R. (2009) Establishing and developing strategic relationships – the role of operations managers, *International Journal of Operations and Production Management*, vol. 29, no. 6, 564–590; Wyganowska, J. (2008) The top 10 skills of effective operations managers, Recreation Management, http://www.recmanagement.com/200802gc04.php; Operationsmanagers.com (2011) The 5 key personality traits of operations managers, http://careers-in-business.com/omskill.htm

Chapter 2

1. Source: Novozymes annual report, 2014.

2. The phrase 'the triple bottom line' was first used in 1994 by John Elkington, the founder of a British consultancy called SustainAbility. Read Elkington, J. (1997) *Cannibals with Forks: The Triple Bottom Line of 21st Century Business*, Capstone, Oxford. Also good is: Savitz, A.W. and Weber, K. (2006) *The Triple Bottom Line: How Today's Best-Run Companies Are Achieving Economic, Social and Environmental Success – and How You Can Too*, Jossey-Bass, San Francisco.

3. Sources include: The Economist (2012) Firms with benefits: a new sort of caring, sharing company gathers momentum, *The Economist*, 7 January; Patagonia website, http://www.patagonia.com/

4. Sources: Holcim press releases. (Note that, since this was written, Holcim has merged with another similar company, Lafarge.)

5. Jensen, M.C. (2001) Value maximization, stakeholder theory, and the corporate objective function, *Journal of Applied Corporate Finance*, vol. 14, no. 3, 7–21.

6. Sources include: Nestlé press release (2015) Expect the unexpected: why food safety depends on staying one step ahead, 30 March, http://www.nestle.com/media/newsandfeatures/; Stewart, E. (2014) Quality Street chocolates ranked from worst to best, Metro.co.uk, 24 December; Nestlé Corporate website (2014), Nestlé quality policy, March.

7. Sources include: Kelly, S. (2015) Technology speeds up the air ambulance, BBC News, 28 April, http://www.bbc.co.uk/news/technology-32484151; London's Air Ambulance Service (2015) Our services, https://londonsairambulance.co.uk; Marlinson, C. (2006) The golden hour, *Sunday Times*, 21 September.

8. Sources include: Levitz, J. (2011) Inside UPS's weather machine, *Wall Street Journal*, 23 December.

9. Sources include: mymuesli website, http://uk.mymuesli.com/muesli/

10. Source: John Hendry-Pickup of Aldi.

11. Sources include: Moore, M. (2012) 'Mass suicide' protest at Apple manufacturer Foxconn factory, *Daily Telegraph*, 12 January; The Economist (2010) Suicides at Foxconn, *The Economist*, 27 May.

12. Source: Miles, A. and Baldwin, T. (2002) Spidergram to check on police forces, *The Times*, 10 July.

13. Kaplan, R.S. and Norton, D.P. (1993) *The Balanced Scorecard*, Harvard Business School Press, Boston, MA.

14. Skinner, W. (1985) *Manufacturing: The Formidable Competitive Weapon*, Wiley, Chichester.

15. We are grateful to the management of the Penang Mutiara for permission to use this example.

Chapter 3

1. Sources include: Cookson, C. (2015) Guildford's SSTL leads world in small satellite supply, *Financial Times*, 12 June; The Economist (2015) The pioneer of small satellites is laying plans for the infrastructure and services needed for travel to other planets, *The Economist*, 30 May; SSTL (2015) Corporate brochure: changing the economics of space – SSTL is the world's premier provider of small satellite missions and services.

2. Hayes, R.H. and Wheelwright, S.C. (1984) *Restoring our Competitive Edge*, Wiley, Chichester.

3. For a more thorough explanation, *see* Slack, N. and Lewis, M. (2015) *Operations Strategy*, 4th edn, Pearson, Harlow.

4. Mintzberg, H. and Waters, J.A. (1995) Of strategies: deliberate and emergent, *Strategic Management Journal*, July/September.

5. Sources include: Poeter, D. (2011) Apple Stores' secret sauce spilled, PC Mag.com, 15 June; Lipschutz, K. (2011) Apple's retail philosophy: employees reveal calculated culture, *Adweek*, 15 June; Johnson, R. (2011) What I learned building the Apple Store, HBR Blog network, 21 November.

6. Hill, A. and Hill, T. (2009) *Manufacturing Operations Strategy*, Palgrave Macmillan, Basingstoke.

7. There is a vast literature which describes the resource-based view of the firm. For example, *see* Barney, J. (1991) The resource-based model of the firm: origins, implications and prospect, *Journal of Management*, vol. 17, no. 1, 97–98; or Teece, D.J. and Pisano, G. (1994) The dynamic capabilities of firms: an introduction, *Industrial and Corporate Change*, vol. 3, no. 3, 537–556.

8. Barney, J. (1991) 'The resource-based model of the firm: origins, implications and prospect', *Journal of Management*, vol. 17, no. 1, 97–98.

9. Sources include: Satariano, A. and Burrows, P. (2011) Apple's supply-chain secret? Hoard lasers, *Bloomberg Business week*, 3 November; Elmer-DeWitt, P. (2011) How Apple became a monopsonist, CNN News, 5 July; Lariviere, M. (2011) Operations: Apple's secret sauce?, *The Operations Room*, 4 November.

10. Adapted from Slack, N. and Lewis, M.A. (2015) *Operations Strategy*, 4th edn, Pearson, Harlow.

11. Sources include: Birkinshaw, J. (2013) Why corporate giants fail to change, CNN Money, 8 May; Magazine, A. (2013) Two lessons learned from Nokia's downfall, Techwell.com, 24 October; Hessman, T. (2013) The road to failure: Nokia, Blackberry and…Apple, *Industry Week*, 6 September.

12. Weick, K.E. (1990) Cartographic myths in organizations, in A. Huff (ed.) *Managing Strategic Thought*, Wiley, Chichester.

13. Sources include: Whipp, L. (2015) McDonald's to slim down in home market, *Financial Times*, 18 June: Smith, T. (2015) Where's the beef?, *Financial Times*, 22 May; Whipp, L. (2015) McDonald's may struggle to replicate British success, *Financial Times*, 5 May; Kroc, R.A. (1977) *Grinding it Out: The Making of McDonald's*, St Martin's Press, London; Love, J. (1995) McDonald's Annual Report, 2014; Upton, D. (1992) McDonald's Corporation – case study, Harvard Business School; Cooper, L. (2015) At McDonald's the burgers have been left on the griddle far too long, *The Times*, 24 August.

Chapter 4

1. Trott, P. (2011) *Innovation Management and New Product Development*, Pearson, Harlow.

2. Sources include: Heisler, Y. (2013) Apple's iPhone: the untold story, *Network World*, 1 September; Vogelstein, F. (2013) And then Steve said, 'Let There Be an iPhone', *New York Times Magazine*, 4 October; Ahmed, M. (2012) Apple nearly ditched the iPhone, designer admits, *The Times*, 31 July; Breillatt, A. (2012) You can't innovate like Apple, http://www.pragmaticmarketing.com

3. Henderson, R.M. and Clark, K.B. (1990). Architectural innovation: the reconfiguration of existing product technologies and the failure of established firms, *Administrative Science Quarterly*, vol. 35, no. 1, 9–22.

4. These benefits of design are based on: The Design Council (2015) *Leading Business by Design – Why and how business leaders invest in design*, A report by Pietro Micheli of Warwick Business School and The Design Council, UK.

5. The Design Council (2012) *Report on the benefits of good design*, The Design Council, UK.

6. Sources include: The Economist (2012) The last Kodak moment? *The Economist*, 14 Janusary; Wright, M. (2010) Kodak develops: a film giant's self-reinvention, *Wired Magazine*, 15 February.

7. Sources: Many thanks to Mark Taber for his advice; The Economist (2006) Open, but not as usual, *The Economist*, 16 March; Kisiel, R. (2008) BMW wants joint effort to develop open-source in-vehicle platform, *Automotive News Europe*, 23 October.

8. Sources include: The Economist (2008) A people business print edition, *The Economist*, 25 September; de Castella, T. (2010) Should we trust the wisdom of crowds?, *BBC News Magazine*, 5 July.

9. For example, see Leiponen, A. and Hefalt, C.E. (2006) Innovation objectives, knowledge sources, and the benefits of breadth, *Strategic Management Journal*, vol. 31, no. 22, 224–236.

10. Sources include: BBC (2001) Square fruit stuns Japanese shoppers, BBC website, Friday, 15 June; Poulter, S. (2006) Square melons on the way, *Daily Mail*, 3 August.

11. Sources include: Marsh, P. (2011) Dyson heater seen as the key to tech refocus, *Financial Times*, 15 September; Dyson website, www.dyson.co.uk

12. Goodwin, L. (2015) How to bust the biggest myths about the circular economy, *Guardian*, 12 March; Clegg, A. (2015) Sustainable innovation: shaped for the circular economy, *Financial Times*, 26 August; Company website, Newlife Paints, http://www.newlifepaints.com/

13. Sources include: Jervell, E. (2013) The long, slow process of IKEA design, *Wall Street Journal*, 14 October.

14. Bennis, W. and Biederman, P.W. (1997) *Organizing Genius: The Secrets of Creative Collaboration*, Basic Books, New York; new edn, Nicholas Brealey, London, 1998.

Chapter 5

1. Christopher, M. (2011) *Logistics and supply chain management*, Financial Times, London.

2. Sources include: Burton, G. (2013) ARM vs Intel: a battle of business models, *Computing*, 29 May; Turley, J. (2014) Intel vs. ARM: two titans' tangled fate, InfoWorld.com, 27 February.

3. For further details of the origin of this concept *see* Moore, J.F. (1993) Predators and prey: a new ecology of competition, *Harvard Business Review*, May–June.

4. Ibid.

5. Sources include: Blakely, R. (2010) Britain can learn from India's assembly-line heart operations, says doctor, *The Times*, 14 May; The Economist (2011) Economies of scale

made steel – the economics of very big ships, *The Economist*, 12 November.

6. Sources include: The Economist (2011) Clusters flustered – global competition seems to be weakening the benefits of being in a cluster, *The Economist*, 14 April; Deutsche Bank Research (2010) Global financial centres after the crisis, 2 August; The Economist (2009) Britain and Formula 1 – cluster champs, *The Economist*, 22 October; Wendling, M. (2011) Can 'Silicon Roundabout' challenge Silicon Valley? BBC News website, 8 September.

7. Sources include: Clover, C. (2015) HTC shares tumble after slashed sales forecast, *Financial Times*, June 9; The Economist (2009) HTC, upwardly mobile, *The Economist*, 9 July.

8. Definition from: http://searchcio.techtarget.com/definition/outsourcing

Supplement to Chapter 5

1. Linstone, H.A. and Turoof, M. (1975) *The Delphi Method: Techniques and Applications*, Addison-Wesley, Reading, MA.

2. Hogarth, R.M. and Makridakis, S. (1981) Forecasting and planning: an evaluation, *Management Science*, vol. 27, 115–138.

3. Ibid.

4. Armstrong, J.S. and Grohman, M.C. (1972) A comparative study of methods for long-range market forecasting, *Management Science*, vol. 19, no. 2, 211–221.

Chapter 6

1. Sources include: Board, J. and Loke Kok Fai (2015) More airlines, facial recognition technology planned for Changi's Terminal 4, channelnewsasia.com, 9 July; Airport Technology (2014) Terminal 4, Changi International Airport, Singapore, airporttechnology.com; SAA Architects (2013) South East Asia aviation hub development – design led Changi Airport Terminal 4, Singapore, http://www.saaarchitects.com.sg, 6 November; Driver, C. (2014) And the winners are…Singapore crowned the best airport in the world (and Heathrow scoops top terminal), Mail online, 28 March; Talwar, R. (2012) Airport 2025 – rethinking the customer experience, futuretravelexperience.com, 24 November.

2. Takt time was originated by Toyota, the automobile company. It is an adaptation of the German word *taktzeit*, originally meaning 'clock cycle'.

3. Sources include: Oches, S. (2015) The drive-thru performance study, *QSR magazine*, October; Horovitz, A. (2002) Fast food world says drive-through is the way to go, *USA Today*, 3 April.

4. Associated Press (2012) Standardised bed chart 'could prevent hundreds of hospital deaths', *Guardian*, 27 July.

5. Sources include: Ecover website, http://www.the-splash.co.uk/; Osborne, H. (2006) Spick'n'span ethics, *Guardian*, 17 November.

6. Source: Hirschkorn, J. (2014) At the coalface: behind the scenes at a real costume drama, *The Times*, 18 December.

7. The product–process matrix was an idea originally presented in a form similar to this in Hayes, R.H. and Wheelwright, S.C. (1984) *Restoring our Competitive Edge*, Wiley, Chichester.

8. One note of caution regarding this idea: although logically coherent, it is a conceptual model rather than something that can be 'scaled'. Although it is intuitively obvious that deviating from the diagonal increases costs, the precise amount by which costs will increase is very difficult to determine.

9. Sources include: The Economist (2015) Capitalism begins at home – providing better and more affordable housing could be the next 'capitalist achievement', Schumpeter column, *The Economist*, 10 January; Davey, J. (2010) Today we built a house every hour, *The Sunday Times*, 31 January; Persimmon company website; Brown, G. (2010) Space4 growth gives boost to former car sector workers, *Birmingham Post*, 27 August.

10. Source: BBC News site (2014) Sainsbury's store in 'spend more' poster gaffe, 30 September

11. The Workflow Management Coalition (2009), www.wfmc.org

12. Sources include: Schmidt, G. (2005) Applicability of the OM triangle to health care, Paper from the David Eccles School of Business, University of Utah; Heskett, J.L. (2003) Shouldice Hospital Limited, Harvard Business Publishing Case 9-683-068.

Chapter 7

1. Sources include: Hirasuna, D. (2012) VW's transparent factory, *@issue Journal of Business and Design*, 19 March; Markus, F. (2003) VW's transparent factory, *Car and Driver*, September 2003; Segran, E. (2015) Designing a happier office on the super cheap, *Fast Company*, 30 March; Hickey, S. (2014) Death of the desk: the architects shaping offices of the future, *Guardian*, 14 September.

2. Carr-Brown, J. (2005) French factory surgeon cuts NHS queues, *Sunday Times*, 23 October.

3. Koontz, C. (2012) Retail interior layout for libraries, Info Today, 27 January, http://www.infotoday.com/mls/jan05/koontz.shtml

4. Gurman, M. (2012) Apple Store coming to London's world-famous Harrods department store, *inShare.32*, 19 January.

5. Dawson, C. (2011) For Toyota, patriotism and profits may not mix, *Wall Street Journal*, 29 November.

6. Sources: Interviews with company staff and Johnston, R., Chambers, S., Harland, C., Harrison, A. and Slack, N. (2003) *Cases in Operations Management*, 3rd edn, Financial Times Prentice Hall, Harlow.

7. Sources include: Nestlé's Media Room (2014), Flexible, fast and functional: Nestlé to adopt modular factories, http://www.nestle.com/media/, 4 July.

8. Schein, E.M. (1999). The *Corporate Culture Survival Guide – Sense and nonsense about culture change*, Jossey-Bass, San Francisco.

9. Savage, M. (2014) Workplace aesthetics – not just perks & paint, *J Walter Thompson Inside*, July 28.

10. Quoted in: AGSM (2010) Workspace design: will aesthetics give your business the edge?, University of New South Wales, 5 October.

11. Miller, H. (2008) Home sweet office comfort in the workplace, www.hermanmiller.com

12. Reported in: Waber, B., Magnolfi, J. and Lindsay, G. (2014) Workspaces that move people, *Harvard Business Review*, October.

13. Sources include: Saval, N. (2014) A brief history of the dreaded office cubicle, *Wall Street Journal*, 9 May; The Economist (2015) Inside the box: how workers ended up in cubes – and how they could break free, *The Economist*, 3 January.

14. Bitner, M.J. (1992) Servicescapes: the impact of physical surroundings on customers and employees, *Journal of Marketing*, vol. 56, 57–71.

15. Source: Bremmer, C. (2015) Passengers face each other as airlines pack more into economy, *The Times*, July 14.

Chapter 8

1. Sources include: The Economist (2011) I, robot-manager, Schumpeter column, *The Economist*, 31 March; The Economist (2011) Marathon machine – unskilled workers are struggling to keep up with technological change, *The Economist*, 19 November; Brynjolfsson, E. and McAfee, A. (2011) *Race Against The Machine: How the Digital Revolution is Accelerating Innovation, Driving Productivity, and Irreversibly Transforming Employment and the Economy*, Digital Frontier Press; Kageyama, Y. (2012) Canon moves toward robots-only production for digital cameras, *Toronto Star*, 14 May.

2. Sources include: The Economist (2014) The future of jobs: previous technological innovation has always delivered more long-run employment, not less. But things can change, *The Economist*, 18 January; The Economist (2013) Schumpeter – the age of smart machines, *The Economist*, 25 May; Finkelstein, D. (2013) Machines are becoming cheaper than labour, *The Times*, 6 November; Groom, B. (2014) Automation and the threat to jobs, *Financial Times*, 26 January; Frey, C.B. and Osborne, M.A. (2013) The future of employment: how susceptible are jobs to computerisation?, Oxford Martin School Working Paper, 17 September; Brynjolfsson, E. and McAfee, A. (2014) *The Second Machine Age: Work, Progress, and Prosperity in a Time of Brilliant Technologies*, W. W. Norton, New York.

3. Loh Den (2008) My new favorite barber: QB House, denniland.com, June 25th.

4. Sources include: Moskvitch, K. (2011) Internet of things blurs the line between bits and atoms, BBC news website, 3 June; Chui, M., Löffler, M. and Roberts, R. (2010) The Internet of Things, *McKinsey Quarterly*, March; Evans-Pughe, C. (2011) M2M and the Internet of Things, *Engineering and Technology*, vol. 6, issue 9, 12 September.

5. SAP IOT definition, SAP Research, internet.eu/images/1/16/A4_Things_Haller.pdf.

6. Sources include: http://www.news-medical.net/; http://www.telemedicine.com; Studstill, K. (2010) Future of health: remote diagnostics, PSFK Consulting, 2 August.

7. Staff Columnist (2012) Barriers to telemedicine limit patient access to quality care, *Patient Safety and Quality Healthcare*

(PSQH), 22 January, http://www.psqh.com/barriers-to-telemedicine-limit-patient-access-to-quality-care.html

8. Sources include: West, K. (2011) Turn up the heat with Marmite, *Sunday Times*, 2 October; Unilever's sustainable living report (2012), http://www.unilever.co.uk/sustainable-living/

9. Dosi, G., Teece, D. and Winter, S.G. (1992) Towards a theory of corporate coherence, in Dosi, G., Giametti, R. and Toninelli, P.A. (eds) *Technology and Enterprise in a Historical Perspective*, Oxford University Press, Oxford.

10. Sources include: Helm, T. and Campbell, D. (2014) NHS hit by new tech failure as it scraps patient booking system, *Observer,* 10 May; Ashford, W. (2014) NHS to scrap £356m outpatient booking system, *Computer Weekly*, 12 May; Conlan, T. (2014) BBC considering keeping 40-year-old system after £100m DMI failure, *Guardian*, 5 February; Daniel, E. and Ward, J. (2014) BBC's DMI project failure is a warning to all organisations, www.computerweekly.com/; Conlan, T. and Arthur, C. (2013) BBC suspends technology officer after Digital Media Initiative failure, *Guardian*, 24 May.

11. Walley, P. and Amin, V. (1994) Automation in a customer contact environment, *International Journal of Operations and Production Management*, vol. 14, no. 5, 86–100.

12. The Economist (2002) Help! There's nobody in the cockpit, *The Economist*, 21 December.

13. Chew, W.B., Leonard-Barton, D. and Bohn, R.E. (1991) Beating Murphy's Law, *Sloan Management Review*, vol. 5, Spring.

Chapter 9

1. Schein, E.M. (1999) *The Corporate Culture Survival Guide – Sense and nonsense about culture change*, Jossey-Bass, San Francisco.

2. Sources include: Company website; The Sunday Times Best Companies to work for (2009) W.L. Gore & Associates (UK), *The Sunday Times*, 8 March; Caulkin, S. (2008) Gore-Tex gets made without managers, *Observer*, Sunday 2 November; Smith, N. (2008) Profile: WL Gore, *The Institution of Engineering and Technology Knowledge network*, 21 October.

3. Slack, N. (2016) *The Operations Advantage*, Kogan Page, London.

4. Source: Accenture website, www.accenture.com

5. Ulrich, D. (1997) *Human Resource Champions: The next agenda for adding value and delivering results*, Boston, MA: Harvard Business School Press.

6. The Health and Safety Executive (HSE) of the UK government, www.hse.gov.uk/stress

7. Morgan describes these and other metaphors in Morgan, G. (1986) *Images of Organization*, Sage, London.

8. Source: Bone, J., Robertson, D. and Pavia, W. (2010) Plane rumpus puts focus on crews' growing revolution in the air, *The Times*, 12 August.

9. Hoxie, R.F. (1915) *Scientific Management and Labour*, D. Appleton, Washington, DC.

10. Hackman, J.R. and Oldham, G. (1980) *Work Redesign*, Addison-Wesley, Reading, MA.

11. Bowen, D.E. and Lawler, E.E. (1992) The empowerment of service workers: what, why, how and when, *Sloan Management Review*, vol. 33, no. 3, 31–39.

12. Sources include: Lavey-Heaton, M. (2014) Working from home: how Yahoo, Best Buy and HP are making moves, *Guardian*, 10 March; Surowiecki, J. (2013) Face time, *The New Yorker*, 18 March; The Economist (2013) Mayer culpa, *The Economist*, 2 March.

13. Kobrick, J.L. and Fine, B.J. (1983) Climate and human performance, in Osborne, D.J. and Gruneberg, M.M. (eds) *The Physical Environment and Work*, Wiley, New York.

14. Ibid.

15. Sources include: Jones, A. (2015) The riff: dangers of music at work, *Financial Times*, 5 August; Ciotti, G. (2014) How music affects your productivity, *Fast Company*, 11 July; BBC (2013) Does music in the workplace help or hinder? *Magazine Monitor*, 9 September.

Chapter 10

1. Source: Interview with Joanne Cheung, Steve Deeley and other staff at Godfrey Hall, BMW Dealership, Coventry.

2. Sources: Farman, J. (1999) Les coulisses du vol, Air France. Talk presented by Richard E. Stone, NorthWest Airlines, at the IMA Industrial Problems Seminar, 1998.

3. Sources include: Swisher, K. (2014) Man and Uber Man, *Vanity Fair*, December; The Economist (2012) Taxis and technology – dispatching the middleman, The Economist Babbage Science Blog; The Economist (2015) Taxis v Uber – substitutes or complements? *The Economist*, 10 August.

4. The concept of *P:D* ratios comes originally from Shingo, S. (1981) *Study of Toyota Production Systems*, Japan Management Association, Tokyo, and was extended by Mather, K. (1988) *Competitive Manufacturing*, Prentice Hall, Upper Saddle River, NJ.

5. Sources include: The Economist (2011) Please be seated: a faster way of boarding planes could save time and money, *The Economist*, 3 September; Palmer, J. (2011) Tests show fastest way to board passenger planes, BBC News website, 31 August.

6. Source: Thanks to Lawrence Wilkins for this example.

7. Goldratt, E.Y. and Cox, J. (1984) *The Goal*, North River Press, Great Barrington, MA.

8. Based on an original model described in Hofstede, G. (1981) Management control of public and not-for-profit activities, *Accounting, Organizations and Society*, vol. 6, no. 3, 193–211.

9. The original version of this case appears in Slack, N., Brandon-Jones, A., Johnston, R. and Betts, A. (2012) *Operations and Process Management*, 3rd edn, Pearson, Harlow.

Chapter 11

1. Sources include: Equants (2012) London Heathrow airport – economic and social impact, Equants.com/2012_LHR.aspx; Heathrow Airport Holdings Company (2014) Heathrow Airport Holdings Company Information, 12 October.

2. Sources include: The Economist (2009) A piece of cake: panettone season arrives, *The Economist*, 10 December; Bauli website, September 2015, http://www.bauligroup.it/en/

3. Sources include: The Economist (2011) Amazon: the Wal-Mart of the web, *The Economist*, 1 October; Amazon website (2011); Ralph, A. (2011) Too many unhappy returns, *The Times*, 26 November.

4. Sources include: Horticulture Week (2010) Grower guide tackles problem of building sustainable workforces, *Horticulture Week*, 14 May; Growing jobs website, September 2015, http://growingjobs.org/

5. Sources include: Wessel, D. (2013) Gaming the system to beat rush-hour traffic, *Wall Street Journal*, 31 August.

6. Kimes, S. (1989) Yield management: a tool for capacity-constrained service firms, *Journal of Operations Management*, vol. 8, no. 4, 348–363.

7. Sources include: Levenson, E. (2012) SeatGeek 'Bleacher Bum Economics': a fan guide to dynamic pricing at Wrigley Field, operationsroom.files.wordpress.com

8. Flyn, C. (2011) Queuing pinpointing our happiest moments, *The Sunday Times*, 6 November.

Chapter 12

1. Sources include: Farrell, S. (2014) Ocado dismisses fears over Waitrose supply deal, *Guardian*, 11 September: Pratley, N. (2012) Ocado: buy two problems get one free, *Guardian*, 23 January.

2. Sources include: The North Face website; http://uk.thenorthface.com/blog/uk/en/sustainability

3. Sources include: Smithers R (2015) Bangladesh Rana Plaza fund finally meets target, Guardian, 8th june; Butler S (2014) Rana Plaza disaster marked by Oxford Street demonstration, The Guardian, Thursday 24 April; Economist (2013) Disaster at Rana Plaza - A gruesome accident should make all bosses think harder about what behaving responsibly means, May 4th; Economist (2013) Bangladesh's clothing industry- Bursting at the seams, Oct 26th

4. Fisher, M.L. (1997) What is the right supply chain for your product?, *Harvard Business Review*, March–April.

5. Adapted from Kraljic, P. (1983) 'Purchasing must become supply management', *Harvard Business Review*, September.

6. Sources include: The Economist (2011) Broken links – the disruption to manufacturers worldwide from Japan's disasters will force a rethink of how they manage production, *The Economist*, 31 March; BBC (2011) Sony considers two-week shutdown due to power shortages: production at some of Japan's biggest companies has been affected by power shortages, BBC News website, 11 April; BBC (2011) Toyota motors has suspended production at most of its plants in Japan and also reduced output at its North American and European factories, BBC News website, 11 April.

7. Harland, C.M. (1996) Supply chain management relationships, chains and networks, *British Journal of Management*, vol. 1, no, 7, S63–S80.

8. Minahan, T. (2003) Global sourcing: what you need to know to make it work. CIO.com, 11 August.

9. Source: http://www.levistrauss.com/sustainability/

10. Lee, H.L., Padmanabhan, V. and Whang, S. (1997) The bullwhip effect in supply chains, *Sloan Management Review*, Spring.

11. Thanks to Stephen Disney at Cardiff Business School, UK, for help with this section.

12. Source: Lee, H.L. and Whang, S. (2001) Demand chain excellent: a tale of two retailers, *Supply Chain Management Review*, 3 January.

Chapter 13

1. Sources include: BBC News Website (2011) Blood bank 'perfect storm' threat for 2012, 28 December; Stanger, S.H.W, Wilding, R., Yates, N. and Cotton, S. (2012) What drives perishable inventory management performance? Lessons learnt from the UK blood supply chain, *Supply Chain Management: An International Journal*, vol. 17, issue 2, 107–123.

2. Source: The Economist (2012) Energy storage, *The Economist Technology Quarterly*, 3 March.

3. Sources include: Hipwell, D. (2013) Age is no virtue for Treasury Wine Estates, which has a massive American hangover, *The Times*, 17 July; Baab-Muguira, C. (2013) Treasury Wine down over 10% on writedown news, *Motley Fool*, 15 July.

4. Sources include: BBC Magazine website (2012) How do they know when to grit roads? 18 December; Grimm, E. (2009) Prepare for winter, *Daily Chronicle*, 30 November.

5. Sources include: Duke, S. (2014) He knows what you want – before you even want it, *The Sunday Times*, 2 February; Murad Ahmed (2014) Amazon will know what you want before you do, *The Times*, 27 January.

Chapter 14

1. Sources include: Allan, K. (2009) Butcher's Pet Care relies on IT that can co-ordinate its ERP, *Engineering & Technology Magazine*, 21 July; Company website.

2. For a good explanation of this and similar issues, see MacCarthy, B.L. (2006) Organizational, systems and human issues in production planning, scheduling and control, in Hermann, J. (ed.) *Handbook of Production Scheduling*, International Series in Operations Research and Management Science, Springer, New York.

3. Based on MacCarthy, ibid.

4. Wight, O. (1984) *Manufacturing Resource Planning: MRP II*, Oliver Wight Ltd.

5. Koch, C. and Wailgum, T. (2007) ERP definition and solutions, www.cio.com

6. Source: Company website, www.sap.com

7. Source: Thanks to Lawrence Wilkins for this example.

8. Brynjolfsson, E. (1994) Technology's true payoff, *Information Week*, October.

9. This categorization is described in McAffee, A. (2007) *Managing in the Information Age*, Harvard Business School, Teaching note 5-608-011.

10. Based on a review of the research in this area by Finney, S. and Corbett, M. (2007) ERP implementation: a compilation and analysis of critical success factors, *Business Process Management Journal*, vol. 13, no. 3, 329–347.

11. Kanaracus, C. (2008) Waste Management sues SAP over ERP implementation, *InfoWorld*, 27 March.

12. Turbit, N. (2005) ERP implementation – the traps, The Project Perfect White Paper Collection, www.projectperfect.com.au

Chapter 15

1. Example written and supplied by Janina Aarts and Mattia Bianchi, Department of Management and Organization, Stockholm School of Economics.

2. Corbett, S. (2004) Applying lean in offices, hospitals, planes, and trains, Presentation at the Lean Service Summit, Amsterdam, 24 June.

3. Sources include: McKinsey (2014) When Toyota met e-commerce: lean at Amazon, *McKinsey Quarterly*, no. 2; Liker, J. (2004) *The Toyota Way*, McGraw-Hill Professional, New York.

4. Sources include: Interview with Edward Kay, Tom Dyson and Olly Willans of Torchbox, January 2012; Torchbox website, http://www.torchbox.com/blog/kanban-project-management; we are grateful to everyone at Torchbox for their help and allowing us access to their operation.

5. Set-up time reduction is also called single-minute exchange of dies (SMED), because this was the objective in some manufacturing operations.

6. The 5Ss.

7. Goldratt, E.M. and Cox, J. (1986) *The Goal*, North River Press, Great Barrington, MA.

8. Goldratt, E.M. (1990) *What Is This Thing Called Theory of Constraints and How Should it Be Implemented?* North River Press, Great Barrington, MA.

9. Based on: Rattner, S. (2009) What is the theory of constraints, and how does it compare to lean thinking?, The Lean Enterprise Institute, at http://www.leanvs.com/tocvsleanthinking.pdf

10. Voss, C.A. and Harrison, A. (1987) Strategies for implementing JIT, in Voss, C.A. (ed.) *Just-in-Time Manufacture*, IFS/Springer, Berlin.

11. This case is based on the work of several real hospitals, in Scandinavia and the rest of the world, that have used the concepts of lean operations to improve their performance. However, all names and places are fictional and no connection is intended to any specific hospital.

Chapter 16

1. Carroll, L. (1871) *Through the Looking Glass*, Macmillan, London.

2. Imai, M. (1986) *Kaizen – The Key to Japan's Competitive Success*, McGraw-Hill, New York.

3. Sources: Gawande, A. (2010) *The Checklist Manifesto: how to get things right*, Profile Books, London; Aaronovitch, D. (2010) The Checklist Manifesto: review, *The Times*, 23 January.

4. Vasagar, J. (2014) Experiment with a bit of anarchy, *Financial Times*, 28 January.

5. International Organization for Standardization (1986) ISO 8402.

6. Dale, B.G. (1994) Quality management systems, in Dale, B.G. (ed.) *Managing Quality*, Prentice Hall, Upper Saddle River, NJ.

7. Sources include: Company website, http://www.heinekeninternational.com

8. Davenport, T. (1995) 'Reengineering – the fad that forgot people', *Fast Company*, November.

9. Based on an example in Kruse, G. (1995) Fundamental innovation, *Manufacturing Engineer*, February.

10. Note: These defects per million (DPM) figures assume that the mean and/or standard deviation (SD) may vary over the long term, so the 3 sigma DPM is actually based on 1.5 sigma

and 6 sigma on 4.5 sigma. These distributions are assumed to be 'one-tailed' as the shift is usually in one direction.

11. Ibid.

12. Sources include: Sharma, M., Pandla, K. and Gupta, P. (2014) A case study on Six Sigma at Wipro Technologies: thrust on quality, Working Paper, The Jaipuria Institute of Management; Wipro website, www.wipro.com

13. There are many books and publications that explain the benefits of combining lean and Six Sigma. For example, see Byrne, G., Lubowe, D. and Blitz, A. (2007) *Driving operational innovation using Lean Six Sigma*, IBM Institute for Business Value; Brue, G. (2005) *Six Sigma for Managers: 24 Lessons to Understand and Apply Six Sigma Principles in Any Organization*, McGraw-Hill Professional, New York.

14. Deming, W.E. (1982) *Quality, Productivity and Competitive Position*, MIT Center for Advanced Engineering Study, Cambridge, MA.

15. Deming, W.E. (1986) *Out of Crisis*, MIT Center for Advanced Engineering Study, Cambridge, MA.

16. Schein, E.M. (1999). *The Corporate Culture Survival Guide – Sense and nonsense about culture change*, Jossey-Bass, San Francisco.

17. Bessant, J. and Caffyn, S. (1997) High involvement innovation, *International Journal of Technology Management*, vol. 14, no. 1, 7–28. The authors write specifically about continuous improvement, but their points apply more generally.

18. Shenkar, O. (2010) *Copycats: How Smart Companies Use Imitation to Gain a Strategic Edge*, Harvard Business Review Press, Boston, MA.

19. Argyris, C. and Schon, D. (1978) *Organizational Learning*, Addison-Wesley, Reading, MA.

20. Sources include: West, K. (2011) Formula One trains van drivers, *The Times*, 1 May; f1network.net, http://www.f1network.net/main/s107/st164086.htm

21. The authors gratefully acknowledge the valuable assistance of Teo Yi Wen, Department of Industrial and Systems Engineering, NUS. The authors would like to thank the interviewees for their participation in this project and Johnson Paul and Sharon Foo for facilitating the research. All Rights Reserved, National Library Board Singapore and the Authors, 2009.

Chapter 17

1. Parasuraman, A., Zeithaml, V.A. and Berry, L.L. (1985) A conceptual model of service quality and implications for future research, *Journal of Marketing*, vol. 49, Fall, 41–50; and Gummesson, E. (1987) Lip service: a neglected area in services marketing, *Journal of Services Marketing*, vol. 1, no. 1, 19–23.

2. Sources include: Boyd, E.A. (2012) Award-winning analytics, *Analytics Magazine*, May/June; Poppelaars, J. (2012) Supply chain wide optimization at TNT Express, Proceedings of the Euroma Conference, Amsterdam, 2–4 July 2012; TNT Corporate website (2015) TNT Express win the 2012 Edelman Award.

3. Sources include: Vitaliev, V. (2009) The much-loved knife, *Engineering and Technology Magazine*, 21 July; Zuber, F. (2015) The Victorinox quality system, Victorinox website.

4. Source: Interview with Michael Purtill, the General Manager of the Four Seasons Hotel Canary Wharf in London. We are grateful for Michael's co-operation (and for the great quality of service at his hotel!).

5. Berry, L.L. and Parasuraman, A. (1991) *Marketing Services: Competing Through Quality*, Free Press, New York.

6. Based on Parasuraman, A., ibid.

7. Ferdows, K. and de Meyer, A. (1990) Lasting improvement in manufacturing performance, *Journal of Operations Management*, vol. 9, no. 2, 168–184.

8. Sources include: The Economist (2013) Ryanair's future – oh really, O'Leary?, *The Economist Print Edition*, 19 October; BBC News site (2010) OFT watchdog says Ryanair payment policy is 'puerile", Sunday, 3 January.

9. Sources include: Markillie, P. (2011) They trash cars, don't they? *Intelligent life magazine*, Summer.

10. Sources include: Wheatley, M. (2010) Filling time on the production line, *Engineering and Technology magazine*, 8 November.

11. Feigenbaum, A.V. (1986) *Total Quality Control*, McGraw-Hill, New York.

12. Kaynak, H. (2003) The relationship between total quality management practices and their effects on firm performance, *Journal of Operations Management*, vol. 21, 405–435.

13. Sources include: The Economist (2013) Overtired, and overdrawn, *The Economist Print Edition*, 15 June; Wilson, H. (2014) Fat-fingered trader sets Tokyo alarms ringing, *The Times*, 2 October.

14. ISO website, http://www.iso.org/iso/iso_9000_essentials

15. Based on Kolk, A. (2000) *The Economics of Environmental Management*, Financial Times Prentice Hall, Harlow. Also see www.globalreporting.org

16. This case is based on a real situation, but data has been changed for reasons of commercial confidentiality.

Chapter 18

1. Sources include: Raconteur (2013) Business Risk Strategies, 7 May; BBC News (2013) Findus beef lasagne contained up to 100% horsemeat, FSA says, 7 February.

2. Christopher, M. (2002) Business is failing to manage supply chain vulnerability, *Odyssey*, issue 16, June.

3. Szu Ping Chan, and agencies (2013) Timeline: how G4S's bungled Olympics security contract unfolded, *Telegraph*, 21 May; Neate, R. (2013) G4S profits tumble on Olympic failings, *Guardian*, 13 March.

4. Information for this section is based partly on a private communication from Ben Betts of ht2.com

5. Sources include: Blastland, M. and Spiegelhalter, D. (2013) *The Norm Chronicles: Stories and Numbers About Danger*, Profile Books, London; Spiegelhalter, D. (2014) The power of the MicroMort, *British Journal of Obstetrics and Gynaecology*, vol. 121, 662–663; The Economist (2013) Making sense of the statistics that riddle our days, *The Economist*, 22 June.

6. Sources include: Interview with Dr Emma Brandon-Jones, University of Bath; Piersen, K. and Sterman, J. (2013) Cyclical dynamics of airline industry earning, *System Dynamics Review*, vol. 29, no. 3, 129–156.

7. Nahajima, S. (1988) *Total Productive Maintenance*, Productivity Press, New York.

8. Sources include: Nelson, G. (2013) How data mining helped GM limit a recall to four cars, *Automotive News*, 28 October; Valdes-Dapena, P. (2014) GM: steps to a recall nightmare, CNN News, 20 October; Pollock, L. (2014) What you need to know about the GM recalls, *Wall Street Journal*, 2 April; Bennett, J. (2014) GM to recall 8.45 million more vehicles in North America, *Wall Street Journal*, 30 June.

Chapter 19

1. Sources include: Boyes, W. (2011) David Van Wyk shares the Disney Imagineering project management process, controlglobal.com, 29 June; Hoske, M.T. (2011) What do Walt Disney Imagineering and NASA space travel have in common? Engineering inspiration. *Control Engineering*, 22 September, http://www.controleng.com/

2. This example was written and kindly supplied by Mattia Bianchi, Department of Management and Organization, Stockholm School of Economics.

3. Sources include: raconteur.net (2015) Project management, 2 August; World Health Organization malaria programme, http://www.who.int/topics/malaria/en/

4. Shenhar, A.J. and Dvir, D. (2007) *Reinventing Project Management: The Diamond Approach to Successful Growth and Innovation*, Harvard Business School Press, Boston, MA.

5. D'Herbemont, O. and César, B. (1998) *Managing sensitive projects: A lateral approach*, English version adapted by Cutrin, T. and Etcheber, P., Routledge, New York.

6. Sources include: The Scottish Parliament website, www.scottish.parliament.uk; BBC News (2004) Holyrood price tag rises to £430 million, 24 February, retrieved 29 October 2014, http://news.bbc.co.uk/1/hi/scotland/3517225.stm; http://www.playthegame.org/news/news-articles/2014/the-lost-legacy-of-brazil%E2%80%99s-world-cup/; http://engineeringsport.co.uk/2010/04/30/whats-wrong-at-wembley/

7. Sources include: Davis, D. (2011) The MacLeamy curve, Digital Morphogenesis, Evolving architecture through computation, The blog of NZ Architecture, posted 15 October.

Useful websites

There are obviously many websites that will help you to investigate topics in *Operations Management* further. Not all of them give totally trustworthy information. However, the following sites (organised by the four parts of this text) provide a good (but not comprehensive) starting point for exploring the subject.

Part 1 - Direct

www.myomlab Virtual learning lab to be used in conjunction with this book – crammed full of quizzes, movie clips, revision tips, animated diagrams, cases to help your learning.

http://operationsroom.wordpress.com/ Stanford University's take on topical operations stories.

www.iomnet.org The Institute of Operations Management site. One of the main professional bodies for the subject.

www.poms.org A US academic society for production and operations management. Academic, but some useful material, including a link to an encyclopedia of operations management terms.

www.sussex.ac.uk/users/dt31/TOMI/ One of the longest established portals for the subject. Useful for academics and students alike.

www.ft.com Good for researching topics and companies.

http://www.economist.com/ The Economist's site, well written and interesting stuff of business generally

www.worldbank.org Global issues. Useful for international operations strategy research.

www.weforum.org Global issues, including some operations strategy ones.

www.cfsd.org.uk The centre for sustainable design's site. Some useful resources, but obviously largely confined to sustainability issues.

www.conceptcar.co.uk A site devoted to automotive design. Fun if you like new car designs!

www.betterproductdesign.net A site that acts as a resource for good design practice. Set up by Cambridge University and the Royal College of Art. Some good material that supports all aspects of design innovation.

www.ocw.mit.edu/OcwWeb/Sloan-School-of-Management Good source of open courseware from MIT.

www.design-council.org.uk Site of the UK's Design Council. One of the best sites in the world for design related issues.

www.locationstrategies.com Exactly what the title implies. Good industry discussion.

www.cpmway.com American location selection site. You can get a flavour of how location decisions are made.

www.transparency.org A leading site for international business (including location) that fights corruption.

www.outsourcing.com Site of the Institute of Outsourcing. Some good case studies and some interesting reports, news item, etc.

http://www.balancedscorecard.org/ Site of an American organisation with plenty of useful links.

Part 2 - Design

www.bpmi.org Site of the Business Process Management Initiative. Some good resources including papers and articles.

www.bptrends.com News site for trends in business process management generally. Some interesting articles.

www.iienet.org The American Institute of Industrial Engineers site. They are an important professional body for process design and related topics.

www.waria.com A Workflow and Reengineering association website. Some useful topics.

www.strategosinc.com/plant_layout_elements Some useful briefings, mainly in a manufacturing context.

www.bls.gov/oes/ US Department of Labour employment statistics.

www.fedee.com/hrtrends Federation of European Employers guide to employment and job trends in Europe.

Part 3 - Deliver

http://www.bpic.co.uk/ Some useful information on general planning and control topics.

http://www.apics.org The American professional and education body that has its roots in planning and control activities.

http://www.inventoryops.com/dictionary.htm A great source for information on Inventory Management and Warehouse Operations.

http://www.mapnp.org/libary/opsmgnt/opsmgnt.htm General 'private' site on operations management, but with some good content.

http://www.cio.com/research/erp/edit/erpbasics.html Several descriptions and useful information on ERP related topics.

http://www.erpfans.com/ Yes, even ERP has its own fan club! Debates and links for the enthusiast.

http://www.sap.com/index.epx *'Helping to build better businesses for more than three decades',* SAP has been the leading worldwide supplier of ERP systems for ages. They should know how to do it by now!

http://www.sapfans.com/ Another fan club, this one is for SAP enthusiasts.

http://www.lean.org/ Site of the lean enterprise institute, set up by one of the founders of the Lean thinking movement, James Womack.

http://www.dti.gov.uk/er/index Website of the Employment Relations Directorate who have developed a framework for employers and employees which promotes a skilled and flexible labour market founded on principles of partnership.

http://www.worksmart.org.uk/index.php This site is from the Trades Union Congress. Its aim is 'to help today's working people get the best out of the world of work'.

Part 4 – Develop

https://www.instituteofcustomerservice.com The Institute of Customer Service is an independent, professional body for customer service.

http://www.quality-foundation.co.uk/ The British Quality Foundation is a not-for-profit organisation promoting business excellence.

http://www.juran.com The Juran Institute's mission statement is to provide clients with the concepts, methods and guidance for attaining leadership in quality.

http://www.asq.org/ The American Society for Quality site. Good professional insights.

http://www.quality.nist.gov/ American Quality assurance Institute. Well-established institution for all types of business quality assurance.

http://www.gslis.utexas.edu/~rpollock/tqm.html Non-commercial site on Total Quality Management with some good links.

http://www.iso.org/iso/en/ISOOnline.frontpage Site of the International Standards Organisation that runs the ISO 9000 and ISO 14000 families of standards. ISO 9000 has become an international reference for quality management requirements.

http://www.processimprovement.com/ Commercial site but some content that could be useful.

http://www.kaizen-institute.com/ Professional institute for kaizen. Gives some insight into practitioner views.

http://www.imeche.org.uk/mx/index.asp The Manufacturing Excellence Awards site. Dedicated to rewarding excellence and best practice in UK manufacturing. Obviously manufacturing biased, but some good examples.

http://www.ebenchmarking.com Benchmarking information.

http://www.quality.nist.gov/ American Quality assurance Institute. Well-established institution for all types of business quality assurance.

https://www.apm.org.uk/ The Association for Project Management's site, that is 'committed to developing and promoting project and programme management'.

http://www.pmi.org/ The American equivalent of the above.

https://www.controlrisks.com Control Risks is an independent, global risk consultancy. It specialises in managing political, integrity and security risks in 'complex and hostile environments'. Gives a good idea of what is involved in doing business in risky parts of the World.

https://www.theirm.org Site of the Institute of Risk Management. An independent, not-for-profit professional body for risk management.

http://www.sra.org Site of the Society for Risk Analysis (SRA). It 'provides an open forum for anyone interested in risk analysis'.

http://www.industryweek.com/operations/lean-six-sigma A sub-section of the Industry Week website that has a number of interesting articles on lean and six sigma implementation.

http://www.processexcellencenetwork.com/ Lots of articles and comment pieces on approach to improvement here. Use the search tool to find articles on lean.

Glossary

5 S's: a simple housekeeping methodology to organize work areas. Originally translated from the Japanese, they are generally taken to mean sort, strengthen, shine, standardized, and sustain. The aim is to reduce clutter in the workplace.

ABC inventory control: an approach to inventory control that classes inventory by its usage value and varies the approach to managing it accordingly.

Acceptance sampling: a technique of quality sampling that is used to decide whether to accept a whole batch of products (and occasionally services) on the basis of a sample; it is based on the operation's willingness to risk rejecting a 'good' batch and accepting a 'bad' batch.

Activity: as used in project management, it is an identifiable and defined task, used together with event activities to form network planning diagrams.

Aggregated planning and control: a term used to indicate medium-term capacity planning that aggregates different products and services together in order to get a broad view of demand and capacity.

Agility: the ability of an operation to respond quickly and at low cost as market requirements change.

Allowances: term used in work study to indicate the extra time allowed for rest, relaxation and personal needs.

Andon: a light above a workstation that indicates its state, whether working, waiting for work, broken down, etc.; andon lights may be used to stop the whole line when one station stops.

Annual hours: a type of flexitime working that controls the amount of time worked by individuals on an annual rather than a shorter basis.

Anthropometric data: data that relate to people's size, shape and other physical abilities, used in the design of jobs and physical facilities.

Anticipation inventory: inventory that is accumulated to cope with expected future demand or interruptions in supply.

Appraisal costs: those costs associated with checking, monitoring and controlling quality to see if problems or errors have occurred, an element within quality-related costs.

Attributes of quality: measures of quality that can take one of two states, for example, right or wrong, works or does not work, etc.

B Corps: an abbreviation for Benefit Corporations; those that have a clear and unequivocal social benefit.

Back-office: the low-visibility part of an operation.

Backward scheduling: starting jobs at a time when they should be finished exactly when they are due, as opposed to forward scheduling.

Balanced scorecard (BSC): in addition to financial performance, the balanced scorecard also includes assessment of customer satisfaction, internal processes and innovation and learning.

Balancing loss: the quantification of the lack of balance in a production line, defined as the percentage of time not used for productive purposes with the total time invested in making a product.

Bar code: a unique product code that enables a part or product type to be identified when read by a bar-code scanner.

Basic time: the time taken to do a job without any extra allowances for recovery.

Batch processes: processes that treat batches of products together, and where each batch has its own process route.

Bath-tub curve: a curve that describes the failure probability of a product, service or process and indicates relatively high probabilities of failure at the beginning and at the end of the life cycle.

Behavioural job design: an approach to job design that takes into account individuals' desire to fulfil their needs for self-esteem and personal development.

Benchmarking: the activity of comparing methods and/or performance with other processes in order to learn from them and/or assess performance.

Bill of materials (BOM): a list of the component parts required to make up the total package for a product or service together with information regarding their level in the product or component structure and the quantities of each component required.

Blueprinting: a term often used in service design to mean process mapping.

Bottleneck: the capacity-constraining stage in a process; it governs the output of the whole process.

Bottom-up: the influence of operational experience on operations decisions.

Brainstorming: an improvement technique where small groups of people put forward ideas in a creative free-form manner.

Break-even analysis: the technique of comparing revenues and costs at increasing levels of output in order to establish the point at which revenue exceeds cost, that is, the point at which it 'breaks even'.

Breakthrough improvement: an approach to improving operations performance that implies major and dramatic change in the way an operation works; for example, business process re-engineering (BPR) is often associated with this type of improvement, also known as innovation-based improvement, contrasted with continuous improvement.

Broad definition of operations: all the activities necessary for the fulfilment of customer requests.

Buffer inventory: an inventory that compensates for unexpected fluctuations in supply and demand; can also be called safety inventory.

Bullwhip effect: the tendency of supply chains to amplify relatively small changes at the demand side of a supply chain such that the disruption at the supply end of the chain is much greater.

Business continuity: the procedures adopted by businesses to mitigate and recover from the effects of major failures.

Business process outsourcing (BPO): the term that is applied to the outsourcing of whole business processes; this need not mean a change in location of the process, sometimes it involves an outside company taking over the management of processes that remain in the same location.

Business process re-engineering (BPR): the philosophy that recommends the redesign of processes to fulfil defined external customer needs.

Business processes: processes, often that cut across functional boundaries, which contribute some part to fulfilling customer needs.

Business strategy: the strategic positioning of a business in relation to its customers, markets and competitors, a subset of corporate strategy.

Capacity: the maximum level of value-added activity that an operation, or process, or facility is capable of over a period of time.

Capacity lagging: the strategy of planning capacity levels such that they are always less than or equal to forecast demand.

Capacity leading: the strategy of planning capacity levels such that they are always greater than or equal to forecast demand.

Cause–effect diagrams: a technique for searching out the root cause of problems, it is a systematic questioning technique, also known as Ishikawa diagrams.

Cell layout: locating transforming resources with a common purpose such as processing the same types of product, serving similar types of customer, etc., together in close proximity (a cell).

Centre-of-gravity method of location: a technique that uses the physical analogy of balance to determine the geographical location that balances the weighted importance of the other operations with which the one being located has a direct relationship.

Chase demand: an approach to medium-term capacity management that attempts to adjust output and/or capacity to reflect fluctuations in demand.

Cluster analysis: a technique used in the design of cell layouts to find which process groups fit naturally together.

Clusters: where similar companies with similar needs locate relatively close to each other in the same geographical area.

Co-creation: where the customer or customers play an important part in the character of the product or service offering.

Combinatorial complexity: the idea that many different ways of processing products and services at many different locations or points in time combine to result in an exceptionally large number of feasible options; the term is often used in facilities layout and scheduling to justify non-optimal solutions (because there are too many options to explore).

Commonality: the degree to which a range of products or services incorporate identical components (also called 'parts commonality').

Community factors: those factors that are influential in the location decision that relate to the social, political and economic environment of the geographical position.

Competitive factors: the factors such as delivery time, product or service specification, price, etc. that define customers' requirements.

Component structure: *see* 'Product structure'.

Computer-aided design (CAD): a system that provides the computer ability to create and modify product, service or process drawings.

Computer-integrated manufacturing (CIM): a term used to describe the integration of computer-based monitoring and control of all aspects of a manufacturing process, often using a common database and communicating via some form of computer network.

Concept generation: a stage in the product and service design process that formalizes the underlying idea behind a product or service.

Contracting relationships: relationship between operations in a supply network that rely on formal and/or legal contracts that specify obligations and roles.

Concurrent engineering: *see* 'Simultaneous development'.

Condition-based maintenance: an approach to maintenance management that monitors the condition of process equipment and performs work on equipment only when it is required.

Content of strategy: the set of specific decisions and actions that shape the strategy.

Continuous improvement: an approach to operations improvement that assumes many, relatively small, incremental improvements in performance, stressing the momentum of improvement rather than the rate of improvement; also known as 'kaizen', often contrasted with breakthrough improvement.

Continuous processes: processes that are high-volume and low-variety; usually products made on a continuous process are produced in an endless flow, such as petrochemicals or electricity.

Continuous review: an approach to managing inventory that makes inventory-related decisions when inventory reaches a particular level, as opposed to period review.

Control: the process of monitoring operations activity and coping with any deviations from the plan; usually involves elements of replanning.

Control charts: the charts used within statistical process control to record process performance.

Control limits: the lines on a control chart used in statistical process control that indicate the extent of natural or common-cause variations; any points lying outside these control limits are deemed to indicate that the process is likely to be out of control.

Co-opetition: an approach to supply networks that defines businesses as being surrounded by suppliers, customers, competitors, and complementors.

Core functions: the functions that manage the three core processes of any business: marketing, product/service development and operations.

Corporate social responsibility: how business takes account of its economic, social and environmental impacts.

Corporate strategy: the strategic positioning of a corporation and the businesses within it.

CRAFT: Computerized Relative Allocation of Facilities Technique, a heuristic technique for developing good, but non-optimal, solutions.

Crashing: a term used in project management to mean reducing the time spent on critical path activities so as to shorten the whole project.

Create-to-order: *see* 'Make-to-order'.

Critical path: the longest sequence of activities through a project network, it is called the critical path because any delay in any of its activities will delay the whole project.

Critical path method (CPM): a technique of network analysis.

Crowdsourcing: the act of taking an activity traditionally performed by a designated agent and outsourcing it to a large group of people in the form of an open call.

Customer contact skills: the skills and knowledge that operations staff need to meet customer expectations.

Customer relationship management (CRM): a method of learning more about customers' needs and behaviours by analysing sales information.

Customization: the variation in product or service design to suit the specific need of individual customers or customer groups.

Cycle inventory: inventory that occurs when one stage in a process cannot supply all the items it produces simultaneously and so has to build up inventory of one item while it processes the others.

Cycle time: the average time between units of output emerging from a process.

Decision support system (DSS): a management information system that aids or supports managerial decision-making; it may include both databases and sophisticated analytical models.

De-coupling inventory: the inventory that is used to allow work centres or processes to operate relatively independently.

Delivery: the ativities that plan and control the transfer of products and services to customers.

Delivery flexibility: the operation's ability to change the timing of the delivery of its services or products.

Demand management: an approach to medium-term capacity management that attempts to change or influence demand to fit available capacity.

Demand side: the chains of customers, customers' customers, etc. that receive the products and services produced by an operation.

Dependability: delivering, or making available, products or services when they were promised to the customer.

Dependent demand: demand that is relatively predictable because it is derived from some other known factor.

Design acceptability: the attractiveness to the operation of a process, product or service.

Design capacity: the capacity of a process or facility as it is designed to be, often greater than effective capacity.

Design concept: the set of expected benefits to the customer encapsulated in a product or service design.

Design feasibility: the ability of an operation to produce a process, product or service.

Design funnel: a model that depicts the design process as the progressive reduction of design options from many alternatives down to the final design.

Design package: the component products, services and parts within a product or service design that provide the benefits to the customer.

Design screening: the evaluation of alternative designs with the purpose of reducing the number of design options being considered.

Development: a collection of operations activities that improve products, services and processes.

Directing: operations activities that create a general understanding of an operation's strategic purpose and performance.

Disaster recovery: term is used in a similar way to business continuity, but is concerned largely with action plans and procedures for the recovery of critical information technology and systems after a natural or human-induced disaster.

Diseconomies of scale: a term used to describe the extra costs that are incurred in running an operation as it gets larger.

Disintermediation: the emergence of an operation in a supply network that separates two operations that were previously in direct contact.

Disruptive technologies: technologies which in the short term cannot match the performance required by customers but may improve faster than existing technology to make that existing technology redundant.

Distributed processing: a term used in information technology to indicate the use of smaller computers distributed around an operation and linked together so that they can communicate with each other, the opposite of centralized information processing.

Division of labour: an approach to job design that involves dividing a task down into relatively small parts, each of which is accomplished by a single person.

DMAIC cycle: increasingly used improvement cycle model, popularized by the Six Sigma approach to operations improvement.

Do or buy: the term applied to the decision on whether to own a process that contributes to a product or service, or, alternatively, outsource the activity performed by the process to another operation.

Downstream: the other operations in a supply chain between the operation being considered and the end customer.

Drum, buffer, rope: an approach to operations control that comes from the theory of constraints (TOC) and uses the bottleneck stage in a process to control materials movement.

Earned-value control: a method of assessing performance in project management by combining the costs and times achieved in the project with the original plan.

E-business: the use of internet-based technologies either to support existing business processes or to create entirely new business opportunities.

E-commerce: the use of the internet to facilitate buying and selling activities.

Economic batch quantity (EBQ): the amount of items to be produced by a machine or process that supposedly minimizes the costs associated with production and inventory holding.

Economic bottom line: the part of the triple bottom line that assesses an organization's economic performance, usually in financial terms.

Economic order quantity (EOQ): the quantity of items to order that supposedly minimizes the total cost of inventory management, derived from various EOQ formulae.

Economy of scale: the manner in which the costs of running an operation decrease as it gets larger.

Effective capacity: the useful capacity of a process or operation after maintenance, changeover and other stoppages and loading have been accounted for.

Efficient frontier: the convex line which describes current performance trade-offs between (usually two) measures of operations performance.

EFQM excellence model: a model that identifies the categories of activity that supposedly ensure high levels of quality; now used by many companies to examine their own quality-related procedures.

Electronic marketplaces: also sometimes called infomediaries or cybermediaries, websites that offer services to both buyers and sellers, usually in B2B markets.

Emergent strategy: a strategy that is gradually shaped over time and based on experience rather than theoretical positioning.

Empowerment: a term used in job design to indicate increasing the authority given to people to make decisions within the job or changes to the job itself.

End-to-end business processes: processes that totally fulfil a defined external customer need.

Enterprise project management (EPM): software that integrates all the common activities in project management.

Enterprise resource planning (ERP): the integration of all significant resource planning systems in an organization that, in an operations context, integrates planning and control with the other functions of the business.

Environmental bottom line: the element of the triple bottom line that assesses an organization's performance in terms of how it affects the natural environment.

E-procurement: the use of the Internet to organize purchasing; this may include identifying potential suppliers and auctions as well as the administrative tasks of issuing orders etc.

Ergonomics: a branch of job design that is primarily concerned with the physiological aspects of job design, with how the human body fits with process facilities and the environment; can also be referred to as human factors, or human factors engineering.

Ethernet: a technology that facilitates local-area networks that allows any device attached to a single cable to communicate with any other devices attached to the same cable; also now used for wireless communication that allows mobile devices to connect to a local-area network.

European Quality Award (EQA): a quality award organized by the European Foundation for Quality Management (EFQM), it is based on the EFQM excellence model.

Events: points in time within a project plan; together with activities, they form network planning diagrams.

Evidence-based problem solving: using statistical methods and hard data as a basis for improvement.

Expert systems (ES): computer-based problem-solving systems that, to some degree, mimic human problem-solving logic.

External failure costs: those costs that are associated with an error or failure reaching a customer, an element within quality-related costs.

Extranets: computer networks that link organizations together and connect with each organization's internal network.

Facilitating products: products that are produced by an operation to support its services.

Facilitating services: services that are produced by an operation to support its products.

Fail-safeing: building in, often simple, devices that make it difficult to make the mistakes that could lead to failure; also known by the Japanese term 'poka-yoke'.

Failure analysis: the use of techniques to uncover the root cause of failures; techniques may include accident investigation, complaint analysis, etc.

Failure mode and effect analysis (FMEA): a technique used to identify the product, service or process features that are crucial in determining the effects of failure.

Failure rate: a measure of failure that is defined as the number of failures over a period of time.

Fault tree analysis: a logical procedure starts with a failure or potential failure and works backwards to identify its origins.

Finite loading: an approach to planning and control that only allocates work to a work centre up to a set limit (usually its useful capacity).

First-tier: the description applied to suppliers and customers that are in immediate relationships with an operation with no intermediary operations.

Fixed cost break: the volumes of output at which it is necessary to invest in operations facilities that bear a fixed cost.

Fixed-position layout: locating the position of a product or service such that it remains largely stationary, while transforming resources are moved to and from it.

Flexibility: the degree to which an operation's process can change what it does, how it is doing it, or when it is doing it.

Flexible manufacturing systems (FMS): manufacturing systems that bring together several technologies into a coherent system, such as metal cutting and material handling technologies; usually their activities are controlled by a single governing computer.

Flexi-time working: increasing the possibility of individuals varying the time during which they work.

Focus group: a group of potential product or service users, chosen to be typical of its target market who are formed to test their reaction to alternative designs.

Forward scheduling: loading work onto work centres as soon as it is practical to do so, as opposed to backward scheduling.

Four-stage model of operations contribution: model devised by Hayes and Wheelwright that categorizes the degree to which operations management has a positive influence on overall strategy.

Front-office: the high-visibility part of an operation.

Functional layout: layout where similar resources or processes are located together (sometimes called process layout).

Functional operations: the idea that every function in an organization uses resources to produce products and services for (internal) customers, therefore, all functions are, to some extent, operations.

Functional strategy: the overall direction and role of a function within the business; a subset of business strategy.

Gantt chart: a scheduling device that represents time as a bar or channel on which activities can be marked.

Gemba: also sometimes called Gamba, term used to convey the idea of going to where things actually take place as a basis for improvement.

Globalization: the extension of operations' supply chain to cover the whole world.

Heijunka: see 'Levelled scheduling'.

Henderson–Clark Model: innovation theory that distinguishes between knowledge of the components of an idea and knowledge of how the components fit together.

Heuristics: 'rules of thumb' or simple reasoning short cuts that are developed to provide good but non-optimal solutions, usually to operations decisions that involve combinatorial complexity.

Hierarchy of operations: the idea that all operations processes are made up of smaller operations processes.

High-level process mapping: an aggregated process map that shows broad activities rather than detailed activities (sometimes called an 'outline process map').

Hire and fire: a (usually pejorative) term used in medium-term capacity management to indicate varying the size of the workforce through employment policy.

House of quality: see 'Quality function deployment'.

Human factors engineering: an alternative term for ergonomics.

Human resource strategy: the overall long-term approach to ensuring that an organization's human resources provide a strategic advantage.

Immediate supply network: the suppliers and customers that have direct contact with an operation.

Importance–performance matrix: a technique that brings together scores that indicate the relative importance and relative performance of different competitive factors in order to prioritize them as candidates for improvement.

Improvement cycles: the practice of conceptualizing problem solving as used in performance improvement in terms of a never-ending cyclical model, for example the PDCA cycle or the DMAIC cycle.

Independent demand: demand that is not obviously or directly dependent on the demand for another product or service.

Indirect process technology: technology that assists in the management of processes rather than directly contributes to the creation of products and services, for example information technology that schedules activities.

Indirect responsibilities of operations management: the activities of collaborating with other functions of the organization.

Infinite loading: an approach to planning and control that allocates work to work centres irrespective of any capacity or other limits.

Information technology (IT): any device, or collection of devices, that collects, manipulates, stores or distributes information, nearly always used to mean computer-based devices.

Infrastructural decisions: the decisions that concern the operation's systems, methods and procedures and shape its overall culture.

Innovation: the act of introducing new ideas to products, services, or processes.

Innovation S-Curve: the curve that describes the impact of an innovation over time.

Input resources: the transforming and transformed resources that form the input to operations.

Intangible resources: the resources within an operation that are not immediately evident or tangible, such as relationships with suppliers and customers, process knowledge, new product and service development.

Interactive design: the idea that the design of products and services on one hand, and the processes that create them on the other, should be integrated.

Internal customers: processes or individuals within an operation that are the customers for other internal processes or individuals' outputs.

Internal failure costs: the costs associated with errors and failures that are dealt with inside an operation but yet cause disruption; an element within quality-related costs.

Internal suppliers: processes or individuals within an operation that supply products or services to other processes or individuals within the operation.

Internet of Things: the integration of physical objects into an information network where the physical objects become active participants in business processes.

Inventory: also known as stock, the stored accumulation of transformed resources in a process; usually applies to material resources but may also be used for inventories of information; inventories of customers or customers of customers are usually queues.

ISO 9000: a set of worldwide standards that established the requirements for companies' quality management systems; last revised in 2000, there are several sets of standards.

ISO 14000: an international standard that guides environmental management systems and covers initial planning, implementation and objective assessment.

Job design: the way in which we structure the content and environment of individual staff members' jobs within the workplace and the interface with the technology or facilities that they use.

Job enlargement: a term used in job design to indicate increasing the amount of work given to individuals in order to make the job less monotonous.

Job enrichment: a term used in job design to indicate increasing the variety and number of tasks within an individual's job; this may include increased decision-making and autonomy.

Job rotation: the practice of encouraging the movement of individuals between different aspects of a job in order to increase motivation.

Jobbing processes: processes that deal with high variety and low volumes, although there may be some repetition of flow and activities.

Just-in-time (JIT): a method of planning and control and an operations philosophy that aims to meet demand instantaneously with perfect quality and no waste.

Kaizen: Japanese term for continuous improvement.

Kanban: Japanese term for card or signal; it is a simple controlling device that is used to authorize the release of materials in pull control systems such as those used in JIT.

Keiretsu: a Japanese term used to describe a coalition of companies which form a supply network around a large manufacturer and can include service companies such as banks as well as conventional suppliers.

Lead-time usage: the amount of inventory that will be used between ordering replenishment and the inventory arriving, usually described by a probability distribution to account for uncertainty in demand and lead time.

Lean: (also known as Lean Synchronization) an approach to operations management that emphasizes the continual elimination of waste of all types, often used interchangeably with just-in-time (JIT); it is more an overall philosophy whereas JIT is usually used to indicate an approach to planning and control that adopts lean principles.

Lean Sigma: a blend of improvement elements from lean and Six Sigma.

Less important factors: competitive factors that are neither order-winning nor qualifying; performance in them does not significantly affect the competitive position of an operation.

Level capacity plan: an approach to medium-term capacity management that attempts to keep output from an operation or its capacity constant, irrespective of demand.

Levelled scheduling: the idea that the mix and volume of activity should even out over time so as to make output routine and regular, sometimes known by the Japanese term 'heijunka'.

Life-cycle analysis: a technique that analyses all the production inputs, life-cycle use of a product and its final disposal in terms of total energy used and wastes emitted.

Line balancing: the activity of attempting to equalize the load on each station or part of a line layout or mass process.

Line layout: a more descriptive term for what is technically a product layout.

Line of fit: an alternative name for the 'natural' diagonal of the product process matrix.

Little's law: the mathematical relationship between throughput time, work-in-process and cycle time (throughput time equals work-in-process × cycle time).

Loading: the amount of work that is allocated to a work centre.

Local-area network (LAN): a communications network that operates, usually over a limited distance, to connect devices such as PCs, servers, etc.

Location: the geographical position of an operation or process.

Logistics: a term in supply chain management broadly analogous to physical distribution management.

Long-term capacity management: the set of decisions that determine the level of physical capacity of an operation in whatever the operation considers to be long-term; this will vary between industries, but is usually in excess of one year.

Long thin process: a process designed to have many sequential stages, each performing a relatively small part of the total task; the opposite of short fat process.

MacLeamy curve: a model that conveys the idea that, as projects move forward, the cost of making changes to the original project plan increases but the ability of project managers to influence the project goes down.

Maintenance: the activity of caring for physical facilities so as to avoid or minimize the chance of those facilities failing.

Make-to-order: operations that produce products only when they are demanded by specific customers.

Make-to-stock: operations that produce products prior to their being demanded by specific customers.

Management information systems (MIS): information systems that manipulate information so that it can be used in managing an organization.

Manufacturing resource planning (MRP II): an expansion of materials requirement planning to include greater integration with information in other parts of the organization and often greater sophistication in scheduling calculations.

Market requirements: the performance objectives that reflect the market position of an operation's products or services, also a perspective on operations strategy.

Matrix organizational forms: hybrids of M form and U form organizations.

Mass customization: the ability to produce products or services in high volume, yet vary their specification to the needs of individual customers or types of customer.

Mass processes: processes that produce goods in high volume and relatively low variety.

Mass services: service processes that have a high number of transactions, often involving limited customization, for example mass transportation services, call centres, etc.

Master production schedule (MPS): the important schedule that forms the main input to material requirements planning, it contains a statement of the volume and timing of the end products to be made.

Materials requirement planning (MRP): a set of calculations embedded in a system that helps operations make volume and timing calculations for planning and control purposes.

Mean time between failures (MTBF): operating time divided by the number of failures; reciprocal of failure rate.

Method study: the analytical study of methods of doing jobs with the aim of finding the 'best' or an improved job method.

M-form organization: an organizational structure that groups together either its resources needed to produce a product or service group, or those needed to serve a particular geographical area in separate divisions.

Milestones: term used in project management to denote important events at which specific reviews of time, cost and quality can be made.

Mitigation: a term used in risk management to mean isolating a failure from its negative consequences.

Mix flexibility: the operation's ability to produce a wide range of products and services.

Modular design: the use of standardized sub-components of a product or service that can be put together in different ways to create a high degree of variety.

MRP netting process: the process of calculating net requirements using the master production schedule and the bills of materials.

Muda: all activities in a process that are wasteful because they do not add value to the operation or to the customer.

Mura: a term meaning lack of consistency or unevenness that results in periodic overloading of staff or equipment.

Muri: waste because of unreasonable requirements placed on a process that will result in poor outcomes.

Multi-skilling: increasing the range of skills of individuals in order to increase motivation and/or improve flexibility.

Multi-sourcing: the practice of obtaining the same type of product, component, or service from more than one supplier in order to maintain market bargaining power or continuity of supply.

Network analysis: overall term for the use of network-based techniques for the analysis and management of projects; for example, includes critical path method (CPM) and programme evaluation and review technique (PERT).

N-form organization: networked organizational structures where clusters of resources have delegated responsibility for the strategic management of those resources.

Off-shoring: sourcing products and services from operations that are based outside one's own country or region.

Open sourcing: products or services developed by an open community, including users.

Operations function: the arrangement of resources that are devoted to the production and delivery of products and services.

Operations management: the activities, decisions and responsibilities of managing the production and delivery of products and services.

Operations managers: the staff of the organization who have particular responsibility for managing some or all of the resources which compose the operation's function.

Operations resource capabilities: the inherent ability of operations processes and resources; also a perspective on operations strategy.

Operations strategy: the overall direction and contribution of the operation's function with the business; the way in which market requirements and operations resource capabilities are reconciled within the operation.

Optimized production technology (OPT): software and concept originated by Eliyahu Goldratt to exploit his theory of constraints (TOC).

Order fulfilment: all the activities involved in supplying a customer's order, often used in e-retailing but now also used in other types of operation.

Order-winners: the competitive factors that directly and significantly contribute to winning business.

Outline process map: *see* 'High-level process mapping'.

Outsourcing: the practice of contracting out to a supplier work previously done within the operation.

Overall equipment effectiveness (OEE): a method of judging the effectiveness of how operations equipment is used.

Pareto law: a general law found to operate in many situations that indicates that 20 per cent of something causes 80 per cent of something else, often used in inventory management (20 per cent of products produce 80 per cent of sales value) and improvement activities (20 per cent of types of problems produce 80 per cent of disruption).

Partnership: a type of relationship in supply chains that encourages relatively enduring co-operative agreements for the joint accomplishment of business goals.

Parts commonality: *see* 'Commonality'.

Parts family coding: the use of multi-digit codes to indicate the relative similarity between different parts, often used to determine the process route that a part takes through a manufacturing operation.

PDCA cycle: stands for Plan, Do, Check, Act cycle, perhaps the best known of all improvement cycle models.

P:D ratio: a ratio that contrasts the total length of time customers have to wait between asking for a product or service and receiving it (D) and the total throughput time to produce the product or service (P).

Performance management: similar but broader to performance measurement but also attempts to influence decisions behaviour and skills development so that individuals and processes are better equipped to meet objectives.

Performance measurement: the activity of measuring and assessing the various aspects of a process or whole operation's performance.

Performance objectives: the generic set of performance indicators that can be used to set the objectives or judge the performance of any type of operation; although there are alternative lists proposed by different authorities, the five performance objectives as used in this book are quality, speed, dependability, flexibility and cost.

Performance standards: a defined level of performance against which an operation's actual performance is compared; performance standards can be based on historical performance, some arbitrary target performance, the performance of competitors, etc.

Periodic review: an approach to making inventory decisions that defines points in time for examining inventory levels and then makes decisions accordingly, as opposed to continuous review.

Perpetual inventory principle: a principle used in inventory control that inventory records should be automatically updated every time items are received or taken out of stock.

Physical distribution management: organizing the integrated movement and storage of materials.

Pipeline inventory: the inventory that exists because material cannot be transported instantaneously.

Planning: the formalization of what is intended to happen at some time in the future.

Plant-within-a-plant: a similar term to a cell layout but sometimes used to indicate a larger clustering of resources, *see also* 'Shop-within-a-shop'.

Poka-yoke: Japanese term for fail-safeing.

Polar diagram: a diagram that uses axes, all of which originate from the same central point, to represent different aspects of operations performance.

Predetermined motion–time systems (PMTS): a work measurement technique where standard elemental times obtained from published tables are used to construct a time estimate for a whole job.

Preliminary design: the initial design of a product or service that sets out its main components and functions, but does not include many specific details.

Prevention costs: those costs that are incurred in trying to prevent quality problems and errors occurring, an element within quality-related costs.

Preventive maintenance: an approach to maintenance management that performs work on machines or facilities at regular intervals in an attempt to prevent them breaking down.

Principles of motion economy: a checklist used to develop new methods in work study that is intended to eliminate elements of the job, combine elements together, simplify the activity or change the sequence of events so as to improve efficiency.

Processes: an arrangement of resources that produces some mixture of products and services.

Process capability: an arithmetic measure of the acceptability of the variation of a process.

Process design: the overall configuration of a process that determines the sequence of activities and the flow of transformed resources between them.

Process distance: the degree of novelty required by a process in the implementation of a new technology.

Process hierarchy: the idea that a network of resources form processes, networks of processes form operations, and networks of operations form supply networks.

Process layout: alternative (misleading) name for functional layout.

Process mapping: describing processes in terms of how the activities within the process relate to each other (may also be called 'process blueprinting' or 'process analysis').

Process mapping symbols: the symbols that are used to classify different types of activity; they usually derive either from scientific management or from information-systems flow-charting.

Process of operations strategy: how operations strategies are put together, often divided into formulation, implementation, monitoring and control.

Process outputs: the mixture of goods and services produced by processes.

Process technology: the machines and devices that create and/or deliver goods and services.

Process types: terms that are used to describe a particular general approach to managing processes; in manufacturing these are generally held to be project, jobbing, batch, mass and continuous processes; in services they are held to be professional services, service shops and mass services.

Production flow analysis (PFA): a technique that examines product requirements and process grouping simultaneously to allocate tasks and machines to cells in cell layout.

Process variability: the degree to which activities vary in their time or nature in a process.

Productivity: the ratio of what is produced by an operation or process to what is required to produce it, that is, the output from the operation divided by the input to the operation.

Product layout: locating transforming resources in a sequence defined by the processing needs of a product or service.

Product–process matrix: a model derived by Hayes and Wheelwright that demonstrates the natural fit between volume and variety of products and services produced by an operation on one hand, and the process type used to produce products and services on the other.

Product/service flexibility: the operation's ability to introduce new or modified products and services.

Product/service life cycle: a generalized model of the behaviour of both customers and competitors during the life of a product or service; it is generally held to have four stages: introduction, growth, maturity and decline.

Product structure: diagram that shows the constituent component parts of a product or service package and the order in which the component parts are brought together (often called components structure).

Product technology: the embedded technology within a product or service, as distinct from process technology.

Professional services: service processes that are devoted to producing knowledge-based or advice-based services, usually involving high customer contact and high customization; examples include management consultants, lawyers, architects, etc.

Programme: as used in project management, it is generally taken to mean an ongoing process of change comprising individual projects.

Programme evaluation and review technique (PERT): a method of network planning that uses probabilistic time estimates.

Project: a set of activities with a defined start point and a defined end state which pursue a defined goal using a defined set of resources.

Project manager: competent project managers are vital for project success.

Project processes: processes that deal with discrete, usually highly customized, products.

Prototyping: an initial design of a product or service devised with the aim of further evaluating a design option.

Pull control: a term used in planning and control to indicate that a workstation requests work from the previous station only when it is required, one of the fundamental principles of just-in-time planning and control.

Purchasing: the organizational function, often part of the operations function, that forms contracts with suppliers to buy in materials and services.

Push control: a term used in planning and control to indicate that work is being sent forward to workstations as soon as it is finished on the previous workstation.

Qualified worker: term used in work study to denote a person who is accepted as having the necessary physical attributes, intelligence, skill, education and knowledge to perform the task.

Qualifiers: the competitive factors that have a minimum level of performance (the qualifying level) below which customers are unlikely to consider an operation's performance satisfactory.

Quality: there are many different approaches to defining this. We define it as consistent conformance to customers' expectations.

Quality characteristics: the various elements within the concept of quality, such as functionality, appearance, reliability, durability, recovery, etc.

Quality function deployment (QFD): a technique used to ensure that the eventual design of a product or service actually meets the needs of its customers (sometimes called 'house of quality').

Quality loss function (QLF): a mathematical function devised by Genichi Taguchi that includes all the costs of deviating from a target performance.

Quality-related costs: an attempt to capture the broad cost categories that are affected by, or affect, quality, usually categorized as prevention costs, appraisal costs, internal failure costs and external failure costs.

Quality sampling: the practice of inspecting only a sample of products or services produced rather than every single one.

Quality variables: measures of quality that can be measured on a continuously variable scale, for example length, weight, etc.

Queuing theory: a mathematical approach that models random arrival and processing activities in order to predict the behaviour of queuing systems (also called 'waiting line theory').

Rating: a work study technique that attempts to assess a worker's rate of working relative to the observer's concept of standard performance – controversial and now accepted as being an ambiguous process.

Received variety: the variety that occurs because the process is not designed to prevent it.

Recovery: the activity (usually a predetermined process) of minimizing the effects of an operation's failure.

Red Queen effect: the idea that improvement is relative; a certain level of improvement is necessary simply to maintain one's current position against competitors.

Redundancy: the extent to which a process, product or service has systems or components that are used only when other systems or components fail.

Relationship chart: a diagram used in layout to summarize the relative desirability of facilities to be close to each other.

Reliability: when applied to operations performance, it can be used interchangeably with 'dependability'; when used as a measure of failure it means the ability of a system, product or service to perform as expected over time; this is usually measured in terms of the probability of it performing as expected over time.

Reliability-centred maintenance: an approach to maintenance management that uses different types of maintenance for different parts of a process depending on their pattern of failure.

Remainder cell: the cell that has to cope with all the products that do not conveniently fit into other cells.

Re-order level: the level of inventory at which more items are ordered, usually calculated to ensure that inventory does not run out before the next batch of inventory arrives.

Re-order point: the point in time at which more items are ordered, usually calculated to ensure that inventory does not run out before the next batch of inventory arrives.

Repeatability: the extent to which an activity does not vary.

Repetitive strain injury (RSI): damage to the body because of repetition of activities.

Research and development (R&D): the function in the organization that develops new knowledge and ideas and operationalizes the ideas to form the underlying knowledge on which product, service and process designs are based.

Resource distance: the degree of novelty required of an operation's resources during the implementation of a new technology or process.

Resource-based view (RBV): the perspective on strategy that stresses the importance of capabilities (sometimes known as core competences) in determining sustainable competitive advantage.

Resource-to-order: operations that buy-in resources and produce only when they are demanded by specific customers.

Reverse engineering: the taking apart or deconstruction of a product or service in order to understand how it has been produced (often by a competing organization).

Robots: automatic manipulators of transformed resources whose movement can be programmed and reprogrammed.

Rostering: a term used in planning and control, usually to indicate staff scheduling, the allocation of working times to individuals so as to adjust the capacity of an operation.

Run-to-breakdown maintenance: an approach to maintenance management that only repairs a machine or facility when it breaks down.

SAP: a German company which is the market leader in supplying ERP software, systems and training.

Scheduling: a term used in planning and control to indicate the detailed timetable of what work should be done, when it should be done and where it should be done.

Scientific management: a school of management theory dating from the early twentieth century; more analytical and systematic than 'scientific' as such, sometimes referred to (pejoratively) as Taylorism, after Frederick Taylor who was influential in founding its principles.

SCOR model: a broad but highly structured and systematic framework of supply chain improvement developed by the Supply Chain Council.

Second-tier: the description applied to suppliers and customers who are separated from the operation only by first-tier suppliers and customers.

Sequencing: the activity within planning and control that decides on the order in which work is to be performed.

Service level agreements (SLAs): formal definitions of the dimensions and levels of service that should be provided by one process or operation to another.

Servicescape: a term used to describe the look and feel of the environment within an operation.

Service shops: service processes that are positioned between professional services and mass services, usually with medium levels of volume and customization.

Set-up reduction: the process of reducing the time taken to change over a process from one activity to the next; also called 'single-minute exchange of dies' (SMED) after its origins in the metal pressing industry.

Seven types of waste: types of waste identified by Toyota, they are overproduction, waiting time, transport, process waste, inventory, motion and defectives.

Shop-within-a-shop: an operations layout that groups facilities that have a common purpose together; the term was originally used in retail operations but is now some-times used in other industries, very similar to the idea of a cell layout.

Short fat processes: processes designed with relatively few sequential stages, each of which performs a relatively large part of the total task; the opposite of long thin processes.

Simulation: the use of a model of a process, product or service to explore its characteristics before the process, product or service is created.

Simultaneous development: overlapping these stages in the design process so that one stage in the design activity can start before the preceding stage is finished, the intention being to shorten time to market and save design cost (also called 'simultaneous engineering' or 'concurrent engineering').

Single-minute exchange of dies (SMED): alternative term for set-up reduction.

Single-sourcing: the practice of obtaining all of one type of input product, component, or service from a single supplier, as opposed to multi-sourcing.

Six Sigma: an approach to improvement and quality management that originated in the Motorola Company but which was widely popularized by its adoption in the GE Company in America. Although based on traditional statistical process control, it is now a far broader 'philosophy of improvement' that recommends a particular approach to measuring, improving and managing quality and operations performance generally.

Skunkworks: a small, focused development team who are taken out of their normal working environment.

Social bottom line: the element of the triple bottom line that assesses the performance of a business in relation to the people and the society with which it has contact; and/or environmental mission and a legal responsibility to respect the interests of workers, the community and the environment as well as shareholders.

Social responsibility: the incorporation of the operation's impact on its stakeholders into operations management decisions.

Spatially variable costs: the costs that are significant in the location decision that vary with geographical position.

Speed: the elapsed time between customers requesting products or services and their receiving them.

Stakeholders: the people and groups of people who have an interest in the operation and who may be influenced by, or influence, the operation's activities.

Standardization: the degree to which processes, products or services are prevented from varying over time.

Standard performance: term used in work measurement to indicate the rate of output that qualified workers will achieve without over-exertion as an average over the working day provided they are motivated to apply themselves, now generally accepted as a very vague concept.

Standard time: a term used in work measurement indicating the time taken to do a job and including allowances for recovery and relaxation.

Statistical process control (SPC): a technique that monitors processes as they produce products or services and attempts to distinguish between normal or natural variation in process performance and unusual or 'assignable' causes of variation.

Stock: alternative term for inventory.

Strategic decisions: those which are widespread in their effect, define the position of the organization relative to its environment and move the organization closer to its long-term goals.

Structural decisions: the strategic decisions which determine the operation's physical shape and configuration, such as those concerned with buildings, capacity, technology, etc.

Subcontracting: when used in medium-term capacity management, it indicates the temporary use of other operations to perform some tasks, or even produce whole products or services, during times of high demand.

Supplier quality assurance (SQA): the activity of monitoring and improving levels of quality of the products and services delivered by suppliers; also used to assess supply capability when choosing between alternative suppliers.

Supply chain: a linkage or strand of operations that provides goods and services through to end-customers; within a supply network several supply chains will cross through an individual operation.

Supply chain dynamics: the study of the behaviour of supply chains, especially the level of activity and inventory levels at different points in the chain; its best known finding is the bullwhip effect.

Supply chain risk: a study of the vulnerability of supply chains to disruption.

Supply network: the network of supplier and customer operations that have relationships with an operation.

Supply side: the chains of suppliers, suppliers' suppliers, etc. that provide parts, information or services to an operation.

Support functions: the functions that facilitate the working of the core functions, for example accounting and finance, human resources, etc.

Sustainability: the ability of a business to create acceptable profit for its owners as well as minimizing the damage to the environment and enhancing the existence of the people with whom it has contact.

Synthesis from elemental data: work measurement technique for building up a time from previously timed elements.

Systemization: the extent to which standard procedures are made explicit.

Taguchi method: a design technique that uses design combinations to test the robustness of a design.

takt time: (similar to cycle time) the time between items emerging from a process, usually applied to 'paced' processes.

Tangibility: the main characteristic that distinguishes products (usually tangible) from services (usually intangible).

Telemedicine: the ability to provide interactive healthcare utilizing modern telecommunications technology.

Teleworking: the ability to work from home using telecommunications and/or computer technology.

Theory of constraints (TOC): philosophy of operations management that focuses attention on capacity constraints or bottleneck parts of an operation; uses software known as 'optimized production technology' (OPT).

Three-D printing: also known as additive manufacturing, a technology that produces three-dimensional objects by laying down layer upon layer of material.

Throughput efficiency: the work content needed to produce an item in a process expressed as a percentage of total throughput time.

Throughput time: the time for a unit to move through a process.

Time study: a term used in work measurement to indicate the process of timing (usually with a stopwatch) and rating jobs; it involves observing times, adjusting or normalizing each observed time (rating) and averaging the adjusted times.

Time to market (TTM): the elapsed time taken for the whole design activity, from concept through to market introduction.

Top-down: the influence of the corporate or business strategy on operations decisions.

Total productive maintenance (TPM): an approach to maintenance management that adopts a similar holistic approach to total quality management (TQM).

Total quality management (TQM): a holistic approach to the management of quality that emphasizes the role of all parts of an organization and all people within an organization to influence and improve quality; heavily influenced by various quality 'gurus', it reached its peak of popularity in the 1980s and 1990s.

Total supply network: all the suppliers and customers who are involved in supply chains that 'pass through' an operation.

Trade-off theory: the idea that the improvement in one aspect of operations performance comes at the expense of deterioration in another aspect of performance, now substantially modified to include the possibility that in the long term different aspects of operations performance can be improved simultaneously.

Transformation process model: model that describes operations in terms of their input resources, transforming processes and outputs of goods and services.

Transformed resources: the resources that are treated, transformed or converted in a process, usually a mixture of materials, information and customers.

Transforming resources: the resources that act upon the transformed resources, usually classified as facilities (the buildings, equipment and plant of an operation) and staff (the people who operate, maintain and manage the operation).

Triple bottom line: (also known as people, plants and profit) the idea that organizations should measure themselves on social and environmental criteria as well as financial ones.

Two-handed process chart: a type of micro-detailed process map that shows the motion of each hand used in an activity on a common timescale.

U-form organization: an organizational structure that clusters its resources primarily by their functional purpose.

Upstream: the other operations in a supply chain that are towards the supply side of the operation.

Usage value: a term used in inventory control to indicate the quantity of items used or sold multiplied by their value or price.

Utilization: the ratio of the actual output from a process or facility to its design capacity.

Valuable operating time: the amount of time at a piece of equipment or work centre that is available for productive working after stoppages and inefficiencies have been accounted for.

Value-added throughput efficiency: the amount of time an items spends in a process having value added to it expressed as a percentage of total throughput time.

Value engineering: an approach to cost reduction in product design that examines the purpose of a product or service, its basic functions and its secondary functions.

Value stream map: a mapping process that aims to understand the flow of material and information through a process or series of processes, it distinguishes between value-added and non-value-added times in the process.

Variation: the degree to which the rate or level of output varies from a process over time, a key characteristic in determining process behaviour.

Variety: the range of different products and services produced by a process, a key characteristic that determines process behaviour.

Vertical integration: the extent to which an operation chooses to own the network of processes that produce a product or service; the term is often associated with the 'do or buy' decision.

Virtual operation: an operation that performs few, if any, value-adding activities itself, rather it organizes a network of supplier operations, seen as the ultimate in outsourcing.

Virtual prototype: a computer-based model of a product, process or service that can be tested for its characteristics before the actual process, product or service is produced.

Visibility: the amount of value-added activity that takes place in the presence (in reality or virtually) of the customer, also called 'customer contact'.

Visual management: an approach to making the current and planned state of an operation or process transparent to everyone.

Voice of the customer (VOC): capturing a customer's requirements, expectations and perceptions and using them as improvement targets within an operation.

Volume: the level or rate of output from a process, a key characteristic that determines process behaviour.

Volume flexibility: the operation's ability to change its level of output or activity to produce different quantities or volumes of products and services over time.

Waiting line theory: an alternative term for queuing theory.

Web-integrated ERP: enterprise resource planning that is extended to include the ERP-type systems of other organizations such as customers and suppliers.

Weighted-score method of location: a technique for comparing the attractiveness of alternative locations that allocates a score to the factors that are significant in the decision, and weights each score by the significance of the factor.

Wide-area networks (WANs): similar to local-area networks (LANs) but with a greater reach, usually involving elements outside a single operation.

Work breakdown structure: the definition of, and the relationship between, the individual work packages in project management; each work package can be allocated its own objectives that fit in with the overall work breakdown structure.

Work content: the total amount of work required to produce a unit of output, usually measured in standard times.

Workflow: process of design of information-based processes.

Work-in-progess (WIP): the number of units within a process waiting to be processed further (also called 'work-in-process').

Work measurement: a branch of work study that is concerned with measuring the time that should be taken for performing jobs.

Work study: the term generally used to encompass method study and work measurement, derived from the scientific management school.

World Wide Web (WWW): the protocols and standards that are used on the Internet for formatting, retrieving, storing and displaying information.

Yield management: a collection of methods that can be used to ensure that an operation (usually with a fixed capacity) maximizes its potential to generate profit.

Zero defect: the idea that quality management should strive for perfection as its ultimate objective even though in practice this will never be reached.

Index